Architectural Competitions 1950–Today

Architektur Wettbewerbe 1950–Heute

Concours d'Architecture 1950 à nos jours

Cees de Jong | Erik Mattie

Architectural Competitions 1950–Today

Architektur Wettbewerbe 1950–Heute

Concours d'Architecture 1950 à nos jours

Benedikt Taschen

Printed in Germany
English cover:
ISBN 3-8228-8900-8 (cloth-bound)
ISBN 3-8228-8901-6 (leather-bound)
German cover:
ISBN 3-8228-8929-6 (cloth-bound)
ISBN 3-8228-9242-4 (leather-bound)
French cover:
ISBN 3-8228-9291-2 (cloth-bound)
ISBN 3-8228-9292-0 (leather-bound)

Contents

Townhall and Church, Seinäjoki, Finland, 1950

6

Project

Town Hall

Site

Town centre, Seinäjoki, Finland

Dates

First round closing date 6 October 1950
Second round closing date December 1958

Number of entries

First round 42 *Second round* 5

Jury

Olavi Piha (Mayor), Olli Kivinen, Erik Krakström (both architects), Antti K. Huttunen (civil engineer), Kalle Koskinen (building contractor), Eino Rosti (technical engineer), Reino Hautala (council secretary)

Result

First prize Elissa & Alvar Aalto *Second prize* Pekka Pitkänen *Third prize* Mona & Lars Hedman; Timo Penttilä & Kari Virta; Erkki Pasanen

Commissioned by

The Municipality of Seinäjoki

Construction

1962 to 1965

Architect

Alvar Aalto (1898–1976)

Project

Church

Site

Town centre, Seinäjoki, Finland

Dates

Closing date 1 October 1951

Number of entries

45 (4 entries were disqualified because they did not meet the conditions)

Jury

I.V. Ahonen (teacher, elementary school), Reino Ala-Kulju (teacher, secondary school), Oskari Herttua (financial advisor), Viljo Rewell, Martti Välikangas (architects)

Result

First prize Pekka Pitkänen & Olli Vahtera *Second prize* Christer Bärlund *Third prize* Eero Eerikäinen & Martti Jaatinen *Honourable mention* A. Hytönen & R.V. Luukkonen; Risto Sammalkorpi; Alvar Aalto

Commissioned by

The Lutheran Church

Construction

1958 to 1960

Architect

Alvar Aalto (1898–1976)

Competitions in architecture and town planning since 1792

Town Hall and Church, Seinäjoki, Finland, 1950

Town Hall and Church, Seinäjoki, Finland, 1950

Town Hall and Church, Seinäjoki

Alvar Aalto was the most influential Finnish architect of the twentieth century and was one of the world's leading Modernists. He produced an extensive œuvre during a career spanning fifty years. His pre-war work, which included high points such as the Paimo sanatorium, was among the best that this heroic Functionalist period had to offer. After the Second World War, Aalto not only remained one of the world's leading architects, but also left his mark on architectural history with his urban development projects. The centre of the Finnish town of Seinäjoki is the product of a unique combination of his talents.

Alvar Aalto

Town Hall and Church from the yard

Church from north-west

Illustrious predecessors

Aalto's illustrious predecessors were Eliel Saarinen, Lars Sonck and Sigurd Frosterus. Saarinen had shown how an architect could be attracted to both Finnish, national, rural architecture and to a more international, modern style: Jugendstil. Frosterus had participated in the competition for Helsinki Station and leaned more towards pure Jugendstil, whereas Sonck incorporated Rationalist features in his National-Romanticist designs. Obviously, there were also other architects in Finland, but the three mentioned above determined the architectural climate in which Aalto grew up. Furthermore, the rate of technological development during Aalto's lifetime was astounding, and these developments, together with the specific Finnish cultural heritage, all had an influence on Aalto[1], although it was his personal genius that made him one of the most creative and productive architects of this century.

Aalto developed an affinity for Functionalism early on in his career. He and other architects such as Le Corbusier, Martin Gropius and Johannes Duiker had started to construct buildings in this modern style while others were still experimenting on a small scale, or contemplating the theoretical aspects of Functionalism. His œuvre includes the TB sanatorium in Paimo (1929–33) and the Turun Sanomat newspaper printing house and office block in Turku (1927–29). At this point Aalto was still keeping pace with Western European developments, and his buildings would not have looked out of place in Berlin or Rotterdam. However, this certainly did not apply to his later work. After the war, Aalto's style became more personal and moved away from the angular forms of dogmatic Functionalism. In addition, his choice of building materials was no longer based on the preferences of his foreign colleagues and he returned to more traditional Finnish materials, such as brick and wood.

Two competitions

After the Second World War, the Finnish authorities focused their architectural policy upon new housing and urban development projects. The Soviet Union – whose occupation of the country had ended fifty years before – had annexed a number of areas on the eastern borders of Finland, and many Finns had fled to the western

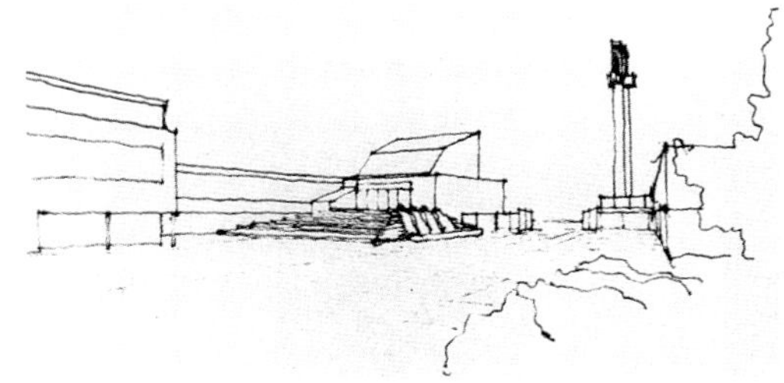

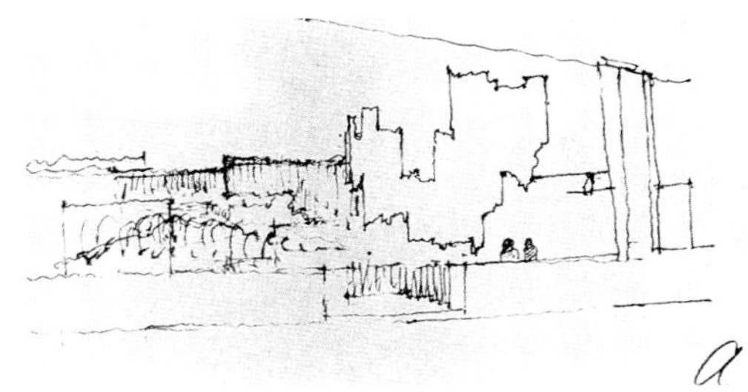

Alvar Aalto **sketch of Church and Town Hall, c. 1961**

Alvar Aalto **sketch of the organ in the Church, c. 1958**

part of the country. In addition, the authorities wanted to boost national productivity.

One of the country's urban development hubs was Seinäjoki, situated in the Ostrobothnia region of central Finland. Even though it had a population of only 20 000, Seinäjoki had an important regional function. The town was situated at an intersection of various transport routes and was the most important religious centre in the region. Because the urban facilities had not kept pace with the rapid growth of the town, two competitions were organised in order to provide the necessary facilities. The first competition, for a new town hall, was organised in 1950. The following year, architects were invited to submit designs for a church which would enhance Seinäjoki's status as a religious centre.

It is not surprising that Aalto decided to compete. He earlier in his career had already designed a Civil Guard House in Seinäjoki, applying a somewhat plain, early Modernist style. Whereas most architects had their hands full with a single competition design, Aalto – who was one of Europe's most productive architects – participated in both competitions. He won the competition for the town hall. It is interesting to note that both competitions were restricted to Finnish participants and that many of the other competing architects were great admirers of Aalto's work. Aalto had time to work on the church design, because it was some time before his town hall design was executed. The Lutheran Church, who had commissioned the project, had stipulated that the church had to blend in with the surrounding architecture, and that it had to be structurally refined and symbolic of the spiritual support offered by the church.

The prizes in the church competition were snatched from under Aalto's nose by three students of architecture. Aalto and two other nominees received an honourable mention. One may see this result as indicative of the quality of Finnish architecture at the time, perhaps even of the quality of the local academy of architecture, but the result was probably most indicative of the jury's competence. The Lutheran Church reviewed the result at length, even after it had been announced, eventually ignoring the official result and appointing Aalto as executive architect. Construction work on the church got under way in 1957. One favourable side-effect of this was that the town council was suddenly spurred into renewed action regarding the competition for the new town hall.

The architectural apple of Aalto's eye

In 1958 the town council decided to organise a second round for the five prize-winning architects from the first round. Aalto also won this round. It is not improbable, and certainly not illogical, that the jury may have been biased towards Aalto's design from the start. Aalto was the undisputed master of Finnish architecture at the time, and it is plausible that certain members of the jury – local dignitaries in particular – were aware of the fact that one or two of his buildings would put Seinäjoki on the world's architectural map. The jury's next step was therefore logical: if Aalto was going to build the town hall and the church, why not let him design the rest as well. Consequently, Aalto produced an urban development plan which included public buildings such as a library (1963–65), a state department building and a town auditorium (1968–69).

Aalto worked on the Seinäjoki project for no less than 26 years. The town became the architectural apple of his eye and he was on site as often as possible, which was not common practice in Finnish architectural circles. Although Aalto was certainly not a fan of the uncompromising dogmas proposed during the CIAM congresses of the Modernists, many of the features of his urban development plan were derived from concepts which were developed during the early years of CIAM. Motorised and pedestrian traffic were kept strictly separate, even though Aalto had to demolish two existing streets in order to achieve this. In addition, the housing and office sectors were also situated in separate areas[2].

Three centres

The town has a religious centre, a cultural and administrative centre and a traffic centre which has parking facilities and is partially concealed, allowing the other centres to come to the fore. The two other centres are closely tied in with one another and, although the colours and building materials used differ considerably, they form an architectural entity. This was largely a result of Aalto's characteristic formal language, which included certain key concepts such as fan-

Interior of the conference hall

Interior of Church

shaped segments in the floor plans, terraces and the rhythmic articulation of the structures.

The religious centre not only boasts the church with its striking tower, but also has a banquet hall, a restaurant, gymnasia, dwellings and other facilities. The light colours used for the religious centre contrast with the dark blue tiling of the town hall, but are in harmony with the library and the town auditorium. The church façade facing the square can be opened up, whereby services can be held for 15 000 people, which is almost the entire population of Seinäjoki. The church and square are surrounded by a park. A second, elongated square connects the church with the cultural-administrative centre. One of the most striking features of the town hall is the council chamber which is perched on top of pillars.

The church was completed first, followed by the town hall, the library, the U-shaped presbytery (1964–1966) and the town auditorium. In the interim Aalto designed numerous extensions. Aalto died in 1976. His creativity declined considerably in his latter years, due to chronic alcoholism and old age. After his death, his wife Elissa, who had worked with Aalto on many projects, completed his favourite project and "pièce de résistance".

1 See chapter on Helsinki Station in this book.

2 It bears mentioning that this division of housing and office sectors had been stipulated in the competition programme.

Rathaus und Kirche, Seinäjoki

Alvar Aalto gilt als der einflußreichste finnische Architekt des 20. Jahrhunderts und zählt international zu den bedeutendsten Vertretern der Moderne. Sein umfangreiches Oeuvre umfaßt einen Zeitraum von mehr als 50 Jahren, und seine Arbeiten aus der Zeit vor dem Zweiten Weltkrieg – mit dem Sanatorium in Paimio als einem der Höhepunkte – gehören zu den herausragenden Beispielen des Funktionalismus. Nach dem Zweiten Weltkrieg verteidigte Aalto seinen Ruf als führender Architekt und drückte dem Bereich der Stadtplanung ebenfalls seinen Stempel auf: Im Stadtzentrum von Seinäjoki gelang ihm eine einzigartige Kombination seiner Talente.

Berühmte Vorgänger

Zu Aaltos berühmten Vorgängern zählten Eliel Saarinen, Lars Sonck und Sigurd Frosterus. Saarinen hatte gezeigt, daß man sich als Architekt sowohl zum finnischen, national-ländlichen Baustil als auch zu internationalen, moderneren Stilrichtungen wie etwa dem Jugendstil hingezogen fühlen konnte. Dagegen galt Frosterus, der sich u.a. an der Ausschreibung für den Hauptbahnhof von Helsinki beteiligt hatte, als reiner Jugendstilarchitekt, während Soncks nationalromantischer Stil auch rationale Einflüsse aufwies. Zwar gab es in Finnland noch andere Architekten, aber diese drei sind exemplarisch für das architektonische Klima, in dem der junge Aalto aufwuchs. Während dieser Zeit wurde er Zeuge der rasanten Entwicklung in allen Bereichen der Technik, die ihn neben seinem finnischen Erbe (siehe das Kapitel zum Hauptbahnhof, Helsinki) formen und beeinflussen sollte. Doch es war sein eigenes Genie, das ihn zu einem der kreativsten und produktivsten Architekten dieses Jahrhunderts machte.

Aalto fühlte sich schon früh zum Funktionalismus hingezogen. Neben Architekten wie Le Corbusier, Martin Gropius und Johannes Duiker war er als einer der ersten in der Lage, Bauwerke in diesem modernen Stil zu realisieren – während andere Baumeister sich damit nur theoretisch oder im kleinen Maßstab befaßten. Das bereits erwähnte TB-Sanatorium in Paimio (1929–1933) sowie das Büro- und Zeitungsgebäude »Turun Sanomat« in Turku (1928–1933) sind nur einige Beispiele für diesen Baustil. In jenen Jahren folgte Aalto den Entwicklungen in (West-)Europa sehr genau, und seine Bauwerke hätten ebensogut in Berlin oder Rotterdam stehen können. Bei seinen späteren Werken änderte sich dies jedoch: Nach Kriegsende wurde Aaltos Baustil persönlicher, denn er wandte sich von den eckigen Formen des dogmatischen Funktionalismus ab. Auch bei der Auswahl der Baumaterialien orientierte er sich weniger an seinen ausländischen Kollegen, sondern griff auf traditionelle finnische Materialien wie Holz und Ziegelstein zurück.

Zwei Ausschreibungen

Nach dem Zweiten Weltkrieg widmete die finnische Regierung ihre ganze Aufmerksamkeit dem Wohnungs- und Städtebau. Die als ständige Bedrohung empfundene Sowjetunion – 50 Jahre zuvor noch Besatzungsmacht – hatte an Finnlands Ostgrenze einige Gebiete annektiert, so daß viele Finnen gezwungen waren, in Richtung Westen umzuziehen. Außerdem sollte die inländische Wirtschaft neue Impulse erhalten.

Eines der urbanen Wachstumsgebiete war Seinäjoki in der Region Ostrobothnia in Mittelfinnland. Dieser Ort erfüllte eine wichtige regionale Funktion, obwohl er kaum 20 000 Einwohner zählte: Seinäjoki war sowohl bedeutender Verkehrsknotenpunkt als auch religiöses Zentrum der Gegend. Die städtischen Einrichtungen hatten mit dem Wachstum der Stadt nicht Schritt halten können, und um diesen Mißstand zu beheben, entschloß man sich zu zwei Ausschreibungen. Der erste Wettbewerb – für das neue Rathaus – fand 1950 statt; ein Jahr später wurden die Architekten eingeladen, ihren Entwurf für eine Kirche einzureichen, die dem religiösen Status Seinäjokis gerecht werden sollte.

Aalto beteiligte sich an beiden Wettbewerben. Er kannte Seinäjoki aus seiner beruflichen Anfängerphase, als er hier ein Wachhaus in frühmodernem Stil entworfen hatte. Die meisten anderen Architekten, von denen viele Aaltos Arbeiten bewunderten, waren bereits mit einem Wettbewerb vollauf ausgelastet. Aalto gewann die Ausschreibung für das neue Rathaus, aber da sich die Ausführung der Konstruktionspläne in die Länge zog, konnte er sich sofort nach seiner Ernennung intensiv der Gestaltung des geplanten Kirchengebäudes widmen. Der Auftraggeber dieses Wettbewerbs, die lutherische Kirche, machte zur Auflage, daß sich die neue Kirche harmonisch in ihre Umgebung einpaßte. Zudem sollte sie ein Symbol geistiger Kraft sein und eine feingliedrige Strukturierung erhalten.

Bei dieser Ausschreibung mußte Aalto drei Studenten über sich auf den ersten bis dritten Plätzen dulden, während er zusammen mit zwei anderen Architekten eine ehrenvolle Erwähnung erhielt. Das Ergebnis sprach für die ausgezeichnete Architektenausbildung in Finnland. Nach der Verkündung des Beschlusses erfolgte eine intensive Debatte innerhalb der lutherischen Kirche, die das offizielle Ergebnis ignorierte und Aalto zum Architekten des neuen Kirchengebäudes ernannte. Zwar konnte erst 1957 mit den Bauarbeiten begonnen werden, doch hatte dies den günstigen Nebeneffekt, daß sich die Stadtverwaltung plötzlich wieder mit dem Bau des Rathauses beschäftigte.

Aaltos Lieblingskomplex

1958 entschloß sich die Stadt zu einer zweiten Ausschreibungsrunde mit den besten fünf Architekten des ersten Wettbewerbs. Auch diese Ausschreibung gewann Aalto. Es wäre durchaus denkbar und keineswegs unlogisch, daß die Jury schon im Vorfeld von Aaltos Entwurf beeindruckt war, da er zu diesem Zeitpunkt als unangefochtener Großmeister der finnischen Architektur galt. Ein oder zwei von ihm entworfene Gebäude würden Seinäjoki internationale Aufmerksamkeit garantieren. Diese Überlegung spielte bei der Entscheidung der Jurymitglieder – hauptsächlich Honoratioren des Ortes – sicherlich eine Rolle, und sie zog einen weiteren Schritt nach sich: Wenn Aalto schon die Kirche und das Rathaus errichtete, dann sollte er sich auch um die weiteren Bauvorhaben kümmern. Dieser Gedanke wurde direkt in die Tat umgesetzt, wobei Aalto nicht nur für die anderen öffentlichen Gebäude – Stadtbibliothek (1963–1965), Regierungsbüro und Stadthalle (1968–1969) –, sondern auch für die städteplanerische Struktur des gesamten Komplexes verantwortlich zeichnete.

Seinäjoki entwickelte sich zu Aaltos Lieblingsprojekt, an dem er 26 Jahre arbeitete und für das er von all seinen Werken den größten Stolz empfand. Beispielsweise verbrachte er sehr viel mehr Zeit auf der Baustelle, als für einen Architekten üblich. Obwohl Aalto nicht zu den Verfechtern der rigorosen Dogmen zählte, die während der Tagungen der modernistischen Architektenorganisation CIAM (Congrès Internationaux d'Architecture Moderne) aufgestellt wurden, ging sein städteplanerischer Entwurf für das Zentrum von Seinäjoki sehr wohl auf die Ideen aus der Anfangszeit dieser Kongresse zurück. Straßen- und Fußgängerverkehr sind streng voneinander getrennt, wofür Aalto zwei bereits bestehende Straßen opfern mußte. Für Wohnen und Arbeiten gibt es gesonderte Bereiche. Diese Trennung gehörte zu den Auflagen der Ausschreibung für die Stadtanlage.

Drei Stadtkerne

Das Stadtzentrum von Seinäjoki ist in drei Bereiche unterteilt: ein religiöser Kern, ein kulturell-administrativer Kern sowie ein Verkehrskern, der zugunsten der beiden anderen Bereiche eher versteckt wurde, aber genügend Parkmöglichkeiten bietet. Die beiden anderen Teile sind eng miteinander verbunden und bilden trotz der unterschiedlichen Farbgebung und Fassadengestaltung eine städtbauliche Einheit, die durch Aaltos typische Formensprache unterstrichen wird. Hierbei spielen Fächersegmente im Grundriß, Terrassen und eine starke rhythmische Gliederung eine wichtige Rolle.

Das religiöse Zentrum umfaßt neben der Kirche mit ihrem auffallenden Turm einen Festsaal, ein Restaurant, Turnhallen, Wohnungen sowie andere Nebengebäude und bildet mit seiner hellen Farbgebung einen Kontrast zur dunkelblauen Kachelverkleidung des Rathauses. Hingegen harmoniert es farblich mit der Bibliothek und der Stadthalle. Eine Wand der Kirche läßt sich zum Platz hin öffnen, so daß 15 000 Besucher am Gottesdienst teilnehmen können. Die Kirche befindet sich in einer parkähnlichen Anlage und ist durch einen zweiten, langgestreckten Platz mit dem kulturell-administrativen Zentrum verbunden. Zu den wichtigsten Merkmalen des Rathauses gehört der auf Pilotis ruhende Sitzungssaal.

Als erstes Gebäude wurde die Kirche fertiggestellt. Danach folgten das Rathaus, die Bibliothek, das U-förmige Kirchengemeindehaus und die Stadthalle. Während der gesamten Bauzeit nahm Aalto noch weitere Veränderungen vor. Jahrelanger Alkoholmißbrauch und die üblichen Alterserscheinungen raubten ihm jedoch viel von seiner Kreativität. 1976 starb er. Nach seinem Tod vollendete seine Frau Elissa, mit der er eng zusammengearbeitet hatte, Aaltos Lieblingskomplex und »pièce de resistance«.

L'Hôtel de Ville et l'église, Seinäjoki

Alvar Aalto, dont la carrière a duré cinquante ans, est le plus influent architecte finlandais du vingtième siècle et l'un des plus importants représentants du Modernisme. Son travail d'avant-guerre, comme son célèbre sanatorium de Paimo, est sans doute la plus remarquable réalisation des débuts héroïques du fonctionnalisme. Après la Seconde Guerre mondiale, il demeura non seulement l'un des plus grands architectes du monde mais apposa sa marque sur des projets d'urbanisme. Le centre de la ville finlandaise de Seinäjoki est né de la conjonction de ses deux talents.

De grands prédécesseurs

Aalto fut précédé par d'illustres architectes finlandais comme Eliel Saarinen, Lars Sonck ou Sigurd Frosterus. Saarinen avait montré qu'un architecte pouvait être à la fois attiré par une source locale d'inspiration rurale et par un style plus actuel et international, le Jugendstil. Frosterus avait participé au concours pour la gare d'Helsinki et s'était converti au pur style Jugendstil alors que Sonck intégrait déjà des éléments rationalistes à ses plans d'esprit national-romantique. D'autres architectes opéraient bien entendu en Finlande, mais ces trois grands praticiens déterminèrent le climat qui contribua à la formation d'Aalto. L'accélération confondante du progrès technique durant sa vie et l'héritage culturel finnois exercèrent également sur lui une profonde influence[1] – même si c'est à son génie personnel que l'on doit l'une des œuvres architecturales les plus créatives et les plus riches de ce siècle.

Aalto s'intéressa très tôt au fonctionnalisme. Comme Le Corbusier, Martin Gropius ou Johannes Duiker, il avait commencé à construire dans ce style d'avant-garde alors que d'autres en étaient encore restés au stade de l'expérimentation modeste ou se contentaient de réfléchir aux aspects théoriques de cette nouvelle tendance. Avec le sanatorium pour tuberculeux de Paimo (1929), les bureaux et l'imprimerie du journal Turun Sanomat à Turku (1928), Aalto travaillait dans l'esprit de ce qui se faisait en Europe, et ses bâtiments n'auraient pas été déplacés à Berlin ou à Rotterdam, ce que l'on ne peut pas dire de ses réalisations ultérieures. Après la guerre, son style devint plus personnel et s'éloigna des formes anguleuses d'un fonctionnalisme dogmatique. Ses choix de matériaux se différencièrent de ceux de ses confrères étrangers et il en revint à des éléments plus finlandais comme la brique et le bois.

Deux concours

Après la Seconde Guerre mondiale, les autorités finlandaises orientèrent leur politique architecturale vers le logement et l'urbanisme. La menaçante Union Soviétique, dont l'occupation avait pris fin en 1917, avait annexé un certain nombre de territoires à la frontière orientale et de nombreux Finlandais s'étaient réfugiés dans la partie ouest du pays. Par ailleurs le gouvernement voulait redynamiser l'économie.

L'un des centres d'expansion urbaine du pays était la petite ville de Seinäjoki, en Ostrobothnie, à l'ouest du pays. Bien qu'elle ne compta alors qu'une population de 20 000 habitants, Seinäjoki remplissait une importante fonction régionale. Elle était située à l'intersection de plusieurs voies de communication et jouait un rôle religieux. Ses équipements n'ayant pas suivi sa rapide croissance, deux concours furent organisés pour rattraper ce retard. Le premier, pour l'hôtel de ville, fut lancé en 1950 et le second pour une église affirmant le rôle religieux de la cité, l'année suivante. Tous deux étaient réservés aux architectes finlandais et de nombreux concurrents étaient de grands admirateurs de l'œuvre d'Aalto.

Il n'est pas surprenant que celui-ci y ait participé puisqu'il avait en effet conçu quelques années auparavant l'hôtel de police pour Seinäjoki, dans un style moderniste primitif assez neutre. Aalto, déjà l'un des architectes les plus productifs de son temps, participa aux deux compétitions et remporta immédiatement celle de l'hôtel de ville. Il eut en fait tout loisir de travailler sur le projet de l'église car un certain temps s'écoula avant que l'hôtel municipal ne soit exécuté. L'Eglise luthérienne qui était à l'origine du projet, souhaitait que ce nouveau lieu de culte reste en harmonie avec l'environnement, soit de qualité et symbolise le soutien spirituel de la religion.

Les trois premiers prix de ce deuxième concours furent ravis à Aalto par trois étudiants en architecture. Le maître et un autre participant ne reçurent que des mentions honorables. On peut se demander si ce palmarès reflétait la qualité de l'architecture finlandaise, celle de l'école des Beaux-Arts de la ville ou tout simplement les limites de la compétence du jury. L'Eglise luthérienne ignora les résultats du concours, désigna Aalto architecte de son projet et la construction commença en 1957. L'une des conséquences de cet événement fut de tirer le conseil municipal de sa torpeur.

La dernière passion de l'architecte

En 1958, la municipalité décida donc d'organiser un second concours entre les cinq architectes qui avaient été retenus au premier. Aalto remporta cette nouvelle épreuve. Il n'est ni improbable ni illogique que le jury ait préféré dès le départ les plans d'Aalto. Il était le maître incontesté de l'architecture finlandaise et certains membres du jury – les notables locaux, en particulier – devaient sentir que posséder un ou deux bâtiments signés d'un aussi grand nom serait une contribution prestigieuse à l'image architecturale de la ville. L'étape suivante fut donc logique: si Aalto devait construire l'hôtel de ville et l'église, pourquoi ne pas lui confier l'ensemble des autres projets? Il fut donc chargé du plan d'urbanisme comprenant une bibliothèque (1963–1965), un bâtiment administratif et une salle de concert (1968–1969).

Aalto travailla ainsi pour Seinäjoki pendant vingt six-ans. La petite ville devint sa principale préoccupation et il se rendit sur place aussi souvent que possible, ce qui n'était guère courant dans les pratiques des architectes finlandais. Bien qu'il n'ait jamais été un inconditionnel des dogmes des CIAM, de nombreux aspects de ses conceptions urbanistiques sont issus de concepts mis au point lors de leurs cénacles. La circulation des voitures et celle des piétons furent strictement séparées même si, pour y arriver, il fallut démolir deux rues. Les zones de logement et de travail furent également différenciées.

Trois centres

La ville possède maintenant une centre religieux, un centre administratif et culturel et un centre de parkings, partiellement enterré, permettant à l'ensemble de fonctionner. Les deux premiers centres sont étroitement imbriqués et bien que leurs couleurs et leurs matériaux soient très différents, ils forment une seule entité. Ce résultat est largement dû au langage formel de l'architecte qui faisait appel à des concepts comme la segmentation en éventail des plans de masse, les terrasses et l'articulation rythmique des structures.

Le centre religieux peut s'enorgueillir non seulement de l'église et de son remarquable clocher, mais également d'une salle pour banquets, d'un restaurant, de gymnases, de logements et d'autres équipements. Leurs coloris clairs contrastent avec la couverture sombre de l'hôtel de ville, mais sont en harmonie avec la bibliothèque et la nouvelle salle de concert. La façade de l'église, sur la place, s'ouvre entièrement pour accueillir des cérémonies réunissant 15 000 personnes, presque toute la population de la ville. L'église et la place sont entourées d'un parc tandis qu'une seconde place allongée relie l'église au centre administratif et culturel. L'un des éléments les plus frappants de l'hôtel municipal est la salle du conseil perchée sur des piliers.

L'église fut la première à être terminée, suivie de l'hôtel de ville, de la bibliothèque, du presbytère en forme de U (1964–1966) et de la salle de concert. Entre-temps, Aalto avait conçu de nombreuses extensions. Il mourut en 1976 mais sa créativité avait beaucoup décliné dans ses dernières années. Après sa mort, sa femme Elissa, qui avait beaucoup travaillé avec lui, termina son projet favori, sans doute son œuvre majeure.

1 *Voir le chapitre sur la gare d'Helsinki.*

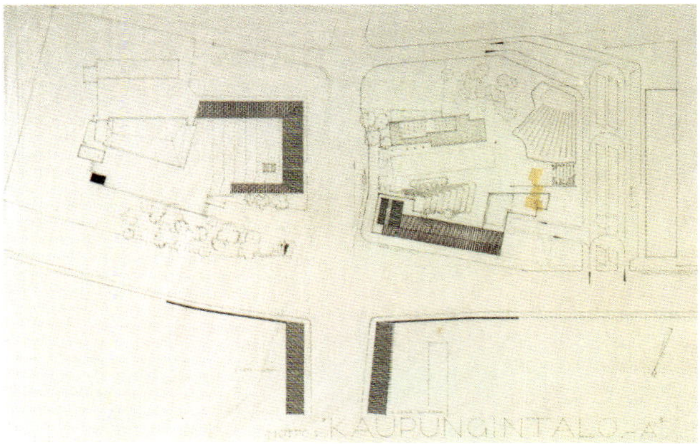

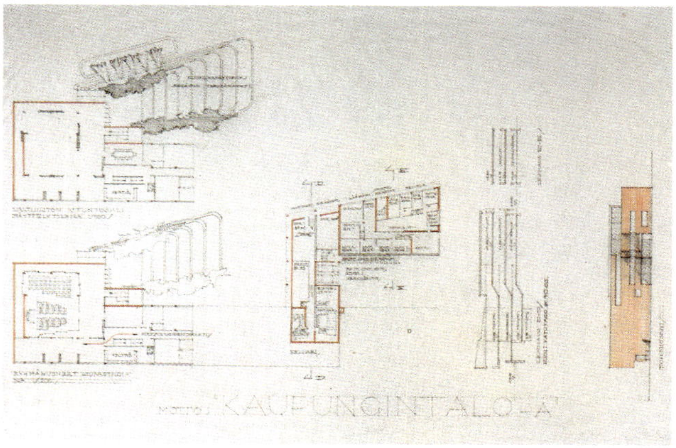

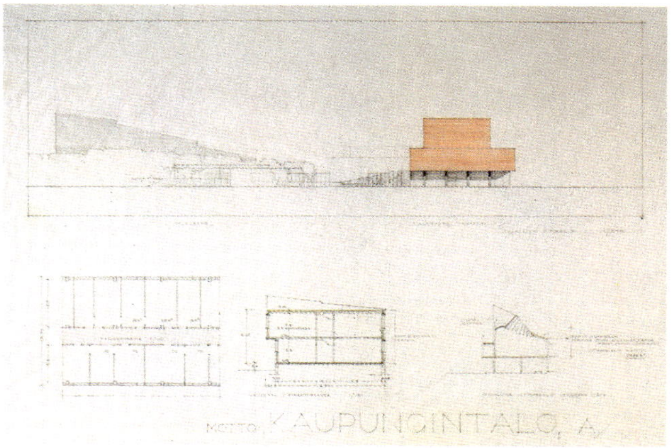

Elissa & Alvar Aalto the second round competition design for the Town Hall, 1958, above: exterior view from south, below: roof plan, first prize

Elissa & Alvar Aalto the second round competition design for the Town Hall, 1958, site plan, first prize

Elissa & Alvar Aalto the second round competition design for the Town Hall, 1958, from above left: plan of public hall (as exhibition hall), plan of public hall (as assembly hall), section of the office (D, D, E-E), west elevation, first prize

Elissa & Alvar Aalto the second round competition design for the Town Hall, 1958, above: east elevation, below left: plan of office sector, below right: section, first prize

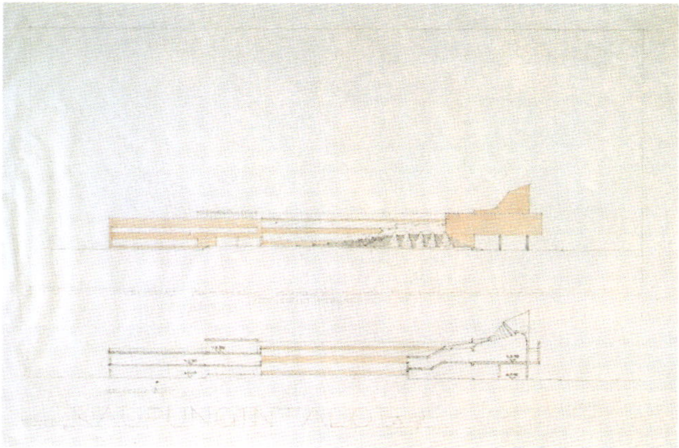

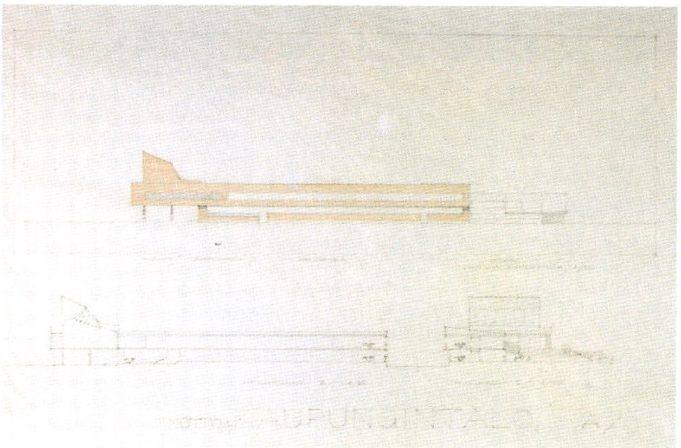

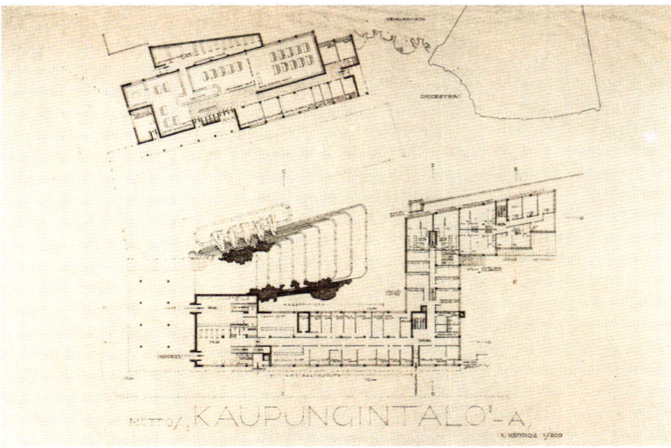

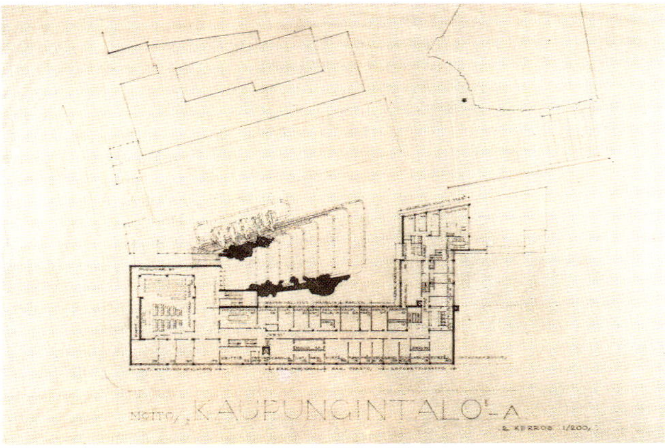

Elissa & Alvar Aalto the second round competition design for the Town Hall, 1958, above: south elevation, below: east-west section, first prize

Elissa & Alvar Aalto the second round competition design for the Town Hall, 1958, above: north elevation, below left: east-west section, below right: north-south section, first prize

Elissa & Alvar Aalto the second round competition design for the Town Hall, 1958, ground floor plan, first prize

Elissa & Alvar Aalto the second round competition design for the Town Hall, 1958, first floor plan, first prize

Town Hall and Church, Seinäjoki, Finland, 1950

16

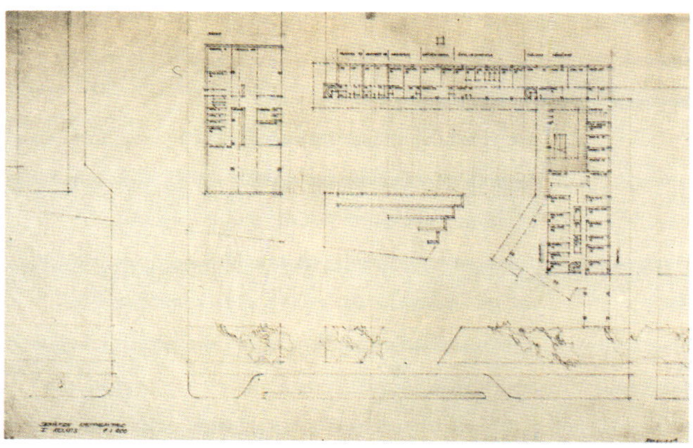

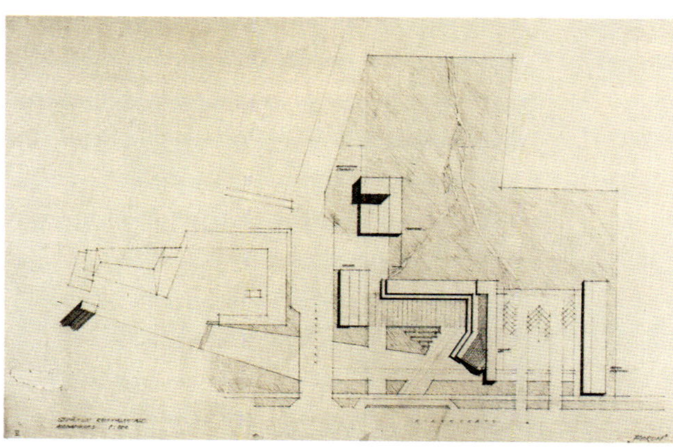

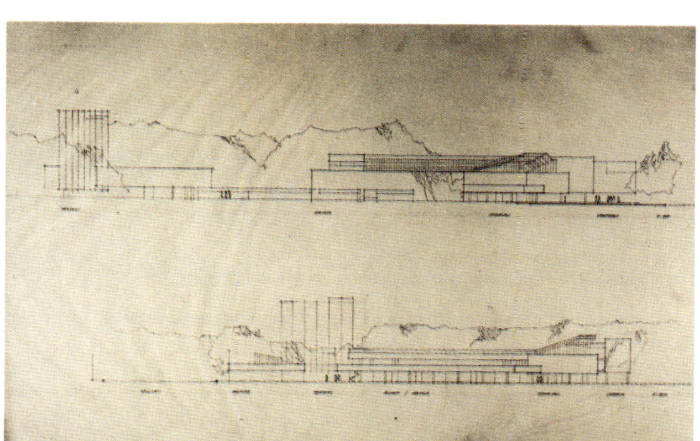

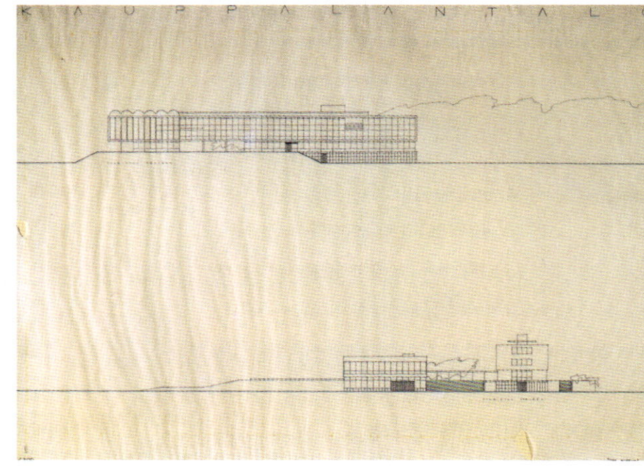

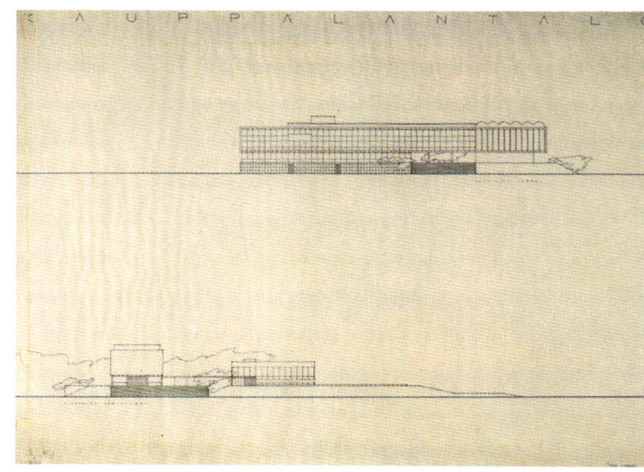

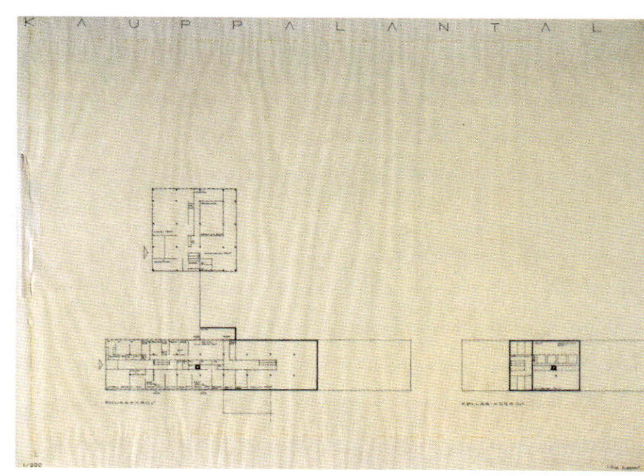

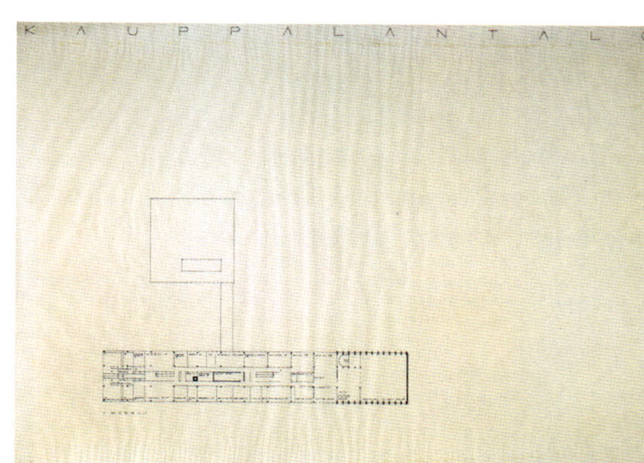

Timo Penttilä & Kari Virta the second round competition design for the Town Hall, 1958, exterior view from north-east, third prize

Timo Penttilä & Kari Virta the second round competition design for the Town Hall, 1958, ground floor plan, third prize

Timo Penttilä & Kari Virta the second round competition design for the Town Hall, 1958, site plan, third prize

Timo Penttilä & Kari Virta the second round competition design for the Town Hall, 1958, above: east elevation, below: north elevation, third prize

Erkki Pasanen the second round competition design for the Town Hall, 1958, above: west elevation, below: south elevation, third prize

Erkki Pasanen the second round competition design for the Town Hall, 1958, above: east elevation, below: north elevation, third prize

Erkki Pasanen the second round competition design for the Town Hall, 1958, left: ground floor plan, right: basement plan, third prize

Erkki Pasanen the second round competition design for the Town Hall, 1958, third floor plan, third prize

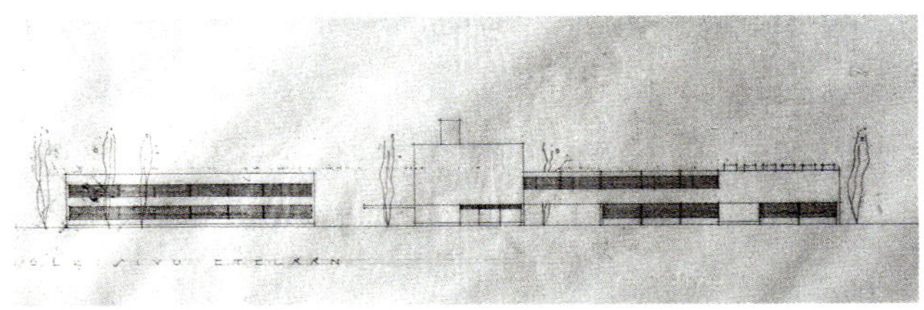

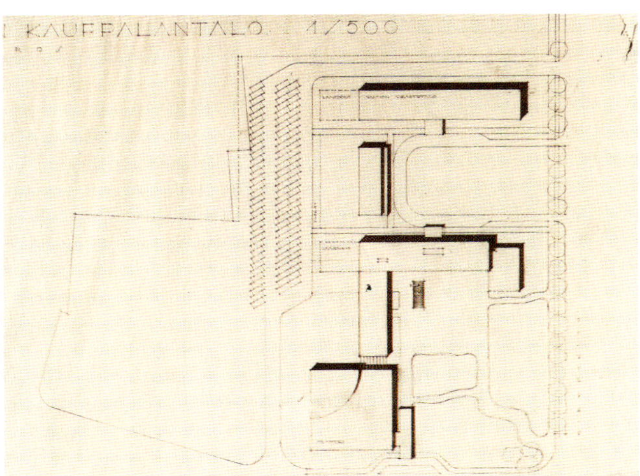

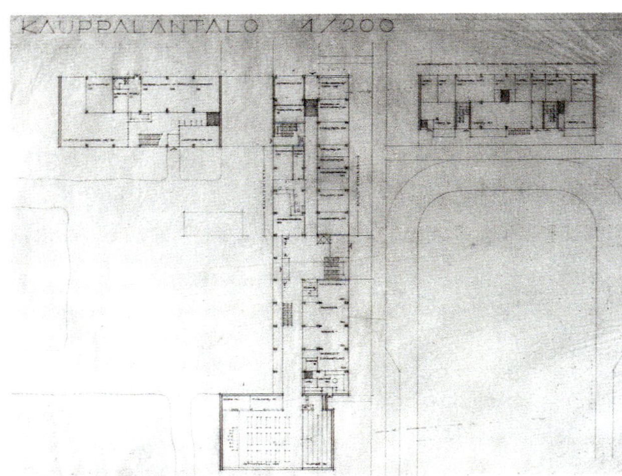

Pekka Pitkänen the second round competition design for the Town Hall, 1958, east elevation, second prize

Pekka Pitkänen the second round competition design for the Town Hall, 1958, south elevation

Pekka Pitkänen the second round competition design for the Town Hall, 1958, site plan, second prize

Pekka Pitkänen the second round competition design for the Town Hall, 1958, ground floor plan, second prize

Mona & Lars Hedman the second round competition design for the Town Hall, 1958, exterior view from north-east, third prize

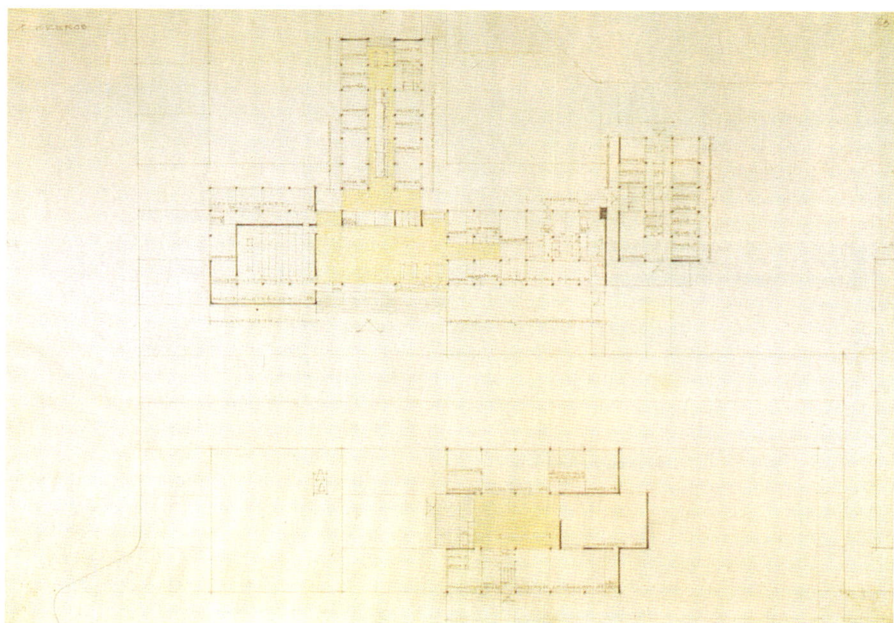

Mona & Lars Hedman the second round competition design for the Town Hall, 1958, site plan, third prize

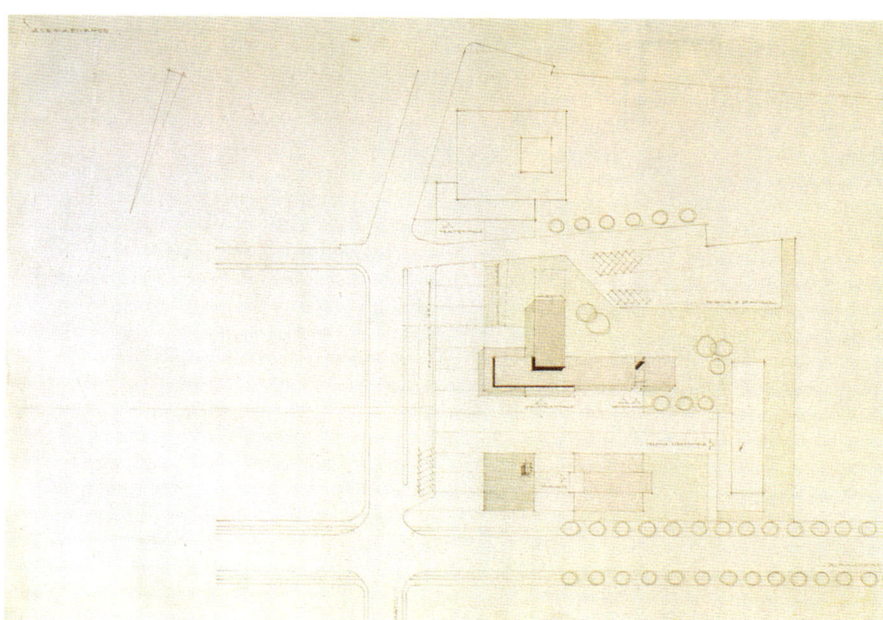

Mona & Lars Hedman the second round competition design for the Town Hall, 1958, ground floor plan, third prize

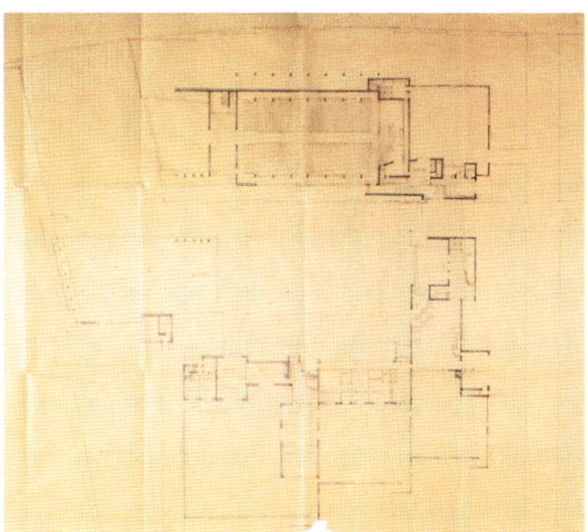

Christer Bärlund competition design for the Church, 1951, exterior view from north-west, second prize

Christer Bärlund competition design for the Church, 1951, ground floor plan, second prize

Christer Bärlund competition design for the Church, 1951, site plan, second prize

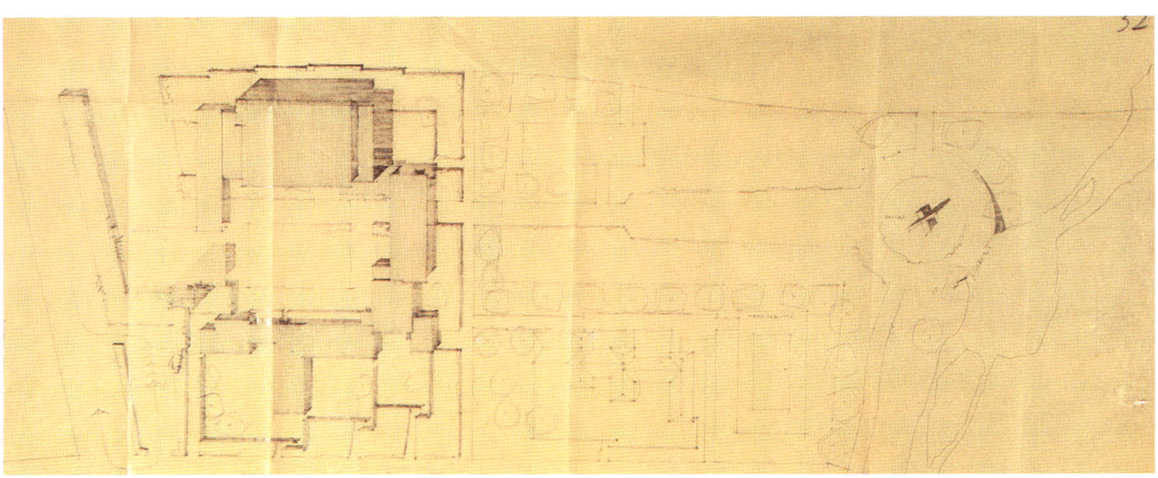

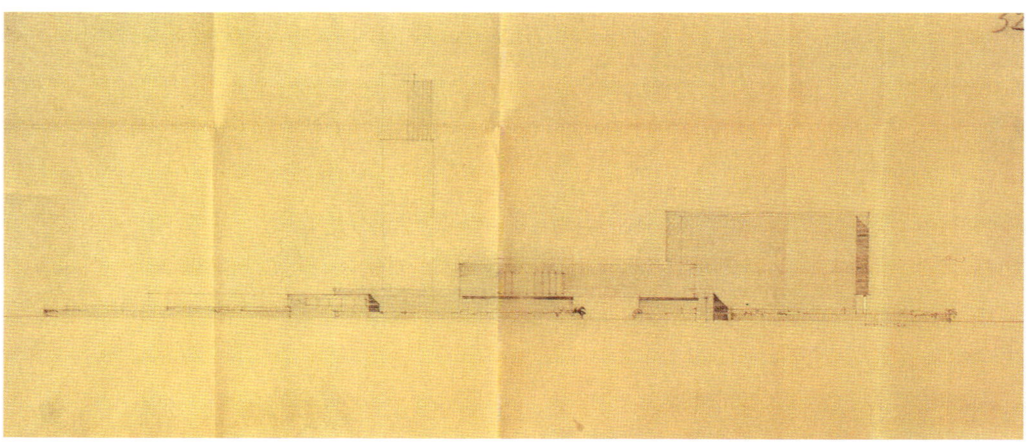

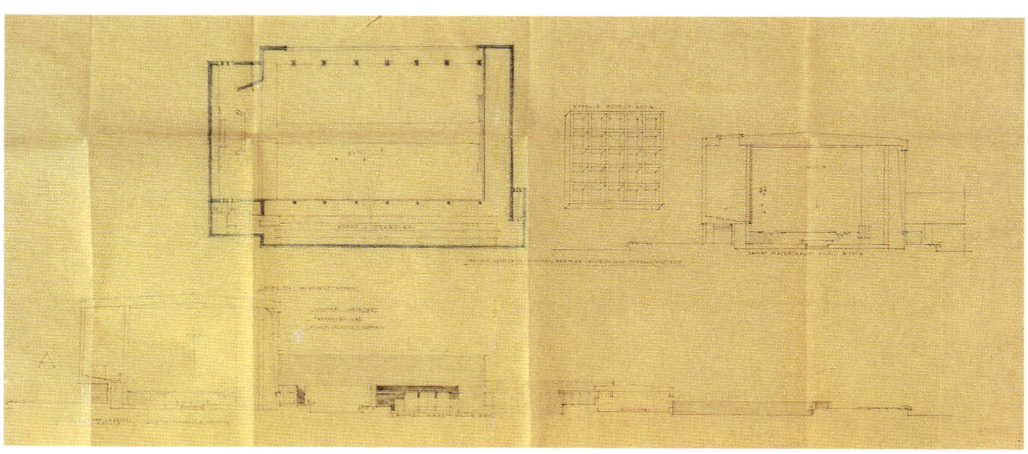

Christer Bärlund competition design for the Church, 1951, east-west section (north-side), second prize

Christer Bärlund competition design for the Church, 1951, interior view of the Church, second prize

Christer Bärlund competition design for the Church, 1951, east elevation, second prize

Christer Bärlund competition design for the Church, 1951, above left: plan of the Church, above right: north-south section of the Church, below: north-south section, second prize

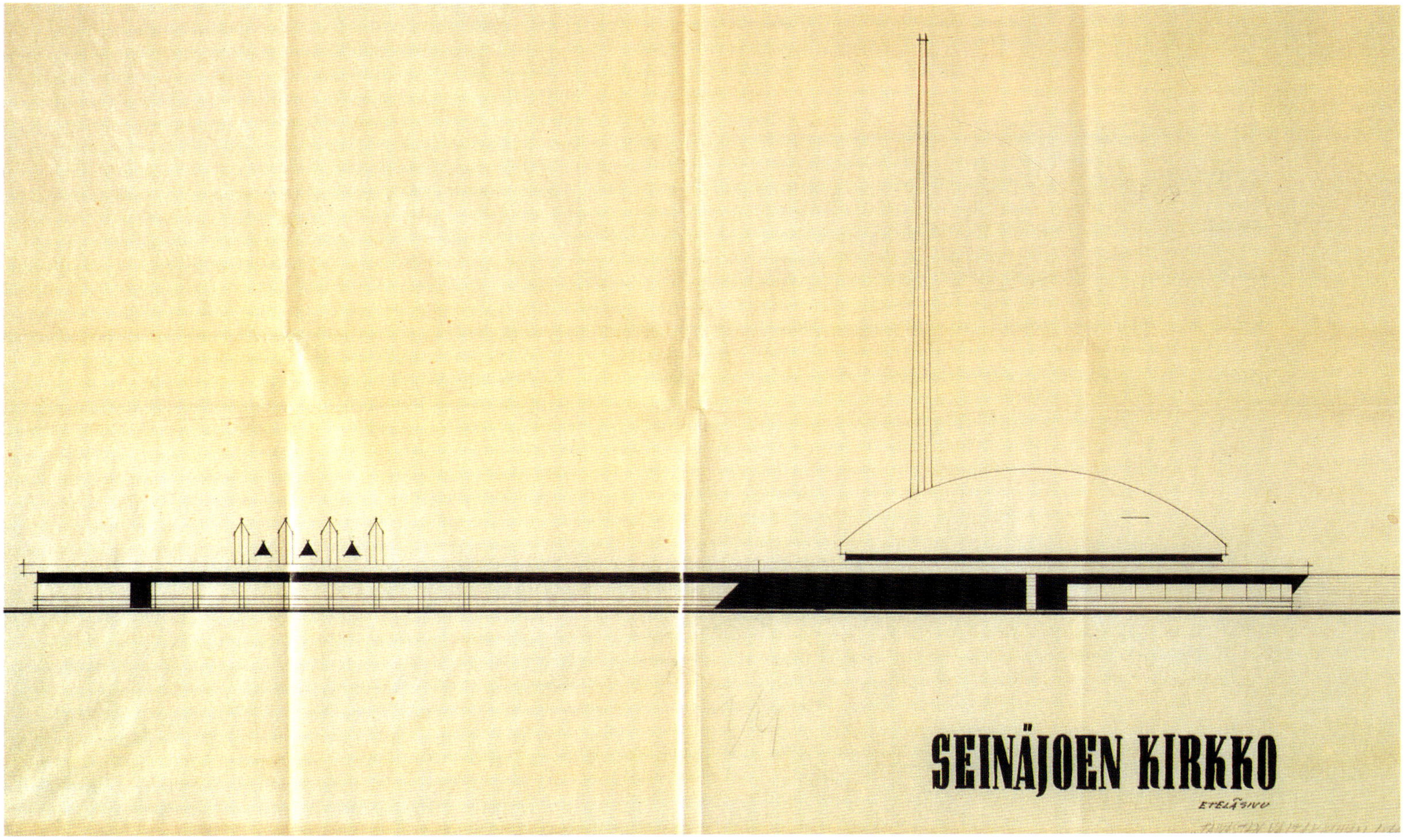

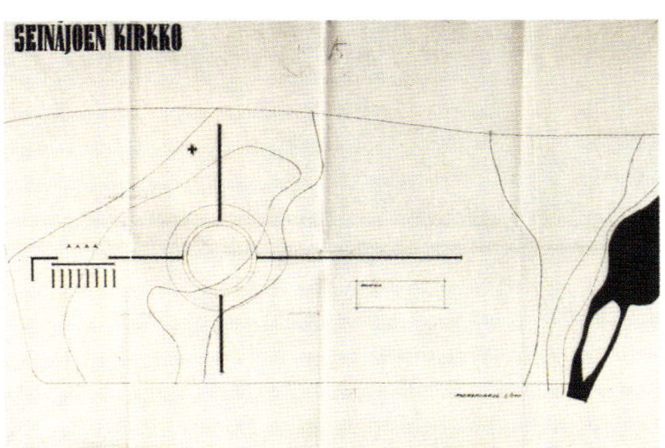

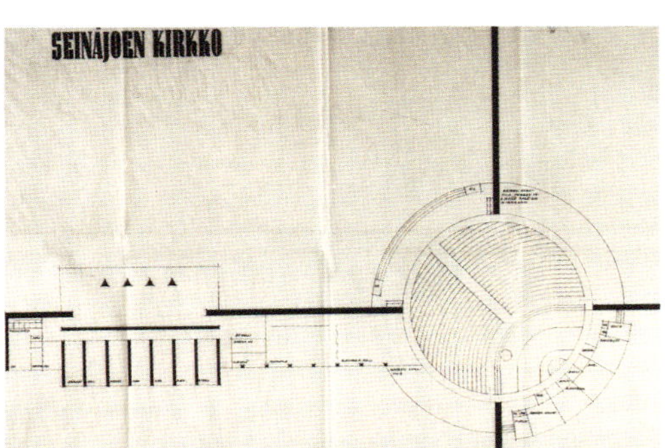

Eero Eerikäinen & Martti Jaatinen
competition design for the Church,
1951, third prize

Eero Eerikäinen & Martti Jaatinen
competition design for the Church,
1951, site plan, third prize

Eero Eerikäinen & Martti Jaatinen
competition design for the Church,
1951, ground floor plan, third prize

Risto Sammalkorpi competition design for the Church, 1951, elevation, honourable mention

Risto Sammalkorpi competition design for the Church, 1951, interior perspective of the Church, honourable mention

Risto Sammalkorpi competition design for the Church, 1951, elevation, honourable mention

Risto Sammalkorpi competition design for the Church, 1951, ground floor plan, honourable mention

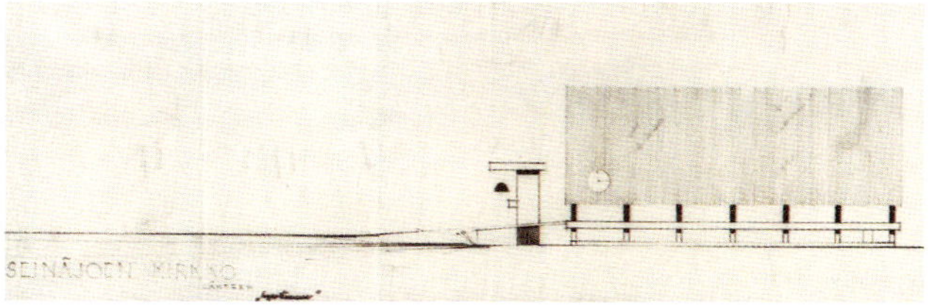

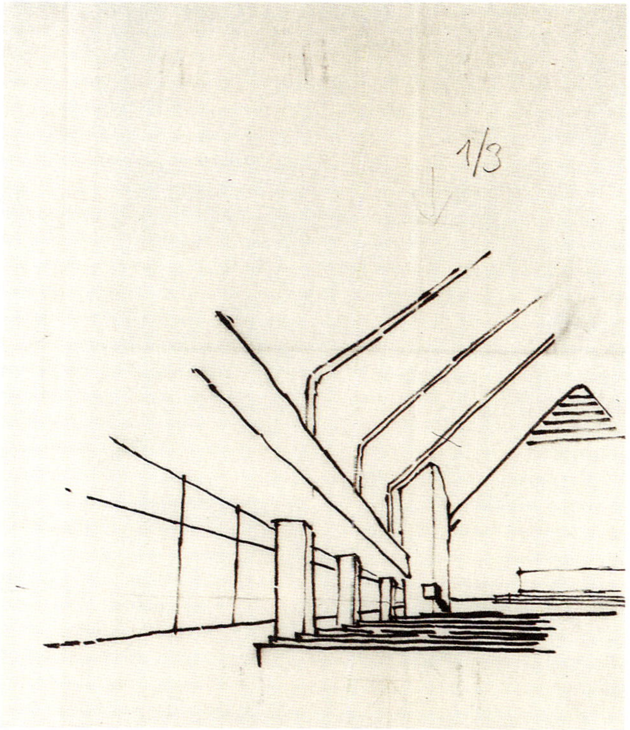

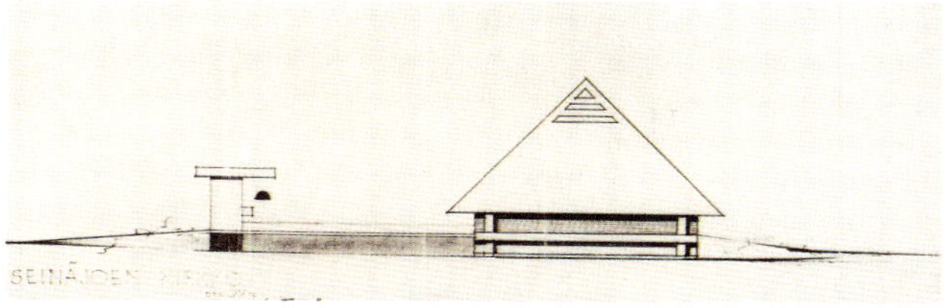

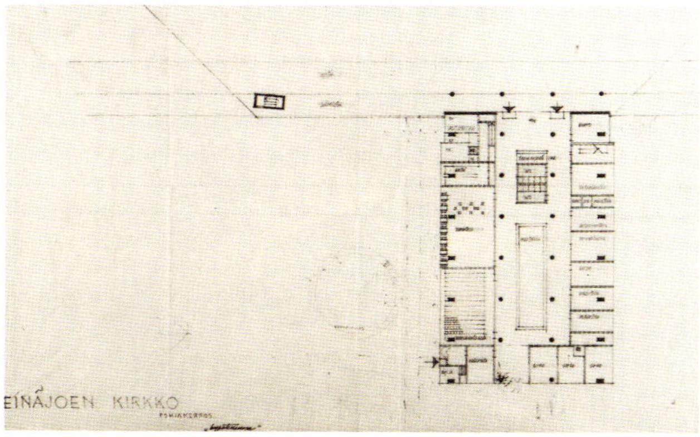

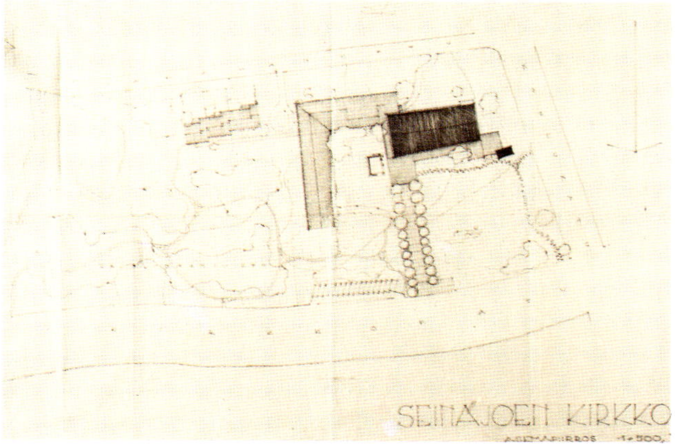

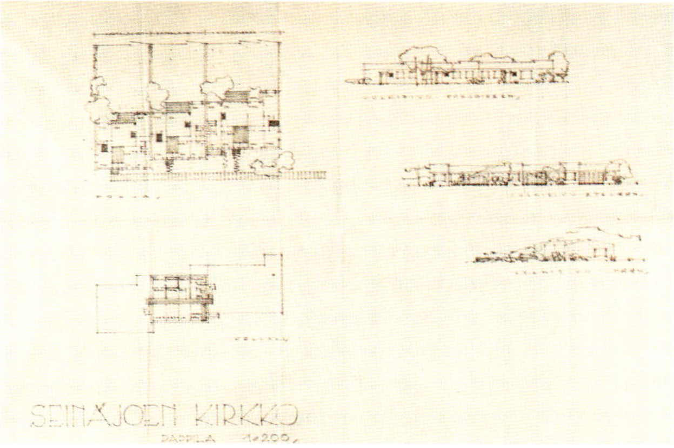

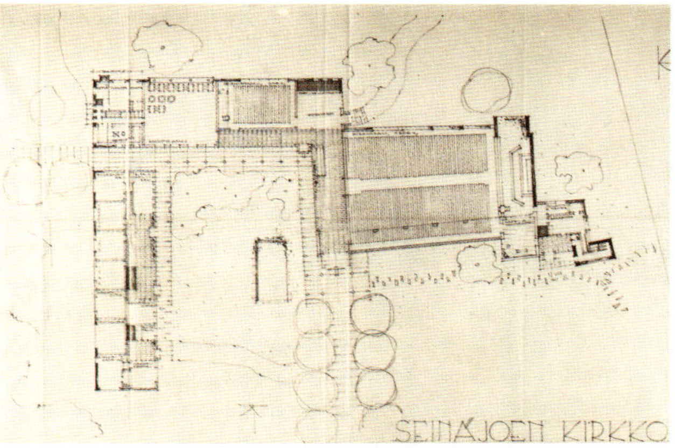

Alvar Aalto competition design for the Church, 1951, site plan, honourable mention

Alvar Aalto competition design for the Church, 1951, interior view of the Church, honourable mention

Alvar Aalto competition design for the Church, 1951, above left: ground floor plan, below left: basement plan, above right: north elevation, middle right: south elevation, below right: east elevation, honourable mention

Alvar Aalto competition design for the Church, 1951, ground floor plan, honourable mention

Opera House, Sydney, 1956–1957

24

Project

Opera house and concert hall

Site

Bennelong Point, Sydney

Dates

Competition announced May 1956 *Closing date* December 1956 *Result announced* 29 January 1957

Number of entries

233

Jury

Eero Saarinen (United States, architect), Gobden Parkes (Head of the Public Works Department, New South Wales), J.L. Martin (Cambridge University, architect), Henry Ingham Ashworth (Australia, architect)

Result

First prize Jørn Utzon *Second prize* Joseph Marzella, Leon Loschetter, W.W. Cunningham, Walter Weissman, Melvin Brecher, Robert Geddes & George Qualls (a team of American architects) *Third prize* Paul Boissevain & Barbara Joan Osmond (England)

Commissioned by

A committee appointed by J.J. Cahill, prime minister of New South Wales

Construction

1957 to 1973

Architects

Jørn Utzon *After 1966* Peter Hall, Lionel Todd and David Littlemore

Construction cost

C. 50 000 000 Australian dollars

Opera House, Sydney, 1956–1957

Jørn Utzon drawing from the "Red Book", 1958, sketch

Opera House, Sydney

When the Sydney Opera House opened its doors to the public in 1973, the entire population of Australia and one Dane breathed a sigh of relief. The construction of Jørn Utzon's masterpiece had taken much longer than expected, it had been a political nightmare for successive governments, and construction costs had eventually rocketed to almost fifty million Australian dollars. Following a period marred by controversy, Utzon had resigned and returned to Denmark long before the project was completed. Fortunately, his design later received the acclaim it justly deserved.

A gift

The initiative for the Sydney Opera House was taken by Eugene Goossens, the director of the Music Conservatory, and J.J. Cahill, the prime minister of New South Wales, who hoped to win votes for the Labour Party by presenting this gift to the city. A site was designated in 1954: Bennelong Point, a spit of land in Port Jackson harbour. Two years later an open, international competition was organised. The building would not only be a venue for opera but would also stage other theatrical and art events. The main auditorium was to seat 3500 people, the smaller auditorium 1200 people. Due to the multi-functional nature of the building, it would also obviously require a restaurant, a café and other secondary facilities. The jury had 233 designs to choose from, all of them line drawings as had been requested. The most influential member of the jury was Eero Saarinen, who ran a successful architectural firm in the United States together with his father Eliel. It is rumoured that one of the rejected designs caught Saarinen's eye, perhaps because its daring structure coincided with his own approach to architecture[1]. Upon returning the design to the jury for assessment, he is known to have said: *"Gentlemen, here is the winner"*. The design had been submitted by the Danish architect Jørn Utzon.

From left: Jørn Utzon, Erik Andersson (Utzon's right-hand man), Robert Quentin (general manager, Elizabethan Trust Opera Co.), 1957

Bird's-eye view, north-west

Concert hall

Third-generation Modernist

Having graduated from the Royal Academy of Art in Copenhagen, Utzon (Copenhagen, 1913) became a pupil of the world's leading architects. He worked for Alvar Aalto in 1946 and for Frank Lloyd Wright in 1949, both of whom made an indelible impression on the young architect. He also travelled through Africa and Europe, where he met Le Corbusier. During a tour of Central America, he developed a particular fascination for Aztec and Mayan art.

Utzon's style evolved during the 1950s, when pre-war Modernism began to develop more poetic features. The way had, of course, been paved by the master himself: Le Corbusier had designed the chapel in Ronchamp in 1952. Subsequently, a second generation of Modernists stepped into the limelight, among them Louis Kahn and Hans Scharoun, whose Philharmonic building in Berlin (1956) heralded a breakthrough in concert-hall architecture. Utzon, a member of the next generation, was to benefit from these developments.

Prior to the Sydney competition, Utzon had mostly designed housing complexes, his projects consisting primarily of rows of single-family dwellings. His designs were clearly influenced by the works of Mies van der Rohe and Alvar Aalto; he used similar materials and also applied the concept of organic structure. Utzon saw architecture as a self-contained entity, and not merely as the product of a drawing-board. Human existence and architecture were governed by the same physical laws. The Sydney Opera House was clearly a product of Utzon's belief that buildings are organic entities, but the construction of the building also underscored the fact that the organic approach inevitably led to structural problems.

Striking designs

Utzon was not the only architect to submit a remarkable design. Laurence Prynn's design was grouped around a cylinder supported by overhead arches. The cylinder was bisected and served as a stage tower for both auditoria. Prynn received an honourable mention for his opera building, which was situated in an eerie, organic landscape. An American team, captained by Joseph Marzella, also submitted a cylindrical design with a spiral-shaped floor plan for which they were awarded second prize. Third prize went to the team of Paul Boissevain and Barbara Joan Osmond. Their design was less spectacular: two separate structures housing the auditoria, mounted on a platform. The architectural team of Terence Bliss and Michael Le Pelley also submitted a design with two separate blocks.
Other architects applied a more uncompromising variant of the Modernist style. Hugh D. Krall, for example, limited his design to a simple block form. Derek A. Cobb & Wilhelm Holzbauer tried to marry the poetic and rigid Modernist varieties by placing a striking, arched, shell roof on top of a simple block. They received an honourable mention for their unwieldy effort. Robert A. Dunster & Peter S. Straughton also based their design on a "box" shape. However, their design is remarkably original because the façades have been left "open", so that the auditoria are clearly visible.

Parts of the same imaginary sphere

As with Cobb and Holzbauer's design, Utzon's design was also topped with a characteristic shell structure. However, in Utzon's design the shell roof and its sub-structure formed an organic entity. The shells, which all form part of the same imaginary sphere, are an architectural echo of Sydney's harbour, where the sails of thousands of yachts are silhouetted against the sky. Utzon took the view that no building constructed on the designated site could have a flat roof, and saw the roof of his building as a fifth façade, which was as important as the four lateral façades. The shell structure also obviated the problem of the stage towers, each of which was housed in a shell which neatly fitted in amongst the other shells. The jury ruled that this solution had a greater aesthetic appeal than the cube-on-a-block approach taken by many other participants. The shells were to be coated with glazed tiles and, according to Utzon, the roof would be reminiscent of a sculpture or a Gothic church.
The construction of the shells proved to be a major problem. Utzon had not yet found a satisfactory solution when he submitted his so-called "Red Book", which contained his first designs. Ove Arup's engineering bureau was also unable to find a solution to the problem, and eventually Utzon came up with the idea that prefabricated elements, which formed part of a single sphere, should be used for the construction of the shells. This solution was described in the so-called "Yellow book".
However, by the time Utzon had solved the problem, construction was already well under way, urged on by the project's spiritual father, Cahill, who thus increased the tension between the architect and the commissioning authorities. Moreover, Utzon was given little time to mull over any of the other problems, one of which was the seating capacity. Utzon never did find a solution. The political pressure eventually became more than he could bear and he resigned in 1966, leaving the project in the hands of Australians Peter Hall, David Littlemore and Lionel Todd. Their solution to the problem of seating capacity can best be described as a weak compromise. They decided

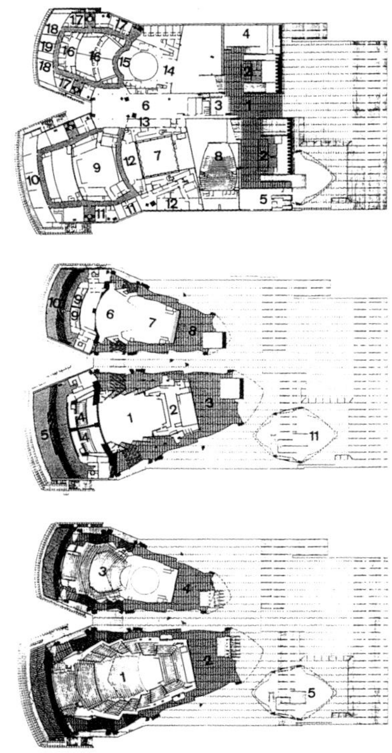

From above: first floor plan, third floor plan, auditorium-level plan

North-south section

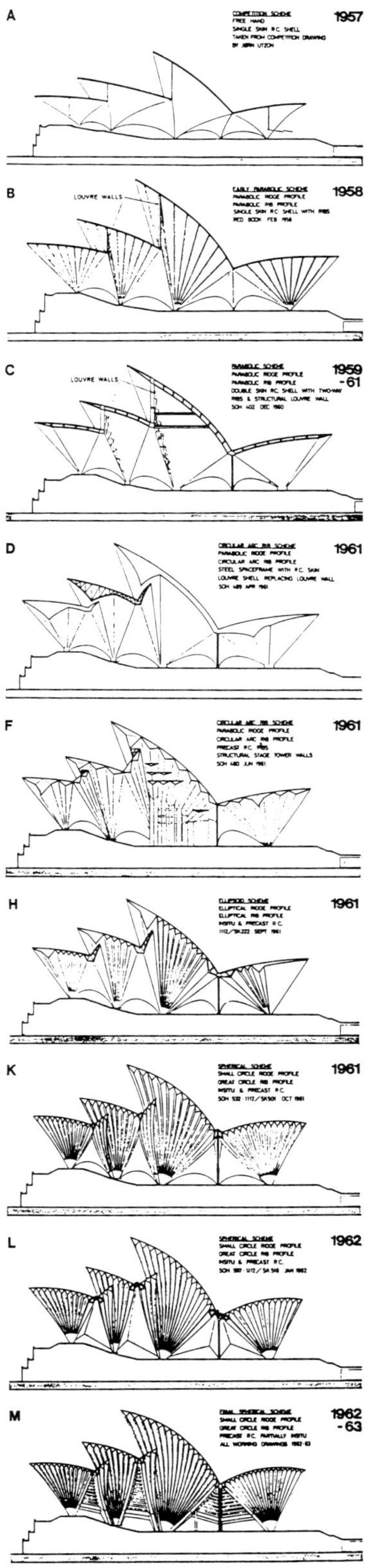

Changes of the roof structure

that the building would not serve as a venue for opera in the future, but that it would only be used to stage concerts, therefore the size of the stage could be reduced, leaving space for extra rows of seats. This compromise made Utzon's stage-tower solution look ridiculous and, as a result, his brilliantly conceived structure was not only complicated and expensive, it had also been rendered useless. The Sydney Opera House became the Sydney Concert Hall. Nevertheless, Utzon had put Sydney on the architectural map. He gave the city a new face and conceived a roof which had a new form and function, a fact often neglected by Modernists.

Although Utzon's masterpiece was completed by other architects, it shows a clear affinity to the work of Alvar Aalto: it has the same organic, flowing shapes and similar rhythmic vertical elements. It is unfortunate that Utzon did not see the project through to completion. It is also intriguing to contemplate a concrete version of Utzon's auditoria, even though his successors certainly cannot be accused of shoddy workmanship. Their efforts seem to have been guided by leading first and second-generation Modernists, such as Poelzig and Scharoun, whose names are often listed alongside Utzon's.

Fifty million Australian dollars

Cahill's hopes that the Opera House would bring prosperity to Sydney and win support for the Labour Party were never realised. On the contrary, Labour lost the 1965 elections and left the continuing problem of the Opera House to their successors. As a precautionary measure, a number of civil servants were charged with the supervision and execution of the project. Utzon saw this subtle form of control as proof of the fact that the authorities had little confidence in his ability, and tendered his resignation. Perhaps this was an over-hasty move, because his resignation was immediately accepted. However, Utzon's departure solved few problems and by the time the Opera House was officially opened, seven years after Utzon's return to Denmark, it had taken sixteen years to build and had cost more than seven times the original estimate.

1 *It is interesting to note that the structure of the TWA building at Kennedy International Airport in New York is similar to that of the Sydney Opera House. The TWA building, built between 1956 and 1962, was designed by Eero Saarinen.*

Opera House, Sydney

Als das Sydney Opera House 1973 seine Tore öffnete, seufzten ein Däne und die gesamte Bevölkerung Australiens erleichtert auf. Der Bau von Jørn Utzons Meisterwerk hatte viel länger gedauert als erwartet, mehreren australischen Regierungen politisches Kopfzerbrechen bereitet und schließlich fast 50 Mio. australische Dollar verschlungen. Utzon selbst war zu diesem Zeitpunkt schon längst wieder in Dänemark, wohin er sich nach heftigen Auseinandersetzungen zurückgezogen hatte. Erst dort erhielt er die volle Anerkennung für seinen Entwurf.

Ein kleines Geschenk

Die Initiative zum Bau einer neuen Oper in Sydney ging aus von E. Goossens, dem Direktor des Konservatoriums, und J.J. Cahill, dem Premierminister von Neusüdwales. Cahill versprach sich von diesem Geschenk an die Stadt Unterstützung für seine Labour-Party. 1954 fand man ein geeignetes Baugelände: Bennelong Point, in herrlicher Lage direkt am Hafen (Port Jackson). Zwei Jahre später wurde der Wettbewerb international ausgeschrieben. Neben Opernaufführungen sollten im neuen Opernhaus Kunstausstellungen und andere Darbietungen stattfinden können; die Bauauflagen forderten einen großen Saal mit einer Kapazität von 3000 bis 3500 Plätzen und einen kleinen Saal für 1200 Personen. Zu dem multifunktionellen Gebäude gehörten auch ein Restaurant, ein Cafe sowie weitere Nebenräume.
Die Jury hatte die Wahl unter 233 Beiträgen, die alle – wie gefordert – als Linearzeichnungen eingesandt worden waren. Bedeutendstes Jurymitglied war Eero Saarinen, der zusammen mit seinem Vater Eliel schon seit Jahren eines der bekanntesten Architekturbüros in den Vereinigten Staaten leitete. Angeblich war Saarinen von einem der bereits abgelehnten Entwürfe besonders beeindruckt – vielleicht aufgrund des kühnen Formenspiels, das seinen eigenen Auffassungen von Architektur besonders nahe kam. Das von ihm errichtete TWA-Terminal des internationalen Flughafens in Idlewild, New York (1956–1962) besitzt eine dem Opera House vergleichbare Struktur. Saarinen brachte die Zeichnungen erneut vor die Jury und sagte zu den anderen Mitgliedern: »*Meine Herren, dies ist der erste Preis*«. Der so gelobte Entwurf stammte von Utzon.

Modernist der dritten Generation

Der 1913 in Kopenhagen geborene Utzon hatte nach dem Besuch der Königlichen Kunstakademie seine Ausbildung bei den Großen seiner Zunft fortgesetzt. 1946 arbeitete er für Alvar Aalto und 1949 für Frank Lloyd Wright; beide hinterließen bei ihm bleibenden Eindruck. Zudem unternahm Utzon ausgedehnte Reisen durch Afrika, Europa – dort traf er mit Le Corbusier zusammen – und Amerika, wo er sich besonders von der Kunst der Mayas und Azteken beeindruckt zeigte.
Utzon entwickelte seinen persönlichen Stil in den 50er Jahren, zu einer Zeit, als der Modernismus der Vorkriegsphase poetischere Züge annahm. In diesem Punkt ging der Meister allen anderen voraus: 1952 zeichnete Le Corbusier seine Entwürfe für die Wallfahrtskirche von Ronchamp; aber die Architekten der »zweiten Generation« folgten ihm auf dem Fuße: Louis Kahn und Hans Scharoun, dessen Berliner Philharmonie von 1956 einen Durchbruch auf dem Gebiet der Konzertsäle bedeutete. Diese Entwicklung war auch für Utzon, der bereits der »dritten Generation« von Modernisten angehörte, von Vorteil.
Vor seiner Teilnahme am Wettbewerb für das Opera House in Sydney hatte sich Utzon vornehmlich mit dem Wohnungsbau beschäftigt. Bei den von ihm realisierten Projekten handelte es sich hauptsächlich um Reihensiedlungen mit Einfamilienhäusern. In seinen Wohnungsbauentwürfen sind die Einflüsse von Mies van der Rohe und Alvar Aalto (Materialgebrauch, organische Anordnung) erkennbar. Architektur war für Utzon kein reines Produkt des Zeichenbretts, sondern ausgestattet mit einer eigenen »Existenz«. Alle für den Menschen gültigen physikalischen Gesetze galten auch für die Baukunst. Er sah ein Gebäude immer als eine organische Einheit, was im Entwurf des Sydney Opera House deutlich zur Geltung kommt. Allerdings führen derartige Ansätze häufig zu Konstruktionsproblemen.

Herausragende Entwürfe

Neben Utzons markantem Entwurf gab es eine Reihe weiterer bemerkenswerter Beiträge. So entwarf Laurence Prynn einen Zylinder, gestützt von Strebpfeilern, als Grundform. Dieser Zylinder war in zwei Teile unterteilt und diente als doppelter Bühnenturm für beide Säle. Prynn hatte rund um sein Operngebäude einen wenig ansehnlichen organischen Landschaftspark geplant; er erhielt für seinen Beitrag eine ehrenvolle Erwähnung.
Ein amerikanisches Architektenteam unter Leitung von Joseph Marzella reichte einen zylindrischen Entwurf mit einem spiralförmigen Grundriß ein, der mit dem zweiten Preis ausgezeichnet wurde. Der dritte Preis ging an Paul Boissevain und Barbara Joan Osmond, deren weniger spektakuläre Konstruktion aus zwei voneinander getrennten Gebäuden bestand, die auf einer Plattform standen. Auch Terence Bliss und Michael Le Pelley entwarfen zwei separate Schachtelkonstruktionen.
Andere Architekten vertraten die etwas rigidere Richtung der Moderne und beließen es – wie beispielsweise Hugh D. Krall – bei einer einfachen Blockform. Dagegen versuchten Derek A. Cobb und Wilhelm Holzbauer, die poetische und die »steifere« Richtung der modernen Bewegung zu vereinigen, indem sie auf ihre Blockform eine interessante Schalenkonstruktion setzten. Auch dieser Versuch erhielt eine ehrenvolle Erwähnung. Im Ansatz schachtelförmig ist ebenso der Entwurf von Robert A. Dunster und Peter S. Straughton. Dennoch wirkt ihre Konstruktion originell: Die Seitenwände sind »geöffnet«, wodurch die Saalformen deutlich erkennbar bleiben.

Teile derselben imaginären Kugel

Ebenso wie beim Entwurf von Cobb und Holzbauer steht bei Utzon die Schalenkonstruktion im Vordergrund. Doch seine Konstruktion geht mit dem Unterbau eine harmonische Verbindung ein. Die Schalen – alles Teile derselben imaginären Kugel – bilden eine architektonische Antwort auf den Hafen von Sydney, wo sich die Segel zahlloser Schiffe scharf vom Horizont abheben. Utzon war der Ansicht, daß ein Gebäude an dieser Stelle kein flaches Dach haben dürfe. Das Dach sollte eher zu einer fünften Fassade werden und mindestens so auffällig sein wie die anderen vier. Dadurch löste sich für ihn auch das Problem der Bühnentürme: Jeder erhielt seine eigene Schale, die nahtlos zwischen die anderen Schalen eingefügt wurde. Nach Auffassung der Jury war diese Lösung ästhetisch ansprechender als ein Kubus auf einem Block wie bei vielen anderen Einsendungen. Utzon selbst verglich die Schalen, die mit Majolikaplatten bedeckt werden sollten, mit einer Skulptur und dem Gesamteindruck einer gotischen Kirche.
Die Konstruktion der Schalen bildete eine der größten Schwierigkeiten beim Bau der Oper. Als Utzon seine ersten Entwürfe vorstellte – zusammengefaßt im sog. Red Book – hatte er für die Schalen noch keine adäquate Lösung anzubieten. Auch die Planungsfirma von Ove Arup fand zunächst keinen Ausweg. Schließlich kam Utzon auf die Idee, die Teile der imaginären Kugel mit Hilfe vorgefertigter Elemente zu bauen. Diese Elemente zeichnete er im sog. Yellow Book vor.
Während sich Utzon noch mit diesem Problem befaßte, war der Bau bereits in vollem Gang – ganz nach dem Wunsch des Initiators Cahill. In der Folge verstärkten sich die Spannungen zwischen Architekt und Auftraggeber. Auch bei anderen Schwierigkeiten – etwa in der Frage der Saalkapazität – erhielt Utzon kaum Zeit zum Nachdenken. Als der Druck der Politik auf ihn immer größer wurde, kündigte Utzon 1966, und die Australier Peter Hall, David Littlemore und Lionel Todd übernahmen den Weiterbau. Sie fanden in der Frage der Saalkapazität keine Lösung, sondern einigten sich auf einen »faulen« Kompromiß: In Zukunft sollten in dem Gebäude keine Opern aufgeführt werden, sondern nur Konzerte stattfinden. Wenn man die Bühne verkleinerte, ließ sich der neu entstandene freie Raum mit Stühlen auffüllen. Diese Variante machte Utzons Lösung für den Bühnenturm zunichte, so daß seine meisterliche Konstruktion nicht nur kompliziert und teuer, sondern auch noch sinnlos war. Das Sydney Opera House verwandelte sich in die Sydney Concert Hall. Dennoch machte Utzons Entwurf Sydney zu einem festen Punkt auf der Weltkarte der Baukunst. Der Däne gab der Stadt ein neues Gesicht und sorgte dafür, daß das in der Moderne häufig vernachlässigte Dach neue Formen und Inhalte erhielt. Überall dort, wo sich Utzon noch selbst mit dem Bauwerk beschäftigen konnte, fällt die Verwandtschaft seiner Arbeiten zu den Werken Aaltos auf – die gleichen organischen, fließenden Formen und rhythmischen vertikalen Elemente. Leider hat Utzon sein Bauwerk nicht vollenden können, und es bleibt die Frage, wie die Säle sonst ausgesehen hätten. Glücklicherweise lieferten seine Nachfolger gute Arbeit. Ihre Beiträge zeigen Einflüsse großer Vertreter der »ersten« und »zweiten Generation« der Moderne: Hans Poelzig und Hans Scharoun.

50 Mio. australische Dollar

Ursprünglich hatte Cahill gehofft, mit dem Bau der Oper in Sydney Stimmen für die Labour-Party zu gewinnen. Aber genau das Gegenteil war der Fall: Seine Partei verlor die Wahlen 1965. Die neue Regiering sah sich durch den Bau der Oper vor große Probleme gestellt. Vorsorglich stellte die Administration Utzon einige Beamte zur Seite und beauftragte sie mit der Kontrolle über die Ausführung der Bauarbeiten. Dieses offene Mißtrauen war für den Dänen Anlaß, seinen Rücktritt anzubieten. Zwar wurde dieses – etwas voreilige – Angebot sofort akzeptiert, aber auch ohne ihn waren die offenen Fragen noch lange nicht gelöst. Erst sieben Jahre nach Utzons Demission konnte die Oper feierlich eröffnet werden. Der Bau hatte insgesamt 17 Jahre gedauert, und das Gebäude hatte mehr als das Siebenfache der ursprünglich veranschlagten Summe verschlungen.

L'Opéra de Sydney

A l'inauguration de l'opéra de Sydney en 1973, l'entière population de l'Australie et un architecte danois respirèrent. La construction du chef-d'œuvre de Jorn Utzon qui avait duré beaucoup plus longtemps que l'on ne pensait, avait nourri les cauchemars de plusieurs gouvernements successifs et son coût avait allègrement grimpé pour atteindre presque cinquante millions de dollars australiens. Après une période marquée par d'incessantes controverses, Utzon avait démissionné et s'en était retourné au Danemark avant la fin des travaux. Il fallut attendre plusieurs années avant que la qualité de son projet ne soit enfin reconnue.

Un don

L'initiative de l'opéra de Sydney est due à Eugene Goossens, le directeur du conservatoire de musique et à J.J. Cahill, alors Premier ministre des Nouvelles-Galles-du-Sud, qui espéraient ainsi attirer de nouveaux électeurs au parti travailliste. Un site fut choisi dès 1954, Bennelong Point, une langue de terre s'avançant dans la baie de Port Jackson et deux ans plus tard, un concours international fut lancé. L'édifice prévu devait pouvoir accueillir aussi bien un opéra que d'autres types de spectacles et manifestations. La grande salle devait avoir une capacité de 3 500 places, la petite de 1 200. Cette multiplicité de fonctions s'accompagnait évidemment d'équipements comme un restaurant, un café, etc.

Le jury fut chargé de choisir parmi 233 projets présentés, selon le règlement, sous forme de dessins au trait. Le juré le plus célèbre était Eero Saarinen qui, à l'époque, dirigeait avec son père, Eliel, un cabinet prospère aux Etats-Unis. On raconte que l'un des projets rejetés dont l'audace structurelle coïncidait avec sa propre approche architecturale du moment avait attiré son intention. Le remettant au jury, il aurait déclaré: «*Messieurs, voici le gagnant*». C'était la proposition de l'architecte danois Jørn Utzon.

Un moderniste de la troisième génération

Diplômé de l'Académie Royale des Arts de Copenhague, Utzon, né dans cette ville en 1913, avait été l'élève de certains des plus grands architectes de ce siècle. Il avait travaillé pour Alvar Aalto en 1946 et pour Frank Lloyd Wright en 1949, qui tous deux exercèrent une profonde influence sur lui. Il voyagea en Afrique et en Europe où il rencontra Le Corbusier et, pendant un périple en Amérique Centrale, s'intéressa de très près aux arts mayas et aztèques.

Le style de Utzon évolua pendant les années 50 lorsque le Modernisme d'avant-guerre commença à favoriser une approche plus poétique. Le chemin avait été tracé par le maître lui-même, Le Corbusier, qui avait dessiné la chapelle de Ronchamp en 1952. Une seconde génération de modernistes apparut alors en pleine lumière avec Louis Kahn et Hans Scharoun dont la Philharmonie de Berlin (1956) annonçait une révolution dans la conception des salles de concert. Utzon, membre de la troisième génération, allait plus tard bénéficier de ces avancées.

Avant le concours de Sydney, il avait surtout conçu des immeubles de logement, ses projets consistant essentiellement en alignements de rangées de logements individuels. Ses travaux étaient nettement influencés par ceux de Mies van der Rohe et Alvar Aalto. Il se servait des mêmes matériaux et appliquait également le concept d'organicité. Il concevait l'architecture comme une entité autonome et non seulement comme le produit d'une recherche sur la planche à dessin. L'existence humaine et l'architecture répondaient aux mêmes lois physiques. L'opéra de Sydney reflétait sa conception selon laquelle une structure doit être une entité organique, mais sa construction souligna cruellement que l'approche organique conduit souvent à des problèmes structurels insolubles.

Des dessins surprenants

Utzon ne fut pas le seul architecte à soumettre un projet étonnant. L'opéra de Laurence Prynn était resserré autour d'un énorme cylindre coupé en deux qui servait de tour des cintres aux deux salles et était soutenu par une arcature. Prynn reçut une mention honorable pour son projet qu'il avait dessiné au milieu d'un paysage organique fantastique. Une équipe américaine, animée par Joseph Marzella, proposa elle aussi un projet cylindrique avec un plan de masse en spirale qui lui rapporta le second prix. Le troisième alla à l'équipe de Paul Boissevain et Barbara Joan Osmond. Leurs plans étaient beaucoup moins spectaculaires: deux bâtiments séparés abritaient les deux salles montées sur plate-forme. Terence Bliss et Michael le Pelley soumirent également un projet en deux parties.

D'autres architectes appliquèrent une variante plus stricte du style moderniste. Hugh D. Krall, par exemple, limita son dessin à un bloc de forme massive. Derek A. Cobb et Wilhelm Holzbauer essayèrent de marier les variantes poétique et dogmatique du Modernisme en installant un curieux toit en forme de coquille au-dessus de leur parallélépipède. Robert A. Dunster et Peter S. Straughton utilisèrent eux aussi une forme de «boîte» mais en laissant des façades ouvertes qui laissaient entrevoir les salles.

Les éclats d'une même sphère imaginaire

Comme dans le cas du projet Cobb et Holzbauer, Utzon avait couronné son opéra d'une structure en forme de coquilles très caractéristiques mais qui s'unissaient organiquement à l'infrastructure et masquaient les tours des cintres. Réunies, elles auraient pu former une sphère, et elles faisaient écho au jeu des voiles des centaines de yachts qui sillonnent la baie de Sydney ou pouvaient également évoquer une sculpture ou une église gothique. Elles devaient être recouvertes de tuiles vernissées. Pour Utzon, aucun édifice sur ce site ne pouvait se contenter d'un simple toit plat et il conçut le sien comme une cinquième façade tout aussi importante que les quatre autres. Le jury trouva cette solution plus esthétique que les approches cubistes des autres participants.

Leur construction souleva un problème majeur. L'architecte n'avait pas encore trouvé de solution satisfaisante lorsqu'il livra son «Livre rouge» qui contenait ses premiers plans. Le bureau d'ingénierie d'Ove Arup fut tout aussi incapable de trouver une issue. Finalement, Utzon proposa d'utiliser des éléments préfabriqués formant une sphère imaginaire, solution décrite dans son «Livre jaune».

En attendant, la construction était déjà très avancée, et même pressée par le père spirituel du projet, Cahill, ce qui accrut la tension entre l'architecte et l'administration. Utzon n'eut pas davantage de temps pour réfléchir à d'autres problèmes, dont celui de la capacité des salles pour laquelle il ne trouva d'ailleurs jamais de solution. La pression politique devenant insupportable, il démissionna en 1966, laissant le projet aux mains des Australiens Peter Hall, David Littlemore et Lionel Todd. Leur façon de résoudre le problème de capacité fut un triste compromis. Ils décidèrent que l'édifice ne serait plus un opéra mais simplement une salle de concerts ce qui permettait de réduire la taille de la scène et donc d'ajouter des rangées de sièges. Ce compromis rendait inutile la coûteuse solution de la dissimulation des cintres dans les coques et le Sydney Opera House devint le Sydney Concert Hall. Néanmoins, Utzon avait apporté une notoriété et un nouveau visage à la ville. Il avait imaginé un toit qui offrait à la fois une forme et une fonction, fait souvent négligé par les Modernistes.

Bien que le chef-d'œuvre d'Utzon ait été achevé par d'autres, il présente une évidente affinité avec le travail d'Aalto: mêmes formes organiques, fluides et mêmes éléments rythmiques verticaux. Il est dommage que l'architecte n'ait pu surveiller la finalisation de son projet. La réalisation en béton des salles, par exemple, est un peu décevante même si l'on ne peut accuser ses successeurs de manque de soin. Leurs efforts semblent avoir été guidés par les grands maîtres de la première et de la seconde génération modernistes tels Poelzig et Scharoun.

50 millions de dollars

Les espoirs de Calhill de voir l'opéra apporter la prospérité à sa ville et la victoire des Travaillistes ne furent jamais réalisés. Au contraire, le parti travailliste perdit les élections de 1965 et abandonna l'opéra à ses vainqueurs. De multiples fonctionnaires avaient été chargés de superviser le projet et d'en assurer la réalisation, situation vécue par Utzon comme une forme subtile de contrôle et la preuve que les autorités n'avaient guère confiance en ses capacités d'où sa démission rageuse immédiatement acceptée. Son départ résolut peu de problèmes et au moment où l'opéra fut inauguré, six ans après le départ de son architecte, pas moins de seize années s'étaient écoulées depuis la pose de la première pierre. Le coût de construction, de son côté, avait été multiplié par sept...

1 *La structure du terminal TWA de l'Aéroport Kennedy (New York) que construisit Saarinen de 1956 à 1962 est en effet similaire à celle de l'opéra de Sydney.*

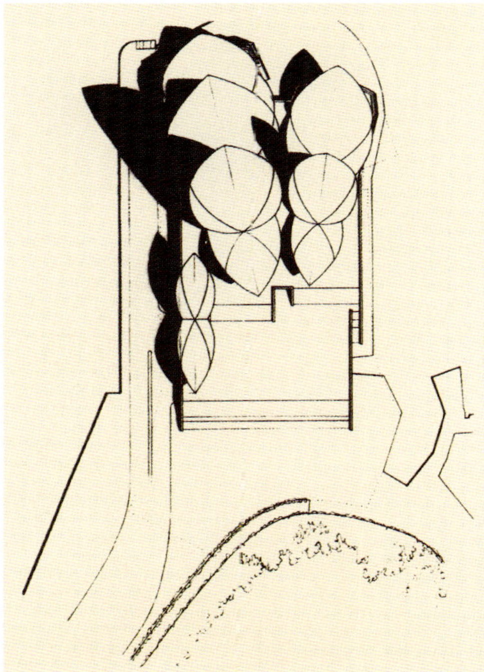

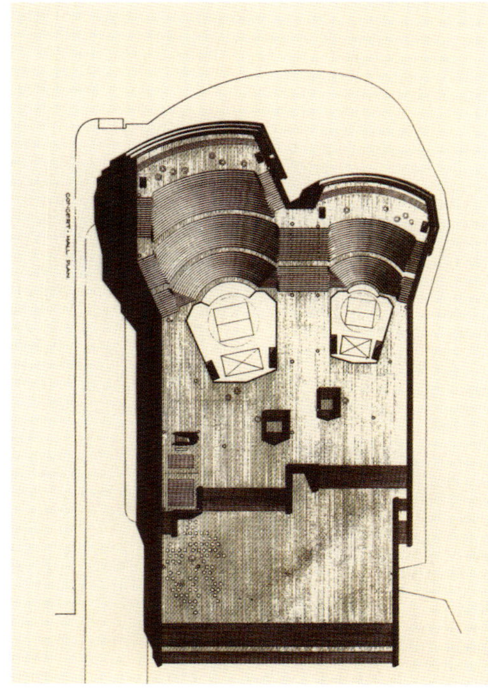

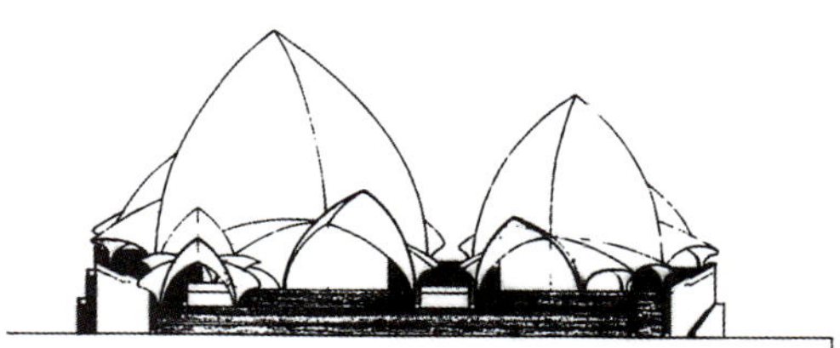

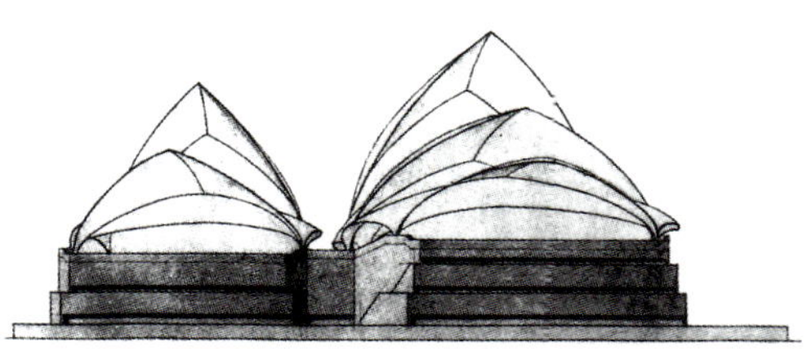

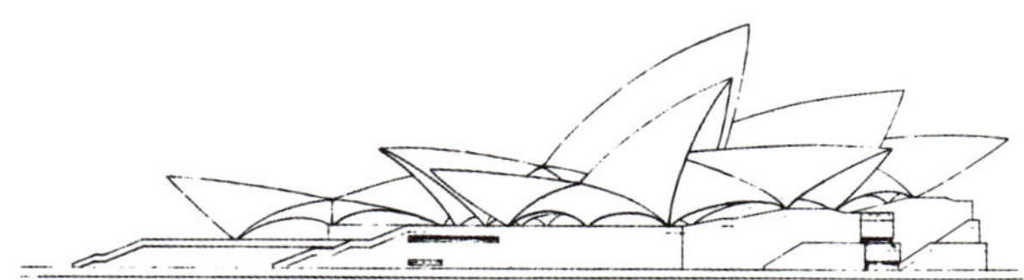

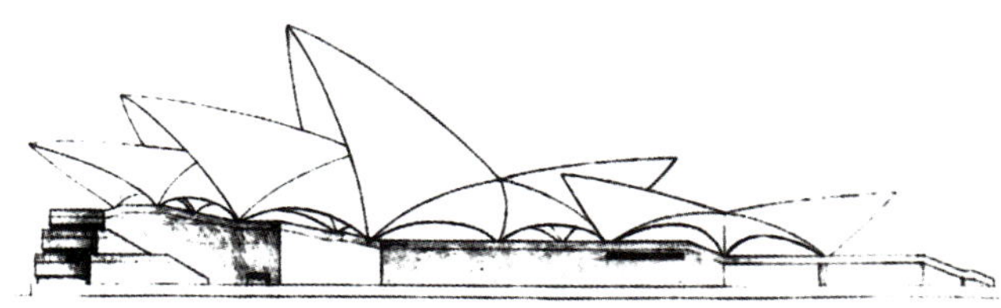

Jørn Utzon drawing from "Red Book" (1958), site plan

Jørn Utzon drawing from "Red Book" (1958), plan of the Concert Hall Level

Jørn Utzon drawing from "Red Book" (1958), north elevation

Jørn Utzon drawing from "Red Book" (1958), south elevation

Jørn Utzon drawing from "Red Book" (1958), east elevation

Jørn Utzon drawing from "Red Book" (1958), west elevation

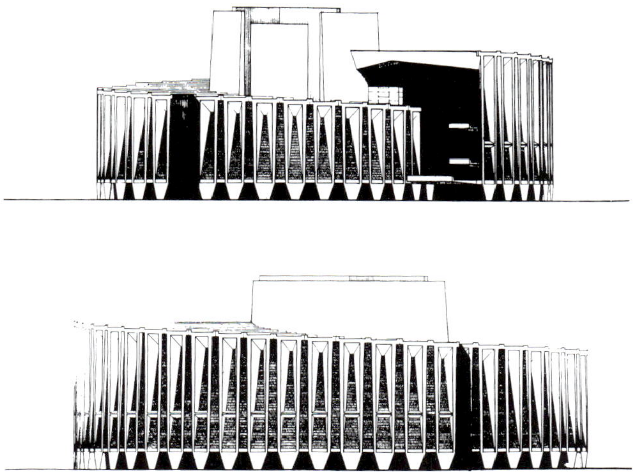

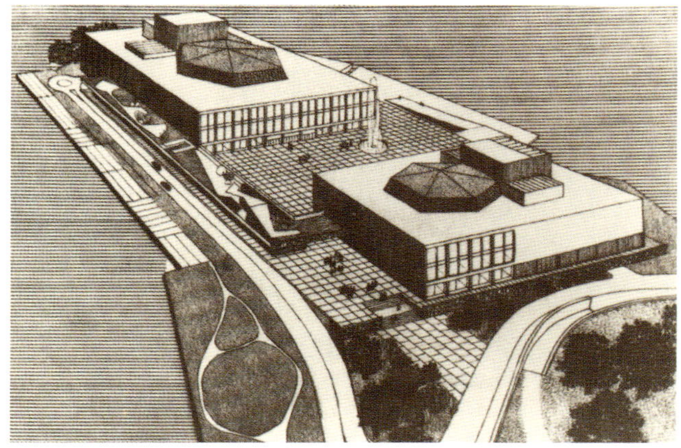

Joseph Marzella, Leon Loschetter, W.W. Cunningham, Walter Weissman, Melvin Brecher, Robert Geddes & George Qualls competition design, 1956, exterior view from south, second prize

Paul Boissevain & Barbara Joan Osmond competition design, 1956, bird's eye view, third prize

Paul Boissevain & Barbara Joan Osmond competition design, 1956, plan of auditorium level, third prize

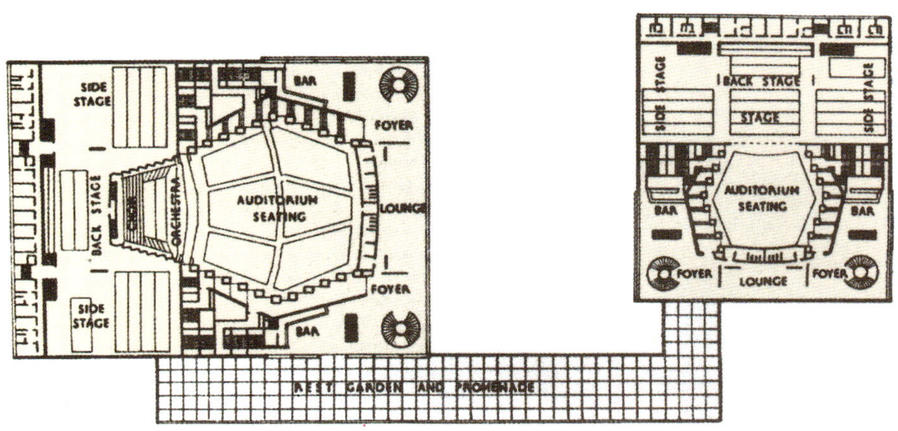

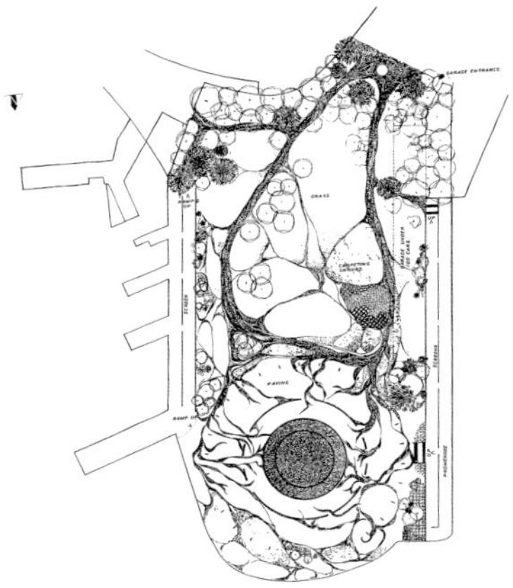

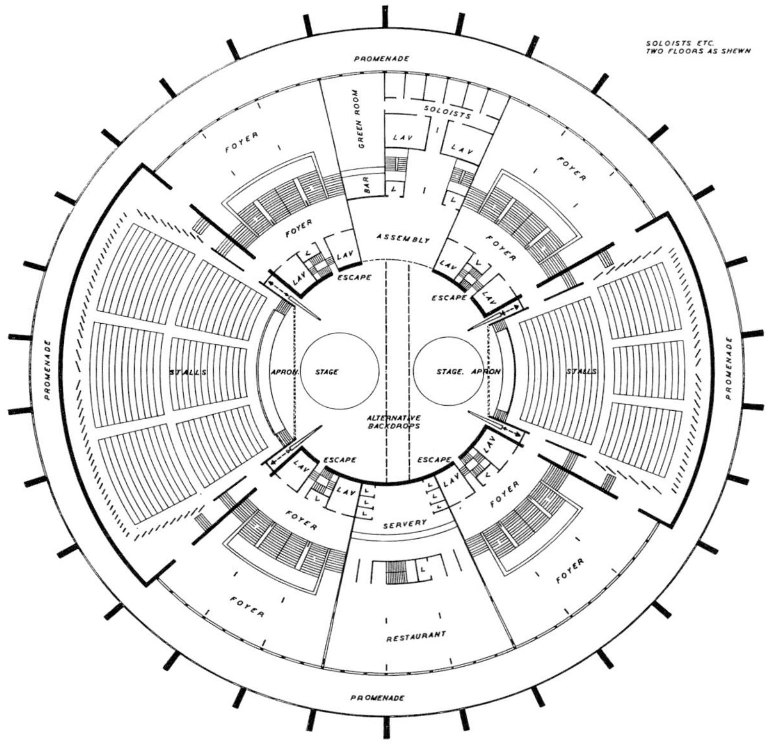

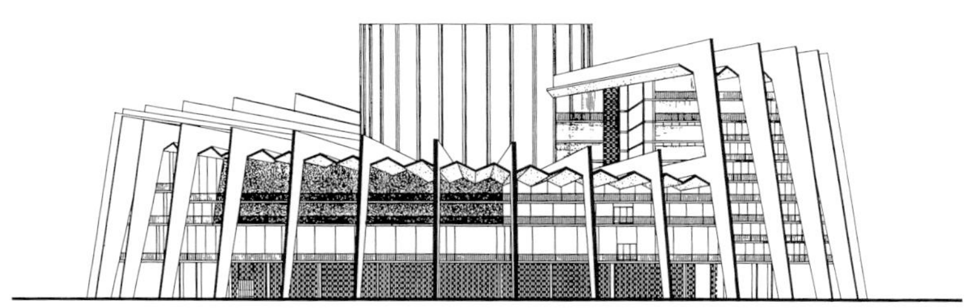

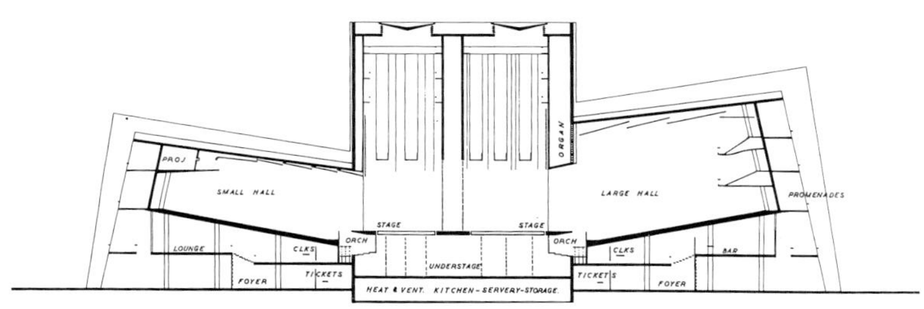

Laurence Prynn competition design, 1956, site plan, honourable mention

Laurence Prynn competition design, 1956, second floor plan, honourable mention

Laurence Prynn competition design, 1956, west elevation, honourable mention

Laurence Prynn competition design, 1956, north-south section, honourable mention

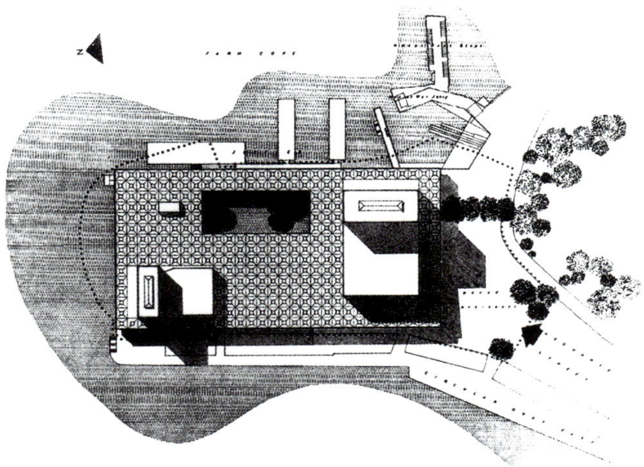

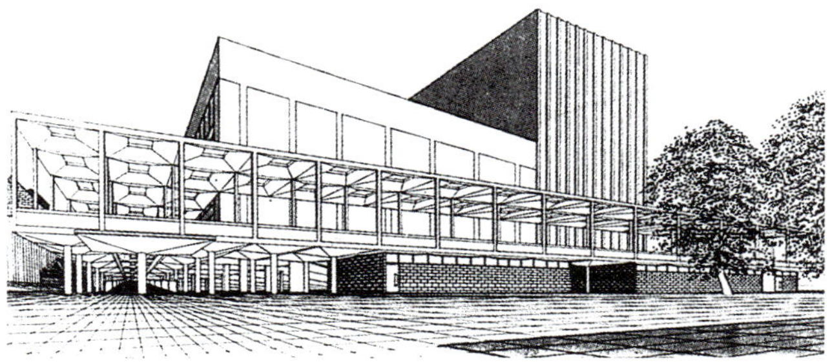

Hugh D. Krall competition design, 1956, exterior view from south, honourable mention

Hugh D. Krall competition design, 1956, site plan, honourable mention

Hugh D. Krall competition design, 1956, from top: north-south section through large hall, north-south section through small hall, east-west section through small hall, east-west section through large hall, honourable mention

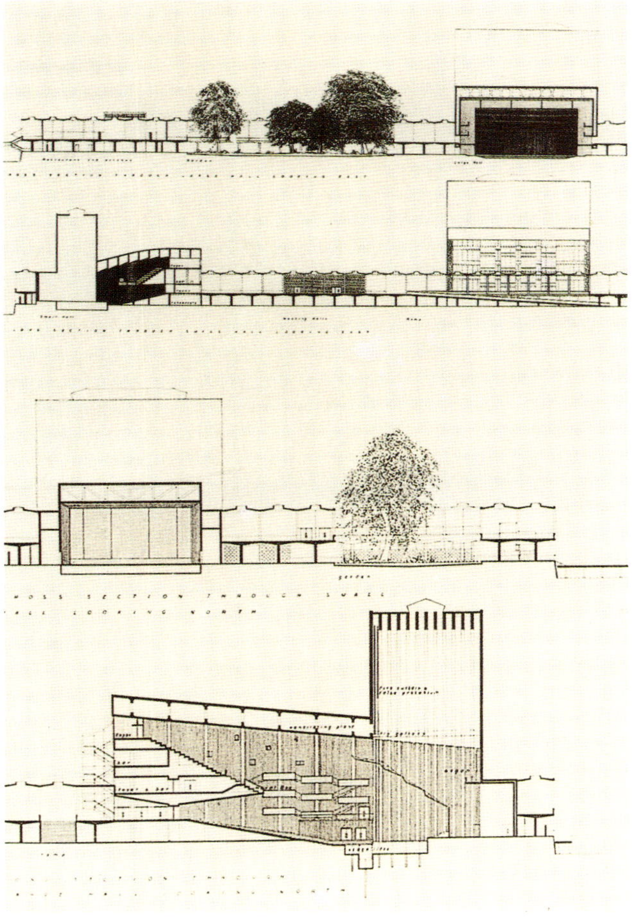

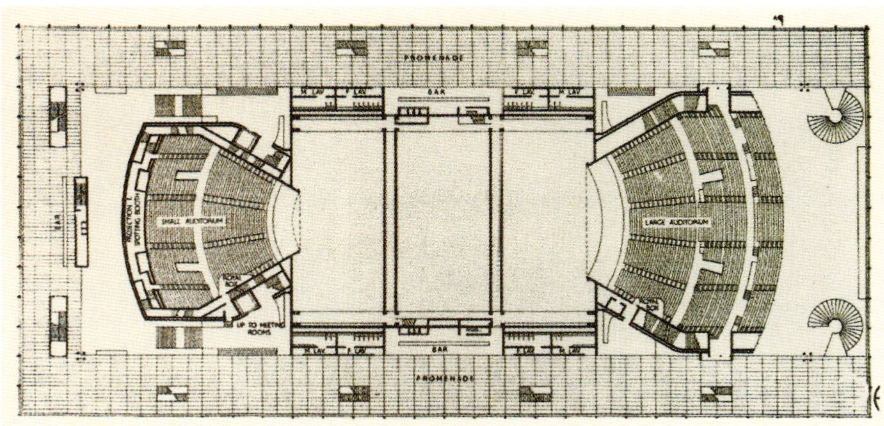

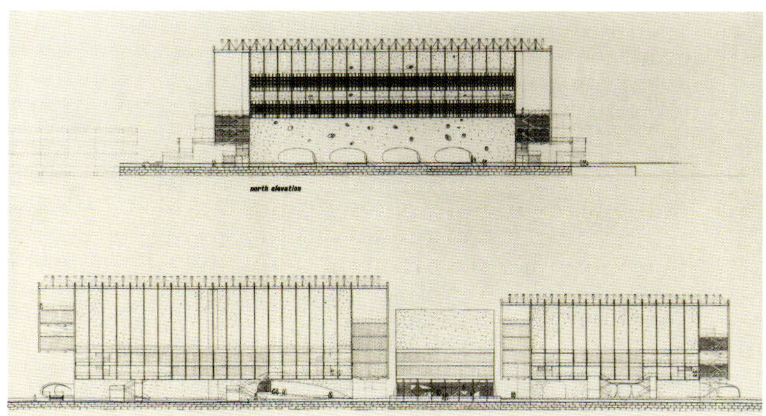

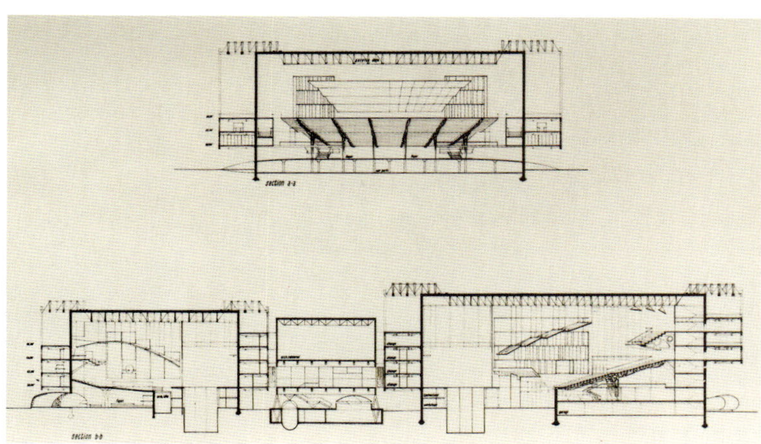

Robert A. Dunster & Peter S. Straughton competition design, 1956, exterior view from south, honourable mention

Robert A. Dunster & Peter S. Straughton competition design, 1956, plan of auditorium level, honourable mention

Terence Bliss & Michael Le Pelley competition design, 1956, above: north elevation, below: west elevation, honourable mention

Terence Bliss & Michael Le Pelley competition design, 1956, above: perspective section of large hall, below: north-south section, honourable mention

Derek A. Cobb & Wilhelm Holzbauer
competition design, 1956, exterior view from north-west, honourable mention

Project

Pilot plan for the new federal capital of Brazil

Site

Federal District of Brasilia, Goias State

Dates

Competition announced 19 July 1956 *Closing date* 11 March 1957 *Result announced* 16 March 1957

Number of entries

26

Jury

Israel Pinheiro da Silva (chairman without a vote, director Novacap), Oscar Niemeyer (Novacap), Stamo Papadaki (United States, Novacap), Paulo Antunes Ribeiro (Brazilian Institute of Architects), Horta Barbosa (Society of Engineers), André Sive (Paris, urban planner), William Holford (London, urban planner)

Result

First prize Lúcio Costa *Second prize* Ney Fontes Gonçalves, Baruch Milman & João Henrique Rocha *Joint third prize* Rino Levi; MMM Roberto *Fifth prize* Henrique Ephin Mindlin & Giancarlo Palanti; Carlos Cascaldi, Joan Villanova Artigas & Mario Wagner Vieira da Cunha & Paulo de Camargo e Almeida; Construtécnica S.A. Comercial en Construtora (headed by Milton Ghiraldini)

Commissioned by

Companhia Urbanizadora da Nova Capital do Brasil (Novacap)

Construction

October 1956 to 21 April 1960 and thereafter

Architects

Lúcio Costa (*1902, urban planning design), Oscar Niemeyer (*1907, architectural design), Israel Pinheiro da Silva (engineering)

Brasilia Urbanisation Plan, 1956–1957

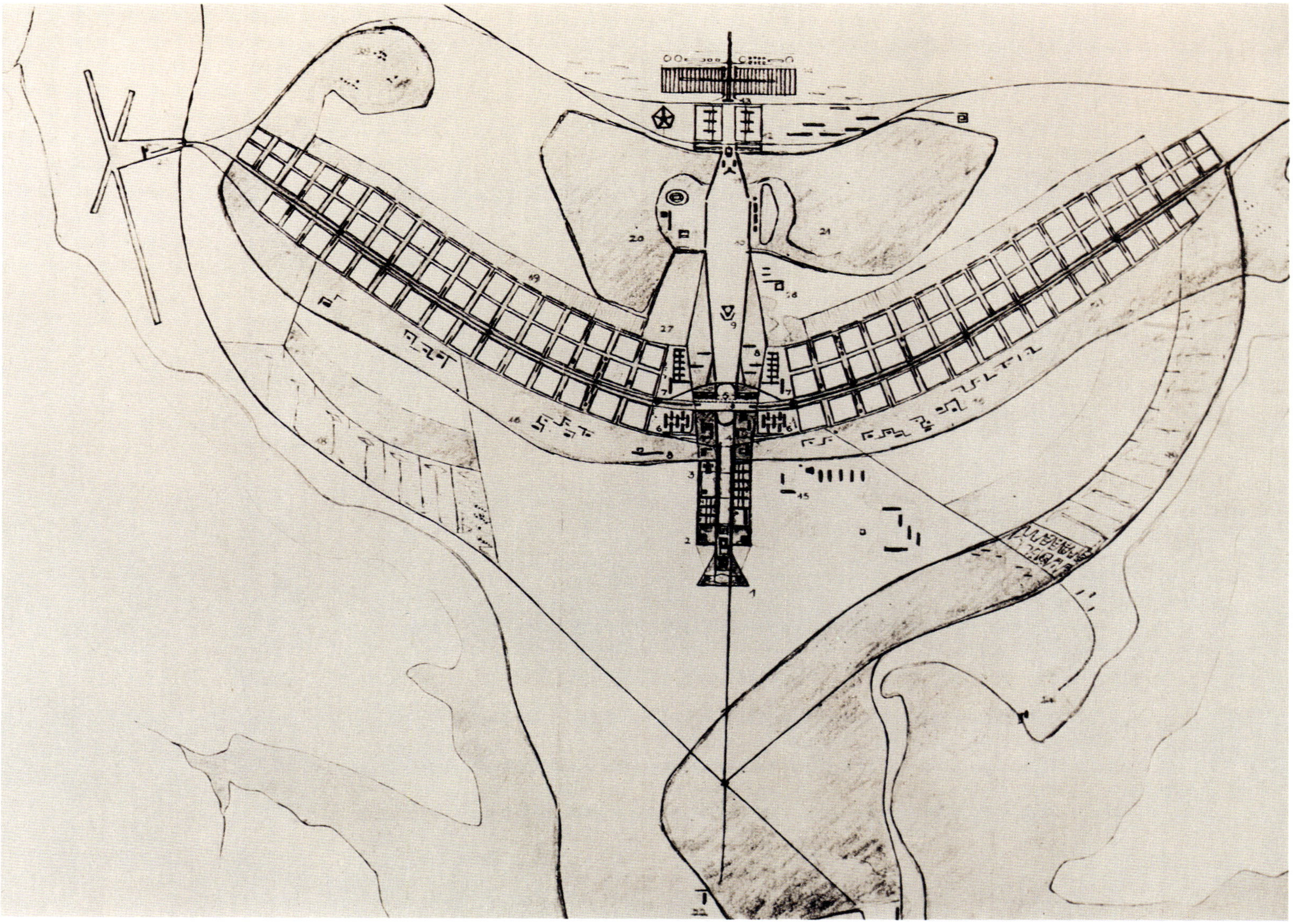

Lúcio Costa competition design, 1957, pilot plan, first prize

Brasilia Urbanisation Plan

If prizes were to be awarded for delays and postponements, then the project to build a new federal capital in the Brazilian interior would win hands down. The plan was first proposed in 1789 by the radical party "Inconfidentes Mineros", who suggested that the capital be moved to the federal district where the party had its headquarters: Minais Gerais. However, it was to be one hundred and seventy years before the capital was eventually relocated.

A long run-up

Brazil has always been characterised by the stark contrast between its prosperous coastal regions and poverty-stricken interior. The reasons for this may be traced back to the country's colonial past, when both Portuguese and Dutch colonial forces established their colonies along the coast, and rarely ventured into the densely-wooded interior. The coastal region, with its modern cities, is still oriented towards Europe, whereas the interior is poor and sparsely populated. Over the centuries, the country had always been aware that its massive resources were being only partially exploited and that a forceful impulse was required to correct this imbalance. The new capital Brasilia, which was to arise in the federal state of Goias, was to provide this impulse.
Following a lengthy period during which many plans were produced and discarded, the matter suddenly gained momentum in 1937 when the plan to relocate the federal capital to a central point was added to the national constitution. The president was called upon to form a commission which would designate a suitable site. However, this only came to pass when the ruling dictator, Getulio Vargas, was overthrown. In 1946 his successor, Dutro, appointed a commission which found a suitable site the following year, although another six years were to pass before the commission's decision was ratified by parliament. During that same year (1953) an American company, Donald J. Belcher & Associates, was commissioned to survey and specify the site.
By that time the former dictator Vargas had returned to power; this time he had been legally elected. However, his term of office was short-lived, his regime was toppled and he committed suicide. Subsequently Juscelino Kubitschek de Oliveira became president (1955) and he personally took charge of the new capital during his term of office. Before the year's end, funds were made available to purchase the necessary property, the first machines arrived on site and a planning commission was appointed. A national competition, organised by the Companhia Urbanizadora da Nova Capital do Brasil (Novacap), was announced on 19 July 1956.

More than enough room

The conditions listed in the competition programme were not very complicated. There was more than enough room to build the city which, in a short time, was to increase its population from 5000 to 500 000. The participants' designs had to include proposals for urban infrastructure, division into districts and municipal services such as

Lúcio Costa sketch for Brasilia

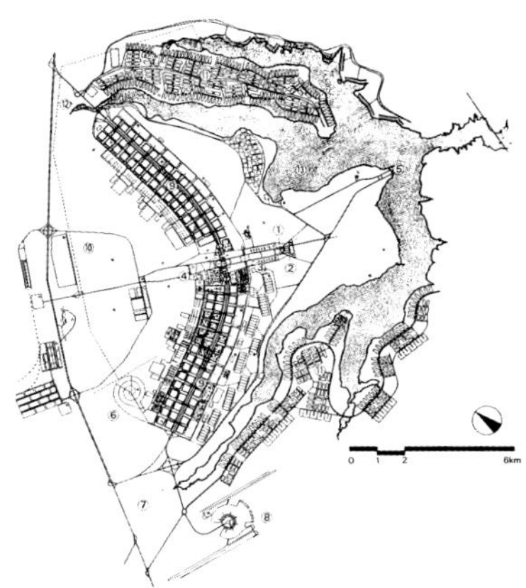

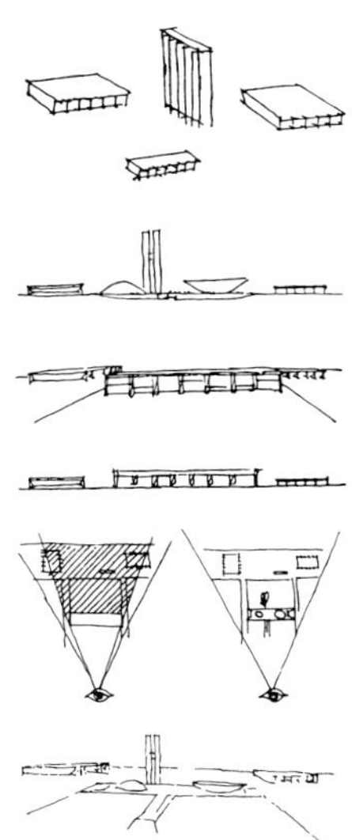

electricity, water and telephone lines. Although the opportunity to design an entirely new city was the chance of a lifetime, only 26 designs were submitted. This was probably due to the fact that eight months was not a long enough period in which to design an entire city, though another contributing factor may have been that the competition was restricted to national participants. Many of the designs were based on the pre-war Modernist principles developed during CIAM congresses. Le Corbusier's urban planning approach was evidently particularly popular. The approach taken by the Brazilian architects and urban planners followed the international trend of the day, and their designs compare favourably to Kenzo Tange's design for the urban expansion project in Tokyo.

The influence of Modernism

Housing, offices and traffic were all kept strictly separate in the Modernist-oriented designs. There were lush, green areas between the housing blocks, allowing sufficient daylight to enter the dwellings. These basic urban planning principles, which had been drafted at the 1933 CIAM congress in Athens, were particularly evident in the design submitted by Ney Fontes Gonçalves, Baruch Milman and João Henrique Rocha, which won second prize. They had divided Brasilia into three districts: a housing district for government officials and civil servants, and separate districts for trade and industry. Three different types of dwellings were spread over these three districts: two kinds of high-rise buildings and single-family dwellings. Their design, however, was rather monotonous and seemed to widen the rift between the social classes: the civil servants' dwellings were to be splendidly situated on the banks of a lake, whereas the workers would be packed together in giant housing blocks. Naturally, this plan was not likely to produce an ideal capital for the new Brazil, which was to be prosperous and free of corruption.

Rino Levi's design was more democratic in that all the dwellings had a view of the lake. At first glance, Levi's plan also seems to have been derived from the models developed during the 1930s, though on closer inspection one sees that the housing blocks are in fact urban sub-centres which can accommodate up to sixteen thousand people. Each block has eight interconnected skyscrapers, which are 300 metres high and have four sets of twenty floors. Levi's plan has six clusters of three of these mega-structures; each cluster having its own services centre, and the six clusters are grouped around the government centre.

The design submitted by Henrique Ephin Mindlin and Giancarlo Palanti features a freer application of Le Corbusier's principles. Although the smaller units have a characteristic layout, the plan as a whole, with its flowing shapes, is more dynamic than many of the other entries.

The field also included participants whose designs were not quite so clearly based on Modernist principles. The design submitted by the brothers Marcelo, Milton and Mauricio Roberto, for example, featured web-like structures reminiscent of the designs submitted for the

Brasilia Shopping Centre seen from the TV tower

Oscar Niemeyer

Oscar Niemeyer Cathedral in Brasilia

Canberra urban development project[1]. There was, however, one notable difference between the Robertos' design and designs such as that submitted by W. Scott Griffiths for Canberra, in that the Brazilian plan was based on equal, non-hierarchical, largely independent urban hubs, whereas the elements of Griffiths' design had been grouped around the city's most important buildings.

Cross, crucifix, kite

In the end, the jury discarded all of the above plans in favour of that submitted by the grand old man of Brazilian Modernism, Lúcio Costa, who based his design on a cross, which later evolved into a crucifix or, less reverently, a kite. As in Mindlin and Palanti's design, one of the axes was curved due to the geographic features of the site. Costa said that the cross shape was a reference to the age-old symbol used to mark appropriated land, but the inherently religious symbolism was of course fortuitous, certainly in a country such as Brazil.

The jury had been particularly impressed by the monumentality of Costa's city. The two arms of the cross denote the two main traffic arteries which link the housing and office districts to one another, while the dwellings are situated in high-rise blocks, surrounded by expansive green areas. Costa had planned three matching buildings for the three main authorities: the supreme court, the presidential palace and the parliament stood side by side in his design. The ministries

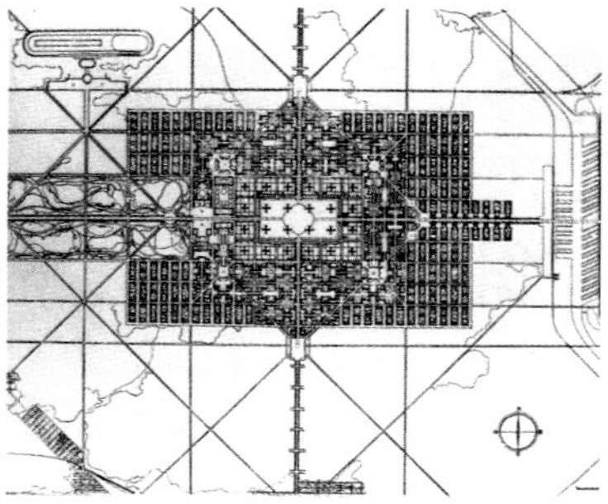

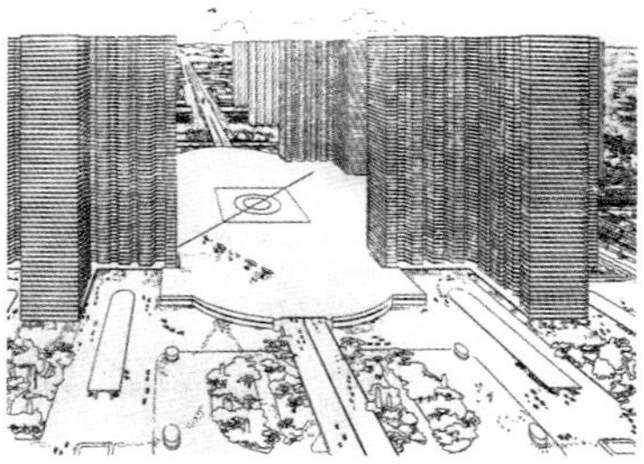

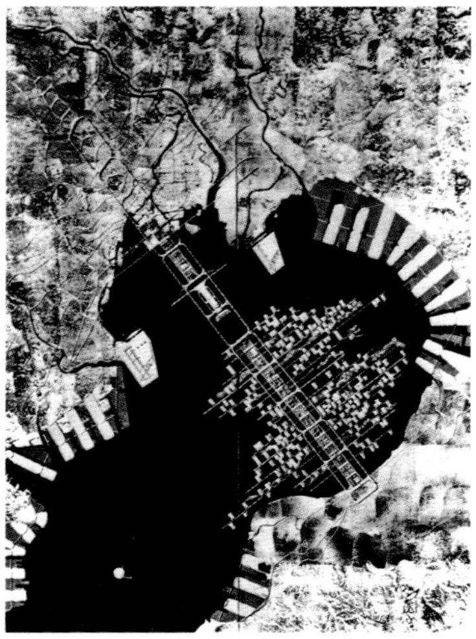

were situated along the monumental main axis, which leads to the government square. He used the on-site gradient to emphasise the monumental stature of certain buildings.

UNESCO monument

Kubitschek wanted Costa's design for Brasilia to be executed as soon as possible. Consequently, the city was constructed at a speed which did not allow time for necessary alterations and, naturally, this had a detrimental effect on the project. The problems which arose were therefore dealt with at a later stage, by which time only partial solutions could be found. Nevertheless, Kubitschek attained his objective: the project was completed before his term of office ended. On 21 April 1960 Brasilia officially became the capital of Brazil.
Regardless of its shortcomings, Brasilia may unreservedly be termed a monument to Modernist urban planning. It was for this reason that the status of UNESCO World Monument was conferred upon the capital in 1986. This status, unique for such a young city, comes with the proviso that all projected changes in urban design have to be ratified by a special commission. The governor of Goias State has a seat on this commission, together with Lúcio Costa and the former jury member, Oscar Niemeyer.

As chief architect, Oscar Niemeyer played an important part in the construction of Brasilia. His designs for the cathedral, the presidential palace and the congress building have won him worldwide acclaim. His concrete fantasies were perfectly suited to Brasilia's monumental character and its wide, open spaces. Both Niemeyer and Costa were given a free hand, although this brought with it certain disadvantages. From the start Brasilia had been a pretty picture, rather than an interdisciplinary product contrived by a co-operative of urban planners, economists and other experts. This artistic freedom caused a city to materialise along the lines of the principles propounded by European Modernists since CIAM was established in 1928 and, more specifically, since the Athens Charter was drafted; it is nevertheless debatable whether the inhabitants of Brasilia have benefited from this architectural status, considering the number of people who escape the city by flying to Rio de Janeiro or São Paulo for the weekend.

Le Corbusier urban plan for the Ville Couteau poraire, site plan

Le Corbusier urban plan for the Ville Couteau poraire, bird's-eye view, 1921–1922

Kenzo Tange plan for Tokyo, toward a structural organization, 1959–1960

1 *See chapter on the Canberra project*

Städtebauplan für Brasilia

Es gibt kaum ein Architekturprojekt, dessen Durchführung so lange auf sich warten ließ wie der Bau der neuen Hauptstadt im Landesinneren Brasiliens. Die ersten Forderungen nach einer solchen Stadt wurden 1789 geäußert: Damals schlug die radikale Partei »Inconfidentes Mineros« vor, die Hauptstadt in den Bundesstaat zu verlegen, in dem sie selbst die meisten Anhänger hatte: Minais Gerais. Aber es sollten noch 170 Jahre vergehen, bis tatsächlich eine neue brasilianische Metropole entstand.

Ein langer Anlauf

Brasilien ist von jeher gekennzeichnet durch große Gegensätze zwischen den wohlhabenden Küstengebieten und dem armen Binnenland. Die portugiesischen – und kurzfristig die niederländischen – Kolonialisten erbauten ihre Niederlassungen an der Küste und wagten sich nur selten in das dichtbewaldete Landesinnere. Auch heute noch sind die Küstenregionen europäisch orientiert. Moderne Metropolen bestimmen dort das Bild, während das Binnenland arm und spärlich bevölkert ist. Durch die Jahrhunderte hindurch wurde nur ein geringer Teil des flächenmäßig großen Landes »benutzt«. Um dieses Ungleichgewicht auszugleichen, war ein starker Impuls nötig: Diesen sollte die neue Hauptstadt Brasilia im Bundesstaat Gôias geben.
Nach vielen theoretischen Überlegungen wurde das Vorhaben erstmals 1937 vorangetrieben, als ein Passus in die Verfassung kam, der die Verlegung der brasilianischen Hauptstadt auf einen zentralen Punkt im Landesinneren vorsah. Der Präsident erhielt den Auftrag, eine Kommission ins Leben zu rufen, die ein geeignetes Baugelände finden sollte. Diktator Getúlio Vargas lehnte dieses Ansinnen ab, so daß erst sein Nachfolger Präsident Dutro 1946 ein entsprechendes Gremium benannte: Bereits ein Jahr später war ein passendes Gelände gefunden. Allerdings dauerte es noch bis 1953, bevor das brasilianische Parlament den Kommissionsvorschlag annahm und eine amerikanische Firma (Donald J. Belcher & Ass.) mit der Vermessung des Bauplatzes begann. Schließlich stellte 1955 Präsident Juscelino Kubitschek de Oliveira die zum Ankauf der Grundstücke benötigten Geldmittel zur Verfügung, beorderte die ersten Baumaschinen auf das Gelände und berief eine Planungskommission ein. Am 19. Juli 1956 wurde ein nationaler Architekturwettbewerb ausgeschrieben.

Platz genug

Brasília – so der Name der neuen Hauptstadt – sollte in kürzester Zeit von 5000 vorläufigen Einwohnern auf 500 000 Einwohner anwachsen. Dementsprechend mußten die Entwürfe geeignete Lösungen für die städtische Infrastruktur, eine Einteilung der Stadt in Sektoren und Vorschläge für die Versorgung mit Strom, Wasser und Telefon bieten. Die Planung einer völlig neuen Stadt bot den Architekten eine einmalige Gelegenheit; dennoch gab es nur 26 Einsendungen, da der vorgegebene Zeitraum von acht Monaten für den Entwurf einer vollständigen Stadt wahrscheinlich zu knapp bemessen war. Zudem handelte es sich um eine rein nationale Ausschreibung. Viele der eingesandten Entwürfe waren beeinflußt von den CIAM-Kongressen der Vorkriegszeit und den stadtplanerischen Ideen eines Le Corbusier.

Der Einfluß der Moderne

Die durch den Einfluß der Moderne gekennzeichneten Entwürfe sahen eine klare Trennung der Wohn-, Arbeits- und Verkehrsbereiche vor, mit viel Licht und Grün zwischen den Wohntürmen. Diese stadtplanerischen Prinzipien entsprachen den Forderungen, die der Kongreß der CIAM 1933 aufgestellt hatte. Insbesondere die Gewinner des zweiten Preises (Ney Fontes Gonçalves, Baruch Milman und João Henrique Rocha) folgten diesen Anforderungen in ihrem Entwurf weitestgehend. Ihr Konzept sah eine Dreiteilung der Stadt vor: ein Sektor für die Verwaltung und die Wohnungen der Beamten, ein Sektor für den Handel und ein Bereich für die Industrie. Über diese drei Zonen verteilten sich drei Wohnungstypen: Zwei Arten von Hochbauten sowie Einfamilienhäuser. Der Gesamtentwurf wirkt relativ eintönig und ließ von vornherein soziale Unterschiede deutlich werden. Während die Beamtenwohnungen in angenehmer Lage direkt am See geplant waren, sollten die Arbeiter in langweiligen Wohnsilos eng zusammenleben. Diese Konzeption entsprach in keinster Weise dem Ideal einer neuen Stadt, die zu einem zukünftigen, wohlhabenden und korruptionsfreien brasilianischen Staat passen sollte.
Etwas »demokratischer« fiel der Entwurf von Rino Levi aus, bei dem alle Wohnungen Ausblick auf den See hatten. Bei flüchtigem Hinsehen wirkte auch Levis Plan wie eine Variation der Modelle, die seit den 30er Jahren immer populärer wurden. Aber der Schein trog: Bei Levis Appartementhäusern handelte es sich um eigene Stadtteilzentren, die je 16 000 Bewohnern Platz boten. Pro Block wurden acht Wolkenkratzer mit je vier mal zwanzig Etagen und einer Höhe von 300 Metern aneinander gekoppelt. Insgesamt umfaßte Levis Plan sechs Gruppen von je drei solcher Megastrukturen, wobei jede Gruppe über ein separates Versorgungszentrum verfügen sollte. Diese sechs »Stadtteile« wollte Levi rund um das Regierungsviertel plazieren.
Eine etwas freiere Interpretation der Prinzipien Le Corbusiers bot der Beitrag von Henrique Ephin Mindlin und Giancarlo Palanti. Obwohl die kleineren Wohneinheiten eine durchaus übliche Einteilung zeigten, wirkte der Entwurf mit seinen leicht gerundeten Formen weniger statisch als viele andere Einsendungen.
Nicht alle Entwürfe waren stark von der Moderne beeinflußt. Beispielsweise erinnerte der Vorschlag der Gruppe MMM Roberto (eine Zusammenarbeit der Gebrüder Marcelo, Milton und Mauricio Roberto) mit seinen spinnwebartigen Kernstrukturen eher an ein Konzept im Stil der Stadtplanung für Canberra. Allerdings bestand ein bedeutender Unterschied zwischen dem Beitrag von MMM Roberto und W. Scott Griffiths Entwurf für Canberra: Während der brasilianische Plan von gleichwertigen, nicht hierarchischen und nahezu autonomen Stadtteilkernen ausging, plazierte Griffith seine Stadtteile rund um die wichtigsten Gebäude der Stadt.

Kreuz, Kruzifix, Flugzeug

Die Jury prämierte den Beitrag des »großen alten Mannes« der brasilianischen Moderne: Lúcio Costa. Sein Konzept sah als Grundform der Stadt ein Kreuz vor. Dieses Kreuz entwickelte sich im Laufe der Planung zu einem Kruzifix oder – etwas weniger ehrerbietig – zu einem Flugzeug. Dabei entstand die gebogene Form der Flügel – die auch im Entwurf von Mindlin und Palanti zu finden waren – als Folge geographischer Voraussetzungen. Costa selbst verglich das Kreuz mit dem uralten Symbol der Inbesitznahme neuen Landes: Wer ein Grundstück mit einem Kreuzzeichen markierte, erhob damit Anspruch auf diesen Boden.
Costas Entwurf beeindruckte die Jury aufgrund seiner Monumentalität. Die Achsen des Kreuzes werden von den wichtigsten Verkehrsadern gebildet, die die Funktionsbereiche Wohnen und Arbeiten miteinander verbinden. Als eigentliche Wohneinheiten dienen Hochbauten, zwischen denen ausgedehnte Grünanlagen liegen. Für die drei Regierungsgewalten schwebten Costa drei gleichwertige Gebäude vor, und er setzte das Oberste Bundesgericht, den Regierungspalast (Palácio do Planalto) und den Nationalkongreß auf dem »Platz der drei Gewalten« direkt nebeneinander. Die Ministerien liegen entlang der monumentalen Hauptachse, die zum Regierungssitz führt.

UNESCO-Weltkulturdenkmal

Da Präsident Kubitschek sein Brasília so schnell wie möglich entstehen sehen wollte, wurde die Stadt nach Costas Plänen in kürzester Zeit aus dem Boden gestampft. Das Tempo der Bauarbeiten war so hoch, daß für Modifizierungen der Pläne keine Zeit mehr blieb. Erst in einem späteren Stadium ging man auf neu entstandene Probleme ein und versuchte, Lösungen zu finden. Aber auch diese Änderungen glückten nur zum Teil. Dennoch erreichte Kubitschek das von ihm selbst gesetzte Ziel: Noch innerhalb seiner Amtszeit wurde Brasília am 21. April 1960 offiziell zur Hauptstadt Brasiliens erklärt. Trotz einiger Mängel kann die Metropole mit Recht als ein Monument des modernen Städtebaus bezeichnet werden. Aus diesem Grund entschloß sich die UNESCO 1986, der Stadt den Status eines Weltkulturdenkmals zu verleihen – eine einzigartige Auszeichnung für eine so junge Stadt. Als Folge dieses Ausnahmestatus' muß heute jede städtebauliche Änderung von einer Sonderkommission genehmigt werden.
Oscar Niemeyer spielte als verantwortlicher Architekt bei der Entstehung Brasílias eine entscheidende Rolle. Seine Entwürfe für die Kathedrale, den Palast des Präsidenten und die Nationalversammlung wurden weltberühmt, denn wie kein anderer verstand er, mit seinen Betonphantasien die Größe und die ausgedehnten Räume der Stadt zu unterstreichen. Ebenso wie Costa besaß Niemeyer völlige Handlungsfreiheit, was immer wieder Anlaß zu Kritik gab. Seit ihrer Gründung war Brasília eher ein schöner Traum als ein interdisziplinäres Produkt von Städteplanern, Volkswirten und anderen Wissenschaftlern. Andererseits konnte nur so im Landesinneren Brasiliens eine Stadt entstehen, wie sie den europäischen Vertretern der Moderne seit der Gründung des CIAM 1928 und seit der Charta von Athen vorgeschwebt hatte. Allerdings scheint dieser Gedanke die Einwohner der Stadt kaum zu beglücken – ein Blick auf die Massenflucht, die jedes Wochenende von Brasília aus in die Küstenstädte Rio de Janeiro und Saô Paulo einsetzt, genügt.

Le plan de Brasilia

Si un prix devait être accordé pour les retards et les annulations sur un même projet, la nouvelle capitale du Brésil l'emporterait haut la main. C'est en effet en 1789 que le parti radical des «Inconfidentes Mineros» proposa le transfert de la capitale dans l'Etat du Minais Gerais où le mouvement avait son siège. Mais il fallut attendre cent soixante dix ans avant que ce projet ne se réalise, dans une autre région.

Un long cheminement

Le Brésil a toujours été marqué par un fort contraste entre la prospérité des régions côtières et la pauvreté de l'intérieur, dont les raisons remontent en partie à son passé colonial. Les Portugais et les Néerlandais avaient établi leurs colonies au bord de la côte sans s'aventurer vers l'intérieur des terres souvent recouvert de très denses forêts. La côte et ses villes modernes regardent encore aujourd'hui vers l'Europe alors que l'intérieur reste pauvre et peu peuplé. Au cours des siècles, le pays a toujours été conscient de la sous-exploitation de ses énormes ressources naturelles et de la nécessité de créer une dynamique pour corriger ce déséquilibre. Brasilia, la nouvelle capitale, créée dans l'état de Goias, avait pour but de provoquer ce choc salutaire.

Après une longue période au cours de laquelle de multiples plans furent proposés et rejetés, le sujet revint brusquement au premier plan de l'actualité en 1937 lorsque le déplacement de la capitale vers l'ouest fut inscrit dans la constitution. Le président devait former une commission pour choisir un site, mais il fallut attendre la chute du dictateur Getulio Vargas pour que son successeur, Dutro, désigne, en 1946, la commission qui trouva le site en un an. Six années furent encore nécessaires pour que ce choix soit ratifié par le parlement mais, dans le même temps, une société américaine, Donald J. Belcher & Associates, réalisait les premières études topologiques.

Vargas était entre-temps revenu au pouvoir en se faisant élire démocratiquement mais n'alla pas au bout de son mandat et, devant les difficultés qui l'assaillaient, se suicida. Juscelino Kubiteischek de Oliveira fut élu président en 1955 et prit le problème en mains. En moins d'un an, les fonds pour l'achat des terres furent dégagés, les premières machines arrivèrent sur le terrain, une commission d'urbanisme fut nommée et un concours national fut lancé par la Companhia Urbanizadora da Nova Capital do Brasil (Novacap), le 19 juillet 1956.

Aucun problème d'espace

Les conditions du cahier des charges n'étaient guère compliquées. Il y avait largement la place de construire une ville dont la population allait rapidement passer de 5 000 à 500 000 habitants. Les projets devaient comprendre des propositions pour les infrastructures, la division en quartiers et la distribution des principaux services publics comme l'électricité, l'eau et le téléphone. Exceptionnel par ses ambitions, ce concours n'attira que 26 participants sans doute parce que les délais de remise de travaux étaient relativement courts – 8 mois – et que la participation était réservée aux Brésiliens. De nombreux projets s'inspiraient des principes modernistes d'avant-guerre élaborés lors des congrès des CIAM, et l'approche urbaine de Le Corbusier était à l'évidence très appréciée. Les travaux des architectes et des urbanistes brésiliens reflétaient les tendances internationales du moment et leurs propositions pouvaient se comparer favorablement à celles d'un Kenzo Tange pour Tokyo.

Influence du modernisme

Les plans modernistes séparaient strictement les différentes fonctions: travail, habitation, circulation. De vastes espaces verts entouraient les blocs d'appartements, laissant pénétrer partout l'air et la lumière. Ces principes d'urbanisme mis au point lors du congrès des CIAM à Athènes en 1933 apparaissaient nettement dans les propositions de Ney Fontes Gonçalves, Baruch Milman et João Henrique Rocha qui remportèrent le second prix. Ils avaient divisé Brasilia en trois zones: une pour les fonctionnaires et deux pour le commerce et l'industrie. Trois types de logements, deux énormes immeubles et une maison individuelle, étaient prévus. Ce plan assez monotone risquait d'élargir les fossés entre les classes: les villas des fonctionnaires étaient merveilleusement situées sur les rives d'un lac tandis que les travailleurs se retrouvaient parqués dans des immeubles géants. Un tel plan avait peu de chance de donner naissance à la capitale idéale d'un nouveau Brésil qui se voulait prospère et libéré de la corruption.

Le plan de Rino Levi était plus démocratique, ne serait-ce que parce que tous ses logements donnaient sur le lac. A première vue, son plan peut paraître inspiré de modèles des années trente mais en y regardant de plus près, on voit que ses unités d'habitation étaient en fait des sous-centres urbains, conçus pour seize mille habitants. Chacune était composée de huit tours de 300 mètres de haut faites de quatre blocs de vingt étages interconnectés. Le plan de Levi montre six regroupements de trois de ces structures géantes, chacun ayant ses propres équipements de services et tous étant rassemblés autour du centre gouvernemental.

Le projet d'Henrique Ephin Mindlin et Giancarlo Palanti est un exercice libre à partir des principes de Le Corbusier. Malgré le dessin très original des unités d'habitation relativement petites, son plan aux formes douces est plus séduisant dans l'ensemble que ceux de la plupart des concurrents.

Certaines propositions n'avaient rien à voir avec le modernisme. Celle des frères Marcelo, Milton et Mauricio Roberto, par exemple, faisait appel à une organisation en toile d'araignée rappelant quelques-uns des plans du concours de Canberra[1]. On peut noter une importante différence entre le plan Roberto et celui de W. Scott Griffiths pour Canberra. Le projet brésilien repose sur des noyaux urbains égaux, non hiérarchisés, quasi indépendants alors que ceux de Griffiths étaient regroupés autour des bâtiments les plus importants de la capitale.

Croix et cerf-volant

Le jury finit par se prononcer en faveur du grand maître du modernisme brésilien, Lúcio Costa, qui proposa un plan en forme de croix, ou, pour certains, de cerf-volant. Comme dans les projets de Mindlin et de Palanti, l'un des axes était incurvé pour tenir compte de la topographie. Costa déclara que cette croix était une référence à l'ancien symbole d'appropriation des terres, mais ce symbolisme n'était peut-être pas un hasard dans un pays aussi religieux que le Brésil.

Le jury fut particulièrement impressionné par la monumentalité de la cité imaginée par Costa. Les deux bras de la croix représentent les deux grandes artères qui relient les zones de bureaux et celles de logement, situées dans de grands immeubles entourés de vastes espaces verts. Costa avait prévu trois édifices, traités en harmonie, pour les trois principaux pouvoirs, la cour suprême, le palais du président et le parlement. Il implanta les ministères le long du principal axe monumental qui mène à la place du Gouvernement et utilisa habilement la dénivellation du terrain pour accroître la monumentalité de certains bâtiments.

Un monument classé par l'Unesco

Kubitschek voulait que le plan de Costa soit réalisé le plus rapidement possible et cette précipitation empêcha certaines mises au point nécessaires. Les problèmes qui en découlèrent ne purent être résolus que partiellement et avec le temps. Mais le président avait atteint son objectif d'inaugurer la capitale avant la fin de son mandat. Le 21 avril 1960, Brasilia devint officiellement la capitale du Brésil.

En dépit de quelques faiblesses, Brasilia est incontestablement un chef-d'œuvre d'urbanisme moderniste. C'est pour cette raison que le statut de Monument du monde, protégé par l'Unesco, lui a été accordé en 1986. Cette distinction exceptionnelle pour une ville aussi récente, entraîne pour chaque modification du plan d'origine l'accord d'une commission où siègent le gouverneur de l'Etat de Goias ainsi que Lúcio Costa et l'architecte Niemeyer.

Architecte en chef de Brasilia, Oscar Niemeyer joua bien évidemment un rôle fondamental dans l'édification de la cité. Ses plans pour la cathédrale, le palais présidentiel et le parlement lui ont valu une célébrité mondiale. Sa créativité dans le maniement du béton était parfaitement adaptée au caractère monumental de la capitale et à ses vastes espaces ouverts. Niemeyer et Costa bénéficièrent d'une grande liberté ce qui n'alla pas sans quelques conséquences malheureuses. Dès le départ, Brasilia était davantage une splendide vision que le fruit du travail commun d'urbanistes, d'économistes et de sociologues. Cette liberté artistique a donné naissance à une cité fidèle aux principes du modernisme européen et de la Charte d'Athènes. On peut néanmoins se demander si les Brasiliens sont réellement satisfaits de leur ville lorsque l'on voit le nombre de ceux qui passent leurs week-ends à Rio ou à São Paulo.

1 *Voir le chapitre sur Canberra*

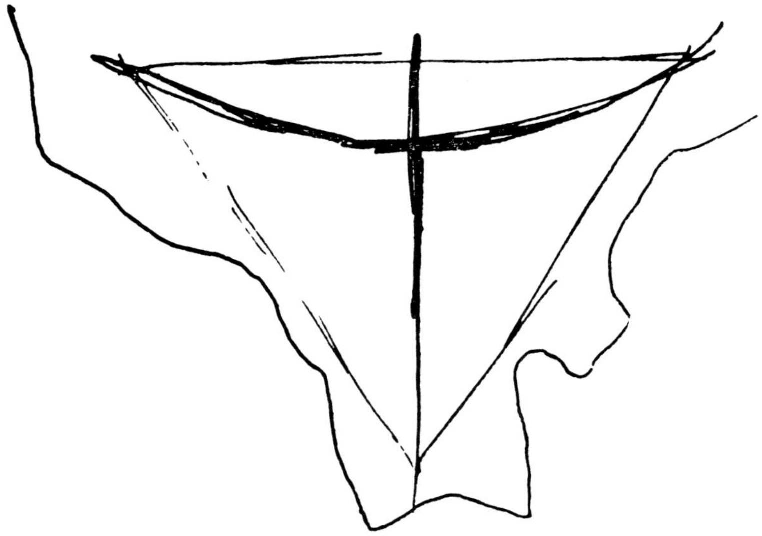

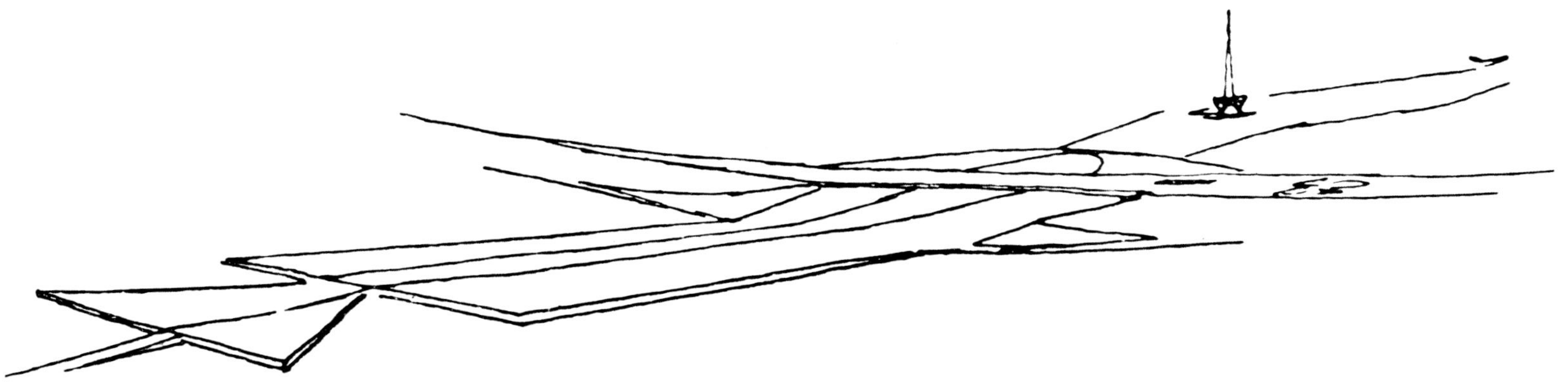

MMM Roberto competition design, 1957, pilot plan, joint third prize

MMM Roberto competition design, 1957, plan of the rural district urban zone, joint third prize

MMM Roberto competition design, 1957, plan of an urban unit, third prize

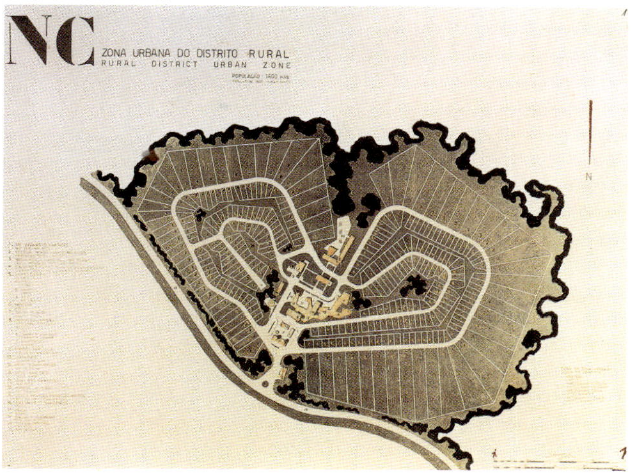

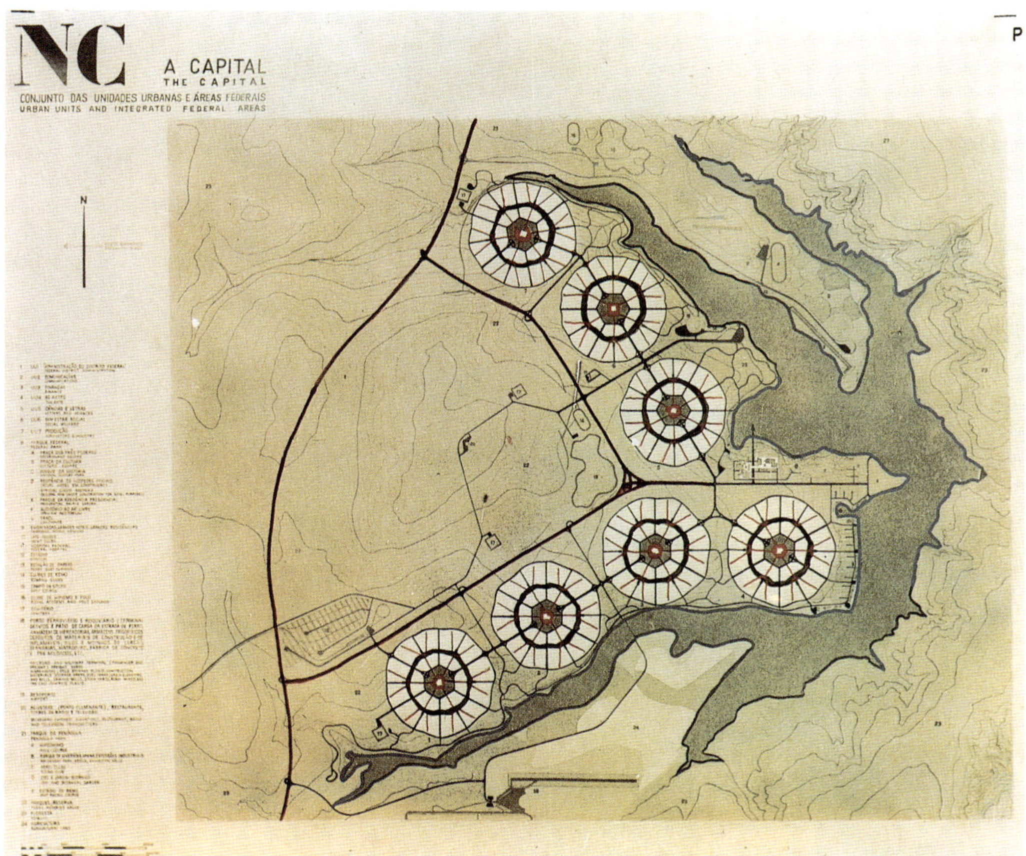

Lúcio Costa competition design, 1957, sketch, first prize

Lúcio Costa competition design, 1957, sketch for the general plan, first prize

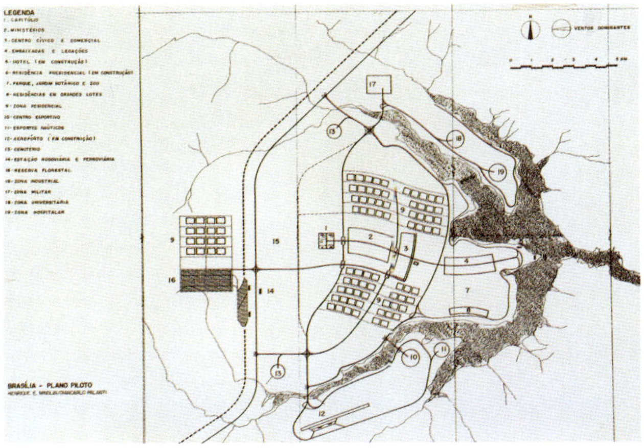

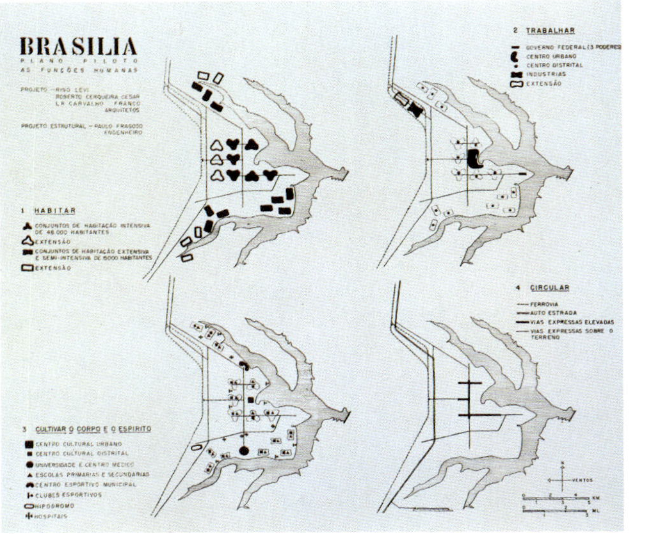

Rino Levi competition design, 1957, pilot plan, joint third prize

Rino Levi competition design, 1957, plan with several urban functions, joint third prize

Henrique Ephin Mindlin & Giancarlo Palanti competition design, 1957, pilot plan, fifth prize

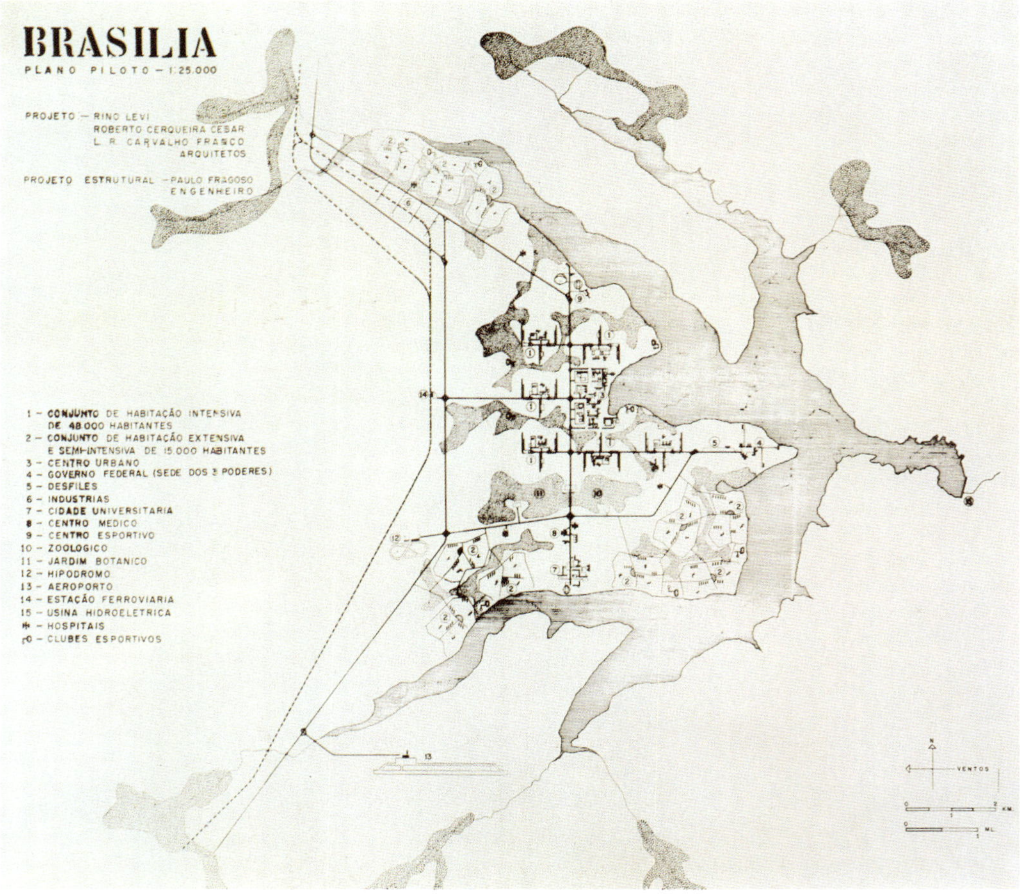

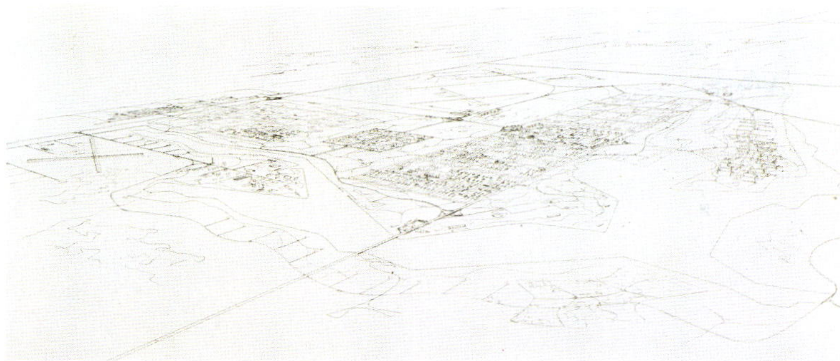

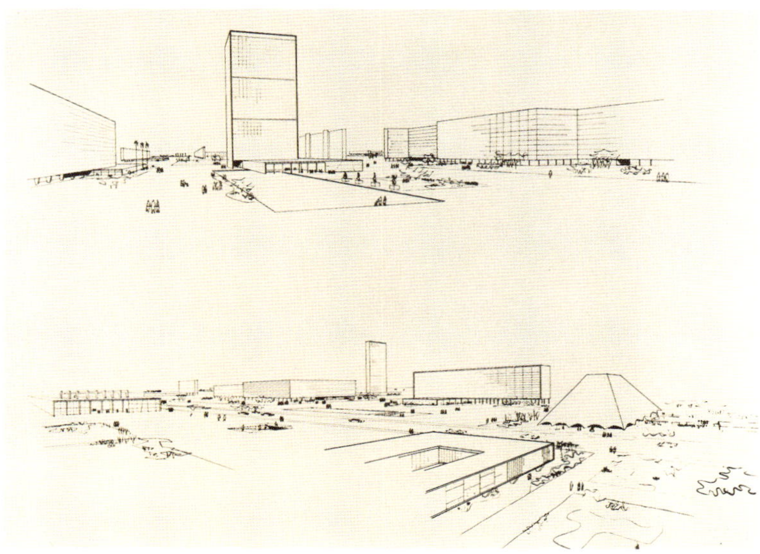

Ney Fontes Gonçalves, Baruch Milman, João Henrique Rocha competition design, 1957, bird's-eye view, second prize

Ney Fontes Gonçalves, Baruch Milman, João Henrique Rocha competition design, 1957, pilot plan, second prize

Ney Fontes Gonçalves, Baruch Milman, João Henrique Rocha competition design, 1957, bird's-eye view, second prize

Supreme Court, Tokyo, 1968–1969

Project

Supreme Court

Site

13-1 Hayabusa-cho, Chiyoda-ku, Tokyo

Dates

Competition announced 29 March 1968 *Closing date* 20 December 1968
Result announced 7 February 1969

Number of entries

217

Jury

Shigeru Ito, Junzo Sakakura, Eika Takayama, Togo Murano, Yasumi Yositake, Isoya Yoshida (all architects), Toru Iwano, Tsunetaka Ueda (director, Mainichi Newspapers), Kogoro Uemura (Federation of Economic Organisations), Michiaki Kawakita (curator, Art Museum), Yoshinori Maeda, Kisaburo Yokota (former Chief Justice of the Supreme Court), Masahiko Yokoyama (director-general, Government Buildings Bureau)

Result

First prize Shin-ichi Okada *Second prize* Yukio Sano; Sueji Suzuki; Kenzo Tange; Yoji Watanabe

Commissioned by

The Ministry of Construction, the Secretariat Architectural Competition Supreme Court and the Government Building Bureau

Construction

June 1971 to March 1974

Architect

Shin-ichi Okada

Construction cost

7 800 000 000 yen

Supreme Court, Tokyo, 1968–1969

Shin-ichi Okada competition design, 1968, exterior view from south-east, first prize

Supreme Court, Tokyo

The competition for the Supreme Court in Tokyo marked the end of an era which is sometimes referred to as the "Golden Age" of Japanese architectural competitions. During the 1960s, the face of Japanese architecture was determined by three major national architectural competitions. The competition for the Supreme Court was the last in this series. It was preceded by the competitions for the National Theatre, also in Tokyo, and the International Conference Hall in Kyoto.

Post-war metamorphosis

A year after the competition for the Supreme Court was announced in 1968, a minor competition was held for an International Tourist Centre in Hakone. However, it was not until the 1980s that a new generation of Japanese architects were given a chance to prove that they were also capable of producing original designs.
Japan had experienced a period of unprecedented economic growth during the 1950s and 60s. The 1964 Olympic Games in Tokyo had been a perfect showcase for this prosperity. The entire city underwent a metamorphosis and the world marvelled at the Olympic venues, which included a spectacular stadium designed by Kenzo Tange. Tokyo's post-war reconstruction had gained momentum during the 1950s when the necessary building materials were no longer in short supply. The reconstruction reached its height with the completion of the subway and highways.
Regrettably, the reconstruction of the city was not always in the hands of architectural visionaries. Rapid construction and high profits were the main objectives, and the competitions organised by the state had a negligible effect on this state of affairs. The only areas in the city which had a coherent structure were the Olympic district and the golden strip around the Imperial Palace. It was here that the Supreme Court was to be built.

International acclaim

In contrast to the competitions organised before 1960, the three major competitions of the "Golden Age" were of national rather than regional significance. This had several positive side-effects. The status of the nominated architects was enhanced and a list of general competition regulations was drawn up, along with guidelines for the execution of a project. These factors, coupled with the reconstruction of Tokyo and other Japanese cities, brought Japanese architecture into the international limelight, where it received the acclaim it deserved.
The competition for the Supreme Court was announced in March 1968 and closed on 20 December of that same year. No fewer than 217 architects submitted designs. The jury chairman was Shigeru Ito, from the University of Tokyo, who had made a favourable impression as a member of the competition jury for the International Congress Building in Kyoto. The jury included five other architects and seven jury members from various professional communities.
The participating architects were faced with the task of designing a prestigious building for one of the most important sites in the city, situated close to the Imperial Palace, surrounded by parks and overlooking the Japanese parliamentary building. It was stressed that the building should exude an aura of dignity befitting a Supreme Court. More than half of the designated site was to be left vacant, to allow for the layout of a park. In addition to the actual courtrooms, the architects had to include areas for a library and for the judicial administration.
The general quality of the entries was rather disappointing, probably due to the fact that contemporary Japanese architecture was still at an embryonic stage. For more than five decades, Japanese architects had sought a balance between their own national style and international influences. European neo-styles had been popular in Japan for a while,

National Gymnasia for the Tokyo Olympics

as they had been in Western countries. Around the turn of the century, Japan developed closer contacts with European countries, especially Germany, England, France and Italy, and these countries subsequently set the trend for Japanese architecture.
Foreign architects were invited to work in Japan. The German architects Hermann Ende & Wilhelm Böckmann submitted designs for the Japanese parliamentary building (never executed), the Ministry of Justice (1895, destroyed) and the old Supreme Court (1896). Ende & Böckmann, who had won second prize in the Reichstag competition, applied every possible neo-style in their designs. Other, more talented foreign architects were also popular, especially Le Corbusier and Frank Lloyd Wright, who built the Imperial Hotel in Tokyo between 1919 and 1922. Le Corbusier made his contribution to Japanese architecture after the war when he designed the National Museum for Western Art in Tokyo (1957–1959). His earlier work was also well-known amongst his Japanese colleagues.

Metabolism

During the latter half of the 1950s, Japanese architecture embraced the more poetic variety of Le Corbusier's Modernism, which is characterised by flowing rather than angular shapes. This trend continued during the 1960s, when the dynamic shapes were enlivened even more.
In 1960, a movement developed based on change and variation, rather than form and function. Metabolism became the leading architectural movement in Japan. Kenzo Tange and his pupil Arata Isozaki became members of this movement in 1964. Although Tange was only joint runner-up in the Supreme Court competition, he was already famous when he joined the movement and later became Japan's leading post-war architect.
The 1960s also heralded the breakthrough of high-rise buildings in Japan. The Kasumigaseki building, which had thirty-six floors, was completed in 1968. This was a rather daring project, because Tokyo had been plagued by earth tremors since time immemorial.

The Supreme Court competition was won by Shin-ichi Okada and his Kajima Corporation team. The other Kajima team, captained by Yukio Sano, was also nominated. They were joint runners-up alongside Tange, Yoji Watanabe and the Sueji Suzuki team of the Shimizu Corporation.
It is interesting to note that quite a number of the prize-winners were company architects. The main reason for this is that the larger Japanese construction companies have in-house design departments, ensuring close co-operation between the contractor, the architect and the engineer. However, this system also hampers architects who want to work independently. During the Supreme Court competition, the architectural community raised objections to this system and it was therefore decided that architects would be allowed to participate while still in the company's employ, but that they would have to establish an independent firm in order to be commissioned. Okada therefore left the Kajima corporation and established his own firm.

Outside wall beside the main entrance

Monumental designs

Okada's design is striking in that the structural elements of the building have been stacked in an apparently asymmetrical manner, so that no one part of the building has been particularly accentuated. This contrasts sharply with the designs of the other prize-winners, all of which featured symmetrical, hierarchical structures. Nevertheless, Okada's design is no less monumental, with its massive blind walls of stacked stone blocks. The anti-hierarchical structure of Okada's building mirrored the contemporary constitutional principles of post-war Japan, where a totalitarian imperial regime had been replaced by a modern constitutional state.
Kenzo Tange had clearly been influenced by Le Corbusier. His design certainly met the required standard of grandeur and was more monumental and impressive than Okada's. The magnificent hallway leading to the main courtroom is reminiscent of the gates of an impregnable fortress.

Above: entrance hall, below: grand court

Watanabe's design seems to have been derived from a new type of building which Tange had introduced towards the end of the 1950s: the town hall-cum-administration building. One of the most striking features of Watanabe's design is the enormous entrance hall in which the corridors have been suspended from massive pillars. The hall occupies almost half of the building's entire volume and the courtrooms are consequently no more than "boxes within a box". Suzuki's design features a symmetrical and rather monotonous complex, consisting of three blocks. The entrance hall makes a particularly closed and grim impression, reminiscent of the party offices in the former Soviet Union. Yukio Sano's design is completely different. His building is characterised by the use of coloured stone, by the way it opens out and by its rhythmic variation of forms. The exterior façades are charming but they are less varied than the interior.

Although the general quality of the designs was disappointing, the winning designs underscored the fact that Japanese architects were an even match for their European counterparts. Their designs compare favourably with the designs for the second Amsterdam Town Hall competition, even though the two buildings had different purposes. Since the 1960s Japan has occupied a leading position in the international architectural community, which is truly remarkable considering the fact that there was not a single school of architecture in the country ninety years before.

Oberster Gerichtshof, Tokio

Die Ausschreibung für den Obersten Gerichtshof von Tokio setzte einen Schlußstrich unter eine Epoche der japanischen Architektur, deren Bild in den 60er Jahren von drei großen nationalen Ausschreibungen geprägt wurde: den Wettbewerben für das Nationaltheater (ebenfalls in Tokio), die Internationale Konferenzhalle in Kyoto (Kyoto International Conference Hall) und den Obersten Gerichtshof. Die 60er Jahre gelten daher auch als das »goldene Zeitalter« der japanischen Architekturwettbewerbe.

Nachkriegs-Metamorphose

Während der 50er und 60er Jahre hatte Japan einen ungeahnten Wachstumsschub erfahren und präsentierte sich mit den Olympischen Sommerspielen 1964 in Tokio der Weltöffentlichkeit. Es entstanden nicht nur die Olympiabauten, wie etwa das von Kenzo Tange entworfene Stadion, sondern die ganze Stadt wurde einer Metamorphose unterzogen. So bildeten die Untergrundbahn und die Autobahn den Höhepunkt der Tokioter Nachkriegsarchitektur, deren Aufschwung erst in den 50er Jahren begonnen hatte, als die benötigten Baumaterialien wieder im vollen Umfang erhältlich waren.

Allerdings ging der Wiederaufbau der Stadt nicht immer Hand in Hand mit architektonischer Weitsicht. Viel wichtiger waren schnell zu errichtende Konstruktionen und größtmöglicher Gewinn. Auch die von der Regierung ausgeschriebenen Architekturwettbewerbe konnten daran nicht viel ändern. Die einzigen halbwegs durchstrukturierten Bereiche der Stadt befanden sich im Olympischen Viertel und rund um den Kaiserpalast, in dessen Nähe auch der Oberste Gerichtshof entstehen sollte.

Internationale Anerkennung

Die Wettbewerbe früherer Jahre sowie die drei großen Ausschreibungen in den 60er Jahren unterschieden sich insofern voneinander, als es sich bei letzteren nicht um regionale Bauten, sondern um Bauwerke von nationaler Bedeutung handelte. Dadurch wuchs das Interesse, denn die Karriere und der Status des prämierten Architekten erfuhren einen beachtlichen Schub. Außerdem entstanden erstmals allgemeine Regeln zur Organisation einer Ausschreibung und zur Durchführung von Projekten. Aufgrund dieser Entwicklung und des Wiederaufbaus zahlreicher Städte rückte Japans Architektur in den Mittelpunkt des internationalen Interesses und erhielt endlich die verdiente Anerkennung.

Die Ausschreibung für den Obersten Gerichtshof wurde im März 1968 bekanntgegeben; Einsendeschluß war der 20. Dezember desselben Jahres. Während dieser Zeit gingen 217 Beiträge ein, die den 13 Jurymitgliedern (sechs Architekten und sieben Vertreter anderer Berufsgruppen) zur Begutachtung vorlagen. Den Vorsitz der Jury übernahm der Architekt Shigeru Ito, der als Jurymitglied bei der Ausschreibung für die Internationale Konferenzhalle in Kyoto bereits einen guten Eindruck hinterlassen hatte.

Die teilnehmenden Architekten sahen sich vor die Aufgabe gestellt, ein repräsentatives Gebäude für einen der wichtigsten Standorte der Stadt zu entwerfen – in unmittelbarer Nähe zum Kaiserpalast mit seinen großzügigen Gartenanlagen und mit direkter Sicht auf den Sitz des japanischen Parlaments. Die Auflagen forderten, den Charakter des Obersten Gerichtshofes zu berücksichtigen und dem neuen Gebäude eine entsprechend würdevolle Ausstrahlung zu verleihen. Dabei durfte nur etwa die Hälfte des zur Verfügung stehenden Geländes bebaut werden; auf der anderen Hälfte sollte ein Park entstehen. Das neue Gerichtsgebäude mußte genügend Raum für Bibliotheks- und Verwaltungsraum aufweisen. Die Qualität der Beiträge ließ jedoch zu wünschen übrig – möglicherweise, weil sich die moderne japanische Architektur noch in der Entwicklungsphase befand. Bereits 50 Jahre zuvor hatten Japans Architekten eine Symbiose aus einem eigenen, nationalen Stil und ausländischen Einflüssen angestrebt. Auch hier kannte man – genau wie in den westlichen Ländern – eine Periode, die europäische Neo-Stilrichtungen propagierte. Gegen Ende des 19. Jahrhunderts nahmen die Kontakte zu Ländern wie Deutschland, England, Frankreich und Italien, die eine Vorbildfunktion für den Baustil der nachfolgenden Jahre inne hatten, zu.

Ausländische Architekten erhielten die Chance, in Japan zu bauen: So entwickelten die deutschen Architekten Hermann Ende und Wilhelm Böckmann Konstruktionspläne für das Parlamentsgebäude (nicht ausgeführt), für das Justizministerium (1895, zerstört) sowie für das alte Gebäude des Obersten Gerichtshofs (1896). Ende und Böckmann verwendeten in ihren Entwürfen alle ihnen bekannten Neo-Stilrichtungen. Aber auch andere ausländische Baumeister wie Frank Lloyd Wright, der zwischen 1919 und 1922 das Imperial Hotel in Tokio errichtete, und Le Corbusier trafen den japanischen Geschmack. Le Corbusier entwarf zwischen 1957 und 1959 das Nationalmuseum für Westliche Kunst, zudem waren seine früheren Werke bei den japanischen Fachkollegen wohlbekannt.

Der Metabolismus

Ab der zweiten Hälfte der 50er Jahre folgte die japanische Architektur dem eher poetischen Modernismus Le Corbusiers mit seinen geschwungenen statt rechteckigen Formen. Dieser Trend setzte sich auch in den 60er Jahren fort, als die bereits dynamischen Formen noch lebendiger gestaltet wurden.

1960 entstand der »Metabolismus«, eine Bewegung, die statt Form und Funktion Veränderung und Variation bevorzugte. Dieser Gruppe junger Architekten traten 1964 Kenzo Tange und sein ehemaliger Student und Mitarbeiter Arata Isozaki bei. Obwohl Tange bei der Ausschreibung für den Obersten Gerichtshof nur einen zweiten Platz errang – den er sich auch noch teilen mußte –, entwickelte sich der Metabolismus zu einer der wichtigsten Architekturströmungen Japans in den 60er Jahren. Der zum Zeitpunkt seines Beitritts bereits bekannte Baumeister Kenzo Tange avancierte zum bedeutendsten japanischen Architekten der Nachkriegszeit.

Neben dem Metabolismus sahen die 60er Jahre in Japan den Durchbruch des Hochbaus: 1968 wurde das Kasumigaseki-Gebäude mit seinen 36 Stockwerken vollendet – eine kühne Glanzleistung der Technik angesichts der schweren Erdbeben, die Tokio seit Menschengedenken heimsuchen.

Die Ausschreibung für den Obersten Gerichtshof gewannen Shin-ichi Okada und sein Mitarbeiterstab der Kajima Corporation, deren zweites Firmenteam unter Leitung von Yukio Sano zusammen mit Kenzo Tange, Yoji Watanabe und Sueji Suzukis Team der Shimizu Corporation den geteilten zweiten Platz errang.

Unter den Preisträgern befanden sich auffallend viele Firmenarchitekten, denn die großen Bauunternehmen verfügen häufig über eine eigene Entwurfsabteilung. Auf diese Weise können Bauunternehmer, Architekt und Ingenieur perfekt zusammenarbeiten. Allerdings bereitete diese enge Kooperation denjenigen Architekten große Probleme, die selbständig arbeiten wollten. Gegen diese Praxis erhoben sich daher zur Zeit des Wettbewerbs für den Obersten Gerichtshof Proteste, woraufhin man beschloß, daß der prämierte Architekt nicht von einer Firma abhängig sein durfte. Firmenarchitekten wurden zwar nicht ausgeschlossen, doch der Gewinner der Ausschreibung mußte sich selbständig machen. So kam es, daß Okada die Kajima Corporation verließ und sein eigenes Architekturbüro gründete.

Monumentale Entwürfe

Okadas Konzept zeichnet sich durch die scheinbar asymmetrische Anhäufung von Bauelementen aus. Diese sind auf eine Weise gestapelt, die jegliche Betonung eines einzelnen Elements ausschließt – ganz im Gegensatz zu den anderen Preisträgern, deren symmetrische Konstruktionspläne einen hierarchischen Aufbau besitzen. Zweifellos handelt es sich bei Okadas Entwurf mit seinen geschlossenen, massiven Wänden aus Natursteinblöcken um ein monumentales Bauwerk. Die anti-hierarchische Formgebung paßt gut zum Japan der Nachkriegszeit, das sich eher durch die Entwicklung eines modernen Rechtsstaates als durch die Traditionen des absolutistischen Kaiserreichs auszeichnet.

Kenzo Tanges Pläne wirken imposanter und eindrucksvoller als Okadas Entwurf. Die Eingangshalle zum Saal des Gerichtshofes erweckt den Eindruck eines nahezu uneinnehmbaren Festungstors. Watanabes Konzept scheint stärker von einem Gebäudetypus – Rathaus nebst Verwaltungszentrum – beeinflußt, den Tange gegen Ende der 50er Jahre eingeführt hatte. Tange wiederum orientierte sich stark an Le Corbusiers Ideen. An Watanabes Konstruktionsplänen fällt besonders die riesige Halle mit ihren an massiven Pfeilern aufgehängten Korridoren auf, die etwa die Hälfte des gesamten Gebäudes in Anspruch nimmt. Dadurch werden die Gerichtssäle zu »Schachteln in einer Schachtel« herabgewürdigt.

Suzukis Entwurf sieht einen symmetrischen, aus drei Blöcken bestehenden und relativ monotonen Gebäudekomplex vor. Die Eingangshalle erzeugt einen geschlossenen, grauen Eindruck. Von diesem Konzept hebt sich Yukio Sanos Beitrag deutlich ab. Das äußere Erscheinungsbild seines Gerichtshofes ist geprägt von farbenfrohem Naturstein, einem abwechslungsreichen Formenspiel und verschiedenen Öffnungen zum umliegenden Park. Allerdings wirken die Außenfassaden weniger variationsreich als die Ausstattung der Innenräume.

Auch wenn die Qualität der Beiträge nicht unbedingt allerhöchstes Niveau erreichte, bewiesen die prämierten Entwürfe, daß Japan auf architektonischem Gebiet nicht hinter Europa zurückstecken mußte. Seitdem ist Japan nicht mehr aus der Architekturwelt wegzudenken, obwohl der Berufszweig des Architekten in diesem Land noch 90 Jahre zuvor völlig unbekannt war.

La Cour suprême, Tokyo

Le concours pour la Cour suprême de Tokyo annonça la fin d'une ère parfois qualifiée d'âge d'or des concours d'architecture du Japon. Pendant les années 60, l'architecture japonaise fut profondément marquée par trois compétitions majeures pour le Théâtre national, également à Tokyo, le Centre international de conférences de Kyoto et enfin la Cour suprême.

Les métamorphoses de l'après-guerre

Un an après l'annonce du concours pour la Cour suprême (1968), une mise en compétition de moindre importance fut organisée pour un Centre international de tourisme à Hakone, mais il fallut attendre 1980 pour qu'une nouvelle génération d'architectes japonais ait l'occasion de prouver à l'occasion de grands projets qu'elle était, elle aussi, capable d'une production originale.

Le Japon avait connu une période de croissance économique sans précédent pendant les années 50 et 60, et les Jeux Olympiques de Tokyo de 1964 avaient servi de vitrine à cette nouvelle prospérité. La ville avait été métamorphosée et le monde entier s'était émerveillé devant les stades olympiques dont celui si spectaculaire de Kenzo Tange. La reconstruction du Tokyo d'après-guerre avait trouvé son rythme pendant les années 50, dès la fin du rationnement des matériaux de construction. Les travaux avaient culminé avec la construction du métro et du réseau d'autoroutes urbaines.

Malheureusement, ce nouvel urbanisme n'était pas toujours inspiré par des architectes visionnaires. Les principaux objectifs étaient de construire vite en réalisant d'énormes profits et les concours officiels n'exercèrent que peu d'influence sur le niveau qualitatif de l'architecture. Les seules zones dans lesquelles la ville fit preuve d'un peu de cohérence furent le district olympique et les environs du Palais impérial et c'est à cet endroit que la Cour suprême devait être construite.

L'approbation internationale

A la différence des appels d'offre d'avant 1960, les trois grands concours de l'âge d'or revêtirent une importance nationale plutôt que régionale, ce qui entraîna des conséquences positives. Le statut des architectes fut rehaussé et une sorte de réglementation-type pour les concours et l'exécution des projets fut établie. Tout ceci, conjugué à l'accélérateur économique de la reconstruction de Tokyo et d'autres grandes villes, fit émerger l'architecture japonaise de son obscurité.

Le concours de la Cour suprême fut annoncé en mars 1968 et clos le 20 décembre de la même année. Pas moins de 217 architectes y participèrent. Le président du jury était Shigeru Ito, de l'Université de Tokyo, qui s'était fait remarquer comme juré pour le concours du Palais des congrès internationaux de Kyoto. Cinq autres architectes et sept membres de diverses professions faisaient également partie du jury.

Les participants étaient confrontés à la tâche délicate de concevoir un édifice de prestige sur l'un des sites les plus en vue de la capitale, à proximité immédiate du palais impérial, de ses parcs et du parlement. On souhaitait vivement que son architecture traduise la dignité de sa fonction, et plus de la moitié du terrain devait être réservée à un nouveau parc. Outre les salles nécessaires, des espaces devaient être prévus pour une bibliothèque et l'administration judiciaire.

La qualité des propositions fut en général assez décevante, sans doute parce que l'architecture japonaise en était encore à un stade embryonnaire. Au tournant du siècle, le Japon avait multiplié les contacts avec les pays européens, en particulier avec l'Allemagne, la Grande-Bretagne, la France et l'Italie, et était allé y chercher ses modèles architecturaux. Pendant plus de cinquante ans, les Japonais avaient ainsi cherché un équilibre entre leur propre style et diverses influences internationales. Des architectes étrangers avaient même été invités à venir travailler à Tokyo. C'est ainsi que les Allemands Hermann Ende et Wilhelm Böckmann, second prix du concours pour le Reichstag et adeptes des styles «néo» les plus variés, proposèrent des plans (non réalisés) pour le Parlement, le ministère de la justice (détruit) et l'ancienne Cour suprême (1896). D'autres étrangers de plus de talent étaient heureusement tout aussi appréciés comme Le Corbusier et Frank Lloyd Wright auquel on doit l'Imperial Hotel (1919–1922). Le Corbusier intervint après la guerre et dessina le Musée National d'Art Occidental de Tokyo de 1957 à 1959. Ses travaux antérieurs étaient cependant bien connus de ses confrères japonais.

Métabolisme

Pendant la seconde moitié des années 50, l'architecture japonaise adopta le modernisme lyrique de Le Corbusier aux formes arrondies plutôt qu'anguleuses. Cette tendance persista pendant toutes les années 60, faisant même preuve d'un dynamisme formel encore plus affirmé. En 1960, un mouvement reposant sur le changement et la variation plutôt que sur la forme et la fonction fit son apparition – le métabolisme – qui devint le principal mouvement architecural. Kenzo Tange et son élève Arata Isozaki s'y rallièrent en 1964. Bien que Tange n'ait été que second lors du concours de la Cour suprême, il était déjà très connu à cette époque et allait s'imposer comme le plus célèbre des grands architectes japonais.

Les années 60 marquent également l'apparition des immeubles de grande hauteur au Japon. L'immeuble Kasumigaseki de trente-six étages, terminé en 1968 à Tokyo, ne manquait pas d'audace pour une ville soumise à d'incessants tremblements de terre.

Le concours de la Cour suprême fut remporté par Shin-ichi Okada et son équipe de Kajima Corporation. La seconde équipe Kajima, animée par Yukio Sano, fut également récompensée et arriva en deuxième position ex-aequo avec Tange, Yoji Watanabe et l'équipe Sueji Suzuki de Shimizu Corporation.

Un certain nombre de lauréats étaient en effet les employés de puissants groupes immobiliers. Les grandes sociétés de construction japonaises possédaient des départements d'architecture, ce qui présentait l'avantage d'une coopération étroite entre le promoteur, l'architecte et l'ingénieur mais freinait la créativité des architectes. A l'occasion du concours, beaucoup d'entre eux s'élevèrent contre ce système et l'on décida de permettre à des architectes salariés de participer, à condition qu'ils créent leur propre cabinet en cas de succès. Okada quitta ainsi Kajima Corporation pour s'installer à son compte.

Des plans monumentaux

Le plan d'Okada est remarquable: les éléments de la structure de soutien ont été empilés de façon apparemment asymétrique de telle manière qu'aucune partie de l'immeuble ne semble privilégiée. Cette solution contraste fortement avec celles des autres lauréats qui avaient tous travaillé sur des constructions symétriques et hiérarchisées. Le plan d'Okada n'en est pas moins monumental avec ses massifs murs aveugles constitués d'un entassement de blocs de pierre. Sa composition libre faisait écho aux nouveaux principes constitutionnels du Japon qui voyaient le pouvoir impérial s'effacer au profit d'une organisation démocratique moderne.

Kenzo Tange avait clairement été influencé par Le Corbusier et sa proposition répondait habilement à l'attente de «grandeur» de l'administration. Elle était plus monumentale et plus impressionnante encore que celle d'Okada. Son hall magnifique conduisant à la pièce principale rappelle l'atmosphère d'une forteresse imprenable.

La proposition de Watanabe semblait reprendre l'idée d'un nouveau type de bâtiment que Tange avait introduit vers la fin des années 50: l'hôtel de ville/immeuble de bureaux. L'une de ses caractéristiques les plus frappantes était l'énorme hall d'entrée parcouru de couloirs suspendus à des piliers massifs. Ce hall occupe presque la moitié du volume intérieur et les chambres ne sont guère plus que des «boîtes dans une boîte».

Le plan de Suzuki décrivait un ensemble symétrique et assez monotone en trois blocs. Son hall d'entrée donnait une impression particulièrement fermée et maussade, rappelant presque certaines administrations soviétiques.

Le projet Yukio Sano était entièrement différent. Il se singularisait par l'utilisation d'une pierre colorée ainsi que par son ouverture et son rythme. Bien que ses façades ne manquassent pas de charme, elles étaient moins animées que son espace intérieur.

Malgré la déception provoquée par la qualité moyenne des propositions, les plans retenus confirmaient que les architectes japonais pouvaient maintenant se poser en concurrents de leurs confrères européens. Leurs projets peuvent ainsi être favorablement comparés à ceux du second concours pour l'hôtel de ville d'Amsterdam, même si les deux édifices n'avaient pas la même fonction. Depuis les années 60, le Japon occupe une place de premier plan dans l'architecture internationale, situation d'autant plus remarquable qu'il n'existait pas une seule école d'architecture dans ce pays quatre-vingt-dix ans plus tôt.

Shin-ichi Okada competition design, 1968, model (south elevation), first prize

Shin-ichi Okada competition design, 1968, site plan, first prize

Shin-ichi Okada competition design, 1968, ground floor plan, first prize

Shin-ichi Okada competition design, 1968, first floor plan, first prize

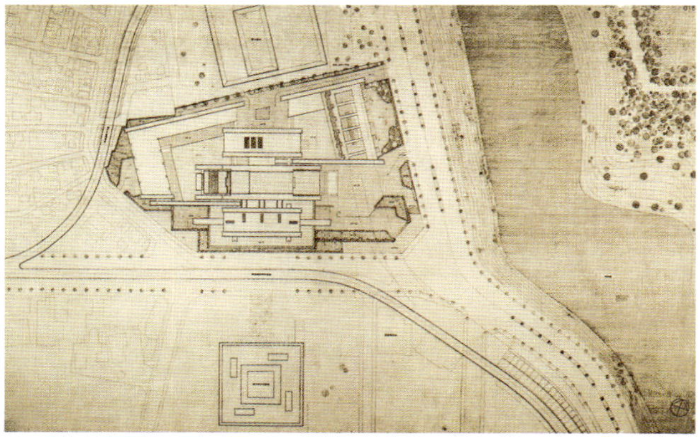

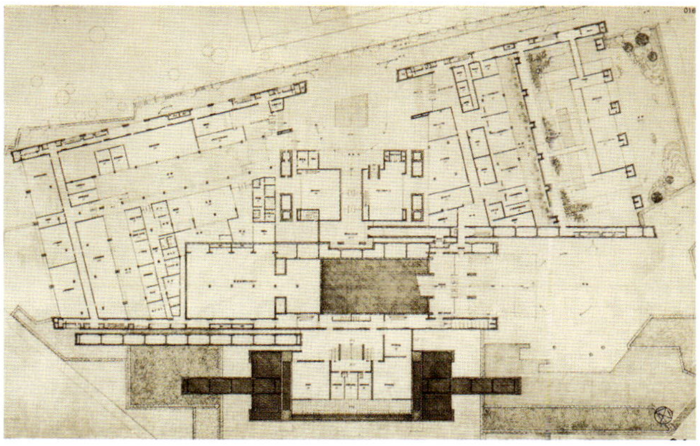

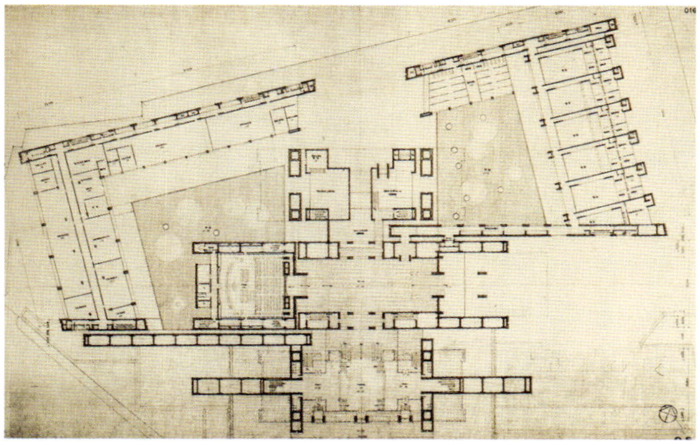

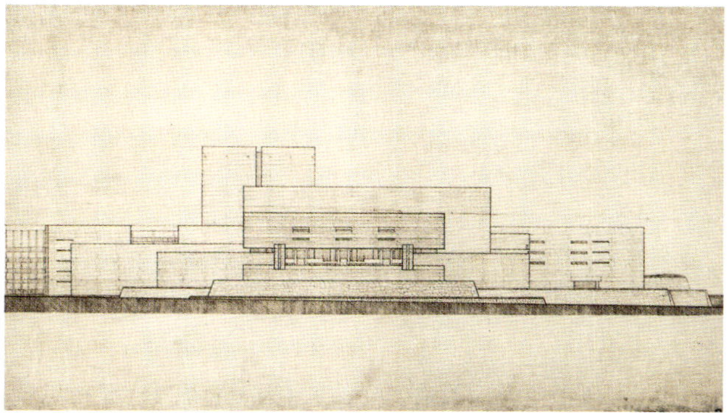

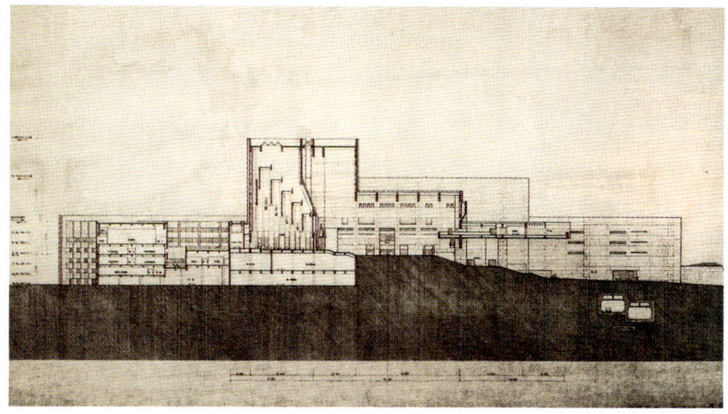

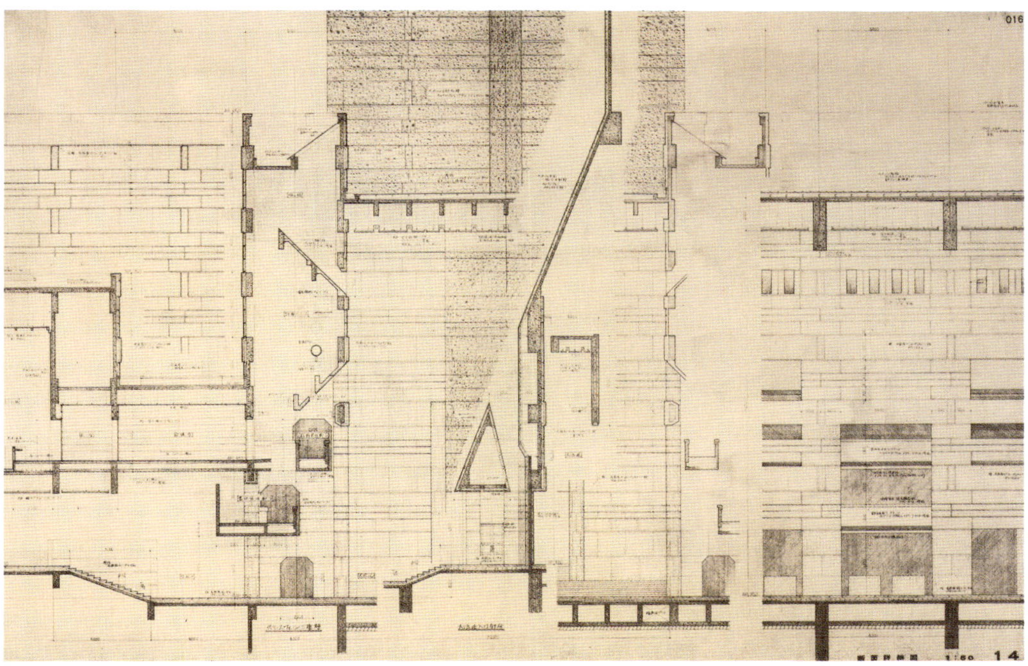

Shin-ichi Okada competition design, 1968, south elevation, first prize

Shin-ichi Okada competition design, 1968, east-west section, first prize

Shin-ichi Okada competition design, 1968, section details, first prize

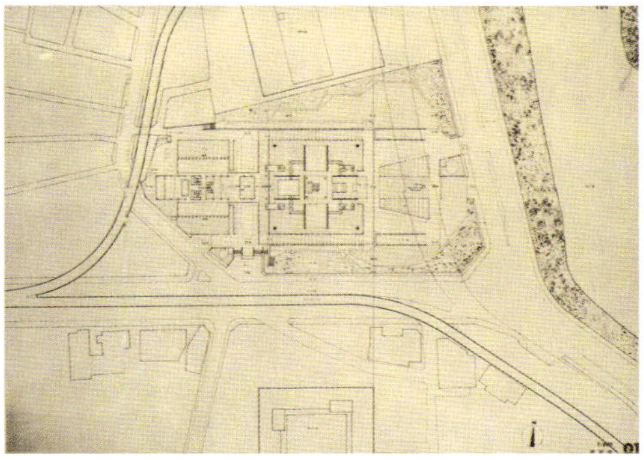

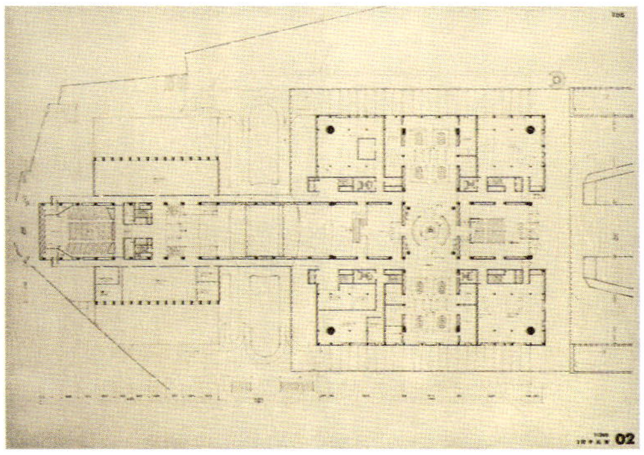

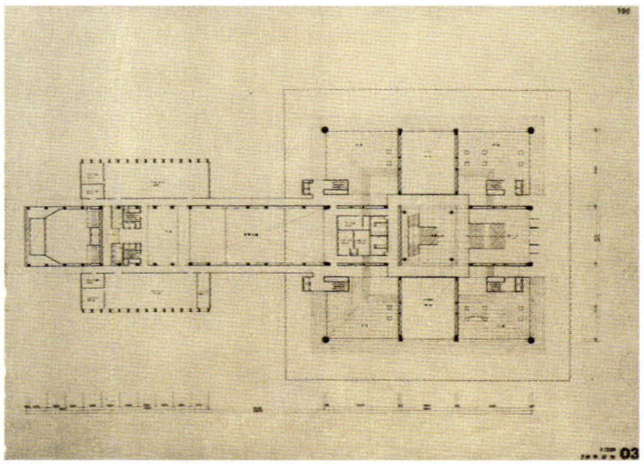

Kenzo Tange competition design, 1968, exterior view from east, second prize

Kenzo Tange competition design, 1968, site plan, second prize

Kenzo Tange competition design, 1968, ground floor plan, second prize

Kenzo Tange competition design, 1968, first floor plan, second prize

Kenzo Tange competition design, 1968, interior view of entrance hall, second prize

Kenzo Tange competition design, 1968, interior view of grand court, second prize

010

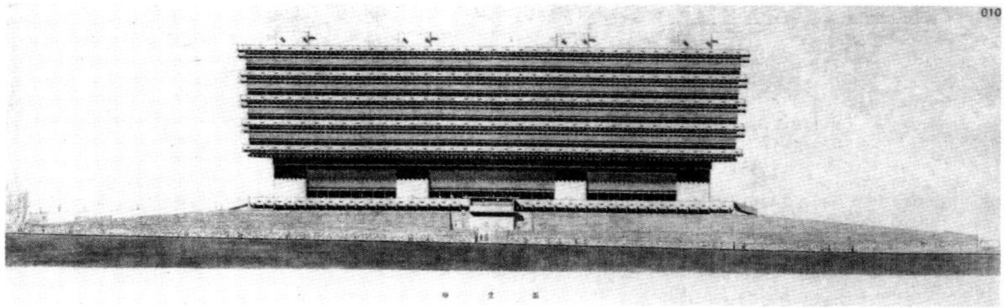

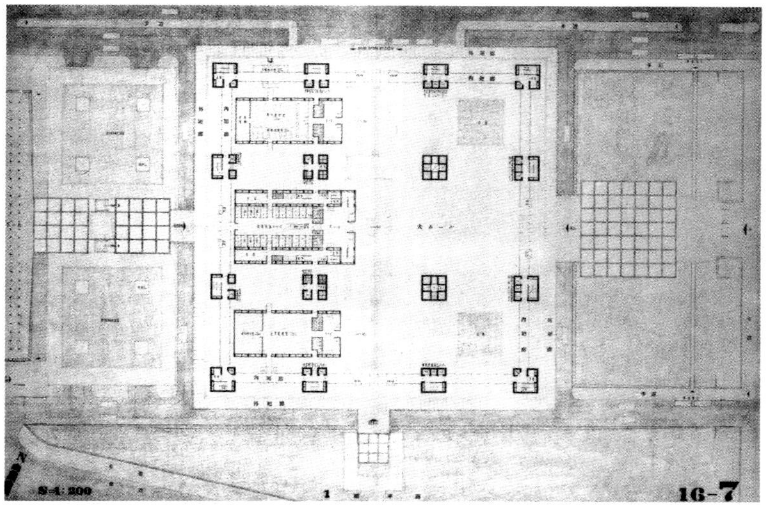

Yoji Watanabe competition design, 1968, south elevation, second prize

Yoji Watanabe competition design, 1968, ground floor plan, second prize

Yoji Watanabe competition design, 1968, east elevation, second prize

Yoji Watanabe competition design, 1968, east-west section, second prize

Yoji Watanabe competition design, 1968, north-south section, second prize

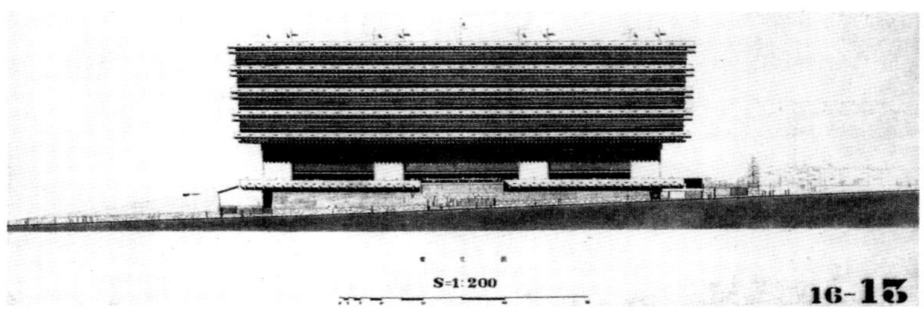

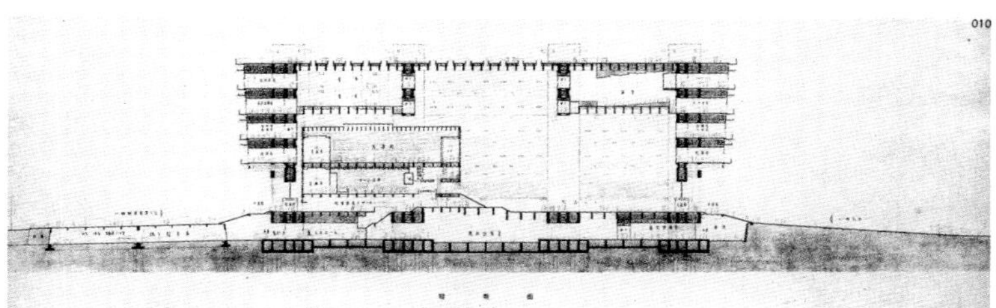

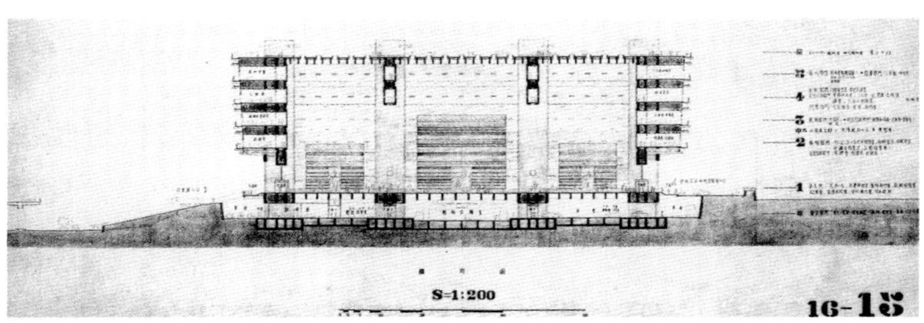

Yoji Watanabe competition design, 1968, exterior view from east, second prize

Yoji Watanabe competition design, 1968, section view of grand hall, second prize

Yoji Watanabe competition design, 1968, interior view of grand court, second prize

Yukio Sano competition design, 1968, interior view of grand court, second prize

Yukio Sano competition design, 1968, interior view of entrance hall, second prize

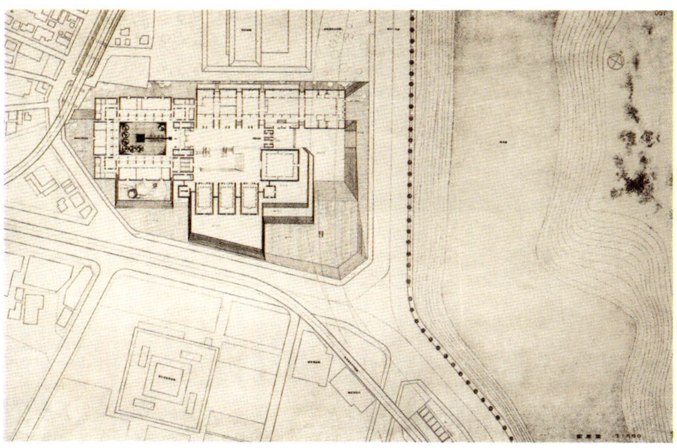

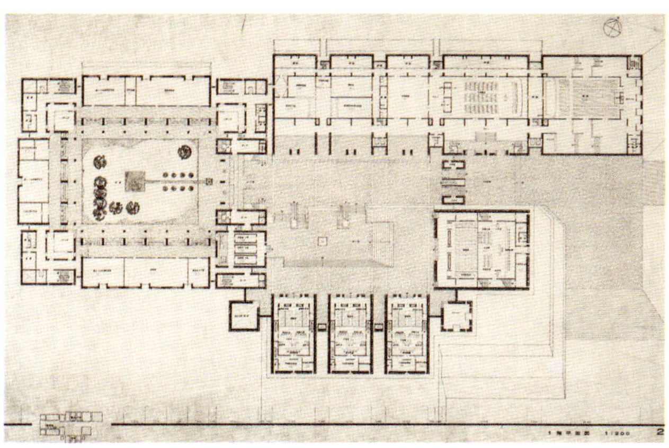

Yukio Sano competition design, 1968, exterior view from south, second prize

Yukio Sano competition design, 1968, site plan, second prize

Yukio Sano competition design, 1968, ground floor plan, second prize

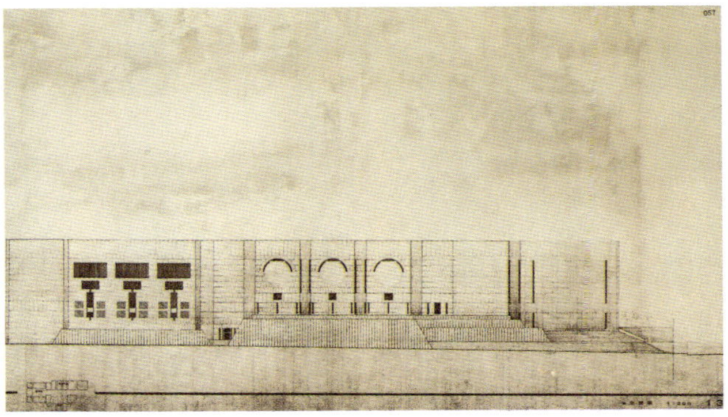

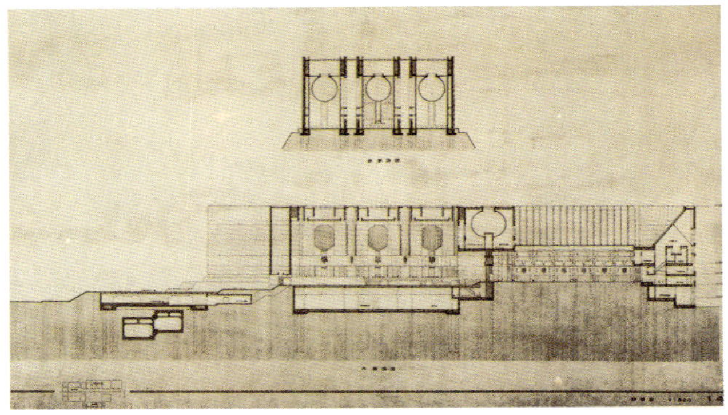
14

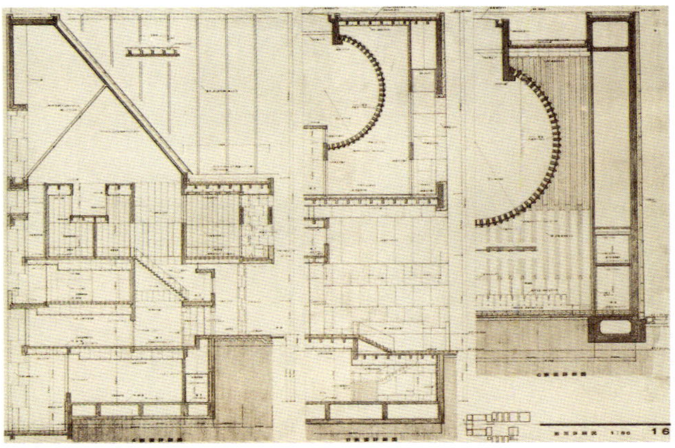
16

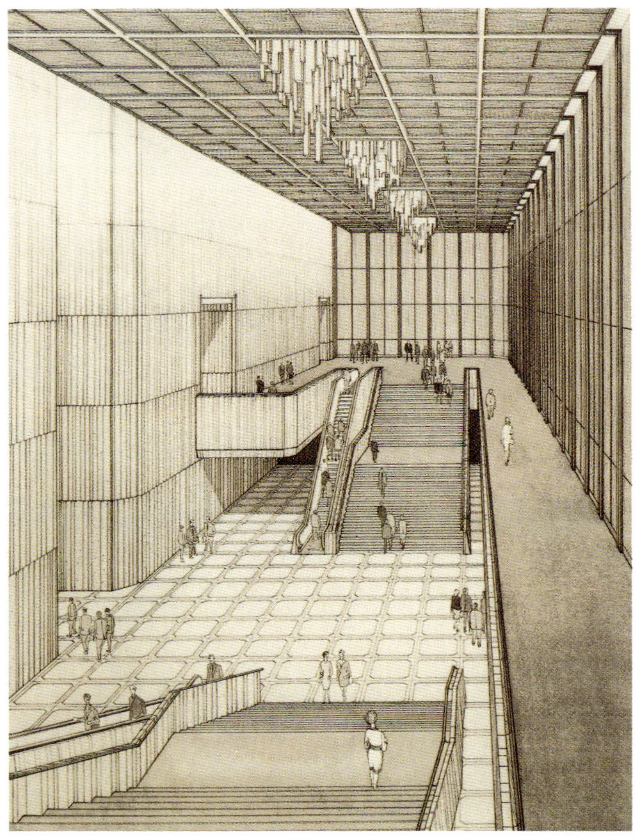

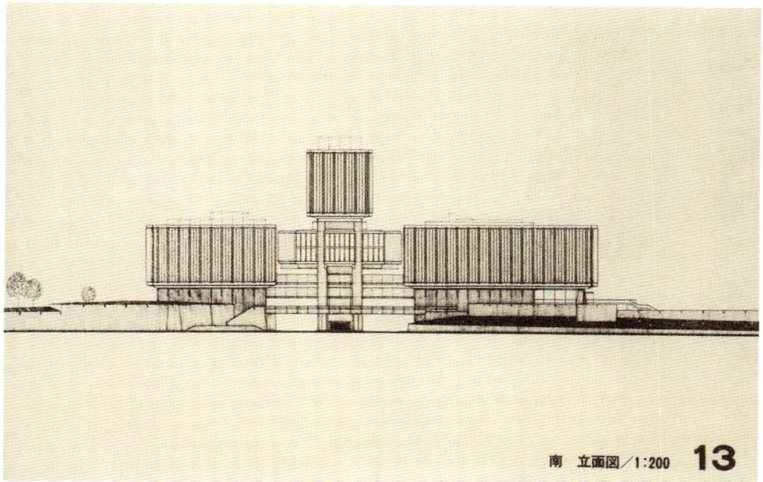

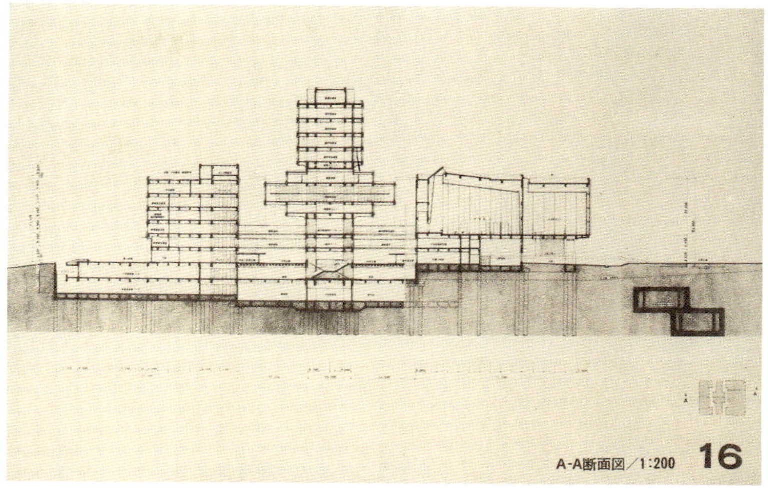

Yukio Sano competition design, 1968, south elevation, second prize

Yukio Sano competition design, 1968, above: section of small court, below: east-west section, second prize

Yukio Sano competition design, 1968, section details, second prize

Sueji Suzuki competition design, 1968, interior view of entrance hall, second prize

Sueji Suzuki competition design, 1968, exterior view from east, second prize

Sueji Suzuki competition design, 1968, interior view of grand court, second prize

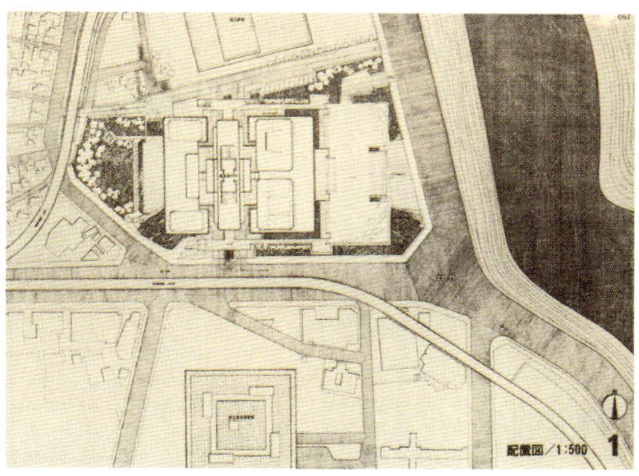

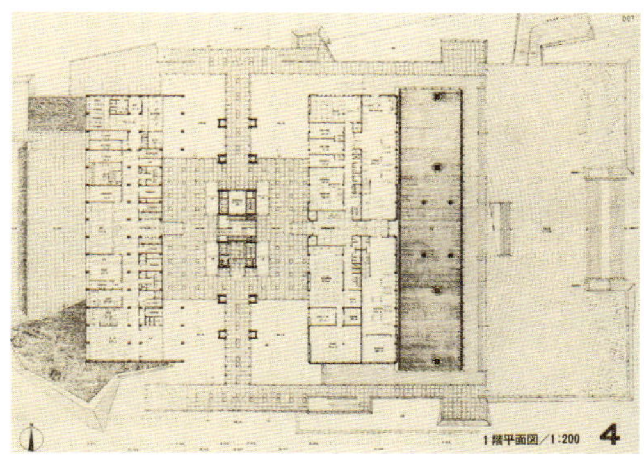

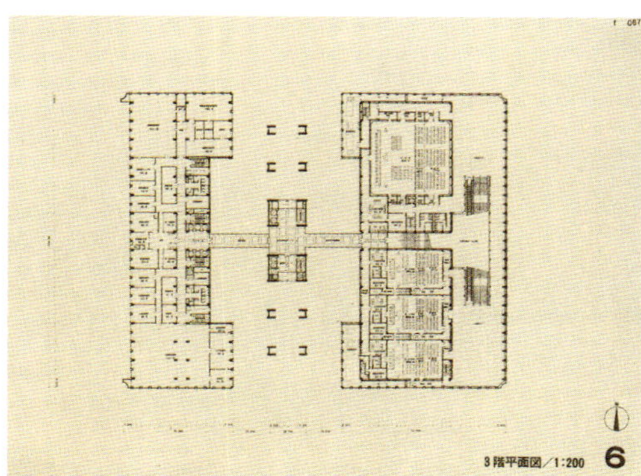

Sueji Suzuki competition design, 1968, south elevation, second prize

Sueji Suzuki competition design, 1968, east-west section, second prize

Sueji Suzuki competition design, 1968, site plan, second prize

Sueji Suzuki competition design, 1968, ground floor plan, second prize

Sueji Suzuki competition design, 1968, second floor plan, second prize

Project

Entertainment Centre

Site

Strip of land between Avenue Princesse Grace and the Mediterranean Sea in Monte Carlo

Dates

Competition announced 5 May 1969 *Closing date* October 1969 *Result announced* Spring 1970

Number of entries

12

Jury

Pierre Vago, Ove Arup, Michel Ragon, René Sarger

Result

First prize Archigram – Peter Cook, Dennis Crompton, Colin Fournier, David Greene, Ron Harrow, Ken Akinson, Tony Pickardi, Frank Newby (technical advisor)

Construction

Never built

Entertainment Centre, Monte Carlo, 1969–1970

Entertainment Centre, Monte Carlo, 1969–1970

70

Archigram competition design, 1969, collage diagram, first prize

Entertainment Centre, Monte Carlo

Monte Carlo is the capital of Monaco, that famous, sun-drenched city state on the Mediterranean coast, whose few residents can afford to enjoy the finer things in life to their hearts' content. In an effort to pander to the tastes of the residents, twelve architects and architectural teams were invited to submit a design for an entertainment centre. The jury awarded first prize to the Archigram team, who had submitted a plan for an underground complex for this carefree and frivolous city.

New architectural challenges

European society experienced a period of growing prosperity during the 1960s. This went hand in hand with more leisure time, which presented new architectural challenges. Society was undergoing radical change and there was an increasing demand for entertainment facilities.

In May 1969, the Monaco Department of Public Works decided that the time was ripe to build an entertainment centre for the chic inhabitants of the mini state. A suitable site was hard to find, because Monaco was almost completely built-up. Eventually, however, a strip of land between the Mediterranean and the Avenue Princesse Grace was prepared for construction. The building assignment was certainly not an easy one. The entertainment centre was to be surrounded by a park, and was to include an exhibition area, a sports hall (ice hockey) and a circus. In addition, the centre was to seat between 1500 and 2000 people, as well as providing a suitable venue for theatrical performances and banquets.

What was surprising was that, in addition to the temporary functions listed above, the centre had to have certain permanent facilities, the details of which were to be decided by the architects. The programme therefore appeared to give the architects a free hand. However, this freedom itself later proved to be a hindrance, since it was almost impossible to tie in the permanent facilities with the temporary facilities, which were of cardinal importance.

The jury consisted of Pierre Vago, who was one of the leading French architects at the time, Ove Arup, the engineer involved in the Sydney Opera House and other daring creations, Michel Ragon, an art historian, and René Sarger. They were given twelve designs to assess and from these they chose the most spectacular entry: the design submitted by the architectural team Archigram. It was the most radical plan a jury had ever selected and it was clear that great things were afoot in the world of architecture.

Site view, Monte Carlo

Archigram

Archigram was founded in London in 1961 by a group of young, frustrated architectural graduates. The name Archigram is a variation on words such as telegram and aerogram. Within the Archigram group, championed by Peter Cook, there existed an inherent and essential contradiction: although they were influenced by a rapidly developing modern society – technological innovation had a

particularly significant influence upon Archigram's designs – it was also clear that the members of the group viewed the superficial, modern world with certain reservations.
Archigram introduced a number of key concepts which embodied their ambivalent opinions concerning consumer society, and it is necessary to elaborate upon these concepts in order to gain a better understanding of their Monte Carlo design.
The first concept requiring attention is the "plug-in city". Archigram was fascinated by the deluge of electrical appliances which flooded the market during the 1960s. The plug-in city was a mega-structure, imaginative and carefully thought out, involving movable buildings, cranes, supply pipelines and other futuristic elements. The plug-in city was able to function efficiently through the use of electrical systems, cranes and robots. This pioneering optimism was clearly a product of the years preceding the energy crisis of the 1970s.
Another Archigram project was the "blow-out village". This was even more exciting than the plug-in city. The blow-out village consisted of a main mast with a number of arms, to which the actual housing units were attached. The entire structure could rotate and looks like a giant fairground attraction.
Archigram took a completely different approach in the collages which expressed their views on urban society. Whereas the plug-in city and blow-out village are large-scale projects based on technological innovation, the collages and photomontages are more intimate and directed towards the individual user. In fact, these collages can be compared with the psychedelic art which was popular during the same period, appearing on record sleeves in England, and in the Beatles' film "Sgt. Pepper's Lonely Heart's Club Band".
Other Archigram concepts include the "walking city", "drive-in houses" and the "instant city". The instant city is a particularly imaginative concept consisting of a vertical, movable structure, to which urban facilities have been attached. Consumerism and entertainment form integral parts of the instant city, which is both surrealistic and terrifying. Archigram incorporated many of these elements in their design for the Monte Carlo entertainment centre.

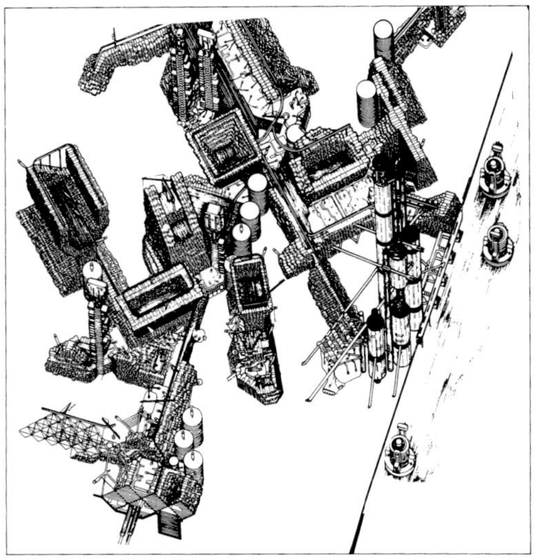

Archigram **plug-in city, axonometric, 1964**

A place in the sun

The Archigram team, with their ambivalent approach to consumer society, seemed perfectly cut out for the Monte Carlo competition. Peter Cook formulated their approach as follows: *"To all of us, the name of Monte Carlo has conjured up Glamour, Money, Indolence and Exotic – unreality as real-life – Marienbad-in-California – cream suits and white Rolls Royces – and, at last, a place in the sun for Archigram"*. It was as if the features of the instant city, the collages and all the other imaginative concepts fell into place in Monte Carlo. Features which had seemed alien in previous designs now seemed logical. Naturally, imaginative drawings alone were not enough to impress the jury. The fact that the Archigram architects were truly competent was borne out by their floor plans and cross-sectional drawings, and by the diversity of the temporary facilities they incorporated in their design. These included facilities for space research, ice hockey and Grand Prix car races. Naturally, all the elements were movable. The complex as a whole was to be subterranean, which left enough room for a fair-sized park in built-up Monte Carlo. None of the other teams had come up with an underground solution. It goes without saying that the rest of their design was also unique.

The features of Archigram's design were characteristic of the late 1960s and early 1970s. In 1970, Arata Isozaki had designed a giant robot for the Osaka Expo, which would undoubtedly have been to Archigram's liking. Robots had also been planned for the Entertainment centre, for example, the masts in the ice-hockey arena. These robot-buffets were to provide spectators with drinks and ice-creams.
It is debatable whether Cook and his team took the competition seriously, and one might also question whether the fanciful elements in their design were not a little excessive. Regrettably, the Monte Carlo centre shared the fate of so many other Archigram projects: it was never built. Apparently, the client had developed reservations

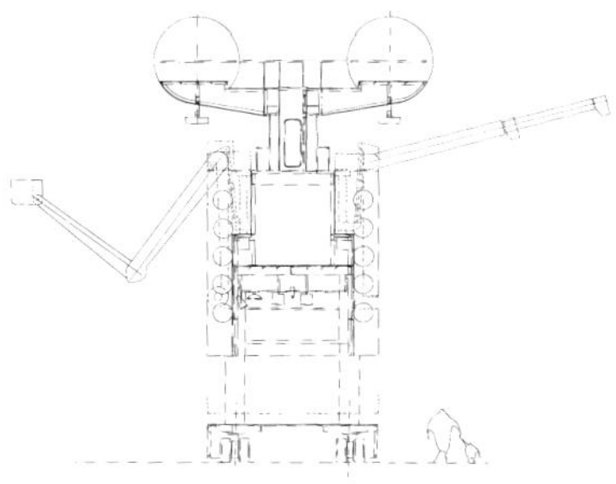

Arata Isozaki robot in the Festival Plaza, Expo 1970

about Archigram's competence. Peter Cook clearly did not think highly of his client, as is borne out by the following quotation: *"Monaco is prepared to try new things so long as they don't frighten away the rich mums and the European rich in general. So no hippies and not too much noise; fireworks as displays and games that are sporty rather than sweaty."* By this time the project had already been cancelled.

Other entries

Due to Archigram's awe-inspiring design, most of the other participants were undeservedly pushed into the background. The Finnish architect Reima Pietilä also submitted an extraordinary design consisting of an expressively developed, organic structure which projected out over the bay, and in which the bay actually formed part of the interior. Beneath the fantastic exterior lay a rational structure which provided space for various activities on different floors.

Frei Otto's design was of a completely different calibre. This architectural engineer designed a roofing structure which was both remarkable and complex, and though the jury may initially have had doubts about the technical feasibility of the plan, these doubts proved to be unfounded. Frei Otto, who wrote "Das hängende Dach" (The hanging roof, 1954) later saw his roofing structure materialise over the Olympic Stadium in Munich, which was completed in 1972 and received worldwide acclaim.

Though Archigram's architectural designs were greatly admired, designs alone are not enough. Architectural immortality is reserved for those whose visionary concepts become real.

Sommerkasino, Monte Carlo

Monte Carlo ist die Hauptstadt Monacos, dessen Bewohner sich an der begünstigten geographischen Lage des kleinen Stadtstaates am Mittelmeer erfreuen können. Um dem steigenden Bedürfnis nach Unterhaltung und Vergnügung zu entsprechen, luden die Stadtväter zwölf Architekten und Architekturbüros ein, Entwürfe für ein Sommerkasino vorzulegen. Den spektakulärsten Vorschlag reichte die Architektengemeinschaft Archigram ein – einen unterirdischen Komplex.

Neue architektonische Herausforderungen

Der wachsende Wohlstand in Europa und der damit verbundene Freizeitzuwachs stellten die Architektur in den 60er Jahren vor neue Herausforderungen. Die Gesellschaft war starken Veränderungen unterworfen, die Nachfrage nach Räumen und Möglichkeiten für die Freizeitgestaltung nahm beständig zu.

Im Mai 1969 gelangte Monacos Dezernat für Öffentliche Bauten zu der Einsicht, daß der Kleinstaat ein Unterhaltungs- und Vergnügungszentrum gebrauchen könne. Allerdings gestaltete sich die Suche nach einem geeigneten Baugelände in der bereits dichtbesiedelten Stadt schwierig, ehe man sich auf ein gerade erst bebaubar gemachtes Grundstück zwischen der Mittelmeerküste und der Avenue Princesse Grace einigte. Das geplante Bauvorhaben war schwierig: Das Sommerkasino sollte in einem Park liegen, gleichzeitig als Ausstellungsgebäude, (Eishockey-) Sporthalle sowie als Zirkus dienen und 1500 bis 2000 Besuchern Platz bieten. Darüber hinaus sahen die Bauauflagen eine Verwendung als Veranstaltungsort für Theateraufführungen und Bankette vor.

Als Problem erwies sich, daß das Gebäude neben seinen temporären Funktionen auch eine permanente Nutzung erfahren sollte. Für diese Nutzung machte die Stadt keine Vorschriften, sondern überließ es den Architekten, entsprechende Vorschläge zu unterbreiten.

Die Jury bestand aus Pierre Vago (einem zu diesem Zeitpunkt führenden französischen Architekten), Ove Arup (Inhaber einer Planungsfirma, die durch ihre Beteilung an der Ausschreibung für das Sydney Opera House und andere kühne Konstruktionen bekannt war), dem Kunsthistoriker Michel Ragon und René Sarger. Die Jurymitglieder entschieden sich für den spektakulärsten Entwurf unter den zwölf eingesandten Beiträgen: das Konzept der Architektengemeinschaft Archigram. Noch nie zuvor hatte eine derart ungewöhnliche Zeichnung eine Ausschreibung gewonnen.

Archigram

Archigram war 1961 in London von einer Gruppe frisch examinierter Architekten gegründet worden, die mit der Bezeichnung »Archigram« auf Worte wie »Telegramm« »Aerogramm« anspielten. Die Architektengemeinschaft mit ihrem Protagonisten Peter Cook stand einerseits unter dem Einfluß der sich rasch entwickelnden modernen Gesellschaft – insbesondere technische Innovationen flossen in die Arbeiten ein –, andererseits zeigten die Archigram-Mitglieder eine gewisse Zurückhaltung gegenüber der allzu materialistischen Komponente der modernen Welt.

Archigram propagierte einige Kernbegriffe, die ihre ambivalente Haltung gegenüber der Konsumgesellschaft zum Ausdruck brachte. Ein solcher Kernbegriff ist »Plug-in City«. Archigram war fasziniert von der sprunghaften Verbreitung von Elektrogeräten, die sich während der 60er Jahre in den Haushalten vollzog. Plug-in City stellt eine Mega-Struktur dar – phantasievoll und durchdacht, aus beweglichen Gebäuden, Hebekränen, Versorgungsschächten und anderen futuristischen Elementen. In der ganzen Stadt sorgen elektrische Systeme, Kräne und Roboter für einen effizienten Ablauf. Dieser Fortschrittsoptimismus stammte eindeutig aus der Zeit vor der sog. Energiekrise Anfang der 70er Jahre. Ein weiteres Archigram-Projekt umfaßt das »Blow-out Village«, das aus einem Großmast besteht, dessen Rahen die eigentlichen Wohnungen tragen und der in sich beweglich ist. Das Ganze erinnert an eine Kirmesattraktion.

Einen völlig anderen Ansatz zeigen Archigrams Collagen, die eine eigene Sichtweise des städtischen Zusammenlebens wiedergeben. Während Plug-in City und Blow-out Village von der neuen Technologie ausgehen, wirken die Collagen und Fotomontagen intimer und mehr auf den individuellen Menschen als Benutzer bezogen. Archigrams Collagen sind den psychedelischen Kunstströmungen vergleichbar, die sich u.a. auf diversen Plattencovern und in dem Beatles-Film »Sgt. Pepper's Lonely Heart's Club Band« äußerten.

Zu den weiteren Modellen von Archigram zählen u. a. »Walking City« und »Drive-in Houses« sowie die »Instant City«, die besonders phantasievoll gestaltet wurde. Hierbei handelt es sich um eine vertikale, transportable Struktur, an der die städtischen Einrichtungen buchstäblich aufgehängt sind. Konsum und Vergnügen gelten als unverzichtbare Bestandteile der Instant City, die zugleich irreal und beängstigend wirkt. Viele dieser Elemente finden sich auch in dem Entwurf für das Sommerkasino in Monte Carlo.

Ein Platz an der Sonne

Die Monte-Carlo-Ausschreibung war dem Team von Archigram mit seiner Einstellung gegenüber der Konsumgesellschaft wie auf den Leib geschrieben. Peter Cook formulierte es so: *»Für jeden von uns steht der Name Monte Carlo für Glamour, Geld, Müßiggang und Exotik, für eine Unwirklichkeit, die als wahres Leben ausgegeben wird, es ist gleichbedeutend mit Marienbad in Kalifornien, cremefarbenen Kostümen und weißen Rolls Royces – und bedeutet schließlich einen Platz an der Sonne für Archigram.«*

Es schien, als fänden alle Elemente von Instant City, den Collagen und den anderen Modellen in Monte Carlo endlich ihren richtigen Platz. Die fachkundige Jury ließ sich von spektakulären Bildern nicht blenden. Das hervorragende Können der Archigram-Architekten zeigte sich auch anhand der mitgeschickten Grundrisse und Längsschnitte sowie in den diversen Vorschlägen für die zeitweiligen Aufgaben des Zentrums. Der gesamte Komplex sollte unterirdisch angelegt werden, damit im dicht bebauten Monte Carlo noch genügend Platz für einen Park zur Verfügung stand. Archigram hatte sich als einziges Architektenteam zu einer unterirdischen Lösung entschlossen, was die Einzigartigkeit ihrer Konstruktionspläne erneut unterstreicht.

Archigrams Entwurfsmethodik ist kennzeichnend für die späten 60er und frühen 70er Jahre. Zum Vergleich: 1970 entwarf Arata Isozaki für die Weltausstellung in Osaka einen riesigen Roboter, den das Team von Cook sicher zu würdigen gewußt hätte. Auch Archigrams Plan für das Unterhaltungs- und Vergnügungszentrum sah verschiedene Roboter vor, z.B. sollten die unteren Teile der Masten der Eishockey-Halle für Erfrischungsgetränke und Eis sorgen (Roboter-Buffet). Sicherlich stellt sich die Frage, inwiefern Cook und seine Kollegen die Ausschreibung ernst nahmen und ob die spielerischen Elemente nicht zu sehr überwogen. Wie viele andere Archigram-Projekte wurde auch der Entwurf für das Sommerkasino in Monte Carlo nicht verwirklicht. Offensichtlich setzten die Auftraggeber bei näherer Betrachtung kein allzu großes Vertrauen in das fachmännische Können der Archigram-Architekten. Cook hatte wiederum keine hohe Meinung von seinen Auftraggebern, wie das folgende Zitat belegt: *»Monaco ist offen für Innovationen, solange sie nicht die reichen alten Damen oder den europäischen Jetset im allgemeinen verscheuchen. Also gibt es keine Hippies und nicht zuviel Lärm, Feuerwerk nur im Schaukasten und Spiele sind eher sportiv als schweißtreibend.«* Zu diesem Zeitpunkt hatten Monte Carlos Stadtväter den Auftrag bereits zurückgezogen.

Die anderen Entwürfe

Aufgrund der ungestümen Formensprache der Archigram-Architekten gerieten die Beiträge der anderen Teilnehmer etwas ins Hintertreffen. Doch auch der Entwurf des Finnen Reima Pietilä hob sich aus der Masse hervor: Sein organisch strukturiertes und expressiv ausgearbeitetes Unterhaltungs- und Vergnügungszentrum ragt über die Bucht hinaus und läßt sie sogar nach innen dringen. Unter den bizarren Formen der Außenseite verbirgt sich eine Konstruktion, die den diversen Aktivitäten auf verschiedenen Ebenen Raum bietet.

Der Ingenieur-Architekt Frei Otto entwarf hingegen eine außergewöhnliche und komplizierte Überdachung. Möglicherweise zweifelte die Jury an der technischen Durchführbarkeit. Diese Bedenken waren jedoch nicht gerechtfertigt, denn Frei Otto – zugleich Autor von »Das hängende Dach« (1954) – realisierte einige Jahre später die Überdachung des Olympiastadions in München (1972 fertiggestellt), die allgemeine Bewunderung hervorrief. Auch die visionären Zeichnungen von Archigram erhielten die verdiente Bewunderung und Anerkennung. Allerdings: Unsterblichen Ruhm erlangen Architekten erst durch die Ausführung ihrer Konzepte.

Centre de Loisirs, Monte-Carlo

Monte-Carlo est la capitale de Monaco, la célèbre petite principauté méditerranéenne dont les résidents sont généralement assez fortunés pour profiter sans restriction de tous les plaisirs de la vie. Pour ajouter encore à leur bonheur, douze architectes ou équipes d'architectes furent conviés à soumettre des propositions pour un centre de loisirs. Le jury attribua le premier prix à Archigram qui avait imaginé une construction souterraine.

Nouveaux défis architecturaux

La prospérité croissante que connut l'Europe au cours des années 60 entraîna de nombreux bouleversements sociaux. La société des loisirs fit son apparition, donnant naissance du même coup à de nouveaux besoins architecturaux.
En mai 1969, le ministère des Travaux publics de Monaco décida que le moment était venu de construire un centre de loisirs pour les habitants de ce mini-Etat. Bien que Monaco soit déjà saturé de constructions, un site fut trouvé: une étroite bande de terre entre l'avenue de la Princesse Grace et la mer. Le programme du concours n'était pas facile: le centre, entouré d'un parc, devait comprendre un espace d'exposition, une salle de sport (hockey sur glace) et un cirque. Il devait offrir de 1 500 à 2 000 places assises et permettre de recevoir des tournées théâtrales et des banquets.
En dehors de ces structures d'accueil pour des activités temporaires, les architectes pouvaient proposer des activités permanentes. Cette liberté se révéla un inconvénient tant il était difficile de marier le permanent à un temporaire d'importance majeure pour les promoteurs du projet.
Le jury était composé de Pierre Vago, l'un des grands architectes français de l'époque, d'Ove Arup, célèbre pour son intervention sur l'opéra de Sydney et d'autres projets spectaculaires, de Michel Ragon, historien d'art, et de René Sarger. Ils reçurent douze projets et retinrent le plus étonnant, celui de l'équipe d'Archigram. C'était le plan le plus radical jamais sélectionné par un jury et ce choix signifiait du même coup au monde que l'architecture était en train de changer.

Archigram

Archigram avait été fondé à Londres en 1961 par quelques jeunes diplômés, frustrés par l'état de l'architecture de leur époque. Le nom d'Archigram vient de la contraction d'architecture et du grec graphein, écriture. La philosophie de ce groupe, animé par Peter Cook, n'était pas sans ambiguïté. D'une part, il était sensible aux changement rapides qu'insufflait la modernité dans la société (l'innovation technologique le fascinait, comme il le montra dans ses projets), d'autre part il n'était pas sans exprimer des réserves politiques sur le caractère superficiel de ce même monde moderne.
Archigram mit au point un certain nombre de concepts clés illustrant l'ambivalence de leurs attitudes par rapport à la société de consommation. Ils permettent de mieux apprécier leur projet pour Monte-Carlo.
Le premier concept est celui de la «cité branchée». Archigram était fasciné par la masse de nouveaux appareils électriques qui inondait le marché pendant les années 60. La «cité branchée» était une méga-structure, pleine d'invention mais réfléchie avec soin, qui comprenait des immeubles mobiles, des grues, des tuyaux d'alimentation apparents et de multiples composants futuristes. Elle fonctionnait grâce à un ensemble de grues et de robots. Cet optimisme technologique était fréquent dans les années précédant la crise de l'énergie des années 70.

Le «village éclaté» était un concept encore plus audacieux. Il consistait en un mât central doté de bras auquel les unités d'habitation se trouvaient attachées. Toute la structure pouvait pivoter sur elle-même et faisait un peu penser à une attraction foraine.
Dans une approche complètement différente, Archigram exprima également ses vues sur la société urbaine à travers une série de collages. Alors que la «cité branchée» et le «village éclaté» sont des projets à grande échelle s'appuyant sur l'innovation technologique, ces collages et photo-montages sont plus intimes, plus proches de l'individu. Ils peuvent être rapprochés de l'art psychédélique très populaire en Grande-Bretagne à la même période (pochettes de disques, films des Beatles comme «Sergeant Pepper's Lonely Heart's Club Band», etc.).
Parmi les autres concepts d'Archigram, la «cité qui marche», les «maisons drive-in» et la «cité instantanée» sont tout aussi étonnants. La «cité instantanée» consiste en une structure verticale mobile à laquelle les services urbains sont attachés. Consumérisme et loisirs font partie intégrante de cette cité à la fois surréaliste et terrifiante. Archigram incorpora plusieurs de ces éléments dans son projet pour Monaco.

Une place au soleil

L'équipe d'Archigram, et son approche ambiguë de la société de consommation, semblait parfaitement convenir au concours de Monte-Carlo. Peter Cook présenta leur approche de la façon suivante:
«Pour chacun d'entre nous, le nom de Monte-Carlo signifiait sophistication, argent, oisiveté et exotisme, la non-réalité vécue comme vie réelle, Marienbad-in-Californie, costumes blancs et Rolls Royces blanches, et, enfin, une place au soleil pour Archigram.»
C'était comme si la «cité instantanée», les collages et tous ces autres concepts si inventifs pouvaient enfin prendre corps. Des détails qui avaient pu sembler bizarres dans certains projets semblaient maintenant logiques. Mais des idées aussi créatives soient-elles n'étaient pas suffisantes pour impressionner le jury. La compétence des architectes d'Archigram se confirmait dans leurs plans de masse et de coupe et la diversité des activités qu'ils avaient réussi à intégrer. On trouvait par exemple des équipements pour un centre sur l'espace, pour le hockey sur glace et le Grand Prix de Monaco. Tous ces éléments étaient mobiles. Le complexe était essentiellement souterrain, ce qui laissait en surface toute la place nécessaire à un parc de bonnes dimensions, luxe appréciable dans une ville aussi construite que Monte-Carlo. Aucune autre équipe n'avait pensé à la solution souterraine. L'ensemble de ces plans sortait totalement de l'ordinaire de l'architecture.
Les caractéristiques des plans d'Archigram étaient typiques de la fin des années 60 et du début des années 70. En 1970, Arata Isozaki avait conçu un robot géant pour l'Exposition universelle d'Osaka qui avait dû plaire à Archigram, et le centre de loisirs était équipé de nombreux robots. Dans les mâts du stade de hockey, par exemple, des robots-buffets proposaient aux spectateurs des boissons et des glaces.
On peut se demander si Cook et son équipe prirent réellement ce concours au sérieux et si certaines fantaisies de leurs plans n'étaient pas excessives. Leur centre connut le sort de la plupart de leurs autres projets et ne fut jamais construit. Le client émit de plus en plus de réserves sur la compétence des architectes, et l'opinion de Peter Cook sur la principauté n'était pas très positive si l'on en juge par une autre de ses déclarations: *«Monaco est prêt à la nouveauté, dans la mesure où elle n'effraye pas les vieilles dames riches et les riches Européens en général. Pas de hippies et pas trop de bruit; juste des feux d'artifices et des sports agréables à regarder et sans sueur.»*

Les autres participations

Confrontés au superbe projet d'Archigram, la plupart des plans des autres concurrents furent injustement éclipsés. Le Finlandais Reima Pietilä avait proposé une structure organique très expressive qui se projetait au-dessus de la mer. Sous cette apparence fantastique se cachait un plan très rationnel qui offrait sur plusieurs niveaux toutes les surfaces nécessaires aux différentes activités.
Le projet de Frei Otto était d'un calibre très différent. Cet ingénieur spécialisé en architecture avait conçu un toit tendu aussi étonnant que complexe. Le jury avait peut-être douté à tort de sa faisabilité puisque Frei Otto, auteur de «Das hängende Dach» (Le toit suspendu, 1954) vit plus tard ses propositions prises au sérieux pour le stade olympique de Munich, qui fut réalisé en 1972 à l'admiration de tous.
Hautement appréciées, les conceptions architecturales d'Archigram montrent que la pure qualité des plans ne suffit pas toujours. L'immortalité architecturale est réservée à ceux dont les visions ont la chance d'être réalisées.

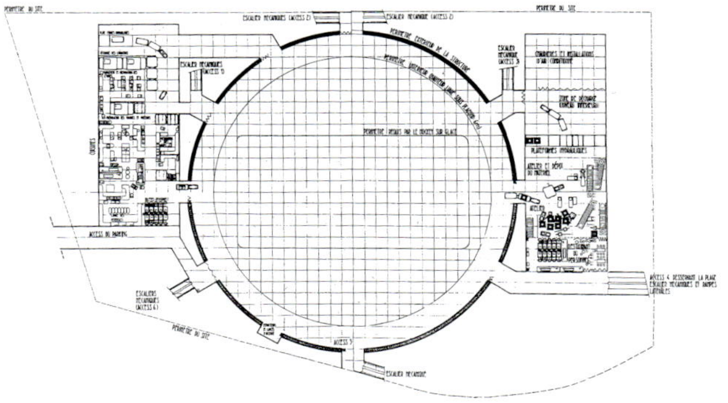

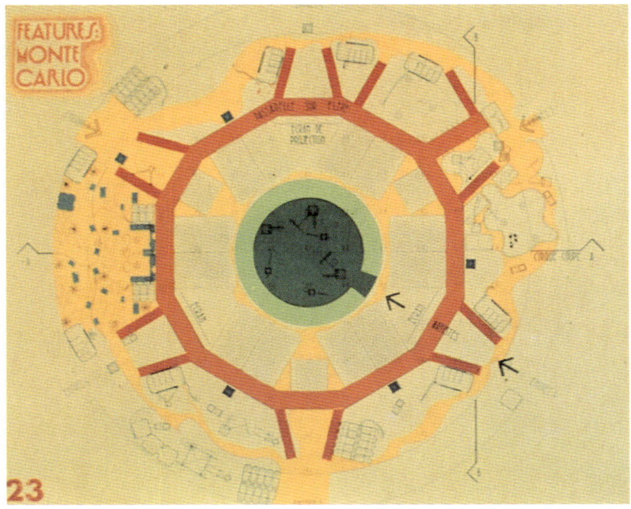

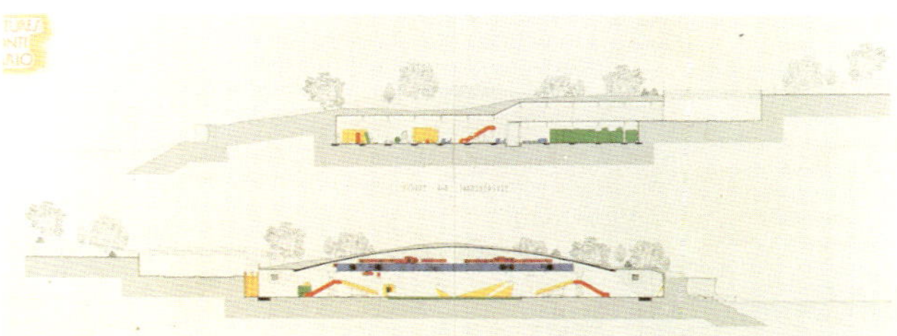

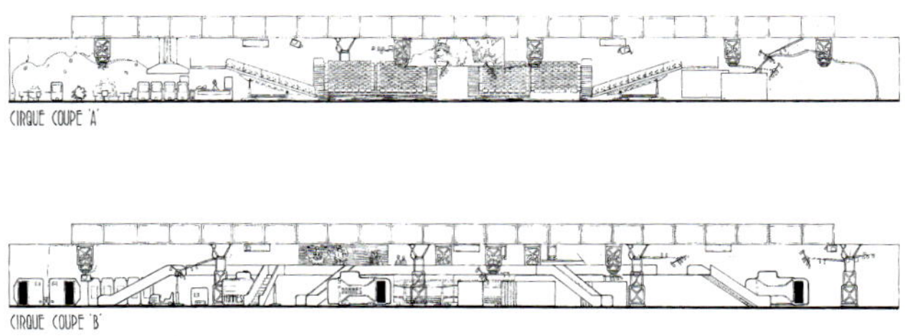

Archigram: competition design, 1969 collage of "Land Beach", first prize

Archigram competition design, 1969, basic plan, first prize

Archigram competition design, 1969, above: east-west section (north side), below: east-west section (south side), first prize

Archigram competition design, 1969, collage of "Circus variation", first prize

Archigram competition design, 1969, plan of "Circus variation", first prize

Archigram competition design, 1969, sections of "Circus variation", first prize

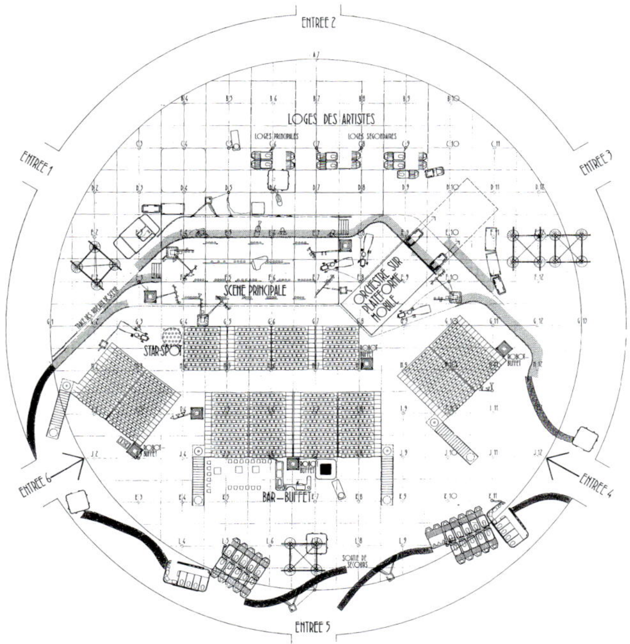

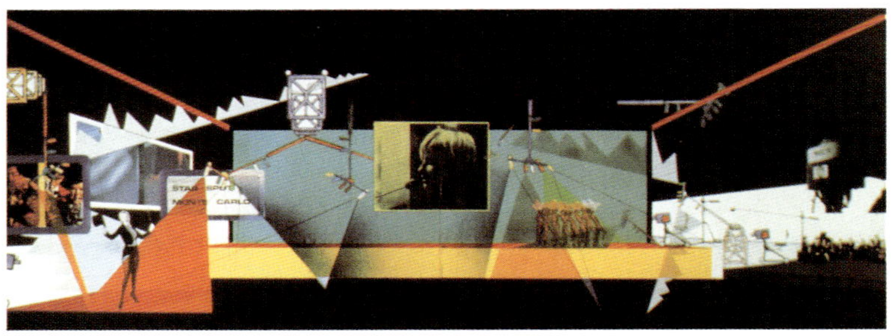

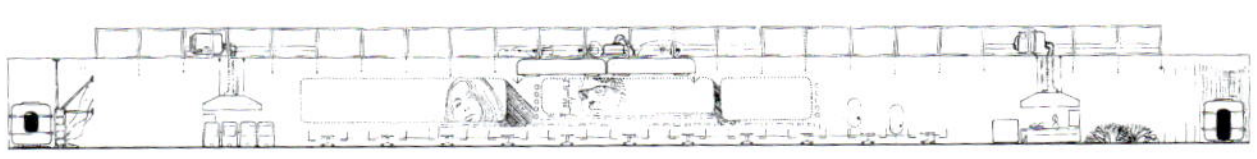
BANQUET COUPE A

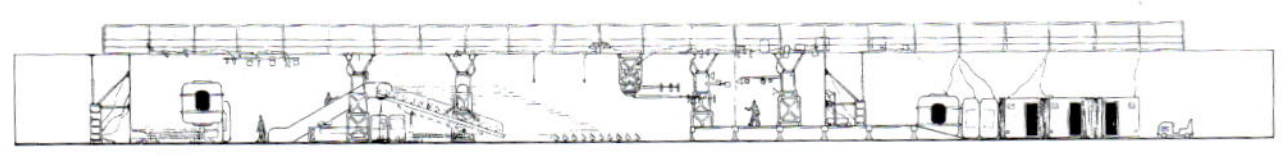
SPECTACLE DE VARIÉTÉS COUPE 'A'

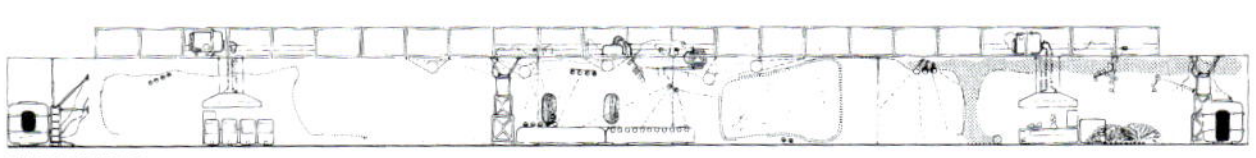
BANQUET COUPE B

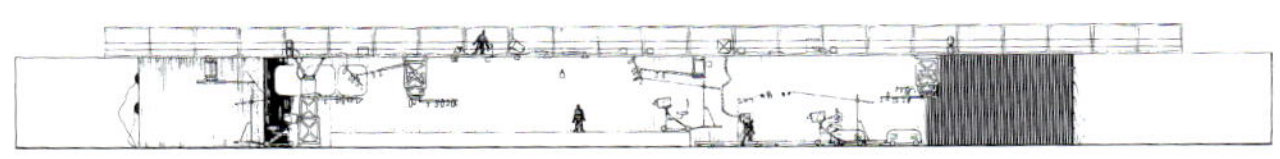
SPECTACLE DE VARIÉTÉS COUPE 'B'

Archigram **competition design, 1969, collage of "Variety Show variation", first prize**

Archigram **competition design, 1969, plan of "Variety Show variation", first prize**

Archigram **competition design, 1969, sections of "Variety Show variation", first prize**

Archigram **competition design, 1969, collage of "Banquet variation", first prize**

Archigram **competition design, 1969, plan of "Banquet variation", first prize**

Archigram **competition design, 1969, sections of "Banquet variation", first prize**

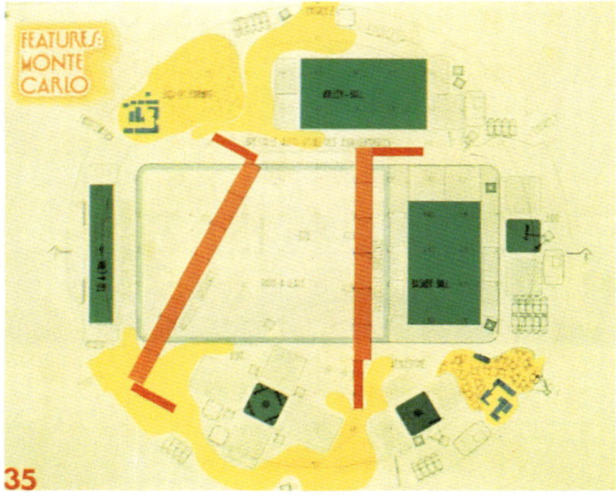

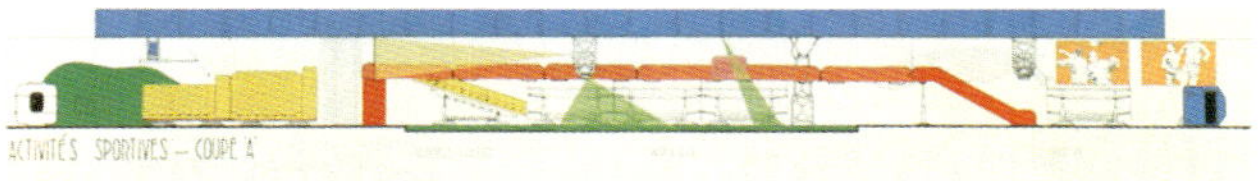

Archigram competition design, 1969, collage of "Sports Activities variation", first prize

Archigram competition design, 1969, plan of "Sports Activities variation", first prize

Archigram competition design, 1969, sections of "Sports Activities variation", first prize

Archigram competition design, 1969, collage of "Ice Hockey variation", first prize

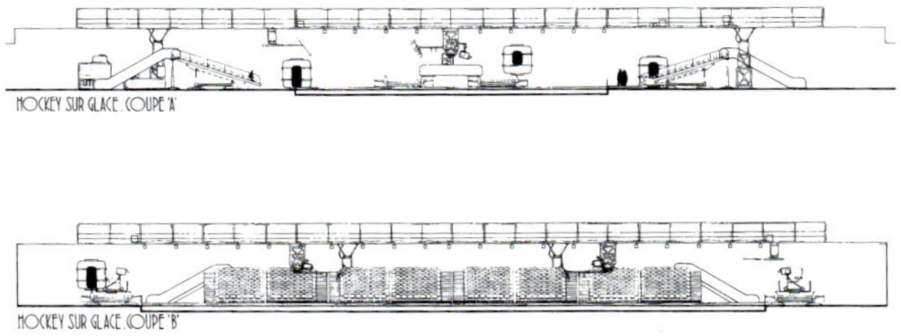

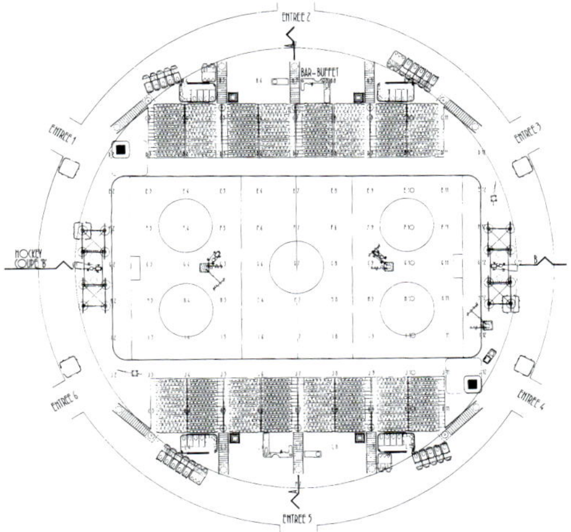

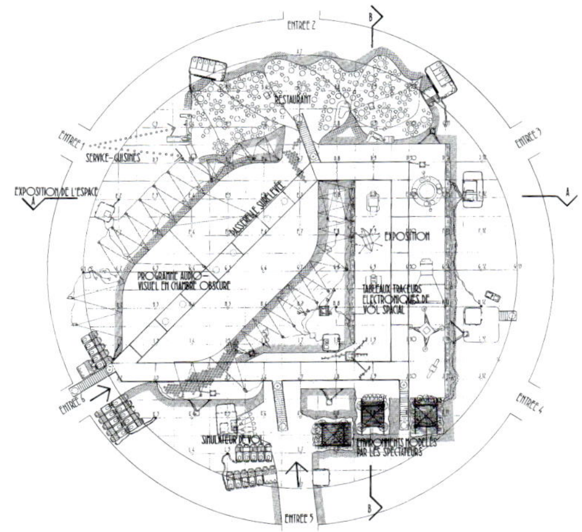

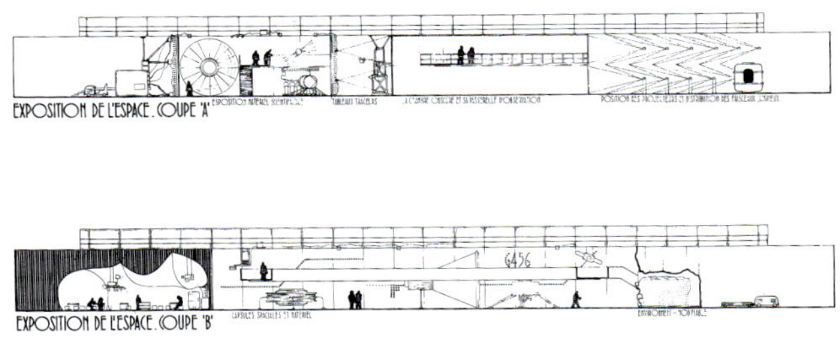

Archigram competition design, 1969, sections of "Ice Hockey variation", first prize

Archigram competition design, 1969, plan of "Ice Hockey variation", first prize

Archigram competition design, 1969, sections of exhibition of "Space Exploration variation", first prize

Archigram competition design, 1969, plan of exhibition of "Space Exploration variation", first prize

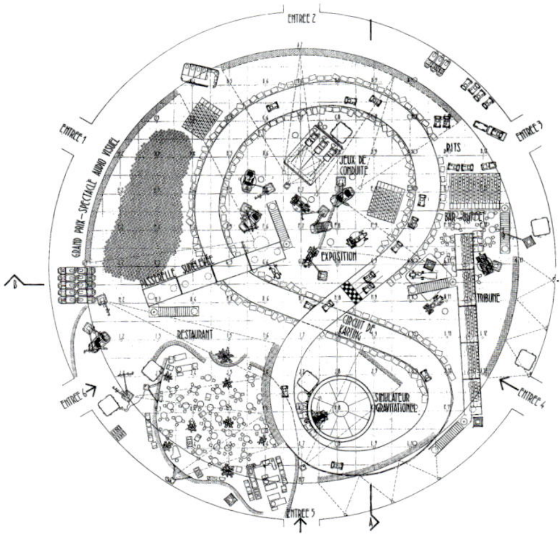
RESTAURANT
EXPOSITION
TRIBUNE

Shell

GRAND PRIX COUPE 'A'

GRAND PRIX COUPE 'B'

FEATURES: MONTE CARLO
43

Archigram competition design, 1969, plan of exhibition of "F1 Monte Carlo Grand-Prix variation", first prize

Archigram competition design, 1969, collage of exhibition "F1 Monte Carlo Grand-Prix variation", first prize

Archigram competition design, 1969, sections of exhibition "F12 Monte Carlo Grand-Prix variation", first prize

Archigram competition design, 1969, plan of "Cultural Event variation", first prize

Archigram competition design, 1969, collage of "Cultural Event variation", first prize

Frei Otto competition design, 1969, photomontage of Monte Carlo

Frei Otto competition design, 1969, model

Frei Otto competition design, 1969, photomontage

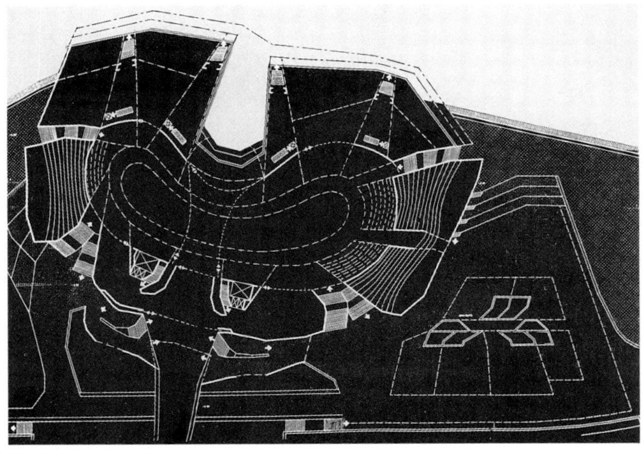

Reima Pietilä competition design, 1969, site plan

Reima Pietilä competition design, 1969, plan

Reima Pietilä competition design, 1969, east-west section (south side)

Reima Pietilä competition design, 1969, east-west section (south side)

Reima Pietilä competition design, 1969, north-south section (east side)

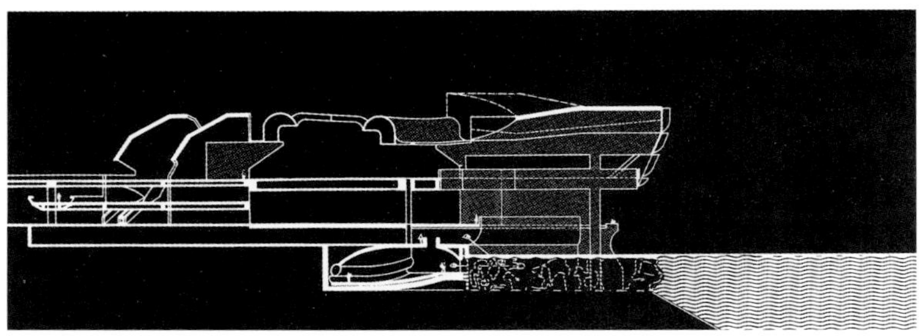

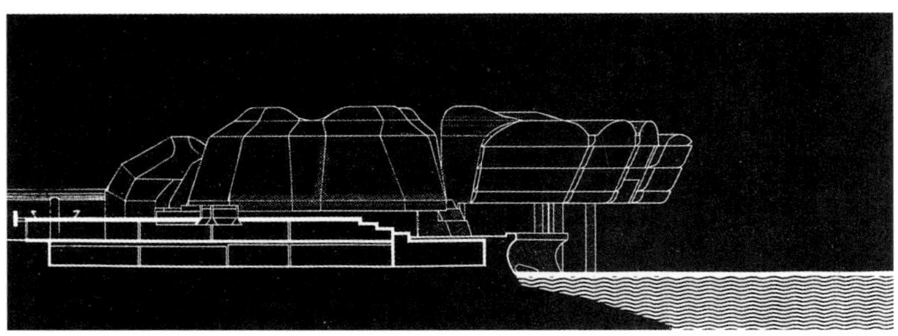

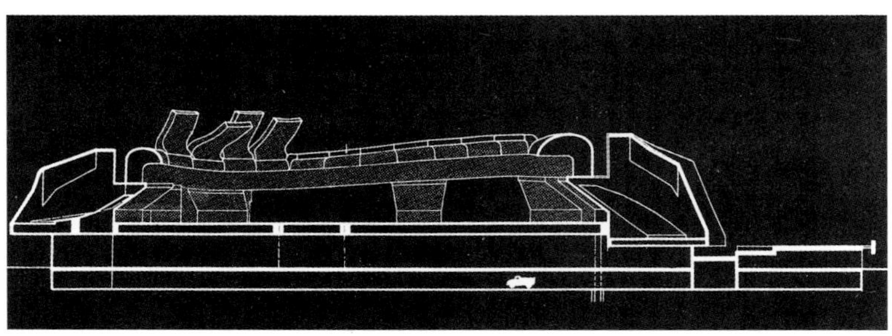

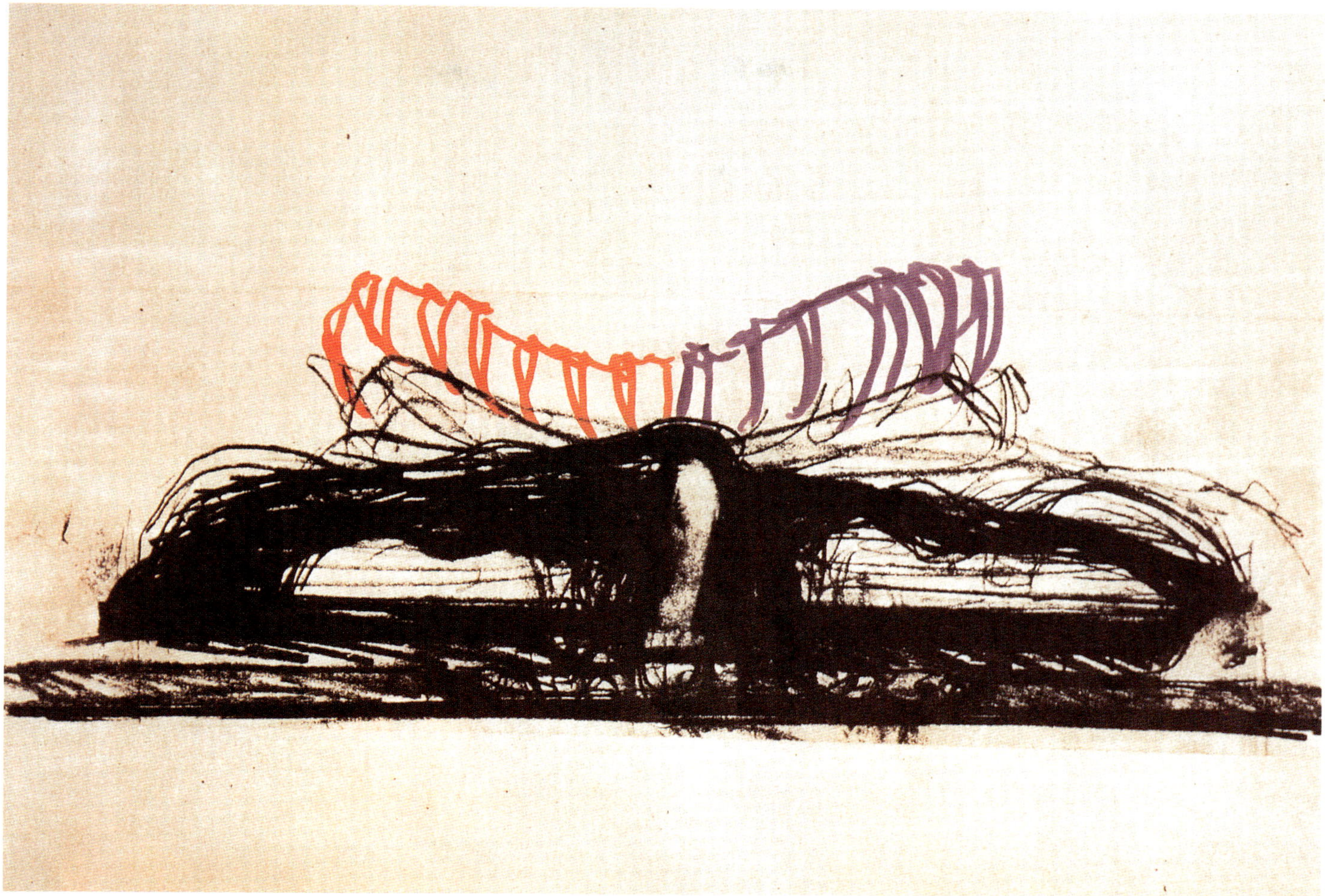

Reima Pietilä competition design, 1969, drawing

Reima Pietilä competition design, 1969, drawing

Project

Museum and centre for culture and information

Site

Rue du Renard, Rue Rambuteau, Rue St. Martin and Rue St. Mérri: Plateau Beaubourg

Dates

Competition announced December 1970 *Closing date* 1 June 1971 *Result announced* 15 July 1971

Number of entries

681

Jury

Jean Prouvé (chairman, architect), Gaëtan Picon (former director-general of the Ministère des Beaux Arts), Sir Frank Francis (honorary director of the British Museum), Michel Laclotte (chief curator of the Louvre), Herman Liebaers (director of the Royal Library in Brussels), Willem Sandberg (former director of the Stedelijk Museum in Amsterdam), Emille Aillaud, Philip Johnson, Oscar Niemeyer (all architects) and Robert Regard (technical advisor)

Result

First prize Renzo Piano & Richard Rogers, together with Gianfranco Franchini and Ove Arup & Associates *Honourable mention* J.L.C. Choisy, R. Ouendag & G. Martens; Manfred Schiedhelm; Moshe Safdie; Robert Stones & Wolfgang Pearlman; Dennis Crompton & William Alsop; Ahmet Gulgonen; K. Kurokawa; and 23 other architects

Commissioned by

The Ministry of Cultural Affairs

Construction

March 1972 to January 1977

Architects

Renzo Piano & Richard Rogers, Ove Arup & Associates

Construction cost

480 000 000 francs

Centre Pompidou, Paris, 1970–1971

Renzo Piano & Richard Rogers
competition design, 1971, west elevation, first prize

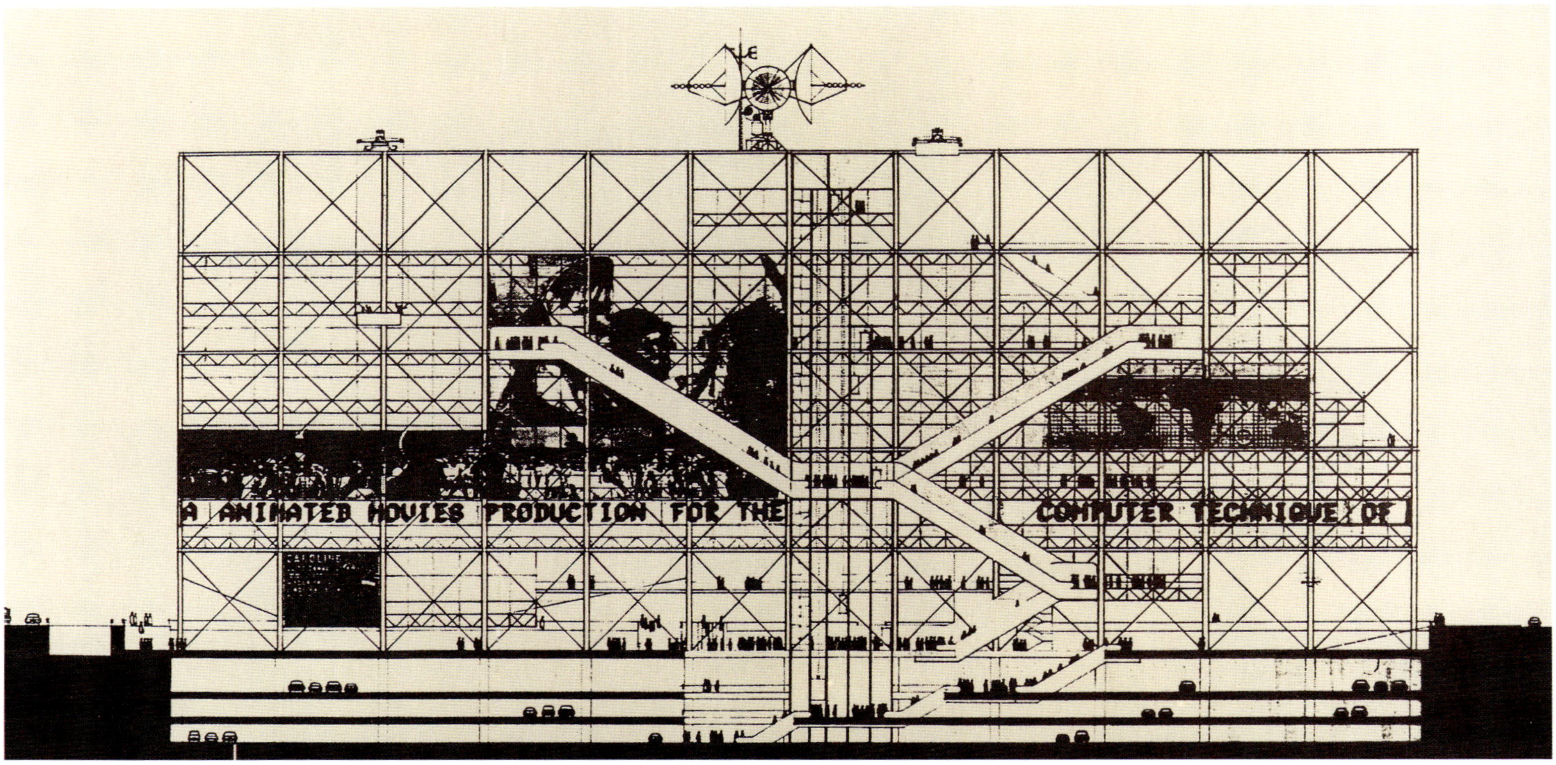

Centre Pompidou, Paris

The genesis of the Centre Georges Pompidou is as illustrious as that of the Eiffel Tower. Both structures are situated in the centre of Paris and, in a sense, they are both high-tech. After the initial critical rumpus had died down, both the Eiffel Tower and the Centre Pompidou became important Parisian tourist attractions. Moreover, they unquestionably represent the best that modern architecture has to offer.

Presidential ambition

It has become customary in France for the ruling president to spend large portions of the taxpayers' money on prestigious projects, in an effort to guarantee his own architectural immortality. In a sense they are perpetuating a tradition started by their illustrious royal predecessors. President Georges Pompidou will go down in history as the man who got the ball rolling although, in terms of scale, his efforts have since been overshadowed by those of the current president, François Mitterrand[1]. The fact that neither the "Grande Arche" nor any of the projects bears his name probably attests to the president's modesty.

Although the project for the cultural centre had officially been commissioned by the Ministry of Cultural Affairs, the driving force behind it was Pompidou himself, who wanted to have something to show for his seven-year term of office. The president and his wife, who were great admirers of modern art, wanted to build a centre which would become a venue for all forms of art and, more importantly, would attract many visitors. Although the old museum of modern art on the Avenue Président Wilson had a magnificent collection, it drew few visitors.

The architects Renzo Piano and Richard Rogers, who initially limited themselves to the design of a new museum, clearly understood the wishes of the president. The museum would not be built along traditional lines, with the kind of imposing façade that makes a threatening rather than inviting impression on the "man in the street". The architects had something completely different in mind. As Renzo Piano put it: *"Breaking through the wall of suspicion between the general public and modern art, by constructing a building which is both as familiar as a factory, and as intriguing as a space ship – in other words, it evokes the desire to enter the building in order to find out what is going on inside."*

Even though Pompidou appeared to have found kindred spirits in architecture, he was less than charmed by Rogers and Piano's original designs which had won first prize. However, he accepted the jury's decision because he had faith in their expertise. It took a while for the general public, the target group, to do the same, but once their initial suspicion had faded, they arrived in droves. Thus Pompidou achieved what he had set out to do: millions of people now knew his name.

Although the costs were high – the maintenance costs are still astronomical – the end glorified the means. The fact that some people persistently refer to the centre as Beaubourg – the centre is situated on the Plateau Beaubourg – has done little to tarnish Pompidou's dream.

Les Halles, 1854

Philip Johnson, architect, explains the project of Renzo Piano & Richard Rogers to other members of the jury

An untidy parking area

The Centre National d'Art et de Culture (CNAC) resulted from a competition for a completely different project. The entire district where the Plateau Beaubourg and the central market were situated was to be redeveloped. A project had been initiated before the Second World War, but this had come to an early end. The Plateau Beaubourg was an untidy parking area and the market did not have the capacity to provide food for the whole of France.

In 1967 a handful of French architects were invited to submit plans for the district. At the same time, two new tracks for the high-speed metro (RER) were to be constructed, which were to cross under the market halls. The architects were also asked to include a new business centre, as well as a new building for the Ministry of Finance (which later moved to the Seine), offices, hotels, dwellings and a museum of modern art. Unfortunately for the architects, president Charles de Gaulle was "dethroned" by Pompidou and, with the exception of the museum of modern art, the plans were shelved. A new open, international competition was organised in December 1970, for which no fewer than 681 designs from 50 different countries were duly submitted. A quarter of the participating architects were French.

The project was extremely complicated, because various art forms had to be gathered under a single roof. The complex was to contain a museum of modern art, a centre for industrial design, a library, and a

music centre. The latter was later housed in the IRCAM institute, which is situated diagonally opposite the Centre Pompidou and which was also designed by Piano & Rogers[2]. The centre was to focus upon the research and integration of the arts. Because this was a totally new concept, the architects were expected to come up with an innovative plan. In an effort to avoid complicating matters further, the form and estimated costs were left up to the architects.
As was to be expected the competition drew a wide variety of entries and the jury, which included such renowned architects as Jean Prouvé, Oscar Niemeyer and Philip Johnson, had a difficult task in picking a winner. After lengthy deliberation, they decided to award first prize to Piano & Rogers. Thirty other architects received an honourable mention and 10 000 francs.

A partnership

Renzo Piano (b. Genoa 1937) was already an experienced architect when he left for Paris. He had worked together with his father and F. Albini in Italy, with Louis Kahn in Philadelphia and with Z.S. Makowski in London. He had worked with Rogers since the CNAC competition in 1971. It is worth mentioning here that this sort of partnership is not unusual on a project of this magnitude. However, partnership does not imply that two diligent and enthusiastic architects sit down at their drawing-boards and each design half a building; architectural firms which engage in partnerships usually have a large staff and at the time of the competition, Piano's firm had offices in Genoa, Paris and London.
Rogers, on the other hand, did not have many buildings to his name when he engaged in partnership with Piano, although he was later to become one of the top three architects in England, together with Norman Foster and James Stirling.
The structural aspects of the design were in hands of the engineering firm Ove Arup & Partners, with whom Piano had regularly worked in the past. No fewer than 2000 people worked for Arup's firm.

High-tech prototype

The Centre Pompidou is the product of a fruitful partnership and has a special place in architectural history, because it is considered to be the prototype of the high-tech style which developed during the 1980s. The term "high-tech" is a combination of the terms "high-style" and "technology", thus implying that the movement was interested in both design and structure.
The term was first coined in 1978 by Joan Kron and Suzanne Slesin in their book High-Tech: The Industrial Style and Source Book for the Home (New York, 1978). Design and structure are not separate entities, but form an integrated whole, where the aesthetic features of an object are determined by its technical structure, which may or may not be prefabricated. The technical structure is preferably provided by some industrial object which was designed for purposes other than those projected by the architect. The structure and technical elements of the building are clearly visible, and are prominent features of the building as a whole. That is to say, they are conspicuous and striking, rather than merely visible.
The high-tech movement was particularly popular in Great Britain, the home country of its proponents Rogers, Foster, Grimshaw and Hopkins. The architects of the Archigram group, who developed "technological" plans for "plug-in cities" and other imaginative projects, are seen as the visionary predecessors of the movement[3], though it is also possible that the high-tech architects were influenced by Soviet architecture of the 1920s and 1930s. The stylistic background may be even broader, yet the Centre Pompidou was the first building in which all structural aspects of the building are visible. Features such as escalators, air-conditioning ducts and antennae are all conspicuous elements of the design.
Once again a comparison with the Eiffel Tower can be made. However, the structural aspects of the tower are dominant and the aesthetic features are no more than architectural embellishments which have no structural function, as is the case in most examples of utilitarian building. The Centre Pompidou would have been even more "turned inside-out", had it not been for the fact that fire regulations necessitated alterations to the original design, as a result of which the entire east side, where Rogers and Piano had projected a glass façade, had to be "closed".

Renzo Piano & Richard Rogers
Centre Pompidou, view of the west façade and the piazza

Renzo Piano & Richard Rogers
Centre Pompidou, view of the façade on Rue du Renard

A slap in the face

Today it is hard to imagine that the Centre Pompidou met with such vehement protest only twenty-five years ago. In those days many Parisians experienced its bright colours and daring structure as a slap in the face, and the complex was seen as an architectural tumour in the historical heart of Paris.
However, the tumour was not malignant. Rogers and Piano had used only half of the Plateau Beaubourg. The other half became a square, similar to the Campo in Sienna. An extension of the Centre Pompidou, it is a space in which (semi-) cultural productions and performances are held, which enhanced the urban function of the entire district. The IRCAM and the magnificent fountain designed by Jean Tinguely and Niki de Saint-Phalle all contribute to the aura of culture envisaged by Pompidou. The surrounding district has also benefited from the complex. The nearby market halls, which were the subject of the original competition, were eventually transformed into a less interesting complex by Claude Vasconi and Georges Pencreac'h.

In contrast to the striking view from the square, the interior of the Centre Pompidou is remarkably austere. The visitor is indeed lured into the building to find out what is going on inside, only to discover that the answer is nothing. The real events take place outside. Naturally one can view wonderful exhibitions and collections, but the works of art are rather carelessly displayed against movable partitions. In addition, another wall was also closed off in order to meet the fire regulations. As a result, the concept of a glass box suspended in a steel structure is less conspicuous than was originally intended. However, these are marginal comments, considering the multitude of outstanding features which the building does possess.

Fantastic plans

The margin of artistic freedom gave architects the opportunity to concoct the most fantastic plans, the wildest of which was executed. Consequently, a number of architects deserve a special mention. Manfred Schiedhelm designed a futuristic, transparent dome which covered the entire Plateau Beaubourg and the complex. Moshe Safdie also used all the available space: his building had characteristic underground levels and a large hole in the middle, above which he projected a stepped, overhanging structure.
Dennis Crompton's design, which was also partially situated underground, was actually drawn by the third-year student William Alsop. Crompton's name undoubtedly contributed to the fact that they received an honourable mention. A number of Dutch architects, including Jan Hoogstad and J.L.C. Choisy, also participated. Hoogstad's design is characterised by an excellent spatial sub-division. Different facilities were separated by open spaces, whereby the dominant presence of the concrete complex is tempered considerably.
Robert Stones and Wolfgang Pearlman designed a structure which consisted of elements which had twelve identical surfaces. Visitors would have required a system of signposts and a map to get from one side of the building to the other. Nevertheless, they received an honourable mention for their design. Other notable entries came from Japan (Yutaka Murata, Kisho Kurokawa, Minoru Takeyama), Belgium (Charles Vandenhove) and Turkey (Ahmet Gulgonen).

Renzo Piano & Richard Rogers
Centre Pompidou, National Museum of Modern Art on the fourth floor

Renzo Piano & Richard Rogers
Centre Pompidou, Library

1 *See chapters on the "Grands Projets" elsewhere in this book.*
2 *IRCAM, the Institut de Recherche et Coordination Acoustique-Musique, was built between 1973 and 1977.*
3 *See chapter on the Entertainment Centre in Monte Carlo elsewhere in this book.*
4 *See chapters on the "Grands Projets" elsewhere in this book.*

Centre Pompidou, Paris

Das Centre Georges Pompidou und der Eiffelturm haben viele Gemeinsamkeiten: Beide Bauwerke stehen im Zentrum von Paris, besitzen eine turbulente Entstehungsgeschichte und sind in gewisser Weise »High-Tech«. Nachdem sie anfangs auf starken Widerstand stießen, zählen heute sowohl der Eiffelturm als auch das Centre Pompidou zu den bedeutendsten Touristenattraktionen der französischen Hauptstadt und zu den Höhepunkten der modernen Baukunst.

Präsidiale Geltungssucht

Obwohl das Ministère des Affaires Culturelles als offizieller Auftraggeber fungierte, war der eigentliche Initiator und Motor dieses Projekts Staatspräsident Georges Pompidou, der seine siebenjährige Amtszeit krönen wollte. Wie seine Frau galt auch er als begeisterter Liebhaber moderner Kunst. Ihm schwebte ein Zentrum für alle Künste vor, das große Menschenmengen anziehen sollte, denn das bisherige Museum für moderne Kunst an der Avenue du Président Wilson erfreute sich trotz einer großartigen Sammlung nur geringen Zuspruchs.
Die zunächst nur mit der Planung für ein Museum beauftragten Architekten Renzo Piano und Richard Rogers teilten die Ansichten des Staatspräsidenten: Es sollte kein Museum im klassischen Sinne entstehen, vielmehr schwebte den Architekten ein Ansatz vor, den Renzo Piano so umschrieb: »*Man muß die Mauern des Mißtrauens zwischen dem breiten Publikum und der modernen Kunst niederreißen durch ein Gebäude, das einerseits vertraut erscheint – wie eine Fabrik –, aber andererseits auch fasziniert – wie ein Raumschiff. Es soll den Wunsch erwecken, hineinzugehen und sich alles darin anzusehen.*« Pompidou zeigte sich von Rogers und Pianos Entwürfen, von der Jury mit dem ersten Preis ausgezeichnet, keinesfalls überzeugt. Da er den Sachverstand der Jury anerkennen mußte, akzeptierte er ihr Urteil. Es sollte noch einige Jahre dauern, bis sich auch die angestrebte Zielgruppe – das breite Publikum – diesem Urteil anschloß.

Ein ungepflegter Parkplatz

Das Centre National d'Art et de Culture (CNAC) ist Ergebnis eines Architekturwettbewerbs, der ursprünglich zu einem ganz anderen Zweck ausgeschrieben worden war: Ein ganzes Stadtviertel, in dem auch das Plateau Beaubourg und die Markthallen lagen, sollte völlig neu bebaut werden. Obwohl schon vor dem Zweiten Weltkrieg die ersten Pläne für die Sanierung entstanden waren, hatte sich nicht viel verändert. Das Plateau Beaubourg diente als Parkplatz für Lastwagen. Die Markthallen waren nicht mehr groß genug.
1967 wurden einige französische Architekten eingeladen, Pläne für ein neues Viertel auszuarbeiten. Zwei Trassen für die Untergrundschnellbahn (RER) sollten sich bei den Hallen kreuzen. Die Architekten wurden gebeten, in ihre Entwürfe ein Geschäftszentrum, ein neues Finanzministerium (das später an der Seine entstand), Büros, Hotels, Wohnungen und ein Museum für moderne Kunst zu integrieren.
Als der damalige Staatspräsident Charles De Gaulle zurücktrat, verschwanden diese Pläne wieder in der Versenkung – Ausnahme: das Museum für moderne Kunst. Abermals schrieb die Regierung einen Architekturwettbewerb aus (Dezember 1970). Dabei handelte es sich um eine internationale Ausschreibung, an der sich 681 Einsender aus 50 Ländern beteiligten. Gut ein Viertel der Beiträge stammte aus Frankreich.
Die Anforderungen an die Architekten waren besonders hoch, da in einem einzigen Baukomplex Raum für die verschiedensten Künste geschaffen werden mußte. Neben einem Museum für moderne Kunst sah die Ausschreibung auch ein Zentrum für industrielles Design, eine Bibliothek und eine Musikabteilung vor. Diese Abteilung fand ihren Platz schließlich im ebenfalls von Piano und Rogers gebauten IRCAM-Institut, das dem Centre Pompidou schräg gegenüberliegt. Im Mittelpunkt des Projekts sollte die Integration der Künste stehen. Dieser ungewöhnliche Ansatz erforderte von den Architekten neuartige Ideen und Entwürfe. Um die Aufgabe nicht noch zu vergrößern, blieben Form und Baukosten des Projekts unspezifiziert.
Die unterschiedlichsten Wettbewerbsbeiträge trafen ein, so daß sich die Aufgabe der Jury schwierig gestaltete. Nach langwierigen Beratungen entschlossen sich die Mitglieder – darunter große Namen wie Jean Prouvé, Oscar Niemeyer und Philip Johnson – den ersten Preis an den Entwurf von Piano und Rogers zu vergeben. 30 weitere Teilnehmer erhielten eine ehrenvolle Erwähnung und je 10 000 Francs.

Ein Gemeinschaftsprodukt

Der 1937 in Genua geborene Renzo Piano konnte bereits vor seiner Arbeit in Paris auf langjährige Erfahrungen zurückblicken: Er hatte in Italien mit seinem Vater und F. Albini zusammengearbeitet, in Philadelphia mit Louis Kahn und in London mit Z.S. Makowski. Niederlassungen Pianos befanden sich in Genua, Paris und London. Mit der Ausschreibung für das CNAC 1971 begann seine Zusammenarbeit mit Rogers. Die Konstruktionspläne wurden durch das Ingenieurbüro Ove Arup & Partners erstellt, mit dem Piano häufig zusammenarbeitete, und für das etwa 2 000 Mitarbeiter tätig waren. Rogers dagegen hatte vor seiner Zusammenarbeit mit Piano deutlich weniger Bauprojekte zu verzeichnen. Im Laufe der Jahre entwickelte er sich jedoch neben Norman Foster und James Stirling zu einem der »Großen Drei« der englischen Architektur.

Prototyp des High-Tech

Das Centre Pompidou ist ein herausragendes Beispiel für eine erfolgreiche Zusammenarbeit zweier Architekten. Es nimmt einen besonderen Platz in der Architekturgeschichte ein, denn es gilt als Prototyp einer Bewegung, die in der Baukunst der 80er Jahre Furore machen sollte: »High-Tech«. Der Ausdruck entstand aus der Kombination der Begriffe »high-style« und »technology« und stellt damit nicht nur den Entwurf, sondern auch die Konstruktion in den Mittelpunkt.
Der Ausdruck selbst wurde 1978 eingeführt von Joan Kron und Suzanne Slesin in ihrem Buch »High-Tech: The Industrial Style and Source Book for the Home« (New York) eingeführt. Form und Konstruktion stehen nicht isoliert nebeneinander, sondern bilden ein integratives Ganzes, wobei die technische Form als ästhetischer Ausgangspunkt dient. Bei der Formenwahl erfolgt vorzugsweise ein Rückgriff auf Industrieprodukte, die ursprünglich für ganz andere Zwecke gedacht waren. Konstruktion und Technik lassen sich am Gebäude ablesen und übernehmen im Gesamtentwurf eine zentrale Rolle. Die High-Tech-Bewegung konnte sich vor allem in der englischen Architektur durchsetzen. Als bekannteste Vertreter gelten Rogers und Foster sowie Nicolas Grimshaw und Michael Hopkins. Ein phantasievoller Vorgänger dieser Strömung ist die Gruppe Archigram (siehe das Kapitel über das Sommerkasino, Monte Carlo) mit ihren »technischen« Entwürfen für die »Plug-in City«. Auch die sowjetische Architektur der 20er und 30er Jahre läßt sich als mögliche Inspirationsquelle für die Architekten des High-Tech heranziehen. Im Gegensatz zu diesen und weiteren möglichen Vorbildern ist das Centre Pompidou das erste Bauwerk, bei dem die Technik durchgängig sichtbar bleibt und Elemente wie Rolltreppen, Versorgungsleitungen (Belüftungsschächte u.ä.) und Kommunikationsmittel (Antennen, Lichtzeitung) ausdrücklich zum Gesamtentwurf gehören.
Ein Vergleich mit dem Eiffelturm drängt sich auf. Allerdings überwiegt bei diesem Bauwerk – ähnlich wie bei reinen Zweckbauten – die technische Seite; seine Formgebung besteht nur aus architektonischen Ausschmükkungen, die der eigentlichen Konstruktion nichts mehr hinzufügen. Wenn es die feuerpolizeilichen Vorschriften zugelassen hätten, wäre beim »Centre Pompidou« das Innerste nach außen gekehrt worden. Diesen ersten Entwurf mußten Rogers und Piano jedoch abändern: Aus Sicherheitsgründen blieb die gesamte Ostseite, für die ursprünglich eine gläserne Wand vorgesehen war, geschlossen.

Ein Schlag ins Gesicht

Viele Pariser Bürger empfanden die grellen Farben und die gewagte Konstruktion als einen Schlag ins Gesicht und als Angriff auf das historische Zentrum der Stadt. Aber diese Befürchtungen erwiesen sich als unbegründet. Der Entwurf von Rogers und Piano füllte nur die eine Hälfte der Place Beaubourg aus. Auf der anderen Hälfte entstand ein Platz, der dem Campo von Siena nachempfunden war. In der Verlängerung des Centre Pompidou war somit ein Forum für (sub-)kulturelle Veranstaltungen, die den volksnahen Charakter des Komplexes stärker betonen sollten, angesiedelt. Durch die Kombination mit dem IRCAM und dem faszinierenden Brunnen von Jean Tinguely und Niki de Saint-Phalle erhielt die Place Beaubourg genau jene Ausstrahlung, die Pompidou vorgeschwebt hatte.

Phantastische Pläne

Die offene Ausschreibung führte zu einer Reihe phantastischer Wettbewerbsbeiträge – von denen der kühnste realisiert wurde. Manfred Schiedhelm entwarf beispielsweise eine futuristische, durchsichtige Kuppel, die nicht nur das Gebäude überspannen, sondern sich im Gegensatz zum Entwurf von Rogers und Piano auch über den gesamten Platz ausdehnen sollte. Ebenso machte Moshe Safdie in seinem Beitrag von der Gesamtfläche des Geländes Gebrauch. Sein Entwurf wird charakterisiert durch mehrere unterirdische Geschosse rund um einen großen Mittelschacht; darüber erhebt sich eine stufenweise auskragende Konstruktion.
Ebenfalls teilweise unterirdisch angelegt ist der Beitrag von Dennis Crompton, den eigentlich der Architekturstudent William Alsop anfertigte: Das »Ausleihen« eines bekannten Namens verhalf ihm zu einer ehrenvollen Erwähnung. Robert Stones und Wolfgang Pearlman entwarfen eine Konstruktion, deren Elemente aus jeweils zwölf gleichen Flächen bestehen. Auffällig ist, daß unter den 30 ausgezeichneten Projekten kaum französische Entwürfe zu finden sind.

Le Centre Pompidou, Paris

L'histoire de la naissance du Centre Pompidou est aussi mouvementée que celle de la tour Eiffel. Les deux édifices sont situés au centre de Paris et illustrent le style high tech. Après que les clameurs crititiques se soient tues, tous deux devinrent d'étonnantes attractions touristiques et constituent deux des meilleurs exemples d'architecture moderne de leur époque respective.

Ambition présidentielle

Les présidents français disposent d'importants pouvoirs et la décision ultime de construire de grands équipements de prestige relève généralement de leur autorité. Dans un sens, ils perpétuent une tradition illustrée par leurs prédécesseurs royaux. Georges Pompidou restera dans l'histoire comme l'homme qui a relevé cette tradition bien que ses efforts aient été éclipsés par ceux du président Mitterrand[1].

Bien que la construction du futur Centre National d'Art et de Culture ait été placée sous le contrôle du ministère des Affaires culturelles, G. Pompidou accorda toujours beaucoup d'attention à ce dossier. Le président souhaitait édifier un centre qui accueille toutes les formes de création artistique. L'ancien Musée d'Art Moderne de l'avenue du président Wilson n'attirait que peu de visiteurs.

Les architectes Renzo Piano et Richard Rogers comprirent les vœux du chef de l'Etat. Ils écartèrent toute approche classique, en particulier toute façade imposante risquant de détourner l'homme de la rue, et proposèrent une idée complètement différente. Comme l'écrivit Renzo Piano: *«Faire éclater le mur de suspicion entre le grand public et l'art moderne, en construisant un bâtiment qui soit aussi familier qu'une usine, aussi étonnant qu'un vaisseau spatial, en d'autre mots qui fasse naître le désir d'y pénétrer pour y découvrir ce qui se trouve à l'intérieur.»*

Le Président ne fut pas vraiment enthousiasmé par les plans de Piano et Rogers qui avaient remporté le premier prix, mais il entérina néanmoins le choix du jury auquel il faisait confiance.

Un affreux terrain vague

Le Centre National d'Art et de Culture (CNAC) est issu d'un appel d'offres pour un projet entièrement différent. Le quartier sur lequel se trouvaient le plateau Beaubourg et les Halles devait être entièrement rénové. Un projet avait été mis au point avant la Seconde Guerre mondiale puis abandonné: le plateau Beaubourg n'était plus qu'un affreux parking et les Halles engorgées ne remplissaient plus leur fonction parisienne et nationale.

En 1967, quelques architectes français furent invités à proposer des projets pour le quartier en tenant compte des deux nouvelles lignes du RER qui allaient se croiser sous les Halles. On leur demanda de prévoir un centre d'affaires, un nouveau bâtiment pour le ministère des Finances (qui plus tard s'installa à Bercy, au bord de la Seine), des bureaux, des hôtels, des logements et un musée d'art moderne.

Le général de Gaulle quitta le pouvoir en 1969 et, à l'exception du musée, ces plans furent écartés. Un nouveau concours international fut organisé en décembre 1970 qui n'attira pas moins de 681 projets de 50 pays, un quart des participants seulement étant français.

Le projet était extrêmement complexe dans la mesure où plusieurs formes d'expression artistique allaient se trouver rassemblées sous un seul toit: un musée d'art moderne, un centre de design, une bibliothèque et un centre de recherche musicale, l'IRCAM[2], qui fut par la suite installé dans un bâtiment souterrain à quelques mètres du Centre Pompidou. Le CNAC avait pour objectifs la recherche artistique et l'intégration des différentes formes d'art. Le concours attira des projets de toute sorte et le jury qui comprenait des professionnels aussi renommés que Jean Prouvé, Oscar Niemeyer et Philip Johnson eut beaucoup de mal à désigner un vainqueur. Il décida d'attribuer le premier prix à Piano et Rogers tandis que trente autres architectes recevaient une mention honorable et 10 000 francs chacun.

Un partenariat

Renzo Piano (né à Gênes en 1937) était déjà un architecte expérimenté lorsqu'il s'installa à Paris. Il avait travaillé en Italie avec son père et F. Albini, à Philadelphie avec Louis Kahn et à Londres avec Z.S. Makowski. Il s'associa avec Rogers pour le concours du Centre Pompidou. Rogers n'avait encore que peu d'immeubles à son actif mais il allait devenir assez rapidement connu, en compagnie de James Stirling et de Norman Foster. Les aspects techniques du projet étaient confiés à Ove Arup & Partners, un cabinet d'ingénierie qui employait plus de 2 000 personnes et avec lequel Piano avait déjà collaboré.

Un prototype High Tech

Le Centre Pompidou est né d'un partenariat particulièrement fructueux et occupe une place spéciale dans l'histoire de l'architecture car il est considéré comme le prototype du style high tech qui allait se développer tout au long des années 80. Le terme de high tech est une combinaison de «high-style» et «technology» traduisant le double penchant de ce mouvement pour l'importance des structures et la qualité du dessin. Le terme fut utilisé pour la première fois par Joan Kron et Suzanne Slesin dans leur livre: High Tech: The industrial Style and Source Book for the Home, New York 1978. Dans ce cadre, la conception et la structure ne sont pas des entités séparées mais forment un tout intégré dans lequel le caractère esthétique d'un objet est déterminé par sa structure technique, préfabriquée ou non. Le mouvement high tech a été particulièrement populaire en Grande-Bretagne, pays de ses principaux initiateurs, Rogers, Foster, Grimshaw et Hopkins. Les membres du Groupe Archigram qui mirent au point des plans «technologiques» pour des «cités branchées» et d'autres projets créatifs sont souvent considérés comme les précurseurs de ce mouvement[3], bien qu'il soit possible que l'architecture soviétique des années 20 et 30 ait aussi exercé sur lui une influence et que ses sources stylistiques soient encore plus riches. Le Centre Pompidou est le premier édifice pouvant revendiquer ce style dans lequel tous les aspects structurels sont mis en évidence. Escaliers mécaniques, canalisations de conditionnement d'air, antennes participent à l'esthétique du projet.

Dans le cas de la Tour Eiffel, si les éléments structurels dominent, d'autres sont purement décoratifs et sans aucune fonction. Le Centre Pompidou aurait encore été plus provocant si les règlements de sécurité n'avaient imposé certaines modifications, comme la fermeture de la façade Est que les architectes avaient à l'origine prévue en verre.

Une gifle

Il est difficile d'imaginer 25 ans plus tard, la véhémence des protestations qui accueillirent le Centre Pompidou. Beaucoup de Parisiens vécurent ses couleurs vives et ses audaces comme un camouflet, un cancer moderne au cœur du vieux Paris.

Et pourtant, Piano et Rogers n'avaient utilisé que la moitié du plateau Beaubourg. L'autre partie fut aménagée en place en creux, un peu comme le Campo de Sienne, et se transforma vite en une sorte d'extension non-officielle du centre. L'IRCAM et la superbe fontaine de Jean Tinguely et Niki de Saint-Phalle participent également à l'ensemble, et le quartier environnant a été profondément modifié par l'irruption de cet énorme vaisseau. Après bien des années d'hésitations, le trou des Halles (détruites dès 1968) a été comblé par un vaste centre commercial souterrain beaucoup moins intéressant que le CNAC et signé Claude Vasconi et Georges Pencreac'h.

L'intérieur du Centre Pompidou est plus austère que ses façades. En entrant dans l'immense atrium, le visiteur peut même ressentir une impression de vide. Il trouvera cependant vite le chemin du Musée d'Art Moderne, de la Bibliothèque Publique d'Information, de multiples salles d'expositions temporaires, d'un théâtre, d'un cinéma, d'une librairie, d'une boutique de design et d'une cafétéria en terrasse. L'installation intérieure du musée, placée sous le signe de la mobilité des cloisonnements a déjà été revue deux fois et ne donne toujours pas entièrement satisfaction. Le concept de «boîte de verre» suspendue à l'intérieur d'une structure d'acier a été quelque peu mis à mal par la fermeture d'une façade.

Retour du fantastique

La liberté donnée aux architectes déboucha sur des plans totalement fantastiques. Un certain nombre de projets méritent une mention spéciale. Manfred Schiedhelm dessina un dôme futuriste transparent qui recouvrait tout le plateau Beaubourg et le complexe culturel. Moshe Safdie occupa aussi tout l'espace: son projet s'articulait autour de niveaux souterrains, percés d'une sorte de cratère au-dessus duquel était suspendu une structure en gradins.

La proposition de Dennis Crompton, en partie souterraine, fut en fait dessinée par une étudiant en architecture de troisième année, William Alsop et c'est sans doute le nom de Crompton qui la fit bénéficier d'une mention honorable. Plusieurs architectes néerlandais envoyèrent des projets dont Jan Hoogstad et J.L.C. Choisy. Le plan de Hoogstad se distinguait par une excellente répartition de l'espace et une séparation des différentes activités par des zones ouvertes qui atténuaient l'omniprésence du béton.

Robert Stones et Wolfgang Pearlman imaginèrent une structure composée d'éléments identiques à douze faces. Les visiteurs auraient eu besoin d'un plan et d'un fléchage détaillé pour s'y retrouver, ce qui n'empêcha pas le jury de leur accorder une mention honorable. Du Japon (Yutaka Murata, K. Kurokawa, Minoru Takeyama), de Belgique (Charles Vandenhove) et de Turquie (Ahmet Gulgonen) arrivèrent plusieurs intéressants projets.

La fin de la construction du Centre Pompidou annonça la renaissance de l'architecture en France[4]. Grâce aux efforts de G. Pompidou, la France retrouvait ainsi une place importante dans l'architecture internationale.

1 *Voir, dans cet ouvrage, le chapitre sur les «Grands projets».*

2 *IRCAM, Institut de Recherche et Coordination Acoustique-Musique, fut construit de 1973 à 1977 et agrandi en 1990.*

3 *Voir le chapitre sur le Centre de Loisirs de Monte-Carlo.*

4 *Voir le chapitre sur les «Grands Projets».*

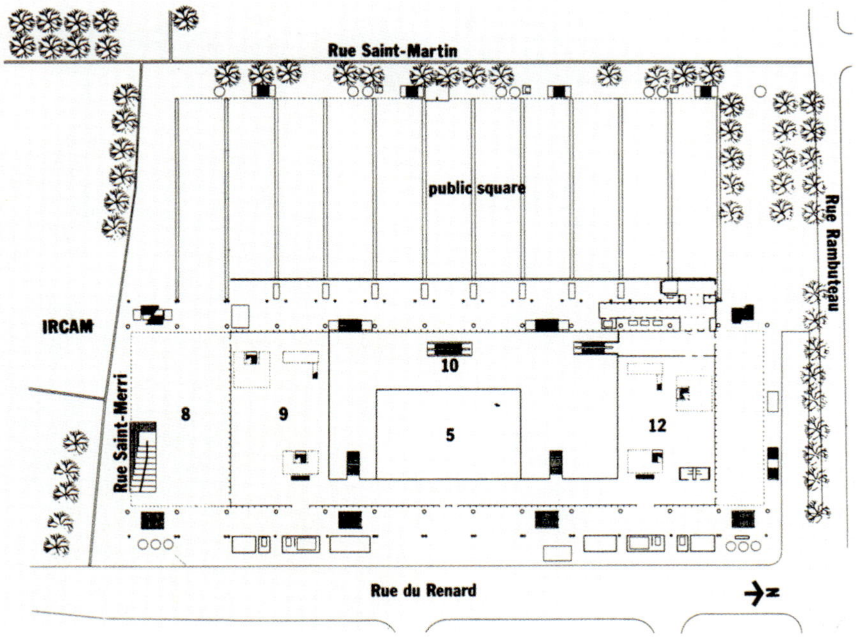

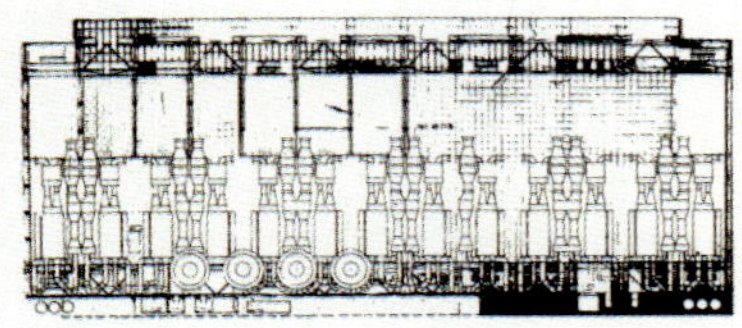

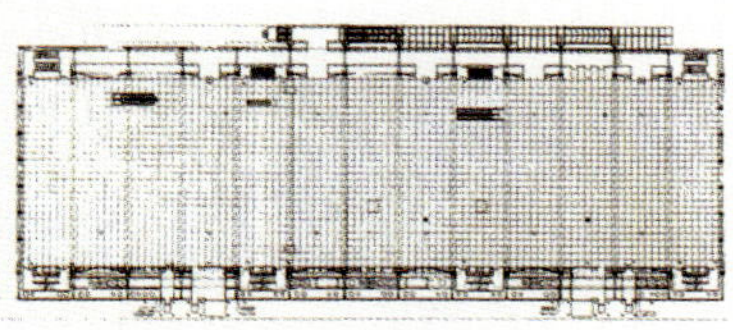

Renzo Piano & Richard Rogers
competition design, 1971, diagram, first prize

Renzo Piano & Richard Rogers
competition design, 1971, above: roof plan, below: third floor plan, first prize

Renzo Piano & Richard Rogers
competition design, 1971, piazza level plan, first prize

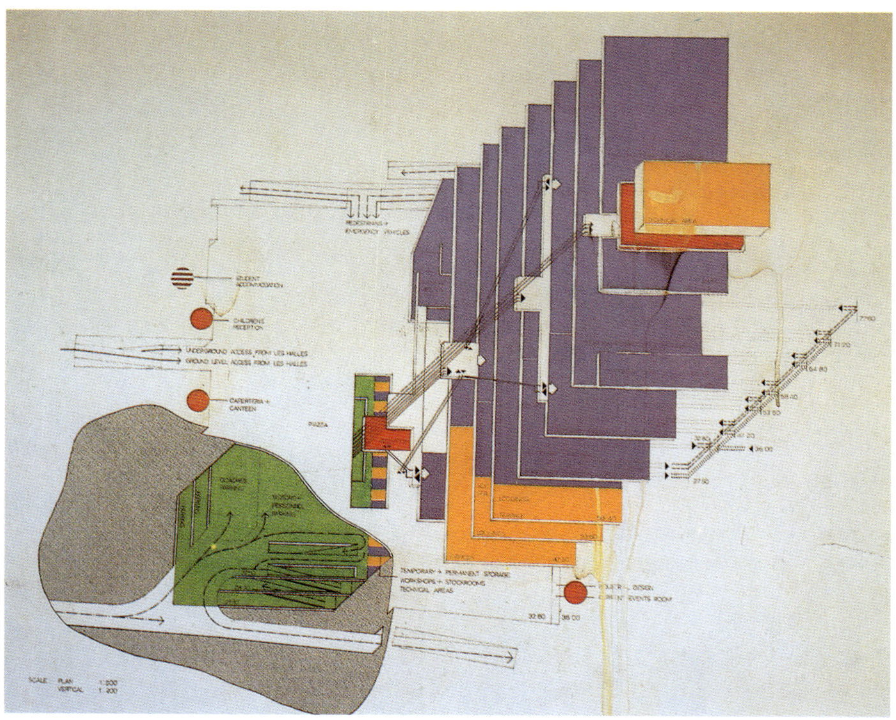

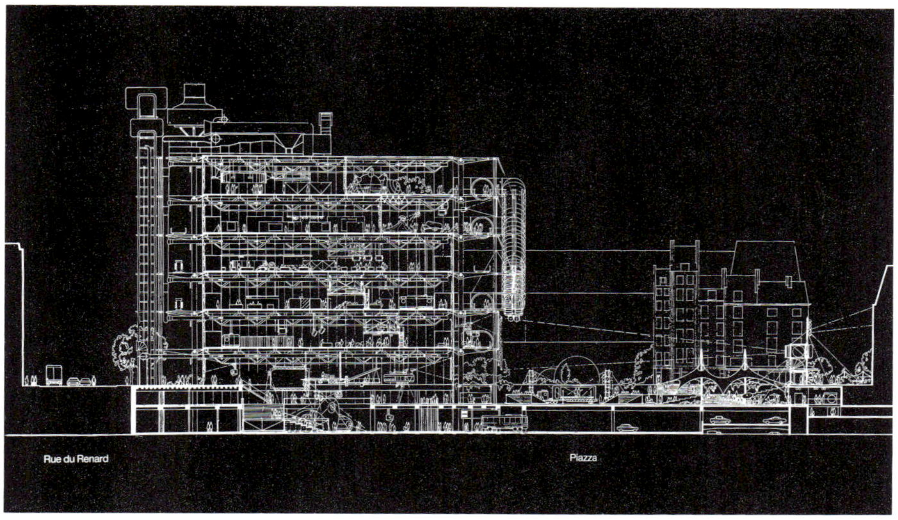

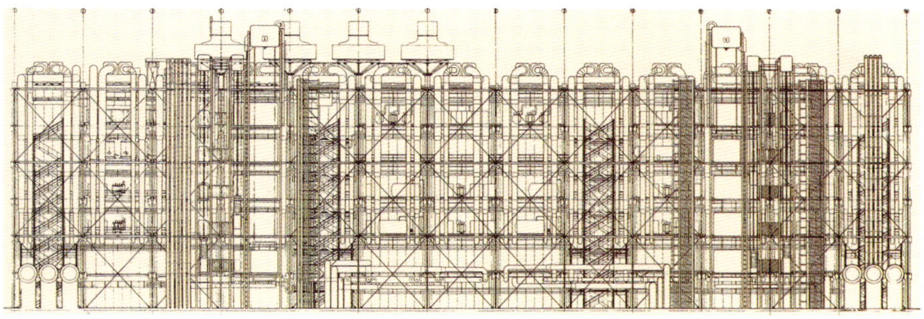

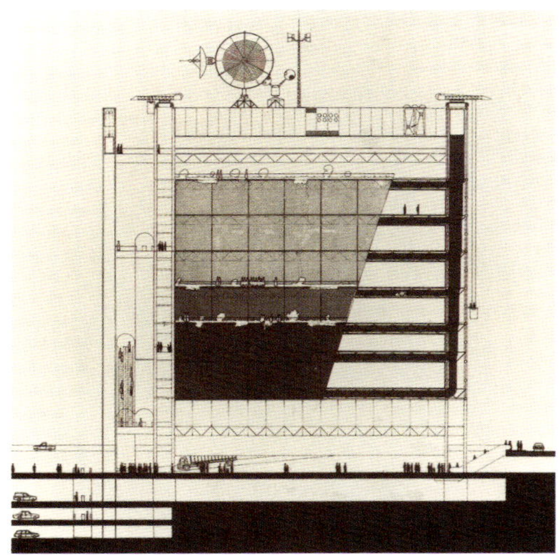

Renzo Piano & Richard Rogers
competition design, 1971, east-west section (south side), south elevation, first prize

Renzo Piano & Richard Rogers
competition design, 1971, east-west section (north side), first prize

Renzo Piano & Richard Rogers
presentation design, 1971, isometric sketch

Renzo Piano & Richard Rogers
execution design, 1971, elevation on Rue du Renard

Renzo Piano & Richard Rogers
execution design, 1971, section through the escalator system

Renzo Piano & Richard Rogers
competition design, 1971, model, first prize

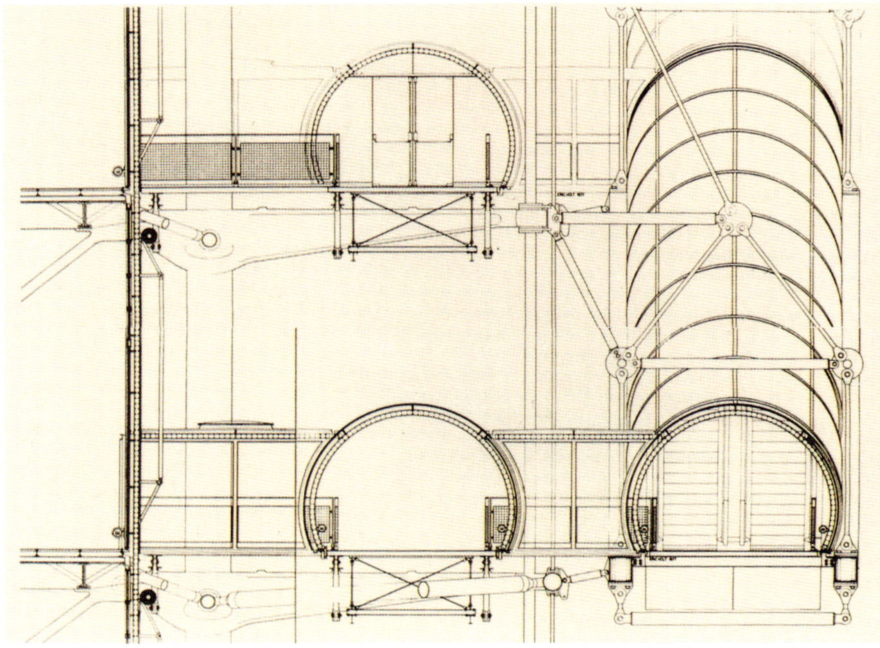

Manfred Schiedhelm competition design, 1971, model, special reward

Manfred Schiedhelm competition design, 1971, typical floor plan, special reward

Manfred Schiedhelm competition design, 1971, north-south section (west side), special reward

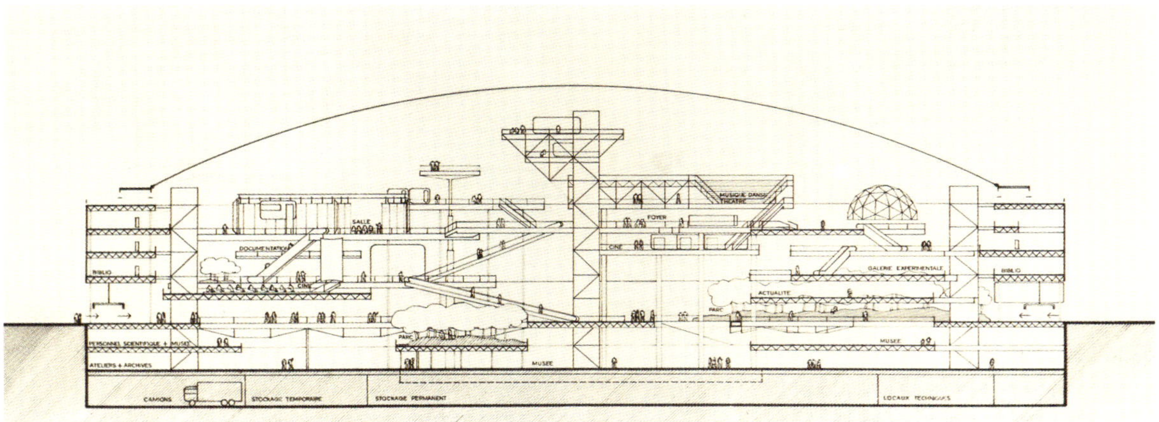

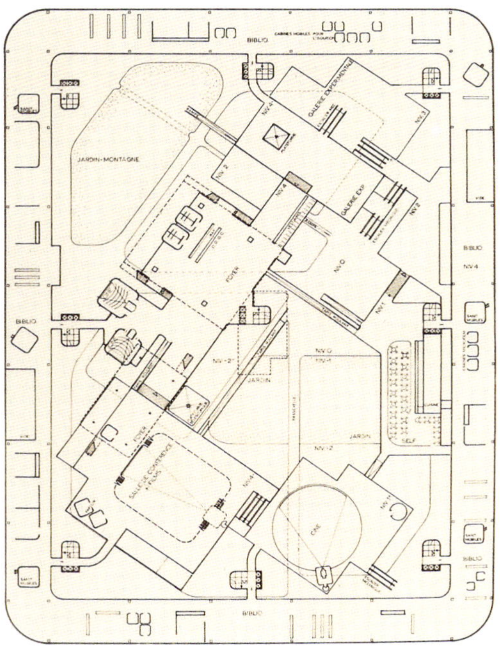

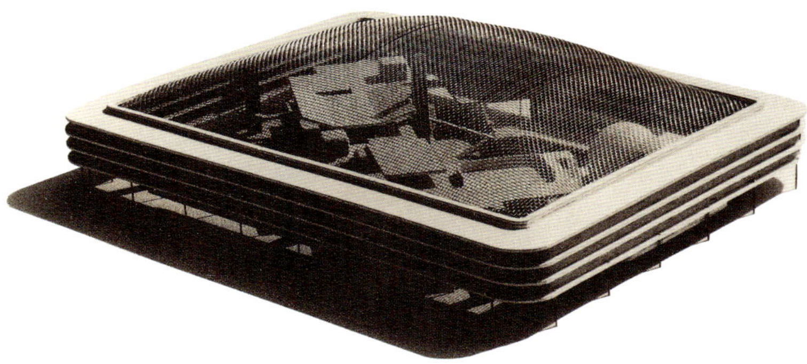

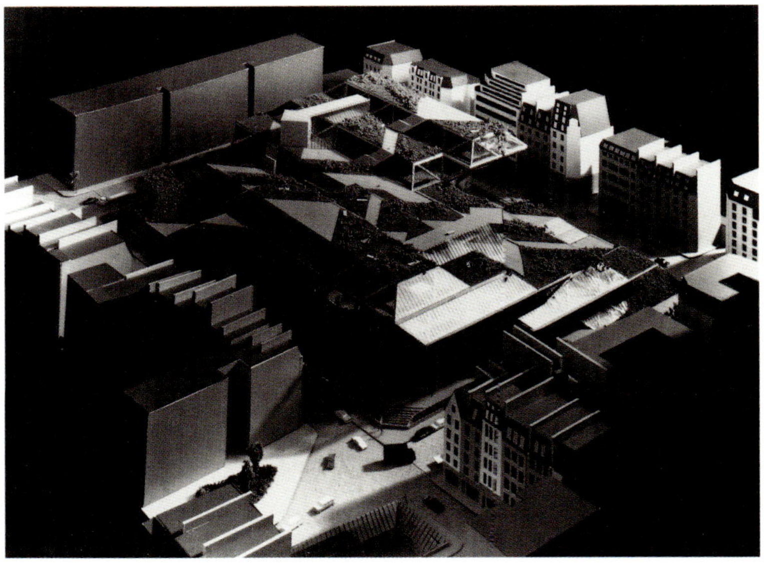

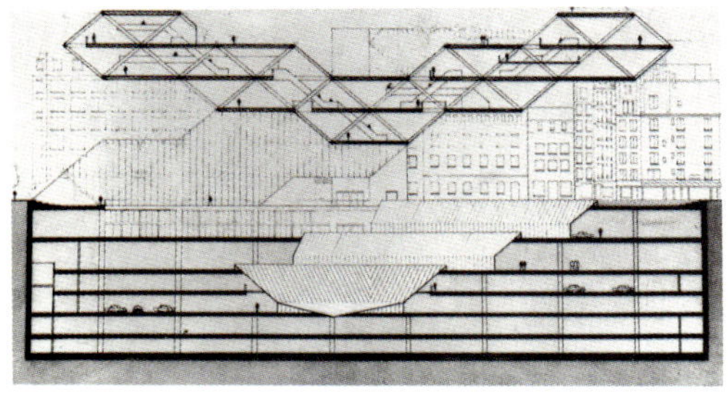

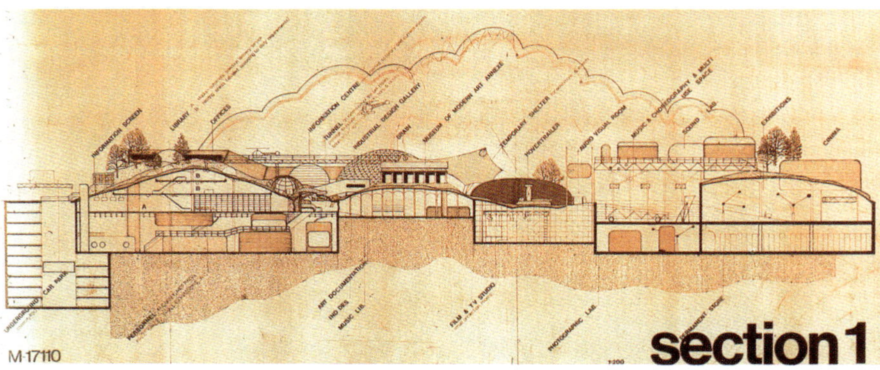

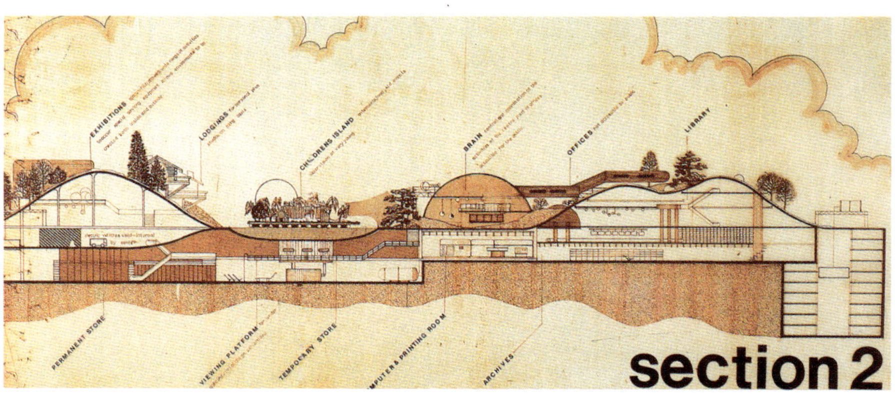

Moshe Safdie competition design, 1971, model, honourable mention

Moshe Safdie competition design, 1971, above: east-west section (south side), below: model, honourable mention

Dennis Crompton & William Alsop competition design, 1971, section, honourable mention

Dennis Crompton & William Alsop competition design, 1971, section, honourable mention

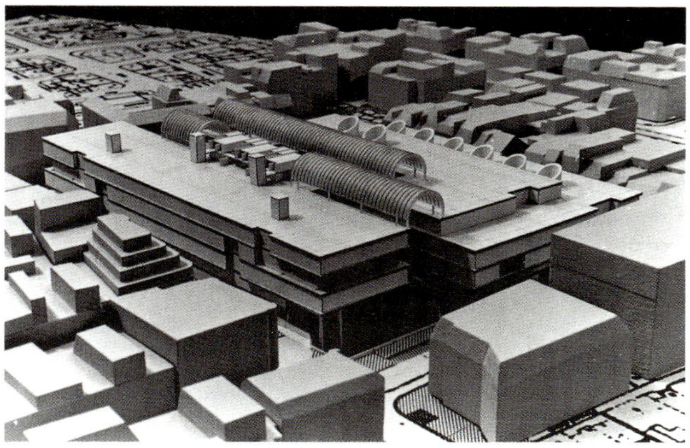

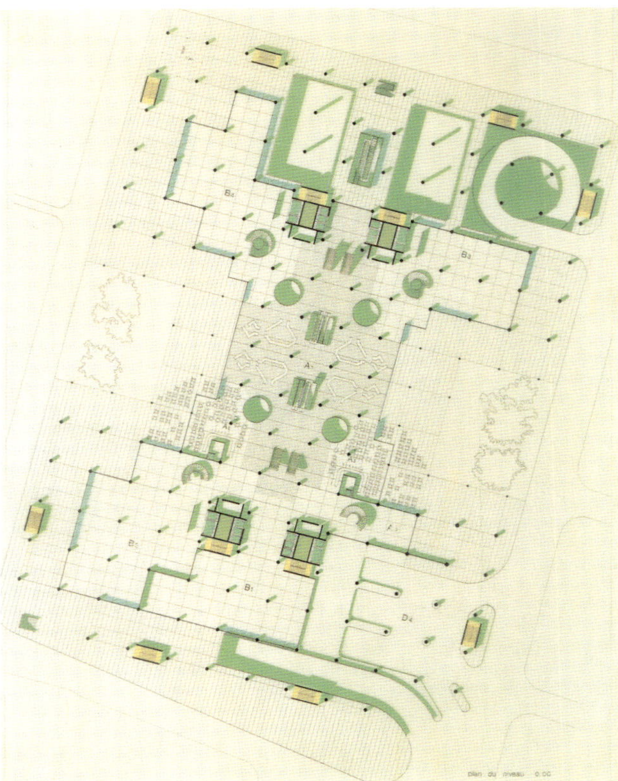

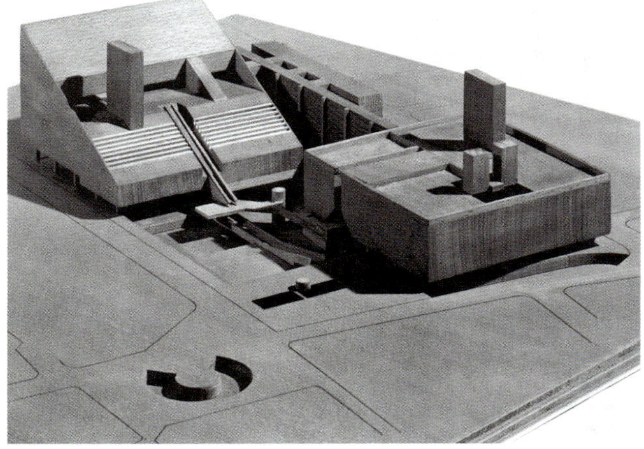

J.L.C. Choisy, R. Ouendag & G. Martens competition design, 1971, model, honourable mention

J.L.C. Choisy, R. Ouendag & G. Martens competition design, 1971, section model, honourable mention

Jan Hoogstad competition design, 1971, model

Charles Vandenhove competition design, 1971, ground floor plan

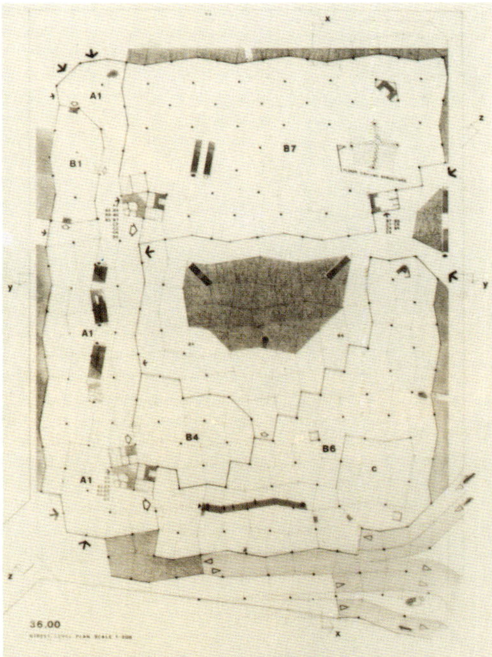

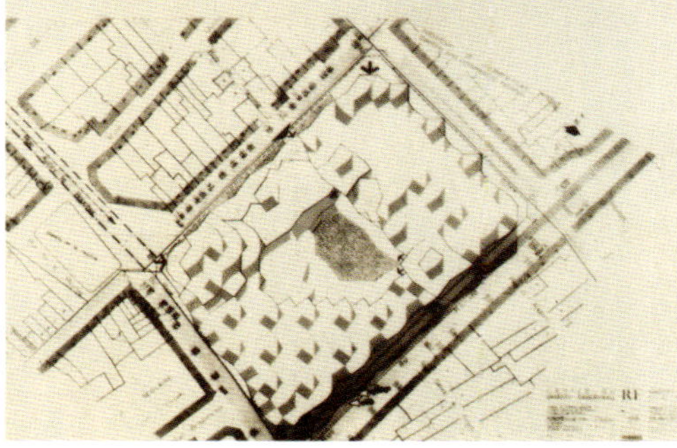

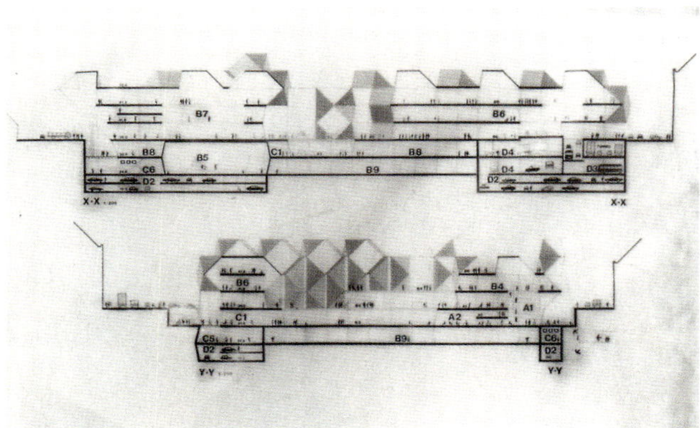

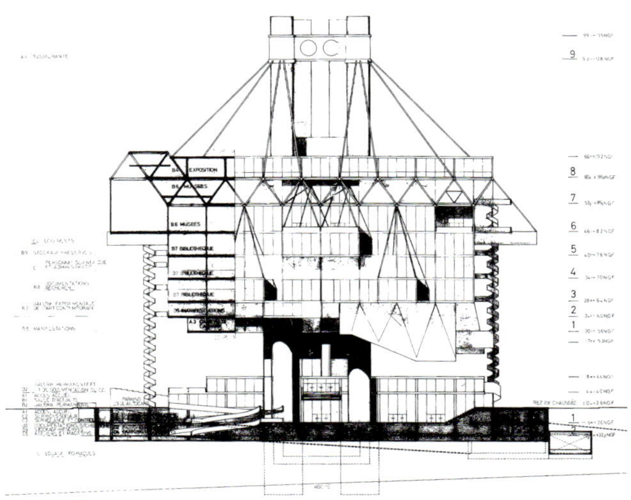

RUE DU RENARD

Robert Stones & Wolfgang Pearlman competition design, 1971, above: ground floor plan, below: site plan, honourable mention

Robert Stones & Wolfgang Pearlman competition design, 1971, model, honourable mention

Robert Stones & Wolfgang Pearlman competition design, 1971, above: north-south section (west side), below: east-west section (north side), honourable mention

Yutaka Murata competition design, 1971, east-west section

Yutaka Murata competition design, 1971 site plan

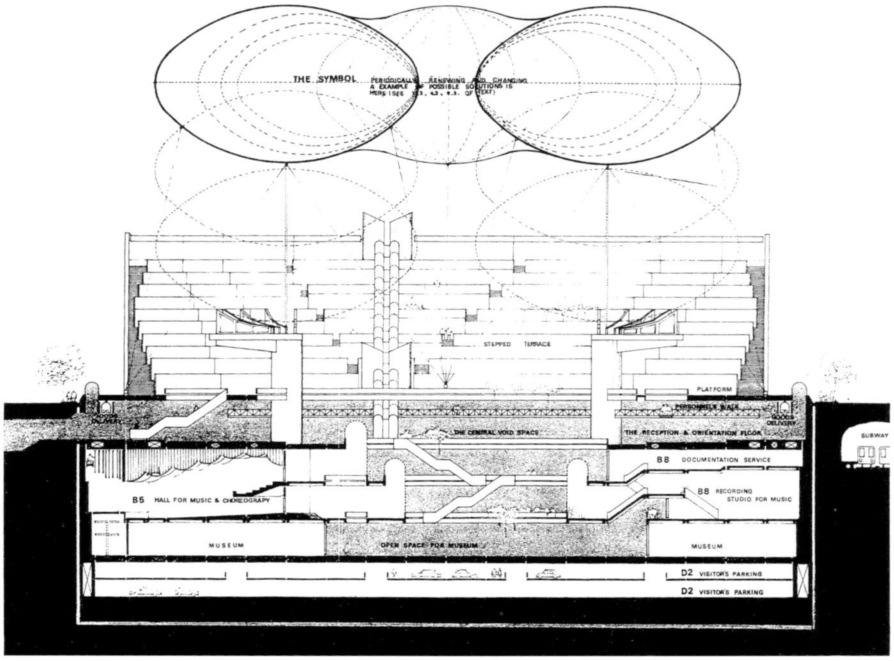

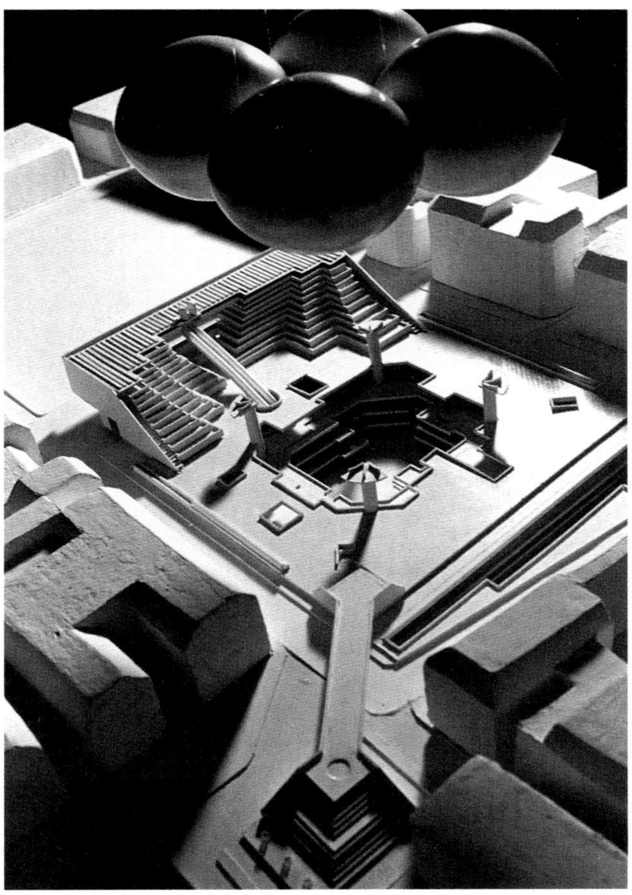

Minoru Takeyama competition design, 1971, model

Minoru Takeyama competition design, 1971, east-west section (south side)

Project

Cemetery

Site

To the east of the old San Cataldo Cemetery, north of Modena, Italy

Dates

Competition announced 6 May 1971 *First round closing date* 2 November 1971 *Result announced* 10 June 1972 *Second round closing date* 8 September 1973 *Result announced* 20 April 1974

Number of entries

First round 51 *Second round* 3

Jury

Rubes Triva (chairman, Mayor of Modena), Mario Pergetti (secretary), Paolo Sorzia, Pietro Guerzoni, Umberto Bisi, Alfredo Mango (all city councillors), Carlo Melograni, Carlo Aymonino, Paolo Portoghesi, Emirio Montessori, Pier Luigi Cervellatti (all architects), Athos Baccarini, Allesandro Magni, Mario Ghio, Glauco Gresleri, Ugo Cavazzutti, Teodosio Greco, Ermete Bortolotti

Result

First round, First prize Aldo Rossi & Gianni Braghieri *Second prize* Constantino Dardi, Michele Rebora, Ariella Zattera & Giovanni Morabito *Third prize* Fabio Lunelli, Beppe Cerutti, Federico Colombo & Roberto Giamberini *Purchased* Franca Stagi & Cesare Leonardi; Adriano Campioni, Giulio Dubbini, Francesco Pierobon, Leonardo Rampazzi & Piero de Pra; Lorenzino Cremonini, Tullio Zini & Paolo Banaiuto; Alberto Caruso & Bruno Giromella; Paola Marzoli, Marco Vigi & Guglielmo Veronesi; Gianfranco Moneta, Andrea Jovene & Valeriano Trubbiani *Second round* No prizes awarded

Commissioned by

The Municipality of Modena

Construction

Started in 1974

Architects

Aldo Rossi & Gianni Braghieri

Construction cost

The most recent extension cost 1 500 000 000 million lire

San Cataldo Cemetery, Modena, 1971–1974

Aldo Rossi & Gianni Braghieri

conceptual drawing, 1973

San Cataldo Cemetery, Modena

Less than one hundred years after its consecration, Modena's municipal cemetery had become too small and was in dire need of extension. The careful planning which preceded the extension was characteristic of all urban development projects in Modena. During the 1960s and 70s many Northern Italian cities experienced explosive growth, and planning and regulation became key concepts.

A cautious competition procedure

In 1967, officials put their heads together and concluded that it would be best to draw up a multi-phased development scheme for the new cemetery, rather than executing ad hoc extensions over the years. However, another four years passed before a competition was cautiously organised. There were to be two rounds. Italian architects were invited to submit conceptual designs for the open first round, indicating how they envisaged the new cemetery and how it would tie in with the old cemetery. Detailed plans were not required at this stage. It was decided that the ideas would first be published, before a second round was organised, during which selected plans could be developed.
However, events took a different course. Following a lengthy knock-out procedure, the jury selected nine of the 51 designs. Three were awarded prizes and six others were purchased. First prize was awarded to a design entitled "l'azzurro del cielo" (the blue of the sky). It is possible that some members of the jury recognised the characteristic hand of Aldo Rossi (*1931) in this anonymously submitted design, since the architects and jury members Carlo Aymonino and Paolo Portoghesi both knew Rossi quite well. In any event, the designs were not presented to the public as planned. The three prize-winners met again in the second round, which was won by Rossi.

The nineteenth-century cemetery

Rossi's design was striking not only in its style of drawing, but also in its development, which differed from that of the other competition designs. Rossi had clearly tried to relate his design to the existing cemetery, which had been designed by Cesare Costa in the second half of the nineteenth century. Costa's cemetery was rectangular and surrounded by galleries. It had pavilions halfway along the length of the rectangle and had been built in a simple Palladian style. Beyond the walls, on the western side, lay the Jewish cemetery.
Most of the other architects paid scant attention to the architectural detail of the existing nineteenth century cemetery. Adriano Campioni and his team, whose design had also been purchased, had grouped the columbaria irregularly. They were asymmetrically and apparently arbitrarily based on two axes, which stood at right angles to one another. The entrance was situated at the head of the longer axis and although the old and the new cemetery were situated side by side, Campioni had clearly ignored Costa's creation. The same may be said of the design submitted by Constantino Dardi's team (second prize),

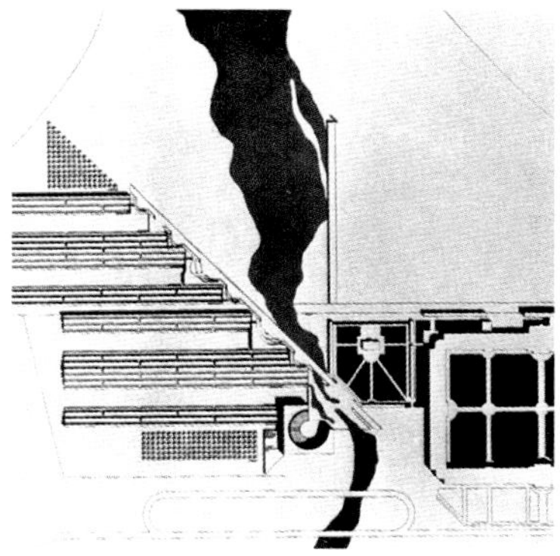

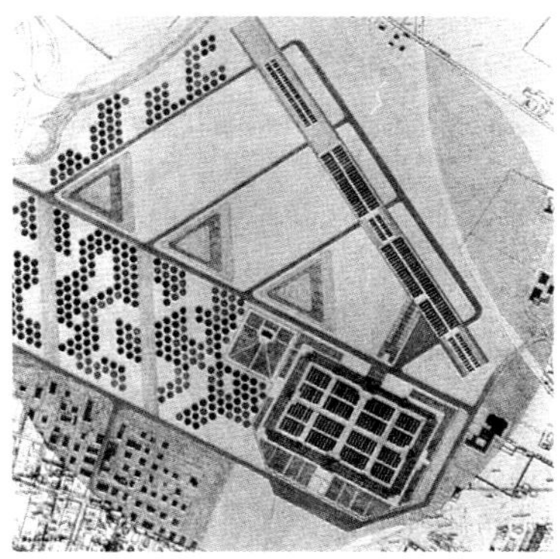

Constantino Dardi et al. competition design, 1971, "DOM" site plan

Fabio Lunelli et al. competition design, 1971, "Il muro" site plan

which showed a cemetery built in several strips, and of Fabio Lunelli's design (third prize) which was characteristically speckled.

Rossi's rationalism

Rossi took a completely different approach in that he deliberately based his design on the old cemetery. However, in order to fully understand the specific features of Rossi's design, the architect and his "rational" approach to architecture must first be discussed.
In contrast to many of his colleagues, who saw Functionalism as the only acceptable form of architecture, Rossi was more receptive to the styles of bygone eras. Any discussion of post-Modernist architecture would be incomplete without a chapter on Rossi, his influential theories and his imaginative creations. However, Rossi had a limited architectural curriculum when he was commissioned, although he had published many articles, most notably on the subject of architectural history. As an editor of the magazine "Casabella", his articles had focused upon Lombard neo-classicism, Italian urban planning and the cultural basis of his own architecture. In 1965 he published his most significant work, "l'Architettura della città", in which he discussed his approach to urban planning and voiced his objections to Functionalism, which was the dominant architectural style at the time. Rossi's broad historical interest, ranging from Andrea Palladio to Adolf Loos, and his criticism of uncompromising Functionalism, made him one of the most important post-Modernist theoreticians. Rossi's own style has often been labelled "Rationalist".

Logical and precise

According to Rossi, architecture should be limited to precise, theoretical structures. The architect must base his designs on logical principles, which apply under all circumstances. This is the main point of Rationalist deviation from Functionalism, which strives to find the best solution for a specific problem. Rationalists consider each problem to be unique and that the solution of the problem depends on the individual architect. A Rationalist strives to find the best solution for a wide variety of problems: a general "framework" to which architectural principles are fastened.
The Rationalist approach blurs typological differences. A solution is generally applicable, regardless of the type of building, and the various architectural forms are reduced to a basic type. This interchangeability also characterises Rossi's approach to urban planning, which bears a certain similarity to the work of the Dutch Structuralists. The house is the city, the passage is the street and the courtyard is the square. The San Cataldo cemetery was designed along these lines.
Criticism of Rossi's approach has centred upon the fact that his theories are impracticable and that his passage/street is unrealistic. Due to the monumental character of his buildings and the magnificent interplay of light and shadow, Rossi's work has been compared to the paintings of Giorgio de Chirico. A similar sense of menace and desolation prevails, as if both artists have brought a dream world to life.

Aldo Rossi & Gianni Braghieri
Columbaria

Aldo Rossi & Gianni Braghieri
Sanctuary

The design

More than twenty years after the competition, two thirds of the cemetery was completed. It was based partly on Rossi's original design and partly on later designs and alterations. As mentioned above, Rossi tied his design in with the nineteenth century neo-Palladian cemetery. Both cemeteries are surrounded by a gallery and are designed on a grid system. Visitors to Rossi's cemetery can view the old cemetery from a variety of angles. The gate-houses of both cemeteries are situated on the lateral axis. The longitudinal axis of Costa's design runs parallel to a connecting road, past the centrally-situated Jewish cemetery, and joins one of the two longitudinal axes in Rossi's design. Rossi's design also contained many other references to the old cemetery and architectural examples from the past, including the gallery mentioned above, which did not have round classical columns crowned with a capital, but consisted of prefabricated concrete slabs. These slabs have been set up like dominoes in the inner U-shaped gallery and in the gallery facing the nineteenth-century cemetery. They present the passer-by with a striking interplay of shadows. Rossi had previously incorporated a similar feature in the Gallaratese district in Milan, emphasising the interchangeability of universal forms.
There are columbaria above the gallery, in an area covered by an elongated saddle roof constructed from pre-painted blue aluminium sheets. A double gallery with an enclosed street has been built on the eastern side, replacing the single gallery in the original design. The two galleries are connected by foot-bridges on the upper level. The

Franca Stagi & Cesare Leonardi
competition design, 1971,
axonometric "Abracadabra"

bridge railings, consisting of square frames with a St. Andrew's cross, are again reminiscent of the Milanese housing complex.
The concrete walls have been plastered in pale pink and the austere, square openings in the walls have been fitted with cross-bar frames. The square is one of the basic shapes which Rossi repeatedly and deliberately uses in his designs.

The interior design

Although Rossi's original interior design was only partially executed, a description of its features will clarify certain aspects of the final design.
In the original design the inner U-shaped gallery formed an enclosed street, which was bisected by the lateral axis of the cemetery, forming two squares. The lateral axis is the most important element of Rossi's design and connects two other basic elements which may be universally applied: the cube and the cone. It goes without saying that a cube is made up of squares. The cone, on the other hand, is less in evidence in Rossi's work, although it is a recurrent thematic element, which Rossi used in his designs for the Primary School in Varese (1972), the School of Architecture in Miami (1986) and Borgoricco Town Hall (1983). The cone shape was also an important element of his competition design for Muggio Town Hall near Milan.
Other features of this last design are also reminiscent of the San Cataldo cemetery. The designs have similar buildings in the background, a factory and chimneys. This again is characteristic of typological interchangeability. The cone in the Modena design has a symbolic function: a factory's chimney stops smoking when work has come to an end. The "chimney" in Modena is symbolic of life that has come to an end. The cone gives access to concentric stairways which lead down to the communal grave.
The columbaria between the cone and the cube form a herringbone pattern. It has been suggested that the herringbone is an allusion to Christ, though this view seems a little far-fetched. Granted, the fish is an accepted symbol of Christianity, but it is debatable whether a herringbone symbolises the death of Christ. A more probable explanation is that the pattern represents a skeleton. Rossi was involved in a serious car accident just before he submitted his competition design, and while in hospital he discovered that the structure of his body resembled a series of fractures which had to be put together again.
The columbaria along the lateral axis may be seen as two triangles, one of which forms part of the floor plan; the other is formed by the columbaria which become higher and higher as they approach the communal grave. The highest columbarium is also the narrowest, and the lowest is the widest. The link between the cube and the cone is therefore both logical and rational: a (double) triangle, on a floor plan made up of squares. The cube is also symbolic of life that has come to an end. It contains the charnel house, which has neither floors nor a roof.

Deviation from Functionalism

The design as a whole is symmetrical, axial and hierarchical in composition, and is reminiscent of Costa's cemetery, Lombard neo-classicism and Palladian architecture. The concrete slabs which form the galleries are of Classicist origin and are characteristic examples of Rossi's deviation from 1960s Functionalism. Although Rossi had previously attempted to bring about the architectural embodiment of his theories, the chances had been few and far between[1]. He had participated in competitions since 1961, but had never been commissioned for anything bigger than San Cataldo cemetery. Twenty years later, while the San Cataldo cemetery was still under construction, Rossi was commissioned to design the cemetery at Rozzano.

1 *He did, however, build the Gallaratese housing complex in Milan and a war memorial in Cuneo.*

Friedhof San Cataldo, Modena

Modenas städtischer Friedhof war kaum 100 Jahre nach seiner Fertigstellung erneut zu klein und bedurfte einer Erweiterung. Allerdings erforderte der Ausbau des Friedhofs – genau wie die Erweiterung der Stadt Modena – eine sorgfältige Planung. »Regulierung« und »Planung« galten als Schlüsselworte in den 60er und 70er Jahren, als zahlreiche norditalienische Städte einen explosiven Bevölkerungszuwachs verzeichneten.

Eine sorgfältig geplante Ausschreibung

1967 entschied sich der Stadtrat von Modena bei der Planung des neuen Friedhofs für ein Ausbauschema, das stufenweise realisiert werden sollte; von sporadisch wiederkehrenden spontanen Ausbauvorhaben distanzierte man sich. Allerdings dauerte es vier Jahre, bevor es zu einer Ausschreibung kam, die dann jedoch sorgfältig geplant wurde. Der Wettbewerb sollte über zwei Runden gehen. Bei der ersten Ausschreibungsrunde waren alle italienischen Architekten eingeladen, ihre Vorschläge und Ideen für einen neuen Friedhof einzusenden. Dabei sollten sie das Verhältnis zwischen der alten und der neuen Begräbnisstätte berücksichtigen. Detaillierte Konstruktionspläne wurden nicht benötigt. Alle Vorschläge sollten veröffentlicht werden; erst danach war eine zweite Ausschreibungsrunde geplant, in der die prämierten Architekten ihre Vorschläge weiter ausarbeiten sollten. Es kam jedoch anders. Die Jury wählte aus den 51 eingesandten Beiträgen nach einem langwierigen Verfahren neun Entwürfe, von denen drei prämiert und die restlichen sechs angekauft wurden. Das Konzept »l'azzuro del cielo« (Das Blau des Himmels) erhielt den ersten Preis. Es ist durchaus denkbar, daß einige Jurymitglieder bei diesem Entwurf Aldo Rossis typischen Zeichenstil wiedererkannten, obwohl die Pläne anonym eingesandt wurden. Die Veröffentlichung der Konstruktionspläne blieb aus, statt dessen mußten die mit dem ersten bis dritten Platz ausgezeichneten Entwürfe in einer zweiten Runde erneut gegeneinander antreten. Am Schluß erhielt Rossi den Bauauftrag.

Der Kirchhof aus dem 19. Jahrhundert

Rossi hatte eine Verbindung zu dem bereits bestehenden, von Cesare Costa in der zweiten Hälfte des 19. Jahrhunderts entworfenen, Friedhof angestrebt. Diese Begräbnisstätte bestand aus einem von Laubengängen umrahmten Rechteck, besaß auf der Hälfte der Längsseiten kleine Pavillons und zeichnete sich durch einen sorgfältigen palladianischen Stil aus. Westlich davon, außerhalb der Friedhofsmauern, lag der jüdische Friedhof. Die meisten Architekten berücksichtigten diese Anlage kaum in ihren Beiträgen. Beispielsweise sah der – von der Stadt angekaufte – Entwurf von Adriano Campioni und seinem Team eine unregelmäßige Anordnung der Kolumbarien vor: Asymmetrisch und scheinbar willkürlich von zwei zueinander rechtwinklig verlaufenden Achsen durchschnitten. Als Eingang diente der Anfang der längsten Achse. Obwohl der alte und der neue Komplex friedlich nebeneinander lagen, ignorierte Campionis Entwurf Costas Werk. Auch Constantino Dardi und sein Team, für ihren Streifenbau mit dem zweiten Platz ausgezeichnet, sowie Fabio Lunelli, der mit seinem Team für einen Tupfenbau den dritten Platz erhielt, konnten mit dem Kirchhof aus dem 19. Jahrhundert wenig anfangen.

Logisch und präzise

Laut Rossi handelt es sich bei der Architektur um ein Fachgebiet, bei dem nur »präzise theoretische Konstruktionen« gestattet sind. Der Architekt muß in seiner Arbeit logische Prinzipien entwickeln, die sich jederzeit anwenden lassen. Hierin besteht der große Unterschied zum Funktionalismus. Der Funktionalist sucht die beste Lösung für ein bestimmtes Problem und nähert sich diesem auf individualistische und einzigartige Weise. Der Rationalist sucht dagegen eine Lösung, die sich auf eine Reihe von Problemen anwenden läßt – ein allgemeingültiges System, an dem die architektonischen Prinzipien festgemacht werden.
Kritiker warfen Rossi immer wieder vor, daß sich seine Theorien in der Praxis weniger gut bewährt hätten. Aufgrund des monumentalen Charakters und des einzigartigen Spiels von Licht und Schatten werden seine Bauwerke mit den Gemälden Giorgio de Chiricos verglichen: Die gleiche Bedrohung, die gleiche Einsamkeit – beide Künstler erwecken eine Traumwelt zum Leben.

Der Entwurf

Ungefähr 20 Jahre nach der Ausschreibung waren etwa zwei Drittel des Friedhofes fertiggestellt, teils anhand von Rossis prämiertem Entwurf, teils anhand von späteren Zeichnungen und Ergänzungen. Rossis Plan basierte ebenso wie der neopalladianische Friedhof des 19. Jahrhunderts auf einem Rastermuster und ist von Laubengängen umgeben. Rossi gestattet von seinem Friedhof aus verschiedene Ausblicke auf die Anlage des Vorgängers. Sogar seine »Eingangsgebäude« befinden sich wie bei Costas Entwurf auf der Querachse. Hingegen geht Costas Längsachse über einen Verbindungsweg entlang des zentral gelegenen jüdischen Friedhofs in eine von zwei Längsachsen aus Rossis Entwurf über.
Auch beim Aufriß erweist Rossi den historischen Vorbildern seine Referenz. Die bereits erwähnten Laubengänge bestehen bei Rossi jedoch nicht aus runden klassischen Säulen mit einem Kapitell, sondern aus vorgefertigten Betonplatten, die beim inneren U-förmigen Laubengang und dem Säulengang mit Blick auf den alten Friedhof wie Dominosteine aufgestellt wurden. So bieten sie den Passanten ein eindrucksvolles Schattenspiel.
Die Urnennischen befinden sich über den Laubengängen in einem Raum, der von einem langgezogenen Satteldach aus vorlackierten blauen Aluminiumplatten überdeckt wird. Die Ostseite des Friedhofs ziert ein doppelter Laubengang mit einem überdachten Weg – der ursprüngliche Entwurf sah nur einen einfachen Laubengang vor. Beide Laubengänge sind auf Höhe des Obergeschosses durch eine Fußgängerbrücke miteinander verbunden, deren Geländer aus einem quadratische Raster mit einem Andreaskreuz bestehen. Die Betonwände sind hellrosa verputzt und von schlichten, quadratischen Öffnungen durchbrochen, in denen sich Kreuzsteckfenster befinden. Das Quadrat zählt zu den Grundformen, die Rossi häufig einsetzt.

Die Bebauung der Innenfläche

Die ursprünglich vorgesehene Bebauung der Innenflächen des Friedhofs wurde nur teilweise realisiert.
Der innere U-förmige Laubengang war als überdachter Gang geplant und wird in der Mitte durch die Querachse des Kirchhofs in zwei Quadrate unterteilt. Diese Querachse bildet das wichtigste Element in Rossis Entwurf. Die Achse verläuft wiederum zwischen zwei Basiselementen, die sich universell einsetzen lassen: Kubus und Kegel. Der Kubus besteht aus Quadraten. Der Kegel findet sich in Rossis Werk zwar seltener, aber doch häufig genug, um ihn als wiederkehrendes Thema zu bezeichnen – wie etwa bei der Grundschule von Varese (1972), der School of Architecture in Miami (1986) und beim Rathaus von Borgoricco (1983). Im Kegelinneren führen konzentrische Treppen hinunter zum Gemeinschaftsgrab. Vom Kegel verläuft eine Fischgräte aus Kolumbarien zum Kubus, wobei man die Gräte als Christussymbol deuten könnte. Diese Symbolik geht allerdings recht weit. Viel wahrscheinlicher ist die Annahme, daß es sich bei dieser Konstruktion um eine Art Gerippe handelt. Rossi hatte kurz vor seiner Teilnahme an der Ausschreibung einen schweren Autounfall gehabt. Im Krankenhaus entdeckte er, daß die Struktur seines Körpers einer Serie von Brüchen glich, die wieder an ihren richtigen Platz gesetzt werden mußten.
Die Urnenhallen entlang der Querachse bilden ein doppeltes Dreieck. Das erste Dreieck entsteht auf dem Grundriß, während das zweite durch das langsame Ansteigen der Kolumbarien gebildet wird, je weiter sich diese dem Gemeinschaftsgrab nähern. Die schmalste Urnenhalle ist zugleich die höchste, und die breiteste Halle zugleich die niedrigste. Daher bildet ein (doppeltes) Dreieck die Verbindung zwischen Kubus und Kegel auf einem quadratischen Grundriß

Bruch mit dem Funktionalismus

Die gesamte Anlage ist streng symmetrisch, axial und hierarchisch im Aufbau – genau wie Costas Friedhof, wie der lombardische Klassizismus und die Werke Palladios. Auch die Betonplatten der Laubengänge sind klassizistisch und kennzeichnend für Rossis Entfremdung vom Funktionalismus der 60er Jahre. Rossi hatte zwar bereits zuvor versucht, seine Theorien zu realisieren, aber dazu nur wenig Gelegenheit erhalten. Seit 1961 beteiligte er sich an zahllosen Ausschreibungen, ein solch großes Projekt wie der Cimitero di San Cataldo hatte er jedoch noch nie realisiert. 20 Jahre nach der Erteilung des Bauauftrags – Rossi arbeitete noch immer an der Verwirklichung der Konstruktionspläne – erhielt er den Auftrag für den Friedhof von Rozzano.

Le cimetière de San Cataldo, Modène

Moins d'un siècle après sa consécration, le cimetière municipal de Modène avait sérieusement besoin d'être agrandi. Le soin porté à la préparation de son extension est caractéristique des projets d'urbanisme de cette municipalité. Pendant les années 60 et 70, de nombreuses cités de l'Italie du Nord connurent une croissance explosive et les notions de programmation et de régulation devinrent des instruments de gestion courants.

Une procédure prudente

En 1967, les responsables municipaux conclurent que la meilleure solution serait de prévoir un plan global de développement du nouveau cimetière en plusieurs phases, plutôt que de réaliser des extensions au coup par coup. Quatre années passèrent cependant avant qu'un concours en deux étapes ne soit lancé. Au premier tour, les architectes italiens étaient invités à soumettre des plans non détaillés exposant leur conception du nouveau cimetière et son articulation avec l'ancien. Ces premières ébauches seraient rendues publiques avant le second tour qui permettrait la mise au point des projets retenus.

Les événements ne respectèrent pas cette savante organisation. Après de longues délibérations, le jury sélectionna 9 propositions sur 51. Trois furent primées et 6 autres acquises. Le premier prix fut attribué au projet intitulé «L'azzurro del cielo» (le bleu du ciel), dans lequel il est probable que des membres du jury comme Aymonino et Portoghesi avaient reconnu le style caractéristique d'Aldo Rossi (né en 1931) malgré l'anonymat requis. Contrairement à ce qui avait été prévu, les projets ne furent pas exposés et les trois architectes primés participèrent à un second tour dont Rossi sortit vainqueur.

Un cimetière du XIXème siècle

Le projet de Rossi était frappant non seulement pour son style mais également dans ses développements très différents de ceux de ses concurrents. Il avait tenté de relier son projet à l'ancien cimetière rectangulaire et entouré de galeries conçu par Cesare Costa dans la seconde moitié du XIXème siècle. Costa avait élevé des pavillons de style palladien simplifié sur l'axe longitudinal de son rectangle.

La plupart des autres architectes ne prêtèrent que peu d'attention aux détails architecturaux du cimetière existant. Adriano Campioni et son équipe (plans acquis) avaient regroupé leurs columbariums de façon irrégulière sur deux axes asymétriques et apparemment arbitraires qui se coupaient à angle droit. L'entrée était située en tête de l'axe longitudinal, et bien que l'ancien et le nouveau cimetière soient situés côte à côte, le travail de Costa avait été ignoré. La même critique pouvait s'adresser à l'équipe de Constantino Dardi (second prix) et à son cimetière en bandes et à celui de Fabio Lunbelli (troisième prix), très éclaté.

Le rationalisme de Rossi

Rossi suivit une approche toute différente et choisit délibérément de s'inspirer de l'ancien cimetière. Ce choix peut s'expliquer par l'approche rationaliste très personnelle qui est la sienne.

A la différence de beaucoup de ses confrères pour lesquels le fonctionnalisme est la seule architecture acceptable, Rossi est beaucoup plus ouvert aux formes du passé. Toute étude sur l'architecture post-moderne serait incomplète sans un chapitre sur ses théories influentes et ses créations inventives. Il reste que son curriculum architectural était bien mince lorsqu'il fut choisi. Auteur de nombreux articles, essentiellement sur l'histoire de l'architecture, éditeur du magazine Casabella, ses contributions traitaient essentiellement du néo-classicisme lombard, de l'urbanisme en Italie et des fondements culturels de ses propres recherches. En 1965, il publia l'un de ses écrits les plus importants «L'architettura della città» dans lequel il exposait sa conception de l'urbanisme et précisait ses objections au fonctionnalisme, style dominant à l'époque. La variété des intérêts architecturaux de Rossi, allant de Palladio à Loos et sa critique d'un fonctionnalisme rigide ont fait de lui l'un des plus importants théoriciens du post-modernisme. Son propre style a souvent été étiqueté de rationaliste.

Logique et précis

Selon Rossi, l'architecture devrait se limiter à l'emploi de structures théoriques bien définies. L'architecte doit s'appuyer dans ses plans sur des principes logiques valables en toutes circonstances. C'est là une déviation essentielle du rationalisme par rapport au fonctionnalisme qui s'efforce au contraire de trouver la meilleure solution spécifique à un problème donné. Un rationaliste s'efforce de trouver la meilleure solution pour une vaste gamme de problèmes à partir d'un cadre général sur lequel viennent se greffer les principes architecturaux. L'approche rationaliste efface les différences typologiques. Il existe toujours une solution applicable, quel que soit le type de construction, et les diverses formes architecturales sont réduites à des expressions basiques. Cette interchangeabilité caractérise l'approche de l'urbanisme de Rossi qui n'est pas sans similarité avec les travaux des structuralistes néerlandais. La maison est la cité, le couloir la rue et la cour la place. Le cimetière de San Cataldo s'inspire de ces idées. Le caractère monumental des immeubles de Rossi et le magnifique jeu de la lumière et de l'ombre qu'il maîtrise à merveille ont souvent fait comparer ses travaux aux peintures métaphysiques de Giorgio De Chirico. Un sens identique de menace et de désolation y prévaut, comme si les deux artistes s'étaient efforcés de matérialiser un rêve.

Le plan

Plus de vingt ans après le concours, les deux tiers du cimetière ont été réalisés, en partie selon les plans originaux de Rossi et en partie d'après des plans ultérieurs ou des modifications. Rossi avait tenu compte de la réalisation néo-palladienne du XIXème siècle. Les deux cimetières sont ainsi entourés d'une galerie et dessinés sur une trame. Les deux pavillons d'entrée des deux cimetières sont situés sur le même axe transversal. L'axe longitudinal du plan de Costa, parallèle à une route, dépasse le cimetière juif situé maintenant entre les deux, et rejoint l'un des deux grands axes de Rossi.

Rossi avait au départ utilisé un système similaire pour son immeuble du quartier de Gallaratese (Milan) qui mettait l'accent sur l'interchangeabilité de formes universelles. Les colombariums sont situés au-dessus de la galerie et recouverts d'un toit incurvé de forme allongée en tôle d'aluminium peinte en bleu. Une double galerie formant une ruelle a été élevée sur le côté est, remplaçant la galerie unique du plan original. Les deux galeries sont réunies par des passerelles au niveau supérieur. Leurs parapets sont constitués de cadres carrés à croix de Saint-André qui rappellent l'immeuble de Milan. Les murs de béton ont été recouverts d'enduit rose pâle, et les ouvertures carrées des murs sont fermées par des grilles en croix. Le carré est l'une de ces formes simples que Rossi aime à utiliser dans ses projets.

La conception intérieure

Dans le plan de départ, les galeries intérieures formaient un passage fermé coupé par l'axe transversal du cimetière qui délimitait deux carrés. Cet axe court est le plus important élément du plan. Il réunit deux autres éléments de base «universels», le cube et le cône. Le cube est fait de carrés, le cône, quant à lui, bien que moins présent dans l'œuvre de Rossi est cependant l'un de ses éléments thématiques récurrents favoris. Il l'a utilisé dans ses plans pour l'école primaire de Varese (1972), pour l'école d'architecture de Miami (1986) et l'hôtel de ville de Borgorico (1983). Cette forme jouait également un rôle important dans sa participation au concours pour l'hôtel de ville de Muggio, près de Milan. Dans ce dernier projet (1972) se retrouvent d'autres points communs avec le cimetière de San Cataldo. Le cône de Modène possède une fonction symbolique: de même qu'une cheminée d'usine s'arrête de fumer lorsque le travail est terminé, de même la «cheminée» de Modène symbolise-t-elle la fin de la vie. Le cône donne accès à un escalier concentrique qui descend vers la fosse commune.

Les columbariums, situés entre le cône et le cube, sont implantés selon un dessin en arête. On a pu suggérer que c'était une allusion au christianisme dont le poisson a été la représentation symbolique, mais cette idée de l'évocation de la mort du Christ est sans doute excessive. Une autre explication, plus plausible, veut que ce dessin évoque un squelette. Rossi avait été victime d'un grave accident de voiture peu de temps avant de remettre ses plans et pendant qu'il était à l'hôpital, il avait trouvé que la structure de son corps ressemblait à une série d'éléments brisés qu'il fallait remettre en forme.

Les colombariums, le long de l'axe transversal, peuvent également être perçus comme une composition sur le thème du triangle, à la fois dans le plan de masse et dans leur forme. Ils deviennent de plus en plus hauts au fur et à mesure que l'on s'approche de la fosse commune. Le colombarium le plus élevé est aussi le plus étroit, et le moins haut le plus large. Le lien entre le cube et le cône est ainsi logique et rationnel: un (double) triangle, sur un plan de masse composé de carrés.

Une déviation du fonctionnalisme

Le plan dans son ensemble est symétrique, axé, hiérarchisé et rappelle celui de Costa, le néo-classicisme lombard et l'architecture palladienne. Les dalles de béton des galeries d'inspiration classique sont typiques de la façon dont Rossi sait s'éloigner du fonctionnalisme des années 60. Bien qu'il ait tenté à de nombreuses reprises de mettre en pratique ses théories, les occasions concrètes avaient été jusque-là rares et espacées[1]. Il avait participé à un certain nombre de concours depuis 1961 mais n'avait jamais reçu de commande plus importante que ce cimetière. Vingt ans plus tard il fut choisi pour en construire un autre, à Rozzano.

1 *Il avait cependant déjà construit l'immeuble de logement à Milan et le monument aux morts de Ségrate.*

88
L'azzurro del cielo
Cimitero di Modena . prospettiva . Aldo Rossi 72.

Aldo Rossi & Gianni Braghieri
bird's-eye view, 1988

Aldo Rossi & Gianni Braghieri
competition design, 1971, bird's-eye view, first prize

Aldo Rossi & Gianni Braghieri
sketch, 1980

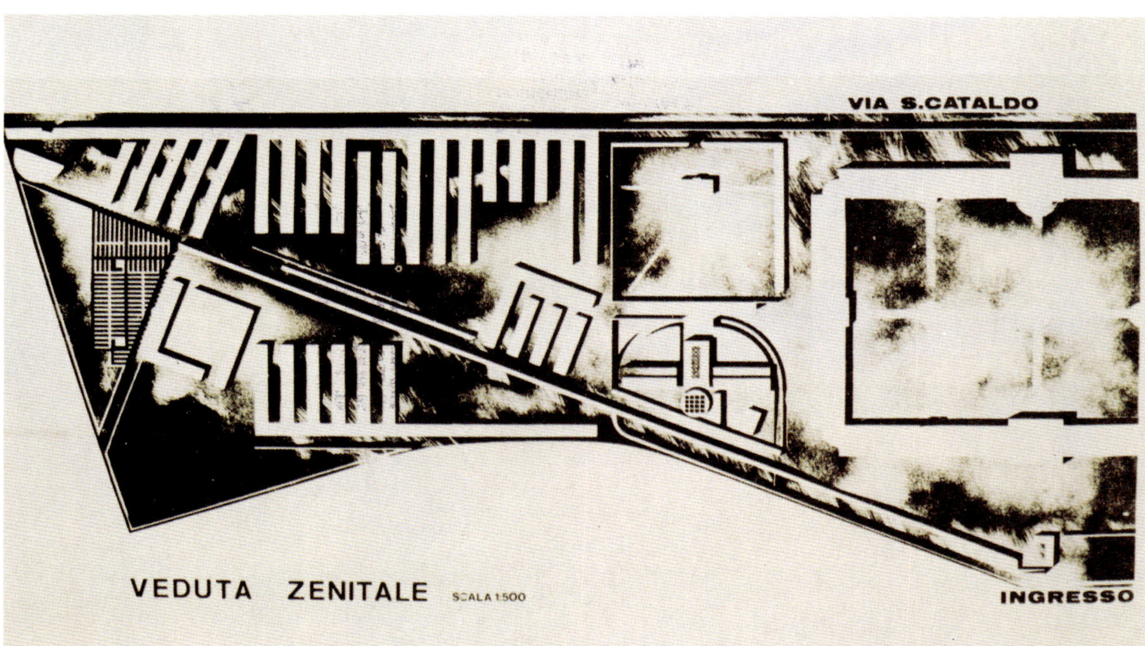

Adriano Campioni, Giulio Dubbini, Francesco Pierobon, Leonardo Rampazzi & Piero de Pra bird's-eye view sketch, 1973

Adriano Campioni, Giulio Dubbini, Francesco Pierobon, Leonardo Rampazzi & Piero de Pra bird's-eye view sketch

Adriano Campioni, Giulio Dubbini, Francesco Pierobon, Leonardo Rampazzi & Piero de Pra competition design, 1971, site plan, purchased

Adriano Campioni, Giulio Dubbini, Francesco Pierobon, Leonardo Rampazzi & Piero de Pra sketches of several details

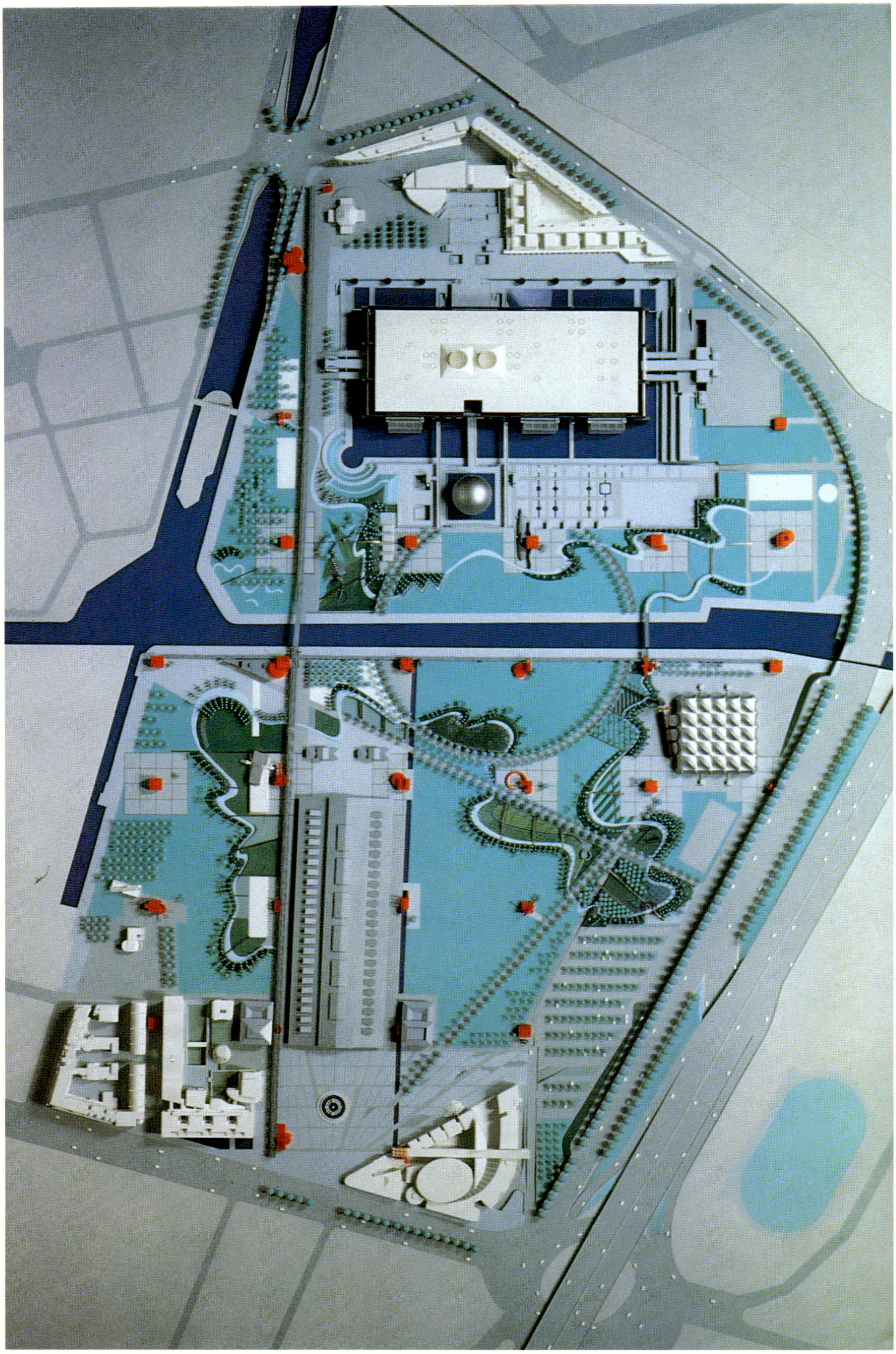

Project

Public park

Site

La Villette, north-east Paris

Dates

First round announced 8 April 1982 *Closing date* August 1982 *Result announced* 13 December 1982 *Second round, result announced* 25 March 1983

Number of entries

First round 471 *Second round* 9

Jury

Roberto Burle Marx (chairman, landscape architect), Pierre Dauvergne (landscape architect), Vittorio Gregotti, Arata Isozaki, Renzo Piano (all architects) and sixteen others

Result

First prize Bernard Tschumi *Second prize* Rem Koolhaas *Third prize* Sven Ingvar Andersson; Alexandre Chemetoff; Bernard Lassus; Gilles Vexlard; Andreu Arriola; Bakker & Bleeker; Jacques Gourvennec and others

Commissioned by

Établissement Public du Parc de la Villette (EPPV)

Construction

First period 1984 to 1987 *Second period* as of 1987

Architect

Bernard Tschumi (*1944)

Construction cost

850 000 000 francs (1984, including La Grande Halle)

Parc de la Villette, Paris, 1976–1982

Bernard Tschumi competition design, 1982, site plan, first prize

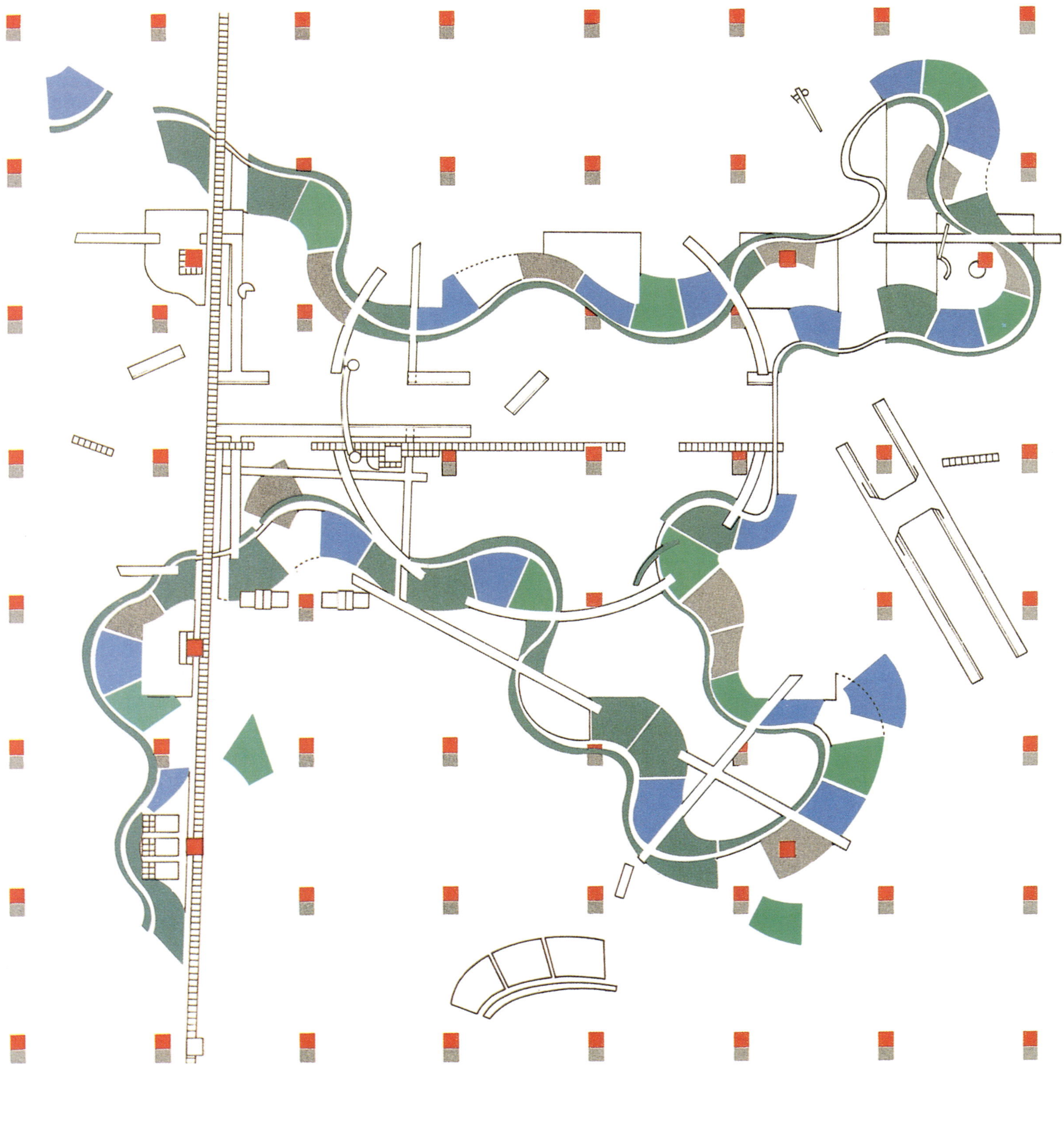

Parc de la Villette, Paris

The histories of the competitions for the Parc de la Villette and the Cité des Sciences et de l'Industrie are inextricably intertwined[1]. Following the first competition in 1976, aimed at a broad transformation of the la Villette abattoir district, the French president, Valéry Giscard d'Estaing, intervened, and in 1980 a second competition for the creation of an entirely new breed of rescentional and arts complet, the Parc de la Villette, was held. This was won by Adrien Fainsilber. However, when François Mitterrand came to power, the Parc and the Cité became separate projects and a new competition was organised in 1982. The conditions stipulated in the competition programme were complex and sometimes contradictory, the most important of them being that the architects had to take into account a number of existing buildings, including the Cité de la Musique which was to be built on the same site.

An impressive site

The most important building on the site requiring consideration was of course the former meat auction-cum-abattoir, which Fainsilber had transformed into a centre for science, technology and industry. The only other remaining annex of the abattoir, designed by Baltard and Janvier in 1867, is situated on the other side of the canal which bisects the grounds. This building had been transformed into an exhibition hall by Bernard Reichen and Philippe Robert, who had also submitted a design for the Cité des Sciences et de l'Industrie. In addition, the participating architects had to incorporate a number of smaller pavilions into their designs, including the Rotonde des Vétérinaires, which was designed by Claude Nicolas Ledoux and dates from 1775. It was on these grounds, which cover an impressive 55 hectares, that the Parc de la Villette was to be laid out.

During the first round, 9 of the 471 participants were jointly awarded first prize and 21 architects received an honourable mention. A number of the nominated architects were reimbursed for their efforts, others were not. Although, initially, there had been no plans for a second round, the nine winning architects were asked to develop their plans further. This was necessary due to the diversity of the designs, and the jury's inability to reach a unanimous decision.

A 21st-century park

The main reason for the diversity of the designs was undoubtedly that the park was envisaged as a complex combination of landscape, architectural and urban planning elements. Consequently, the field of participants included experts from a variety of architectural backgrounds. The winning architect was to be appointed project supervisor. He would be in charge of the general layout of the complex from start to finish, and would personally design the main architectural elements.
The commissioning body wanted to return to the age-old concept of the park as a recreational and social urban facility: a place where all people could meet, regardless of race and class, and not only children with their guardians, and old people. The commission saw the predominance of the latter groups as proof of the declining significance of parks as urban facilities. In order to underscore this newly-conceived function, the park was to have open-air theatres, restaurants, galleries, music and art workshops, sports and recreation facilities, and facilities for video and computer demonstrations. Furthermore, the architects had to incorporate a number of "theme gardens". In combination with the existing facilities and the Cité de la Musique, the park was to become a venue with an unprecedented socio-cultural significance.

François Mitterrand, president

Interior of La Grande Halle

A variety of solutions

Rem Koolhaas (*1935) and Bernard Tschumi had submitted the most complex second round designs. These were consequently spotlighted by the jury. Both architects have been ranked as Deconstructivists, even though there are as many similarities in their work as there are differences. We will return to Tschumi later on.

Koolhaas' plan, which won second prize, was at least as theoretical as Tschumi's, and actually showed a more systematic design. The elements of his park are laid out in strips which run parallel to the canal, and the entire site is covered by a grid system. There are three "layers" of design: the first of these is formed by the infrastructure, which consists of a straight north-south axis, criss-crossed by a system of smaller paths, the second layer contains the major architectural elements, such as the existing buildings and the projected facilities, whilst the third links the complex to its surroundings. As was the case with many other designs, Koolhaas based the layout of the different elements mainly on the orientation of the canal, Baltard and Janvier's abattoir and the auction building.

Koolhaas was evidently intent on getting away from the traditional concept of parks as landscaped gardens. His design was free of meandering paths and other irregular forms, and its asymmetrical layout was a far cry from Baroque and Renaissance gardens. Although the different layers within it are distinct, the design forms an integrated whole, and resembles a Suprematist composition. This is characteristic of the Deconstructivist style, which is largely based on the classic Modernist styles.

The French landscape architects Alexandre Chemetoff, Bernard Lassus and Gilles Vexlard clearly based their designs on the park's vegetation. Chemetoff secluded La Villette from its surroundings by planning a dense perimeter of foliage around the park. In his design, the main axis runs from Ledoux's Rotonde to the nineteenth-century abattoir. A parallel axis runs along the east side of the park, where the theme gardens are situated. The central part of the park is left open, giving an unimpeded view of the abattoir and Fainsilber's Cité des Sciences. Although Lassus also left the central part of the park open, he concealed the Cité behind high trees. He grouped the required buildings in three compact complexes, leaving most of the park free of construction. The perimeter was also left open, which meant that a noise-muffling wall was required between the park and the belt road. In Chemetoff's design the trees formed a natural noise barrier. Vexlard's park had the densest foliage, which even made the Cité des Sciences look like a background feature. As was the case in Tschumi's design, Vexlard left an open space behind the Cité – a city square on the "wrong" side of the complex. Nearly all of the park's main facilities are situated along the north-south axis, which is based on the orientation of the canal and the abattoir, opening the park up to the surroundings. There is a footbridge in the upper region of the grounds, which provides a panoramic view of the park. By utilising the gradient of the park, Vexlard had incorporated both artificial and natural aspects of orientation. This had been stipulated in the competition programme: the Parc de la Villette was to be a synthesis of architectural and natural features.

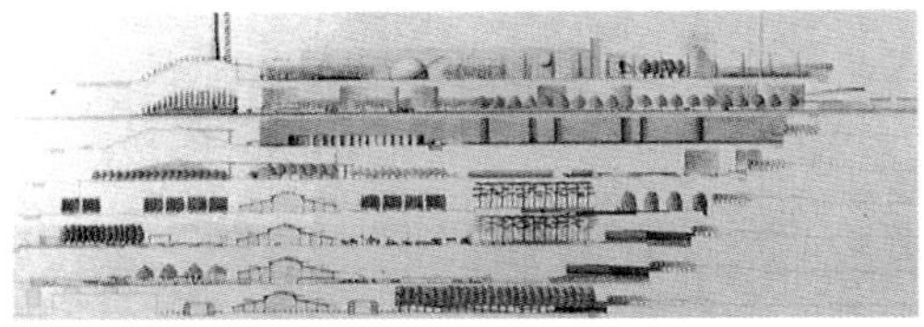

Rem Koolhaas **Parc de la Villette, séquence, 1982**

Bernard Tschumi **series of follies**

Christian de Portzamparc **La Cité de la Musique, isometric projection**

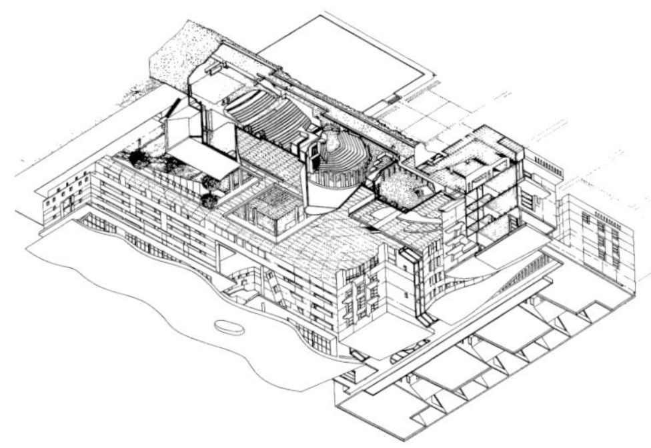

It was evident that both Vexlard and Lassus were true landscape architects. However, they took a back seat to the "structural" architects Tschumi and Koolhaas in the second round. It has been suggested that the composition of the jury, which included both landscape and structural architects, led to discord during adjudication, with both sides trying to promote their own particular protégés. However, this seems unlikely considering the quality of the thirty nominated designs, and the fact that Koolhaas and Tschumi received seventeen votes in the final round, whereas Lassus and Vexlard got only four.

A Deconstructivist victory

The fact that Tschumi was given the opportunity to execute his design was seen as a major victory for the Deconstructivists. Deconstructivism is certainly not a uniform style, but there are obvious similarities between the designs of Koolhaas and Tschumi. Both were inspired by the "Big Apple": Koolhaas' book Delirious New York was published in 1978, and Tschumi published a book entitled Manhattan Transcripts in 1981. Both architects submitted competition designs based on a provisional programme in which activities and forms had been stipulated. Both submitted designs in which the whole is the sum of independent systems. And finally, it is probably coincidental that

Jean Nouvel "La Galérie des jeux informatiques", model

1 Jean Nouvel 2 John Hejduk 3 Peter D. Eisenman & Jacques Derrida 4 Fuijiko Nakaya 5 Henri Gaudin 6 Gilles Vexlard 7 Gaetano Pesce 8 Claes Oldenburg 9 Cedric Price 10 Alexandre Chemetoff & Daniel Buren 11 Kathryn Gustafson 12 Jean Magerand 13 Paysages 14 Kathryn Gustafsog

neither Koolhaas nor Tschumi seemed to consider the belt road a problem, since neither architect bothered to include a noise-muffling wall in his design.

Tschumi's independent systems have become famous over the years: planes denote events, lines denote movement and dots denote meeting places. The planes fit into the existing floor plan, following the lines of the rectangles formed by the abattoir, Fainsilber's building and the course of the Canal d'Ourcq. Tschumi added a circle and a triangle to this system.

Tschumi also included a dot-patterned grid, which is a recurrent element in his designs. In this case the pattern denotes an element of landscape architecture: the folly. However, Tschumi's follies were designed along completely different lines to those in traditional landscape architecture, which are built in a variety of styles and positioned irregularly. As one might expect, the follies in Tschumi's design, all of them spray-painted red, are positioned at regular intervals, 120 metres apart. The only style which may have been a source of inspiration was Russian Constructivism. The basic element is a cube measuring ten by ten metres, which is fragmented, dissected and supplemented with additional elements here and there. This design procedure is characteristically Deconstructivist.

The lines denoting movement also form an independent system. They generally follow the contours of the planes, but now and again they form separate structures, such as the cinematic promenade. Some of the lines denote paths and canals, others tree-lined promenades and footbridges. The route linking the theme gardens is denoted by an irregular, meandering line.

A number of the theme gardens were designed by architects who had participated in the competition. Alexandre Chemetoff designed the Bamboo Garden together with the artist Daniel Buren, and Peter D. Eisenman, another Deconstructivist, formed a design team with Jacques Derrida. One of the other runners-up, Vexlard, was commissioned to design a garden which had "the art of gardening" as its theme. Many other architects, of varying renown, contributed to the design of La Villette: Jean Nouvel, John Hejduk and Gaetano Pesce, to name but three. One of the facilities which deserves a special mention is Le Zenith, an enormous stage designed by Philippe Chaix and Jean-Paul Morel, where pop concerts are held.

An extraordinary number of architects contributed to La Villette, for the simple reason that a project of this magnitude was far too great a task for a single architect. During the first phase (1984–1987) Tschumi's firm alone produced more than four thousand drawings and seventy models. Tschumi has referred to the Parc de la Villette as *"the largest discontinuous building in the world"*.

1 *See chapter on the Cité des Sciences et de l'Industrie elsewhere in this book.*

Parc de la Villette, Paris

Die Geschichte der Ausschreibung zum Parc de la Villette verlief parallel zum Wettbewerb für das Wissenschafts-, Technik- und Industriemuseum (La Cité des Sciences et de l'Industrie). Die Ausschreibung des Jahres 1976 hatte aufgrund der Einmischung von Präsident Valéry Giscard d'Estaing zu keinem Ergebnis geführt, und anfänglich schien es, als trage der Architekt Adrien Fainsilber die alleinige Verantwortung für den gesamten Komplex von La Villette. Nach dem Regierungsantritt von François Mitterrand wurden die Gestaltung des Parks und der Cité des Sciences voneinander getrennt und 1982 ein neuer Wettbewerb ausgeschrieben. Die Auflagen verlangten die Berücksichtigung einiger bereits bestehender Gebäude sowie des neu geplanten Musikzentrums (La Cité de la Musique).

Ein beeindruckender Standort

Das wichtigste Gebäude, das die Architekten in ihre Planung einbeziehen mußten, war der alte Schlachthof samt Viehmarkt, mit dessen Umgestaltung Fainsilber beauftragt war. Auf der anderen Seite des Canal de l'Ourcq, der das Gelände unterteilt, befindet sich noch die letzte der alten, von Baltard und Janvier 1867 errichteten Hallen. Diese Halle wurde von Bernard Reichen und Philippe Robert, die sich ebenfalls an der Ausschreibung für die Cité des Sciences et de l'Industrie beteiligt hatten, zu einem Ausstellungsgebäude umgebaut. Darüber hinaus erhielten die Architekten die Auflage, mehrere kleine Pavillons und die Rotonde des Véterinaires (1775 von Claude Nicolas Ledoux erbaut) zu integrieren. Von den 471 eingegangenen Beiträgen prämierte die Jury neun mit dem ersten Platz und weitere 21 mit einer ehrenvollen Erwähnung, wobei nur ein Teil ein Preisgeld erhielt. Die neun Architekten der ausgewählten Einsendungen wurden gebeten, ihre Entwürfe weiter auszuarbeiten. Diese zweite Ausschreibungsrunde war ursprünglich nicht vorgesehen, aber der Jury blieb aufgrund interner Meinungsverschiedenheiten und unterschiedlicher Konzepte keine andere Wahl.

Ein Park für das 21. Jahrhundert

Die Vielschichtigkeit der Einsendungen hing ohne Zweifel mit der Aufgabe zusammen, einen Park zu entwerfen, der nicht nur landschaftliche, sondern auch architektonische und städtebauliche Komponenten enthielt. Gesucht wurde ein Projektleiter, der das komplexe Bauprogramm von Anfang bis Ende überwachen und die Ausführung der wichtigsten architektonischen Elemente selbst übernehmen sollte. Daher beteiligten sich an dem Wettbewerb neben Landschaftsarchitekten auch Städteplaner und Architekten.
Den Auftraggebern schwebte ein Park vor, der genau wie die Gartenanlagen vergangener Epochen neben seiner Aufgabe als Erholungsstätte eine soziale Funktion besaß: ein Treffpunkt für alle Rassen und Klassen – und nicht nur für ältere Menschen und Eltern mit Kinder. Um diese Funktion des Parks hervorzuheben, sollte der Entwurf u. a. mehrere Freilichtbühnen, Restaurants, Galerien, Sport- und Spielplätze sowie Räumlichkeiten für Video- und Computerdemonstrationen sowie für diverse Workshops bieten. Desweiteren sahen die Auflagen eine Reihe thematischer Gartenanlagen vor.

Verschiedene Lösungen

Von den neun Preisträgern erhielten die komplexen Konstruktionspläne von Rem Koolhaas (1935) und Bernard Tschumi die meiste Aufmerksamkeit. Obwohl sie nur wenige Gemeinsamkeiten verbanden, gehörten beide Architekten zu den Dekonstruktivisten. Koolhaas' Entwurf errang den zweiten Platz. Charakteristisch sind der streifenförmige Aufbau parallel zum Kanal sowie das Rastermuster, das sich über das gesamte Terrain erstreckt. Bei den drei »Ebenen« handelte es sich erstens um die Infrastruktur (eine gerade Nord-Süd-Achse und ein etwas bescheidenerer Fußweg aus schrägen und geraden Abschnitten), zweitens um die Ebene der großen Komponenten (bestehende und geplante Gebäude) sowie drittens um die Anbindung an die Umgebung. Wie bei vielen anderen Entwürfen bestimmen der Kanal, Baltards und Janviers alte Schlachthalle sowie die Viehmarkthalle die Lage der verschiedenen Elemente.
Koolhaas nahm mit seinem Konzept nachdrücklich Abstand von den Parkanlagen der Vergangenheit. Er distanzierte sich von den Landschaftsgärten, indem er auf gewundene Wege und andere unregelmäßige Formen verzichtete, ebenso wie von den Barock- und Renaissancegärten, denn sein Park war asymmetrisch aufgebaut. Die verschiedenen Ebenen bildeten ein zusammenhängendes Ganzes, das – ganz im Stil der Dekonstruktivisten (die sich bei der modernen Klassik bedienen) – an eine dominante Komposition erinnerte. Die französischen Landschaftsarchitekten Alexandre Chemetoff, Bernard Lassus und Gilles Vexlard nahmen die Grünanlagen des Parks als Ausgangspunkt für ihren Entwurf. Chemetoffs Konzept isolierte La Villette von der urbanen Umgebung, indem er die Randgebiete des Parks dicht bepflanzte. Die Hauptachse verlief von Ledoux' Rotonde zur Schlachthalle aus dem 19. Jahrhundert; eine weitere Achse erstreckte sich parallel zur Ostseite des Parks mit den thematischen Gärten. Die mittlere Fläche sollte größtenteils unbepflanzt bleiben und freie Sicht auf die Schlachthalle und Fainsilbers Cité des Sciences bieten.
Auch Lassus verzichtete auf eine dichte Bepflanzung der Parkmitte, setzte aber genau vor die Cité mehrere hohe Bäume. Die in den Auflagen geforderte Bebauung stand in drei Gruppen dicht beieinander, so daß der Park eher leer wirkte. Außerdem waren die Randgebiete zur Stadt hin nicht bepflanzt, wodurch ein Lärmschutzwall zwischen dem Park und der Périphérie notwendig wurde. Bei Chemetoffs Entwurf übernahmen die Bäume diese Funktion.
Vexlards Konzept sah eine sehr dichte Bepflanzung vor, die sogar die Cité des Sciences im Hintergrund verschwinden ließ. Genau wie Tschumi entwarf Vexlard auf der Rückseite der Cité eine offene Fläche: so entstand ein städtischer Platz auf der »falschen« Seite. Die wichtigsten Einrichtungen des Parks befanden sich fast alle entlang der Nord-Süd-Achse, die sich ebenfalls nach dem Verlauf des Kanals und an der Lage der Schlachthalle ausrichtet und zugleich die zentrale Zufahrtsstraße zum Park bildete. Über die Straße führte eine Fußgängerbrükke, von der aus der gesamte Park zu überblicken war. Ferner orientierte sich Vexlard an den Höhenlinien des Terrains und bezog sich, neben den künstlichen Vorgaben, auch auf natürliche Orientierungspunkte – ganz im Sinne der Ausschreibung – der Parc de la Villette als sowohl urbaner wie auch natürlicher Raum.
Bei Vexlards und Lassus' Entwürfen handelte es sich eindeutig um Konzepte von Landschaftsarchitekten. In der letzten Ausscheidungsrunde unterlagen die beiden den »gewöhnlichen« Architekten Tschumi und Koolhaas. Gerüchteweise kam es in der Jury aus Landschaftarchitekten zu einer kontroversen Diskussion, in deren Verlauf beide Berufsgruppen ihre Protegés durchzusetzen versuchten.

Ein Sieg des Dekonstruktivismus

Die Tatsache, daß Tschumi seine Konstruktionspläne verwirklichen durfte, bedeutete einen großen Sieg für die Bewegung des Dekonstruktivismus, zu der auch Koolhaas als zweiter Preisträger gerechnet werden darf. Sicherlich kann man diese Stilrichtung nicht als einheitlich bezeichnen, dennoch finden sich Übereinstimmungen zwischen Koolhaas und Tschumi. In ihren Beiträgen gingen beide Architekten von einem vorläufigen Programm aus, das sich aus Aktivitäten und Formen zusammensetzte. Beide Pläne bestanden aus einer Addition selbständiger Systeme. Interessanterweise betrachtete weder Koolhaas noch Tschumi die Périphérie als besonders problematisch: Keiner der beiden Entwürfe sah eine Lärmschutzmauer vor.
Tschumis selbständige Systeme haben inzwischen Berühmtheit erlangt: Flächen (Ereignisse), Linien (Bewegung) und Punkte (Begegnungspunkte). Die Flächen richten sich nach dem bestehenden Grundriß. Ihre Ausrichtung ist ebenso wie bei vielen anderen Einsendungen durch die Rechtecke der Schlachthalle und Fainsilbers Gebäude sowie den Canal d'Ourcq vorgegeben. Tschumi fügt dem Ganzen einen Kreis und ein Dreieck hinzu. Darüber liegt das Punktraster der als »Folies« bezeichneten Pavillons, einem Element aus der Landschaftsarchitektur. Während die Folies in den klassischen Parkanlagen unregelmäßig plazierte Bauwerke aus verschiedenen Stilepochen darstellten, setzt Tschumi seine Pavillons in einem regelmäßigen Abstand von 120 Meter aneinander und orientiert sich stilistisch ausschließlich am russischen Konstruktivismus. Sein Basiselement ist ein Würfel von zehn Metern Kantenlänge, teilweise fragmentiert, zergliedert oder mit zusätzlichen Formen ergänzt. Diese Entwurfsmethode gilt als charakteristisch für den Dekonstruktivismus. Alle Folies sind in einem leuchtenden Rotton gehalten.
Das letzte selbständige System ist das der Linien, die teils den Konturen der Flächen folgen, teils – wie im Falle der Cinematic Promenade – eigene Strukturen entstehen lassen. Einige Linien werden durch Wege oder Kanäle gebildet, andere durch Baumalleen oder Fußgängerbrücken. Eine unregelmäßige, gewundene Linie dient als Verbindungsroute zwischen den thematischen Gärten.
Die Gärten wurden zum Teil von anderen Architekten entworfen, die sich ebenfalls an der Ausschreibung beteiligt hatten: Alexandre Chemetoff (der Bambusgarten, zusammen mit dem bildenden Künstler Daniel Buren) und dem Dekonstruktivisten Peter D. Eisenman (zusammen mit Jacques Derrida). Der unterlegene Vexlard erhielt den Auftrag zur Gestaltung eines Gartens zum Thema »Die Kunst der Gartenarbeit«. Weitere Architekten, die an La Villette mitarbeiteten, waren u. a. Jean Nouvel, John Hejduk und Gaetano Pesce. Besondere Erwähnung verdient »Le Zenith«, eine Zelthalle für Popkonzerte, von Philippe Chaix und Jean-Paul Morel entworfen.
Für einen Architekten allein wäre das Projekt La Villette ohnehin zu umfangreich geworden. Allein in der ersten Bauphase von 1984 bis 1987 fertigte Tschumis Architekturbüro 4000 Zeichnungen und 70 Modelle an.

Le Parc de la Villette, Paris

Les deux compétitions pour le Parc de la Villette et la Cité des Sciences et de l'Industrie sont inextricablement mêlées[1]. La Cité faisait à l'origine partie du concours de 1976 pour le Parc de la Villette dont les résultats ne furent pas jugés satisfaisants par le président Giscard d'Estaing. Adrien Fainsilber fut désigné pour concevoir la totalité du complexe de la Villette mais à l'arrivée de François Mitterrand au pouvoir, le Parc et la Cité devinrent deux projets séparés et un nouveau concours fut lancé en 1982. Les clauses de ce nouvel appel d'offres étaient compliquées et même parfois contradictoires, la plus contraignante étant la nécessité de prendre en compte un certain nombre de bâtiments existants ou en projet comme la Cité de la Musique.

Un site impressionnant

L'édifice ancien le plus notable était évidemment l'ancien abattoir-salle des ventes aux enchères que Fainsilber avait transformé en musée de la science, de la technologie et de l'industrie. Par ailleurs, la grande Halle aux bœufs de Baltard et Janvier (1867) située de l'autre côté du canal divisant le terrain, avait été aménagée en centre d'expositions par Bernard Reichen et Philippe Robert, également auteurs d'un projet pour la Cité des Sciences. Les participants devaient de plus tenir compte de quelques anciens pavillons plus petits, dont la rotonde des vétérinaires, construite par Claude-Nicolas Ledoux en 1775. C'est sur ces bases que le Parc de la Villette, de plus de 55 ha de superficie, devait être conçu.
A l'issue du premier tour, 9 des 471 participants se virent attribuer un premier prix ex-aequo et 21 une mention honorable. Certains architectes reçurent des dédommagements, d'autres non. Bien qu'un second tour n'ait pas été prévu au départ, les neuf premiers prix furent remis en compétition tant leurs plans étaient différents et tant le jury était incapable de se mettre d'accord sur un vainqueur.

Un parc pour le XXIème siècle

La principale raison de cette diversité tenait indiscutablement à la difficulté de concevoir un ensemble relevant à la fois du paysage, de l'architecture et de l'urbanisme. Des experts de ces trois disciplines s'étaient mis sur les rangs. Il était prévu que l'architecte lauréat serait chargé de proposer un plan de masse, de dessiner les principaux éléments architecturaux et d'animer une équipe pluridisciplinaire.
L'Etablissement public voulait revenir au concept traditionnel du parc, lieu de loisirs et de détente. Cette dernière ne devait pas être privilégiée car on souhaitait un parc vivant, bien inséré dans la vie et les réalités de ces quartiers populaires de l'est parisien. Le parc devait donc être équipé de théâtres de plein air, de restaurants, de lieux d'exposition, d'ateliers pour l'art et la musique, d'équipements de sport et de loisirs, et d'installations vidéo. Des jardins à thème étaient suggérés. Si l'on y ajoute les équipements culturels déjà construits et la future Cité de la musique, le Parc avait toutes les chances de devenir un lieu exceptionnel, sans précédent.

Des solutions variées

Au second tour, Rem Koolhaas (né en 1935) et Bernard Tschumi proposèrent des plans complexes qui furent remarqués par le jury. Tous deux étaient classés parmi les déconstructivistes.
Le projet de Koolhaas, qui remporta le deuxième prix, était tout aussi théorisant que celui de Tschumi et plus systématique encore. Son parc était traité en bandes parallèles au canal existant et la totalité du site obéissait à un système de grille et à une structure en «couches». La première était celle de l'infrastructure, un axe rectiligne nord-sud, traversé par un réseau de sentiers plus étroits; la seconde incluait les principaux éléments architecturaux comme les édifices existants et les équipements projetés; la troisième reliait l'ensemble à son environnement. Koolhaas axait essentiellement son dessin sur l'orientation donnée par le canal, la Grande Halle et la Cité des Sciences.
Koolhaas affichait son intention de rompre avec la conception traditionnelle des parcs publics en tant que jardins paysagers. Son plan ne s'embarrassait ni de chemins sinueux ni de formes irrégulières, et son organisation asymétrique était à mille lieues des idées de la Renaissance ou du Baroque dans ce domaine. Bien que les différentes «couches» soient très identifiables, l'ensemble formait un tout intégré et faisait penser à une composition suprématiste, ce qui est souvent le cas du style déconstructiviste.
Certains participants français comme Chemetov, Lassus et Vexlard utilisaient essentiellement la végétation. Chemetov séparait la Villette de son environnement en prévoyant des plantations d'arbres très denses autour du parc et en faisant aller son axe principal de la rotonde de Ledoux à la Grande Halle du XIXème siècle, avec un axe parallèle le long de la façade Est du parc où étaient aménagés les jardins à thème. La partie centrale restait ouverte pour permettre une vue directe sur la Grande Halle et la Cité des Sciences de Fainsilber.
Bien que Lassus ait également laissé cette zone ouverte, il masquait la vue sur la Cité derrière des arbres de haute futaie. Les constructions demandées étaient regroupées en trois ensembles compacts qui dégageaient la plus grande surface du parc. Le périmètre était tout aussi ouvert, à l'exception d'un mur anti-bruit du côté du boulevard périphérique. Dans le projet Chemetov, les arbres étaient supposés fournir une barrière sonore naturelle.
Le plan Vexlard était le plus arboré et ramenait la Cité des Sciences à un décor de fond. Comme Tschumi, il aménageait un espace ouvert derrière la Cité pour délimiter une place publique sur le côté «neutre» du bâtiment. La quasi totalité des équipements était implantée le long de l'axe nord-sud, selon l'orientation du canal et de la Grande Halle, ouvrant ainsi le parc sur le quartier. Un pont pour piétons permettait d'offrir une vue dominante sur l'ensemble des équipements. En se servant des dénivellations, Vexlard jouait des aspects à la fois artificiels et naturels de l'orientation, ce qui correspondait à une demande du programme du concours: le Parc de la Villette devait être une synthèse de la nature et de l'architecture.
Lassus et Vexlard était d'authentiques architectes-paysagistes. Ils n'en arrivèrent pas moins derrière Koolhaas et Tschumi lors du second tour. Il a été dit que la composition du jury qui comprenait des architectes-paysagistes et des architectes avait entraîné quelques éclats lors des délibérations, chacun essayant d'influencer les votes en faveur de ses protégés. Mais ceci semble peu probable au vu de la qualité des trente projets distingués et du vote final: Koolhaas et Tschumi bénéficièrent de dix-sept voix contre quatre pour Lassus et Vexlard.

Une victoire du Déconstructivisme

La possibilité donnée à Tschumi de réaliser son projet a été saluée comme une grande victoire par les déconstructivistes. Le Déconstructivisme n'est certainement pas un style uniforme, mais on peut trouver des similarités frappantes entre les plans de Koolhaas et de Tschumi. Tous les deux étaient inspirés par New York. Le livre de Koolhaas, Delirious New York («New York délirant») fut publié en 1978 et celui de Tschumi, Manhattan Transcripts («Notes sur Manhattan») en 1981. Tous deux soumirent des projets correspondant au programme préliminaire qui avait précisé les activités et les formes et proposèrent des plans dans lesquels le tout est la somme de systèmes indépendants. Accessoirement, ni l'un ni l'autre ne se préoccupèrent du bruit du boulevard périphérique puisqu'ils ne prévirent pas de mur de protection.
Les systèmes autoréférentiels de Tschumi sont devenus célèbres: les surfaces traduisent des activités, les lignes le mouvement et les points des lieux de rencontre. Les surfaces s'intègrent au plan de masse existant, suivant les lignes des rectangles formés par la Grande Halle, le bâti de Fainsilber et le cours du Canal de l'Ourcq.
Tschumi ajouta à ce système un cercle et un triangle et surtout une grille de points qui figure dans la plupart de ses projets. Pour La Villette, les points signalent un élément d'architecture, une «folie». Ces folies furent conçues de façon très différente de celles de l'architecture paysagée traditionnelle, généralement édifiées dans des styles variés. Celles de Tschumi, toutes laquées de rouge, sont positionnées à 120 m l'une de l'autre selon une trame régulière et dans un seul style, proche du Constructivisme russe. L'élément de base en est un cube de 10 m de côté, fragmenté, déconstruit ou augmenté de composants variés. Cette approche est caractéristique du Déconstructivisme.
Les lignes chargées de souligner le mouvement forment, elles aussi, un système indépendant. Elles suivent généralement le contour des surfaces, mais ici et là constituent des structures indépendantes, comme la promenade cinématique. Certaines lignes marquent des sentiers ou des canaux, d'autres des mails et des passerelles. Le chemin réunissant les jardins à thème suit une ligne irrégulière et sinueuse.
Un certain nombre de jardins à thème ont été conçus par des architectes qui avaient participé à la compétition. Alexandre Chemetov dessina le Jardin des bambous en compagnie de l'artiste Daniel Buren, et Peter D. Eisenman, autre déconstructiviste, fit équipe avec Jacques Derrida. L'un des battus, Vexlard, fut chargé d'un jardin sur le thème de «l'art des jardins». Beaucoup d'autres architectes, très connus ou non, travaillèrent sur le Parc: Jean Nouvel, John Hejduk et Gaetano Pesce, par exemple. L'une des réalisations les plus remarquables est le Zénith, vaste salle de concerts conçue par Philippe Chaix et Jean-Paul Morel. Si autant d'architectes travaillèrent sur ce projet, c'est sans doute, que son importance et sa complexité interdisaient à un seul homme d'en être le maître d'œuvre. Pendant la première phase de construction, le seul cabinet de Tschumi produisit plus de 4000 dessins et 70 maquettes. Tschumi a pu qualifier le Parc de la Villette de *«plus grand édifice discontinu du monde»*.

1 Voir le chapitre sur la Cité des Sciences et de l'Industrie.

Bernard Tschumi "cinematic promenade of gardens", diagram, 1982

Bernard Tschumi "superimposition of three systems", isometric projection, 1982

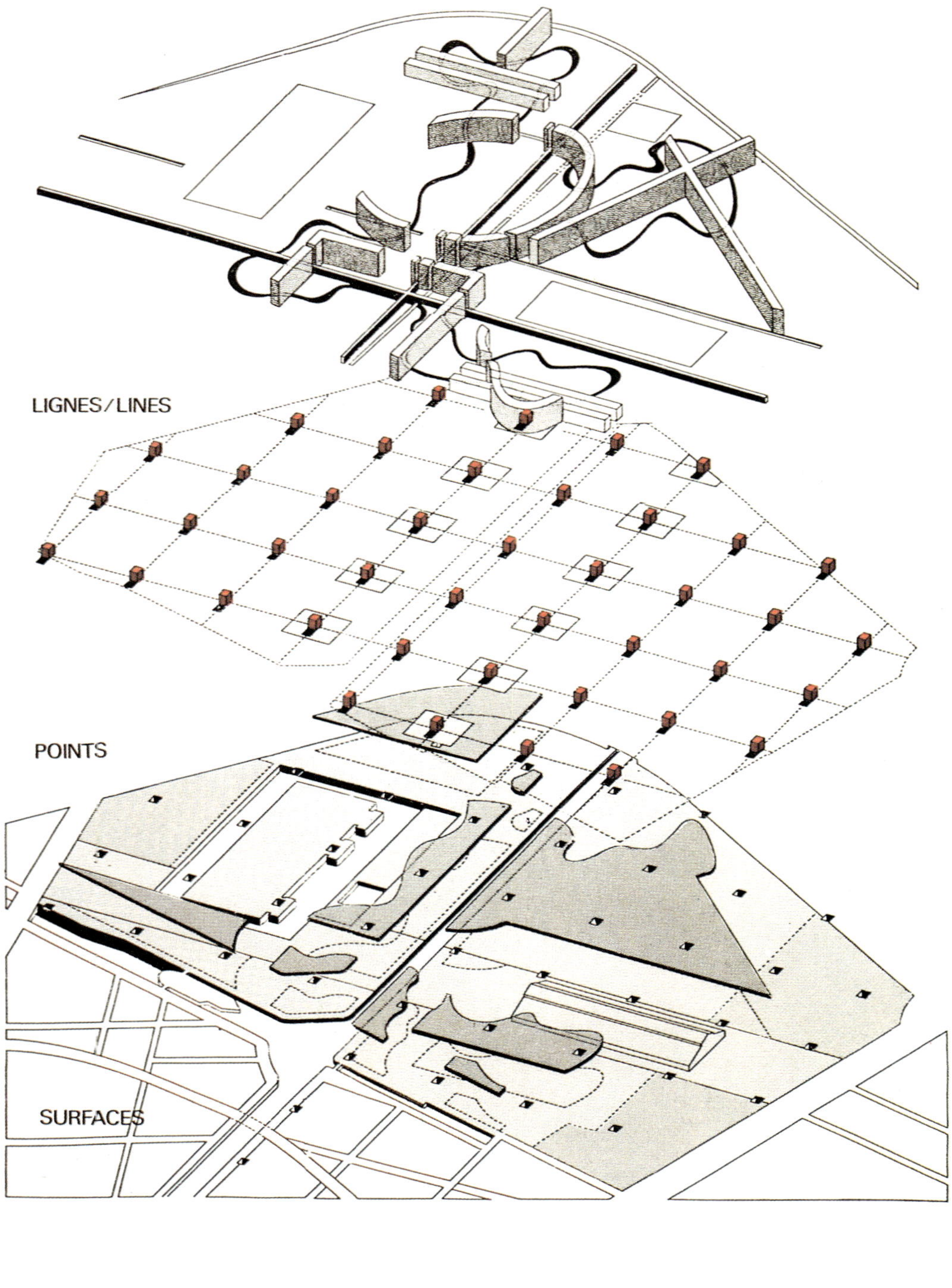

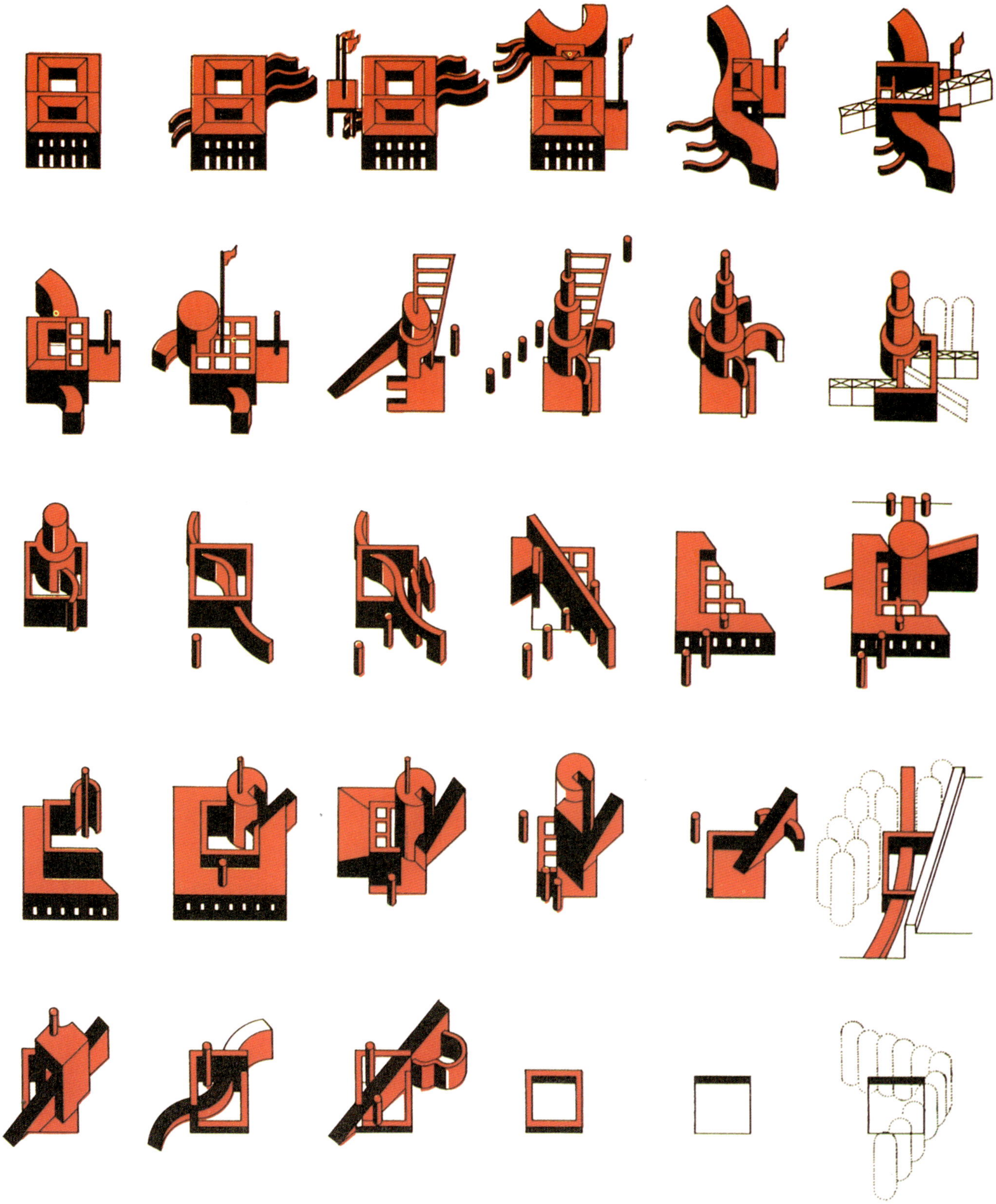

Bernard Tschumi "combination and transformation of architectural elements from the point grid of follies", isometric projection, 1982

Bernard Tschumi view of "Séquences", 1984, first prize

Bernard Tschumi view of "Séquences", 1984, first prize

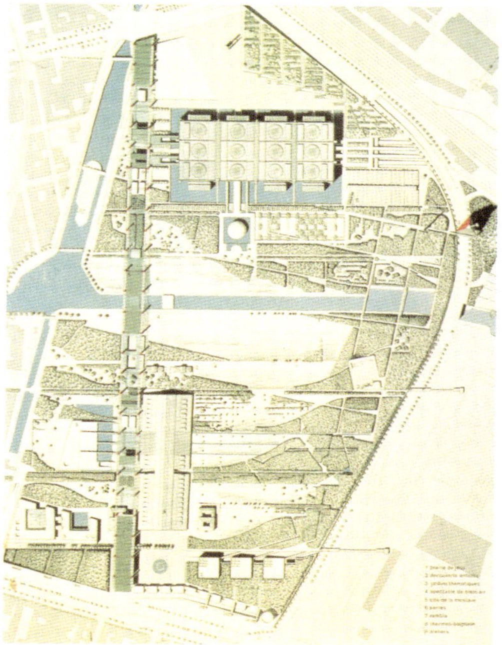

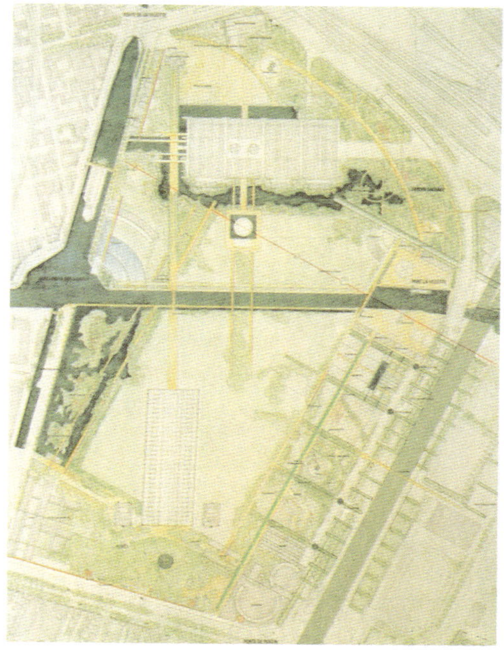

Rem Koolhaas competition design, 1982, site plan, second prize

Rem Koolhaas competition design, 1982, drawing, second prize

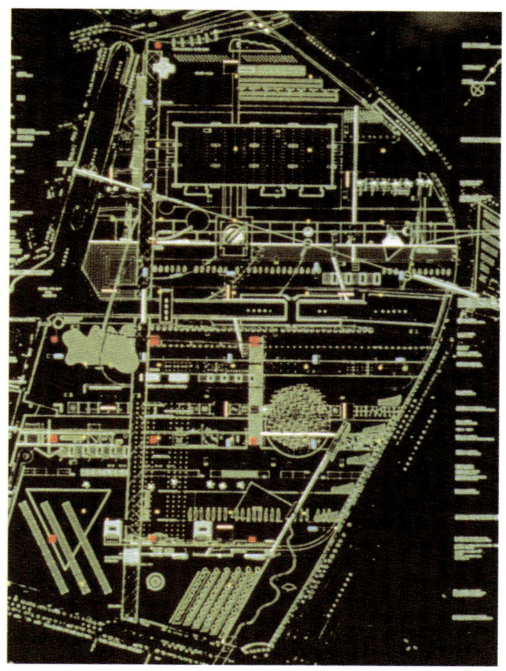

Gilles Vexlard competition design, 1982, site plan, third prize

Alexandre Chemetoff competition design, 1982, site plan, third prize

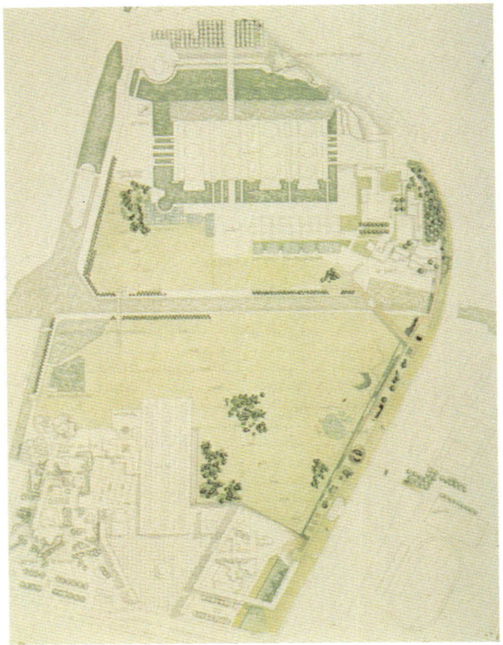

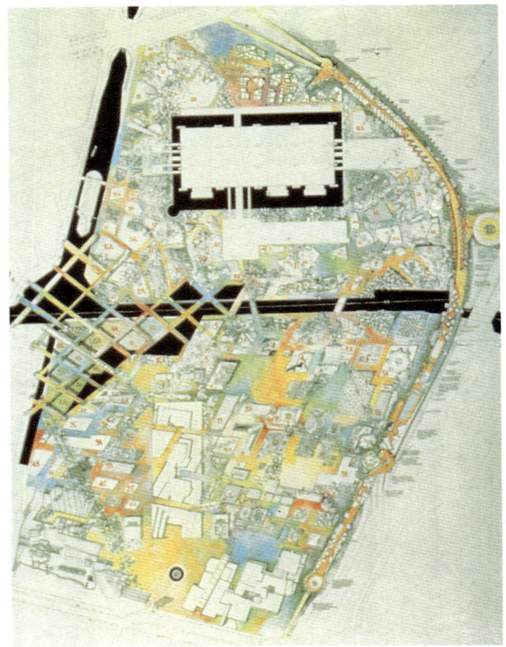

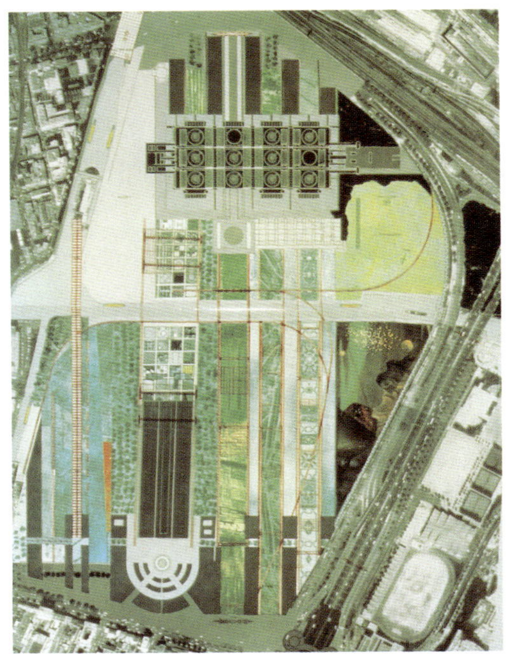

Bernard Lassus competition design, 1982, site plan, third prize

Gaetano Pesce competition design, 1982, site plan, honourable mention

Jean Nouvel competition design, 1982, site plan, honourable mention

Hiroshi Hara competition design, 1982, model, purchased

Hiroshi Hara competition design, 1982, model, purchased

Peter D. Eisenman & Jacques Derrida conceptual design of the Parc de la Villette, 1982, model

Alexandre Chemetoff & Daniel Buren execution design of Jardins thématiques: séquence, 1982, painted photo

Alexandre Chemetoff & Daniel Buren execution design of Jardins thématiques: séquence 4, 1982, painted photo

126

John Hejduk execution design of "Les chaises du Diable", 1982, elevation

John Hejduk execution design of "Les chaises du Diable", 1982, site plan

John Hejduk execution design of "Les chaises du Diable", 1982, details

John Hejduk execution design of "Les chaises du Diable", 1982, details of the fence and steps

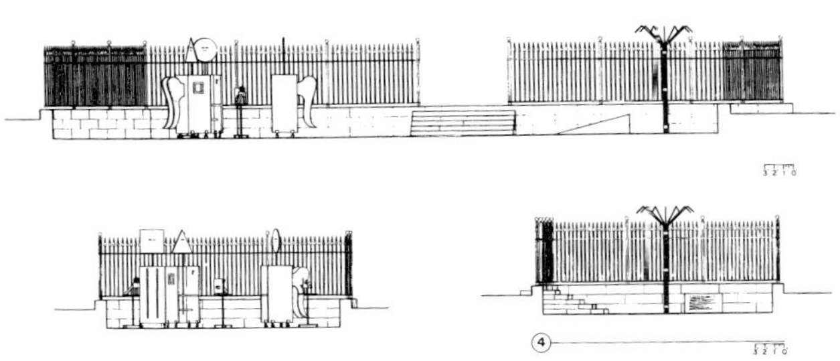

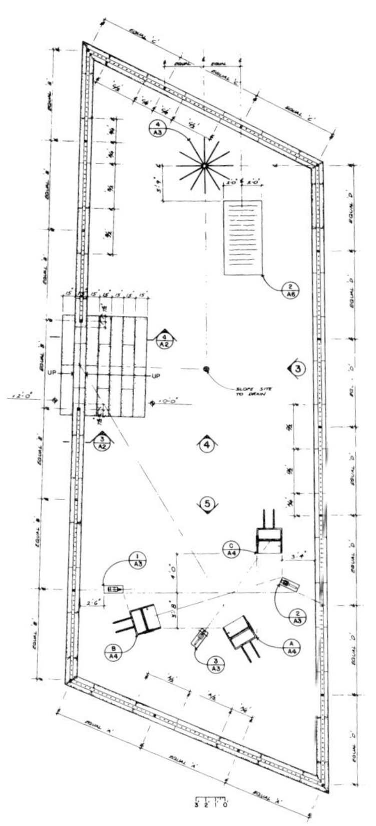

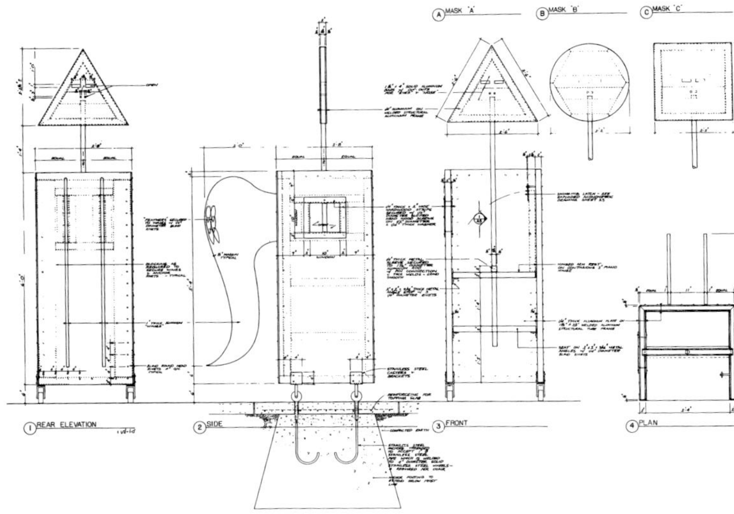

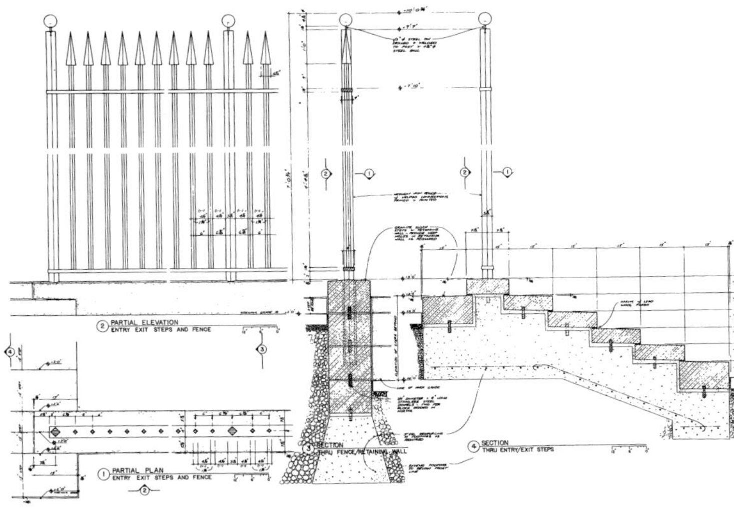

Gaetano Pesce execution design of "La maison des enfants", 1986, site plan

Gaetano Pesce execution design of "La maison des enfants", 1986, model

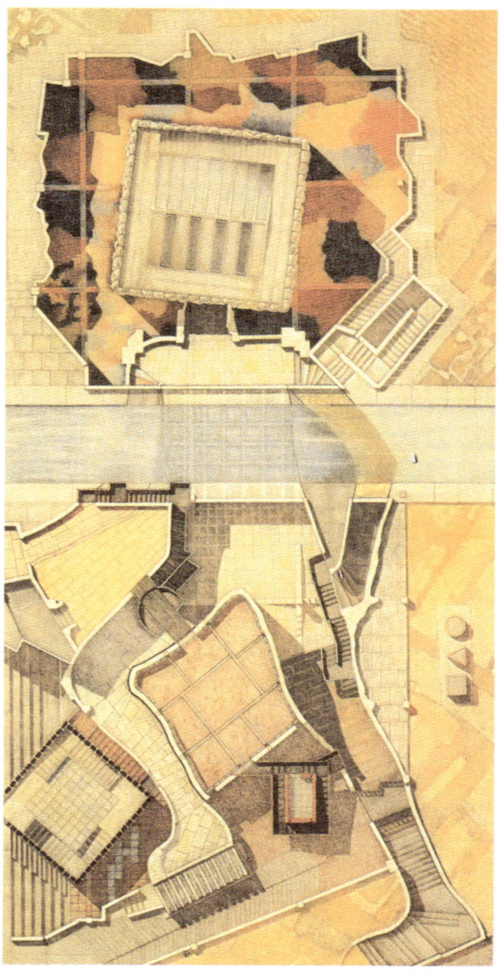

Hongkong and Shanghai Bank, Hong Kong, 1979

Project

Headquarters of the Hongkong and Shanghai Banking Corporation

Site

Queen's Road, Hongkong

Dates

Competition announced 14 June 1979 *Closing date* 8 October 1979 *Result announced* 13 November 1979

Number of entries

7: Foster Associates (Great Britain); Hugh Stubbins & Associates (USA); Palmer & Turner (Hong Kong); Yuncken Freeman (Australia); Harry Seidler & Associates (Australia); Yorke, Rosenberg, Mardall (Great Britain); Skidmore Owings & Merrill (USA)

Jury

Gordon Graham (architectural advisor HSBC), Roy Munden (HSBC), David Thornburrow (architect), PA Management Consultants

Result

First prize Foster Associates

Commissioned by

Hongkong and Shanghai Banking Corporation

Construction

January 1983 to November 1985

Architect

Foster Associates

Construction cost

5 000 000 000 Hong Kong dollars

Hongkong and Shanghai Bank, Hong Kong, 1979

Foster Associates competition design, 1979, 1980, 1981, sketches

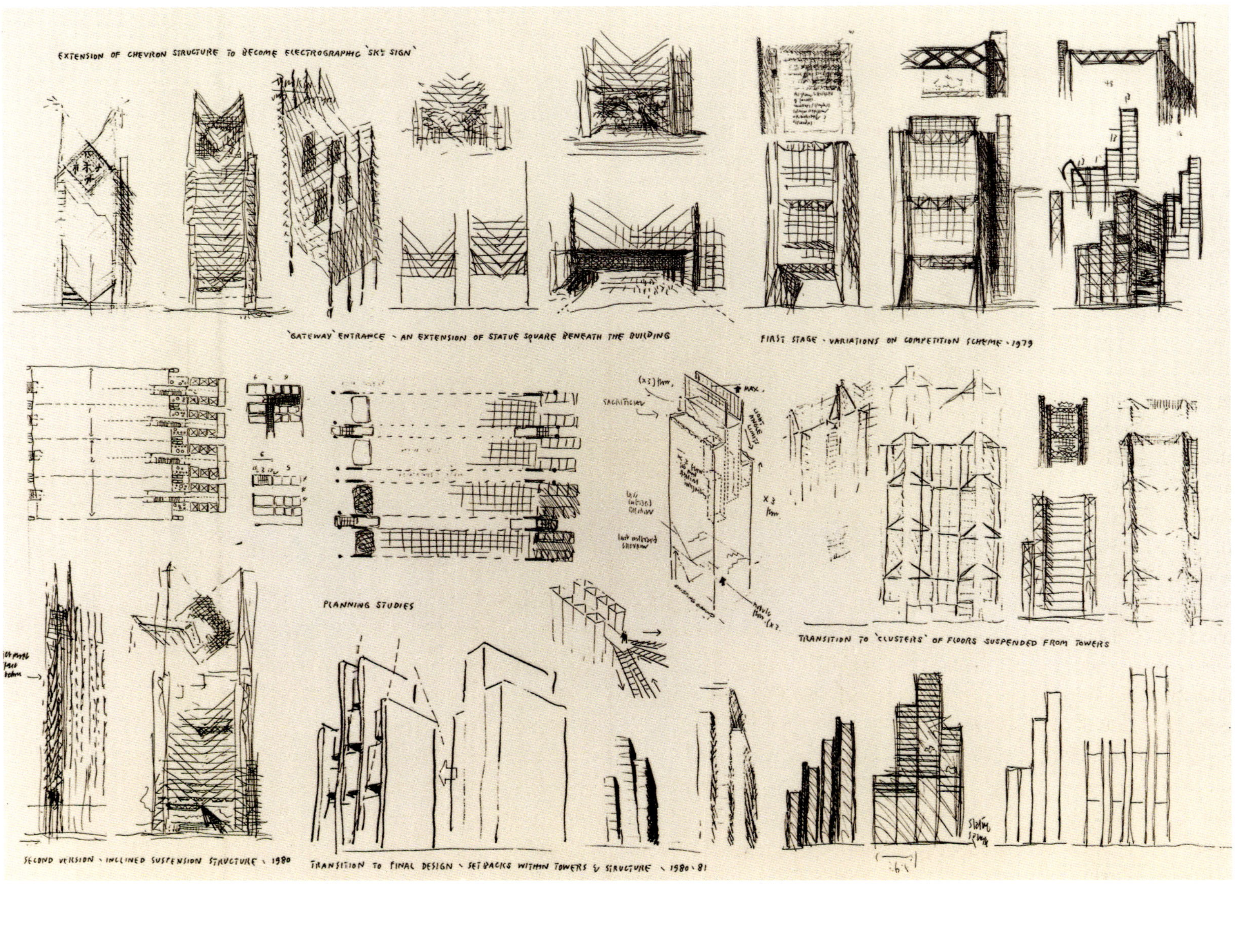

Hongkong and Shanghai Bank, Hong Kong

The Hongkong Bank, established in 1865 by English merchant colonists, had to live up to its high pioneering reputation. Over the years it became the largest foreign bank on the Asian continent, owing to its involvement in the construction of the Chinese railways, and its financing of the Chinese reparation payments to Japan after the war of 1894–1895.

The Bank, the Jockey Club and the Governor

In 1866 the Hongkong Bank became one of the first foreign banks to open a branch in Japan. Having established branches in Calcutta, Bombay, Saigon, Jakarta, Singapore and the Chinese harbour cities. Its New York office was opened in 1880. The Bank became a force to be reckoned with in Hong Kong. As the saying went: Hong Kong is ruled by the Bank, the Jockey Club and the Governor. In that order. The bank building in Hong Kong became the symbol of solvency and was used on bank notes, letterheads and in many other ways. The old bank building had been designed by G.L. "Tug" Wilson, who was employed by Palmer & Turner, a firm established by the English architect Clement Palmer, which the Bank had previously commissioned for a number of projects. In this instance the Bank wanted a striking head quarters, at whatever expense, and Wilson's building, constructed between 1933 and 1935, received international attention, but not for its aesthetic qualities alone.

Wilson based his design on American skyscrapers, which were constructed in a wide variety of Neo-styles[1]. Wilson's building was no exception to the rule. He incorporated various Egyptian, Art Deco and Classicist motifs, as well as elements of local Chinese architecture. However, the building owed much of its fame to the fact that it stood like a giant amongst dwarfs in the distant colony. The steel frame and most of the other materials had been prefabricated in the mother country and imported. The building was air-conditioned and "autogiros" could land on the roof. It was therefore hardly surprising that the bank became a symbol of wealth and prosperity.

After the war the bank outgrew its premises, partly due to the fact that it had financed the urbanisation of Hong Kong, which became a major Asian metropolis; by the 1970s the shortage of space was becoming acute. In the light of its architectural background, it was obvious that the new headquarters would have to have the same symbolic status as Wilson's building. The local population had such faith in the Bank that foundlings were even left on the steps. Over the years, the hands of passers-by had worn down the claw of one of the bronze lions; they believed that by touching the lion's claw, a little of the Bank's prosperity would rub off on them. The new bank building had to convey a similar feeling, but this would be more difficult to realise than it had been in the 1930s. Property had become even more scarce and merely constructing a high building would not suffice, because, by the 1970s, the city's skyline was dominated by American-style skyscrapers .

Around 1970, 95% of the buildings in Hong Kong were less than 25 years old, which illustrates the unprecedented rate of construction and development. The former giant had become a dwarf, overshadowed by massive concrete skyscrapers which had been built during the 1960s and 70s. The existence of a plan to construct the most beautiful bank in the world was seen as a clear sign that Hong Kong had complete

Norman Foster conceptual sketches for the competition, 1979

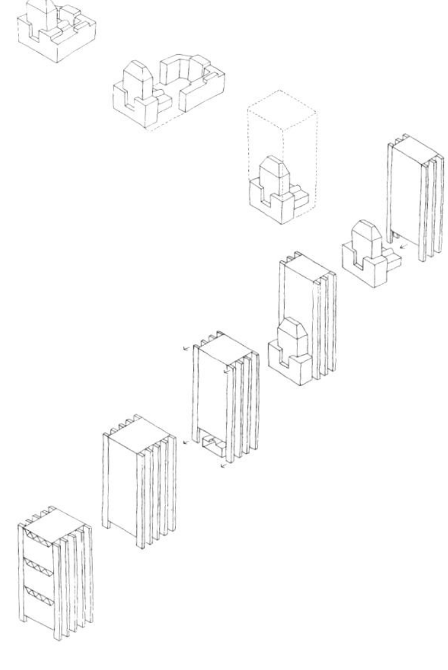

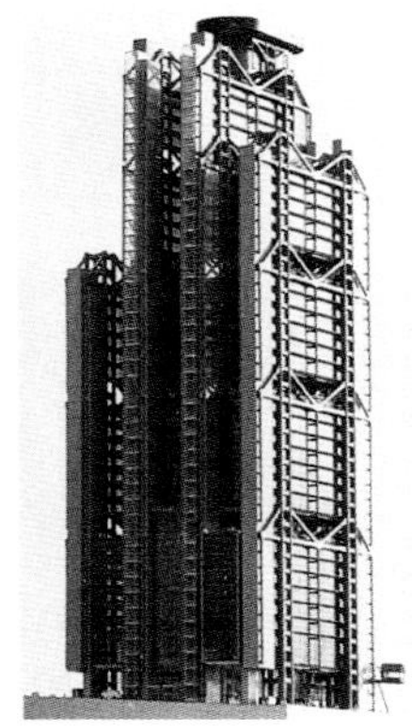

faith in the future, even though the fact that the British crown colony is to be handed over to China in 1997 has left financial institutions unsure as to whether they will have the same operational freedom in the future as they have had in the past.

A new building on a familiar site

The Bank started to develop plans for a new building in 1978.
A commission visited Lloyds in London in order to find out how they had selected an architect for their new building in the heart of the City. A number of other problems also had to be solved in advance.
A suitable site had to be found and, more significantly for Hong Kong, the bank had to be relocated without disturbing the "feng-shui", so as to avoid the danger of upsetting the perfect balance which had guaranteed prosperity in Hong Kong for so many decades. This belief, based on the struggle between good and evil spirits, prevails in all facets of daily life in Hong Kong.
For the above reasons, and because the Bank's directors preferred to retain the tried and trusted site, it was decided that the entire Bank would move to the north wing, whilst the south wing was demolished, reconstructed and made ready for use. The Bank would then move to the south wing, while the north wing was demolished and reconstructed. This approach was more efficient than housing the different banking departments in various offices throughout the city.

A closed competition

Having found a suitable site, the Bank next had to select a suitable architect. The engineering firm which was to take charge of the structural aspects of construction had already been approached: Ove Arup & Partners. It was decided to invite architects who had experience with skyscrapers and, more particularly, who had designed banking towers in the past. Moreover, the architect would have to supervise construction at a distance, as it was assumed that he would not be prepared to move to Hong Kong for six and a half years, which was the estimated construction time.
The Bank initially invited the following architectural firms, all of which had a branch in Hong Kong: Skidmore Owings & Merrill (USA); Gollins, Melvin & Ward (Great Britain) and Yuncken Freeman (Australia). Naturally, they also extended an invitation to the firm of Palmer & Turner. Having visited Lloyds in London, a number of other architectural firms were also invited: Hugh Stubbins & Associates (Boston), Harry Seidler & Associates (Sydney) and Norman Foster Associates (London), who had been specially recommended. The latter firm had also participated in the Lloyds competition. Minoru Yamasaki (USA) and Yorke, Rosenberg & Mardall were invited as reserves. The latter British firm replaced Gollins, Melvin & Ward, who were involved in other projects at the time.
The official invitations were posted on 14 June 1979. It is interesting to note that the British architects had little experience with high-rise buildings. Foster himself had never even built a high-rise building or designed a bank, and he had had no experience in Hong Kong. The Americans and Australians were more experienced. Stubbins & Associates undoubtedly owed their invitation to the striking, 59-storey Citicorp Centre which they had built in New York (1977).
The main aim of the competition was to select a suitable architect. The Bank considered it unlikely that any of the competition designs would comply with the city's strict building regulations. The architects were asked to ponder the problem of the site and to suggest solutions for other problems. For example, the north and south tower had to form an integrated whole upon completion, and the banking activities were not to be disturbed by construction, et cetera. The architects were also asked to consider other options in which the old bank would be only partially demolished. Otherwise, the architects were given a free hand and little other information, other than the stipulation that the building was to be an architectural masterpiece.

The runners-up

Almost all of the participants submitted a single option. A notable exception was the British firm Yorke, Rosenberg & Mardall, who submitted three options and left it up to the bank to decide which one they preferred. In two of the options Wilson's building was retained, whereas the third was based on the two-phased plan (demolish half and

Norman Foster models for competition design

The Hongkong and Shanghai Bank under construction

reconstruct, after which the other half would be demolished and reconstructed).
Stubbins' design projected a complete redevelopment of the site. Wilson's bank would be replaced by a low-rise building for the cashiers, and a concave tower would be constructed on the south side. Seidler & Associates first intended to retain the old bank and build a tower on the south side. However, this plan was later scrapped in favour of multi-phased construction. During the last phase the old bank would be replaced by a skyscraper. Palmer & Turner also submitted a multi-phased proposal: a high-rise building – which was to be the highest in Hong Kong – would first be built on the south side, the old building on the north side would later be replaced by a lower block. Yuncken Freeman had projected no less than six phases to guarantee smooth-running construction.
In Skidmore Owings & Merrill's solution the entire site was to be utilised and the old bank was to be immediately demolished. Their building was suspended from two piles, whereby the ground floor was left open and could be used as a public area. The central banking hall was suspended above this area. The building would be given a majestic aura by using dark and expensive materials for the exterior.
Their efforts were to no avail. Roy Munden, the Bank's assistant general manager who had been charged with the task of selecting the most suitable candidate, had visited all of the participating architects in September 1979 and had been most impressed by Foster's concept. The seven other members of the jury were also satisfied with Munden's choice and on 13 November 1979 Foster was officially commissioned to design the new Hongkong and Shanghai Bank.

A high-tech design

Even though he had never built a building higher than four storeys, Foster was already a reputable architect when he was invited to participate. He had designed the IBM building in Hampshire (1971) and the Sainsbury Centre for the Arts (University of East Anglia, 1977), both of which had attracted international attention. Foster had established the firm Foster Associates in 1967, together with his wife Wendy Cheeseman Foster. He belonged to the same generation of British high-tech architects as Richard Rogers[2]. He had even worked together with Rogers, Cheeseman and Wolton (1963–1967) in a group called Team 4. It is interesting to note that neither Rogers nor Foster see themselves as high-tech architects, preferring – like most artists – not to belong to any group.
Foster's Hongkong Bank consists of eight clusters of four steel masts, from which the floors have been suspended. The "coat hangers" by which the floors are attached to the masts are visible from the outside. The prefabricated elements were hauled up to the top of the building by cranes and assembled. The necessary rigidity is provided by the massive St. Andrew's crosses in the central banking hall, which is suspended above a plaza, as was the case in Skidmore Owings & Merrill's design. The upper floors had neither a set layout nor a specific function, which provided the necessary flexibility of arrangement. The secondary facilities, such as toilets, lifts and the like, are situated towards the sides.
During construction the main offices were moved to an annex which had been built in 1966, while the remaining offices were demolished. The bronze lions were moved to the entrance of the annex during construction. There was a brief crisis when problems arose concerning the main sub-contract for the required steel; the bank almost torpedoed Foster's plan, but changed its mind just in time. The new Hongkong and Shanghai Bank building was completed within six years, when once again assumed its dominant position overlooking the waters of the city and became the new trademark on the Hong Kong dollar.

1 *See chapter on the Chicago Tribune Tower elsewhere in this book.*

2 *See chapter on the Centre Pompidou elsewhere in this book.*

Hongkong and Shanghai Bank, Hongkong

Die Hongkong and Shanghai Bank kann auf eine ruhmreiche Vergangenheit zurückblikken. Von englischen Kaufleuten 1865 in der neuen Kolonie gegründet, entwickelte sie sich im Laufe der Jahre zur größten ausländischen Bank auf asiatischem Boden. Die Hongkong Bank beteiligte sich am Bau der chinesischen Eisenbahn und finanzierte u. a. die Reparationszahlungen, die China nach dem Krieg von 1894/95 an Japan zu leisten hatte.

Die Bank, der Jockey Club und der Gouverneur

Die spätere Hongkong and Shanghai Bank gehörte 1866 zu den ersten Banken, die eine Filiale in Japan eröffneten. Als 1880 die Niederlassung in New York gegründet wurde, besaß die Hongkong Bank bereits Filialen in Kalkutta, Bombay, Saigon, Jakarta, Singapur und einigen chinesischen Hafenstädten. Innerhalb Hongkongs entwickelte sie sich zu einem bedeutenden Machtfaktor: Eine Redewendung besagt, daß Hongkong regiert wird von der Bank, dem Jockey Club und dem Gouverneur und zwar in dieser Reihenfolge.
Das alte Hauptgebäude der Bank in Hongkong wurde zwar von G.L. »Tug« Wilson vom Architekturbüro Palmer & Turner, entworfen. Dieses vom englischen Architekten Clement Palmer gegründete Büro hatte bereits früher Aufträge der Hongkong Bank bearbeitet.
Wilson hatte sich bei seinem 1933–1935 realisierten Entwurf von den amerikanischen Wolkenkratzern inspirieren lassen, die in einer Vielzahl von Neo-Stilen erbaut worden waren (siehe das Kapitel zum Chicago Tribune Tower). Neben verschiedenen Motiven im ägyptischen, klassizistischen und Art déco-Stil integrierte Wilson auch Elemente der lokalen chinesischen Baukunst. Allerdings erregte weniger die Außenfassade des Gebäudes Aufmerksamkeit als vielmehr seine Höhe: In der weit abgelegenen Kolonie wirkte es wie ein imposanter Riese inmitten von Zwergen Das Stahlskelett und ein Großteil der Baumaterialien mußten als vorgefertigte Teile aus England importiert werden.
Nach dem Zweiten Weltkrieg wuchs die Bank rapide weiter, vor allem durch die Finanzierung der Stadtentwicklung Hongkongs, das sich zu einer der bedeutendsten asiatischen Metropolen entwickelte. In den 70er Jahren wurde der Neubau des Hauptgebäudes unumgänglich. Doch Baugelände war sehr knapp geworden, und um Aufmerksamkeit zu erregen, reichte der Faktor Höhe allein nicht mehr aus: Schon seit den 70er Jahren beherrschten Wolkenkratzer amerikanischen Ausmaßes die Skyline der Stadt. Um 1970 waren 95% aller Gebäude weniger als 25 Jahre alt. Der ehemalige Riese stand mittlerweile wie ein bescheidenes Häuschen im Schatten von Wolkenkratzern der 60er und 70er Jahre.

Neubau auf vertrautem Grund

Ab 1978 begann die Bank mit den Planungen eines Neubaus. Auf einer Informationsreise zu Lloyd's in London hielt man nach einem Architekten Ausschau, der in der Lage war, einen bedeutenden Auftrag mitten im Herzen der City zu realisieren. Am alten Standort der Bank wollte man festhalten und entschied, mit dem Unternehmen zunächst in den Nordflügel des alten Gebäudes zu ziehen. Anschließend sollte der Südflügel abgerissen, neu aufgebaut und komplett eingerichtet werden, so daß die Bank sich dort einrichten konnte. Zum Schluß wollte man den alten Nordflügel niederreißen und auf diesem Gelände den neuen Nordturm bauen.

Eine geschlossene Ausschreibung

Nachdem das Baugelände feststand, mußte der geeignete Architekt gefunden werden. Die Auftraggeber hatten sich schon auf ein Ingenieursbüro festgelegt, welches die Konstruktionszeichnungen anfertigen sollte: Ove Arup & Partners. Die Bank beschloß die Ausschreibung eines geschlossenen Wettbewerbs, wobei nur Baumeister eingeladen werden sollten, die bereits Erfahrungen mit Hochhausarchitektur vorzuweisen hatten. Desweiteren sollte der Architekt in der Lage sein, den Bau aus der Entfernung zu überwachen.
Eingeladen wurden die Büros von Skidmore, Owings & Merrill (USA), Gollins, Melvin & Ward (Großbritannien) und Yuncken Freeman (Australien), die alle eine Filiale in Hongkong besaßen. Auch das Büro Palmer & Turner wurde zur Teilnahme aufgefordert. Darüber hinaus boten die Bauherren nach dem Informationsbesuch bei Lloyd's einer Reihe weiterer Architekten eine Beteiligung an: Hugh Stubbins & Associates (Boston), Harry Seidler & Associates (Sydney) und – auf besondere Empfehlung – Norman Foster Associates aus London; dieses Büro hatte sich auch am Wettbewerb für die Zentrale von Lloyd's beteiligt. Auf der Reserveliste standen Minoru Yamasaki (USA) sowie Yorke, Rosenberg, Mardall. Das britische Architektenteam nahm später den Platz von Gollins, Melvin & Ward ein, die aus Zeitgründen absagen mußten. Die offiziellen Einladungen wurden am 14. Juni 1979 versandt. Von den englischen Teilnehmern besaß niemand Erfahrung mit derart hohen Gebäuden, z. B. hatte Foster weder ein Hochhaus realisiert noch jemals ein Bankgebäude entworfen. Die Amerikaner und Australier dagegen wiesen weitaus größere Vorkenntnisse auf – man denke nur an das markante Citicorp Center (New York, 1977), ein 59 Stockwerke hohes Bankgebäude von Stubbins & Associates. Da die Bank sich keinerlei Hoffnungen machte, daß einer der vorgelegten Entwürfe den strengen Bauvorschriften Hongkongs in allen Punkten entsprechen könnte, bat sie die Architekten, mit dem Problem des Baugeländes zu spielen und Detaillösungen für andere Punkte zu finden: Nord- und Südturm mußten nach der Fertigstellung ein harmonisches Ganzes bilden, die Bauphase durfte die Arbeitstätigkeit der Bank nicht allzu sehr behindern. Die Modelle sollten von einem partiellen Abriß des alten Gebäudes ausgehen.

Die Verlierer

Fast alle Teilnehmer legten sich auf ein Projekt fest; nur das britische Büro Yorke, Rosenberg und Mardall reichte der Jury drei Entwürfe ein und überließ der Bank die endgültige Entscheidung. Zwei dieser Entwürfe behielten das ursprüngliche Gebäude Wilsons bei, während der dritte von der vorgeschlagenen Trennung in zwei Bauphasen ausging. Stubbins' Beitrag sah eine völlige Neugestaltung des zur Verfügung stehenden Baugeländes vor: Anstelle von Wilsons Bankgebäude sollte ein Flachbau für den Publikumsverkehr entstehen sowie ein konkaver Turm an der Südseite. Seidler & Associates hatten zunächst ebenfalls einen Turm an der Südseite geplant, der neben dem alten Bankgebäude entstehen sollte. Später ersetzten sie diese Idee durch einen in mehrere Abschnitte eingeteilten Entwurf, bei dem das alte Bankgebäude im letzten Bauabschnitt einem Wolkenkratzer weichen mußte. Das Projekt von Palmer & Turner sah ebenfalls mehrere Bauphasen vor: Zunächst war ein Hochbau an der Südseite vorgesehen (hier sollte der höchste Turm Hongkongs entstehen) und später ein etwas kleineres Gebäude anstelle des alten Bauwerks an der Nordseite. Yuncken Freeman unterteilte seinen Entwurf in nicht weniger als sechs Bauphasen, um einen problemlosen Umzug zu ermöglichen.
Der Beitrag von Skidmore, Owings & Merrill sah einen sofortigen vollständigen Abriß des ursprünglichen Hauses und eine grundlegende Neugestaltung des Baugeländes vor. Das neue Gebäude sollte an zwei Pfeilern aufgehängt werden, so daß statt eines Erdgeschosses ein öffentlicher Platz entstand. Darüber »hing« die zentrale Halle. Zudem war eine Verkleidung der Außenfassaden mit dunklen, edlen Materialien geplant, um dem Gebäude ein majestätisches Äußeres zu verleihen.
Doch auch dieser Kunstgriff nützte den Amerikanern nichts. Roy Munden, Assistant General Manager der Hongkong and Shanghai Bank und beauftragt mit der Wahl des geeigneten Architekten, war im September 1979 auf Informationsreise gegangen, um alle Teilnehmer noch einmal zu begutachten. Dabei hatten ihn die Entwürfe von Norman Foster am stärksten beeindruckt. Als sich auch die anderen sieben Jurymitglieder mit Fosters Konzept zufrieden zeigten, ernannte man ihn am 13. November 1979 offiziell zum Architekten des neuen Verwaltungsgebäudes.

Ein High-Tech Entwurf

Obwohl Norman Foster zum Zeitpunkt des Wettbewerbs noch kein Projekt realisiert hatte, das höher als vier Stockwerke gewesen war, eilte ihm ein beachtlicher Ruf voraus. Sein IBM-Gebäude in Hampshire (1971) und das Sainsbury Centre for the Arts (University of East Anglia, 1977) hatten weltweit für Aufsehen gesorgt. Foster, seit 1967 zusammen mit seiner Frau Wendy Cheeseman Foster Inhaber des Architekturbüros Foster Associates, gehörte ebenso wie Richard Rogers (siehe Kapitel Centre Pompidou) zu den englischen Vertretern des High-Tech. Von 1963 bis 1967 hatte er mit Rogers, Cheeseman und Georgie Wolton unter dem Namen »Team 4« zusammengearbeitet.
Die Konstruktion der Hongkong Bank beruht auf einem Konzept von acht Masten aus jeweils vier Röhren, die das Gebäude tragen. An den Masten der Außenfassade sind deutlich die aussteifenden Rahmen in Form von Kleiderbügeln zu erkennen, von denen die einzelnen Geschosse abgehängt sind. Die vorfabrizierten Elemente wurden mit Hilfe von auf dem Gebäude montierten Kränen hochgehoben und an Ort und Stelle montiert. Das Gebäude erhält seine Stabilität u. a. durch die überdimensionalen Andreaskreuze in der zentralen Halle. Wie beim Entwurf von Skidmore, Owings & Merrill befindet sich diese Halle auf der ersten Ebene des Gebäudes, direkt über einem offenen Erdgeschoß (Plaza). Die einzelnen Stockwerke lassen sich frei einteilen und in ihrer Funktion verändern. Dadurch entsteht ein hohes Maß an Flexibilität. An den Seiten des Gebäudes befinden sich Versorgungsräume wie Toiletten und Aufzüge.
Während der ersten Bauphase wurden die wichtigsten Geschäftsräume in einen bereits 1966 errichteten Anbau verlegt, danach alle anderen Büros abgerissen. Die Bronzelöwen erhielten einen Platz vor dem Eingang. Das neue Domizil der Bank konnte innerhalb der geplanten Bauzeit von sechs Jahren fertiggestellt werden. Heute steht das Verwaltungsgebäude der Hongkong and Shanghai Bank nicht nur wieder auf seinem angestammten Platz am Wasser, sondern präsentiert sich auch als stolzes Markenzeichen auf dem Hongkong-Dollar.

La Hong Kong and Shanghaï Bank, Hong Kong

Créée en 1865 par des négociants britanniques, la Banque de Hong Kong se devait de se montrer digne de sa réputation. Au cours des années, elle était en effet devenue la plus importante banque étrangère d'Asie, grâce à son activité dans le financement des chemins de fer chinois et des réparations chinoises au Japon après la guerre de 1894-1895.

La banque, le Jockey Club et le gouverneur

En 1866, la banque qui allait devenir plus tard la Hong Kong and Shanghaï Bank fut l'un des premiers établissements financiers étrangers à ouvrir une représentation au Japon. Après s'être installée à Calcutta, Bombay, Saïgon, Djakarta, Singapour et dans les grands ports chinois, elle ouvrit un bureau à New York en 1880. A Hong Kong, elle était une puissance avec laquelle il fallait compter. On disait même que la ville était dirigée par la banque, le Jockey Club et le gouverneur. Dans cet ordre.

Son premier siège social important avait été conçu par G.L. «Tug» Wilson, employé de Palmer & Turner, un cabinet créé par l'architecte britannique Clement Palmer qui avait travaillé à de nombreuses reprises pour la banque. Celle-ci avait souhaité un édifice de prestige, quel qu'en soit le prix, et l'immeuble édifié par Wilson entre 1933 et 1935 était plus connu pour ce qu'il représentait que pour ses qualités esthétiques. Wilson s'était inspiré des gratte-ciel américains construits alors dans toutes sortes de styles «néo». Il se servit d'éléments égyptiens, Art-Déco, classiques, et même chinois. Le prestige de l'immeuble tenait aussi à ce qu'il se dressait seul de son espèce au milieu de nains. La structure d'acier et la plupart des matériaux de construction avaient été fabriqués dans la mère-patrie et importés. Il était climatisé et des hélicoptères pouvaient se poser sur son toit. Après la guerre, la banque se trouva de plus en plus à l'étroit dans ses locaux. Elle participait à l'urbanisation de Hong Kong qui devenait rapidement l'une des grandes métropoles d'Asie et il devint évident au cours des années 70 que l'immeuble ne suffisait plus à ses besoins. Elle souhaitait que son nouveau siège reflète aussi bien son image et sa puissance que celui de Wilson. La population locale avait une telle foi dans la banque que parfois même des enfants étaient abandonnés sur ses marches. Les mains des passants avaient usé la patte de l'un des lions de bronze de l'entrée, dans l'espoir que ce geste leur apporte un peu de la prospérité de la banque. Le nouvel immeuble devait donc tenir compte de ces relations très particulières, ce qui était moins facile que dans les années 30. Les terrains étaient devenus rares et construire une tour de plus ne signifiait plus rien car, dès les années 70, le paysage urbain s'était hérissé de multiples gratte-ciel d'esprit américain. A cette époque, 95% des immeubles de la ville étaient construits depuis moins de 25 ans, ce qui illustre la rapidité du développement de la colonie. L'ancien géant était devenu un nain, à l'ombre de massifs gratte-ciel de béton des années 60 et 70. Enfin, l'intention de construire la plus belle banque du monde serait interprétée comme le signe que Hong Kong croyait en son futur, malgré l'échéance de 1997 de remise de l'ancienne colonie à la Chine, qui ne pouvait qu'inquiéter des institutions financières habituées à la plus grande liberté.

Un nouvel immeuble sur un site ancien

La banque commença à travailler à son projet en 1978. Une commission rendit visite aux Lloyd's de Londres pour savoir de quelle façon la société avait sélectionné son architecte pour son nouveau siège de la City. Mais quelques problèmes devaient être résolus. Il fallait trouver un terrain adéquat et faire en sorte que la reconstruction de la banque ne dérange pas le «feng-shui», l'esprit préservant le parfait équilibre qui garantit la prospérité de Hong Kong depuis tant d'années. Cette croyance dans la réalité du combat entre les esprits du bien et ceux du mal détermine tous les aspects de la vie quotidienne des habitants de la colonie. Pour ces raisons il fut décidé que les services s'installeraient dans l'aile nord pendant la démolition de l'aile sud qui serait reconstruite dans un deuxième temps. Cette approche semblait plus rationnelle que de disperser les services aux quatre coins de la ville.

Un concours restreint

La banque se mit alors à la recherche de son architecte après avoir choisi la société d'ingénierie qui devait prendre en charge les aspects techniques de la construction: Ove Arup & Partners. Elle était décidée à faire appel à un praticien ayant déjà l'expérience des tours et même mieux, de tours pour des banques.

Dans un premier temps, furent conviés des cabinets d'architectes représentés sur place: Skidmore Owings & Merrill (USA), Gollins, Melvin & Ward (Grande-Bretagne), et Yuncken Freeman (Australie) et bien sûr Palmer & Turner. Après la visite à Londres, d'autres architectes furent approchés: Hugh Stubbins & Associates (Boston), Harry Seidler & Associates (Sydney) et Norman Foster Associates (Londres), chaudement recommandé et qui avait participé au concours des Lloyd's. Minoru Yamasaki (USA) et Yorke, Rosenberg, Mardall (Grande-Bretagne) furent tenus en réserve, ces derniers remplacèrent Gollins, Melvin & Ward qui étaient débordés.

Les invitations officielles furent envoyées le 14 juin 1979. Il est intéressant de noter que les Britanniques n'avaient que peu d'expérience des immeubles de grande hauteur. Foster lui-même n'avait pas plus construit de tour que de banque et ne connaissait pas Hong Kong. Les Américains et les Australiens étaient plus expérimentés et Stubbins & Associates devaient leur invitation au remarquable immeuble de 59 étages qu'ils avaient élevé pour Citicorp à New York (1977).

Le but principal du concours était de sélectionner un architecte. La banque ne pensait pas que les premiers projets puissent obéir à la très stricte réglementation locale. Les architectes furent conviés à ne pas attacher trop d'importance au site et à suggérer des solutions pour d'autres problèmes. Ils devaient également étudier une solution qui évite la démolition totale de l'ancien immeuble. Par ailleurs, ils avaient toute liberté: on leur demandait surtout d'imaginer un vrai chef-d'œuvre d'architecture.

Les refusés

Presque tous les participants ne traitèrent qu'une seule option à l'exception de Yorke, Rosenberg et Marsall qui en proposèrent trois et laissèrent le choix au comité. Dans deux options, l'immeuble de Wilson était conservé alors que la troisième prévoyait des travaux en deux temps (démolition puis reconstruction). La proposition de Stubbins entraînait un redéveloppement complet du site. La banque de Wilson était remplacée par un bâtiment bas pour les guichets et une tour concave sur le côté sud du terrain. Seidler & Associates voulurent d'abord conserver l'ancienne banque et construire une tour au sud, puis se rabattirent sur une reconstruction totale en plusieurs temps. Pendant la dernière phase, l'ancienne banque était remplacée par une tour. Palmer & Turner proposèrent de même d'élever d'abord une tour, la plus haute de Hong Kong vers le sud, puis de remplacer l'ancien immeuble par un bâtiment bas. Yuncken Freeman n'avait pas prévu moins de six phases pour assurer une transition particulièrement douce. Skidmore, Owings & Merrill démolissaient immédiatement le vieil immeuble et occupaient la totalité du site. Leur bâtiment était suspendu à deux piles qui libéraient le sol aménagé en espace public. Le hall principal de la banque était accroché au-dessus de cette place et des matériaux sombres et coûteux conféreraient à l'ensemble une majesté visible. Leurs efforts furent vains. Roy Munden, le directeur général adjoint de la banque chargé de la sélection du meilleur candidat avait rendu visite à tous les architectes en septembre 1979 et avait été très impressionné par les idées de Foster. Les sept autres jurés approuvèrent son choix et le 13 novembre 1979, le Britannique fut officiellement chargé de concevoir la nouvelle Hong Kong and Shanghaï Bank.

Un plan high tech

Bien qu'il n'ait jamais construit de bâtiment de plus de quatre étages, Foster avait déjà une réputation enviée lorsqu'il fut retenu par la banque de Hong Kong. Il avait réalisé un immeuble pour IBM (Hampshire, 1971) et le Sainsbury Centre for the Arts (University of East Anglia, 1977) qui avaient attiré sur lui les regards de la presse internationale. Il avait créé sa firme, Foster Associates en 1967, avec sa femme Wendy Cheeseman Foster et appartenait à la même génération d'architectes high tech que Rogers[1]. Il avait même travaillé avec ce dernier, Cheeseman et Wolton dans un groupe baptisé Team 4 (1963-1967). Ni lui ni Rogers ne se considèrent d'ailleurs comme des spécialistes du high tech, refusant, comme beaucoup de créateurs, toute étiquette.

La Hong Kong Bank de Foster est composée de huit ensembles de quatre mâts d'acier auxquels sont suspendus les niveaux. Les «portemanteaux» auxquels sont attachés les étages sont visibles de l'extérieur. Les éléments préfabriqués ont été montés par des grues et assemblés par le haut. La rigidité nécessaire est apportée par de massives croix de Saint André du hall central suspendu au-dessus d'un espace public, comme dans le projet de Skidmore, Owings & Merrill. Les niveaux supérieurs n'avaient aucune fonction prédéterminée au départ, ce qui permettait des aménagements très libres. Le nouveau siège de la Hong Kong and Shanghaï Bank a été terminé en six ans. Il domine de nouveau les eaux de la baie et illustre dorénavant les billets de banque de Hong Kong.

1 *Voir le chapitre sur le Centre Pompidou.*

Foster Associates competition design, 1979, north elevation, first prize

Foster Associates competition design, 1979, from left: banking hall plan, banking hall plan (alternative layout), upper basement plan, ground level plan, first prize

Foster Associates competition design, 1979, south elevation, first prize

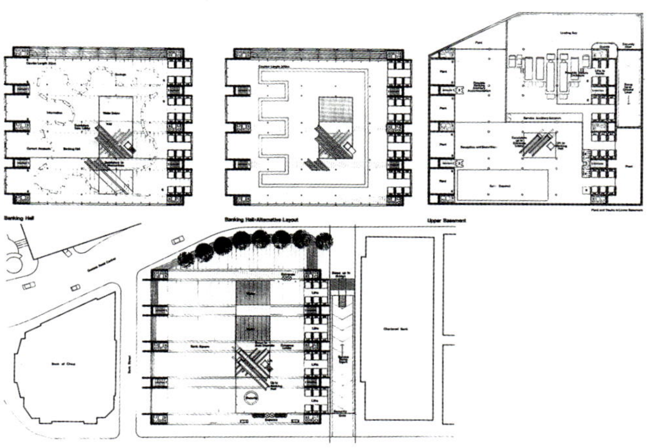

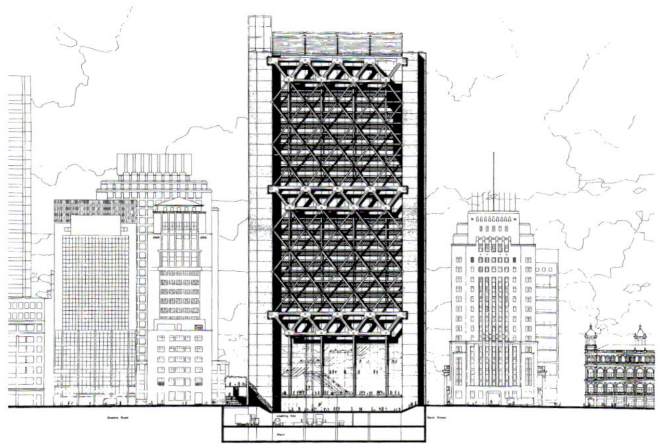

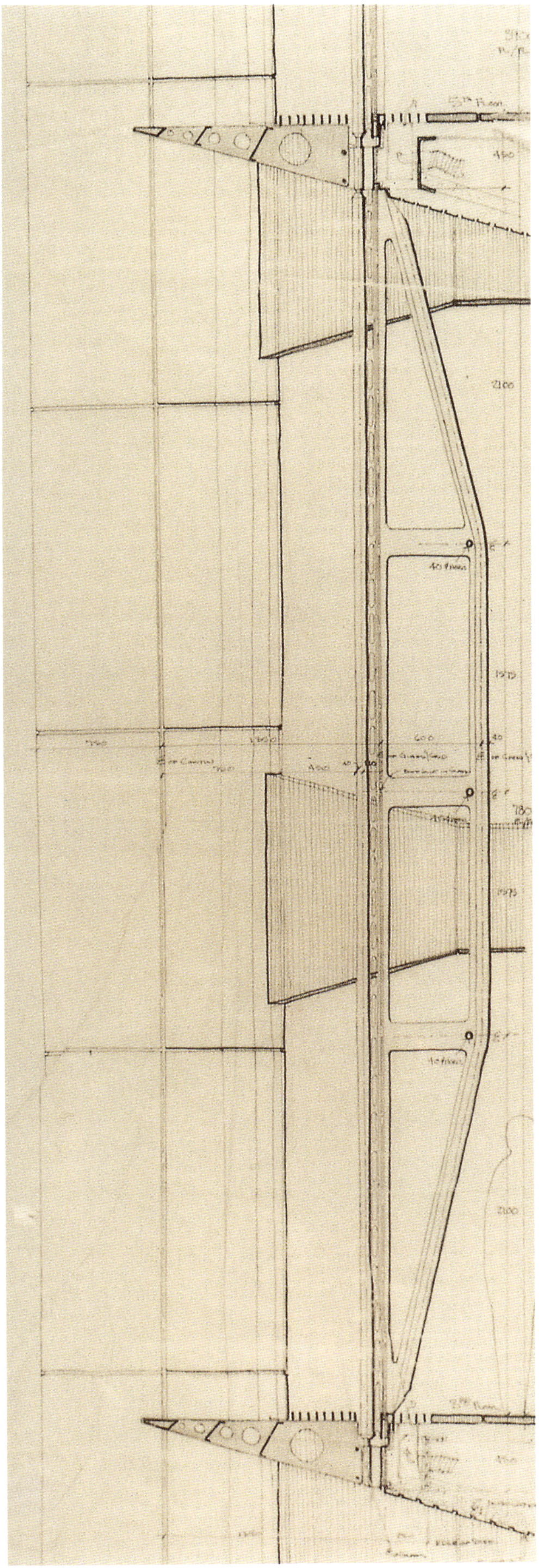

Foster Associates competition design, 1981, drawing of construction detail

Foster Associates competition design, 1980 interior perspective of the atrium

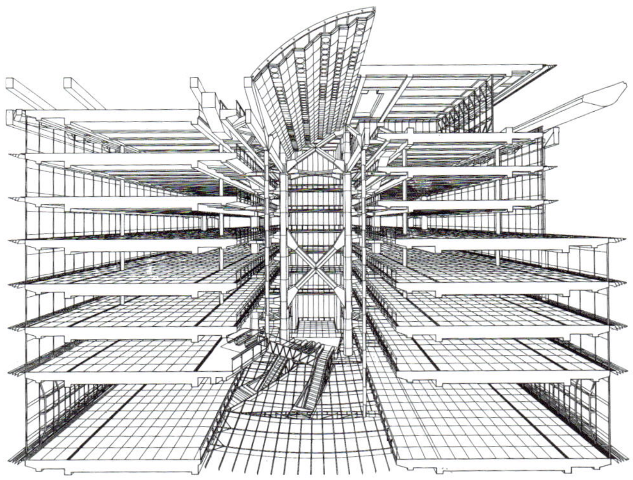

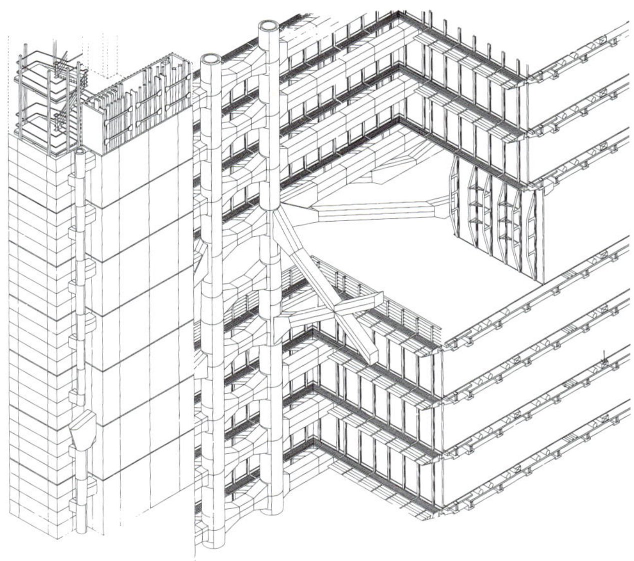

Foster Associates competition design, 1980, isometric drawing

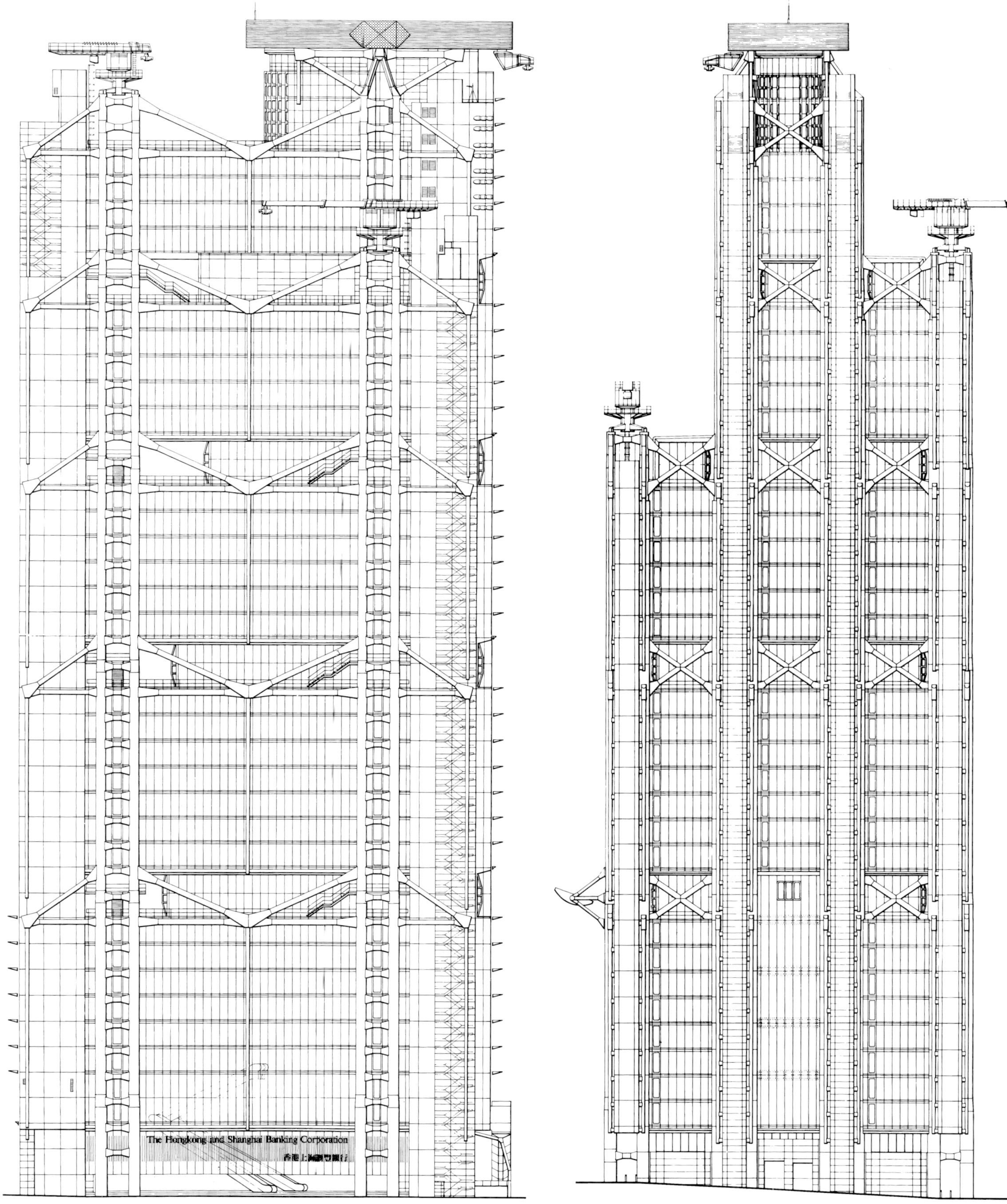

Foster Associates execution design, 1982, left: north elevation, right: east elevation

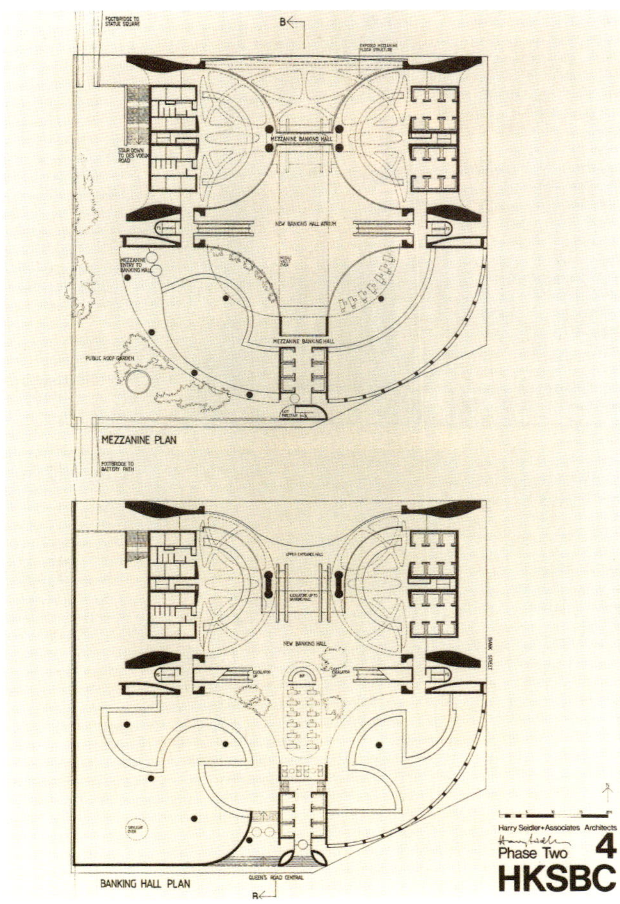

Harry Seidler & Associates competition design, 1979, photomontage

Harry Seidler & Associates competition design, 1979, above: mezzanine plan, below: banking hall plan

Harry Seidler & Associates competition design, 1979, photomontage

Palmer & Turner competition design, 1979, elevation from Statue Square

Palmer & Turner competition design, 1979, model

142

Yorke, Rosenberg, Mardall
competition design, 1979, exterior
view from Statue Square

Yorke, Rosenberg, Mardall
competition design, 1979, exterior
view from Statue Square

Yorke, Rosenberg, Mardall
competition design, 1979, exterior
view from Statue Square

Hugh Stubbins & Associates competition design, 1979, exterior perspective from Statue Square

Yuncken Freeman competition design, 1979, model

Skidmore, Owings & Merrill competition design, 1979, photomontage

Project

National museum for science, technology and industry

Site

The former abattoir and the surrounding grounds in La Villette, Paris

Dates

First round, selection announced 8 February 1980 *Second round* 20 May to 12 September 1980

Number of entries

First round 28 (4 participants withdrew) *Second round* 7 (Adrien Fainsilber & Sylvain Mersier; Daniel Badani; B. Bonnier; Alexandre Chemetoff; P. Lajus; Philippe Robert & Bernard Reichen; A. Zublena)

Jury

Paul Delouvrier (chairman Commission de Classement, director Établissement Public de Parc de la Villette). President Giscard d'Estaing selected the winner from 7 entries nominated by the Commission de Classement.

Result

First prize Adrien Fainsilber & Sylvain Mersier

Commissioned by

Établissement Public du Parc de la Villette (EPPV)

Construction

1983 to 1986

Architects

Adrien Fainsilber (*1932) & Sylvain Mersier

Construction cost

4 450 000 000 francs (June 1984)

La Cité des Sciences et de l'Industrie, Paris, 1980

Adrien Fainsilber presentation design, section through entrance hall

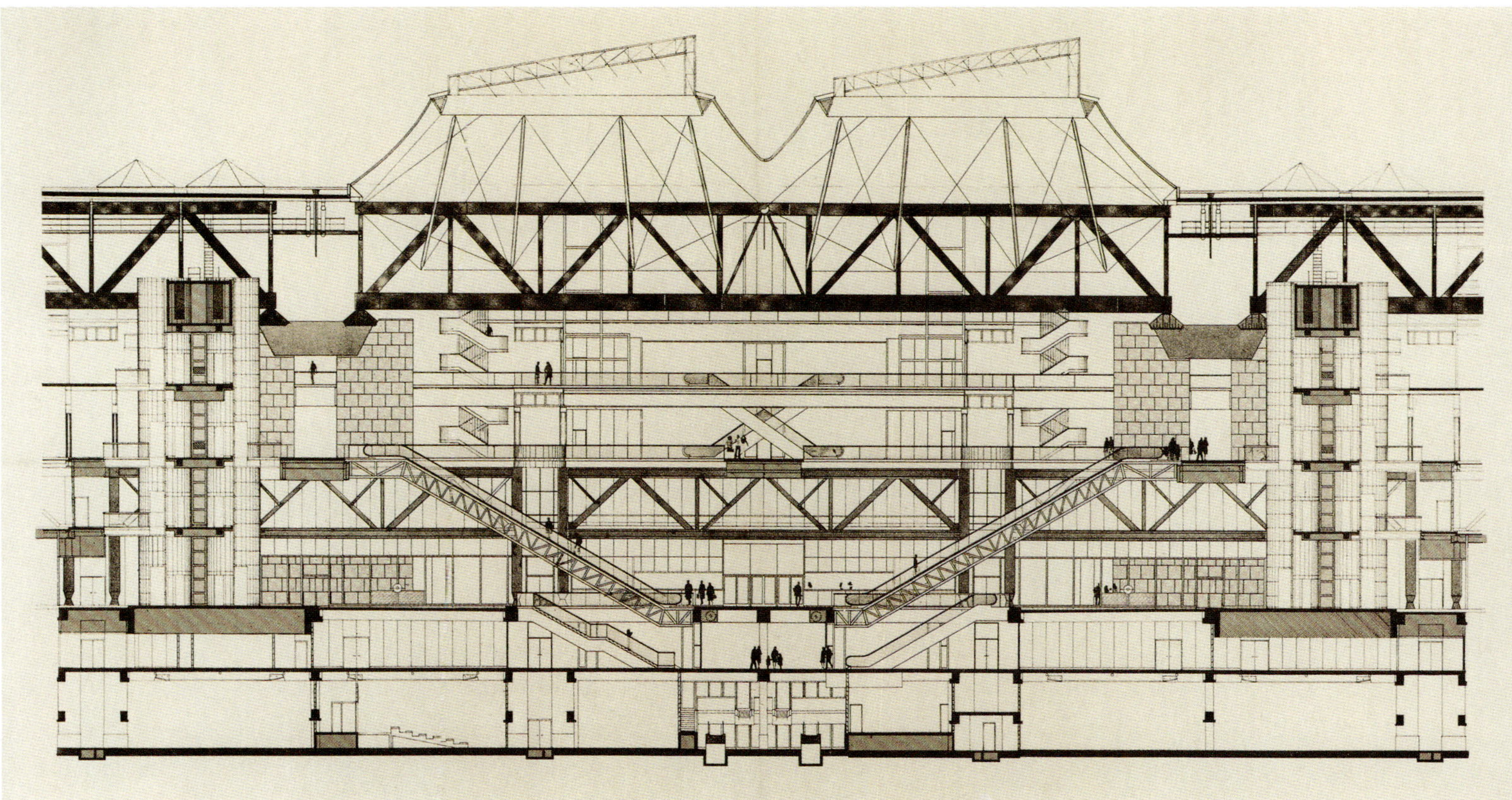

La Cité des Sciences et de l'Industrie, Paris

When François Mitterrand became president of France in 1981, he was determined to leave his mark on the French capital, just as Georges Pompidou had done with the Centre Pompidou in 1977. During the 1980s Mitterrand became the driving force behind the "Grands Projets", an unprecedented series of prestigious projects. In the case of the competition for the revitalisation of the La Villette district of Paris, however, it was his predecessor Valéry Giscard D'Estaing who originally set the ball rolling.

Mitterrand's Grands Projets

The Parc de la Villette was not the only project Mitterrand took over from his predecessor. Giscard was also unable to take full credit for transforming the former Gare d'Orsay into a museum. By rounding off running projects and initiating new ones, Mitterrand gave Paris a number of new landmarks within a relatively short period of time. The competitions for the Ministry of Finance and the Parc de la Villette were announced in 1982, and in 1983 Ieoh Ming Pei was commissioned to build a pyramid in front of the Louvre. During that same year competitions for La Tête Défense and the Opéra Bastille were announced[1], followed a year later by the competition for the Cité de la Musique, which was to be located in the Parc de la Villette. The open competitions drew a great many entries: no less than 750 for the Opéra Bastille, 424 for La Grande Arche (at La Tête Défense) and 471 for the Parc de la Villette.

The former abattoir complex, La Villette

Adrien Fainsilber Cité des Sciences et de l'Industrie

Adrien Fainsilber Cité des Sciences et de l'Industrie

From abattoir to museum

Giscard's decision to transform the grounds around the old abattoir of La Villette into a cultural centre came as a godsend to the district. In the past, the district had been a village on the outskirts of the old centre. In the mid-nineteenth century, La Villette was selected as the site for the central slaughterhouse by Baron Haussmann (1807–1891). The abattoir, designed by Baltard and Janvier, was completed in 1867. Baltard had also designed Les Halles, the market halls in the city centre.

By 1920, the abattoir and the surrounding grounds were in drastic need of modernisation, and a first architectural competition organised in 1923. This competition did not have a satisfactory outcome, and it was not until 1950 that the subject of the abattoir was raised again. The competition organised in 1957 was won by the architects Semichon, Walrand, Vigouroux and Mirquet, with a proposal for a massive meat auction-cum-abattoir. They worked on La Villette from 1959 to 1969 and were almost finished, when the city decided to move all Paris's market halls, including those in La Villette, to Rungis, south of the capital. The abattoir, which had hardly been used, became a deserted complex and La Villette a desolate quarter.

Rice, Francis, Ritchie glasshouse

Rice, Francis, Ritchie interior view of glasshouse

In 1976 a new competition was organised with the objective of establishing recreational facilities in La Villette. A number of French architects were invited to submit designs. At this point president Giscard d'Estaing started to take an active interest in the proceedings. He subsequently ignored the result of the 1976 competition and appointed Roger Taillibert as project architect. In 1978 Taillibert published his plan to transform the old abattoir into a national museum for science. The term "museum" was soon dropped in favour of "city", because the emphasis was to be on state-of-the-art technology – particularly French developments – rather than on technological innovations from the past. The main object of the project was to convince people that modern science and technology were a blessing, to stimulate the conscientious use of the products of innovation and to serve as an incentive for further innovation. The Cité des Sciences et de l'Industrie would become eventually the world's largest centre of its kind, four times the size of the Centre Pompidou.

A shrinking brief

The Établissement Public du Parc de la Villette (EPPV) was established in 1977. The EPPV organised a closed competition for the Cité des Sciences et de l'Industrie in 1980, inviting 28 architects to take part. Taillibert was thanked for his preparatory work and dismissed. Four of the selected architects withdrew, including the offended Taillibert; the EPPV then selected seven of the remaining 24 designs and presented them to Giscard. On the advice of the EPPV chairman, Paul Delouvrier, on 12 September 1980, the president selected Adrien Fainsilber's design. Because the EPPV was not completely satisfied with Fainsilber's design, preliminary research was required to determine its feasibility.

Six months after the result had been announced, Giscard lost the elections and Mitterrand came to power, which meant that the plans had to be revised once again, even though research was well under way.

The 1980 competition had been for the site as a whole, including the scientific centre, the auditorium and all the other buildings. The resultant plans had never been executed, however, and the City of Paris authorities continued to put forward their own ideas on how best to exploit what was officially a state-owned site. Mitterrand eventually acceded to the City's wish to build a housing complex and a music centre on the site in addition to the original Cité.

Fainsilber was thus obliged to cede part of the site to Gérard Thurnauer and Christian de Portzamparc, who won the competitions for the housing complex and the music centre respectively.

Fainsilber's main building was to be constructed behind the abattoir, where the housing complex was planned. He had designed it in such a way that visitors would discover the building bit by bit, rather than all at once. Thurnauer's housing complex was eventually built further back and does not form part of the greater La Villette concept.

Fainsilber lost the rest of the site in 1982 when Mitterrand decided to organise a competition for a 21st century park: Parc de la Villette. This competition was won by Bernard Tschumi[2]. The trees in Tschumi's design partially obscured the view of the Cité. Thus Fainsilber's broader architectural concept was gradually pared down. The rear façade, which is not obscured, became the most important facet of the Cité.

The three projected axes (water, vegetation and light) were never realised, and all that remained of Fainsilber's original plan were the Cité and "La Geodé", a spherical theatre.

In order to realise Fainsilber's design, the abattoir had to be almost completely demolished, leaving only the foundations, the roof and twenty pillars. His design included three structures on the longer, south-east side, resembling glass verandas. Each of these verandas was 32 metres high and covered an area of more than 1000 square metres. Due to the structural complexities involved, Fainsilber called in the English engineers Peter Rice, Ian Ritchie and Martin Francis. This team also designed the two movable skylights and a number of other structural novelties; in fact the plans for additional skylights were subsequently scrapped, because the museum curators preferred to use artificial light. To add insult to injury, part of the Cité itself was also snatched from under Fainsilber's nose. The enormous halls within the building were decorated by various designers – including Philip Starck –

Adrien Fainsilber Cité des Sciences et de l'Industrie, atrium

Adrien Fainsilber La Géode

Adrien Fainsilber interior view of La Géode

who were all intent on leaving their mark on the building and generally neglected to consult Fainsilber. Fainsilber's complex ecosystems, designed to provide natural air conditioning within the building, never materialised.

An architectural challenge

From the outset it had been evident that the project was fraught with architectural problems. The enormous meat-auction hall, with its set parameters, was a challenge in itself. The existing structure, which included twenty support pillars, necessitated a subdivision into four bays. However, a building which was 270 metres long, 110 metres wide and 47 metres high required a lot more than a simple subdivision to bring about an acceptable proportional harmony.
Architects such as B. Bonnier and Alexandre Chemetoff, who chose to use blind walls in their designs, produced buildings which had an uninviting, factory-like appearance. Other architects, such as Robert & Reichen and Badani, tried to obviate this problem by designing an "open" structure, which included four gigantic trestles.
Fainsilber's solution was more complex. By digging a canal around the building and by placing eight-metre-high framework girders on top of the existing pillars, the building's length and height were brought into proportional harmony. The length of the façade is split up by the three glass verandas, which stand in staggered relation to one another. The fourth bay was reserved for La Géode, which accentuated the longitudinal axis in the original plan.

La Géode

La Géode was the only other element of Fainsilber's plan that he managed to retain. The theatre is spherical due to the concave projection screen and the rounded area inside, which has a diameter of 26 metres. Fainsilber, a poet by nature, has said that the stainless-steel casing and the water basin in which La Géode appears to float increase the dimensions of the structure and reflect the changing skies over the Ile-de-France. The clouds reflected on the sphere are like continents; they are symbolic of the universe and give the observer a constantly changing view of the surroundings. Fainsilber deliberately used the theatre's spherical shape to soften the harsh, linear character of the long façade. La Géode consists of two separate structures: the first structure is an unadorned, reinforced concrete pillar, to which the interior core with the screen has been attached; the second structure is a steel-tubing frame to which the exterior casing, consisting of 6433 convex triangles, has been attached. The area between the two structures is packed with technical facilities.

Even though Fainsilber's design underwent many changes, the building which eventually materialised is particularly striking. The enormous halls are impressive in their own right, even though the interior designers went to great lengths to conceal them. Construction was still under way when Mitterrand officially opened the building in 1986. A quarter of the Cité will remain vacant for the time being, to allow for future development. Fortunately, Fainsilber was soon able to put the project, and all the unwanted interference, behind him. He was later commissioned to build two other museums of less magnificent proportions: the Musée d'Art Moderne et Contemporaine in Strasbourg and the Musée des Beaux-Arts in Clermont-Ferrand, the latter preceded by a competition.

1 *See chapters on La Grande Arche and the Opéra Bastille elsewhere in this book.*

2 *See chapter on the Parc de la Villette elsewhere in this book.*

La Cité des Sciences et de l'Industrie, Paris

Als François Mitterrand 1981 zum französischen Staatspräsidenten gewählt wurde, war er fest entschlossen, der Hauptstadt Paris ebenso »seinen Stempel aufzudrücken«, wie es sein Vorgänger Georges Pompidou 1977 mit dem Centre Beaubourg getan hatte. Unter Mitterrand entwickelten sich die 80er Jahre zu einem Jahrzehnt der »Grands Projets«. Allerdings gebührt Valéry Giscard d'Estaing die Ehre, den Wettbewerb für den Parc de la Villette ins Leben gerufen zu haben.

Mitterands »Grands Projets«

Der Parc de la Villette war nicht das einzige Projekt, das Mitterrand von seinem direkten Vorgänger übernahm: Auch den von ihm angeregten Umbau des alten Gare d'Orsay in ein Museum mußte Giscard seinem Nachfolger überlassen. Durch die Fortführung dieser bereits begonnenen Bauvorhaben und den gleichzeitigen Beginn neuer Projekte gelang es Mitterrand, Paris in kurzer Zeit ein neues Gesicht zu geben. 1982 schrieb man die Wettbewerbe für das Finanzministerium und – erneut – für den Parc de la Villette aus. Im folgenden Jahr erhielt Ieoh Ming Pei den Auftrag zum Bau der Pyramide im Louvre, und die Ausschreibungen für das Viertel La Défense (siehe das Kapitel zur Grande Arche) sowie die Opéra Bastille (siehe gleichnamiges Kapitel) wurden veröffentlicht. 1984 fand ein Wettbewerb für die Cité de la Musique statt – ebenfalls im Parc de la Villette gelegen – den Christian de Portzamparc gewann.
Die Resonanz auf die Ausschreibungen war riesig: 750 Einsendungen für die Opéra de la Bastille, 424 für La Grande Arche und 471 für den Parc de la Villette. Unter den Teilnehmern fanden sich allerdings kaum bekannte Namen, da – wie immer bei offenen Ausschreibungen – die renommierten Architekturbüros das Risiko eines Gesichtsverlustes scheuten.

Von Wettbewerb zu Wettbewerb

Als sich Giscard entschloß, das Gelände rund um den ehemaligen Schlachthof im Pariser Viertel La Villette einer neuen Bestimmung zuzuführen, brauchte die Gegend dringend eine städtebauliche Aufwertung. Das ehemals am Stadtrand von Paris gelegene Dorf hatte Baron Haussmann (1807–1891) zum Standort der zentralen Fleischhallen bestimmt. 1867 entstand der Schlachthof nach einem Entwurf von Janvier und Baltard, der auch die Hallen im Stadtzentrum gebaut hatte.
1923 kam es zur ersten Ausschreibung. Allerdings blieb der Wettbewerb ohne Erfolg, und erst 1950 beschäftigte man sich wieder mit der Sanierung des Geländes. Nach einer weiteren Ausschreibung erhielten 1957 die Architekten Semichon, Walrand, Vigouroux und Mirquet den Auftrag, La Villette neuzugestalten. Als der Komplex mitsamt Schlachthof und Auktionsgebäude kurz vor der Fertigstellung stand, entschlossen sich die Stadtväter, alle Pariser Hallen – also auch die von La Villette – nach Rungis, südlich von Paris zu verlegen. Der kaum genutzte Komplex verfiel, und La Villette blieb in einem desolaten Zustand zurück.
1976 wurde ein neuer Wettbewerb ausgeschrieben, um La Villette in einen Freizeitpark umzuwandeln. Als die ersten französischen Architekten Pläne ausarbeiteten, zog Präsident Giscard d'Estaing die Initiative an sich und benannte Roger Taillibert als verantwortlichen Architekten. 1978 trat er mit dem Plan an die Öffentlichkeit, die alten Auktionshallen in ein nationales Wissenschaftsmuseum zu verwandeln. Dabei wurde die Bezeichnung »Museum« recht schnell fallengelassen: Nicht die technischen Erfindungen der vergangenen Jahrhunderte, sondern die neuesten Entwicklungen der Wissenschaft – unter besonderer Berücksichtigung der Rolle Frankreichs – sollten im Vordergrund stehen. Die »Cité des Sciences et de l'Industrie« sollte die weltgrößte Ausstellung dieser Art werden – etwa viermal so groß wie das Centre Pompidou.

Eine dezimierte Preisfrage

1977 wurde das Établissement Public du Parc de la Villette (EPPV) ins Leben gerufen, das 1980 für 28 ausgewählte Architekten einen erneuten Wettbewerb ausschrieb. Zuvor hatte man Taillibert für seine vorbereitende Arbeit gedankt und ihn entlassen. Von den 28 Eingeladenen zogen sich der gekränkte Taillibert und drei weitere Architekten aus dem Wettbewerb zurück. Aus den 24 übrigen Beiträgen wählte das EPPV sieben aus und legte sie Giscard vor. Auf Anraten des Vorsitzenden des EPPV, Paul Delouvrier, entschied sich der Präsident am 12.9.1980 für Adrien Fainsilbers Konzept; allerdings mußten noch zahlreiche Details geklärt werden.
1981, ein halbes Jahr nach Bekanntgabe des Ausschreibungsergebnisses verlor Giscard die Wahlen gegen Mitterrand. Dies bedeutete eine erneute Überprüfung von Fainsilbers Plänen. Der Wettbewerb von 1980 hatte sich auf die Neugestaltung des gesamten Geländes sowie den Bau eines Wissenschaftszentrums, eines Auditoriums und sämtlicher anderer Gebäude bezogen. Dagegen wollte die Stadt Paris auf diesem Gelände lieber Wohnungen und ein Musikzentrum bauen, und Mitterrand kam ihr entgegen. Zwar galt der Staat als offizieller Eigentümer des Terrains, aber da er nur zögernd von seinem Eigentumsrecht Gebrauch machte, nutzte die Stadt die Zeit für immer neue Pläne.
So fiel ein Teil von Fainsilbers Plänen Gérard Thurnauer und Christian de Portzamparc zum Opfer, die die Ausschreibungen für die Wohnbauten bzw. das Musikzentrum gewannen. Ursprünglich hatte Fainsilber die Bebauung an der Rückseite der Viehhalle so anlegen wollen, daß die Besucher die Größe der Halle nach und nach entdeckten. Auch die Gestaltung des übrigen Geländes wurde Fainsilbers Federführung entzogen. 1982 entschloß sich Mitterrand, für den Parc de la Villette erneut einen Wettbewerb auszuschreiben, den Preis für den Park des 21. Jahrhunderts. Gewinner wurde der Schweizer Architekt Bernard Tschumi (siehe das Kapitel zum Parc de la Villette). Tschumi verstellte einen Teil der Gesamtansicht der Cité, indem er eine Reihe von Bäumen davor anpflanzen ließ. All diese Veränderungen höhlten Fainsilbers städteplanerisches Konzept fast vollständig aus: Während die frei einsehbare Rückseite zum wichtigsten Blickfang des Gebäudes wurde, verlor die Vorderfront stark an Bedeutung, und auch das Basiskonzept der drei Grundelemente (Wasser, Vegetation und Licht) kam nicht wie beabsichtigt zur Geltung. Nur der Auftrag für die Cité und »La Géode«, ein kugelförmiges Theater, blieb bestehen.
Sogar die Konstruktion der Cité wurde Fainsilber zum Teil entzogen. Sein ursprünglicher Entwurf sah eine nahezu vollständige Demontage der ehemaligen Verkaufshalle vor, von der nur das Fundament, das Dach und 20 Pfeiler beibehalten werden sollten. An der langen Südostfassade hatte Fainsilber drei treibhausähnliche Glaskästen von je 32 Metern Länge und Breite sowie 8 Metern Höhe geplant. Die schwierige Aufgabe zum Bau dieser Glaskästen übernahm das englische Ingenieurbüro von Peter Rice, Ian Ritchie und Martin Francis, das auch für die Konstruktion zweier drehbarer Lichtkuppeln und einiger anderer technischer Feinheiten verantwortlich zeichnete. Weitere, von Fainsilber geplante Lichtkuppeln mußten den Forderungen der Museumseinrichter weichen, die Kunstlicht dem Tageslicht vorzogen. Die enormen Räume innerhalb des Gebäudes wurden verschiedenen Designern, u. a. Philip Starck überlassen. Auch der ursprüngliche Plan, mit Hilfe komplizierter Ökosysteme das Klima im Gebäude zu regeln, geriet völlig in Vergessenheit.

Eine bautechnische Herausforderung

Von Anfang an war abzusehen, daß die Realisierung des Projektes für alle eingeladenen Architekten mit großen Schwierigkeiten verbunden sein würde. Schon die gigantische Auktionshalle erwies sich als problematische Aufgabe für die Teilnehmer. Die vorgegebene Konstruktion von 20 tragenden Pfeilern zwang zu einer Aufteilung in vier Gewölbeabschnitte. Bei der Verwendung geschlossener Wände entsteht rasch der Eindruck eines abweisenden Fabrikgebäudes, wie die Entwürfe von B. Bonnier und Alexandre Chemetoff vermitteln Andere Architekten, wie etwa Philippe Robert und Bernard Reichen sowie Daniel Badani, lösten dieses Problem recht erfolgreich mit Hilfe einer »offenen« Konstruktion aus vier enormen Jochen. Fainsilbers Lösung ist dagegen noch komplexer: Durch das Ausheben eines Wassergrabens rund um das Gebäude und die Plazierung offener, acht Meter hoher Fachwerkträger auf die bereits bestehenden Pfeiler schuf er ein harmonisches Verhältnis zwischen Länge und Höhe. Drei Glasvorbauten durchbrechen die Fassade der Länge nach. In der vierten, offenen Travée steht die Kugel »La Géode« zentral ausgerichtet, wodurch die Längsachse akzentuiert wird.

La Géode

Bei »La Géode« handelt es sich um das einzige landschaftliche Element, das Fainsilber – dem ursprünglichen Auftrag entsprechend – realisieren durfte. Das Gebäude ist kugelförmig und enthält neben einer Halbkugelleinwand einen Raum von 26 Metern Durchmesser. Der Architekt selbst beschrieb seine Konstruktion in poetischen Worten: *»Die spiegelnden, rostfreien Stahldreiecke und das Wasserbassin, in dem La Géode zu treiben scheint, vergrößern die Abmessungen der Kugel und reflektieren den sich ständig ändernden Himmel über der Ile-de-France, während die Wolken – als Symbole des Universums – sich wie Kontinente auf der Kugel widerspiegeln und dem Betrachter ein immer neues Bild seiner Umwelt vermitteln«.* Fainsilber verwendete bewußt eine Kugelform, um den linearen Gesamteindruck der langen Außenfassade der Halle zu durchbrechen. La »Géode« besteht aus zwei Teilen: Ein nackter Pfeiler aus Stahlbeton trägt den Kern mit dem Kinosaal. Die davon unabhängige Außenhülle in Kugelform besteht aus einem Rahmen aus Stahlröhren, auf dem 6433 konvexe Stahldreiecke angebracht sind. Der Raum zwischen der Innen- und Außenhülle ist der Technik des Gebäudes vorbehalten.
Das Gebäude wurde 1986, noch vor der Bauabnahme, von Mitterrand persönlich eröffnet. Ein Viertel der Cité steht bis heute leer, um genügend Raum für zukünftige Erweiterungen der Ausstellung zu bieten. Fainsilber benötigte nur kurze Zeit, um sich über die vielen unerwünschten Eingriffe in sein Projekt hinwegzutrösten. Kurz nach der Fertigstellung erhielt er Aufträge für zwei weitere, allerdings etwas kleinere Museumsbauten: das Musée d'Art Moderne et Contemporaine in Straßburg und das Musée des Beaux-Arts in Clermont-Ferrand.

La Cité des Sciences et de l'Industrie, Paris

Le Président de la République en 1981, François Mitterrand s'intéressa immédiatement aux grands projets architecturaux en cours ou à venir qui allaient modifier le visage de la capitale, à l'image de ce que Georges Pompidou avait fait pour le Centre Beaubourg. Les «Grands Projets» portent la marque du président socialiste mais c'est son prédécesseur, Valéry Giscard d'Estaing, qui eut la tâche délicate de trancher le nœud gordien du Parc de la Villette.

Les grands projets mitterrandiens

Le Parc de la Villette n'est pas le seul projet dont Mitterrand hérita puisque Giscard d'Estaing avait également été à l'origine de la transformation de la gare d'Orsay en musée. Les concours pour le ministère des Finances et le Parc de la Villette furent annoncés en 1982 et, en 1983, Ieoh Ming Pei fut désigné pour construire la pyramide et les espaces souterrains du Louvre. La même année furent lancés les appels d'offre pour la Tête Défense et l'Opéra Bastille[1] et un an plus tard, celui de la Cité de la Musique du Parc de la Villette que remporta Christian de Portzamparc (né en 1944).

Ces concours ouverts attirèrent un grand nombre de participants: pas moins de 750 pour l'Opéra Bastille, 424 pour la Grande Arche (à la Défense) et 471 pour le Parc de la Villette.

L'une des conséquences du dynamisme de cette politique fut de redonner à l'architecture française un essor longtemps attendu. Sans exception, les projets furent couverts par toute la presse internationale et les initiatives parisiennes incitèrent les villes de province à lancer des projets similaires. Si la réalisation la plus importante des années 70, le Centre Pompidou, fut l'œuvre d'un Italien et d'un Anglais, la France de l'architecture redevint sous la présidence Mitterrand un pays avec lequel il fallait compter.

D'un concours à l'autre

La décision de Giscard d'Estaing de transformer les abattoirs de La Villette en un vaste ensemble culturel fit l'effet d'une divine surprise sur le quartier. Village de la banlieue parisienne, La Villette avait été choisi par le baron Haussmann (1807–1891) pour recevoir les abattoirs centraux qui furent conçus par Baltard, l'architecte des Halles au cœur de Paris, et terminés en 1867.

En 1923, un premier concours pour la modernisation de ces installations fut lancé. Ses résultats ne donnèrent aucune solution satisfaisante et ce n'est qu'en 1950 que le sujet fut de nouveau abordé. Le concours de 1957 fut remporté par Semichon, Walrand, Vigouroux et Mirquet qui travaillèrent sur La Villette de 1959 à 1969. La construction était pratiquement terminée lorsque la ville et l'Etat décidèrent de transférer tous les marchés professionnels de produits frais de Paris, y compris celui de La Villette, à Rungis, au sud de la capitale. Les abattoirs qui venaient d'entrer en service furent abandonnés et La Villette devint un quartier orphelin.

En 1976, un nouveau concours fut organisé pour créer un équipement de loisirs à La Villette et un certain nombre d'architectes français furent invités à y réfléchir. C'est à ce moment que le président de la République commença à s'intéresser au projet. Il ignora les résultats du concours de 1976 et choisit Roger Taillibert. En 1978, celui-ci révéla ses plans de transformation des anciens abattoirs en Musée National des Sciences, terme vite abandonné puisque le nouvel équipement devait essentiellement présenter l'état contemporain des techniques, en particulier françaises. L'idée était de réconcilier les visiteurs avec la science et la technologie pour promouvoir et stimuler l'utilisation de produits. La Cité des Sciences et de l'Industrie devint la plus grande institution mondiale de ce type, quatre fois plus grande que le Centre Pompidou.

Un projet richement doté

Créé en 1977, l'Etablissement Public du Parc de la Villette (EPPV) organisa un concours restreint pour 28 architectes en 1980. Taillibert fut remercié pour ses études préparatoires et déchargé de ses responsabilités. Quatre des architectes sélectionnés se retirèrent ainsi que Taillibert, blessé. L'EPPV sélectionna sept des projets restants et les présenta au chef de l'Etat qui se rangea à l'avis du président de l'Etablissement public et choisit le projet d'Adrien Fainsilber le 12 septembre 1980. L'EPPV, qui avait quelques doutes sur la faisabilité du projet, réclama cependant des études complémentaires.

Six mois après la proclamation de ce résultat, Giscard d'Estaing perdit les élections et Mitterrand arriva au pouvoir ce qui entraîna de nouvelles révisions des plans, bien que les études aient déjà été très avancées. Le concours de 1980 concernait le site dans son ensemble, y compris le musée, l'auditorium et les autres constructions. L'Etat ne réalisant ses plans qu'avec lenteur, la ville exerça des pressions pour les modifier, et Mitterrand accepta finalement de laisser construire des immeubles de logement et un complexe consacré à la musique.

Fainsilber fut donc forcé d'abandonner une partie du site à Gérard Thurnauer et à Christian de Portzamparc qui remportèrent les concours pour les logements et la Cité de la musique. Les immeubles de Thurnauer furent édifiés en arrière du bâtiment de Fainsilber et ne font ainsi pas réellement partie de l'ensemble de La Villette. Fainsilber perdit une autre partie du projet en 1982, lorsque l'administration décida d'organiser un concours pour un parc du XXIème siècle, le Parc de la Villette, que remporta Bernard Tschumi[2]. Les plantations du projet de Tschumi occultèrent en partie la vue sur la Cité des Sciences et le grand projet architectural de Fainsilber fut peu à peu affaibli. La façade arrière de sa Cité se retrouva très en vue alors que la façade principale perdait de sa force, brouillée par les interférences de Tschumi. Les trois axes projetés (eau, végétation et lumière) ne furent jamais réalisés et seules furent conservées la Cité des Sciences et la salle sphérique de la Géode. Pour mener à bien le projet Fainsilber, les anciens abattoirs furent presque entièrement détruits à l'exception des fondations, du toit et de vingt piliers. La nouvelle façade sud-est, était divisée en quatre ouvertures, trois étant aménagées en énormes serres. Pour résoudre certains problèmes de structure, Fainsilber fit appel aux ingénieurs britanniques Peter Rice, Ian Ritchie et Martin Francis qui conçurent également deux coupoles rotatives et un certain nombre d'éléments originaux. Les projets pour les autres coupoles furent par la suite annulés, les conservateurs de la Cité préférant la lumière artificielle. Pour rendre les choses encore plus pénibles pour Fainsilber, l'aménagement des énormes halls lui échappa et fut confiés à divers décorateurs, dont Philip Starck, qui avaient bien l'intention de laisser leur marque sur le projet et négligèrent généralement de consulter l'architecte.

Un défi

Dès le départ il était évident que ce projet serait difficile à mettre en œuvre. L'énorme salle des ventes à la criée représentait à elle seule un défi. La structure existante qui comprenait vingt piliers de soutien pouvait bien être répartie en quatre volumes, il fallait plus qu'une simple division pour prétendre harmoniser les proportions d'un bâtiment de 270 m de long, 110 de large et 47 de haut. Des architectes comme B. Bonnier et Alexandre Chemetov choisirent la solution de façades aveugles qui donnaient à leur projet l'allure d'une usine assez peu avenante. D'autres, comme Robert et Reichen, ou Badani, essayèrent de contourner le problème en concevant une structure ouverte à quatre gigantesques tréteaux.

La solution de Fainsilber était plus complexe. En creusant un canal autour de son bâtiment et en posant un cadre de poutres métalliques de huit mètres de haut au-dessus des piliers existants, il retrouvait des proportions harmonieuses. La longueur de la façade est rythmée par les trois serres et la quatrième ouverture de l'entrée et de la Géode qui accentuent l'impression d'allongement de la construction.

La Géode

La Géode fut heureusement sauvée du plan original de Fainsilber. C'est une salle sphérique de 26 m de diamètre qui accueille un énorme écran de projection concave. Poète, l'architecte aime à faire remarquer que la couverture en acier inoxydable et le bassin sur lequel semble flotter cette sphère accroissent visuellement ses dimensions et mirent le ciel changeant de l'Ile-de-France. Les nuages reflétés sur la paroi sphérique figurent des continents et symbolisent l'univers. Ils donnent au spectateur une vision perpétuellement changeante de l'environnement. Fainsilber utilisa délibérément cette forme ronde pour adoucir la linéarité un peu sèche de sa façade. La Géode est réalisée en deux structures indépendantes. La première, en béton armé, supporte les aménagements intérieurs dont l'écran, et la seconde consiste en un cadre tubulaire sur lequel est posée la couverture d'acier composée de 6 433 triangles convexes. L'espace entre les deux structures sert de passage aux conduites techniques.

Bien que les plans de Fainsilber aient été profondément modifiés, le bâtiment de la Cité reste remarquable. Ses énormes halls sont impressionnants, même si quelques décorateurs ont dépensé beaucoup d'énergie pour les faire oublier. La construction n'était pas encore terminée lorsque F. Mitterrand l'inaugura en 1986. Un quart des surfaces est encore inemployé, réservé à une extension à venir. Fainsilber réussit finalement à mener à bien son projet et reçut par la suite plusieurs commandes de musées importants, bien que de moindres proportions: le Musée d'Art Moderne de Strasbourg et le Musée des Beaux-Arts de Clermont-Ferrand, ce dernier remporté à l'issue d'un concours.

1 *Voir les chapitres sur La Grande Arche et l'Opéra Bastille.*

2 *Voir le chapitre sur le Parc de la Villette.*

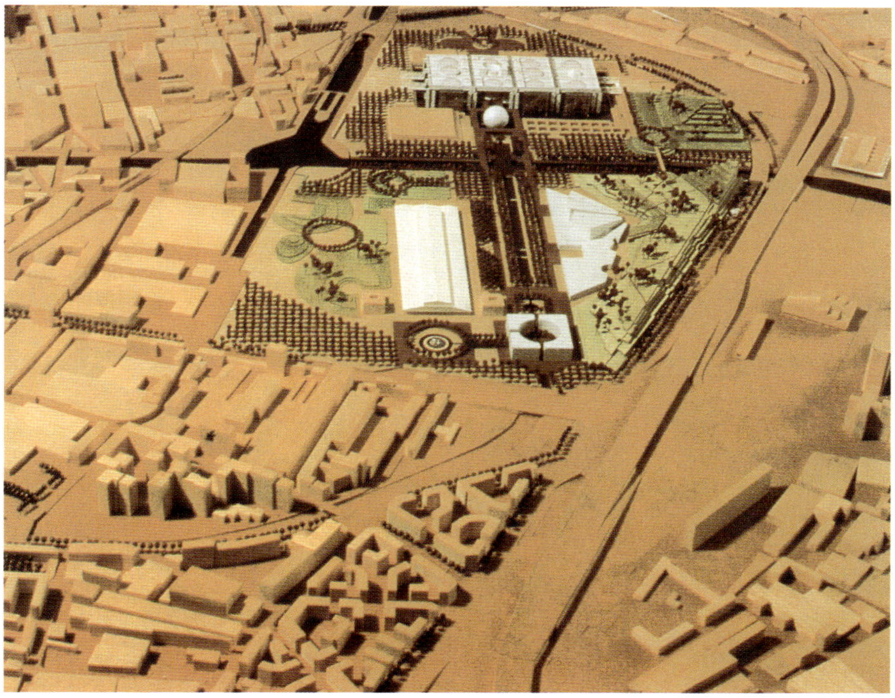

Adrien Fainsilber competition design, 1980, model, first prize

Adrien Fainsilber competition design, 1980, site plan, first prize

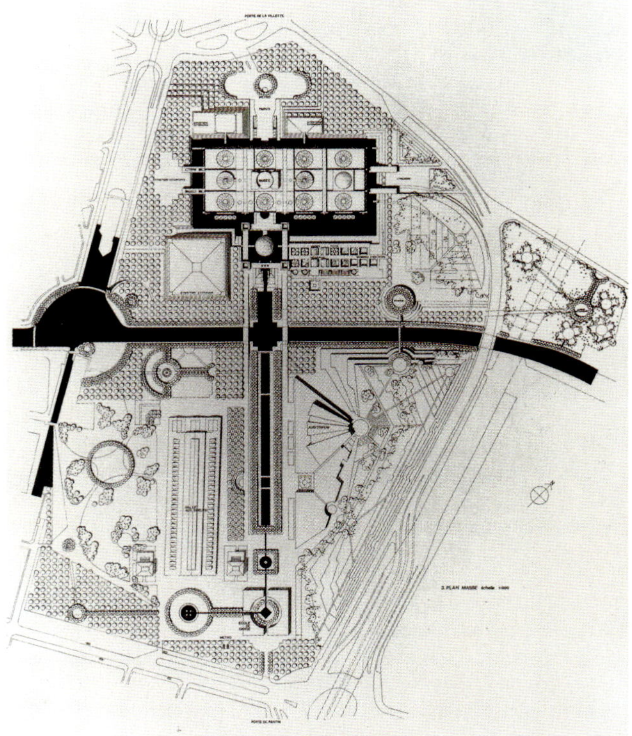

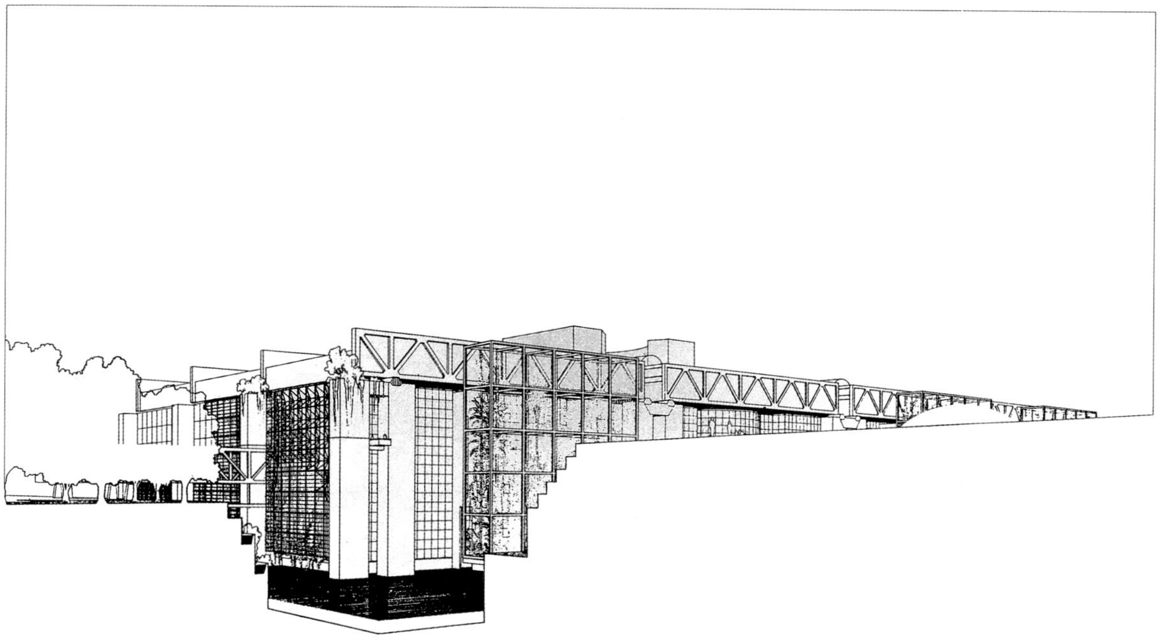

Adrien Fainsilber competition design, 1980, exterior view from south, first prize

Adrien Fainsilber competition design, 1980, exterior view from west, first prize

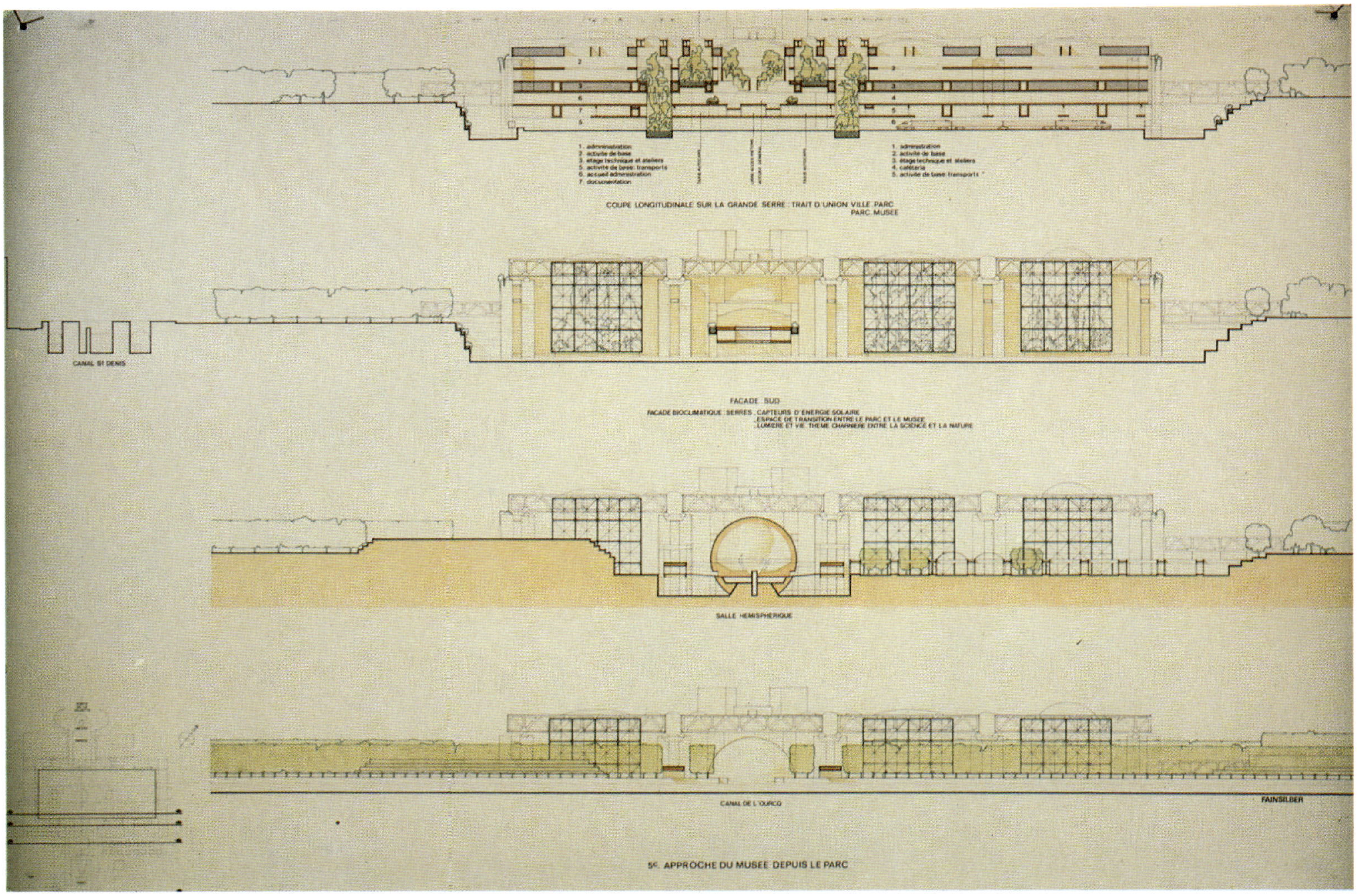

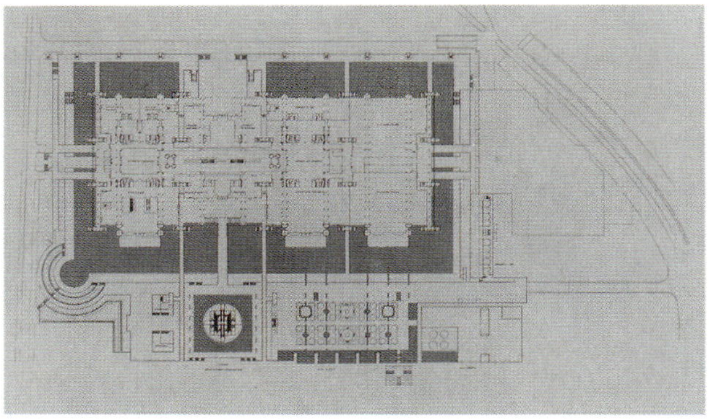

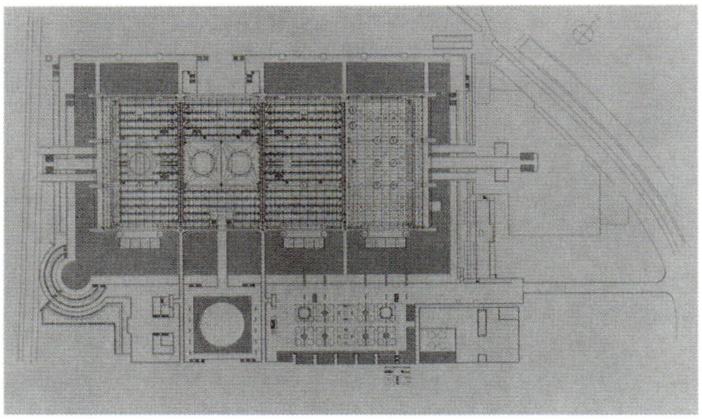

Adrien Fainsilber competition design, 1980, from top: longitudinal section, south elevation, section through La Géode, elevation on the canal, first prize

Adrien Fainsilber presentation design, roof plan

Adrien Fainsilber presentation design, entrance floor plan

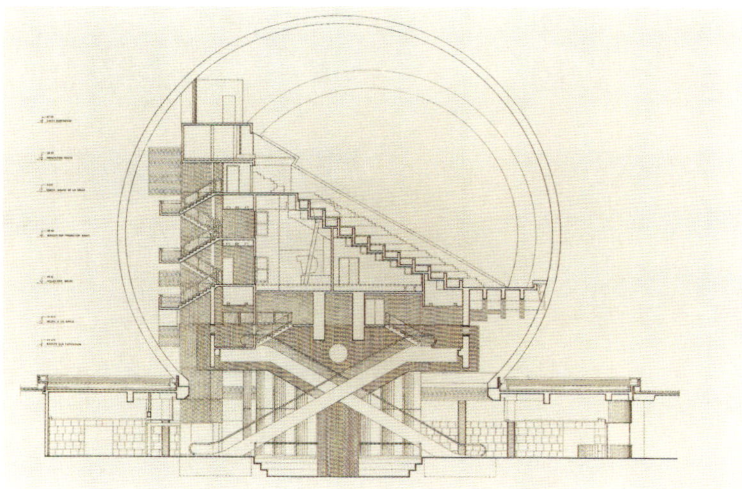

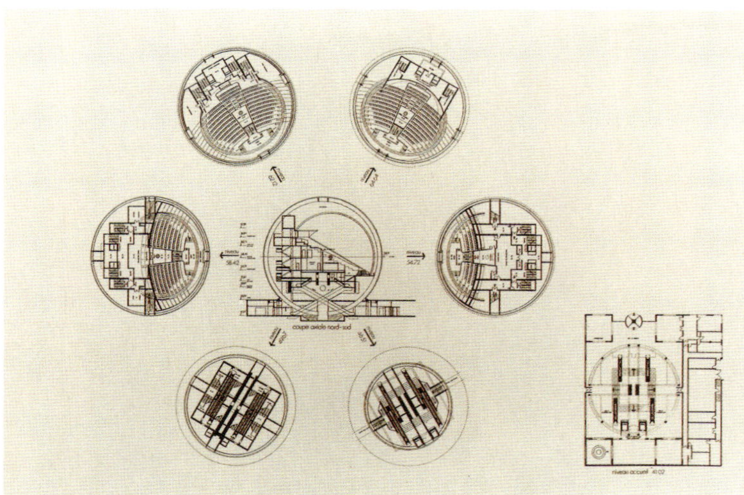

Adrien Fainsilber execution design, 1983, section model

Adrien Fainsilber presentation design, 1981, model

Adrien Fainsilber competition design, 1980, north-south section of La Géode (east side), first prize

Adrien Fainsilber competition design, 1980, north-south section (east side), first prize

Daniel Badani competition design, 1980, model

P. Lajus competition design, 1980, model

Alexandre Chemetoff competition design, 1980, model

B. Bonnier competition design, 1980, model

Philippe Robert & Bernard Reichen competition design, 1980, model

A. Zublena competition design, 1980, model

Project

International communications centre

Site

La Tête Défense, Paris

Dates

First round announced July 1982 *Closing date* 15 March 1983 *Result announced* 27 April 1983 *Second round* 28 April to 25 May 1983

Number of entries

First round 424 *Second round* 4

Jury

Robert Lion (chairman), Oriol Bohigas, Kisho Kurokawa, Richard Meier, Richard Rogers, Antoine Grumbach, Gerard Thurnauer, Bernard Zehrfuss (all architects), Mahdi Elmandjra, E. Tierno Galvan, Ada Louise Huxtable, Serge Antoine, Louis Moissonnier, François Lombard (technical advisor)

Result

First prize Johan Otto von Spreckelsen *Second prize* Jean-Paul Viguier & Jean-François Jodry *Third prize* Jean Nouvel, Pierre Soria, Architecture Studio, Jean-Marc Ibos & Didier Laroque *Fourth prize* James Carscallen Crang & George Elliot Boake; D.M. Robertson, J. Szabo & D. Vokac *Honourable mention* Yves Lion, Bernard Althabegoity & François Leclercq; Vittorio Gregotti, Augusto Cagnardi & Pierluigi Cerri; Stanislas Fiszer & Witold Zandfos; Chaix, Confino, Delanne, Duval & Morel; Salomon, Chabert & Maddalena; Studio 7; Georges Pencreac'h; Roland Castro; Guy Autran & Michel Macary; Bernard Tschumi; Françoise-Hélène Jourda & Gilles Perraudin; A.J. Diamond Associates

Commissioned by

EPAD (l'Etablissement Public pour l'Aménagement de la Region de la Défense), Robert Lion

Construction

1985 to July 1989

Architects

Johan Otto von Spreckelsen (1929–1987) and Paul Andreu (*1938)

Construction cost

3 400 000 000 francs

Competitions in architecture and town planning since 1792

Grande Arche, Paris, 1982–1983

Johan Otto von Spreckelsen
competition design, 1983, exterior view from east, first prize

Grande Arche, Paris

The competition for the international communications centre at "La Tête Défense" may be seen as an end point, for more reasons than one. In temporal terms the competition marked the end of a period during which contemporary Parisian urban development reached its height. In architectural terms the building, viewed from the centre of the city, forms a boundary for La Défense, the new suburb north-east of Paris. And finally there was the key question as to whether the communications centre at La Tête Défense should form the end point of the historical axis which runs from the Louvre, through the Arc du Carrousel, across Place de la Concorde, through the Arc de Triomphe on Place Charles de Gaulle, through the middle of La Défense to La Tête Défense.

Johan Otto von Spreckelsen

Paul Andreu

La Défense, 1976

A deserted office district

For many years Paris was engaged in a love-hate relationship with La Défense, a district lying only a few metro stations beyond the Arc de Triomphe, and which was constructed according to the urban development principles of Functionalists such as Le Corbusier and van Eesteren. In fact, Le Corbusier had envisaged a plan for the whole of Paris along the lines of La Défense: separate districts for different urban activities, high-rise buildings interspersed with large parks, and separate routes for motorised traffic and pedestrians. However, the Athens Charter, the unofficial minutes of the fourth CIAM congress, had been drafted in 1933, whereas La Défense was developed during the 1950s.

The plan to build housing units in amongst the office blocks was soon forgotten, and in less than twenty years the 800 000 square metres of office space stipulated in the original plan was doubled, at the expense of housing. La Défense became an office district which was completely deserted at night. Moreover, the aesthetic features of the office blocks which shot up like mushrooms ten years after the first plans were submitted, were food for thought for many Parisians. The Paris skyline seemed set to undergo radical change, much to the distress of the local population. Furthermore, the skyscrapers posed another problem for the city, because even though there was a drastic shortage of office space in the city centre, many of the office blocks in La Défense remained vacant. The source of this problem lay in the impersonality of the skyscrapers built during the 1970s[1]. To make matters worse, La Défense experienced a general slump during the oil crisis, and neither president Georges Pompidou nor president Valéry Giscard d'Estaing was able to turn the tide. The present president, François Mitterrand, has been more successful.

Architectural chaos

Officially La Défense was an independently-managed project. In 1958 a public body, EPAD (l'Etablissement Public pour l'Aménagement de la Région de la Défense), was formed to run the project. However, it achieved only marginal success. The fact that La Tête Défense, the starting-point of the project, remained an architectural mess for more than 25 years is indicative of the critical state of affairs.

The Centre National des Industries et Techniques (CNIT), designed by Zehrfuss, Camelot and de Mailly, was built on this site in 1958. This exhibition building, which had a triangular floor plan, boasted the world's largest roofing surface at the time. In 1958 and 1960 the same architects submitted plans for the site opposite the CNIT, which lay on the historical axis. These plans were never executed and for many years nothing happened, until Ieoh Ming Pei was approached in 1970. He designed two office towers on either side of the historical axis, which were joined by a parabola-shaped block, thereby forming an optical boundary to the axis, but without shutting it off completely.
A few years later Emile Aillaud submitted a design for two concave office blocks which were to bound the axis completely .
This triggered a debate and the term "La Tête Défense" came into vogue. A competition was organised, backed by Pompidou, and more plans were submitted. Aillaud altered his plans so that the office blocks were no longer visible from the Place d'Étoile, but once again the plan was rejected. The oil crisis caused general stagnation for a few years, until new initiatives were developed towards the end of the 1970s. For some time the main architectural contenders for the design of La Tête Défense were Emile Aillaud and Jean Willerwal. The latter was the favourite, because Aillaud was not very popular with people in high places, particularly the president. It was therefore not surprising that Willerwal was appointed on 28 January 1981. However, the Minister for Urban Planning, Roger Quillot, unexpectedly short-circuited the procedure and Willerwal, learned via the press that his plan had been rejected.

The Gang of Four

"Mitterrand decapitates La Tête Défense", screamed the newspaper headlines. But nothing could stop Quilliot and the three other officials who had been commissioned to improve the quality of French architecture. This "Gang of Four", appointed in 1981, also included the Minister of Culture, Jack Lang, the Presidential Advisor, Paul Guimard, and Premier Mauroy's right-hand man, Robert Lion. Jack Lang was in charge of the new Opéra, Lion was in charge of the international communications centre which was to be built at La Tête Défense.
Both projects were preceded by a competition, though initially the architectural community seemed disinterested in the latter competition, which was a lot less interesting than the competition for the Opéra. However, 424 designs were eventually submitted. The adjudication procedure was completed in less than eight days. Although the jury included a number of relatively renowned architects, Lion and president Mitterrand evidently had a great deal of influence on the final decision.
The first round winner was Johan Otto von Spreckelsen, who was completely unknown in France, although he was a respected architect in his home country of Denmark. Von Spreckelsen was better versed in the theoretical rather than in the practical aspects of architecture and, although he had already designed a number of churches, none of his structures had been as daring as his open cube for La Défense. Funnily enough, von Spreckelsen was probably one of the last people in Denmark to receive the good news.The result was announced while he was on a three-day holiday in the wilds of Jutland, and no-one in his party the news on the radio.

Ieoh Ming Pei **project for La Tête Défense, 1971**

Emile Aillaud **project for La Tête Défense, model, 1972**

Johan Otto von Spreckelsen Peter Rice **"nuage" under construction**

Jean-Pierre Buffi **project for Les Collines Nord-Sud, above: exterior perspective, below: plan**

Art work neighboring La Grande Arche

The third triumphal arch

Von Spreckelsen's design was a deserving winner. His open cube "La Grande Arche" gave a monumental accent to the historical axis without closing it off. Von Spreckelsen had added a third arch to the axis, which was already marked by the Arc du Carrousel and the Arc de Triomphe. However, his arch was truly contemporary, certainly in comparison to Ricardo Bofill's design, which was little more than a blown up triumphal arch made of steel and glass. This post-modernist effort was not nearly as striking as the cube submitted by the "unknown" Dane. Having received news of the result, Von Spreckelsen immediately went into retreat for six months to work on the structural aspects of his design.
La Grande Arche is an almost perfectly hollow cube, measuring 110 metres in height and 106 metres in width. The central cavity is 90 metres high and 70 metres wide; large enough to house Nôtre-Dame. The structure consists of four outsized frames positioned at 21 metre intervals. This structure supports the upper part of the cube; a grid

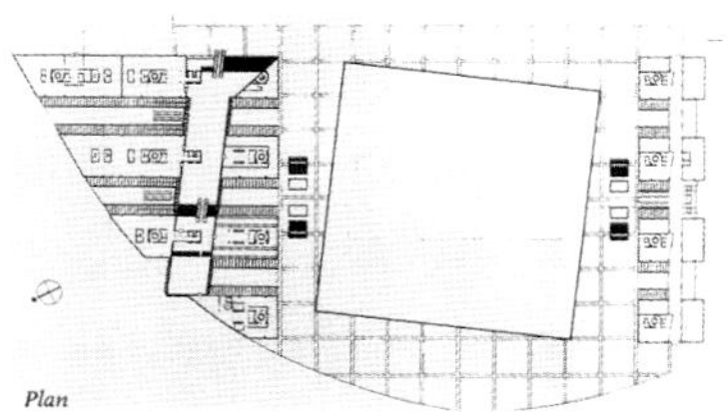

Plan

lying east to west, which counteracts the force exerted by the wind. The cube as a whole rests on twelve enormous underground piles, each of which carries the weight of four Eiffel towers. Theoretically, the building as a whole can be tilted to either side. It is an autonomous structure.

Due to subterranean structures, such as the high-speed RER metro, the twelve piles could not be sunk along the historical axis. Von Spreckelsen came up with an elegant solution to this problem: he turned the Arche 6°30' from the axis. The building's angle to the axis is now the same as that of the Louvre's Cour Napoleon III. It is hard to imagine a greater gesture of deference towards Parisian architectural heritage.

The walls of the building are faced with glass and white Carrara marble. In order to soften the building's angular features, von Spreckelsen designed a tent roof, "le nuage" (the cloud), within the cube. The technical realisation of this structure was in hands of the Englishman Peter Rice, who had also worked on the Cité des Sciences et de l'Industrie[2]. The technical realisation of the cube itself was entrusted to Paul Andreu, the architect who designed the Aéroport de Paris.

The smooth, shining walls of the cube represent a micro-chip with its circuits laid bare. Symbolism of this sort is an embodiment of von Spreckelsen's view that La Grande Arche was a window on the world, a view to the future. It also symbolised his hope that the world would one day be at peace with itself. Unfortunately, a year after construction had started, the plan for the international communications centre was cancelled (April 1986) and a new purpose had to be found for the building. Irritated by these circumstances and the constant bickering about the structural aspects of building his design, von Spreckelsen tendered his resignation in August 1986. He left Andreu in charge and died on 17 March 1987.

Other designs

Construction proceeded along the lines of von Spreckelsen's original design. However, this did not apply to the surrounding plot of land, Les Collines. Jean-Pierre Buffi submitted an entirely new design for this small corner of the site, which lies opposite the so-called Triangle de la Folie. La Grande Arche was completed in 1987. During that same year Jean Nouvel (*1945) won a new competition with his spectacular design for a glass tower.

Undoubtedly, Jean Nouvel believed that justice had finally been done. He had won third prize in the original competition back in 1983. In both designs Nouvel had a happy medium. Although the block in his earlier design stood squarely on the axis, only the sides were closed; the central part of the structure was open. It was this feature which had distinguished not only Nouvel and von Spreckelsen but also Stanislas Fiszer & Witold Zandfos from the other prize-winners, who had envisaged La Tête Défense as the end point of the historical axis. The Dutch architects Ton Alberts and Max van Huut were not amongst the prize-winners. Their design seemed to be a free interpretation of Ieoh Ming Pei's design of 1971, although it had a more expressionistic appearance.

However, none of these designs can truly match the simplicity of La Grande Arche, which is probably one of the most remarkable buildings in Paris. It has the potential – partially due to its artistically decorated surroundings – to become one of the new architectural attractions of the French capital. Although various organisations occupy offices in the building, the lifts and the top floor are still in hands of the state. The fact that the International Foundation for Human Rights and Sciences is now established here would undoubtedly have met with von Spreckelsen's approval.

---

1 *The skyscrapers of the 1970s form part of the so-called second generation (Fiat tower, R. Saubot & F. Jullien, 1974). These of the first generation, built during the 1960s, were smaller and less forbidding. The skyscrapers of the third generation, built during the 1980s, is oriented more towards the individual and towards saving energy (Elf tower, R. Saubot & F. Jullien, 1985).*

2 *See chapter on the Cité des Sciences et de l'Industrie elsewhere in this book.*

Grande Arche, Paris

Die Ausschreibung für das internationale Kommunikationszentrum in La Défense beendete den vollständigen Ausbau dieses Pariser Neubauviertels. Die Grande Arche schließt La Défense und ist gleichzeitig der würdige Endpunkt der historischen Königsachse – einer Achse, die vom Louvre und dem Arc du Carrousel über die Place de la Concorde und die Place Charles de Gaulle mit dem Arc de Triomphe quer durch La Défense bis zur Grande Arche verläuft.

Eine leere Bürostadt

Die Stadt Paris verbindet eine langjährige Haßliebe mit La Défense. Das Viertel liegt nur wenige Metrostationen vom Arc de Triomphe entfernt und entstand nach den Prinzipien der schon 1933 von Le Corbusier formulierten »Charta von Athen«. Dieses Dokument faßte die städtebaulichen Prinzipien funktionalistischer Architekten zusammen. La Défense war im Grunde nichts anderes als ein Bild, das Le Corbusier für ganz Paris vorschwebte: voneinander getrennte städtische Funktionen, Hochbauten mit viel Grün dazwischen und separate Wege für Fußgänger und Autofahrer.
Sehr schnell stellte sich heraus, daß beim Bau von La Défense zwar viele Bürogebäude, aber keine Wohnsektoren entstanden. In weniger als 20 Jahren verdoppelte sich die ursprünglich geplanten 800 000 m² Bürofläche auf Kosten geplanter Appartementhäuser. La Défense wurde zu einer Bürostadt, die jeden Abend ausstarb. Ein weiteres Problem stellte die unpersönliche Ausstrahlung der Wolkenkratzer dar. Dies galt vor allem für die Bauten der 70er Jahre, der sog. zweiten Generation. Sie waren größer und dominanter als die Hochhausbauten der 60er Jahre und gleichzeitig weniger individuell konzipiert als die Bauten der dritten Generation, die ein Jahr später entstanden. Folge: In La Défense standen riesige Büroflächen leer, obwohl es im Zentrum an Büroräumen mangelte.

Städtebauliches Chaos

Offiziell war La Défense von Stadt und Staat unabhängig. 1958 hatte man zu diesem Zweck eine öffentliche Körperschaft ins Leben gerufen, die EPAD (l'Etablissement Public pour l'Aménagement de la Région de la Défence). Doch über mehr als 25 Jahre endeten alle Planungen für das Gelände im Chaos. 1958 entstand das Centre National des Industries et Techniques (CNIT) nach einem Entwurf von Zehrfuss, Camelot und Jean de Mailly. Diese Messehalle mit ihrem dreieckigen Dach besaß lange Zeit das größte Gewölbe der Welt. Die selben Architekten reichten 1958 und 1960 Pläne für ein Gebäude gegenüber dem CNIT auf der berühmten historischen Achse ein. Aber weder diese noch weitere Entwürfe kamen zur Ausführung. Erst 1970 wandte man sich an Ieoh Ming Pei. Er entwarf zwei Bürotürme, die zu beiden Seiten der Achse einander gegenüberstehen und durch einen parabolförmigen Block miteinander verbunden sind. Auf diese Weise erhielt die Achse einen optischen Endpunkt, ohne jedoch endgültig abgeschlossen zu sein (1971). Einige Jahre später legte Emile Aillaud einen Entwurf für zwei konkav gewölbte Bürogebäude vor, die den Abschluß der Achse bilden sollten.
Zu dieser Zeit entstand auch der Ausdruck »la Tête Défense« (der Kopf von La Défense). Präsident Georges Pompidou entschied sich für eine Ausschreibung, weitere Pläne entstanden. Aillard veränderte seinen Entwurf dahingehend, daß die Büroblöcke von der Place d'Étoile aus nicht sichtbar waren. Aber wieder gerieten die Planungen ins Stocken – diesmal bis Ende der 70er Jahre. Eine Zeitlang schien es, als werde der Kampf um die Bebauung von »la Tête Défense« ausschließlich zwischen Emile Aillaud und Jean Willerwal ausgetragen. Dabei besaß letzterer die besseren Chancen, da Aillaud nicht bei allen – insbesondere nicht beim Präsidenten – beliebt war. Am 28.1.1981 fiel die Wahl erwartungsgemäß auf Willerwal. Doch Bauminister Roger Quillot lehnte eine Umsetzung der Pläne ab.

Die »Viererbande«

»Mitterrand köpft la Tête Défense«, lauteten die Schlagzeilen. Quilliot aber wollte, zusammen mit drei anderen Politikern, der französischen Architektur zu neuem Ruhm verhelfen. Diese »Viererbande« formierte sich 1981 und bestand neben Quillot aus Kultusminister Jack Lang, Paul Guimard, einem Berater des Präsidenten, und Robert Lion, engster Vertrauter von Premierminister Mauroy. Lang sollte sich mit dem Bau der neuen Opéra beschäftigen und Lion die Planung des neuen, internationalen Kommunikationszentrums in La Défense übernehmen.
Für beide Projekte schrieb man einen Architekturwettbewerb aus. Dabei erwies es sich zunächst als schwierig, die internationale Architektenwelt für eine Ausschreibung zu interessieren, die weniger vielversprechend zu sein schien als der Wettbewerb für die neue Oper. Dennoch kamen 424 Entwürfe, die die Jury in acht Tagen beurteilte. Den stärksten Einfluß auf die Entscheidung hatten Lion und Präsident Mitterrand.
Nach einer ersten Vorauswahl prämierte die Jury den in Frankreich unbekannten Dänen Johan Otto von Sprekelsen, der bis dahin nur in seinem Heimatland als Architekt anerkannt war, wo er einige Kirchen realisiert hatte. Noch nie war er mit einer so gewagten Konstruktion an die Öffentlichkeit getreten wie mit dem offenen Kubus für »La Tête Défense«. Übrigens zählte von Sprekelsen zu den letzten, die von der Wahl erfuhren: Als die Entscheidung der Jury bekanntgegeben wurde, befand er sich auf einer dreitägigen Ferienreise in einem Dorf in Jütland, wo niemand den Bericht im Radio gehört hatte.

Ein dritter Triumphbogen

Von Spreckelsens Entwurf war ein würdiger Gewinner. Der offene Kubus, La Grande Arche, bildete eine monumentale Krönung der Königsachse, ohne diese endgültig abzuschließen. Neben dem Arc du Carrousel und dem Arc de Triomphe ergänzte von Spreckelsen diese Achse um einen dritten Triumphbogen, der allerdings wesentlich zeitgemäßer ausfiel als der Entwurf von Ricardo Bofill, der lediglich einen übergroßen Triumphbogen aus Glas und Stahl vorsah. Das postmoderne Projekt Bofills besaß nur wenig von der Eigenständigkeit, die der Kubus des Dänen ausstrahlte. Unmittelbar nachdem er das Ergebnis der Ausschreibung erfahren hatte, zog sich von Spreckelsen für sechs Monate zurück, um die Konstruktion seines Entwurfs genauer auszuarbeiten.
La Grande Arche ist ein nahezu perfekter hohler Würfel von 110 Metern Höhe und 106 Metern Breite. Der Hohlraum ist etwa 70 Meter breit und 90 Meter hoch, so daß die Kathedrale Notre Dame mühelos darin Platz finden würde. Sein Skelett besteht aus vier Megastrukturen, viereckigen Rahmen, die in einem Abstand von 21 Metern zueinander stehen. Quer dazu liegt auf der Oberseite des Würfels ein Gitter in Ost-West-Ausrichtung, das die Windströmungen ausgleichen soll. Das gesamte Gebäude ruht auf zwölf im Untergeschoß verankerten Pfeilern, von denen jeder viermal das Gewicht des Eiffelturms trägt.
Da beim Bau Rücksicht auf die bereits bestehenden Verkehrswege im Untergrund genommen werden mußte, konnten die zwölf Pfeiler nicht genau in einer Linie zur Königsachse ausgerichtet werden. Von Spreckelsen löste dieses Problem sehr elegant: Er drehte La Grande Arche sechs Grad und dreißig Minuten von der Achse weg und gab ihr damit genau denselben Winkel, in dem der Cour Napoleon III. des Louvre zur Königsachse steht. Deutlicher läßt sich der Respekt vor der Pariser Stadtgeschichte kaum bezeugen.
Die Wände des Quaders sind mit Glas und weißem Carrara-Marmor verkleidet. Um die harten Formen des Kubus ein wenig abzuschwächen, entwarf von Spreckelsen inmitten des Würfels das Zeltdach Le Nuage (die Wolke). Für die technische Durchführung zeichnete der Engländer Peter Rice verantwortlich, der auch schon beim Bau der Cité des Sciences et de l'Industrie mitgewirkt hatte. Für die technische Leitung beim Bau des Kubus konnte von Spreckelsen Paul Andreu, den Architekten des Aéroports de Paris, gewinnen. Die glatten, glänzenden Außenwände der Grande Arche symbolisieren einen Mikrochip mit offenliegenden Schaltkreisen.
Eine derartige Symbolik entsprach ganz den Vorstellungen von Spreckelsens, der die Grande Arche als Fenster zur Welt sah, als einen Blick in die Zukunft und ein Sinnbild der Hoffnung auf ein friedliches Miteinander. Sehr zum Ärger des dänischen Architekten wurde jedoch im April 1986, kaum ein Jahr nach Baubeginn, die Idee eines internationalen Kommunikationszentrums fallengelassen. La Grande Arche sollte eine neue Bestimmung erhalten. Diese Entscheidung und ständige Meinungsverschiedenheiten über Fragen der Konstruktion veranlaßten von Spreckelsen, im August 1986 um seine Entlassung zu bitten und die Fertigstellung der Arbeiten Andreu zu überlassen. Der Däne starb im März des folgenden Jahres.

Die übrigen Entwürfe

Von Spreckelsens Bauwerk wurde soweit wie möglich nach den ursprünglichen Plänen fertiggestellt. Dies galt jedoch nicht für das umliegende Gelände, »Les Collines« genannt. Hierfür entwarf Jean-Pierre Buffi völlig neue Pläne. Ein weiterer Wettbewerb präsentierte 1987, im Jahr der Bauabnahme der Grande Arche, den Architekten Jean Nouvel (1945) als Gewinner: Er hatte für das Gelände einen spektakulären gläsernen Turm entworfen.
Dieser Preis stellte für Nouvel, der mit seinem Vorschlag für »la Tête Défense «1983 nur einen dritten Preis gewonnen hatte, eine Art ausgleichender Gerechtigkeit dar. Damals hatte sich Nouvel für den vermeintlich goldenen Mittelweg entschieden: Zwar plazierte er den Block mitten auf die Achse, ließ aber nur die Seiten des Gebäudes geschlossen, während der Mittelteil eine offene Struktur besaß. Mit dieser Konzeption unterschieden sich die Entwürfe Nouvel, von Spreckelsen sowie Stanislas Fiszer und Witold Zandfos von denen aller anderen Preisträger. Die übrigen Gewinner sahen »La Tête Défense« hauptsächlich als Endpunkt der historischen Königsachse.
Keines der erwähnten Projekte kann La Grande Arche das Wasser reichen. In ihrer Schlichtheit zählt sie zu den bemerkenswertesten Bauwerken von Paris. Nicht zuletzt dank ihrer kunstvoll gestalteten Umgebung hat sie sich mehr und mehr zu einer Touristenattraktion der französischen Hauptstadt entwickelt. Verschiedene Institutionen haben inzwischen Teile des Gebäudes bezogen. Nur die Aufzüge und das Dachgeschoß befinden sich noch in Händen des Staates. Hier hat die Fondation International des Droits de l'Homme et des Sciences Humaines (Internationale Gesellschaft für Menschenrechte und Humanwissenschaften) ihre Büroräume – eine Ansiedlung, die ganz im Sinne von Spreckelsens gewesen wäre.

La Grande Arche, Paris

Le concours pour le Centre international de communication de la Tête Défense marque la fin d'une période qui a vu le paysage urbain parisien se modifier profondément. En termes d'urbanisme, l'édifice, aperçu du centre de Paris semble, mettre un point final à La Défense, le plus récent des quartiers d'affaires de Paris. En fait, que la Grande Arche ferme ou non l'axe historique qui va du Louvre à la Défense en passant par l'Arc du Carrousel, la place de la Concorde et l'Arc de Triomphe reste une question toujours... ouverte.

Un quartier de bureaux

Pendant de longues années, Paris vécut une relation complexe avec La Défense un quartier de bureaux situé à quelques stations de métro de l'Arc de Triomphe et construit selon des principes fonctionnalistes que n'auraient pas reniés Le Corbusier ou Van Eesteren. Le Corbusier avait d'ailleurs imaginé avant-guerre un plan pour Paris sur les principes que l'on allait appliquer à La Défense: spécialisation des quartiers en fonction de leur activité, immeubles de grande hauteur isolés dans des parcs et séparation des circulations automobile et piétonnière. Mais la Charte d'Athènes, compte rendu officieux du quatrième congrès des CIAM, datait de 1933, alors que La Défense ne sortit de terre qu'à la fin des années 50.
Le projet de construire des immeubles de logement au milieu des tours de sièges sociaux fut bientôt oublié et en moins de vingt ans, les 800 000 mètres carrés de bureaux du plan original furent doublés aux dépens des appartements. La Défense devint un quartier d'affaires actif le jour et désert la nuit. Le style discutable des tours qui avaient poussé comme des champignons n'enthousiasmait guère les Parisiens qui acceptaient mal les changements radicaux apportés au caractère de la ville. L'impersonnalité de ces gratte-ciel des années 70 y était pour quelque chose[1]. Pour aggraver encore la situation, La Défense connut un véritable passage à vide pendant la crise du pétrole. Malgré ses aides et sa bonne volonté, l'Etat ne put rétablir l'équilibre financier de l'opération et il fallut attendre le premier septennat de F. Mitterrand pour que le mouvement s'inverse.

Un chaos architectural

Officiellement La Défense était un projet autonome, mais piloté par un organisme public, EPAD. Pendant longtemps, l'opération végéta et la Tête Défense, l'extrémité du quartier, resta dans les nimbes pendant plus de 25 ans.
Le Centre National des Industries et des Techniques (CNIT), conçu par Zehrfuss, Camelot et de Mailly avait été construit sur le site même, dès 1958. Ce lieu d'expositions de forme triangulaire pouvait se flatter à l'époque de posséder la plus vaste voûte sans pilier du monde. En 1958 et 1960, les mêmes architectes soumirent des plans pour la zone faisant face au CNIT, juste sur la perspective historique de Paris. Ils ne furent jamais exécutés et rien ne se passa pendant de longues années jusqu'à ce que Ieoh Ming Pei (né en 1917) ne soit consulté en 1970. Il dessina deux tours de bureaux de chaque côté de l'axe historique, reliées par un immeuble parabolique fermant optiquement l'axe mais sans le clore réellement (1971). Quelques années plus tard, Émile Aillaud proposa deux tours concaves qui, elles, devaient totalement obturer la perspective.
De là naquit un vaste débat et la «Tête Défense» devint le sujet de conversation à la mode. Un concours fut organisé, avec l'appui du président Pompidou, et de nouveaux plans furent produits. Aillaud modifia ses dessins pour que ses immeubles ne soient plus visibles de la place de l'Etoile, mais une fois encore, ses plans furent rejetés. La crise du pétrole entraîna un gel de tous les projets de ce type et il fallut attendre la fin des années 70 pour que de nouvelles initiatives se fassent jour. Longtemps, les principaux candidats en lice avaient été Aillaud et Jean Willerwal devenu favori, car le premier n'avait plus l'oreille du président Giscard d'Estaing. Le 28 janvier 1981, Willerwal fut donc nommé responsable du projet. Mais après les élections qui virent l'arrivée des socialistes au pouvoir, le ministre Roger Quillot court-circuita la procédure et Willerwal apprit par la presse que son plan ne serait jamais réalisé.

La bande des quatre

«Mitterrand décapite la Tête Défense» titrèrent les journaux! Mais rien ne pouvait arrêter Quillot et les trois personnalités qui avaient été chargées d'améliorer la qualité de l'architecture française. Cette «bande des quatre», nommée en 1981, comprenait également le ministre de la Culture, Jack Lang, un conseiller de l'Élysée, Paul Guimard et le chef de cabinet du Premier ministre, Robert Lion. Jack Lang s'occupait plus particulièrement du nouvel opéra et Lion du Centre international de communication que l'on projetait dorénavant de construire à la Tête Défense.
Les deux projets firent donc l'objet d'un concours, mais la communauté architecturale sembla se désintéresser de La Défense qui semblait moins prestigieuse que l'Opéra Bastille. 424 projets furent néanmoins soumis. La procédure d'adjudication se déroula en à peine huit jours. Bien que le jury ait inclus nombre de grands architectes, Lion et le Président Mitterrand exercèrent une forte influence sur la décision finale.
Le vainqueur du premier tour fut Johan Otto von Spreckelsen, un architecte danois inconnu en France, mais très respecté dans son pays. Spreckelsen était plus versé dans la théorie que dans la pratique et, bien qu'il ait déjà construit quelques églises, aucune de ses réalisations n'était aussi audacieuse que le cube ouvert qu'il imagina pour

Un troisième arc de triomphe

Le plan de Spreckelsen méritait de gagner. Son cube ouvert «la Grande Arche» confirmait la monumentalité de l'axe historique, sans le fermer. Il s'agissait en quelque sorte d'un troisième arc succédant en perspective à celui du Carrousel et de la place de l'Etoile. En même temps cette arche était réellement contemporaine, à la différence de celle de Ricardo Bofill qui n'était guère plus qu'une sorte d'arc de triomphe enflé en verre et en acier dont le post-modernisme était loin d'être aussi convaincant que le cube de l'architecte danois «inconnu».
La Grande Arche est un cube creux presque parfait de 110 m de haut et 106 de large. L'ouverture centrale mesure 90 m de haut et 70 de large, et Notre-Dame de Paris pourrait facilement s'y abriter. La structure est composée de quatre gigantesques cadres positionnés à 21 m d'intervalle qui soutiennent la partie supérieure, une grille orientée est-ouest équilibrant les forces exercées par le vent. Le cube repose sur douze énormes piles souterraines. Structure autonome, l'édifice peut théoriquement s'incliner de n'importe quel côté.
L'existence d'équipements souterrains comme la gare du métro express régional empêchant de couler les piles symétriquement à l'axe historique, l'architecte trouva une solution élégante et fit pivoter l'Arche de 6°30', retrouvant ainsi l'orientation de la Cour Napoléon III du palais du Louvre.
Les murs sont recouverts de verre et de marbre de Carrare blanc. Pour adoucir quelque peu la sécheresse de l'ensemble, Spreckelsen conçut une sorte de tente, «le nuage», suspendue dans l'ouverture du cube dont la réalisation technique fut confiée à l'ingénieur britannique Peter Rice qui avait déjà travaillé sur la Cité des Sciences et de l'Industrie[2]. La réalisation technique du cube lui-même fut confiée à Paul Andreu, l'architecte des Aéroports de Paris.
Le dessin des façades représente une puce électronique aux circuits mis à nu. Ce symbolisme illustre la vision de Spreckelsen selon laquelle La Grande Arche symbolise une fenêtre sur le monde, une vision du futur et également l'espoir que le monde soit un jour en paix avec lui-même. Malheureusement, un an après le début des travaux, le projet de Centre international de communication fut abandonné (avril 1986) et une nouvelle fonction dut être trouvée. Irrité de cette situation et par les innombrables querelles sur ses capacités techniques, Spreckelsen démissionna en août 1986 et laissa Andreu en charge du projet. Il mourut le 17 mars 1987.

Les autres projets

Les terrains avoisinant connurent une histoire plus mouvementée. Jean-Pierre Buffi proposa de nouveaux plans pour le reste du site sur la zone dite des Collines. L'année de la fin des travaux de la Grande Arche, Jean Nouvel (né en 1945) remporta un autre concours avec son projet spectaculaire de «Tour sans fin» toute proche. Nouvel pouvait penser que justice lui était enfin rendue. Il avait remporté le troisième prix lors du concours de 1983. Si son bâtiment était à cheval sur l'axe historique, seuls les façades latérales étaient fermées. La partie centrale restait ouverte. Cette caractéristique distinguait non seulement les projets de Spreckelsen et de Nouvel mais également ceux de Stanislas Fiszer et Witold Zanfos de ceux des autres lauréats qui avaient envisagé la Tête Défense comme le point final de la grande perspective historique. Par exemple, les Néerlandais Ton Alberts et Max van Huut avaient proposé une interprétation libre des plans de Ieoh Ming Pei de 1970 dans un style plus expressif.
La Grande Arche devient peu à peu l'une des grandes attractions architecturales de la capitale, grâce également à son environnement très soigné. Bien que de nombreuses sociétés et un ministère se soient installées dans le bâtiment, le toit et les ascenseurs extérieurs sont restés la propriété de l'Etat. Que la Fondation internationale pour les Droits de l'Homme et les Sciences Humaines y ait trouvé son siège eut certainement plu à Spreckelsen.

1 *Les tours des années 70 appartiennent à la «seconde génération» d'immeubles de La Défense (Tour Fiat R. j155 Saubot, F. Jullien, 1974). Les immeubles de la première génération, édifiée dans les années 60 étaient plus petits et moins sinistres. La troisième génération, celle des années 80, fut respectua davantage les besoins de l'individu et de l'environnement, en particulier dans le domaine de l'énergie (Tour Elf, R. Saubot et F. Jullien, 1985).*

2 *Voir le chapitre sur la Cité des Sciences et de l'Industrie.*

Grande Arche, Paris, 1982–1983

166

Johan Otto von Spreckelsen
competition design, 1983, sketches, first prize

Johan Otto von Spreckelsen
presentation design, 1983, site plan

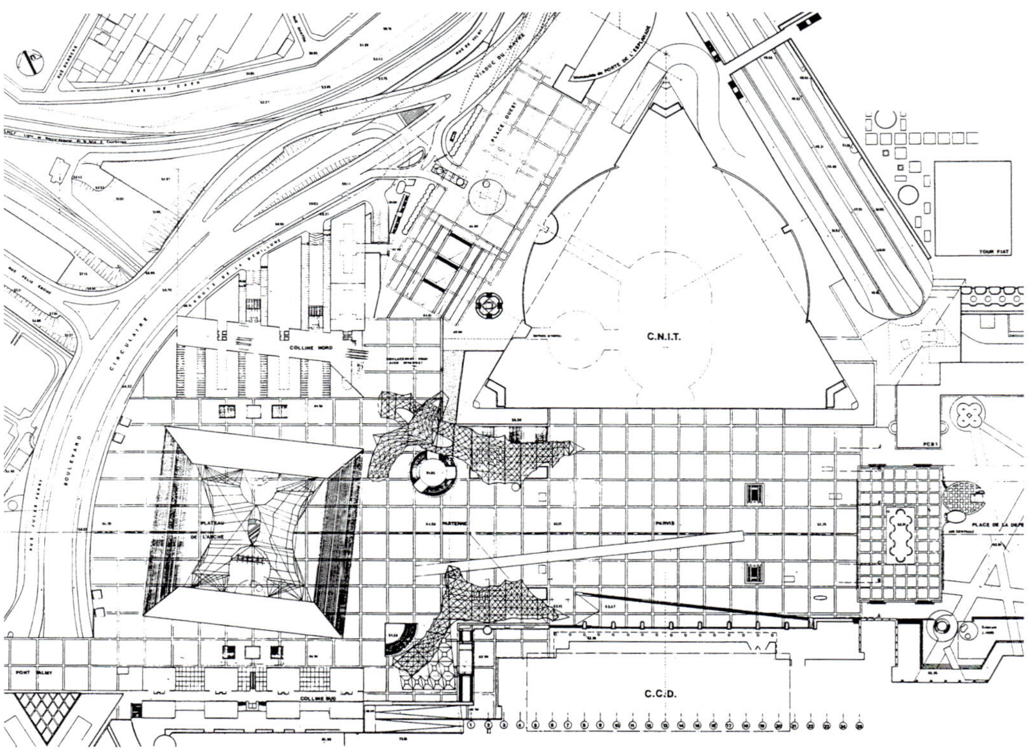

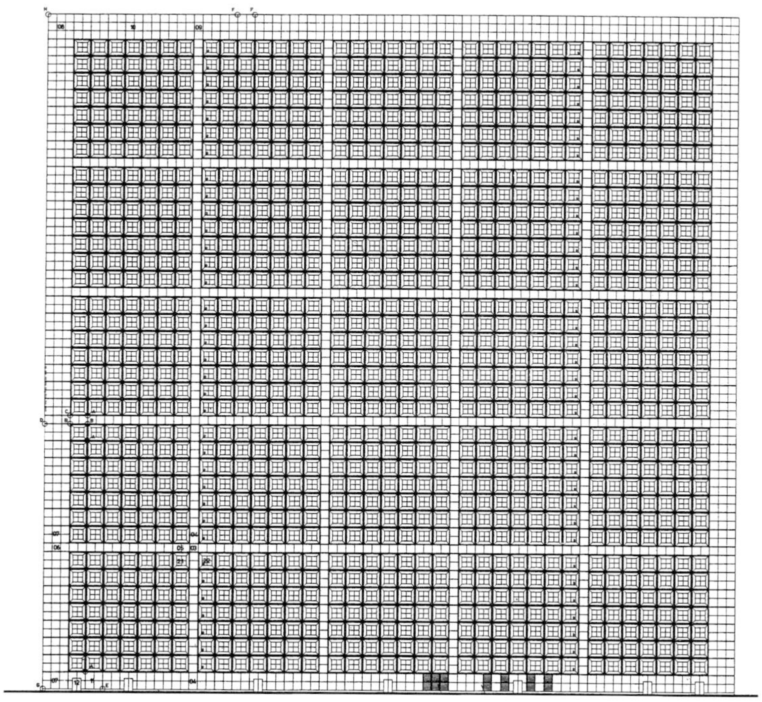

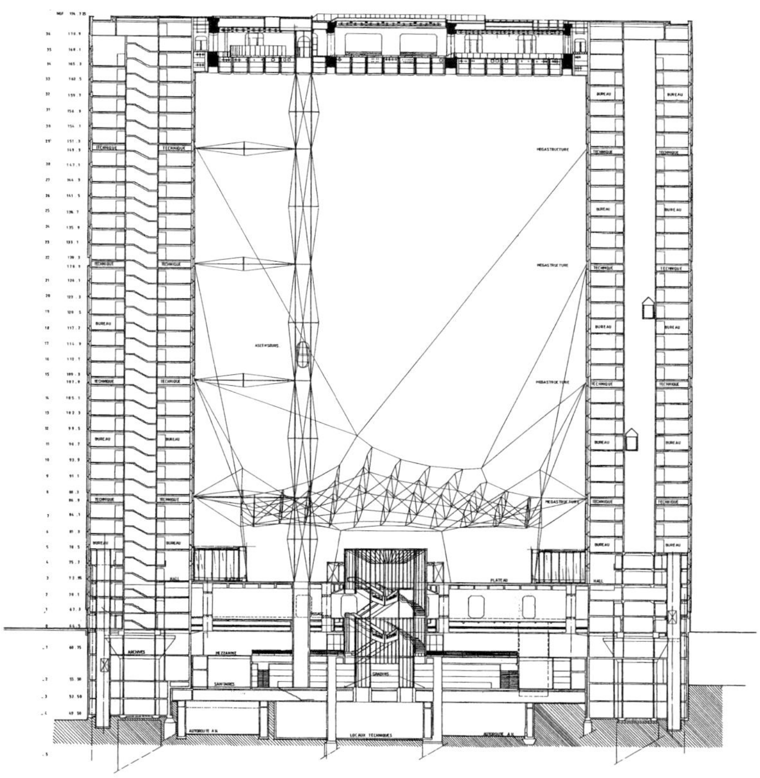

Johan Otto von Spreckelsen
presentation design, 1983, elevation

Johan Otto von Spreckelsen
presentation design, 1983, north-south section (east side)

Jean-Paul Viguier & Jean-François Jodry competition design, 1983, bird's-eye view from north-east, second prize

Jean-Paul Viguier & Jean-François Jodry competition design, 1983, exterior view from east, second prize

Jean-Paul Viguier & Jean-François Jodry competition design, 1983, interior view of the atrium, second prize

Jean-Paul Viguier & Jean-François Jodry competition design, 1983, bird's-eye view from west, second prize

James Carscallen Crang & George Elliot Boake competition design, 1983, study of exterior, fourth prize

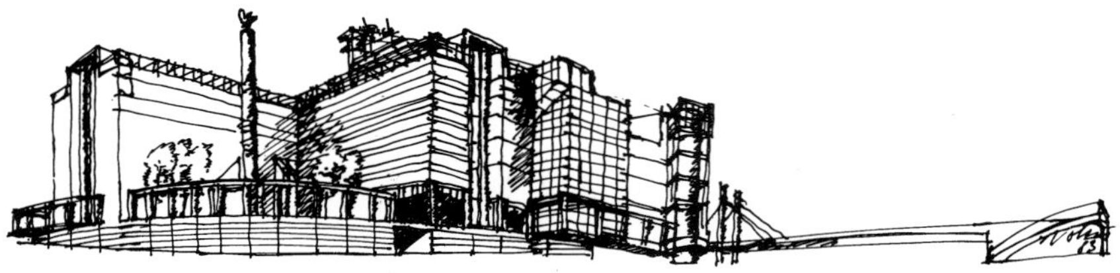

James Carscallen Crang & George Elliot Boake competition design, 1983, study of exterior, fourth prize

James Carscallen Crang & George Elliot Boake competition design, 1983, study of exterior, fourth prize

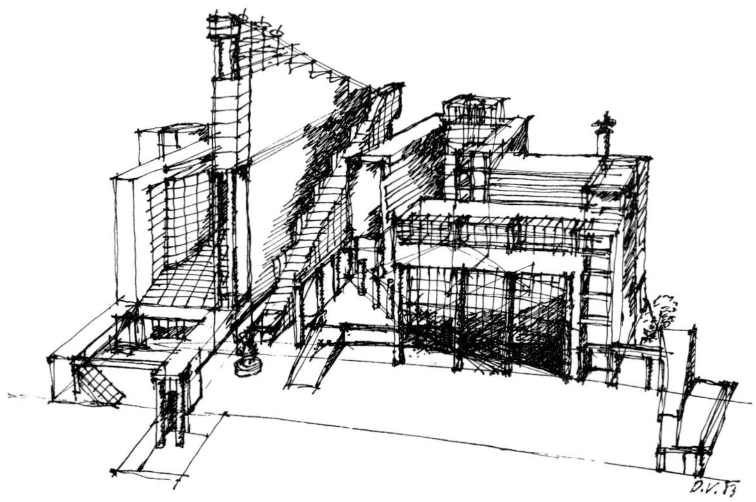

James Carscallen Crang & George Elliot Boake competition design, 1983, study of elevation, fourth prize

James Carscallen Crang & George Elliot Boake competition design, 1983, exterior view from east, fourth prize

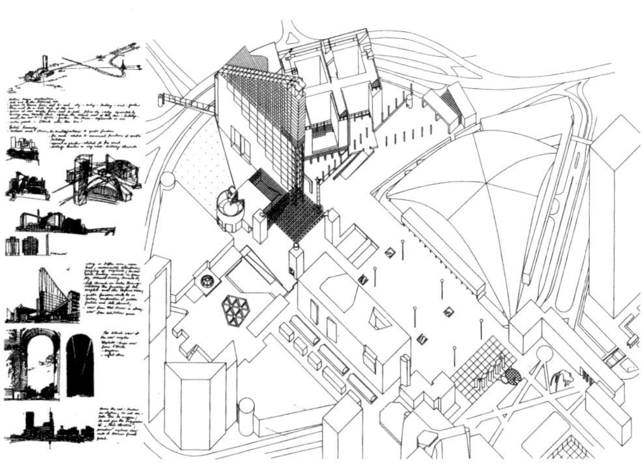

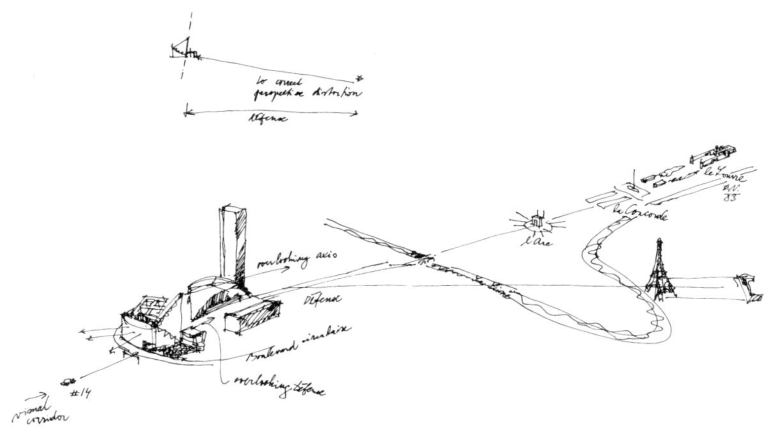

James Carscallen Crang & George Elliot Boake competition design, 1983, axonometric sketches, fourth prize

James Carscallen Crang & George Elliot Boake competition design, 1983, conceptual sketch, fourth prize

James Carscallen Crang & George Elliot Boake competition design, 1983, study of exterior, fourth prize

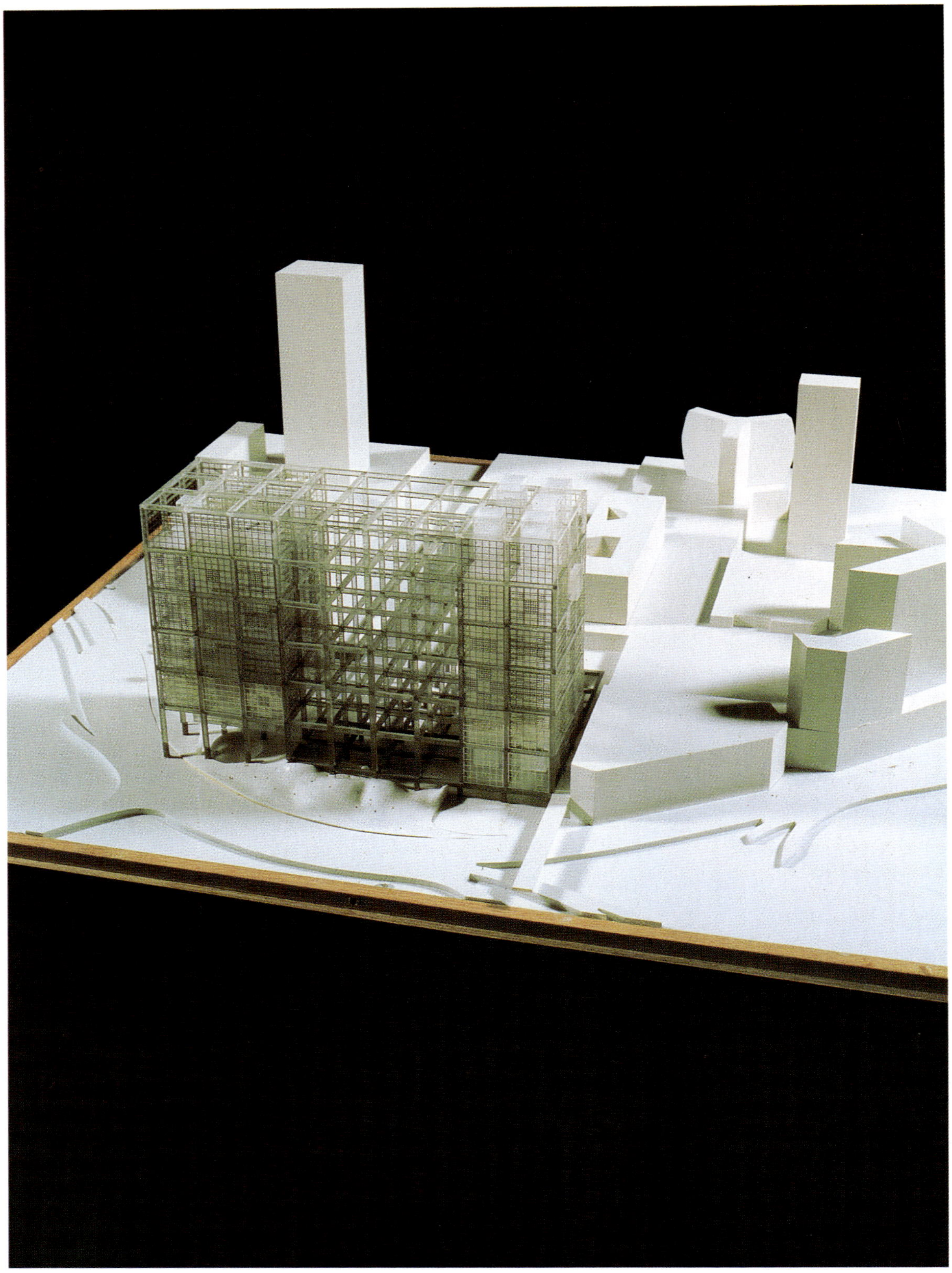

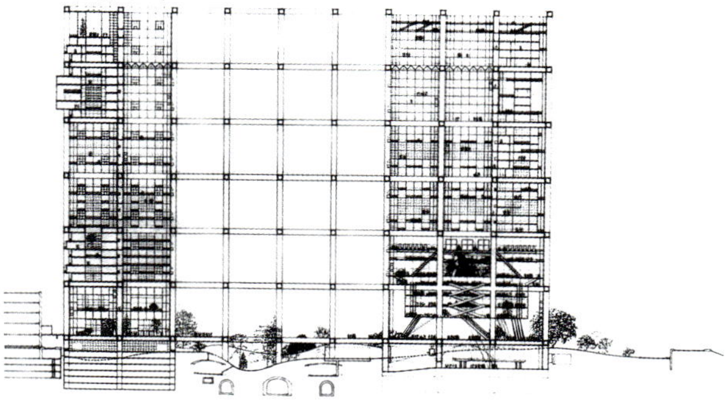

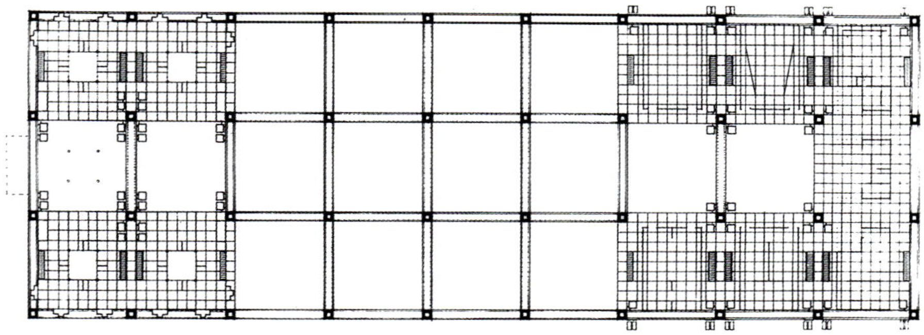

Jean Nouvel, Pierre Soria Architecture Studio, Jean-Marc Ibos & Didier Laroque competition design, 1983, model, third prize

Jean Nouvel, Pierre Soria Architecture Studio, Jean-Marc Ibos & Didier Laroque competition design, 1983, north-south section (east side), third prize

Jean Nouvel, Pierre Soria Architecture Studio, Jean-Marc Ibos & Didier Laroque competition design, 1983, typical floor plan, third prize

Jean Nouvel, Pierre Soria Architecture Studio, Jean-Marc Ibos & Didier Laroque competition design, 1983, east elevation, third prize

Yves Lion, Bernard Althabegoity & François Leclercq competition design, 1983, axonometric, honourable mention

Yves Lion, Bernard Althabegoity & François Leclercq competition design, 1983, from top: east elevation, north-south section (east side), east-west section (south side), honourable mention

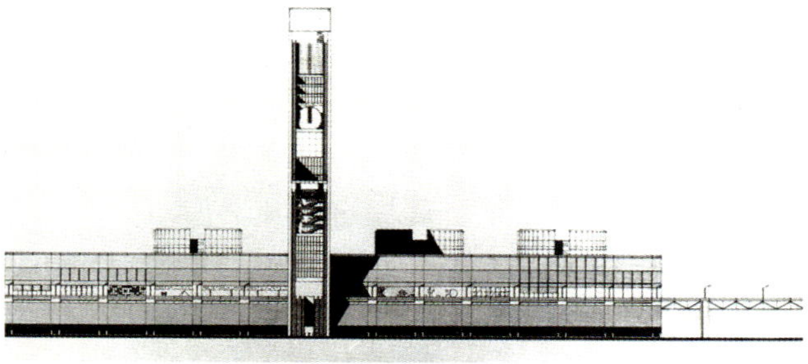

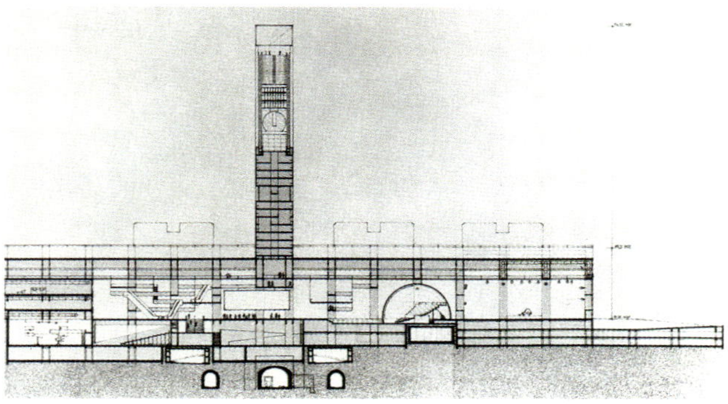

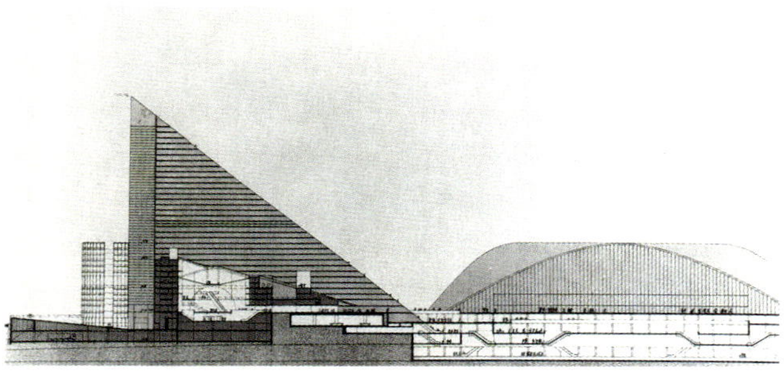

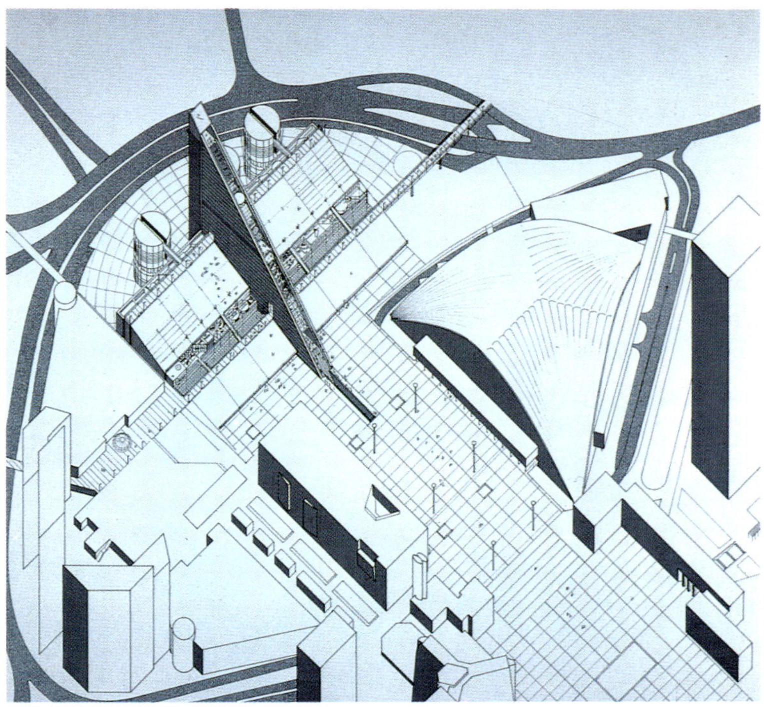

Stanislas Fiszer & Witold Zandfos competition design, 1983, exterior view from east, honourable mention

Stanislas Fiszer & Witold Zandfos competition design, 1983, exterior view from east, honourable mention

Ton Alberts & Max van Huut competition design, 1983, exterior view from east

Ton Alberts & Max van Huut competition design, 1983, bird's-eye view from north-east

Ricardo Bofill competition design, 1983

La Tour d'Argent
27 28 29
JUILLET 1830

Project

Opera house

Site

Place de la Bastille, between Rue de Lyon and Rue de Charenton, Paris

Dates

Competition announced November 1982 *First round closing date* 13 May 1983 *Result announced* 3 July 1983 *Second round* 5 July 1983 to 1 September 1983 *Final result announced* 10 November 1983

Number of entries

787 (including 31 disqualified entries)

Jury

François Bloch-Lainé (chairman, director of the Mission Opéra Bastille), Carlo Aymonino, Massimo Bogianckino (both vice-chairman), Mario Botta, Horst Birr, Christian Dupavillon, Herman Hertzberger, Jean Nouvel, Gustav Peichl, Dennis Sharp, Clorindo Testa, Oswald Mathias Ungers (all architects), Jean-Pierre Duport, Louis Erlo, Maurice Fleuret, Michäel Hampe, Pierre-Yves Ligen (architectural experts), Denys Pradelle, Michèle Audon (advisors) and Paul Puaux, Pierre Boulez, (composer)

Result

Preliminary round, winners Nicolas Hare; Dan Monteanu, Odile Perreau Hamburger, Teodor Georgesco, Alice Tufan & Teodor Tufan; Carlos Ott; Christian de Portzamparc; Jean-Paul Viguier & Jean-François Jodry; Rocco S.K. Yim *Special mention* Kajima Corporation *Honourable mention* Kenji Fukuzawa & Akira Komiyama *Final result, first prize* Carlos Ott (Canada) *Second prize* Rocco S.K. Yim (Hong Kong) *Third prize* Dan Monteanu, Odile Perreau Hamburger, Teodor Georgesco, Alice Tufan & Teodor Tufan (France)

Commissioned by

Mission Opéra Bastille (research team), later renamed Etablissement Public Opéra Bastille (EPOB), under the auspices of the French Ministry of Culture

Construction

1985 to 1989

Architect

Carlos Ott (*1946) in collaboration with Saubot & Julien and the EPOB

Competitions in architecture and town planning since 1792

The Opéra Bastille, Paris, 1982–1983

Carlos Ott competition design, 1983, from above left: axonometric projection, site plan, from above middle: plan, elevation on Rue de Lyon, plans, elevation on Place de la Bastille, from above right: plans, sections, section view, first prize

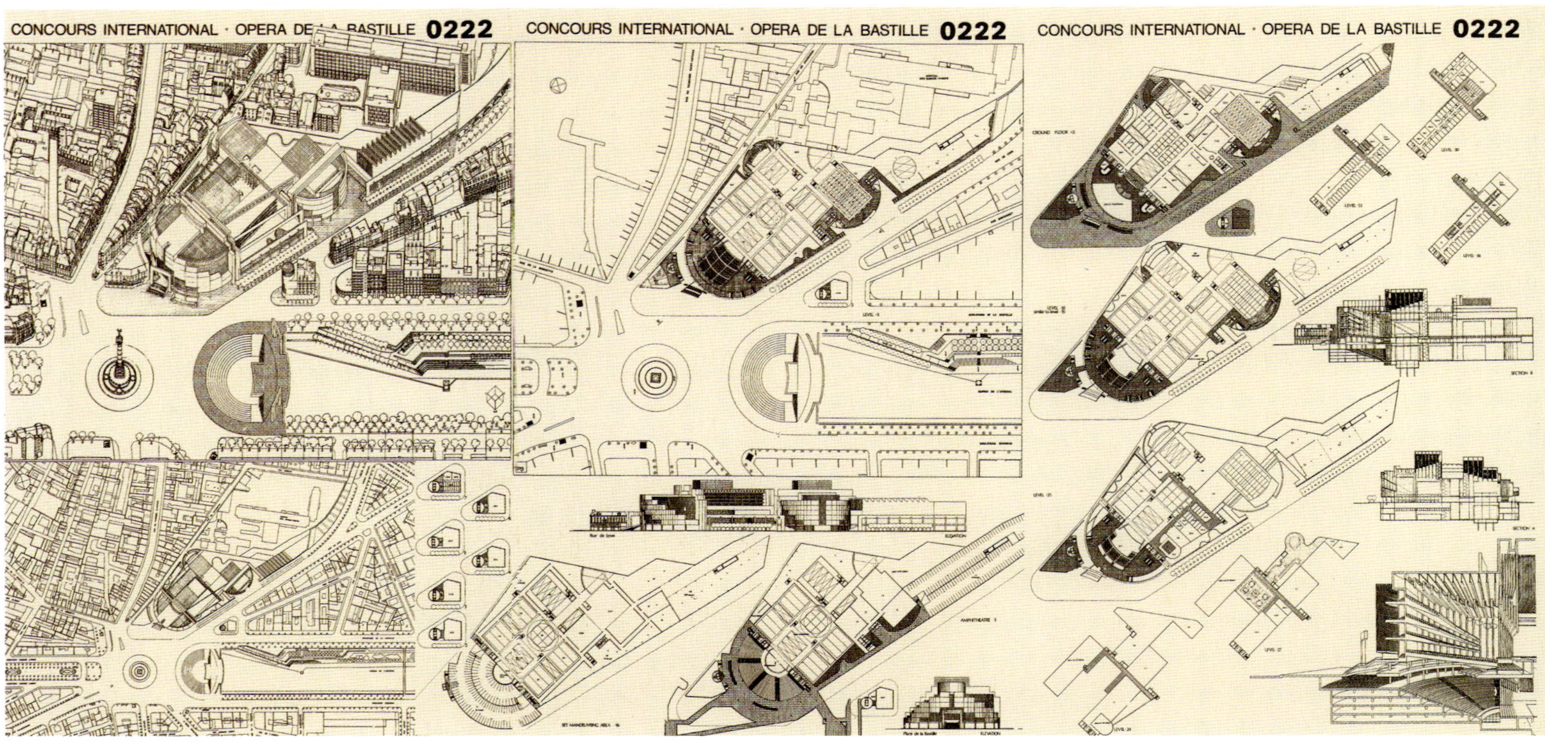

The Opéra Bastille, Paris

Napoleon III had two objectives in mind when he decided to build a new opera house during the 1850s. He wanted to leave the city a magnificent building which would be associated with his name, whilst at the same time presenting wealthy citizens with a place where they could enjoy music and, of course, each other. The Opéra Bastille was also seen as a project to increase the prestige of those in power, the French Socialists, and this meant giving as many people as possible the opportunity to participate in Parisian musical life, at a reasonable price.

An opera house for the general public

Garnier's opera house[1] was mainly visited by the wealthy élite, who were generally more interested in each other than in the music itself. Four hundred of the nineteen hundred seats in the Opéra Garnier have an inadequate view of the stage, and there are no separate rehearsal areas for the performers. One hundred years on, the approach to opera and cultural accessibility had changed considerably. The prevailing view was that the general public should be given the opportunity to witness developments in the world of music, and at a reasonable price. Consequently, on 9 March 1982 the French cabinet, advised by Jean Vilar and Pierre Boulez, approved the plans to build a new opera house. A report had been published six years before, in which François Bloch-Lainé, who was later appointed jury chairman, concluded scathingly:
"The Palais Garnier combines all the prerequisites necessary to ensure the least possible democracy at the highest possible cost, the most magnificent productions for the smallest audiences."
A research team, the Mission Opéra Bastille, was appointed to prepare the project. The commission concluded that a new opera house with a seating capacity of 3000, preferably situated in central Paris, was essential. Another factor which fuelled the desire for a new opera house was France's ambition to become one of leading countries in the world of music. This implied that the new building would have to be a suitable venue for a wide variety of productions. More productions and larger audiences meant lower costs. However, more productions also meant that a large number of companies would have to rehearse in the same complex, and that other facilities would also have to be close at hand[2].

Metropolitan Opera House, New York

Old Bastille station

A diagrammatic floor plan

The competition programme, which was made available in November 1982, contained a diagrammatic floor plan in which the most important facilities had been indicated. These included rehearsal areas and workshops for the production of sets and costumes. There was a large auditorium which could seat between 2700 and 3000 people, and a smaller auditorium which could be adapted to seat between 600 and 1000 people, depending on the nature of the production. The latter hall was reserved for experimental theatre and all its features had to be convertible in order to meet the needs of various directors. Special attention was to be paid to supporting technical facilities, so that the productions would run smoothly.

The greater part of the complex was reserved for permanent and temporary staff, such as musicians, technicians, singers and the like. It was estimated that a professional staff of between 800 and 1000 people would be present on a daily basis. Although a possible merger with the Academy of Music had been allowed for in the original concept, the Academy was in fact later housed in a separate building in the Parc de la Villette.

After lengthy deliberation, the commission decided that Place de la Bastille was the most suitable site for the new opera house. There were plans to hold a World Exhibition there to celebrate the bicentenary of the French Revolution on 14 July 1989, and as the planned event was to coincide with the inauguration of the Opéra Bastille, this would ensure that the Opéra would become a monument to socialism. The World Exhibition was subsequently cancelled, but the inauguration of the Opéra did form part of the festivities during the "Bicentenaire".

Dark horse winner

The jury received no less than 787 entries, 31 of which were disqualified immediately. Adjudication took place in three phases; first round designs which had been nominated at least four times went through to the second round. The jury were disappointed by the general quality of the entries but, after lengthy deliberation, they selected six designs for the final round. It is interesting to note that the design submitted by Dan Monteanu and his team, which later won second prize, was initially eliminated but was later subsequently added to the field of finalists.

It is said that some members of the jury recognised the hand of Richard Meier in one of the anonymously submitted designs. The jury awarded first prize to this design on the assumption that it had indeed been submitted by this famous architect, although it later became apparent that the design had in fact been submitted by Carlos Ott, a relatively unknown Canadian-Uruguayan architect who ran a successful firm in Toronto. Initially, the critics were not enthusiastic. Ott was neither famous nor French. Nevertheless, he had successfully incorporated all the necessary elements into his design.

The design

The main problem was, of course, the layout of the facilities. The competition had stipulated that the various groups within the building should not get in one another's way, and at the same time that the complex division of facilities should not hamper efficiency. The stage tower of the main auditorium is situated at the heart of the Opéra. This auditorium forms part of a semicircular block which also contains the ticket office, foyers, bars, et cetera. There is a rotating platform behind the stage and both platform and stage are surrounded by storerooms. Ott himself came up with the idea for the 500-seat amphitheatre which is situated under the auditorium.

There is another semicircular block on the Rue de Lyon, containing the convertible auditorium. The third primary facility, the large rehearsal studio, is situated on the other side of the building on the Rue de Charenton. Ott also took into account the need to transport sets from one area to another. The sets, props and costumes are stored in the workshop area on the Rue de Lyon, which is attached to the main building like a tail. In addition, there is a 280-seat studio which was not specified in the original programme, but which developed more or less by chance.

One of the buildings which stood in the way of the new Opéra was the restaurant "La Tour d'Argent", which was situated in the only pre-revolutionary building on the square. Due to its historical value, it was decided that this building should be reconstructed close to the original site, and that it should become one of the opera's facilities. Ott designed the floors above the restaurant for use as a studio. Another restaurant, separated from the main stage by a patio, is situated on the Rue de Lyon. This triangular restaurant provided Ott with a solution for the problem created by the wedge-shaped building site.

Carlos Ott isometric projection of l'Opéra Bastille

Carlos Ott interior view of l'Opéra Bastille

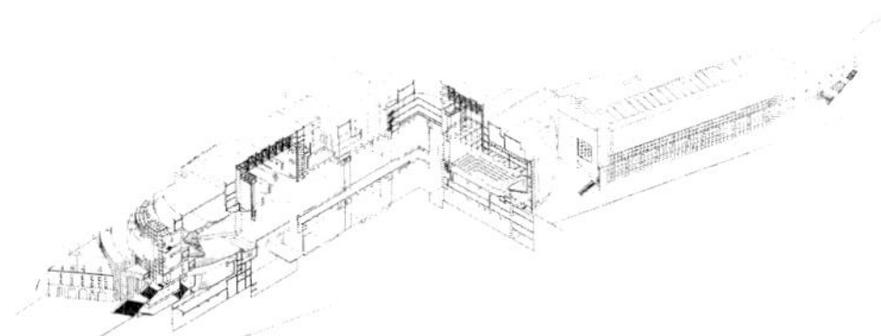

All the seats in the main auditorium have an equally good view of the stage and, although the view may not be as spectacular as that in New York's Metropolitan Opera, the seats are certainly an improvement on those in the Opéra Garnier. The new opera was also more accessible. As well as a main entrance, the opera can also be reached via an underground passage which leads from the Metro station.

The main entrance is accentuated by a free-standing, Lanhelin granite portal, the double arch of the portal serving as a hinge-point between the square and the semi-circular Opéra. The opening is square, as are the other features on the façade. Ott based this part of the design on a ninety-by-ninety centimetre matrix. The transparent façade offers visitors a magnificent view of the city from the foyers and bars, and visitors have free access to this outer shell of the building, even when there are no performances.

In contrast to Garnier, his illustrious predecessor, Ott included almost no decorative elements in his design. However, the costly building materials used for the Opéra are embellishments in themselves: Lanhelin granite, light Valreuil limestone, grey-blue Breccia marble, various sorts of wood and, of course, vast quantities of glass. Ott sought to find a balance between the building's purpose as a public entertainment facility and the fact that it was a well-oiled machine measuring 150 000 square metres: a balance between efficiency of production and the glitter and glamour of performance.

An efficient opera factory

For the most part, Ott's design has lived up to high-flown expectations. The Opéra Bastille has all the prerequisites necessary to provide a varied, top-class and, at the same time, experimentally innovative programme. The theatrical facilities offered are the best and the experiments with acoustics were rigorously tested. In short, nothing was left to chance.

The projected figures are impressive: 250 productions in the main auditorium, 120 in the "salle modulable" (never built) with an annual audience capacity of 775 000. These figures do not include the concerts in the studio and the amphitheatre, and visitors to the restaurants, bars, cafés, shops, et cetera. The Opéra Garnier staged no more than 110 productions per year, generally for season ticket holders.

In comparison to the Opéra Garnier, which now serves as a venue for ballet and musical performances, the Opéra Bastille lacks grandeur. This will undoubtedly be something of a disappointment to many Parisians, who have retained their affinity for grandeur in spite of the wave of democratisation that has washed over the city. However, Ott is not wholly to blame for this: the square which the participants also had to include in their design has yet to be completed, consequently the site does not yet provide the ideal setting for France's premier temple of music.

Carlos Ott, Jack Lang (Minister of Culture), François Mitterrand (President of France), et al.

Place de la Bastille

---

1 See chapter on this building elsewhere in this book.

2 More productions were necessary to guarantee a continuous programme. A taxing aria cannot be sung by the same person on two consecutive nights.

Opéra Bastille, Paris

Als Napoleon III. sich in den 50er Jahren des vorigen Jahrhunderts zum Bau einer neuen Pariser Oper entschloß, verfolgte er mit dieser Entscheidung zwei Ziele: Einerseits beabsichtigte er, der Stadt ein beeindruckendes Bauwerk zu hinterlassen, mit dem sein Name unauslöschlich verbunden war, andererseits wollte er dem Bürgertum Gelegenheit geben, neben großartigen musikalischen Darbietungen vor allem sich selbst zu bewundern. Beim Bau der Opéra Bastille spielte zudem der Prestigegewinn der Regierenden, in diesem Falle der Sozialisten, eine entscheidende Rolle: Möglichst viele Menschen sollten gegen einen geringen Eintrittspreis am musikalischen Leben von Paris teilhaben können.

Eine Oper für das Volk

Garniers Opéra (siehe Kapitel »Oper, Paris«) wurde zu ihrer Zeit hauptsächlich von einer kleinen, wohlhabenden Elite besucht. Von den 1 900 Sitzen boten nur 1 500 eine gute Sicht auf die Bühne, Proberäume für Künstler und Musiker fehlten. Im Laufe der nächsten 100 Jahre veränderte sich die Einstellung zur Oper und deren Zugänglichkeit für das breite Publikum: Jedermann sollte die Möglichkeit erhalten, die Entwicklungen auf musikalischem Gebiet zu einem angemessenen Preis miterleben zu können.
Am 9. März 1982 beschloß der französische Ministerrat, u. a. auf Anraten von Jean Vilar und Pierre Boulez, den Plänen zum Bau einer neuen Opéra zuzustimmen. Bereits sechs Jahre zuvor war eine Untersuchung veröffentlicht worden, in der der spätere Jury vorsitzende François Bloch-Lainé zu einem niederschmetternden Urteil kam: *»Das Palais Garnier bietet alle Voraussetzungen für die geringste Demokratie zu den höchsten Kosten und der kleinsten Zuschauerzahl zu den schönsten Aufführungen.«*
Die aus diesem Anlaß gegründete Studiengruppe »Mission Opéra Bastille« gelangte zu der Ansicht, daß ein neues Operngebäude mit etwa 3 000 Plätzen mitten im Zentrum von Paris unverzichtbar sei. Es sollte ausreichend Platz für eine Vielzahl unterschiedlicher Aufführungen bieten. Gleichzeitig würde eine größere Zahl von Vorstellungen die Zuschauerzahlen ansteigen lassen und damit die Kosten senken. Mehr Vorstellungen bedeuteten aber auch, daß im selben Gebäudekomplex mehr Proberäume und in direkter Nachbarschaft andere, für das Theater notwendige Einrichtungen zur Verfügung stehen mußten.

Ein schematischer Grundriß

Die im November 1982 ausgeschriebene Preisfrage enthielt ein Diagramm eine Art schematischen Grundriß mit den wichtigsten Funktionsbereichen einer neuen Oper. In diesem Diagramm nahmen die Probenräume und die Arbeitsplätze für Dekorateure und Kostümbildner viel Platz ein. Neben einem großen Saal mit ca 3 000 Plätzen war ein flexibler Saal mit 600 bis 1 000 Plätzen vorgesehen, der je nach Art der Vorstellung verändert werden konnte. In diesem Raum sollte hauptsächlich experimentelles Theater stattfinden. Um einen reibungslosen Ablauf des Spielbetriebs zu gewährleisten, wurde auch auf die technische Ausstattung des Hauses besonderes Augenmerk gelegt.
Den meisten Raum innerhalb des Komplexes benötigten die festangestellten Mitarbeiter: Musiker, Techniker, Sänger. Bei den Berechnungen war man von 800 bis 1000 Mitarbeitern pro Tag ausgegangen. Das ursprüngliche Konzept hatte auch einen eventuellen Zusammenschluß mit dem Konservatorium in Betracht gezogen, aber dieser Ausbildungszweig wurde letztendlich von der Oper abgekoppelt und fand seinen Platz im Parc de la Villette. Nach einigem Suchen fiel die Wahl auf die Place de la Bastille als geeignetes Gelände für die neue Oper. Auf diesem historischen Platz war zur Feier des 200. Jahrestages der französischen Revolution eine große Weltausstellung geplant, deren Eröffnung am 14.7.1989 zeitgleich mit der offiziellen Einweihung der Opéra Bastille stattfinden sollte. Dadurch wäre die Oper zu einem Monument des Sozialismus geworden. Zwar ließ sich die Idee der Weltausstellung nicht umsetzen, aber die Eröffnung der Oper fand im Rahmen der Feierlichkeiten zum »Bicentenaire« statt.

Ein unbekannter Gewinner

Die Jury sichtete 787 Beiträge, von denen sie 31 sofort disqualifizierte. Die Beurteilung erfolgte in drei Wettbewerbsrunden. In der ersten Runde wurden die Entwürfe ausgewählt, die mindestens vier Stimmen erhalten hatten. Dabei beklagte die Jury die geringe Qualität der Beiträge, die dazu führte, daß sie nur mit Mühe sechs Teilnehmer für die letzte Runde fand. Es ist bezeichnend für den Wettbewerb, daß der spätere Gewinner des zweiten Preises, das Team von Dan Monteanu, eigentlich schon ausgeschieden war und nur mangels Alternativen in die letzte Runde kam.
Einige Jury-Mitglieder glaubten, in einem der anonym eingesandten Beiträge Zeichnungen von Richard Meier zu erkennen. In der Hoffnung, diesen berühmten Architekten für das Projekt zu gewinnen, erhielt der Entwurf den ersten Preis. Es stellte sich jedoch heraus, daß man Carlos Ott, einen Architekten kanadisch-uruguayischer Abstammung, der in Toronto ein großes und angesehenes Architekturbüro leitete, ausgezeichnet hatte. Die Kritiker zeigten sich zunächst nicht allzu begeistert, denn Ott war weder berühmt noch Franzose.

Der Entwurf

Das größte Problem für den Architekten bildete die Aufteilung der Räume: Einerseits sollten sich die Benutzer der Oper nicht gegenseitig behindern, andererseits machte eine effiziente Auslastung der Säle eine komplexe Funktionsverteilung erforderlich. Den Kern der Oper bildet daher der Theaterturm mit dem Großen Saal. Dieser Saal befindet sich in einem halbrunden Gebäudeteil, wo auch der Kassen, die Foyers und die Bars untergebracht sind. Hinter der Bühne befindet sich eine drehbare Plattform, deren umliegende Räume als Lagerräume dienen. Unter dem Auditorium entstand ein Amphitheater mit 500 Plätzen.
An der Rue de Lyon liegt ein weiterer halbrunder Gebäudeteil, der den flexiblen Saal enthält. Auf der anderen Seite, zur Rue de Charenton hinaus, ist der dritte Schwerpunkt des Komplexes, der große Übungssaal, angesiedelt. Ott achtete besonders auf genügend Raum für den Transport von Dekorationen zwischen diesen drei Bereichen: Bühnenbilder, Requisiten und Kostüme kommen aus den Werkstätten an der Rue de Lyon. Darüber hinaus schuf Ott noch einen Studiosaal mit 280 Plätzen, der ursprünglich nicht vorgesehen war.
Eines der Gebäude, das der neuen Oper weichen mußte, war das Restaurant »La Tour d'Argent«. Es lag im einzigen Haus an der Place de la Bastille aus vorrevolutionärer Zeit. Das Haus wurde in der Nähe seines ursprünglichen Platzes wieder aufgebaut, das Restaurant zum Theaterrestaurant umfunktioniert. Die über der Gaststätte liegenden Stockwerke nutzte Ott für seinen Studiosaal. An der Rue de Lyon entstand ein weiteres Restaurant, das durch einen Patio vom großen Theatersaal getrennt wurde. Mit der dreieckigen Grundform löste Ott das Problem des spitzzulaufenden Baugeländes. Alle Plätze im Großen Saal bieten eine hervorragende Sicht auf die Bühne – eine deutliche Verbesserung im Vergleich zu Garniers Opéra. Auch wurde die Zugänglichkeit der Oper erleichtert: Außer durch den Haupteingang können die Besucher durch die Metrostation auf unterirdischem Wege direkt hineingelangen.
Der Haupteingang wird gekennzeichnet durch ein freistehendes Portal aus Lanhelin-Granit, dessen doppelte Kurve als Verbindungspunkt zwischen dem Platz und dem halbrunden Operngebäude dient. Ebenso wie der eigentliche Eingang und die anderen Fassadenelemente ist das Portal viereckig. Ott verwendete als Basiseinheit ein Modul von 90 x 90 cm. Die durchsichtigen Fassadenelemente bieten aus den Bars und Foyers eine großartige Aussicht. Diese äußere Hülle ist auch für Besucher geöffnet, wenn keine Vorstellungen stattfinden.
Ott beließ sein Gebäude nahezu ohne jede Dekoration. Einziges Luxus – die Verwendung von Materialien wie Lanhelin-Granit, leichtem Valreuil-Kalkstein, graublauem Brecciamarmor, edlen Hölzern und natürlichem Glas.

Eine effiziente Opernfabrik

Die Opéra Bastille erfüllt alle Voraussetzungen, um ein qualitativ hochstehendes, vielfältiges und gleichzeitig experimentelles Programm bieten zu können. Die Einrichtungen für die Theatermacher und die Akustik der Säle sind auf dem neuesten Stand. Auch die Zahlen sprechen für sich: 250 Vorstellungen im Großen Saal, 120 im »Salle Modulable« bei jährlich 775 000 Besuchern. Nicht enthalten in dieser Zahl sind die Zuschauer der Konzerte im Studiosaal, des Amphitheaters unter dem Großen Saal sowie die Besucher der Restaurants, Bars, Cafés und Geschäfte. Dennoch fehlt der Opéra Bastille etwas, über das Garniers Opéra im Überfluß verfügte: Grandeur. Allerdings trifft dieser Vorwurf nur zum Teil Ott, da die in der Ausschreibung als Baugelände vorgesehene Place de la Bastille auch unter städtebaulichen Aspekten nicht unbedingt der geeignete Ort für Frankreichs größten Musiktempel ist.

L'Opéra Bastille, Paris

Napoléon III avait deux objectifs en tête lorsqu'il décida de construire un nouvel opéra dans les années 1850. Il souhaitait laisser à la capitale une prestigieuse trace de son règne et offrir aux classes dirigeantes de l'époque un lieu où elles pourraient écouter des opéras et se retrouver entre elles. L'Opéra Bastille avait pour but, quant à lui, d'offrir au plus grand nombre possible de spectateurs la possibilité d'assister à des spectacles de qualité dans les meilleures conditions. Mais il devait également témoigner de la capacité du nouveau pouvoir socialiste, féru de culture, à résoudre le problème de la construction d'un nouvel opéra posé depuis des décennies, celui de Garnier étant obsolète.

Un opéra pour le grand public

L'opéra de Garnier[1] était resté en grande partie réservé à une certaine élite sociale. 400 des 1900 sièges offraient une mauvaise visibilité, et les interprètes ne disposaient d'aucune salle de répétition. En un siècle, l'approche de l'opéra avait profondément changé. Le grand public s'intéressait de plus en plus à cette forme d'expression artistique et l'Etat souhaitait lui donner accès à des spectacles de qualité, faire connaître un répertoire plus moderne et tout cela à des prix de places accessibles.
Le 9 mars 1982, le gouvernement, conseillé par Jean Vilar et Pierre Boulez, approuva le projet de construction d'un nouvel opéra. Dans un rapport publié six ans plus tôt, François Bloch-Lainé, futur président du jury du concours, avait pu écrire: *«Le Palais Garnier accumule toutes les défauts nécessaires pour assurer le moins de démocratie possible au prix le plus élevé possible, monter les plus splendides productions pour les plus faibles audiences.»*
Un autre facteur joua également dans la décision du gouvernement: l'ambition française de retrouver un rôle important dans le monde musical international. Par ailleurs, la possibilité de donner davantage de spectacles pour un public plus large devait permettre d'abaisser les coûts de fonctionnement de la nouvelle salle. Pour cela, il fallait prévoir toute une organisation permettant l'alternance des spectacles et donc une concentration des équipements techniques en un même lieu. Un groupe d'étude, la Mission Opéra Bastille, fut constitué pour préparer le projet et conclut qu'il fallait construire un nouvel opéra de 3 000 places, de préférence au centre de Paris.

Un plan de masse-programme

Le programme du concours, publié en novembre 1982, contenait un plan de masse sur lequel les équipements les plus importants étaient indiqués, dont des salles de répétition et des ateliers pour la production des décors et des costumes. La grande salle devait contenir entre 2 700 et 3000 personnes et une salle plus petite, «modulable», de 600 à 1000 personnes, selon sa configuration et la nature du spectacle. Elle serait réservée à des productions expérimentales et devait pouvoir être transformée en fonction des besoins des metteurs en scène. Une attention particulière serait portée aux équipements techniques pour faciliter l'alternance des spectacles.
Le plus grand de la surface était réservé aux personnels permanents et temporaires: musiciens, chanteurs, techniciens, etc. On estimait que 800 à 1000 personnes travailleraient chaque jour dans les locaux. On imagina même un moment une fusion avec la Cité de la Musique qui s'installa plus tard à la Villette.
Après de longues délibérations, la commission décida que la place de la Bastille était le site idéal. A cette époque, on espérait encore organiser une Exposition Universelle à Paris à l'occasion du Bicentenaire de la Révolution et l'inauguration conjointe de l'Opéra Bastille aurait constitué un événement supplémentaire. L'Exposition fut annulée mais l'inauguration du nouvel Opéra consitua l'un des temps forts de ces festivités.

Un vainqueur masqué

Le jury ne reçut pas moins de 787 projets dont 31 furent disqualifiés immédiatement. La sélection se déroula en trois temps. Les propositions du premier tour, qui avaient été retenues par au moins quatre jurés, pouvaient participer au second tour. Le jury fut déçu par la qualité des projets en général mais, après de longues délibérations, sélectionna quatre envois pour le tour final. Dan Montéanu et son équipe qui allaient remporter le second prix furent éliminés puis repêchés au dernier moment.
L'histoire court que quelques membres du jury crurent reconnaître la main de Richard Meier dans l'un des projets anonymes et qu'ils lui auraient attribué le premier prix pour cette raison. Il s'agissait en fait de celui de Carlos Ott, un canadien-uruguayen peu connu qui dirigeait néanmoins un cabinet florissant à Toronto. Les critiques ne furent guère enthousiastes au départ d'autant plus que Ott n'était ni célèbre ni même français. Mais il avait eu le talent de réussir à intégrer les multiples contraintes du programme.

Le plan

Le principal problème résidait dans l'implantation des équipements. D'un côté il était stipulé que les activités des différentes équipes ne devaient pas empiéter les unes sur les autres mais, d'un autre côté, la répartition des équipements ne devait pas faire obstacle à l'efficacité. La salle principale est située au cœur de l'opéra et fait partie d'un bloc semi-cylindrique qui contient également entre autres la billetterie, les foyers et les bars. Une plate-forme tournante aménagée derrière la scène est entourée de cinq espaces de dégagement pour les décors. Ott lui-même proposa d'installer un amphithéâtre supplémentaire de 500 places sous la grande salle.
Un autre bloc semi-cylindrique sur la rue de Lyon devait contenir la salle modulable. Le troisième grand pôle, la grande salle de répétitions, est situé à l'opposé, sur la rue de Charenton. Ott prit également en compte les transports des décors d'une scène à l'autre. Décors, praticables et costumes sont stockés dans la zone de l'atelier qui prolonge le bâtiment principal sur la rue de Lyon. Un studio (salle de 280 places) non prévu dans le programme a pu être créé grâce à une opportunité inattendue: l'un des immeubles du XVIIIème siècle, qui entourait la place de la Bastille et gênait le développement de la façade de l'opéra, était occupé par un restaurant qui s'appelait alors La Tour d'Argent. Pour «préserver» ce témoin du passé, il fut décidé de le démolir et de le reconstruire pratiquement au même endroit et de l'intégrer à l'opéra. Le restaurant se réinstalla et le studio de l'opéra fut aménagé dans le volume restant. Un second restaurant, séparé de la grande salle par une cour, a été implanté rue de Lyon, au pied d'une aile de bureaux assurant la continuité rectilinéaire de la façade sur la rue de Lyon.
Toutes les places de la grande salle disposent d'une excellente vue de la scène, bien que parfois un peu trop en plongée, à la différence du Metropolitan Opera de New York qui est d'une capacité similaire. Pour les spectateurs, le progrès est néanmoins considérable par rapport à l'opéra Garnier. Comme son ancêtre, le nouvel opéra est accessible par métro, mais plus directement encore, et dispose de parkings souterrains.
L'entrée principale est marquée par un imposant portique de granit noir, dont la double-arche fait le lien entre la façade semi-circulaire et la forme de la place de la Bastille. Son ouverture est carrée comme tous les éléments apparents de la façade montée sur une trame carrée de 90 cm de côté. A l'entracte, les spectateurs peuvent profiter d'une vue magnifique sur Paris à partir des foyers et des bars et pendant la journée, les touristes ont accès à la partie extérieure du bâtiment.
L'opéra de Ott ne comporte pratiquement aucun ornement, à la différence de celui de Garnier, mais les coûteux matériaux utilisés forment en eux-mêmes un décor: granit de Lanhelin, pierre calcaire de Valreuil, marbre gris bleu de Breccia, plusieurs essences de bois et bien sûr énormément de verre. Ott a cherché à trouver un juste milieu entre un lieu de spectacle ouvert au grand public et un énorme équipement technique de plus de 150 000 mètres carrés, à créer un équilibre entre l'efficacité et la magie du spectacle.

Une efficace usine à opéra

Pour l'essentiel, le projet de Ott a répondu aux attentes, malgré quelques difficultés dues à la sophistication des techniques. L'Opéra Bastille offre toutes les facilités pour assurer une programmation de haut niveau. Les équipements théâtraux d'avant-garde et l'acoustique excellente n'ont rien laissé au hasard.
Les chiffres sont impressionnants: 250 représentations ont lieu chaque année dans la grande salle pour 750 000 spectateurs, sans compter les concerts, la programmation du studio et de l'amphithéâtre, les visiteurs, les clients des restaurants, des bars, des cafés, de la boutique. Par comparaison, l'Opéra Garnier ne donnait que 110 représentations annuelles en privilégiant les abonnés. L'Opéra Bastille n'est évidemment pas encore chargé du même prestige historique que Garnier, mais les Parisiens l'ont dans l'ensemble adopté. Les nouveaux aménagements de la place de la Bastille permettent enfin de mieux l'inscrire dans ce site marqué par l'histoire même s'il n'évoque en rien les fastes d'une époque, comme avaient su si bien le faire Garnier et Haussmann au service de Napoléon III.

1 Voir le chapitre sur l'Opéra de Paris.

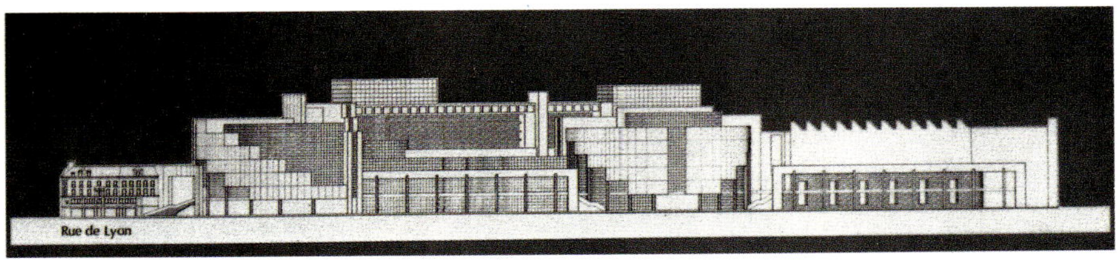

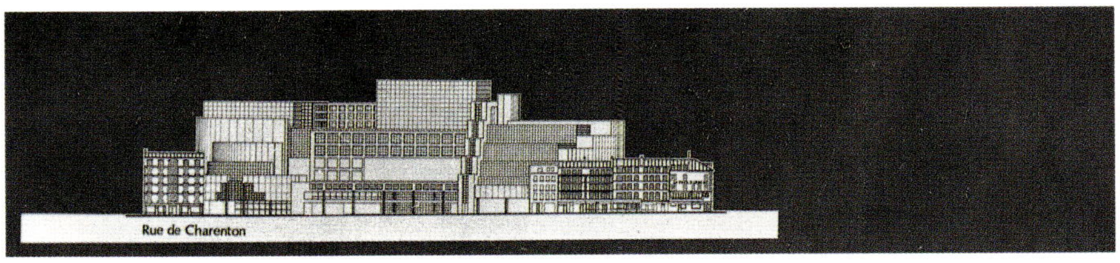

Carlos Ott competition design, 1983, elevation on Rue de Lyon, first prize

Carlos Ott competition design, 1983, elevation on Rue de Charenton, first prize

Carlos Ott competition design, 1983, site model, first prize

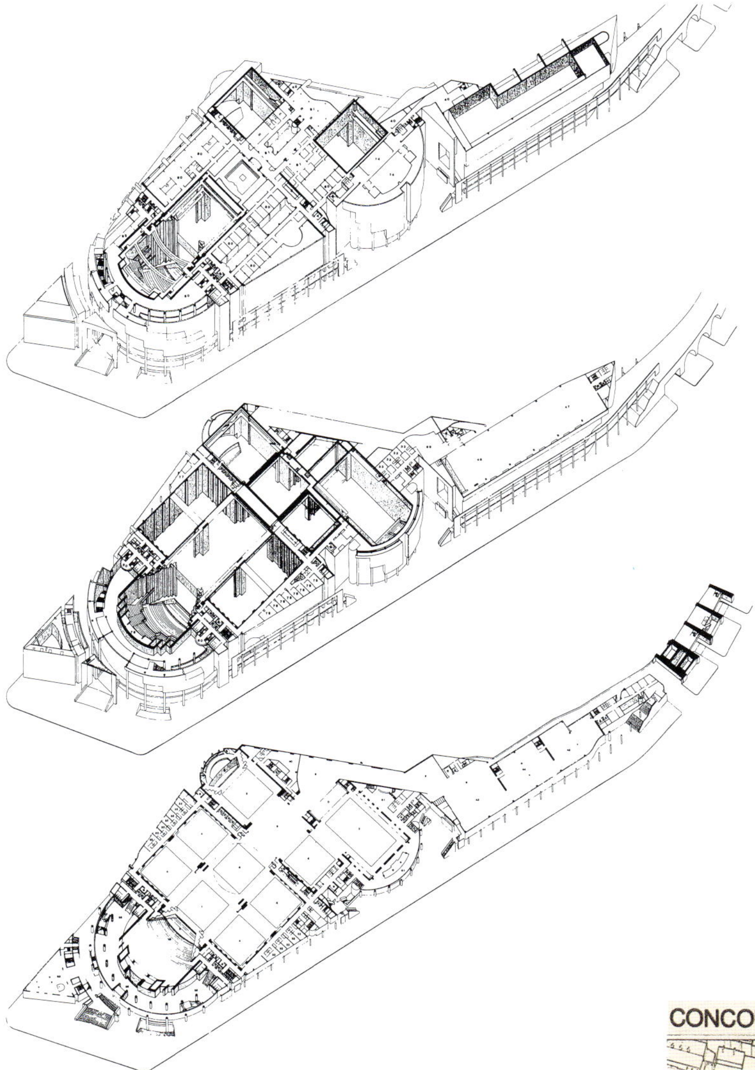

Carlos Ott competition design, 1983, axonometric projection, first prize

Rocco S.K. Yim competition design, 1983, axonometric projection, second prize

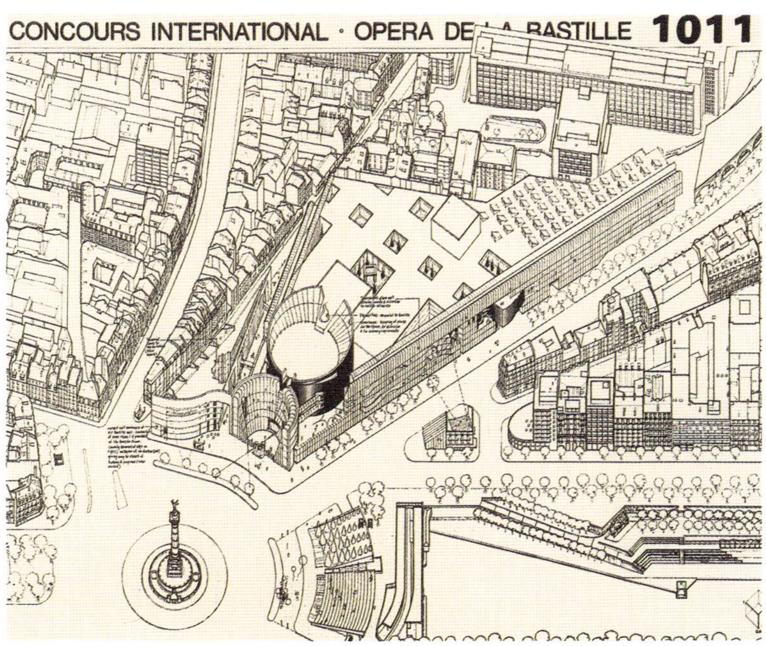

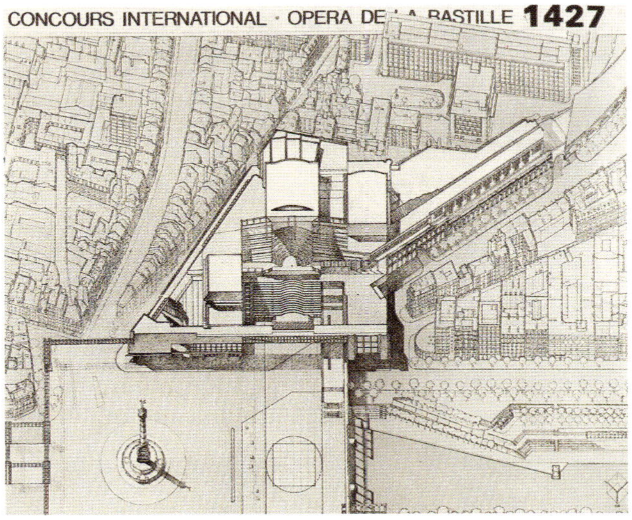

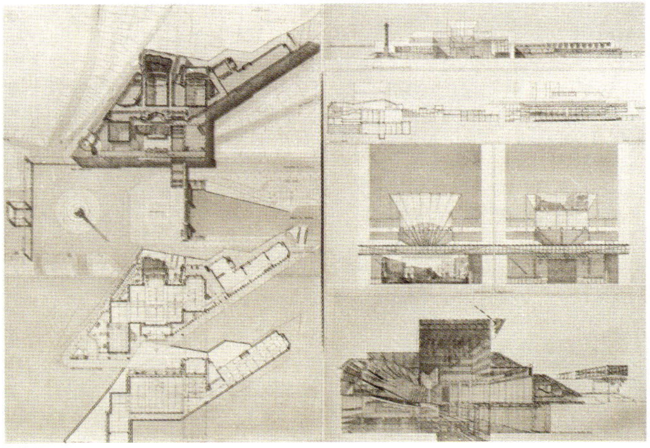

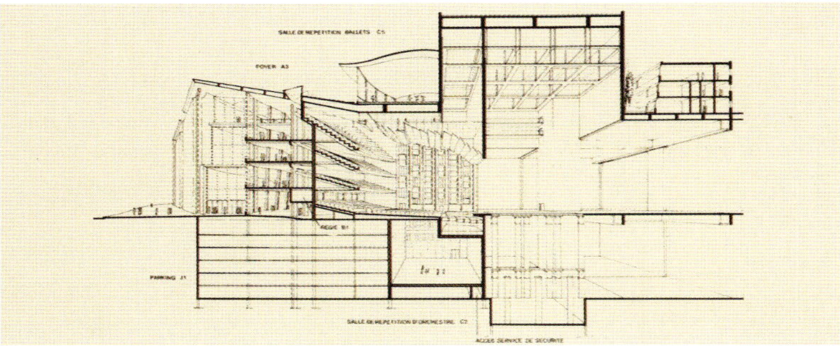

Dan Monteanu, Odile Hamburger, Teodor Georgesco, Alice & Teodor Tufan competition design, 1983, left: plans, from above right: elevation on Place de la Bastille, section, views of the Gate, sectional view through the theatre, third prize, first round winner

Christian de Portzamparc competition design, 1983, above: elevation on Rue de Lyon, below: sectional view through the theatre, first round winner

Christian de Portzamparc competition design, 1983, exterior view on Place de la Bastille, first round winner

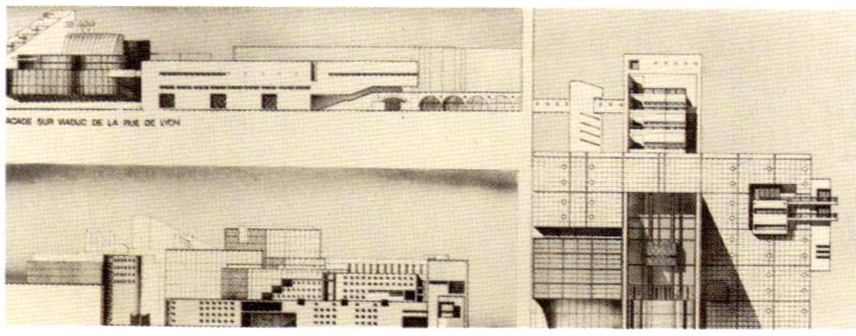

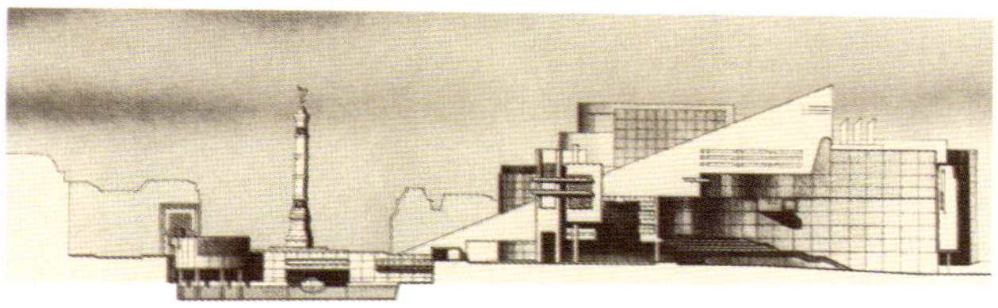

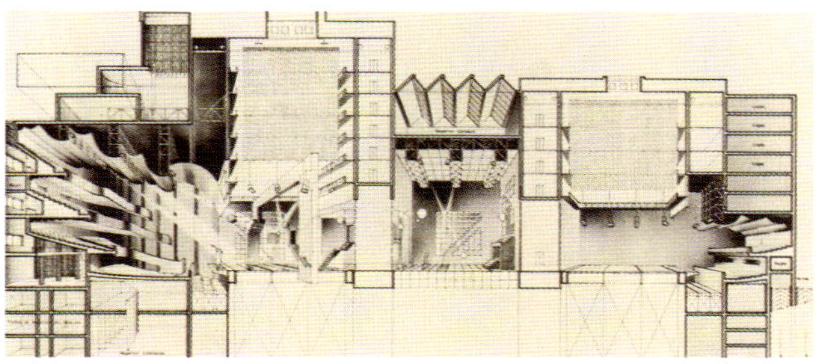

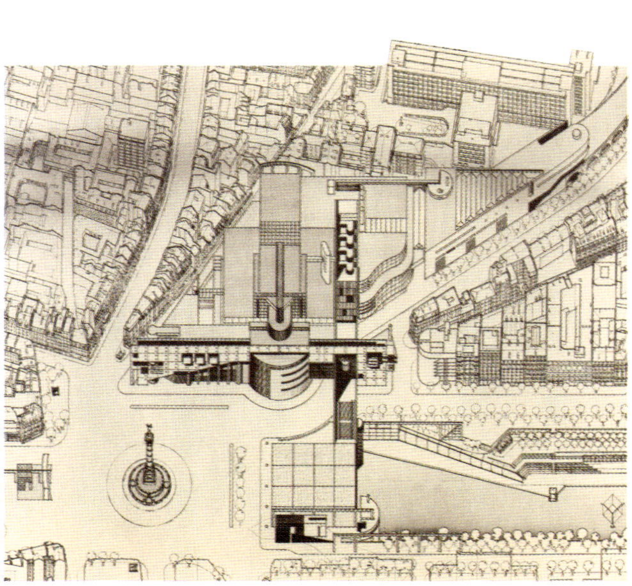

Jean-Paul Viguier & Jean-François Jodry competition design

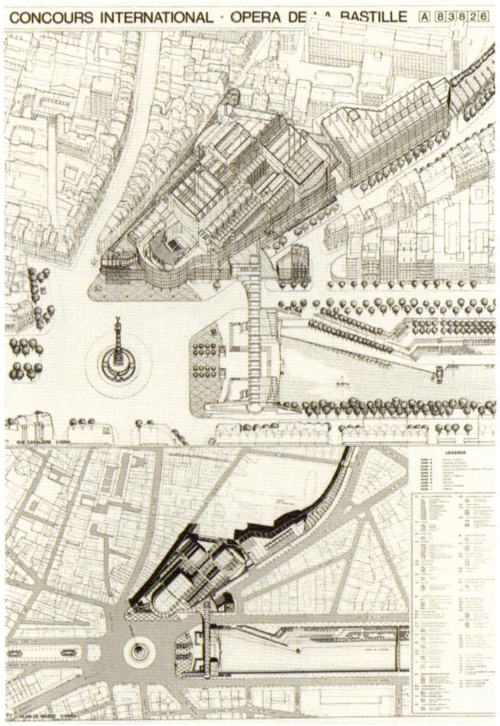
CONCOURS INTERNATIONAL · OPERA DE
BASTILLE
A 83826

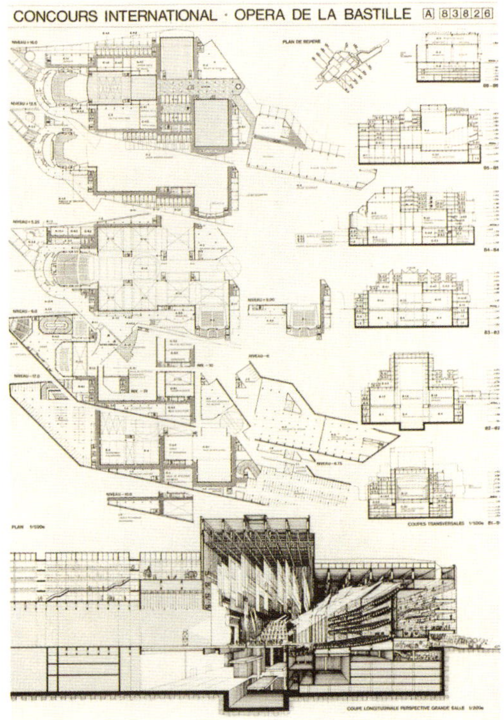
CONCOURS INTERNATIONAL · OPERA DE LA BASTILLE
A 83826

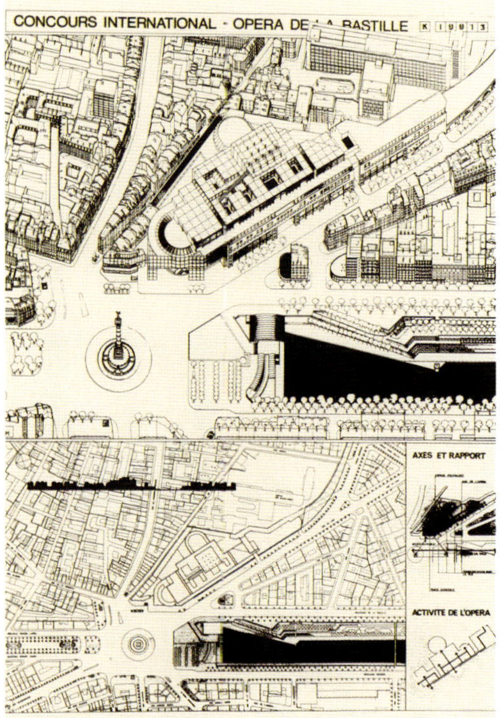
CONCOURS INTERNATIONAL · OPERA DE
BASTILLE
K 19913
AXES ET RAPPORT
ACTIVITE DE L'OPERA

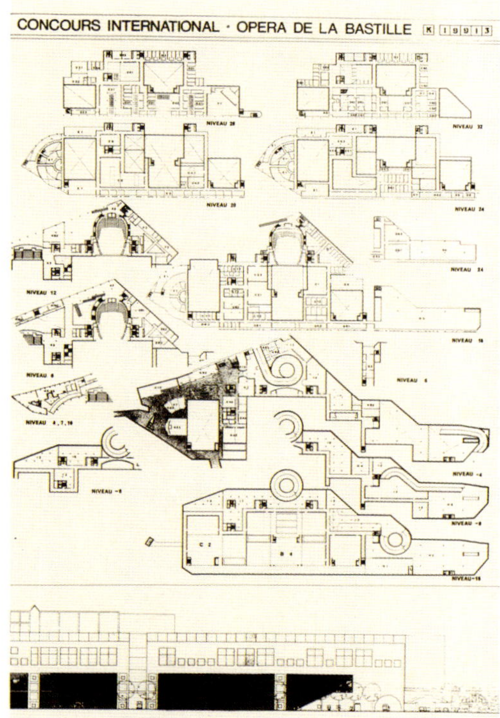
CONCOURS INTERNATIONAL · OPERA DE LA BASTILLE
K 19913

Kajima Corporation competition design, 1983, above: axonometric projection, below: site plan, honourable mention

Kenji Fukuzawa & Akira Komiyama competition design, 1983, above: axonometric projection, site plan, honourable mention

Kajima Corporation competition design, 1983, from top: plans, sections, sectional view through the theatre, honourable mention

Kenji Fukuzawa & Akira Komiyama competition design, 1983, from top: plans, elevation, honourable mention

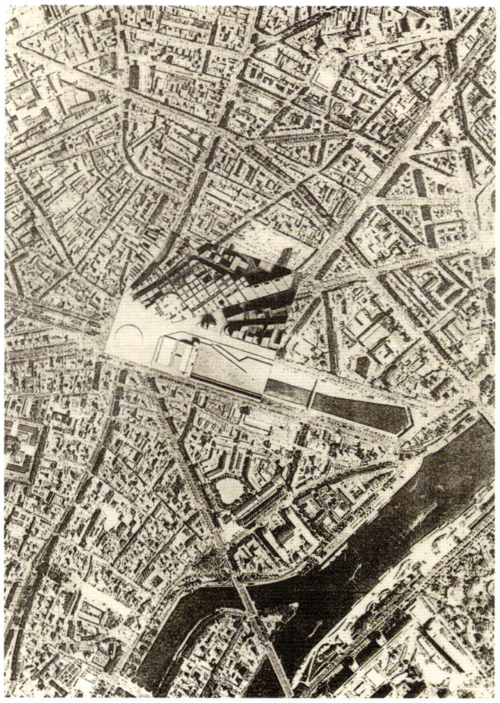

George Ranalli competition design, 1983, photomontage

George Ranalli competition design, 1983, photomontage

George Ranalli competition design, 1983, site model

Project

Luxury apartments and clubhouse

Site

Mount Austin Road, near the top of Victoria Peak, Hong Kong

Dates

Competition announced June 1982 *Closing date* 1 November 1982 *Result announced* March 1983

Number of entries

539

Jury

John Andrews (chairman, architect), Arata Isozaki, Gabriel Formoso (architects), Ronald Poon (director of the Hong Kong Institute of Architects), Alfred Siu (OLS Property Development Ltd.)

Result

First prize Zaha M. Hadid *Second prize* Barrington Charles Marshall *Third prize* Edmund Baylon Burke; John S. Hagmann & David Hannaford Mitchell

Commissioned by

OLS Property Development Ltd.

Construction

Never built

The Peak, Hong Kong, 1982–1983

Zaha M. Hadid presentation design, 1982, exploded isometric projection

The Peak, Hong Kong

Zaha Hadid became world-famous virtually overnight upon winning the competition for The Peak. Her unique drawings were a milestone in the history of the nascent Deconstructivist movement, a movement which only received full recognition and the attention it deserved in 1988, with exhibitions in London and New York.

Zaha Hadid and Deconstructivism

The Iraqi architect Zaha Hadid was just 32 years old when she won the competition for The Peak. At that time the greater part of her œuvre existed only on paper. It was hardly surprising therefore that many people doubted the feasibility of her "suspended" creations. Their doubts were probably born out of ignorance, because Hadid is an exceptionally talented mathematician whose ambition to become an architect developed at the tender age of eleven. Furthermore, she obtains structural advice for her designs from the renowned engineering firm Ove Arup & Partners.
However, such doubts are understandable, considering the fact that no architect had ever won a competition with designs which deviated so radically from the norm. Hadid's designs were even more extreme than those submitted by the Archigram group for the Entertainment Centre in Monte Carlo[1]. An interesting historical detail is that the Archigram architect Peter Cook also took part in the competition for The Peak. Hadid graduated from the London Academy of Architecture (AA), which was the most progressive architectural institute in the world at that time. She was tutored by Bernard Tschumi, Rem Koolhaas and Elia Zenghelis. During his period at the Academy, Tschumi, who was then one of the leading architectural theoreticians, spent most of his time writing. His design for the Parc de la Villette was the first Deconstructivist design ever executed. This design was based on a grid system which he had developed according to literary-philosophical principles – hence his references to this project as "Joyce's garden". Koolhaas continued to encourage Hadid after her graduation from the Academy[2]. She was employed by Koolhaas' bureau, OMA, for six months. The Dutch architect also introduced her to the Russian Constructivism of Ivan Leonidov and she later developed an affinity for the Suprematism of Kasimir Malevich. She based one of her Academy projects on his work, and her later designs, which feature "suspended" geometric figures, resemble Suprematist compositions.

An abstract painting

In contrast to literary Deconstructivists, such as Tschumi and Eisenman, Hadid's work has not been influenced by the philosophy of Jacques Derrida. However, her designs are clearly Deconstructivist, because they feature a characteristic blend of architecture and fine art. A Deconstructivist design may be interpreted as a precisely dissected piece of architecture or as an abstract painting. Each architect is inspired by a different period or movement in modern art. Deconstructivism rejects existing architectural dogmas, turns them

View from Victoria Peak

Zaha M. Hadid

Zaha M. Hadid exterior view

upside-down and tries to redefine the norms.
Until recently, the movement had made little headway, probably on account of the unusual Deconstructivist design technique. Tschumi's commission for the Parc de la Villette presented one of the first opportunities to put Deconstructivist principles into practice. During that same period Eisenman and Jacquelin Robertson won the competition for Block 5 (Kochstrasse) of the International Building Exhibition[3] in Berlin, and Hadid won the competition for The Peak.

An elite club

Victoria Peak or Che Kei Shan is one of the most beautiful places in Hong Kong. It is high and rocky, and offers a magnificent view of the bay. However, due to its inaccessibility, the peak had been neglected for many years. The site was owned by OLS Property Development, a family business headed by Alfred Siu.
In June 1982, Alfred Siu organised an open, international competition for The Peak. The participants were asked to submit designs for a club, forty guest apartments with studios, and a residence for the Siu family. Amongst other facilities, the club was to have a swimming pool, squash courts, restaurant, bar and library. Whilst the club would serve primarily as a recreational facility for the company's business partners, it would also be a home for the Siu family where they could conduct business in a relaxed atmosphere. One of the most important conditions was that the "Feng-shui", the spirits of good and evil, should not be disturbed[4].
Alfred Siu had a seat on the jury, along with three renowned architects and a local dignitary. The architects were John Andrews, Arata Isozaki and Gabriel Formoso, who replaced Richard Meier. The fifth member of the jury was Ronald Poon, chairman of the Hong Kong Institute of Architects. The prize money for the competition was no less than $ 300 000, which possibly accounts for the fact that 539 architects submitted designs. In order to whittle the field down, the jury asked a number of the company's technical advisors, including Ove Arup, to make a preliminary selection, which resulted in the elimination of four hundred designs.
However, the jury were not satisfied with this preliminary selection and they decided to review the eliminated designs. Surprisingly, Arata Isozaki nominated one of these, the design submitted by Zaha Hadid, for first prize. Most of the jury members rejected Isozaki's selection and nominated a different winner. The only member of the jury who supported Isozaki's selection was Alfred Siu. Zaha Hadid won the competition.

A Suprematist composition

Hadid started by changing the face of the landscape. A section of the peak would be excavated and the uncovered mass of granite would be polished on the spot and incorporated into the design. The main structural elements of Hadid's design are four "beams", stacked on top of one another at slightly different angles.

Zaha M. Hadid isometric projection of apartments, exterior view of penthouse, view from library

Between the second and third beams there is an open space, which is about thirteen metres high and contains various club facilities. The lower beam is partly underground and contains fifteen two-storey studio-apartments, linked by a passage on the ground floor and by a balcony on the upper floor. The second beam rests on the lower beam and contains twenty, two-storey apartments. Most of the club facilities are situated on the roof of this beam.
The overhanging third beam is supported by pillars from which platforms have been suspended. These platforms form part of the club facilities, and contain fitness areas, the bar, the library and other facilities. The swimming pool is situated on the club "floor". The other club facilities, such as the sauna, the restaurant and the squash courts, are situated in areas which have been partially hewn out of the granite of the mountainside. The third and fourth beams contain additional apartments, including those for the Siu family, and other creature comforts, such as a private pool.

Like so many of Hadid's other projects, her design for The Peak was shelved indefinitely. It is therefore impossible to compare theory and practice, which is a pity, because Hadid's designs are particularly intriguing, even though they appear to be unfeasible. Elements seem to float through infinite space, the basic elements of the structure have been laid bare and, at first glance, it looks as though the architecture is subordinate to her mathematical Suprematist composition. Her work is also reminiscent of the Futurism of such architects as Umberto

Rem Koolhaas (OMA competition design Dutch House of Parliament

Bernard Tschumi Joyce's Garden\

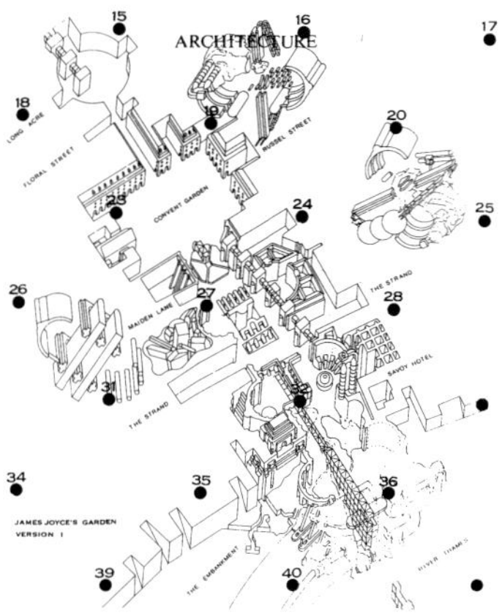

Boccioni. Her drawings sometimes contain elements resembling snow storms or explosions. In one of her other drawings the building's beams seem to have swooped down and collided with the mountain. Her designs are tremendously dynamic, and it always takes some time to figure them out.

However, she always includes "normal" drawings, such as floor plans and cross sections to clarify her intentions. Her designs have been executed on a number of occasions, proving that they are indeed feasible and may be converted into a tangible form. She will undoubtedly provide further evidence to this effect in the future, in spite of the fact that the project for The Peak was cancelled.

Other contenders

The design favoured by the other jury members was submitted by Barrington Charles Marshall. His design featured a rather gloomy complex, shut off from the outside world, where most of the facilities were grouped on the roof, out of sight. It was therefore in stark contrast with the open character of Hadid's club. The joint third-prize winners had submitted somewhat vague, Modernist designs, not unlike Marshall's, and although these designs were not undeserving of nomination, they were probably not spectacular enough to impress the Siu family's guests.

Nevertheless, there were a number of other outstanding designs besides Hadid's. The sacral cylinders, for example, submitted by Akira Kuryu's team, which were probably considered a little too bombastic for a clubhouse. And, of course, there was the design submitted by the Archigram architect Peter Cook and his wife Christine Hawley. However, their design seemed almost respectable and mundane in comparison to Hadid's, in spite of the significant contribution that Archigram had made to postwar, avant-garde architecture.

1 *See chapter on the Monte Carlo Entertainment Centre elsewhere in this book.*

2 *Hadid was also a lecturer at the Academy for some time.*

3 *See chapter on the International Building Exhibition elsewhere in this book.*

4 *For more information about the "Feng-shui" see chapter on the Hongkong and Shanghai Bank elsewhere in this book.*

The Peak, Hongkong

Durch den Gewinn des Architekturwettbewerbs für The Peak wurde Zaha Hadid bekannt. Ihre einzigartigen Zeichnungen bedeuteten einen Meilenstein in der noch jungen Geschichte des Dekonstruktivismus, einer Strömung, die erst ab 1988 durch Ausstellungen in London und New York in den Blickpunkt der Öffentlichkeit trat.

Hadid und der Dekonstruktivismus

Die Irakerin Zaha Hadid war erst 32 Jahre alt, als sie den Wettbewerb für The Peak gewann. Ihr Oeuvre hatte bis zu diesem Augenblick vornehmlich aus Arbeiten auf Papier bestanden. Folglich äußersten einige Kritiker Zweifel an ihren schwebenden Konstruktionen. Doch Hadid, die seit ihrem elften Lebensjahr Architektin werden wollte, verfügt über ein ausgeprägtes mathematisches Talent. Bei der Realisierung ihrer Entwürfe läßt sie sich vom Ingenierbüro Ove Arup & Partners beraten. Hadid erhielt ihre Ausbildung an der Londoner Academy of Architecture (AA), die zu den progressivsten Lehrinstituten der Baukunst zählt. Zu ihren Dozenten gehörten Bernard Tschumi, Rem Koolhaas und Elia Zenghelis. Tschumi galt zu dieser Zeit als einer der bedeutendsten theoretischen Architekten der Welt. An der Academy of Architecture widmete er sich vorwiegend dem Verfassen von Aufsätzen und kam erst durch seine Arbeiten am Parc de la Villette zur Realisierung dekonstruktivistischer Bauwerke. Tschumis Entwürfe für den Park entstanden nach einem Rastermuster, das er selbst nach literarisch-philosophischen Prinzipien entwickelt hatte. Er nannte das Projekt »Joyce's Garden«.
Nach dem Studium arbeitete Hadid sechs Monate lang für Koolhaas' Büro O.M.A. Durch ihn kam sie in Kontakt mit dem russischen Konstruktivismus von Iwan Leonidow und wandte sich später mehr dem Suprematismus Kasimir Malewitschs zu. Malewitschs Arbeiten bildeten die Grundlage eines ihrer Projekte für die AA in London, und ihre späteren Entwürfe aus »schwebenden« geometrischen Figuren.

Ein abstraktes Gemälde

Im Gegensatz zu Tschumi und Peter Eisenman, den beiden literarischen Dekonstruktivisten, ist Zaha Hadid nicht durch die Philosophie Jacques Derridas beeinflußt. Ihre Gemeinsamkeit mit den übrigen Dekonstruktivisten liegt in der charakteristischen Entwurfsmethode, die eine Gratwanderung zwischen Bau- und bildender Kunst darstellt. Ein dekonstruktivistisches Projekt läßt sich sowohl als ein bis ins letzte Detail zergliedertes Bauwerk auffassen wie auch als ein abstraktes Gemälde, wobei sich jeder Architekt durch eine andere Periode der modernen Kunst inspirieren läßt. Der Dekonstruktivismus löst sich bewußt von den Selbstverständlichkeiten der Baukunst, stellt sie in Frage und versucht, zu einer neuen Definition von Normen zu gelangen.
Mit diesem Ansatz verbindet sich auch ein eigenwilliger Zeichenstil, der den Dekonstruktivisten bis vor einigen Jahren Ablehnung einbrachte. Der von Tschumi entworfene Parc de la Villette war eines der ersten realisierten dekonstruktivistischen Bauwerke, bei dem die Theorie in der Praxis überprüft werden konnte. Zur gleichen Zeit gewannen Eisenman und Jacquelin Robertson bei der Internationalen Bauausstellung in Berlin die Ausschreibung für die Gestaltung von Block 5 an der Kochstraße (siehe das Kapitel zur IBA, Berlin) und Hadid den Wettbewerb für The Peak.

Ein kultivierter Club

Der Victoria Peak, Che Kei Shan, felsig und hoch über der Stadt gelegen, gehört mit seiner herrlichen Aussicht über die Bucht von Kowloon zu den schönsten Gebieten Hongkongs. Eigentümer war die Firma OLS Property Development, geführt von der Familie Siu, an deren Spitze Alfred Siu stand. Siu schrieb im Juni 1982 einen offenen internationalen Architektenwettbewerb aus.
Die Teilnehmer mußten einen Entwurf einreichen für einen Club, 40 Appartements und Studios für Gäste sowie für eine Residenz der Familie Siu. Der Club selbst sollte mit einem Schwimmbad, Squashcourts, Restaurant, Bar, Bibliothek usw. ausgestattet und hauptsächlich den Geschäftsfreunden von OLS zur Verfügung stehen. Weitere Auflage: Das Fengshui, der lokale Aberglaube, durfte nicht gestört werden.
Die Jury sollte sich zusammensetzen aus Alfred Siu, drei berühmten Architekten und einer angesehenen Persönlichkeit Hongkongs. Die Architekten waren John Andrews, Arata Isozaki und – anstelle von Richard Meier – Gabriel Formoso; als fünftes Jurymitglied gewann man Ronald Poon, den Vorsitzenden des Hong Kong Institute of Architects. Angelockt durch das hohe Preisgeld von 300 000 Dollar reichten 539 Architekten ihre Entwürfe ein. Daraufhin bat die Jury die technischen Berater des Wettbewerbs, unter denen sich auch Ove Arup befand, um eine Vorauswahl, der 400 Beiträge zum Opfer fielen.
Da die Jury mit der Vorauswahl nicht zufrieden war, ging sie sämtliche Einsendungen noch einmal durch. Dabei entdeckte Isozaki der bereits ausgeschiedenen Entwürfe den Beitrag von Zaha Hadid und nominierte ihn für den ersten Preis. Die anderen Jurymitglieder schlossen sich dieser Meinung nicht an und benannten einen Gegenkandidaten. Obwohl Isozaki als einziger Architekt der Jury Hadids Entwurf mit dem ersten Preis belohnen wollte, gab es ein Argument, das seiner Stimme besonderes Gewicht verlieh: Alfred Siu teilte Isozakis Ansicht – und Zaha Hadid gewann den Wettbewerb.

Eine suprematistische Komposition

Hadid befürwortete einen einschneidenen Eingriff in die Landschaft: Sie schlug vor, die Bergspitze abzutragen und die darunterliegenden Granitfelsen zu polieren, um sie in den Entwurf einzubeziehen. Der wichtigste Teil ihrer Konstruktion bestand aus vier Balken, die sie in einem leicht veränderten Winkel stapelte.
Zwischen dem zweiten und dritten Balken befindet sich ein offener Raum von etwa 13 Metern Höhe für die verschiedenen Einrichtungen des Clubs. Der unterste Balken liegt zum Teil unter der Erde und beherbergt 15 doppelstöckige Studio-Appartements, die durch einen Gang im Erdgeschoß und einen durchgehenden Balkon auf der ersten Etage miteinander verbunden sind. Direkt darauf ruht der zweite Balken, in dem sich 20 ebenfalls doppelstöckige Appartements befinden. Auf deren Dach liegen die meisten Einrichtungen des Clubs.
Die Pfeiler, auf denen der stark auskragende dritte Balken ruht, werden in die Aktivitäten des Clubs einbezogen: An ihnen hängen verschiedene Plattformen, auf denen sich die Bar, die Bibliothek und die Fitneßräume befinden. Der Platz des Schwimmbads ist das »Erdgeschoß« des Clubs. Dagegen liegen die anderen Räume des Clubs, die Saunen, Restaurants und Squashcourts im wahrsten Sinne des Wortes weiter bergeinwärts: Sie sind in den Granit des Berges hineingehauen. Der dritte und vierte Balken sind wiederum Appartements vorbehalten; dort befindet sich auch die Residenz der Familie Siu, ausgestattet mit einem Privatschwimmbad und weiteren Annehmlichkeiten.
Bedauerlicherweise wurde The Peak, ebenso wie die meisten anderen Arbeiten Hadids, nicht realisiert. Ein Vergleich zwischen der Theorie, die die Phantasie des Betrachters reizt, und der bautechnischen Praxis blieb folglich aus.
Körper schweben durch einen unendlichen Raum; die Konstruktion ist bis auf die Grundelemente zergliedert, so daß die Architektur auf den ersten Blick einer mathematischen, suprematistischen Komposition völlig untergeordnet erscheint. Der Vergleich mit dem Futurismus eines Umberto Boccioni drängt sich auf. Manchmal scheinen Hadids Zeichnungen eine Explosion oder einen Schneesturm darzustellen; ein anderes Mal wirken die Balken von The Peak, als ob sie nach einem Gleitflug gegen die Felsspitze geprallt wären. In sämtlichen Skizzen herrscht Bewegung, in manchen Fällen ist es schwierig, den eigentlichen Entwurf zu erkennen.
Doch es gibt auch »gewöhnliche« Architekturzeichnungen mit Grundrissen und Querschnitten. Die wenigen nach Hadids Entwürfen entstandenen Bauten zeigen, daß sich ihre Zeichnungen durchaus in konkrete Bauformen übertragen lassen.

Die übrigen Entwürfe

Der von der Jury-Mehrheit favorisierte Beitrag stammte von Barrington Charles Marshall. Er hatte einen relativ abweisenden, nach außen geschlossenen Komplex entworfen, bei dem sich die meisten Aktivitäten auf dem Dach des von außen nicht einsehbaren Gebäudes abspielen sollten. Dieser Ansatz stand dem offenen Charakter von Hadids Club diametral entgegen. Ebenso wie Marshall hatten sich auch die beiden Gewinner des dritten Preises für einen vage modernistischen Stil entschieden, der jedoch für die ausgesuchte Kundschaft von OLS Property Development nicht exklusiv genug war.
Neben Hadids Projekt gingen noch weitere extravagante Beiträge ein, wie z.B. die sakralen Zylinder des Teams um Akira Kuryu, die für ein Clubgebäude sicherlich etwas zu bombastisch ausfielen. Auch Peter Cook und seine Frau Christine Hawley reichten einen Entwurf ein. Obwohl beide mit Archigram einen der wichtigsten Beiträge für die avantgardistische Baukunst der Nachkriegszeit geliefert hatten, mutet ihr Projekt im Vergleich zu Hadids Zeichnungen fast brav und bieder an.

The Peak, Hong Kong

Née en 1950, Zaha Hadid parvint brusquement à la célébrité en remportant le concours pour «The Peak». Ses plans et leur style marquent les débuts «officiels» du Déconstructivisme, un mouvement qui n'attira réellement l'attention des médias qu'à partir de 1988 et des expositions qui lui furent consacrées à Londres et à New York.

Zaha Hadid et le Déconstructivisme

L'architecte irakienne Zaha Hadid n'avait que 32 ans lorsqu'elle remporta ce concours. A cette époque, l'essentiel de son œuvre n'existait que sur le papier. La faisabilité de ses créations «suspendues» soulevait d'ailleurs de nombreux doutes tenant sans doute à l'ignorance de la critique, puisque l'architecte est une brillante mathématicienne. Par ailleurs elle se faisait conseiller par la célèbre société d'ingénierie Ove Arup & Partners. Ce manque de confiance peut se comprendre lorsque l'on sait qu'aucun architecte ne remporta jamais de compétition avec des plans aussi éloignés des normes architecturales en vigueur. Ceux de Hadid étaient encore plus extrémistes que les propositions d'Archigram pour le centre de loisirs de Mont-Carlo[1] (Peter Cook, d'Archigram, participa d'ailleurs à la compétition de Hong Kong).

Hadid est diplômée de la London Academy of Architecture (AA) qui était à l'époque une des écoles les plus progressistes du monde. Elle eut pour enseignants Bernard Tschumi, Rem Koolhaas et Elia Zenghelis. Le Parc de la Villette de Tschumi, déjà théoricien reconnu, fut la première œuvre déconstructiviste jamais réalisée. Ses plans reposaient sur une trame inspirée de principes littéraires et philosophiques. Il appelait d'ailleurs son projet: «Le jardin de Joyce».

Koolhaas continua à encourager Hadid après son diplôme[2]. Elle travailla dans son cabinet, O.M.A. pendant six mois et il l'initia au constructivisme russe d'Ivan Leonidov. Plus tard, elle s'intéressa particulièrement au Suprématisme de Malévitch et s'appuya sur son œuvre à l'occasion de l'un de ses projets pour l'Academy. Ses plans ultérieurs, «suspendus», font penser à des compositions suprématistes.

Comme une peinture abstraite

A la différence de celles des déconstructivistes «littéraires» comme Tschumi et Eisenman, les recherches de Hadid n'ont pas été influencées par la philosophie de Jacques Derrida. Ses plans se caractérisent par une fusion étroite entre architecture et création artistique. Un plan déconstructiviste peut être interprété, disséqué, comme un morceau d'architecture ou une peinture abstraite. Chaque architecte s'inspire d'une période différente ou mouvement de l'art moderne. Le Déconstructivisme rejette les dogmes existants, les démonte, les retourne, à la recherche de nouvelles normes. Jusqu'à récemment, le mouvement n'a guère rencontré de succès, ce qui tient peut-être à ses rendus très inhabituels. Après la commande du Parc de la Villette enlevée par Tschumi, Eisenman et Jacquelin Robertson remportèrent cependant le concours du Block 5 (Kochstrasse) de l'IBA à Berlin[3] et Hadid celui de Hong Kong.

Un club pour l'élite

Victoria Peak, ou Che Kei Shan, est l'un des plus beaux sites de Hong Kong. Ce pic élevé et rocailleux qui offre une vue magnifique sur la baie avait été longtemps laissé à l'abandon. Le vaste terrain était la propriété de OLS Property Development, une société familial dirigée par Alfred Siu.

En juin 1982, ce dernier organisa un concours international ouvert pour la construction d'un club, de quarante appartements d'hôtes et d'une résidence personnelle, le tout accompagné d'une piscine, de courts de squash, d'un restaurant, d'un bar et d'une bibliothèque. Lieu de détente pour ses partenaires, le club servirait également de résidence pour la famille Siu d'où elle pourrait mener ses affaires dans une atmosphère détendue. L'une des conditions à respecter était de ne déranger en rien les «Feng-shui», les esprits du bien et du mal[4].

Alfred Siu siégeait au jury, en compagnie de trois grands architectes, John Andrews, Arata Isozaki et Gabriel Formoso (remplaçant Richard Meier) et d'un représentant de l'élite locale. Le cinquième juré était Ronald Poon, président du Hong Kong Institute of Architects. Le prix mis en jeu était de 300 000 $, ce qui explique sans doute la participation empressée de 539 concurrents! Pour alléger sa tâche, le jury demanda à des conseillers techniques de la société, dont Ove Arup, de faire une première sélection qui élimina 400 projets.

Le jury décida cependant de revoir les plans écartés et, à la surprise générale, Arata Isozaki choisit comme vainqueur la proposition de Zaha Hadid. Il ne fut pas suivi par les autres jurés, à l'exception d'un seul, le plus important, Alfred Siu. Zaha Hadid remporta ainsi le concours.

Une composition suprématiste

Hadid avait commencé par modifier le paysage. Elle creusait une section du pic et polissait le granit découvert. La structure de son plan reposait sur quatre «poutres» empilées les unes sur les autres selon divers angles. Entre la seconde et la troisième poutre s'inscrivait un espace ouvert de 13 m de haut contenant divers équipements du club. La poutre inférieure, en partie enterrée, réunissait 15 duplex reliés par un passage au niveau du sol et par un balcon au niveau supérieur. La seconde poutre accueillait vingt appartements en duplex et recevait sur son «toit» la plupart des services et équipements.

La troisième poutre en porte-à-faux était soutenue par des piliers auxquels étaient suspendues des plate-formes faisant partie du club et accueillant, entre autres, une salle de sport, le bar et la bibliothèque. La piscine était située au niveau du club et le sauna, le restaurant et les courts de squash profitaient de l'espace gagné sur la montagne. Les troisième et quatrième poutres contenaient d'autres appartements dont la résidence Siu et divers équipements, comme une piscine privée.

Comme beaucoup des projets de Hadid, la construction du Peak fut indéfiniment retardé. Il est donc malheureusement impossible de comparer la théorie et la réalisation de ces plans qui peuvent paraître, à certains égards, irréalistes. Les éléments semblent flotter dans l'espace et l'architecture se soumettre à un ordre mathématique ou à une composition d'esprit suprématiste. On peut également penser à l'architecture futuriste d'un Boccioni, par exemple, et certains dessins évoquent presque des tempêtes ou des explosions. Dans l'un d'entre eux, les poutres semblent s'être effondrées et être entrées en collision avec la montagne. Ces dessins incroyablement dynamiques ne sont pas toujours très faciles à lire. Hadid joint cependant toujours des plans «normaux» (plans de masse, et coupes) qui éclaircissent ses intentions. Plusieurs réalisations ont d'ailleurs prouvé la faisabilité de ses conceptions.

Les autres concurrents

Le plan apprécié par les autres membres du jury était celui de Barrington Charles Marshall avait proposé un ensemble un peu terne, fermé sur l'extérieur et qui regroupant toute la partie club sur le toit. Il était donc très différent du projet Hadid. Le troisième prix était une proposition assez vague d'esprit moderniste, non sans ressemblance avec celle de Marshall. Mais ces deux projets, non dénués de qualités, n'étaient sans doute pas assez spectaculaires pour impressionner les hôtes de la famille Siu.

D'autres propositions étaient cependant assez remarquables, mêmes comparées à celle de Zaha Hadid. Les cylindres sacrés de l'équipe d'Akira Kuryu, par exemple, furent probablement trouvés un peu trop ampoulés pour un clubhouse. Peter Cook et sa femme, Christine Hawley, proposèrent un projet presque respectable et mondain, loin des contributions provocantes qu'Archigram avait jadis apportées à l'architecture d'avant-garde.

1 *Voir le chapitre sur le Centre de loisirs de Monte-Carlo dans cet ouvrage.*

2 *Hadid fut également assistante à l'Academy pendant quelque temps.*

3 *Voir le chapitre sur l'Internationale Bauaustellung dans cet ouvrage.*

4 *Voir également à ce sujet le chapitre sur la Hong Kong and Shangai Bank, dans cet ouvrage.*

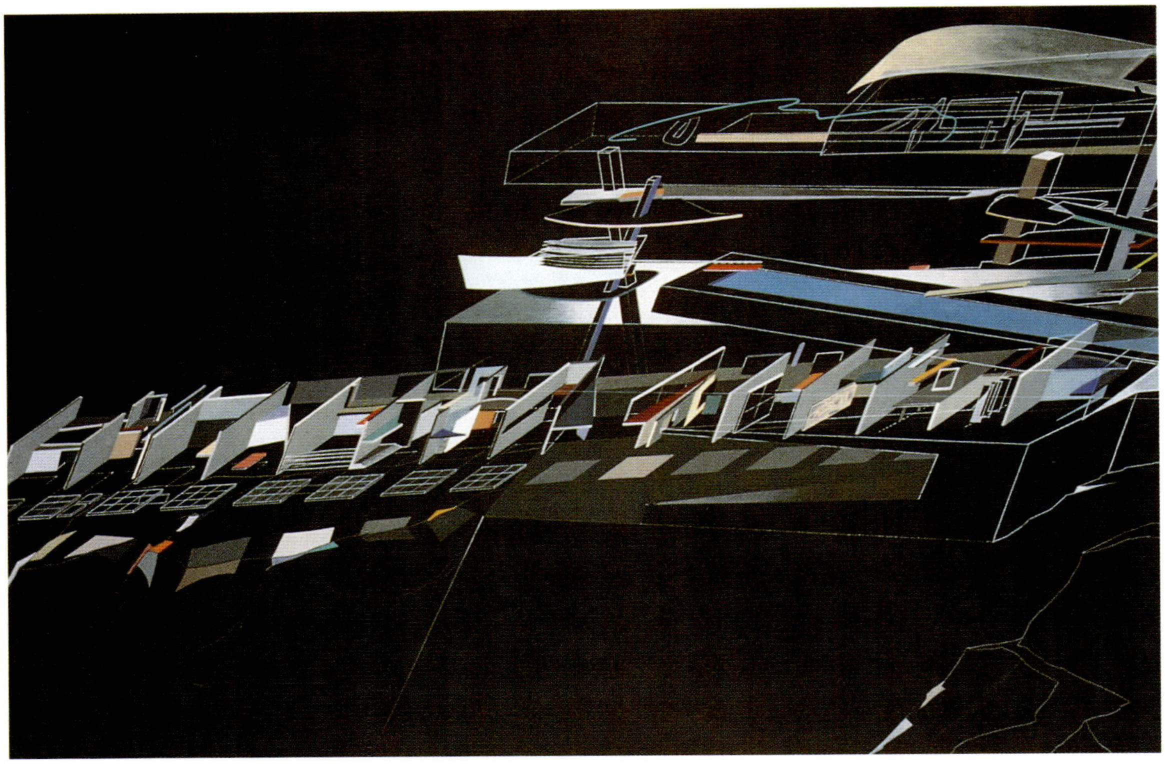

Zaha M. Hadid presentation design, 1982, isometric projection (studio apartment)

Zaha M. Hadid competition design (revised), 1982, site plans, first prize

Zaha M. Hadid presentation design, 1982, exterior view (approach by ramp)

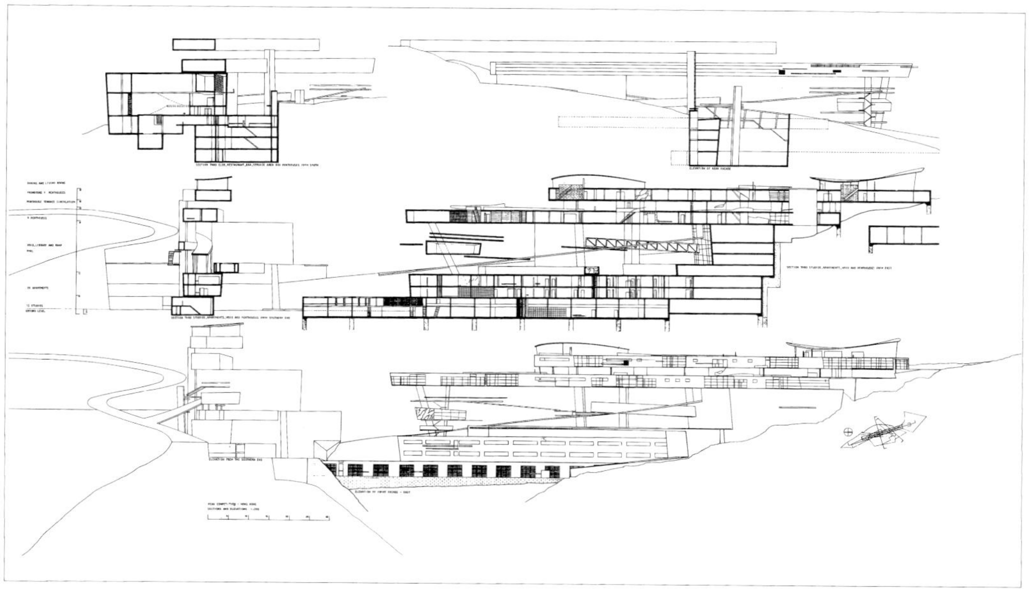

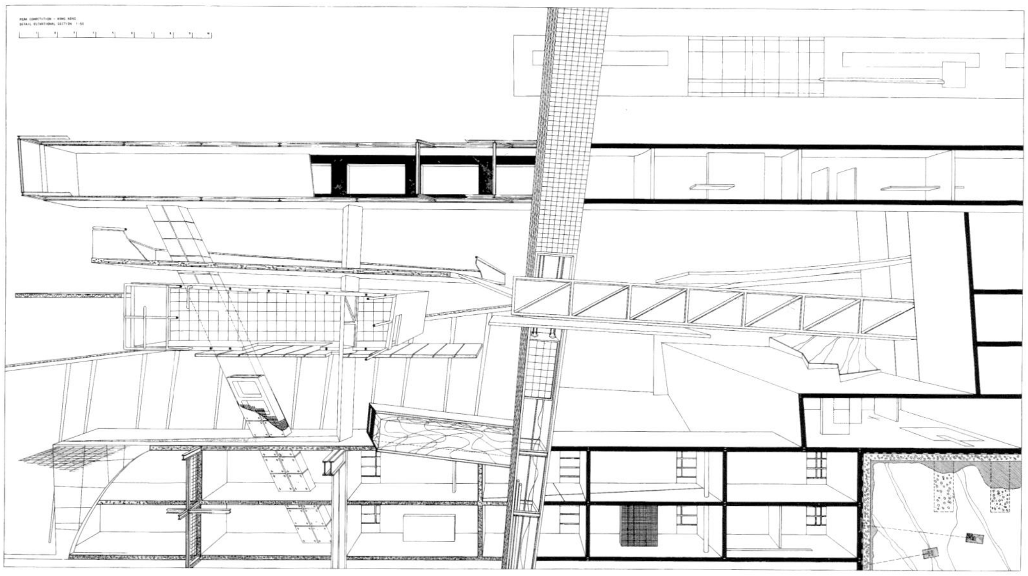

Zaha M. Hadid competition design (revised), 1982, above left: east-west section (north side), middle left: east-west section (south side), below left: south elevation, above right: north-south section (west side), middle right: north-south section (east side), below right: east elevation, first prize

Zaha M. Hadid competition design, 1982, sectional view, first prize

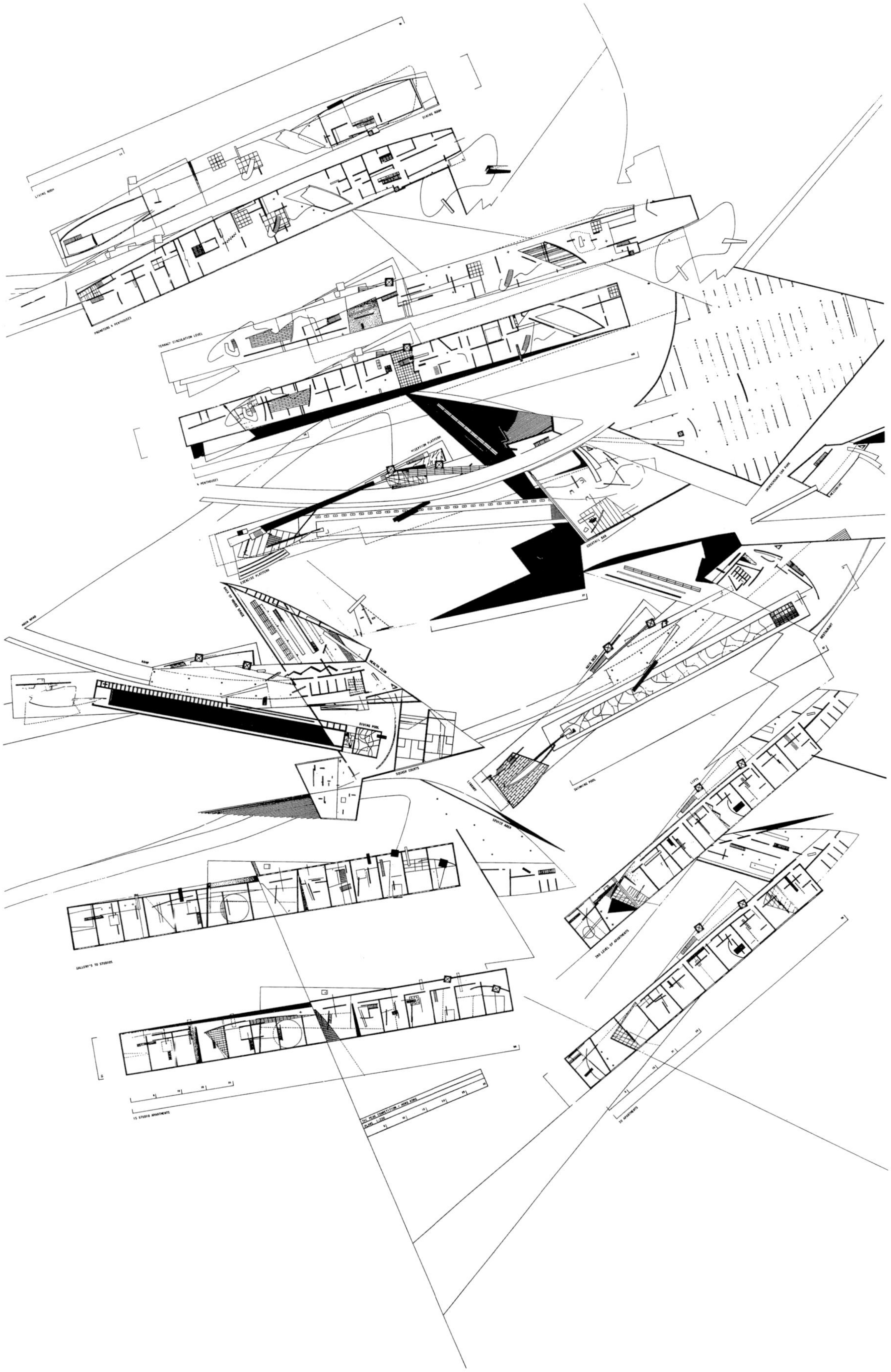

Zaha M. Hadid competition design, 1982, plans, first prize

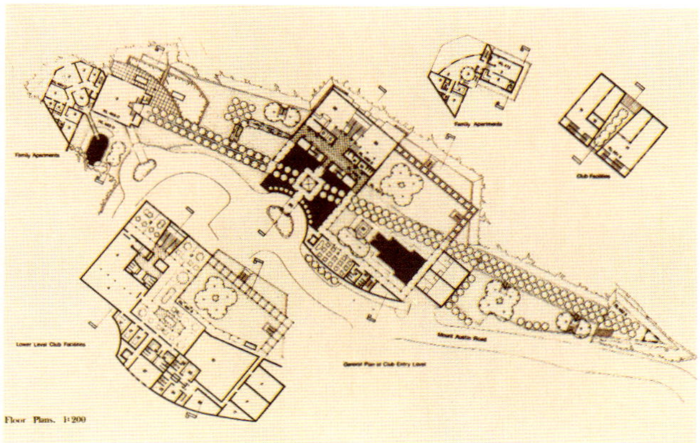

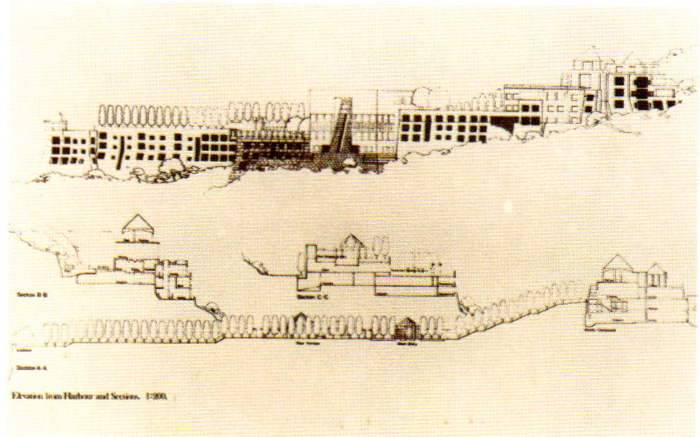

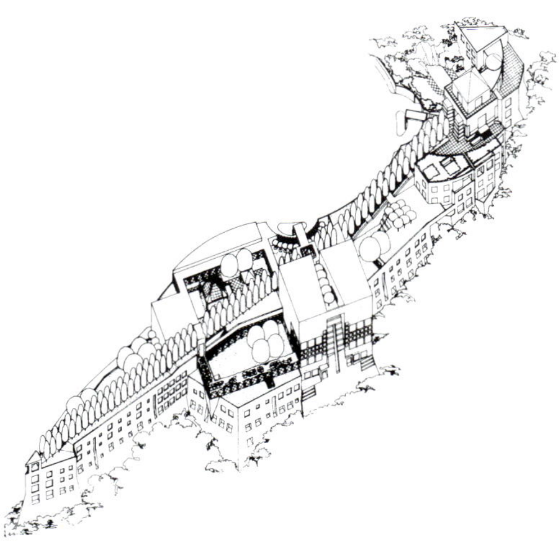

Barrington Charles Marshall
competition design, 1982, floor plans, second prize

Barrington Charles Marshall
competition design, 1982, above: east elevation, below: sections, second prize

Barrington Charles Marshall
competition design, 1982, perspectival sketches, second prize

Barrington Charles Marshall
competition design, 1982, axonometric projection, second prize

Peter Cook & Christine Hawley competition design, 1982, east elevation

Peter Cook & Christine Hawley competition design, 1982, axonometric projection

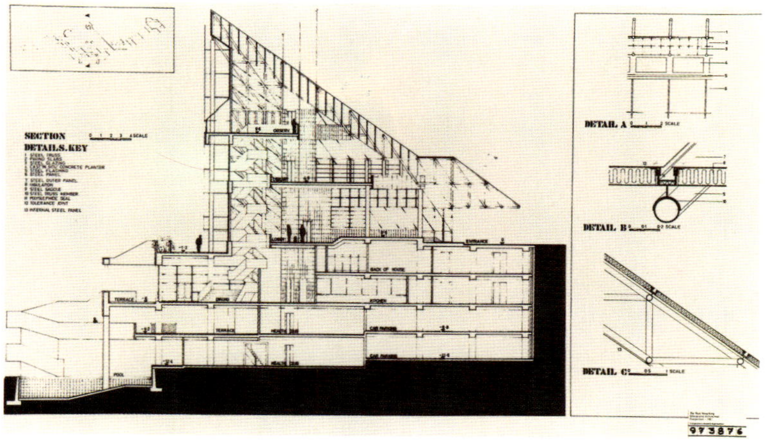

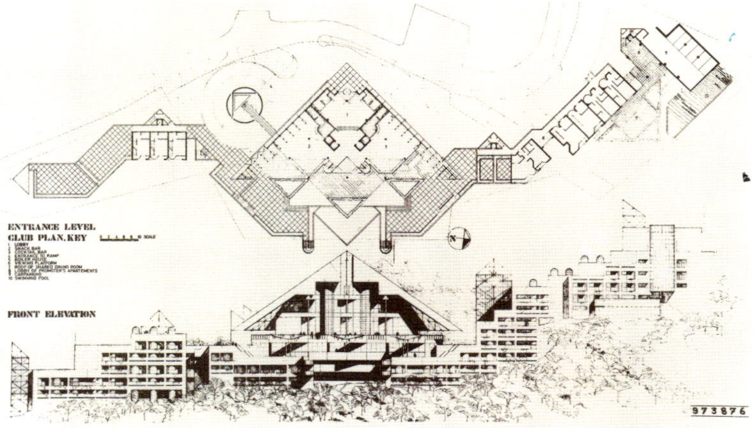

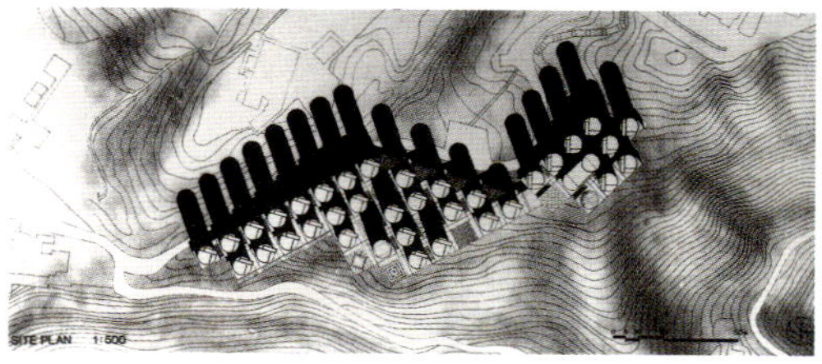

Edmund Baylon Burke competition design, 1982, bird's-eye view, third prize

Edmund Baylon Burke competition design, 1982, above: ground floor plan, below: east elevation, third prize

John S. Hagmann & David Hannaford Mitchell competition design, 1982, above: ground floor plan, below: first floor plan, third prize

John S. Hagmann & David Hannaford Mitchell competition design, 1982, above: east elevation, middle: west elevation, below: north-south section (west side), third prize

Akira Kuryu, Koichi Tanaka, Kenichi Nakamura, Kenji Sato, Akira Uenishi & Tetsuya Uekubo competition design, 1982, site plan

Akira Kuryu, Koichi Tanaka, Kenichi Nakamura, Kenji Sato, Akira Uenishi & Tetsuya Uekubo competition design, 1982, model

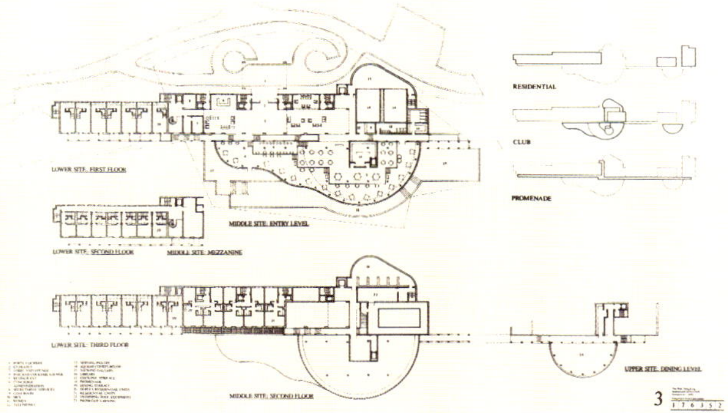

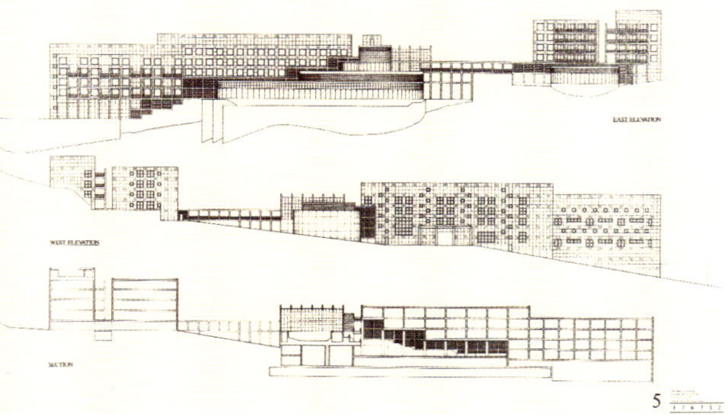

Project

Mediatheque (information centre and library) and museum of contemporary art

Site

Place de la Comédie, Nîmes

Dates

First round result announced 16 August 1984 *Second round closing date* 15 October 1984 *Result announced* December 1984

Number of entries

10: *First round* Christian de Portzamparc (Paris); Alvaro Siza (Portugal); Paul Andreu (Paris); Aldo Rossi (Milan); Hans Hollein (Vienna); Cesar Pelli (New Haven); Jean Nouvel (Paris); Frank O. Gehry (Los Angeles); Norman Foster (London) and Arata Isozaki (Tokyo) *Second round* 5: Cesar Pelli; Jean Nouvel; Frank O. Gehry; Norman Foster and Arata Isozaki (who later withdrew)

Jury

Jean Bousquet (chairman, Mayor of Nîmes), Robert Calle (who later became director of the museum of contemporary art), Jean-Pierre Dufoix, Daniel Mazet, Jean-Remy Negre, Roland Simounet, Alain Sarfati, James Stirling (all architects), Martial Raysse (artist), P. Schoots (director of the Public Library in Rotterdam) and others

Result

First prize Norman Foster *Honourable mention* Jean Nouvel

Commissioned by

The Municipality of Nîmes

Construction

January 1988 to June 1992

Architect

Norman Foster (*1935)

Construction cost

Approximately 222 600 000 francs

Carré d'Art, Nîmes, 1984

Norman Foster competition design, 1984, sketch (section of north side), first prize

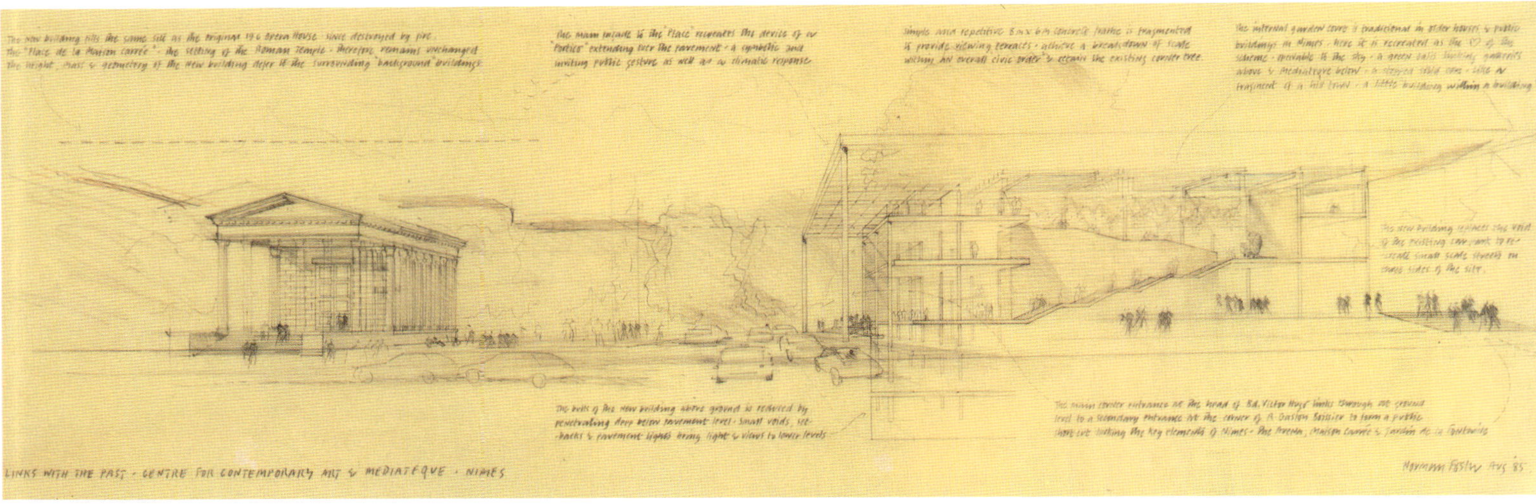

Carré d'Art, Nîmes

Nîmes was to become the Beaubourg of the South. At least, that was the heartfelt wish of the town's mayor, Jean Bousquet. According to the critics, the project was an intolerable attack on French cultural heritage. The mediatheque-cum-museum of contemporary art stirred up a controversy. However, the building which eventually materialised was clearly designed with respect for its venerable neighbour and has become an architectural asset to the city of Nîmes.

Classicist Mecca

The Maison Carrée in Nîmes and the Pantheon in Rome are two of the best preserved Roman temples in existence. The Maison Carrée dates from the Augustinian period and, together with the Pont du Gard and the amphitheatre, it has made Nîmes a Mecca for classically-oriented architects. The nineteenth-century theatre, which was situated directly opposite the west side of the Maison Carrée, was also classically inspired. This building was almost completely destroyed by fire in 1952. All that remained was the eastern portico and the square to which it lent its name: Place de la Comédie. It was on this square, which was directly linked to the famous amphitheatre, that Bousquet would build his architectural contribution to the city.

The mayor's sudden cultural enthusiasm was shared by authorities throughout France during the 1980s. The extent of government involvement in the Centre Pompidou in Paris had sent a shock wave through the hitherto unspectacular world of French architecture. Although the capital was well ahead of the field with its "Grands Projets", the city of Nîmes, which had a population of just 130,000, also took an early lead. Daring projects were later also initiated and carried out in Villeurbanne (a library by Mario Botta), Lille (a housing district by Rem Koolhaas), Amiens (a housing district by Robert Krier) and many other cities and towns.

A far-reaching decentralisation programme, initiated by the French president Valéry Giscard d'Estaing and developed further by his successor François Mitterrand, had simplified administrative procedure and served as a catalyst for cultural developments. If someone had proposed building a modern centre for the arts on the same square as the Maison Carrée ten years before, they would have been branded a madman. Naturally, certain people were still opposed to the plan in 1984, but the climate had become a lot more favourable.

Hub of cultural life

The mayor and aldermen of Nîmes decided to boost cultural life in the city, partly influenced by the fact that the city was becoming a veritable artist's colony. By 1970 the city could boast the highest concentration of painters and sculptors in all France. Many of these artists enjoyed national and even international fame. Moreover, the Ecole des Beaux-Arts in Nîmes was one of the most dynamic art schools in the country. Nîmes had the potential to become the hub of cultural life in southern France[1].

The existing museums of archaeology, fine arts and urban history were to be housed in the new centre, which would also be home to a sizeable collection of French modern art, a total of 150 works which the city had on loan from private collectors. The centre would also have an area for temporary exhibitions, where an annual "exposition de prestige" would be held during the summer.

The mediatheque was to be situated in another wing of the complex. The existing municipal library had become inadequate and was unable to cope with the public's changing tastes. The new mediatheque would provide both written works and visual material. New facilities would include a department with various auditory devices, a department for video material (specialising in dramatic arts), a theatre booking office and an art library. The new complex would also enhance Nîmes' status as a tourist centre.

Couvertures des Arènes

Jean Bousquet, Maire de Nîmes

Jean-Michel Wilmotte **(interior), Musée des Beaux-Arts**

A closed competition

With the above objectives in mind, a competition for a mediatheque-cum-museum of contemporary art was organised in 1984. Twelve internationally renowned architects were invited to participate, ten of whom submitted plans. Richard Meier and James Stirling were too busy. However, the latter did accept a seat on the jury, which outnumbered the competition entrants by almost two to one. Naturally, Jean Bousquet was the self-appointed chairman. He was assisted by Robert Calle, who had contributed part of his collection to the museum and later became its director. From the outset, Calle had supported Bousquet in his endeavour to boost cultural life in Nîmes[2]. The rest of jury consisted of civil servants, architects and architectural experts. The renowned artist Martial Raysse also had a seat on the jury. The designs would be judged not only on their quality but also on the way in which they related to the Maison Carrée. The architects were asked to submit preliminary sketches and a prospectus for the first round. They were free to decide what they would do with the remaining portico of the burnt-down theatre. Initially they all suggested demolition. Five of the ten architects were selected and asked to develop their plans further. Arata Isozaki was taken ill, which left Norman Foster, Frank Gehry, Jean Nouvel and Cesar Pelli. The local community were indignant that only one of the finalists was French, though actually his presence in a field of this stature can also be seen as a great honour.
The French finalist, Jean Nouvel, received an honourable mention for his underground complex and Norman Foster was awarded first prize. This was not surprising considering the popularity of high-tech in France at the time. The works of Renzo Piano, Richard Rogers and Peter Rice had all contributed to the growing popularity of this style. However, the jury asked Foster to incorporate the portico of the old theatre in his new design. He was also asked to alter the façade. He did so no less than ten times, until he eventually came up with a design that was to everyone's satisfaction.
Foster paid clearly respect to the site's cultural nuances. He expressed his deference in a number of ways, which is almost unique when one considers the rest of his œuvre. Undoubtedly, Foster's deference had a lot to do with the fact that this was his first chance to realise a project on a site of such historical significance.

Carré d'Art

The area occupied by Foster's Carré d'Art is not much bigger than that of the forum containing the Maison Carrée. The result was two equal architectural units on either side of the Boulevard Victor Hugo. In order to maintain the harmony between the two Carrés, no parking areas were planned around the newer building.
The architectural harmony between the east side of the temple and the west side of Foster's mediatheque is even greater. Instead of extending the main façade, Foster moved the mediatheque outward in its entirety. The proportions of the mediatheque's façade mirror those of the closed, eastside of the Maison Carrée without entablature. The proportions of the closed side of the temple with entablature mirror those of the mediatheque, up to and including the roof. And finally, the proportions of the lateral façade of the temple are equal to those of Foster's main façade as a whole.
There is a terrace on top of the mediatheque, providing a magnificent view of the city. However, Foster's true stroke of genius was his high-tech version of the Roman peristyle. In contrast to Greek temples, Roman temples are not entirely surrounded by a free-standing peristyle; they consist of an open and a closed part. In Foster's version of the Roman peristyle – which is actually of Etruscan origin – the free-standing "columns" are slender pillars which support the awning above the terrace. The awning forms an integral part of the roofing structure. The "closed" part of Foster's structure is formed by glass walls in which the support pillars are clearly visible. They mirror the Corinthian embedded columns in the walls of the Maison Carrée.
In this way Foster brought about a perfect synthesis between the old and the new. He respected and even enhanced the historical splendour of the Maison Carrée, but also presented Nîmes with a piece of modern architecture which is of outstanding significance. In an earlier, far less original design, Foster had incorporated the remaining portico of the old theatre into the new façade. The stairs and the stylobate, the platform on which the temple is built, are also recognisable in Foster's design. As well as these classical Roman features, there are also traces of more modern influences, such as Pierre Chareau's Maison de Verre

Kisho Kurokawa & François Fontes

Colisée

Jean Nouvel Nemausus, first sketch

Norman Foster Carré d'Art, under construction

in Paris as well as of traditional Japanese architecture in the subdivision of the windows.
Even though the centre had to house a wide variety of facilities, it is not out of proportion, because half of the building was situated underground. Two of the four underground levels are open to the public. The library is situated on one of these floors. The museum is situated on the upper floors. Due to the purpose of the rooms in this area, windows were not essential. The mediatheque and the library can be viewed from the central hall, where the stairways and lifts are situated.

An unfair comparison

Obviously it is not completely fair to compare Foster's final design to those of the other participants. When construction was almost completed, Foster added three pillars to the corbelling roof, whereby the harmony with the Maison Carrée was enhanced. Most architects are not given the opportunity to develop their designs, and few if any expect to see their original competition designs materialise. However, it is only fair to say that the other entries also contained interesting features. Gehry's Deconstructivist edifice, for example, seemed to have been designed with total disregard for the historical surroundings. Nouvel's underground cultural centre had a roof formed by transparent road surfacing overhead. Cesar Pelli's design was the least appealing: his building crossed the road and approached the Maison Carrée – a little too close for comfort.

Naturally, it was highly unlikely that the world's finest architects would not produce at least one practicable design. Nevertheless, there was a risk that the delicate historical balance on site might be rudely disturbed by a new mega-structure in the area. Foster succeeded in bringing about a perfect synthesis between the venerable past and the best that modern architecture had to offer.

1 *Other sectors also experienced this wind of change. Shin Takamatsu and Kisho Kurokawa designed a new trade centre and Vittorio Gregotti designed a new station.*
2 *The designer Jean-Michel Wilmotte had also supported Bousquet from the outset.*

Carré d'Art, Nîmes

Ein »Beaubourg des Südens« sollte die Stadt Nîmes erhalten – das war zumindest der Wunsch des Bürgermeisters Jean Bousquet. Als untragbaren Angriff auf das kulturelle Erbgut Frankreichs beurteilten hingegen die Kritiker das Projekt bereits im Vorfeld. Das Zentrum für zeitgenössische Kunst samt Mediathek brachte die Gemüter im ganzen Land in Wallung. Dabei zeigt das letztlich realisierte Gebäude nicht nur Respekt vor seinen altehrwürdigen Nachbarn, sondern ist auch zu einer architektonischen Bereicherung der Stadt Nîmes geworden.

Wallfahrtsort der Klassizisten

Das Maison Carrée in Nîmes gehört neben dem Pantheon in Rom zu den am besten erhaltenen römischen Tempeln. Dieses Bauwerk aus der augusteischen Epoche, der Pont du Gard und das Amphitheater lassen Nîmes (Nemausus) zu einem Wallfahrtsort für den klassizistisch orientierten Architekten werden. Auch das aus dem 19. Jahrhundert stammende Theater, das dem Maison Carrée auf der Westseite direkt gegenüberlag, war deutlich von klassischen Vorbildern inspiriert. 1952 vernichtete ein Brand das Theater bis auf die östliche Kolonnade. Auf der Place de la Comédie, dem einstigen Standort des Theaters, wollte Bousquet seinen architektonischen Beitrag für das Stadtbild entstehen lassen.

In den 80er Jahren wurden im ganzen Land aufsehenerregende Architekturprojekte begonnen. Zwar übertraf Paris mit den »Grands Projets« alle anderen Städte, doch auch Nîmes gehörte zu den Vorreitern dieser Welle. Später folgten kühne Architekturprojekte u. a. in Villeurbanne (Bibliothek von Mario Botta), Lille (Wohnviertel von Rem Koolhaas) und Amiens (Wohnviertel von Robert Krier). Diese Projektwelle wurde verwaltungstechnisch ermöglicht durch ein Dezentralisierungsprogramm, das von Präsident Valéry Giscard d'Estaing ins Leben gerufen worden war und von dessen Nachfolger François Mitterrand weitergeführt wurde. Noch zehn Jahre zuvor wäre der Bau eines modernen Kunstzentrums neben dem Maison Carrée undenkbar gewesen. Zwar gab es auch 1984 noch Widerstände, aber das allgemeine Klima hatte sich gewandelt.

Zentrum des kulturellen Lebens

Als der Bürgermeister und die Beigeordneten von Nîmes sich entschlossen, dem kulturellen Leben der Stadt neue Impulse zu verleihen, geschah dies vor dem Hintergrund, daß sich in Nîmes ab etwa 1970 eine der größten Künstlerkolonien Frankreichs gebildet hatte, deren Mitglieder – Maler und Bildhauer – teilweise von nationalem bzw. internationalem Rang waren. Die örtliche Kunsthochschule zählte zu den progressivsten Ausbildungsstätten für junge Künstler in Frankreich. Nîmes besaß gute Chancen, sich zum kulturellen Zentrum des Südens zu entwickeln. Die bestehenden Museen für Archäologie, Kunst und Stadtgeschichte sollten in einem neuen Komplex zusammengefaßt werden. Auch eine repräsentative Sammlung moderner französischer Kunst, die etwa 150 Exponate umfaßte und der Stadt von verschiedenen Sammlern als Leihgabe zur Verfügung gestellt worden war, hätte in diesen Komplex aufgenommen werden können. Außerdem sollte das neue Gebäude Räumlichkeiten für Wechselausstellungen bieten, wobei als jährlicher Höhepunkt eine im Sommer stattfindende »Exposition de Prestige« geplant war.

Als ein weiterer Schwerpunkt des Komplexes war eine Mediathek vorgesehen, da die alte Stadtbibliothek den veränderten Ansprüchen ihrer Benutzer nicht mehr genügte. Die neue Mediathek sollte nicht nur als Bibliothek, sondern auch als audiovisuelles Zentrum dienen. Neu waren u. a. eine Abteilung mit verschiedenen Arten von Tonträgern, eine Abteilung für Videobänder – mit besonderem Augenmerk für das Theater –, eine Vorverkaufsstelle für Theaterkarten und eine Artothek. Darüber hinaus sollte der neu zu schaffende Komplex die Stadt Nîmes um eine touristische Attraktion ergänzen.

Eine geschlossene Ausschreibung

1984 wurde ein Wettbewerb für eine Mediathek und ein Zentrum für zeitgenössische Kunst ausgeschrieben. Die Stadtväter luden zwölf international renommierte Architekten ein, von denen schließlich zehn einen Beitrag vorlegten. Richard Meier und James Stirling mußten aus Zeitgründen absagen. Allerdings nahm Stirling einen Platz in der Jury ein, die beinahe doppelt soviel Mitglieder zählte wie die Anzahl der teilnehmenden Architekten. Jean Bousquet übernahm den Vorsitz. Er ließ sich u. a. beraten durch Dr. Robert Calle, den späteren Direktor des Museums. Bousquets Bemühungen, der Stadt Nîmes neues Leben einzuhauchen, waren bei Calle von Anfang an auf fruchtbaren Boden gefallen. Bei den anderen Jury-Mitgliedern handelte es sich um städtische Beamte, Architekten und Fachleute, zu denen auch der Künstler Martial Raysse gehörte.

Bei der Auswahl der Entwürfe spielte nicht nur deren architektonische Qualität eine Rolle, sondern auch ihr Verhältnis zum Maison Carrée. Den Architekten war freigestellt, ob sie die Kolonnade des abgebrannten Theaters in ihre Pläne aufnehmen wollten. Alle Teilnehmer gingen jedoch zunächst von einem Abriß aus. Die Jury erwartete in diesem Planungsstadium nicht mehr als eine Vorstudie mit dazugehörigen Erläuterungen und wählte von den zehn eingereichten Beiträgen fünf zur weiteren Ausarbeitung aus. Von den fünf Teilnehmern dieser zweiten Runde zog sich Arata Isozaki aus Krankheitsgründen zurück, so daß Norman Foster, Frank Gehry, Jean Nouvel und Cesar Pelli den Preisträger unter sich ausmachten. Die Tatsache, daß nur einer der vier Architekten Franzose war, rief zunächst einige Empörung hervor.

Jean Nouvel erhielt letztendlich eine ehrenvolle Erwähnung für seine originelle Lösung, den gesamten Komplex unterirdisch anzulegen. Der erste Preis ging an Norman Foster, was aufgrund der damaligen Popularität des High-Tech in Frankreich nicht weiter verwundert – einer Popularität, die neben Foster vor allem Renzo Piano, Richard Rogers und Peter Rice zu verdanken war. Die Jury bat Foster, detaillierte Pläne auszuarbeiten und dabei die Kolonnade des alten Theaters in den Komplex zu integrieren. Desweiteren sollte er die Vorderfront des Entwurfs verändern. Foster entsprach den Wünschen der Jury und änderte seine Zeichnungen so lange ab – insgesamt zehnmal– bis eine Version entstand, die alle Beteiligten zufriedenstellte. Sein endgültiger Entwurf zeugt in zahllosen Details von großer Sensibilität und Respekt gegenüber den umliegenden Bauten und ihrer Geschichte – ein in Fosters Œuvre einmaliger Vorgang.

Carré d'Art

Die Fläche, die Fosters Carré d'Art einnimmt, ist nicht wesentlich größer als das Forum mit dem Maison Carrée. Auf diese Weise entstanden zwei gleichwertige städtebauliche Einheiten, die zu beiden Seiten des Boulevard Victor Hugo liegen. Bewußt wurde auf einen Parkplatz verzichtet, um das Gleichgewicht der beiden Carrées nicht zu zerstören.

Diese Einheit begegnet dem Betrachter ebenfalls zwischen der Ostseite des Tempels und der Mediathek auf der Westseite von Fosters Gebäude. Statt einer durchgängigen Außenfassade rückte Foster diesen Gebäudeteil völlig nach außen, wodurch die Proportionen der Fassade der Mediathek exakt mit denen der geschlossenen Ostseite des Maison Carrée übereinstimmen. Die Abmessungen der gesamten Seitenfassade des Tempels entsprechen genau den Maßen der Vorderfront.

Über der Mediathek wurde eine Terrasse mit herrlicher Aussicht angelegt. Foster Geniestreich aber ist seine eigene High-Tech-Interpretation eines römischen Peristyls. Im Gegensatz zu den griechischen Tempeln waren die römischen Tempel nur selten allseitig von Säulen umschlossen; statt dessen besaßen sie einen offenen und einen geschlossenen Teil. Diese ursprünglich etruskische Bauweise führte Foster weiter: Seine freistehenden Säulen sind schlanke Pfeiler, auf denen das Sonnendach über der Terrasse ruht. Dieser Sonnenschutz bildet einen integralen Bestandteil der Dachkonstruktion. Der geschlossene Teil des Gebäudes besteht aus gläsernen Wänden, durch die die Tragpfeiler ebenso deutlich zu erkennen sind wie die korinthischen Halbsäulen im Innern des Maison Carrée.

Auf diese Weise erfüllte Foster zwei Voraussetzungen: Zum einen zeigt und betont sein Entwurf den Eigenwert des Maison Carrée, zum anderen wurde die Stadt Nîmes um ein Bauwerk von internationaler Geltung reicher. Dagegen ist eine seiner früheren Lösungen, nach der der ehemalige Portikus des Theaters in die neue Fassade integriert werden sollte, weitaus weniger originell. In Fosters Entwurf sind auch die Treppen und das Stylobat, der Unterbau des antiken Tempels, wiederzufinden. Neben diesen klassisch römischen Charakteristika weist das Gebäude eine Reihe moderner Einflüsse auf: Es erinnert an das von Pierre Chareau in Paris gebaute Maison de Verre und macht in der Unterteilung der Fenster Anleihen bei der traditionellen japanischen Baukunst.

Da eine Hälfte des Gebäudes unterirdisch angelegt wurde, fiel das »Carré d'Art« trotz seiner vielfältigen Funktionen nicht überproportional aus. Zwei der vier Kellergeschosse sind für den Publikumsverkehr geöffnet, u. a. befindet sich hier die Bibliothek. Die oberen Stockwerke enthalten den musealen Teil des Komplexes und bestehen aus Sälen mit geschlossenen Wänden. Dagegen sind die Mediathek und die Bibliothek von der Haupthalle mit ihren Treppen und Aufzügen aus durchgehend zu überblicken.

Ein unehrlicher Vergleich

Ein Vergleich zwischen Fosters letztem Entwurf und den anderen Wettbewerbsbeiträgen wäre mehr als ungerecht. Buchstäblich in letzter Minute ergänzte Foster seine überkragende Dachkonstruktion um drei weitere Pfeiler, wodurch die Wechselwirkung mit dem Maison Carrée noch stärker hervortrat. Auch die anderen Wettbewerbsbeiträge besitzen durchaus ihre Qualitäten: Gehrys dekonstruktivistischer Entwurf zeigte sich von der historischen Umgebung unbeeindruckt, Nouvel entwarf ein unterirdisches Kulturzentrum mit einem durchsichtigen Dach zur Straße hin, und Cesar Pelli schuf ein Gebäude, das die Straße überspannen und sich bis dicht an das Maison Carrée herandrängen sollte.

Der Vergleich mit den anderen Entwürfen offenbart jedoch eines: Norman Foster ist eine perfekte Symbiose zwischen altehrwürdiger Vergangenheit und dem Besten der Gegenwart gelungen.

Le Carré d'Art, Nîmes

Si l'idée du maire de Nîmes, Jean Bousquet, n'était rien moins que de construire le Beaubourg du midi, son projet architectural fut vécu par certains critiques comme une atteinte à l'héritage culturel national. Et pourtant, cette médiathèque-musée d'art contemporain si controversée a été construite dans le respect de son environnement historique et fait aujourd'hui partie des richesses de la ville.

Un haut-lieu du classicisme

La Maison Carrée de Nîmes et le Panthéon de Rome sont les deux temples romains les mieux conservés au monde. La Maison Carrée date d'Auguste et, avec le pont du Gard et les Arènes, elle fait de Nîmes (Nemausus) un lieu de pélerinage obligé pour les architectes classiques. Le théâtre, construit au XIXème siècle à l'ouest de la Maison Carrée, était bien entendu d'inspiration néo-classique. En 1952, il fut presque complètement détruit par un incendie qui n'en laissa qu'un lourd portique en bordure de la place de la Comédie, et c'est sur ses ruines que le maire souhaitait édifier son grand projet.

Le soudain enthousiasme de l'élu pour la culture fut le lot commun de la plupart des autorités municipales françaises pendant les années 80. L'implication massive de l'Etat dans le Centre Pompidou avait réveillé un monde architectural assez endormi. Bien que la capitale ait pris de l'avance grâce à la politique des «Grands Projets», la ville de Nîmes (130 000 habitants) joua également un rôle pilote dans ce mouvement qui vit des réalisations audacieuses menées à bien à Villeurbanne (bibliothèque de Mario Botta), Lille (des logements par Rem Koolhaas), Amiens (un quartier d'habitation par Robert Krier) et dans de nombreuses autres villes.

Un programme de décentralisation initié par V. Giscard d'Estaing et développé par son successeur à l'Élysée avait simplifié les procédures administratives et servi de catalyseur aux initiatives culturelles. Si quelqu'un avait proposé de construire un centre culturel à deux pas de la Maison Carrée dix ans plus tôt, il aurait immédiatement été traité de fou. Même si le projet rencontra une forte opposition en 1984, le climat général lui était cependant beaucoup plus favorable.

Un creuset culturel

Le maire et les conseillers municipaux de Nîmes décidèrent de faire porter leurs efforts sur l'animation culturelle de leur cité, en partie parce qu'elle était peu à peu devenue une colonie d'artistes[1]. En 1970, elle pouvait se flatter de posséder la plus forte concentration de peintres et de sculpteurs en dehors de Paris. Beaucoup de ces artistes étaient nationalement et même internationalement connus, et l'Ecole des Beaux-Arts était l'une des plus dynamiques du pays. Nîmes avait le potentiel pour devenir le creuset culturel du midi de la France. Les musées existants, archéologie, Beaux-Arts et histoire de la ville, devaient être regroupés dans le nouveau centre qui accueillerait également une importante collection de 150 œuvres d'art moderne françaises prêtées à la ville par des collectionneurs privés. Un espace serait prévu pour des expositions temporaires et une exposition de prestige estivale.

La bibliothèque municipale obsolète avait du mal à s'adapter à l'évolution des goûts du public, d'où l'idée d'une médiathèque installée dans une autre partie du complexe en compagnie d'un département audio, d'un département vidéo (axé sur les arts dramatiques), d'un théâtre et d'une bibliothèque artistique. L'ensemble devait contribuer à améliorer l'image de la ville auprès des nombreux touristes.

Un concours fermé

Ces objectifs précisés, le concours fut organisé en 1984. Douze grands architectes internationaux furent invités à participer, ce qu'acceptèrent dix d'entre eux, Richard Meier et James Stirling étant trop occupés par ailleurs. Stirling accepta cependant de participer au jury dont la composition faisait ainsi la part belle aux architectes, présents à deux contre un. Jean Bousquet avait tenu à présider ce jury, assisté par le Dr. Robert Calle qui avait offert une partie de sa collection au musée dont il allait devenir le directeur. Dès l'origine, il avait soutenu le maire dans ses efforts pour ranimer la vie culturelle locale. Les autres membres du jury étaient des fonctionnaires, des architectes et des experts en architecture ainsi qu'un artiste renommé, Martial Raysse.

Les plans ne devaient pas être seulement jugés sur leur qualité mais sur la façon dont ils prenaient en compte la proximité de la Maison Carrée. Pour le premier tour, chaque architecte devait envoyer des dessins préliminaires et un exposé d'intention. Chacun était libre de décider du sort du portique de l'ancien théâtre et tous souhaitèrent le démolir. Cinq des dix architectes furent retenus pour le second tour mais Isozaki étant souffrant, il ne restait plus en compétition que Norman Foster, Frank Gehry, Jean Nouvel et Cesar Pelli. Les Nîmois étaient furieux qu'un seul Français fasse partie des finalistes, même si l'on pouvait penser qu'il était tout à fait honorable d'avoir été sélectionné au milieu de tels concurrents.

Jean Nouvel reçut une mention pour ses plans souterrains et Norman Foster se vit attribuer le premier prix, ce qui n'était guère surprenant, vu la popularité du style high-tech à cette époque en France, où les travaux de Renzo Piano, Richard Rogers et Peter Rice avaient contribué à le faire apprécier. Le jury demanda néanmoins à Foster d'incorporer l'ancien portique à son projet et de modifier sa façade. Il le fit dix fois de suite jusqu'à ce qu'il trouve une solution qui emporte l'assentiment général.

Indéniablement, les derniers plans de Foster prennent mieux en compte les aspects culturels du site que les premiers. Ils illustrent avec brio son respect du passé, surtout dans le contexte de son œuvre habituelle. C'était aussi la première fois qu'il se trouvait confronté à un site d'une telle sensibilité culturelle et historique.

Le Carré d'Art

La surface occupée par le Carré d'Art de Foster n'est pas plus importante que celle du forum et de la Maison Carrée: les deux monuments de volume apparemment égal se retrouvent ainsi presque face à face de chaque côté du boulevard Victor Hugo. Le stationnement des voitures ayant été éliminé, une réelle harmonie se crée entre les deux «carrés».

Elle est encore plus grande entre la façade Est du temple et la façade Ouest de la médiathèque de Foster. Au lieu d'avancer sa façade principale, Foster la recula dans sa totalité vers l'intérieur. Les proportions de la façade de la médiathèque font écho à celles de la façade Est de la Maison Carrée, hors entablement qui, entablement compris, rappellent celles de la médiathèque, toit compris. Une terrasse abritée offre une vue superbe sur la vieille ville. Le trait de génie de Foster fut d'inventer la version high tech d'un péristyle romain. A la différence des temples grecs, les temples romains n'étaient pas entièrement entourés de colonnes. Dans sa version «romaine» – en fait d'origine étrusque – Foster a remplacé les colonnes par de fins piliers soutenant le vaste auvent de la terrasse qui forme partie intégrante du toit. Les marches d'accès et le stylobate (plate-forme sur laquelle est construite le temple) sont également identifiables dans son dessin. La partie «fermée» du bâtiment est en murs de verre accrochés entre les piliers clairement visibles qui évoquent les pilastres de la Maison Carrée. De cette façon, Foster a réalisé une parfaite synthèse entre le – très – ancien et le nouveau. Il a respecté et même mis en valeur la splendeur historique de la Maison Carrée en offrant à Nîmes un chef-d'œuvre d'architecture contemporaine. En dehors du classicisme, des traces d'influences plus récentes peuvent s'observer comme celle de la Maison de verre de Pierre Chareau ou de l'architecture traditionnelle japonaise pour la subdivision des ouvertures.

Bien que le bâtiment abrite de nombreuses activités, il demeure de proportions harmonieuses, car la moitié de ses surfaces sont en fait souterraines. Deux niveaux souterrains seulement sont ouverts au public, dont celui de la bibliothèque pour laquelle la lumière du jour n'était pas essentielle. La médiathèque et la bibliothèque s'aperçoivent du hall central d'où partent les escaliers et les ascenseurs.

Une comparaison injuste

La plupart des architectes n'ont pas l'occasion de mettre au point leurs projets et peu d'entre eux s'attendent même à ce que leurs premières propositions de concours soient acceptées telles quelles. Il n'est donc pas très juste de comparer le projet final de Foster à ceux de ses concurrents. Alors que la construction était pratiquement terminée, il rajouta même trois piliers au toit en porte-à-faux pour renforcer la parenté visuelle avec la Maison Carrée… Les autres projets étaient néanmoins intéressants. La médiathèque déconstructiviste de Gehry, par exemple, ne semblait pas se préoccuper une seule seconde de l'environnement historique. Le centre culturel souterrain de Nouvel avait un toit de verre sur lequel pouvaient passer voitures et piétons. La proposition de Cesar Pelli était la moins séduisante car son bâtiment traversait la rue et se rapprochait de beaucoup trop près de la Maison Carrée. On pouvait imaginer dès le départ que de la participation de quelques-uns des plus célèbres architectes du monde sortirait une solution satisfaisante, mais le risque de voir un site aussi sensible défiguré par un bâtiment de grande taille était réel. Foster réussit à réaliser une synthèse parfaite entre un passé vénéré et le meilleur de ce que l'architecture moderne sait offrir.

1 *D'autres secteurs connaissaient également un regain de dynamisme: Shin Takamatsu et Kisho Kurokawa créèrent un nouveau centre d'affaires et Vittorio Gregotti construisit une nouvelle gare.*

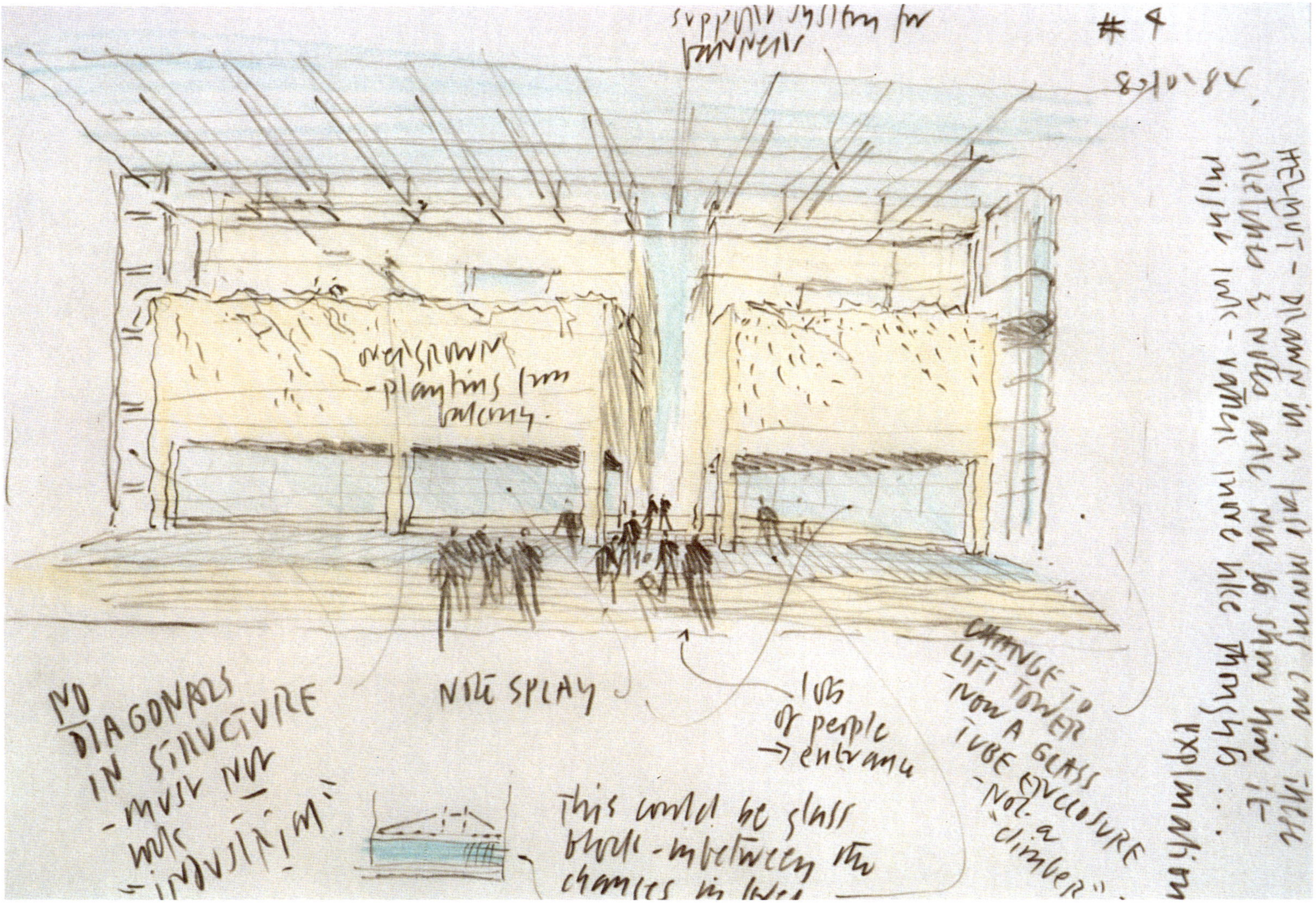

Norman Foster competition design, 1984, analytical sketches, first prize

Norman Foster final design, 1985, sectional model (north side), first prize

Norman Foster final design, 1985, sectional model (south side), first prize

Norman Foster final design, 1985, east-west section (south side), first prize

Norman Foster final design, 1985, model (entrance), first prize

Norman Foster final design, 1985, isometric projection, first prize

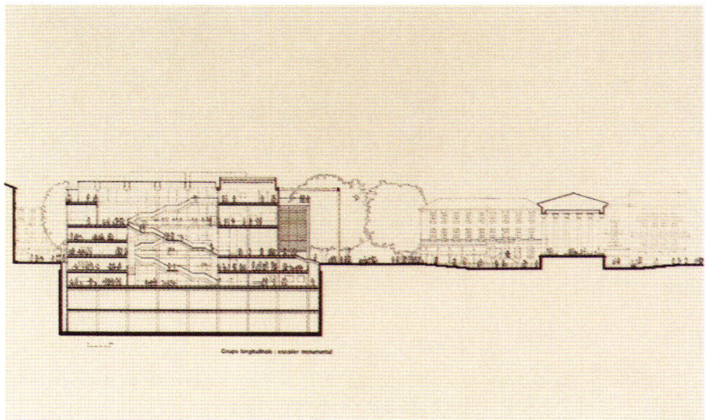
Coupe longitudinale : escalier monumental

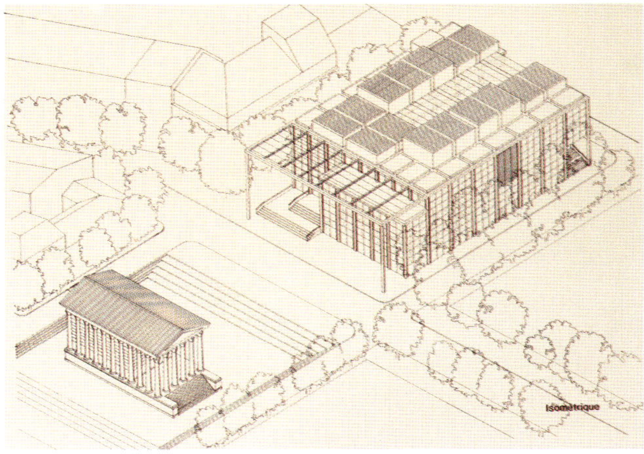
Isométrique

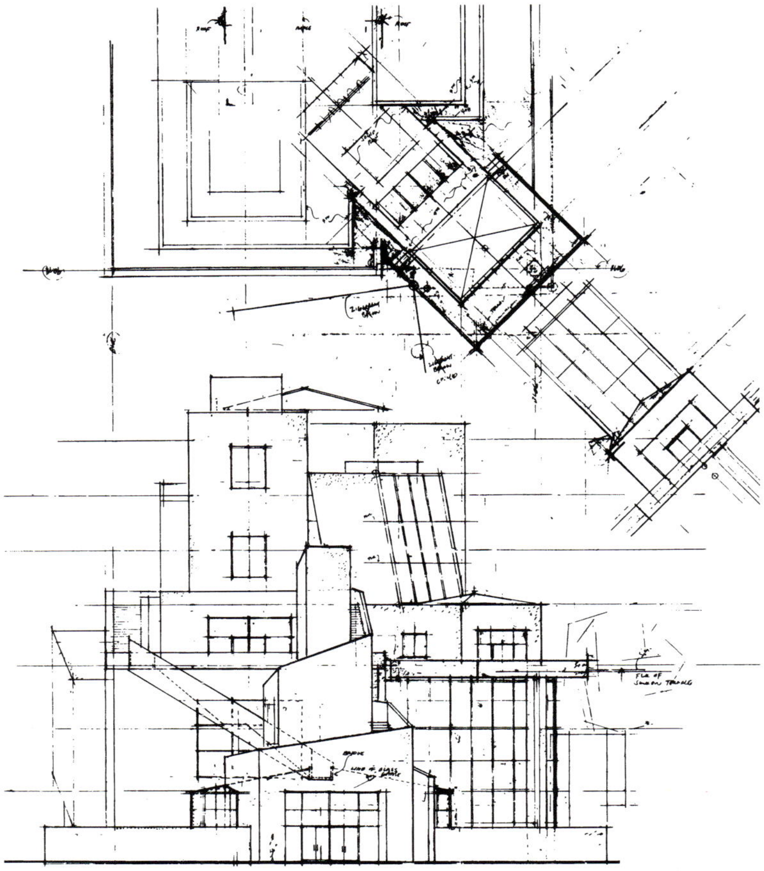

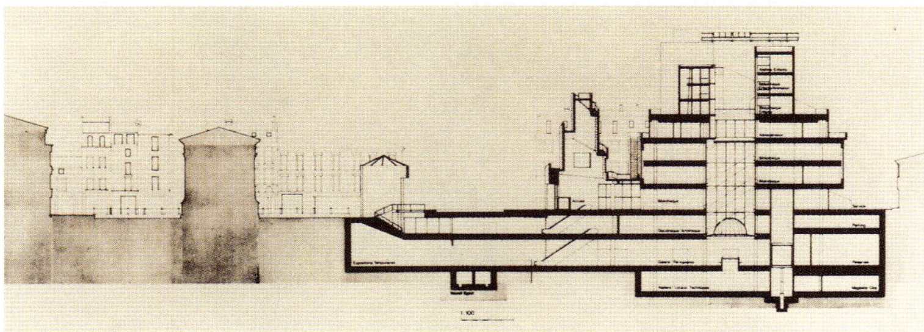

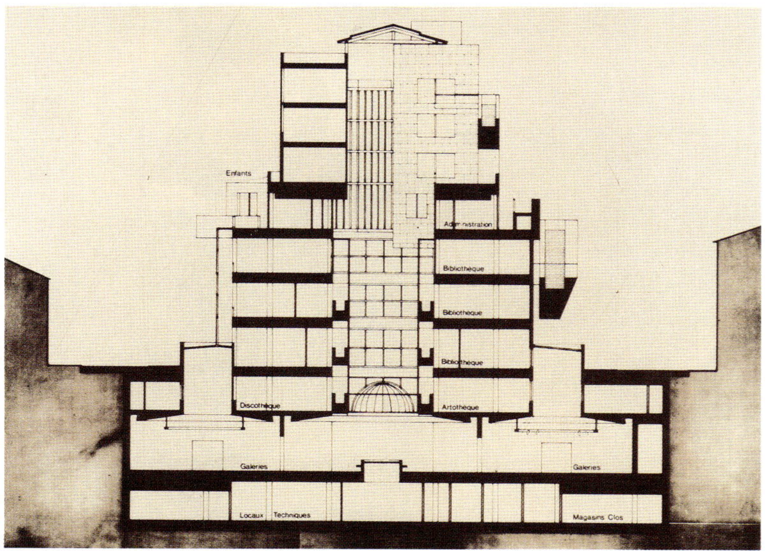

Frank O. Gehry **competition design, 1984, sketches: above: roof plan and elevation (north side), below: east elevation**

Frank O. Gehry **competition design, 1984, east-west section (north side)**

Frank O. Gehry **competition design, 1984, north-south section (west side)**

Frank O. Gehry competition design, 1984, model (north-west side)

Frank O. Gehry competition design, 1984, model (north side)

Frank O. Gehry competition design, 1984, model

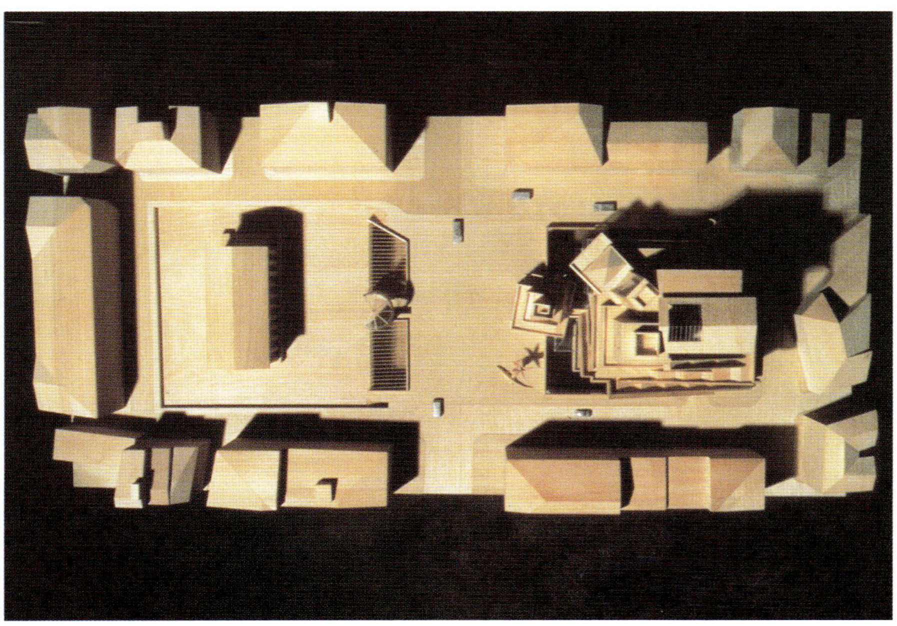

Cesar Pelli competition design, 1984, model (north side)

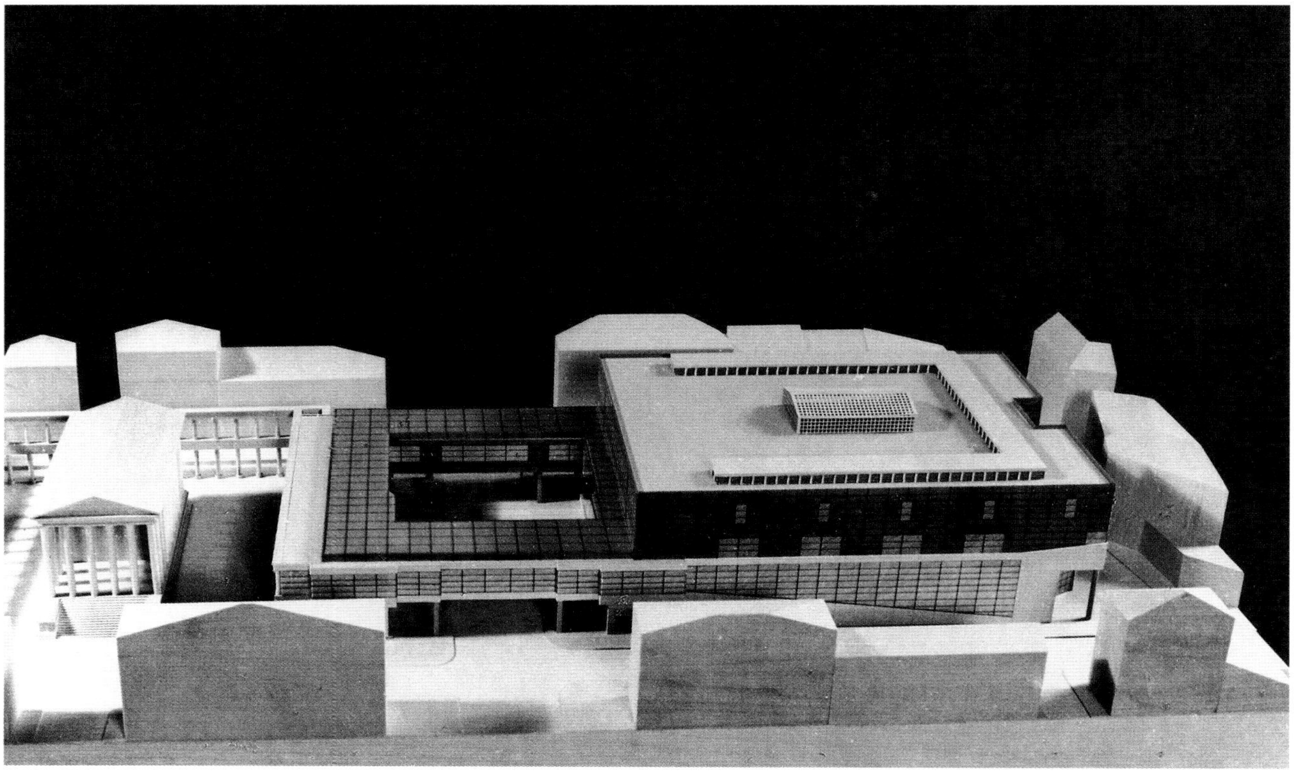

Jean Nouvel competition design, 1984, north-south section (west side), honourable mention

Jean Nouvel competition design, 1984, interior view of entrance, honourable mention

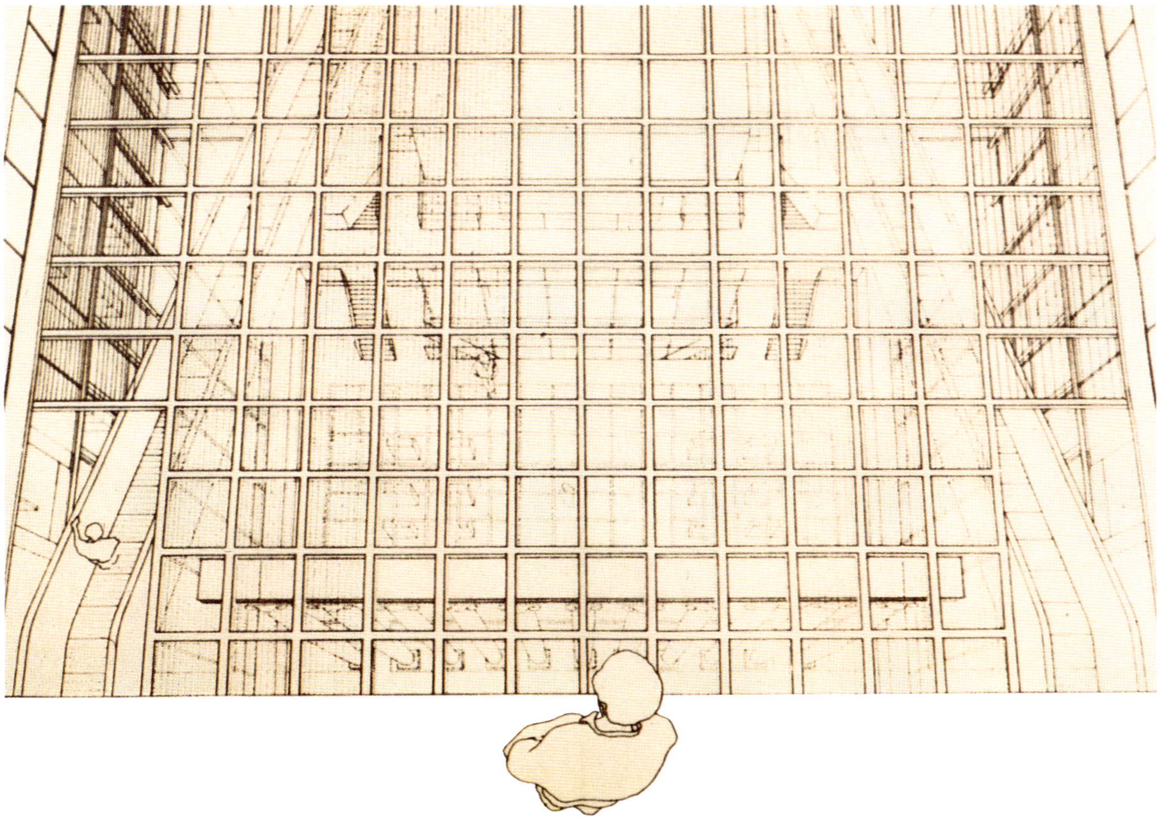

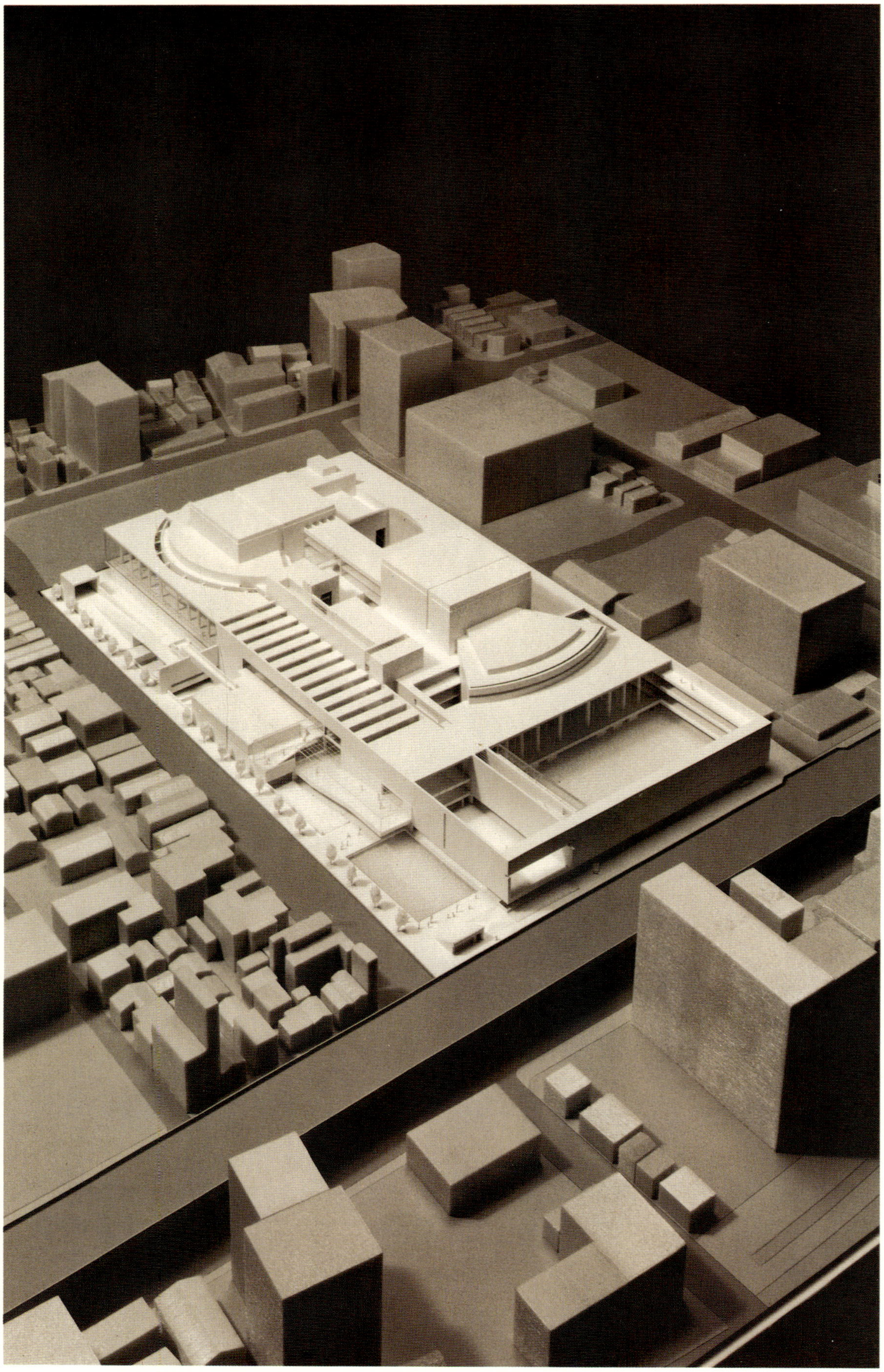

Project

Theatre for contemporary performing arts

Site

Hon-cho, Shibuya-ku, Tokyo

Dates

Competition announced 26 July 1984 *Closing date* 1–15 April 1985 *Result announced* 28 May 1985

Number of entries

228 (168 Japanese entries and 60 foreign entries from 22 different countries).

Jury

Yasumi Yoshitake (chairman, architect), Yoshinobu Ashihara, Arata Isozaki, Ichiro Ebihara, Hiroshi Oe, Kazuo Ota, Sakae Omi (all architects), Naoshi Inumaru (director-general of the National Theatre of Japan), Asakazu Sakamoto, Koreya Senda, Kazuyuki Toyama, Naohiko Hishi, Isamu Yamashita and twelve other technical advisors.

Result

First prize Takahiko Yanagisawa and team (Harald Deilman, Adolf Zotzmann, Hidemi Ito, Hiroshi Yoshiuchi, Hisao Nagai, Edeltraud Jauster, Shouichi Ito, Kenichi Tokiwa, Michiko Nojima, Naomi Matsuura, Yoshio Kono, Chihiro Mizuuchi, Yoshiyuki Okubo, Akira Ikegami, Kenji Kageyama, Yukiya Tokuriki) *Second prize* Hisao Wakamatsu and team (Tomohisa Yuri, Masato Tanaami, Tadashi Sugano); Hans Hollein; Bernard Tschumi; Osamu Ogasawara *Honourable mention* Kan Izue; Peter D. Eisenman; Tadayoshi Fujiki and team (Shunichi Nakamura, Yoshiaki Tsuboi, Takeo Morimura, Hiroshi Ezaki); Kaichi Naruse; Tomohisa Yuri and team (Hisao Wakamatsu, Hiroyuki Sakamoto, Norio Kita); Yoichi Okugawa

Commissioned by

The Ministry of Construction and the Bureau of Cultural Affairs

Construction

Due 1996

Architect

Takahiko Yanagisawa & Tak Ass. (Engineering bureau)

New National Theatre, Tokyo, 1984–1985

Rep. Takahiko Yanagisawa

competition design, 1985, exterior view from south-west, first prize

New National Theatre, Tokyo

The design and construction of a new opera house has always appealed to the imagination of architects and the public. This appeal is fuelled by the magnitude and prestige of such projects, and fanned by the public's anticipation of the spectacular productions that are to be staged there. The construction of opera houses in Vienna, Sydney and Paris all had a similar appeal. The construction of the New National Theatre in Tokyo had an added dimension: it was to be the first major Japanese theatre that would not stage traditional, Japanese performing arts, but would be purpose-built for the performance of Western opera productions.

A growing interest in Western culture

For many years Western opera and other performing arts had been far less popular in Japan than Noh theatre and Kabuki performances. There was not a single theatre in the country that was suitable for the performance of foreign productions, and for many years the authorities had remained indifferent to this state of affairs. However, the intensification of Japan's economic ties with the West went hand in hand with a growing interest in Western culture, an interest which began to develop during the Meiji era, in the latter half of the nineteenth century, and continued into the twentieth century. During the twentieth century Japanese architects developed an affinity for Western architecture; Frank Lloyd Wright and Le Corbusier became important sources of inspiration. However, it was to be some time before Western performing arts gained a similar status.
It was not until the 1970s and 80s that plans for the construction of theatres for Western performing arts were developed on a grand scale. The first projects were initiated by private enterprise, because the authorities still harboured certain reservations. Over the years the Japanese business community has continued to promote Western culture and has funded a number of cultural projects, including the Casals Hall in Tokyo, designed by Arata Isozaki and completed in 1987. It is, of course, significant that the concert hall was named after a famous Western cellist.
Eventually, the national government, notorious for its cultural lethargy, had to admit to some embarrassment at the fact that an economic superpower – which could match any Western, industrialised country in most fields and surpassed many – did not have its own opera house, a building steeped in prestige. Consequently, the authorities developed plans to build a theatre that would not only serve as a venue for opera and ballet, but would also stage experimental theatre. The necessary funds for the New National Theatre were made available by the authorities and a site was eventually designated in Hatsudai, Shinjuku, on the grounds of the former Tokyo Industrial Laboratory. This site was easily accessible, but the surrounding district was a little run down, a fact which caused some objections to be raised. However, these objections proved unwarranted because plans to redevelop the entire district were well under way. The new Tokyo Metropolitan Hall was also later built in this district[1].

Hiroshi Ohe, National Noh Theatre, 1983

Takenaka Corporation, National Theatre, 1966

A Japanese tussle

The Ministry of Construction and the Bureau of Cultural Affairs, who were in charge of the project, decided to organise an open international competition to select an architect. The competition was announced on 26 July 1984 and the closing date was 15 April 1985. The participants were asked to include three auditoria in their designs: the main auditorium, with 1 900 seats, would be reserved for opera and ballet; the second auditorium, with 1 000 seats, would be used to stage drama, modern dance and smaller opera productions, while the third auditorium, with 400 seats, would be used to stage experimental theatre.

The authorities' decision to organise an open competition – a novelty in Japan – was possibly prompted by widespread criticism of Japanese protectionism. Sixty foreign architects eventually submitted designs and the jury ranked Hans Hollein, Bernard Tschumi and Peter Eisenman amongst the best of the 228 participants. However, their decision to award first prize to a Japanese team was sharply criticised, because the jury were all Japanese and because the international regulations for architectural competitions, drafted by the Union Internationale d'Architectes, and intended for use as a guideline, had in this case been ignored. The competition for the Western-oriented opera house therefore became a tussle between Japanese architects. A few years later, an open international competition for the Kansai airport in Osaka was won by a foreign architect[2]

Japanese traditions

Japan has had mixed feelings about its own architectural traditions since Western architecture was brought to the country in the nineteenth century. On the one hand, Western traditions were studied and copied, while, on the other hand, the age-old Japanese architectural traditions were still revered. Most of the traditional structures were made of rice paper and wood, with no doors or windows, and had open, uncluttered rooms divided by movable partitions. Space and light were, and still are, amongst the most important aspects of Japanese design. Foreign architects not only introduced a new style, but also brought with them new materials and techniques. Those who shared the Japanese affinity for space and light, were particularly popular, which explains why Le Corbusier's open floor plans, his emphasis upon the interplay of light and shadow and many other characteristic features of his designs still have an influence on Japanese architecture.
The step from Le Corbusier to European Functionalism was a small one. After the Second World War, Modernism became the style of the future and it was not until the 1960s that a unique, Japanese style developed. This style was developed by the Metabolists and was based on traditional values and the human aspects of architecture. Many leading Metabolists produced designs for the 1970 Expo in Osaka[3], an early highlight in the movements history.

Arata Isozaki Casals Hall, section, 1987

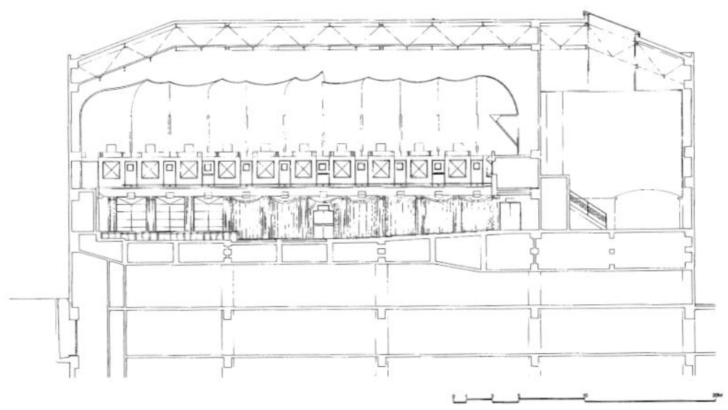

Arata Isozaki Casals Hall, section, 1987

Japanese Modernism has produced many magnificent buildings. During the 1970s and 80s – when the New National Theatre was built – Japanese architects kept pace with the post-Modernist styles of their European and American counterparts. At first sight, Post-Modernism seemed particularly suited to the tastes of Japanese architects with their affinity for tradition, because it derived its features from the styles of bygone eras. However, the Japanese Post-Modernists did not only delve into their own past, but also derived features from European traditions.

This gave rise to a counter-current in Japanese architecture, which brought forth a new generation of architects, including Toyo Ito and Itsuko Hasegawa[4]. The movements described above existed more or less side-by-side at the time of the competition – some were in decline and others were still developing – which explains the stylistic diversity of the designs submitted for the New National Theatre.

A missed chance

In contrast to many other competitions, the winning design was not the most spectacular entry. A number of foreign participants were spotlighted. The New National Theatre would probably have received worldwide publicity if the jury had selected either one of the Deconstructivist designs submitted by Tschumi and Eisenman. Hollein, the third foreign nominee, had also submitted an outstanding design, which would almost certainly have produced one of Tokyo's most striking buildings. A number of the Japanese entries, all of which were submitted by teams, were also remarkable. Kan Izue's design featured "mountainous" stage towers and an undulating roof line. Tomohisa Yuri submitted a Modernist design. One of his drawings is enlivened by a scene from Verdi's "Aïda".

Takahiko Yanagisawa's winning design was styled according to run-of-the-mill Modernist principles. It was a collection of ordered facilities and, as a result, the design as a whole is rather boring, certainly in comparison to the "chaotic" products of the Deconstructivists. Yanagisawa sited the auditoria well away from the nearby freeway and the subway, in order to prevent disturbances. The focal points of his design are the subsidiary facilities and the technical structure. However, the winning team did not lose sight of the theatre's purpose as a public facility, and included a number of public areas.

Although Yanagisawa's design has produced a solid piece of architecture, Japan's first national opera house lacks that something extra which would have put it on a par with the operas in Paris and Vienna. And that, undoubtedly, must have been a disappointment to the authorities.

---

1 *See chapter on the Tokyo Metropolitan Hall elsewhere in this book.*

2 *See chapter on Kansai Airport elsewhere in this book.*

3 *Contributors included Arata Isozaki, Kisho Kurokawa and Kiyonori Kikutake, founding menbers of Metabolism in 1960, who designed pavilions, and Arata Isozaki and Kenzo Tange, who designed the Festival Plaza.*

4 *See chapter on the Shonandai Cultural Centre elsewhere in this book.*

Neues Nationaltheater, Tokio

Ein Architekturwettbewerb für eine neue Oper sorgt stets für Aufmerksamkeit – einerseits wegen des großen Auftragsvolumens und andererseits wegen des zu erwartenden Spektakels rund um die Ausschreibung (man denke nur an die Opern von Wien und Sydney oder an beide Pariser Opern). Das Neue Nationaltheater in Tokio fügte eine neue Dimension hinzu: Es sollte das erste Theater von Rang in Japan sein, das speziell für westliche Opernproduktionen eingerichtet wurde.

Interesse an westlicher Kultur

Jahrhundertelang waren westliche Opern und Theaterstücke in Japan weit weniger populär als Noh-Theater und Kabuki-Spiele. In ganz Japan gab es nicht ein einziges Gebäude, das zur Aufführung ausländischer Stücke geeignet gewesen wäre – und diese Politik war ganz im Sinne der Regierung. Erst als sich Japan wirtschaftlich dem Westen zu öffnen begann, entstand auch ein Interesse an westlicher Kultur. Diese Tendenz war bereits in der Meiji-Ära in der zweiten Hälfte des 19. Jahrhunderts spürbar und setzte sich im 20. Jahrhundert fort. Auch auf dem Gebiet der Architektur richtete sich ab dem 19. Jahrhundert der Blick nach Westen: Frank Lloyd Wright und Le Corbusier galten als wichtige Inspirationsquellen und Vorbilder. Nur die darstellenden Künste mußten noch auf ihre Anerkennung in Japan warten.
Erst in den 70er und 80er Jahren begann man mit Bauvorhaben größeren Stils, die die Aufführung ausländischer Theater- und Musikproduktionen ermöglichen sollten. Die staatlichen Stellen beobachteten diese Aktivitäten mit einiger Zurückhaltung, so daß die Initiativen ausschließlich von privaten Investoren ausgingen, die sich intensiv um die Verbreitung westlicher Kultur in Japan bemühten. Unter diesen Voraussetzungen entstand 1987 der Casals-Saal in Tokio – benannt nach dem berühmten spanischen Cellisten – nach einem Entwurf von Arata Isozaki. Schließlich begann sogar der japanische Staat umzudenken, der auf kulturellem Gebiet traditionell schwerfällig reagierte. Einige Regierungsstellen sahen es als einen bedenklichen Mangel an, daß eine wirtschaftliche Großmacht, die sich in allen Belangen mit den westlichen Industrieländern messen konnte und die meisten von ihnen überholt hatte, immer noch kein eigenes Operngebäude besaß.
Aus diesem Grund beschloß die Regierung den Bau eines Neuen Nationaltheaters, in dem neben Oper- und Ballettaufführungen auch experimentelles Theater stattfinden sollte. Nachdem die benötigten finanziellen Mittel zur Verfügung standen, fand man ein geeignetes Baugelände in Hatsudai, Shinjuku, auf dem Gelände des ehemaligen Industrie-Laboratoriums Tokio. Bedenken gegen den Bauort, der trotz seiner zentralen Lage in einem ziemlich heruntergekommenen Viertel lag, wurden von kommunalen Sanierungsplänen für das gesamte Stadtviertel entkräftet.

Japanische Vetternwirtschaft

Der Bau des neuen Theaters sollte unter Federführung des Bauministeriums und des Büros für kulturelle Angelegenheiten entstehen. Den geeigneten Architekten wollten die Behörden im Rahmen einer offenen internationalen Ausschreibung finden, die am 26. Juli 1984 begann und am 15. April 1985 endete. Die Zulassung ausländischer Architekten war für Japan ungewöhnlich und geschah aufgrund politischen Drucks anderer Nationen, die dem japanischen Protektionismus ein Ende bereiten wollten. Auch der spätere Wettbewerb für den Kansai International Airport bei Osaka wurde international ausgeschrieben und sogar von einem Ausländer gewonnen. So weit war man beim Neuen Nationaltheater noch nicht, obwohl Hans Hollein, Bernard Tschumi und Peter Eisenman zu den 228 teilnehmenden Architekten gehörten, von denen insgesamt 60 aus Übersee kamen.
Die Entscheidung der Jury, den ersten Preis an eine japanische Architektengruppe zu vergeben, sorgte für einige Proteste, da die ausschließlich aus Japanern zusammengesetzte Jury die internationalen Ausschreibungsbedingungen ignoriert hatte, die unter Mithilfe der Union Internationale d'Architects verfaßt worden waren und als Richtschnur dienen sollten. Dadurch geriet der Wettbewerb für ein westlich orientiertes Operngebäude zu einem typischen Beispiel japanischer Vetternwirtschaft. Außer einem großen Saal mit 1 900 Plätzen hatten die Teilnehmer Entwürfe für einen zweiten Saal mit etwa 1 000 Sitzen und einen kleinen Saal für 400 Zuschauer vorzulegen. Der große Saal war ausschließlich für Opern- und Ballettaufführungen gedacht, während im kleinen Saal experimentelles Theater und im mittleren Saal Theateraufführungen, kleinere Opernaufführungen und moderne Tanzvorstellungen stattfinden sollten.

Japanische Traditionen

Seit der Einführung der westlichen Baukunst im 19. Jahrhundert hat die japanische Kultur ihrer eigenen architektonischen Tradition mit einer gewissen Ambivalenz gegenübergestanden: Während man westliche Formen studierte und übernahm, wurde gleichzeitig die jahrhundertealte japanische Formsprache gepflegt und weiterentwickelt. Offene, leere Räume mit beweglichen Wänden aus transparentem Reispapier und Holzkonstruktionen ohne Fenster und Türen gehören zu den typischen äußeren Merkmalen dieser Bautradition. Auch heute noch sind Raum und Licht die wichtigsten Elemente einer japanischen Konstruktion. Von den ausländischen Entwürfen, die neben den westlichen Stilformen auch neue Materialien und Techniken nach Japan brachten, fanden nur diejenigen Beachtung, die sich ebenfalls dieser Elemente bedienten.
Entsprechend wurden Le Corbusiers freier Grundriß, sein Spiel mit Licht und Schatten ebenso begeistert aufgenommen wie seine übrigen Bauprinzipien, die bis heute großen Einfluß auf die japanische Architektur ausüben. Nach Le Corbusier war es nur noch ein kleiner Schritt zu einer funktionalistischen Architektur europäischen Zuschnitts, und nach dem Zweiten Weltkrieg galt die Moderne als Stil der Zukunft. Erst mit dem Metabolismus der 60er Jahre, der die Betonung auf traditionelle Werte und die menschlichen Aspekte der Architektur legte, wurde ein eigenständiger, japanischer Weg eingeschlagen. Diese Phase fand ihren baulichen Höhepunkt auf der Expo 1970 in Osaka, wo die bedeutendsten Vertreter des Metabolismus ihre Vorstellungen realisieren konnten[1]. Auch die japanische Moderne hat Gebäude von verblüffender Schönheit hervorgebracht. In den 70er und 80er Jahren – der Periode der Musiksäle und des Neuen Nationaltheaters – folgten die Architekten ihren europäischen und amerikanischen Kollegen in die Postmoderne. Diese Stilrichtung, die sich ungehemmt der Stile der Vergangenheit bedient, schien wie geschaffen für die traditionsbewußten Japaner. Doch die japanischen Postmodernisten griffen auf Bauten und Stile aus dem westlichen Kulturkreis zurück: Die Welt stand Kopf.
Auf diese Entwicklung folgte eine Gegenbewegung, die eine Generation von Architekten wie Toyo Ito und Itsuko Hasegawa (siehe das Kapitel zum Shonandai Kulturzentrum) hervorbrachte. Zum Zeitpunkt des Wettbewerbs standen all diese Strömungen gleichberechtigt nebeneinander, einige auf dem Vormarsch, andere auf dem Weg in die Vergessenheit. Dadurch erklären sich auch die stilistischen Unterschiede der eingesandten Entwürfe.

Verpaßte Chancen

Im Gegensatz zu vielen anderen Architekturwettbewerben war der preisgekrönte Entwurf bei weitem nicht der spektakulärste Beitrag; eine Anzahl von Teilnehmern aus Übersee erregte weit mehr Aufmerksamkeit. Wenn sich die Jury für einen der dekonstruktivistischen Entwürfe Tschumis oder Eisenmans entschieden hätte, wäre das Neue Nationaltheater in die Schlagzeilen der Weltpresse geraten. Auch Holleins Beitrag war außergewöhnlich und hätte sicher zu einem von Tokios auffälligsten Bauwerken geführt. Aus Japan selbst kamen interessante Entwürfe wie der von Kan Izue mit seinen bergartigen Theatertürmen und einer wellenförmigen Firstlinie. Dagegen mutet der Vorschlag von Tomohisa Yuri modernistisch an. In seiner Atmosphärezeichnung ist als markantes Detail eine Szene aus Verdis »Aida« zu sehen. Die japanischen Einsendungen entstanden übrigens – nach guter japanischer Sitte – sämtlich in Teamarbeit; so auch das preisgekrönte Projekt von Takahiko Yanagisawa. Yanagisawas Entwurf steht in der Tradition der Moderne und wirkt wie eine Addition geordneter Funktionen. Der Gesamteindruck vermittelt daher eher Langeweile, insbesondere im Vergleich mit den dekonstruktivistischen Entwürfen anderer Teilnehmer. Yanigasawa plazierte seine Säle so, daß sie kein Hemmnis für die nahegelegenen Auto- und Untergrundbahnen darstellen. Technik und Versorgungsfunktionen spielen in seinem Entwurf eine besondere Rolle; darüber hinaus konzipierte das Siegerteam zahlreiche unterschiedliche öffentliche Räume.
Das Neue Nationaltheater ist sicher ein solides Bauwerk geworden, dennoch fehlt der Schuß Genialität, der das erste nationale Operngebäude Japans auf eine Stufe mit den Opern von Paris und Wien gebracht hätte. Allerdings hatte man dies ursprünglich erreichen wollen.

1 *Die Gründer (um 1960) dieser Bewegung waren Arata Isozaki, Kisho Kurokawa und Kiyonori Kikutake. Kurokawa und Kikutake bauten Pavillons für die Expo 1970; der später zu den Metabolisten gestoßene Kenzo Tange entwarf zusammen mit Isozaki die zentrale Festival Plaza.*

Le Nouveau Théâtre National, Tokyo

La conception et l'édification d'un nouvel opéra parlent à l'imagination des architectes et du grand public. Cette fascination tient à la fois au prestige de tels projets et à l'anticipation du plaisir des nouveaux spectacles qu'ils annoncent. La construction des opéras de Vienne, Sydney et Paris illustre ce phénomène. Celle du Nouveau Théâtre National de Tokyo offrait une dimension supplémentaire, puisqu'il s'agissait du premier grand théâtre construit au Japon à ne pas être consacré aux spectacles traditionnels mais à la représentation d'œuvres occidentales.

Un intérêt grandissant pour la culture de l'Occident

Jusqu'à une date récente, l'opéra, comme tous les types de spectacles occidentaux, était beaucoup moins populaire au Japon que le théâtre Nô ou Kabuki. Il n'existait pas une seule salle capable d'accueillir correctement des productions venues de l'Ouest et, longtemps, les autorités officielles étaient restées indifférentes à cet état de fait. Et pourtant, l'intensification des liens économiques entre le Japon et l'Ouest avait suscité un intérêt grandissant pour la culture occidentale dès l'ère Meiji, intérêt qui s'était affirmé de plus belle au XXème siècle. Au XIXème siècle, l'architecture européenne avait exercé une réelle influence sur un Japon en pleine modernisation et au XXème, Frank Lloyd Wright et Le Corbusier y furent souvent pris pour modèles. Mais il fallut encore attendre longtemps pour que les arts du spectacle occidentaux puissent prétendre à un statut équivalent.
A partir des années 1970, des projets d'initiative privée de construction de théâtres à l'occidentale se développèrent rapidement. Ce furent plutôt des grandes entreprises ou des hommes d'affaires qui assurèrent la promotion de l'art occidental et financèrent de nombreux projets dont la Salle Casal, à Tokyo, dessinée par Arata Isozaki. Ce n'est pas un hasard si son nom est celui d'un célèbre violoncelliste européen.
Le gouvernement, dont l'inaction culturelle est notoire, finit par admettre avec un peu d'embarras qu'il était anormal qu'une superpuissance économique ne possède même pas un opéra, édifice de prestige par excellence. Un projet de bâtiment pouvant accueillir à la fois des opéras et des représentations de théâtre expérimental fut donc ébauché. Les financements nécessaires furent débloqués et un site fut trouvé à Hatsudai, Shinjuku, sur les terrains de l'ancien Laboratoire de l'Industrie. L'emplacement était facilement accessible, mais le quartier environnant était un peu déclassé, ce qui souleva quelques oppositions vite apaisées par un projet de rénovation du quartier. Le nouvel hôtel de ville[1] fut d'ailleurs édifié non loin de là quelque temps après.

Une chasse gardée

Le ministère de la Construction et le bureau des Affaires culturelles chargé du projet décidèrent d'organiser un concours international ouvert. Il fut annoncé le 26 juillet 1984 et clos le 15 avril 1985. Les participants devaient prévoir trois salles: une de 1 900 places, réservée à l'opéra et au ballet; une seconde, de 1 000 places, pour le théâtre, la danse contemporaine et de petites productions d'opéra; la troisième, 400 places, affectée au théâtre expérimental.
La décision des autorités de lancer un concours international – une nouveauté pour le Japon – était peut-être une réponse aux critiques de plus en plus vives contre le protectionnisme japonais. 60 architectes étrangers participèrent et le jury classa les propositions de Hans Hollein, Bernard Tschumi et Peter Eisenman parmi les meilleures. Mais sa décision d'accorder le premier prix à une équipe japonaise fut fortement critiquée car le jury était entièrement composé de Japonais et la réglementation des concours internationaux de l'Union Internationale des Architectes avait été ignorée. Le concours pour un opéra occidental devint ainsi une chasse gardée au bénéfice des seuls architectes japonais.
Signe de changement, quelques années plus tard le concours international pour l'aéroport de Kansai à Osaka allait être remporté par un étranger[2].

Traditions japonaises

Les sentiments des Japonais par rapport à leur architecture sont assez ambigus. D'un côté, les pratiques occidentales ont été étudiées et copiées depuis le XIXème siècle, et d'un autre, les traditions locales anciennes sont toujours révérées. En introduisant de nouveaux styles, les architectes étrangers apportèrent également des techniques et des matériaux nouveaux. La plupart des constructions traditionnelles nippones sont de bois et de papier de riz, sans porte ni fenêtre, et possèdent un plan intérieur très ouvert, divisé par des cloisons mobiles. L'espace et la lumière sont encore les éléments les plus importants des plans des maisons japonaises. Ceux d'entre eux qui partageaient la sensibilité locale pour l'espace et la lumière, comme Le Corbusier, furent particulièrement appréciés ce qui explique que ses plans de masse très ouverts, ses jeux d'ombre et de lumière et de multiples aspects de ses recherches exercent encore une influence au Japon.
Passer de Le Corbusier au fonctionnalisme européen ne demanda pas beaucoup d'effort et le modernisme japonais peut se flatter de nombreuses réussites.
Pendant les années 70 et 80 – à l'époque de la construction du Théâtre National – les architectes japonais restèrent en phase avec les styles de l'après-modernisme de leurs confrères européens et américains. A première vue, un certain Post-modernisme à base d'éléments tant européens que nippons pouvait même sembler correspondre à leur goût pour la tradition.
Ce ne fut pas avant la fin des années 60 que l'on vit naître un style japonais moderne authentique, le Métabolisme. Il reposait sur les valeurs traditionnelles et une analyse des rapports entre l'homme et l'architecture. Plusieurs grands métabolistes se firent remarquer lors de l'exposition universelle d'Osaka (1970), une des dates marquantes de l'histoire de ce mouvement qui révéla une nouvelle génération d'architectes (dont Toyo Ito et Itsuko Hasegawa[3]).
Modernisme et métabolistes coexistaient avec plus ou moins de bonheur à l'époque du concours du Nouveau Théâtre National, ce qui explique la diversité stylistique des projets soumis.

Une chance manquée

A la différence de ce qui s'était passé dans de nombreux autres concours, le projet primé n'était pas le plus spectaculaire. Certains concurrents étrangers furent brillants et l'on peut penser que ce Nouveau Théâtre National aurait fait parler de lui dans le monde entier si les propositions déconstructivistes de Tschumi ou d'Eisenman avaient été retenues. Hollein avait envoyé des plans remarquables qui auraient certainement donné à Tokyo l'un de ses plus remarquables édifices. D'autres projets japonais étaient tout aussi intéressants. Celui de Kan Izue s'articulait à partir de deux tours de cintres «montagneuses» et d'un toit ondulé tandis que Tomohisa Yuri proposait un projet moderniste et animait l'un de ses dessins à l'aide d'une scène de l'Aïda de Verdi.
Le projet vainqueur, celui de Takahiko Yanagisawa, respecte les principes modernistes classiques. Il aligne sagement les divers équipements demandés et semble un peu ennuyeux, surtout par rapport aux «chaos» organisés des déconstructivistes. Les salles sont implantées loin des autoroutes urbaines pour limiter les interférences sonores. Les points forts du projet sont les aménagements secondaires et la structure technique, même si les espaces publics sont bien conçus.
Si les plans de Yanagisawa sont solides, le premier opéra construit au Japon manque de ce «plus» qui pourrait le rapprocher des salles de Paris et de Vienne. En leur for intérieur, les responsables japonais ont sans doute été déçus.

1 *Voir le chapitre sur l'hôtel de ville de Tokyo, dans cet ouvrage.*
2 *Voir le chapitre sur l'aéroport de Kansai, dans cet ouvrage.*
3 *Ses participants comprenaient les membres fondateurs des années 60, Arata Isozaki, Kisho Kurokawa et Kiyonori Kikutake. Kurokawa et Kikutake dessinèrent des pavillons pour l'Exposition Universelle de 1970 et Isozaki le «Festival Plaza» avec Kenzo Tange, qui rejoignit plus tard le mouvement.*

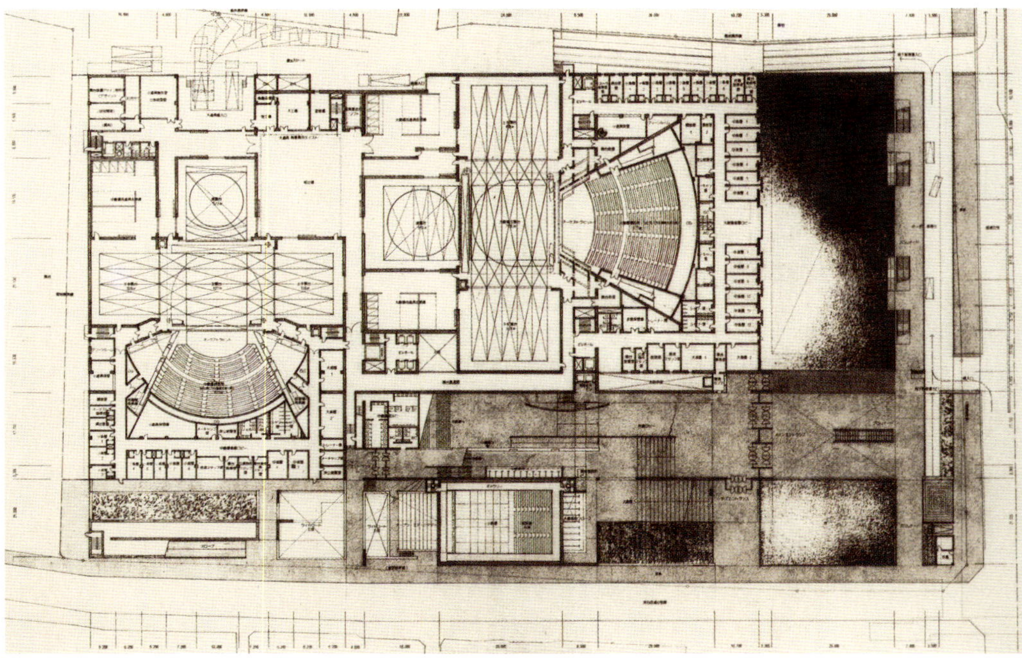

Takahiko Yanagisawa and team
competition design, 1985, interior view of communal lobby, first prize

Takahiko Yanagisawa and team
competition design, 1985, interior view, left: main theatre, right: medium theatre, first prize

Takahiko Yanagisawa and team
competition design, 1985, ground floor plan, first prize

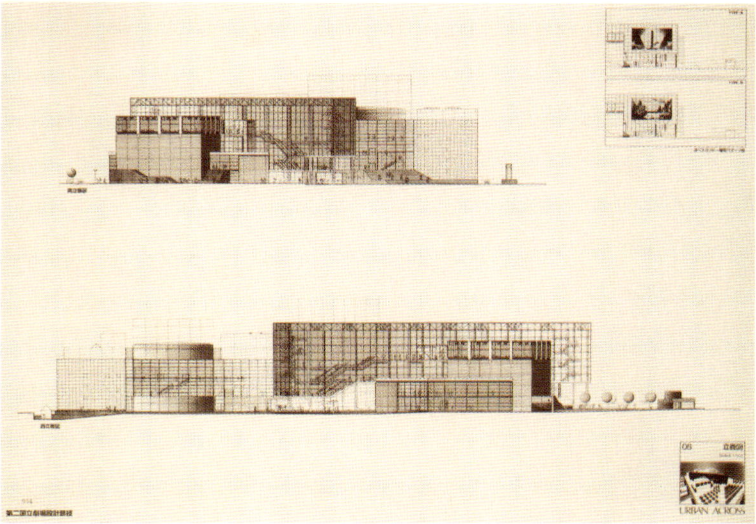

Hisao Wakamatsu and team
competition design, 1985, above: south elevation, below: west elevation, second prize

Hisao Wakamatsu and team
competition design, 1985, exterior view from south-west, second prize

Hisao Wakamatsu and team
competition design, 1985, interior view of communal lobby, second prize

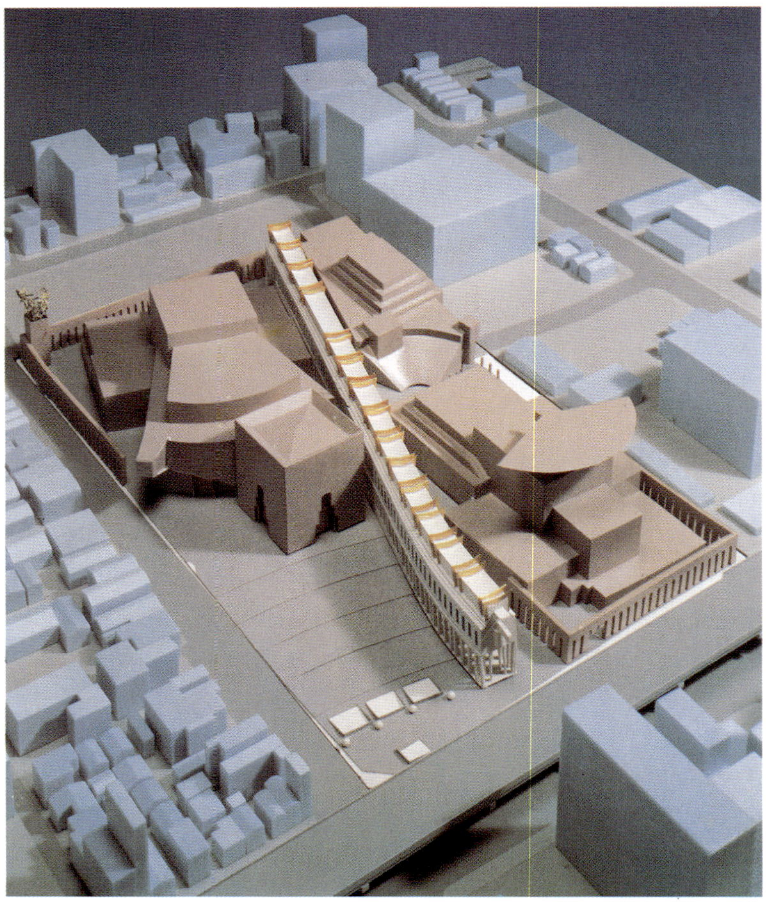

Hans Hollein competition design, 1985, interior view of the theatre, second prize

Hans Hollein competition design, 1985, model (south-west), second prize

Bernard Tschumi competition design, 1985, left: interior view of main theatre, right: sectional view of medium theatre, second prize

Bernard Tschumi competition design, 1985, exterior view from south-west, second prize

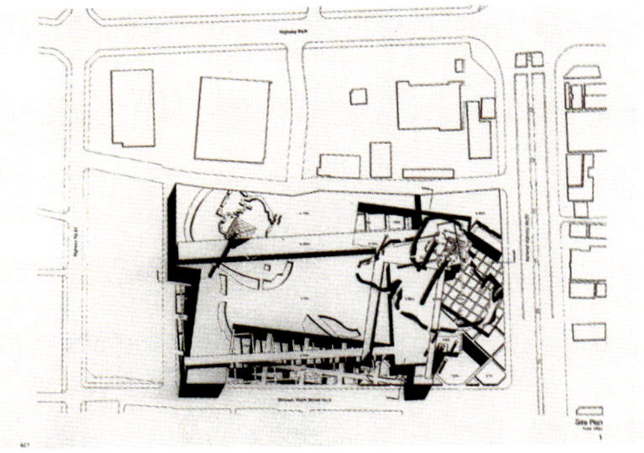

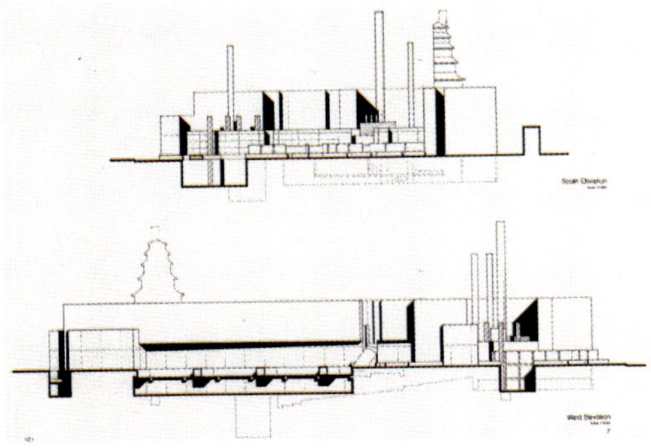

Peter D. Eisenman competition design, 1985, site plan, honourable mention

Peter D. Eisenman competition design, 1985, above: south elevation, below: west elevation, honourable mention

Peter D. Eisenman competition design, 1985, interior view of main lobby, honourable mention

Peter D. Eisenman competition design, 1985, exterior view from south-west, honourable mention

Kan Izue competition design, 1985, exterior view, honourable mention

Kan Izue competition design, 1985, interior view of communal lobby, honourable mention

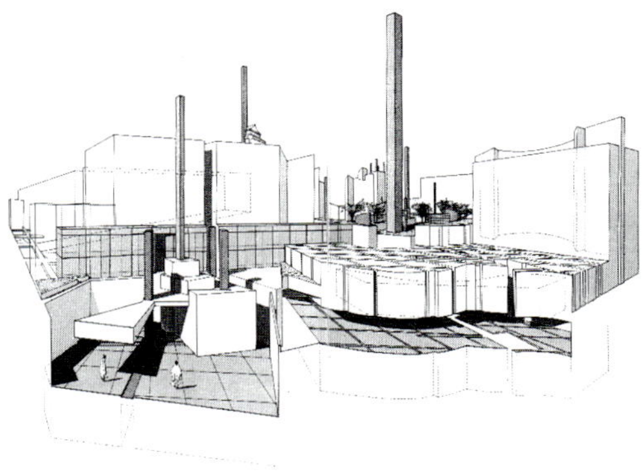

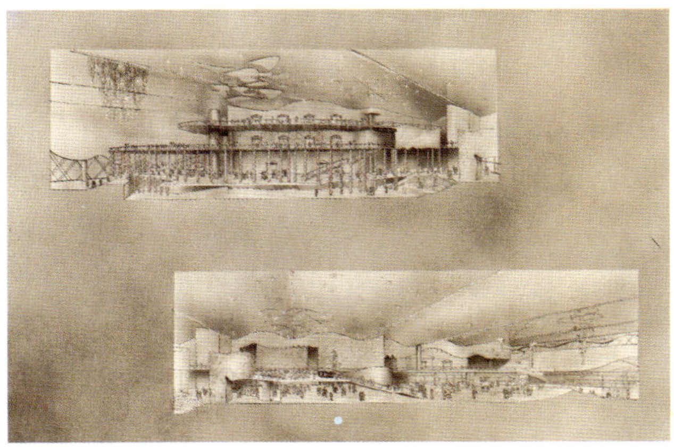

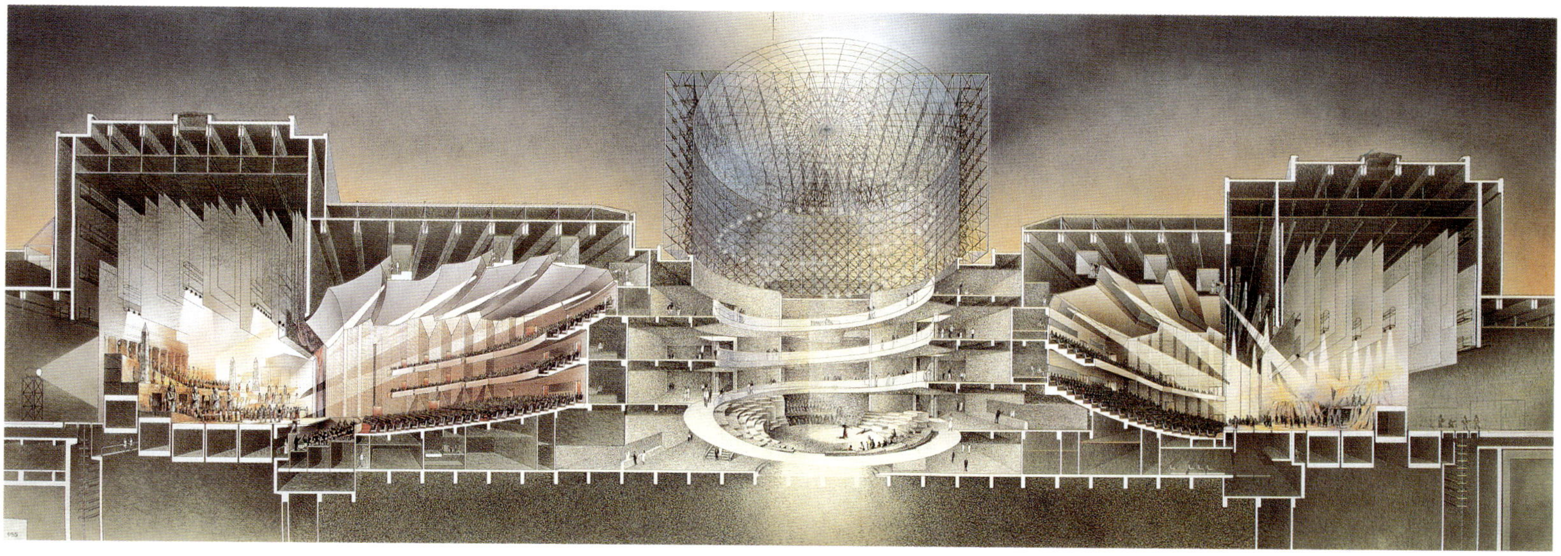

Tomohisa Yuri competition design, 1985, sectional view of theatres, honourable mention

Tadayoshi Fujiki competition design, 1985, interior view of communal lobby, honourable mention

Tadayoshi Fujiki competition design, 1985, interior view above: main theatre, below: medium theatre, honourable mention

Shonandai Cultural Centre, Fujisawa, 1985–1986

Project

Municipal cultural centre

Site

Shonandai 1–8, Fujisawa

Dates

Competition announced 2 October 1985 *Closing date* 17 January 1986 *Result announced* February 1986

Number of entries

215

Jury

Kiyoshi Seike (chairman, Professor of Fine Arts and Music, Tokyo National University), Arata Isozaki (architect), Matsuo Uchida (chairman of the Fujisawa Town Council), Akiyoshi Ogata (Yokohama National University), Shun Hayama (mayor of Fujisawa), Fumihiko Maki (professor, Tokyo University), Shozo Kanbe

Result

First prize Itsuko Hasegawa (Itsuko Hasegawa Studio) *Runners-up* Katsuhiro Kobayashi & Kiyoshi Sei Takeyama (Amorphe); Shin Takamatsu *Honourable mention* Kensuke Yoshida (Yoshida Architectural Work Room); Kunihiko Hayakawa & Associates; Kazunari Sakamoto (Tokyo Technological Institute, Sakamoto Studio); Hajime Yatsuka (Urban Project Machine); Kazumasa Furuichi & Takuro Hoshino

Commissioned by

A special commission appointed by the Municipality of Fujisawa

Construction

First phase July 1987 – June 1989 *Second phase* December 1988 – July 1991

Architect

Itsuko Hasegawa (*1941)

Shonandai Cultural Centre, Fujisawa, 1985–1986

Itsuko Hasegawa execution design, 1990, model

Shonandai Cultural Centre, Fujisawa

Over the years the old Japanese coastal town of Fujisawa had developed into an enormous dormitory suburb of Tokyo, fifty kilometres away. However, Fujisawa lacked the recreational and cultural facilities that are usually found in a medium-sized provincial town with 300 000 inhabitants.

A shortage of facilities

During the 1960s a network of rapidly expanding dormitory towns had developed along the Bay of Sagami in the Shonan region, all satellites to nearby Tokyo. However, the infrastructure and urban facilities of these towns had not kept pace with the rapidly increasing number of inhabitants.

Fujisawa was one of the towns which required a structured urban development plan. The town is roughly divided into three parts: the coastal strip, where the main recreational facilities are situated; the district around the JR and Odakyu stations, where the main commercial activities are centred; and the northern district, which has a characteristic mix of housing and cultural facilities.

From the beginning of the 1970s, the newly-appointed mayor of Fujisawa, Shun Hayama, took charge of the town's development. He commissioned the renowned architect Fumihiko Maki to design a new complex for sport and culture in the northern part of the city. The complex was completed in 1984. Hayama initiated many other projects, including the development of a new city centre, which was to be based on three main themes: children, community and communication. In order to realise these plans, an open competition for a cultural centre was organised in 1985.

This cultural centre for children was to be built close to Odakyu Shonandai station. One of its main attractions would be a planetarium which could accommodate two hundred visitors. This fact alone made the competition something special and also meant that the participants would have to make a special effort to identify with the target audience. A civic hall and auditorium were planned for the adult population. These three main facilities, corresponding with the three themes, children, community and communication, were to be grouped around a square. The area beneath the complex would serve as a car-park, with space for one hundred cars.

The official competition programme caused a certain amount of confusion, because it requested "design proposals", but that did not prevent more than two hundred architects from submitting plans. The field of contenders was whittled down during five rounds of adjudication. As a safeguard against over-hasty decisions, those architects who were eliminated in the first round were given a second chance. Only eight architects remained after the fourth round. Five received an honourable mention and three were awarded prizes. This trio of finalists went through to the final round, which was won by Itsuko Hasegawa.

Hasegawa's success was remarkable because she was not employed by

Fumihiko Maki Akibadai Arts and Gymnastics Hall, 1984

Nobuaki Furuya competition design, 1986, view of plaza

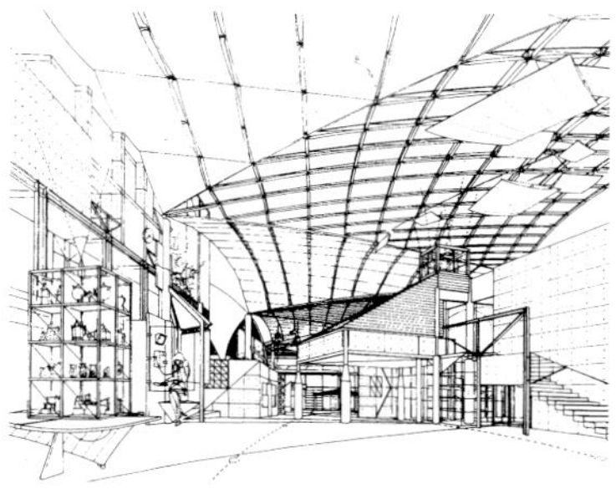

a major architectural firm, but formed part of a new and younger generation of architects, as did many of the other fourth and fifth-round contenders. It was hailed as a victory for the avant-garde, for architects with innovative ideas who worked independently and were not employed by architectural firms in collaboration with commercial construction companies.

Nature as master of the arts

Hasegawa (*1941) was not only young and independent, she was also a woman, and had had little experience with projects of this magnitude. Her victory is all the more remarkable in view of the fact that the Japanese architectural world is male-dominated, and may serve as an incentive for other women working in the field. Hasegawa's language of forms is abstracted from nature, her main source of inspiration: the hills, trees and mountains of the surrounding landscape are represented as architectural elements, an approach which clearly shows the influence of her mentor Kazuo Shinohara, with whom she worked for several years.

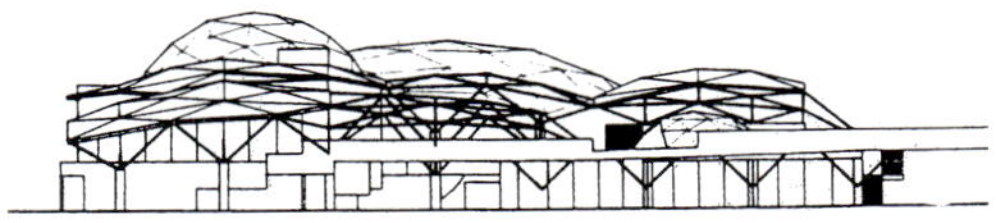

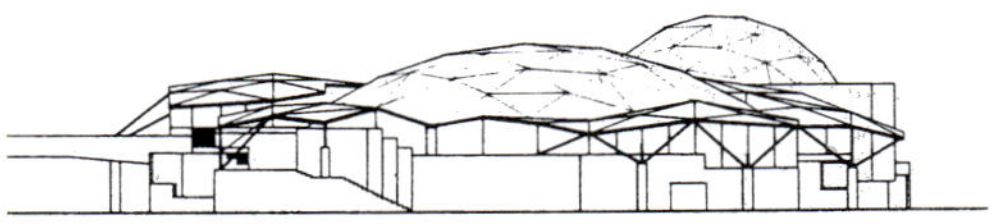

Shinohara is one of the masters of post-war Japanese architecture. Initially part of the Metabolism movement, he soon developed a personal architectural idiom based on nature and tradition, and became one of the spiritual fathers of a new Japanese architectural movement, characterised by wild, primitive, and especially anti-hierarchical features. This movement, sometimes referred to as post-Structuralism, glorifies rustic pleasures and simplicity and is a classic example of similar trends which have emerged in the arts throughout history. However, only in Japan, where harmony between art and nature has always been considered important, could a movement of this sort produce results with such a strong imaginative appeal. Hasegawa and Toyo Ito are two of the most important exponents of this approach.

Winning the competition gave Hasegawa the perfect opportunity to put her principles into practice. She had been able to do so on a smaller scale in the past, but a project of this magnitude naturally offered a wider range of architectural possibilities.

An artificial landscape

Hasegawa designed an aluminium and concrete landscape for the Shonandai Cultural Centre. Aluminium, preferably perforated, is one of her favourite materials. The complex resembles a valley with rock gardens, a stream, trees and a variety of other irregular elements. It had been her intention to create an environment in which visitors both young and old would feel at ease. The most striking elements of the landscape are the enormous domes of the planetarium and auditorium (seating capacity 800), which resemble two suns setting behind the mountainous "horizon" of the complex, formed by the roofs of the workshops and the foyer. From inside, the view is dominated by "woods" and "pastoral hamlets". One of the domes is also a globe, emphasising the fact that planet earth is part of the universe.

Haijme Yatsuka competition design, 1986, model, honourable mention

Kazunari Sakamoto competition design, 1986, south elevation and north elevation, honourable mention

Shin Takamatsu competition design, 1986, model, runner-up

Itsuko Hasegawa Shonandai Cultural Centre, 1990

The complex has many diverse and dynamic faces. Architecture is presented as an alternative form of nature; not governed by principles, but original and organic. As Hasegawa put it: *"Apparently the nature of the Japanese people harbours an ideal, which has found expression throughout the extended history of this rural community. It should be a natural stage, with jutting mountains, streaming rivers, rice fields, lakes and seas, dotted with houses, temples and shrines. Various architectural symbols of Western or Japanese origin are used in commercial housing, but I try to create a natural stage with the aid of natural symbols. The roofs of houses, grouped in a circle, resemble mountains. Mountains and a sea of trees form a shadowy image on the sheer surfaces."*

Although Hasegawa had undoubtedly submitted the most provocative design, the competition's true victor was architecture itself. The competition attracted many daring and original entries, including the light and dynamic design submitted by Hasegawa's kindred spirit Toyo Ito, and the more hierarchic and imposing design submitted by Atsushi Ueda. There is a similar contrast between Katsuhiro Kobayashi and Kiyoshi Sei Takeyama's monumental design and the more irregular, natural design submitted by Kensuke Yoshida.

Lunar fairy-tale village

The Shonandai Cultural Centre is certainly a hit as far as children are concerned. During an instructive school outing, they can play with electronic gadgets to their hearts' content, or simply marvel at the shows in the planetarium. Hasegawa's approach to architecture has been described as childish, intuitive and irrational. If this is so, she was perfectly cut out to identify with the perceptions of the younger visitors to this "lunar fairy-tale village"[1].

1 Hajime Yatsuka, architecture critic.

Shonandai-Kulturzentrum, Fujisawa

Im Laufe der Jahre hatte sich der japanische Küstenort Fujisawa zu einer riesigen Schlafstadt für das 50 km entfernte Tokio entwickelt. Doch den rund 300 000 Einwohnern fehlten sämtliche rekreativen und kulturellen Einrichtungen, die eine mittelgroße Provinzstadt dieser Größe im Sinne zufriedenstellender Lebensqualität benötigte.

Mangel an Einrichtungen

Im Gebiet von Shonan an der Bucht von Sagami entstand ein Netz schnell wachsender Schlafstädte, in denen Beschäftigte aus dem nahegelegenen Tokio übernachteten. Infrastruktur und öffentliche Einrichtungen der Städte hatten sich nicht proportional zur explosiven Bevölkerungszunahme entwickelt.

Fujisawa ist in drei Teile gegliedert – den Küstenstreifen, mit dem größten Angebot an Freizeiteinrichtungen, das Gebiet rund um die Bahnhöfe JR und Odakyu, das den kommerziellen Sektor beherbergt, sowie den Nordteil mit gemischtem Charakter (Wohnen und Kultur).

In den 70er Jahren nahm Bürgermeister Shun Hayama die Entwicklung Fujisawas in die Hand: Er beauftragte den bekannten Architekten Fumihiko Maki mit dem Bau eines neuen Sport- und Kulturkomplexes im Norden, der 1984 fertiggestellt wurde. Neben vielen anderen Projekten bemühte sich Hayama auch um die Bildung eines neuen Stadtzentrums unter den Schlagworten: »Kinder, Gemeinschaft und Kommunikation«. Aus diesem Grund beschlossen die Behörden 1985 den Bau eines Kulturzentrums, das in der Nähe des Odaky-Shonandai-Bahnhofs entstehen sollte; den geeigneten Architekten wollte man in einem offenen Wettbewerb ermitteln.

Als wichtigster Bestandteil des neuen Komplexes galt ein kulturelles Zentrum für Kinder mit einem Planetarium für 200 Besucher. Diese Auflage machte die Ausschreibung für alle Teilnehmer äußerst anspruchsvoll und verlangte großes Einfühlungsvermögen. Für die Erwachsenen waren ein Bürgerzentrum und ein Auditorium geplant. Die drei Gebäude sollten rund um einen Platz gruppiert werden; unter dem neuen Gebäudekomplex war eine Tiefgarage für 100 Autos vorgesehen.

Die Bezeichnung »Vorschlag für einen Entwurf« in der offiziellen Ausschreibung sorgte für einige Unklarheit unter den Teilnehmern, was rund 200 Architekten jedoch nicht davon abhielt, ihre Pläne einzureichen. Die Beiträge wurden von der Jury in fünf Runden bewertet und aussortiert. Als zusätzliche Versicherung gegen überhastete Beschlüsse erhielten die »Verlierer« der ersten Runde eine zweite Chance. Nach der vierten Ausschreibungsrunde waren noch acht Entwürfe in der engeren Auswahl, von denen schließlich drei einen Preis und fünf eine ehrenvolle Erwähnung bekamen. Den ersten Preisbekam Itsuko Hasegawa zugesprochen. Dieser Entschluß der Jury sorgte für einiges Aufsehen, da die Architektin – ebenso wie viele andere Teilnehmer der vierten und fünften Runde – nicht aus einem der großen Büros kam, sondern zu einer neuen Generation junger Architekten gehörte. Man betrachtete die Entscheidung für Hasegawa allgemein als Triumph der Avantgarde, als Erfolg unabhängiger Architekten mit frischen Ideen.

Die Natur als Lehrmeister der Kunst

Hasegawa besaß wenig Erfahrung mit Aufträgen dieser Größenordnung. Für die stark von Männern beherrschte japanische Architekturwelt bedeutete der Sieg einer Frau eine bemerkenswerte Leistung und neue Motivation für andere Architektinnen. Hasegawa besinnt sich in ihren Entwürfen auf das Vorbild der Natur: Ihre Gebäude folgen natürlichen Formen wie Hügeln, Bäumen oder Bergen, die mit Hilfe architektonischer Formen abstrahiert und symbolisiert werden. Dieser Ansatz zeigt deutlich den Einfluß ihres Mentors Kazuo Shinohara, mit dem sie einige Jahre zusammenarbeitete.

Der 1925 geborene Shinohara gilt als einer der bedeutendsten Architekten der japanischen Nachkriegszeit. Zunächst vom Metabolismus beeinflußt, entwickelte er schnell eine eigene Formensprache, bei der Natur und Tradition die zentralen Ausgangspunkte bilden. Damit stand Shinohara am Anfang einer neuen Bewegung innerhalb der japanischen Architektur, die sich zu einem wilden, primitiven und anti-hierarchischen Baustil bekannte. Mit ihrer Verherrlichung alles Schlichten und Ländlichen gehört die unter dem Namen »Post-Strukturalismus« bekannte Strömung in eine Gruppe von Stilrichtungen, die in unregelmäßigen Abständen immer wieder in der Welt der Kunst auftauchen. Gerade in Japan führt ein solcher Stil zu phantasievollen Ergebnissen, da hier die Harmonie zwischen Kunst und Natur eine zentrale Rolle spielt. Neben Hasegawa gilt auch Toyo Ito als bedeutender Vertreter dieser Richtung. Für Hasegawa stellte der Gewinn des Wettbewerbs eine einzigartige Gelegenheit dar, ihre Vorstellungen in die Praxis umzusetzen. Dies war ihr bislang nur in kleinerem Maßstab gelungen.

Eine künstliche Landschaft

Hasegawa entwarf das Shonandai-Kulturzentrum als eine Landschaft aus Aluminium und Beton, wobei Aluminium – meist in Form von Lochblechen – zu ihren Lieblingsmaterialien gehört. Der Komplex erinnert an ein Tal mit Felsgruppen, einem Bach, Bäumen und verschiedenen unregelmäßigen Elementen. Es sollte ein Ort entstehen, an dem sich jeder Besucher, Kinder wie Erwachsene, wohlfühlen konnte. Die auffälligsten Elemente dieser Landschaft sind die beiden riesigen Kugeln, die das Planetarium bzw. ein Auditorium mit 800 Plätzen enthalten und wie doppelte Sonnen hinter dem bergigen Horizont des Komplexes untergehen. Der Horizont in Form einer Bergkette besteht aus den Dächern u. a. der Workshops und des Foyers. Aus dem Inneren blickt man jedoch auf »Wälder« und »Bauernhäuser«. Zusätzlich dient eine der Kugeln als Globus und erinnert an den Kosmos und seine Planeten.

Auf diese Weise offenbart der Komplex immer neue Gesichter und wirkt abwechslungsreich und dynamisch – Architektur als andere Form der Natur, nicht vom Verstand gelenkt, sondern ursprünglich, organisch gewachsen. Dazu erklärt Hasegawa: »*Offensichtlich besitzt das japanische Volk ein Ideal, was sich in der langen Geschichte seiner ländlichen Gemeinschaft äußert. Dabei muß es sich um eine Art natürlicher Bühne handeln, mit steilen Bergen, strömenden Flüssen, Reisfeldern, Seen und Meeren, dazwischen ein paar Häuser, Tempel und Schreine. Verschiedene dieser Symbole westlichen oder japanischen Ursprungs sind auch in am Markt orientierten Häusern zu finden, aber ich versuche, mit Hilfe natürlicher Symbole eine natürliche Bühne zu schaffen. Ein Kreis von mehreren kleinen Dächern läßt das Bild einer Bergkette entstehen. Berge und ein Meer von Bäumen stehen wie ein Schattenriß auf einer lotrechten Fläche.*«

Zweifellos hatte Hasegawa den phantasievollsten Entwurf eingereicht, aber der große Gewinner der Ausschreibung war die Architektur selbst: Unter den Einsendungen befanden sich eine ganze Reihe origineller und kühner Zeichnungen wie z. B. die luftigen, beweglichen Formen von Hasegawas Geistesverwandtem Toyo Ito und der hierarchische, imposante Entwurf von Atsushi Ueda. Ein vergleichbares Paar bilden der verspielte, natürliche Beitrag von Kensuke Yoshida und das monumentale Projekt von Katsuhiro Kobayashi und Kiyoshi Sei Takeyama.

Märchendorf auf dem Mond

Kinderfreundlich ist das Shonandai-Kulturzentrum in jedem Falle: Im Rahmen eines Schulausflugs können die Kinder sich mit elektronischen Spielereien beschäftigen oder das Planetarium besuchen. Hasegawas Architektur erscheint einigen Betrachtern als kindlich, intuitiv und irrational – doch gerade dadurch ist sie wie geschaffen für die Erlebniswelt der kleinen Besucher dieses »Märchendorfs auf dem Mond«, so der Architekturkritiker Hajime Yatsuka.

Le Centre Culturel de Shonandai, Fujisawa

La banlieue de Tokyo s'est beaucoup développée depuis quelques décennies, en particulier au bord de la baie de Sagami (Shonan). Au fil des années, l'ancienne petite ville côtière de Fujisawa, à cinquante kilomètres seulement de la capitale, s'est transformée en une énorme commune-dortoir. L'urbanisme n'ayant pas suivi au même rythme, Fujisawa manquait jusqu'à une époque très récente des équipements culturels et de loisirs que l'on devrait pouvoir trouver dans une ville de 300 000 habitants.

Le manque d'Institution

La ville est à peu près divisée en trois parties: le front de mer, où se trouvent les principaux équipements de loisirs, la zone des gares de JR et Odakyu, qui concentre les commerces, et le quartier nord comprenant aussi bien des logements que des équipements culturels.
Dès le début des années 70, le nouveau maire de Fujisawa, Shun Hayama, prit en main le redéveloppement de sa cité. Il chargea le célèbre architecte Fumihiko Maki de concevoir pour le nord de la ville un nouveau complexe culturel et sportif qui fut achevé en 1984. Il lança plusieurs autres projets dont la rénovation du centre-ville à partir de trois thèmes principaux: les enfants, la communauté et la communication, et organisa en 1985 un concours pour un centre culturel. Ce centre destiné aux enfants et comprenant un planétarium de 200 places devait être édifié près de la gare d'Odakyu Shonandai. L'objet du concours était donc assez particulier et demandait aux participants un réel effort d'identification au public visé. Une salle commune et un auditorium étaient d'autre part prévus pour les adultes. Ces trois grands équipements, illustrant les trois thèmes déjà cités, seraient regroupés autour d'une place dont les sous-sols serviraient de parking pour cent voitures.
En demandant des «propositions de concepts» le programme provoqua une certaine confusion qui n'empêcha pas cependant plus de deux cents architectes de concourir. Leur nombre se réduisit au cours de cinq tours mais, pour éviter des décisions trop hâtives, une seconde chance fut donnée aux éliminés du premier tour. Seuls huit architectes restèrent en lice pour le cinquième tour. Cinq reçurent une mention honorable et trois furent primés. Ce trio de finalistes participa au dernier tour, remporté par Itsuko Hasegawa.
Le succès d'Hasegawa est remarquable dans la mesure où elle ne travaillait pas pour un grand cabinet d'architecture et faisait partie d'une nouvelle jeune génération d'architectes comme plusieurs des concurrents des deux derniers tours. Il fut salué comme une victoire de l'avant-garde et des architectes créatifs indépendants, non liés à des groupes de construction immobilière.

La nature, maîtresse de tous les arts

Hasegawa n'était pas seulement jeune et indépendante, elle était aussi femme et n'avait guère d'expérience de projets de cette ampleur. Sa victoire est d'autant plus étonnante que le monde de l'architecture au Japon est essentiellement masculin et à ce titre, elle a valeur de modèle. Hasegawa s'inspire essentiellement de la nature et représente sur un mode architectural des collines, des arbres et des montagnes, approche qui témoigne de l'influence de son mentor, Kazuo Shinohara, avec lequel elle travailla plusieurs années.
Shinohara est l'un des maîtres de l'architecture japonaise d'après-guerre. Membre du mouvement métaboliste, il développa rapidement son propre vocabulaire architectural à partir de la nature et de la tradition, et devint l'un des pères spirituels d'un nouveau mouvement japonais, caractérisé par des éléments naturels, voire primitifs et son opposition à toute organisation hiérarchique. Ce mouvement, parfois appelé Post-structuralisme, rend hommage aux plaisirs et à la simplicité de la ruralité et rappelle plusieurs mouvements artistiques similaires qui se sont développés au cours des siècles. Mais ce n'est qu'au Japon, où l'harmonie entre l'art et la nature a toujours été considérée comme importante, qu'un mouvement de cette sorte pouvait aboutir à des résultats aussi séduisants. Hasegawa et Toyo Ito sont les deux plus importants représentants de cette approche.
Ce concours offrit à Hasegawa l'opportunité exceptionnelle de mettre ses principes en pratique. Elle avait réussi à le faire à petite échelle dans le passé, mais le centre culturel de Shonandai lui donnait beaucoup plus de possibilités.

Un paysage artificiel

C'est ainsi qu'elle conçut tout un paysage d'aluminium et de béton, l'aluminium, de préférence perforé, étant l'un de ses matériaux favoris. L'ensemble évoque une vallée avec des rochers, une rivière, des arbres et de multiples éléments de forme libre. Son intention était de créer un environnement dans lequel les visiteurs, jeunes et vieux, se sentiraient à l'aise. Les points marquants de ce paysage recréé sont les énormes dômes du planétarium et de l'auditorium (800 places), qui font penser à deux soleils émergeant derrière l'«horizon» montagneux formé par le toit des ateliers et du foyer. De l'intérieur, la vue est dominée par des «bois» et des «hameaux de pasteurs». L'un des dômes est en fait une sphère, image de la planète terre.
L'ensemble est dynamique et varié, et l'architecture est ici une alternative organique et originale à la nature. Comme Hasegawa a pu l'écrire: «*Apparemment, pour le peuple japonais, la nature nourrit un idéal qui a trouvé son expression tout au long de l'histoire de cette communauté humaine d'origine rurale. Cette idéal pourrait être représenté par une scène naturelle avec des montagnes élevées, des rivières écumantes, des champs de riz, des lacs et des mers, parsemée de maisons, de temples et de tombeaux. Divers symboles architecturaux d'origine japonaise ou occidentale sont utilisés dans les immeubles d'aujourd'hui, mais j'essaye de recréer une certaine nature à l'aide de symboles naturels. Les toits des maisons, groupés en cercle, font ainsi penser à des montagnes. Les montagnes et la mer des arbres se reflètent sur les façades lisses.*»
Bien que Hasegawa ait indubitablement proposé le plan le plus provocant, le vrai gagnant de ce concours fut l'architecture elle-même. La compétition suscita de nombreux projets audacieux dont les plans aériens et mouvementés d'un proche d'Hasegawa, Toyo Ito et ceux plus imposants et rationnels d'Atsushi Ueda. On trouve un contraste similaire entre les projets monumentaux de Katsuhiro Kobayashi et Kiyoshi Sei Takeyama et le plan irrégulier et «naturel» de Kensuke Yoshida.

Un village de contes de fées sur la lune

Le centre culturel de Shonandai est très apprécié par les enfants. Lors de leurs sorties de classe, ils peuvent jouer autant qu'ils le veulent avec des gadgets électroniques ou simplement admirer les programmes du planétarium. L'approche architecturale d'Hasegawa a été parfois qualifiée d'infantile, d'intuitive et d'irrationnelle, ce qui explique peut-être qu'elle soit si bien perçue par les jeunes visiteurs. Un critique, Hajime Yatsuka, a pu décrire Shonandai comme «un village de contes de fées sur la lune».

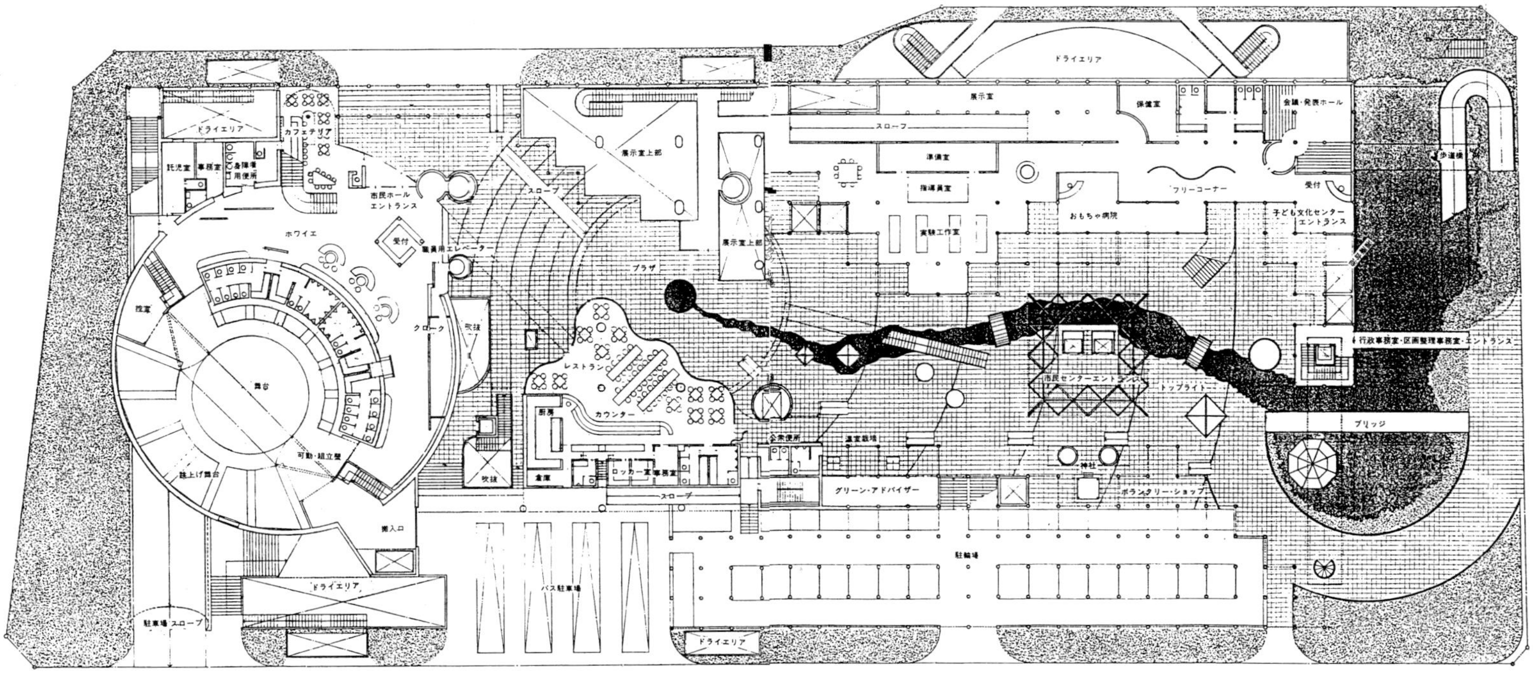

Itsuko Hasegawa competition design, 1986, ground floor plan, first prize

Itsuko Hasegawa competition design, 1986, above from left: west elevation, north elevation, middle from left: south elevation, east elevation, below from left: north-south section (east side), east-west section (south side), first prize

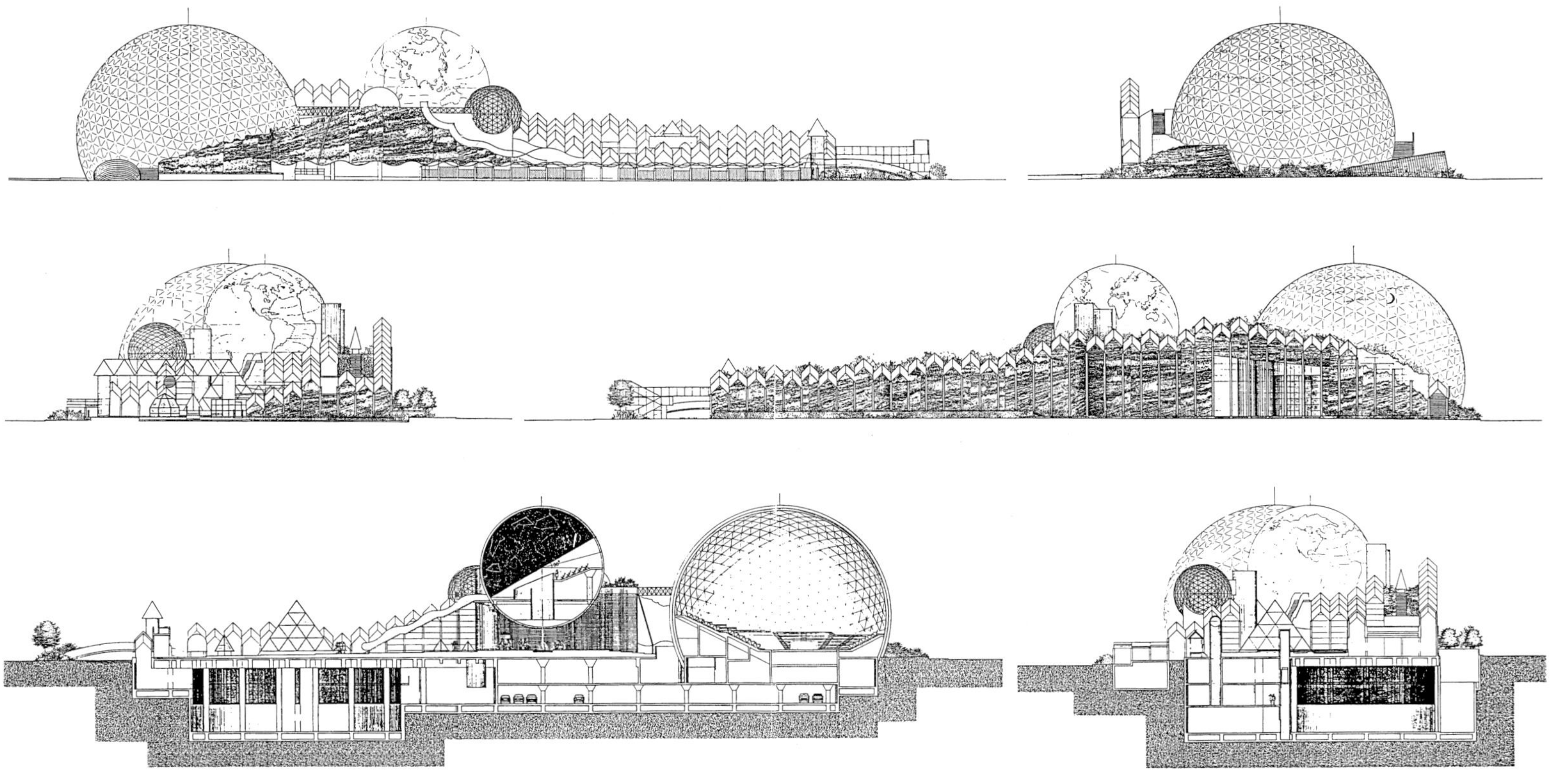

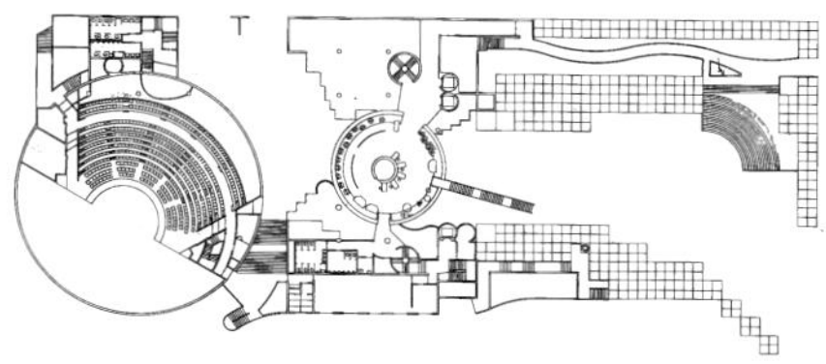

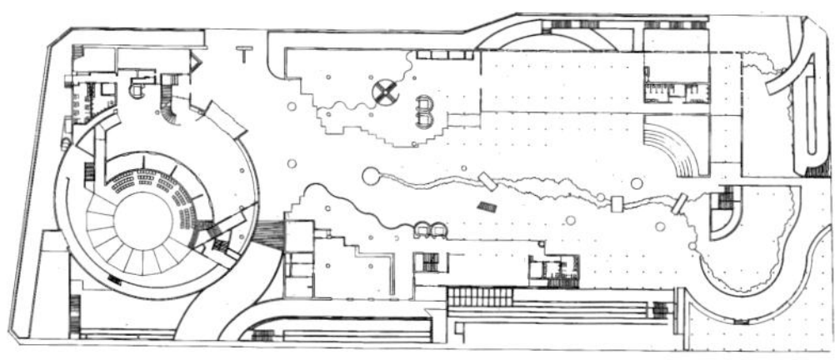

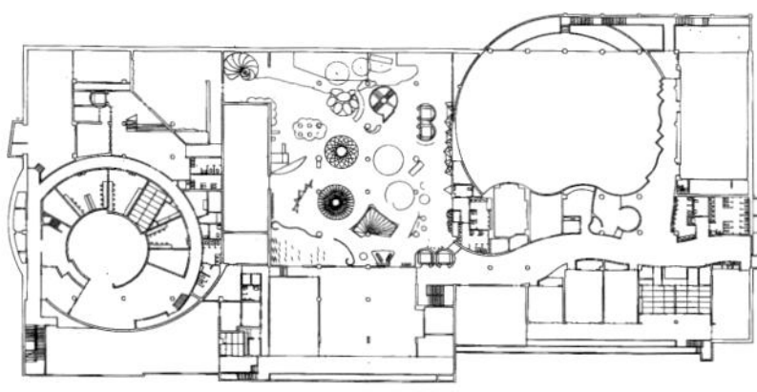

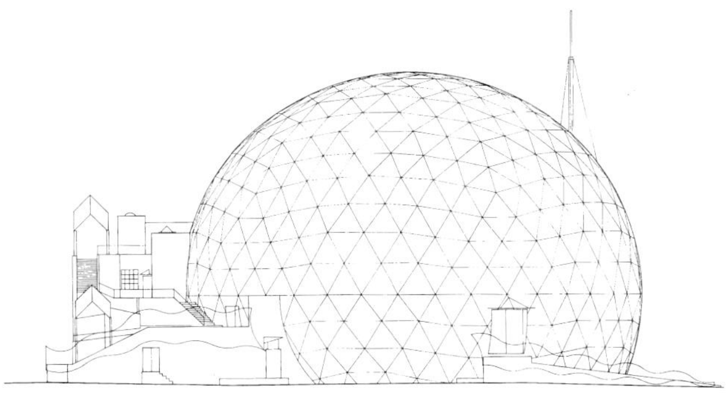

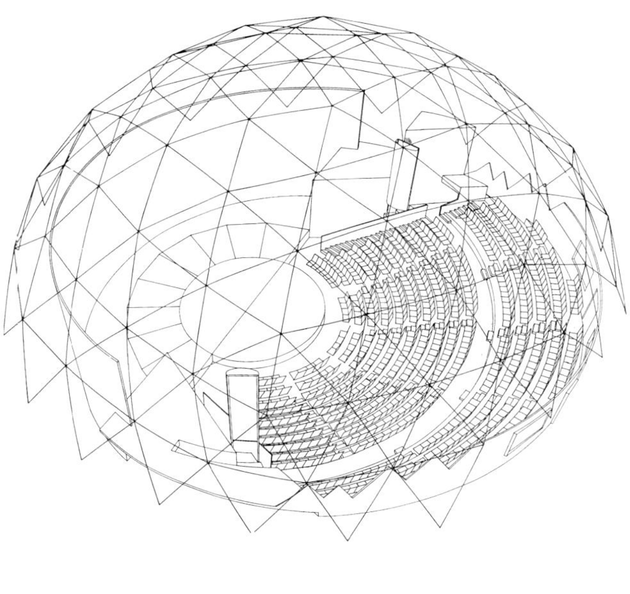

Itsuko Hasegawa execution design, 1990, from top: first floor plan, ground floor plan, basement floor plan

Itsuko Hasegawa execution design, 1990, north elevation

Itsuko Hasegawa execution design, 1990, interior view of civic theatre

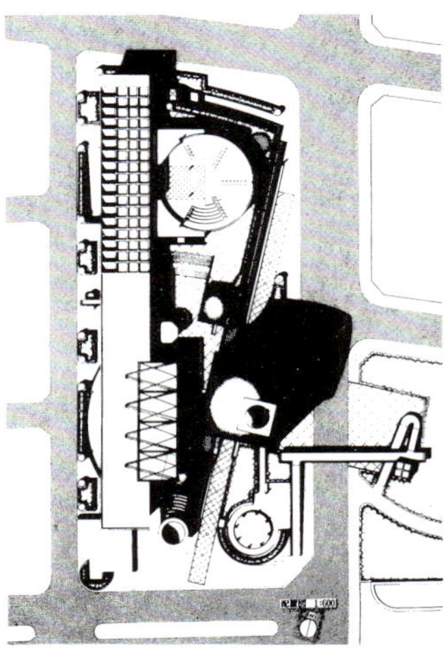

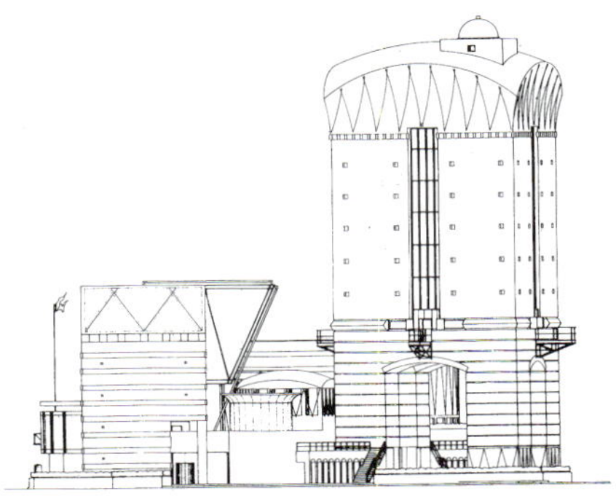

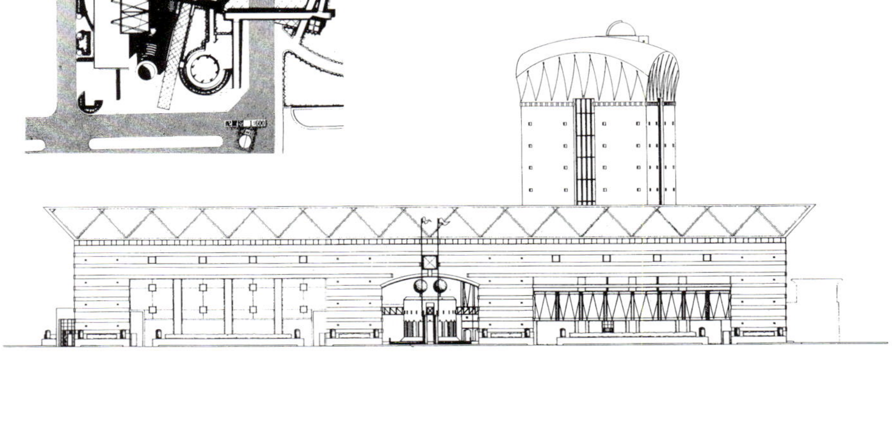

Shin Takamatsu competition design, 1986, model, runner-up

Shin Takamatsu competition design, 1986, above from left: site plan, south elevation, below: west elevation, runner-up

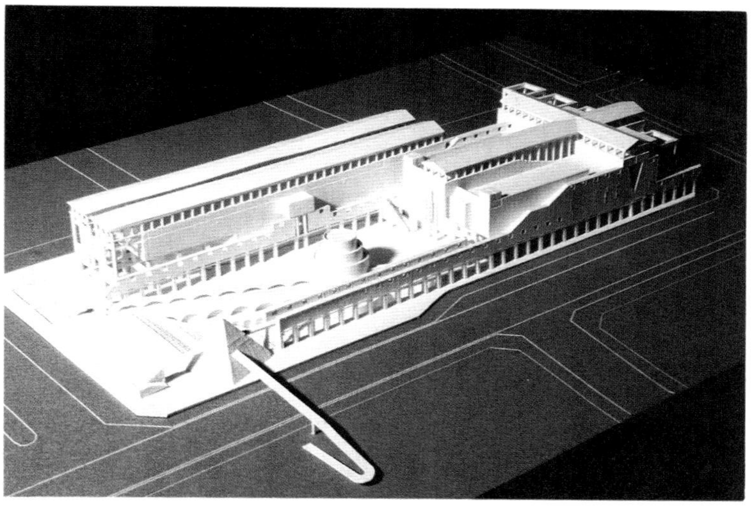

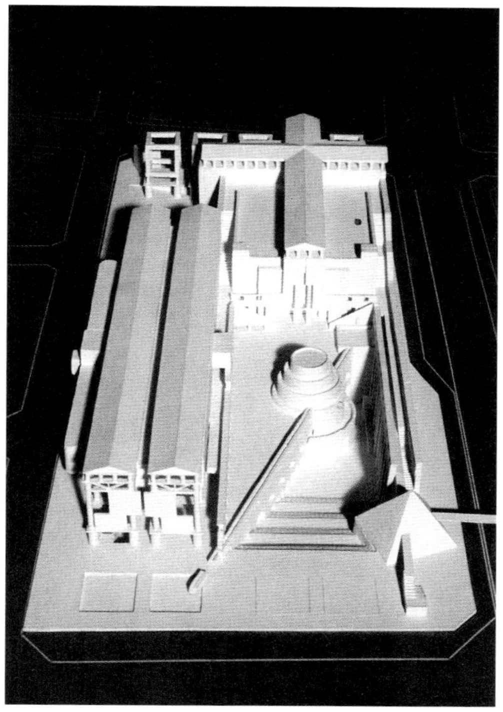

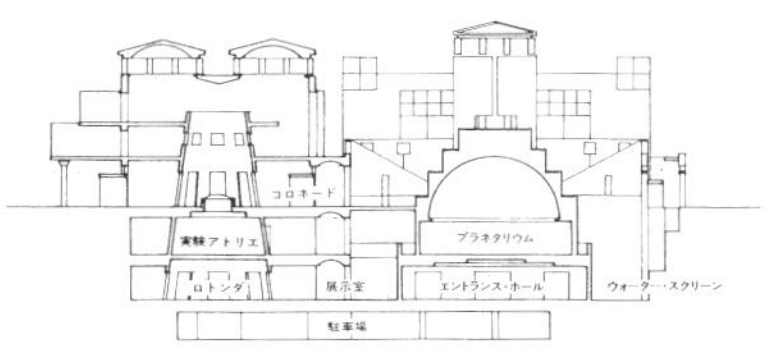

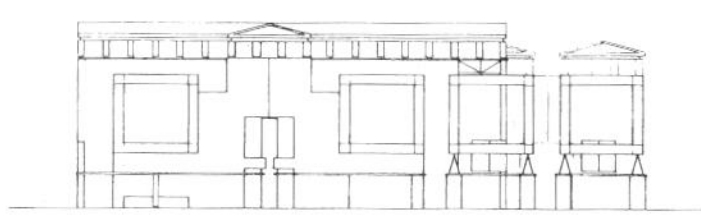

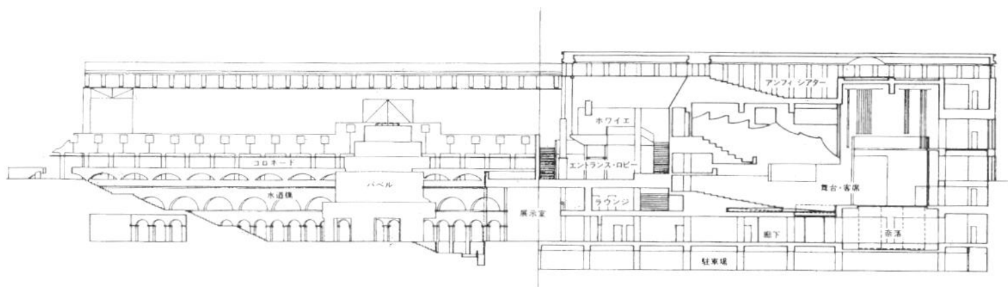

Katsuhiro Kobayashi & Kiyoshi Sei Takeyama competition design, 1986, model, runner-up

Katsuhiro Kobayashi & Kiyoshi Sei Takeyama competition design, 1986, model, runner-up

Katsuhiro Kobayashi & Kiyoshi Sei Takeyama competition design, 1986, above left: east-west section (south side), above right: north elevation, below: north-south section (east side), runner-up

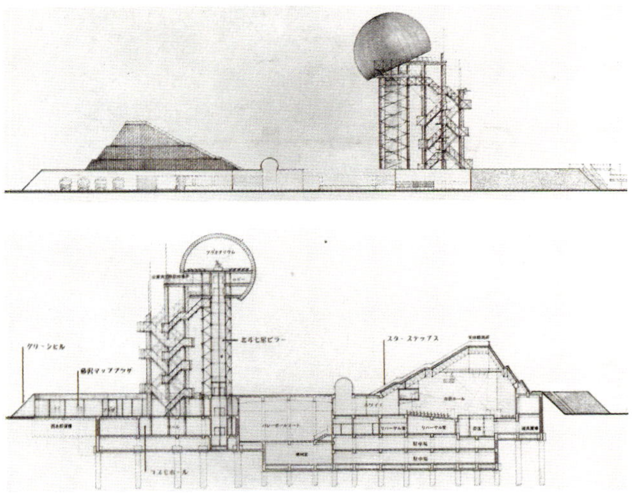

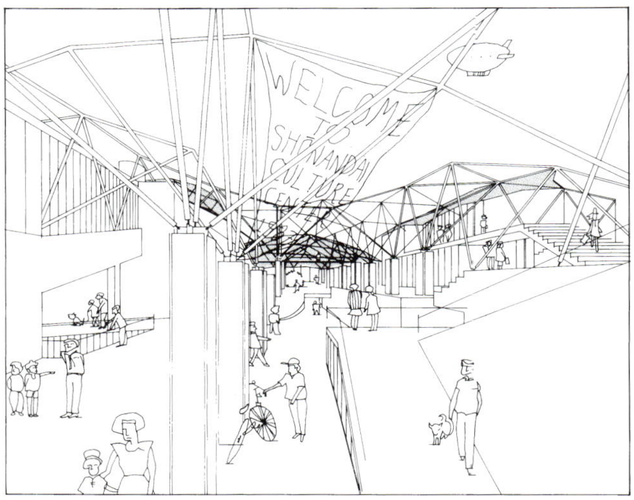

Kensuke Yoshida competition design, 1986, model, honourable mention

Kazunari Sakamoto competition design, 1986, view of civic plaza, honourable mention

Kensuke Yoshida competition design, 1986, above: west elevation, below: north-south section (east side), honourable mention

Kazunari Sakamoto competition design, 1986, model, honourable mention

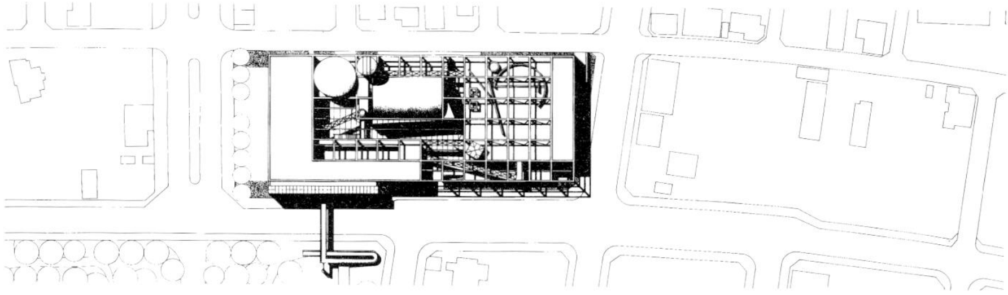

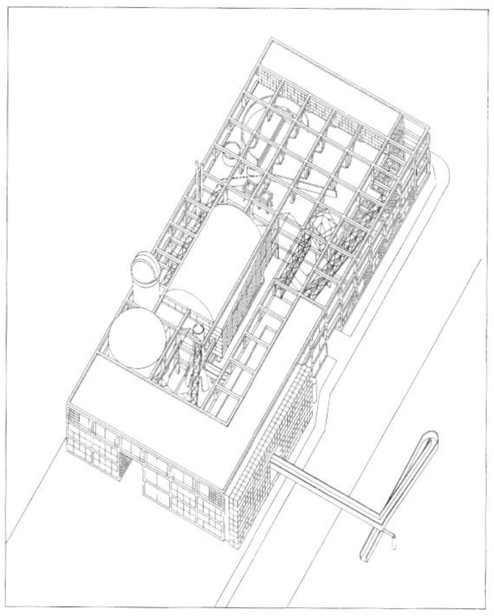

Kunihiko Hayakawa competition design, 1986, site plan, honourable mention

Kunihiko Hayakawa competition design, 1986, axonometric projection, honourable mention

Kunihiko Hayakawa competition design, 1986, interior view of promenade, honourable mention

Kunihiko Hayakawa competition design, 1986, ground floor plan, honourable mention

Kunihiko Hayakawa competition design, 1986, first floor plan, honourable mention

Kunihiko Hayakawa competition design, 1986, second floor plan, honourable mention

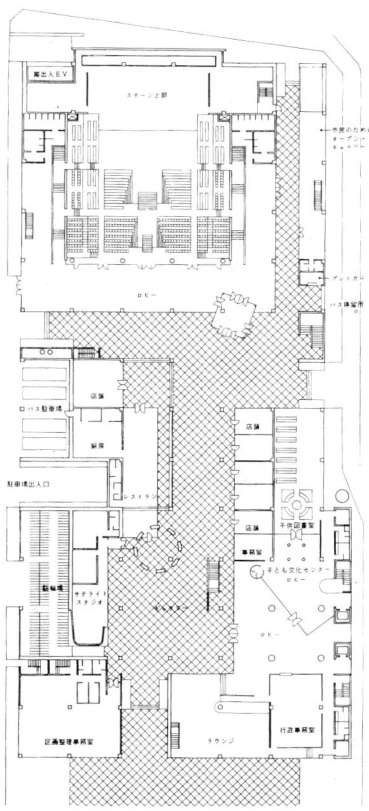

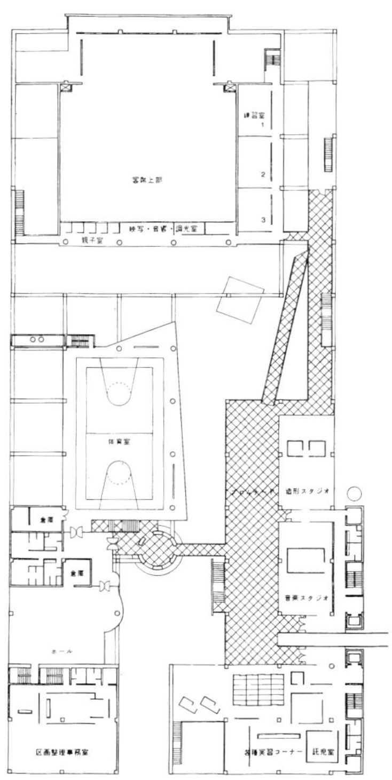

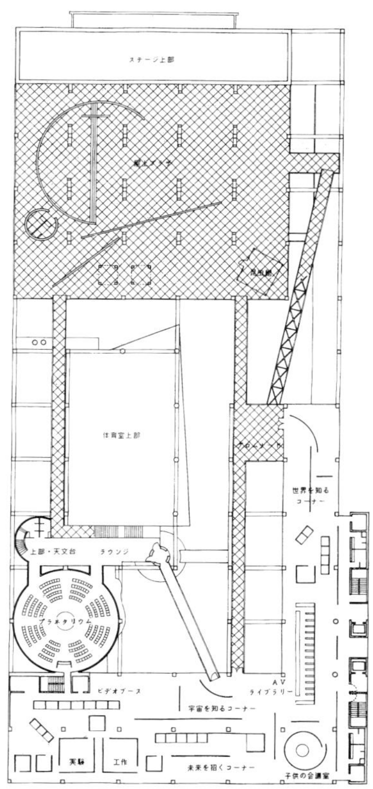

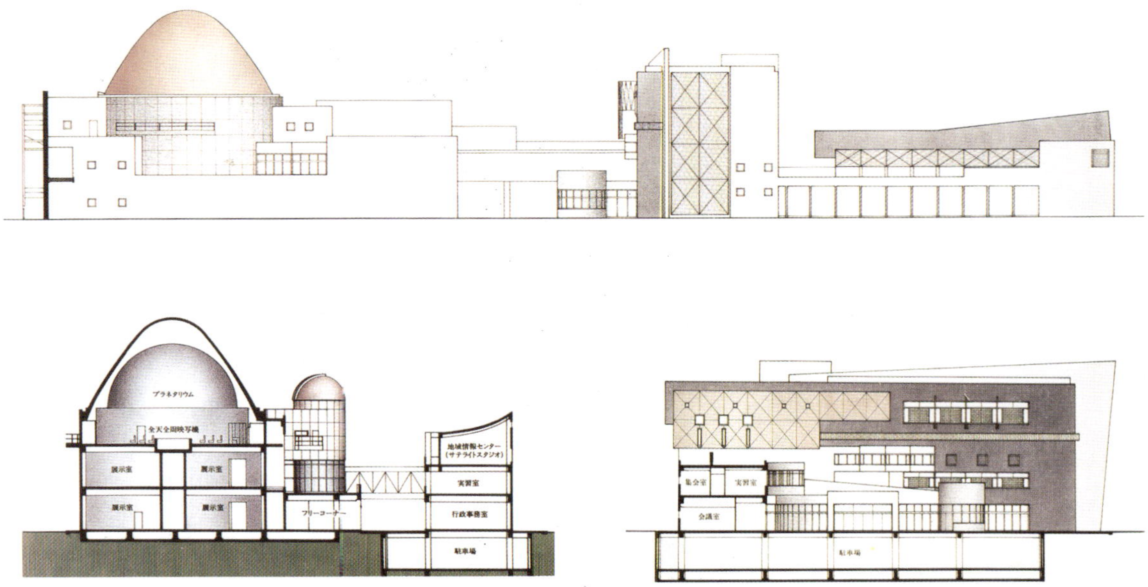

Hajime Yatsuka competition design, 1986, south elevation, honourable mention

Hajime Yatsuka competition design, 1986, above: east elevation, below from left: east-west section (north side), east-west section (south side), honourable mention

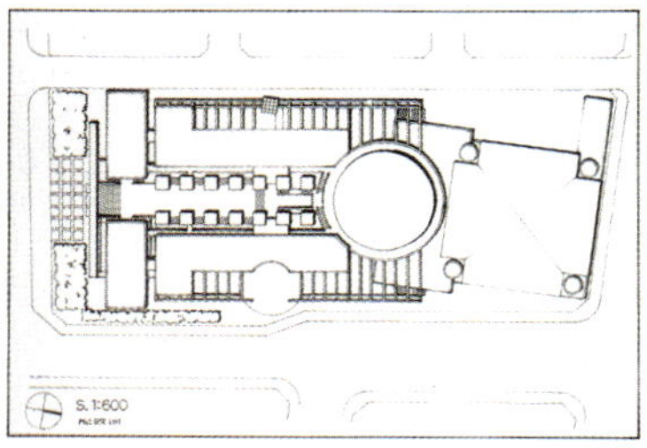

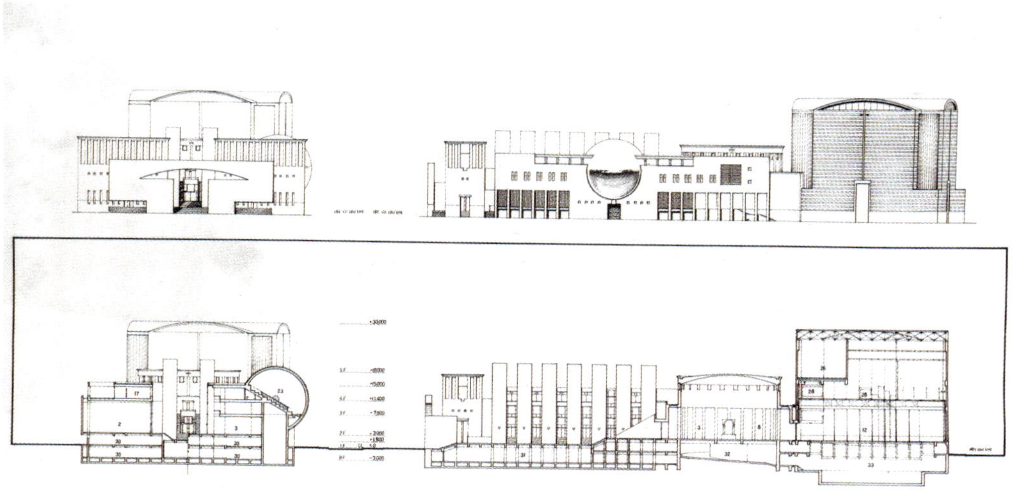

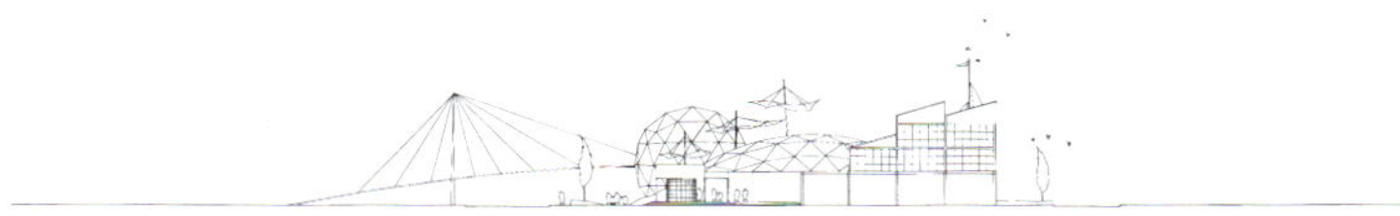

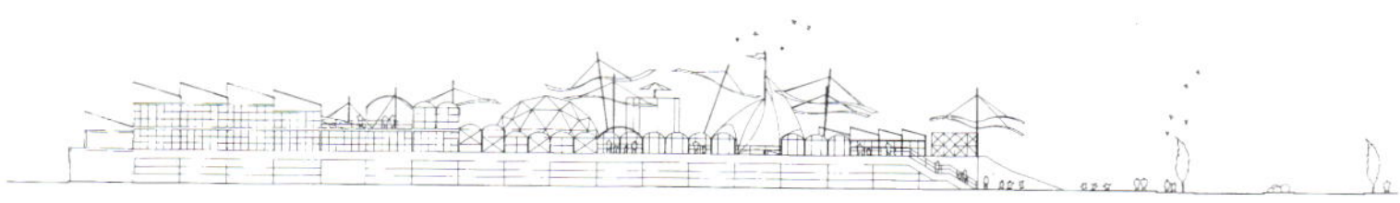

Kazumasa Furuichi & Takuro Hoshino competition design, 1986, site plan, model, honourable mention

Kazumasa Furuichi & Takuro Hoshino competition design, 1986, above from left: south elevation, east elevation, below from left: east-west section (south side), north-south section (east side), honourable mention

Toyo Ito competition design, 1986, from top: model, north elevation, west elevation

Itsuo Kamiya competition design, 1986, sectional model, honourable mention

Itsuo Kamiya competition design, 1986, basement floor plan, honourable mention

Itsuo Kamiya competition design, 1986, ground floor plan, honourable mention

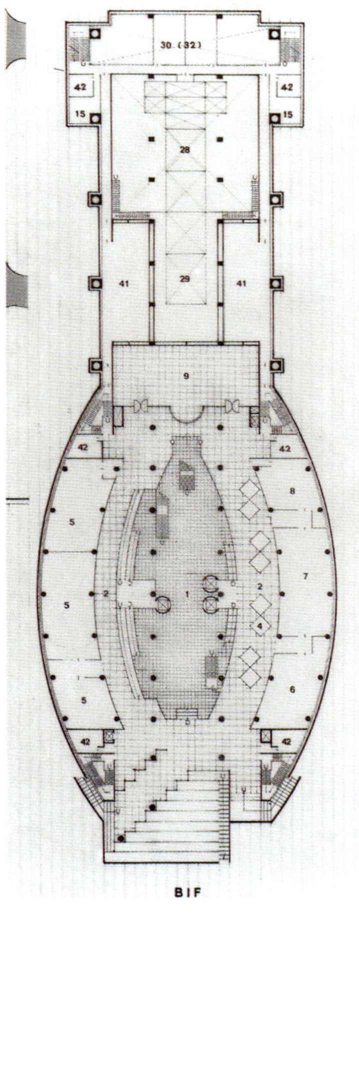

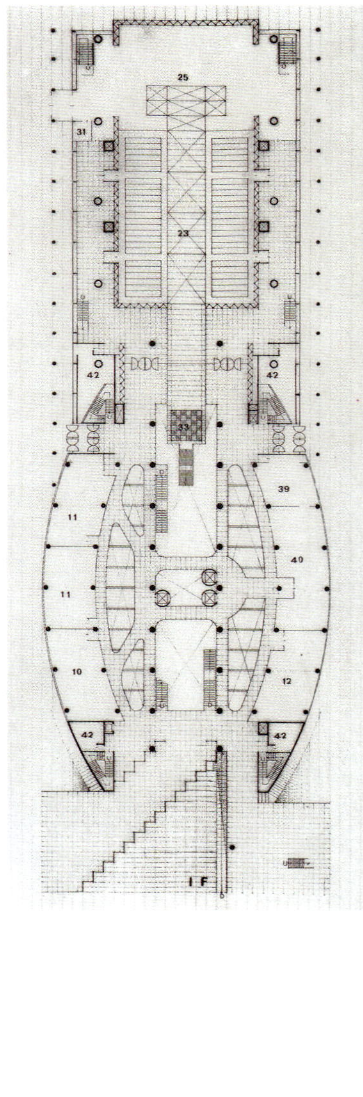

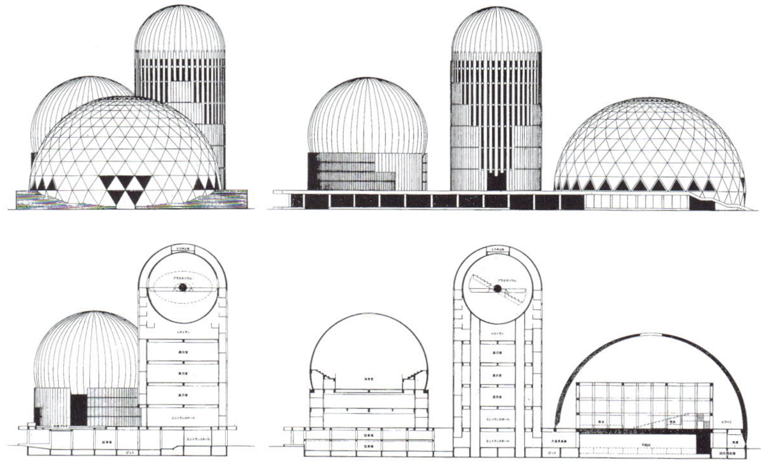

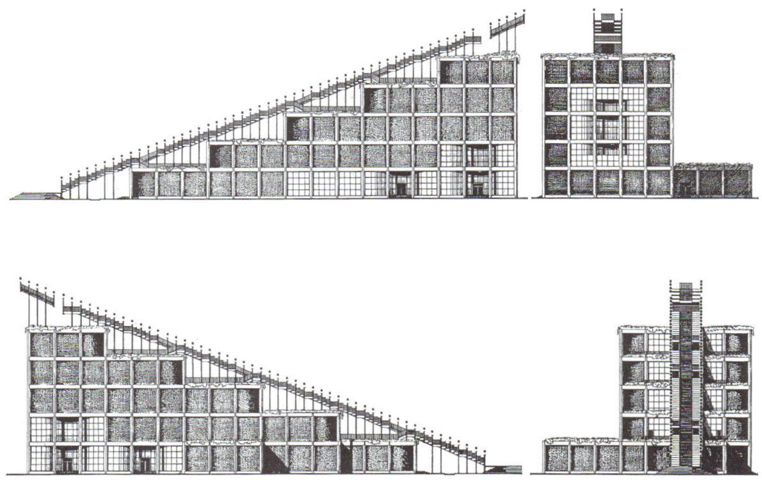

Yasufumi Kijma competition design, 1986, computer graphic

Atsushi Ueda competition design, 1986, model

Yasufumi Kijma competition design, 1986, above from left: south elevation, west elevation, below from left: east-west section (south side), north-south section (west side)

Atsushi Ueda competition design, 1986, above from left: east elevation, north elevation, below from left: west elevation, south elevation

Metropolitan Hall, Tokyo, 1985–1986

Project

Metropolitan Hall

Site

Nishishinjuku, Shinjuku-ku, Tokyo

Dates

Competition announced 8 November 1985 *Closing date* 25 February 1986
Result announced 7 April 1986

Number of entries

9

Jury

Kenji Adachi (chairman, director of the National Museum of Modern Art, Tokyo), Teiji Ito, Sakae Ohmi (architectural historians), Yoshinobu Ashihara, Ryohei Amamiya, Taneo Oki, Kiyonori Kikutake, Minoru Takeyama, Nobuo Hozumi (all architects), Hiroshi Hasegawa (Tokyo Municipality)

Result

First prize Kenzo Tange Associates

Commissioned by

Tokyo Municipality

Construction

April 1988 to March 1991

Architects

Kenzo Tange Associates

Metropolitan Hall, Tokyo, 1985–1986

Kenzo Tange Associates
competition design, 1986, east elevation of Tower I, first prize

Metropolitan Hall, Tokyo

The new Metropolitan Hall in Tokyo rivals most of the world's parliamentary buildings in its size and grandeur. In fact, the Tokyo municipal administration is housed in better quarters than Japan's national government. The new Metropolitan Hall is an indication of the growing economic power and influence of major cities throughout the world.

A well-oiled machine

In order to regulate life in a densely-populated city, a large and efficient municipal administration is required, with accommodation to match. In the past, Tokyo's municipal departments had been housed in various buildings in the Yurakucho district, where the old Metropolitan Hall, designed by Kenzo Tange, was also situated. Tange had won the 1957 competition for the Metropolitan Hall, and from then on his design had served as a prototype for other Japanese city halls and administrative offices. His prototype hinted at the well-oiled administrative machine inside and expressed an aversion to bureaucratic pomposity. His design was clearly Modernist-inspired; Le Corbusier's influence was particularly evident.
Early on in his career, Tange (* 1913) developed an affinity for Le Corbusier's work. It was therefore not surprising that his 1957 Metropolitan Hall was supported by "pilotis", a feature introduced by Le Corbusier. During the Second World War, Tange developed a life-long affinity for urban planning, which he approached three-dimensionally. In the early sixties, he joined the Metabolism movement and gradually changed his approach to architecture. Over the years, Tange has become one of the world's most influential architects. In 1991 he added the new Tokyo Metropolitan Hall to his extensive oeuvre.

The new Metropolitan Hall was built in record time, partly due to the perseverance of Tokyo's governor, Shun'ichi Suzuki. The governor had first proposed its construction in 1980, because Tange's 1957 complex, which had never been properly completed, seemed ready to burst at the seams. An Advisory commission was subsequently appointed on 27 January 1982. The commission's main task was to find a suitable site, but it was also asked to submit a preliminary construction report.
The commission's report, presented on 25 December 1983, prompted the city council's decision to locate the building in the Shinjuku district, on the grounds of the former Yodobashi water purification plant. This site borders on the Shinjuku Central Park and is surrounded by skyscrapers on three sides. The fact that Shinjuku is situated in the urban periphery, outside the old city centre, caused critics to grumble, but Suzuki managed to smooth ruffled feathers by including other districts in his ambitious plan to change the face of Tokyo. The eastern part of the city was subsequently enriched with an aquarium, the Tokyo Sea Life Park, based on a design (1989) by Yoshio Taniguchi, and the old city hall, in the Yurakucho district, was transformed into an international congress centre.

Kenzo Tange old Metropolitan Hall, Tokyo, 1957

Suzuki had valid reasons for hastening the completion of the project: his term of office was set to end in 1991, and a new city hall seemed to be an appropriate parting gift.

On the threshold of the 21st century

On 8 November 1985 the municipality announced that a closed, national competition would be held to select an architect for the new Metropolitan Hall. A total of nine architects and architectural firms were invited to submit plans for this prestigious project, which was to embody the development of culture and autonomy in Tokyo on the threshold of the 21st century. Moreover, the building would exemplify Tokyo's new image as both a place of residence and a metropolis. Although this objective seemed rather contradictory, it was a clear indication that the authorities had developed a new policy which differed radically from that of the 1950s and early 1960s.
One of the priorities stipulated in the competition programme was that the complex should have both administrative and cultural facilities. Other stipulated facilities included an information bureau and a contingency planning centre. The municipal staff would be provided with a state-of-the-art computer system, underscoring Japan's leading position on the computer market. The public areas warranted special attention. One of the focal points of the project was a plaza surrounded by a number of housing blocks, the blocks being situated on four lots, divided lengthways by a number of freeways.
The participants had only three months in which to complete their designs. However, this was not an insurmountable problem, because

Shun'ichi Suzuki Governor of Tokyo

Yoshio Taniguchi Tokyo Sea Life Park, 1989

most were experienced architects who ran sizeable architectural firms. The only architect who experienced problems with the stipulated conditions was Arata Isozaki, who had been added to the field as an afterthought, to safeguard against uniformity. He had never designed a government building before and his main problem was the stipulated proportional relationship between surface area and cubic content. Nevertheless, he submitted one of the most original designs, which survived the first round of elimination, along with designs submitted by Tange, Yamashita Architects & Engineers and Sakakuru Associates. Isozaki and Sakakuru were eliminated after the second round, and Tange beat Yamashita in the final round.

A 21st-century cathedral

The dominant feature of Tange's design is a super-block, Tower I, consisting of twin towers connected by a mid-section which is 150 metres high. Tower I has the silhouette of a medieval cathedral, a clear indication that Tange had moved away from the anti-hierarchical approach he adopted in 1957.
The second block, Tower II, has three towers, which are not as high as the twin towers of the first block but are oriented in the same manner. The third block is a low-rise building with a conference hall on the upper floor, it overlooks the semicircular plaza and is connected to Tower I by two footbridges. The last quarter of the site has been left vacant for a new metro station, due to be completed in 1995. Tower I, which is 243 metres high and has 48 floors, contains the governor's office. Tower II is less formidable than the twin towers; it is 163 metres high and has 33 floors. Both towers border on the park.

As mentioned above, Tower II consists of three towers, which decrease in size towards Tower I and have a similar orientation. The two main towers of the complex are linked by a promenade, which in turn links up with the covered footbridges leading to the low-rise block housing the conference hall. Although the complex is enclosed, it is easily accessible via footbridges, which are carried across the surrounding freeways on monumental pillars.
The conference hall in the low-rise block serves as a show-case for the rest of the complex. It overlooks the semi-circular plaza; an open space which counterbalances the density of the surrounding architecture. The block itself is not straight, but concave, tying it in more directly with the plaza. It is linked to footbridges on either side, and thus embraces the plaza, creating a secluded haven where exhausted civil servants can enjoy a moment's peace away from the rat-race. The plaza slopes down towards a small stage near the towers and is reminiscent of Greek amphitheatres and the Campo in Siena.

The façades of the complex have a dual significance. The horizontal and vertical elements of the façade form a stylised image of traditional Japanese wooden architecture in reference to Tokyo's illustrious past as Edo, the "Eastern capital". However, the façades are also reminiscent of the integrated circuits of a computer, reflecting Tokyo's status as

one of the world's most powerful cities. Granite was used for the façades; the dark slabs were imported from Sweden, the lighter slabs are of Spanish origin. The interior, the exterior, the façade and the floor plan have all been designed with the utmost care. No trouble or expense was spared to make Metropolitan Hall a magnificent and impressive piece of architecture, and thanks to Kenzo Tange's winning design, the city of Tokyo has got exactly what it asked for.

Arata Isozaki

The other participants had also given their best. One, Arata Isozaki, a former student of Tange's who had been associated in the 60s with the Metabolism movement, had deviated from the stipulated conditions. His design consisted of one immense block which covered half of the available site and was traversed by two passageways of equally magnificent proportions. The design was based on a geometric pattern of squares, which is a characteristic element of Isozaki's work. The most striking features of the design are the sphere and the pyramid mounted on the roof.

Façade of Metropolitan Hall tower

Notre-Dame, Paris

New Tokyo Metropolitan Hall under construction

The Tokyo Metropolitan Hall has a special place in the history of architectural competitions. The participants completed their designs on time, Tange's appointment did not lead to a national scandal, and the building was brought into use three years after construction began. In the end, Suzuki's drive to complete the project before his term of office ended proved to be unnecessary, because the governor – whose career has been marked by scandals – was unexpectedly re-elected for a fourth term of office.

Rathaus, Tokio

Das neue Rathaus der Stadt Tokio steht in Größe und Monumentalität den Regierungsgebäuden vieler anderer Länder in nichts nach. Ganz sicher besitzt die Tokioter Stadtverwaltung ein wesentlich eleganteres Domizil als die japanische Regierung. Das Rathaus gehört zu den Bauten, die als Zeichen für Macht und Einfluß der Metropole auf die Weltwirtschaft gelten.

Eine gut geölte Maschine

Damit das Leben der Millionenstadt Tokio in geregelten Bahnen verläuft, ist ein effizient arbeitender Verwaltungsapparat unabdingbar. Die Stadtverwaltung aber war seit Jahren über das gesamte Stadtviertel Yurakucho, in dem auch das alte Rathaus lag, verstreut. Das Gebäude, nach einem Wettbewerb entstanden, den Kenzo Tange im Jahre 1957 für sich entschieden hatte, galt seither als Prototyp für japanische Verwaltungszentren: Ein Rathaus als gut geölte Maschine, ohne jede bürokratische Selbstverherrlichung und vom modernen Baustil eines Le Corbusier beeinflußt.

Seit seiner Jugend galt Tange (*1913) als Bewunderer Le Corbusiers. Daher war es auch nicht verwunderlich, daß sein Rathausentwurf von 1957 auf den berühmten »Pilotis« ruhte. Während des Zweiten Weltkriegs entdeckte Tange den Städtebau, eine Disziplin, die ihn den Rest seines Lebens nicht mehr loslassen sollte. Zu Beginn der 60er Jahre schloß er sich den Metabolisten an und veränderte seine architektonischen Vorstellungen. In den folgenden 30 Jahren erwies sich Tange immer wieder als einer der bedeutendsten Neuerer der japanischen und internationalen Baukunst. Sein Tokioter Rathaus stellt den Höhepunkt seines bisherigen Schaffens dar.

Die Fertigstellung des neuen Rathauses in Rekordzeit ist in erster Linie dem Durchsetzungsvermögen von Schun'ichi Suzuki, Gouverneur von Tokio, zu verdanken. Der hohe Beamte entwickelte bereits 1980 Pläne zum Bau eines neuen Verwaltungssitzes, da das (übrigens niemals völlig fertiggestellte) alte Gebäude von Tange aus dem Jahre 1957 aus allen Nähten zu platzen drohte. Am 27. Januar 1982 wurde ein Ausschuß eingesetzt, der eine vorbereitende Baustudie erstellen und ein geeignetes Baugelände finden sollte. Am 25. Dezember 1983 legte die Kommission ihre Ergebnisse vor.

Der Stadtrat beschloß, das neue Rathaus auf dem Gelände der ehemaligen Kläranlage Yodobashi zu bauen. Dieses Terrain, das auf drei Seiten von Wolkenkratzern umgeben war und zu einer Seite an den Shinjuku Central Park grenzte, lag im Stadtteil Shinjuku. Das Viertel befindet sich zwar außerhalb des alten Tokio (dem früheren Edo) in einem Außenbezirk der Stadt; da Tokio jedoch ein neues städtebauliches Gesicht erhalten sollte, nahmen die Honoratioren dies in Kauf. Im Osten der Stadt war ein neues Aquarium geplant, der sog. Tokyo Sea Life Park, den Yoshio Taniguchi entwarf (1989). Darüber hinaus wollte man das alte Rathaus in ein internationales Kongreßzentrum verwandeln.

Auf dem Weg Ins 21. Jahrhundert

Suzuki wollte seine Pläne so schnell wie möglich durchsetzen, denn seine Amtsperiode lief im Frühjahr 1991 aus, und er hatte vor, seinen Abschied in einem neuen Rathaus zu feiern.

Der Architekt für das neue Rathaus sollte im Rahmen einer geschlossenen nationalen Ausschreibung ermittelt werden, die am 8. November 1985 veröffentlicht wurde. An neun Architekten und Architekturbüros erging die Einladung, einen Entwurf für dieses prestigeträchtige Projekt einzureichen, das als Symbol für die kulturelle und autonome Entwicklung Tokios auf dem Weg ins 21. Jahrhundert stand. Gleichzeitig sollte das neue Rathaus das zukünftige Bild der Stadt als Wohnort und Metropole bestimmen. Der Komplex mußte ausreichend Platz für Verwaltungsbehörden wie auch für kulturelle Aktivitäten bieten. Darüber hinaus waren ein Informations- und ein Katastrophenschutz-Zentrum vorgesehen, ausgestattet mit hochwertigen Computersystemen, die den Status Japans als führende Computernation unterstreichen sollten. Außerdem verlangte man von den Teilnehmern ausdrücklich den Entwurf eines Rathausplatzes, angelegt als öffentlicher Raum zwischen den Baublöcken des Rathauses. Diese Blöcke sollten auf vier Parzellen verteilt werden, die der Länge nach von Autostraßen durchschnitten wurden.

Die Teilnehmer hatten nur drei Monate Zeit, um ihre Pläne einzureichen, Alle erfüllten die geforderten Bedingungen bis auf Arata Isozaki. Er besaß keine Erfahrung mit Regierungsgebäuden und war wegen seiner oft originellen Ideen eingeladen worden. Sein größtes Problem bestand im festgelegten Verhältnis der Grundflächen zum angestrebten Bauvolumen. Letztendlich zählte sein Entwurf zu den augenfälligsten Beiträgen und wurde zusammen mit den Plänen von Tange, Yamashita Architects & Engineers und Sakakuru Associates in die engere Wahl aufgenommen. Bei einer zweiten Ausscheidung blieben nur Yamashita und Tange übrig, dem die Jury schließlich den ersten Preis zusprach.

Kathedrale des 21. Jahrhunderts

Tanges Rathausentwurf wird von einem »Superblock« – Turm I – dominiert. Zwillingstürme sind durch ein 150 m hohes Mittelstück miteinander verbunden, was dem Entwurf das Aussehen einer mittelalterlichen Kathedrale verleiht. Dies ist bereits ein deutliches Zeichen dafür, wie weit sich Tange mit seinem neuen Rathaus von den eigenen anti-hierarchischen Auffassungen des Jahres 1957 entfernt hat.

Der zweite Block, Turm II, besteht aus drei etwas niedrigeren Türmen, die ebenso ausgerichtet sind wie der Zwillingsturm des ersten Blocks. Den dritten Teil von Tanges Entwurf bildet ein niedriger Block, auf dem der Sitzungssaal liegt und der über zwei Fußgängerbrücken mit Turm I verbunden ist. Von hier aus blickt man auf eine halbrunde Plaza. Das letzte Viertel des Baugeländes blieb einer Metrostation vorbehalten, die bis 1995 fertiggestellt sein soll. Turm I ist mit 243 m Höhe und 48 Stockwerken eines der höchsten Gebäude Japans; er beherbergt u.a. das Büro des Gouverneurs. Der 163 m hohe Turm II, ebenso wie Turm I unmittelbar am Park gelegen, verfügt hingegen nur über 33 Etagen.

Turm II besteht, wie beschrieben, aus drei einzelnen Türmen, die der Größe nach in Richtung Turm I ausgerichtet sind, wobei sie zum Zwillingsturm hin niedriger werden. Zwischen den beiden Turmkomplexen entstand eine Promenade, die ihrerseits wieder mit den überdachten Spazierwegen zum Sitzungssaal verbunden ist. Auf monumentalen Pfeilern ruhende Wege überqueren die Autobahnen, so daß ein umschlossener und dennoch räumlich offener Gesamteindruck entsteht.

Der Block mit dem Sitzungssaal, dem bedeutendsten Repräsentationsraum des Komplexes, blickt auf eine halbrunde Plaza, die zur Seite hin abfällt und am tiefsten Punkt an einer kleinen Bühne endet. Durch diesen Anblick drängt sich ein Vergleich mit griechischen Theatern oder dem Campo von Siena auf: Auch dort grenzt ein halbrunder, abfallender Platz – in diesem Fall in umgekehrter Richtung – an das Rathaus, den Palazzo Pubblico. Während seiner Studentenzeit hatte Tange, ein großer Bewunderer Michelangelos, die Schönheit der italienischen Renaissance entdeckt.

Allerdings ist das Tokioter Rathaus keineswegs eine Nachahmung des Palazzo Pubblico: Der Block mit dem Sitzungssaal ist nicht gerade, sondern konkav gewölbt, wodurch der Anschluß an den Platz unmittelbar gegeben ist. Die Spitzen des Gebäudes laufen auf die Spazierwege aus und scheinen den Platz förmlich zu »umarmen«. Dadurch entstand ein intimer öffentlicher Raum zur Erholung der städtischen Bediensteten.

Die Fassaden des Komplexes sollten zum einen an die ruhmreiche Edo-Vergangenheit erinnern, zum anderen den heutigen Status Tokios als einer der mächtigsten Städte der Welt unterstreichen. Ersteres erreichte Tange durch die Verbindung horizontaler und vertikaler Fassadenelemente, deren Muster eine stilisierte Form alter japanischer Holzbauweise darstellt. Gleichzeitig erinnern die Fassaden an die Schaltkreise eines Computers (Integrated Circuits, Large Scale Integration).

Als Baumaterial verwendete Tange Granit – dunkle Platten aus Schweden, helle aus Spanien. Die Stadt scheute bei der Ausführung des Baus weder Kosten noch Mühen und sah am Ende alle ihre Erwartungen an das neue Gebäude erfüllt.

Arata Isozaki

Auch die Entwürfe der anderen Teilnehmer brauchten einen Vergleich mit dem Sieger nicht zu scheuen. Arata Isozakis Entwurf ging von einem einzigen riesigen Baublock aus, der die Hälfte des Baugeländes ausgefüllt hätte. Dieser Block sollte von zwei Straßen von ebenfalls enormen Ausmaßen durchkreuzt werden. Charakteristisch für Isozakis Entwurf ist sein geometrisches Viereckmuster; eine Kugel und eine Pyramide auf dem Dach gehören zu den auffälligsten Elementen.

Das Rathaus der Stadt Tokio stellt in der Geschichte der Architekturwettbewerbe eine Ausnahme dar: Die Teilnehmer reichten pünktlich und in kurzer Zeit ihre Beiträge ein, es gab keinen nationalen Skandal nach Bekanntgabe des Sieges von Tange, und drei Jahre nach Baubeginn konnte das neue Rathaus bezogen werden – noch vor dem Ende der Amtszeit Suzukis. In gewisser Hinsicht hätte man sich diese Eile sparen können, denn obwohl seine Person nicht von Skandalen verschont blieb, wurde er – entgegen aller Voraussagen – für eine vierte Amtsperiode gewählt.

L'Hôtel de Ville, Tokyo

Par ses dimensions et sa monumentalité, le nouvel hôtel de ville de Tokyo rivalise avec la plupart des sièges des grandes institutions démocratiques du monde. L'administration municipale de la capitale est en fait aujourd'hui mieux installée que le gouvernement japonais. Cet immeuble impressionnant est un signe supplémentaire de la croissance de l'influence économique et du pouvoir des grandes métropoles.

Une machine bien huilée

Une cité aussi densément peuplée que Tokyo nécessite une administration puissante qui a besoin d'outils de travail adaptés pour fonctionner. Par le passé, les services municipaux de la capitale étaient dispersés dans plusieurs immeubles du quartier de Yurakucho où se trouvait l'ancien hôtel de ville déjà conçu en 1957 par Kenzo Tange après concours. Son projet, étudié pour améliorer l'efficacité de l'administration et refusant toute pompe bureaucratique, avait depuis pratiquement servi de prototype à de nombreux autres immeubles municipaux et administratifs dans tout le Japon. Il était d'inspiration moderniste et l'influence de Le Corbusier n'était pas loin.

Très tôt dans sa carrière, Tange (né en 1913) s'était senti en affinité avec les recherches de Le Corbusier. Son premier hôtel de ville fut ainsi monté sur pilotis, solution corbuséenne par excellence. Pendant la Seconde Guerre mondiale, il s'intéressa à l'urbanisme dans une approche tridimensionnelle et, au début des années 60, se rallia au mouvement métaboliste avant de modifier peu à peu sa pratique architecturale. Au cours des années, il s'est imposé comme l'un des plus influents architectes du monde et son nouvel hôtel de ville pour Tokyo était donc très attendu.

L'énorme immeuble fut construit en un temps record grâce en partie à la pugnacité du gouverneur de Tokyo, Shun'ichi Suzuki qui avait proposé la construction d'un nouvel hôtel municipal, celui de 1957 (partiellement inachevé) étant au maximum de ses possibilités. Il tenait à mener le projet à bien avant la fin de son mandat prévue pour 1991.

La municipalité créa une commission consultative le 27 janvier 1982 afin de trouver un site et de proposer une réflexion préliminaire.

Son rapport du 25 décembre 1983 concluait à la construction du nouvel hôtel municipal dans le quartier de Shinjuku, sur les terrains de l'ancienne usine de traitement des eaux de Yodobashi. Le site, entouré sur trois côtés par des tours, se trouve en bordure du Parc central de Shinjuku. Cette situation excentrée par rapport au centre historique (Edo) souleva quelques critiques que Suzuki apaisa en dotant les autres quartiers de nouveaux équipements. L'Est de la ville reçut ainsi un aquarium – le Parc de la vie marine – d'après un projet de Yoshio Taniguchi (1989), et l'ancien hôtel de ville du quartier de Yurachuko fut transformé en centre international de congrès.

Au seuil du XXIème siècle

Le 8 novembre 1985, la municipalité annonça le lancement d'un concours restreint national pour la désignation d'un architecte. Neuf architectes furent invités à soumettre des plans pour ce prestigieux projet d'importance primordiale pour l'affirmation de la personnalité culturelle et de l'autonomie de Tokyo. Il s'agissait de donner une meilleure image de la ville, à la fois comme lieu de vie et grande métropole. Ce souci des autorités différait beaucoup de ceux qui avaient présidé à la construction du précédent siège de la municipalité. L'appel d'offre précisait que le nouvel immeuble devait abriter des activités administratives et culturelles, dont un bureau d'information et un centre d'urgence. Le personnel municipal serait évidemment doté d'un système informatique d'avant-garde, le moins que l'on puisse attendre de la part du Japon. Les espaces publics devaient être particulièrement soignés, en particulier une place entourée d'immeubles d'habitation construits sur quatre parcelles séparées longitudinalement par des autoroutes urbaines.

Les participants n'avaient que trois mois pour remettre leurs plans, ce qui n'était pas vraiment un problème puisque l'on avait retenu des architectes expérimentés disposant d'équipes importantes. Le seul concurrent auquel le programme posa quelques difficultés fut Arata Isozaki, rajouté à la sélection au dernier moment pour éviter une trop grande uniformité des projets. Il n'avait jamais conçu de bâtiments administratifs et eut du mal à respecter le rapport entre les surfaces et les volumes stipulé dans l'appel d'offres. Son projet, l'un des plus originaux, passa néanmoins le cap du premier tour en compagnie de ceux de Tange, de Yamashita Architects & Engineers et Sakakuru Associates. Isozaki et Sakakuru furent éliminés au second tour et Tange battit Yamashita au tour final.

Une cathédrale du XXIème siècle

L'élément dominant du projet de Tange est un «super-bloc», Tower 1, composé de deux tours jumelles réunies jusqu'à 150 m de haut. Cette Tower 1 n'est pas sans évoquer la silhouette d'une cathédrale médiévale et montre à quel point l'architecte s'est éloigné de ses principes antihiérarchiques de 1957.

Le second bloc, Tower 2, est constitué de trois éléments dont la hauteur décline en se rapprochant de Tower 1, mais qui sont orientés sur le même axe que celle-ci. Le troisième bloc est un bâtiment bas possédant une salle de conférence à son niveau supérieur et dominant la place semi-circulaire. Il est relié à Tower 1 par deux passerelles. Le dernier quart du terrain est dégagé pour faire place à une nouvelle station de métro prévue pour 1995. Tower 1, qui contient le bureau du gouverneur, est avec ses 48 niveaux et ses 243 m un des plus hauts immeubles du Japon. Tower 2, avec 33 étages et 163 m de haut est moins formidable. Toutes deux donnent sur un parc. Les deux principales tours sont reliées par une promenade connectée aux passerelles couvertes qui conduisent au bâtiment bas et à sa salle de conférence. Bien que le complexe soit fermé sur lui-même, il est d'accès facile grâce à des passerelles qui franchissent les autoroutes sur des piliers monumentaux.

La salle de conférence domine la place dont l'espace ouvert équilibre la densité des bâtiments environnants. Le sol s'abaisse vers une sorte de petite scène au pied des tours, qui n'est pas sans rappeler un Campo de Sienne inversé. La découverte par le jeune Tange des splendeurs de la Renaissance italienne – et en particulier de Michel-Ange – explique peut-être cette évocation siennoise. L'immeuble de la salle de conférence n'est pas rectiligne mais concave, et avec ses passerelles, semble encercler la place en délimitant un havre de calme où les fonctionnaires ont sans doute plaisir à venir se détendre.

Le dessin des façades de l'hôtel de ville peut être interprété comme une stylisation des constructions de bois traditionnelles du pays (référence à l'ancienne Edo) ou comme des circuits intégrés d'ordinateur, évoquant ainsi la puissance de l'une des plus grandes villes du monde.

Les plaques de granit sombre qui recouvrent les façades viennent de Suède, celles de granit clair d'Espagne. Le plan de masse, les aménagements extérieurs ou intérieurs ont été dessinés avec un soin extrême. Aucune peine, aucune dépense n'a été épargnée pour faire de cet hôtel de ville une œuvre aussi forte que magnifique. Grâce à Kenzo Tange, la ville de Tokyo s'est dotée de l'instrument de prestige qu'elle souhaitait.

Arata Isozaki

Les autres participants avaient également très bien travaillé. Comme il a été mentionné plus haut, Arata Isozaki s'était quelque peu affranchi des stipulations du programme. Ancien élève de Tange, il appartenait également au mouvement métaboliste. Son projet consistait en un immense ensemble couvrant la moitié du site et traversé par deux passerelles de proportions superbes. Il avait utilisé une trame carrée, caractéristique de son style et posé sur le toit deux éléments surprenants: une sphère et une pyramide.

L'hôtel de ville de Tokyo occupe une place à part dans l'histoire des concours d'architecture puisque les participants rendirent leurs projets dans les délais, que la désignation de Tange ne déclencha aucun scandale et que le bâtiment fut inauguré trois ans seulement après la pose de la première pierre. Pour l'anecdote, l'anxiété de Suzuki de terminer la construction avant la fin de son mandat se révéla sans objet puisque de façon inattendue, il fut réélu pour un quatrième mandat.

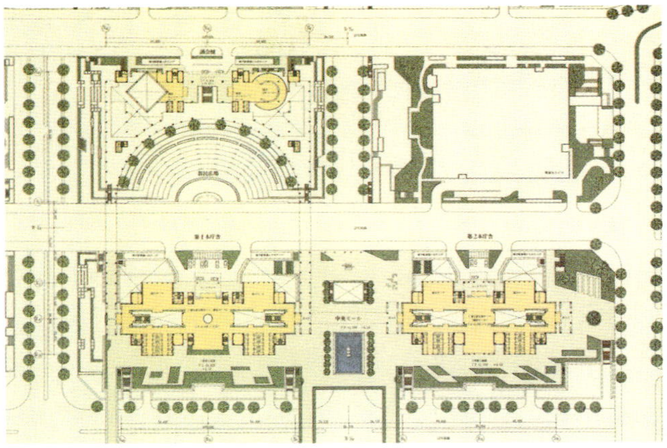

Kenzo Tange Associates
competition design, 1986, ground floor plan of Tower I, first prize

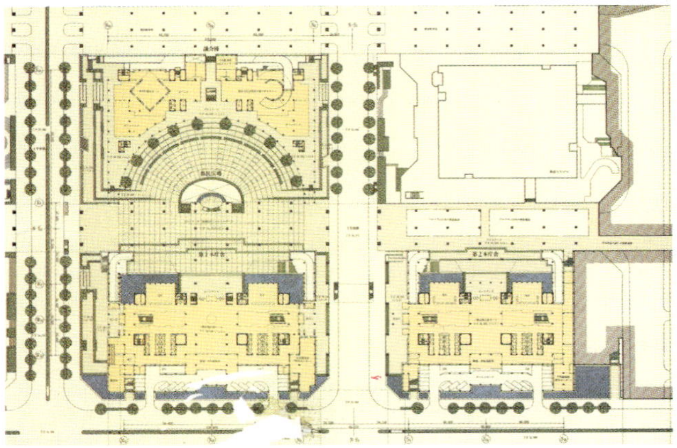

Kenzo Tange Associates
competition design, 1986, ground floor plan of Tower I, first prize

Kenzo Tange Associates
competition design, 1986, model, first prize

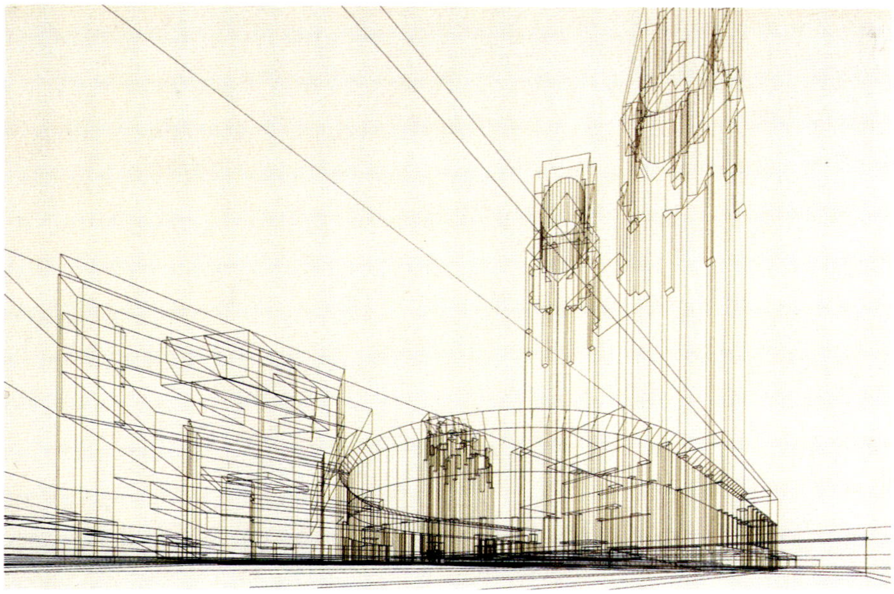

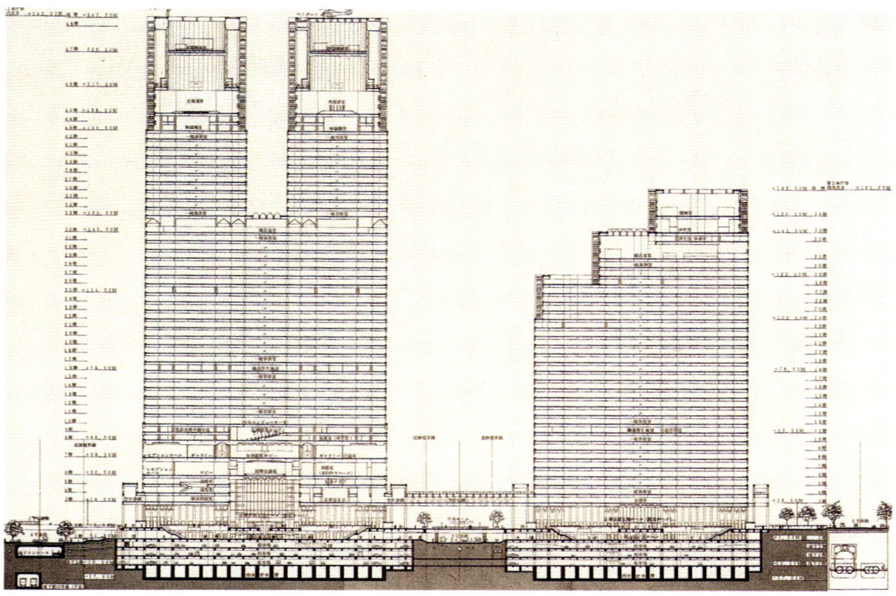

Kenzo Tange Associates
competition design, 1986 exterior view from Avenue 4 (computer graphic), first prize

Kenzo Tange Associates
competition design, 1986, exterior view from Shinjuku Central Park (computer graphic), first prize

Kenzo Tange Associates
competition design, 1986, north-south section (west side), first prize

Sakakuru Associates competition design, 1986, west elevation of Tower I

Sakakuru Associates competition design, 1986, north elevation of Tower I

Sakakuru Associates competition design, 1986, south elevation of main hall in area 1

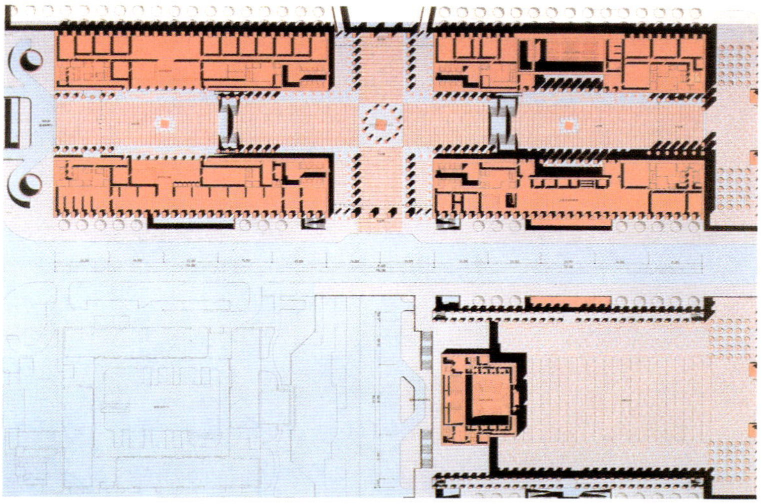

Arata Isozaki & Associates competition design, 1986, second floor of Tower I

Arata Isozaki & Associates competition design, 1986, north-south elevation (east side) of Tower I

Arata Isozaki & Associate
competition design, 1986, "The space of Heaven, Earth and Man", interior view

Arata Isozaki & Associates
competition design, 1986, view from north-east (computer graphic)

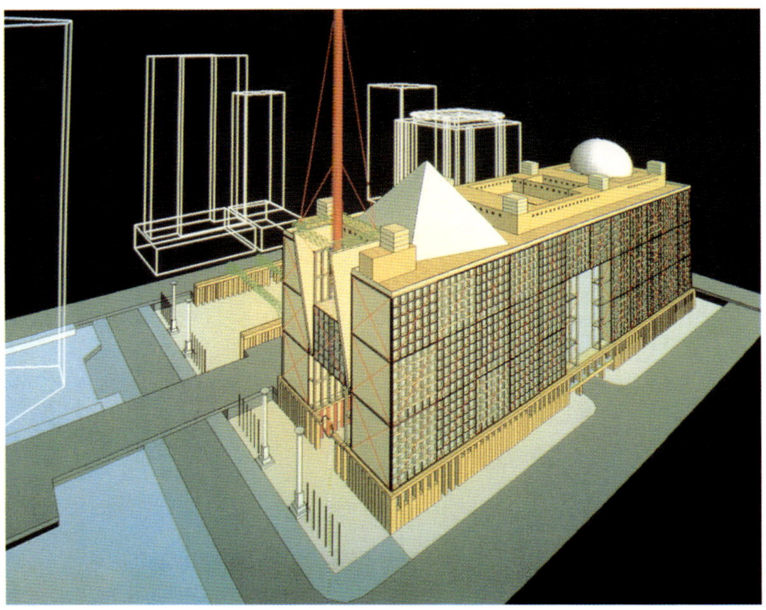

Nikken Sekkei competition design, 1986, exterior view (computer graphic)

Nihon Architects, Engineers & Consultants, Inc. competition design, 1986, interior view of the atrium

Nihon Architects, Engineers & Consultants, Inc. competition design, 1986, model

Kunio Mayekawa Architects & Associates competition design, 1986, ground floor plan of Tower I

Kunio Mayekawa Architects & Associates competition design, 1986, model

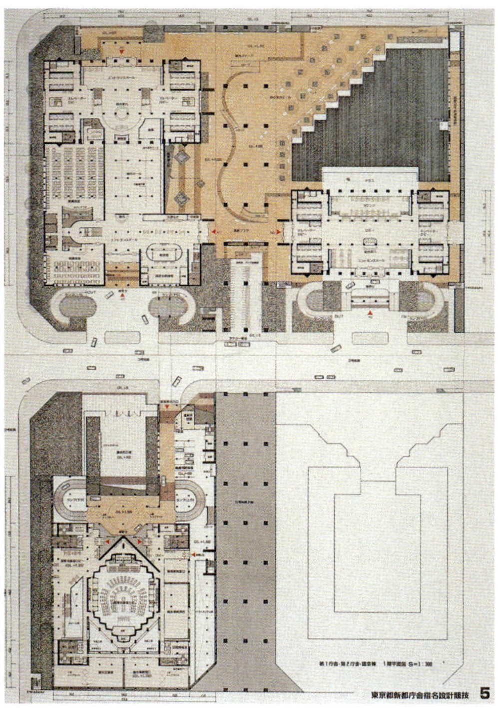

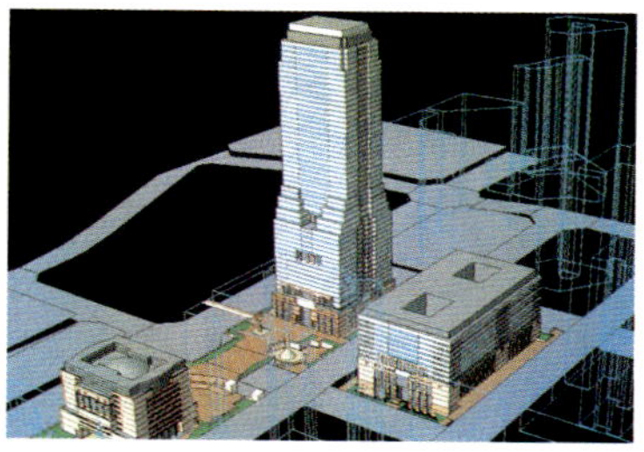

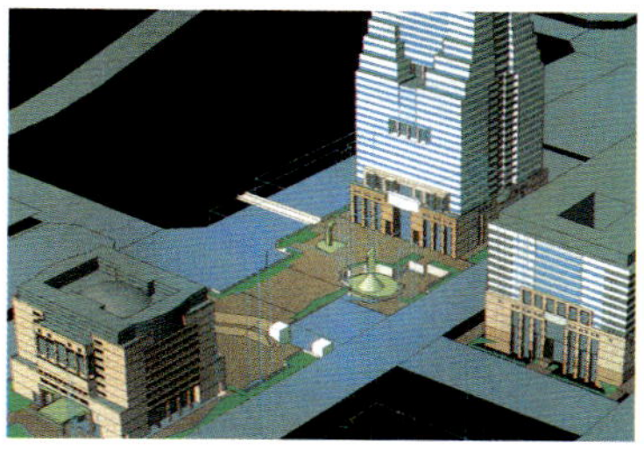

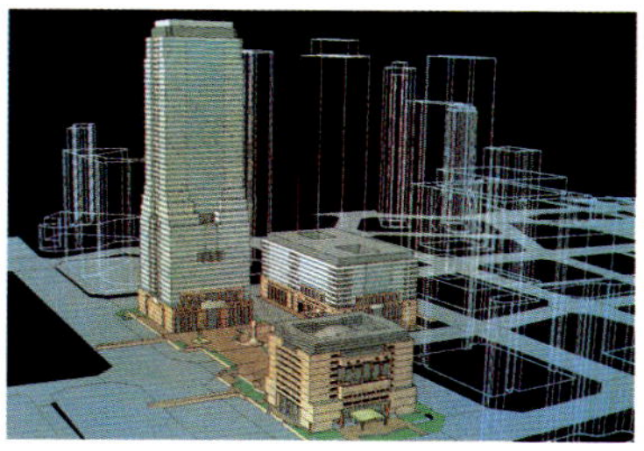

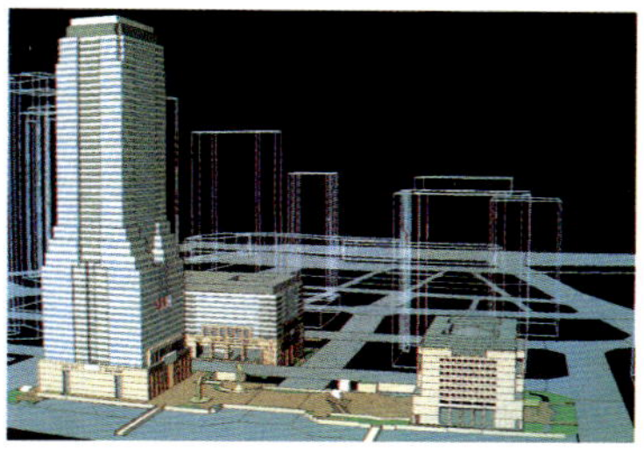

MHS Planners, Architects & Engineers competition design, 1986, bird's-eye view (computer graphic)

Yasui Architects & Engineers Inc. competition design, 1986, bird's-eye view from north

Yamashita Architects & Engineers Inc. competition design, 1986, photomontage

Project

City hall and library

Site

Spui-kwartier, The Hague

Dates

Competition announced 3 June 1986 *Closing date* 1 December 1986 *Result announced (jury)* 20 January 1987 *(city council)* July 1989

Number of entries

Five project developers were invited to submit a design and a construction budget, in collaboration with an architect: Hans Boot (van den Broek & Bakema) & Mabon Bouwontwikkeling; Helmut Jahn (Murphy & Jahn) & Wilma Vastgoed; Richard Meier (Richard Meier & Partners) & Ontwikkelingscombinatie Stadhuis; Saubot & Julien (WZMH) & Haags Projecten Consortium; Norman Foster (Foster Associates) & MAB, replaced in October by Rem Koolhaas (OMA) & Multi Vastgoed.

Jury

S. Herweijer (chairman), H. van der Cammen (secretary), J. van Beuzekom (council secretary, The Hague), Aldo van Eijck, Herman Hertzberger, Sjoerd Schamhart, Yap Hong Seng, P. Hakkesteegt, J.G. Lambooy, A. Batenburg, Marthe Röling, Pierre Jansen, U. Klaassen, W.M. Renes, C. Weeber

Result

First prize Rem Koolhaas *(jury)* Richard Meier *(public)* Richard Meier *(city council)*

Commissioned by

The Municipality of The Hague

Construction

July 1990 to 1995

Architect

Richard Meier (*1934), in collaboration with Projectbureau Stadhuis

City Hall, The Hague, 1986–1989

Richard Meier competition design, 1986, axonometric projection, first prize

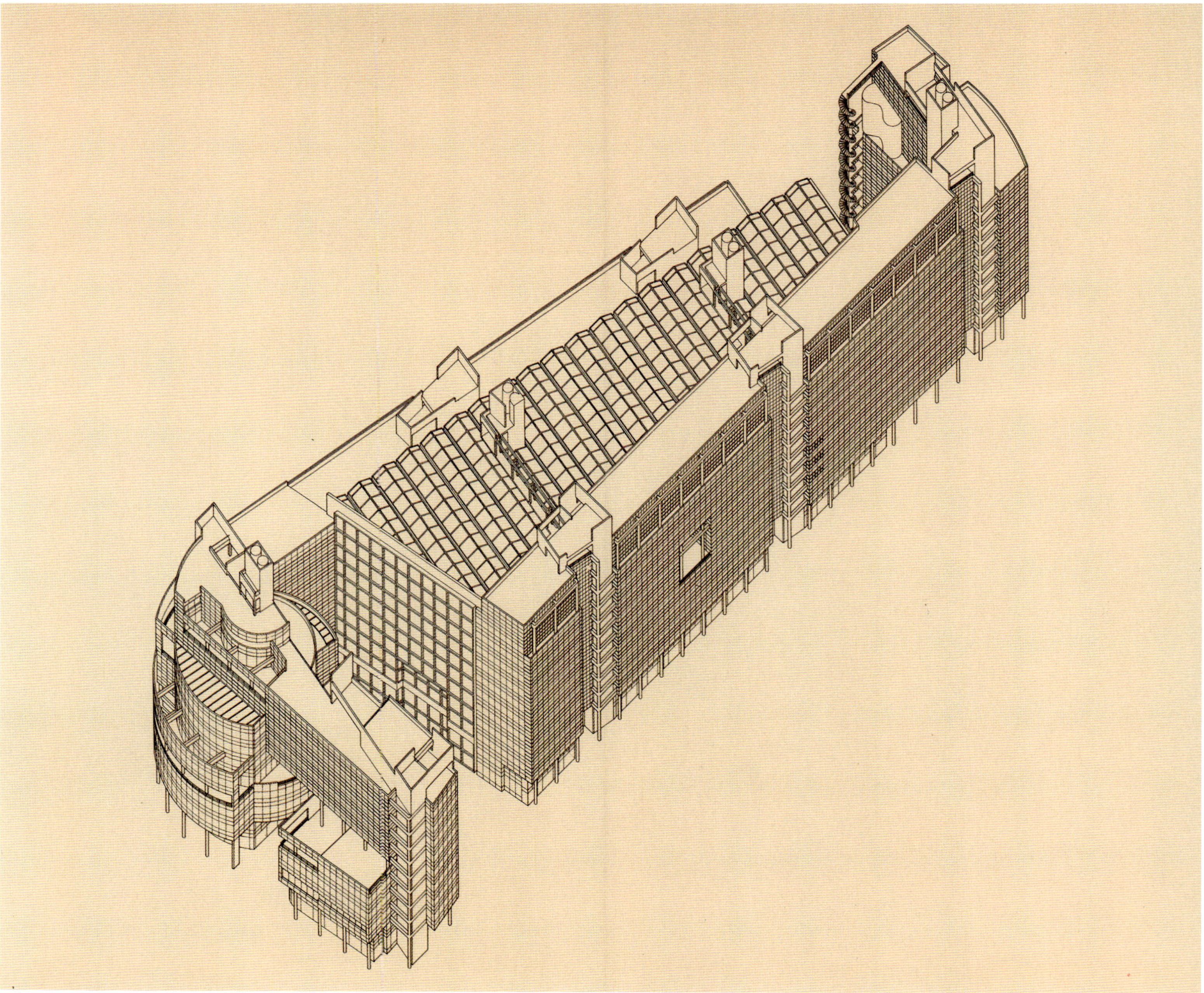

City Hall, The Hague

Although The Hague is not the capital of the Netherlands, it is the seat of the Dutch government and the place of residence of the Queen Beatrix. As court-capital, The Hague has always had a reputation for being a rather prim and proper city; despite being the third-largest city in the Netherlands, it possessed little in the way of entertainment facilities and night life. Compared to cities such as Rotterdam, Amsterdam and Utrecht, The Hague lacked a pulsating urban heart, and in an effort to make good this deficiency, a number of projects to reanimate the city were initiated during the early eighties.

A city without a heart

The Hague lacks the hustle and bustle of an urban night life, a deficiency which starkly illustrates the city's provincialism. The cultural and entertainment centres are spread around the city and are more often than not situated on the outskirts. The old city hall was also built far from the city centre, on the Burgemeester de Monchyplein, and the public library was equally remotely situated on the Bilderdijkstraat. The city's main theatres and museums are situated far from one another and, within a short period, a number of cinemas closed down. In short, the city was in dire need of a pulsating heart featuring a variety of entertainment facilities.

There was no shortage of suitable sites in The Hague which, while it lacks entertainment facilities, does boast a wealth of monuments. However, the city had not always been consistent in caring for its cultural heritage, and during the period of "city-forming" – a Dutch architectural policy which put progress before architectural heritage – the city centre lost its cohesive character. The needs for a new urban core soon became painfully obvious.

From 1980, the authorities tried to call a halt to the gradual process of disintegration. A new bureaucratic term, "crossways compromise", was coined, referring to the city's plans to rejuvenate the old city centre. One of the main objectives was the redevelopment of the Spui, one of The Hague 's more attractive areas, which had degenerated rapidly over the years.

Initially there had only been plans to build new accommodation for the Residentie Orchestra and the national ballet company, Nederlands Danstheater. However, plans were later also developed to group a variety of urban facilities around the Spui, including the Marge theatre, the Kijkhuis cinema, the public library, and a number of restaurants, thus making this square the heart of the city. The Nederlands Danstheater was the first building on the Spui to be completed. This building, designed by Rem Koolhaas, was opened in 1987 and drew the attention of the architectural world much to the delight of the local city council who wanted to give new impetus to architecture in The Hague.

The socialist councillor for urban planning and renewal, Adri Duivesteijn, was one of the champions of architectural rejuvenation in The Hague. He was also the driving force behind the competition for the city hall-cum-public library. The authorities envisaged a fresh, new, transparent, efficient and austere city hall, with an international cachet.

Rem Koolhaas (OMA) **Nederlands Danstheater, 1987**

Ricardo Bofill **housing project for the Burgemeester de Monchyplein**

Having consulted the necessary literature on the subject, the authorities invited five teams to submit designs for the city hall-cum-library. The teams would consist of an architect and a contractor of his or her choice, which was an excellent idea, because both the architect and contractor would be involved in the project from the start. It also meant that a more accurate estimate of the construction costs could be made, limiting the chance that the budget would be exceeded, as had been the case with the construction of the City Hall in Amsterdam[1].
At least, that was the plan. Unfortunately, the city council were unable to call a halt to the gradually increasing costs. The project eventually led to an almighty row between Duivesteijn and the councillor responsible for finance, both of whom tendered their resignations long before construction was completed. At present Duivesteijn is director of the Netherland's Architecture Institute, but it is rumoured that he will return to the Dutch political arena in the near future.

An international competition

The city's desire to improve the quality of local architecture prompted the decision to invite a number of renowned foreign architects to participate in the competition. Although famous Dutch architects such as Jan Duiker, Hendrik Petrus Berlage and J.J.P. Oud had left their mark on the city's architecture in the past, more recent additions to the city lacked character and stature. It was for this reason that Alvaro Siza, Neave Brown and Ricardo Bofill were asked to develop housing projects at the time of the competition.
The foreign entrants in the City Hall competition were Saubot & Julien (France), Helmut Jahn, and Richard Meier (both USA). The Dutch invitees were Rem Koolhaas and Hans Boot, of the renowned firm van den Broek and Bakema. Rem Koolhaas replaced Norman Foster, who had withdrawn from the competition. Each of the participants developed their designs in collaboration with a Dutch construction company.

Koolhaas had only been added to the field in October 1986 and therefore had less time than the other architects to submit the preliminary sketches and construction budget required. Nevertheless, he managed to submit a sound design. The construction site posed a problem, because it was an elongated strip, surrounded by modern office blocks and historical buildings. Koolhaas solved this problem by designing two "discs" which reflected the surroundings. The discs, which are of different heights, form an artificial skyline and have been placed behind one another, extending across the entire length of the site.
Helmut Jahn's State of Illinois Center had proved that he was more than capable of designing an open, modern structure, which was what the council had in mind. His design for the City Hall was based on its public function. One of his priorities had been to tie the building in with the square. Koolhaas'design, on the other hand, had emphasised the building's municipal-administrative function.

Helmut Jahn **State of Illinois Center, 1985**

A characteristic feature of Boot's design is its conceptual clarity. The city hall, the library and the restaurant are clearly separate entities in his design. The city hall section is roughly rectangular and contains an elongated atrium. The wedge-shaped library penetrates the city hall structure. The business facilities are situated in a triangle which has been appended to the city hall section. The different sections of the building are accessible via passages and the atrium, which is a public area. The city hall section consists of high office towers, which are interconnected and are vaguely reminiscent of 1920s and 30s Soviet architecture. The library is easily recognisable because it is a low-rise building, and because the colour scheme and building materials used in its construction differ from those used for the rest of the complex.
Saubot and Julien, who are well-known for their high-rise projects in the Parisian district of La Défense, designed a Modernist block in combination with an articulated office tower.
The jury, which included the renowned Dutch architects Aldo van Eijck and Herman Hertzberger, were most impressed by the design submitted by the Dutch architect Rem Koolhaas. However, a public survey indicated that Richard Meier's design was the most popular. Consequently, the city council, who were apparently in a democratic mood, decided to set aside the experts' decision and commission Meier for the project.

A European American

Richard Meier was one of the world's leading architects when he submitted his design for the City Hall in The Hague. He is one of a

Richard Meier interior view of the atrium

group of architects referred to as the New York Five or the Whites, a reference to their favourite colour. The other members of this group are Peter Eisenman, Michael Graves, Charles Gwathmey and John Hejduk. He had made a name for himself in Europe with his Museum für Kunsthandwerk in Frankfurt am Main (1979–1985), and was subsequently contracted for a great number of projects in Germany, France and also the Netherlands. In consequence, he has been referred to as the most European of the American architects. His popularity in Europe probably stems from his efforts to forge a link between his own style and that of the classic European Modernists, particularly Le Corbusier.

Meier's City Hall is a fairly colossal building, structured around a huge atrium. The walls throughout the building are faced with white slabs, a characteristic feature of Meier's work. The layout of the building is based on logically-ordered, geometric shapes. Although Meier's design seeks to forge a link with the past, it will only be possible to ascertain the success of his efforts once the city hall and library are in use. The city council will then also be able to determine whether or not they have succeeded in creating a new urban heart for The Hague.

A number of new buildings have already been completed on the Spui. These include the Nederlands Danstheater, the Anton Philips Hall for the Residentie Orchestra and the Theatre Centre, which was completed in 1993 and contains the Haagse Filmhuis. The latter was constructed between 1986 and 1993, after a design by Herman Hertzberger. The most important historical building on the square is the seventeenth-century Nieuwe Kerk (New Church).

These buildings, together with the City Hall, will serve as a backdrop for the reanimation of The Hague's night life and will also prove that, in future, one will not need to travel to Amsterdam or Rotterdam to see the best in Dutch architecture.

1 *See chapter on the Amsterdam City Hall (Stopera) elsewhere in this book.*

Rathaus, Den Haag

Obwohl nicht die Hauptstadt der Niederlande, befinden sich in Den Haag der Wohnsitz der Königin Beatrix und der Sitz der niederländischen Regierung. Allerdings hatte die »Hofstadt« schon immer den Ruf, etwas steif zu sein, obwohl das Kultur- und Vergnügungsangebot der drittgrößten Stadt der Niederlande als besonders interessant galt. Im Gegensatz zu Metropolen wie Amsterdam, Rotterdam und Utrecht fehlte Den Haag ein lebhaftes, pulsierendes Zentrum. Um diesen Mangel zu beheben, unternahm man zu Beginn der 80er Jahre mehrere Versuche, der Stadt neues Leben einzuhauchen.

Eine Stadt ohne Herz

Die verschiedenen Kultur- und Freizeitzentren sind über die Stadt verstreut und liegen häufig in den Vororten. Auch das alte Rathaus stand weitab vom Zentrum am Burgemeester de Monchyplein, und die Stadtbibliothek war in der noch abgelegeneren Bilderdijkstraat angesiedelt. Auch bedeutende Theater und Museen verteilten sich über die ganze Stadt, obwohl Den Haag über zahlreiche Plätze, die sich als Mittelpunkt geeignet hätten, verfügt. Zudem hatte die Stadt zahlreiche Monumente aufzuweisen. Allerdings war man mit dem Denkmalbestand nicht immer sorgfältig umgegangen: Im Zuge der »City-Bildung« – einer speziell niederländischen Erscheinung, hatte man historische Stadtzentren architektonisch zerrissen. Ab 1980 steuerte die Verwaltung diesem Zerfallsprozeß aktiv entgegen. Der neue verwaltungstechnische Ausdruck »dwarswegcompromis« (Seitenstraßenkompromiß) bezeichnete die Sanierung der alten Innenstadt. Im Vordergrund der Den Haager Planung stand die Aufwertung des Spui, ursprünglich einer der schöneren Plätze, der im Lauf der Jahre jedoch arg verbaut worden war.
Ursprünglich war nur die Errichtung eines neuen Hauses für das »Residentie Orkest« und die Ballettgruppe des Nederlands Danstheater geplant gewesen. Später entstand der Plan, auch das Margetheater, das Filmtheater »Kijkhuis«, ein neues Rathaus, die Stadtbibliothek, Restaurants sowie weitere städtische Einrichtungen rund um den Spui anzusiedeln. Hier sollte das neue Herz Den Haags entstehen. Das Nederlands Danstheater, Heimstatt der gleichnamigen Ballettgruppe, war das erste Gebäude, das am Spui entstand. Gebaut nach einem Entwurf von Rem Koolhaas und 1987 eröffnet, erregte es weltweite Aufmerksamkeit.
Vor allem der für Raumordnung und Stadterneuerung zuständige sozialistische Beigeordnete Adri Duivesteijn versuchte, neuen Schwung in die Den Haager Architektur zu bringen. Duivesteijn war Initiator des Architekturwettbewerbs für das neue Rathaus, das er in einem Komplex zusammen mit einer öffentlichen Bibliothek entstehen lassen wollte. Das Gebäude sollte internationales Format besitzen, innovativ sein und gleichzeitig transparent, effizient und nüchtern wirken.
Fünf Teams erhielten die Einladung, Entwürfe für das neue Rathaus mit Bibliothek auszuarbeiten. Die Gruppen setzten sich aus je einem Architekten und einem Bauunternehmer ihrer Wahl zusammen. Durch die enge Zusammenarbeit erhoffte man sich, bereits im Planungsstadium die späteren Baukosten besser vorausberechnen zu können. Auf diese Weise sollte ein Überschreiten der Kostenvoranschläge wie beim Bau der Amsterdamer Stopera (einer Kombination aus Rathaus und Oper, siehe gleichnamiges Kapitel) ausgeschlossen werden.
Allerdings gelang es auch der Haager Stadtverwaltung nicht, die Kosten im Rahmen zu halten, was noch lange vor der eigentlichen Bauabnahme zum Austritt zweier erzürnter Beigeordneter aus dem Stadtrat führte.

Internationale Ausschreibung

Da die Stadt auf architektonischem Gebiet zu altem Glanz zurückfinden wollte, wurden auch ausländische Architekten zu dem Wettbewerb eingeladen. In der Vergangenheit hatten berühmte Baumeister wie Jan Duiker, Hendrik Petrus Berlage und J.J.P. Oud mit ihren Bauten Den Haag verschönert. Zeitgleich zur Ausschreibung des Wettbewerbs für das Rathaus bat die Stadt daher Alvaro Siza, Neave Brown und Ricardo Bofill an, in Den Haag Wohnungsbauprojekte zu realisieren.
Bei den zur Wettbewerbsteilnahme eingeladenen ausländischen Architekten handelte es sich um Saubot & Julien aus Frankreich sowie um Helmut Jahn und Richard Meier aus den USA. Die Niederlande waren mit Rem Koolhaas und Hans Boot vom Architekturbüro Van den Broek en Bakema vertreten. Koolhaas sprang für Norman Foster ein, der sich aus dem Wettbewerb zurückgezogen hatte. Alle Teilnehmer arbeiteten mit niederländischen Baugesellschaften zusammen.
Der erst im Oktober 1986 dazugestoßene Koolhaas hatte nur wenig Zeit für die Anfertigung der geforderten Skizzen und die Berechnung der Baukosten. Dennoch legte er einen angemessenen Entwurf vor. Als problematisch erwies sich das Baugelände, ein langgestrecktes Grundstück, das sowohl von modernen Bürogebäuden als auch von historischen Bauten umgeben war. Kohlhaas stellte zwei Scheiben hintereinander auf, die sich über die gesamte Länge des Geländes ziehen und ihre Umgebung zu reflektieren scheinen. Beide Scheiben sind in der Höhe unregelmäßig versetzt, wodurch der Eindruck einer künstlichen Skyline entsteht.
Helmut Jahn, der mit seinem State of Illinois Centre bereits eine moderne, offene Konstruktion geschaffen hatte, ging bei seinem Entwurf von der Öffentlichkeitsfunktion des Rathauses aus und bezog den Platz in seine Pläne ein. Im Vergleich dazu betonte Kohlhaas' Entwurf die verwaltungstechnischen und bürokratischen Funktionen des Gebäudes.
Der Beitrag von Boot bestich durch seine konzeptionelle Klarheit: Rathaus, Bibliothek und Restaurant sind deutlich voneinander getrennt. Der Rathausteil bildet ein angedeutetes Rechteck mit einem langgezogenen Atrium, in das die Bibliothek keilförmig hineinragt. Die kommerziellen Bereiche des Komplexes befinden sich in einem baulichen Dreieck, das am Rathausteil »klebt«. Passagen und die öffentliche Halle des Atriums verbinden die einzelnen Gebäudeteile des Komplexes miteinander. Der Rathausbereich besteht aus mehreren hohen Bürotürmen, die untereinander ebenfalls Verbindungswege besitzen und an die Sowjetarchitektur der 20er und 30er Jahre erinnern. Die Bibliothek hebt sich von den übrigen Gebäudeteilen durch unterschiedliche Farben und Materialien ab. Die für ihre Hochbauprojekte im Pariser Vorort La Défense bekannten französischen Architekten Saubot & Julien legten den Plan für einen modernistischen Baublock in Kombination mit einem abgestuften Büroturm vor.
Die Jury, der u.a. Aldo van Eyck und Herman Hertzberger angehörten, entschied sich für den Entwurf des Niederländers Koolhaas. Dagegen sprachen sich in einer öffentlichen Umfrage die meisten Teilnehmer für den Beitrag von Richard Meier aus. Aus diesem Grund entschloß sich die Stadtverwaltung, das Urteil der Fachleute zu ignorieren und Meier den Auftrag zu erteilen.

Ein europäischer Amerikaner

Richard Meier zählte mit Peter Eisenman, Michael Graves, Charles Gwathmey und John Hejduk zu den sog. New York Five, die nach ihrer Lieblingsfarbe auch als »The Whites« bezeichnet wurden.
In Europa war er mit seinem Museum für Kunsthandwerk in Frankfurt am Main (1979–1985) bekannt geworden und hatte in der Folge eine Reihe von Aufträgen in Deutschland, Frankreich und in den Niederlanden erhalten. Durch diese Arbeiten erwarb er sich den Ruf des europäischsten aller amerikanischen Architekten. Meiers Bauten erinnern an die klassische europäische Moderne und an Le Corbusier, was wohl seinen Erfolg in Europa zum Teil erklärt.
Der Entwurf für das Den Haager Rathaus zeigt ein kolossales Bauwerk rund um ein riesiges Atrium. Die Fassadenverkleidung besteht aus weißen Platten. Auch das übrige Gebäude ist in Weiß gehalten. Der Komplex setzt sich aus geometrischen Flächen und Formen, die auf logische Weise geordnet erscheinen, zusammen. Meier versuchte, mit seinem Entwurf einen Anschluß an die historische Umgebung zu finden. Ob ihm dies geglückt ist, läßt sich erst feststellen, wenn Rathaus und Stadtbibliothek für den Publikumsverkehr geöffnet werden. Erst dann wird sich auch herausstellen, ob es der Stadtverwaltung gelungen ist, Den Haag ein neues Herz zu geben. Außer dem Nederlands Danstheater befinden sich am Spui der Anton Philipszaal für das Residentie Orkest sowie ein 1993 fertiggestelltes Theaterzentrum, in dem auch das Haagse Filmhuis untergebracht ist. Dieser Komplex wurde zwischen 1986 und 1993 von Herman Hertzberger realisiert. Das bedeutendste historische Gebäude am Spui ist die aus dem 17. Jahrhundert stammende Nieuwe Kerk. Zusammen mit dem neuen Rathaus sollen diese Gebäude einen würdigen Rahmen für ein neues Kultur- und Nachtleben bilden und zeigen, daß niederländische Architektur nicht nur in Amsterdam und Rotterdam bewundert werden kann.

L'Hôtel de Ville, La Haye

Bien que La Haye ne soit pas la capitale des Pays-Bas, elle est le siège du gouvernement et le lieu de résidence de la reine Beatrix et de la cour. Ville agréable et propre, elle n'offre pas les activités de loisirs ou nocturnes auxquelles la troisième ville des Pays-Bas pourrait prétendre. Comparée à des cités comme Rotterdam, Amsterdam ou Utrecht, elle manque d'un véritable centre animé. Un certain nombre de projets virent le jour pendant les années 80 pour remédier à cette situation.

Une cité «sans cœur»

Sans réelle vie nocturne, La Haye souffre encore d'un esprit provincial. Les équipements culturels ou de loisirs sont dispersés et très souvent situés en banlieue.
L'ancien hôtel de ville se trouvait loin du centre, sur le Burgemeester de Monchyplein, et la bibliothèque municipale s'était retrouvée exilée Bilderdijkstraat. Les principaux théâtres et musées sont éloignés les uns des autres et plusieurs cinémas ont fermé au cours de la dernière décennie. En bref, la ville avait besoin de se refaire un cœur.
La ville n'avait pas toujours su protéger son héritage culturel et pendant la période dite de «city-forming», politique d'urbanisme spécifique aux Pays-Bas et faisant passer le progrès avant la préservation du patrimoine, la ville perdit de sa cohérence et de son caractère.
Les sites ne manquaient pas pour recréer un centre car La Haye est riche de multiples monuments. A partir de 1980, les autorités essayèrent de mettre fin au processus de sa dégénérescence urbaine à travers une nouvelle politique: le «cross-wise compromise». Mise au point pour revitaliser l'ancien centre, elle était en vigueur lors de l'apparition des premiers projets de construction de lieux culturels. L'un de ses principaux objectifs était la rénovation du Spui, l'une des places les plus agréables de la ville qui s'était dégradée au cours des années.
A l'origine, les plans ne concernaient que de nouveaux bâtiments pour le Residentie Orkest et la compagnie de ballet du Nederlands Danstheater. Mais rapidement s'y ajoutèrent d'autres équipements dont le Théâtre Marge, le Cinema Kijkhuis, la bibliothèque publique et quelques restaurants. Tout laissait espérer que cette place allait devenir le cœur de la cité. Le Nederlands Danstheater fut le premier édifice à s'y élever. Conçu par Rem Koolhaas, il ouvrit ses portes en 1987 et attira l'attention du monde entier, à la grande satisfaction des édiles qui souhaitaient donner une impulsion nouvelle à l'architecture locale.
Le conseiller municipal socialiste pour l'urbanisme et la rénovation urbaine, Adri Duivesteijn, fut l'un des champions de cette nouvelle orientation architecturale et l'un des principaux animateurs du concours pour l'hôtel de ville que les autorités voulaient sobre et efficace, mais de qualité architecturale internationale.
Après mûre réflexion, la municipalité invita cinq équipes à travailler sur les plans d'un hôtel de ville-bibliothèque. Ces équipes se composaient d'un architecte et d'une entreprise de construction de son choix, ce qui permettait de faire travailler ensemble dès le départ créateurs et techniciens. Cette formule présentait également l'avantage de permettre une estimation plus précise des devis et de limiter les dépassements qui avaient marqué, par exemple, la construction du Stopera d'Amsterdam[1].
C'était du moins le projet... En fait, le conseil municipal fut incapable de contenir les coûts et l'on assista à d'incroyables confrontations entre Duivesteijn et l'adjoint aux Finances qui donnèrent tous deux leur démission bien avant que les travaux ne soient terminés. Duivesteijn est aujourd'hui directeur de l'Institut Néerlandais d'Architecture, mais il est déjà question de son retour dans l'arène politique.

Un concours international

Le souhait municipal d'améliorer le niveau de l'architecture locale conduisit à inviter un certain nombre d'architectes étrangers. Bien que dans le passé, de célèbres architectes néerlandais comme Jan Duiker, Hendrik Petrus Berlage et J.J.P. Oud aient laissé leur marque sur la ville, les réalisations les plus récentes manquaient de caractère et de prestige. C'est pour remédier à cette situation qu'Alvaro Siza, Neave Brown et Ricardo Bofill avaient été chargés de concevoir des immeubles de logement en parallèle au concours.
Les invités étrangers furent Saubot et Julien (France), Helmut Jahn et Richard Meier (USA) qui concoururent avec les Néerlandais Rem Koolhaas et Hans Boot, du célèbre cabinet Van den Broek et Bakema. Koolhaas remplaçait Norman Foster qui s'était retiré.
Koolhaas, qui n'avait été appelé qu'en octobre 1986, eut moins de temps que ses confrères pour étudier à la fois des plans préliminaires et un devis, ce qui ne l'empêcha pas de soumettre une proposition solide. Le site choisi n'était pas facile. De forme allongée, il était entouré d'immeubles de bureaux modernes et de constructions historiques. Koolhaas résolut le problème en dessinant deux «disques» de hauteurs différentes qui reflétaient leur environnement et se détachaient sur le ciel. Ils étaient placés l'un derrière l'autre et couvraient la totalité de la longueur du terrain.
Le State of Illinois Centre d'Helmut Jahn avait prouvé que celui-ci était plus que capable de dessiner un bâtiment moderne et convivial du style de ce que le conseil municipal avait en tête. Son projet reposait sur une analyse des fonctions publiques de l'édifice qu'il voulait étroitement lier à la place. Koolhaas avait, quant à lui, plutôt privilégié les fonctions administratives.
Une des caractéristiques du projet Boot était sa lisibilité conceptuelle. L'hôtel de ville, la bibliothèque et le restaurant étaient clairement séparés. La section hôtel de ville, pratiquement rectangulaire, contenait un atrium tout en longueur. La bibliothèque en forme de coin pénétrait dans le bloc de la mairie et les services accessoires étaient installés dans un bâtiment triangulaire attenant. Les différentes sections étaient accessibles par des passages et l'atrium était largement ouvert au public. L'hôtel de ville lui même était composé de tours de bureaux reliées entre elles et rappelant un peu l'architecture soviétique des années 20 et 30. Le bâtiment bas de la bibliothèque se différenciait par ses couleurs et ses matériaux de construction de ceux utilisés pour le reste de l'ensemble.
Saubot et Julien, très connus pour leurs tours du quartier de la Défense, à Paris, conçurent un bloc moderniste associé à une tour de bureaux de forme complexe. Le jury, qui comprenait les grands architectes néerlandais Aldo van Eijck et Herman Hertzberger, fut très impressionné par les plans de Koolhaas. Mais une enquête auprès du public montra que le projet de Meier était mieux reçu. Très démocratiquement, le conseil municipal décida de se passer de l'avis des experts et nomma Meier architecte du projet.

Un Euro-américain

Richard Meier était déjà un architecte respecté dans le monde entier lorsqu'il proposa son projet pour La Haye. Avec Peter Eisenman, Michael Graves, Charles Gwathmey et John Hejduk, il avait fait partie du célèbre groupe des New York Five ou Whites, par référence à leur couleur favorite. Il s'était fait connaître en Europe grâce à son Musée des Arts Décoratifs de Francfort (1979–85), et fut par la suite appelé sur de nombreux projets en Allemagne, en France et aux Pays-Bas. Il passa vite pour le plus européen des architectes américains, sans doute au titre de ses efforts pour forger un lien entre son propre style et celui des classiques du modernisme européen, en particulier Le Corbusier.
L'hôtel de ville de Meier est une construction assez colossale, structurée autour d'un atrium géant. Les façades sont recouvertes des dalles blanches caractéristiques de son travail. Le plan de masse s'articule à partir de formes géométriques organisées avec beaucoup de logique. Bien que Meier s'inspire souvent de solutions éprouvées, ce n'est qu'à l'usage que l'on saura si cette réalisation «fonctionne». C'est également avec le temps que le conseil municipal saura s'il a réussi à donner un nouveau cœur à sa cité.
Un certain nombre d'édifices ont déjà été achevés tout autour du Spui: le Nederlands Danstheater, l'Anton Philipszaal pour le Residentie Orkest et le Centre Théâtre de Herman Hertzberger, terminé en 1993 et qui contient une cinémathèque, mais le plus important monument historique de la place reste la Nieuwe Kerk (nouvelle église) qui date du XVIIème siècle.
Ces nouveaux développements architecturaux animeront peut-être la vie culturelle et nocturne de La Haye mais d'ores et déjà ils signifient que l'amateur n'est plus obligé d'aller à Amsterdam ou Rotterdam pour admirer une architecture de qualité.

1 *Voir le chapitre sur le Stopera dans cet ouvrage.*

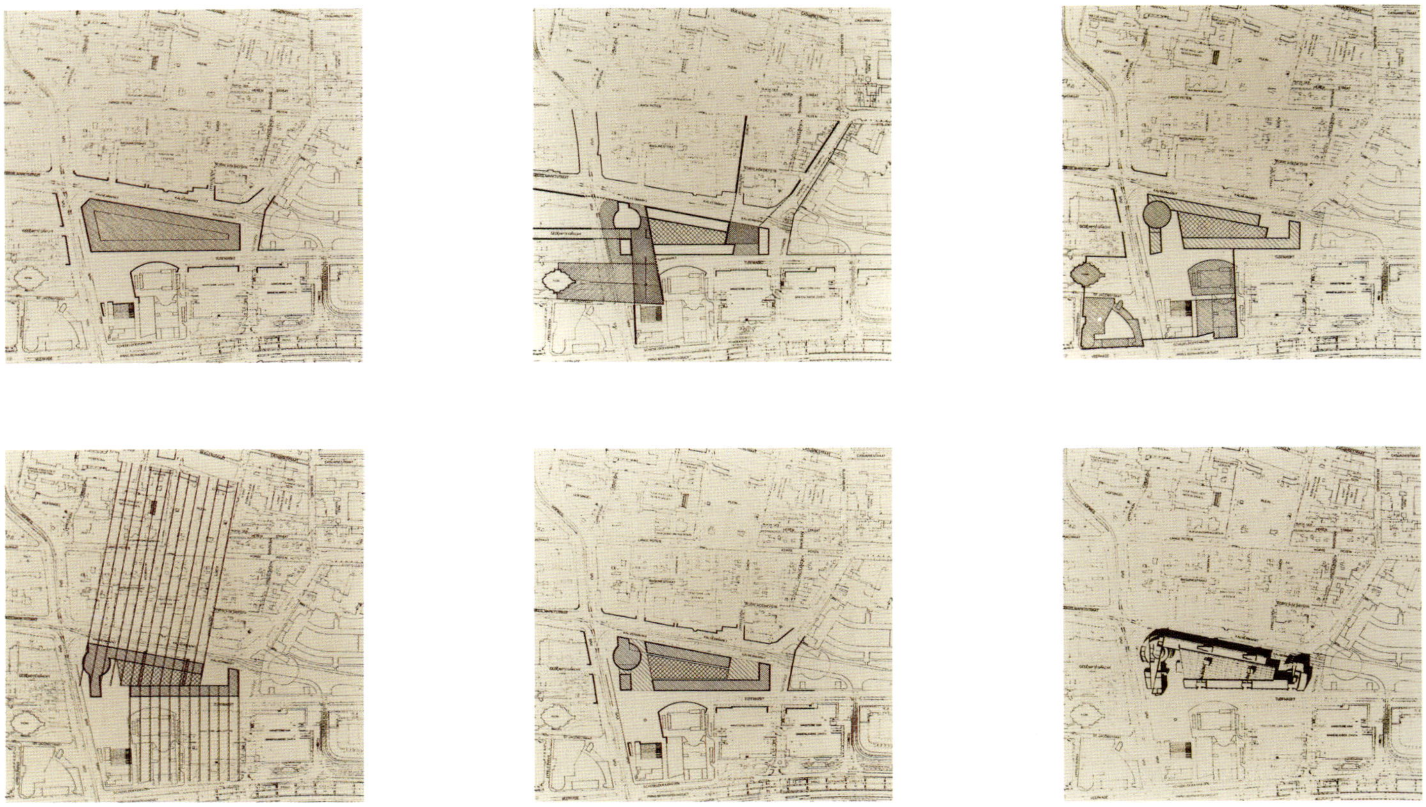

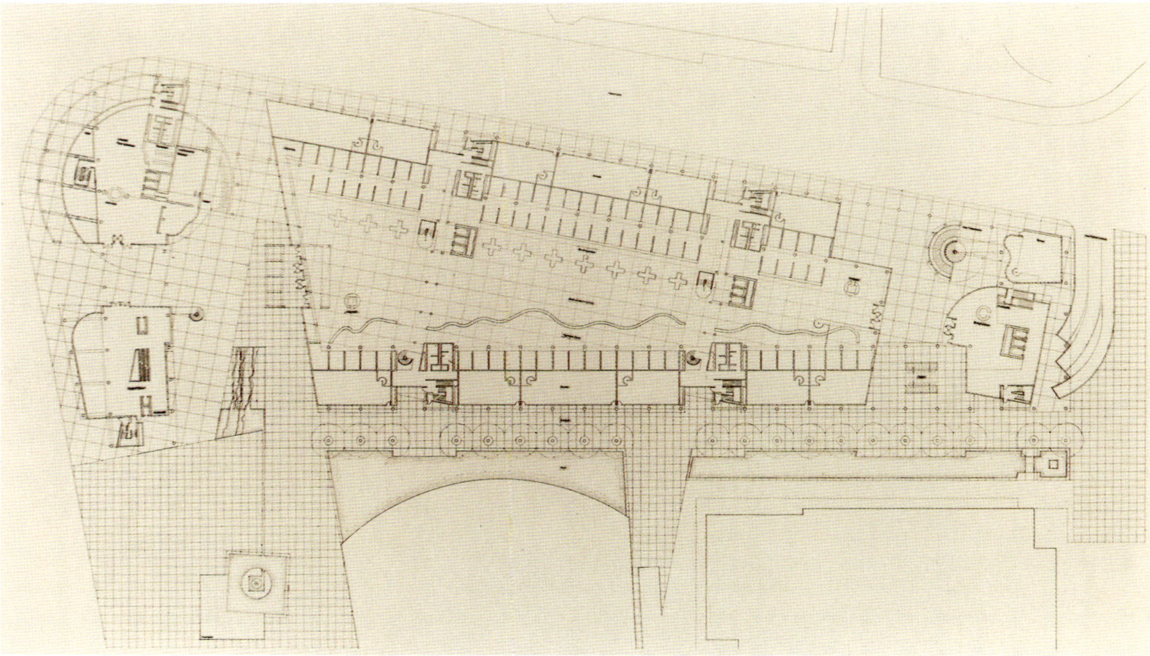

Richard Meier competition design, 1986, analytical diagrams of the site, first prize

Richard Meier competition design, 1986, ground floor plan, first prize

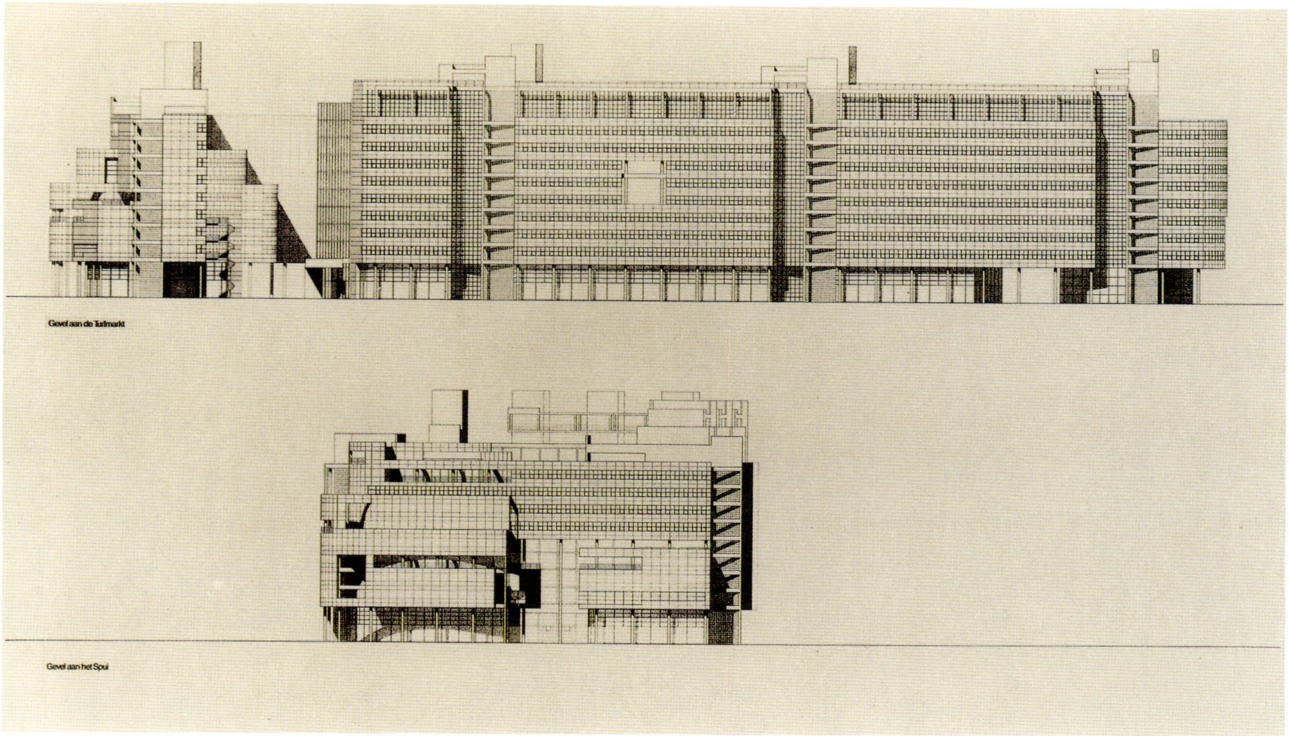

Richard Meier competition design, 1986, above: south elevation, below: west elevation, first prize

Richard Meier competition design, 1986, interior view, first prize

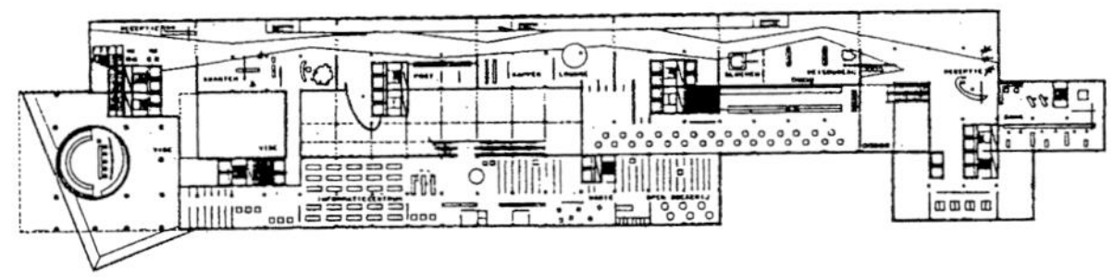

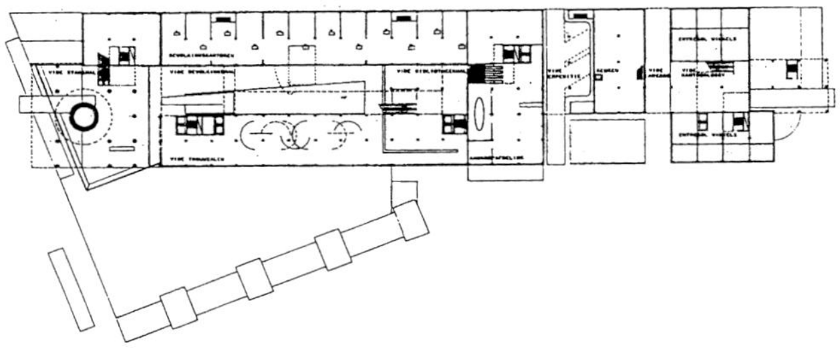

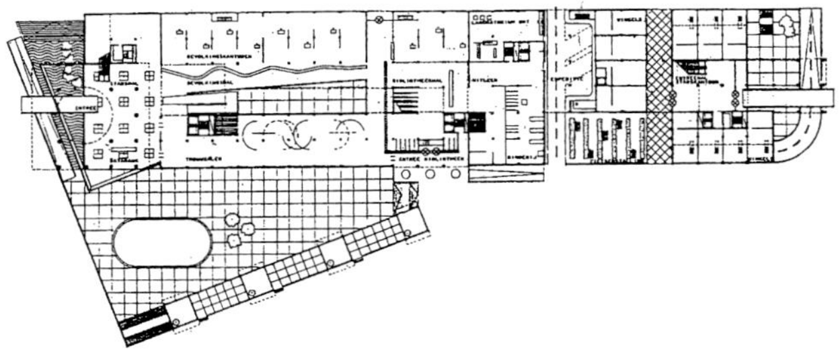

Rem Koolhaas (OMA) competition design, 1986, from top: second floor plan, first floor plan, ground floor plan

Rem Koolhaas (OMA) competition design, 1986, from above left: north-south section (west side), north-south section (east side), east-west section (south side)

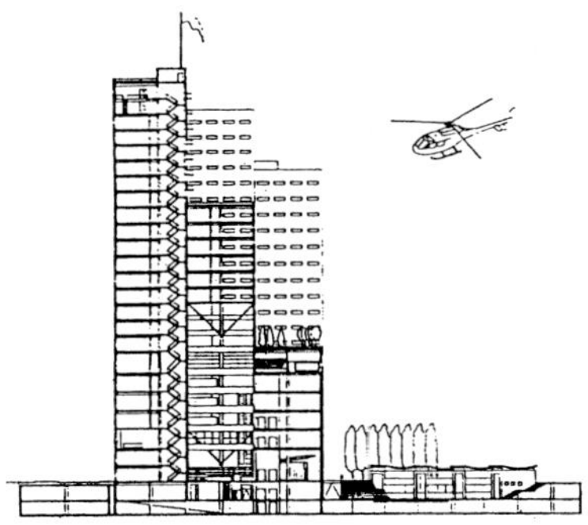

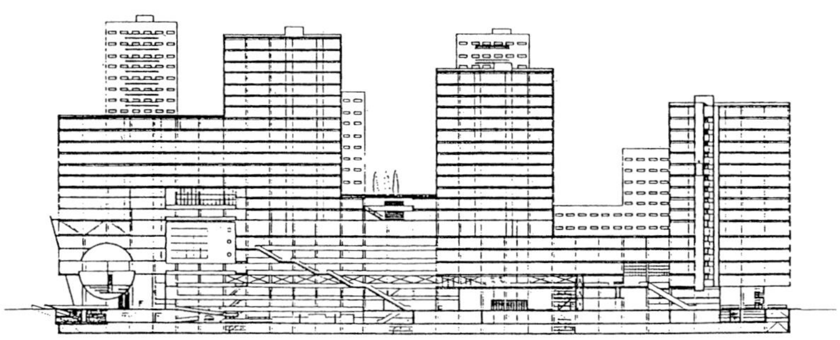

Rem Koolhaas (OMA) competition design, 1986, interior view

Rem Koolhaas (OMA) competition design, 1986, interior view of the hall

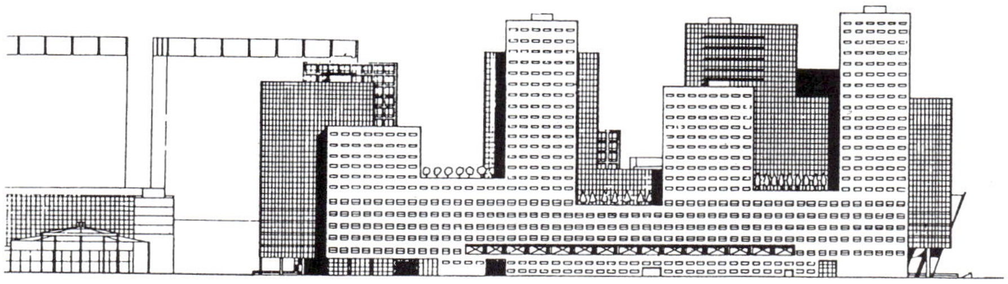

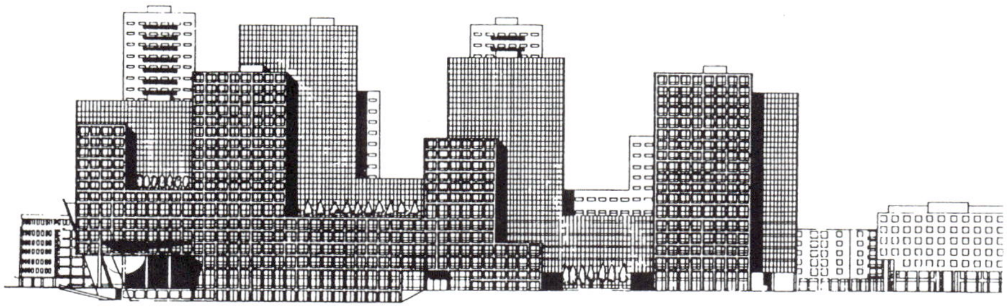

Rem Koolhaas (OMA) competition design, 1986, above: north elevation, below: south elevation

Rem Koolhaas (OMA) competition design, 1986, model

Helmut Jahn competition design, 1986, sketches (study for plans and exterior)

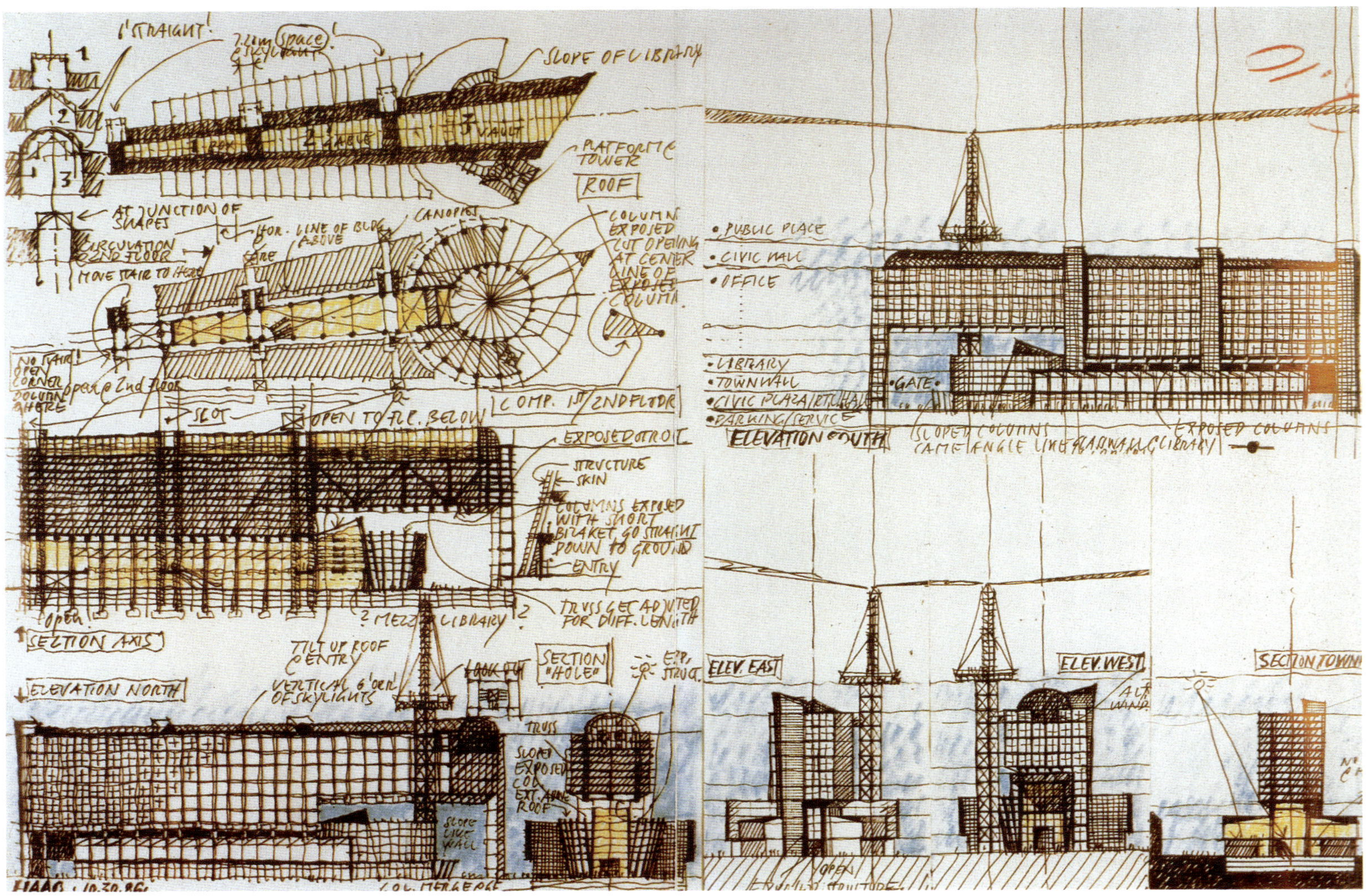

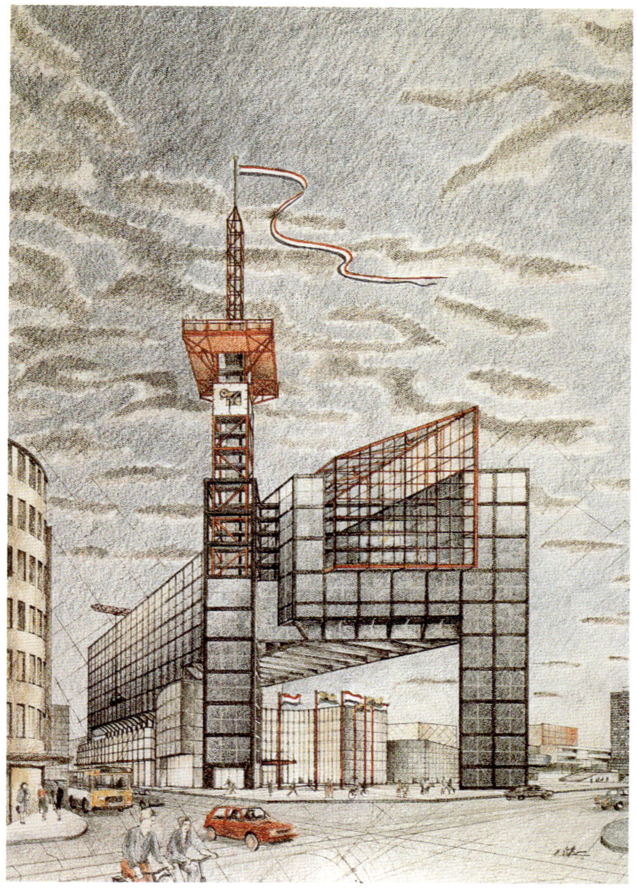

Helmut Jahn competition design, 1986, interior view

Helmut Jahn competition design, 1986, exterior view on the Spui

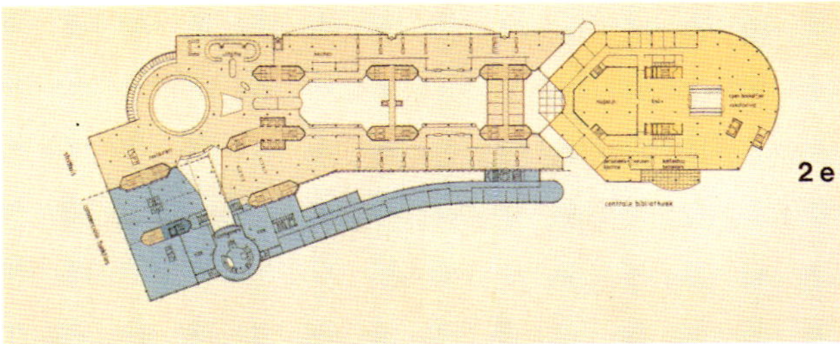

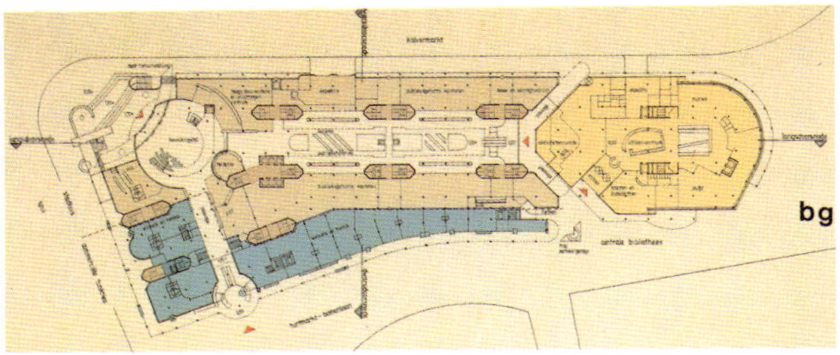

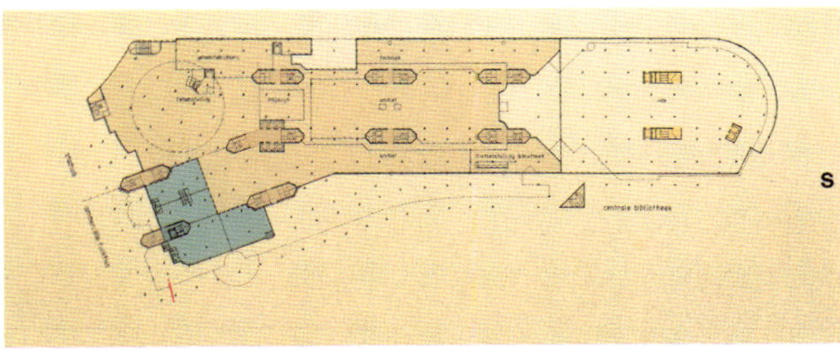

Hans Boot competition design, 1986, above: second floor plan, middle: ground floor plan, below: basement floor plan

Hans Boot competition design, 1986, north elevation

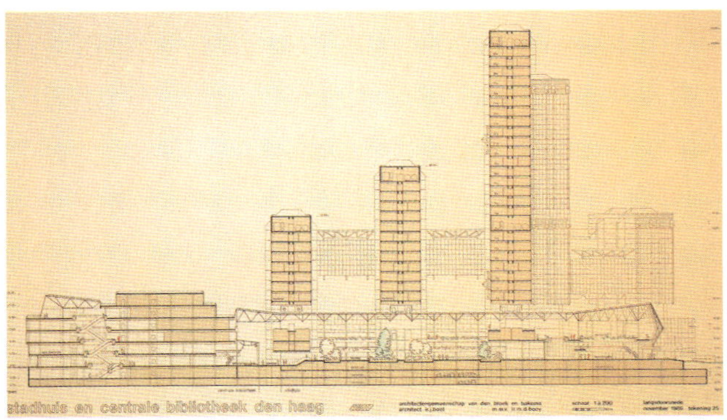

Hans Boot competition design, 1986, east-west section (north side)

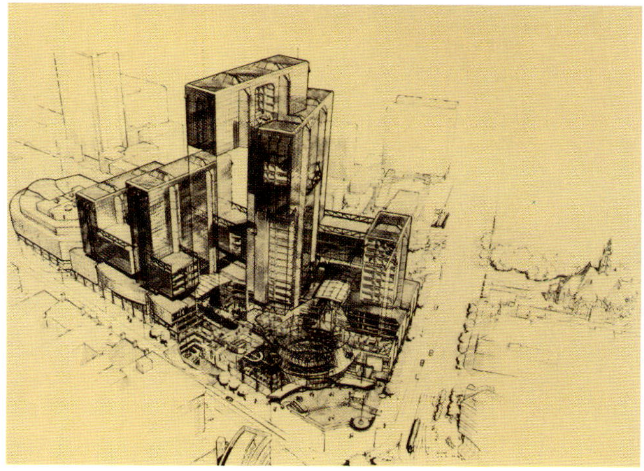

Hans Boot competition design, 1986, bird's-eye view

Hans Boot competition design, 1986, model

Roger Saubot & François Julien competition design, 1986, model

Roger Saubot & François Julien competition design, 1986, model

Tegel

Project

Redevelopment of the harbour, including recreational and housing facilities

Site

Tegel harbour, Berlin-Reinickendorf

Dates

First round announced May 1980 *Closing date* September 1980 *Result announced* October 1980 *Second round announced* 1981

Number of entries

9

Jury

Harald Deilmann (chairman), Kenneth Frampton, Josef Paul Kleihues, Heinrich Klotz, Rem Koolhaas (replaced Aldo van Eijck), Hans C. Müller, Gottfried Böhm, Gustav Peichl, Richard Meier.

Result

First prize Charles Moore, John Ruble & Buzz Yudell *Second prize* Stavoprojekt Liberec; Studio 2 Ralph Erskine *Third prize* Arata Isozaki *Honourable mention* Leon Krier

Commissioned by

Bauausstellung Berlin GmbH

Construction

1987 (harbour and island), 1988 (library and housing blocks)

Architects

Charles Moore, John Ruble & Buzz Yudell (urban development plan, library and housing); Poly; Steinebach & Weber (housing); Dietrich Bangert, Bernd Jansen, Stefan Scholz, Axel Schultes (housing); John Hejduk (housing); Antoine Grumbach (housing); Paolo Portoghesi (housing); Stanley Tigerman (housing); Robert Stern (housing); Cornelia Müller, Elmar Knippschild; Jan Wehberg (gardens)

Friedrichstadt

Design
Housing and offices

Site
Block 4, 5, 10 and 11 in Friedrichstadt South, Berlin-Kreuzberg

Dates
Competition announced September 1980 *Closing date* January 1981 *Result announced* February 1981

Number of entries
47

Jury
Max Bächer (chairman), Vittorio Gregotti, Josef Paul Kleihues, Rob Krier (replaced John Hejduk), Vittorio Magnago Lampugnani (replaced Oswald Mathias Ungers), Hans C. Müller, Paolo Portoghesi

Result
Block 4, First prize Oriol Bohigas, David John Mackay & Josep Martorell *Block 5, First prize* Peter D. Eisenman & Jaquelin Robertson *Block 10, First prize* Aldo Rossi & Gianni Braghieri *Block 11, First prize* Marie-Claude Betrix, Eraldo Consolascio, Bruno Reichlin & Fabio Reinhart

Commissioned by
Bauausstellung Berlin GmbH

Construction
Block 4 largely completed in 1990 *Block 5* Peter D. Eisenman: completed in 1986; Hans Kammerer: completed in 1985 *Block 10* Aldo Rossi: completed in 1988; Dietmer Grötzebach: completed in 1990 *Block 11* John Hejduk: completed in 1988; Raimund Abraham: completed in 1987; Schudnagis & Hameyer: completed in 1991

Architect
Block 4 Oriol Bohigas, David John Mackay & Josep Martorell; Herbert Pfeiffer; Joachim Schürmann; Burkhard Grashorn; Peter Faller, Christian Muschalek, Hermann Schröder; Ernst Bartels, Christoph Schmidt-Ott; Rem Koolhaas & Elia Zenghelis *Block 5* Peter D. Eisenman & Jaquelin Robertson; Hans Kammerer & Walter Belz *Block 10* Aldo Rossi; Dietmer Grötzebach, Günter Plessow & Reinhold Ehlers *Block 11* John Hejduk; Raimund Abraham; Schudnagis & Hameyer

Prinz-Albrecht-Palais

Project
Park and monument to the Holocaust

Site
Block 3, Friedrichstadt South, Berlin-Kreuzberg

Dates
Competition announced June 1983 *Closing date* January 1984 *Result announced* March-April 1984

Number of entries
196

Jury
Eberhard Roters (chairman), Jaap Engel, Waldemar Grzimek, Josef Paul Kleihues, Vittorio Magnago Lampugnani (replaced Aldo Rossi), Wolfgang Ludwig, Walter Rossow, Herbert Sandberg (replaced Colin Rowe), Ionel Schein (replaced Bruno Zevi).

Result
First prize Jürgen Wenzel & Nikolaus Lang *Second prize* Giorgio Grassi *Third prize* Reinhold Grübl *Fourth prize* Peter Bayerer, Rainer Heidenreich & Wolfgang Schuster *Fifth prize* Werner Seligman, Esteban Senney & Bruce Coleman; Ronald Zeytunian; Daniel Kocheniewski

Commissioned by
Bauausstellung Berlin GmbH

Construction
Never built

Tiergarten

Project
Housing and offices

Site
Block 228 / 240 in Berlin-Tiergarten

Dates
Competition announced February 1987 *Closing date* April 1987 *Result announced* May 1987

Number of entries
6

Jury
Christoph Sattler (Chairman), Josef Paul Kleihues, Hans Kollhoff, Fritz Neumeyer

Result
First prize Daniel Libeskind *Second prize* Simon Ungers & Walter Arno Noebel *Third prize* Gerd Neumann

Commissioned by
Bauausstellung Berlin GmbH

Construction
Never built

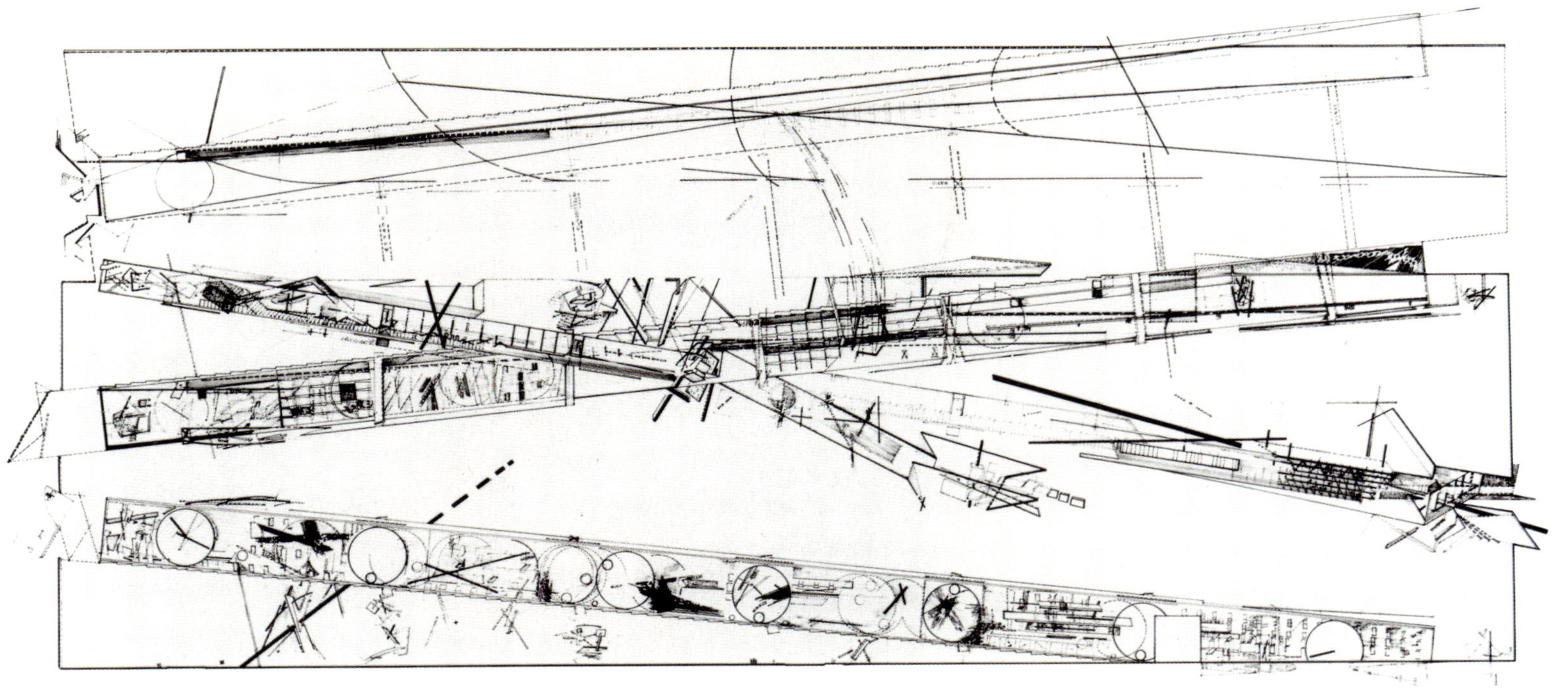

Daniel Libeskind design of the competition City Edge, 1987, plans, sections of Cloud Prop, first prize

Daniel Libeskind design of the competition City Edge, 1987, site model, first prize

International Building Exhibition, Berlin

Over the years Berlin has gained a reputation for its architectural competitions and exhibitions, particularly in the housing sector. The city therefore had every reason to plan and execute the urban renewal projects of the 1980s with the utmost care and, to this end, the Bauausstellung Berlin GmbH was founded in 1979. This body's main task was to organise an international building exhibition, the IBA (Internationale Bauausstellung), based on the theme: "Die Innenstadt als Wohnort" (the inner city as a place of residence).

Previous history

Prior to the Second World War, Berlin had initiated a series of housing projects which had drawn the world's attention. Examples include the Freie Scholle Siedlung in Tegel (1924–1926) designed by Bruno Taut, Siemensstadt (1929–1931) designed by Hans Scharoun and Otto Bartning, and Lindenhof (1918–1919) in Kreuzberg designed by Martin Wagner. In 1931, a major building exhibition was organised in Berlin with progressive architecture as the focal point of the exhibition, particularly the housing of the Weimar Republic, developed by architects such as Walter Gropius, Hugo Häring and Ludwig Mies van der Rohe.

The Modernists had to wait till after the war before they could take up the thread of their development. The Marshall Plan, initiated in 1947, gave rise to the Wirtschaftswunder (economic miracle), which went hand in hand with widespread reconstruction. It was natural that housing projects in the larger cities should merit extra attention: when the first International Building Exhibition (Interbau) was organised in Berlin in 1954, the greater part of the city still lay in ruins.

One of the first exhibition competitions was for the reconstruction of the Hansaviertel, which formed part of the devastated Tiergarten district. This competition was won by Willy Kreuer, Gerhard Jobst and Wilhelm Schiesser, whose urban development plan completely ignored the pre-war street pattern and the city's traditional housing blocks with their enclosed courtyards. Instead, their design elaborated on the avant-garde styles of the 1920s and 30s, echoing ideals developed during the fourth CIAM congress: high-rise buildings, extensive green areas and separate urban functions (traffic, recreation, housing and work). The buildings in the district were designed by renowned architects, such as Alvar Aalto, Oscar Niemeyer and Walter Gropius.

Reconstruction with respect for the past

The design for the Hansaviertel deviated radically from traditional architecture. In contrast, the 1979 Internationale Bauausstellung (IBA) was based on the idea that the new buildings should be tied in with the old city; an approach that was reminiscent of traditional urban planning. Projècts such as that for the Hansaviertel were considered to be too large-scale. The IBA would ensure that the new housing projects would not go to extremes. The primary objective was reconstruction, which does not imply that an exact copy of pre-war Berlin would be constructed, but rather that the reconstruction would be effected with respect for the past and with an eye for quality.

As early as 1974, the district between Tiergarten and the Landwehr Canal had been designated as a future building site. This IBA site was further specified in 1980. The project was roughly divided into two types of activity: new building and urban redevelopment. New buildings would be constructed in the Tegel and Pragerplatz districts, and in the southern parts of Tiergarten and Friedrichstadt. Urban redevelopment would take place around Luisenstadt and the district SO 36 in eastern Kreuzberg. Both Friedrichstadt-Süd and Luisenstadt are also situated in Kreuzberg, to the north of the Landwehr Canal.

Charles Moore **residential building on Tegel harbour, 1988**

Daniel Libeskind City Edge, competition design, 1987, model

Aldo Rossi residential building on Block 10, Friedrichstadt-Süd, 1988

Tegel

The first major competition was for Tegel and the banks of the Tegeler See (lake). This area is situated far from the other IBA areas around the Landwehr Canal, and was targeted for the development of housing projects and recreational facilities. In contrast to Kreuzberg and Tiergarten, Tegel is situated in a rural area which is a popular weekend destination for nature-loving urbanites. Before the fall of the Berlin Wall, areas of this sort were scarce in and around the city. The policy for the Tegel project was therefore completely different to that developed for the Hansaviertel. The motto for the project was indicative of the change that had taken place: *"mit Kind und Kegel auf nach Tegel"* (off to Tegel with the whole family), which implied that Tegel was fun for everyone, and not just for a few architecture buffs. Unfortunately, there was one major drawback: the poor quality of the water in the Tegeler See. Because the water which flowed into the lake from North Berlin was rich in nutrients, the lake was infested with algae. In order to combat this problem, the IBA decided to build a water purification plant. The construction of this "Phosphateliminationsanlage" (PEA) was to be combined with the redevelopment of the harbour, which would include housing and recreational facilities.

Gustav Peichl was commissioned to design the PEA and a competition was organised for the redevelopment of the harbour. A total of eleven German and foreign architects were invited to submit designs, nine of whom accepted the invitation. This competition was of the alternative type described above. Each of the participants would be reimbursed for their efforts, and although prizes would be awarded, the runners-up would also be commissioned for parts of the project.

Stanley Tigerman, John Hejduk, Robert Stern and a number of other renowned architects designed 150 of the 320 housing units. The remaining 170 units were designed by Moore, Ruble and Yudell (Santa Monica, USA), who were also asked to submit an urban development plan for the harbour and a design for the library. The colour scheme and the building materials were binding elements of the design. The redevelopment was competed in 1988, in a style which Charles Moore described as Industrial Baroque, although the project may also be described as Post-Modernist.

Friedrichstadt

Friedrichstadt had remained reasonably intact throughout the war, until allied bombers completely destroyed the district in February 1945. Most of the remaining buildings were demolished soon after the war to make way for urban development projects. Only a few buildings were left standing in this desolate quarter, among them the tourist attraction Checkpoint Charlie.

There was so little left of Friedrichstadt (in Kreuzberg) that total reconstruction was the only solution. To this end, a competition for the redevelopment of Kochstrasse and Friedrichstrasse was organised in 1980. The project was divided into four blocks, numbered 4, 5, 10 and 11. Six architects were invited to submit designs for each block; two from Berlin, two from West Germany and two from other countries. All that remained of Friedrichstadt was the Baroque street plan, all other historical features having been obliterated.

An architectural cross-section

The competition for Friedrichstadt was also of the alternative variety. All the participants were reimbursed for their efforts. The winners received additional prize money and were assigned to various project sectors, as were most of the other participants. The alternative competitions ensured stylistic diversity, in keeping with the policy of critical reconstruction. The architects were not necessarily assigned to those project sectors for which they had submitted plans. The winners of the Block 11 competition refused their commission and were replaced by John Hejduk, who had not been amongst the 24 architects invited to participate. Friedrichstadt and the other IBA projects presented a cross-section of contemporary architectural movements together with their leading representatives. One of the most striking consequences of this architectural blend was that a Deconstructivist design by Peter Eisenman could materialise opposite a block designed by Aldo Rossi. The block was Rossi's first project outside Italy.

It was evident that Rossi had understood what Kleihues had in mind: his design, which features brickwork and monumental corner structures, clearly echoes Berlin's pre-war architecture. The fact that

Oswald Mathias Ungers **Friedrichstadt-Süd, Block 1, competition design, 1986, axonometric projection**

Rossi applied his own language of forms within the historical surroundings tied in perfectly with Kleihues' critical reconstruction policy: the architects were not only asked to take historical features into account, but were also urged to give the city a new and unique identity.
Eisenman designed his block along completely different lines. He had incorporated the nearby Berlin Wall into his design, unaware of the fact that it would be torn down a few years after the competition. Opposite the Wall, Eisenman had planned another wall, which formed part of a grid pattern representing the earth's meridians. At a lower level there is second grid pattern, clearly visible from the footpaths on the upper grid, which mirrors the district's former street plan. Eisenman had included the second grid to remind local inhabitants of the past. As requested, he had incorporated the three remaining historical buildings into his design. However, his approach clearly differed from that of the other participants, in that he did not create a continuous façade on all four sides of the block, but structured the block symbolically.

Prinz-Albrecht-Palais

One of the other competitions was for the Prinz-Albrecht-Palais, which was also part of Friedrichstadt. A park and a Holocaust Memorial had been projected for this district. The open competition drew no less than 196 entries, six of them invited. This clearly illustrates the difference between the various types of competition. Although the general quality of the designs was satisfactory, it is interesting to note that only a few renowned architects submitted designs for the Prinz-Albrecht-Palais competition, preferring instead to concentrate on the competitions for which they were invited. As a result, the competition was won by the relatively unknown architects Jürgen Wenzel and Nikolaus Lang.
Nevertheless, there were a number of famous participants. Giorgio Grassi, for example, who was one of the leading Rationalist architects, after Rossi of course. His design features a combination of austere, angular shapes and fragments of classical ruins. John Hejduk and José Rafael Moneo also submitted plans. Neither was amongst the prize-winners.

Tiergarten

The last competition organised by the IBA was for an abandoned tract of land situated near the Wall in the Tiergarten district. This district, known for its residential character, also houses the Kulturforum and the Zoo, which was initially designed as a park by Peter Joseph Lenné. The competition was won by the Deconstructivist Daniel Libeskind. The Deconstructivists are famous for their spectacular designs and Libeskind's was no exception. In fact, his design was so spectacular that the jury doubted whether the gigantic "suspended" beam was technically feasible, and appointed a technical jury to ascertain whether the design could actually be executed. If the jury's report was negative, the runners-up, Ungers & Noebel and Gerd Neumann, would be commissioned. In the end the entire project was cancelled. Libeskind later won the competition for the Jewish Museum in Berlin[1].
The cancellation of Libeskind's project did not detract from the success of the other Tiergarten projects, which included Rossi's housing project for Rauchstrasse and Oswald Mathias Ungers' design for the Lützowstrasse project.

A successful project

When the project commissions were disbanded in 1987, it was concluded that, on the whole, the International Building Exhibition had been a resounding success. The project areas had, for the greater part, been provided with housing of an exceptional quality and the urban infrastructure had developed as planned. It is worth mentioning that the IBA was merely an organisational body and that the Berlin senate was the driving force behind the project. The urban renovation in Kreuzberg is proceeding according to plan. In this district the IBA has been replaced by the S.T.E.R.N. (Gesellschaft der behutsamen Stadterneuerung GmbH), a body formed to safeguard the continuity of urban renovation.

1 *See chapter on the Jewish Museum elsewhere in this book.*

Internationale Bauausstellung, Berlin

Da die Stadt Berlin auf dem Gebiet der Architekturwettbewerbe und -ausstellungen sowie im Wohnungsbau einen guten Ruf zu verteidigen hatte, wurde die Stadtsanierung in den 80er Jahren sorgfältig betreut. Zu diesem Zweck war bereits 1979 die Bauausstellung Berlin GmbH gegründet worden, deren Aufgabe in der Organisation einer Internationalen Bauausstellung (IBA) unter dem Motto »Die Innenstadt als Wohnort« bestand.

Vorgeschichte

Während der Vorkriegsjahre wurden in Berlin zahlreiche Wohnungsbauprojekte realisiert, die internationales Interesse erweckten – z. B. die Freie Scholle Siedlung (1924–1926) in Tegel von Bruno Taut, Siemensstadt (1929–1931) von Hans Scharoun und Otto Bartning sowie Lindenhof (1918–1919) in Kreuzberg von Martin Wagner. 1931 organisierte die Stadt eine große Bauausstellung, deren Schwerpunkt auf der progressiven Architektur lag und die sich hauptsächlich mit dem Wohnungsbau der Weimarer Republik und Architekten wie Walter Gropius, Hugo Häring und Ludwig Mies van der Rohe befaßte. Allerdings führte diese Ausstellung mit ihren Wohnungsmodellen im Maßstab 1:1 zu keinen nennenswerten Ergebnissen. Erst nach dem Zweiten Weltkrieg nahmen die Anhänger der Moderne die Ideen ihrer Vorgänger wieder auf. Der Marshall Plan und das daraus resultierende Wirtschaftswunder bewirkten eine enorme Zunahme der Bauaktivitäten, wobei die besondere Förderung dem Wohnungsbau in den Großstädten galt. 1954 fand im zerstörten Berlin, wo die Kriegsfolgen immer noch sichtbar waren, die erste Internationale Bauausstellung – kurz »Interbau« – statt. Den für das Hansaviertel im schwer zerstörten Stadtteil Tiergarten ausgeschriebenen Sanierungs-Wettbewerb gewannen Willy Kreuer, Gerhard Jobst und Wilhelm Schiesser. Ihr städtebaulicher Plan für das Viertel ignorierte die Straßenzüge und die tradionell geschlossenen Wohnblöcke der Vorkriegszeit. Statt dessen führten sie die avantgardistische Architektur der 20er und 30er Jahre fort und entwarfen ein städtebauliches Programm im Stil des vierten CIAM-Kongresses: Hochbau, ausgedehnte Grünanlagen und getrennte Funktionsbereiche (Verkehr, Freizeit, Wohnen und Arbeiten). Renommierte Architekten wie Alvar Aalto, Oscar Niemeyer und Walter Gropius befaßten sich mit der Ausgestaltung des Viertels.

Wiederaufbau mit Respekt vor der Vergangenheit

Die Gestaltung des Hansaviertels bedeutete einen abrupten Bruch mit der Vergangenheit. Dagegen ging die Internationale Bauausstellung (IBA) 1979 von einer Anpassung an die alte Stadt aus und kehrte damit teilweise zur traditionellen Stadtplanung zurück. Die Rekonstruktion stand im Vordergrund, wobei man keine exakten Kopien des Berlins der Vorkriegszeit anstrebte. Bereits seit 1974 war der Stadtteil zwischen Tiergarten und Landwehrkanal als zukünftiges Baugelände ausgewiesen, 1980 erfolgte im Rahmen der IBA eine detaillierte Aufschlüsselung des Terrains, das in zwei Hauptgebiete geteilt werden sollte. Ein Bereich war als Neubaugebiet vorgesehen, mit den Schwerpunkten Tegel, Pragerplatz, dem südlichen Teil von Tiergarten sowie dem Süden von Friedrichstadt, während für das andere Gebiet – Luisenstadt und der Ortsteil SO 36 im Osten Kreuzbergs – eine Stadtsanierung geplant wurde.

Tegel

Die erste große Ausschreibung befaßte sich mit dem Stadtteil Tegel und dem Uferbereich am Tegeler See. Dieses Terrain ist weit von den anderen IBA-Gebieten am Landwehrkanal entfernt und war für Wohnbauten und Erholungsgebiete bestimmt. Im Gegensatz zu den Stadtvierteln Kreuzberg und Tiergarten liegt Tegel in einer ländlichen Umgebung. Vor dem Fall der Mauer waren diese Naturgebiete nur spärlich gesät, weshalb man Tegel nicht wie seinerzeit das Hansaviertel bebauen wollte. Allerdings wies das Gelände einen Nachteil auf: Das Wasser des Tegeler Sees war aufgrund der Abwassereinleitung aus Nord-Berlin von schlechter Qualität. Aus diesem Grund sah die IBA für Tegel zwei Hauptziele vor: erstens, eine Umstrukturierung des Hafens und zweitens, die Errichtung einer Kläranlage, der Phosphateliminationsanlage (PEA).
Den Auftrag für den Bau der PEA erhielt Gustav Peichl, während für das Hafengebiet eine sog. alternative Ausschreibung erfolgte: Jeder Teilnehmer wurde für seine Arbeit bezahlt, und trotz Preisvergabe bekamen alle Architekten – auch die nicht prämierten – den Auftrag für einen Teilbereich. 150 der 320 Wohnbaueinheiten wurden u. a. von Stanley Tigerman, John Hejduk und Robert Stern realisiert. Die restlichen 170 Einheiten sowie die Bibliothek und der städtebauliche Plan für den Hafen entstanden unter Leitung von Moore, Ruble und Yudell (Santa Monica, USA). Farbe und Material bildeten das Verbindungsglied zwischen den einzelnen Bereichen in Tegel. Charles Moore beschrieb das 1988 fertiggestellte Viertel als »industriellen Barock.«

Friedrichstadt

Der Süden Friedrichstadts hatte die ersten Kriegsjahre relativ unbeschadet überstanden, bis im Februar 1945 die Bomber der Allierten den Stadtteil in Schutt und Asche legten. Die stehengebliebenen Gebäude fielen nach dem Krieg der Stadtsanierung zum Opfer. 1980 erfolgte für die Kochstraße und die Friedrichstraße eine Ausschreibung, die sich mit den Wohnblöken 4, 5, 10 und 11 befaßte. Für jeden Wohnblock wurden zwei Berliner Architekten, zwei westdeutsche Baumeister sowie zwei Architekten aus dem Ausland eingeladen.
Die kritische Rekonstruktion ist eines der Grundprinzipien der IBA; dieser Begriff, geprägt von Kleihues, beinhaltet den Wiederaufbau der Stadt unter Berücksichtigung historischer Gegebenheiten. Im Falle von Koch- und Friedrichstraße bedeutete dies, daß die alten Häuserfluchten erhalten werden mußten, Baulüken gestopft, eventuelle historische Gebäude restauriert und die Straßen wieder zu alten Ehren gelangen sollten. Ein weiterer, erheblicher Unterschied zum Städtebau der 50er und 60er Jahre zeigte sich in der Auflage an die Architekten, neben Wohnungen auch kleine Geschäftsräume zu entwerfen. Auch die Ausschreibung für Friedrichstadt erfolgte nach dem »alternativen« IBA-Modell. Alle Teilnehmer wurden für ihren Beitrag entlohnt, wobei die Jury die prämierten Entwürfe in der Rangstufe der Plätze zusätzlich vergütete. Nach Bekanntgabe des Ergebnisses ernannte man die ausführenden Architekten. Die Wettbewerbsgewinner als auch die meisten anderen Beteiligten erhielten einen Auftrag, der sich aber nicht notwendigerweise auf den Block bezog, für den sie ihre Konstruktionspläne eingereicht hatten. Lediglich die Gewinner der Ausschreibung zu Block 11 wurden nicht an der baulichen Durchführung des Projekts beteiligt. An ihre Stelle trat John Hejduk, der nicht zu den 24 eingeladenen Architekten gezählt hatte.
Wie die übrigen IBA-Projekte ist Friedrichstadt ein Abbild der zeitgenössischen Architekturströmungen und ihrer wichtigsten Vertreter. Als herausragende architektonische Leistung können der dekonstruktivistische Entwurf von Peter Eisenman und auf der anderen Straßenseite der Wohnblock von Aldo Rossis Konzept genannt werden, der in Berlin seinen ersten Auftrag außerhalb Italiens realisierte. Er integrierte die nahegelegene Berliner Mauer in sein Konzept, ohne zu ahnen, daß diese wenige Jahre nach der Ausschreibung verschwinden würde. Gegenüber der Mauer plazierte er eine andere Mauer, die wiederum Bestandteil eines Rasters war, das die Meridiane der Erde darstellt. Auf einer darunterliegenden Ebene legte Eisenman ein weiteres Raster an, das sich parallel zum Straßenverlauf des alten Viertels erstreckt.
Die drei noch existierenden historischen Gebäude ließ er stehen und integrierte sie in seinen Entwurf, indem er eine symbolische Struktur über den Block legte und auf eine durchgehende Bebauung entlang der vier Straßenzüge verzichtete.

Prinz-Albrecht-Palais

Friedrichstadt war Schauplatz einer weiteren Ausschreibung, des Wettbewerbs für das Prinz-Albrecht-Palais. In dem Viertel waren ein Park und ein Denkmal für die Opfer des Holocaust geplant. An der offenen Ausschreibung beteiligten sich 196 Architekten, darunter sechs auf Einladung. Deutlich trat der Unterschied zu den geschlossenen Wettbewerben zutage: Es waren kaum große Namen vertreten, so daß weniger bekannte Vertreter ihres Fachs, Jürgen Wenzel und Nikolaus Lang den Wettbewerb gewannen.

Tiergarten

Die letzte, von der IBA organisierte Ausschreibung betraf ein vergessenes Areal entlang der Mauer im Bezirk Tiergarten, der für seine parkähnliche Anlage bekannt ist und zu dem auch das Kulturforum und der seinerzeit von Peter Joseph Lenné als Stadtpark konzipierte Tiergarten gehören. Den Wettbewerb gewann der Dekonstruktivist, Daniel Libeskind, doch die Jury bezweifelte die technische Durchführbarkeit seines gewaltigen »schwebenden« Balkens und verlangte eine sorgfältige Prüfung. Falls sich Libeskinds Entwurf nicht realisieren ließe, sollte der Auftrag an die Gewinner des zweiten und dritten Platzes gehen: Ungers und Noebel sowie Gerd Neumann. Schließlich kam jedoch das Aus für das gesamte Projekt. Kurze Zeit später gewann Libeskind die Ausschreibung für das Jüdische Museum (siehe gleichnamiges Kapitel) in Berlin. Trotz der Streichung dieses Vorhabens entwickelten sich die anderen Projekte im Bezirk Tiergarten – z. B. an der Rauchstraße mit Wohnungen von Rossi und an der Lützowstraße mit der von Oswald Mathias Ungers konzipierten Bebauung – zu einem großen Erfolg.

Ein gelungenes Projekt

Insgesamt kann die IBA, die sich 1987 ihrem Ende zuneigte, als erfolgreiches Projekt bezeichnet werden. Große Teile der vier ausgewählten Gebiete wurden mit Wohnungen von außergewöhnlicher Qualität versehen; unter städtebaulichen Aspekten erfüllen die Projekte alle an sie gestellten Erwartungen. Auch die Stadtsanierung im Bezirk Kreuzberg verläuft reibungslos; hier hat die S.T.E.R.N (Gesellschaft der behutsamen Stadterneuerung GmbH) den Platz der aufgelösten IBA übernommen, um die Kontinuität der Sanierung zu gewährleisten.

L'Internationale Bauausstellung

Au cours de ces dernières années , Berlin s'est fait un nom dans le domaine des concours et des grandes manifestations architecturales, en particulier dans le secteur du logement. La ville, faut-il le rappeler, avait toutes les raisons de se lancer dans des projets de rénovation urbaine qui furent menés avec le plus grand soin, et c'est dans ce but que fut fondée la Bauausstellung Berlin GmbH, en 1979. Cet organisme avait pour tâche principale d'organiser une exposition internationale d'architecture, l'Internationale Bauausstellung (IBA), sur le thème de «Habiter la ville».

Un peu d'histoire

Avant la Seconde Guerre mondiale, Berlin avait lancé des opérations de construction de logements qui avaient déjà attiré l'attention internationale avec, par exemple, la Freie Scholle Siedlung à Tegel (1924–26), de Bruno Taut, Siemensstadt (1929–31), de Hans Scharoun et Otto Bartning et Lindenhof (1918–19), à Kreuzberg, conçu par Martin Wagner. En 1931, une grande manifestation fut organisée sur le thème de l'architecture progressiste, en particulier autour de la politique du logement de la République de Weimar, à laquelle avaient collaboré des architectes comme Walter Gropius, Hugo Häring et Ludwig Mies van der Rohe. Les participants y avaient présenté des modèles d'appartements grandeur nature.
Les modernistes durent attendre longtemps après la guerre avant de pouvoir réintervenir. Le plan Marshall de 1947 et une politique économique audacieuse permirent le «miracle économique allemand» qui s'accompagna d'un énorme effort de reconstruction. Les plus importants projets de construction de logements étaient réservés aux grandes villes quasiment détruites: la première exposition internationale de construction (Interbau) fut donc organisée dans un Berlin encore en ruines.
L'un des premiers concours qui l'accompagna fut celui de la reconstruction du quartier de la Hanse (Hansaviertel), au bord du Tiergarten dévasté. Il fut remporté par Willy Kreuer, Gerhard Jobst et Wilhelm Schiesser, dont le plan d'urbanisme ignorait la voirie d'avant-guerre et le principe de construction berlinoise du «block» à cour centrale. Leur plan s'appuyait sur les styles avant-gardistes des années 20 et 30 et rappelait les idéaux des congrès des CIAM: immeubles de grande hauteur, vastes espaces verts et séparation des fonctions urbaines (circulation, loisirs, habitation et travail). Les immeubles furent dessinés par des architectes aussi renommés que Alvar Aalto, Oscar Niemeyer et Walter Gropius.
Ce quartier n'était pas seulement une référence au Berlin progressiste et culturel de l'avant-guerre mais également une forme de critique du classicisme pompeux des nazis et des jungles de béton que l'on élevait en Allemagne de l'Est. Ces dernières années, ce quartier a été très critiqué et les concours des années 80 ont pris des orientations toutes différentes.

Reconstruire dans le respect du passé

Le projet du Hansaviertel s'éloignait radicalement de l'architecture traditionnelle. L'IBA de 1979 s'articulait au contraire sur l'idée de la nécessité d'intégrer les nouvelles constructions dans l'existant, une conception plus proche de celle de l'urbanisme classique. Les projets comme ceux de la Hanse étaient jugés trop gigantesques et la nouvelle IBA voulait éviter de tomber dans ces extrêmes. L'objectif principal était la reconstruction, ce qui n'impliquait pas la copie du Berlin d'avant-guerre, mais plutôt un certain respect du passé et le souci de la qualité.
Dès 1974, le quartier entre le Tiergarten et le Landwehrkanal avait été retenu comme futur site de reconstruction, la zone attribuée à l'IBA étant précisée en 1980. Le projet était divisé en deux types d'intervention: nouveaux immeubles et rénovation urbaine. Les nouveaux immeubles seraient construits dans le Tegel et autour de la Pragerplatz au sud du Tiergarten et de Friedrichstadt et la rénovation centrée autour de Luisenstadt et de la zone SO36 de Kreuzberg-Ost. Friedrichstadt-Süd et Luisenstadt se trouvent également sur Kreuzberg, au nord du Landwehrkanal.

Tegel

Le premier grand concours concerna Tegel et les rives du Tegeler See (lac), secteur éloigné des autres zones de l'IBA groupées autour du Landwehrkanal. Il était programmé pour des logements et des équipements de loisirs. A la différence de Kreuzberg et du Tiergarten, Tegel est situé dans une zone encore semi-rurale où les citadins aiment à se retrouver en fin de semaine. Avant la chute du mur de Berlin, les lieux de cette sorte étaient rares pour les habitants de l'Ouest. La politique choisie fut donc totalement différente de celle retenue pour le Hansaviertel. Le slogan *«Mit Kind und Kegel auf nach Tegel»* (Allons à Tegel, avec les enfants et les quilles) impliquait que le secteur devait être accessible à tous et non pas aux seuls aficionados d'architecture.
Un obstacle majeur se révéla malheureusement très vite: la qualité insuffisante de l'eau du Tegeler See, chargée d'engrais et envahie d'algues. L'IBA décida de construire une usine de traitement des eaux, la «Phosphateliminationsanlage» (PEA) dont fut chargé Gustav Peichl.
Onze architectes allemands ou étrangers furent invités à participer au concours pour la rénovation du secteur et neuf acceptèrent. Il s'agissait d'un concours «alternatif». Chaque candidat recevrait un dédommagement et même si aucun prix n'était prévu, les vaincus pourraient participer à certaines parties du projet.
Stanley Tigerman, John Hejduk, Robert Stern et un certain nombre d'architectes de renom dessinèrent 150 des 320 unités d'habitation prévues. Les 170 restantes furent confiées à Moore, Ruble & Yudell (USA), ainsi qu'un plan d'aménagement urbanistique du port et un projet de bibliothèque. Le programme commun de coloration et de matériaux de construction servait d'élément unificateur à l'ensemble du projet. La rénovation fut achevée en 1988 dans un style que Charles Moore a pu décrire comme «baroque industriel» mais que l'on a également qualifié de «Friedrichstadt post-moderne».

Friedrichstadt

Friedrichstadt avait échappé aux bombardements de la guerre jusqu'en février 1945. La plupart des bâtiments restants avaient été démolis peu après le conflit, pour laisser la place aux projets de rénovation, et les quelques immeubles sauvegardés n'amélioraient en rien l'apparence désolée de ce quartier rendu célèbre par le sinistre Checkpoint Charlie.
Seul le réseau de voirie baroque subsistait mais tous les éléments historiques avaient disparu. Une reconstruction totale était la seule solution. A cette fin, un concours pour la rénovation de la Kochstrasse et de la Friedrichstrasse fut lancé en 1980. Le projet était divisé en quatre blocs numérotés 4, 5, 10 et 11. Six architectes invités soumirent des plans pour chaque bloc: deux de Berlin, deux d'Allemagne de l'Ouest et deux étrangers.

Prinz-Albrecht-Palais

Le secteur du Prinz-Albrecht-Palais faisait également partie de Friedrichstadt et c'est là qu'avaient été prévus un parc et un monument à l'Holocauste. Le concours ouvert n'attira pas moins de 196 participants, six d'entre eux étant invités. Il est intéressant de noter que les «grands» architectes ne s'y intéressèrent pas, se réservant pour les appels d'offre auxquels ils étaient conviés. Le concours fut ainsi remporté par deux architectes relativement peu connus, Jürgen Wenzel et Nikolaus Lang.
Parmi les concurrents plus notables figurait Giorgio Grassi, l'un des principaux représentants du Rationalisme, après Rossi bien sûr. Son projet austère faisait appel à des fragments de ruines classiques. John Hedjuk et José Rafael Moneo proposèrent également des plans, Moneo étant primé.

Tiergarten

Le dernier concours de l'IBA concernait un terrain abandonné non loin du mur, dans le secteur du Tiergarten. C'est dans ce quartier, de caractère résidentiel, que se trouvaient le Kulturforum et le zoo, dessiné à l'origine par Peter Joseph Lenné. Le concours fut remporté par Daniel Libeskind dont les plans déconstructivistes étaient, comme de bien entendu, spectaculaires. En fait, telle était son originalité que le jury douta de la faisabilité de cette énorme poutre «suspendue» et demanda l'avis d'un jury technique. En cas de conclusions négatives, la commande serait attribuée à Ungers & Noebel et Gerd Neumann. Finalement, le projet fut annulé et Libeskind remporta ultérieurement le concours du Musée Juif de Berlin[1]. Cette annulation ne ternit cependant pas le succès des autres projets pour le Tiergarten, dont l'immeuble d'appartements de Rossi pour la Rauchstrasse et celui d'Oswald Mathias Ungers pour la Lützowstrasse.

Un projet réussi

Les diverses commissions de l'IBA, organisme administratif piloté en fait par le Sénat de Berlin, furent dissoutes en 1987 et il apparut en conclusion que l'opération avait été un grand succès. Les divers secteurs intéressés se virent dotés de constructions d'une qualité exceptionnelle et l'infrastructure urbaine fut modernisée comme prévu. La rénovation urbaine de Kreuzberg est en cours selon les plans choisis. Dans ce quartier, l'IBA a été remplacée par le S.T.E.R.N. (Gesellschaft der behutsamen Stadterneueerung GmbH), un organisme constitué pour sauvegarder l'unité des programmes de rénovation de la capitale.

1 Voir le chapitre sur le Musée Juif dans cet ouvrage.

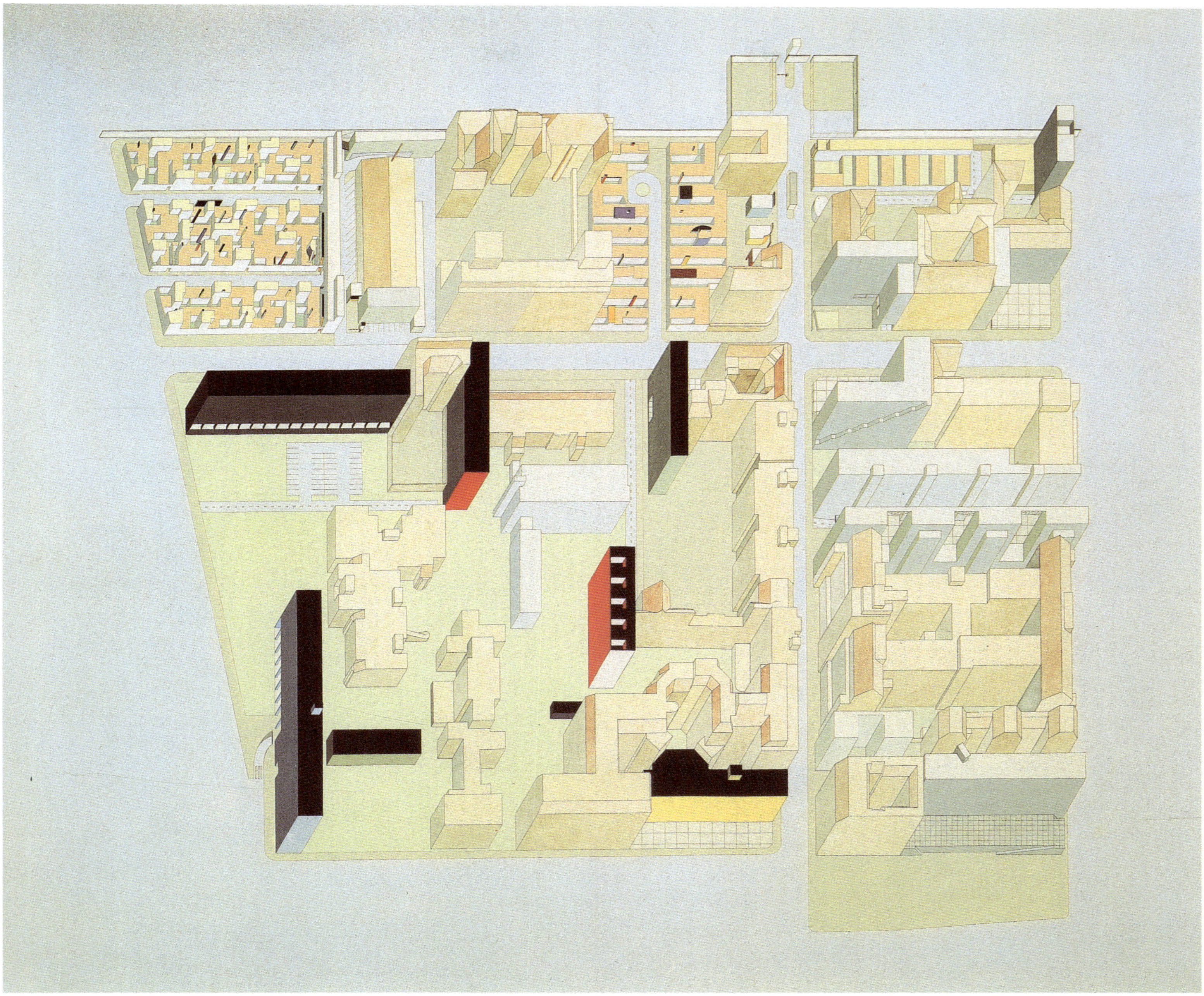

Charles Moore, John Ruble & Buzz Yudell design for the competition "Wohnen und Freizeit am Tegeler Hafen", 1980, bird's-eye view, first prize

Charles Moore, John Ruble & Buzz Yudell design for the competition "Wohnen und Freizeit am Tegeler Hafen", 1981, bird's eye view, first prize

Rem Koolhaas & Stefano de Martino design for the competition "Wohnen und Arbeiten in der Südlichen Friedrichstadt", 1981, axonometric design of the concept "Kochsstraße, Friedrichsstraße", Block 4, 5, 10, 11, purchased

Aldo Rossi & Gianni Braghieri
design for the competition "Wohnen und Arbeiten in der Südlichen Friedrichstadt", 1981, above: elevation on Wilhelmstrasse, below: ground floor plan, Block 10, first prize

Aldo Rossi & Gianni Braghieri
design for the competition "Wohnen und Arbeiten in der Südlichen Friedrichstadt", 1980, isometric sketch, Kochsstraße, Friedrichsstraße, Block 10, first prize

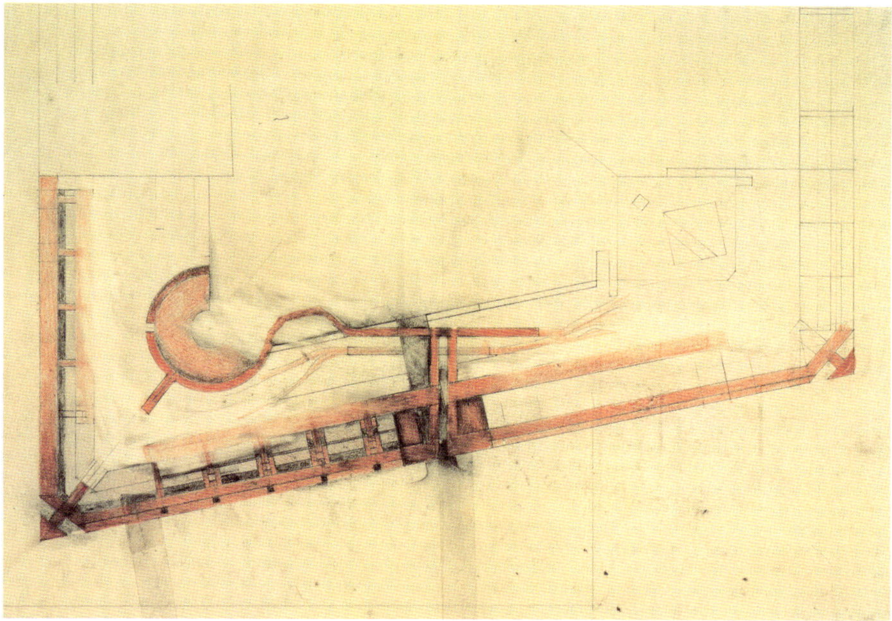

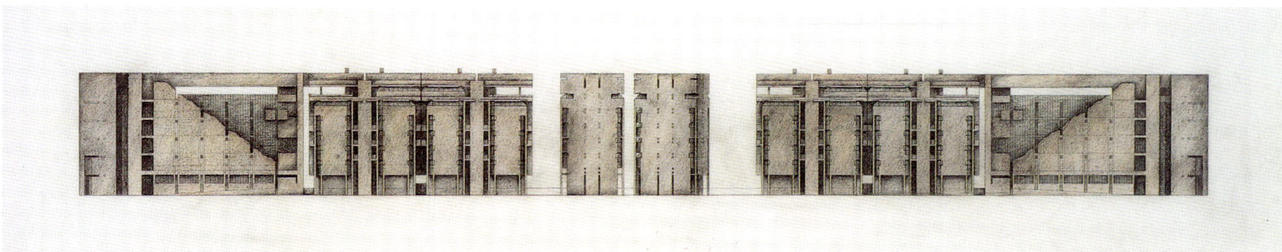

Raimund Abraham design for the competition "Wohnen und Arbeiten in der Südlichen Friedrichstadt", 1981, study sketch for the site plan of the block bordered by Kochstrasse, Wilhelmsstrasse, Puttkamerstrasse, Block 10, award

Raimund Abraham design for the competition "Wohnen und Arbeiten in der Südlichen Friedrichstad", 1981, elevation on Wilhelmstrasse, Block 10, award

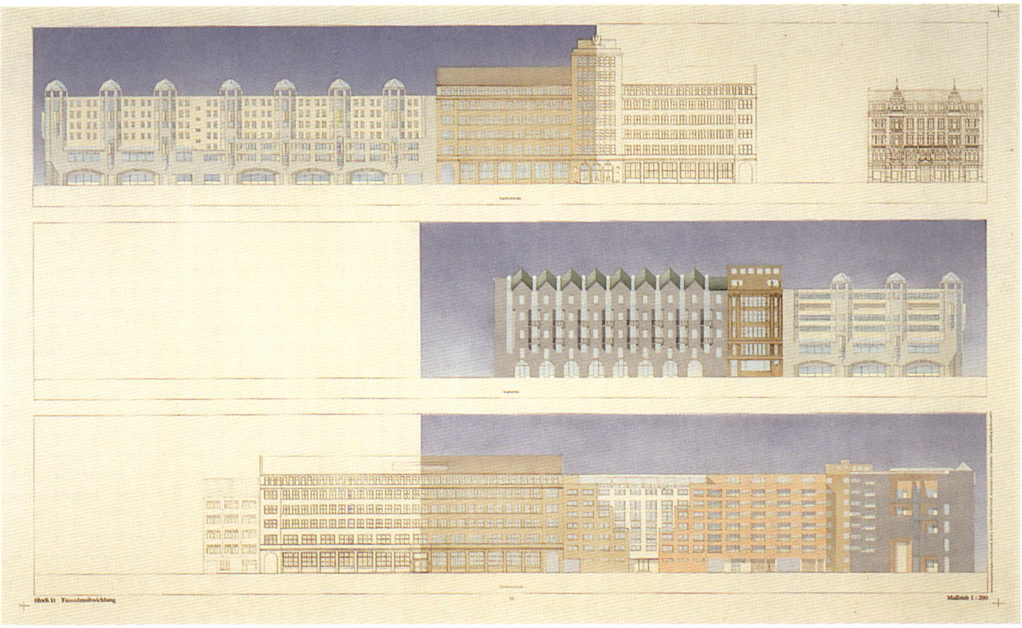

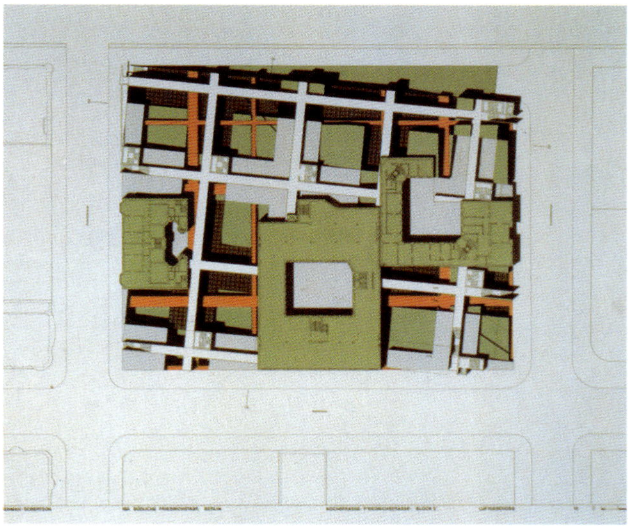

Marie-Claude Betrix, Eraldo Consolascio, Bruno Reichlin & Fabio Reinhart design for the Friedrichstadt redevelopment competition, 1981, above: elevation on Friedrichstrasse, middle: elevation on Kochstrasse, below: elevation on Charlottenstrasse, Block 11, first prize

Josep Martorell, Oriol Bohigas & David Mackay design for the Friedrichstadt redevelopment competition, 1985, view of Kochstrasse, Zimmerstrasse, Block 4, first prize

Peter Eisenman & Jacquelin Robertson design for the Friedrichstadt redevelopment competition, 1981, typical floor plan, "Kochstrasse, Friedrichstrasse", Block 5, first prize

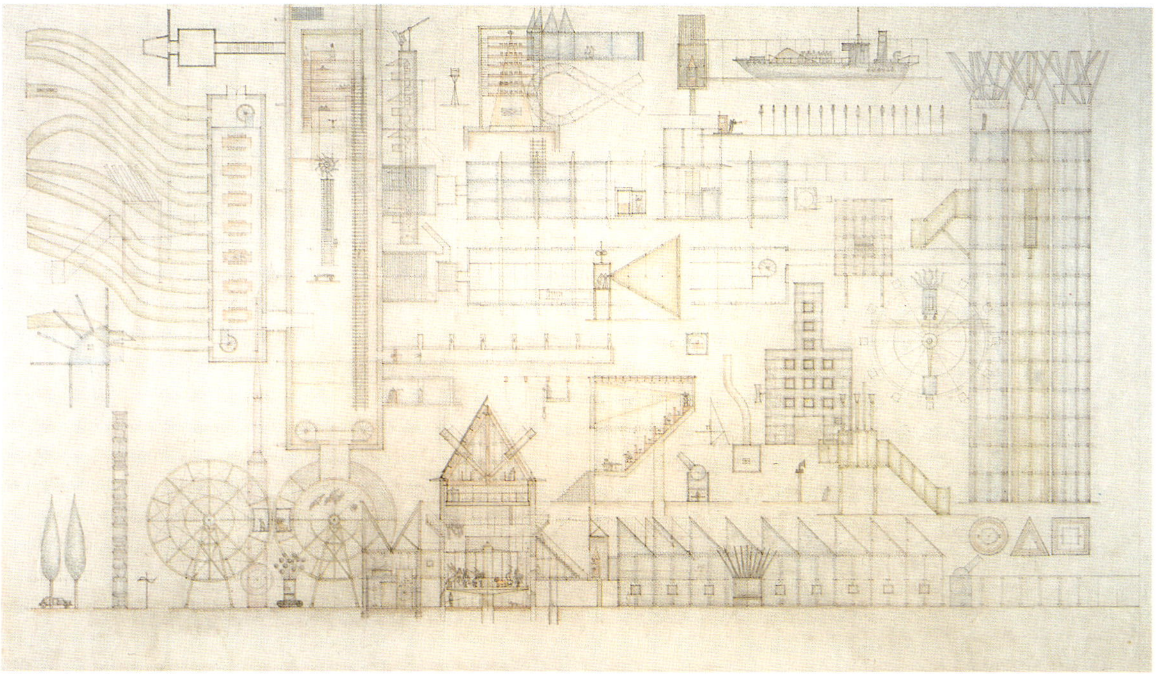

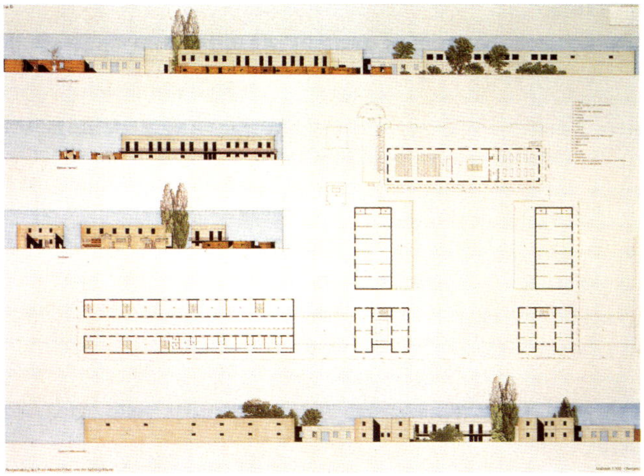

John Hejduk design for the Prinz-Albrecht-Palais site development competition, 1984, structural drawing, purchased

Giorgio Grassi design for the Prinz-Albrecht-Palais site development competition, 1984, from top: west elevation, east elevation on garden, north elevation, first floor plan, east elevation on Wilhelmstrasse, second prize

Raimund Abraham design for the Prinz-Albrecht-Palais site development competition, 1984, from top: north-south section (west side), north-south section (east side), east-west section (south side), below left: site model (south-east side), purchased

Elisabeth Lux & Martin Wiedemann design for the Prinz-Albrecht-Palais site development competition, 1984, analytical plan, purchased

José Rafael Moneo design for the Prinz-Albrecht-Palais site development competition, 1984, above left: roof plan, below left: elevation, right: section,

José Rafael Moneo design for the Prinz-Albrecht-Palais site development competition, 1984, above left: ground floor plan, below left: section, right: section

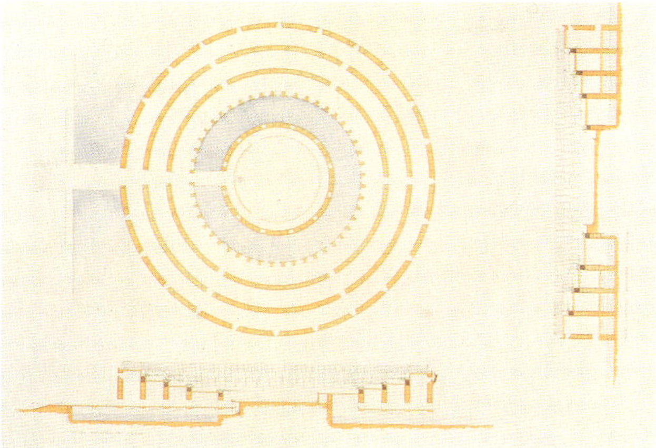

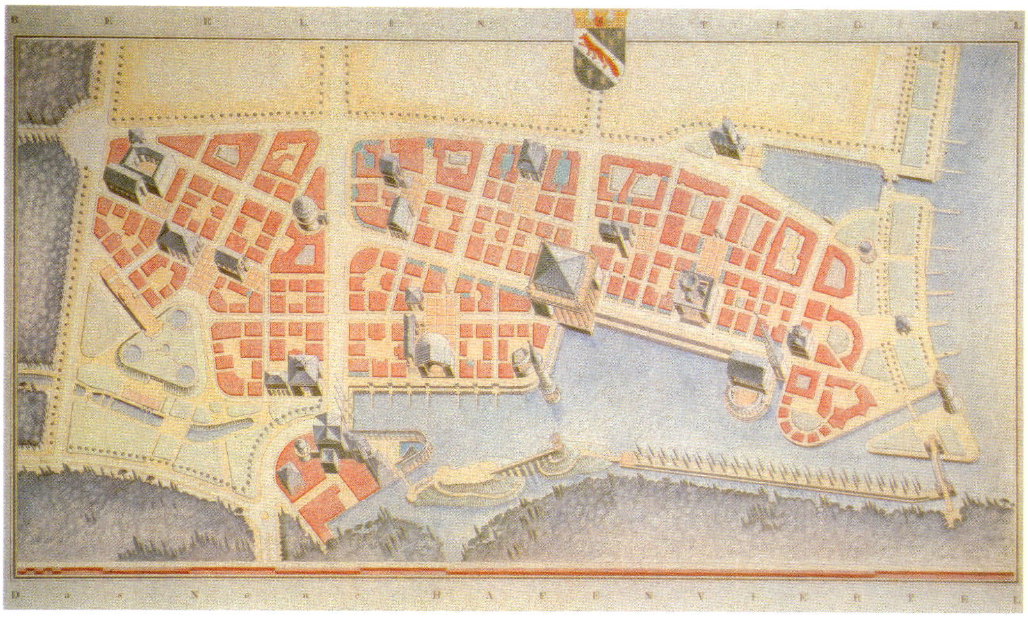

Leon Krier Tegel lakeside development, 1980, tourist plan of "Das neue Hafenviertel", honourable mention

Stavoprojekt Liberec, Studio 2 Tegel lakeside development, 1980, bird's-eye view from north, second prize

Arata Isozaki Tegel lakeside development,1980, view on Tegeler Hafen, third prize

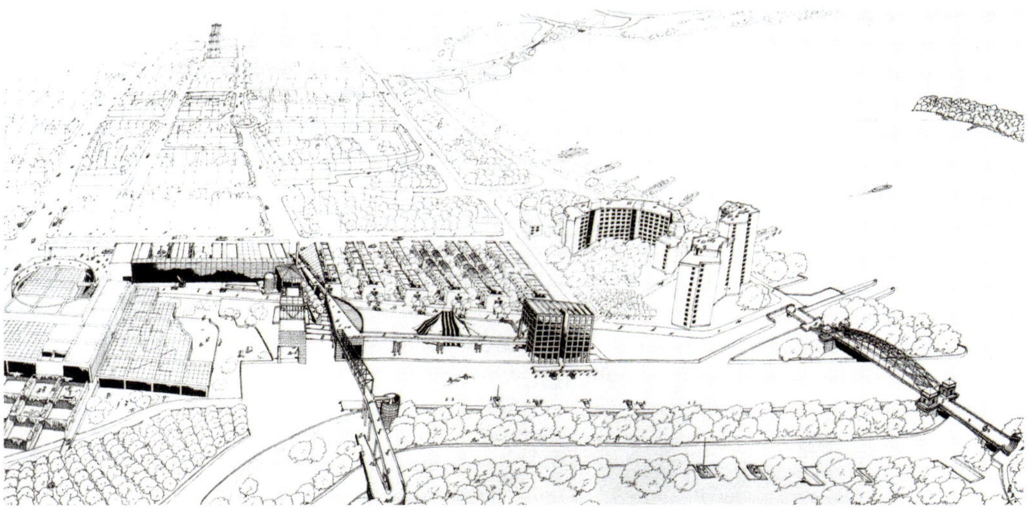

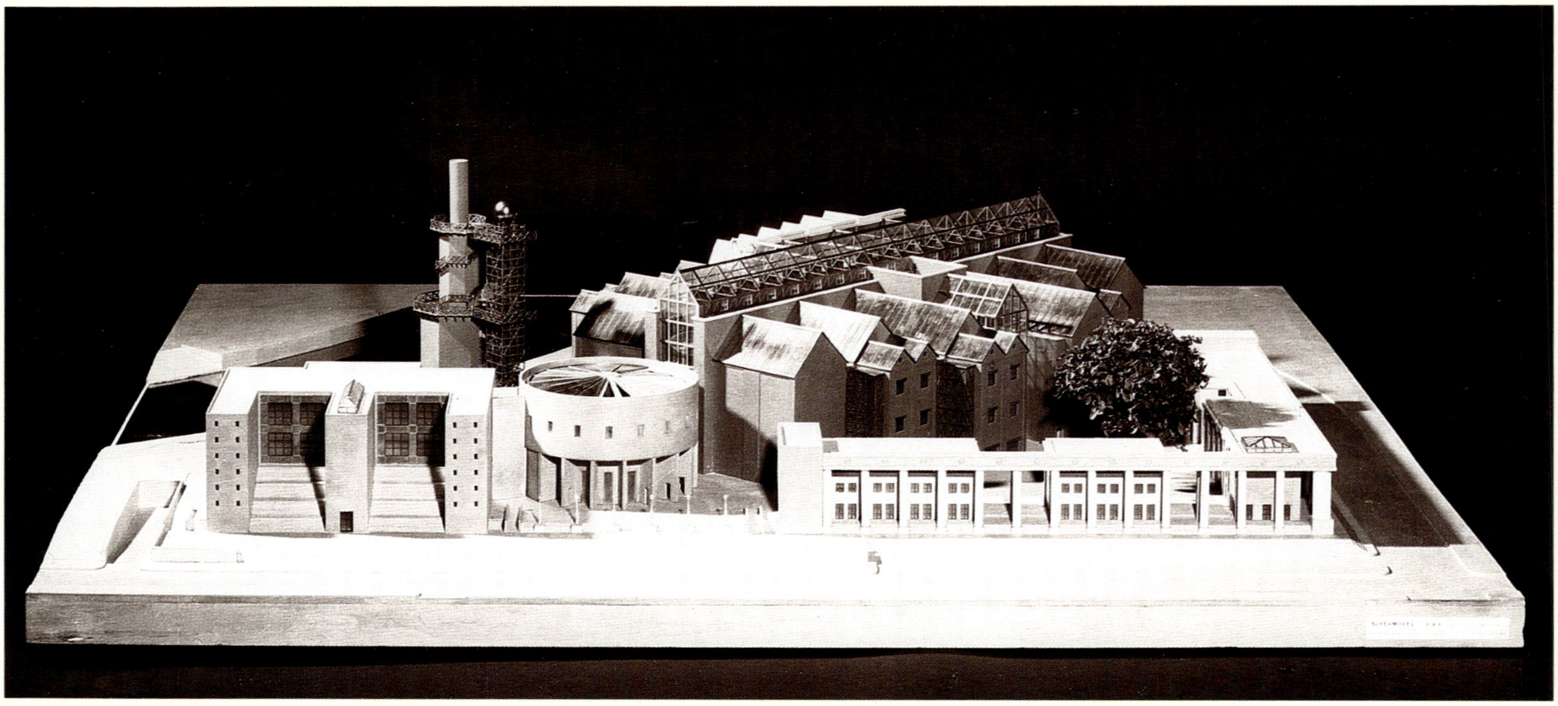

Project

German Historical Museum

Site

Spreebogen (bend in the river Spree), Berlin

Dates

Competition announced 3 August 1987 *Closing date* 3 March 1988 (drawings), 17 March 1988 (models) *First selection* 17–19 May 1988 *Second selection* 7–9 June 1988

Number of entries

220 (including seven disqualified entries)

Jury

Max Bächer (Chairman), Otto Casser (Ministry of Public Works), Joachim Darge, Harald Deilman (both from the Municipality of Berlin), Fritz M. Sitte, Klaus Humpert, Ingeborg Kuhler, Gustav Peichl, Karl Josef Schattner, Luigi Snozzi, Eberhard Weinbrenner

Result

First prize Aldo Rossi & Massimo Scheurer *Second prize* Schweger & Partner *Third prize* Axel Schultes (Bangert, Jansen, Scholz & Schultes) *Fourth prize* Florian Musso *Fifth prize* Gerber & Partner *Sixth prize* Wilhelm Holzbauer & Ernst Mayer *Purchased* Friedrich Trautmann; Lothar Eckhardt, Goldapp & Klumpp; Hensel & Bechtloff; Bollmann & Friedemann; Schneider, Schumacher & Köhler; Manfred Anthony; Oswald Mathias Ungers; Markus Loffler; A.P.B. Planen & Bauen; Jürgen Leitner

Commissioned by

The Ministry of Public Works and the Federal Building Authority

Construction

Never built

German Historical Museum, Berlin, 1987–1988

Aldo Rossi competition design, 1987, exterior view from south-east and collage, first prize

German Historical Museum, Berlin

In modern times, museums have replaced cathedrals and palaces as symbols of national or dynastic consciousness. This development is welcomed by patrons of the arts and is particularly evident in Germany. The German Historical Museum (Deutsches Historisches Museum) in Berlin was projected as an interim high point in this pursuit of national consciousness.

Modern museums

Long before the fall of the Berlin Wall, many cities and provincial towns in West Germany set about purchasing striking designs which would allow them to build the most beautiful museum in the country. Their efforts are reminiscent of those undertaken during the nineteenth century, when museums were seen as temples of the arts. However, there are important differences. Nineteenth-century museums strove to imbue visitors with respect for the exhibited objects and, more often than not, the monumental, neo-classicist style was thought to provide the most appropriate architectural environment for this endeavour.

In modern museums, however, there is a far greater emphasis on education and research. Modern museums are dynamic rather than static, they encourage active participation rather than passive contemplation. Aldo Rossi's views on museum architecture are perfectly in line with this approach. He does not see museums as mere *"clinics for history and art, structures consisting of white, aseptic walls".* However, although museums are no longer the product of stylistic prescription, the desire to build a beautiful environment for the objects lives on. As a result, museums themselves often rival the splendour of their collections.

Hans Hollein's Post-Modernist design for the Museum Abteiberg in Mönchengladbach (1972) is sometimes seen as the starting point of recent developments. Contemporary museums were later also built in Stuttgart (James Stirling), Frankfurt am Main (Oswald Mathias Ungers, Günther Behnisch, Hans Hollein and a handful of other architects), Bonn (Axel Schultes, Gustav Peichl) and in many other towns and cities. Naturally, Berlin did not want to lag behind in these developments. In view of the construction costs incurred by the International Building Exhibition, however, it was obliged at least for the moment to take a back seat. Naturally, the fact that Berlin already boasted a great number of museums was another significant factor. The city had been a world leader in the development of museum architecture since the nineteenth century, starting with the Altes Museum (1824–1830), designed by Karl Friedrich Schinkel, and ending with the New National Gallery (1962–1968), designed by Ludwig Mies van der Rohe. Forunately, the blow to the city's status as a leader in the development of contemporary museum architecture was softened somewhat by the designs for the German Historical Museum and the Jewish Museum.

A museum without a collection

In contrast to the Jewish Museum, the German Historical Museum did

Front: *Hans Scharoun* Staatsbibliothek, below left: *Mies van der Rohe*, New National Gallery, below right: *Hans Scharoun* Philharmonic Hall

Pilot plan: 1 Staatsbibliothek, 2 New National Gallery, 3 Church, 4 Philharmonic Hall

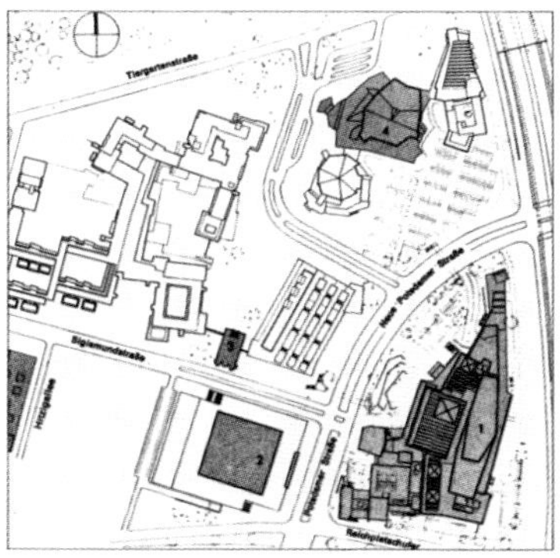

not have a collection when it was founded in 1987[1]. This became one of the main points of criticism against the museum, because there was a threat that it might trigger the so-called Getty effect: a wealthy museum will purchase objects at any cost in order to obtain the best possible collection as quickly as possible. As a result, prices rocket and smaller provincial museums cannot afford to add to their collections.
The designated site for the new museum was a bend in the river Spree (the Spreebogen), where the General Staff Headquarters had been situated, overlooking the Reichstag. The competition, jointly organised by the national and municipal authorities, was announced on 3 August 1987. It was an open, national competition which attracted entries from 201 architects. In addition, 19 international architects were specially invited to participate. Seven participants were immediately disqualified, because their designs did not meet the competition conditions. 34 of the remaining 213 architects went through to the second and final round, for which they were asked to build a model. After lengthy deliberation the jury selected the design submitted by Aldo Rossi and Massimo Scheurer by a majority of two-to-one. The jury's decision probably surprised Rossi most, as he had expected his design to be judged "politically incorrect". This was rather naïve of the famous architect, whose name was written on the design in boldface capitals and who might have foreseen that Berlin would want a celebrated architect to design their new museum.
It is a telling fact that a foreign architect was commissioned to design the museum, a building of national significance which was to be built on a site steeped in history. A foreign architect, Norman Foster, had also been commissioned for the alteration of the nearby Reichstag building, even though there were many German participants who were equally competent. Although the fact that foreign architects were commissioned to design these buildings was undoubtedly motivated by the desire to draw international attention to the projects, there may have been another contributing factor: the latent fear that nationalist sentiments might be aroused if a German architect was to design a building of such significance.
However, nationalist sentiments proved to be unavoidable and, in spite of the fact that Rossi had designed buildings in Berlin in the past[2], the result caused a storm of protest. Although the main points of criticism concerned the design itself and the high costs of construction, the nationality of the architect was certainly also of tacit significance.

A multifaceted design

Rossi and Scheurer's design was literally multifaceted: they envisaged their museum as an urban complex consisting of diverse elements, and loaded their design with symbolic imagery.
The most striking example of this symbolic imagery is the rectangular block facing the Reichstag, which contains the directors' offices and the restaurant. The colonnade is clearly a reference to Schinkel's Altes Museum, situated in what was formerly East Berlin. The cylinder or rotunda, which contains the foyer, and the monumental stairway are

Mies van der Rohe New National Gallery

also references to nineteenth-century museum architecture. The main corridor of the complex has a glass saddle roof and opens out into the rotunda. This was a reference to the Galleria Vittorio Emanuele in Milan, which Rossi considered to be one of the most important architectural monuments. It was a textbook example of a synthesis between architecture and urban planning, a synthesis which Rossi perpetually strove to incorporate in his designs.
The urban-planning aspect of the design is accentuated by the saddle-roofed "maisonettes", which contain the exhibition halls and stand at right angles to the "galleries". Besides the galleries, the right-angled block and the rotunda, the complex has a fourth block which houses educational facilities. Its style is reminiscent of 1920s' and 30s' Berlin housing architecture. Rossi was inspired by German architects such as Mies van der Rohe, Bruno Taut, Eric Mendelsohn and Peter Behrens. The San Ambroglio Church in Milan was also a source of inspiration for his design, which included a small tower overlooking the Spree.
As discussed in the chapter on the San Cataldo Cemetery elsewhere in this book, Rossi's work contains recurrent elements which give his designs a certain consistency. One example is the rotunda in the Carlo Felice Theatre in Genoa (1983), which does not contain the foyer, but is situated within it; another is the galleries in the Centro Torri shopping mall in Parma (1985), which he also used for a housing block in The Hague (1988). In his Centro Città a design for the central business district in Gifu (Japan, 1988), Rossi even went so far as to include a variety of elements from his Berlin design, including a small tower

Karl Friedrich Schinkel Altes Museum, elevation

consisting of stacked, octagonal elements. The tower was eventually built as a monument in Zaandam (The Netherlands, 1989). The monument also has a mini-gallery and is proof of Rossi's architectural talent, albeit on a small scale.

Few of the other prize-winners were renowned architects, with the notable exception of Axel Schultes of Bangert, Jansen, Scholz & Schultes. He won third prize with his design, which was considerably less striking than Rossi's from the outside, and was later commissioned to build the Kunst- und Ausstellungshalle in Bonn. The Danish architects Dissing and Weitling, who had contributed designs for the International Building Exhibition, submitted an outstanding design, as did Friedrich Trautmann. The designs of two of the more renowned architects, Wilhelm Holzbauer and Oswald Mathias Ungers, were also prize-winners.

Unexecuted projects

During his career Rossi has become well-known for his unexecuted projects. The German Historical Museum was added to this list. This prestigious project was cancelled because Berlin has been designated the capital of united Germany, and new government buildings are to be built on the Spreebogen site. The German Historical Museum is now housed in the 300-year-old Zeughaus on Unter den Linden. The museum will be officially opened in 1996 after the building has been renovated.

1 *The West German government decided to establish the German Historical Museum in Berlin in honour of the city's 750th anniversary.*

2 *See chapter on the International Building Exhibition elsewhere in this book.*

Deutsches Historisches Museum, Berlin

Während in früheren Zeiten Kathedralen und Paläste das Selbstbewußtsein einer Nation oder Dynastie ausdrückten, wird jene Funktion heute von Museumsbauten übernommen. Diese für den Kunstliebhaber erfreuliche Entwicklung kommt in Deutschland immer stärker zum Ausdruck. Ihr vorläufiger Höhepunkt sollte mit dem Bau des Deutschen Historischen Museums in Berlin erreicht werden.

Das moderne Museum

Schon lange vor dem Fall der Mauer bemühten sich zahlreiche kleine und große westdeutsche Städte mit aufsehenerregenden Entwürfen darum, das schönste Museum Deutschlands für sich beanspruchen zu können. Auf den ersten Blick drängt sich ein Vergleich mit dem 19. Jahrhundert auf, als Museen »Tempel der Kunst« waren. Dennoch sind einige bedeutende Unterschiede festzustellen. Das Museum des 19. Jahrhunderts war darauf ausgerichtet, dem Besucher Ehrfurcht vor den ausgestellten Objekten zu vermitteln. Entsprechend äußerte sich die Architektur in einem monumentalen Klassizismus. Das moderne Museum dagegen legt sehr viel mehr Wert auf wissenschaftliche Schwerpunkte; es ist nicht statisch, sondern dynamisch und verlangt von seinen Besuchern aktive Anteilnahme statt kontemplativer Passivität. Mit diesem Ansatz läßt sich Aldo Rossis Auffassung über Museumsarchitektur in Einklang bringen. Er möchte das Museum nicht auf eine *»Klinik für Geschichte und Kunst, eine Einheit, zusammengestellt aus weißen, aseptischen Wänden«* reduzieren.
In der heutigen Zeit existieren keine vorgeschriebenen Stilrichtungen für Museumsbauten mehr. Geblieben ist nur der Wunsch, den Menschen ein außergewöhnliches Bauwerk zu schaffen – und nicht selten stehen die Bauten in Konkurrenz mit der darin ausgestellten Kunst. Diese Entwicklung nahm 1972 mit Hans Holleins postmodernem Entwurf für das Städtische Museum Abteiberg in Mönchengladbach ihren Anfang. Später folgten Museumsbauten in Stuttgart (James Stirling), Frankfurt am Main (Oswald Mathias Ungers, Günther Behnisch, Hollein, et al) Bonn (Axel Schultes, Gustav Peichl) und anderen Städten. Berlin wollte nicht länger hintanstehen. Bisher hatten insbesondere die Bauaktivitäten der Internationalen Bauausstellung (IBA) enorme Summen verschlungen und damit das Entstehen zeitgenössischer Museumsbauten verhindert. Zudem existierten in Berlin bereits eine ganze Reihe weltberühmter Museen. Die Stadt hatte für den Typus des Museumsbaus und seine Entwicklung im 19. Jahrhundert eine wichtige Rolle gespielt, beginnend beim Alten Museum (1824–1830) von Karl Friedrich Schinkel bis hin zu Mies van der Rohes Neuer Nationalgalerie (1962–1968).

Ein Museum ohne Sammlung

Als das Deutsche Historische Museum 1987 gegründet wurde, besaß es noch keine eigene Sammlung[1]. Dies wurde später zu einem der wichtigsten Kritikpunkte am geplanten Neubau, da man sich vor dem sogenannten Getty-Effekt fürchtete, d. h. Vervollständigung der Sammlung in kürzester Zeit, indem ein reiches Museum Objekte um jeden Preis ankauft. Die kleineren Museen hätten den mit einer solchen Einkaufspolitik einhergehenden Preissteigerungen nicht folgen und keine weiteren Objekte für ihre eigenen Sammlungen mehr erstehen können.
Als Baugelände wählte man ein Stück Land direkt an der Spree – den Spreebogen, das ehemalige Gelände des Oberkommandos der Wehrmacht mit Aussicht auf den Reichstag. Die Ausschreibung wurde von Stadt und Staat gemeinsam am 3. August 1987 veröffentlicht. Es handelte sich um einen offenen nationalen Wettbewerb, an dem sich 201 Architekten beteiligten. Daneben lud man weitere 19 Architekten von internationalem Rang zur Teilnahme ein. Sieben Beiträge schieden sofort aus, da sie den Auflagen nicht genügten. Von den übrigen 213 Entwürfen wählte die Jury 34 für die zweite und entscheidende Ausschreibungsrunde aus und bat die Architekten, eine Maquette anzufertigen.
Nach langen Beratungen entschied sich die Jury mit Zweidrittelmehrheit für den Entwurf von Aldo Rossi und Massimo Scheurer – eine Entscheidung, die Rossi selbst am meisten überraschte, da er seinen Entwurf für »politisch inkorrekt« hielt. Diese Haltung eines berühmten Architekten mutet recht naiv an, denn sein Name stand in Großbuchstaben auf dem Entwurf, und es war anzunehmen, daß die Berliner nur zu gern eine Berühmtheit mit der Ausführung ihres Museums beauftragen würden. Die Wahl eines Ausländers für ein solch sensibles Bauwerk wie ein Nationalmuseum – noch dazu an dieser Stätte läßt einige Schlüsse zu. Auch der Umbau des nahegelegenen Reichstagsgebäudes wurde von einem Ausländer, Norman Foster, durchgeführt, obwohl sich unter den deutschen Teilnehmern genügend Architekten von Rang und Namen befanden. Aus dieser Entscheidung spricht zweifellos der Wunsch, die internationale Aufmerksamkeit auf sich zu ziehen. Gleichzeitig schien die Angst groß, durch die Auftragsvergabe an einen deutschen Architekten nationalistische Gefühle zu stärken. Genau das Gegenteil war der Fall: Obwohl Rossi bereits früher in Berlin gearbeitet hatte (siehe das Kapitel zur Internationalen Bauausstellung), erhob sich nach der Bekanntgabe der Entscheidung ein Sturm der Entrüstung. Die Kritik richtete sich zwar in erster Linie gegen den Bau selbst und die damit verbundenen hohen Kosten, unterschwellig aber spielte sicherlich auch die Nationalität des Architekten eine Rolle.

Ein vielseitiger Entwurf

Der Entwurf von Rossi und Scheurer ist im wahrsten Sinne des Wortes vielseitig: Zum einen präsentiert sich das Museum als städtischer Komplex, zusammengesetzt aus verschiedenen Elementen, zum anderen haben Rossi und Scheurer ihr Projekt mit einer Unmenge symbolischer Bedeutungen versehen. Bestes Beispiel hierfür ist der von Rossi entworfene Museumsblock, der im rechten Winkel auf das Reichstagsgebäude weist und in dem sich der Direktionsflügel und das Restaurant befinden. Seine Kolonnade erinnert an Schinkels Altes Museum im ehemaligen Ostberlin. Auch der Zylinder oder die Rotunde, in der sich das Foyer befindet, und die monumentalen Treppen lehnen an Museumsbauten des 19. Jahrhunderts an. Auf die Rotunde führt der wichtigste Weg des gesamten Komplexes zu, überdacht mit einem gläsernen Satteldach. Mit dieser Konstruktion verweist Rossi auf die Galleria Vittorio Emanuele in Mailand, die seiner Meinung nach zu den bedeutendsten Monumenten der Baukunst zählt und ein Schulbeispiel für eine Mischung aus Städtebau und Architektur ist. Diesen Ansatz strebte Rossi immer an. Quer zur Galleria liegen einige Häuser mit Satteldächern, die den städtebaulichen Aspekt des Entwurfs unterstreichen sollen und in denen sich die Ausstellungssäle befinden. Das vierte Element des Komplexes – neben Galleria, Rotunde und Winkel – besteht aus einem Block, der in seiner Form an den Berliner Wohnungsbau der 20er und 30er Jahre erinnert. Rossi ließ sich bei seinem Entwurf von deutschen Architekten wie Mies van der Rohe, Bruno Taut, Erich Mendelsohn und Peter Behrens inspirieren, nahm aber auch Eindrücke der Mailänder Sant' Ambrogio-Kirche in seine Arbeit auf. Das letzte Element dieses Komplexes ist ein freistehender kleiner Turm mit Blick über die Spree.
Rossi arbeitet mit wiederkehrenden Elementen, die er als konstante Faktoren einsetzt – beispielsweise die Rotunde im Theater Carlo Felice in Genua (hier nicht als Foyer, sondern im Innern desselben eingesetzt, 1983), die Galleria im Einkaufszentrum Centro Torri in Parma (1985) und in einem Wohnblock in Den Haag (1988). In Rossis Projekt »Centro Città«, einem Geschäftszentrum für die japanische Stadt Gifu, finden sich mehrere Elemente seines Berliner Entwurfs, darunter ein kleiner Turm aus aufeinander gestapelten oktagonalen Elementen (1988). Diesen Turm realisierte Rossi als städtisches Denkmal in Zaandam (1989).
Unter den anderen Preisträgern befanden sich nur wenig große Namen. Axel Schultes aus der Architektengemeinschaft Bangert, Jansen, Scholz & Schultes war einer der wenigen bekannten Teilnehmer. Er gewann den dritten Preis mit einem Entwurf, der schon von seinem Äußeren her wesentlich weniger auffiel als Rossis Beitrag. Später erhielt er mit der Planung der Kunst- und Ausstellungshalle in Bonn den Auftrag für einen anderen repräsentativen Museumsbau. Weitere bemerkenswerte Pläne kamen von den Dänen Dissing und Weitling, die auch für die IBA tätig gewesen waren, sowie von Friedrich Trautmann. Wilhelm Holzbauer und Oswald Mathias Ungers gehörten zu den Architekten, deren Beiträge angekauft wurden.

Nicht realisierte Projekte

Rossi ist bekannt für eine große Anzahl nicht realisierter, prestigeträchtiger Projekte, zu denen auch das Deutsche Historische Museum gehört. Als Berlin neue Hauptstadt des wiedervereinigten Deutschlands wurde, reservierte man den Spreebogen als Gelände für die neu zu schaffenden Regierungsgebäude. Das Deutsche Historische Museum fand seinen Platz im 300 Jahre alten Zeughaus an der Straße Unter den Linden. Nach einem Umbau soll es 1996 offiziell eröffnet werden.

1 *Die Bundesregierung schenkte der Stadt Berlin das Deutsche Historische Museum zur Feier ihres 750jährigen Bestehens.*

Le Musée de l'Histoire Allemande, Berlin

Les musées sont aujourd'hui en voie de remplacer les cathédrales et les palais dans les consciences nationales ou historiques. Celui de l'Histoire Allemande, à Berlin, est parfaitement représentatif de cette évolution.

Les musées modernes

Longtemps avant la chute du mur de Berlin, de nombreuses villes d'Allemagne de l'Ouest se sont lancées dans une politique souvent audacieuse et même concurrentielle de construction de musées. Leurs efforts rappellent ceux du XIXème siècle et de la première vague de construction de musées, mais avec néanmoins une différence importante.
Les musées du siècle dernier voulaient insuffler le respect de l'art et de l'œuvre à leurs visiteurs et la plupart du temps, le style néo-classique monumental leur paraissait seul capable de répondre à cet objectif. Dans les musées contemporains, l'accent est davantage mis sur l'éducation et la recherche grâce à des politiques dynamiques qui encouragent la participation plutôt que la contemplation passive. Les conceptions d'Aldo Rossi sur l'architecture muséale correspondent à cette approche. Il ne considère pas du tout les musées comme de simples *«cliniques pour l'histoire et l'art, bâtiments essentiellement composés de murs blancs et aseptisés»*. Si les musées ne sont plus aujourd'hui soumis à des a priori stylistiques, le désir de créer un environnement de qualité pour leurs collections subsiste malgré tout. Certains édifices rivalisent même de splendeur avec leurs trésors.
Le musée municipal de l'Abteiberg à Mönchengladbach (1972) conçu par Hans Hollein est parfois pris pour point de départ de cette évolution nouvelle de l'architecture muséale, jalonnée par ailleurs par les nouvelles galeries de Stuttgart (James Stirling), Francfort-sur-le-Main (Oswald Mathias Ungers, Günther Behnisch, Hollein, et d'autres), Bonn (Axel Schultes, Gustav Peichl) et de nombreuses villes.
Berlin avait, elle aussi, d'importants besoins dans ce domaine, mais se devait de patienter tant les coûts de l'Internationale Bauausstellung (IBA) étaient astronomiques. La capitale possède déjà de nombreux grands musées et avait même été une ville-modèle dans ce domaine dès le XIXème siècle avec la création de l'Altes Museum (1824–1830) par Karl Friedrich Schinkel. Plus récemment, la Neue Nationalgalerie (1962–1968) de Mies van der Rohe avait également marqué son époque.
L'amertume de ne pas participer à ce grand mouvement de renaissance des musées fut quelque peu adoucie par les projets pour le Musée de l'Histoire Allemande et du Musée Juif.

Un musée sans collection

A la différence du Musée Juif, le Musée de l'Histoire Allemande ne possédait pas de collection lorsqu'il fut fondé en 1987[1]. Cette grave lacune entraîna de nombreuses critiques car on craignait un «effet Getty», c'est-à-dire l'interventionnisme d'un riche musée prêt à acheter à n'importe quel coût pour se constituer la meilleure collection possible dans les meilleurs délais. Les prix du marché explosent alors et les petits musées de province ne peuvent plus suivre.
Le site choisi était une courbe de la Spree (Spreebogen) tout près du Reichstag. Le concours national ouvert, organisé conjointement par les autorités nationales et municipales, fut annoncé le 3 août 1987 et attira 201 participants dont 19 étrangers invités en direct. Sept projets furent immédiatement disqualifiés pour non-conformité avec le règlement et 34 des 213 candidats restants accédèrent au second et troisième tour, à l'issue duquel il leur fut demandé de soumettre une maquette. Après de longues délibérations, le jury se décida à deux contre un pour la proposition de Aldo Rossi et Massimo Scheurer. Cette décision surprit probablement Rossi qui pensait que ses plans n'étaient pas dans la ligne politique officielle. Cette idée ne l'avait pas empêché d'écrire son nom en grandes capitales sur ses plans en espérant peut-être que Berlin souhaiterait s'attacher un architecte célèbre. Il n'avait pas facilité la tache du jury pour autant et sa réflexion était compliquée voire acrobatique.
Ainsi un architecte étranger recevait-il la commande d'un nouveau musée d'importance nationale à édifier sur un site historique. Au même moment, un autre étranger, Norman Foster, était chargé de la rénovation du Reichstag voisin, en dépit du nombre élevé d'excellents concurrents allemands. Si le choix d'étrangers a pu être motivé par le désir d'attirer l'attention internationale sur les plus importants projets de la ville, les craintes latentes de se voir accuser de nationalisme expliquent peut-être les décisions des autorités allemandes.
Ces sentiments chauvins se révélèrent inévitables et bien que Rossi ait déjà travaillé à Berlin, sa victoire provoqua un concert de protestations. Les critiques portaient essentiellement sur le projet lui-même et son coût élevé, mais la nationalité de l'architecte y était certainement pour quelque chose.

Un projet à facettes

Le projet de Rossi et Scheurer était une œuvre à facettes. Ils avaient conçu leur musée comme un ensemble urbain composite et surchargé leurs plans de toute une imagerie symbolique.
L'exemple le plus frappant en est le bâtiment rectangulaire, face au Reichstag, qui contient les bureaux de la direction et le restaurant. La colonnade est un hommage à l'Altes Museum de Schinkel situé dans l'ancien Berlin-Est. Le cylindre, ou rotonde, qui contient le foyer et l'escalier monumental fait également référence à l'architecture muséale du siècle dernier. Le couloir principal est surmonté d'un toit galbé transparent et s'ouvre sur la rotonde, rappel de la galerie Vittorio Emanuele de Milan, que Rossi considère comme un très grand monument. L'ensemble est une sorte de manuel de synthèse de l'architecture et de l'urbanisme, un thème qui lui est cher.
Les aspects urbanistiques du plan sont accentués par des «maisonnettes» à toit voûté, perpendiculaires aux galeries, qui contiennent les salles d'exposition. Le complexe comprend également un quatrième bloc qui abrite les services éducatifs, et dont le style rappelle celui des immeubles d'appartements berlinois des années 20 et 30. Rossi s'est beaucoup inspiré ici d'architectes allemands comme Mies van der Rohe, Bruno Traut, Eric Mendelsohn et Peter Behrens, mais l'église de San Ambrogio de Milan a également laissé quelques traces comme, par exemple, une petite tour indépendante dominant la Spree.
L'œuvre de Rossi se caractérise par des éléments récurrents qui rendent ses projets facilement identifiables. Par exemple, la rotonde du théâtre Carlo Felice de Gênes (1983), qui ne contient pas le foyer mais est au contraire contenue par lui, ou les galeries du centre commercial Centro Torri de Parme (1985) qu'il réutilise sous forme d'immeubles d'habitation à La Haye (1988). Dans son projet «Centro città» pour le quartier des affaires de Gifu (Japon, 1988), il est même allé jusqu'à reprendre plusieurs des composants de son projet pour Berlin, dont la petite tour faite d'un empilement d'éléments octogonaux. Elle réapparaît sous forme de monument à Zaandam (Pays-Bas, 1989) et sert de mini-galerie d'exposition prouvant la maîtrise de l'architecte, même à petite échelle.
Peu d'architectes de grande notoriété figurèrent parmi les vainqueurs, à l'exception notable d'Axel Schultes (Bangert, Jansen, Scholz & Schultes). Il remporta le troisième prix avec un projet moins surprenant que celui de Rossi et reçut plus tard la commande de la Kunst- und Austellungshalle de Bonn. Les Danois Dissing et Weitling, qui avaient participé à l'IBA, soumirent un plan remarquable, de même que Friedrich Trautmann. Les plans de deux des architectes allemands les plus connus, Wilhelm Holzbauer et Oswald Mathias Ungers, ne furent pas retenus.

Une fois encore, un projet sans suite

Rossi est célèbre pour ses projets non exécutés et le Musée de l'Histoire Allemande doit malheureusement être ajouté à cette liste. Ce projet de prestige fut annulé parce que Berlin avait retrouvé sa fonction de capitale de l'Allemagne réunifiée et que des bâtiments gouvernementaux devaient être construits sur ce même site du Spreebogen. Le Musée s'installera dans la Zeughaus, vieille de trois siècles et située sur Unter den Linden. Il ouvrira officiellement en 1996 après la rénovation complète de l'édifice.

1 *Le gouvernement ouest-allemand avait décidé de créer un Musée de l'Histoire Allemande à Berlin à l'occasion du 750ème anniversaire de la naissance de la ville.*

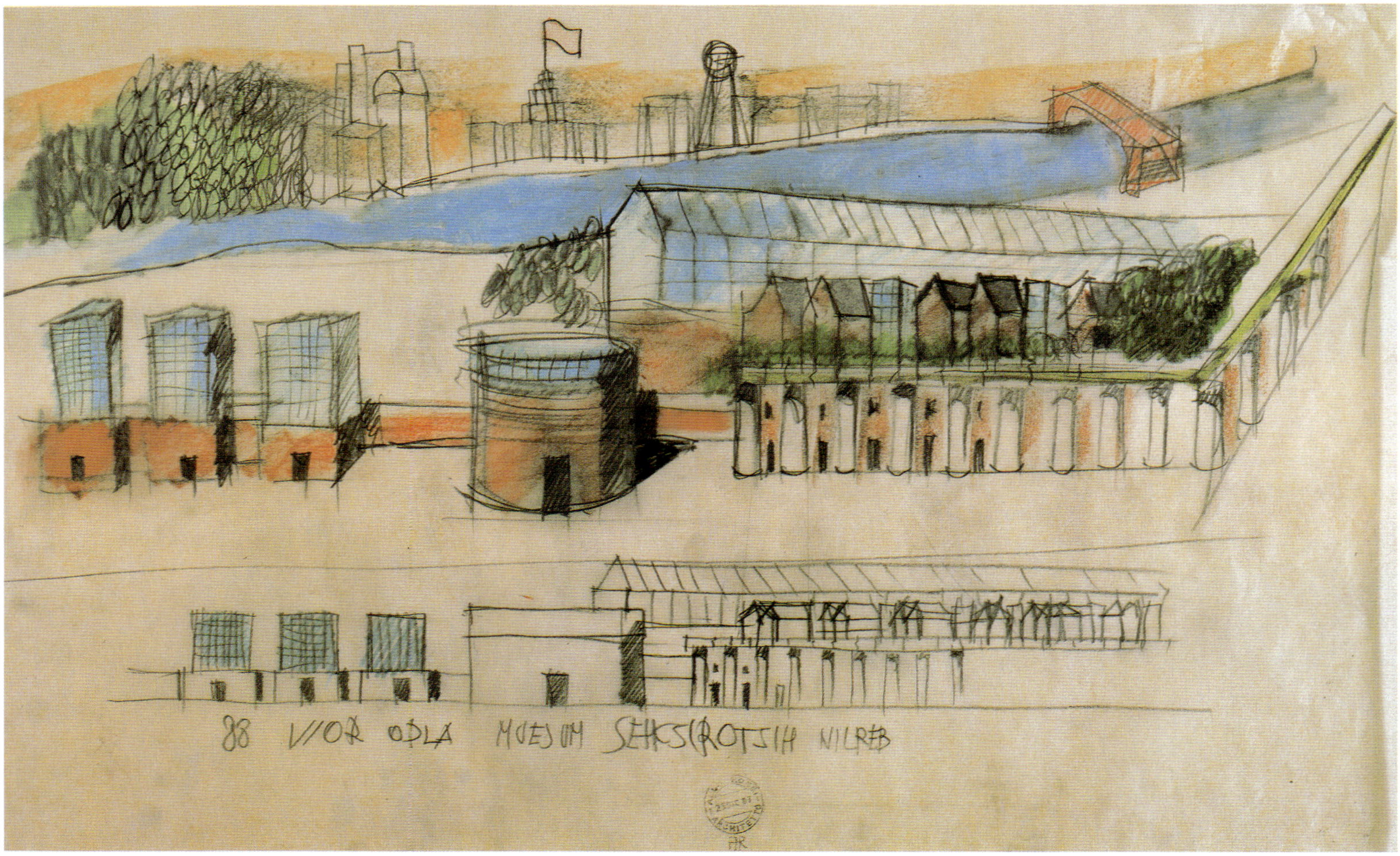

Aldo Rossi competition design, 1987, sketch, first prize

Aldo Rossi competition design, 1987, sketch, first prize

Aldo Rossi competition design, 1987, sketch, first prize

Aldo Rossi competition design, 1987, sketch, first prize

Aldo Rossi competition design, 1987, from top: south elevation, east-west section, east elevation, north-east elevation, first prize

Aldo Rossi competition design, 1987, from top: sections, north-west elevation, section (south-east side), south-east elevation, first prize

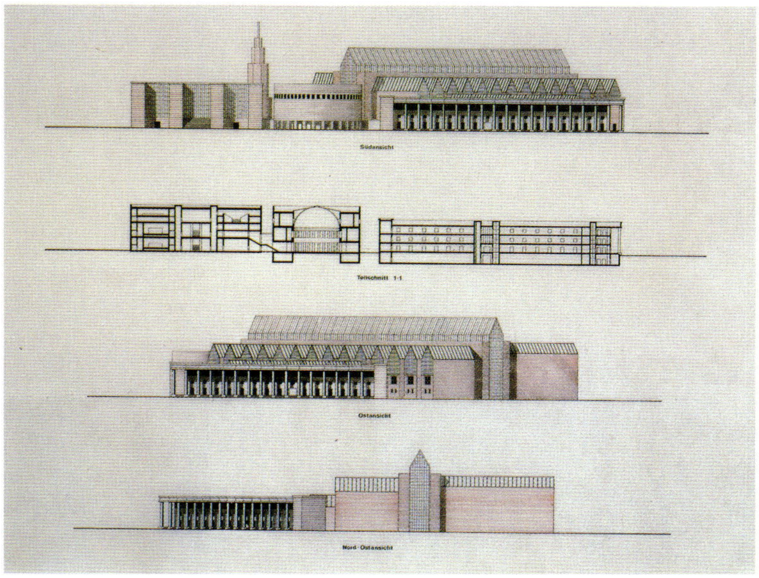

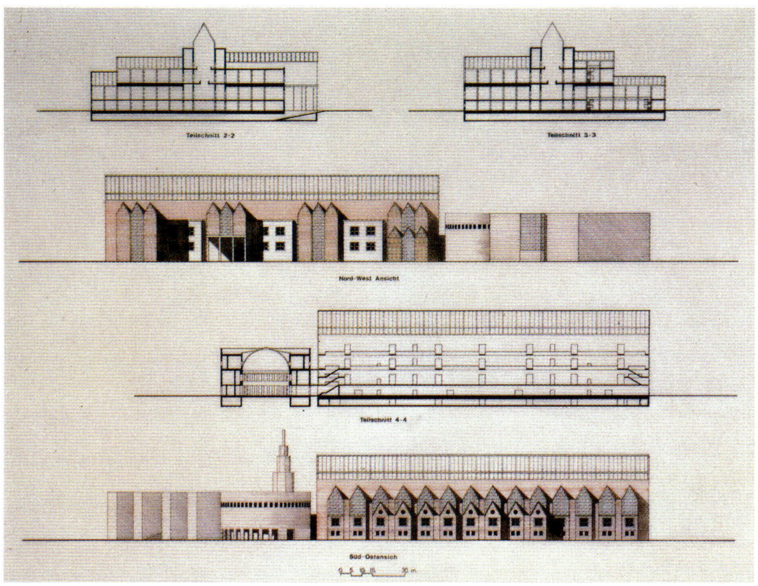

Aldo Rossi competition design, 1987, above left: section of administrative building, above right: section, axonometric projection of administrative building, middle: south elevation, below: ground floor plan, first prize

Gerber & Partner competition design, 1987, model, fifth prize

Dissing & Weitling competition design, 1987, model

Ansicht und Schnitt

Axonometrische Darstellung mit Schnitt

Südansicht

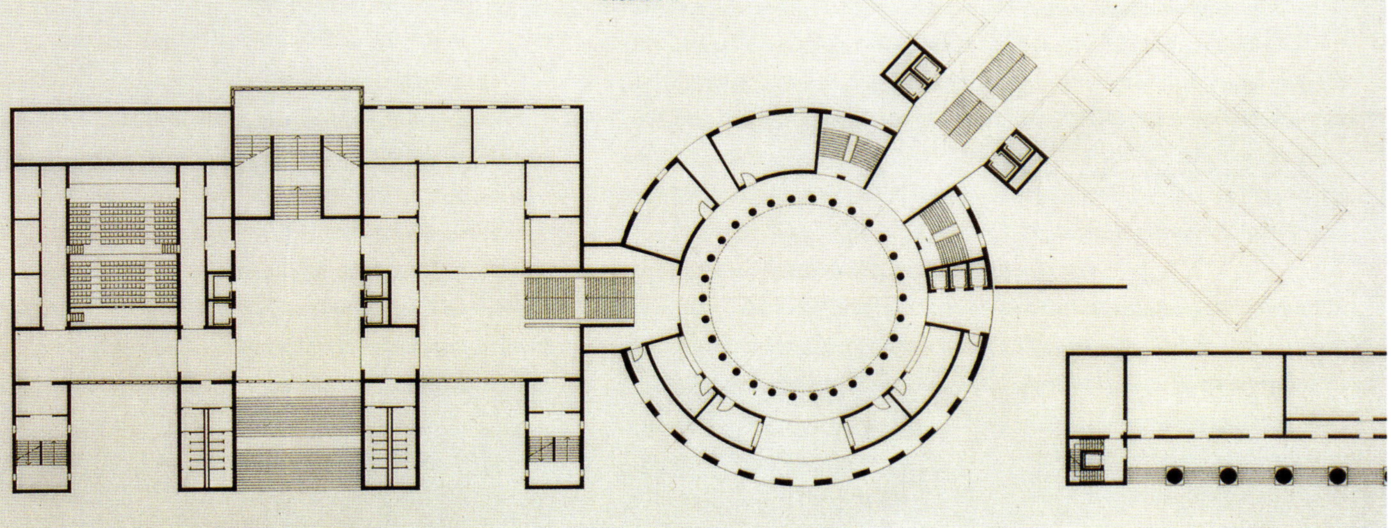

Grundrissplan

0 1 2 3 4 5 10 15

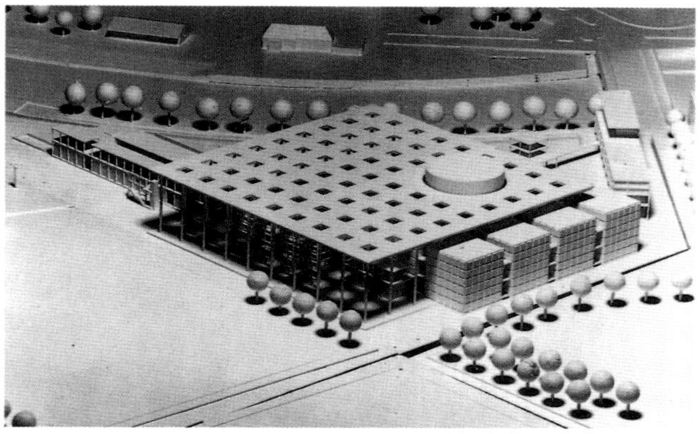

1053

1215

1024

1168

Project

A park with dwellings and facilities for media productions, for information and communications technology, for software production, and for art and entertainment

Site

To the north-west of Cologne city centre, on the grounds of the former Gereon freight depot

Dates

First round announced 2 February 1987 *Closing date* 21 August 1987 (drawings and prospectus) 4 September 1987 (models) *Result announced* December 1987 *Second round result announced* March 1988

Number of entries

103

Jury

Fred Angerer, Hans Adrian, Wilhelm Holzbauer, Gerhard Lohmann, Erich Schneider-Wessling, Thomas Sieverts, Donata Valentien, Herbert Wiesemann (architects), Jürgen Noppel, Gerhard Meyer, Hartmut Strube, Norbert Burger, Kurt Rossa, Rüdiger Göb, Wolfgang Keil (civil servants), Friedrich Nowottny, Gerhard Schmidt, Hans Beck, Franz Arnold, Jaap Engel, Karla Fohrbeck, Wolf Schöde (architectural experts), a number of municipal representatives and members of the Baugruppen Köln, who were in charge of the pre-examination

Result

First round, first prize Eberhard H. Zeidler *Runners-up* Miroslav Volf; Michael Müller-Born; Oswald Mathias Ungers; Kei Minohara, Hiroshi Hara, NTT, Shimizu Corporation and others; Rolf Schuster *Purchased* William Alsop & John Lyall; Kölner Planwerkstatt; Stjepan Čadež & Ivo Ruić; Busmann & Haberer *Second round* Eberhard H Zeidler (Block 1; subsequently replaced by Jean Nouvel); Kölner-Bucht (Block 2), Joachim Schürmann (Block 3), Miroslav Volf (Block 4), Hermann Hertzberger (Block 5), O. Steidle (Block 6)

Commissioned by

Cologne City Council

Architect

Eberhard H. Zeidler

Media Park, Cologne, 1987–1988

Eberhard H. Zeidler competition design, 1987, site plan, first prize, first round

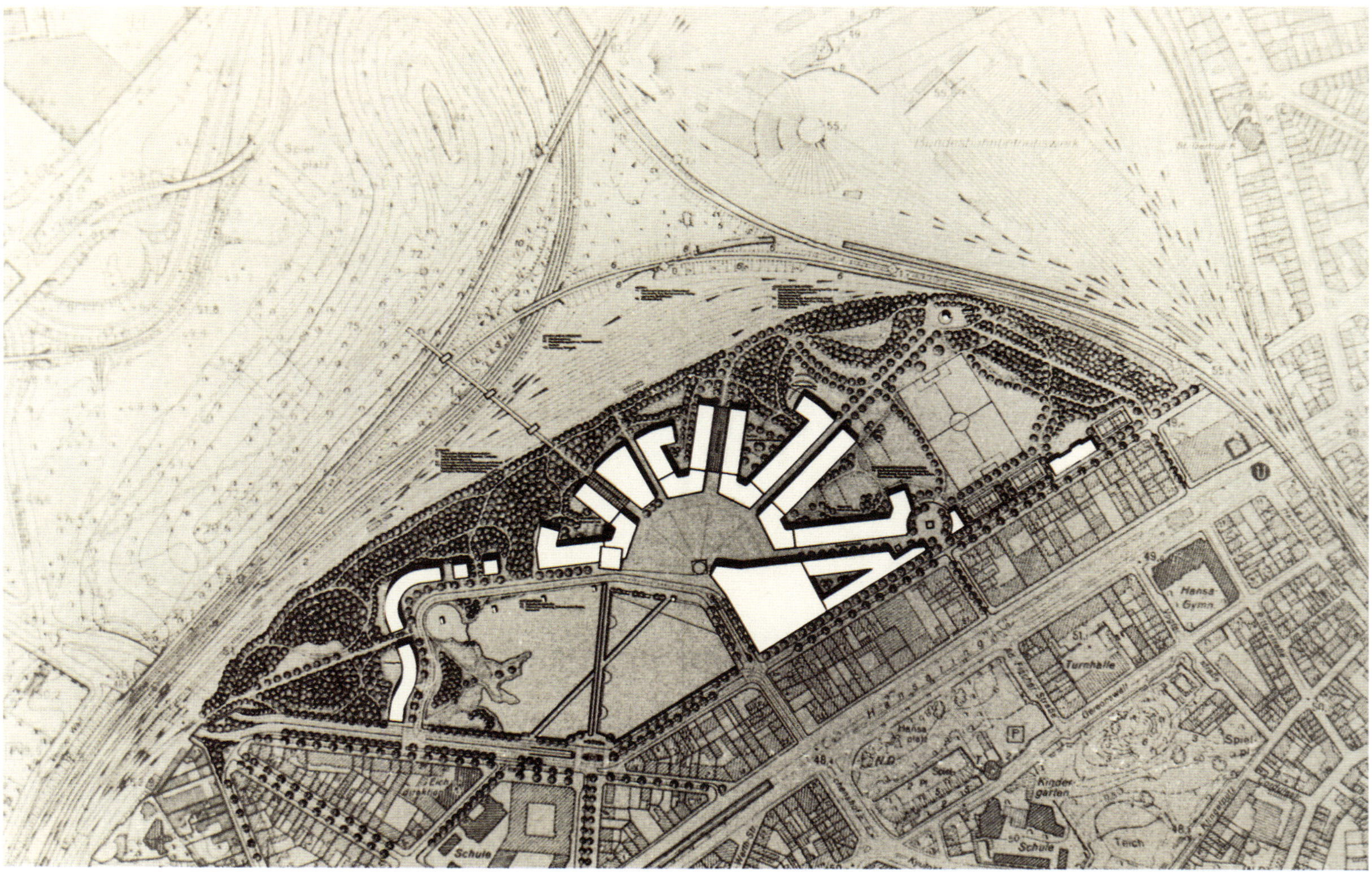

Media Park, Cologne

The Media Park in Cologne is a prime example of the harmonious co-operation which is possible between the authorities and private enterprise. Initially, the site designated for the Media Park looked set to fall into the hands of a profiteering project developer. However, timely intervention by the Media Park Development Association (MPK) ensured that nothing would stand in the way of the joint venture.

IIA centre for media and communication

The MPK, which was jointly established by the city of Cologne and the federal government in 1988, is a private organisation, partly controlled by the authorities. This arrangement allows sufficient opportunity for private initiatives, whilst at the same time safeguarding the interests of the general public.

At first, the MPK seemed destined for an early grave. The municipality had almost sold the twenty-hectare site of the former Gereon freight depot to the "Gewerbe im Park" (GiP) construction company. Due to its position close to the old centre, which boasts the Wallraf-Richartz-Museum and the Cologne's famous cathedral, the potential profits were enormous. The city had projected a complex on this site which would boost the local economy and stimulate future development. Cologne was to become Germany's media and communications capital.

Just as this ambitious dream was about to be shattered by the sale of the site to the GiP construction company, the MPK succeeded in finding two investors, an insurance company and a cinema operator, who were prepared to buy a quarter of the available property. The press conference organised to announce the new investors, on 7 November 1989, gave an indication of the Media Park's future potential. Journalists were informed of the details of the sale via a direct satellite link between Cologne and New York. The MPK had subdivided the site into lots, with the aim of developing an architecturally diverse complex. A further control – evidence of the guiding hand of the authorities – was the proviso that all new designs had to be approved by the MPK.

As a safeguard against speculation, investors had to adhere to the original functional concept of the complex for at least fifteen years. This left a certain margin of freedom for the development of a variety of housing, trade and recreational projects. However, each project had to be linked to media and technology in one way or another, thus providing the necessary urban development structure, and ensuring that non-profit projects would receive extra attention.

Another important aspect of the development scheme was that a large part of the site had been designated a green area. The term "Media Park" must, therefore, be interpreted more literally than, for example, the term "amusement park".

The first competition

The first competition for the Media Park had already been held by the time the first investors were brought in. This competition had been

Cologne cathedral

organised by the Municipality of Cologne and was held before the establishment of the MPK. The competition was announced in February 1987 and was open to all German architects, but in order to make the competition a little more prestigious, ten renowned local and foreign architects were also invited to participate, including the acclaimed German architect Oswald Mathias Ungers, and the Japanese team captained by Kei Minohara and Hiroshi Hara. First prize, however, was snatched from under their noses by the German-Canadian architect Eberhard Zeidler. Five additional prizes were awarded and four other designs purchased.
Zeidler's plan was based on a fan-shaped development subdivided into six tapered construction blocks grouped around a central square. Zeidler had also provided for the future addition of a small lake. The blocks were to house a variety of facilities such as a giant cinema complex and offices. Dwellings were also planned which would wind outwards from the western edge of the fan, their point of attachment being marked by a high tower which formed the centre of the Media Park and was therefore the most important building. More than half of the site was left vacant to allow for the development of green areas and squares. These features of Zeidler's design made it one of the competition's most "user-friendly" plans. Many of the other participants concentrated on the architecture and merely filled the remaining part of the design with green areas, or designed a separate park instead of an integrated whole. Zeidler therefore deservedly won first prize. However, a number of the other designs also warrant description.
The design submitted by William Alsop and John Lyall, for example, was based on a long, thin construction and was partly sited underground; a wall of technology facing the single-family apartments. The high-tech design submitted by Čadež and Ruić was also remarkable, if only for its bird's-eye view of the complex. In their design, the district between the Media Park and the cathedral has been replaced by an airport which, due to its central position, would undoubtedly have been an asset for international aviation.

Separate competitions

The most logical sequel to the competition was that Zeidler would be invited to develop his outstanding tower design. However, events took a different course. The MPK organised a separate, restricted competition for each facility or block.
A number of architects, including Zeidler, Günther Behnisch, Werner Finke and Jean Nouvel, were invited to submit designs for Block 1, which featured the tower. The architects were given few specifications, but were asked to include a four-star hotel with 220 rooms, offices, apartments, shops, restaurants and a pharmacy. In addition, the complex required schools and a parking area for 220 cars.
Nouvel was also asked to submit a design for Block 5, which would house the Leonardo Centre for Arts and Culture. This competition was eventually won by the renowned Dutch architect, Herman Hertzberger. The competitions for the other blocks were won by the Kölner-Bucht team (Block 2), Joachim Schürmann (Block 3), O. Steidle (Block 6) and Miroslav Volf (Block 4), who had also participated in the first competition.
The competition for the main block (Block 1) was won by Zeidler, much to the dissatisfaction of the local press, who preferred the design submitted by Nouvel and his team. Herbert Hillebrand, the property developer for Block 1, also preferred Nouvel's design and therefore rejected the jury's decision and commissioned the French architect.

An individualistic design

Nouvel's design for the office tower was far more spectacular than Zeidler's. This was hardly surprising considering the unique nature of Nouvel's œuvre and his work method. Nouvel sets a personal objective for each project, which he then pursues without reverting to stock patterns. For example, when he was commissioned to design a housing block in Nîmes, his personal objective was to increase the specified surface area for each dwelling by thirty per cent. In order to stay within the stipulated construction budget, he designed a rough and simple structure using industrial materials. He also left the walls and ceilings unplastered.

The site of the former Gereon freight depot

This unique approach to architecture, and the use of extraordinary materials, are characteristic features of Nouvel's designs. His work is also characterised by an attention to detail and to the surroundings; a unique approach to flat surfaces, together with a positive reassessment of two-dimensional features; and an obsession for light and transparency. Good examples of the latter are Nouvel's remarkable tower design for La Défense, which becomes increasingly slender and transparent towards the top, and his prize-winning design for the head offices of the publishers DuMont-Schauberg in Cologne. Nouvel also incorporated these elements into his design for the Media Park tower. Nouvel used dark-grey glass façades, which also show which facilities and activities are to be found on each floor. Dynamic elements, such as the lifts and the panels indicating which floor the lift is on, are brightly coloured. He also applied line patterns resembling bar-codes, which he derived from the works of the artists Daniel Buren and Patrick Raynaud, whom he greatly admires. The bar-code pattern is a symbolic data-carrier, and is reminiscent of a similar feature incorporated into the walls of the Grande Arche in La Défense, which resemble microchips (see chapter on La Grande Arche elsewhere in this book). Nouvel has described his tendency to derive features from the works of other artists as a form of kleptomania. He creates novel features by combining existing elements, which is of course one of the basic principles of art.

The tower, which Nouvel describes as an exploded block, forms part of a complex made up of four blocks. The 134-meter-high tower tapers towards the top, where the best offices are situated. Although the execution of Hertzberger's design has been indefinitely postponed due to financial problems, Nouvel's tower is due to be completed in the spring of 1996.

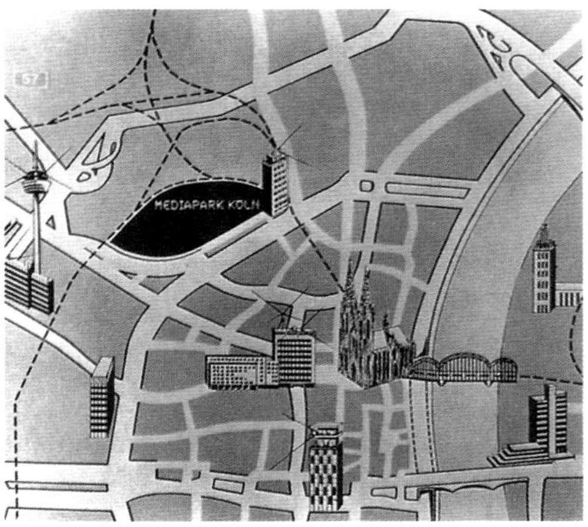

Illustration of the Media Park, Cologne

Mediapark, Köln

Der Mediapark Köln ist ein Beispiel für die harmonische Zusammenarbeit zwischen Verwaltungsbehörden und Privatunternehmen. Obwohl es zunächst danach aussah, als sollte das für den Mediapark vorgesehene Baugelände durch die Spekulationen eines Baulöwen an den Meistbietenden abgegeben werden, stand nach der erfolgreichen Intervention der Media Park Entwicklungsgesellschaft GmbH (MPK) einer geregelten Projektentwicklung nichts mehr im Wege.

Zentrum für Medien und Kommunikation

Die MPK wurde 1988 von der Stadt Köln und dem Bundesland Nordrhein-Westfalen ins Leben gerufen. Es handelt sich um eine Gesellschaft in privater Trägerschaft, an der der Staat zur Hälfte beteiligt ist. Auf diese Weise bleibt genügend Spielraum für private Initiativen, ohne daß dabei das Wohl der Allgemeinheit aus den Augen verloren wird.

Es hätte nicht viel gefehlt, und die MPK wäre eines leisen Todes gestorben: Die Stadt hatte das fast 20 ha große Gelände des ehemaligen Güterbahnhofs Gereon an die Baugesellschaft »Gewerbe im Park« (GiP) des Philipp-Holzmann-Konzerns verkauft. Aufgrund der erstklassigen Lage in direkter Nähe des Zentrums, wo sich u.a. das Wallraf-Richartz-Museum und der Kölner Dom befinden, konnte der Rat eine hohe Kaufsumme verlangen. Ursprünglich war ein Projekt geplant, daß der Stadt neue wirtschaftliche Impulse geben und in seiner Art zukunftsweisend sein sollte: Köln als deutsche Medienhauptstadt.

Als diese Zukunftsträume durch den Verkauf an GiP zu zerplatzen drohten, gelang es der MPK, in letzter Minute zwei Versicherungsgesellschaften und eine Filmtheaterkette als erste Investoren zu gewinnen, die etwa ein Viertel des Geländes ankauften. Die Bekanntgabe der Investoren am 7. November 1989 war ein kleiner Vorgeschmack auf das, was der zukünftige Mediapark zu bieten haben würde: Über eine direkte Satellitenverbindung zwischen New York und Köln konnten die anwesenden Journalisten Einzelheiten der Kaufverhandlungen erfahren. Die MPK hatte das Gelände in der Absicht, ein architektonisch vielfältiges Ganzes zu entwickeln, in Parzellen unterteilt. Als zusätzliche Qualitätskontrolle – darin äußerte sich der Einfluß der staatlichen Stellen – mußten die Architekten ihre Entwürfe im Vorfeld der MPK vorlegen.

Um sich vor Spekulanten zu schützen, verlangte man von den Investoren, sich 15 Jahre lang an ein vorgegebenes funktionelles Konzept zu binden. Dieses Konzept erlaubte zwar die Entwicklung allgemeiner städtischer Aktivitäten wie Wohnen, Arbeiten und Erholung, verlangte aber gleichzeitig, daß all diese Aktivitäten mit Medien oder Technik in Verbindung stehen mußten. Dadurch sollte das urbane Wachstum in geordnete Bahnen gelenkt werden und genügend Raum für Projekte bleiben, die nicht unbedingt auf Gewinnmaximierung ausgerichtet waren. Aus diesen Gründen sollte auch Raum für öffentliche Grünanlagen freigehalten werden.

Die erste Ausschreibung

Als die ersten Investoren für die Entwicklung des Mediaparks gefunden wurden, war die erste Ausschreibung für das Gelände bereits vergessen. Dieser Wettbewerb hatte im Februar 1987 noch vor Gründung der MPK unter Leitung der Stadt Köln stattgefunden. Er stand allen deutschen Architekten offen. Um dem Wettbewerb zusätzlichen Glanz zu verleihen, wurden zehn in- und ausländische Architekten von Rang zur Teilnahme eingeladen, darunter der deutsche Oswald Mathias Ungers und die Gruppe um die Japaner Kei Minohara und Hiroshi Hara. Der erste Preis ging an den in Kanada lebenden Deutschen Eberhard Zeidler. Desweiteren wurden fünf zusätzliche Preise vergeben und vier Entwürfe angekauft.

Zeidlers Plan ging von einer fächerförmigen Verteilung des Geländes in sechs spitzzulaufende Baublöcke aus, die an einem zentralen Platz zusammenkommen sollten. Von diesem Platz aus blickte man auf einen kleinen, künstlich angelegten See. Die Blöcke selbst sollten größtenteils Büros und Einrichtungen wie einen Filmpalast aufnehmen. Wohngebäude wollte Zeidler in einer Reihe sich windender Häuserblöcke am äußersten westlichen Rand des Weihers anlegen. Dieser Übergang wurde durch einen hohen Turm gekennzeichnet, der das Zentrum des Mediaparks und damit das bedeutendste Gebäude darstellte. Über die Hälfte des Geländes blieb unbebaut und war für Grünanlagen und Plätze bestimmt.

Zeidlers Entwurf gehörte zu den am stärksten auf Freizeitgestaltung ausgerichteten Konzepten. Andere Teilnehmer gingen von einer eher urbanen Bebauung aus und füllten die Zwischenräume mit Grünanlagen, oder sie entwarfen einen Park, der vom baulichen Gesamtkonzept wie losgelöst schien.

Der Beitrag von William Alsop und John Lyall ging von einem langen, schmalen bebauten Streifen aus, der sich teilweise unterirdisch fortsetzte und wie eine technische Mauer einer Reihe von Einfamilienwohnungen gegenüberlag. Bemerkenswert war auch High-Tech-Entwurf von Čadež und Ruić, wenn auch nur aufgrund seiner beigelegten Zeichnungen in der Vogelflugperspektive: Zwischen dem Mediapark und dem gerade noch sichtbaren Dom sollte die städtische Bebauung einem Flugplatz weichen, der unzweifelhaft internationalen Ansprüchen genügt hätte – vor allem wegen seiner zentralen Lage.

Zusätzliche Ausschreibungen

Üblicherweise wäre Zeidler nach Ende des Wettbewerbs dazu aufgefordert worden, seinen Entwurf für den markanten Turm weiter auszuarbeiten. Aber die Entwicklungen nahmen einen anderen Verlauf: Die MPK schrieb für jeden Block einen eigenen, begrenzten Wettbewerb aus. Für Block 1 – auf diesem Gelände sollte auch der Turm stehen – wurden neben Zeidler noch Günther Behnisch, Werner Finke und Jean Nouvel eingeladen. Die Formulierung der Ausschreibung blieb recht allgemein: Vorgesehen waren ein Vier-Sterne-Hotel mit 220 Zimmern, Büros, Wohnungen, Geschäfte, Restaurants und eine Apotheke, dazu kamen Schulen sowie Parkmöglichkeiten für 220 Autos. Nouvel wurde außerdem noch für den Wettbewerb um Block 5 eingeladen, in dem das Leonardo-Zentrum für Kunst und Kultur entstehen sollte. Diese Ausschreibung gewann der niederländische Architekt Herman Hertzberger, während die übrigen Blöcke von der Gruppe Kölner Bucht (Block 2), Joachim Schürmann (Block 3), O. Steidle (Block 6) und Miroslav Volf (Block 4) realisiert wurden, wobei letzterer sich schon am ersten Wettbewerb beteiligt hatte.

Den bedeutendsten Teil der Ausschreibung – die Bebauung von Block 1 – gewann erneut Zeidler, sehr zum Ärger der Lokalpresse, die den Entwurf von Jean Nouvel, Cattani & Associés favorisiert hatte. Auch der für Block 1 zuständige Bauherr, Herbert Hillebrand, war dieser Ansicht und beschloß daher, die Entscheidung der Jury außer acht zu lassen und Nouvel mit der Planung zu beauftragen.

Ein eigenwilliger Entwurf

Nouvels Entwurf für den Büroturm fiel wesentlich spektakulärer aus als Zeidlers Vorhaben. Nouvel ist für seine eigenwilligen Projekte bekannt: Bei jedem Auftrag setzt er sich ein neues Ziel, das er zu verwirklichen versucht, ohne dabei den üblichen Mustern zu folgen. Als er in Nîmes einen Wohnblock bauen sollte, nahm er sich vor, die Wohnfläche jeder Wohnung über den vorgegebenen Wert hinaus um etwa 30% zu vergrößern. Da er die veranschlagte Bausumme nicht überschreiten wollte, entwarf er eine grobe, einfache Konstruktion und griff auf Materialien aus dem Industriebau zurück, Wände und Decken des Hauses ließ er unverputzt.

Diese individuellen Prinzipien und sein ungewöhnlicher Materialgebrauch sind ebenso typisch für Nouvel wie sein Blick für die Umgebung und für Details, die eigensinnige Behandlung der Ebene, die damit zusammenhängende Neubewertung des Zweidimensionalen sowie seine Vorliebe für Licht und Transparenz. Gute Beispiele für Nouvels Stil sind der für La Défense entworfene Turm, der zur Spitze hin immer transparenter wird, sowie der prämierte Entwurf für die Zentrale des DuMont-Schauberg Verlags in Köln.

Nouvel entwarf transparente Fassaden, die gleichzeitig als Informationsträger dienen: An jeder dieser Flächen ist abzulesen, wo und in welchem Stockwerk sich die Benutzer befinden. Die Fassaden bestehen aus anthrazitgrauem Glas; dynamische Elemente wie Aufzüge oder Fahrstuhlanzeigen sind dagegen farbig gehalten. Das Streifenmuster, das den Betrachter an einen Strichcode erinnert, entlehnte Nouvel den Werken von ihm bewunderter Künstler wie Daniel Buren und Patrick Raynaud. In dieser Hinsicht erinnert sein Entwurf an die Grande Arche (siehe gleichnamiges Kapitel), deren Fassaden Mikrochips als Kommunikationsträger symbolisieren. In Bezug auf andere Künstler sieht Nouvel sich selbst als eine Art Kleptomanen: Er trägt Vorhandenes zusammen und läßt daraus etwas Neues entstehen – eines der Grundprinzipien der Kunst.

Nouvels Gebäudekomplex für den Mediapark umfaßt neben dem Turm (laut Nouvel ein »explodierter Block«) noch drei weitere Gebäude. Der 134 m hohe Turm verjüngt sich zur Spitze hin, wo auch die schönsten Büroräume geplant sind. Hertzbergers Entwürfe wurden aus finanziellen Gründen bis auf weiteres zurückgestellt. Die Bauabnahme von Nouvels Büroturm ist dagegen für das Frühjahr 1996 geplant.

Le Mediapark, Cologne

Le Mediapark de Cologne est l'exemple même d'une coopération harmonieuse entre des autorités officielles et le secteur privé. A l'origine, le site choisi devait revenir à un promoteur immobilier lorsqu'une intervention à point nommé de l'organisme créé pour promouvoir Mediapark (MPK) permit de préserver le futur de ce grand projet.

Un centre pour les médias et la communication

Le MPK, créé conjointement par la ville de Cologne et le gouvernement fédéral en 1988, est un organisme privé, en partie contrôlé par les autorités. Cette formule permet de laisser une certaine liberté aux initiatives privées tout en sauvegardant les intérêts publics.
Au début, le MPK semblait pourtant en mauvaise posture. La ville avait en effet pratiquement vendu les vingt hectares du site de l'ancienne gare de marchandises de Gereon à une société immobilière «Gewerbe im Park» (GiP, Philipp Holzmann Konzern). Leur situation, non loin du centre ancien, laissait entrevoir une opération très rentable. Mais la ville avait également projeté de créer au même endroit un complexe plus potentiellement intéressant pour l'économie locale et qui ferait de Cologne la capitale des médias et de la communication de l'Allemagne.
Au moment où ce rêve ambitieux allait s'écrouler et où la vente du site à GiP avait presque été signée, le MPK réussit à trouver deux investisseurs, une compagnie d'assurance et un producteur de cinéma, disposés à acheter un quart du terrain. La conférence de presse qui annonça cette bonne nouvelle, le 7 novembre 1989, permit de faire saisir tout l'intérêt du projet de Mediapark. Les journalistes apprirent par exemple les détails de la vente par une liaison satellite directe entre New York et Cologne. Le MPK avait divisé le terrain en lots pour favoriser la construction d'un ensemble architecturalement diversifié, mais son contrôle, et par là même celui des autorités, sur les plans, restait garanti.
Pour protéger le projet de la spéculation, les investisseurs durent s'engager à respecter les principes fondateurs du complexe pour une durée d'au moins quinze ans. Une certaine marge de liberté était laissée dans la construction des logements, des commerces et deséquipements de loisirs. Mais chaque projet devait être lié d'une façon ou d'une autre aux médias et à la technologie. Les projets sans but lucratif seraient particulièrement bien accueillis.
Une grande partie du site devait être aménagée en espaces verts pour justifier ainsi pleinement le nom de Mediapark.

Le premier concours

Le premier concours avait déjà eu lieu lorsque les investisseurs firent leur apparition. En fait, il avait été organisé par la municipalité avant même la création du MPK. Lancé en 1987, il était réservé aux architectes allemands mais afin de donner un peu plus de prestige à l'événement, dix architectes célèbres, allemands ou étrangers, avaient été invités, en particulier Oswald Mathias Ungers ainsi qu'une équipe japonaise animée par Kei Minohara et Hiroshi Hara. Le premier prix leur fut cependant ravi par le germano-canadien Eberhard Zeidler. Cinq autres prix furent attribués et quatre autres plans acquis.
Le plan de Zeidler reposait sur le développement en éventail de six blocs regroupés autour d'une place centrale et qui devaient accueillir différents équipements, dont un cinéma géant et des bureaux. Un lac était également prévu pour le futur. Les logements étaient réunis dans les blocs de l'extrémité ouest de l'éventail, annoncés par une tour de grande hauteur marquant le centre du parc et constituant son plus important édifice. Plus de la moitié du site restait disponible pour les espaces verts.
Le plan de Zeidler était l'un des plus conviviaux du concours. De nombreux autres participants s'étaient concentrés sur l'architecture et contentés de remplir les espaces restants avec des jardins ou avaient créé un parc indépendant des constructions. Le premier prix attribué à Zeidler était donc mérité, même si plusieurs autres propositions méritent que l'on s'y arrête.
Le projet de William Alsop et John Lyall, par exemple, basé sur un bâtiment long et étroit, était en partie souterrain, un mur «technologique» faisant face aux logements. Le plan high tech soumis par Cadež et Ruić était encore plus étonnant, surtout en vue aérienne. Ils étaient allés jusqu'à remplacer le quartier entre Mediapark et la cathédrale par un aéroport...

Des concours séparés

La suite logique du concours était de demander à Zeidler de mettre au point son projet de tour. En fait, le MPK organisa un autre concours restreint pour chaque équipement ou immeuble.
Un certain nombre d'architectes, dont Zeidler, Günther Behnisch, Werner Finke et Jean Nouvel furent invités à travailler sur le Block 1, celui de la tour. Le programme était succinct mais portait sur un hôtel quatre étoiles de 220 chambres, des bureaux, des appartements, des boutiques, des restaurants, une pharmacie, des écoles et un parking pour 220 voitures.
Nouvel fut également chargé de proposer un plan pour le Block 5, celui du Centre Leonardo pour les Arts et la Culture. Le concours fut remporté par le célèbre architecte néerlandais Herman Hertzberger. Ceux des autres blocs furent gagnés par l'équipe Kölner-Bucht (Block 2), Joachim Schürmann (Block 3), O. Steidle (Block 6) et Miroslav Volf (Block 4), qui avait déjà pris part au premier concours.
La partie principale, le «Block 1» fut attribuée à Zeidler au grand déplaisir de la presse locale qui préférait le projet de Nouvel et de son équipe. Herbert Hillebrand, le promoteur du «Block 1» préférant également Nouvel, rejeta la décision du jury et passa commande à l'architecte français.

Un plan très personnel

Le projet de Nouvel pour la tour de bureaux était beaucoup plus spectaculaire que celui de Zeidler, ce qui n'est pas surprenant lorsque l'on connaît son œuvre et ses méthodes. Nouvel se donne un objectif personnel pour chacun de ses projets et le poursuit jusqu'au bout. Par exemple, chargé de concevoir un immeuble de logements à Nîmes, il se donna pour but d'augmenter la surface spécifiée de chaque appartement de 30%. Pour respecter les contraintes financières, il conçut un bâtiment simple et dénudé à base de matériaux industriels et laissa les murs et les plafonds bruts de décoffrage.
Cette approche originale et le recours à des matériaux hors de l'ordinaire sont caractéristiques de son style. Il porte également une grande attention aux détails et à l'environnement; c'est un adepte des surfaces lisses, de la lumière et de la transparence et de la mise en valeur des plans bidimensionnels. Deux exemples de ce style sont fournis par son projet de tour pour La Défense qui devient de plus en plus translucide vers son sommet ou son siège social pour les éditions DuMont-Schauberg à Cologne. Nouvel incorpora ces éléments dans ses plans pour la tour de Mediapark.
Il dessina des façades gris foncé qui laissent entrevoir les activités intérieures et les équipements de chaque étage. Les éléments dynamiques comme les ascenseurs et leurs indicateurs sont brillamment colorés. Il utilise également des motifs en bande faisant penser à des codes à barre ou aux œuvres des artistes Daniel Buren et Patrick Raynaud qu'il admire. Le code à barre est un porteur d'information symbolique par excellence et n'est pas sans rappeler le motif des façades latérales de la Grande Arche de la Défense inspiré de la structure d'une puce électronique. Nouvel parle volontiers de «kleptomanie» dans sa façon d'emprunter certains éléments à ses amis artistes.
La tour, que Nouvel décrit comme un «bloc explosé» fait partie d'une ensemble composé de quatre blocs. De 134 m de haut, elle s'amincit vers son sommet où sont implantés les meilleurs bureaux. Bien que le projet d'Hertzberger ait été retardé pour une durée indéterminée à la suite de difficultés financières, la tour de Nouvel devrait être achevée en 1996.

Eberhard H. Zeidler competition design, 1988, exterior view from Erftstrasse, first prize, first round

Eberhard H. Zeidler competition design, 1987, model, first prize, first round

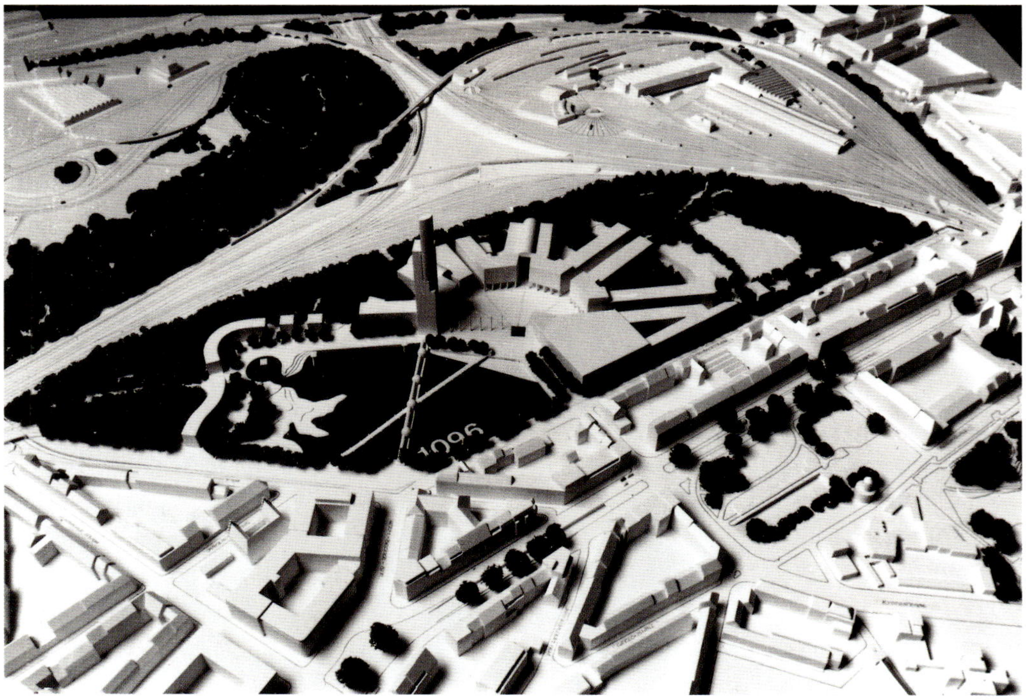

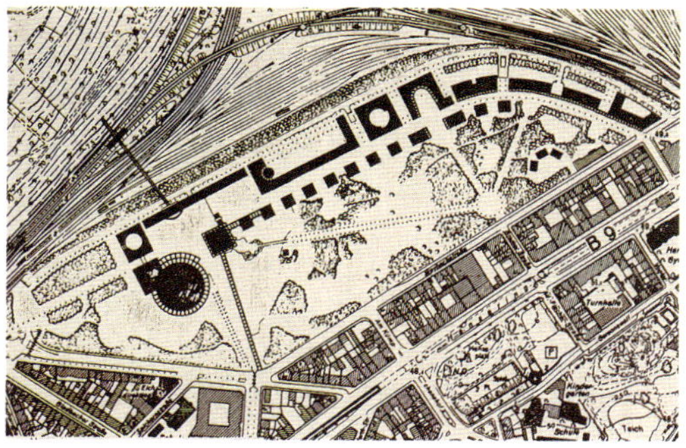

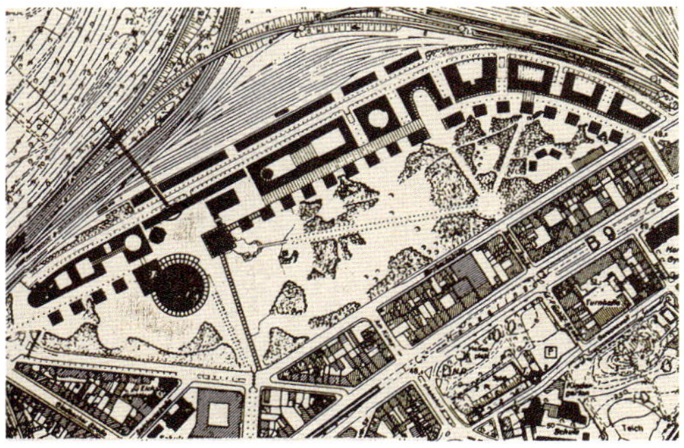

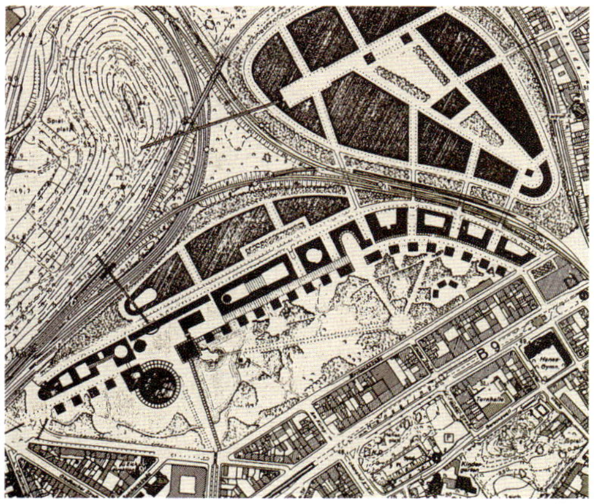

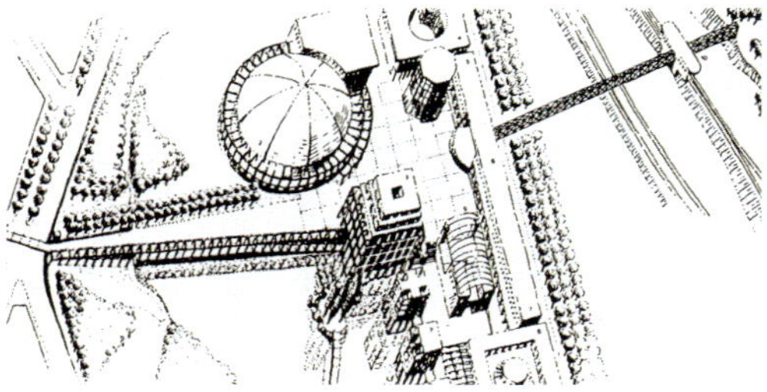

Miroslav Volf competition design, 1987, runner-up, first round

Miroslav Volf competition design, 1987, from top: view from park, interior view, runner-up, first round

Miroslav Volf competition design, 1987, model, runner-up, first round

Michael Müller-Born competition design, 1987, conceptual drawings, runner-up, first round

Michael Müller-Born competition design, 1988, perspective drawing of exterior, runner-up, first round

Michael Müller-Born competition design, 1987, model, runner-up, first round

Michael Müller-Born competition design, 1987, axonometric projection, runner-up, first round

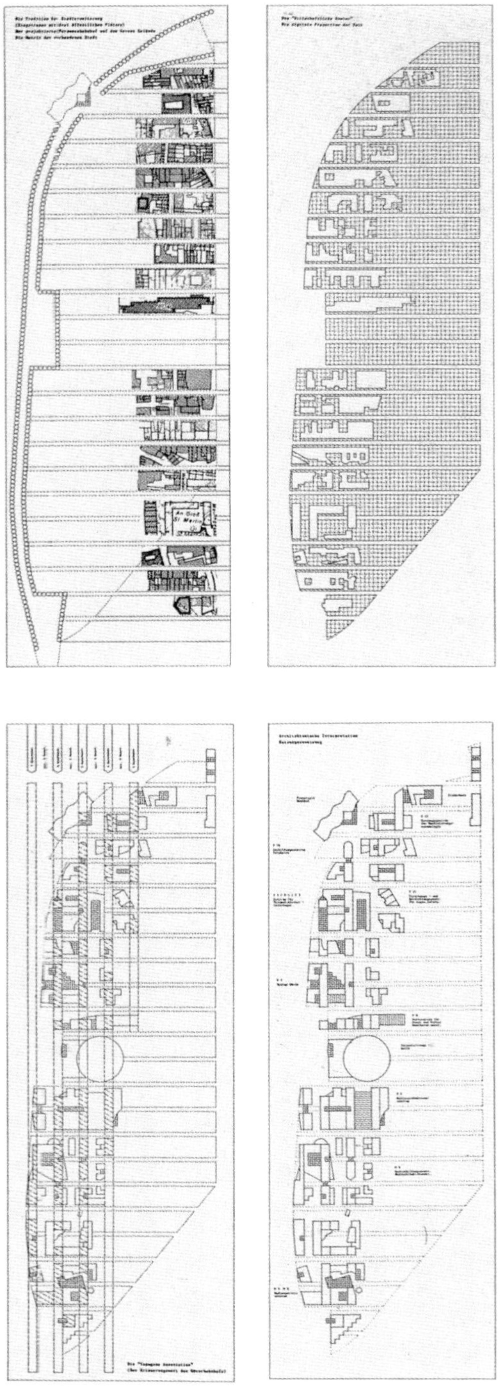

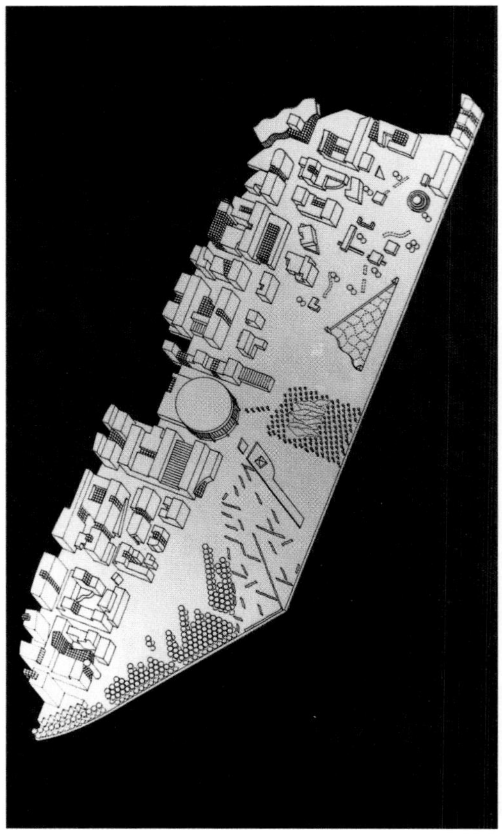

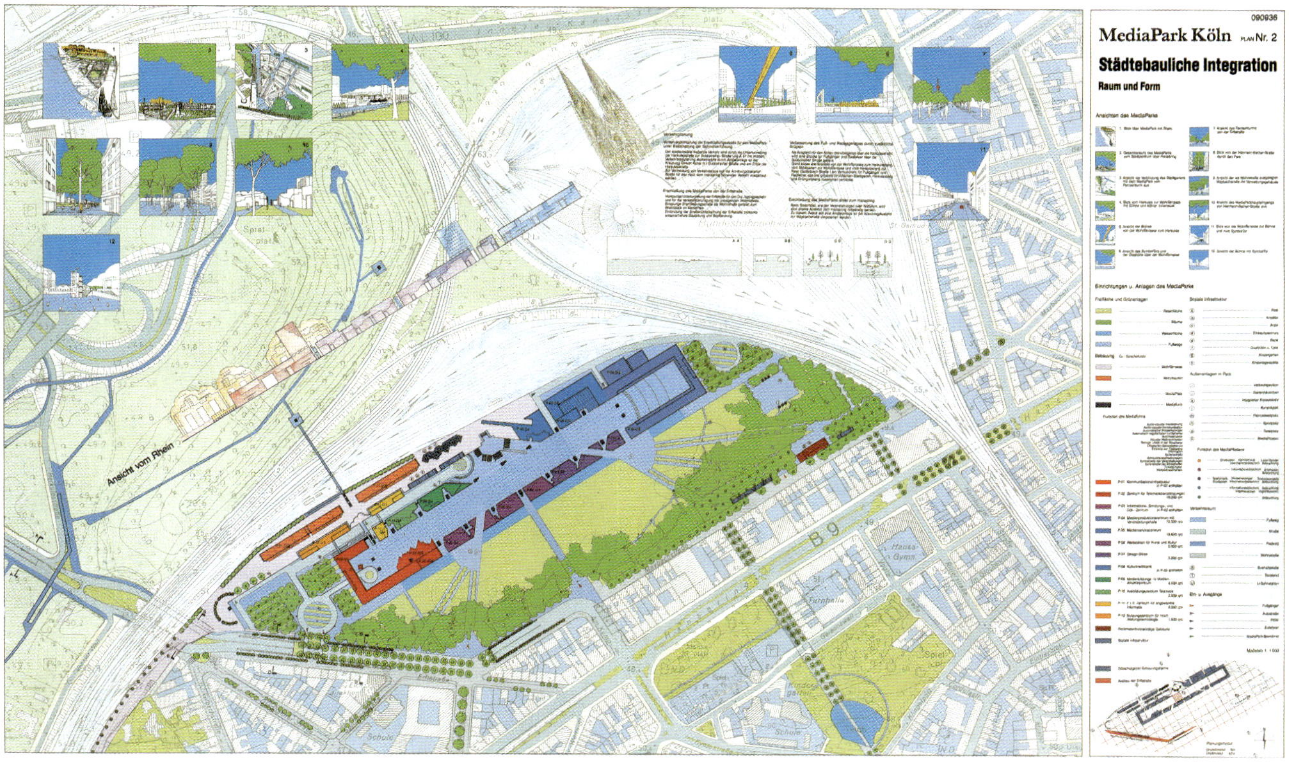

Kei Minohara, Hiroshi Hara, NTT,
Shimizu Corporation et al.
competition design, 1987, space and form, runner-up, first round

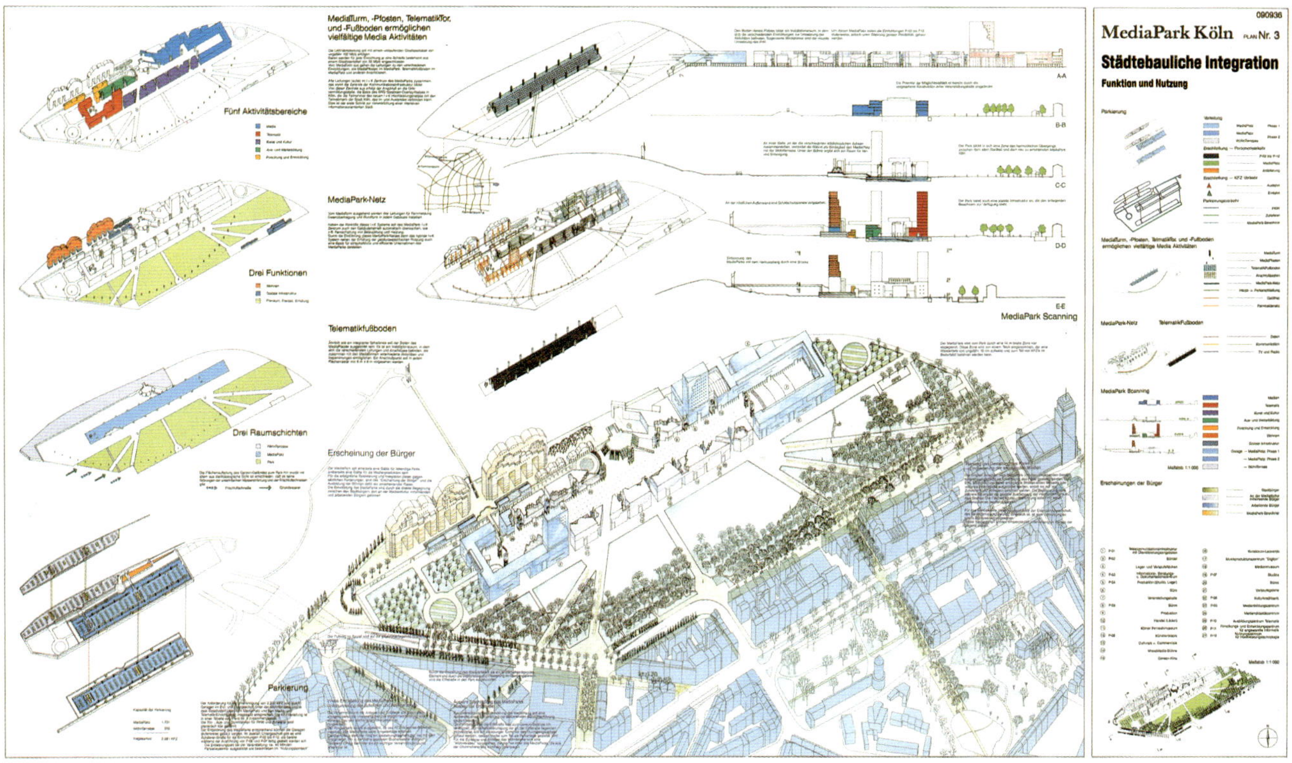

Kei Minohara, Hiroshi Hara, NTT,
Shimizu Corporation, et al.
competition design, 1987, function and use, runner-up, first round

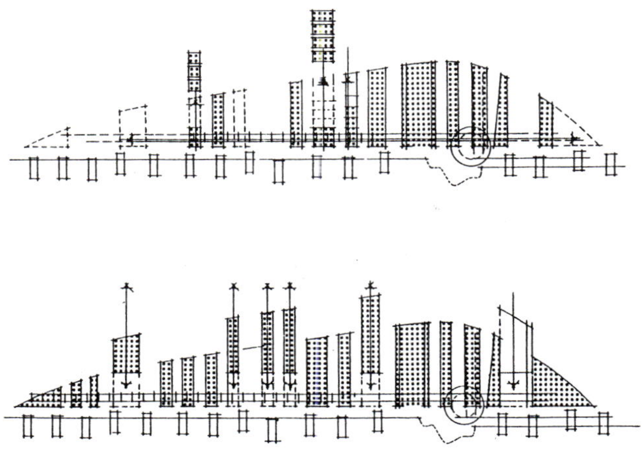

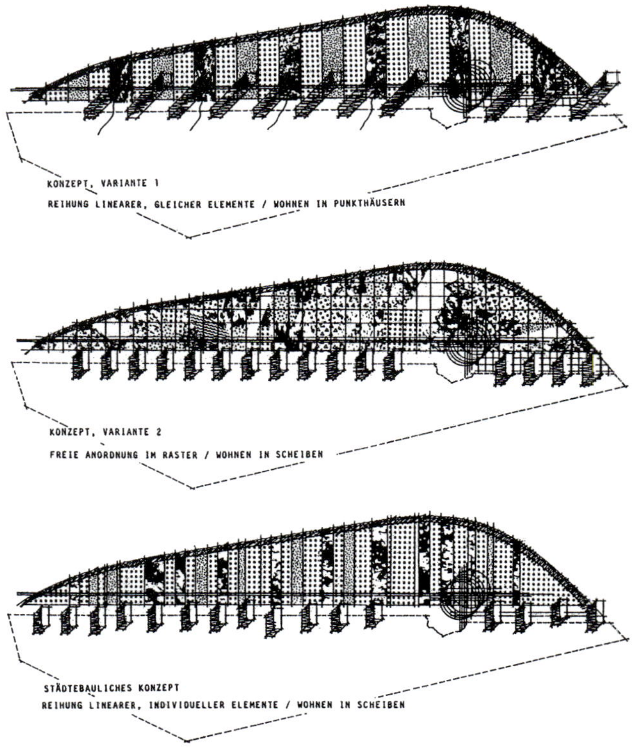

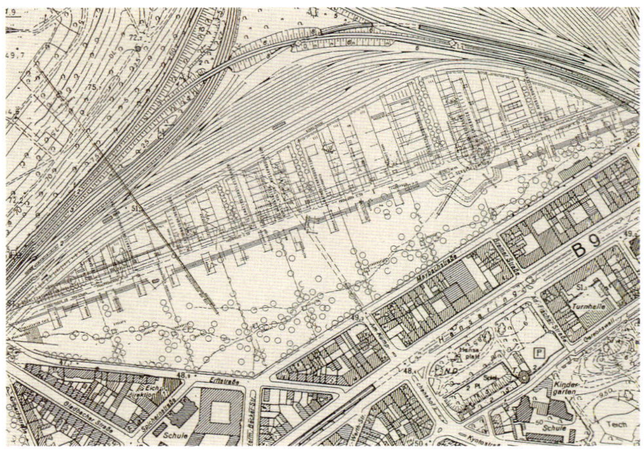

Rolf Schuster competition design, 1987, process of growth, evolution and change, runner-up, first round

Rolf Schuster competition design, 1987, model, runner-up, first round

Rolf Schuster competition design, 1987, concept of arrangement and variation, runner-up, first round

Rolf Schuster competition design, 1987, site plan, runner-up, first round

William Alsop & John Lyall
competition design, 1987, north-south section (west side), purchased

William Alsop & John Lyall
competition design, 1987, model, purchased

Stjepan Čadež & Ivo Ruić
competition design, 1987, bird's-eye view, purchased

Stjepan Čadež & Ivo Ruić
competition design, 1987, site plan, purchased

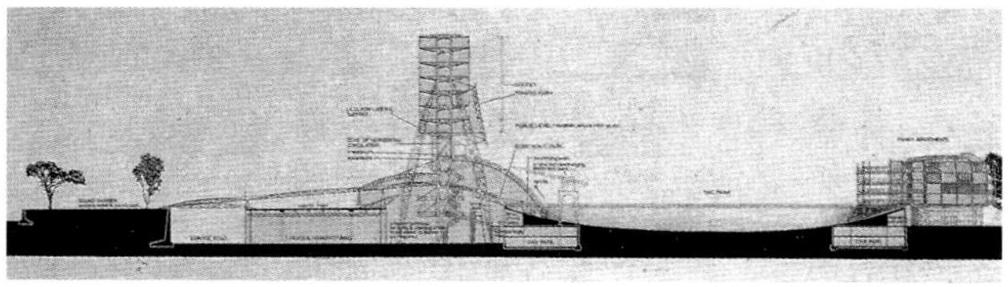

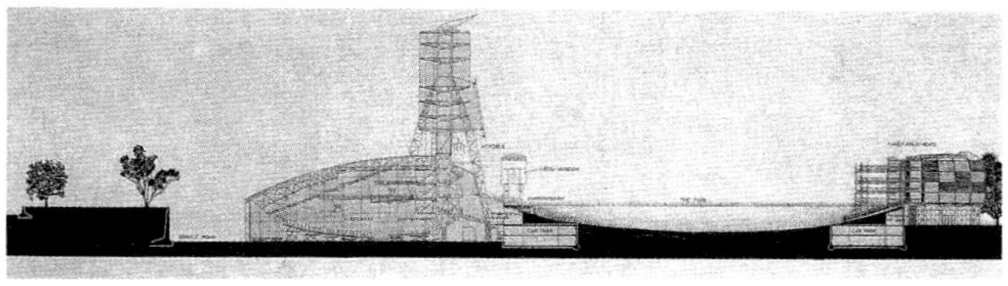

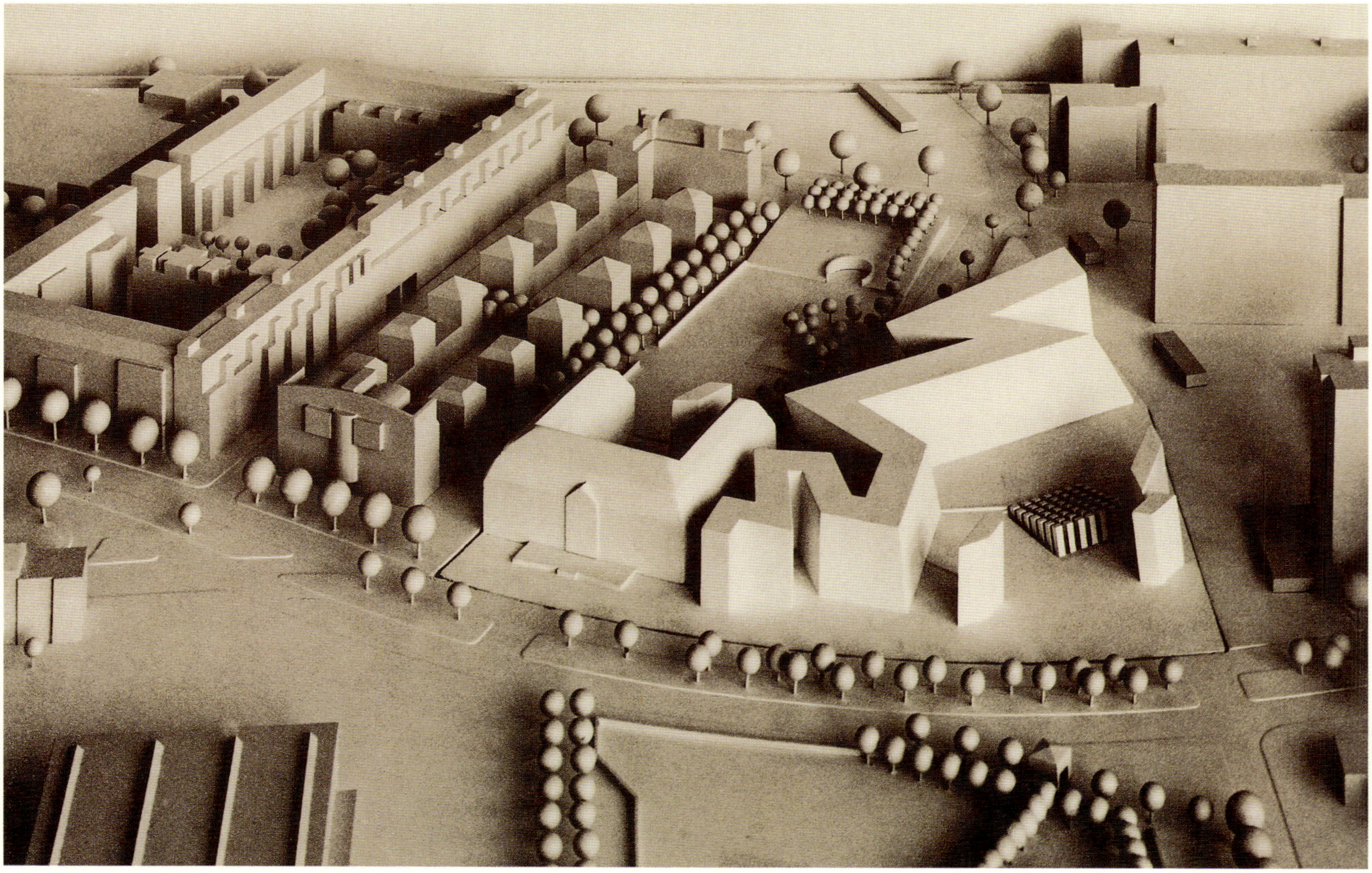

Project

Jewish Museum

Site

Friedrichstadt-South, Berlin, south of the Berlin Museum

Dates

Competition announced December 1988 *Closing date* 28 April 1989 (drawings), 12 May 1989 (models) *Result announced* 23 June 1989

Number of entries

165

Jury

Josef Paul Kleihues (chairman), Harald Deilman, Christoff Hackelsberger, Heinz W. Hallmann, Herman Hertzberger, Klaus Humpert, Isaak Luxemburg, Peter P. Schweger (architects), Joachim Darge, Hans Kirchner, Karl Heinz Wuthe, Günter Kokott, Rolf Bothe (director of the Berlin Museum), Edward van Voolen (director of the Jewish Historical Museum, Amsterdam), Wolfgang Schäche (cultural historian)

Result

First prize Daniel Libeskind *Second prize* Raimund Abraham *Third prize* Lange-Ulrich & Partner *Fourth prize* Thomas Langenfeld & Markus Torge *Fifth prize* Axel Schultes (BJSS) *Purchased* Harald Graff; Helge Bofinger & Partner; Ernst Klein; Gerd Dirichlet; Gisela Glass & Robert Niess

Commissioned by

The Municipality of Berlin

Construction

Due 1995; collection on display 1996

Architect

Daniel Libeskind (*1946)

Jewish Museum, Berlin, 1988–1989

Daniel Libeskind competition design, 1989, from left: ground floor plan, site plan, basement floor plan, second floor, first prize

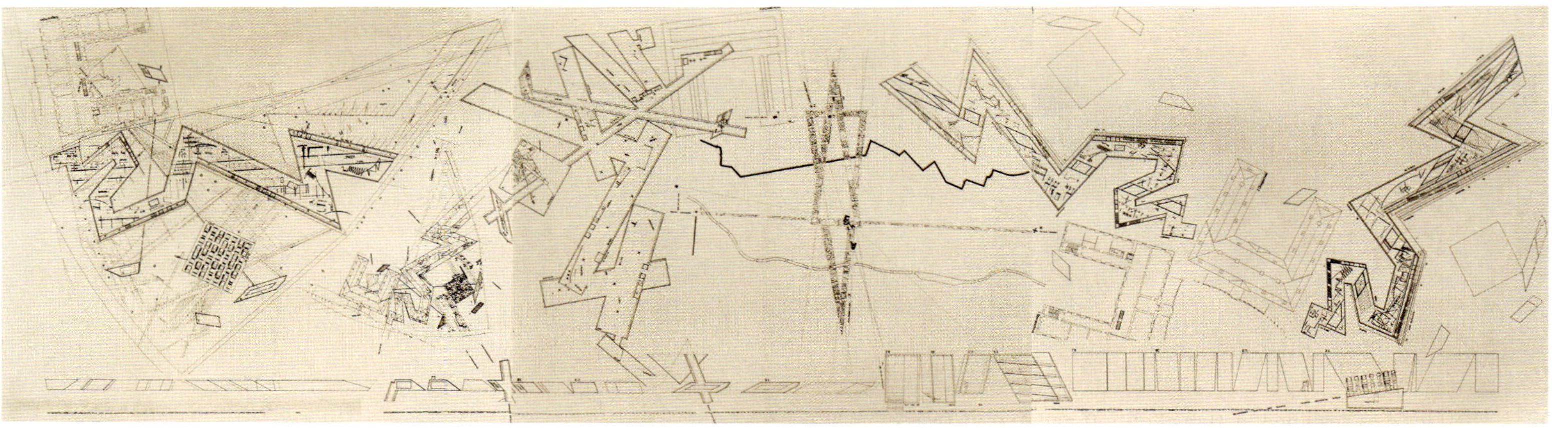

Jewish Museum, Berlin

In spite of a controlled acquisition policy, the Berlin Museum had become too small to house its collection. The departments of fashion, theatre and Jewish history seemed ready to burst at the seams, which prompted a decision to increase the available exhibition space in December 1988.

Expansion plans

The Berlin Museum is a historical museum founded by private investors in 1962. Since 1969 the collection has been housed in the former Kammergericht (Supreme Court), designed by Philippe Gerlach in the early eighteenth century. The Kammergericht was the only building in Friedrichstadt-South to survive both Second World War bombing and the subsequent period of drastic, post-war reconstruction.
When the Berlin Museum moved to the Kammergericht, the Jewish Museum became an independent department, a collection within a collection. It still formed part of the Berlin Museum when the municipality assumed responsibility for both museums two years later (1971). This was more or less a question of necessity, because plans to house the collection in the Palais Ephraim had failed. This baroque urban palazzo, which had been dismantled and placed in storage, had once been the property of a wealthy Jewish financier. Unfortunately, the Palais Ephraim had been reconstructed in East Berlin, which meant that an alternative museum building had to be found. The fact that the Jewish Museum's collection had previously been housed in two different buildings, the Kollegienhaus and the Martin-Gropius-Bau, naturally made it difficult to present an overview of the Jewish cultural history of Berlin; a single building for the entire collection was therefore deemed preferable.
The first plans to renovate the Berlin Museum and to build a new annex were developed in 1981. That same year Friedrichstadt was designated an urban redevelopment area for the International Building Exhibition[1]. An urban development plan was also drafted for the triangular area bounded by Hollmannstrasse, Alte Jakobstrasse and Lindenstrasse. A competition was organised for part of this plan, which included a garden designed by Hans Kollhoff and Arthur Ovaska. However, it was subsequently decided that more exhibition space was required inside in the museum, and in 1988 a part of the triangle was made available for the construction of a new wing for the Jewish department of the Berlin Museum.
It was considered imperative that the Jewish department should not be separated from the municipal-history museum, because German and Jewish cultures have always been intertwined in Berlin. The city owes a great deal of its metropolitan status to the Jewish community, whose intellectual, cultural and financial contribution over the years has been enormous.

The Jewish Museum's collection consisted largely of Jewish liturgical objects. Fortunately, many of the most important objects had survived *Kristallnacht* and the war. In addition, the collection included works by Berlin artists, which depicted Jewish life in the city.
The plans for the new museum were comprehensive. The collection was to be divided amongst three departments: the first department would contain Judaica and, more specifically, would focus on Judaism as a whole; the two other departments would present various aspects of Berlin's Jewish cultural history. One department would present the history of various Jewish communities in the city, which culminated in their horrific annihilation, and the other would present the personal histories of Jewish people who had left their mark on the city.

Berlin Museum, housed in the former Kammergericht (Supreme Court) designed by Philipp Gerlach

Palais Ephraim

A mixed competition

In June 1989 the first step towards the realisation of these plans was taken. A mixed competition was organised: it was both open and national (i.e. restricted to West German architects) and closed and international, because eight foreign architects were invited to participate. The competitions for the IBA International Building Exhibition, held during the 1980s, also had a mixed character of this kind. Furthermore, the co-ordinator of the IBA competitions, Josef Paul Kleihues, was also appointed jury chairman for the Jewish Museum competition. Kleihues was assisted by a number of architects, civil servants, and the directors of the Berlin Museum and the Jewish Historical Museum in Amsterdam.

Among the foreign architects participating were Peter Cook and Wilhelm Holzbauer. Cook, who had teamed up with Christine Hawley, had won the competition for the Monte Carlo Entertainment Centre, and Holzbauer had won the Amsterdam City Hall competition[2]. Although most of the foreign architects produced disappointing designs, one of them did win first prize: Daniel Libeskind, a Milan-based, Jewish architect, who was born in Lodz (Poland) in 1946. His design was not only perfectly in line with the Museum's wishes, but was also the most striking of the 165 entries.

A feasible and carefully conceived plan

Libeskind had previously won one of the competitions for the International Building Exhibition with a design so remarkable that its feasibility was doubted. Consequently, the design was never executed. Fortunately for Libeskind, the feasibility of his museum design was not questioned. He was commissioned for the project and joined the select group of Deconstructivist architects who had been given the opportunity to put their principles into practice. Although few of Libeskind's designs had ever been executed prior to the competition – something he shared with the Deconstructivists Zaha Hadid and Bernard Tschumi – he was well-versed in architectural theory. This is certainly evident in the form and content of his design for the Jewish Museum, both of which were exceptionally well thought-out.

Libeskind's design was entitled "Between the lines". One of the lines is the thunderbolt which is a dominant feature of the museum's outer appearance. The other is a straight axis which runs the entire length of the museum and is marked by a series of wells. The wells not only symbolise the void left by the Holocaust, but also the total lack of moral conscience which made the extermination camps possible. In other words, this interrupted axis symbolises the broken spine of the German nation. It is for this reason that the wells are to be left completely empty. The museum curators will not be allowed to fill them with any other symbolic elements.

Libeskind based his design on "irrational" architectural elements, a conscious effort to counteract the rationale which so often leads to war and domination. According to Libeskind, the irrational character of his design is determined by invisible, abstract elements. The wells are one example, but there are others. Inspired by Friedrichstadt's rich Jewish history, he linked the sites of the former houses of famous Jewish inhabitants with a system of triangles which formed an invisible and irrational Star of David.

A second, more complex, invisible element of Libeskind's concept is the uncompleted opera "Moses and Aaron" by Arnold Schönberg, who had also lived in Friedrichstadt. The main theme of this opera is Moses' disappointment at the image of God created by Aaron. Words fail Moses towards the end of the second act; the music fades away and he says: *"O Wort, du Wort, das mir fehlt"* (Word, o word, that fails me). According to Libeskind, Schönberg had no other alternative but to end the opera at this point, instead of adding a third act.

Libeskind has also included a third symbolic void in his design. In this case the void is made tangible by two thick, black telephone directories which list the names of local Jews who were murdered during the Second World War. The fourth and last symbolic element is a text about the urban Apocalypse by Walter Benjamin.

All of the above elements have been incorporated more or less invisibly into Libeskind's design, and this prompted the jury's decision to award

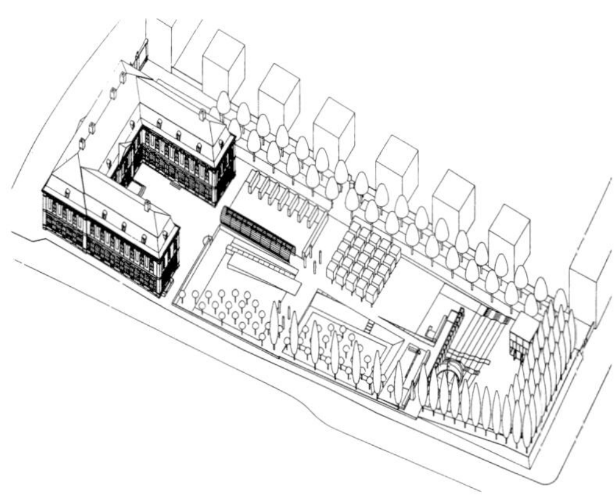

Ernst Gisel **Palais Ephraim, reconstruction project, elevation, 1978–1979**

Hans Kollhoff, Arthur Ovaska **Garden, Berlin Museum**

Daniel Libeskind competition design, 1989, model, first prize

him first prize. The powerful symbolic character of the design exceeded the expectations of the commissioning body, who wanted to build a museum steeped in meaning. The layout of Libeskind's design is also excellent. The collection of Judaica will be housed in the subterranean part of the building and will be accessible via the main entrance of the newly-restored Kammergericht, which will house the other departments of the Berlin Museum. The two other departments of the Jewish Museum will be situated on the upper floors of the new wing. Throughout the building the visitors will encounter the wells as a solemn reminder of the history of the Jewish people.

Other participants

A number of the other entries are certainly worth mentioning – Axel Schultes' design, for example, and the fan-shaped design submitted by Harald Graff. Gerd Dirichlet submitted an exceptionally impressive design, which had a rounded façade bisected by a straight slab marking the division between the two museums. However, none of these designs can match the significance and eloquent symbolism of Libeskind's design.

1 *See chapter on the International Building Exhibition elsewhere in this book.*

2 *See chapters on the Monte Carlo Entertainment Centre and the Amsterdam City Hall elsewhere in this book.*

Jüdisches Museum

Trotz einer zielgerichteten Ankaufspolitik bot das Berlin-Museum im Laufe der Jahre immer weniger Ausstellungsfläche. Als man sich im Dezember 1988 zu einer Erweiterung entschloß, war die Sammlung so weit angewachsen, daß die Abteilungen Mode, Theater und Jüdische Geschichte aus allen Nähten zu platzen drohten.

Erweiterungspläne

Das Berlin-Museum mit seiner historischen Sammlung zur Berliner Stadtgeschichte war 1962 in privater Initiative entstanden und befand sich seit 1969 im alten Kammergericht. Dieses hatte als einziges Gebäude der Umgebung (Friedrichstadt-Süd) sowohl die Bombenangriffe als auch die drastischen Stadtsanierungen nach dem Krieg überlebt. Im Jahr des Umzugs in das ehemalige Kammergerichtsgebäude entstand auch das Jüdische Museum als selbständige Abteilung innerhalb der Sammlung.

Zwei Jahre später übernahm die Stadt Berlin die Leitung des Berlin-Museums. Das Jüdische Museum blieb Teil dieser Sammlungen, nachdem Pläne gescheitert waren, das Palais Ephraim als eigenständigen Museumsbau herzurichten. Dieses barocke Stadtpalais, das ursprünglich einem wohlhabenden jüdischen Bankier gehört hatte, war lange in Einzelteile zerlegt eingelagert gewesen. Da es in Ost-Berlin wieder aufgebaut wurde, mußte sich das Jüdische Museum nach einem neuen Sitz umschauen.

Die ersten Pläne für eine Renovierung des ehemaligen Kammergerichtsgebäudes und den Aufbau einer neuen Abteilung entstanden bereits 1981. Platzmangel führte jedoch zu einer Änderung der Pläne. Etwa zur gleichen Zeit wurde Friedrichstadt als Stadtsanierungsgebiet für die Internationale Bauausstellung ausgewählt (siehe entsprechendes Kapitel). Auch für das Straßendreieck aus Hollmannstraße, Alte Jakobstraße und Lindenstraße entstand ein neues städtebauliches Konzept. Dieses war zum Teil im Rahmen eines Architekturwettbewerbs entwickelt worden und sah u.a. eine von Hans Kollhoff und Arthur Ovaska entworfene Parkanlage vor. 1988 wurde beschlossen, einen Teil des Dreiecks für einen Neubau des Berlin-Museums – genauer gesagt für dessen jüdische Abteilung – zur Verfügung zu stellen.

Die Jüdische Abteilung sollte nicht vollständig vom stadthistorischen Museum abgetrennt werden, denn die Wechselwirkung zwischen deutscher und jüdischer Kultur war seit Jahrhunderten in Berlin spürbar gewesen. Ohne die jüdischen Einflüsse hätte sich Berlin niemals zu einer Weltstadt entwickeln können.

Die Sammlungen des Jüdischen Museums bestanden hauptsächlich aus Judaica und liturgischen Objekten. Glücklicherweise hatten zahlreiche bedeutende Kunstschätze die Reichskristallnacht (November 1938) und den Zweiten Weltkrieg unbeschadet überstanden. Neben diesen Ausstellungsstücken gab es noch eine Reihe von Werken Berliner Künstler, die sich mit dem jüdischen Leben auseinandersetzten.

Das Konzept des neuen Museumsbaus ging über diesen Aspekt hinaus: Die Ausstellung wurde in drei Teile gegliedert, wobei nur der erste Teil die Judaica zeigen und genauer auf die Darstellung des jüdischen Glaubens eingehen sollte. Die beiden anderen Abteilungen präsentierten Stationen der Jüdisch-Berlinerischen Geschichte: Die Entwicklung der verschiedenen Glaubensgemeinschaften in Berlin sowie Darstellungen von Leben und Werk herausragender jüdischer Persönlichkeiten, die die Stadt im Laufe der Jahrhunderte nachhaltig geprägt hatten.

Gemischte Ausschreibung

Um die Pläne endlich zur Durchführung zu bringen, wurde im Juni 1989 ein Wettbewerb ausgeschrieben, an dem sich nur westdeutsche Architekten beteiligten. Zudem erhielten acht ausländische Architekten eine Einladung zur Teilnahme. Vorsitzender der Jury war Josef Paul Kleihues, der bereits die Jury des IBA-Wettbewerbs geleitet hatte. Kleihues erhielt Unterstützung von anderen Architekten, städtischen Beamten sowie den Direktoren des Berlin-Museums und des Joods Historisch Museum in Amsterdam.

Unter den ausländischen Teilnehmern befanden sich so renommierte Architekten wie Peter Cook, der den Wettbewerb für das Sommerkasino in Monte Carlo gewonnen hatte und zusammen mit Christine Hawley antrat, und Wilhelm Holzbauer, der Gewinner der Ausschreibung für die Amsterdamer Stopera. Doch die Beiträge der internationalen Architekten erwiesen sich als eher enttäuschend: Unter den siegreichen Einsendungen befand sich nur ein ausländischer Entwurf – der allerdings erhielt den ersten Preis. Er stammte von Daniel Libeskind, einem nach dem Zweiten Weltkrieg im polnischen Lodz geborenen Juden, der zur Zeit des Wettbewerbs in Mailand lebte. Libeskinds Entwurf erwies sich als der ungewöhnlichste aller 165 Einsendungen.

Durchführbar und durchdacht

Libeskind hatte bereits zu Zeiten der IBA mit einem aufsehenerregenden, aber nicht realisierten Entwurf eine Ausschreibung für sich entschieden (siehe das Kapitel zur IBA). Seine Vorstellungen erwiesen sich als so kühn, daß sie einigen Fachleuten undurchführbar erschienen. Im Falle des Jüdischen Museums waren derlei Befürchtungen unbegründet. Libeskind eilte der Ruf eines theoretisch hervorragenden Architekten voraus, was sein Konzept für das Jüdische Museum bestätigt, da es sowohl formal als auch inhaltlich gut durchdacht erscheint.

Er selbst nannte seinen Entwurf »Between the lines«. Seine erste Linie ist eine durchbrochene Gerade, die sich aus leeren Räumen zusammensetzt. Diese leeren Flächen, die in einer geraden Linie den gesamten Museumsbau durchziehen, symbolisieren die Leere, die der Holocaust hinterlassen hat. Gleichzeitig stehen die gebrochenen Linien für das gebrochene Rückgrat der deutschen Gesellschaft. Aus diesem Grund dürfen die leeren Räume von den Innenarchitekten des Museums keinesfalls verändert oder mit anderen Symbolen ausgestattet werden. Bei der dritten Linie handelt es sich um den Blitzstrahl, der dem Gebäude seine Form gibt.

Libeskind wollte das Irrationale zum Ausgangspunkt seines Entwurfs machen und sich bewußt von der Vernunft abgrenzen, die so häufig zu Krieg und Unterdrükkung führt. Mit »irrational« bezeichnete er das Unsichtbare, Unfaßbare. Nicht nur die leeren Räume stehen stellvertretend für diese Auffassung; Libeskind ließ sich auch durch die reiche, in Teilen jüdische Geschichte von Friedrichstadt inspirieren. Er besuchte die Orte, an denen die Häuser berühmter Bewohner dieses Stadtteils gestanden hatten, und verband diese Punkte durch ein System von Dreiecken, die zusammen einen unsichtbaren, »irrationalen« Davidstern bilden.

Einen zweiten, etwas komplizierteren Ausgangspunkt für Libeskinds Konzept bildet die unvollendete Oper »Moses und Aron« von Arnold Schönberg, der in Friedrichstadt wohnte. Thema der Oper ist die Enttäuschung, die Moses beim Anblick des von Aron geschaffenen Gottesbildes empfindet. Am Ende des zweiten Aktes kann Moses nur noch hervorbringen: *»O Wort, du Wort, das mir fehlt«*. An diesem Punkt – so Libeskind – blieb Schönberg nichts anderes übrig, als die Oper zu beenden; daher fehle auch der dritte Akt.

Der dritte Ausgangspunkt Libeskinds bezieht sich ebenfalls auf den Aspekt der Leere, ist aber greifbar in Form zweier dicker, schwarzer Telefonbücher, die die Namen aller Berliner Juden enthalten, die im Zweiten Weltkrieg ermordet wurden. Ein Text von Walter Benjamin über die städtische Apokalypse bildet den vierten und letzten Bezugspunkt.

All diese Elemente sind sichtbar oder unsichtbar in Libeskinds Museumsentwurf verarbeitet. Mit dem Aufbau der verschiedenen Bedeutungsebenen hatte der Dekonstruktivist den Wunsch der Jury nach einem Bauwerk von hohem Symbolcharakter erfüllt. Auch programmatisch konnte sein Entwurf allen Anforderungen gerecht werden. Die Sammlung von Judaica sollte im unterirdischen Teil des Gebäudes ihren Platz finden. Dieser ist durch den Haupteingang des renovierten Kammergerichtsgebäudes zu erreichen, in dem die Ausstellungsräume für die übrigen Sammlungen des Berlin-Museums liegen. Die beiden anderen Abteilungen des Jüdischen Museums brachte man in den oberen Stockwerken des Neubaus unter. So wird der Besucher im gesamten Gebäude mit leeren Räumen und damit mit der jüdischen Geschichte konfrontiert.

Die übrigen Teilnehmer

Auch unter den übrigen 165 Beiträgen befanden sich einige bemerkenswerte Arbeiten, darunter ein Entwurf von Axel Schultes (Büro Bangert, Jansen, Scholz & Schultes) und ein fächerförmiges Projekt von Harald Graff. Beeindruckend wirkte auch die runde Fassade von Gerd Dirichlet, die von einer geraden Platte durchschnitten wird, die den Übergang zum Berlin-Museum kennzeichnet. Dennoch besaß keiner dieser Entwürfe die gleiche Spannung und symbolische Ausdruckskraft wie das Werk von Daniel Libeskind.

Le Musée Juif, Berlin

En dépit d'une politique d'acquisitions limitée, le Musée de Berlin était devenu trop petit pour abriter ses collections dans de bonnes conditions. Les départements de la mode, du théâtre et de l'histoire juive étaient à la limite de l'implosion quand, en décembre 1988, fut prise la décision de créer de nouvelles surfaces d'exposition.

Plans d'expansion

Le Berlin Museum est un musée d'histoire fondé en 1962 par des personnes privées. Depuis 1969, ses collections sont installées dans l'ancien Kammergericht, seul bâtiment de Friedrichstadt-Süd à avoir échappé aux bombardements de la Seconde Guerre mondiale et aux reconstructions ultérieures. De l'ancienne ville baroque du XVIIIème siècle dessinée par Philipp Gerlach, également architecte de l'ancien Kammergericht, ne subsistait que le réseau de voirie.
Le Musée d'histoire juive devint un département indépendant lorsque le musée s'installa dans l'ancien Kammergericht, mais il faisait encore partie de celui-ci quand la municipalité prit en mains les destinées de l'ensemble deux ans plus tard (1971). Cette mesure était devenue pratiquement inévitable après l'échec des plans de transfert des collections au Palais Ephraïm. Démantelé et entreposé, ce palais baroque avait été jadis la propriété d'un financier juif fabuleusement riche. Malheureusement l'édifice avait été remonté à Berlin-Est d'où la nécessité de trouver un autre lieu. La dispersion des collections pendant un temps entre la Kollegienhaus et le Martin-Gropius-Bau n'était qu'un pis-aller qui rendait difficile une bonne compréhension de l'héritage juif berlinois. La solution d'un bâtiment unique fut préférée.
Les premiers plans de rénovation de l'ancien Kammergericht et de construction d'une annexe furent élaborés en 1981. La même année, Friedrichstadt fut désignée comme zone de rénovation urbaine dans le cadre de l'Internationale Bauaustellung[1]. Un plan d'aménagement du triangle formé par la Hollmannstrasse, la Alte Jakobstrasse et la Lindenstrasse fut établi par concours. Le projet comprenait un jardin dessiné par Hans Kollhoff et Arthur Ovaska. La décision d'extension du musée fit modifier ces plans et, en 1988, une partie du triangle lui fut réservée.
Les responsables voulaient éviter la séparation du département juif du musée de l'histoire de la ville, les cultures allemandes germaniques et juives ayant toujours été étroitement imbriquées. La cité devait beaucoup de sa puissance à la communauté juive dont la contribution intellectuelle, culturelle et financière avait été très importante au cours des siècles.
Les collections du musée consistaient essentiellement en objets religieux qui avaient pu échapper à la «Nuit de Cristal» et à la guerre, et en œuvres d'artistes berlinois décrivant la vie de la communauté juive dans la capitale. Les plans pour le nouveau musée étaient plus ambitieux et globaux. La collection serait divisée en trois départements: le premier comprendrait les objets liés au culte et s'attacherait plus particulièrement au Judaïsme dans sa globalité; le second présenterait la vie des différentes communautés israélites dans la cité jusqu'à leur annihilation par les nazis, et le troisième tracerait le portrait de grandes personnalités juives qui avaient joué un rôle dans l'histoire de Berlin.

Un concours mixte

En juin 1989, la première étape fut franchie avec l'organisation d'un concours mixte, à la fois ouvert et national, c'est-à-dire restreint aux architectes d'Allemagne de l'Ouest. En revanche huit architectes étrangers étaient invités. Les concours de l'IBA avait été tous organisés sur le même principe et leur coordinateur, Josef Paul Kleihues, était président du jury qui comprenait plusieurs architectes, des fonctionnaires et les directeurs du Berlin Museum et du Musée de l'Histoire Juive d'Amsterdam.
Parmi les étrangers invités, figuraient Peter Cook et Wilhelm Holzbauer. Cook, qui faisait équipe avec Christine Hawley, avait remporté le concours pour le Centre de loisirs de Monte-Carlo et Holzbauer celui de l'hôtel de ville d'Amsterdam[2]. Bien que la plupart des concurrents étrangers aient proposé des plans assez décevants, c'est l'un d'entre eux qui remporta le premier prix: Daniel Libeskind, architecte israélite né en Pologne après la guerre et résidant à Milan. Son projet, le plus remarquable des 165 en lice, correspondait parfaitement aux souhaits des organisateurs.

Un plan réalisable et conçu avec soin

Libeskind avait auparavant remporté l'un des concours de l'IBA avec un plan si étonnant que des doutes s'étaient élevés sur sa faisabilité et qu'il ne fut jamais réalisé. Heureusement pour lui, celle de son projet de musée ne fut jamais mise en question. Libeskind faisait partie de ce groupe des déconstructivistes, à la fois très intellectuel et très à la mode, qui pour la première fois voyait l'un des siens avoir la chance de mettre ses idées en pratique. Peu de projets de Libeskind avaient été réalisés avant ce concours – ce qui était le cas des autres déconstructivistes comme Zaha Hadid et Tschumi – mais il maniait avec habileté la théorie architecturale comme le prouvent ses plans pour le musée brillamment réfléchis.
Son projet était intitulé «Entre les lignes». L'une de ces lignes est un axe droit ponctué par une série de puits, qui traverse toute la longueur du musée. Ces puits entièrement vides ne symbolisent pas seulement les manques laissés par l'Holocauste, mais également l'absence de conscience morale qui a rendu possible l'existence des camps de concentration. En d'autres mots, cet axe interrompu est à l'image de la colonne vertébrale brisée de la nation allemande. Les puits ne devront à aucun moment être utilisés par les conservateurs. L'autre ligne est un éclair à l'image de l'apparence extérieure du musée.
Libeskind a basé son plan sur des éléments «irrationnels» en un effort conscient de réaction contre un rationalisme qui conduit souvent à la guerre et à des rapports de domination. Pour lui, ce caractère irrationnel se nourrit d'éléments abstraits et invisibles. Les puits en sont un exemple parmi d'autres. S'appuyant sur l'histoire de la communauté juive de Friedrichstadt, il réunit les emplacements des anciennes maisons de citoyens juifs célèbres par un système de triangles formant une sorte d'étoile de David invisible.
Un autre élément immatériel, plus complexe est «Moïse et Aaron», l'opéra inachevé d'Arnold Schönberg, ancien habitant de Friedrichstadt. Le thème principal de cet opéra est la déception de Moïse devant l'image de Dieu créée par Aaron. Les paroles lui manquent vers la fin du second acte, la musique se dissout et il dit: «*O mot, mot qui me manque.*» Pour Libeskind, Schönberg ne pouvait plus après cela que mettre fin à son œuvre.
L'architecte a également inclus un troisième vide symbolique, matérialisé par deux épais annuaires du téléphone noirs qui donnent la liste des juifs du quartier assassinés pendant la dernière guerre. Le quatrième et dernier élément symbolique est un texte sur l'apocalypse urbaine, de Walter Benjamin.
Tous ces éléments, incorporés de façon plus ou moins évidente dans les plans de Libeskind, incitèrent le jury à lui décerner le premier prix. Le puissant caractère symbolique de ce projet allait au-delà des attentes du commanditaire qui pourtant souhaitait un musée signifiant.
L'organisation interne des plans de Libeskind est également excellente. La collection d'objets culturels est présentée dans la partie souterraine du musée et accessible par l'entrée du Kammergericht restauré. Les deux autres départements occuperont les étages supérieurs de la nouvelle aile. Tout au long de leur visite, les visiteurs seront confrontés aux puits, souvenir de l'histoire du peuple juif.

Les autres participants

Parmi les autres projets intéressants, il faut noter celui d'Axel Schultes et le plan en éventail de Harald Graff. Gerd Dirichlet proposa un projet étonnant à façade arrondie, coupé en deux par une dalle droite marquant la division entre les deux musées. Mais aucune de ces tentatives ne pouvait égaler l'éloquent symbolisme du projet de Libeskind.

1 *Voir le chapitre sur l'Internationale Bauaustellung dans cet ouvrage.*
2 *Voir les chapitres sur le Centre de Loisirs de Monte-Carlo et l'hôtel de ville d'Amsterdam dans cet ouvrage.*

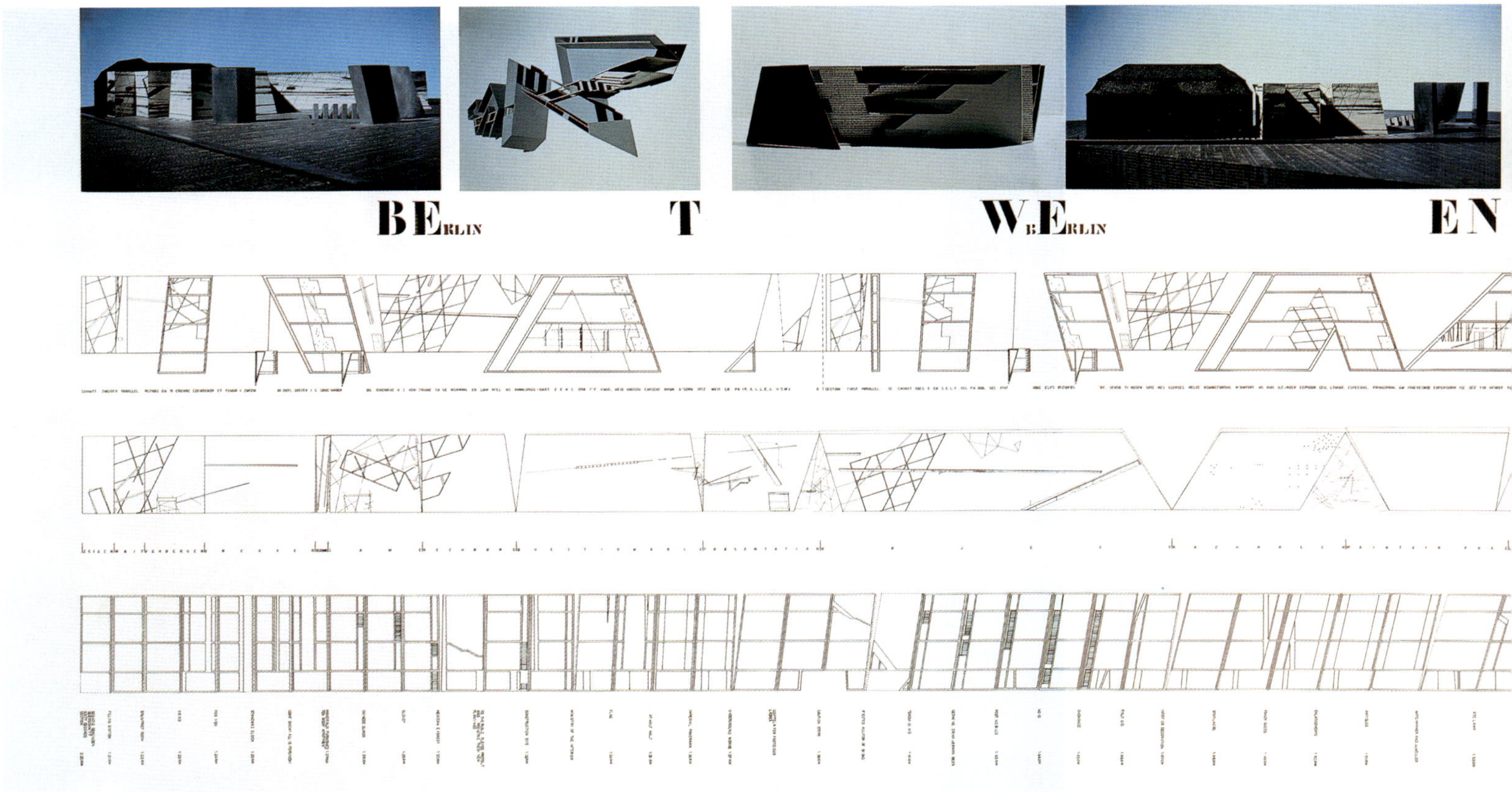

Daniel Libeskind competition design, 1989, from top: model, section of second parallel, section of first parallel, elevation and section of the Jewish Museum, sections indicating the several functions, sections indicating the rooms, first prize

Raimund Abraham competition design, 1989, model, second prize

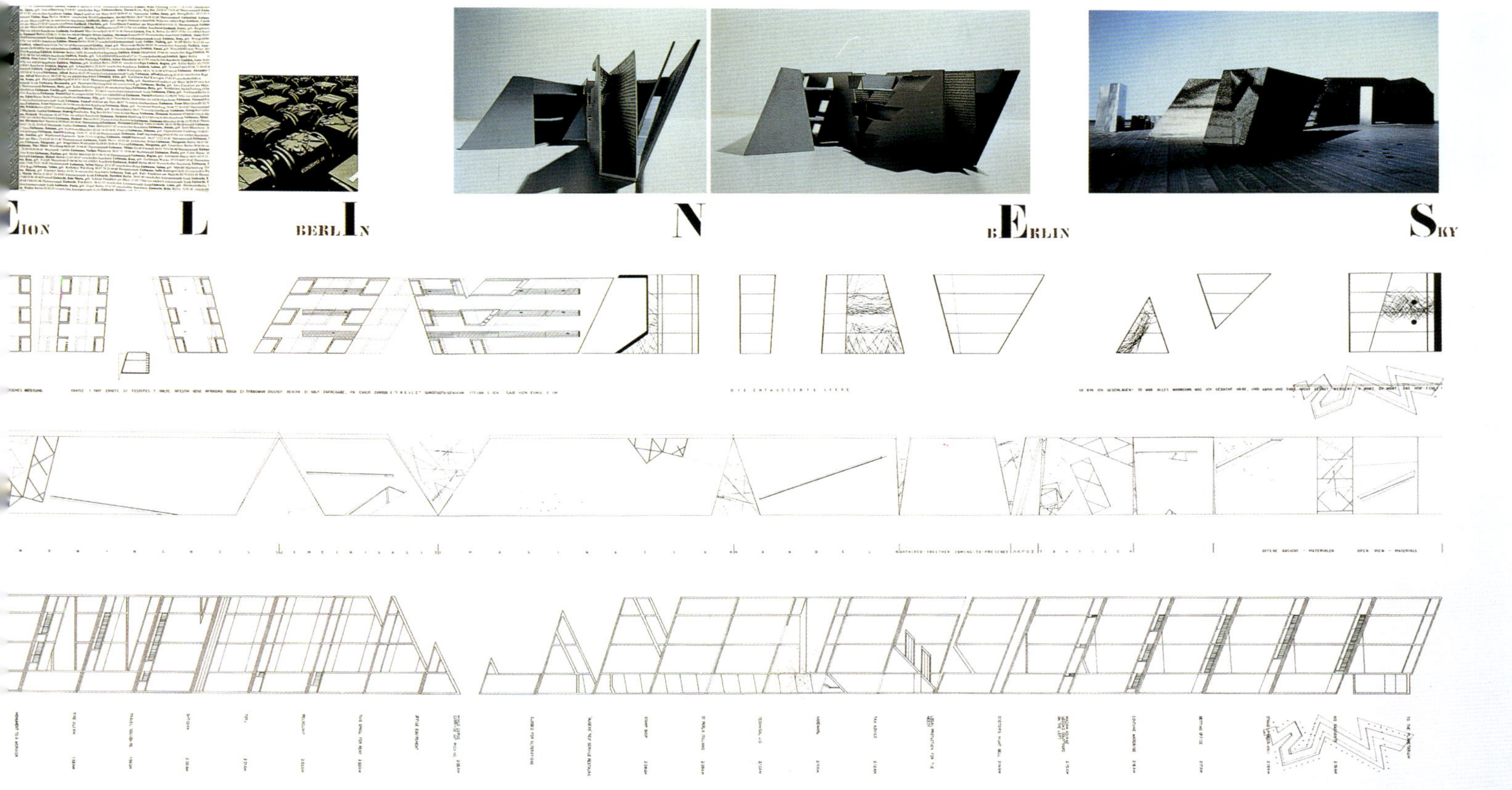

Raimund Abraham competition design, 1989, first floor plan, second prize

Raimund Abraham competition design, 1989, from top: west elevation, south elevation, north elevation, east elevation, east-west section (north side), east-west section (north-east side), second prize

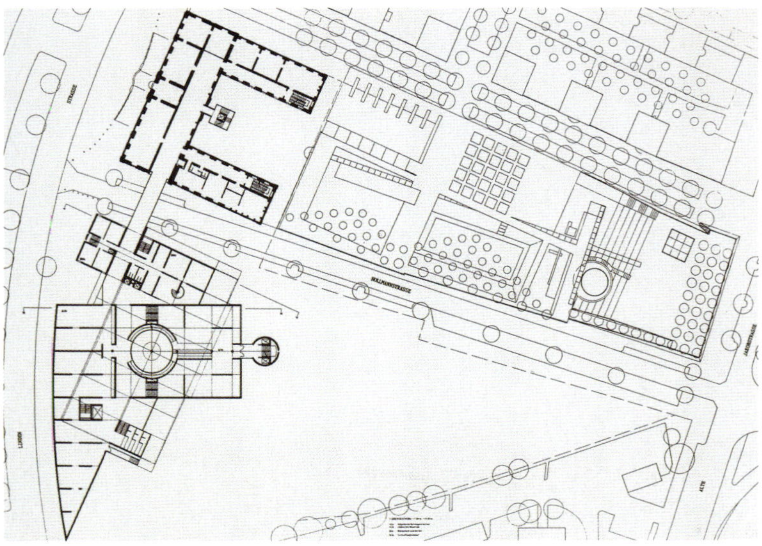

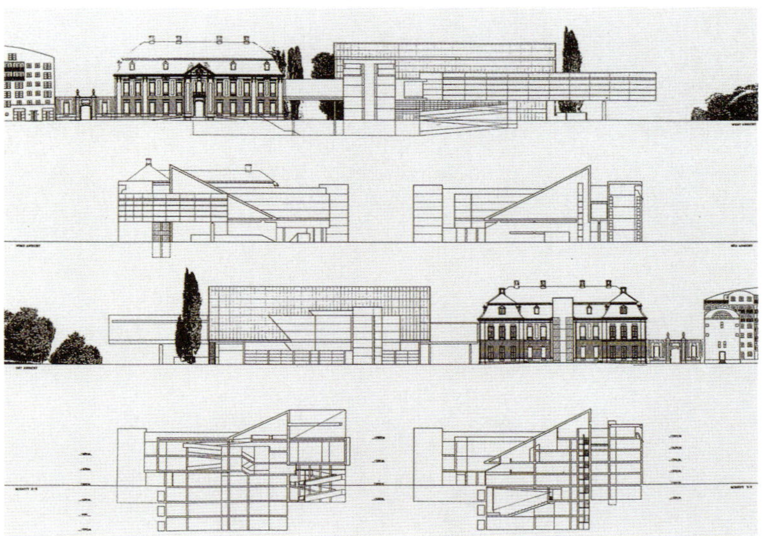

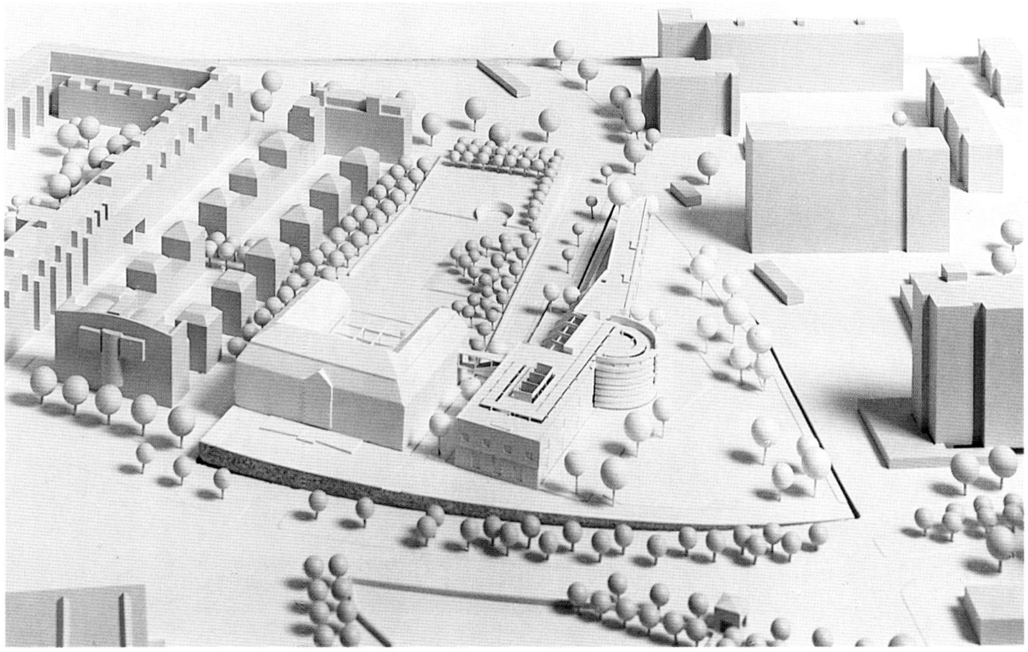

Lange-Ulrich & Partner competition design, 1989, third prize

Lange-Ulrich & Partner competition design, 1989, site plan and concept plan (+3, +6.3, +9.3 level), third prize

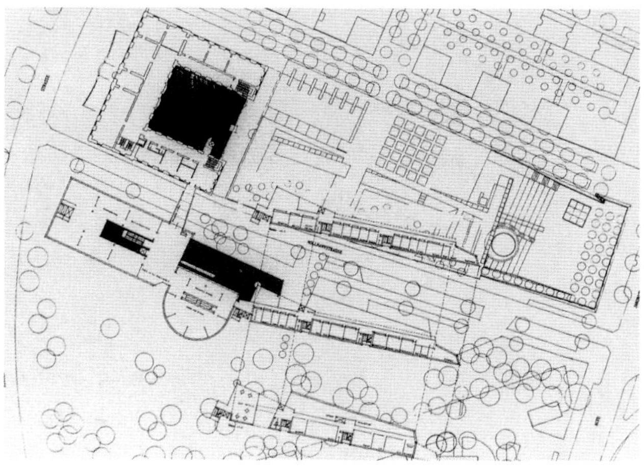

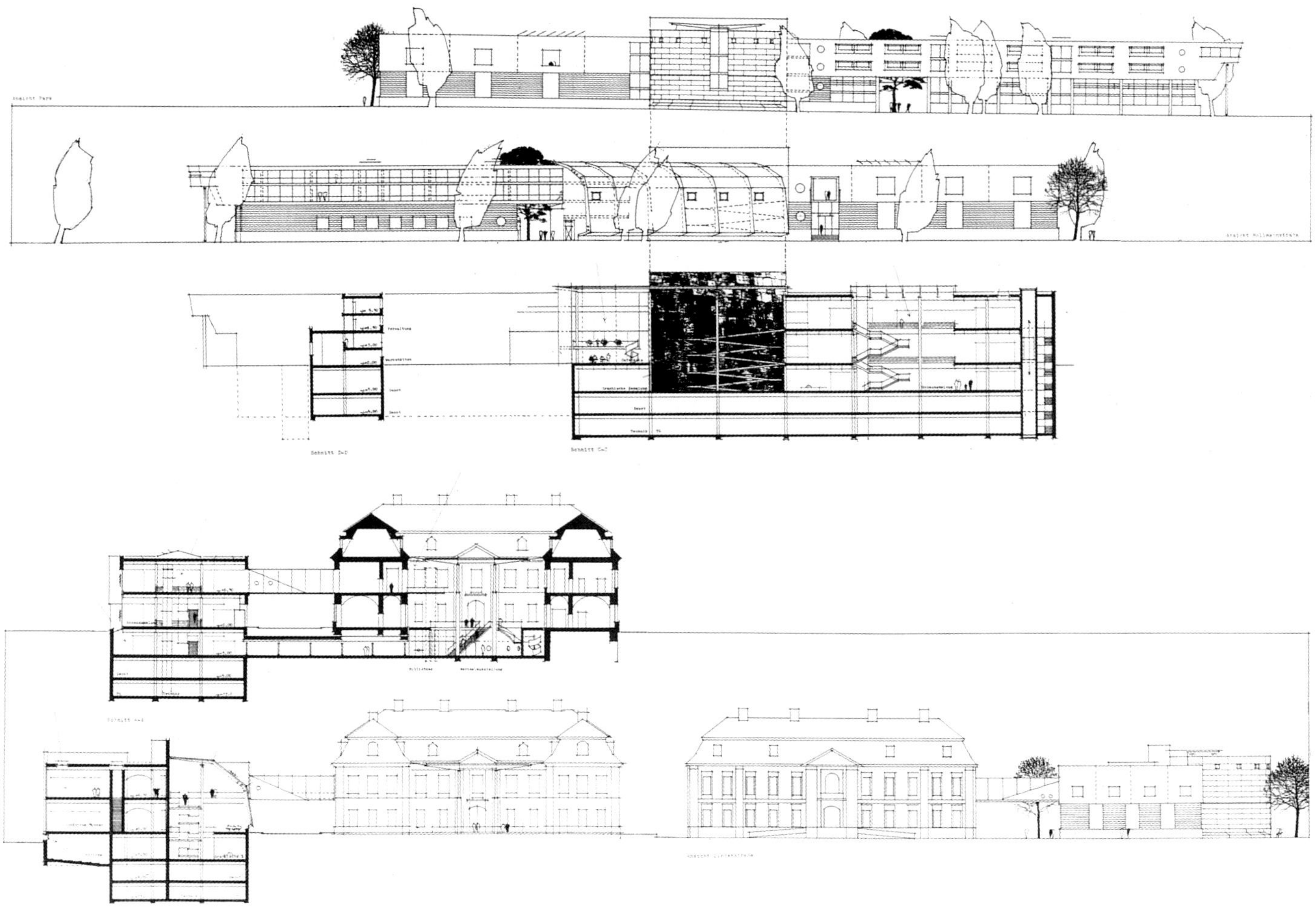

Lange-Ulrich & Partner competition design, 1989, from top: park elevation, Hollmanstrasse elevation, east-west section (north side), north-south section (indicating the connection with the existing facility), north-south section (east side), third prize

Thomas Langenfeld, Markus Torge
competition design, 1989, model, fourth prize

Thomas Langenfeld, Markus Torge
competition design, 1989, first floor plan, fourth prize

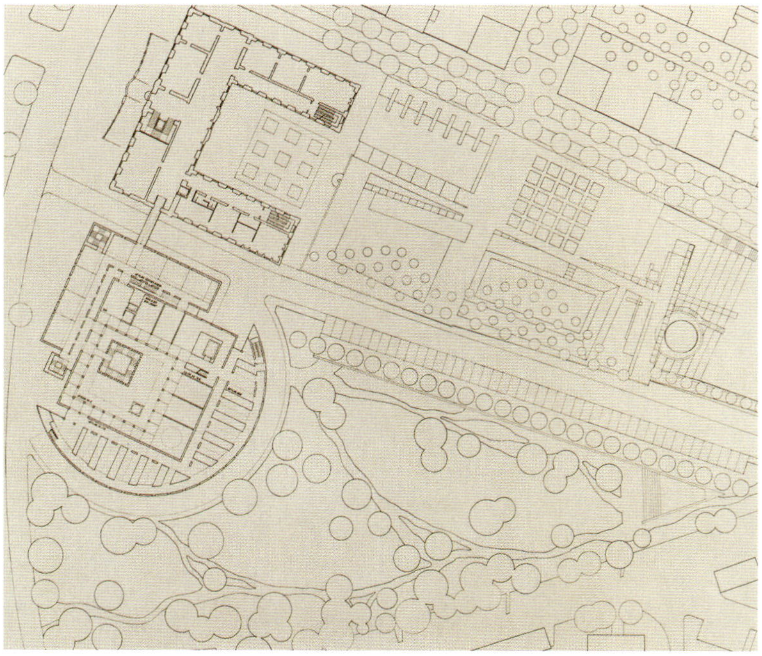

Axel Schultes (BJSS) competition design, 1989, model, fifth prize

Axel Schultes (BJSS) competition design, 1989, sectional model, fifth prize

Axel Schultes (BJSS) competition design, 1989, ground floor plan, fifth prize

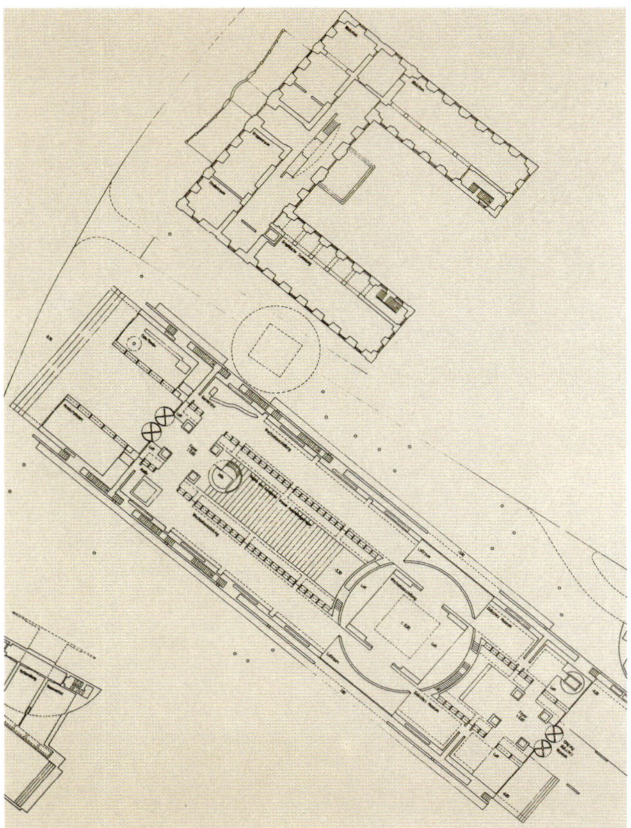

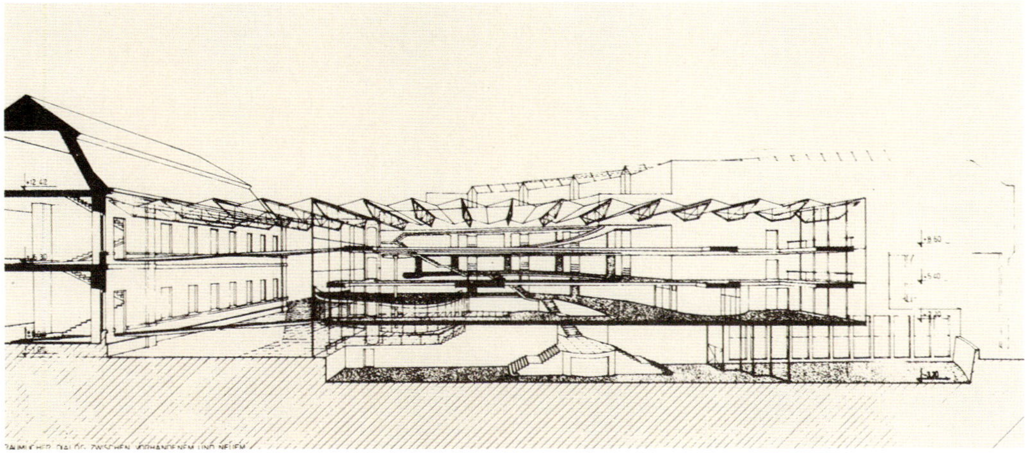

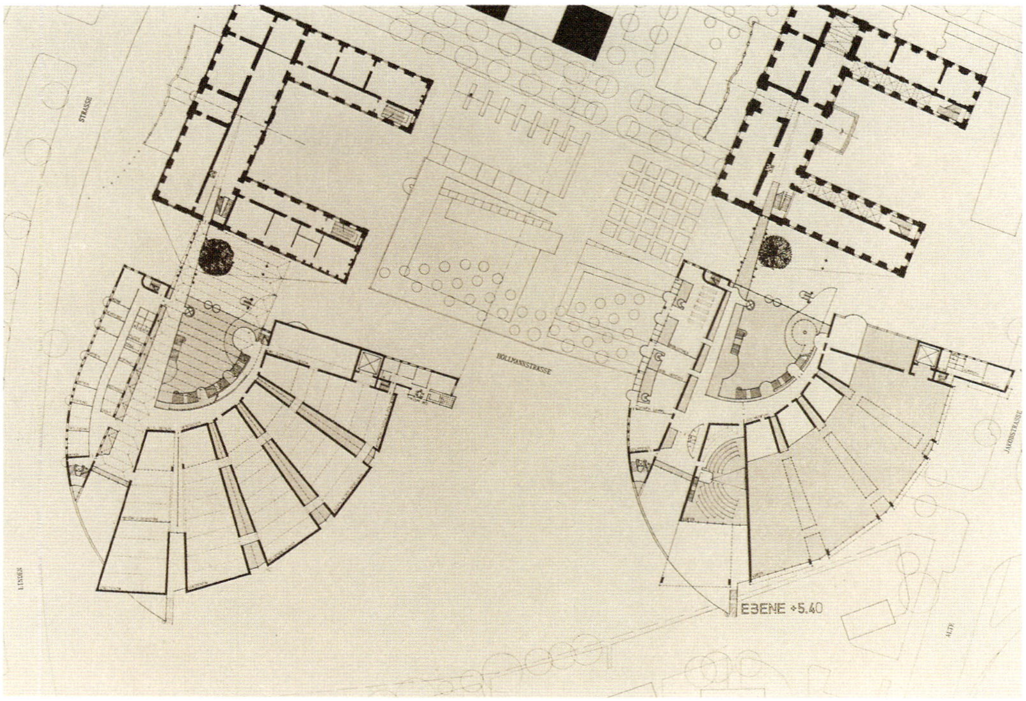

Harald Graff competition design, 1989, sectional view, purchased

Harald Graff competition design, 1989, left: +8.60 level plan, right: +5.40 level plan, purchased

Harald Graff competition design, 1989, model, purchased

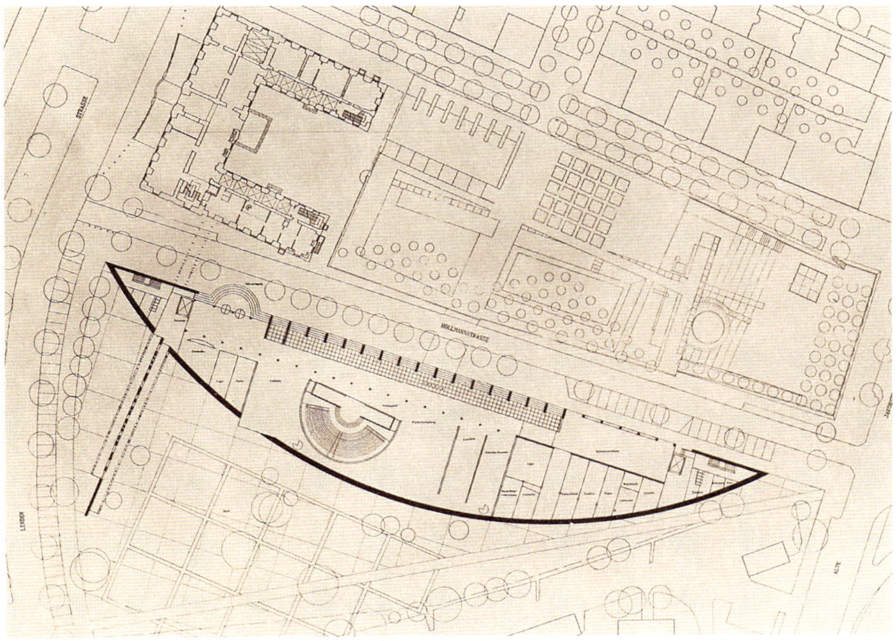

Gerd Dirichlet competition design, 1989, model, purchased

Gerd Dirichlet competition design, 1989, south-west elevation, Hollmannstrasse elevation, purchased

Gerd Dirichlet competition design, 1989, ground floor plan, purchased

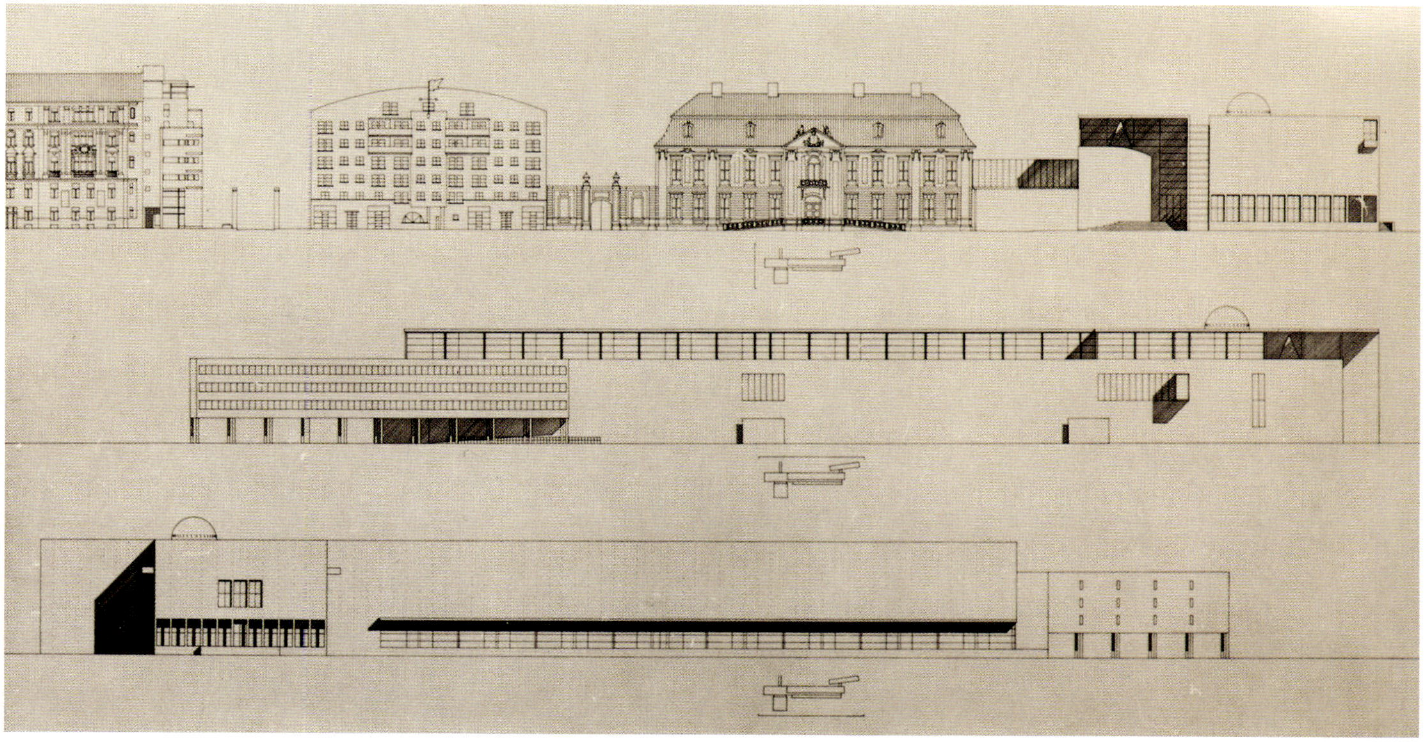

Ernst Klein competition design, 1989, from top: Lindenstrasse elevation, Hollmannstrasse elevation, park elevation, purchased

Ernst Klein competition design, 1989, model, purchased

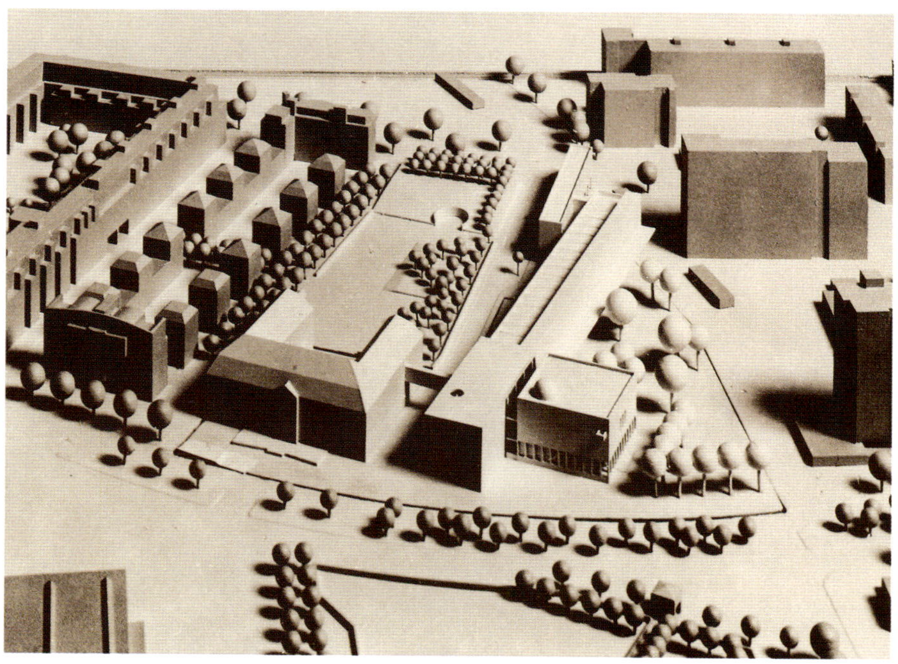

Gisela Glass & Robert Niess
competition design, 1989, from top:
north-south section (east side),
east-west section (north side),
east-west section (south side),
south-west section, ground floor
plan, purchased

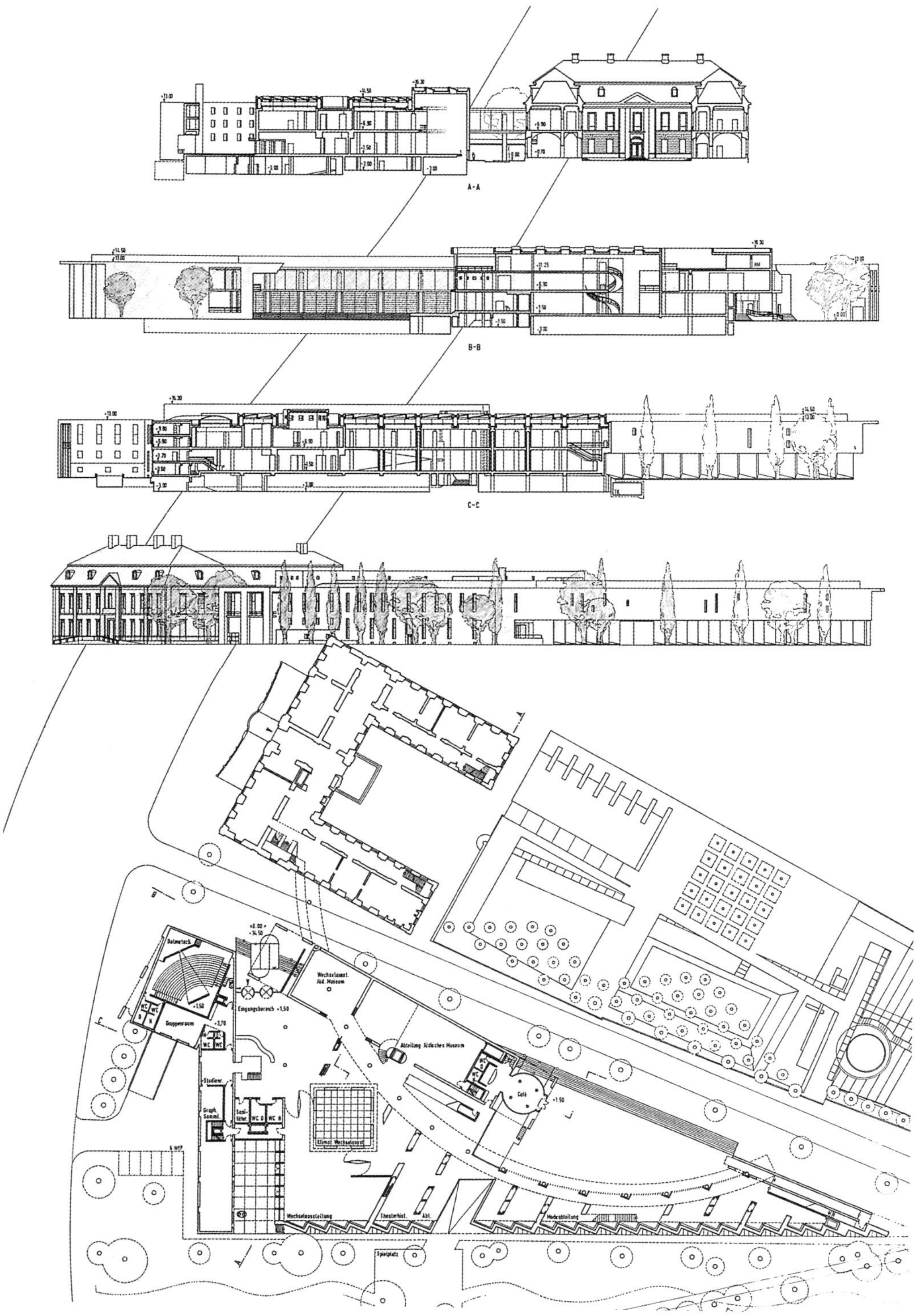

Project

Passenger terminal for an international airport

Site

Man-made island in the south-eastern part of the Bay of Osaka

Dates

First round announced 15 April 1988 *Closing date* 25 May 1988 *Second round nominations* 6 June 1988 *Closing date* 10 November 1988 *Result announced* 9 December 1988

Number of entries

First round 48 *Second round* 15

Jury

Yoshio Takeuchi (chairman, director Kansai International Airport Co. Ltd.), Kisho Kurokawa, Arata Isozaki, Helmut Jahn, Richard Rogers (architects), Kiyoshi Kawasaki (University of Kyoto), Toru Akiyama, Souichi Nishimura

Result

Renzo Piano Building Workshop Paris (Renzo Piano & Noriaki Okabe)

Advisors

Ove Arup & Partners (Peter Rice & Tom Barker)

Commissioned by

Kansai International Airport Co. Ltd.

Construction

Construction of island 1987; construction of terminal 1991–1994

Architect

Renzo Piano Building Workshop Japan K.K., Ove Arup & Partners (advisors), Aéroports de Paris (Paul Andreu), Nikken Sekkei Ltd., Japan Airport Consultants Inc.

Kansai Airport, Osaka, 1988

Renzo Piano Building Workshop Paris competition design, 1988, from top: section of the terminal building, air side elevation of the terminal building, air side elevation, land side elevation, first prize

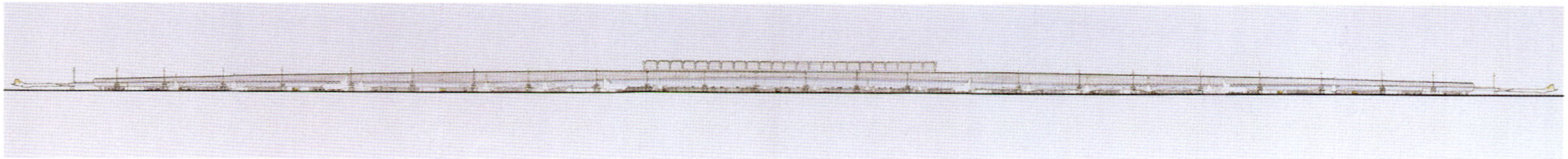

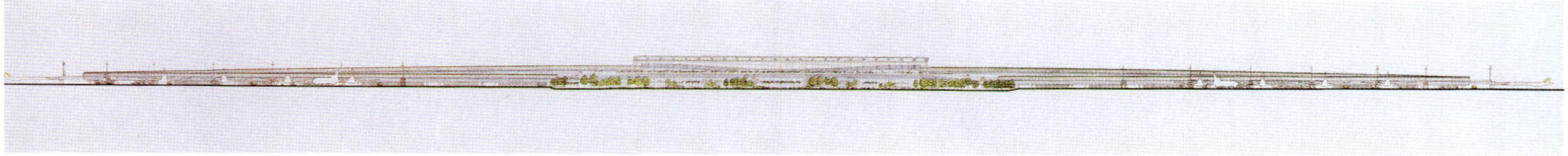

Kansai Airport, Osaka

The main aim of early, pre-war airports and stations was to make travelling more comfortable. Initially, therefore, the buildings were designed to serve this purpose, and airports and stations were travellers' palaces. In later years – particularly during the 1970s – the transport of cargo became more important, and airports increasingly became places where passengers were helped onto and off the planes as efficiently as possible. In recent years, however, the tide has turned.

Small cities

Airports are undergoing rapid development. There has been a constant increase in cargo and passenger transport over the years, which has led to the construction of new airports and the extension and modernisation of existing ones. As a result, modern airports often resemble small cities, and face similar organisational problems. Architects do not merely design a passenger terminal, but take the entire airport into account. A specific type of design is required, which not only ensures the unimpeded flow of passengers and cargo, but which also gives an airport a unique and recognisable character, distinguishing it from other airports.

Oswald Mathias Ungers, a participant in the Kansai Airport competition, has contemplated the airport issue and has openly voiced doubts as to whether it is still possible to express contemporary life stylistically in a world where communication and transport are of paramount importance. One of the main stumbling blocks that he has encountered is the apparent infinity of airports. Furthermore, Ungers has argued that the nineteenth-century railway station approach does not meet modern requirements, and he is equally critical of anonymous, efficiency-oriented buildings, which are the same all the world over, and which give no clues to the traveller as to where he has landed.

As gateways to the cities and the sky, airports have a representative, symbolic function. However, they also have a key function in urban infrastructure, and it is this dual purpose which poses a problem for architects. On the one hand, an airport requires extensive planning and a systematic layout of the necessary facilities; on the other, architects must take into account the airport's style and aesthetic qualities. In recent years, architects have shown that this problem is not insurmountable.

Due to the nature of airports, the most suitable style would seem to be one which reveals the structural and technological features of the architecture. In recent years, the aviation sector has become increasingly competitive, a fact which has led to the construction of a number of new airports, allowing us to gain greater insight into the changing nature of airport architecture. Prime examples include Stansted Airport near London, designed by Norman Foster, and the projected Aeropuerto Sodika in Bilbao, designed by Santiago Calatrava. Many other renowned architects have also had the opportunity to upgrade airports as junctions in urban infrastructure and as rendezvous points for passengers. Aldo Rossi was commissioned to restructure the Milan airport, Linate, and José Rafael Moneo upgraded the San Pablo airport in Seville. Other interesting projects were undertaken by Richard Rogers (extension of the airport in Marseille), Ricardo Bofill (extension of Barcelona airport), Benthem and Crouwel (Schiphol Amsterdam) and Helmut Jahn, who designed the United Airlines Terminal for the world's largest airport (O'Hare, Chicago). And, last but certainly not least, Paul Andreu (Aéroports de Paris), who was involved in the development of Kansai Airport and Roissy-Charles de Gaulle outside Paris.

A man-made island

The airport at Osaka, in Kansai province, was in need of extension. Kansai is an extremely prosperous province and the most densely

Scene of examination

populated region in Japan, after Tokyo. The old Itami airport was situated in a built-up area, which made further expansion impossible. Moreover, night flying was prohibited, so as not to disturb local residents, and public transport link-ups were so inadequate that a trip to Tokyo was faster by train than by plane!

In the early 1980s, when the first plans for expansion were developed, it was decided that a man-made island would by constructed in the Bay of Osaka, five kilometres off the coast. The island would be easily accessible and noise would be kept to a minimum, allowing the airport to stay open day and night. Kansai airport would be Japan's largest and most important airport; a gateway to the world, with 12 million foreign passengers and 13 million domestic passengers passing through it every year[1].

A remarkable comparison may be made between the airport island and the Dutch trading-post Deshima, a man-made island constructed off the coast of Japan in 1635, which facilitated an early cultural exchange between Japan and the West. Kansai airport enhances Japan's accessibility in a similar manner.

Osaka was well aware of the fact that careful planning was required for such a prestigious project. A striking terminal building was needed in order to give foreign passengers a positive first impression of the country upon arriving at the airport, and a competition to select a suitable architect was consequently organised in 1988. The competition guidelines were based on preliminary designs which Paul Andreu had submitted at the request of the Kansai International Airport Company. Andreu and several Japanese firms had already spent two years developing a layout for the airport as a whole.

The open international competition was held over two rounds. Fifteen architects were selected during the first round and were allowed to develop their plans for the second round. A number of architectural heavy-weights had seats on the jury: Kisho Kurokawa, Arata Isozaki, Richard Rogers and the airport expert Helmut Jahn. A number of renowned architects were amongst the finalists: Ricardo Bofill, Oswald Mathias Ungers, Cesar Pelli, Jean Nouvel, Bernard Tschumi and Norman Foster. Almost all of the finalists, both Japanese and European, had developed their plans in collaboration with large construction companies. In the end, Renzo Piano's faith in his own company paid off: he was commissioned for the project. His main opponents in the final round were Foster, Tschumi and Pelli.

Sandwich

At the time of the competition the island existed only on paper. Naturally, the architects had been informed that they would have to take into account an elongated site, measuring 511 hectares. The shape and orientation of the island had also been roughly specified. In addition, the architects had to bear in mind the "sandwich" concept conceived by Andreu. Initially, Andreu had projected separate terminals for domestic and international flights, but this made the incorporation of the train station problematic. Consequently, he

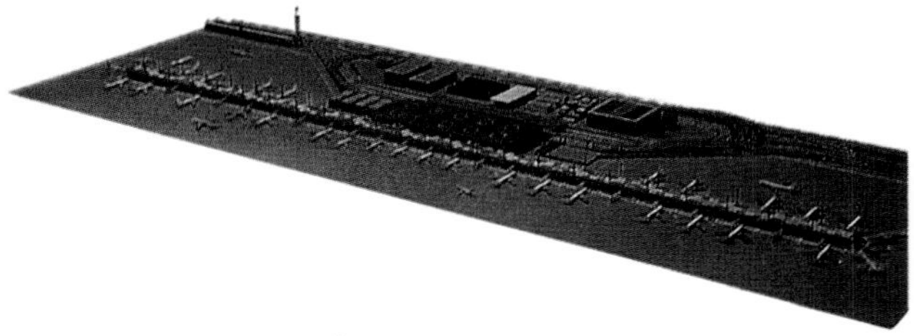

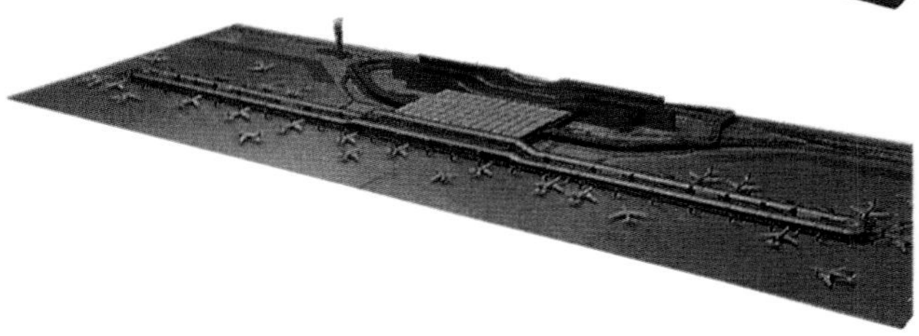

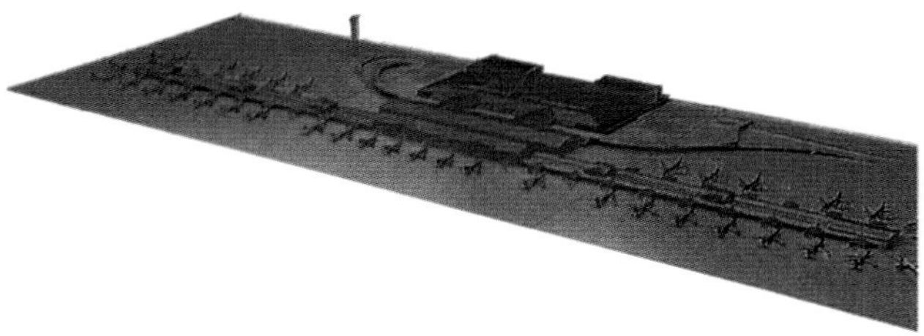

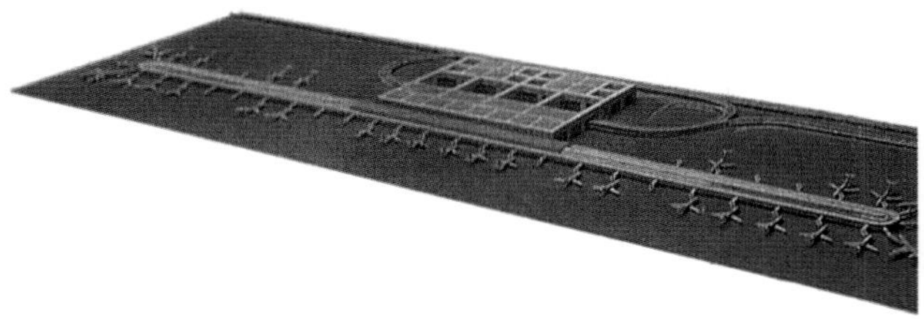

Ricardo Bofill (Taller de Arquitectura) & NACO competition design, 1988, model

Jean Nouvel et Associés SARL competition design, 1988, model

Kijyoshi Seike (Design system) & JD Architekten BDA competition design, 1988, model

Oswald Mathias Ungers competition design, 1988, model

decided to "sandwich" the domestic terminal between the floors for international arrivals and departures.

Piano's terminal is 1.7 kilometres long. It features a centrally-situated main building, attached to a long, straight wing. The departure hall is situated in the main building. It is a glass structure, 28 metres in width, which has plenty of foliage. The lifts, escalators and footbridges are clearly visible. The shape of the terminal's roof takes into account the flow of rising air, allowing for natural ventilation. Nature and technology go hand in hand in Piano's design. The lush foliage and natural ventilation, in combination with high-tech structures, represented a new step forward for airport architecture.

A green zone

According to the jury, the most appealing aspect of Piano's design was his attention to the areas surrounding the buildings and the runways. Piano's terminal stood in the middle of a green zone, which covered almost half of the island and extended into the building itself. Many of the island's fifteen thousand trees were planted in the terminal. Passengers entering the building see the trees from below. Those departing look over the treetops at the noses of the waiting planes. This landscaping concept was also part of Andreu's plan.

Considering the extent of Andreu's contribution, it is a pity that he was not asked to submit a definitive design and that a competition was organised instead. To make matters worse, Andreu was not completely satisfied with the execution of his master plan, although he was extremely pleased with the shape of the roof; a feature which had also appealed to the jury. Piano had designed the undulating roof together with Peter Rice of the engineering firm Ove Arup. The striking shape of the roofs of the main building and the wing distinguish Piano's design from those of the other contenders.

Cesar Pelli's design did not deviate much from Andreu's master plan, but Norman Foster was more inventive. His main building was situated off-centre. The roofs of the main building and the wing consisted of uniform elements. The Kajima Corporation ignored the master plan and designed a triangular terminal building, flanked by two parallel, free-standing wings. Regrettably, none of the designs gives travellers arriving at Kansai Airport any indication that they have set foot in a completely different part of the world.

---

1 *For purposes of comparison (passengers per year): Narita (Tokyo) – 15 million, O'Hare (Chicago) – 60 million, Frankfurt – 25 million (in the near future), Roissy-Charles de Gaulle (Paris) – 43 million after expansion.*

Kansai International Airport, Osaka

Die ersten Vorkriegsflughäfen sollten – genau wie die großen Bahnhöfe jener Zeit – den Reisenden größtmöglichen Komfort bieten. Die Architektur war diesem Ziel unterworfen: Flughäfen und Bahnhöfe sollten »Paläste für den Reisenden« sein. In den 70er Jahren konzentrierte sich die Bahn zunehmend auf den Güterfernverkehr. Der Flughafen entwickelte sich zu einer Durchgangsstation des Reisenden auf dem Weg zwischen Ankunft und Abflug. Erst in den letzten Jahren zeichnete sich ein neues Verständnis von der Funktion des Flughafenterminals ab.

Kleinstädte

Flughäfen erleben zur Zeit einen enormen Aufschwung: Da sowohl der Personen- als auch der Luftfrachtverkehr immer mehr zunimmt, entstehen neue Airports und bereits bestehende werden erweitert und modernisiert. Sie entwickeln sich zu kleinen, isolierten Städten – samt den dazugehörigen Problemen. Ein Architekt muß sich bei seinem Entwurf für einen Flughafen nicht nur mit dem Terminal, sondern mit dem gesamten Flughafengelände auseinandersetzen. Dazu gehört ein Baustil, der nicht ausschließlich auf einen möglichst reibungslosen Durchfluß der Verkehrsströme ausgerichtet ist. Dem Reisenden soll auch das Gefühl vermittelt werden, daß sich dieser Flugplatz von anderen unterscheidet. Oswald Mathias Ungers, der an der Ausschreibung für den Kansai Airport teilnahm, stellte in aller Öffentlichkeit die Frage, ob es möglich sei das Gefühl einer Zeit, in der Kommunikation und Transport von zentraler Bedeutung sind, mit Hilfe von Architektur auszudrükken. Vor allem die scheinbare Unendlichkeit eines Flughafens erschien ihm dabei als unüberwindliches Hindernis. Nach Ungers Meinung eignen sich weder die Bahnhöfe des 19. Jahrhunderts als Terminalgebäude noch die anonymen Bauten, denen man überall auf der Welt begegnet und die dem Reisenden keinen Hinweis darauf geben, in welchem Land er sich gerade befindet. Als Tor zur Stadt oder Zugang zum Luftraum besitzt ein Flughafen eine repräsentative und symbolische Funktion und bildet gleichzeitig einen Knotenpunkt der Infrastruktur. Dieser Zwiespalt stellt die Architekten vor eine schwierige Aufgabe. Trotzdem gelang es ihnen in den letzten Jahren, auch für dieses Problem Lösungen anzubieten.
Aus der Natur der Sache drängt sich ein Stil auf, der die Technik in den Vordergrund stellt. In den letzten Jahren wurden – auch aus Konkurrenzerwägungen – eine ganze Reihe von Flughäfen neu konzipiert, so daß sich der Betrachter heute ein genaues Bild von den Entwicklungen in der Flughafenarchitektur machen kann. Gute Beispiele sind u.a. der von Norman Foster entworfene Stansted Airport bei London und der geplante Bau des von Santiago Calatrava konzipierten Aeropuerto Scdika bei Bilbao. Aber auch andere bekannten Architekten erhielten die Chance, Flughäfen als Begegnungsstätte und Knotenpunkt für Reisende baulich aufzuwerten. So war Aldo Rossi verantwortlich für die Umbaupläne des Flugplatzes Linate bei Mailand, während José Rafael Moneo den Flughafen San Pablo bei Sevilla entwarf. Weitere phantasievolle Umsetzungen entstanden nach Entwürfen von Richard Rogers (Erweiterung Marseille), Ricardo Bofill (Erweiterung Barcelona), Benthem und Crouwel (Schiphol, Amsterdam) und von Helmut Jahn, der neben dem United Airlines Terminal auf dem Chicagoer O'Hare International Airport – dem größten Flughafen der Welt – eine Anzahl weiterer Flughäfen konzipierte. Außerdem darf in dieser Reihe Paul Andreu nicht fehlen, der an den Flughäfen Kansai Airport bei Osaka und Roissy-Charles de Gaulle bei Paris mitgearbeitet hat.

Eine künstliche Insel

Auch der Flughafen von Osaka benötigte dringend einen Ausbau. Die Region Kansai ist nach Tokio das am dichtesten bevölkerte Gebiet Japans und wirtschaftlich von großer Bedeutung. Der alte Flughafen Itami, der inmitten eines dichtbebauten Areals lag, konnte nicht parallel mit der schnellen Entwicklung der Stadt Osaka vergrößert werden. Auch waren von Itami aus Nachtflüge verboten, da sie eine unerträgliche Belastung der Anwohner bedeutet hätten. Dazu kam eine ausgesprochen schlechte Verkehrsanbindung, so daß man schneller mit dem Zug als mit dem Flugzeug nach Tokio reisen konnte.
Aus diesen Gründen plante die Stadt bereits zu Beginn der 80er Jahre eine Erweiterung des Flughafens auf einer künstlichen Insel, die fünf Kilometer vor der Küste in der Bucht von Osaka angelegt werden sollte. Auf diese Weise wollte man einen leicht erreichbaren Flugplatz schaffen, der 24 Stunden am Tag angeflogen werden konnte, die Stadt aber nur mit einem Minimum an Fluglärm belasten würde. Der Airport von Kansai sollte sich zu einem der größten und bedeutendsten Flughäfen Japans entwickeln, einem Tor zum Rest der Welt, mit einer jährlichen Besucherzahl von 12 Millionen inländischen und 13 Millionen ausländischen Fluggästen[1].
Diese Konzeption weist eine verblüffende Ähnlichkeit mit dem Bau des ersten holländischen Handelspostens in Japan auf: Auch Dessima entstand 1635 auf einer künstlichen Insel und bot beiden Kulturkreisen, dem westlichen wie dem japanischen, die Möglichkeit zur gegenseitigen Kontaktaufnahme. Auf ähnliche Weise erleichtert auch Kansai Airport den Zugang zum japanischen Mutterland.
Ein so prestigeträchtiges Projekt mußte mit der nötigen Sorgfalt angegangen werden: Schon bei ihrer Ankunft sollten die Besucher aus Übersee einen positiven Eindruck gewinnen. 1988 wurde ein Wettbewerb für das Abfertigungsgebäude ausgeschrieben. Als Richtlinien für die Teilnehmer galten einige Vorskizzen, die Paul Andreu auf Einladung der Kansai International Airport Company angefertigt hatte. Der Flugplatz selbst war zu dieser Zeit schon seit zwei Jahren im Bau, teilweise unter Federführung einiger japanischer Firmen, teilweise unter Leitung von Andreu.
Der Wettbewerb fand in zwei Ausschreibungsrunden statt: Nach der ersten, international offenen Runde sollten 15 Architekten ausgewählt werden, die ihre Pläne weiter ausarbeiten durften. In der für die Auswahl zuständigen Jury befanden sich Koryphäen wie Kisho Kurokawa, Arata Isozaki, Richard Rogers und Helmut Jahn. Zu den Auserwählten der zweiten Runde gehörten Ricardo Bofill, Oswald Mathias Ungers, Cesar Pelli, Jean Nouvel, Bernard Tschumi und Norman Foster. Die meisten der 15 eingeladenen Architekten arbeiteten ihre Beiträge in Zusammenarbeit mit großen Baufirmen aus Japan und Europa aus. Renzo Piano dagegen vertraute auf das Können seines eigenen Büros – und hatte Erfolg, denn er erhielt den Auftrag. Zuvor hatte er sich jedoch zusammen mit Foster, Tschumi und Pelli einer letzten Ausscheidungsrunde stellen müssen.

Sandwich

Zur Zeit der Ausschreibung existierte die künstliche Insel vor der Küste noch nicht, doch die Architekten kannten deren Ausmaße und wußten, daß sie von einem länglichen Baugelände von 511 Hektar Größe ausgehen konnten. Desweiteren mußten sie sich mit dem von Andreu erdachten »Sandwich«-Konzept auseinandersetzen: Ursprünglich hatte Andreu zwei getrennte Terminals für in- bzw. ausländische Flüge geplant, was zu Schwierigkeiten mit der Integration der Bahnstation führte. Daher legte er die Abfertigungshalle für Inlandflüge zwischen die Ebenen mit den Ankunfts- bzw. Abflughallen für Auslandsflüge.
Die Gesamtlänge des Terminals beträgt 1,7 Kilometer, wobei sich der Komplex in ein zentral gelegenes Hauptgebäude und einen langen, geraden Seitenflügel unterteilt. Im Hauptgebäude befinden sich die Abflughalle, ein 28 Meter breites Treibhaus mit Grünpflanzen sowie die deutlich sichtbaren Transportkanäle (Lifte, Rolltreppen und Laufbrücken). Die Dachform des Terminals wird bestimmt durch die Bewegung der aufsteigenden Luft: Auf diese Weise entsteht eine natürliche Ventilation. Natur und Technik bilden eine Einheit. Diese Kombination von viel Grün, natürlicher Ventilation und High-Tech-Bauten markiert einen neuen Abschnitt in der Entwicklung der Flughafenarchitektur.

Eine grüne Zone

Pianos Entwurf überzeugte die Mitglieder der Jury wegen der durchdachten Konzeption der Räume rund um die Gebäude und Landebahnen. Das Terminal sollte mitten in einer grünen Zone entstehen, die ungefähr die Hälfte der Insel einnahm und bis in das Gebäude selbst vordrang: Der ankommende Reisende blickt auf die Bäume, der abfliegende Passagier schaut über Baumkronen hinweg auf die Cockpits der bereitstehenden Maschinen. Dieses Gartenkonzept stammte ursprünglich ebenfalls von Andreu. Umso bedauerlicher ist daher, daß auf einen Wettbewerb nicht verzichtet und nicht Andreu selbst mit der Ausarbeitung seiner Pläne beauftragt wurde. Verständlicherweise sagte ihm die endgültige Ausführung seiner Ideen nicht zu, allerdings lobte er – wie zuvor schon die Jury – die gelungene Dachkonstruktion. Dieses wellenförmige Dach hatte Piano in Zusammenarbeit mit Peter Rice und dem Ingenieurbüro von Ove Arup entwickelt. Seine besondere Formgebung, die sowohl auf dem Hauptgebäude als auch auf dem Flügel erkennbar ist, zeichnet Pianos Entwurf aus.
Während Cesar Pellis Konzeption genau den Plänen Andreus folgt, beweist Norman Foster mit seiner exzentrischen Plazierung des Hauptgebäudes mehr eigenen Gestaltungswillen. Die Dächer seines Hauptgebäudes und des Flügels bestehen aus Standardelementen. Kajima Corporation ließ Andreus Vorstellungen außer acht und stellte ein dreieckiges Terminalgebäude mit zwei freistehenden parallelen Seitenflügeln vor.

1 *Zum Vergleich: Narita 15 Millionen, Chigago O'Hare 60 Millionen, Frankfurt am Main 25 Millionen, Roissy-Charles de Gaulle nach dem Ausbau 43 Millionen Fluggäste.*

L'Aéroport de Kansai, Osaka

La principale fonction des premiers aéroports et des gares de jadis était de rendre le voyage plus plaisant pour les passagers. A partir des années 70, le transport de fret devenant de plus en plus important, les aéroports évoluèrent vers un simple fonctionnel: charger et décharger au plus vite les avions de leurs passagers. Il semble que depuis peu, la tendance se soit à nouveau inversée.

Comme une petite ville

Le transport aérien connaît un développement rapide. L'augmentation constante du trafic, tant des passagers que du fret pousse à la construction de nouveaux aéroports et à la modernisation des anciens. Les aéroports modernes sont pratiquement devenus des petites villes d'une extraordinaire complexité.
Les architectes ne se contentent plus de concevoir une aérogare mais prennent en charge l'ensemble de l'aéroport. La conception doit prendre en compte de multiples données techniques tout en donnant au bâtiment un caractère distinctif, si possible reflet du pays ou de la ville qu'il dessert.
Oswald Mathias Ungers, participant au concours pour l'aéroport de Kansai, a manifesté ses doutes sur la possibilité d'exprimer stylistiquement la modernité dans un monde où la communication et le transport sont devenus d'importance primordiale. L'un de ses blocages tient au nombre apparemment infini d'aéroports. Il critique l'approche de la gare du XIXème siècle qui ne répond pas aux attentes actuelles, de même que les bâtiments anonymes et purement fonctionnels qui se ressemblent tous et ne laissent aucune chance au voyageur de savoir dans quel pays il se trouve.
Portes des villes et du ciel, les aéroports exercent une fonction symbolique de représentation tout en jouant un rôle majeur dans les infrastructures urbaines. Cette dualité explique les difficultés que rencontrent les architectes. D'un côté, l'aéroport est un «objet» technologique extrêmement complexe, de l'autre il doit présenter des qualités esthétiques distinctives. Ce problème n'est pas insurmontable comme l'ont prouvé de nombreuses réalisations récentes.
Le développement du trafic aérien a entraîné une évolution architecturale rapide. Le style high tech semblerait a priori convenir à la nature des aérogares comme en témoignent Stansted, près de Londres, conçu par Norman Foster et Sodika, à Bilbao, dessiné par Santiago Calatrava.
Aldo Rossi est intervenu sur l'aéroport de Milan, Linate, et José Rafael Moneo a modernisé celui de San Pablo, à Séville. D'autres projets significatifs ont été signés par Richard Rogers (agrandissement de l'aéroport de Marseille), Ricardo Bofill (Barcelone), Benthem et Crouwel (Schiphol, Amsterdam) et Helmut Jahn qui a réalisé le United Airlines Terminal au plus grand aéroport du monde, O'Hare, à Chicago. Enfin, Paul Andreu (Aéroports de Paris) a conçu les nouvelles aérogares de Roissy-Charles de Gaulle et a travaillé sur l'aéroport de Kansai.

Une île artificielle

L'aéroport d'Osaka, dans la province de Kansai, était devenu insuffisant. Cette province très prospère est la région la plus peuplée du Japon après celle de Tokyo. L'ancien aéroport d'Itami était situé dans une zone habitée qui rendait son extension impossible. Par ailleurs, les vols de nuit y étaient interdits afin de ne pas gêner les riverains, et les transports terrestres étaient si mal organisés qu'un voyage à Tokyo durait moins longtemps[1] en train qu'en avion.
Au début des années 80, lorsque les premiers plans d'agrandissement furent mis au point, il fut décidé de construire une île artificielle facilement accessible dans la baie d'Osaka, à cinq kilomètres de la côte. Les nuisances sonores seraient ainsi réduites au minimum pour permettre de faire fonctionner l'aéroport nuit et jour. L'aéroport de Kansai deviendrait le plus important aéroport du Japon et accueillerait chaque année 12 millions de passagers étrangers et 13 millions de nationaux[2]. Une comparaison peut être tracée entre cette île-aéroport et le comptoir hollandais de Deshima qui était déjà une île artificielle construite en face de la côte japonaise en 1635 et qui favorisa les premiers contacts entre le Japon et l'Occident.
La ville d'Osaka était consciente de la difficulté d'un projet aussi ambitieux. Elle souhaitait un terminal spectaculaire pour donner aux passagers une image positive du pays dans lequel ils arrivaient. En 1988, elle organisa un concours pour sélectionner un architecte. A la demande de la Kansai International Airport Company, un programme avait déjà été établi par Paul Andreu et plusieurs entreprises japonaises spécialisées qui avaient passé deux ans à définir l'ensemble du projet.
Le concours ouvert et international se déroula en deux phases. Quinze concurrents furent sélectionnés au premier tour et invités à mettre au point leurs plans pour le second tour. De grands architectes figuraient au jury dont Kisho Kurokawa, Arata Isozaki, Richard Rogers et Helmut Jahn. Plusieurs participants connus restèrent en lice pour le second tour: Ricardo Bofill, Oswald Mathias Ungers, Cesar Pelli, Jean Nouvel, Bernard Tschumi et Norman Foster. Presque tous les finalistes avaient travaillé en liaison avec de grandes entreprises de travaux publics. En final, Renzo Piano remporta l'adjudication devant Foster, Tschumi et Pelli.

Sandwich

Lors du concours, l'île artificielle n'existait toujours que sur le papier mais, bien entendu, les architectes disposaient des plans précis de ses futurs 511 hectares. Ils devaient tenir compte du concept de «sandwich» conçu par Andreu. Celui-ci avait prévu initialement des terminaux séparés pour les vols internationaux et nationaux, ce qui rendait difficile l'intégration de la gare de chemin de fer. Il décida alors de placer le terminal national en sandwich entre les niveaux des arrivées et des départs internationaux.
Le terminal de Piano mesure 1,7 km de long. Il est composé d'un bâtiment principal central auquel se rattache une longue aile droite. Le hall des départs est situé dans le bâtiment principal et consiste en une halle de verre de 28 m de large emplie de végétation. Les ascenseurs, escaliers roulants et passerelles sont tous apparents. La forme du toit tient compte des flux d'air pour assurer une ventilation naturelle. La nature et la technologie se trouvent ainsi étroitement associées dans ce projet qui marque une étape de l'histoire des aérogares.

Un zone verte

Selon le jury, l'aspect le plus séduisant du projet Piano était l'attention qu'il portait aux zones entourant les bâtiments et les pistes. Son terminal s'élèvera dans une zone verte qui couvrira pratiquement la moitié de l'île et jouxtera le bâtiment. 15 000 arbres sont prévus dont un grand nombre dans le terminal lui-même. Les passagers débarquant verront les arbres par en dessous et ceux qui partent les domineront. Ce rôle de l'aménagement paysager était déjà évoqué dans le plan d'Andreu.
L'importance de la contribution d'Andreu fait regretter qu'il n'ait pas eu l'opportunité de prendre en charge la totalité du projet et qu'un concours ait été organisé. Pire encore, Andreu ne fut pas entièrement satisfait de l'exécution de son plan de masse, même s'il apprécia la forme du toit qui avait séduit le jury. Piano avait dessiné une couverture ondulée en collaboration avec Peter Rice, de la société d'ingénierie Ove Arup. Ce toit et la grande aile distinguaient radicalement le projet de Piano de ceux de ses concurrents.
Cesar Pelli s'en tint au plan de masse de Andreu, mais Norman Foster se montra plus inventif. Son bâtiment principal était décentré et ses toits ainsi que ceux des ailes étaient réalisés dans des éléments identiques. La Kajima Corporation ignora le plan de masse et créa un terminal triangulaire flanqué de deux ailes indépendantes parallèles. Aucun de ces projets ne donnait aux voyageurs arrivant à Kansai, la moindre indication sur la partie du monde où ils venaient d'atterrir.

1 *L'aéroport de Naritra, à Tokyo, est également fermé la nuit.*
2 *Narita accueille 15 millions de passagers, O'Hare, 60 millions, Francfort, 25 millions dans un proche futur, Roissy-Charles de Gaulle, 43 millions après agrandissement.*

Renzo Piano Building Workshop Paris competition design, 1988, from top: landscape, bird's-eye view, second floor plan (international departures), first floor plan (domestic arrivals and departures), first prize

Renzo Piano Building Workshop Paris competition design, 1988, detailed structural section of the terminal building, first prize

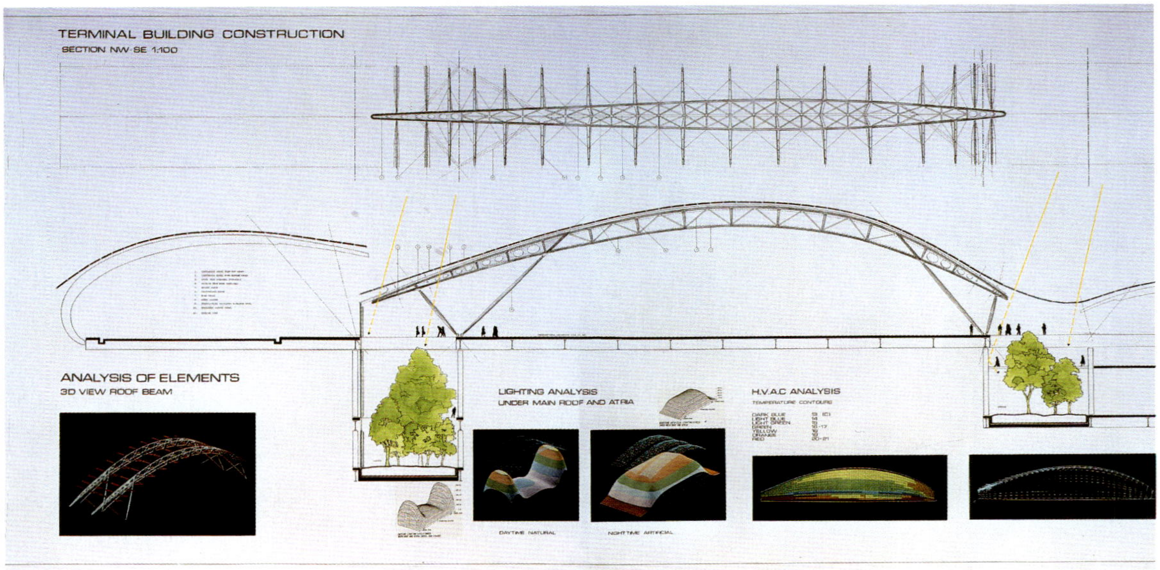

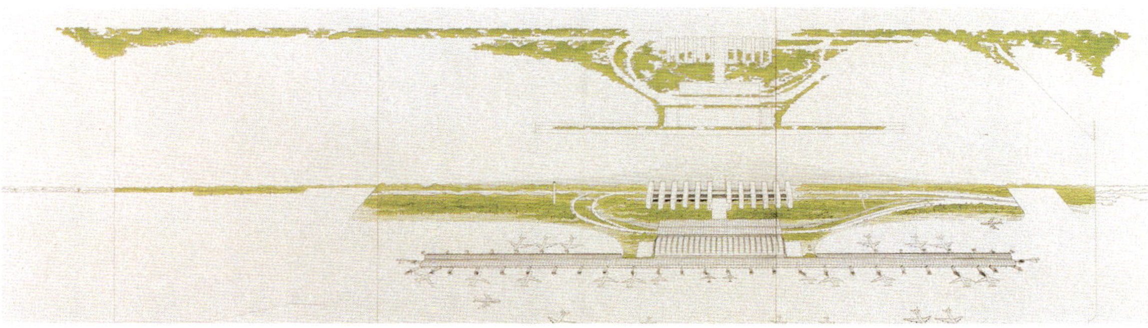

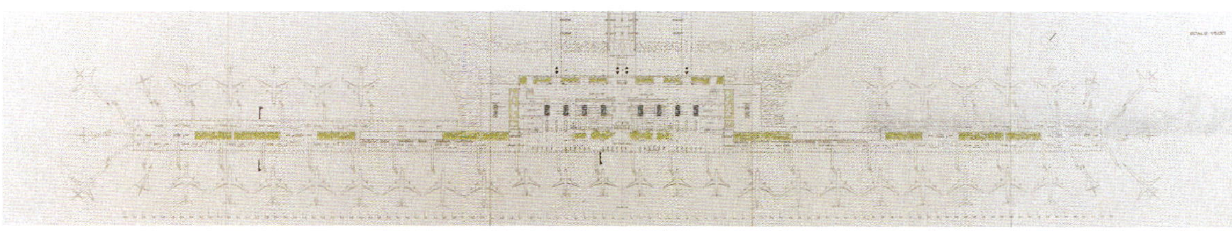

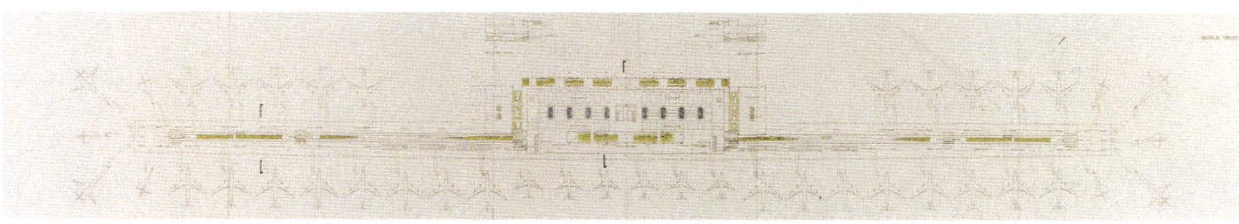

Renzo Piano Building Workshop
Paris competition design, 1988, interior view of the international departure lobby, first prize

Renzo Piano Building Workshop
Paris competition design, 1988, interior view of the wing gate lounge, first prize

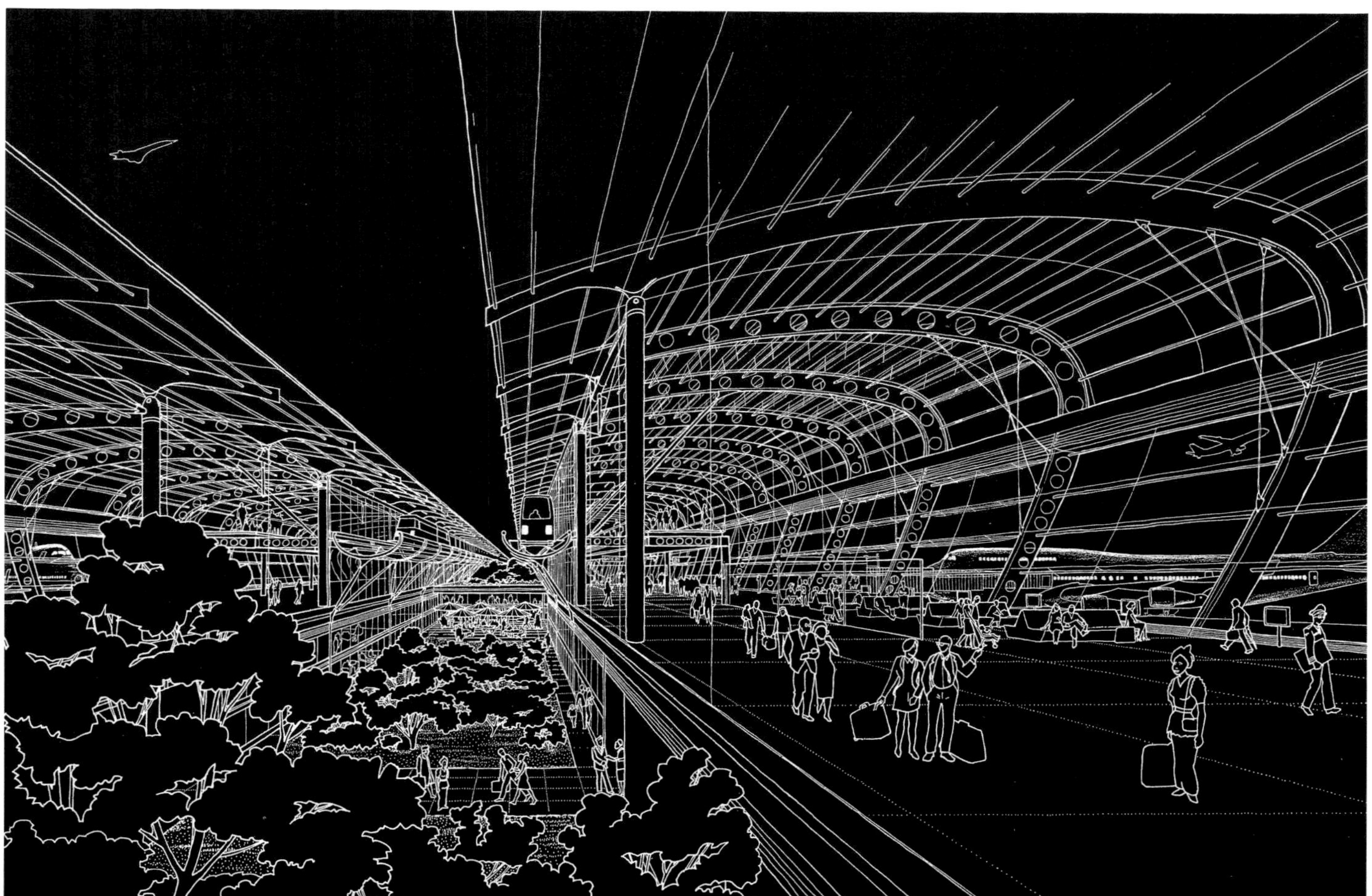

Foster Associates & Obayashi Corporation competition design, 1988, model

Foster Associates & Obayashi Corporation competition design, 1988, model

Foster Associates & Obayashi Corporation competition design, 1988, interior view of the terminal building

Foster Associates & Obayashi Corporation competition design, 1988, bird's-eye view

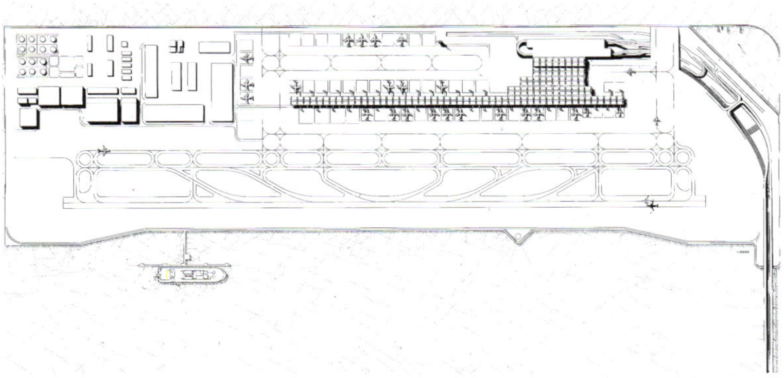

Cesar Pelli & Associates, Takenaka Corporation competition design, 1988, model

Cesar Pelli & Associates, Takenaka Corporation competition design, 1988, exterior view

Cesar Pelli & Associates, Takenaka Corporation competition design, 1988, model

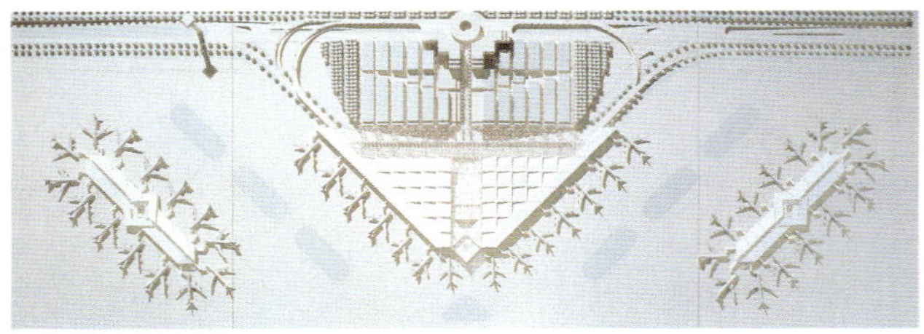

Kajima Corporation, Hellmuth, Obata & Kassabaum Inc. competition design, 1988, model

Kajima Corporation, Hellmuth, Obata & Kassabaum Inc. competition design, 1988, from top: model, elevation, ground floor plan, model

Bernard Tschumi competition design, 1988, models

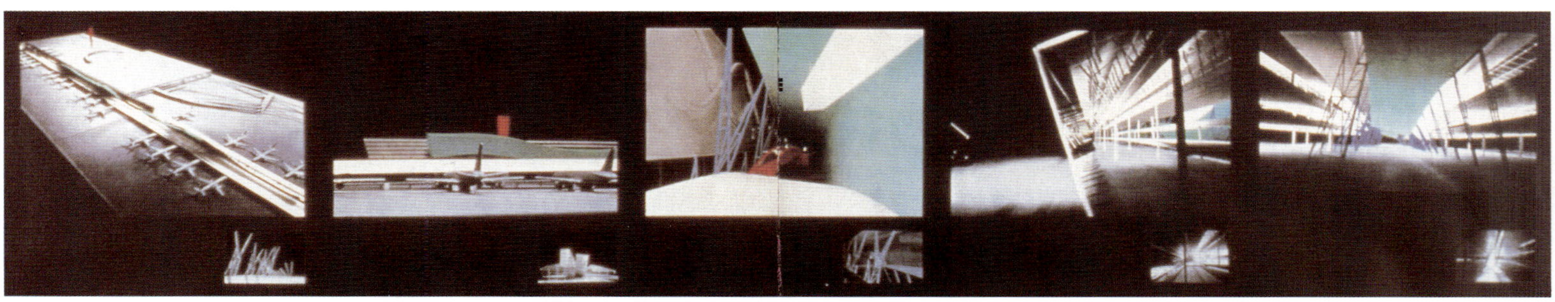

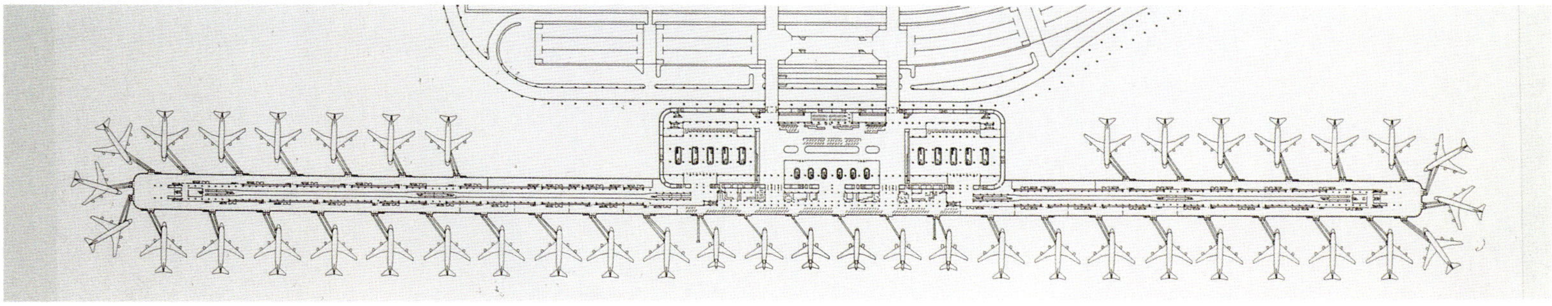

Kiyonori Kikutake & Associates
competition design, 1988, model

Kiyonori Kikutake & Associates
competition design, 1988, first floor plan

Kiyonori Kikutake & Associates
competition design, 1988, model

Project

Centre for Japanese Culture

Site

Between Rue de la Fédération and the Quai Branly, Paris

Dates

Competition announced June 1989 *Closing date* between 24 January and 5 February 1990 *Result announced* 16 March 1990

Number of entries

First round 453

Jury

Robert S. Ingersoll (chairman, USA), Tadao Ando (Japan), Paul Andreu (France), Mario Botta (Switzerland), Fumihiko Maki (Japan), Roland Simounet (France), Alvaro Siza (Portugal), André Larquié (France), Yoshihiro Nakayama (Japan), Bernard Rocher (France), Shuji Takashina (Japan)

Result

First prize Masayuki Yamanaka, Kenneth Armstrong & Jennifer Smith et al *Second prize* Ryoji Suzuki (Hitoshi Kamimura, Toyohiko Yamabe, Hisao Matuura et al) *Third prize* Yoshito Takahashi *Honourable mention* Jean-Paul Deschamps; Hirokazu Kono; Toyo Ito (Takeo Higashi, Masashi Sogabe, Makoto Yokomizo, Nagisa Kidozaki, Hirono Koike et al); Tomohisa Yuri; Riken Yamamoto (Ryo Higashi, Takahiro Tanabe, Andrew Gutteridge, Tomoyuki Suzuki, Yoshifumi Kojima, J. Delafield Cook et al); Bernard Saillol; Katsuhiro Kobayashi (Kobayashi Studio, Tokyo Metropolitan University); Thierry Nguyên-Giac, François Gillard, Michel Hubault & Denis Loesel; Jean-Philippe Vassal; Hiroyuki Sakamoto (Norio Kita, Toru Kajisa, Masayosi Tanabe et al); Kazuyo Sejima (Toshiaki Ishida et al); Tomohito Okudaira; Hiroyasu Sakaguchi; Eric Chazelle, Henri Raynaud, Mounir Soubai & Jean-Pierre Vidal; Mikio Kobayashi *Special mention* Shiro Matsushima; Shin Takamatsu (Jean Michel Wilmotte); Regis Masson, Patrick Charoin & Christian Chopin; Toru Sakata; Takahiko Yanagisawa; Dominique O. Coulon; Pierre Guerin & Hector Pedroza; Daniel Hermet; Nobuaki Furuya

Commissioned by

Les Comités de Parrainage de la Maison de la Culture du Japon à Paris

Construction

June 1994 –

Centre for Japanese Culture, Paris, 1989–1990

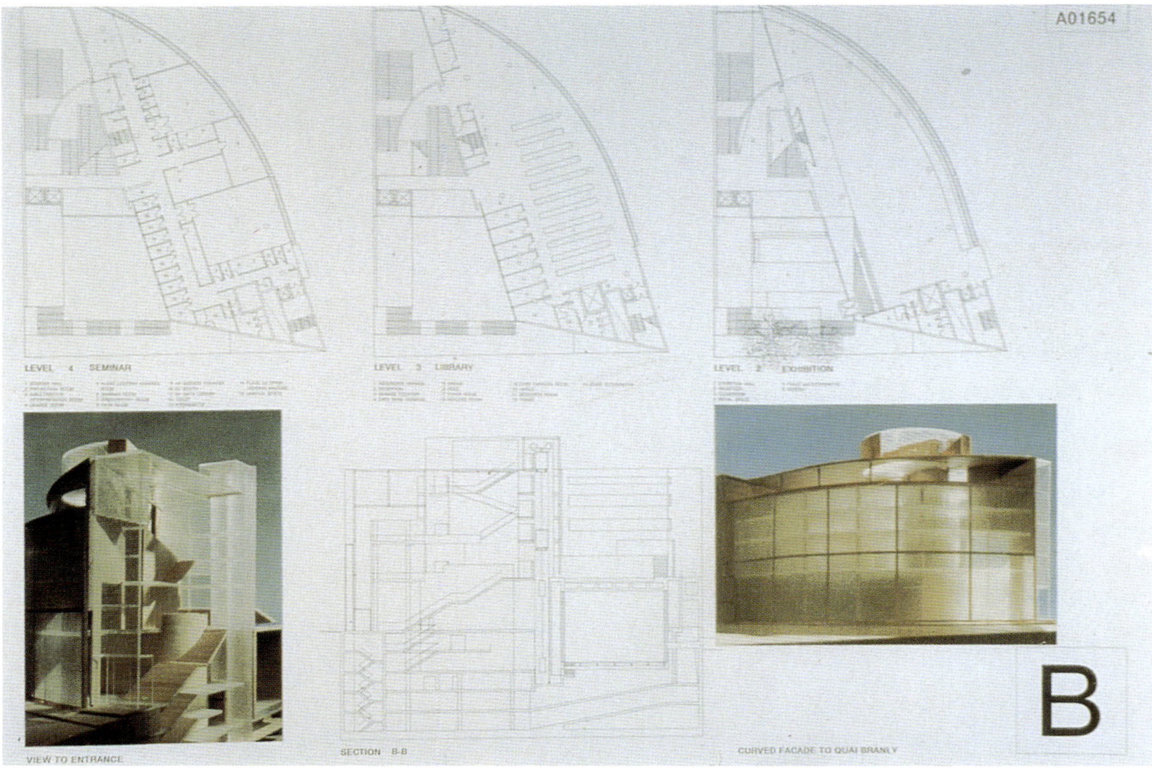

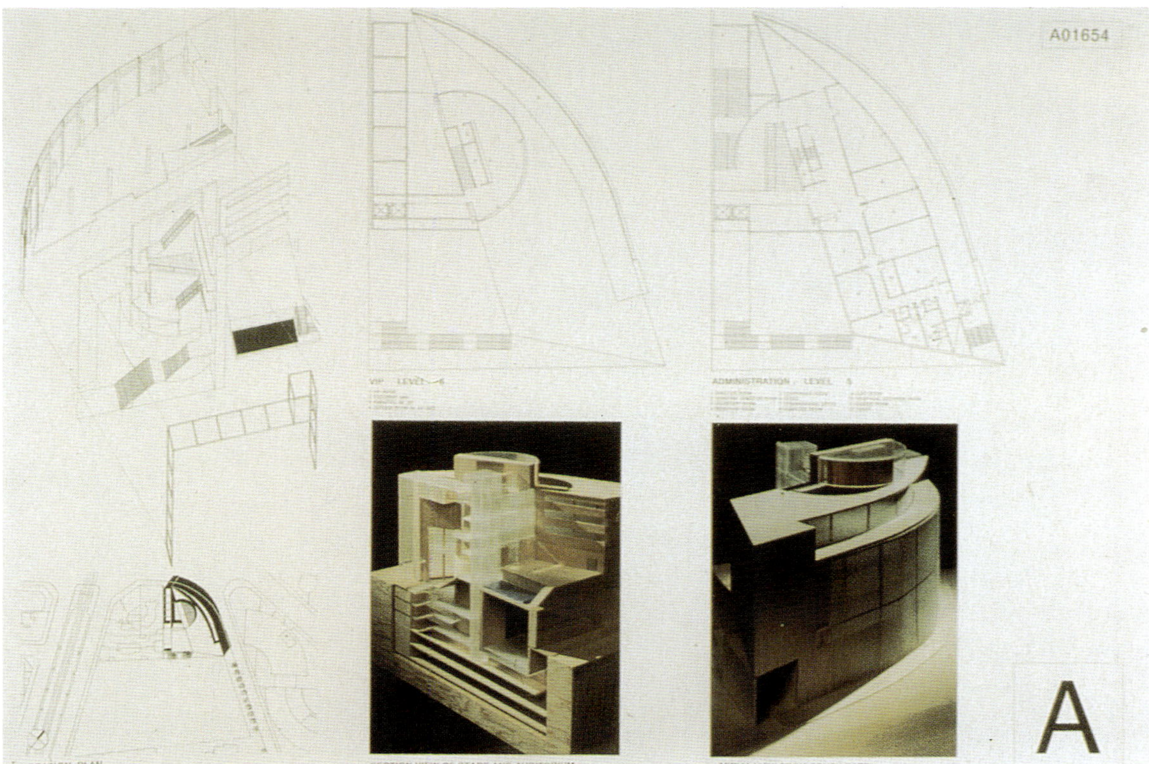

Masayuki Yamanaka, Kenneth Armstrong & Jennifer Smith competition design, 1989, above from left: third floor plan, first floor plan, below from left: sectional model, sectional model, first prize

Masayuki Yamanaka, Kenneth Armstrong & Jennifer Smith competition design, 1989, above from left: fifth floor plan, fourth floor plan, below from left: site plan, sectional model, model, first prize

Centre for Japanese Culture, Paris

Although Japan and France have always maintained close cultural ties, the French capital had lacked a centre for Japanese culture since the Second World War. This cultural deficiency was an embarrassment to the French government, and was heightened by the fact that a series of bilateral cultural institutes had opened in Tokyo during the 1960s.

Mutual interest

For the past three centuries, France has nurtured a latent interest in Japanese culture which has occasionally revealed itself in brief periods of Japanmania. Conversely, during the nineteenth century, the Japanese developed an affinity for French art. This affinity does not appear to have diminished over the years, as indicated by the lengths to which Japanese investors will go to purchase Impressionist masterpieces. However, in spite of this mutual interest in one another's art, the Maison du Japon, which was established in Paris before the Second World War, did little more than provide temporary accommodation for Japanese exchange students.

Although a number of Parisian museums, including the Musée Guimet (est. 1879), held Japanese art in their collections, other aspects of Japanese culture did not receive the attention they deserved. French people who wanted to get a taste of Japanese culture thus had to travel to Japan or to Berlin, which boasted a German-Japanese Cultural Centre. Naturally, this was a blow to French pride, a blow made all the more painful by the fact that institutes such as the Athénée Français and the Institut Franco-Japonais in Tokyo were exporting French culture to Japan. The French business community, intent on protecting Franco-Japanese trade interests, saw their lobbying rewarded in April 1982, when Mitterrand and Suzuki, president and prime minister, agreed to establish institutes for cultural exchange.

A forgotten competition

Seven years after the agreement was signed, competitions for the institutes were held in France and Japan.

The response was overwhelming. More than 1900 architects registered for the competition, 453 of whom eventually submitted designs for the Centre for Japanese Culture. In principle, it was an open, national competition, but the architects had be registered in either France or Japan, which meant that most of the participants hailed from these two countries. Only a handful of renowned architects participated. It is a well-known fact that major international architectural firms, with branches all over the world, are not usually keen to participate in open competitions which attract entries from hundreds of relatively unknown architects.

The French authorities provided a site a mere stone's throw from the Eiffel Tower: a triangular plot in the 15th arrondissement, overlooking the Bir Hakeim Bridge on the Seine. The organisation was in the hands of a specially appointed body, Les Comités Officiels de Parrainage de la Maison de la Culture du Japon à Paris. The committee decided that the

Takamasa Yoshizaka Athénée Français, 1962

centre would be multi-functional: it would not only house a collection of Japanese art, but would also shed light on other aspects of Japanese culture. It was to have exhibition and study areas, a library and auditoria. In short, the new complex would present Japanese culture in the broadest possible sense of the word.

This broad approach met with the particular and emphatic approval of the Japanese business community, who promptly provided a chairman for the organising committee: Gaishi Hiraiwa. The jury appointed by the committee included a number of world-famous architects, such as Tadao Ando, Paul Andreu, Mario Botta and Alvaro Siza. Undoubtedly, the organisers had hoped to boost the prestige of the competition in this way and, judging by the number of entries, the committee's ploy was a success. However, the international press were a lot less enthusiastic. Their coverage of the competition was minimal and the result was doomed to be forgotten; undeservedly so, because many of the entries were outstanding.

The first three prizes were won by Japanese architects. This is an indication of the verve with which Japanese architects have stormed the European and American architectural markets. Their dynamism, in turn, is due to the fact that Japanese architecture is booming. In Japan, hiring an architect, buying expensive materials and paying attention to architectural detail are relatively inexpensive when compared with the country's astronomical property prices. This contrasts sharply with the West, where the architectural aspects of a project are usually the hardest hit by construction cutbacks. Japanese companies are prepared to spend more than their Western counterparts in order to obtain a better result. These factors have all contributed to the boom in Japanese architecture.

A Japanese victory

After four rounds of adjudication, the jury awarded first prize to Masayuki Yamanaka, a Japanese architect based in London. associated with Jennifer Smith and Kenneth Armstrong. The main feature of Yamanaka's design is the transparent, curved façade on Rue de la Fédération. The curve was inspired by the shape of the site, and most of the other designs also featured a curved façade. In Yamanaka's design the exhibition area, library and auditorium are situated above one another behind the curved façade. The semicircular structure on the roof contains a VIP lounge. A transparent stairway is situated at the corner of the block where the cultural facilities are housed. The main auditorium is situated in the remaining corner of the triangular site. The auditorium, which has a well above it, is partly situated underground. Yamanaka also projected three subterranean levels under the main auditorium.

The runner-up, Ryoji Suzuki, submitted a manifestly Deconstructivist design, featuring cryptic drawings and geographical references, which was partly based on a photograph of one of the Eiffel Tower's framework posts under construction. One of the most remarkable features of his design is the monumental stairway, which is bisected by a colonnade.

Rafael Vinoly **Tokyo International Forum, competition design, 1989**

Rafael Vinoly **Tokyo International Forum, competition design, 1989, site plan**

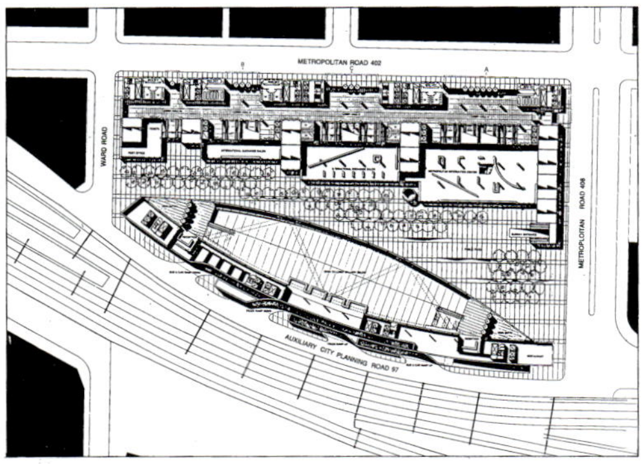

Toyo Ito Centre for Japanese Culture, competition design, 1990, model, honourable mention

There is also an abundance of stairways in Yoshito Takahashi's design, which won third prize. However, in contrast to Suzuki's design, where the stairways seem to invite the public to promenade and visit the cultural centre, Takayashi's stairways lend an almost sacred aura to his design and seem to lead straight to heaven.
Not all of the participants were newcomers. Takahiko Yanagisawa had won the competition for the New National Theatre in Tokyo[1], and Toyo Ito and Shin Takamatsu have gained considerable renown over the years. Masato Kawakami, an architecture critic, once described Takamatsu's work as follows: *"He rejects human warmth and kindness, that which humanists and modern democracies wish to see embodied in architecture. His architecture has an aura of death, ritualism and eroticism"*. Having seen his dark and sombre design for the cultural centre, one can understand the sense of gloom described by Kawakami. Toyo Ito was mentioned briefly in the chapter on the Shonandai Cultural Centre.

Naturally, Japanese architects were not the only participants. A number of French architects received an honourable mention. The team led by Thierry Nguyên-Giac, for example, who submitted one of the few designs which did not follow the curve of Rue de la Fédération. In spite of this original, non-conformist solution, French architects took a back seat in the competition. It is as yet unclear whether this is a result of the boom in Japanese architecture, or a consequence of French architectural exhaustion brought about by the "Grands Projets".

1 *See chapter on the New National Theatre in Tokyo elsewhere in this book.*

Japanisches Kulturzentrum, Paris

Obwohl die kulturellen Beziehungen zwischen Frankreich und Japan von jeher besonders eng waren, existierte in Paris seit dem Zweiten Weltkrieg kein japanisches Kulturinstitut mehr. Dieses Manko wurde in den 60er Jahren umso auffälliger, da zur gleichen Zeit in Tokio zahlreiche neue bilaterale Einrichtungen entstanden.

Gegenseitiges Interesse

Das französische Interesse an der japanische Kultur war in den letzten drei Jahrhunderten zumindest unterschwellig stets vorhanden; dies zeigt die in unregelmäßigen Abständen wiederkehrende Begeisterung für alles Japanische, die in Frankreich Modewellen auslöste. Umgekehrt entwickelten die Japaner ab dem 19. Jahrhundert eine besondere Vorliebe für die französische Kunst, die bis heute anhält – man denke nur an die Preise, die Japaner für Werke französischer Impressionisten zu zahlen bereit sind.

Während die Pariser die japanische Kunst in verschiedenen Museen und Sammlungen ihrer Stadt kennenlernen konnten – wie etwa dem 1879 gegründeten Musée Guimet – waren andere Bereiche der japanischen Kultur in Frankreich völlig unterrepräsentiert. Zu diesem Zweck mußten die Franzosen ins Mutterland selbst oder nach Berlin zum Deutsch-Japanischen Kulturzentrum reisen. Dieser Zustand wurde als unbefriedigend empfunden, zumal die französische Kultur in Tokio durch Einrichtungen wie das Athénée Français und das Institut Franco-Japonais hervorragend vertreten war. Auf zunehmenden Druck seitens der Industrie – Japan und Frankreich sind bedeutende Handelspartner – unterzeichneten die Präsidenten beider Länder, François Mitterrand und Zenko Suzuki, im April 1982 ein Abkommen, das die Gründung von Einrichtungen für einen regelmäßigen Kulturaustausch vorsah.

Eine vergessene Ausschreibung

Zu diesem Zweck schrieb man sieben Jahre später sowohl in Japan wie in Frankreich Architekturwettbewerbe aus. Die Reaktionen waren überwältigend: An der Ausschreibung zum Japanischen Kulturzentrum beteiligten sich 1918 Teilnehmer, von denen 453 einen Entwurf einreichten. Im Prinzip handelte es sich um eine offene internationale Ausschreibung, doch die Teilnehmer mußten entweder in Frankreich oder in Japan registriert sein, so daß sich hauptsächlich Architekten aus diesen beiden Ländern am Wettbewerb beteiligten.

Das vom französischen Staat zur Verfügung gestellte Baugelände – ein dreieckiges Grundstück im 15. Arrondissement mit direktem Ausblick auf die Seinebrücke Bir Hakeim – lag nur einen Steinwurf vom Eiffelturm entfernt. Die Durchführung des Wettbewerbs wurde speziell zu diesem Zweck ins Leben gerufenen Kommissionen übertragen: Les Comités Officiels de Pairainage de la Maison de la Culture du Japon à Paris. Die Vorgaben für die Teilnehmer fielen relativ umfangreich aus: Außer der japanischen Kunst sollten im neuen Kulturzentrum auch alle anderen Teilbereiche der japanischen Gesellschaft zur Geltung kommen. Aus diesem Grunde waren für den neuen Komplex Ausstellungs- und Studienräume, eine Bibliothek und Vortragssäle vorgesehen, damit der Besucher die japanische Kultur in einem breiteren Kontext kennenlernen konnte.

Diese Erweiterung der ursprünglichen Intention stieß auf breite Zustimmung der japanischen Geschäftswelt, die den Vorsitzenden des Organisationskomitees stellte: Gaishi Hiraiwa. In der vom Komitee eingeladenen Jury saßen eine Reihe international bekannter Architekten wie Tadao Ando, Paul Andreu, Mario Botta und Alvaro Siza, deren Beteiligung dem Wettbewerb die nötige öffentliche Aufmerksamkeit sicherte. Allerdings fielen die Reaktionen der internationalen Presse äußerst zurückhaltend aus. Folge: Die Ergebnisse des Wettbewerbs gerieten in Vergessenheit, obwohl viele Einsendungen von hoher Qualität waren.

Die ersten drei Preise gingen an japanische Teilnehmer – eine Tatsache, die bezeichnend ist für den Eifer, mit dem sich japanische Architekten auf die europäische und amerikanische Bauwelt stürzten. Eine solche Entwicklung läßt sich zum Teil auch aus der ungeahnten Blüte der japanischen Architektur dieser Zeit erklären: Durch die enorm gestiegenen Grundstückspreise waren zwar die Baukosten hoch, aber die Kosten für den Architekten und für teure Baumaterialien vergleichsweise gering. Zudem gaben japanische Investoren gern etwas mehr Geld aus, wenn die Architektur ihrer Gebäude interessant und ungewöhnlich ausfiel.

Ein japanischer Sieg

Der Entwurf von Masayuki Yamanaka, eines in London lebenden japanischen Architekten, wurde nach vier Ausschreibungsrunden zum Sieger erklärt. Das beherrschende Merkmal seines Bauwerks ist die gebogene, transparente Fassade an der Rue de la Fédération. Dabei wird der Schwung der Fassade durch die Form des Grundstücks vorgegeben – einer Form, der auch einige andere Entwürfe folgten. Durch die Fassade sind übereinander angeordnet die Ausstellungsräume, die Bibliothek und der Vortragssaal zu erkennen. Auf das Dach des Baukörpers setzte Yamanaka einen halbrunden Aufbau mit Räumlichkeiten für Gäste. An der Spitze dieses Blocks, der die kulturellen Funktionen des Zentrums beherbergt, befindet sich das durchsichtige Treppenhaus. Die übrige freie Fläche füllte Yamanaka mit einem halb unterirdisch angelegten großen Saal; den Raum ließ er bewußt leer. Unter dem großen Saal sollten noch drei weitere Tiefgeschosse entstehen.

Ryoji Suzuki, Gewinner des zweiten Preises, gab sich in seinem Beitrag voller kryptischer Zeichnungen und geografischer Bezüge als überzeugter Dekonstruktivist. Ein Foto, das einen der vier im Bau befindlichen Pfeiler des Eiffelturms zeigt, diente als Ausgangspunkt des Entwurfs. Suzukis Projekt wird von einer monumentalen Kolonnade beherrscht, durch deren Mitte die Eingangstreppe führt. Treppen finden sich auch in Takahashis Entwurf, aber während Suzukis Treppen den Passanten zu einem Bummel und einem Besuch des Kulturzentrums einzuladen scheinen, verleihen Takahashis Treppen dem Gebäude einen sakralen Charakter und erwekken den Eindruck, als würden sie in den Himmel führen.

Nicht alle Teilnehmer waren Unbekannte: Hiroyuki Sakamoto und Takahiko Yanagisawa beispielsweise hatten sich auch an der Ausschreibung zum Neuen Nationaltheater in Tokio beteiligt, und zählten ebenso wie Toyo Ito sowie Shin Takamatsu zu den bedeutenden Vertretern japanischer Architektur. Über Takamatsu sagte der japanische Architekturkritiker Masato Kawakami: *»Er verspottet die menschliche Wärme und Freundlichkeit, die den Wünschen moderner Demokratien und humanistischer Philosophen zufolge das Wesen der Architektur ausmachen soll. Seine Architektur zeigt dagegen Tod, Rituale und Erotik«*. Wer Takamatsus düsteren Entwurf für das Kulturzentrum betrachtet, wird sich dieser Meinung anschließen.

Neben den japanischen Architekten beteiligten sich eine Reihe Franzosen am Wettbewerb, von denen einige mit einer ehrenvollen Erwähnung ausgezeichnet wurden. Dazu gehörte das Team von Thierry Nguyên-Giac, das die Biegung der Rue de la Fédération nicht in seinen Entwurf integrierte. Trotz solcher originellen und nonkonformistischen Lösungen spielten die französischen Architekten im Wettbewerb nur eine Nebenrolle. Ob dies am Aufwind der japanischen Architektur lag oder daran, daß die französischen Architekten bei den Ausschreibungen zu den »Grand Projets« ihre Kreativität verbraucht hatten, wird die Zukunft zeigen.

La Maison de la Culture du Japon, Paris

Bien que la France et le Japon entretiennent depuis longtemps des liens culturels assez étroits et que plusieurs instituts culturels bilatéraux aient été ouverts à Tokyo au cours des années 60, la capitale française ne possédait pas, au début des années 80, de centre consacré à la culture japonaise.

Un intérêt réciproque

Depuis trois siècles et par intermittence, la France se passionne pour le Japon au point même de connaître des poussées de nippomanie. Parallèlement, depuis la fin du XIXème siècle, les Japonais éprouvent une affinité pour l'art français qui ne semble pas avoir diminué avec les années, si l'on en juge par les achats de tableaux impressionnistes de leurs investisseurs. Malgré ces facteurs favorables, la Maison du Japon qui existait à Paris avant la Seconde Guerre mondiale n'était guère plus qu'une structure d'accueil pour les étudiants japonais.
Un certain nombre de musées parisiens, dont le Musée Guimet (fondé en 1879) possèdent bien des collections japonaises, mais les autres aspects de la culture de l'empire ne recevaient pas l'attention qu'ils méritent. Les Français intéressés devaient se rendre à Tokyo ou au centre culturel germano-japonais de Berlin. Les autorités françaises virent donc d'un bon œil le projet d'un centre culturel parisien, ne serait-ce que par réciprocité puisque que l'Athénée Français et l'Institut Franco-Japonais de Tokyo se montraient très actifs dans leurs efforts pour faire connaître la culture française. Des hommes d'affaires français et japonais appuyèrent le projet et, en avril 1982, le président Mitterrand et le premier ministre japonais Suzuki annoncèrent conjointement la création d'un centre à Paris.

Un concours vite oublié

Sept années après la signature de cet accord, deux concours furent lancés simultanément en France et au Japon. La réponse des architectes fut enthousiaste. 1900 d'entre eux s'inscrivirent et 453 envoyèrent des projets. Il s'agissait en principe d'un concours ouvert et national mais les candidats devaient être enregistrés soit en France, soit au Japon, ce qui explique que la plupart des participants aient été originaires de ces deux pays. Seuls quelques architectes connus se lancèrent dans la compétition car très souvent les grands cabinets internationaux n'aiment guère participer à des concours qui attirent des architectes relativement obscurs.
La France offrit un terrain triangulaire à quelques centaines de mètres de la Tour Eiffel, tout près du pont de Bir-Hakeim et de la Seine et l'organisation de l'opération fut confiée aux deux Comités Officiels de Parrainage de la Maison de la Culture du Japon à Paris. Ils décidèrent que le centre serait multifonctionnel et présenterait non seulement une collection d'art japonais mais une vision aussi large que possible de la culture japonaise. Il comprendrait des espaces d'exposition et d'étude, une bibliothèque et des auditoriums. Cette approche reçut l'approbation des milieux d'affaires japonais qui proposèrent un président pour le comité d'organisation: Gaishi Hiraiwa. Le jury comptait plusieurs architectes très connus dont Tadao Ando, Paul Andreu, Mario Botta et Alvaro Siza, ce qui augmentait encore le prestige de la compétition. La presse internationale ne manifesta cependant qu'un enthousiasme limité et les résultats furent vite oubliés, malgré la qualité de nombreuses propositions.
Les trois premiers prix furent remportés par des Japonais, bonne indication du dynamisme avec lequel ils tentent de conquérir les marchés architecturaux européens et américains. Cet activisme fait également écho à l'explosion de l'architecture au Japon où prendre un architecte, acheter des matériaux coûteux et apporter un soin extrême aux finitions reste relativement bon marché par rapport aux prix astronomiques des terrains, alors qu'en Occident de très nombreux programmes sont victimes de restrictions budgétaires. Les sociétés japonaises sont disposées à investir davantage que leurs homologues occidentales pour obtenir un meilleur résultat. Ces facteurs expliquent en grande partie l'expansion rapide du marché de l'architecture dans ce pays.

Une victoire japonaise

A l'issue de quatre tours, le jury accorda le premier prix à Masayuki Yamanaka, un Japonais résident à Londres. Sa proposition s'organise essentiellement autour d'une façade courbe et transparente qui suit la forme du terrain sur la rue de la Fédération.
De nombreux participants s'inspirèrent du même principe. L'espace d'exposition, la bibliothèque et l'auditorium sont implantés les uns au-dessus des autres derrière cette façade, flanquée en angle d'un grand escalier transparent. Une structure semi-circulaire sur le toit contient un salon pour les personnalités. Le principal auditorium, en partie souterrain, se termine par une forme en puits et occupe le terrain restant. Trois niveaux souterrains sont aménagés en dessous de cette salle.
Le battu, Ryoji Suzuki, proposa des plans d'esprit déconstructiviste bardés de dessins sybillins et de références géographiques. Ils reposaient en partie sur une photographie d'un pied de la Tour Eiffel en construction. Son escalier monumental coupé par une colonnade était particulièrement intéressant.
Le projet de Yoshito Takahashi se fit également remarquer par ses nombreuses volées d'escaliers et remporta le troisième prix. Alors que les degrés de Suzuki invitaient le public à parcourir le centre, l'escalier de Takahashi dessinait une sorte d'aura sacrée et semblait mener droit au ciel.
Tous les participants n'étaient pas de nouveaux venus. Takahiko Yanagisawa avait déjà remporté le concours du Nouveau Théâtre National de Tokyo[1] et Toyo Ito et Shin Takamatsu se sont fait amplement connaître en Occident depuis. Masato Kawakami, critique d'architecture, décrivit un jour l'œuvre de Takamatsu de la façon suivante: *«Il rejette la chaleur humaine et l'affabilité, que les humanistes et les démocraties contemporaines voudraient voir incarnées dans l'architecture. Son architecture possède une aura de mort, de rituel et d'érotisme.»* Son projet pour Paris ne démentait pas ces propos.
Les Japonais ne furent pas les seuls à participer. Quelques Français reçurent une mention honorable. L'équipe menée par Thierry Nguyên-Giac, par exemple, soumit l'un des rares projets qui ne suivait pas la courbe de la rue de la Fédération. Malgré cette solution originale et non-conformiste, les Français ne firent pas très bonne figure. Il est difficile de dire si c'était la conséquence de la situation florissante de l'architecture au Japon ou d'une certaine fatigue française après les «Grands Projets».

1 *Voir le chapitre sur cette réalisation dans cet ouvrage.*

Ryoji Suzuki competition design, 1989, model (entrance on Rue de la Fédération), second prize

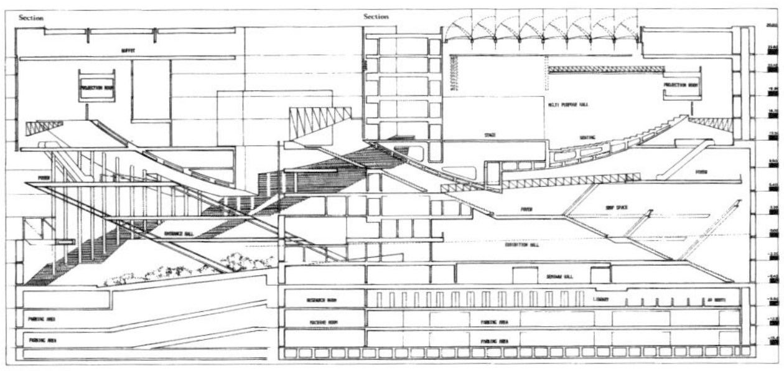

Ryoji Suzuki competition design, 1989, drawing entrance, second prize

Ryoji Suzuki competition design, 1989, left: section (south-west elevation), right: section (north-east elevation), second prize

Line drawn by distance of Paris-Tokyo

Line drawn by Seine = empty space of void

Leg of the Eiffel Tower under construction

Clairière

Multi-purpose hall of open air theatre

Exhibition hall, seminar room and library

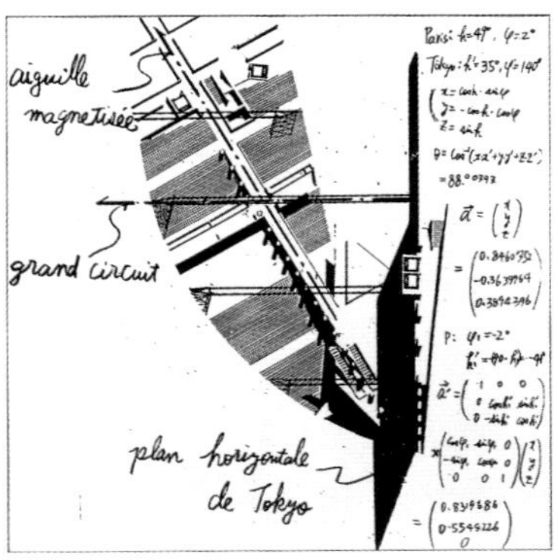

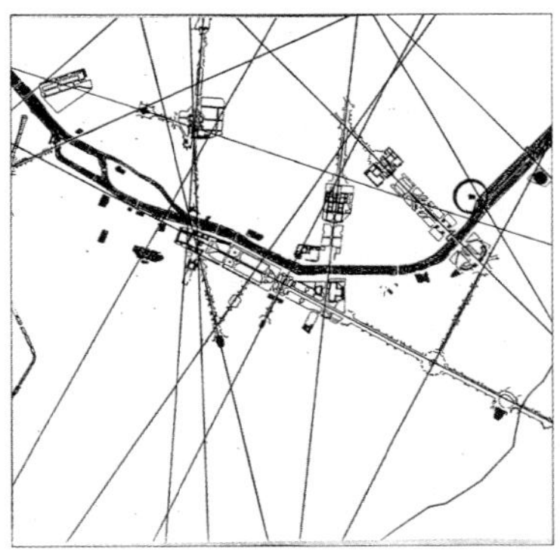

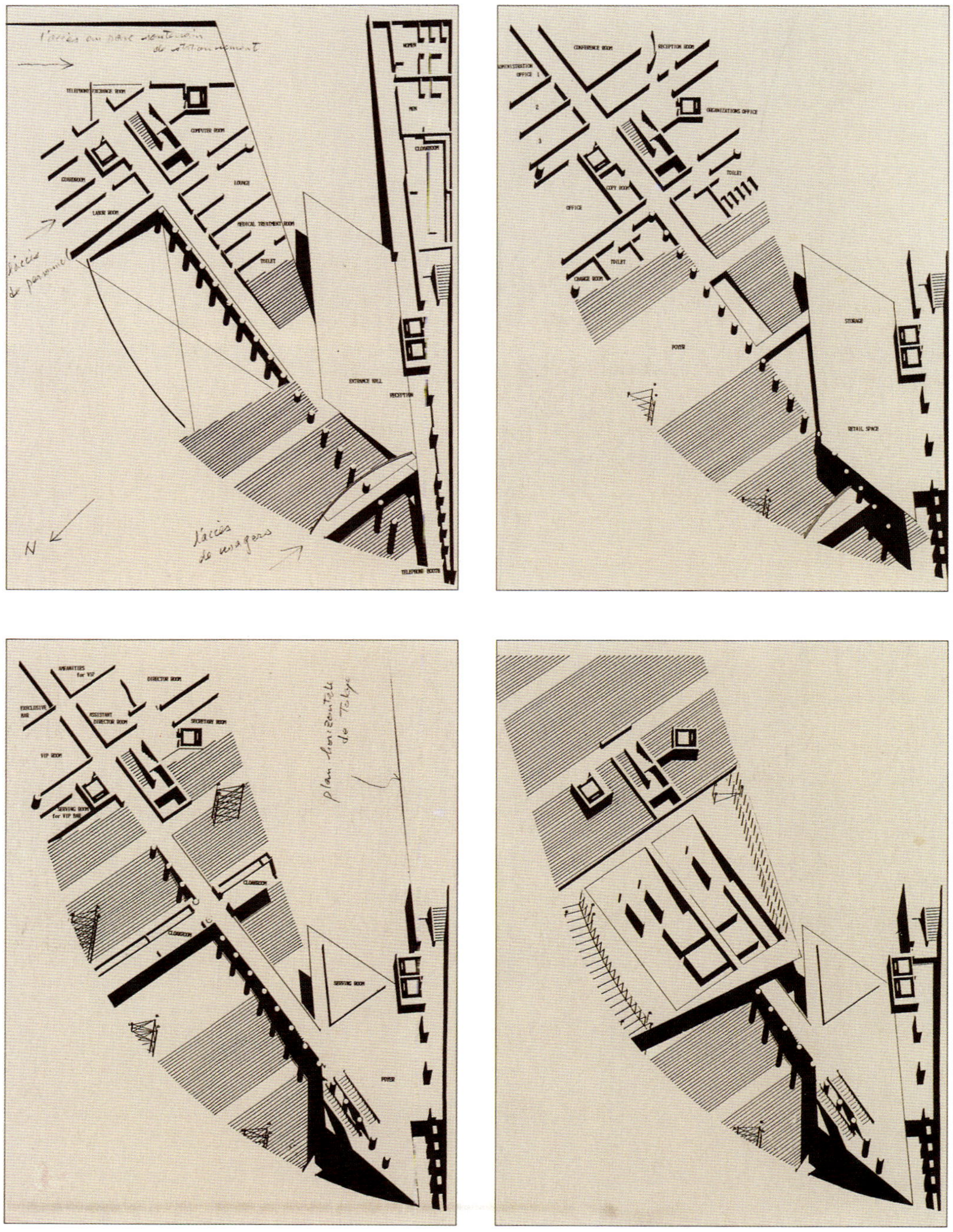

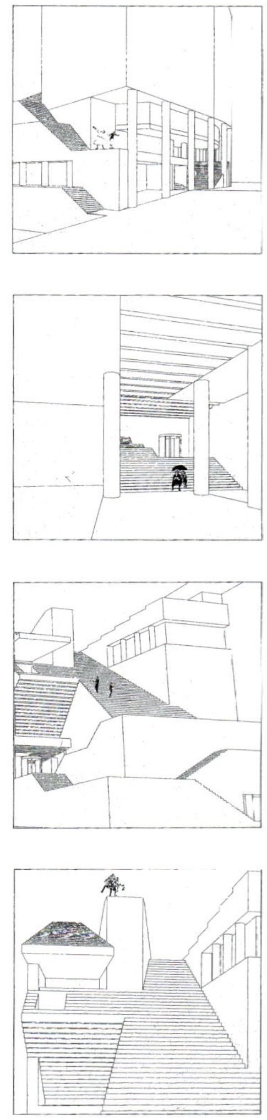

Ryoji Suzuki competition design, 1989, above left: ground floor plan, above right: first floor plan, below left: second floor plan, below right: third floor plan, second prize

Yoshito Takahashi competition design, 1989, from top: exterior view on Rue de la Fédération, interior view of entrance hall, exterior view of main stairs from south-east, third prize

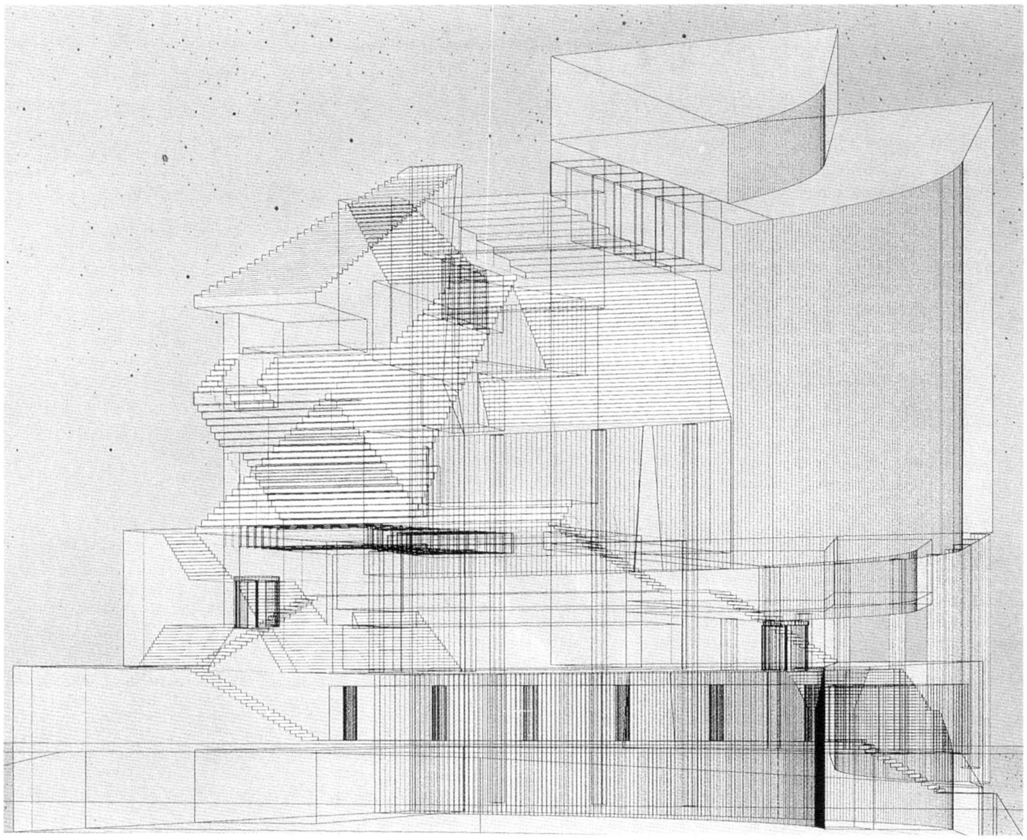

Yoshito Takahashi competition design, 1989, drawing (south-east elevation), third prize

Yoshito Takahashi competition design, 1989, model (east elevation), third prize

Yoshito Takahashi competition design, 1989, model (façade on Rue de la Fédération), third prize

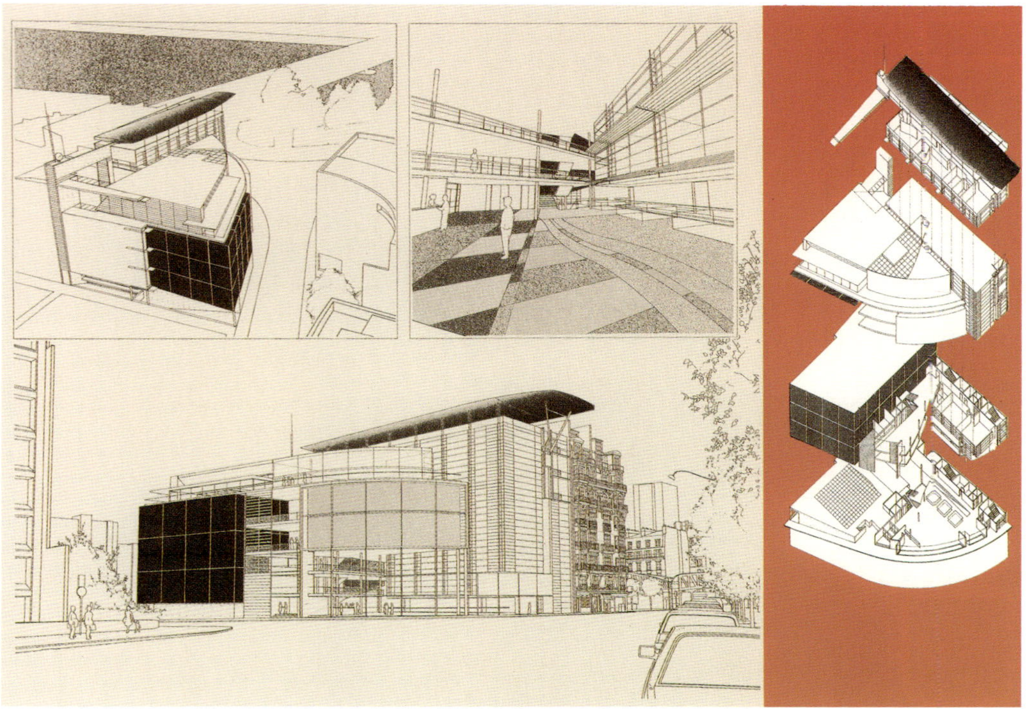

Jean-Paul Deschamps competition design, 1989, above left: exterior view from east, above middle: interior view of entrance hall, below left: exterior view on Quai Branly, right: axonometric projection, honourable mention

Riken Yamamoto competition design, 1989, above left: isometric projection, north-west elevation, north-east elevation, middle left and centre: plan (hall), middle right: detail drawing, isometric projection (garden), below from left: ground floor plan, first floor plan, second floor plan, honourable mention

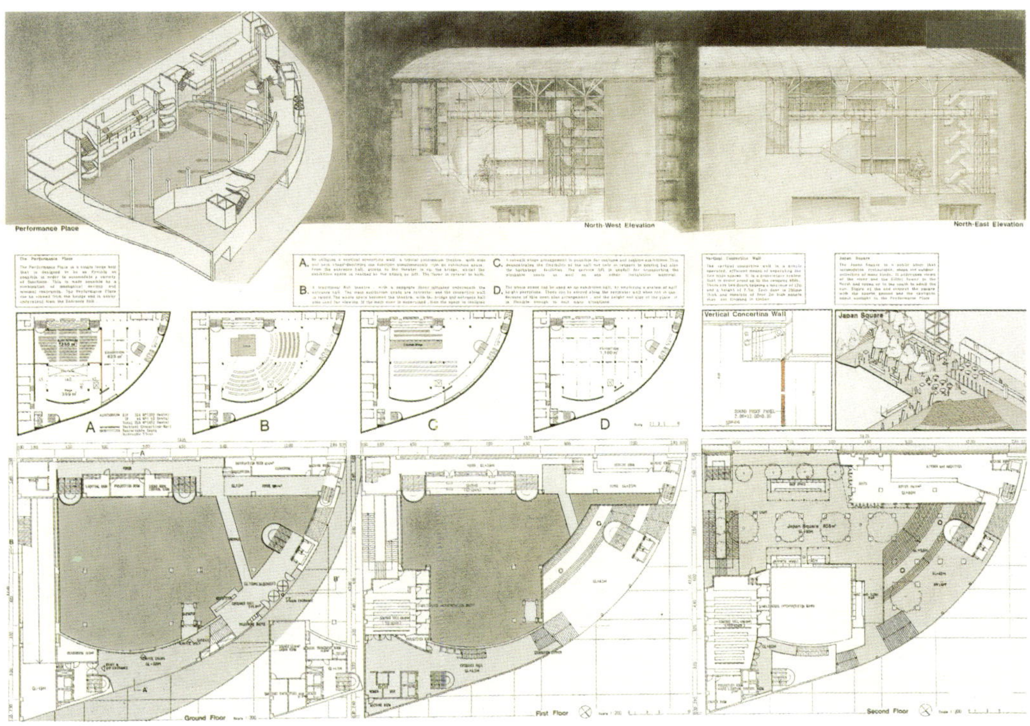

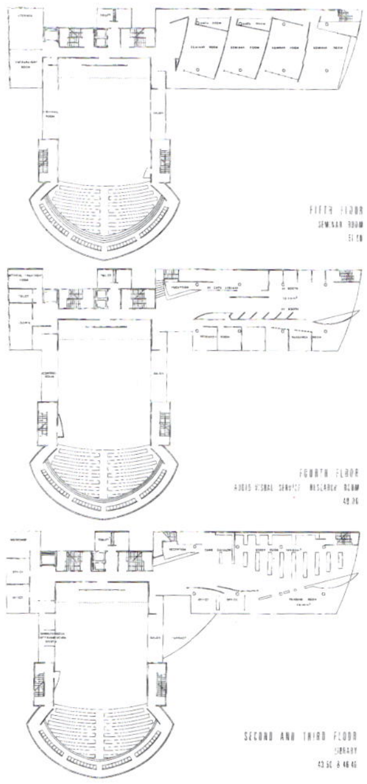

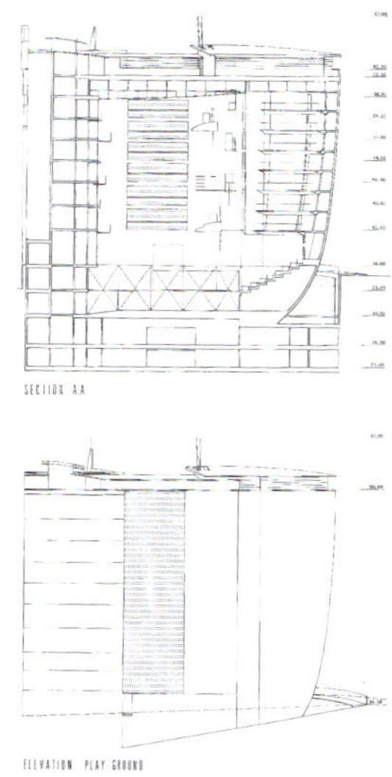

Thierry Nguyên-Giac, François Gillard, Michel Hubault & Denis Loese competition design, 1989, above left: fifth floor plan, below left: second and third floor plan, middle: interior view of the hall, above right: section (south-east elevation), below right: south-east elevation, honourable mention

Thierry Nguyên-Giac, François Gillard, Michel Hubault & Denis Loesel competition design, 1989, sectional view (east elevation), honourable mention

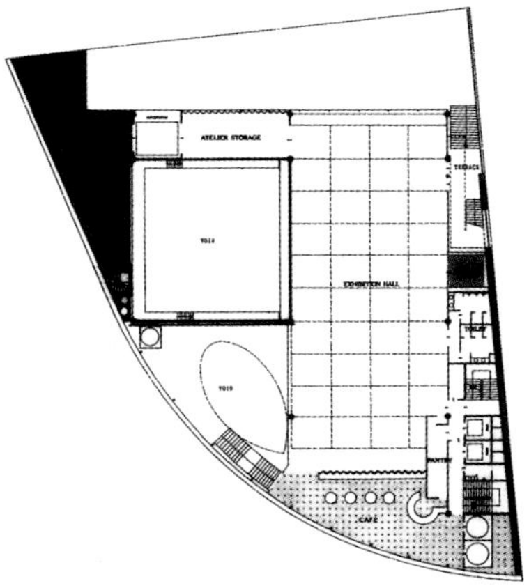

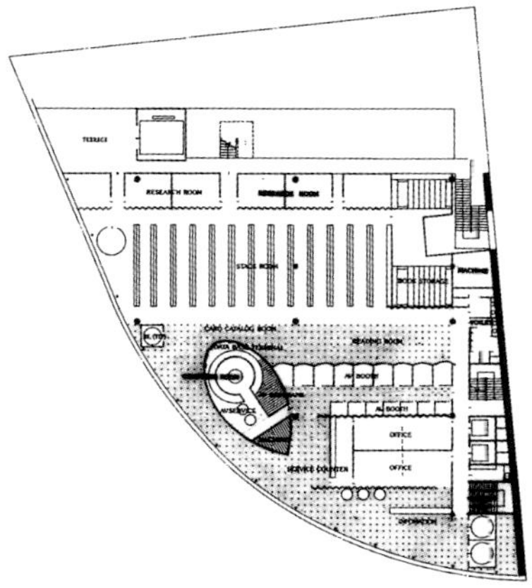

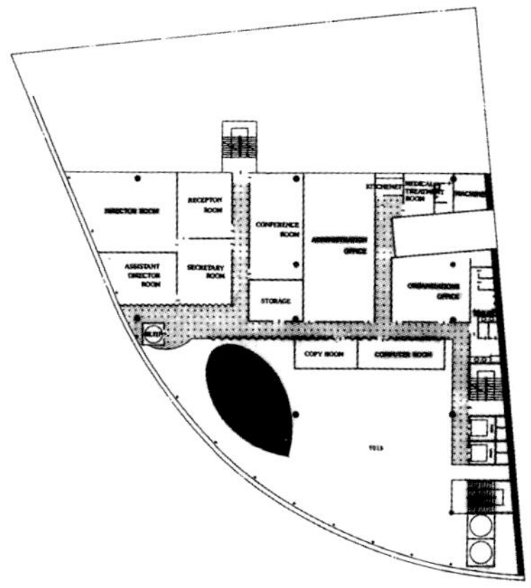

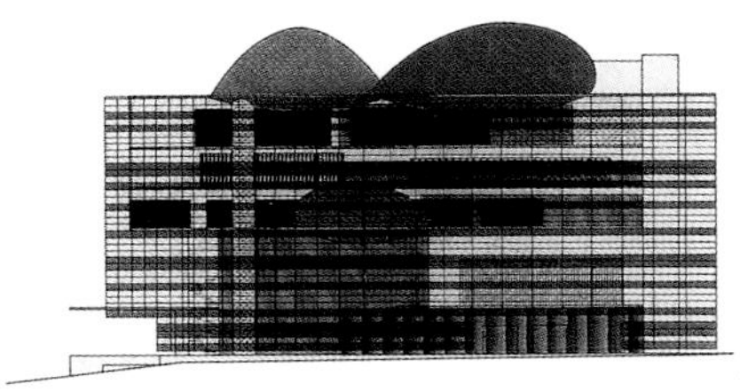

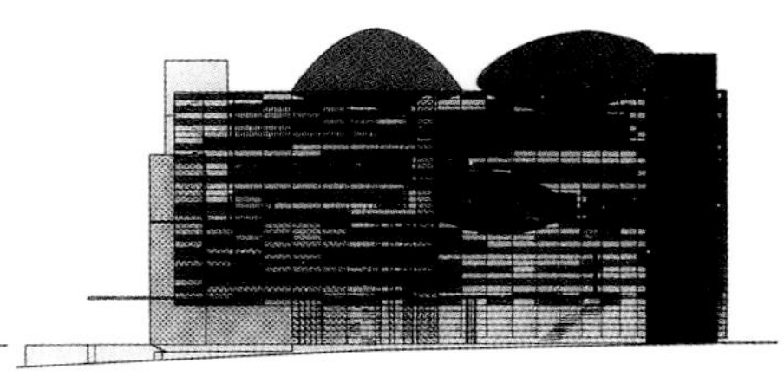

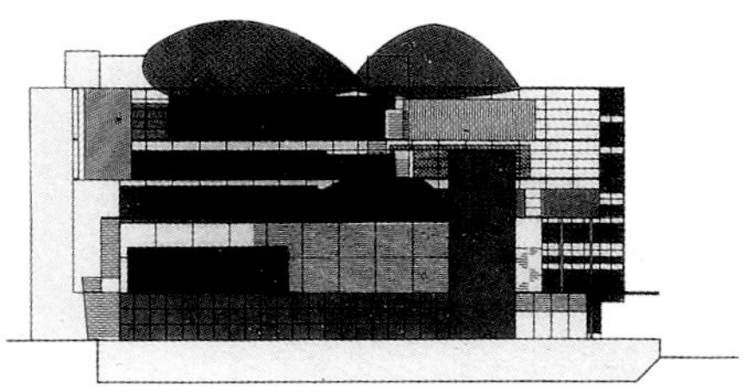

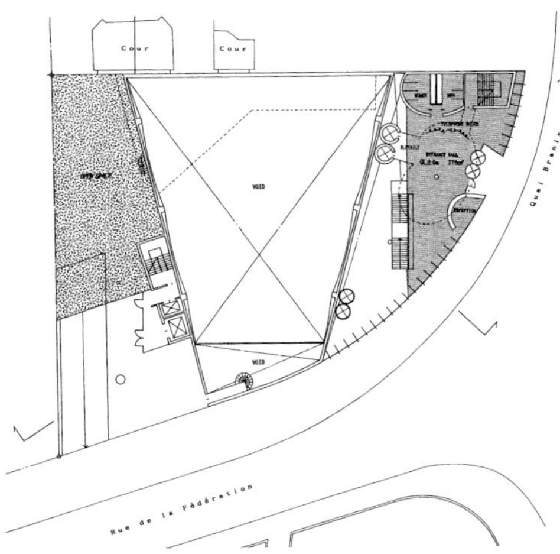
Cour
Cour
Quai Branly
Rue de la Fédération

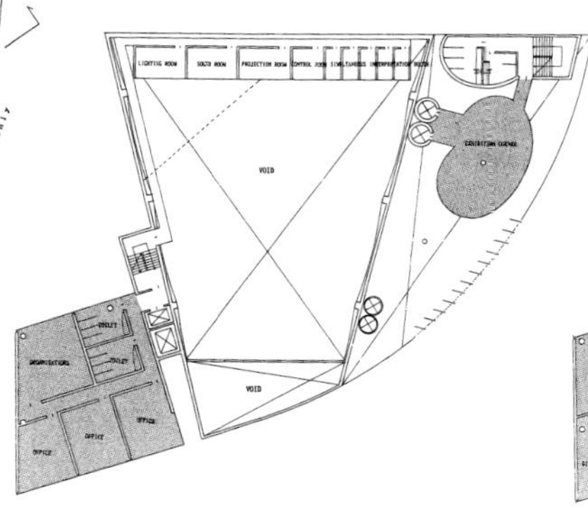

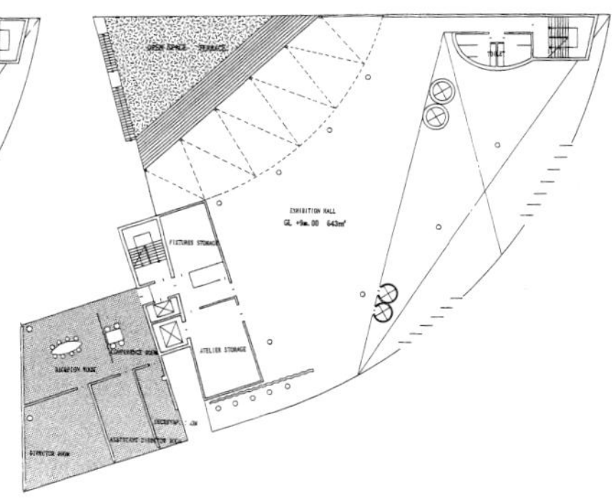

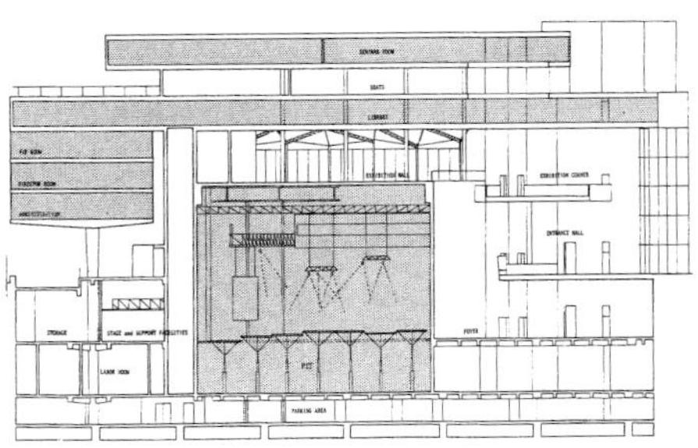

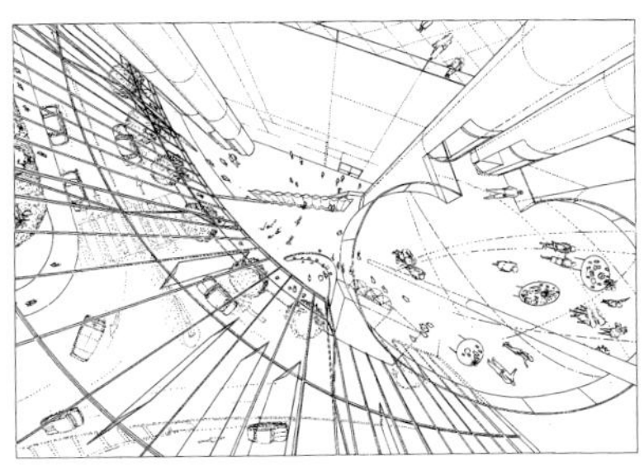

Toyo Ito competition design, 1989, above from left: first floor plan, second floor plan, third floor plan, below from left: north-west elevation, north-east elevation, south-east elevation, honourable mention

Kazuyo Sejima competition design, 1989, above from left: ground floor plan, first floor plan, second floor plan, below from left: section (Rue de la Fédération, Quai Branly side), interior view of the café, interior view of entrance hall, honourable mention

Katsuhiro Kobayashi competition design, 1989, models, honourable mention

Bernard Saillol competition design, 1989, models, honourable mention

Jean-Philippe Vassal competition design, 1989, left: model, right: model (facade on Rue de la Fédération), honourable mention

Hiroyuki Sakamoto competition design, 1989, above: model (façade on Rue de la Fédération), below: interior view of entrance hall, honourable mention

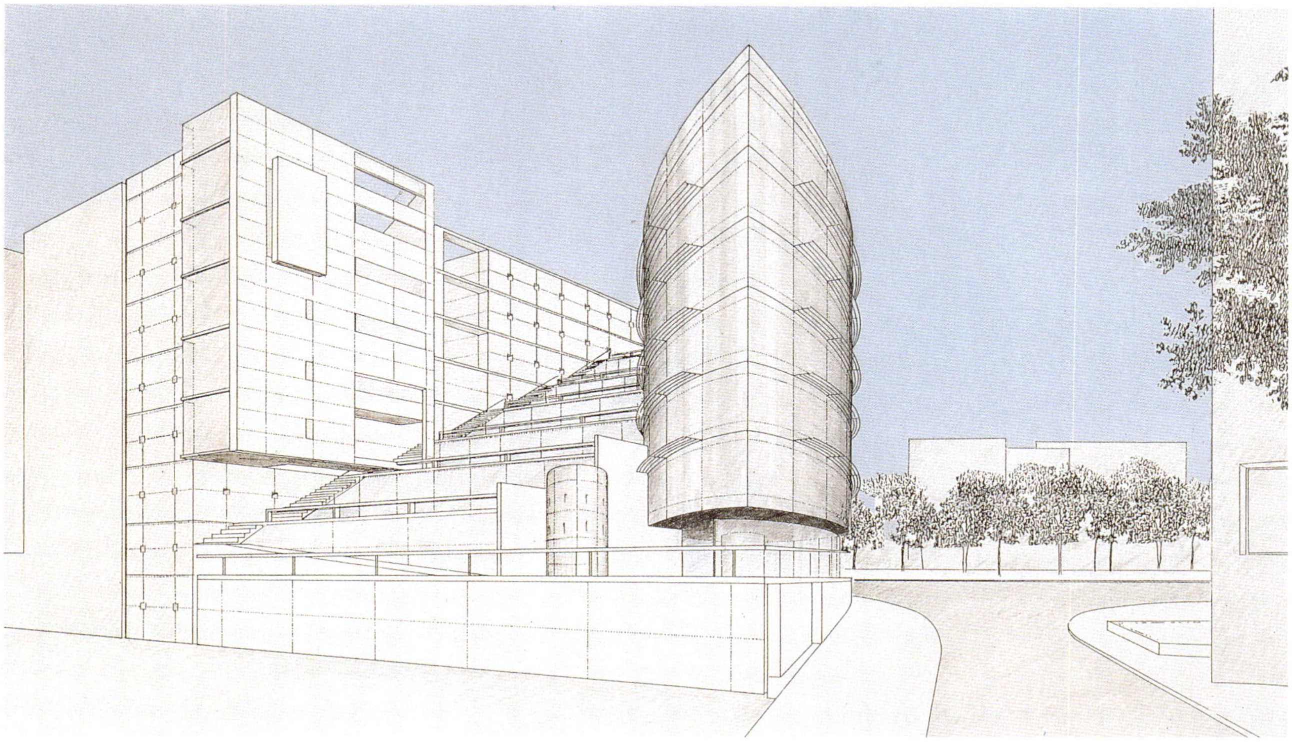

Pierre Guerin & Hector Pedroza competition design, 1989, exterior view from east, special mention

Shin Takamatsu competition design, 1989, elevation on Rue de la Fédération, special mention

Reichstag, Berlin, 1992

Project

Parliament building

Site

Spreebogen, Berlin

Dates

26 June 1992 to 23 October 1992

Number of entries

7

Of the 14 international architects invited to participate, only seven submitted designs: Pi de Bruijn (The Netherlands), Santiago Calatrava (Spain), Norman Foster (Great Britain), Jean Nouvel (France), Jiri Suchomel (Czech Republic), Helmut Jahn (Murphy & Jahn, United States), Coop Himmelblau (Austria)

Jury

Karl Josef Schattner (chairman)

Result

First round, first prize Pi de Bruijn (De Architekten Cie.) *Second prize* Santiago Calatrava; Norman Foster *Second round, first prize* Norman Foster

Commissioned by

The Bundestag (German Parliament) in collaboration with the Berlin company BSM

Construction

Not yet built

Architect

Norman Foster (*1935)

Reichstag, Berlin, 1992

Norman Foster

sectional model

Reichstag, Berlin

On 20 June 1991, the German authorities announced that Berlin would succeed Bonn as the new capital and seat of government of united Germany. This announcement heralded a new episode in the tumultuous history of the Reichstag building. The old Reichstag – built after a competition, sidelined by the Nazis and later shot to pieces – was no more than a relic of a bygone era, a dilapidated monument to the horrors of war. However, on 31 October 1991, the authorities decided that, once it had been completely renovated, the Reichstag would be reinstated as the seat of the German Bundestag (the federal parliament).

Previous history

The Reichstag has been the subject of no less than five previous competitions[1]. The last competition, for the reconstruction of the building, was held in 1960 and won by Paul Baumgarten. Although, in a sense, these competitions were an indication of Germany's desire to give democracy its rightful place, history has taught us that there is often a world of difference between desire and reality. Thus, when the Reichstag was first inaugurated in 1882, the country was still ruled by a Kaiser who openly expressed his aversion to a parliament that interfered in his affairs. In a later, dark chapter of its history, the Reichstag fire of 27 February 1933 gave the Nazis the opportunity to disenfranchise the German nation by sidelining the parliament.
The building's vaunted dome, the *pièce de résistance* of Paul Wallot's original design, did not survive the turmoil of Hitler's thousand-year Reich, and played a significant part in the most recent competition. Having overcome a series of political and structural stumbling blocks, Wallot had placed the original 76-metre-high dome above the main assembly hall, symbolically crowning democracy. Due to its symbolic function, the reconstruction of the dome became a focal point of the 1992 competition. The dome may be seen as a *pars pro toto,* an exemplary part of the whole. Its reconstruction would not only return Wallot's building to its former glory, but would also commemorate the tumultuous history of the German parliament. On the other hand, if the dome was not reconstructed, the old Reichstag would become subordinate to the new design, signifying the new beginnings of a united Germany.

Soon after the Bundestag had decided to move back to Berlin, a variety of commissions were appointed, including a parliamentary building commission which decided that the old Reichstag would not merely be renovated, but that a competition would be organised to obtain an entirely new architectural concept for the building. A Berlin company, BSM, was approached to work out the details of the competition.
This company organised an open national competition, and also invited fourteen internationally renowned architects to participate.
The competition was announced on 26 June 1992: the 151st anniversary of Paul Wallot's birth. At around the same time, a competition was also being held to select a design for the redevelopment of Berlin's Spreebogen district, and some of the jury members had seats on both competitions' juries. Because the Reichstag is also situated in the Spreebogen district, the jury decided to kill two birds with one stone and announced the results of both competitions on 18 February 1993. The three finalists for the Reichstag competition, all of whom were foreigners, were asked to present their designs at a press conference attended by the jury and a number of politicians. The winners of the Spreebogen competition were invited to present their designs at the same time.

Paul Wallot **final design**

It is interesting to note that two of the winning Reichstag designs, de Bruijn's and Foster's, did not tie in with Axel Schultes' winning Spreebogen design. Both architects therefore submitted entirely new second-round designs. Santiago Calatrava only had to make slight alterations in order to tie his design in with Schultes'. The second round was won by Norman Foster, who had also been the jury's first-round favourite. Foster was appointed executive architect, but was told that he had to make certain alterations; more particularly, he was asked to add a dome to his design(!), as Calatrava had done.

Berlin's most popular architect

Calatrava's nomination for the final round came as no surprise. He was, without exaggeration, Berlin's most popular architect. Between August 1991 and August 1992 he had worked on four other designs for Berlin besides the Reichstag[2]. Calatrava's designs form a bridge – in two cases this may be taken literally – between East and West Berlin. The Reichstag and Calatrava's sports park, which are situated in the former border zone, symbolise German unification and are a monument to the end of the Cold War.

Calatrava was one of the few participants who put a new dome on the Reichstag. And a magnificent dome at that! Calatrava is famous for his daring structures and his Reichstag dome was no exception. Wallot had initially planned an 85-metre-high structure, which proved to be technically unfeasible and was replaced by a smaller glass and steel dome. Calatrava designed a lofty structure which would cause the sombre hall of assembly to be bathed in a sea of light. The dome resembles a blossoming flower and is not topped with the usual lantern. It is light, thin and transparent, and has a skeleton-like structure, which Calatrava also intended to use for the rest of the roof. The building's silhouette would roughly resemble its nineteenth-century predecessor – an indication of Calatrava's respect for the historical context.

The interior of Calatrava's Reichstag is, however, both modern and impressive, and would almost certainly have enhanced the German parliament's pride and prestige. The main assembly hall is partially situated underground, making the building even more spacious. Calatrava was, naturally, disappointed that Foster had won the competition. He accused the jury of incompetence and remarked that Foster's design was rather outdated and not worthy of the Reichstag. He thought the same of de Bruijn's design, even though both designs were clearly just as striking as his own.

A foreign affair

It was a strange coincidence that the three finalists were all foreigners who had been invited to take part. However, the other invitees were less successful. Although Coop Himmelblau received a commendation along with thirteen other participants, Helmut Jahn, Jiri Suchomel and Jean Nouvel were amongst the 59 architects eliminated after the first round. Seven other foreign architects – Hans Dissing & Otto Weitling (Denmark), Hans Hollein (Austria), Juha Leiviska (Finland), Fumihiko Maki (Japan), José Rafael Moneo (Spain), I.M. Pei (USA) and Aldo Rossi (Italy) – had turned down the invitation for various reasons.

The Dutch architect, Pi de Bruijn, was the least famous of the three finalists. However, a number of his designs had set tongues wagging in his home country; particularly his new wing for the Concert Hall in Amsterdam. This project rivalled the Reichstag project in its complexity. A new wing, built in a contemporary style, had to be attached to a nineteenth-century Classicist building. De Bruijn had probably received an invitation for the Reichstag competition because he had experience with parliamentary buildings, having been commissioned to design a new wing for the Dutch Lower House in The Hague in 1978. This project had also been preceded by a competition and had required the assimilation of a new building into an old complex.

De Bruijn's design for the Reichstag underscores the growing significance of subsidiary facilities, such as conference halls for commissions and other government bodies. The old building lacked facilities of this sort, because there was little need for them in 1882. In order to accommodate these facilities de Bruijn designed an assembly hall on the square in front of the Reichstag. The hall is situated on a plateau and is shaped like a giant saucer. It is tied in with the old

Ernst von Giese & Paul Weidner
Reichstag, competition design, 1882, exterior view on Königsplatz, third prize

building by a broad wall, which has a number of openings and extends across the entire width of the complex.
The plateau is one of the design's most remarkable features. It is, in fact, an extension of the old stairway which leads to the main entrance. As a result, it looks as though the Reichstag itself is situated on the plateau, which largely conceals the rusticated base of the old building. A number of other facilities are also situated on the plateau, including a hall for visitors, an exhibition area and an auditorium. Calatrava mockingly compared the front view of de Bruijn's design to Oscar Niemeyer's parliamentary building in Brasilia. De Bruijn did not include a dome in his design and, as a result, the old building looks a little pathetic. Stripped of its most important facility, the assembly hall, it merely serves as an annex for its contemporary counterpart. The old Reichstag would serve as an administration building and would house the different party offices. The old conference hall was to be transformed into an open patio, and would no longer serve as a reminder of the Weimar Republic's impotent parliament. Much of the old interior was left unaltered, because de Bruijn had situated most of the new facilities outside the old building. The presidential dining hall is situated in one of the towers, possibly as a vestige of imperial privilege.

Front façade of the Reichstag on Platz der Republik (Königsplatz); recent photograph

Pi de Bruijn radically altered his design for the second round. He scrapped the saucer and the wall, but retained a plateau on one side of the building, facing the Brandenburger Tor. He also returned the assembly hall to the old Reichstag building.

Norman Foster

Foster was one of the world's leading architects when he was invited to participate in the Reichstag competition, and the buildings which he and his firm had built across the globe had already been widely acclaimed[3]. His design for the Reichstag was structured around a centrally-situated assembly hall, which was undeniably monumental, but had no dome. Instead, Foster had come up with an entirely different idea.
He left the exterior of the old Reichstag intact, but covered the entire building with a huge, transparent canopy, fifty metres high. Foster developed four options for the final round. The jury selected the version featuring the canopy – which Foster referred to as the umbrella – but this was not his preferred option. Foster emphasised the Reichstag's historical value and tried to incorporate all the facilities in the existing structure, which meant that most of the inner walls had to be removed. He also proposed to include a museum of German history in the complex.
Naturally, his design was drawn with an eye for detail and finish. He included glass lifts and ensured that sufficient natural light could enter the building. He also planned terraces and a café on the roof of the building, offering visitors a view of east and west Berlin.

A butterfly leaving its cocoon

In spite of Calatrava's criticism, Foster's record seems to guarantee that Berlin will not be presented with an architectural monstrosity. As yet, no definitive design has been presented and it is not known when construction will begin. The Bulgarian-American artist Christo will give the world a preview of the impending metamorphosis by wrapping up the entire building. His project has been 21 years in the making. He finally received permission in 1993, when a small majority of the Bundestag voted in favour of his plans. Christo will personally finance his wrap-work, which is symbolic of the new beginnings of German democracy; a butterfly leaving its cocoon.

1 *See chapter on the Reichstag elsewhere in this book.*
2 *Calatrava's four other designs included: Spandau station, the Kronprinzenbrücke (bridge), Oberbaumbrücke (bridge) and the Jahn sports park. Only the two bridges are to be built.*
3 *See chapters on the Hongkong and Shanghai Bank and the Carré d'Art in Nîmes elsewhere in this book.*

Reichstag, Berlin

Als der Bundestag am 20. Juni 1991 entschied, daß Berlin die neue Hauptstadt und der Regierungssitz des wiedervereinigten Deutschlands werden sollte, rückte das Reichstagsgebäude samt seiner wechselvollen Geschichte wieder in den Blickpunkt der Öffentlichkeit. Lange Jahre schien der Reichstag wie ein Relikt aus einer fernen Vergangenheit – entstanden nach einer Ausschreibung, vernachlässigt, zerbombt und schließlich seine letzten Tage als halbverfallenes Mahnmal an die Schrecken des Kriegs fristend.

Vorgeschichte

Das Reichstagsgebäude war in der zweiten Hälfte des 19. Jahrhunderts entstanden, um der Demokratie in Deutschland wieder einen würdigen Sitz zu geben. Nach zahlreichen politischen und bautechnischen Problemen hatte man 1892 die ursprüngliche Kuppel mit einer Höhe von etwa 76 Metern als symbolische Krone der Demokratie über den Plenarsaal plaziert. Diese vielgelobte Kuppel, die pièce de résistance aus Paul Wallots Entwurf, hatte die nationalsozialistische Herrschaft nicht überdauert. Daher stand bei der Ausschreibung von 1992 die Frage nach einem Wiederaufbau der Kuppel im Mittelpunkt des Interesses. Bei einer Rekonstruktion wären Wallots Gebäude und die turbulente Geschichte der deutschen Parlamentarier zu neuen Ehren gekommen; bei einem Verzicht auf dieses wichtige Kennzeichen wäre der alte Reichstag dem neuen Entwurf untergeordnet und ein Neubeginn des wiedervereinigten Deutschlands zum Ausdruck gebracht worden.

Nach dem Beschluß vom 31.10.1991, den Sitz des Parlaments nach Berlin zu verlegen, wurden verschiedene Kommissionen – darunter auch eine parlamentarische Baukommission – ins Leben gerufen, die einen reibungslosen Ablauf der Arbeiten garantieren sollten. Die Baukommission entschloß sich zu einer Ausschreibung, die sich jedoch nicht mit dem Wiederaufbau des alten Gebäudes, sondern mit dem Entwurf eines neuen architektonischen Konzepts befassen sollte. Eine detaillierte Ausgestaltung des Wettbewerbs übertrug man dem Berliner Unternehmen BSM. Diese Firma gab am 26. Juni 1992 – dem 151. Geburtstag Paul Wallots – eine offene nationale Ausschreibung bekannt, zu der zusätzlich 14 internationale Architekten eingeladen wurden. In der Reichstagsjury befanden sich einige Mitglieder der Jury für die Ausschreibung zur städtebaulichen Entwicklung des Berliner Spreebogens – ein Projekt, unter das auch der Reichstag fiel. Die Ergebnisse beider Wettbewerbe wurden am 18. Februar 1993 veröffentlicht: Drei Entwürfe erreichten das Finale. Die drei, sämtlich aus dem Ausland stammenden Architekten erhielten eine Einladung, ihre Konzepte in Gegenwart von Jury, Presse und Politikern zusammen mit den Gewinnern der Spreebogen-Ausschreibung näher zu erläutern.

Dabei fiel auf, daß sich zwei der prämierten Reichstags-Entwürfe – von Pi de Bruijn und Norman Foster – nicht mit dem preisgekrönten Spreebogen-Konzept von Axel Schultes kombinieren ließen. Bei der erforderlichen Überarbeitung der Pläne brachten beide Architekten völlig neue Ideen ein. Calatrava blieb bei seinem ursprünglichen Konzept, abgesehen von kleineren Änderungen, die aufgrund der Auflagen notwendig wurden. Nach einer kurzen zweiten Ausschreibungsrunde ernannte man Foster zum Gewinner und ausführenden Architekten. Allerdings bat man ihn, seine Pläne zu überarbeiten und eventuell eine Kuppel einzuzeichnen.

Der beliebteste Architekt Berlins

Calatrava war einer der wenigen, die dem Reichstag seine Kuppel zurückgeben wollten. In der Folge avancierte er in der Bevölkerung Berlins zum beliebtesten Architekten. Neben der Ausschreibung zum Reichstagsgebäude arbeitete Calatrava zwischen August 1991 und August 1992 an vier weiteren Projekten innerhalb Berlins.

Mit seinen beiden Entwürfen schlug er eine Brücke zwischen Ost- und Westberlin: Ebenso wie ein von ihm konzipierter Sportplatz befindet sich der Reichstag im ehemaligen Grenzgebiet und ist damit sowohl Symbol der Wiedervereinigung als auch Denkmal für das Ende des Kalten Krieges.

Beim Entwurf der Kuppel zog der für seine gewagten Konstruktionen bekannte Spanier alle Register seines Könnens. Die von Wallot ursprünglich geplante Kuppel mit einer Höhe von 85 Metern hatte sich seinerzeit als technisch nicht durchführbar erwiesen, so daß nur eine etwas gedrungen erscheinende Version aus Glas und Stahl entstanden war. Calatrava dagegen entwarf eine stolze, hohe Konstruktion, die den dunklen Sitzungssaal des Parlaments in ein Meer von Licht tauchen sollte. Die Kuppel scheint sich wie eine Blüte zu öffnen, statt wie üblich von der Beleuchtung gekrönt zu werden. Ihre skelettartige Konstruktion – leicht, dünn und transparent – setzte sich bei den übrigen Überdachungen fort, während das Gebäude von außen einen ähnlichen Anblick bieten sollte wie im 19. Jahrhundert. Dadurch wollte Calatrava der historischen Umgebung Respekt bezeugen. Für das Innere des Reichstags konzipierte er moderne Räume, die dem Deutschen Parlament neue Würde verliehen hätten. Die Absenkung des Sitzungssaals unter das Niveau des Erdgeschosses sollte die plastische Räumlichkeit seines Entwurfs zusätzlich betonen.

Nach der Bekanntgabe der Jury-Entscheidung erwies sich Calatrava als schlechter Verlierer: Er zweifelte nicht nur die Kompetenz des Gremiums an, sondern vertrat auch die Ansicht, daß der Reichstag etwas Besseres verdient habe als Fosters Entwurf, den er – genau wie de Bruijns Konzept – als veraltet bezeichnete.

Ausländischer Erfolg

Die drei nominierten Konzepte stammten alle aus der Gruppe der zusätzlich eingeladenen Architekten. Die anderen ausländischen Teilnehmer waren weniger erfolgreich – immerhin zählten Coop Himmelblau, Helmut Jahn, Jiri Suchomel und Jean Nouvel zu den 59 Architekten, deren Beiträge die erste Runde überstanden. Die übrigen sieben eingeladenen Architekten verzichteten auf eine Teilnahme an dieser Ausschreibung.

Der Niederländer Pi de Bruijn war der unbekannteste der drei Preisträger, obwohl er in den Niederlanden schon verschiedene aufsehenerregende Entwürfe vorgelegt hatte – z. B. den Anbau des Amsterdamer Concertgebouw. Sein Konzept unterstrich die Bedeutung der Nebenfunktionen, der Ausschußsitzungsräume und anderer Aufgaben, die 1882 kaum eine Rolle gespielt hatten. Da das alte Gebäude für diese Anforderungen nicht genügend Platz bot, verlegte er den Plenarsaal auf den Platz vor dem Reichstag. Der auf einem Plateau angesiedelte Sitzungssaal erinnert an eine große Schüssel und ist mit dem alten Gebäude durch eine breite, teilweise unterbrochene Mauer verbunden, die sich über die gesamte Breite des Komplexes erstreckt. Das Plateau ist eine Erweiterung der alten Eingangstreppen. In ihm befinden sich weitere Räumlichkeiten, wie etwa die Besucherhalle, ein Ausstellungsraum sowie ein Vortragssaal. Eine Kuppel fehlt, so daß das alte Gebäude ein wenig armselig wirkt – in Form und Funktion den zeitgenössischen Anbauten untergeordnet, denn der wichtigste Saal befindet sich nicht mehr im historischen Bauwerk aus dem 19. Jahrhundert. Statt dessen beherbergt das alte Reichstagsgebäude zahlreiche Büroräume und bietet den politischen Parteien Räumlichkeiten. Der frühere Sitzungssaal ist in einen offenen Patio umgewandelt, so daß nichts mehr an das machtlose Parlament der Weimarer Republik erinnert. Auf der oberen Ebene in einem der Türme befindet sich der Speisesaal des Präsidenten.

Nachdem Pi de Bruijn den geteilten ersten Preis erhalten hatte, arbeitete er seinen Entwurf vollständig um. Die Schüssel und die Mauer verschwanden, lediglich auf der dem Brandenburger Tor zugewandten Seite blieb ein Podium erhalten, während er den Plenarsaal wieder im alten Reichstagsgebäude unterbrachte.

Norman Foster

Als ihn die Einladung zur Ausschreibung für das Reichstagsgebäude erreichte, zählte Foster bereits zu den berühmtesten Architekten der Welt. Rund um den Globus verteilten sich die von ihm entwickelten, Bauwerke (siehe Kapitel zu Hongkong and Shanghai Bank sowie Carré d'Art, Nîmes). Sein Entwurf für den Reichstag geht von einem zentralen Plenarsaal aus. Die Außenfassade des alten Reichstagsgebäudes bleibt zwar vollständig erhalten, wird aber mit einem gigantischen, 50 Meter hohen, transparenten Überdach versehen. Während der detaillierten Ausarbeitung seiner Pläne entwickelte Foster vier Alternativvorschläge, wobei er seinem Entwurf mit der Kuppel eher zurückhaltend gegenüberstand. Foster betont den historischen Wert des Reichstagsgebäudes und bemühte sich, möglichst alle Funktionen im bestehenden Bau unterzubringen. Dies führte zu einer Entkernung der meisten Innenräume. Der Brite sah gläserne Aufzüge vor und plante für das Dach Terrassen und ein Café mit Blick über Ost- und Westberlin.

Wie ein Schmetterling aus Kokon

Wie und wann Fosters Entwurf realisiert werden wird, ist vorläufig noch ungewiß. Als eine Art Vorgeschmack auf die geplante Metamorphose erhielt der bulgarisch-amerikanische Künstler Christo 1993 vom Parlament endlich die Genehmigung zum Verpacken des Gebäudes – nach 21 Jahren Wartezeit und einer tumultuarischen Abstimmung, die nur mit knapper Mehrheit für die Kunst endete. Das Verpackungskunstwerk, dessen Finanzierung Christo übrigens selbst übernimmt, soll einen Neubeginn der deutschen Demokratie symbolisieren, die dann wie ein Schmetterling aus ihrem Kokon schlüpfen wird.

1 *Dabei handelt es sich um den Bahnhof Spandau, die Kronprinzenbrücke, die Oberbaumbrücke und den Jahn-Sportpark. Allerdings wurden nur die beiden Brücken realisiert.*

Le Reichstag, Berlin

Le 20 juin 1991, les autorités allemandes annoncèrent au monde que Berlin allait redevenir la capitale de l'Allemagne réunifiée et le siège du gouvernement, en lieu et place de Bonn. Cette décision ouvrait un nouvel épisode de la tumultueuse histoire du bâtiment du Reichstag. Construit à l'issue d'un concours, incendié à l'arrivée au pouvoir des nazis et en partie bombardé, l'ancien édifice n'était guère plus qu'une relique d'un passé disparu, un monument aux horreurs de la guerre. Le 31 octobre 1991, les autorités décidèrent de le restaurer pour y installer le parlement, le Bundestag.

Histoire ancienne

L'histoire du Reichstag illustre les déboires et les victoires de la démocratie allemande. Il avait déjà fait l'objet de cinq concours[1], dont le dernier, pour sa reconstruction, avait été remporté par Paul Baumgarten en 1960. Lors de son inauguration, à la fin du siècle dernier, le pays était encore dirigé par un empereur qui haïssait une institution parlementaire prétendant empiéter sur sa politique. Après les troubles de la République de Weimar, les nazis saisirent l'opportunité de l'incendie du bâtiment, le 27 février 1933, pour museler le parlement.

Si la grande coupole, chef-d'œuvre de Paul Wallot, n'a pas survécu au Reich hitlérien, elle continua à couvrir de son ombre le déroulement des derniers concours. Après de longues controverses et d'innombrables modifications de plans, Wallot avait fini par l'installer au-dessus de l'hémicycle en couronnement symbolique de l'institution démocratique. Cette fonction se retrouva au centre des controverses des concours de 1992. Pour certains, la coupole était une partie exemplaire du tout et sa reconstruction seule permettrait de restaurer l'édifice dans sa gloire première et de commémorer l'histoire agitée du parlement. Pour d'autres, si elle n'était pas reconstruite, le parlement donnerait davantage l'image du renouveau politique né de la réunification. Le Reichstag et le Parc des sports, situés dans l'ancienne zone frontalière, se transformaient en quelque sorte en emblèmes de l'unification allemande et de la fin de la guerre froide.

Plusieurs commissions furent constituées par le Bundestag, dont une pour la construction des bâtiments. Elle décida que l'ancien Reichstag ne serait pas purement et simplement restauré et qu'il fallait organiser un concours pour trouver un nouveau concept architectural. Une société berlinoise, BSM, fut contactée pour mettre au point les détails du cahier des charges.

Elle annonça le 26 juin 1992 un concours national ouvert en y invitant quatorze architectes étrangers connus. A peu près en même temps, une autre compétition se déroulait pour les plans de réaménagement du quartier du Spreebogen, et certains jurés siégeaient dans les deux jurys. Comme le Reichstag faisait partie de ce secteur, les résultats des deux concours furent annoncés le même jour, le 18 février 1993. Les trois finalistes du concours du parlement (tous étrangers) et les gagnants de celui du Spreebogen, furent conviés à exposer leurs plans lors d'une conférence de presse en présence des jurys et de responsables politiques.

Deux plans retenus, ceux de De Bruijn et de Foster, durent être entièrement retravaillés pour le second tour car ils n'étaient pas adaptés au projet primé d'Axel Schultes pour le Spreebogen. Seul celui de Santiago Calatrava s'y intégrait assez bien. Le second tour fut remporté par Norman Foster, déjà favori du jury au premier. Il fut nommé responsable du projet mais dut accepter certains changements et en particulier l'ajout d'une coupole (!), ce qu'avait proposé Calatrava.

Le plus célèbre des architectes berlinois

La désignation de Calatrava pour le second tour n'avait pas été une surprise. Il était, sans exagération, le plus populaire des architectes étrangers œuvrant à Berlin. Entre août 1991 et août 1992, il avait travaillé sur quatre autres projets dans la capitale[2] qui formaient un pont – au sens propre et figuré – entre Berlin-Est et Berlin-Ouest.

Calatrava fut l'un des rares participants à proposer une coupole, de plus très impressionnante. L'architecte était célèbre pour ses audaces et sa coupole ne faisait pas exception. Wallot avait à l'origine prévu une structure de 85 m de haut techniquement irréalisable qu'il avait remplacée par une coupole de verre et d'acier nettement moins ambitieuse. Calatrava dessina une forme généreuse qui aurait baigné l'auguste et sombre hémicycle d'un océan de lumière. Sa coupole ressemblait à un bouton de fleur sans le lanterneau habituel. Elle était légère et transparente et reposait sur une structure en squelette reprise sur l'ensemble du toit. La silhouette du bâtiment aurait presque rappelé celle de son prédécesseur du XIXème siècle, témoignant ainsi du respect de son auteur pour le contexte historique.

L'intérieur, à la fois contemporain et impressionnant, aurait certainement ajouté encore au prestige du parlement, et son vaste hémicycle était en partie souterrain pour augmenter les surfaces utiles.

Calatrava fut déçu de se voir battu par Foster. Il accusa le jury d'incompétence et jugea les plans de Foster démodés et indignes du parlement. Il pensait la même chose du projet De Bruijn, même si les propositions de ces deux architectes étaient aussi intéressantes que la sienne.

Une affaire étrangère

Si, curieusement, les trois finalistes étaient d'origine étrangère, beaucoup de candidats étrangers furent cependant écartés. Même si Coop Himmelbau reçut les félicitations du jury avec treize autres participants, Helmut Jahn, Jiri Suchomel et Jean Nouvel partagèrent le sort des 59 éliminés du premier tour. Sept autres invités se désistèrent pour diverses raisons.

L'architecte néerlandais, Pi de Bruijn, était le moins connu des trois vainqueurs même si certains de ses projets avaient fait beaucoup parler d'eux dans son pays, en particulier sa nouvelle aile pour le Concertgebouw d'Amsterdam, extension de style contemporain d'un édifice du XIXème siècle d'esprit classique. Mais De Bruijn avait plutôt été invité pour son plan d'extension de la chambre basse néerlandaise à La Haye, en 1978. Ce projet avait également été précédé par un concours et concernait lui aussi l'intégration de nouveaux bâtiments dans un ensemble ancien.

Les plans de De Bruijn pour le Reichstag prenaient en compte l'importance grandissante d'équipements jusqu'alors considérés secondaires, comme des salles pour les commissions et certains organismes gouvernementaux. L'ancien édifice en manquait car leur rôle n'était pas très développé en 1882. Pour dégager la place nécessaire, l'architecte créa une grande salle en forme de soucoupe géante et posée sur un socle élevé sur la place devant l'ancien Reichstag. La salle était reliée à celui-ci par un large passage à nombreuses ouvertures qui traversait toute la largeur de l'ensemble. Ce socle était en fait une extension de l'ancien escalier de l'entrée principale, ce qui donnait l'impression que l'ancien bâtiment reposait également sur lui puisqu'il masquait en grande partie l'ancien soubassement rustiqué. Un certain nombre de services étaient également installés dans ce socle, dont un hall pour les visiteurs, un espace d'exposition et un auditorium.

En s'en moquant Calatrava compara cette solution aux plans de Niemeyer pour le parlement de Brasilia. Mais sans coupole, l'ancien Reichstag semblait un peu pathétique, et dépouillé de sa grande salle, il n'était tout au plus qu'une annexe du nouveau bâtiment. L'ancien aurait été utilisé pour les bureaux de l'administration et des partis. Le vieil hémicycle était reconverti en patio ouvert et l'intérieur était en général assez peu modifié puisque la plupart des activités nouvelles avaient été installées dans le nouveau bâtiment. La salle à manger présidentielle, vestige d'une autre époque, restait dans une des tours.

Pi de Bruijn modifia radicalement son projet lors du second tour. Il supprima la soucoupe et le mur, mais retint le principe d'un socle sur l'un des côtés du bâtiment face à la porte de Brandebourg et réintégra l'hémicycle dans l'ancien édifice.

Norman Foster

Foster était déjà l'un des plus grands architectes du moment lorsqu'il fut invité à participer à ce concours[3]. Son plan pour le Reichstag se structurait autour d'une grande salle indéniablement monumentale, mais sans coupole. Il proposa à la place une idée entièrement nouvelle.

Il laissa l'extérieur de l'ancien bâtiment intact mais le recouvrit dans sa totalité d'une tente géante de 50 m de haut. Pour le tour final, il développa quatre options. Le jury retint l'alternative de la tente, que Foster appelait le parapluie, bien que ce ne soit pas vraiment sa préférence. Il insistait sur la signification historique du parlement et essaya d'intégrer tous les équipements nécessaires dans le bâtiment existant en démolissant la plupart des cloisonnements intérieurs. Il proposa également d'y créer un musée de l'histoire allemande.

Son projet, avec ses ascenseurs transparents et son étude très fine sur la pénétration de la lumière naturelle, était soigné jusque dans ses moindres détails. Des terrasses et un café sur le toit offraient aux visiteurs une vue panoramique sur la ville.

Un papillon quittant son cocon

Malgré les critiques de Calatrava, l'expertise de Foster peut permettre de penser que Berlin ne se retrouvera pas flanquée d'une monstruosité architecturale. A ce jour, les plans définitifs n'ont pas été présentés et personne ne sait à quelle date la construction commencera. L'artiste bulgaro-américain Christo aura ainsi le temps de mettre à bien son projet d'emballage du Reichstag, vieux maintenant de 21 ans. En 1993, le parlement lui en a donné la permission à une faible majorité . Cette intervention temporaire symbolisera en quelque sorte la mutation de la nouvelle Allemagne, robuste papillon sortant de son cocon.

1 *Voir le chapitre sur le Reichstag, 1872–1882.*

2 *Ces quatre projets comprenaient la gare de Spandau, le pont du Kronprinz, le pont d'Oberbaum et le parc des sports Jahn. Seuls les deux ponts restent à construire.*

3 *Voir chapitres sur la Hong Kong Bank et le Carré d'Art, à Nîmes.*

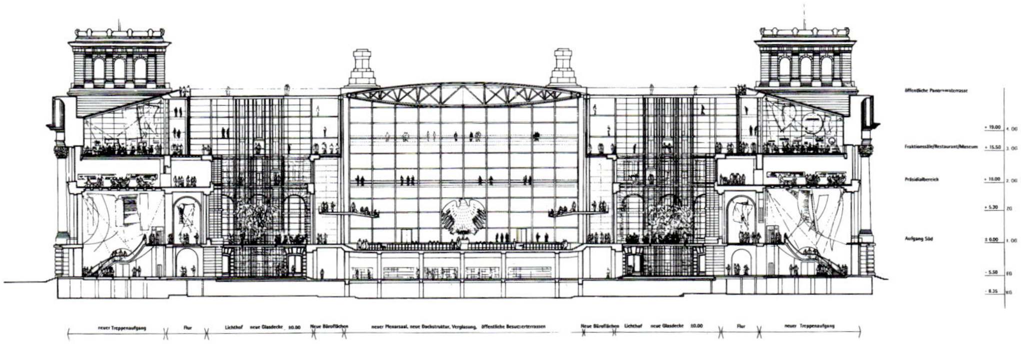

Norman Foster north-south section, west elevation

Norman Foster view of model

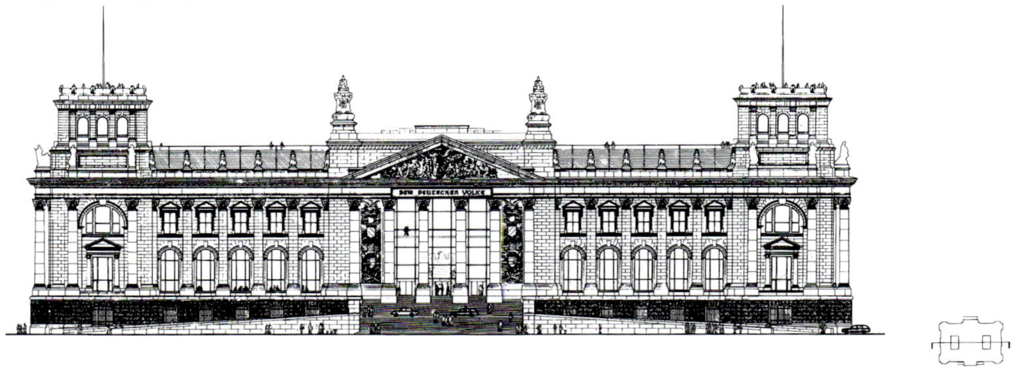

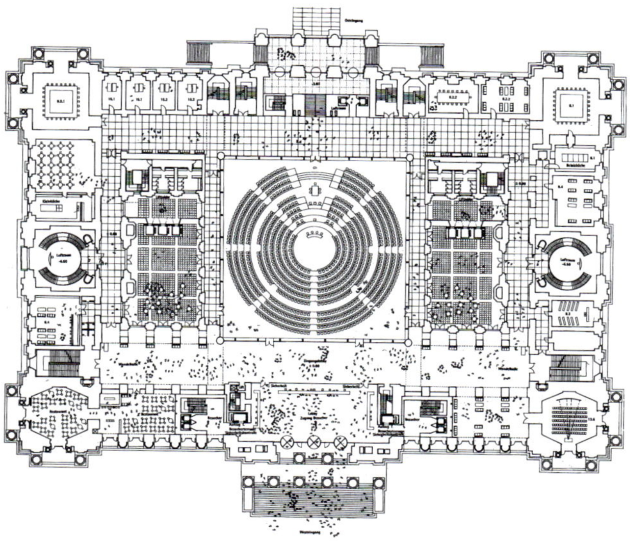

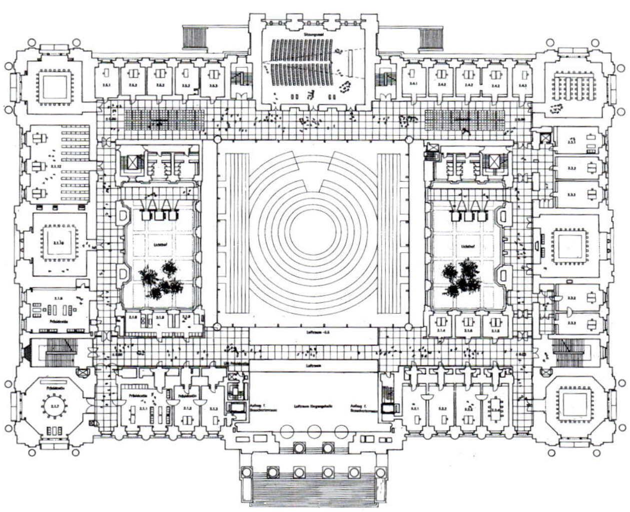

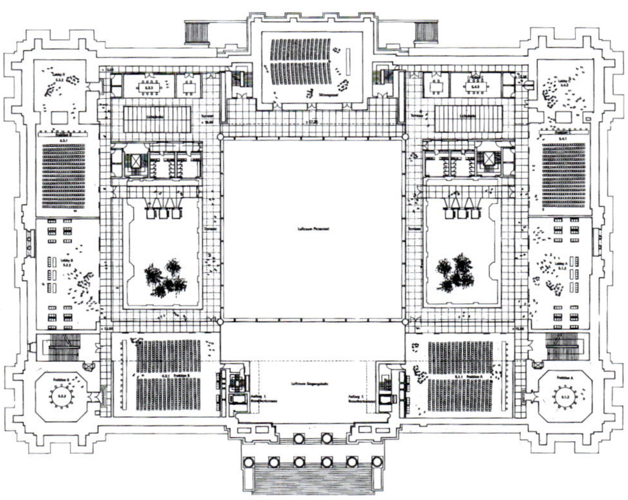

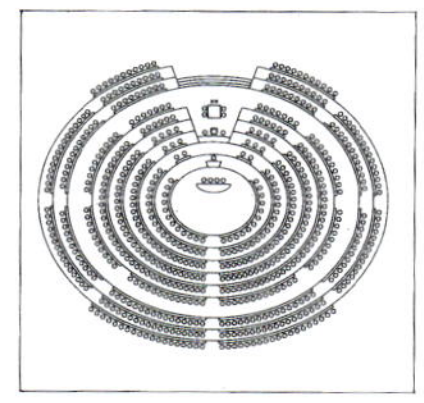

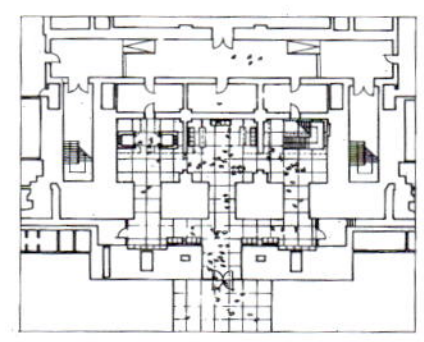

Norman Foster plan of level 1

Norman Foster plan of level 2

Norman Foster plan of level 3

Norman Foster model view of Assembly Chamber

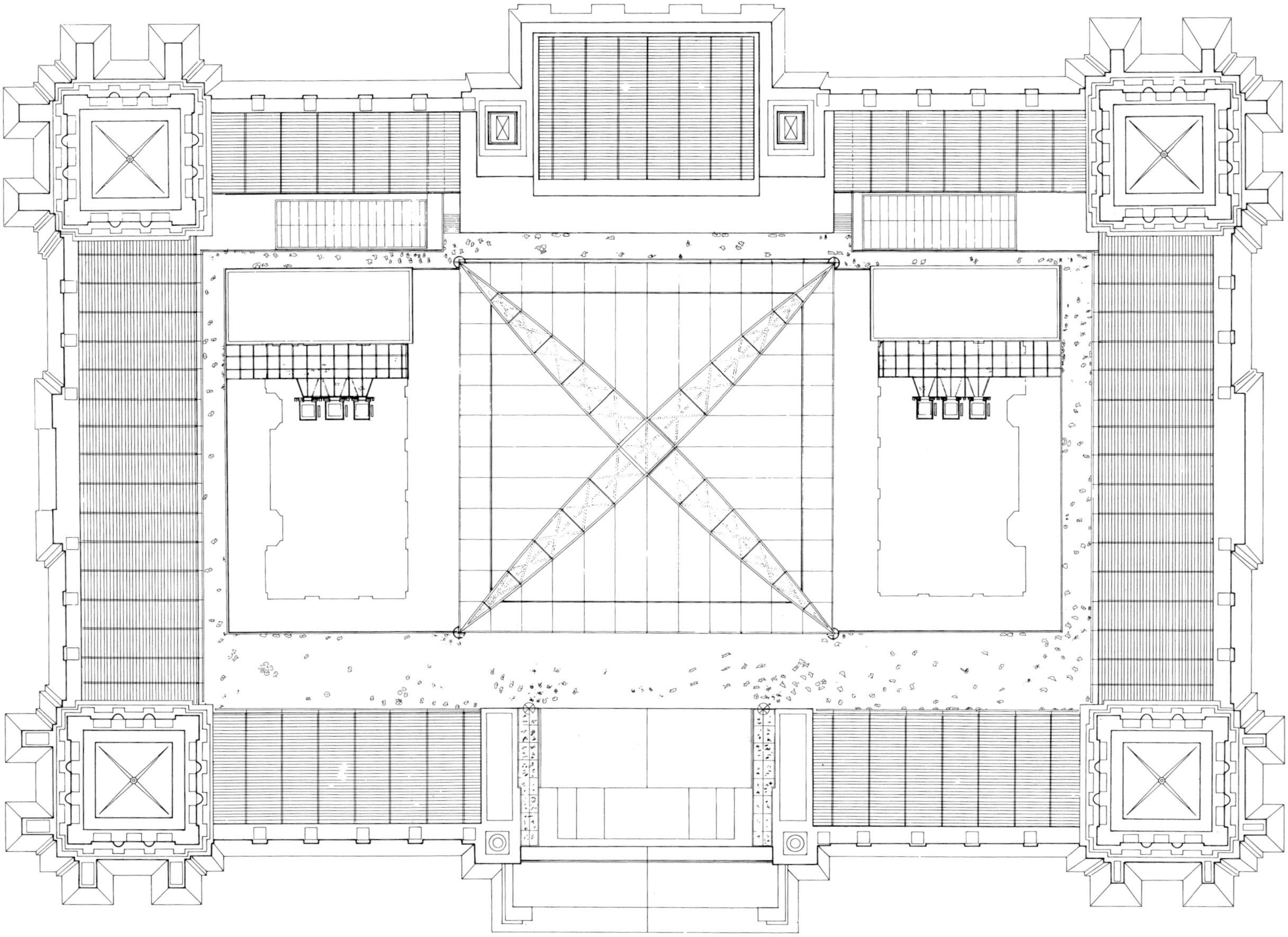

Norman Foster roof plan

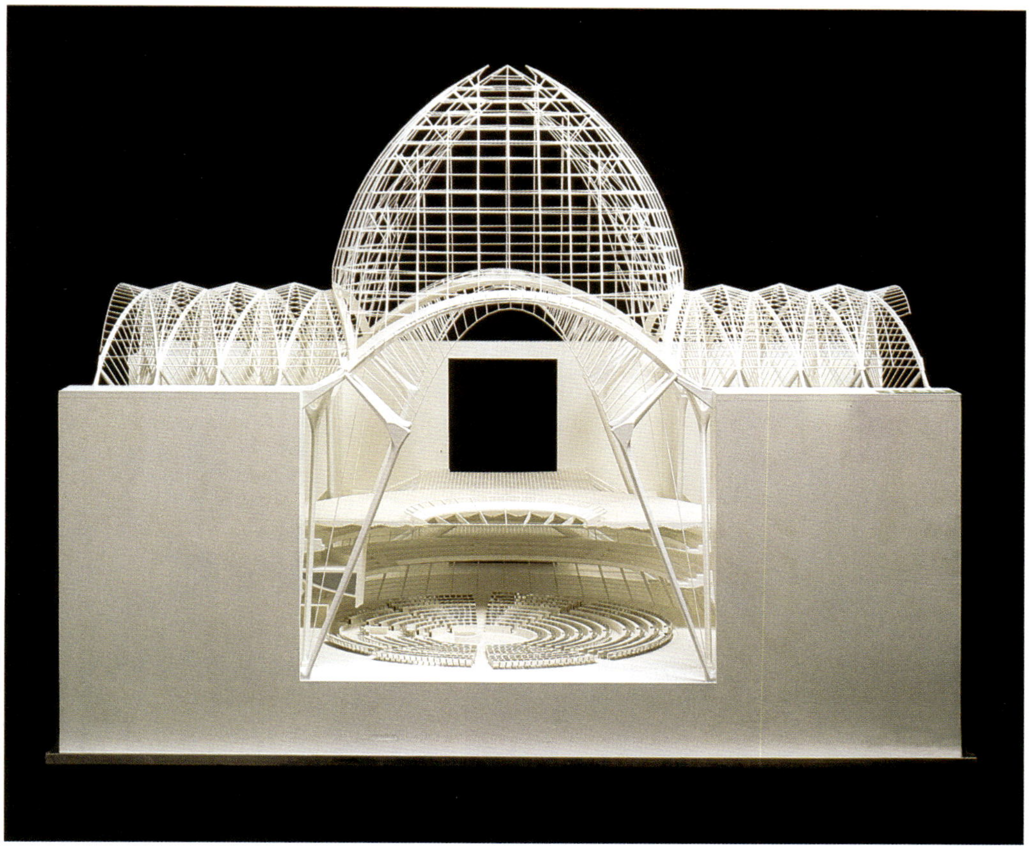

Santiago Calatrava Reichstag surroundings, model

Santiago Calatrava assembly chamber, model

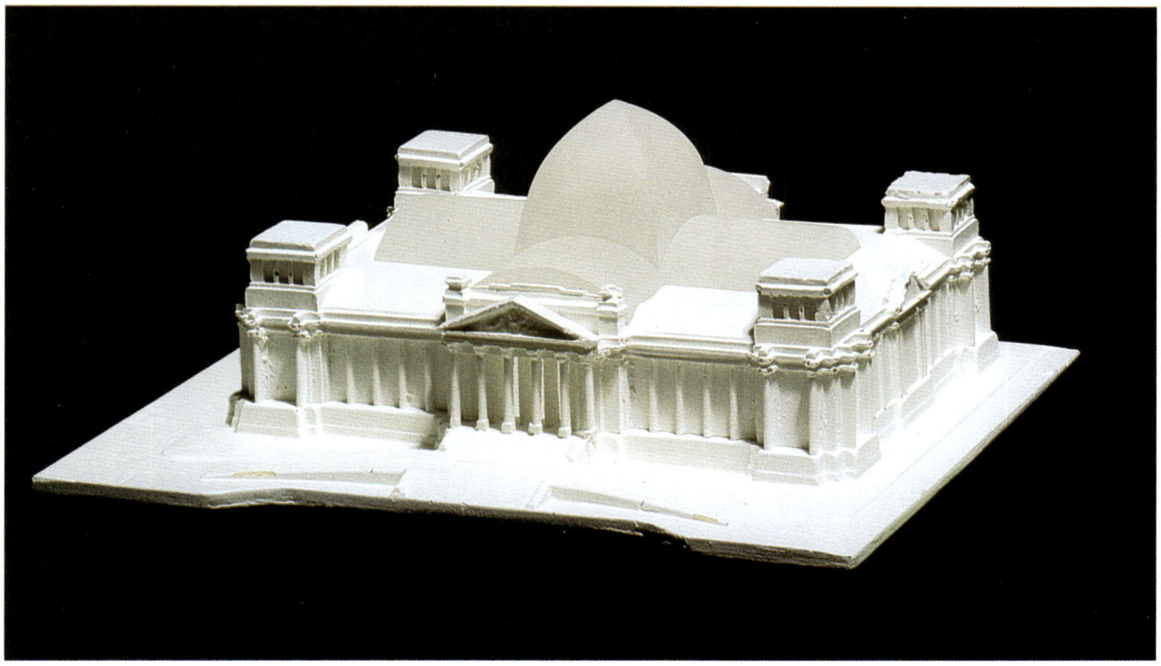

Pi de Bruijn model

Pi de Bruijn groundfloor

Pi de Bruijn first floor

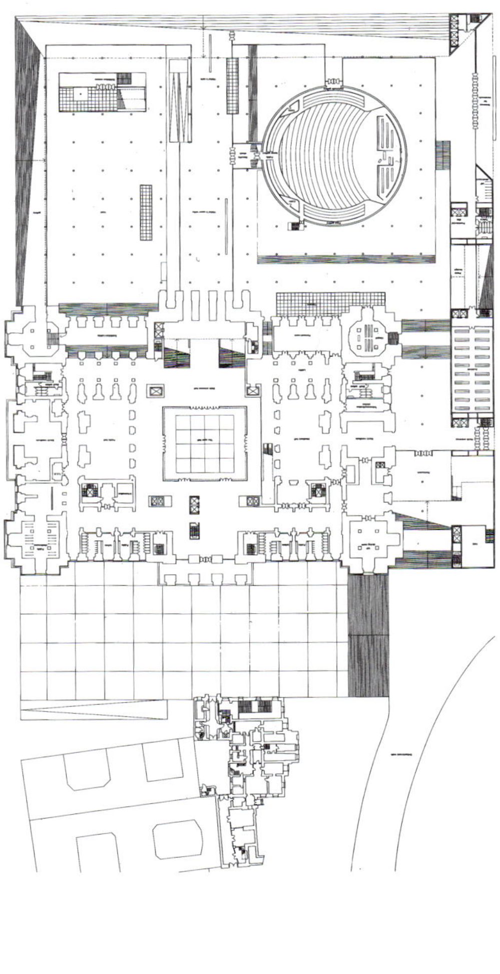

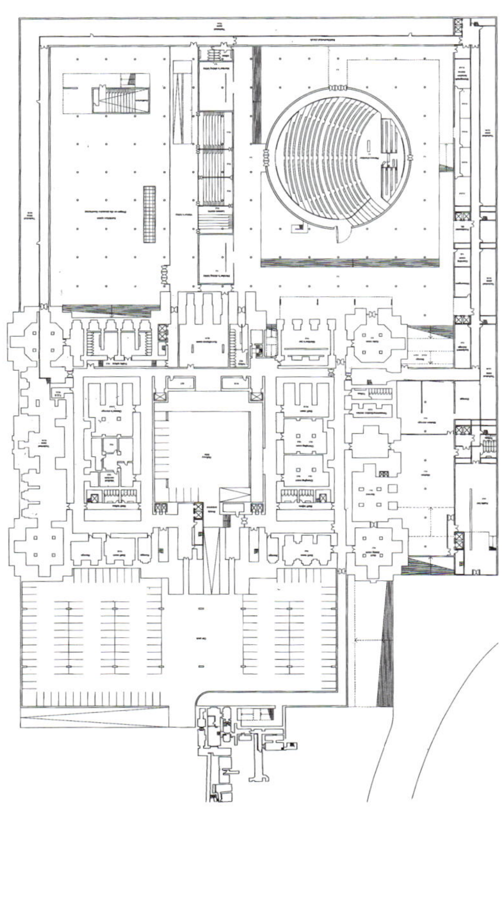

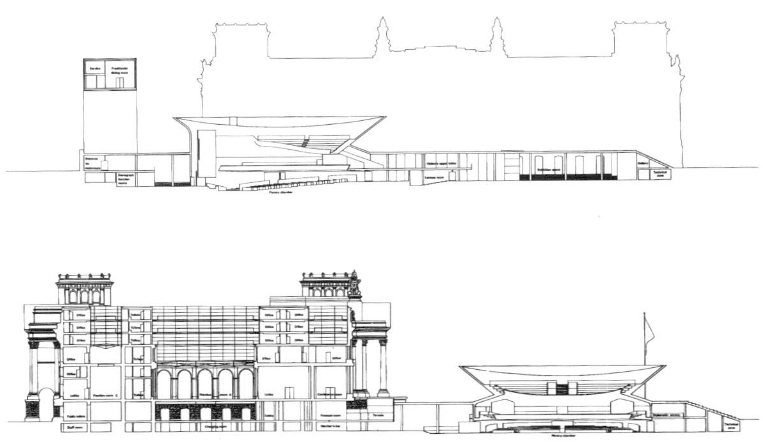

Pi de Bruijn front

Pi de Bruijn front

Pi de Bruijn sections

Bibliography

General bibliography

'Deconstruction, a student Guide', *Journal of Architectural Theory and Criticism*, 1 : 2 : 1991, London 1991

Haan, Hilde de, Ids Haagsma, *Architects in Competition*, New York, 1988

Jödicke, Jürgen, *Architekturgeschichte des 20. Jahrhunderts. Von 1950 bis zur Gegenwart*, Stuttgart 1990

Klotz, Heinrich, *The History of Postmodern Architecture*, Cambridge (Mass.) 1988

Macmillan Encyclopedia of Architects, New York 1982

Middleton, Robin, David Watkin, *Klassizismus und Historismus*, Stuttgart 1987

Mignot, Claude, *Architektur des 19. Jahrhunderts*, Stuttgart 1983

Miyake (ed.), Riichi, Stina van der Ploeg, *Architectural Politics as seen in Competitions*, Tokyo, 1991

Papadakis, Andreas, *Architectuur van nu*, Alphen aan de Rijn 1991

Stewart, David B., *The making of a modern Japanese architecture*, New York / Tokyo 1987

Tafuri, Manfredo, Francesco Dal Co., *Modern Architecture*, New York 1979

Volume 1

The White House, Washington DC, 1792

Borngräber, C., 'Neo-classical Washington', *Architectural design*, profile 23, 48 8–9 (1982)

Hitchcock, H.R. & W. Seale, Temples of Democracy, London (1976)

Roth, L.W., *A Concise History of American Architecture*, New York / London (1980)

Seale, W., *The President's House: A History*, Washington (1986)

The White House: A Historic Guide, Washington (1962)

Valhalla, near Ratisbon, 1814

Fräßle, K., *Carl Haller von Hallerstein* (1774–1817), Freiburg (1971)

Hederer, O., *Leo von Klenze: Persönlichkeit und Werk*, Munich (1964)

Nerdinger, W., *Die Architekturzeichnung*, Munich (1986)

Nerdinger, W., *Klassizismus in Bayern, Schwaben und Franken*, Munich (1980)

Stolz, R., *Die Walhalla: Ein Beitrag zum Denkmalsgedanken im 19.Jahrhundert*, Cologne (1977)

Träeger, J., *Der Weg nach Walhalla*, Regensburg (1987)

Träeger, J., *Walhalla: Idee, Architektur, Landschaft*, Regensburg (1980)

Watkin, D. & Mellinghof, T., *German Architecture and the Classical Ideal 1740–1840*, London (1987)

Houses of Parliament, London, 1835

Clark, K., *The Gothic Revival*, London (1928)

Curl, J.S., *Victorian Architecture*, London (1990)

Eastlake, C., *History of the Gothic Revival*, London (1872)

Ferry, W., *Recollections of A.W.N. Pugin and his father Augustus Pugin*, London (1978)

Jenner, M., *London Heritage*, London (1988)

Pope-Hennesy, J., *The Houses of Parliament*, London (1975)

Port, M.H. (ed.), *The Houses of Parliament*, Yale University (1976)

Turnor, R., *Nineteenth Century Architecture in Britain*, London (1950)

Hofoper, Vienna, 1860

Hoffmann, H-C., W. Krause & W. Kitlitschka, *Das Wiener Opernhaus*, Wiesbaden (1972)

Wulz, F.C., *Stadt in Veränderung: Eine Architektur-politische Studie von Wien in den Jahren 1848–1934*, Stockholm (1976)

L'Opéra, Paris, 1860–1861

Lameyre, Gérard, *Haussmann 'Préfet de Paris'*, Paris (1958)

Mead, C.C., *Charles Garnier's Paris Opéra and the Renaissance of Classicism in Nineteenth Century French Architecture*, Pennsylvania (1986)

Steinhauser, M., *Die Architektur der Pariser Oper*, Munich (1969)

Rijksmuseum, Amsterdam, 1863–1875

Hoogewoud, Guido et al, *P.J.H. Cuypers en Amsterdam*, Den Haag 1985

Catalogus tentoonstelling Rijksmuseum Amsterdam, *Het Nieuwe Rijksmuseum*, Den Haag 1985

Veenland-Heineman, Karen, 'De prijsvragen voor het Muzeüm Koning Willem en het Rijksmuseum 1863–1875', *Nederlands kunsthistorisch Jaarboek 35*, pp. 151–192

Law Courts, London, 1866

Brownlee, D.B., The Law Courts: *The Architecture of George Edmund Street*, New York / Cambridge (1984)

Eastlake, C., *History of the Gothic Revival*, London (1872)

Jenner, M., *London Heritage*, London (1988)

Summerson, J., *Victorian Architecture*, New York / London (1970)

Turnor, R. *Nineteenth Century Architecture in Britain*, London (1950)

Reichstag, Berlin, 1872–1882

Cullen, M. & U. Kieling, *Der Deutsche Reichstag*, Berlin (1992)

Hegemann, W., *Das Steinerne Berlin*, Braunschweig (1976)

Kleihues, J.P., *750 Jahre Architektur und Städtebau in Berlin* (catalogue for IBA-Berlin exhibition 1987), Berlin (1987)

Nerdinger, W., *Die Architekturzeichnung*, Munich (1986)

Raack, H., *Das Reichstagsgebäude in Berlin*, Berlin (1978)

Beurs, Amsterdam, 1884

Bazel, K.P.C. et al, *dr H.P. Berlage en zijn werk*, Rotterdam (1916)

Bock, Manfred, *Anfänge einer neuen Architektur*, Den Haag 1983

Gratama, J., *dr H.P. Berlage Bouwmeester*, Rotterdam (1925)

Hoogewoud, G., 'De Amsterdamse beursprijsvraag van 1884', *Nederlands Kunsthistorisch Jaarboek*, 25 (1974), pp. 277–365

Kloos, M. (ed.), *Berlage in Amsterdam*, Amsterdam (1992)

Polano, S., *Hendrik Petrus Berlage: Het complete werk*, Alphen aan den Rijn (1988)

Retera, W., *Nederlandse Bouwmeesters*, Amsterdam (1947)

Singelenberg, P., *H.P. Berlage: Idea and Style*, Utrecht (1972)

Weissman, A.W., De Amsterdamse Beurs 1835–1903, Amsterdam (1904)

World exhibition, Paris, 1889

Braibant, C., *Histoire de la Tour Eiffel*, Paris (1964)

Chemetov, P. & B. Marey, *Architectures Paris 1848–1914*, Paris (1980)

Cordat, C., *La Tour Eiffel*, Paris (1955)

Friebe, Wolfgang, *Buildings of the World Exhibitions*, Leipzig 1985

Lanoux, Armand (ed.), *La Tour Eiffel*, Paris (1980)

Lemoine, B., *Gustave Eiffel*, Berlin (1988)

'Wereldtentoonstelling', Grafisch Nederland, Christmas Issue (1991)

Henri Loyrette, *Gustave Eiffel, ein Ingenieur und sein Werk*, Stuttgart 1985

Haus eines Kunstfreundes, Darmstadt,1901

Billcliffe, Roger & Peter Vergo, 'Charles Rennie Mackintosh and the Austrian Art Revival', *The Burlington Magazine*, vol. 119, no. 896, 1977, pp. 739–744

Curtis, William J.R., *Modern Architecture since 1900*, London (1982)

Frampton, Kenneth & Yukio Futagawa, *Modern Architecture 1851–1919*, GA Document (2nd special issue), August 1981

Howarth, Thomas, *Charles Rennie Mackintosh and the Modern Movement*, London (1952)

Kossatz, Horst Herbert, 'The Vienna Secession and its Early Relations with Great Britain', *Studio International*, vol. 181, no. 929, 1971, pp. 9–20

Muthesius, Hermann, *Kunstgewerbe und Architektur*, Jena (1907)

Patrick Nuttgens (ed.) *Mackintosh and his conteporaries in Europe and America*, London 1988

Post Office Savings Bank, Vienna, 1903

The architecture of Otto Wagner, London (1989)

Graf, Otto Antonia, *Otto Wager: Das Werk des Architekten*, Vienna (1985)

Horvat Pintaric, Vera, *Vienna 1900*

Kunst, Architektur & Design, Cologne (1987), (Original English edition: New York, 1986)

Lux, Joseph August, *Otto Wagner*, Munich (1914)

Stein, S., Otto Wagner: *Die Österreichischen Postsparkasse*, Vienna (1976–1977)

Varnedoe, Kirk, *Wien 1900*

ZV-Dokumentation, *Otto Wagners Postsparkasse*, Vienna (1977)

City Hall, Stockholm, 1903

Östberg, Ragnar, *The Stockholm Town-hall*, Stockholm (1929)

Paulsson, Thomas, *Scandinavian Architecture*, London (1958)

Helsinki Station, 1903

Donnelly, Marian C., *Architecture in the Scandinavian Countries*, Cambridge, Mass. (1992)

Richards, J.M., *800 Years of Finnish Architecture*, London (1978)

Saarinen in Finland, exhibition catalogue Museum of Finnish Architecture, Helsinki 15 August 1984 – 14 October 1984

Peace Palace, The Hague, 1905

Boer, C.H. de, *Het Vredespaleis*, The Hague (1952)

Eyffinger, Arthur, *The Peace Palace*, The Hague (1988)

Rapport du Jury, Fondation Carnegie, Concours pour le Projet du Palais de la Paix, Amsterdam (1907)

Canberra City Planning, 1911

Fisher, K.F., *Canberra: Myths and Models*, Hamburg (1984)

McKelvey, Blake, *The Urbanization of America (1860–1915)*, New Yersey 1963

Wigmore, Lionel, *The Long View: A History of Canberra, Australia's National Capital*, Melbourne (1963)

Zukowsky, John (ed.), *Chicago Architektur 1872–1922*, München 1987, pp. 323–347

Chicago Tribune Tower, 1922

Chicago Tribune Tower Competition, London (1980)

Condit, Carl W., *The Chicago School of Architecture*, Chicago (1964)

Goldberger, Paul, *The Skyscraper*, New York (1982)

Zukowsky, John (ed.), *Chicago architektur 1872–1922*, München 1987, pp.307–321

League of Nations Building, Geneva, 1926

Le Corbusier (Pierre Jeanneret), *Oeuvre Complet 1910–1929*, Zurich (1960)

Oechslin, Werner (ed.), Le Corbusier & Pierre Jeanneret: *Das Wettbewerbungsprojekt für den Völkerbundspalast in Genf 1927*, Zurich (1988)

Lenin Library, Moscow, 1928

Palace of the Soviets, Moscow, 1931–1933

Peoples' Commissariat of Heavy Industry, Moscow, 1934

'The avant-garde, Russian architecture in the twenties', *Architectural design*, Profile 93, A.D. vol. 61, 1991

Berton, Kathleen, *Moscow. An architectural history*, London 1977

Cooke, Catherine & Igor Kazus, *Soviet Architectural Competitions 1920s–1930s*, London (1992)

Elliot, David, *New worlds. Russian art and society 1900–1937*, London 1986

De Grote Utopie: De Russische Avant-Garde 1915–1932, exhibition catalogue Stedelijk Museum, Amsterdam (6 May 1992)

Kopp, Anatole, *Town and Revolution. Soviet architecture and cityplanning 1917–1937*, New York 1970

Magomedow, Chan, *Pioniere der Sowjetischen Architektur*, Dresden 1983

Palmboom, Frits, *Doel en vermaak in het konstruktivisme*, Sunschrift 142, Nijmegen 1979

'Russian constructivism & Iakov Chernikov', *Architectural design*, 59 no. 7/8

Samona, Alberto (ed.), *Il Palazzo dei Soviet 1931–1933*, Rome (1976)

Voyce, Arthur, *Russian Architecture: Trends in Nationalism and Modernism*, New York (1948)

Zygas, Kestutis Paul, *Form Follows Form: Source Imagery of Constructivist Architecture 1917–1925*, Ann Arbor, Mi. (1981)

Amsterdam City Hall, 1936–1967

Holzbauer, Wilhelm, *Bauten und Projekte 1953–1985*, Salzburg (1985)

Lootsma, Bart, *Cees Dam*, Rotterdam (1989)

Rapport van de Jury, inzake de Openbare en Besloten Prijsvraag voor het Nieuwe Raadhuis van Amsterdam, Amsterdam (1937)

Rooy, Max van & Bas Roodnat, *De Stopera: Een Amsterdamse Geschiedenis*, Amsterdam (1986)

Strauven, Francis, 'Een bovenmaatse gelegenheidscompositie: Het Muziektheater van Holzbauer en Dam', Archis 11, 1986, pp. 6–11

Termini Station, Rome, 1947

Etlin, Richard, *Modernism in Italian architectue 1890–1940*, Cambridge (Mass) 1991

'Railway Terminus at Rome', *Architectural Review*, vol. 109, no. 652, April 1954, pp. 209–215

Volume 2

Town Hall and Church, Seinäjoki, 1950

Fleig, Karl (ed.), *Alvar Aalto*, Zurich (1963)

Hoesli, B. (ed.), *Alvar Aalto Synopsis*, Basel (1970)

Pearson, Paul David, *Alvar Aalto and the International Style*, New York (1978)

Salokorpi, Asko, *Modern Architecture in Finland*, New York (1970)

Tempel, Egon, *New Finnish Architecture*, New York (1968)

Quantrill, Malcolm, *Alvar Aalto, a critical Study*, New York 1983

Opera House, Sydney, 1956

Faber, Tobias, *Geschichte der Architektur in Dänemark*, Copenhagen (1978)

Brasilia Urbanisation Plan, 1956

Arnau, Frank, *Brasilia*, Munich (1960)

Evenson, Norma, *Two Brazilian Capitals: Architecture and Urbanism in Rio de Janeiro and Brasilia*, New Haven / London (1973)

Keijzer, Marcel, Juliette van der Meijden, et al (eds.), *Brasilia: Moderne Stad*, exhibition catalogue Rotterdam, 22 June – 28 July 1989

Meira Penna, J.O. de, *Brazil builds Brasilia*, Rio de Janeiro (1959)

Meurs, Paul et al, 'De moderne stad en het virus van de tijd', *De Architect*, Vol. 20, November 1989

Wirthwein, Holger, 'Brasilia, een symbool als stad', *Platvorm*, no. 8, July 1988

Entertainment Centre, Monte Carlo, 1969

Banham, Reyner, 'Monaco Underground', *The Architects' Journal*, no. 2, September 1970, pp. 506–509

Cook, Peter (ed.), *Archigram*, Basel (1991)

Cook, Peter, *Architecture: Action and Plan*, New York (1969)

'Peter Cook 1961–1989', *A + U*, (extra edition) December 1989

'Peter Cook: Six Conversations', *Architectural Monographs*, no. 28, London (1993)

Architectural Design, vol. XLI, Augustt 1971, Archigram 1970–1971

Centre Pompidou, Paris, 1970

'Centre Pompidou', *A.D. Profiles 2*, London (1977)

Fils, Alexander, *Das Centre Pompidou in Paris*, Munich (1980)

Silver, Nathan, *The making of Beaubourg*, Cambridge (Mass.) London 1994

San Cataldo Cemetery, Modena, 1971

Adjmi, Morri (ed.), *Aldo Rossi, Architecture 1981–1991*, New York (1991)

'Aldo Rossi', *A + U*, November 1982

Braghieri, Gianni, *Aldo Rossi*, Rotterdam (1984)

Moschini, Francesco, *Aldo Rossi: Projects and Drawings 1962–1979*, exhibition catalogue Galleria Pan, 29 March – 28 April 1979, Rome

Rossi, Aldo, *The Architecture of the City*, Cambridge Mass. (1982)

Parc de la Villette, Paris, 1976

'Bernard Tschumi / Jo Coenen', *A + U*, no. 216, September 1989

Boer, Hubert de & Hans van Dijk, 'Het park van de 21ste eeuw', *Wonen / TABK*, 12 / 1983, pp. 8–29

Dijk, Hans van, 'Jury La Villette vlucht voor beslissing', *Wonen / TABK*, 2 / 1983, pp. 2–3

Tschumi, Bernard, *Le Parc de la Villette*, Princeton (1987)

Hongkong and Shanghai Bank, Hong Kong, 1979

Architectural Review, vol. CLXIX, no. 1011, May 1981

Chaslin, François, et al, *Norman Foster*, Paris (1986)

Williams, Stephanie, *Hongkong Bank: The Building of Norman Foster's Masterpiece*, London (1989)

Paris, general bibliography

Architectures Capitales Paris 1979–1989, Paris 1989

Chaslin, François, *Les Paris de François Mitterand*, Paris 1985

Lucan, Jacques, *France Architecture 1965–1988*, Paris 1989

Martin, Hervé, *Guide de l'Architecture à Paris 1900–1990*, Paris 1986

Architectural Review, CLXXXVI, no. 110, August 1989. Theme: Paris 2000

Salat, Serge, Françoise Labbé, *Paul Andreu*, Milan / Paris 1990

La Cité des Sciences et de l'Industrie, Paris, 1980

Dijk, Hans van, 'Triomfalistische non-architectuur', *Archis*, 4, 1987, pp. 47–51

Pélissier, Alain (ed.) et al, Adrien Fainsilber, *La Virtualité de l'Espace: Projects et Architecture 1962–1988*, Paris (1988)

Grande Arche, Paris, 1982

See general bibliography, Paris

The Opéra Bastille, Paris, 1982

Beer, Roland de, 'Zelfs de nagalm is variabel', *de Volkskrant*, 14 February 1986

Charlet, Gerard, *The Opéra Bastille*, Paris (1990)

Kloos, Maarten, 'Een nieuwe opera voor Parijs', *de Volkskrant*, 16 December 1983

Lievaert, Chris, 'Opéra de la Bastille', *Podium*, 2 / 1983, pp. 42–43

Strauven, Francis, 'Een functionele geest in een vreemd lichaam', *Archis*, 4 / 1990, pp. 12–19

The Peak, Hong Kong, 1982

Dijk, Hans van, 'De angst van de duiker voor de waterspiegel', *Archis*, 1987-6, pp. 42-49

El Croquis, 52 Vol. 11 1992, 'Zaha Hadid 1983/1991'

Vision, 4-1983, special edition 'The Peak', including the jury report

Carré d'Art, Nîmes, 1984

Chaslin, François et al, *Norman Foster*, Paris (1986)

Davies, Colin, 'Carré Culturel', *Architectural Review*, Vol. CXCIV, no. 1157, July 1993, pp. 18-31

Glancey, Jonathan, 'Nîmes Schemes', *Architectural Review*, Vol. CLXXVII, no. 1059, May 1985, pp. 31-39

Reglement du jury, published by the Ville de Nîmes, with appendices

New National Theatre, Tokyo, 1985

Meyhöfer, Dirk (ed.), *Contemporary Japanese Architects*, Cologne (1993)

Yanagisawa, Takahiko, 'The New National Theatre', *Japan Architect*, 3 Summer 1991-3, pp. 44-59

Shonandai Culture Centre, Fujisawa, 1985

Bognar, Botond, *Die Neue Japanische Architektur*, New York (1990)

Cook, Peter, 'Shonandai Symbols', *Architectural Review*, August 1990, Volume 188, no. 1122, pp. 30-35

Meyhöfer, Dirk (ed.), *Contemporary Japanese Architects*, Cologne (1993)

Metropolitan Hall, Tokyo, 1985

Boyd, Robin, *New Directions in Japanese Architecture*, London (1968)

Egon Tempel, *Neue Japanische Architektur*, Stuttgart 1969

The new Tokyo City Hall Complex, *Japan Architect*, 1991/3, pp. 6-7

City Hall, The Hague, 1986

Duivesteijn, Adri, *Het Haagse Stadhuis Centraal*, The Hague

Izzo, Ferruccio & Alessandro Gubitosi (Eds.), *Richard Meier, Architecture: Projects 1986-1990*, exhibition catalogue, Palazzo Reale, Naples, 21 June - 21 July 1991

International Building Exhibition, Berlin, 1987

Cramer, Johannes, Gutschow, *Bauaustellungen: eine Architekturgeschichte des 20. Jahrhunderts*, Stuttgart 1984

Hämer, Hardt-Waltherr, Josef Paul Kleihues (eds.), *Idee, Prozess, Ergebnis: Die reparatur und Rekonstruktion der Stadt*, Berlin (1984)

Internationale Bauausstellung Berlin 1984, exhibition catalogue, Bouwcentrum De Doelen, Rotterdam, 3 April - 1 May 1982

Internationale Bauausstellung Berlin 1987: Projektübersicht, Berlin (1987)

Kleihues, Josef Paul (ed.), *Internationale Bauausstellung Berlin 1984: Die Neubaugebiete*, Part 2, Berlin (1984)

Kleihues, Josef Paul (ed.), *Internationale Bauausstellung Berlin 1984-1987: Die Neubaugebiete*, Part 3, Stuttgart (1987)

German Historical Museum, Berlin, 1987

Adjmi, Morris, *Aldo Rossi: Architecture 1981-1991*, New York (1991)

Ferlenga, Alberto (ed.), *Deutsches Historisches Museum Berlin: Aldo Rossis Entwurf im Gefüge der Kulturforen*, Stuttgart (1991), with an article by Werner Oechslin

Giersbergen, Marieke van, 'Een compositie van fragmenten', *Archis*, 1988/9, pp 8-9

Mediapark, Cologne, 1987

Bure, Gilles de, *Jean Nouvel, Emmanuel Cattani and Associates: Four Projects*, Zurich/Munich/London (1992)

Giersbergen, Marieke, 'Mediapark Keulen zonder Nouvel?' *Archis*, 1991-5, pp. 9-10

Kloos, Maarten, '1990-0905/20:30: Een Moment onder woorden', *Archis*, 1990-11, pp. 26-31

Lucan, Jacques, 'Jean Nouvel, een ongedurig optimist', *Archis*, 1990-11, pp. 18-25

Mediapark Pressespiegel, December 1989, MPK Cologne

Mediapark Report 8, December 1989, MPK Cologne

Jean Nouvel 1987-1994, *El Croquis* 65/66, 1994

Jewish Museum, Berlin, 1988

Kristin Feireiss (ed.), *Daniel Libeskind: Erweiterung des Berlin Museums mit Abteilung Jüdisches Museum*, Berlin (1992)

Müller, Alois Martin (ed.), *Daniel Liebeskind, Radix Matrix*, München / New York 1994

Kansai Airport, Osaka, 1988

De Architect, March 1992, Special edition "Luchthavens", including articles by Janny Rodermond and Jos Roodbol

Domus Dossier, special edition "Aeroporti", 1993-1

Labbé, Francoise & Serge Salat, Paul Andreu: *Metamorphosis of the Circle*, Milan/Paris (1990)

Okabe, Noriaki, 'Kansai International Airport Passenger Terminal Building', *Japan Architect*, 11 Autumn 1993-3, pp. 59-70

Centre for Japanese Culture, Paris, 1989

Meyhöfer, Dirk, *Contemporary Japanese Architecture*, Cologne (1993)

Reichstag, Berlin, 1992

Collyer, Stanley, 'Reconstructing Berlin's Urban Fabric', *Competitions*, Summer 1993, Vol. 3 no. 2, pp. 3-11

Cullen, Michael S. & Martin Kieren, *Calatrava Berlin: Fünf Projekte*, Basel (1994)

Oosterman, Arjen, 'Rijksdag wordt Bondsdag', *Archis*, 1993-4, pp. 8-11

Acknowledgements

ABC Press Service c.v. Amsterdam
Alberts & M. van Huut, Amsterdam
A.N.P. Foto Amsterdam
Arata Isozaki & Associates, Tokyo
Archigram Archives, London
Architekten Cie., de, Amsterdam
Architectural Institute of Japan, Tokyo
Architektenburo Herman Hertzberger, Amsterdam
Architekten Kollektief Heydenrijk B.V., Amersfoort
Architektengroep Loerakker, Rijnboutt, Ruyssenaars, Hendriks, Amsterdam
Archives Authority of New South Wales, the, Sydney
Archives Nationales, Service Photographique, Paris
Australian Archives, A.C.T. Reprography Unit
Australian Tourism Industry Association, Canberra

Bauhaus-Archiv – Museum für Gestaltung, Berlin
Bayerische Staatsbibliothek, Munich
BDK Vollmer, Cologne
Berengo Gardin, Gianni
Bianco, Laurent, Geneva
Bibliothèque Administrative Historique de la Ville de Paris
Bibliothèque Nationale, Paris
Bildmedia, Stockholm
Bliss, Terence, London
Bofill / Taller de Arquitectura, Sant Just Desvern, Ricardo, Spain
Boissevain & Osmond, Epsom
British Architectural Library, RIBA, London
Broek & Bakema, van den, Rotterdam
Bundesbaudirektion, Berlin
Bureau voor Bouwkunde, Rotterdam
Busch Reisinger Museum, Harvard University

Charmet, Jean-Loup, Paris
Clementino, Luiz, Brasilia
Collection of the Maryland Historical Society
Coert Peter Krabbe, Vrije Universiteit, Amsterdam
Commune di Modena
Cook & Christine Hawley, Peter

Deutsches Architekturmuseum, Frankfurt am Main
Deutsches Historisches Museum, Berlin
Dubbini, Giulio

Editions du Demi-Cercle, les
Etablissement Public de l'Opéra de la Bastille, Paris
Etablissement Public du Parc de la Villette, Paris
Etablissement Public pour l'aménagement de la région de la Défense, Paris

Fainsilber, Adrien, Paris
Finlands Architektforbund, Helsinki
Fondation Le Corbusier, Paris

Gehry & Associates Inc., Frank O., Santa Monica
Graphische Sammlung Albertina, Vienna
Grossfoto, Berlin

Haags Gemeentemuseum, Den Haag
Hadid, Studio 9, Zaha M., London
Historisch topografische Atlas van het Gemeentearchief van Amsterdam
Historisches Museum der Stadt Wien, Vienna
Holzbauer's Office, Wilhelm, Vienna
Hoogstad en Van Tilburg, Rotterdam
Hunterian Art Gallery, University of Glasgow, Mackintosh Collection

Kansai International Airport Co. LtD
Keijo Sulkko, Seinäjoki
Koninklijk Huisarchief, Den Haag

Laboratoire Photographique du Musée d'Orsay, Paris
League of Nations Archive and Historical Collections Unit, Geneva
Lenneke Büller & Frank den Oudsten, Amsterdam
Lutheran Congregation of Seinäjoki, the, Finland

Massachusetts Historical Society, London
Mediapark, Cologne
Meier & Partners, Richard
Musee d'Art Contemporain, Nîmes
Musée de la Chartreuse, Douai
Musée d'Orsay, Paris
Museum der Stadt Regensburg
Museum of Finnish Architecture, Helsinki

Nederlands Architectuur Instituut, Rotterdam
Nederlandse Spoorwegen, Utrecht
Nouvel, Emmanuel Cattani et associés, Jean, Paris

Ontwikkelingscombinatie Stadhuis Den Haag
Osaka International Peace Foundation
Österreichische Postparkasse, Vienna

P & T Architects & Engineers LtD
Photo Department Sinkenchiku, Japan
Photothèque EPAD, Paris
Plansammlung der Universitätsbibliothek der Technischen Universität, Berlin
Portzamparc, Christian de, Paris
Prynn, Laurence, London

Raili & Reima Pietila, Helsinki
Rau, Uwe, Berlin
Renzo Piano Building Workshop, Osaka
Réunion des Musées Nationaux, Paris
Richard Rogers Partnership, London
Rodier, Agnes, Paris
Royal Commission on the Ancient & Historical Monuments of Scotland, the, Edingburgh
Royal Institute of British Architects, London

Salomon, Jean-Pierre, Paris
Schussev Museum, Moscow
Seidler & Associates, Harry
Senatsverwaltung für Bau- und Wohnungswesen, Archiv Internationale Bauaustellung, Berlin
Service des Bâtiments, Service Information Communication
Shonandai Culture Centre
Sir Norman Foster Associates, London
Skidmore, Owings & Merrill
Société VIP, Paris
Spaarnestad Fotoarchief / Herman Boerrigter, Haarlem
Staatliche Graphische Sammlung, Munich
Stadsmuseum Stockholm
Survey of the Community of Vienna, the

Tate Gallery, London
Technische Universität, Munich

Vandenhove et Associés, Charles, Paris
Victoria & Albert Museum, London
Viguier, Jean François Jodry, Jean Paul, Paris

Weiße, Antonia, Berlin
William Alsop & John Lyell Architects, London

YRM Partnership LTD

Chief editor

Cees de Jong, V+K Publishing, Naarden

Design

Cees de Jong, José K. Vermeulen, V+K Design, Naarden

Illustration research co-ordinator

Emmanuelle Kramps, Naarden

Production co-ordinators

Cees de Jong, Emmanuelle Kramps, Naarden
Jochen Dilling, Cologne

Editor

Erik Mattie, Amsterdam

Assistant editor

Michiel Pestman, Amsterdam

Translator – English

Richard de Nooy, Amsterdam

Translator – German

Franca Fritz & Heinrich Koop, Cologne

Translator – French

Jacques Bosser, Paris

Architectural Competitions is based on an idea developed by Cees de Jong, V+K Publishing, Naarden, The Netherlands.
In 1988, V+K Publishing published an international co-edition *Architects in Competition.*
In 1991, V+K Publishing published *Architectural Politics as seen in Competitions* in a set of seven volumes, especially for the Japanese market.
In 1994, this publication *Architectural Competitions* is completely edited and written by Cees de Jong and Erik Mattie.

Architec tural Competi tions 1792–1949

Archi tektur Wett bewerbe 1792–1949

Concours d'Archi tecture 1792–1949

Cees de Jong | Erik Mattie

Architectural Competitions 1792–1949

Architektur Wettbewerbe 1792–1949

Concours d'Architecture 1792–1949

Benedikt Taschen

Printed in Germany
English cover:
ISBN 3-8228-8900-8 (cloth-bound)
ISBN 3-8228-8901-6 (leather-bound)
German cover:
ISBN 3-8228-8929-6 (cloth-bound)
ISBN 3-8228-9242-4 (leather-bound)
French cover:
ISBN 3-8228-9291-2 (cloth-bound)
ISBN 3-8228-9292-0 (leather-bound)

Competitions in architecture and town planning since 1792

Contents

Grueber interior perspective, 1842, colour lithograph by C. Köppe

Introduction

Architectural competitions have become fairly common events and are interesting for several reasons. One is that the jury reports, the submitted designs, and the reviews in the press and specialist publications contain a wealth of information. Another is the fact that the history of architectural competitions mirrors the history of architecture itself. Renowned and less renowned architects, innovators and conservatives, are all portrayed in a snapshot of architecture taken at a given moment in time. Both the highlights and the peripheral events are significant. The selection of forty-nine competitions from a period spanning almost two centuries, provides a survey of architectural movements and their respective representatives, who were either at loggerheads with one another or worked in peaceful coexistence. Nineteenth-century stylistic issues are discussed alongside the rejection of all styles from bygone eras during the twentieth-century, culminated in proposals to demolish the historical hearts of certain cities. Finally, the history of the architectural competitions themselves will be a recurrent topic of discussion in this book.

In order to maintain a modicum of clarity, the survey has been limited to recent history. Architectural competitions are, of course, a much older phenomenon. A famous early example is the competition for the dome of the Cathedral in Florence, which was won by Brunelleschi. The dome has become one of the most important Renaissance monuments both for its aesthetic achievement and for the sense of pride in their own city that the dome instilled amongst the Florentine population. These two aspects of architecture have been standard ingredients of architectural competitions throughout history to the present day. Kings, emperors, dictators and participating architects shared a common drive for distinction. The latter group had an additional incentive, in that they saw participation as a first step towards architectural immortality.

Two examples – England and the Netherlands

Although this book is limited to highlights of architectural history, architectural competitions are, in fact, an everyday affair. One of the few surveys to have been compiled over the years concerns architectural competitions in Victorian England and Ireland. Its author, Roger Harper, counted no fewer than 2500 competitions during the course of five decades: an average of one per week. London was the undisputed leader with 362 competitions, followed by other British industrial cities such as Manchester, Liverpool, Leeds and Birmingham. One of the main reasons for this spate of architectural competitions was England's rapid economic growth during the nineteenth century, which went hand in hand with a growing need for new buildings for transport, education and health services. However, it was not uncommon for competitions to be organised for the smallest village churches. Initially, local dignitaries sponsored these events in order to obtain inexpensive plans, which they then had executed by a local contractor who finished the job according to the wishes of the organising body. It was also quite common for inexperienced juries to be swayed by pretty, water-coloured pictures, instead of basing their assessment on the architectural merits of a design. Moreover, there were few rules governing the payment of prize money, which meant that architects often gained little more than experience from their participation in competitions. The only real advantage was that the competitions were generally discussed in the British architectural journals.

It was obvious that this dismal state of affairs was in dire need of some form of regulation. Although the Institute of British Architects (IBA) had already drafted a set of rules in 1839, these did not have the weight of the formal regulations drafted by the Royal Institute of British Architects (RIBA) in 1872. In later years, standard regulations were also drafted by the Association of Swiss Engineers and Architects (SIA) and the Union Internationale d'Architects. These regulations were developed in order to put paid to competitions such as that organised for the White House in Washington. In this competition – which is the subject of the first chapter of this book – a jury of amateurs judged designs submitted largely by amateurs and a few architects. Hardly any architectural conditions were stipulated and the architects were granted little time to develop their designs. Furthermore, there was a clear indication that the winning architect, James Hoban, had managed to bias the jury in his favour.

Nevertheless, in spite of the regulations, scandals and rows are still a feature of many of the more prestigious competitions, which makes them all the more intriguing. It is worth mentioning that the increasing body of regulations went hand-in-hand with greater self-esteem amongst the architects and a growing respect for their profession. This development first manifested itself in England, which already boasted a respectable number of architectural journals during the nineteenth century. However, in other countries, such as the Netherlands, the times were also changing, although it must be said that even the winners of well organised competitions were still not always commissioned to execute their designs. In 1842, an association for the advancement of architecture – the Maatschappij tot Bevordering van de Bouwkunst – was established in the Netherlands. Their aim was to improve the quality of architecture and, more specifically, to organise architectural competitions which would stimulate architects to explore the boundaries of their creativity. The association believed that, without the interference of a commissioning body, architects would be capable of achieving great heights at their drawing boards.

The winning design would then serve as a prototype for buildings of its sort; a guideline on how to build a church, a town hall, or any other type of building. Many of the winning architects were instructed to develop their designs further in order to obtain the desired prototype. This type of competition resembled the later conceptual competitions, which will be discussed further on. Obviously, this form of competition presents architectural historians with a rich source of information concerning the architectural ideals of a certain era.

The competitions organised by the Maatschappij were governed by strict regulations concerning prize money and awards. An extended jury report, listing the pros and cons of the submitted designs, was published after the competition, and these jury reports are also an important source of information for researchers with an interest in the complexities of nineteenth century style issues. However, the history of the Peace Palace in The Hague illustrates the fact that not all Dutch competitions were efficiently organised. One of the outstanding features of the jury report for the Peace Palace was its utter triviality, which contributed to the storm of protest that erupted after the result was announced – see the chapter on the Peace Palace for a detailed account –. This underscores the fact that competitions which are run "by the book" are the exception rather than the rule.

Forms of competition

There is a clear distinction between the competitions held in England and those held in the Netherlands during the nineteenth century: a distinction between determinate and indeterminate competitions – this terminology dates back to1844 –: a distinction between competitions which served a concrete purpose, and competitions for the advancement of architecture itself. A more specific distinction can be made between conceptual competitions, which serve to select a suitable architect, and competitions for which detailed designs are requested. Large architectural firms have an edge on other competitors in the latter type of competition, in that these firms can often afford to spend months working on a project which may produce zero results. Moreover, renowned firms are often invited to participate and are then reimbursed for their efforts. In conceptual competitions, which are less time-consuming, the chances are more even.

A parallel distinction may be drawn between open and closed competitions. In closed competitions, the organising body invites a handful of celebrated architects, generally at a more than reasonable fee, who usually help to draw attention to the project and increase the chance that an architectural masterpiece will be erected. An added advantage is that the jury does not drown in a deluge of designs. If there are too many entries, this tends to cloud the jury's assessment capacities. A classic example of this is Utzon's design for the Sydney Opera House, which had already been eliminated by the jury at the start of the competition.

Open competitions attract entries from hundreds of ambitious young architects, who see the competitions as a gateway to immortality, while renowned architects often decline to participate for fear of losing face.

Mixed competitions have also been organised. These are open competitions for which the organising body also invites a number of renowned architects.

A distinction may also be made between national and international competitions. National competitions are often held to keep local architects happy or to obtain designs in a "national style". International competitions are naturally more prestigious. It is interesting to note that during the 19th and early 20th century many architects tried their luck outside their home countries, even though the methods of transport and communication were poor by today's standards. Modern architecture has become an international affair. Whilst nowadays it is not unusual for Japanese architects participate in European competitions and vice versa, in the past, only a few adventurers participated in competitions outside their home country.

Recurrent names

It is interesting to note that the names of a few architects keep popping up, particularly in the records of international competitions. These architects are certainly not desperate novices trying to attract attention, but die-hard, competitive creatures. Some architects participate in every competition while others specialise in certain forms of competition or types of project. Some architects participate as a form of architectural exercise, others participate to earn a living. In general, specialisation usually brings the best results.
Lockwood & Mawson are prime examples of specialist architects in Victorian England. They participated in 30 competitions and won 20. Other contenders include Bellamy & Hardy – 17 out of 35 – and John Johnson – 16 out of 26 –. Here too, the winning architects were not always commissioned to execute their designs. Nevertheless, the list of achievements is still impressive, leading one to surmise that a certain talent is required in order to win a competition. However, it is interesting to note that these successful Victorians generally did not play an important part in architectural history and in most cases their names are not even listed in architectural encyclopædias! This suggests that their special talent really amounted to little more than having a good eye for the preferences of the jury. Needless to say, the juries seldom expressed a preference for the avant-garde or any innovative style; requests for "innovative" designs were generally limited to the major, prestigious competitions.
Nevertheless, specialists are not a dying breed, even though the form of competitions has changed since the Victorian era. Twentieth century specialists include Eero Saarinen – 12 out of 20 – and Alvar Aalto – 25 out of 58 –. There are also examples of contemporary architects whose names repeatedly crop up in international competitions: Rem Koolhaas, Norman Foster and Aldo Rossi. The latter participated in no fewer than 30 competitions, usually to stay in architectural shape, which explains the low success rate. He was rewarded for his efforts on only a few occasions.
It is also interesting to note that jury members seem to develop a taste for their work. Some architects alternately participate in competitions or accept a seat on the jury, and others have seats on one jury after another. Josef Paul Kleihues had a seat on all the competition juries for the IBA in Berlin – see the corresponding chapter –.
England's most popular jury member was Alfred Waterhouse, the RIBA chairman, who accepted seats on 44 juries over the course of a few decades, but participated in "only" seven competitions. However, it must be said that the regulations drafted in 1872 stipulated that all competition juries were to include at least one RIBA member.

The commissioning body

Obviously, a competent jury is a necessity, certainly if the commissioning body intends to construct a prestigious building. Which brings us to the last character in the architectural play: the client or financier, generally a private company or the state. Examples of the former include the Chicago Tribune and the Hongkong and Shanghai Bank, although buildings are usually commissioned by the state. Sometimes the client has a seat on the jury, but in most cases adjudication is left to the experts. Clients have occasionally rejected a jury's decision – usually for good reasons – and have plotted their own course. There have also been instances were the winner was commissioned, but the execution was hampered for a variety of reasons. Examples of both cases have been included in this book. Finally, there are those clients who do not witness the completion of their masterpieces – a tragic fate they share with a number of architects – see chapters on the Law Courts and the Grande Arche –. Tragedy, however, is an integral part of architectural history.

The object of this book is to draw the reader's attention to the significance of competitions for architectural history and it is for this reason that a broad selection of information has been gathered concerning a wide variety of competitions. Naturally it was impossible to include all the available information in each of the written chapters which accompany the designs and other illustrations. However, the bibliographies included in this book will probably still the interested reader's thirst for additional information.

Einführung

Architekturwettbewerbe gehören längst zu den alltäglichen Erscheinungen. Dennoch bieten sie immer wieder neue Perspektiven, denn in ihnen spiegelt sich auch die Geschichte der Architektur. Berühmte und weniger berühmte Architekten, Erneuerer und Traditionalisten sind in einer Momentaufnahme an einem bestimmten Punkt ihrer Entwicklung festgehalten. Die vorliegende Auswahl von Architekturwettbewerben deckt einen Zeitraum von etwa zwei Jahrhunderten ab. Sie bietet einen Überblick über die wichtigsten architektonischen Strömungen dieser Zeit und stellt deren bedeutendste Vertreter vor, die ihre Bauwerke teils in gemeinsamer Arbeit, teils in erbittertem Streit schufen. Dabei kommen die architektonischen Themen des 19. Jahrhunderts ebenso zur Sprache wie die im 20. Jahrhundert aufkommende Ablehnung vergangener Architekturstile, die mit der geplanten Zerstörung historischer Stadtkerne ihren Höhepunkt erreichte. Darüber hinaus gehört die Entwicklung der Architekturwettbewerbe selbst zu den zentralen Themen dieses Buches.

Obwohl sich der Überblick aus Gründen der Übersichtlichkeit auf eine Zeitspanne von zwei Jahrhunderten beschränkt, gehen die Anfänge der Architekturwettbewerbe wesentlich weiter zurück. Ein frühes Beispiel ist der zu Beginn des 15. Jahrhunderts ausgeschriebene Wettbewerb für die Kuppel des Doms in Florenz, den Brunelleschi für sich entschied. Der Dom zählt wegen seiner ästhetischen Komposition und wegen des Stolzes, den er bei den Bürgern der Stadt Florenz weckte, zu den wichtigsten Bauwerken der Renaissance. Beide Aspekte gehören bis heute zu den typischen Merkmalen eines Architekturwettbewerbs. Ob Könige, Kaiser, Diktatoren oder teilnehmende Architekten: Sie alle verbindet ein gemeinsames Streben nach Einzigartigkeit. Zudem betrachten die Architekten ihre Teilnahme als ersten Schritt in die architektonische Unsterblichkeit.

Zwei Beispiele – England und die Niederlande

Zu den wenigen Arbeiten über Architekturwettbewerbe gehört der von Roger Harper zusammengestellte Überblick über die Ausschreibungen im viktorianischen England und Irland. Harper kam auf nicht weniger als 2500 Ausschreibungen innerhalb von fünf Jahrzehnten, was einem Durchschnitt von einem Wettbewerb pro Woche entspricht. Dabei lag London mit 362 Architekturwettbewerben an der Spitze, gefolgt von anderen Industriestädten wie Manchester, Liverpool, Leeds und Birmingham. Einer der Hauptgründe für diese Wettbewerbsflut war das rapide Wirtschaftswachstum im 19. Jahrhundert, das einherging mit einem zunehmenden Bedarf an neuen Gebäuden für Transport, Bildung und Gesundheitswesen. Auch war es üblich, selbst für die kleinste Dorfkirche einen Architekturwettbewerb auszuschreiben. Ursprünglich unterstützten die städtischen Würdenträger solche Pläne, da sie auf diese Weise preisgünstig an Baupläne gelangten, die danach von einem lokalen Bauunternehmer entsprechend den Vorstellungen der Auftraggeber ausgeführt wurden. Die häufig unerfahrenen Jurymitglieder ließen sich oft von hübschen Aquarellen mitreißen, statt ihr Urteil aufgrund der architektonischen Qualitäten eines Entwurfs zu fällen. Es gab nur wenige Regeln bezüglich der Vergabe von Preisgeldern, so daß die Architekten bei ihrer Teilnahme an einem Wettbewerb nur selten mehr als Erfahrung gewannen. Einziger Vorteil: Die Ausschreibungen wurden in der britischen Architekturpresse ausgiebig besprochen.

Dieser unhaltbare Zustand bedurfte dringend einer Reform. Das bereits 1839 vom Institute of British Architects (IBA) verfaßte Regelwerk besaß nicht die Durchsetzungskraft der 1872 vom Royal Institute of British Architects (RIBA) erlassenen Vorschriften. In den Jahren danach verfaßten auch der Schweizer Ingenieur- und Architektenverein (SIA) sowie die Union Internationale d'Architects allgemeine Wettbewerbsregeln. Alle Regelungen sollten dazu dienen, Zustände wie bei der Ausschreibung für das Weiße Haus in Washington zukünftig zu verhindern. Bei diesem Wettbewerb – der im ersten Kapitel näher besprochen wird – beurteilte eine reine Laienjury die ebenfalls von Laien und einigen Architekten eingereichten Entwürfe. Die Teilnehmer bekamen nur wenige Auflagen und hatten entsprechend nur wenig Zeit zur Ausarbeitung ihrer Vorschläge. Deutliche Hinweise zeigen, daß der Gewinner, James Hoban, die Jury zu seinen Gunsten beeinflußte.

Trotz aller Regeln gehören Skandale und Streitigkeiten nach wie vor zu den wichtigsten Merkmalen prestigeträchtiger Ausschreibungen – was sie nur noch faszinierender macht. Parallel zum Anwachsen des Regelwerks nahm das Selbstbewußtsein der Architekten und der Respekt für ihren Berufsstand ständig zu. Diese Entwicklung zeichnete sich zunächst in England ab, wo bereits im 19. Jahrhundert eine ganze Reihe von Architekturzeitschriften erschienen. Andere Länder – wie etwa die Niederlande – folgten diesem Beispiel. Allerdings wurden die Gewinner gut organisierter Wettbewerbe nicht immer mit der Ausführung ihrer Entwürfe beauftragt. 1842 entstand in den Niederlanden die Maatschappij tot Bevordering der Bouwkunst (Gesellschaft zur Förderung der Baukunst), deren erklärtes Ziel eine Verbesserung der Qualität architektonischer Werke war. Insbesondere beschäftigte sie sich mit der Organisation von Ausschreibungen, die die Architekten dazu bringen sollten, die Grenzen ihrer Kreativtität auszuloten. Die Gesellschaft vertrat die Ansicht, daß Architekten nur ohne den Druck eines Auftraggebers zu ihren besten Leistungen am Zeichenbrett fähig wären. Die prämierten Entwürfe sollten als Prototyp für eine Kirche, ein Rathaus oder eine andere Gebäudeart dienen. Die Sieger wurden angehalten, ihre preisgekrönten Beiträge weiterzuentwikkeln, um letztendlich den angestrebten Prototyp zu perfektionieren. Diese Art des Wettbewerbs ähnelte den späteren konzeptionellen Ausschreibungen und dient den heutigen Architekturhistorikern als Informationsquelle über die architektonischen Ideale einer bestimmten Epoche.

Die von der Maatschappij organisierten Ausschreibungen besaßen ein striktes Regelwerk, das die Vergabe der Preisgelder und Auszeichnungen genau festlegte. Ein ausführlicher Bericht der Jury beschrieb die Vor- und Nachteile der eingereichten Entwürfe und wurde nach Ende des Wettbewerbs veröffentlicht. Diese Beurteilungen können als bedeutende Informationsquelle für Architekturhistoriker gelten, die sich mit der komplexen Formensprache des 19. Jahrhunderts beschäftigen. Die Geschichte des Friedenspalastes in Den Haag zeigt jedoch, daß nicht alle niederländischen Ausschreibungen gleich effizient organisiert waren: Der Bericht der Jury zeichnete sich vor allem durch Banalität aus und entfachte einen Sturm der Entrüstung, als das Ergebnis bekannt wurde (siehe das Kapitel über den Friedenspalast, Den Haag). Dies zeigt, daß gutorganisierte Ausschreibungen eher die Ausnahme als die Regel bilden.

Formen des Wettbewerbs

Die Ausschreibungen der vergangenen Jahrhunderte verliefen nicht alle nach dem gleichen Schema. Man unterschied beispielsweise zwischen den sog. bestimmten und unbestimmten Wettbewerben. Diese Terminologie stammte aus dem Jahr 1844 und bezeichnete den Unterschied zwischen Ausschreibungen für ein konkretes Bauwerk und solchen, die dem Fortschritt der Architektur dienen sollten. Eine genauere Klassifizierung bot die Einteilung in konzeptionelle Ausschreibungen zur Auswahl eines geeigneten Architekten und in Wettbewerbe, deren Ziel detailliert ausgearbeitete Konstruktionspläne waren. Bei letzteren waren die großen Architekturbüros im Vorteil, da sie es sich leisten können, mehrere Monate an einem Projekt zu arbeiten, das möglicherweise nicht realisiert wird. Außerdem werden bekannte Firmen häufig zur Teilnahme eingeladen und für ihre Bemühungen entschädigt. Dagegen sind konzeptionelle Ausschreibungen weniger zeitaufwendig, was die Chancengleichheit der Teilnehmer erhöht.

Eine ähnliche Trennlinie läßt sich zwischen offenen und geschlossenen Wettbewerben ziehen. Bei geschlossenen Wettbewerben lädt der Auftraggeber bekannte Architekten ein, die im allgemeinen großzügig honoriert werden und allein durch ihre Teilnahme ein Projekt in den Blickpunkt der Öffentlichkeit rücken. Zudem erhoffen sich die Bauherren ein architektonisches Meisterwerk. Ein zusätzlicher Vorteil dieser Wettbewerbe liegt darin, daß die Jury nicht von einer Flut von Beiträgen überschwemmt wird. Eine zu hohe Anzahl von Einsendungen trübt im allgemeinen die Urteilsfähigkeit, wie beispielsweise im Falle des Sydney Opera House, als man Utzons später prämierten Entwurf in der ersten Ausschreibungsrunde ablehnte. Offene Ausschreibungen ziehen Hunderte von jungen, ehrgeizigen Architekten an, die den Wettbewerb als Tor zur Unsterblichkeit betrachten, während bekannte Architekten aus Angst vor einem Gesichtsverlust auf eine Teilnahme verzichten. Desweiteren finden gemischte Ausschreibungen statt, bei denen der Auftraggeber parallel zur offenen Ausschreibung eine bestimmte Anzahl bekannter Architekten einlädt.

Eine weitere Trennlinie läßt sich zwischen nationalen und internationalen Wettbewerben ziehen, wobei die nationalen häufig der Förderung einheimischer Architekten oder der Pflege eines nationalen Stils dienen, während internationale Ausschreibungen wesentlich prestigeträchtiger sind. Im 19. und zu Beginn des 20. Jahrhunderts suchten viele Architekten ihr Glück im Ausland, obwohl die Transport- und Kommunikationsmittel nach heutigem Ermessen eher mangelhaft waren. Die moderne Architektur hat sich längst zu einer internationalen Angelegenheit entwickelt: Heute ist es keineswegs ungewöhnlich, daß japanische Architekten in Europa bzw. Europäer in Japan arbeiten. In der Vergangenheit hingegen beteiligten sich nur wenige Abenteurer an Wettbewerben außerhalb ihres Heimatlandes.

Bekannte Namen

In internationalen Wettbewerben tauchen einige Namen regelmäßig auf. Bei diesen Architekten handelt es sich keineswegs um nach Aufmerksamkeit heischende Anfänger, sondern um hartgesottene Kämpfernaturen, die auf bestimmte Projektformen spezialisiert sind oder an jedem Wettbewerb teilnehmen. Andere Teilnehmer betrachten eine Ausschreibung als architektonische Fingerübung oder verdienen sich damit ihren Lebensunterhalt. Dabei führt eine Spezialisierung häufig zu den besten Ergebnissen, wie die Arbeiten der Architekten Lockwood & Mawson beweisen, die im viktorianischen England an 30 Ausschreibungen teilnahmen und 20 davon gewannen. Architekten wie Bellamy & Hardy – 17 von 35 – und John Johnson – 16 von 26 – waren ähnlich erfolgreich. Dennoch wurden auch sie nicht immer mit der Ausführung ihrer Entwürfe beauftragt. Die Länge ihrer Erfolgsliste weist jedoch auf ein zweifellos vorhandenes Talent hin. Erstaunlicherweise spielten diese herausragenden viktorianischen Architekten keine bedeutende Rolle in der Architekturgeschichte, ihre Namen sind nur selten in der einschlägigen Literatur zu finden. Vermutlich bestand ihr besonderes Talent darin, die Vorlieben der Jury richtig einzuschätzen. Die Jury ihrerseits legte zumeist wenig Wert auf die Avantgarde und andere innovative Stilrichtungen; die Forderung nach ungewöhnlichen Entwürfen beschränkte sich weitestgehend auf die großen, prestigeträchtigen Wettbewerbe.

Die Spezialisten haben sich bis in die heutige Zeit halten können, auch wenn sich die Formen des Wettbewerbs seit der viktorianischen Epoche sehr verändert haben. Zu den berühmtesten Vertretern des 20. Jahrhunderts zählen Eero Saarinen – 12 Siege bei 20 Wettbewerben – und Alvar Aalto – 25 bei 58 –. Auch bei den heutigen internationalen Ausschreibungen tauchen bestimmte Namen immer wieder auf: Rem Koolhaas, Norman Foster und Aldo Rossi. Rossi beteiligte sich an 30 Wettbewerben – allerdings betrachtete er sie hauptsächlich als architektonisches Training, was seine niedrige Erfolgsquote erklärt. Erstaunlicherweise scheinen auch viele Jurymitglieder Geschmack an ihrer Tätigkeit zu finden: Einige Architekten nehmen abwechselnd an Wettbewerben teil oder sitzen in der Jury, während andere von einer Jury in die nächste wechseln. Josef Paul Kleihues war als Jurymitglied an allen Ausschreibungen der IBA in Berlin (siehe gleichnamiges Kapitel) beteiligt. Englands bekanntestes Jurymitglied hieß Alfred Waterhouse: Der Vorsitzende des RIBA saß im Laufe mehrerer Jahrzehnte in 44 verschiedenen Gremien, nahm als Architekt aber »nur« an sieben Ausschreibungen teil. Allerdings erforderten die 1872 aufgestellten Wettbewerbsregeln, daß sich in der Jury mindestens ein Angehöriger des RIBA befinden mußte.

Der Auftraggeber

Eine kompetente Jury ist eine absolute Notwendigkeit, insbesondere wenn der Bauherr die Errichtung eines prestigeträchtigen Gebäudes beabsichtigt. Zu den privaten Auftraggebern zählten u.a. die Chicago Tribune sowie die Hongkong and Shanghai Bank. Allerdings werden in der Mehrzahl aller Fälle die Bauaufträge vom Staat vergeben. Manchmal sitzt der Auftraggeber in der Jury, doch meist überläßt er die Beurteilung der Entwürfe den Experten. In einigen Fällen setzten sich die Kunden über die Entscheidung der Jury hinweg – meist aus gutem Grund – und verfolgten ihre eigene Politik. Bei anderen Wettbewerben erhielt der Sieger zwar den Bauauftrag, die Ausführung konnte aber aus unterschiedlichen Gründen nicht durchgeführt werden. Daneben gab es noch die Auftraggeber, die die Fertigstellung ihrer Meisterwerke nicht mehr miterleben durften. Dieses tragische Schicksal teilen sie mit einer Reihe von Architekten (siehe die Kapitel zu Law Courts und Grande Arche).

Das vorliegende Buch möchte die Aufmerksamkeit des Lesers auf die besondere Bedeutung der Wettbewerbe im Rahmen der Architekturgeschichte lenken. Aus diesem Grunde wurden bislang wenig bekannte Details über eine ganze Reihe von Wettbewerben zusammengetragen. Natürlich konnten in den Begleittexten zu den Entwürfen und Illustrationen nicht alle verfügbaren Informationen aufgenommen werden, daher unterstützen die bibliographischen Angaben zu Beginn eines jeden Kapitels den Leser bei der Suche nach weiterführender Literatur.

Introduction

Si les concours d'architecture sont aujourd'hui fréquents, ils n'en restent pas moins passionnants et ce pour de multiples raisons. Les projets, les délibérations des jurys et les critiques de la grande presse et des publications spécialisées sont riches de multiples informations. L'histoire des concours d'architecture reflète en fait celle de l'architecture elle-même. Le concours apporte une sorte de photographie instantanée de l'art de bâtir à un moment donné, avec ses participants célèbres ou non, ses innovateurs et ses conservateurs. Les contextes sont aussi révélateurs que les palmarès. Cette sélection de quarante-neuf concours répartis sur une période de presque deux siècles retrace ainsi la succession des grands mouvements architecturaux et de leurs représentants, qui tantôt s'opposèrent violemment tantôt coexistèrent pacifiquement. Les enjeux stylistiques du XIXème siècle y figurent comme le rejet du passé par le vingtième siècle qui atteignit son zénith – ou son nadir – avec les propositions de démolition du cœur historique de certaines villes. Et l'histoire des concours d'architecture elle-même sera un sujet sur lequel nous reviendrons souvent dans ce livre.

Afin de conserver la clarté d'exposition nécessaire, ce survol se limite à l'histoire récente bien que les concours soient un phénomène beaucoup plus ancien. Un exemple historique célèbre est celui de la coupole de la cathédrale de Florence qui fut remporté par Brunelleschi. Cette coupole devint l'un des plus importants monuments de la Renaissance à la fois pour des raisons esthétiques et pour le sentiment de fierté qu'elle fit naître dans des générations de Florentins. Ces deux aspects de l'architecture se retrouvent dans pratiquement tous les concours, de l'antiquité à nos jours. Les rois, les empereurs, les dictateurs, mais aussi les architectes partagèrent une propension commune à se distinguer. Les architectes y étaient d'autant plus incités qu'ils voyaient dans leur victoire un pas de plus vers l'immortalité de leur œuvre.

Deux exemples – la Grande-Bretagne et les Pays-Bas

Bien que ce livre se soit limité à des réalisations marquantes, le concours architectural est en fait une procédure très courante. L'une des rares enquêtes réalisées concerne les appels d'offre de la période victorienne en Grande-Bretagne et en Irlande. Son auteur, Roger Harper, n'a pas compté moins de 2 500 compétitions en un demi-siècle: une par semaine en moyenne! Londres arrivait bien entendu en tête, suivi par les grands villes industrielles comme Manchester, Liverpool, Leeds et Birmingham. L'une des principales raisons de cette avalanche concurrentielle tenait à la rapide croissance économique du royaume pendant le XIXème siècle qui entraîna un besoin grandissant de nouvelles constructions que ce soit pour les transports, l'éducation ou la santé. Mais il n'était pas rare de voir s'organiser un concours pour l'église d'un petit village. A l'origine, les dignitaires locaux finançaient ces mises en compétition afin d'obtenir des plans peu coûteux qu'ils faisaient exécuter par un entrepreneur local plus enclin à se plier aux souhaits des organisateurs. Il était également fréquent de voir un jury inexpérimenté se laisser séduire par de charmantes aquarelles plutôt que par des plans sérieux. De plus, les règles d'attribution des prix en argent étaient très variables, ce qui, dans de nombreux cas, signifiait que les architectes ne gagnaient guère plus qu'une expérience supplémentaire. Leur seul vrai bénéfice était de voir leurs propositions souvent publiées et analysées dans les journaux spécialisés de l'époque.

Il devint peu à peu évident que cette situation devait évoluer. Bien que l'Institute of British Architects ait édicté un ensemble de règles en 1839, elles n'avaient pas le poids de la réglementation formelle du Royal Institute of British Architects (RIBA) de 1872. Plus tard, un règlement standard fut également proposé par l'Association des Architectes et Ingénieurs Suisses et l'Union Internationale des Architectes. Ces règlements furent mis au point pour éviter des expériences comme celle de la Maison Blanche à Washington – premier chapitre de cet ouvrage – où un jury d'amateurs avait jugé des plans essentiellement proposés par des amateurs. Presqu'aucune condition ou indication n'avait été donnée aux concurrents qui n'avaient eu que très peu de temps pour travailler. De plus, il s'avéra que le vainqueur, James Hoban, n'avait rien négligé pour s'attirer les faveurs du jury.

Malgré les réglementations, scandales et querelles ont été le lot commun de nombreux concours parmi les plus prestigieux, ce qui les rend encore plus instructifs.

L'apparition d'un corps réglementaire alla de pair avec une affirmation du sentiment de leur importance par les architectes et la reconnaissance de leur profession. Ces développements se manifestèrent pour commencer en Grande-Bretagne qui posséda dès le XIXème siècle un certain nombre de journaux spécialisés en architecture.

Dans d'autres pays, comme les Pays-Bas, les temps changeaient également, même si les architectes lauréats n'étaient pas toujours retenus pour exécuter leurs plans.

En 1842, une association pour le progrès de l'architecture – le Maatschappij tot Bevordering van de Bouwkunst – fut fondée aux Pays-Bas. Son but était l'amélioration de la qualité de l'architecture et, plus spécialement, l'organisation de concours pour inciter les architectes à aller au bout de leurs possibilités créatives, sans interférence de maîtres d'ouvrage. Les plans primés devaient servir de prototypes pour la construction d'églises, d'hôtels de ville ou de toutes sortes d'édifices et, dans les faits, les projets retenus furent mis au point pour servir de modèles. Ce type de compétition fait penser aux concours d'idées examinés plus loin. Ils offrent à l'historien une véritable mine d'informations sur les conceptions architecturales d'une certaine époque.

Les prix et distinctions accordés à l'occasion des concours du Maatschappij répondaient à des règles strictes. Un rapport du jury faisant état des votes en faveur ou contre chaque projet était publié à leur issue. Ces comptes-rendus sont généralement précieux pour les chercheurs, en particulier dans le domaine des styles, sujet brûlant tout au long du XIXème siècle. L'histoire du Palais de la Paix de La Haye prouve cependant que tous les concours aux Pays-Bas ne furent pas organisés avec la même efficacité. L'un des aspects les plus frappants du rapport de son jury était sa trivialité absolue, qui explique la tempête de protestations que souleva la proclamation des résultats – voir le chapitre sur le Palais de la Paix –. Les concours bien organisés furent en fait souvent l'exception plutôt que la règle.

Les formes des concours

Une distinction claire doit être faite entre les concours organisés au Royaume-Uni et aux Pays-Bas au siècle dernier. Elle a trait aux concours déterminés et indéterminés – terminologie remontant à 1844 –, c'est-à-dire entre les compétitions à but précis et concret et celles lancées au bénéfice du progrès architectural. Une distinction encore plus spécifique peut être tracée au sein de la catégorie des concours d'idées, entre ceux qui servent à sélectionner un architecte et ceux qui sont jugés sur la remise de plans détaillés. Dans ce dernier type de confrontation, les grands cabinets ont un avantage sur leurs concurrents, car ils peuvent se permettre de passer des mois sur un projet dont les chances d'aboutissement sont faibles. De plus, les cabinets renommés sont souvent invités à participer et sont dédommagés financièrement de leurs efforts. Dans les concours d'idées, qui demandent moins de temps, les chances sont plus égales.

Une distinction parallèle s'impose entre les concours ouverts et restreints. Dans les concours restreints, les organisateurs invitent quelques architectes connus – en principe pour des honoraires conséquents – qui généralement attirent l'attention sur le projet et augmentent les chances d'obtenir une œuvre architecturale de grande qualité. Avantage supplémentaire: le jury ne se retrouve pas accablé par un déluge de projets, phénomène, qui, dans certains cas peut troubler le jugement de jurés. Par exemple, Utzon, l'architecte de l'opéra de Sydney avait été éliminé par le jury au début de l'étude des envois des participants.
Les concours ouverts peuvent attirer des centaines de jeunes architectes ambitieux qui y voient des tremplins pour leur carrière alors que des praticiens plus connus hésiteront à mettre leur réputation en jeu sur la place publique. Une autre distinction s'établit entre les concours nationaux ou internationaux. Les appels d'offre nationaux sont souvent organisés pour satisfaire les architectes locaux ou lorsque les organisateurs tiennent à un style «national».
Les concours internationaux sont plus prestigieux. Durant les années 20 et 30, de nombreux architectes tentèrent leur chance à l'étranger, même si les conditions de transports et de communication étaient peu développées par rapport à nos critères actuels. Aujourd'hui, l'architecture moderne s'est internationalisée: il n'est pas inhabituel de voir des Japonais participer à des concours européens et vice-versa. Dans le passé, seuls quelques aventuriers osaient affronter des concurrents étrangers sur leur propre sol.

Des noms connus

Le nom de quelques architectes revient régulièrement dans les listes de participants, en particulier lors des grands concours internationaux. Ce ne sont certainement pas des débutants essayant désespérément d'attirer l'attention sur eux, mais des compétiteurs de profession. Certains participent à tous les concours, d'autres se spécialisent dans certains types de projets. Pour certains, il s'agit d'un exercice de style, pour d'autres, un mode de travail. La spécialisation conduit généralement aux meilleurs résultats. Lockwood & Mason sont de remarquables exemples d'architectes spécialisés de l'époque victorienne. Ils participèrent à 30 concours et en remportèrent 20. Parmi d'autres, Bellamy & Hardy – 17 sur 35 – et John Johnson – 16 sur 26 –. Là encore, les gagnants ne furent pas toujours conservés pour la réalisation de leur projet. Néanmoins, cette liste de succès est impressionnante et laisse supposer qu'un certain talent est nécessaire pour remporter un concours. Il reste que ces Victoriens si souvent primés ne jouèrent pas un grand rôle dans l'architecture de leur temps et que dans la plupart des cas, leurs noms ne figurent même pas dans les encyclopédies d'architecture. Leur talent consistait peut être surtout à savoir ce qui pouvait plaire à un jury. Comme on peut s'y attendre, les jurys exprimèrent rarement un préférence pour l'avant-garde ou un style innovateur. La demande de plans «innovateurs» était la plupart du temps limitée à de grandes compétitions de prestige.
Les spécialistes n'ont pas disparu, même si la forme des concours a beaucoup évolué depuis l'ère victorienne. Parmi ces spécialistes du XXème siècle figurent Eero Saarinen – 12 sur 20 – et Alvar Aalto – 25 sur 58 –. Certains noms reviennent dans de multiples compétitions internationales, comme ceux de Rem Koolhaas, Norman Foster et Aldo Rossi. Ce dernier a participé à 30 concours, le plus souvent pour «rester en forme», ce qui explique son faible taux de réussite.
Certains jurés semblent apprécier leur travail. Quelques architectes participent tantôt à des concours, tantôt à des jurys. Josef Paul Kleihues a été juré dans tous les concours de l'IBA à Berlin – voir plus loin –. Le juré britannique le plus célèbre était Alfred Waterhouse, président du RIBA, qui siégea dans 44 jurys en quelques dizaines d'années, mais ne participa qu'à sept concours. Il est cependant juste de préciser que la réglementation sur les concours de 1872 stipulait que chaque jury devait contenir au moins un membre du RIBA.

La maîtrise d'ouvrage

Un jury compétent est nécessaire, surtout si les maîtres d'ouvrage souhaitent une réalisation prestigieuse. Dans le grand jeu de l'architecture de concours, le client, qu'il soit privé – le Chicago Tribune ou la Hongkong and Shangaï Bank, par exemple – ou l'État, joue un rôle très important. Quelquefois, il siège au jury, mais la plupart du temps, la sélection est laissée aux experts. Les clients rejettent à l'occasion les délibérations de leur jury – souvent pour de bonnes raisons – et reprennent les choses en main. Il arrive aussi que le vainqueur reçoive la commande, mais que son exécution soit empêchée pour de multiples raisons, comme on le verra dans ces pages. Il se peut enfin que certains clients ne vivent pas assez longtemps pour voir le chef d'œuvre dont ils avaient rêvé réalisé. Ce sort est partagé par quelques architectes – Les Law Courts de Londres ou la Grande Arche –. Le sens du tragique fait aussi partie de l'histoire de l'architecture. L'objet de cet ouvrage est d'attirer l'attention du lecteur sur la signification des concours dans l'histoire de l'architecture et c'est pour cette raison qu'un très grand nombre d'informations ont été rassemblées sur de nombreux concours. Il était impossible d'analyser en détail chacune de ces compétitions, mais les bibliographies en tête de chaque chapitre permettront certainement au lecteur intéressé de pousser plus avant ses recherches.

Project

Presidential residence and parliament building (no winner)

Site

Pennsylvania Avenue, Washington DC

Dates

13 March 1792 to 15 June 1792

Conditions

Hardly any specified, newspaper advertisement

Participants

Stephen Hallet, Thomas Jefferson, John Collins, James Diamond, Jacob Small (two designs), Andrew Mayfield Carshore, Philip Hart, James Hoban

Jury

President George Washington, Government Commission for Washington DC (three members)

Winner

James Hoban

Commissioned by

Government Commission for Washington DC

Construction

13 October 1792 (first stone laid) to 1830

Architect

James Hoban (1762–1831)

The White House, Washington DC, 1792

James Hoban final design without date, front elevation on Pennsylvania Avenue

The White House, Washington DC

Following the triumphant War of Independence, New York temporarily became the capital of the United States in 1784. However, six years later, the government decided to build a new capital in the recently established District of Columbia. The French-born architect Pierre Charles L'Enfant, who had previously renovated the old city hall in New York for the federal government, was commissioned to design the city (1790). It had been stipulated that the design should include a residence for the president (President's House) and a building to house the Senate and Congress (Capitol).

L'Enfant chose a site on the river Potomac. During one of his exploratory rambles he came across a hill, called Jenkin's Hill, which he considered to be a suitable building site for the new Capitol. From this point he mapped out a diagonal line of sight to the place where the presidential residence would be built on Pennsylvania Avenue. It is possible that L'Enfant's idea for a "vista" of this sort was based on his father's paintings of landscapes in Versailles. There is a similar axis between the palace at Versailles and the 'Grand Trianon'. L'Enfant designed thoroughfares running parallel and at right angles to the main axis, forming a diamond-shaped pattern. He planned to situate the President's House, the Capitol or a square at the points of intersection. L'Enfant filled the space within this system of axes with a regular grid-pattern street plan. Parks, fountains and monuments were carefully planned. The grand design exuded a French Baroque atmosphere (Versailles and the Château de Marly by J.H. Mansart).

The Frenchman had been under the impression that he would also be commissioned to design the most important public buildings and could thereby make the City of Washington a unique personal project. His arrogance towards everyone, he dealt with everyone except the first president of the United States, George Washington, and his assumption that, as a financially independent architect, he could take the liberty of treating influential people in Washington's circle with lofty disdain made him unpopular. This was not pre-revolutionary France and Thomas Jefferson[1], in particular, quietly relished the thought of seeing the ambitious architect fall. Another aspect of the matter was that Washington wanted to make haste with the completion of the new capital (which would be named after him in 1791). He argued that once the Capitol was under construction no one could stand in the way of the city's completion. Washington's desire to speed things up stemmed mainly from the increasingly fierce political clashes between federalists and anti-federalists. L'Enfant, however, was unable to realise the short-term completion of the city's infrastructure and public buildings.

President's Palace

It is known that L'Enfant had envisaged the President's House as an enormous palace, in keeping with his street plan. "President's Palace" was the term L'Enfant preferred, not "House". The term White House dates from as late as 1901 (owing to the fact that Hoban did not share

Thomas Jefferson, president (1801–1809)

Elbert Peets artist's impression of P.C. l'Enfant's Washington plan

The White House after the fire, 1814

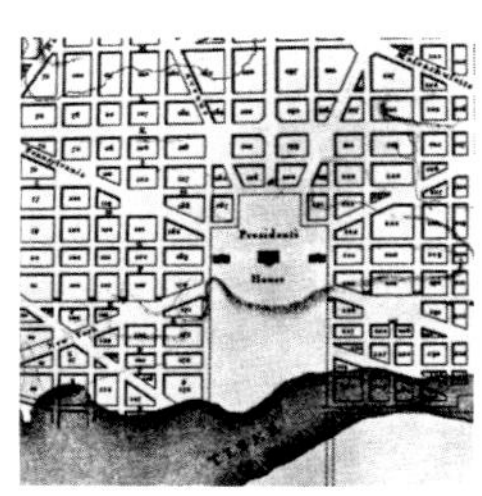

Location of the President's House from Robert King map, 1818

Jefferson's love of brickwork). However, L'Enfant was no longer around to witness all this. Surrounded by enemies who were suspicious of his sense of imperial grandeur, he lost his estate in France which was sequestered by the French revolutionary parliament. With it, he lost his financial independence. He had never asked for, nor received, money for his work on the capital. However, he never lost his arrogance, nor his uncompromising stance. Eventually, even the president could no longer protect him. On 26 January 1792, Jefferson discharged the by then destitute Pierre Charles L'Enfant.

Washington saw work on the federal capital grind to a halt. Meanwhile, New York and Philadelphia, where the government later had its seat, had also built President's Houses in the hope of becoming the capital city. But Washington, supported by Jefferson, pursued his ambitious plan. It was Jefferson who continued where L'Enfant had left off, and it was Jefferson who suggested that a competition should be organised for the President's House and the Capitol. The Commissioners, appointed by Washington to supervise work on the capital announced the competition in a modest newspaper advertisement. The architects were asked to submit floor plans and drawings of elevations and cross sections. Their designs had to be suitable for the selected site and possible future extensions had to be taken into account. Contrary to the president's wishes, Jefferson had seen to it that brick was specified as the basic building material. However, this seems to have had little effect on the participants' designs.

One of the participants was the Irish-born James Hoban, who had been personally introduced to the Commissioners by Washington. Hoban, who was a sociable man, managed to convince the Commissioners of his expertise. He submitted his designs within twenty days. The designs were judged on 16 June. Hoban won first prize[2]. It must be said that the field of competitors was small. In America, the architectural profession was still at a nascent stage of development. The jury received only nine entries: one arrived after the closing date and some had been submitted by hopeful amateurs. Hoban's design seems to have been based on the architecture of his home town of Charleston, South Carolina. The city hall in Charleston was a plain, elongated building, with an Ionic portico in the middle. In his native Ireland there is another building which possibly served as an example: Leinster House in Dublin. However, Hoban's design most closely resembles a drawing in James Gibbs' "Book of Architecture" (1728).

Hoban's design

The composition is almost identical: a rusticated base with windows, an upper floor on which alternate windows have a fronton, and above that a mezzanine, a cornice and a parapet. The Ionic central pilaster strip, the perron and the hipped roof are also identical. However, there are certain differences; Gibbs' drawing has corner pilaster strips and vases on the parapet, giving the building as a whole a more refined

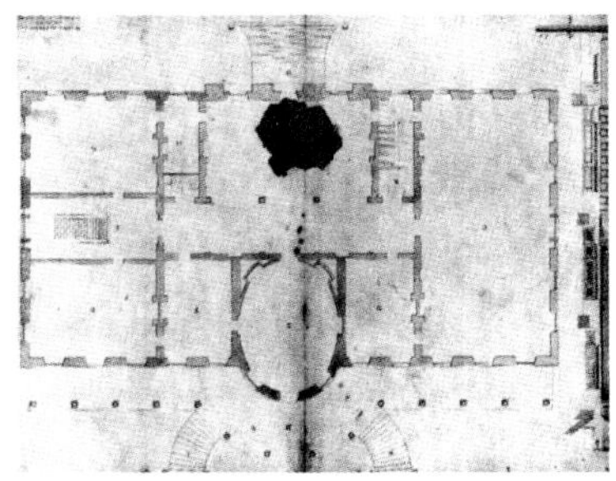

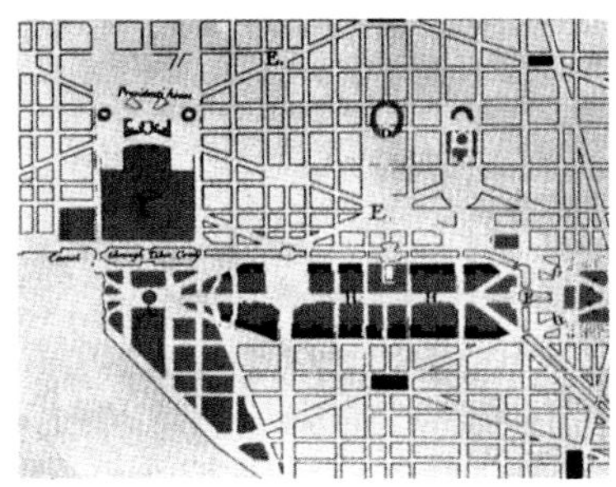

appearance. Apparently twenty days were not enough for Hoban to copy the entire drawing. The eagle on the fronton was a personal touch.

One of the other designs, attributed to Jefferson, vaguely resembled Palladio's Villa Rotonda: a geometric block, with small porticoes on all sides, topped by a disproportionate cupola. The style of James Diamond's design closely resembled Hoban's, but was less expertly drawn. The stairway to the perron resembles that of a staff entrance and the sculpture on the fronton looks like a cross between an eagle and a plucked chicken. His floor plan and cross sections are of a better quality. It is not surprising that the drawings in Gibbs' book served as a source of inspiration. In spite of the country's newly gained independence, American architecture still clearly bore the mark of English influence.

Although Hoban was commissioned, Washington deemed certain alterations necessary. He personally added two bays and some embellishments. In spite of these additions, the White House was much smaller than the palace L'Enfant had initially envisaged. As a result, the building site had to be more precisely specified. Washington took this task upon himself, much to the dissatisfaction of the Commissioners. In comparison to the initial design, the line of sight between the Capitol and the President's House had become less striking. The vista was completely obstructed in 1836, when President Jackson had the Department of the Treasury constructed directly in

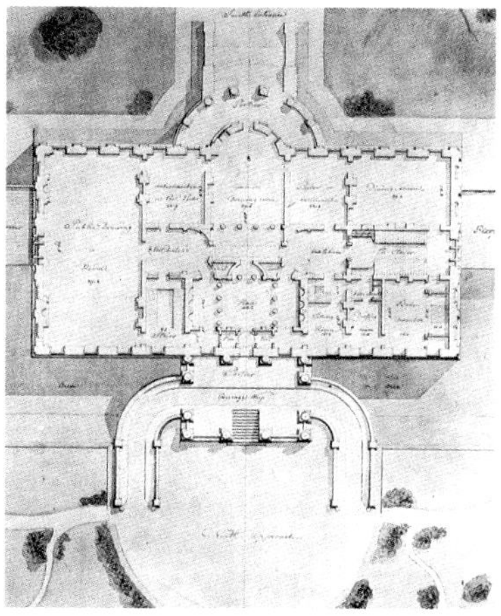

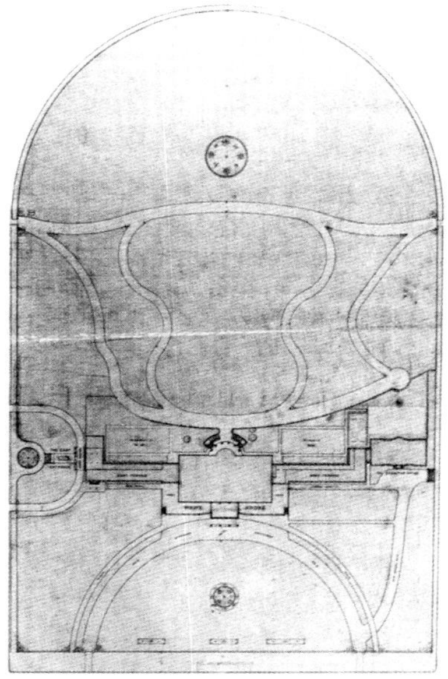

East room of the White House, reception for the Prince of Wales, 1860

James Hoban The White House, first floor plan

Pierre Charles l'Enfant central section of plan of Washington

Benjamin Henry Latrobe proposed alterations, first floor plan, 1807

The White House after the extensions, site plan, 1902

Baroness Hyde de Neuville, the President's "Campus", watercolour, 1820

front of the White House. Washington was also involved in the interior design of the residence. Even though he knew that he would never live there himself, he considered it his duty to bequeath a stately and presentable residence to his successors. Hoban diligently incorporated the President's suggestions. One of the upper floors was scrapped during construction.

Alteration and renovation

After Hoban – who had been permanently appointed by the government – had rounded off his work, the White House was altered several times. As early as 1807, Benjamin Latrobe and Thomas Jefferson designed side pavilions where Hoban had envisaged lateral wings. In truth, Jefferson was pleased with the President's House as it was, and he is known to have said that it was large enough to house two emperors, the pope and the Dalai Lama. In later years, the western pavilion became part of the Treasury and the eastern pavilion was torn down and rebuilt in 1902. Around 1814, the house was extensively renovated by Hoban, after it had been burnt down by the English.

The semi-circular addition on the southern side, based on the Château de Rustignac (Périgord), was built in 1824. The central pilaster strip on the northern side gradually became a portico (1829). Both additions were designed by Hoban. Around 1903, the renowned American architect Charles Follen McKim took charge of the building. In 1929, the White House burnt down once again. It was reconstructed between 1948 and 1952. In spite of all the alterations and renovations over the years, the White House still bears the main features of the stately residence envisaged by Washington and Hoban in 1792.

1 *Jefferson was Secretary of State under Washington and went on to become the third president of the United States.*

2 *Only a few designs were submitted for the Capitol.*

Weißes Haus, Washington DC

Nach dem Ende des Unabhängigkeitskriegs wurde New York 1784 zur zeitweiligen Hauptstadt der Vereinigten Staaten ernannt. Aber schon sechs Jahre später beschloß die Regierung, im neu gegründeten Distrikt Columbia eine andere Hauptstadt zu errichten. Den Auftrag für den Entwurf erhielt 1790 der aus Frankreich stammende Pierre Charles L'Enfant, der bereits für die Föderalregierung das alte New Yorker Rathaus umgebaut hatte. Das Projekt umfaßte u.a. einen Amtssitz für den Präsidenten (President's House) sowie ein Gebäude für den Senat und das Repräsentantenhaus (Capitol).

L'Enfant entschied sich für ein Gelände am Fluß Potomac. Bei seinen Begehungen stieß er auf einen Hügel – Jenkin's Hill –, auf dem er das neu zu bauende Capitol plazieren wollte. Von Jenkin's Hill aus plante er eine schräge Sichtachse zum Platz des neuen Amtssitzes: die Pennsylvania Avenue. Die Planung einer derartigen »Vista« hatte L'Enfant noch von seinem Vater gelernt, der Landschaftsmaler in Versailles war. Dort verlief eine vergleichbare Sichtachse zwischen dem Schloß und dem »Grand Trianon«. Die Hauptstraßen entwarf L'Enfant parallel und in rechten Winkeln zu dieser Achse, so daß ein Rautenmuster entstand, auf dessen Schnittpunkten das President's House, das Capitol und verschiedene Plätze lagen. Eine regelmäßige, rechtwinklige Straßenanlage füllte die Flächen zwischen den Achsen. Auch die Parks, Brunnen und Denkmäler wurden sorgfältig geplant. Der ganze Entwurf erinnerte stark an den französischen Barock.
L'Enfant ging davon aus, daß er auch die wichtigsten öffentlichen Bauten entwerfen sollte, so daß die Stadt Washington ein einzigartiges, ganz persönliches Projekt darstellen würde. Doch aufgrund seiner arroganten Haltung hatte er stark an Beliebtheit eingebüßt. Als finanziell unabhängiger Architekt glaubte L'Enfant es sich erlauben zu können, auch einflußreiche Persönlichkeiten im Umfeld des Präsidenten von oben herab zu behandeln. Aber er befand sich nicht mehr im vorrevolutionären Frankreich, und vor allem Thomas Jefferson[1] brannte insgeheim darauf, den ehrgeizigen Architekten zu Fall zu bringen. Hinzu kam, daß es Präsident George Washington es mit der neuen Hauptstadt (die übrigens 1791 nach ihm benannt wurde) sehr eilig hatte. Wenn man erst einmal mit dem Bau des Capitol begonnen hatte, so dachte er, würde niemand mehr die neue Hauptstadt verhindern können. Washingtons Eile entsprang zum Großteil der Tatsache, daß sich Befürworter und Gegner des Föderalismus auf der politischen Bühne immer heftiger bekämpften. Aber L'Enfant war nicht in der Lage, in kürzester Zeit eine ganze Stadt samt öffentlicher Bauten zu errichten.

President's Palace

L'Enfant plante das President's House als ein eindrucksvolles Palais, das sich eng an seine Straßenplanung anschloß. Als Name schwebte ihm »President's Palace« – und nicht »House« – vor. Der Name »White House« (Weißes Haus) dagegen stammt erst aus dem Jahre 190. Aber dies erlebte L'Enfant nicht mehr. Ausschließlich von Gegnern umringt, die seiner Vorliebe für kaiserliche Grandeur mißtrauten, verlor er auch noch seine Besitzungen in Frankreich: Das französische Revolutionsparlament konfiszierte seine Güter und entzog ihm damit seine finanzielle Unabhängigkeit. Für seine Arbeit an der Hauptstadt hatte L'Enfant nie Geld verlangt oder erhalten, und auch jetzt verlor er weder seine Arroganz noch seine kompromißlose Haltung. Aber selbst der Präsident konnte ihn nicht länger schützen, und am 26. Januar 1792 verkündete Jefferson dem zu diesem Zeitpunkt mittellosen L'Enfant seine Entlassung.

Inzwischen sah Washington voller Bedauern, daß die Arbeiten an der Bundeshauptstadt beinahe zum Erliegen kamen. Auch in New York und Philadelphia, wohin die Regierung umgezogen war, hatte man mit dem Bau von President's Houses begonnen, in der Hoffnung, selbst Hauptstadt zu werden. Aber mit Jeffersons Unterstützung verfolgte Washington weiterhin seine ehrgeizigen Pläne. Es war Jefferson, der L'Enfants Pläne fortführte und eine Ausschreibung für das Capitol und das President's House vorschlug. Man setzte eine schlichte Anzeige in die Zeitung, in der die Mitglieder der Kommission, die Washington zur Beaufsichtigung der Arbeiten berufen hatte, die Ausschreibungskriterien veröffentlichten. Die teilnehmenden Architekten sollten Grundrisse, Aufrißzeichnungen und Querschnitte einreichen. Der Entwurf mußte sich für den bereits gewählten Bauplatz eignen und eventuelle spätere Erweiterungen ermöglichen. Jefferson hatte sich – gegen den Willen des Präsidenten – dafür eingesetzt, daß die Bauauflagen Ziegelsteine als Baumaterial vorsahen; allerdings wurde diese Bedingung von den meisten Teilnehmern ignoriert. Zu den Einsendern gehörte der aus Irland stammende James Hoban, der den Mitgliedern der Kommission von Washington persönlich vorgestellt worden war. Der sehr umgängliche Hoban wußte die Kommission von seinen Fähigkeiten zu überzeugen, und innerhalb von 20 Tagen reichte er seine Zeichnungen ein. Als am 16. Juni die Pläne beurteilt wurden, rief man Hoban zum Gewinner der Ausschreibung aus[2]. Allerdings war das Feld der Konkurrenten nicht überwältigend groß, denn der Beruf des Architekten steckte in den USA noch in den Kinderschuhen. Die Jury zählte nur neun Einsendungen (wovon eine zu spät kam), teilweise von engagierten Laien eingereicht. Hobans Entwurf entsprach einem Gebäudetypus, wie er ihn aus seinem Wohnort Charleston in South Carolina kannte. Das Rathaus der Stadt war ein nüchternes längliches Gebäude mit einem zentralen ionischen Portikus, und in seiner Heimat Irland findet sich ein anderes Bauwerk, das ebenfalls als Vorbild gedient haben könnte: Leinster House in Dublin. Dennoch ähnelte Hobans Entwurf am stärksten einer Zeichnung in James Gibbs' »Book of Architecture« (1728).
Der Aufbau ist beinahe identisch: ein Erdgeschoß mit Rustikamauerwerk und Fenstern, jedes zweite Fenster im ersten Stockwerk mit einem Frontispiz verziert, darüber ein Mezzaningeschoß, Karnies und Brüstung. Ebenso identisch sind der ionische Mittelrisalit, der Beischlag sowie das Walmdach. Aber man findet auch Unterschiede: Gibbs' Zeichnung besitzt Eckrisaliten und Vasen auf der Brüstung, was seinem Entwurf mehr Balance und Raffinesse verleiht. Anscheinend war es Hoban in 20 Tagen nicht gelungen, die Zeichnung in allen Details zu kopieren. Sein eigener Beitrag war der Adler in jedem Frontispiz.
Der Jefferson zugeschriebene Entwurf basierte in groben Zügen auf Palladios Villa Rotonda: Ein geometrischer Block mit einem kleinen Portikus an jeder Seite, gekrönt von einer überdimensionalen Kuppel.
James Diamonds Entwurf entsprach in etwa Hobans Beitrag, war aber weniger sorgfältig gezeichnet. Die Treppe zum Beischlag erinnert an einen Eingang für das Personal, und die Skulptur im Frontispiz wirkt wie eine Kreuzung aus einem Adler und einem gerupften Huhn.
Übrigens war es nichts Ungewöhnliches, daß die Zeichnungen in Gibbs' Buch als Inspirationsquelle dienten, denn trotz der eben errungenen Unabhängigkeit trug die amerikanische Architektur immer noch deutlich den Stempel des englischen Mutterlandes.
Obwohl Hoban den Wettbewerb gewonnen hatte, hielt Washington einige Änderungen für notwendig und fügte dem Entwurf eigenhändig zwei Travéen und einige Verzierungen hinzu. Da das Weiße Haus – trotz dieser Erweiterungen – deutlich kleiner zu werden versprach als ursprünglich von L'Enfant beabsichtigt, mußte das Baugelände genauer festgelegt werden. Auch diese Aufgabe übernahm Washington selbst und löste sie auf eine für die Kommissionsmitglieder unbefriedigende Weise: Die Sichtachse zwischen Capitol und President's House wurde im Vergleich zur ursprünglichen Planung deutlich verengt. 1836 verschwand dieser Durchblick völlig, als der damalige Präsident Jackson unmittelbar vor dem Weißen Haus das Finanzministerium erbauen ließ.
Washington befaßte sich auch mit der Gestaltung der Innenräume. Obwohl er wußte, daß er selbst nie dort wohnen würde, wollte er seinen Nachfolgern einen würdigen, repräsentativen Amtssitz hinterlassen. Hoban setzte die Vorschläge des Präsidenten ganz nach dessen Wünschen um. Noch während der Bauzeit würde eines der geplanten oberen Stockwerke gestrichen.

Veränderung und Renovierung

Nachdem Hoban – der von der Regierung fest angestellt worden war – seine Arbeiten beendet hatte, wurde das Weiße Haus noch einige Male umgebaut. Bereits 1807 entwarfen Benjamin Latrobe und Thomas Jefferson die seitlichen Pavillons, wo nach Hobans Vorstellungen Seitenflügel entstehen sollten. Im Grunde war Jefferson auch mit dem President's House in seiner ursprünglichen Form zufrieden und sagte, daß es groß genug sei für zwei Kaiser, den Papst und den Dalai Lama. In späteren Jahren wurde der westliche Pavillon zu einem Teil des Schatzamts. Den östlichen Pavillon riß man zunächst ab, um ihn 1912 wieder aufzubauen. Hoban selbst renovierte das Haus 1814 von Grund auf, nachdem es von den Engländern in Brand gesteckt worden war.
Der halbrunde Anbau auf der Südseite, nach dem Vorbild des Château de Rustignac (Périgord), stammt von 1824. Fünf Jahre später erweiterte man den Mittelrisalit an der Nordseite zu einem Portikus. Beide Entwürfe stammen noch von Hoban.

Hoban's Zeichnung

Um 1903 nahm sich der amerikanische Architekt Charles Follen McKim des Gebäudes an. 1929 brannte das Weiße Haus zum zweiten Mal ab, zwischen 1948 und 1952 erfolgte eine weitere Restaurierung.
Aber trotz aller Veränderungen und Anpassungen stellt das Weiße Haus in den Grundzügen auch heute noch denselben repräsentativen Amtssitz dar, den Washington und Hoban schon 1792 geplant hatten.

1 *Secretary of State und späterer dritter Präsident der USA.*
2 *Die Ausschreibung für das Capitol fand kaum Resonanz.*

La Maison Blanche, Washington DC

En 1784, à l'issue de la guerre d'Indépendance, le siège du nouveau pouvoir se fixa temporairement à New York. Six ans plus tard, le gouvernement décidait d'édifier une nouvelle capitale dans le District de Columbia qui venait d'être créé. L'architecte d'origine française, Pierre Charles L'Enfant, qui avait rénové l'ancien hôtel de ville de New York pour le gouvernement, fut chargé de dessiner la nouvelle ville (1790). Il était stipulé que ce projet devait comprendre une résidence pour le président (President's House) et un édifice pour le Sénat et le Congrès (Capitole).

L'Enfant choisit un site le long du Potomac et, au cours d'une de ses explorations, repéra une colline qui lui parut être idéale pour l'implantation du futur Capitole, Jenkin's Hill. A partir de là, il traça une diagonale qui aboutissait à la résidence présidentielle: Pennsylvania Avenue. Il est possible que cette «vue» lui ait été inspirée par les paysages de Versailles que son père avait réalisés. On trouve en effet un axe similaire entre le palais de Versailles et le Grand Trianon. L'Enfant dessina ensuite un réseau d'avenues selon une trame régulière, parsemé de parcs, de fontaines et de monuments. De ce plan se dégageait une atmosphère de baroque à la française qui rappelait Versailles et Marly de J.H. Mansart.
L'architecte espérait recevoir également la commande des principaux bâtiments publics et faire ainsi de la nouvelle cité son grand œuvre. Malheureusement, il avait oublié qu'il ne vivait plus dans la France d'avant la Révolution et son arrogance, dont tout le monde avait à souffrir sauf le président, le rendit très impopulaire. Parmi ses nombreux ennemis, Thomas Jefferson[1] se préparait discrètement à faire trébucher cet ambitieux qui était de plus son concurrent. Inquiet des incidents politiques de plus en plus vifs qui éclataient entre les fédéralistes et les anti-fédéralistes, Washington souhaitait hâter la construction de la nouvelle capitale (qui prit son nom en 1791) en pensant qu'une fois le Capitole en construction, personne ne pourrait plus y faire obstacle. L'Enfant n'avait tout simplement pas le temps de mener à bien à la fois les infrastructures de la capitale et la construction des vastes édifices officiels.

Le palais du président

L'architecte français avait envisagé un énorme édifice digne des proportions de ses plans d'urbanisme. Il préférait d'ailleurs le terme de «Palais du président» à celui de «Maison du président». Le nom de 'Maison Blanche' ne date que de 1801 lorsqu'Hoban, qui ne partageait pas le goût de Jefferson pour les briques apparentes, les fit enduire. L'Enfant finit par connaître de graves difficultés. Non seulement il s'était fait beaucoup d'adversaires, mais, de plus, ses biens venaient d'être confisqués en France par les révolutionnaires. Il perdait son indépendance financière et ce d'autant plus qu'il ne s'était jamais fait rétribuer pour ses plans de la capitale. Il ne se départit pas pour autant de sa suffisance et, à partir d'un certain moment, même le Président ne fut plus en mesure de le protéger. Le 26 janvier 1792, Jefferson le démit de ses responsabilités. Pendant ce temps Washington voyait avec tristesse les travaux de sa capitale marquer le pas. New York et Philadelphie, où avait siégé un temps le gouvernement, faisaient construire des résidences présidentielles en espérant toujours devenir capitales. Mais Washington tenait ferme et reçut le soutien de Jefferson qui reprit le flambeau de L'Enfant et suggéra que l'on organise un concours pour la «President's House» et le Capitole. Les commissaires nommés par le président annoncèrent le concours dans la presse: les architectes étaient priés de soumettre des plans de masse, des dessins, des élévations et des coupes adaptés aux sites choisis et susceptibles d'extensions ultérieures. Jefferson avait fait préciser que le matériau de base devait être la brique, ce qui ne fut guère respecté.
James Hoban, architecte d'origine irlandaise, avait été personnellement présenté aux commissaires par Washington. Homme sociable, il réussit à les convaincre de ses capacités et soumit son projet dans les vingt jours. La concurrence n'avait pas de quoi effrayer cet architecte habile. En Amérique, la profession se cherchait encore et, d'ailleurs, le jury ne reçut que neuf projets, l'un envoyé après la date de clôture et d'autres soumis par des amateurs. Les propositions furent jugées le 16 juin et Hoban remporta le premier prix[2]. Ses plans paraissaient inspirés de sa ville natale, Charleston, en Caroline du Sud et en particulier de l'hôtel de ville, bâtiment allongé et sobre orné d'un portique ionique en son milieu. Leinster House, une des grandes demeures de Dublin, a pu également lui servir d'exemple. Mais le projet se rapprochait surtout d'un dessin du «Livre d'architecture» de James Gibbs (1728).

Le projet Hoban

La composition était presque identique: un soubassement à bossage rustique percé d'ouvertures, un niveau supérieur avec une fenêtre sur deux surmontée d'un fronton et, au-dessus, un étage de hauteur réduite, une corniche et un parapet. Le ressaut ionique du centre, le perron et le toit de combles étaient presque identiques. Par contre, le dessin de Gibbs présentait des angles en avancée et des vases sur le parapet qui conféraient à l'ensemble un style plus raffiné: apparemment, vingt jours n'avaient pas suffit à Hoban pour bien copier le dessin. L'aigle du fronton était son apport personnel.
Un des autres projets, attribué à Washington, évoquait un peu la villa La Rotonda de Palladio: un bloc central donnant de chaque côté sur un portique et surmonté d'une importante coupole. Le style de James Diamond se rapprochait de celui de Hoban, mais son dessin était moins expressif. L'escalier du perron ressemblait à une entrée de service et la sculpture du fronton faisait autant penser à un aigle qu'à un poulet déplumé. Le plan de masse et les coupes étaient cependant de meilleure qualité. Les idées de Gibbs étaient donc très présentes dans cette jeune architecture américaine encore sous influence britannique en dépit de son indépendance toute fraîche.
Le choix de Hoban acquis, Washington imposa certaines modifications. Il ajouta de lui-même deux baies et quelques embellissements. Malgré cela, la White House était encore beaucoup plus petite que le palais imaginé par L'Enfant, ce qui amena à redéfinir son implantation précise. Washington s'en chargea lui-même au grand déplaisir des commissionnaires. La perspective entre le Capitole et la résidence présidentielle devint ainsi moins évidente et fut même complètement obturée par la construction du département de trésorie en 1836, sous le président Jackson. Washington s'intéressa également à la décoration intérieure. Même s'il savait qu'il n'y habiterait jamais, il considérait de son devoir d'offrir une résidence prestigieuse à ses successeurs. Hoban se plia avec diligence aux souhaits du grand homme. Un des étages supérieurs fut supprimé pendant la construction.

Modifications et rénovation

Après qu'Hoban se soit retiré – il était devenu architecte du gouvernement – la Maison Blanche fut modifiée à plusieurs reprises. Dès 1807, Benjamin Latrobe et Thomas Jefferson créèrent des pavillons latéraux à la place des ailes envisagées par Hoban. En fait, Jefferson était satisfait de sa demeure et l'on raconte qu'il aimait à dire qu'elle était assez grande pour loger deux empereurs, le pape et le dalaï-lama. Plus tard, le pavillon Ouest fut rattaché au Trésor et le pavillon Est abattu et reconstruit en 1902. Vers 1814, la résidence fut rénovée de fond en comble par Hoban après avoir été incendiée par les Britanniques.
L'addition semi-circulaire de la façade sud, inspirée de Rustignac, un château du Périgord, fut élevée en 1824 et le ressaut central de la façade nord se transforma peu à peu en portique (1829). Ces modifications furent exécutées sous la direction d'Hoban. En 1903, le célèbre architecte américain Charles Follen McKim prit le bâtiment en charge. En 1929, la Maison Blanche fut de nouveau victime d'un incendie et reconstruite entre 1948 et 1952.
Malgré toutes ces modifications et ces rénovations, elle offre encore les principales caractéristiques de la résidence de chef d'Etat imaginée par Washington et Hoban en 1792.

1 *Jefferson était Secrétaire d'Etat sous Washington et devint plus tard le troisième président des Etats-Unis.*
2 *Peu de projets avaient été présentés pour le Capitole.*

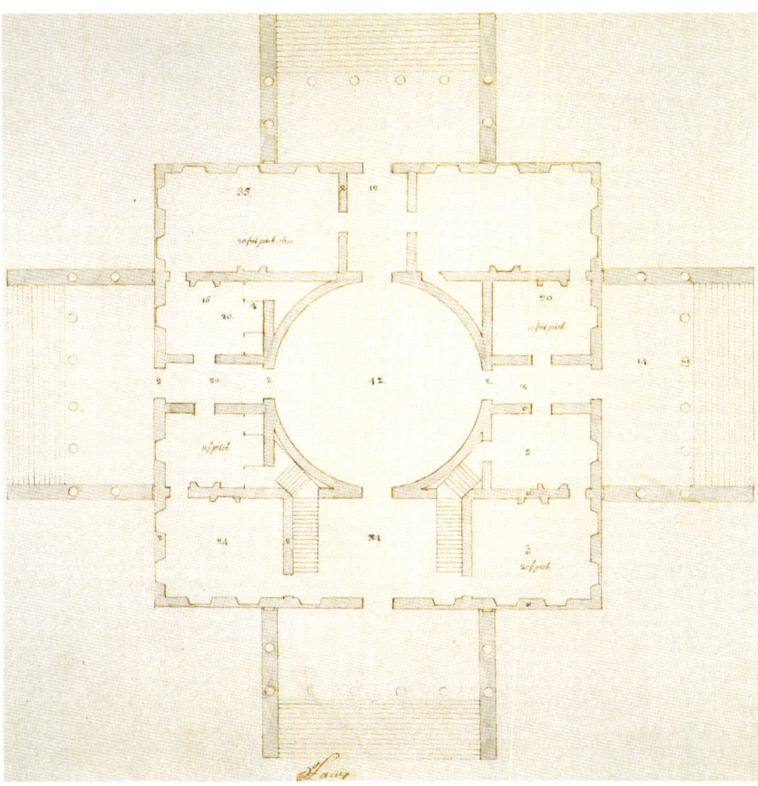

Thomas Jefferson competition design 1792, front elevation on Pennsylvania Avenue

Thomas Jefferson competition design 1792, ground floor plan

James Diamond competition design 1792, top: East-West section, bottom: rear elevation on the south garden

James Diamond competition design 1792, top: front elevation on Pennsylvania Avenue, bottom: first floor plan

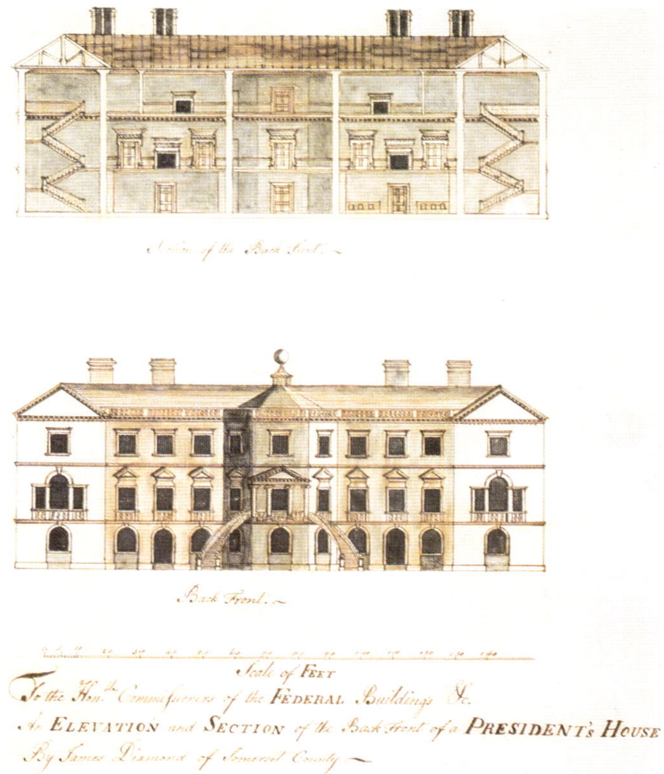

Andrew Mayfield Carshore competition design 1792, top: exterior perspective on Pennsylvania Avenue, front, bottom: ground floor plan

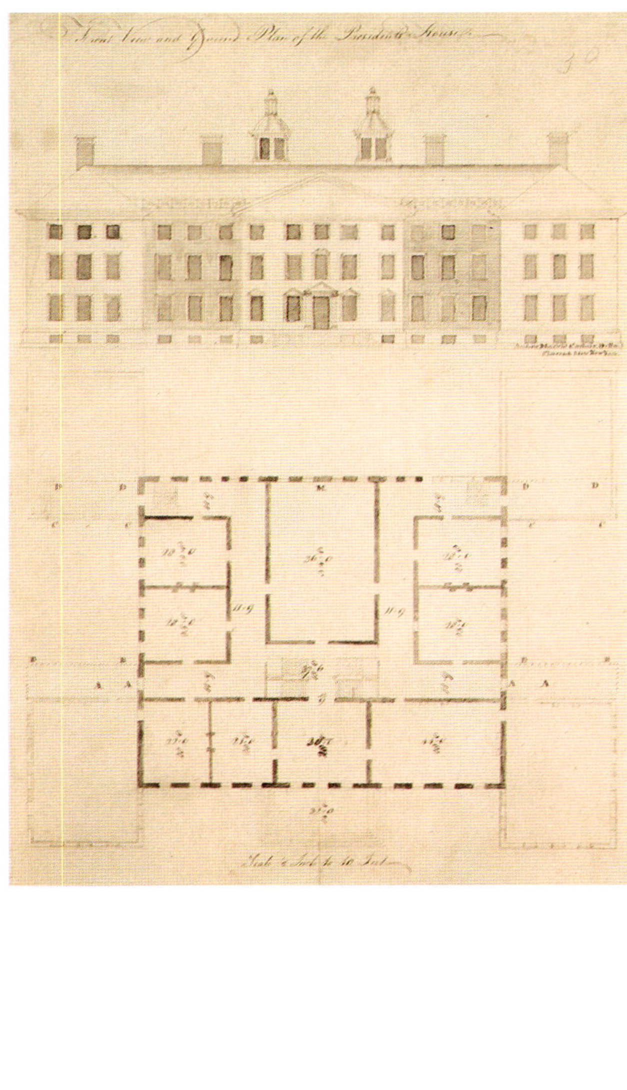

Andrew Mayfield Carshore ground floor plan

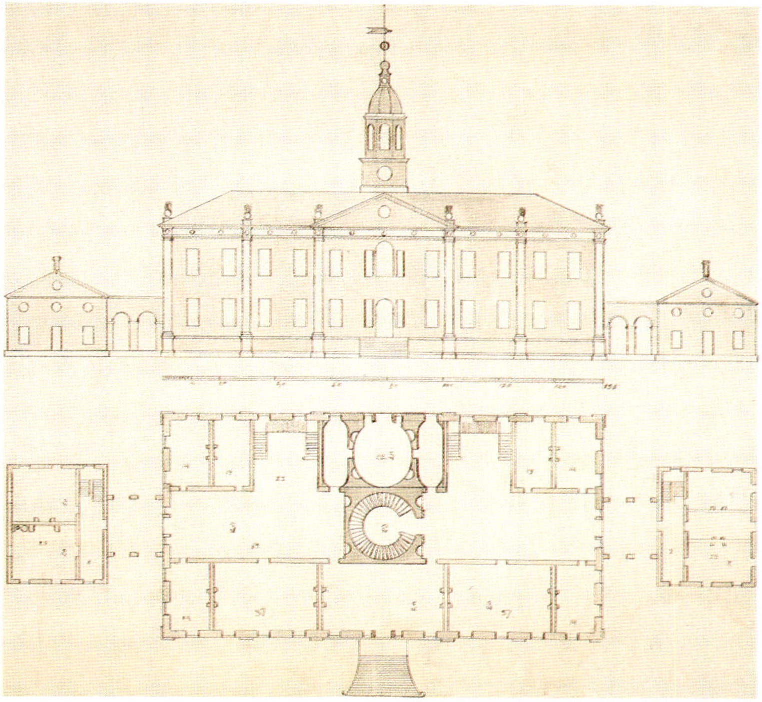

Jacob Small **competition design, alternative A, 1792, front elevation on Pennsylvania Avenue**

Jacob Small **competition design, alternative B, 1792, top: front elevation on Pennsylvania Avenue, bottom: ground floor plan**

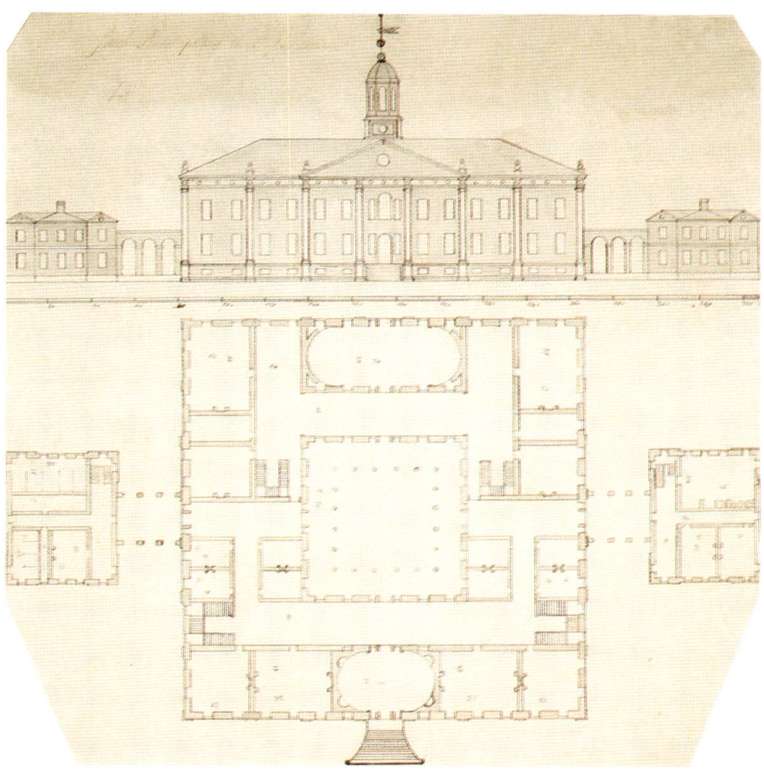

Valhalla, near Ratisbon, 1814

28

Project

Monument. Museum for sculpture

Site

Donaustauf, Regensburg

Dates

Organised 4 February 1814 (Public announcement in the Allgemeine Zeitung: 28 February 1814) *Closing date* 1 January 1815, postponed to 1 January 1816 and later to 1 July 1816

Conditions

Doric style, few further specifications (newspaper advertisement)

Number of entries

51

Jury

Crown prince Ludwig of Bavaria, Carl von Fischer and others

Result

Winner Johann Anton Weiß

Commissioned by

Crown prince Ludwig of Bavaria (crowned in 1825)

Construction

18 October 1830 to 18 October 1842 (the day of Napoleon's defeat at the Völkerschlacht in Leipzig)

Architect

Leo von Klenze (1784–1864)

Valhalla, near Ratisbon, 1814

Valhalla, near Ratisbon, 1814

30

Leo von Klenze altered design, alternative A (centralized type), 1819, elevation

Valhalla, near Ratisbon

The immediate reason for the construction of the Walhalla had much to do with the political situation in Europe at the time. Napoleon reigned and the confidence of most European nations was crippled by their resounding defeat at the hands of the French Army, as at the battles of Ulm and Jena. It was in this time of turmoil that crown prince Ludwig of Bavaria decided, in 1807, to erect a monument in honour of fifty German heroes and heroines.

During his travels abroad, Ludwig had had ample time to view illustrious examples of such monuments built in the recent and distant past. In 1805, he visited the Roman Pantheon – an important source of inspiration for architects over the centuries – and the Pantheon in Paris in 1806. However, before the building was given a definitive form, Ludwig tackled the problem of selecting fifty people (their number was soon raised to a hundred) of whom the Berlin sculptors Schadow, Rauch, Tieck and Wichmann were to make portrait busts. He called in the help of the Swiss historian Johannes von Müller, who worked as his adviser until Müller's death in 1809. It was Müller who suggested the name "Valhalla" to the prince, in reference to the paradise of Germanic-Scandinavian mythology, which was a sanctuary for heroes who had died in battle. Initially, this reference to a "barbaric" past was not particularly popular in Christian, humanist Northern Europe. However, the war against Napoleon was reminiscent of the war between the Germans and the Romans, particularly the illustrious "Hermannsschlacht", where Arminius annihilated three Roman legions in the Teutoburger Forest. This was barbaric behaviour to be proud of.

This history was shared with *"all German-speaking nations"*, as Ludwig put it. He did not envisage a rigidly nationalistic gallery of honour, but strove to include all German-speaking nations in the Valhalla. Not only Goethe, but also the Austrian Mozart and the Dutchman Jan van Eyck. Otto I and Maximillian I would stand side by side with the Anglo-Dutch king and viceroy William III. Ludwig's efforts were characteristic of the early nineteenth century, when vaguely defined ideas concerning peoples and nations were slowly starting to take root in Europe.

The competition

Many years passed before the idea was given a concrete form. Ludwig first had to become king before he could commission a project of this magnitude (1825). However, a competition had already been organised by the Bavarian Akademie der Bildenden Künste on 4 February 1814. The competition was publicly announced in the Allgemeine Zeitung on 28 February of the same year. The initial closing date was 1 January 1815 (later postponed to 1 July 1816). In addition to the design for the Valhalla, architects were asked to submit designs for a home for the disabled and a museum for sculpture (Glyptothek).
The brief was remarkably concise . It is highly likely that Ludwig – who had an interest in architecture but was not hampered by a thorough knowledge of the subject – had taken it upon himself to draw up the competition programme. The stipulations for the monument to German art were as follows: a rectangular floor plan with a peristyle, with one large hall inside and no upper floors. Measurements were not stipulated. One hundred busts had to be housed in the building and therefore the incidence of light was important; the architects were permitted to include a glass roof. The designs had to be drawn in a purely classical style (Ancient Doric). The word "Valhalla" was to be inscribed above the ornate doors. The building did not have to be elegant, as long as it was spectacular. The programme was signed by J.P. Langer and Fr.W.J. Schelling, both from the Akademie der Bildenden Künste.
No less than 51 people submitted designs. Unfortunately, few of their names have been saved for posterity. It is known that the jury member Carl von Fischer submitted a design. Von Fischer had previously made design sketches at Ludwig's request between 1809 and 1810. One of

G.A. Lebsche Valhalla and surroundings, viewed from the ruins of Donaustauf Castle, lithograph

Friedrich Gilly Monument to Friedrich the Great, exterior view, Berlin 1797

these was based on the Roman Pantheon, the other on the Parthenon in Athens. Judging by the competition programme he drafted, Ludwig was very pleased with these classical designs. Other participants included Schinkel, Haller von Hallerstein and Leo von Klenze. Some of the designs submitted by these architects have been retained and in some cases there are records describing the designs. The latter applies to the designs of Daniel Joseph Ohlmüller, who was the only architect who stayed true to his principles, ignoring the competition stipulations and submitting a Gothic Revivalist design. Little or nothing is known of the designs by the architects Malling, Thürmer and Himbsel. It was only discovered later that Peter Speeth of Würzburg had also been a participant.
Like Von Fischer, Haller von Hallerstein had previously been involved in the project. He had even submitted a number of detailed designs, which were later put to good use in the final design. Von Klenze was even in possession of Haller's drawings, most of which have been lost[1]. (Naturally, he only received them after the competition.) The winner was the architect Johann Anton Weiss, who, it later transpired, was a front man for the jury member Carl von Fischer. No prizes were awarded for the other buildings, the home for the disabled and the museum for sculpture. Due to the fact that the jury was under no obligation to execute Weiss' winning design, the competition may be termed a failure.

Leo von Klenze Glyptothek, competition design (Greek style), exterior view, 1815

Karl Friedrich Schinkel palace on the Acropolis, interior view, 1834,

Valhalla, front entrance from south

Style and influence

Ludwig was nevertheless determined to execute his plans. He now informally approached von Klenze (1816), as he had Carl von Fischer and Haller von Hallerstein, which resulted in a lively correspondence and a large number of designs. Von Klenze initially tried to push the Pantheon as a model, but Ludwig objected (1819). Influenced by the Romanticists, so abhorred by von Klenze, Ludwig wanted a design which bore a closer resemblance to Haller's drawings. Von Klenze assented to this request and sent Ludwig, who was then in Rome, two designs (1821): a centralised structure and a rectangular Doric temple on a tripartite substructure and a base. The base, consisting of spider-web rubble walls, had a trapezium-shaped entrance. The latter plan met with Ludwig's approval and later formed the basic structure for the Valhalla. However, it was left untouched for some time, until Ludwig became king in 1825. Another reason for the delay was that Ludwig had given precedence to the Glyptothek, which was also designed by von Klenze.

Von Klenze derived the idea for the Doric temple, in combination with the substructure described above, from Haller's drawings and from Friedrich Gilly's design for the Monument for Frederick the Great[2]. The substructure was of essential significance to the concept which Ludwig had in mind. The temple was to be a place of honour for the world's great historical figures, and the substructure would serve as an antechamber. This concept was initially developed further by Haller and later by von Klenze. The Valhalla was to be a sanctuary for the immortal, in combination with a tomb for the dead. The idea for the tomb, "hypogaion", was based on Etruscan burial chambers. This explains the spider-web rubble walls, the trapezium-shaped entrance and the (groin) vaults. It would house the "comrades" who had been dead less than ten years and whose immortality had yet to be ascertained (this included famous people who were still alive). For those who lived up to the exalted expectations, the deceased, or rather their bust, would be borne upstairs in procession to take up well deserved place in the Valhalla. Ludwig had already toyed with this idea in 1821, but circumstances had forced him to set it aside during construction in 1834, because the statesman Metternich is said to have snidely remarked that Ludwig was probably planning to reserve a place for himself. The trapezium-shaped entrance symbolised the transition to immortality. It is now the rather inappropriate entrance to a storeroom.

The dates marking the beginning and end of construction, 18 October 1830 and 1842, bear witness to Ludwig's romantic heart. It was on that day that Napoleon's French army capitulated at Leipzig (1814).
Besides the Doric temple and the Etruscan burial chamber, other influences are also apparent in von Klenze's design. The stairway had classical predecessors in Persepolis and Praeneste (the Temple of Fortuna Primigenia) while the tripartite substructure was derived from the Tomb of Cyrus at Pasargadai. The most striking aspect of all is that

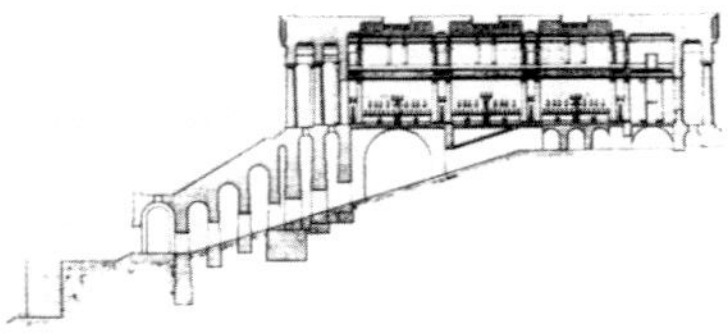

Leo von Klenze Valhalla, longitudinal section, 1842

Leo von Klenze interior view, 1842

von Klenze was inspired by classical architecture and not by German historical architecture, whereas a Germanic monument in Gothic style might have seemed more appropriate.

Justification and symbolism

Von Klenze based the justification of his choice for the Doric style on the so-called Caucasus theory. This theory holds that paradise was once situated somewhere in the Himalayas. All nations, Greek and German included, had at some time departed from this place. The proof of this theory lay in the irregular bonding (Pelasgic or Cyclopean) which one encounters in all cultures, and which was used for the substructure of the Valhalla. According to the Caucasus theory, architectural principles are universal: the Greeks did not invent the Doric style, but were the first to apply it. These universal principles allow architects to borrow freely from Greek, Oriental and Etruscan architecture. The German people had borne these principles with them since the time that the Caucasus was their fatherland. They had settled in Germany after their exodus from paradise.

This rather garbled legend is depicted in a frieze by Martin von Wagner, which shows Caucus helping the Germans across the Danube. However, the reference to history certainly does not end here. The Valhalla was intentionally situated on the Danube and symbolises the founding of the German Reich itself. This gives the Valhalla an added dimension. Von Klenze made two paintings of his creation. In one painting, the emphasis is on the Valhalla and the ruin in the background where Charlemagne is said to have stayed. The scene is bathed in the first light of dawn. In the other painting, bathed in the evening glow, the Salvator Church has been depicted in the foreground. The meaning is evident: the Valhalla symbolises the return to the eternal (Doric) architecture and the growth of a nation. The Salvator Church embodies that which is fleeting and transitory (Gothic).

However universal the architecture may be, the contents of the monument are nationally oriented. Ludwig did not have the world's great historical figures in mind, but the history of the Germanic nations. The sculpted busts of Germans, Austrians and Dutchmen stand side by side in fraternal harmony. Writers, politicians, generals and painters, accompanied by six Valkyries, the mythological female beings who lead the way to Valhalla. An interesting detail is that the sculpted caryatids have a distinctly German look; they have bearskins draped around their shoulders. The sculpture on the tympanum depicts the Hermannsschlacht. Here, too, a historical comparison can be drawn: Caesar Augustus as the predecessor of Emperor Napoleon. Aside from the examples already mentioned, there are many more hidden references to the past in the Valhalla, which, in its style and symbolism, has become one of the most significant monuments in architectural history, despite the fact that von Klenze's classicism was a little outdated, even in his own time.

1 *There is a certain amount of overlap between the informal commission given to Haller von Hallerstein and the competition.*

2 *Gilly's design, which dates from 1796, has long served as a prototype, which was last echoed in Mies van der Rohe's design for the New National Gallery.*

34

Walhalla, bei Regensburg

Der unmittelbare Anlaß zum Bau der Walhalla war eng verknüpft mit der damaligen politischen Situation in Europa. Napoleon herrschte, das Selbstvertrauen der anderen europäischen Völker war schwer erschüttert durch die mühelosen Siege der französischen Armee über ihre Gegner, u.a. in den Schlachten von Ulm und Jena. In dieser hoffnungslosen Zeit entschloß sich Kronprinz Ludwig von Bayern 1807 zur Errichtung eines Monuments zu Ehren der 50 größten Heldinnen und Helden des deutschen Volkes.

Ludwig hatte sich während seiner Auslandsreisen ausführlich über berühmte Vorbilder informiert. So besuchte er 1805 u.a. das römische Pantheon, das durch die Jahrhunderte zahllosen Architekten als Inspirationsquelle gedient hatte, und ein Jahr später das Pantheon in Paris. Noch bevor der Bau konkrete Formen annahm, beschäftigte sich Ludwig mit der Frage, von welchen 50 Personen (schnell wurden 100 daraus) die Berliner Bildhauer Schadow, Rauch, Tieck und Wichmann Porträtbüsten anfertigen sollten. Dabei ließ er sich von dem Schweizer Historiker Johannes von Müller beraten, mit dem er bis zu dessen Tod 1809 einen regen Briefwechsel führte. Von Müller war es auch, der dem Kronprinzen den Namen »Walhalla« vorschlug, nach dem Paradies der germanisch/skandinavischen Mythologie für die in der Schlacht gefallenen Helden. Anfänglich erfreuten sich diese Reminiszenzen an eine »barbarische« Vergangenheit im christlichen und humanistischen Nordeuropa keiner allzu großen Beliebtheit, aber der Kampf gegen Napoleon rief die Erinnerung an den Kampf der Germanen gegen die Römer und an die Hermannsschlacht wach. Man teilte diese Vergangenheit mit *»allen Stämmen Teutscher Sprache«*, wie Ludwig sich ausdrückte. Ihm schwebte keine beschränkte nationalistische Ehrengalerie vor, sondern eine »Walhalla«, in der alle Völker des germanischen Sprachraums vertreten sein sollten: Nicht nur Goethe, sondern auch der Österreicher Mozart und der Niederländer Jan van Eyck, und neben Otto I. und Maximilian I. der englisch/niederländische König und Statthalter Willem III. Diese Gedanken sind typisch für den Beginn des 19. Jahrhunderts, als die Begriffe Volk und Nation in Europa kaum eindeutig definiert waren und erst langsam Fuß zu fassen begannen.

Der Wettbewerb

Bevor diese Ideen in die Tat umgesetzt wurden, vergingen noch einige Jahre. Ludwig mußte zuerst König werden (1825), um einen Bauauftrag dieser Größe erteilen zu können. Aber schon am 4. Februar 1814 schrieb die Bayerische Akademie der Bildenden Künste einen Wettbewerb aus. Die Veröffentlichung erfolgte am 28. Februar desselben Jahres in der Allgemeinen Zeitung; Als Einsendeschluß war der 1. Januar 1815 vorgesehen (später verlängert bis zum 1. Juli 1816). Die Architekten wurden aufgerufen, neben den Plänen für die Walhalla auch Entwürfe für ein Invalidenheim und ein Museum der Bildhauerkunst (Glyptothek) einzureichen.

Die Ausschreibung war äußerst knapp gehalten. Allem Anschein nach hatte Ludwig, der zwar architektonisch interessiert war, aber keine allzu genaue Kenntnis der Materie besaß, die Wettbewerbsbedingungen selbst formuliert. Das Monument der deutschen Kunst sollte wie folgt aussehen: Ein rechteckiger Grundriß mit einem Peristyl, im Innern eine einzige große Halle, keine Obergeschosse. Die genauen Abmessungen waren nebensächlich; das Bauwerk sollte nur Platz für 100 Büsten bieten. Aus diesem Grunde war der Lichteinfall von Bedeutung: Den Architekten wurde erlaubt, ein Glasdach in den Entwurf einzuarbeiten. Darüber hinaus verlangten die Bauauflagen ausschließlich klassische Entwürfe (im dorischen Stil), über den mit Ornamenten verzierten Türen sollte die Inschrift »Walhalla« stehen. Das Bauwerk mußte nicht elegant wirken, sondern groß und aufsehenerregend erscheinen. Unterzeichnet war die Ausschreibung von zwei Mitgliedern der Akademie der Bildenden Künste: J. P. Langer und F. W. J. Schelling.

51 Teilnehmer, von denen nur die wenigsten namentlich überliefert sind, reichten ihre Beiträge ein. Einer seiner Teilnehmer war Carl von Fischer, der gleichzeitig auch als Mitglied der Jury fungierte. Von Fischer hatte schon 1809/10 im Auftrag Ludwigs die ersten Entwurfszeichnungen angefertigt. Eine dieser Zeichnungen basierte auf dem römischen Pantheon, die andere auf dem Parthenon in Athen. Zu den anderen Teilnehmern gehörten Schinkel, Haller von Hallerstein und Leo von Klenze; auch von diesen Architekten sind Zeichnungen erhalten, oder es finden sich zumindest Beschreibungen ihrer Beiträge. Dasselbe gilt für Daniel Joseph Ohlmüller, der – getreu seiner Prinzipien – die Wettbewerbsbedingungen völlig außer acht ließ und einen neugotischen Entwurf einreichte. Nur wenig bis nichts ist über die Pläne der Architekten Malling, Thürmer und Himbsel bekannt, und erst wesentlich später entdeckte man, daß auch Peter Speeth aus Würzburg zu den Teilnehmern zählte.

Ebenso wie von Fischer hatte sich auch Haller von Hallerstein schon vorher mit dem Projekt beschäftigen dürfen und sogar detaillierte Zeichnungen angefertigt, die er in seinem endgültigen Entwurf verwandte. Von Klenze war sogar im Besitz von Hallers Zeichnungen, die heute größtenteils verloren sind[1]. Gewinner wurde der Architekt Johann Anton Weiß, von dem sich wenig später herausstellte, daß er nur als Strohmann des Jurymitglieds Carl von Fischer teilgenommen hatte. Für die anderen Objekte, das Invalidenheim und das Skulpturenmuseum, wurden keine Preise verliehen.

Stil und Einfluß

Ludwig war entschlossen, seine Pläne durchzuführen. Nach Carl von Fischer und Haller von Hallerstein wandte er sich nun inoffiziell an von Klenze (1816), was eine ausgedehnte Korrespondenz und Dutzende von Entwürfen zur Folge hatte. Ursprünglich war von Klenze entschlossen, ein Bauwerk nach dem Vorbild des Pantheon zu schaffen, aber dieser Vorschlag stieß auf den Widerstand Ludwigs (1819). Dieser stand unter dem Einfluß der von Leo von Klenze abgelehnten Romantiker und verlangte einen Entwurf, der den Zeichnungen Hallers ähneln sollte. Von Klenze kam diesem Wunsch nach und schickte Ludwig, der sich zu dieser Zeit in Rom befand, zwei Entwürfe zu (1821): einen Zentralbau und einen rechteckigen dorischen Tempel auf einem dreistufigen Unterbau und einem Sockel. Dieser Sockel sollte aus Haustein-Mauerwerk bestehen und einen trapezförmigen Eingang erhalten. Ludwig stimmte dem letzteren Entwurf zu, der die Grundlage für die spätere Walhalla bildete, aber bis zu Ludwigs Thronbesteigung 1825 zurückgestellt werden mußte. Eine weitere Verzögerung ergab sich durch die Tatsache, daß Ludwig in der Zwischenzeit der Glyptothek den Vorrang gab, die ebenfalls nach einem Entwurf von Klenzes entstand.

Die Idee eines dorischen Tempels, kombiniert mit einem Unterbau, entnahm von Klenze den Zeichnungen Hallers sowie Friedrich Gillys Plänen für das Denkmal Friedrichs des Großen[2]. Dieser Unterbau war von besonderer Bedeutung für das Konzept, das Ludwig vorschwebte. Der Tempel sollte als Ehrenplatz der Großen dieser Erde dienen, der Unterbau übernahm die Funktion eines Vorraums. Diese Idee wurde zunächst durch Haller und danach durch von Klenze weiter ausgearbeitet: Die Walhalla als Ort der Unsterblichen, verbunden mit einer Grabkammer für die Toten. Die Grabkammer – »Hypogaion« – wurde nach etruskischen Vorbildern entworfen, was auch das Haustein-Mauerwerk, den trapezförmigen Eingang und die (Grat-) Gewölbe erklärt. In diesen Kammern sollten die enigen ruhen, die weniger als zehn Jahre tot waren und deren Unsterblichkeit noch nicht feststand (dazu zählten auch noch lebende Berühmtheiten). Nach Ablauf dieser Zeit und nur, wenn er den hochgesteckten Erwartungen entsprochen hatte, wurde die Büste der Verstorbenen in feierlicher Prozession in den Tempel getragen, um einen Ehrenplatz in der Walhalla einzunehmen. Schon 1821 hatte Ludwig mit dieser Idee gespielt; aber er sah sich gezwungen, sie 1834 während des Baus aufzugeben, weil der große Staatsmann Metternich spöttisch bemerkte, daß sich Ludwig selbst anscheinend auch ein Plätzchen reservieren wolle. Der trapezförmige Eingang sollte den Übergang in die Unsterblichkeit symbolisieren; heute bildet er Zugang zu den Lagerräumen. Auch die Anfangs- und Enddaten der Bauzeit – 18. Oktober 1830 bis 18. Oktober 1842 – zeugen von Ludwigs Hang zur Romantik: An diesem Tage hatte Napoleon 1814 in der Völkerschlacht von Leipzig kapituliert.

Rechtfertigung und Symbolismus

So universal sich der Baustil gibt, so volksverbunden ist der Inhalt dieses Monuments: Nicht den Größen der Welt, sondern der Geschichte der germanischen Völker wollte Ludwig ein Denkmal setzen. Hier findet man die Büsten von Deutschen, Österreichern und Niederländern in brüderlicher Harmonie nebeneinander. Schriftsteller, Politiker, Generäle und Maler stehen umrahmt von sechs Walküren, den mythologischen Frauenwesen, die den Toten den Weg nach Walhalla weisen. Besonders auffällig ist das typisch germanische Erscheinungsbild dieser Karyatiden: Sie tragen ein Bärenfell um die Schultern. Das Relief auf dem Tympanon stellt die Hermannsschlacht dar, was weitere historische Vergleiche erlaubt: Der römische Kaiser Augustus als Vorläufer des Konsuls/Kaisers Napoleon. In Stil und Symbolik ist die Walhalla zu den bedeutendsten Monumenten der Architekturgeschichte zu zählen – obwohl von Klenzes Klassizismus bereits zu seinen Lebzeiten als veraltet galt.

1 *Der inoffizielle Auftrag an Haller von Hallerstein und der Beginn des Wettbewerbs gingen zeitlich ineinander über.*

2 *Gillys Entwurf von 1796 gilt als Prototyp, dessen Einflüsse sich noch in Mies van der Rohes Neuer Nationalgalerie finden lassen.*

Le Walhalla, près de Ratisbonne

La première raison qui explique le projet de construction du Walhalla est directement liée à la situation politique en Europe. Napoléon était alors encore au pouvoir et la plupart des nations européennes acceptaient mal leurs défaites répétées devant l'armée française. Ulm et Iéna n'en étaient que quelques exemples parmi trop d'autres. C'est en cette période troublée, en 1807, que le prince héritier Ludwig de Bavière décida d'ériger un monument en l'honneur de cinquante héros et héroïnes allemands.

Lors de ses voyages à l'étranger, il avait pu admirer de nombreux exemples de monuments commémoratifs anciens et récents. En 1805, il avait visité le Panthéon romain – source d'inspiration séculaire de tant d'architectes – et celui de Paris en 1806. Avant de décider du bâtiment, Ludwig avait la lourde tâche de sélectionner cinquante personnages célèbres (nombre bientôt porté à cent) dont les sculpteurs berlinois Schadow, Rauch, Tieck et Wichmann seraient chargés de faire le buste. Il appela à son aide l'historien suisse Johannes von Müller qui le conseilla jusqu'à sa mort en 1809. Ce fut ce dernier qui suggéra le nom de «Walhalla», par référence au paradis de la mythologie germano-scandinave, sanctuaire des héros morts au combat. Au début, ce rappel d'un passé «barbare» ne fut pas particulièrement bien accueilli dans une Europe du Nord humaniste et chrétienne, mais la guerre contre Napoléon rappelait les luttes entre les Germains et les Romains et l'illustre «Hermannsschlacht» où Arminius réduisit à néant trois légions romaines dans les bois de Teutoburg en 9 ap. J. C. Bien que barbare, c'était là un haut fait dont on pouvait être fier.
Cette histoire était *«le patrimoine commun de tous les peuples germanophones»*, comme l'expliquait Ludwig dont le projet ne présentait pas encore de connotations nationalistes. Y figureraient non seulement Goethe, mais également Mozart l'Autrichien et le Néerlandais Jan van Eyck, Otto Ier, Maximilien 1er et le roi anglo-hollandais, Guillaume III. Les préoccupations du prince étaient caractéristiques de ce début du XIXème siècle qui vit se constituer les bases du nationalisme en Europe.

Le concours

De nombreuses années passèrent avant que l'idée ne prenne réellement forme. Ludwig devait d'abord devenir roi avant de pouvoir passer commande d'un projet de cette ampleur, ce qui ne se produisit qu'en 1825. Néanmoins, un concours fut organisé par l'Académie Bavaroise des Arts Appliqués et annoncé dans l'Allgemeine Zeitung du 28 février 1814. La date de remise des projets était fixée au 1er janvier 1815, repoussée ensuite au 1er juillet 1816.
Le programme était étonnamment sommaire. En résumé, le cahier des charges était le suivant: un plan rectangulaire avec péristyle, un grand hall et un seul niveau. Les dimensions n'étaient pas précisées. L'édifice accueillerait cent bustes dont l'éclairage soigné pouvait être obtenu par une verrière. Les projets devaient être traités dans un style inspiré de l'antique – plus précisément dorique – et l'inscription «Walhalla» serait gravée au-dessus de la porte principale. En fait le spectaculaire semblait primer sur l'élégance. Ce programme était signé de J. P. Langer et Fr. W. J. Schelling, tous deux de l'Académie des Arts Appliqués. Pas moins de 51 projets furent présentés. Malheureusement, les noms de la plupart de leurs auteurs ne sont pas passés à la postérité. On sait qu'un des membres du jury, Carl von Fischer, avait proposé un projet, qui prenait la suite des propositons qu'il avait faites, à la demande du prince, en 1809 et 1810. L'une d'entre elles s'inspirait du Panthéon de Rome, l'autre du Parthénon. Ludwig apprécia beaucoup ces idées qui reflétaient ses souhaits. Parmi les autres participants, figuraient Schinkel, Haller von Hallerstein et Leo von Klenze. Certains projets sont parvenus jusqu'à nous, mais beaucoup ne sont connus que par leur description. C'est le cas de ceux de Daniel Joseph Ohlmüller, seul architecte fidèle à ses principes et qui, ignorant délibérément le cahier des charges, proposa un édifice néo-gothique. On ne sait pratiquement rien des propositions de Malling, Thürmer et Himbsel et ce n'est que plus tard que l'on a découvert que Peter Speeth, de Würzburg, avait également participé à cette compétition.
Haller von Hallerstein avait déjà travaillé pour le prince et avait même proposé quelques esquisses détaillées qui lui servirent pour le concours. Von Klenze les eut même entre les mains (après la compétition) mais elles ont malheureusement pour la plupart[1] disparu. Le lauréat fut l'architecte Johann Anton Weiß, qui, comme on le sut plus tard, était l'homme de paille de Carl von Fischer, membre du jury! Aucun prix ne fut attribué pour les autres bâtiments. Comme le jury n'avait nullement l'obligation de faire exécuter les plans de Weiß, le concours peut être considéré comme un échec.

Style et influence

Le prince était cependant décidé à mener à bien son projet. Il approcha officieusement von Klenze, en 1816, comme il avait fait avec Carl von Fischer et Haller von Hallerstein, et leur collaboration donna lieu à une abondante correspondance et à un grand nombre de dessins. Von Klenze avança tout d'abord l'idée que le Panthéon pouvait servir de modèle, mais Ludwig s'y opposa (1819). Influencé par les Romantiques que détestait von Klenze, il souhaitait un projet proche de celui de Haller. L'architecte accepta et envoya à Ludwig, alors à Rome, deux projets: une structure centrale, et un temple dorique rectangulaire sur un soubassement en trois parties et une base. Celle-ci, montée en moellons en appareil polygonal possédait une entrée trapézoïdale. Ce plan plût au prince qui le retint. Puis les choses restèrent en l'état jusqu'à son accession au trône en 1825. Mais Ludwig avait entre-temps fait passer au premier plan de ses préoccupations le musée de sculpture que devait également construire von Klenze. Pour son temple dorique, celui-ci s'inspira des plans de Haller et du projet de Friedrich Gilly pour le monument à Frédéric le Grand[2], auxquels il ajouta le soubassement décrit plus haut. Cet élément revêtait une importance essentielle dans le concept auquel le roi était attaché. Le soubassement servirait en effet d'antichambre au temple selon une idée initialement développée par Haller, puis von Klenze. Le Walhalla devait être à la fois une tombe et un sanctuaire de l'immortalité. L'idée du soubassement-tombeau venait des chambres funéraires étrusques, d'où les murs en appareil polygonal, l'entrée en trapèze et les voutes à arêtes. Il accueillerait les «Genossen», morts depuis moins de dix ans et dont l'immortalité devait encore s'affirmer (ceci incluait également des personnages célèbres encore vivants). Ayant patienté le temps nécessaire et répondu à l'attente générale, le décédé, ou plutôt son buste, serait porté en procession à l'étage supérieur, pour occuper sa place méritée au Walhalla. Ludwig avait déjà joué avec cette idée en 1821, mais les circonstances l'avaient poussé à l'écarter lorsque Metternich avait insidieusement remarqué que le roi s'y réservait probablement une place. La forme trapézoïdale de l'entrée symbolisait le passage vers l'immortalité. Elle sert maintenant d'accès assez peu pratique à un entrepôt.
En dehors du temple dorique et des chambres funéraires étrusques, d'autres influences apparaissent dans le projet de von Klenze. Le grand escalier avait ses antécédents à Persépolis et Praeneste (Temple de la Fortune primigenia) et l'infrastructure en trois parties venait de la tombe de Cyrus à Pasargades. Il est frappant que l'architecte se soit inspiré de l'architecture antique et non pas allemande, alors qu'un style gothique eut semblé parfaitement approprié à un monument aussi germanique.

Justification et symbolisme

Von Klenze justifiait le choix du style dorique par la théorie du Caucase. une construction intellectuelle selon laquelle le paradis se trouvait dans l'Himalaya. Toutes les nations, Grecs et Allemands compris, venaient de ce même lieu. La preuve en était l'appareil de pierre irrégulier (pélagique ou cyclopéen) commun à toutes les cultures et qui servit aux soubassements du Walhalla. Toujours selon cette théorie, les principes de l'architecture sont universels: les Grecs n'inventèrent pas le style dorique, mais furent les premiers à l'appliquer. Cette universalité autorisait les architectes à emprunter leurs modèles dans l'architecture grecque, orientale ou étrusque. Les Allemands portaient en eux ces principes depuis qu'ils avaient quitté leur foyer natal, le Caucase, avant de se fixer en Germanie après leur exil du paradis.
Cette légende fantaisiste est dépeinte dans une fresque de Martin von Wagner montrant Caucus aidant les Germains à traverser le Danube. La référence à l'histoire ne s'arrête d'ailleurs pas là. C'est volontairement que le Walhalla a été situé au bord du Danube pour symboliser la fondation du Reich allemand et conférer ainsi à l'édifice une dimension supplémentaire. Von Klenze réalisa deux peintures de son œuvre. Dans la première, il représente le Walhalla avec, dans le lointain, une ruine où Charlemagne est censé avoir séjourné. La scène est baignée d'une lumière d'aurore. Dans la seconde, illuminée par le crépuscule, l'église du Sauveur apparaît en arrière-plan. La signification est évidente: le Walhalla symbolise le retour à l'architecture éternelle et la naissance d'une nation. L'église du Sauveur, gothique, matérialise ce qui est flottant et transitoire.
César apparaît comme le prédécesseur de Napoléon. De très nombreuses références au passé parsèment l'édifice, ce qui en fait, pour le style et le symbolisme, l'un des plus importants monuments européens pour l'histoire de l'architecture, et cela même si son néo-classicisme était déjà un peu dépassé à l'époque de sa construction.

1 *Il y avait certains points communs entre la commande officieuse passée à Haller von Hallerstein et le concours.*
2 *Les plans de Gilly, qui datent de 1796, ont longtemps servi de prototype, et se retrouvent même dans le projet de Mies van der Rohe pour les nouvelles Galeries Nationales de Berlin.*

Leo von Klenze altered design, alternative B (centralized type) 1819, elevation

Leo von Klenze final design (temple type) 1837, south elevation with foundation, (front)

Leo von Klenze competition design (temple type) 1816, plan

Leo von Klenze competition design (temple type) 1816, elevation

Valhalla, near Ratisbon, 1814

38

Grueber interior perspective, 1842, colour lithograph by C. Köppe

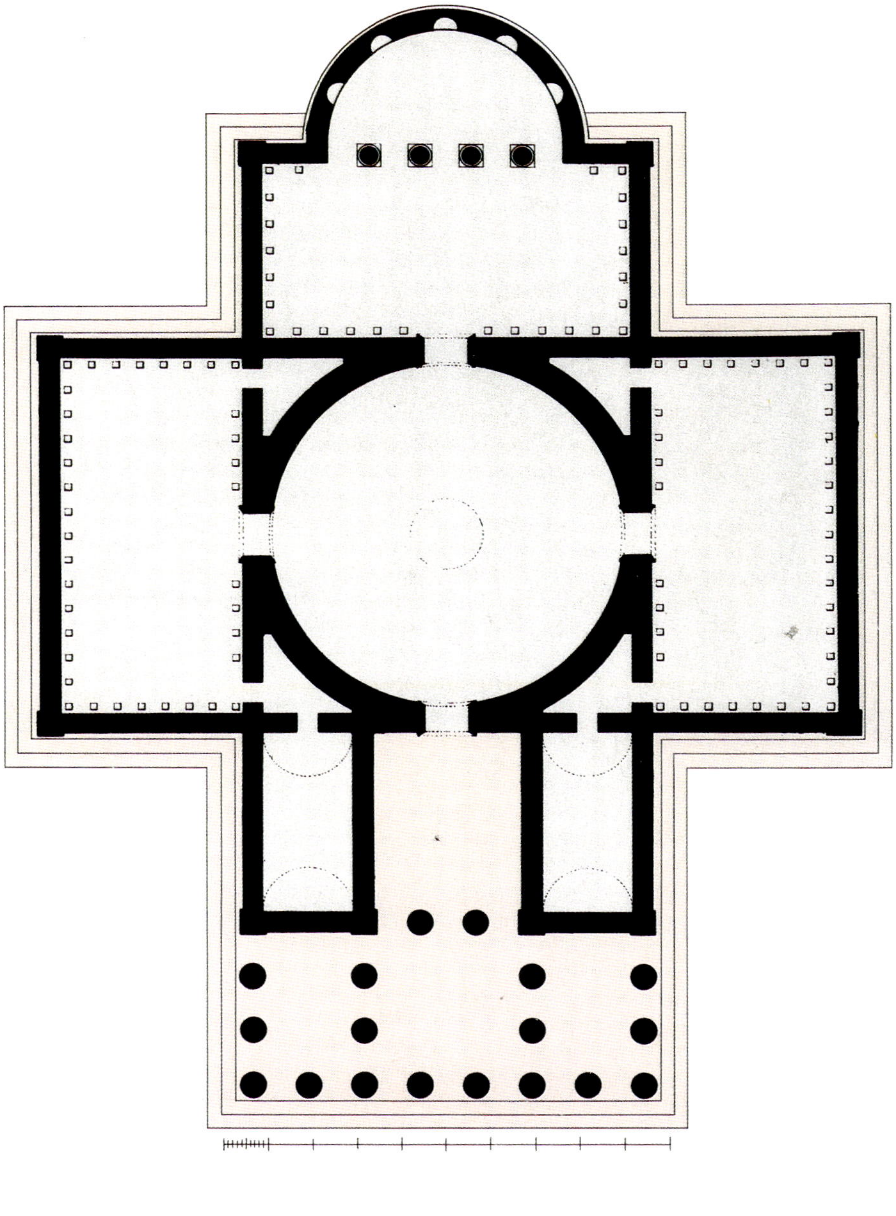

Carl von Fischer alternative A (before competition) 1809, elevation

Carl von Fischer alternative A (before competition) 1809, plan

Carl von Fischer alternative A (before competition) 1809, longitudinal section

Carl von Fischer alternative B (before competition) 1809, front elevation

Carl von Fischer below: alternative B (before competition) 1810, longitudinal section, top: side elevation

Daniel Joseph Ohlmüller front elevation without date

Carl Haller von Hallerstein idealistic situation of Valhalla, 1814, exterior view

Daniel Joseph Ohlmüller transverse section without date

Carl Haller von Hallerstein idealistic situation of Valhalla, 1814–1815, exterior view

Houses of Parliament, London, 1835

Project

Houses of Parliament

Site

New Palace Yard, London

Dates

Competition from 3 June 1835 to 1 November 1835 (postponed to 1 December 1835)

Result announced

31 January 1836

Conditions

Gothic or Elizabethan style

Number of entries

97

Jury

Charles Hanbury Tracy (Chairman, Member of Parliament), Hon. Thomas Lidell (First Commissioner of Woods and Works), Sir Edward Cust (former Member of Parliament, proposed competition), George Vivian (architectural expert, writer)

Result

First prize Charles Barry *Second prize* John Chessel Buckler
Third prize David Hamilton *Fourth prize* William Railton

Commissioned by

Parliament and cabinet

Construction

1835 to 1867

Architects

Charles Barry (1795–1860) and Augustus Welby Northmore Pugin (1812–1852); Edward Barry (1830–1880) following his father's death

Houses of Parliament, London, 1835

Charles Barry final design, 1842, south elevation on Old Palace Yard

Charles Barry competition design, 1836, north elevation on New Palace Yard, first prize

Houses of Parliament, London

London has been the seat of British parliament since time immemorial. The old buildings were grouped around St. Stephen's Chapel, which had been the seat of the House of Commons since 1547. The construction of new buildings had previously been planned in 1692 (Christopher Wren) and in 1733 (William Kent), but shortages of funds, war and other factors had hampered execution. In 1789 the situation had become critical. The buildings were badly ventilated and there was a fire hazard. John Soane was commissioned to design new buildings, but once again the plan was called off and the situation worsened. The industrial revolution had necessitated the passing of new legislation and, with increasing regularity, members of parliament met separately in specialised commissions (transport, labour). Naturally, these commissions required conference halls.

Larger premises had also become a necessity due to the fact that the number of members of the House of Lords and the House of Commons had gradually increased over the years. Soane was approached again in 1820, but it seemed that the time was still not ripe for this grand undertaking. Construction was limited to a few annexes. Soane was also unfortunate in that times had changed. The Gothic Revival had started to gain a firm foothold at the expense of the Classicists.
More plans followed, and this situation would have prevailed were it not that fate took a hand, accommodating parliament's wishes. Piles of wooden tallies, which had been used for administrative purposes in the past, had been stored in the building. These had to be burnt and, in an effort to avoid causing panic in the neighbourhood, they were thrown into the stoves of the House of Lords on 16 October 1834. The stoves had not been cleaned for some time and the lengthy stoking of the fire caused overheating, whereupon fire broke out. The fire destroyed most of the parliamentary buildings. Only Westminster Hall and a part of St. Stephen's survived the flames. This would later become an important aspect of the competition. However, parliament first approached Robert Smirke, who submitted a design in 1835. However, this design met with a storm of criticism and a competition was hastily organised. It was argued that an open competition would be most appropriate for a building which was to house the representatives of the British people.

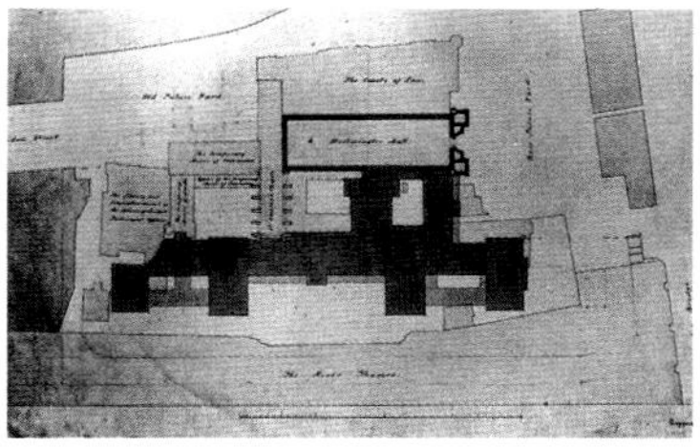

Robert Smirke design for reconstruction of the Houses of Parliament after the fire, site plan, 1835

Augustus Welby Pugin comparative scenes of a Catholic village, 1440 and 1840, showing Gothic style in castle wall and spire of monastery, 1440

Augustus Welby Pugin advent of warehouses and factory stocks, 1840; Pugin advocated the Gothic Revival

Competition announced

On 3 June 1835 the competition was announced. Architects were asked to submit designs for the new houses of parliament, in Gothic or Elizabethan[1] style, under a pseudonym. The jury consisted of well-meaning amateurs, who, it was believed, would harbour no "jalousie de métier". The chairman Charles Hanbury Tracy and Thomas Lidell were both amateur architects of the old school: wealthy and artistic, but lacking specialised training. The jury would award £ 500 to between three and five participants, and an additional £ 1000 to the winning design if the architect was not personally involved in the construction. The use of colour was prohibited, in order to prevent entries from being judged on all sorts of irrelevant æsthetic characteristics. Many participants were also amateurs and not everyone kept to the stipulated conditions. As a result, the jury awarded only four prizes.

Parliament itself had stipulated that the style should be Gothic or Elizabethan. There were various reasons for this. Firstly, the Gothic style was characteristic of the glorious early years of parliament, a period during which Westminster Hall and nearby Westminster Abbey had been built. Moreover, Gothic was seen as a typically British style, which seemed perfectly appropriate for a British national symbol. The parliamentary decision marked a turning point for Gothic Revival. The Gothic style had never quite disappeared in England. Follies in the form of Medieval ruins in English gardens and the architecture of Sir John Vanbrugh and William Kent had all contributed to a fertile breeding ground for Gothic Revival.

Until the early nineteenth century, Gothic had been more or less a prerogative of the elite. This changed in 1818, when the Church Building Commission decided that Gothic was the most appropriate style for religious buildings. The Houses of Parliament were the first monumental public buildings to be built in Gothic style. Naturally, this raised criticism in Classicist circles. However, voices in favour of the Gothic style were predominant. After many years of sober, boring Georgian, the time was ripe for a new style – an English style – which would be more appealing to the senses. Furthermore, Augustus Welby Northmore Pugin (1812–1852) argued in his influential works on architecture that Gothic was the only truly Christian architectural style and that architects were morally obliged to apply this style in their designs. His exhortations received support from the Ecclesiological Society, a religious movement founded around 1841, which wanted to bring about the resurgence of liturgical values. And then there was John Ruskin who, with his "Seven Lamps of Architecture" (1849) and 'Stones of Venice' (1851–1853), was to become the leading architectural theoretician of the nineteenth century[2]. With so many advocates, it is hardly surprising that Gothic Revival became a national style. Even though, after completion of the Houses of Parliament, many public buildings were still built in the Classicist style, by the time the competition for the Law Courts[3] was organised, 25 years after the competition for parliament, the role of the Classicists had become almost completely insignificant, and stations, hospitals, city halls and other public buildings were built in Gothic style.

Problems and solutions

Almost all the participants in the competition for parliament had met the stipulated conditions and had submitted Gothic designs. (C.R. Cockerell (1788–1863), a confirmed Classicist, was a notable exception.) Besides the stipulated style, the architects had to take a number of other factors into account. Firstly, Westminster Hall, which had survived the fire, was to form part of the complex. Westminster Hall was situated on the site and was held in such reverence that it could not be torn down. A similar problem was posed by what remained of St. Stephen's: should it be rebuilt and incorporated, or torn down? Another problem was the characteristically elongated shape of the building site. The façade along the Thames would measure no less than three hundred metres. This brought with it problems of internal circulation, the accessibility of the different quarters and the convenience of the floor plan.

The jury had roughly two categories of designs to judge. The more uniform designs, with a symmetrical Classicist floor plan, and designs of a varied structure, which were asymmetrical with an irregular floor plan. Lewis Nockalls Cottingham (1787–1847) submitted a design of the second category. He expressed his penchant for the Picturesque by enlivening his design with drawings of little boats on the Thames and other totally irrelevant objects. However, the jury did not allow itself to be influenced by picturesque tableaux of this sort. Cottingham was one of many participants who had applied the sixteenth century Gothic (Tudor) style. The designs of Thomas Rickman (1776–1841) and J. Gillespie Graham (1776–1855) may also be listed in the irregular category. This was hardly surprising, because Rickman was one of the

David Hamilton competition design (Elizabethan style), perspectival section of the House of Commons and the House of Lords, third prize

David Hamilton exterior perspective of entrance of the House of Commons and south side of the House of Lords

architects who had rediscovered the true Gothic style of the Middle Ages. In his book "An attempt to discriminate the Styles of English Architecture", published in 1817, he introduced the classic distinction between Early English, Decorated and Perpendicular styles. Gillespie Graham's design had been drawn in collaboration with Pugin, the champion of the Picturesque style in Gothic Revival, who would later also assist Barry in his designs.

Entries of the first category included the designs by J.C. Buckler (1793–1894) and David Hamilton (1768–1843) who were awarded second and third prize respectively. Buckler had chosen the Tudor style and Hamilton was one of the few who had chosen Elizabethan. Hamilton's floor plan would later serve as an example for Barry, after he had won the competition. William Railton's (1801–1877) design had elements of both categories: his floor plan was regular but the vertical elevation was irregular. He was awarded fourth prize for his design. Barry's winning design had one long, uninterrupted, regular façade along the Thames. The libraries and halls of assembly were situated behind this façade. The design followed the slanting lines between Westminster Hall and St. Stephen's, causing a wedge-shaped floor plan to develop.

The Houses of Parliament, interior of the House of Lords

Barry later straightened out the wedge shape with the aid of Hamilton's design. The House of Lords and the House of Commons opened out into a central hall which, in turn, was connected to St. Stephen's (Hamilton had only incorporated Westminster Hall in his design).

Barry and Pugin

The resulting design was far more balanced than Barry's earlier design. In fact, he had initially complicated things for himself. His decision to taper all the courtyards in his first design had been a makeshift solution. The vertical elevation was also extensively altered. In the original design, the north side was dominated by a square tower. This was later literally developed into a bell tower: Big Ben. Besides the alterations already mentioned, the details also deviated from Barry's original drawing. This was largely the result of Pugin's influence. Pugin, the leading Gothic expert, was appointed Barry's advisor after he had been commissioned. Pugin was in charge of the details and the interior decoration: wainscoting, wallpaper, furniture, umbrella stands, ink pots etc.. Meanwhile, he kept his own business running unabated. Pugin was one of the most productive architects of his time. He worked on the Houses of Parliament with Barry from 1835 to 1837 and again from 1844 until his death in 1852. Although their admiration for one another was mutual and their collaboration harmonious, Pugin did not see the Houses of Parliament as a textbook example of the Gothic style he had envisaged. His remark to a friend, while boating on the Thames, has become famous: *"All Grecian, Sir. Tudor details on a classical body".*

1 *Elizabethan can best be described as English late-Tudor Gothic, with a touch of Renaissance influence.*

2 *Within Gothic Revivalism a number of different styles may be distinguished: Early English (13th century), Decorated (1290–1360), Perpendicular (1335–1530), Tudor (1485–1603), Elizabethan (1550–1603), Continental (mainly French, Spanish and Italian forms of Gothic) and Picturesque (typical 19th century Gothic: irregular, asymmetrical, in impression rather than in detail). Additional combinations of the above and personal versions.*

3 *A full account of this competition is given further on in this book.*

Houses of Parliament, London

Der Sitz des britischen Parlaments befand sich von jeher in London. Bereits seit 1547 dienten die alten Parlamentsgebäude, die sich um die Kapelle St. Stephen herum gruppierten, dem Unterhaus (House of Commons) als Tagungsort. Zwar hatte es schon in den Jahren 1692 (Christopher Wren) und 1733 (William Kent) Pläne für einen Neubau gegeben, aber Geldmangel, kriegerische Auseinandersetzungen und anderen Faktoren verhinderten immer wieder die Durchführung. Schließlich hatte sich bis 1789 die Situation aufgrund mangelhafter Belüftung und großer Brandgefahr derartig verschlechtert,daß man John Soane den offiziellen Bauauftrag zum Neubau des Parlamentsgebäudes erteilte; allerdings wurden auch diese Pläne nicht ausgeführt. In der Zwischenzeit nahm der Zustand der Gebäude immer bedrohlichere Formen an. Die Parlamentsmitglieder tagten immer häufiger in speziellen Kommissionen (Transport, Arbeit), die jeweils getrennte Versammlungsräume benötigten.

In Anbetracht der Tatsache, daß Unter- und Oberhaus (House of Lords) seit ihrer Entstehung stetig angewachsen waren, ließ sich eine Erweiterung der Räumlichkeiten nicht mehr verschieben. Erneut wandte man sich an Soane (1820), aber auch dieses Mal war die Zeit noch nicht reif für ein derartig großes Unterfangen. Man ließ ihn lediglich einige kleine Anbauten vornehmen. Darüber hinaus hatte Soane insofern Pech, als sich die Zeiten änderten und sich das »Gothic Revival« auf Kosten des Klassizismus immer mehr durchsetzte.
Es folgten etliche weitere Pläne, doch an der gesamten Situation hätte sich nichts geändert, wenn nicht das Schicksal – ganz im Sinne des Parlaments – eingegriffen hätte. In den alten Gebäuden lagerten noch zahlreiche Stapel mit Holztafeln, die man früher in der Verwaltung verwendet hatte und die nun verbrannt werden sollten. Um die Bewohner der umliegenden Häuser nicht unnötig zu beunruhigen, warf man die Holztafeln am 16. Oktober 1834 in die Öfen des House of Lords. Das stundenlange Heizen in den seit längerer Zeit nicht gereinigten Kaminen verursachte eine Überhitzung der Feuerstellen und führte zu einer verheerenden Feuersbrunst, der fast alle Gebäude auf dem Parlamentsgelände zum Opfer fielen. Nur Westminster Hall und Teile von St. Stephen's Chapel überstanden die Katastrophe. Deren Überreste sollten bei der späteren Ausschreibung eine wichtige Rolle spielen. Zunächst reichte Robert Smirke 1835 auf Bitte des Parlaments ein erstes Konzept für das neue Parlamentsgebäude ein. Diese Pläne stießen jedoch auf derart heftige Kritik, daß man sich hastig zu einem offiziellen Architekturwettbewerb entschloß.

Ausschreibung des Wettbewerbs

Am 3. Juni 1835 wurde die Ausschreibung bekanntgegeben, und die Architektengemeinde war aufgerufen, ihren Entwurf für einen Neubau des Parlamentsgebäudes im gotischen oder elisabethanischen Stil[1] unter einem Pseudonym einzusenden. Die Jury bestand aus engagierten Laien, von denen man annahm, daß ihnen jegliche »jalousie de métier« fremd wäre. Der Vorsitzende der Jury, Charles Hanbury Tracy, und Jurymitglied Thomas Lidell galten als Amateur-Architekten alter Schule: Reich und kunstverständig, aber ohne spezielle Ausbildung auf diesem Gebiet. Als Preis war eine Belohnung von jeweils 500 Pfund für die ersten drei bis fünf Entwürfe vorgesehen; falls man den prämierten Entwurf nicht vom ursprünglichen Architekten ausführen ließ, stand diesem ein zusätzlicher Betrag von 1 000 Pfund zu. Die Konstruktionspläne durften nicht koloriert sein: Auf diese Weise wollte man verhindern, daß die Konzepte aufgrund von stimmungsvollen, nicht sachdienlichen Aspekten beurteilt würden. Bei den meisten Einsendern handelte es sich – wie bei der Jury – um Amateure, und nicht allen gelang eine fachgerechte Umsetzung der Auflagen. Aus diesem Grund entschied sich die Jury schließlich nur für vier Gewinner.
Die Parlamentarier selbst hatten aus mehreren Gründen einen gotischen oder elisabethanischen Stil für das neue Gebäude zur Bauauflage gemacht. Zunächst einmal charakterisierte die Gotik die Epoche der glanzvollen Entstehungsperiode des Parlaments – einer Zeit, aus der auch die angrenzende Westminster Hall und die in der Nähe gelegene Westminster Abbey stammten. Darüber hinaus galt die Gotik als typisch englischer Stil, der sich hervorragend als Symbol für das britische Volk eignete. Dieser Parlamentsbeschluß kennzeichnet einen Wendepunkt des Gothic Revival. In England war die Gotik nie völlig verschwunden: »Follies« (Verrücktheiten) in Form von mittelalterlichen Ruinen in englischen Gärten und die Architektur von Sir John Vanbrugh und William Kent hatten den Boden für die Neugotik bereitet.
Bis zum Beginn des 19. Jahrhunderts war die Gotik mehr oder weniger der Oberschicht vorbehalten gewesen. Dies änderte sich erst 1818, als ein Beschluß der Church Building Commission (Kirchenbaukommission) die Gotik als den passendsten Stil für ein religiöses Bauwerk bezeichnete. Die Houses of Parliament sollten nun das erste große Staatsgebäude im gotischen Stil werden – ein Ansinnen, das die Vertreter des Klassizismus entsprechend kritisierten. Dennoch überwogen die Befürworter des gotischen Stils, die – nach einem Jahrhundert des nüchternen und als langweilig empfundenen Georgian Style – nach Neuem verlangten: nach einem englischen Stil, der stärker an das Gefühl appellieren sollte. Hinzu kam, daß Augustus Welby Northmore Pugin (1812–1852) in seinen einflußreichen Werken die Gotik als einzig wahren christlichen Baustil propagierte und seiner Meinung nach ein Architekt die moralische Pflicht hatte, im gotischen Stil zu bauen. Diese Ansicht unterstützte auch die Ecclesiological Society, eine um 1841 entstandene religiöse Bewegung, die den liturgischen Werten zu neuem Leben verhelfen wollte. Auch John Ruskin – der Verfasser der einflußreichen Werke »Seven Lamps of Architecture« (1849) und »Stones of Venice« (1851–1853) – warf sein Gewicht als bedeutendster englischer Architekturtheoretiker des 19. Jahrhunderts in die Waagschale, so daß es bei derartig vielen Befürwortern nicht verwundert, daß die Neugotik zum nationalen Stil avancierte. Dennoch sollten nach dem Willen des Parlaments auch weiterhin zahlreiche Staatsgebäude im klassizistischen Stil errichtet werden, und erst bei der Ausschreibung für die Law Courts[2] (25 Jahre nach der Ausschreibung für das Parlamentsgebäude) hatte der Klassizismus so weit an Einfluß verloren, daß Bahnhöfe, Hospitäler, Rathäuser und andere öffentliche Gebäude im gotischen Stil erbaut wurden.

Probleme und Lösungen

Nahezu alle Architekten hielten sich an die Vorgabe eines gotischen Entwurfs für das neue Parlamentsgebäude, lediglich der überzeugte Klassizist C.R. Cockerell (1788–1863) kam dieser Auflage nicht nach. Darüber hinaus mußten sich die Einsender mit einer Reihe weiterer Faktoren auseinandersetzen: Zum einen sollte die von den Flammen verschonte Westminster Hall in den neuen Gebäudekomplex integriert werden, da sie sich mitten auf dem Baugelände befand und für eine Schleifung viel zu sehr geschätzt wurde. Zum anderen stellte sich die Frage nach einer weiteren Verwendung der Überreste von St. Stephen's Chapel: Sollte man die Kapelle wieder aufbauen und in die neuen Gebäude einpassen oder sie niederreißen? Das längliche Baugelände entlang der Themse bildete eine weitere Erschwernis, da die dem Fluß zugewandte Fassade des Gebäudekomplexes fast 300 Meter Länge aufweisen würde und sich dadurch Probleme mit der Erreichbarkeit der diversen Räume und der Übersichtlichkeit des Grundrisses ergaben.
Der prämierte Entwurf von Barry zeichnete sich durch eine durchgehende Fassade entlang der Themse aus, hinter der sich die Bibliotheken und Versammlungsräume befanden. Insgesamt orientierten sich die Pläne – von diesen Räumen einmal abgesehen – an den schräg verlaufenden Grundmauern von Westminster Hall und der integrierten St. Stephen's Chapel, so daß ein keilförmiger Grundriß entstand. Später korrigierte Barry – stark beeindruckt von Hamiltons Grundriß – seinen Entwurf. Nun öffneten sich Unter- und Oberhaus zu einer zentralen Halle (Central Lobby) hin, die an St. Stephen's Chapel anschloß (Hamiltons Konzept bezog lediglich Westminster Hall ein).

Barry und Pugin

Diese revidierten Konstruktionspläne waren erheblich ausgewogener als Barrys erster Entwurf, mit dem er sich unnötige Probleme bereitet hatte, da alle Innenhöfe notgedrungen spitz zulaufen mußten. Auch der Aufriß wurde entsprechend abgeändert. Schon im ursprünglichen Konzept beherrschte ein quadratischer Turm die Nordseite, der nun zu einem Glockenturm '»heranwuchs«: Big Ben. Auch die Detailarbeiten unterschieden sich aufgrund Pugins Einfluß stark von Barrys ersten Zeichnungen. Da Pugin als ausgezeichneter Kenner der Gotik galt, war er Barry nach dessen Nominierung zum offiziellen Baumeister der Houses of Parliament als Mitarbeiter zugewiesen worden und beschäftigte sich mit allen Details der Gestaltung der Innenräume und deren Ausstattung, z.B. Vertäfelungen, Tapeten, Mobiliar, Schirmständer, Tintenfässer. Pugin zählte zu den produktivsten Architekten seiner Zeit – an den Aufträgen seines eigenen Architekturbüros arbeitete er unterdessen unvermindert weiter. Die gemeinsame Gestaltung der Parlamentsgebäude erstreckte sich von 1835 bis 1837 und ab 1844 bis zu Pugins Tod im Jahre 1852. Obwohl beide großen Respekt füreinander empfanden und sich ihre Zusammenarbeit sehr harmonisch gestaltete, erachtete Pugin die Houses of Parliament nicht als das Musterbeispiel der Gotik, das ihm eigentlich vorgeschwebt hatte. Während einer Bootsfahrt über die Themse äußerte er sich gegenüber einem Freund so: »*All Grecian, Sir. Tudor details on a classical body*«. (»Alles griechisch, mein Herr. Tudor-Details auf Korpus.«)

1 *»Elizabethan« bezeichnet eigentlich die spätenglische Tudor-Gotik, der ein leichter Einfluß der Renaissance anzumerken war.*

2 *Siehe entsprechendes Kapitel.*

Le Parlement, Londres

Londres a toujours été le siège du Parlement britannique. En 1835, ses bâtiments étaient regroupés autour de la chapelle St. Stephen, lieu de réunion de la Chambre des Communes depuis 1547. La construction de nouvelles installations avait été étudiée dès 1692 (Christopher Wren), puis en 1733 (William Kent), mais le manque de moyens financiers et les guerres, entre autres, avaient empêché leur réalisation. En 1789, la situation était devenue critique. Les divers immeubles étaient mal aérés et le risque d'incendie permanent. John Soane fut désigné pour concevoir de nouveaux édifices mais, une fois encore, le projet fut abandonné alors même que la situation devenait de plus en plus critique. En effet, la révolution industrielle nécessitait la mise au point d'une abondante législation nouvelle et les membres du Parlement se réunissaient de plus en plus souvent dans des commissions spécialisées (transport, travail) qui manquaient de salles.

La Chambre des Lords et la Chambre des Communes qui avaient accru le nombre de leurs membres au cours des années, avaient un urgent besoin d'installations plus vastes. Soane fut encore une fois contacté, puis il apparut que le moment n'était toujours pas propice et les agrandissements furent limités à quelques annexes. Parallèlement, le style néo-gothique commençait à s'imposer, aux dépends du néo-classicisme.
D'autres plans se succédèrent et cet état de choses aurait sans doute perduré si le destin ne s'en était mêlé et n'avait répondu aux souhaits des parlementaires. Des piles de vieilles étiquettes en bois de l'administration avaient été entreposées dans un bâtiment. Elles devaient être brûlées et, pour éviter de provoquer une panique dans le voisinage, furent jetées dans les chaudières de la Chambre des Lords le 16 octobre 1834. Ces installations qui n'avaient pas été nettoyées depuis un certain temps, surchauffèrent et déclenchèrent un incendie. Le feu détruisit la plupart des bâtiments du Parlement à l'exception de Westminster Hall et d'une partie de St. Stephen, élément qui allait jouer un rôle dans le futur concours. Le Parlement fit d'abord appel à Robert Smirke dont le plan (1835) souleva une tempête de critiques telle que l'on décida en hâte d'organiser une compétition. On déclara qu'un concours très ouvert était finalement ce qui convenait de mieux pour un palais appelé à abriter les représentants du peuple britannique.

L'annonce du concours

Le 3 juin 1835, le concours fut donc lancé. Les architectes devaient obligatoirement travailler leurs projets dans le style gothique ou élizabéthain[1], sous un pseudonyme. Le jury était composé d'amateurs éclairés qui, pensait-on, seraient insensibles à toute jalousie professionnelle. Le président, Charles Hanbury Tracy, et Thomas Lidell étaient en réalité tous deux des architectes amateurs de la vieille école, riches et esthètes certes, mais manquant de formation technique. Le jury se proposait de répartir 500 £ entre trois ou cinq participants et 1000 £ supplémentaires étaient prévues pour le vainqueur, s'il ne se chargeait pas personnellement de la construction. Les projets devaient être rendus en noir et blanc, afin d'éviter qu'ils soient jugés sur des critères de qualité de dessin plutôt que d'architecture. De nombreux participants étaient des amateurs et ils ne respectèrent pas tous les stipulations du règlement. Dans ces conditions, le jury ne fut en mesure de n'accorder que quatre prix.
Le Parlement lui-même avait décidé que le style devait être gothique ou élizabéthain pour des raisons très diverses. Tout d'abord, le style gothique rappelait les heures glorieuses de la naissance de l'institution parlementaire, période de construction de Westminster Hall et de Westminster Abbey, tout proches. Le style gothique était perçu comme typiquement britannique et semblait donc parfaitement approprié à un symbole de la «britannité». Cette décision marqua d'ailleurs un tournant pour le «Gothic Revival», le style néo-gothique. Le gothique n'avait en fait jamais totalement disparu en Angleterre et quelques folies en forme de ruines médiévales dans les jardins anglais ou l'architecture de Sir John Vanbrugh et de William Kent avaient préparé le terrain pour sa renaissance.
Cependant, jusqu'au début du XIXème siècle, il était plus ou moins réservé aux demeures de l'élite.
Tout changea en 1818, lorsque la Commission pour la construction des églises, décida que ce style était décidément le plus convenable pour les édifices religieux. Le Parlement fut le premier grand bâtiment civil néo-gothique, ce qui déclencha naturellement de violentes critiques dans les cercles néo-classiques. Mais il semblait bien que l'opinion était en général plutôt favorable au gothique. Après de longues années d'un style géorgien sobre et ennuyeux, on souhaitait une nouvelle approche qui parle davantage aux sens. Par ailleurs, Augustus Welby Pugin (1812–1852) défendait dans ses écrits très suivis l'idée que le gothique était la seule expression architecturale vraiment chrétienne et que les architectes étaient moralement obligés de l'utiliser. Ses exhortations avaient reçu le soutien de l'Ecclesiological Society, association religieuse fondée vers 1841 qui promouvait la résurgence des valeurs liturgiques. John Ruskin, enfin, qui avec ses «Sept lampes de l'architecture» (1849) et «Les pierres de Venise» (1851–1853) était en passe de devenir le plus grand théoricien de l'architecture du XIXème siècle appuyait ce mouvement. Soutenu par tant de brillants avocats, il n'est guère surprenant que le néo-gothique soit devenu une sorte de style national.

Problèmes et solutions

Presque tous les participants au concours avaient respecté les conditions du règlement et soumis un projet gothique. (C. R. Cockerell, 1788–1863 néo-classique déterminé, étant la seule exception notable.) En dehors du style, les candidats devaient prendre en compte plusieurs autres facteurs. Tout d'abord, Westminster Hall, qui avait survécu à l'incendie, devait être intégré à l'ensemble proposé car, pour des raisons historiques, il était impensable de l'abattre. Un problème semblable était soulevé par ce qui restait de l'église St. Stephen. Fallait-il la reconstruire, l'incorporer aux nouvelles constructions ou la détruire? La forme du terrain – trois cents mètres le long de la Tamise – posait enfin des problèmes de circulation interne d'accessibilité des différentes parties et de répartition en général.
Le jury eut à juger deux grandes catégories de projets. Des propositions de plan symétrique ou d'esprit néo-classique et d'autres articulées sur une structure complexe, asymétrique et de plan de masse irrégulier. Lewis Nockalls Cottingham (1787–1847), soumit un plan de cette seconde catégorie et, comme beaucoup, s'était inspiré du gothique du XVIème siècle (Tudor). Il manifesta son penchant pour le style «Picturesque» en animant ses dessins de petits bateaux voguant sur la Tamise et d'autres détails aussi déplacés: le jury ne se laissa pas influencer par ces tableaux de genre. Les projets de Thomas Rickman (1776–1841) et de J. Gillespie Graham (1776–1855) appartenaient également à cette seconde catégorie. Le plan de Gillespie Graham avait été réalisé avec la collaboration de Pugin, héraut du style néo-gothique Picturesque et qui allait plus tard travailler avec Barry.
Les participations de la première catégorie comprenaient les plans de J. C. Buckler (1793–1894) et de David Hamilton (1768–1843) qui reçurent respectivement le deuxième et le troisième prix. Buckler avait opté pour le style Tudor et Hamilton était l'un des rares à avoir choisi l'élizabéthain. Le plan de masse d'Hamilton allait en fait inspirer Barry après qu'il eût remporté le concours. La proposition de William Railton (1801–1877) était au carrefour des deux catégories; son plan de masse était régulier mais son élévation irrégulière. Il reçut le quatrième prix. Le projet vainqueur, celui de Barry, présentait le long de la Tamise une longue façade ininterrompue et régulière derrière laquelle étaient disposées les bibliothèques et les salles de réunion. Le dessin respectait les dénivelés entre Westminster Hall et St. Stephen d'où un plan de masse en forme de coin. Barry redressa plus tard cette forme à partir des plans d'Hamilton. La Chambre des Lords et la Chambre des Communes ouvraient sur un hall central également relié à St. Stephen (Hamilton, lui, n'avait intégré que Westminster Hall).

Barry et Pugin

Le plan définitif de Barry fut beaucoup plus équilibré que son projet initial dans lequel il avait compliqué les choses à plaisir. Sa proposition, par exemple, de recouvrir toutes les cours de verrières en forme de cône n'était qu'un expédient. Son élévation verticale était également exagérée. Dans son plan initial, la façade nord était dominée par une tour carrée qui se transforma plus tard en une sorte de clocher: Big Ben. En dehors de ces changements, d'autres détails furent modifiés, en grande partie sous l'influence de Pugin. Expert du gothique, Pugin avait été nommé conseiller auprès de Barry. Il fut chargé de la décoration intérieure et produisit plus de deux mille dessins de candélabres, boiseries, papiers peints, mobilier, porte-parapluies, encriers, etc, tout en continuant à travailler pour sa propre clientèle. Il intervint sur le Palais de Westminster de 1835 à 1837 et de nouveau de 1844 à sa mort en 1852. Bien que l'admiration réciproque des deux architectes ait été parfaitement partagée et leur collaboration harmonieuse, Pugin ne voyait pas dans cette réalisation l'exemple de référence du style gothique dont il avait rêvé. Sa remarque à un ami, alors qu'ils descendaient la Tamise en bateau, est devenue fameuse: *«Complètement grec, Monsieur. Des détails Tudor sur un corps classique».*

1 *Le style élizabéthain peut être décrit comme un style Tudor gothique tardif, légèrement marqué par l'influence de la Renaissance.*

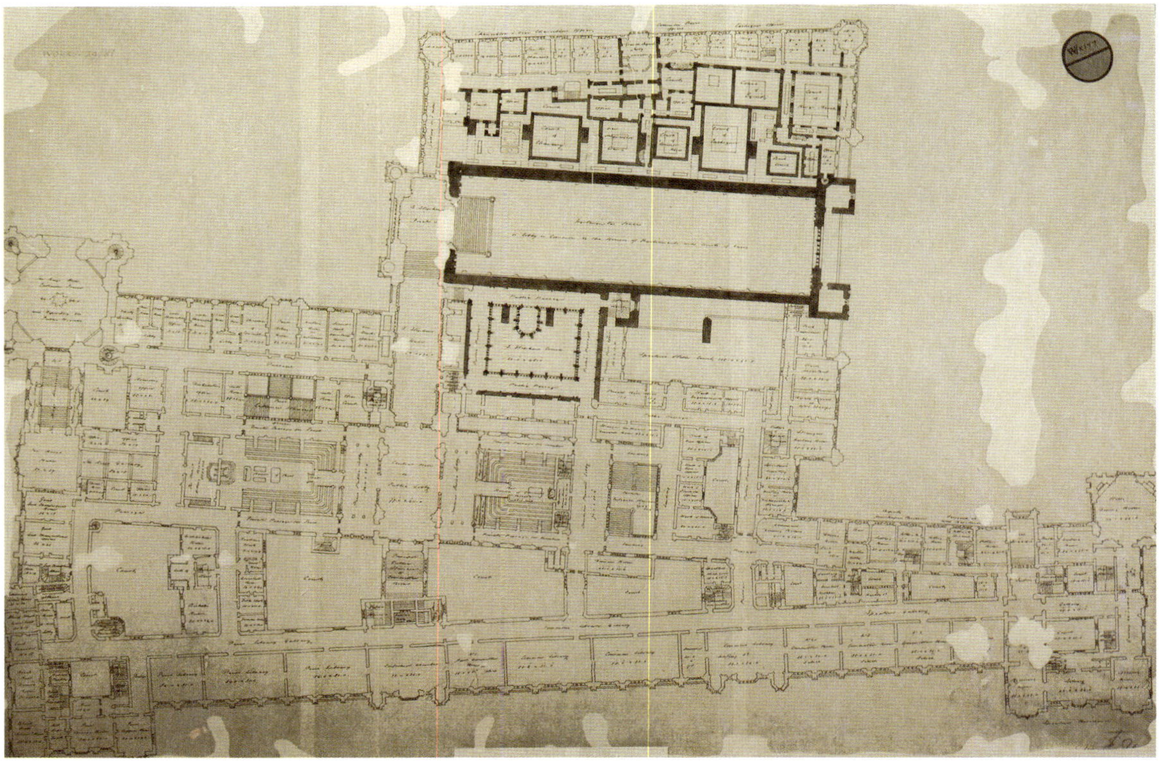

Charles Barry competition design, 1836, ground floor plan, first prize

John Chessell Buckler competition design, 1836, exterior view on the Thames, second prize

John Chessell Buckler competition design, 1836, ground floor plan, second prize, N.B.: anonymous device top right, the "R" and a buckle

Thomas Rickman competition design, 1836, exterior view on the Thames

Thomas Rickman competition design, 1836, exterior perspective

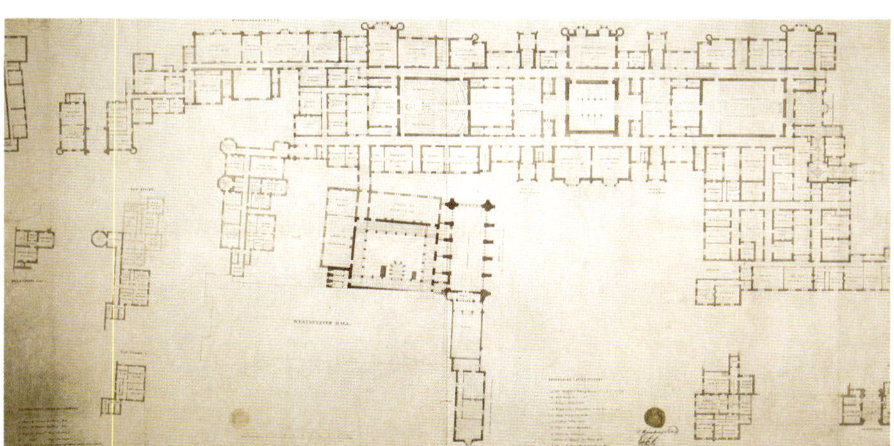

William Railton **competition design, 1836, exterior view on New Palace Yard, fourth prize**

Lewis Nockall Cottingham **competition design, 1836, exterior view**

James Gillespie Graham
competition design, 1836, exterior view on the Thames

James Gillespie Graham
competition design, 1836, interior view of the Assembly Hall in the House of Commons

James Gillespie Graham
competition design, 1836, interior view of the Assembly Hall in the House of Lords

Hofoper, Vienna, 1860

Project

Opera House

Site

Ringstraße, Vienna

Dates

Competition from 10 July 1860 to 10 January 1861

Number of entries

35

Jury

Mathias Konstatin Graf von Wickenburg (Chairman), Draexler, Raymond, Förster, Löhr, Friedrich von Schmidt, Heinrich von Ferstel, Salzmann, Schwendewein, Niernse, Schebeck, Von Matzinger

Result

First prize Eduard van der Nüll & August Sicard von Sicardsburg *Second prize* Ernst von Giese & Bernhardt Schreiber *Third prize* Karl von Hasenaur *Fourth prize* Ferdinand Kirschner *Fifth prize* Karl Guido Ehrig

Commissioned by

Emperor Franz Joseph of Austria & the Obersthofmeisteramt

Construction

December 1861 to 25 May 1869

Architects

Eduard van der Nüll (1812-1868) & August Sicard von Sicardsburg (1813–1868)

Hofoper, Vienna, 1860

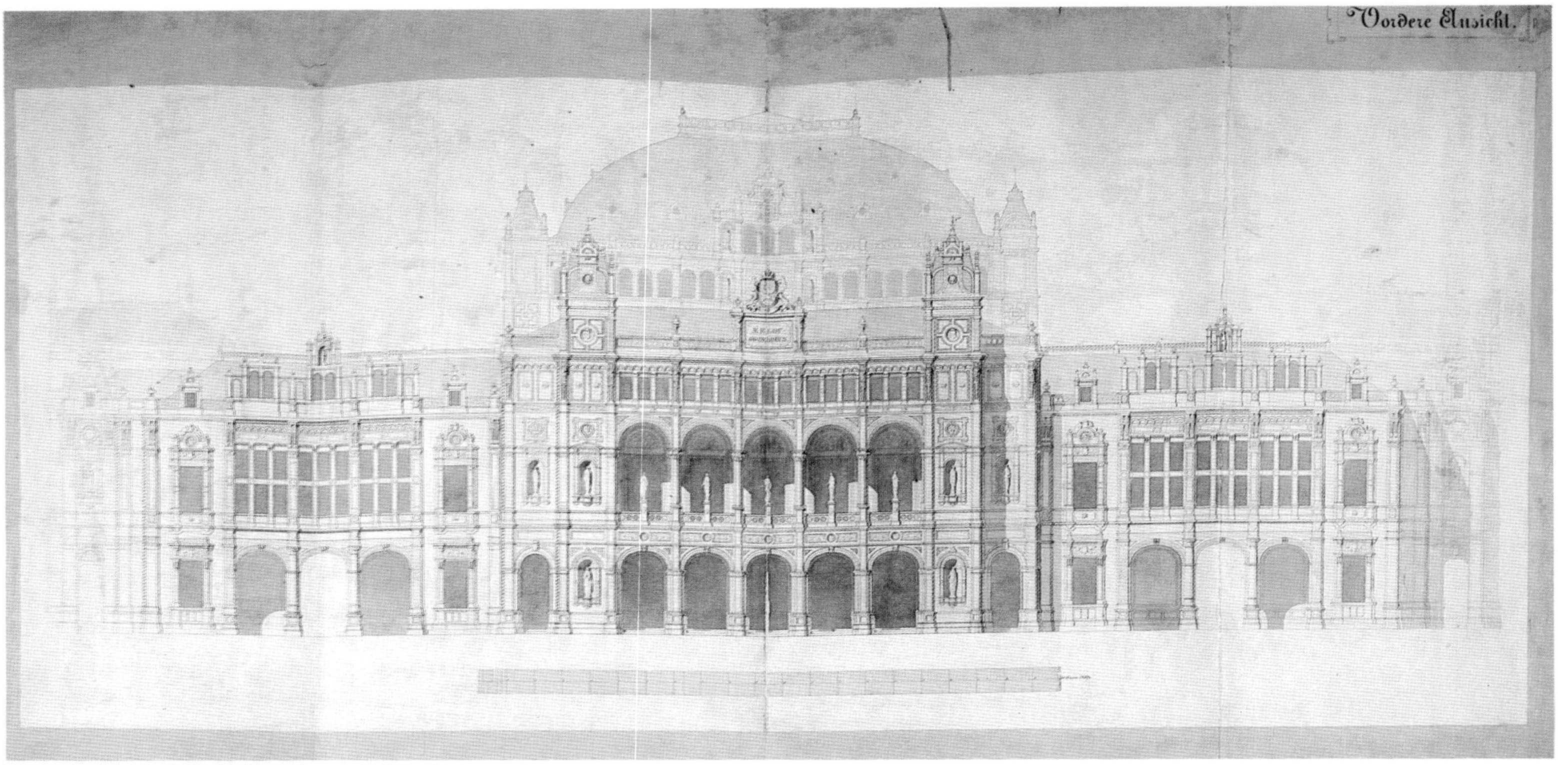

Eduard van der Nüll & August Sicard von Sicardsburg competition design, 1861, front elevation on Ringstraße, first prize

Eduard van der Nüll & August Sicard von Sicardsburg competition design, 1861, rear elevation on Philharmonikerstraße, first prize

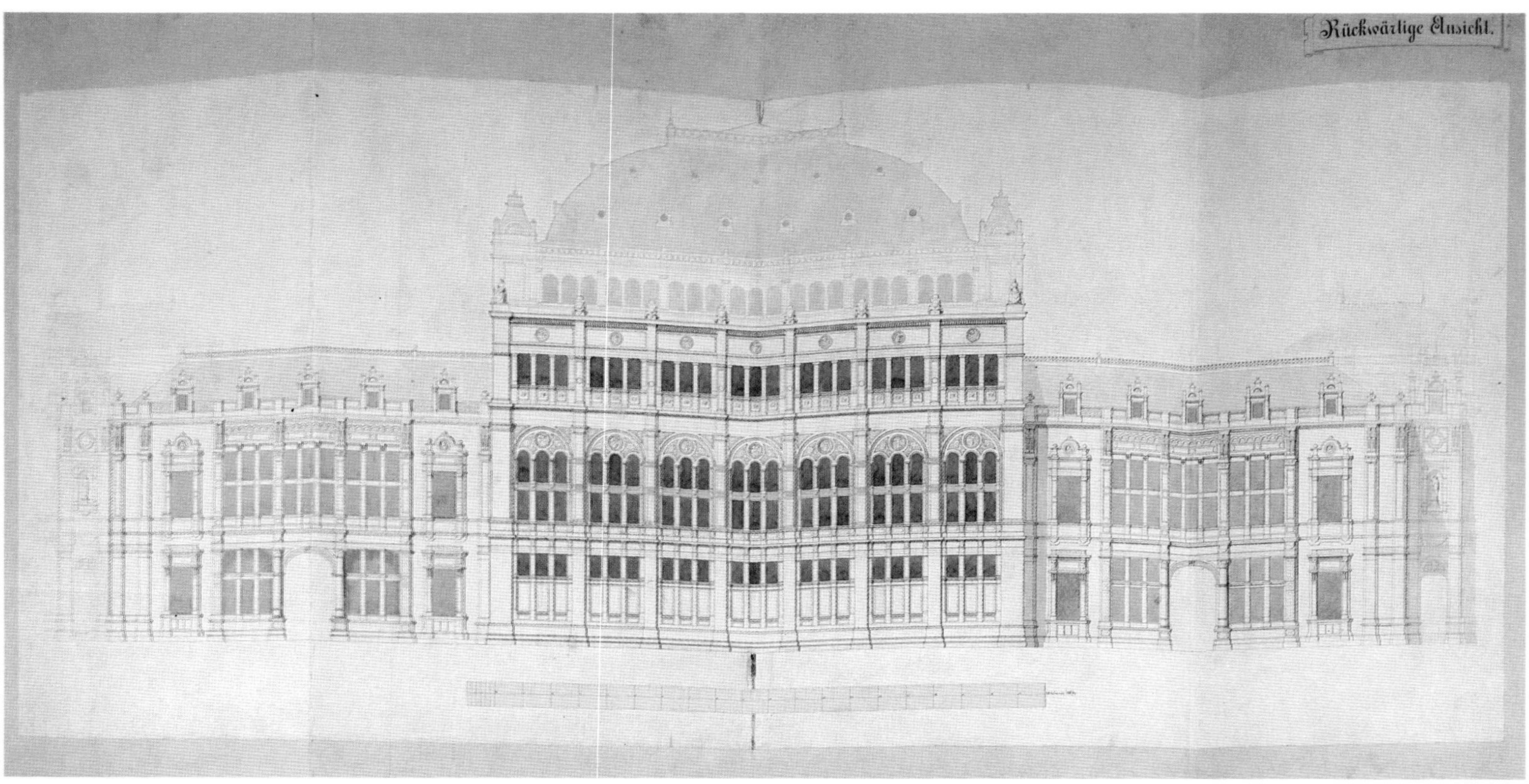

Hofoper, Vienna

The construction of the Hofoper in Vienna should be seen within the context of the events of 1848. During that year it became evident that, although public unrest throughout Europe had been quelled with a heavy hand, the age-old power of the clergy and aristocracy was fading. A new class of wealthy, liberal-minded citizens was demanding a political voice and gaining a prominent position in society. The former was achieved when liberals were elected for seats on the city council, the latter was achieved, amongst other things, by the construction of prestigious buildings on the new Ringstrasse.

The Ringstrasse and the accompanying urban development were the result of the desire of certain people including the Minister of Internal Affairs, Alexander von Bach, to turn Vienna into a true metropolis. A city which could be clearly distinguished from provincial towns. The first step in this direction was made in 1850, when 34 villages and towns in the vicinity were incorporated into Greater Vienna. Linking the new areas with the old city centre (Altstadt) was a complicated matter due to the city walls. The influential military lobby was fervently opposed to the demolition of these walls and the Emperor Franz Joseph I, crowned in 1848, required the support of the army in these times of turmoil.

In 1857, the Emperor eventually did give the order to demolish the walls, thus clearing the way for the realisation of an ambitious development plan around the old city centre. An urban development commission was formed in 1859, to supervise the project. The Ringstrasse was the most important route between the new areas and the old centre. And it was here, where the old Kärntnertor had stood, that a new opera house was planned, that would replace the old theatre which had become too small. To this end, an open competition was organised in 1860, attracting entries from 35 more or less renowned architects. The competition was interesting for more reasons than one. Firstly, at that time the theatre was no longer merely a place to see and be seen. It had become a symbol of the increasing influence of the middle classes, who would now visit the same theatres and other entertainment venues as the aristocracy and the imperial household. A second aspect, related to the first, concerned the fact that architects were given the opportunity to pull out all the stops. There was no reason to skimp and save on such a prestigious building. And, in the third place, the new opera would be the cynosure of the new Vienna, one of Europe's most beautiful cities.

Earlier plans

There had been earlier plans to build a new opera house – since the 1820's to be precise – but due to the shortage of space within the city walls, urban expansion had always been a prerequisite for their execution. Franz Xaver Lösll's project, for example, dating from 1844, in which the opera house formed part of an integrated complex, including a theatre, a concert hall and houses. Other notable designs from the 1844–1848 period include those of Paul Sprenger for the Hofbaurat and Leopold Ernst. The latter submitted a remarkably striking Gothic Revivalist design. After 1848, the military lobby tried to hold off urban expansion for as long as possible, but eventually they could no longer hold back the Altstadt, which seemed ready to burst at the seams. In 1849, Franz Joseph decided to move the city wall near the Kärntnertor and build a new city gate and an opera house. Sprenger was asked to submit a design for the second time, but once again the plans were not executed. The plans to link the Hofoper and the Hofburg (1857) met with the same fate.

Even though these earlier attempts proved fruitless, the Emperor announced the definitive building order on 19 February 1860. In order to draw up the best possible programme of stipulations for the competition, the plans for the opera houses in London, Brussels and Paris were chosen to serve as examples. On 15 March 1860, the commission to organise the competition was formed. The commission consisted of Hofrat Draexler (Obersthofmeisteramt), Hofrat Raymond (Oberstkämmeramt), Steinhauser (manager of the theatre), Hofrat Maltz von Mattenau (Ministry of Public Works), Hofraad Weber von Ebenhof, von Matzinger (for the state), Löhr (Ministry of Finance), von

Eduard van der Nüll & August Sicard von Sicardsburg **competition design, 1861, Ringstrasse (one of the six prize-winning designs)**

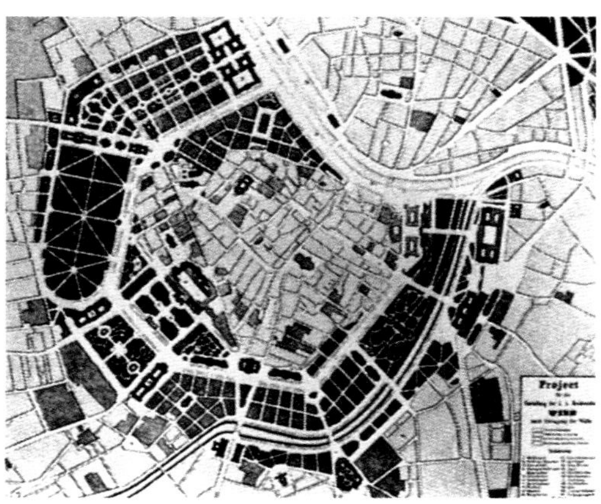

Hermannstal, Mayorys Zelinka and Krones for the City of Vienna and the architects Roesner, Förster and Mayr. The competition was announced on 10 July 1860 and the participants were given six months to submit their designs. The participants were not required to submit a detailed plan. The best designs would be purchased and possibly elaborated upon at a later date. The designs would be judged primarily on their technical qualities and their floor plans, and thereafter on their façade and other architectural features. The entries were submitted anonymously and designs which received a negative evaluation were returned to the participants, without their identity being disclosed. It is for this reason that, of the 35 entries, the names of only a few of the participants can be given with certainty. The plans were submitted under often remarkable mottos, such as *"Das Edelste der Menschen ist sein Geist"* (The noblest facet of man is his spirit), *"Es lebe der Kaiser"* (Long live the Emperor) and *'Ein jeder schafft nach seiner Kraft'* (Every man works to the best of his ability). The latter was judged impracticable.

The winning designs

Eight designs were awarded prize money and five were purchased. The winning designs were submitted by Karl Guido Ehrig, Ferdinand Kirschner, Karl von Hasenauer[1] (third prize, 1 000 florins), Ernst von Giese & Bernhardt Schreiber (second prize, 2 000 florins) and Eduard van der Nüll (1812-1868) & August Sicard von Sicardsburg (1813–1868) (first prize, 3 000 florins). In view of the fact that the submitted plans were extremely detailed, it was decided that there would be no second round and that van der Nüll and von Sicardsburg would be allowed to further develop their design. The winning architects were certainly not unknown in Vienna. They had met as talented students, one at the Academy of Fine Arts and the other at the Polytechnic Institute. In 1838, they had both participated in a competition and had jointly won a gold medal. The accompanying scholarship gave them the opportunity to embark on a European tour, during which they were to study sixteenth century French, Italian and German architecture. They sought a new approach to architecture, an alternative to the styles which were the subject of tuition at the time. Following their tour, they both accepted teaching posts at the Academy of Fine Arts and thereafter they worked together on all the projects that occasionally trickled in. Von Sicardsburg was the engineer and Van der Nüll took charge of the architectural and decorative aspects of the designs. Amongst the buildings they designed were the Schutzengelbrunnen (1843–1846), Sophienbad (1846–1847) and the Arsenal (1849–1856), which they designed with Förster, Hansen and Roesner. Their architectural style has been described as Romantic Historicism, a style which is based on the continuity of architecture, rather than upon a break with the past. The latter had been the case with the Classicism of the revolutionary architects and the Secession in later years. The Hofoper marked the culmination of Romantic Historicism. Thereafter, Historicism became more austere and uniform, disappearing completely during the twentieth century.

However, before the Hofoper could be built, van der Nüll and von Sicardsburg's design had to be perfected. In the original competition programme the architects had been asked to include a storage depot measuring between 1 100 and 1 400 square fathoms (the size of a small football pitch). This large area posed a problem for many architects. Van der Nüll and von Sicardsburg's solution was to attach the lower administrative offices and the storage depots to the opera hall, whereby four small courtyards were formed between the lateral wings and the opera. Sufficient access was provided by entrances at the front and back of the building. The only drawback to this solution was that the building risked becoming an ill-defined structural mass, making it almost impossible to see the roof of the theatre from the side. However, upon consultation with theatre experts, it became clear that only 600 square fathoms would be required in the direct vicinity of the stage and that the basement would provide another 200 square fathoms. The additional storage space was created by altering the Albrechtsbastion. Having solved this problem, the architects returned to the drawing board[2]. Their second design, although clearly based on the original, had undergone some fundamental changes. Two of the four courtyards had been scrapped. Because these two courtyards were at the front, the building's appearance, when viewed from the front and sides, had changed completely. In order to gain an insight into the design procedure, it is necessary to compare the two plans.

A comparison of designs

The Hofoper is situated on the Y-junction between the two main roads leading from the Altstadt. Its entrance faces the Ringstrasse and the new city. The structure around the main entrance consists of five bays, flanked by two slender towers. Seen as a whole, it resembles a Palladian gallery, topped by a loggia, with the superstructure and a parapet above it. The structure juts forward from the entrance hall situated behind it, which, in turn, juts from the wings. The outer ends of the wings have stone cross-windows and harmonise visually with the central entrance due to the ingenious pattern formed by the dormer windows (2 x 3), the side windows (2 x 2) on the upper floors of the wings and an inscription plaque and coat of arms (top centre). All these features are placed in a setting inspired by French Renaissance architecture. Having done away with the two front courtyards, accentuation of this sort became superfluous in the second design. The gallery and loggia were retained, but the flanking towers were shortened. The inscription plaque and coat of arms were scrapped, as were the tripartite cross-windows, which were replaced with two-part, round-arched windows. These windows now completely surrounded the Hofoper, because the cross-windows at the back had also been replaced with round-arched windows. A mezzanine was also added at the back, as an extra floor. The articulation of the central pilaster strip with its seven bays was retained. The mezzanine, topped with a parapet, had also been included at the front and sides. It bears mentioning that the upper floor and the mezzanine did not coincide with the interior floors.

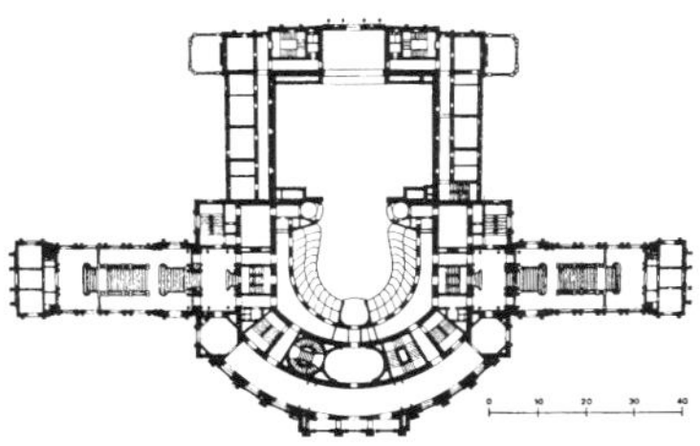

In addition, the jutting pavilions at the sides were reduced to a more modest size.

The design had gained in clarity and lucidity – certainly if viewed at an angle from the front – due to the way the cubic volumes had been placed in relation to one another and due to the programme of decorations[3]. Of course, the two front courtyards had been scrapped in the new floor plan, along with the separate entrance for the Emperor on the right-hand side of the (H-shaped) floor plan. This was replaced by a straight flight of stairs which mirrored the entrance for the Archduke on the left-hand side. The interior is striking with its wide variety of French and Italian motifs. The large stairway for the public was inspired by eighteenth century German Baroque.

Work on the Hofoper began in December 1861 and the inaugural performance was held on 25 May 1869, causing a great scandal, because it was a performance for season ticket holders and not a gala performance. Even Charles Garnier, the architect of the Paris Opera House, who had regularly been consulted by van der Nüll and von Sicardsburg, could not obtain a ticket. The old Kärntnertortheater was closed and demolished in 1870.

Karl von Hasenauer Burgtheater, front elevation

Karl von Hasenauer Burgtheater, plan of balcony with theatre boxes

Staatsoper (Hofoper), detail of front facade

1 Hasenauer was later commissioned to design the smaller Burgtheater.

2 The other prize winners were also asked to find another solution. They received an additional 1 000 florins for their efforts.

3 As a result, the stage, the theatre and the auditorium are of equal height, surrounded by the ancillary areas, which are lower.

Hofoper, Wien

Der Bau des Wiener Hofoperntheaters muß vor dem Hintergrund der Ereignisse des Jahres 1848 betrachtet werden. Damals zeichnete sich ein Ende der alten Machtverteilung zwischen Klerus und Adel ab – auch wenn die Aufstände in ganz Europa mit eiserner Faust niedergekämpft wurden. Eine neue Schicht wohlhabender, liberal denkender Bürger verlangte ein politisches Mitspracherecht und beanspruchte eine herausragende Stellung in der Gesellschaft. Die Mitsprache erreichten sie durch die Berufung liberaler Bürger in den Stadtrat, während ihre zweite Forderung u.a. durch die Errichtung prestigeträchtiger Gebäude an der neuen Ringstraße umgesetzt wurde.

Die Ringstraße und die damit verbundene Stadterweiterung entsprachen dem Wunsch des damaligen Innenministers Alexander von Bach. Er wollte aus Wien eine Metropole machen, die sich deutlich von den umliegenden Provinzstädten abhob. Erster Schritt war die Eingemeindung aller 34 Dörfer und Städte rund um Wien (1850). Allerdings bereitete die Anbindung an das alte Stadtzentrum wegen der noch vorhandenen Stadtmauern einige Probleme. Die einflußreiche Militärlobby lehnte deren Schleifung vehement ab, und der junge Kaiser Franz Joseph I., der 1848 den Thron bestiegen hatte, war auf die Hilfe des Heeres angewiesen.
1857 erteilte er schließlich doch den Befehl zur Schleifung der Stadtmauern und bereitete damit den Weg für die Verwirklichung hochstrebender Stadterweiterungspläne rund um die Altstadt. Zu diesem Zweck wurde 1859 ein Ausschuß gebildet, der den reibungslosen Ablauf des gesamten Projekts zu überwachen und zu gewährleisten hatte. Da die Ringstraße die wichtigste Verbindung zwischen der Altstadt und den neuen Vierteln darstellte, plante man hier (an der Stelle des früheren Kärntnertors) ein Operngebäude, welches das alte, zu klein gewordene Theater ersetzen sollte. 1860 erfolgte die öffentliche Ausschreibung, an der sich 35 Architekten beteiligten.

Frühere Pläne

Seit den 20er Jahren des 19. Jahrhunderts hatte es häufiger Pläne für ein neues Operngebäude gegeben, die aber aufgrund des mangelnden Raumes innerhalb der Stadtmauern stets mit der gewünschten Stadterweiterung verknüpft blieben. Franz Xaver Lössl hatte 1844 beispielsweise einen Gebäudekomplex entworfen, in dem sowohl die Oper als auch ein Theater, ein Konzertsaal sowie ein Mietshaus untergebracht waren. Aus der Zeit zwischen 1844 und 1848 stammt der Entwurf von Paul Sprenger für den Hofbaurat bzw. der Entwurf von Leopold Ernst, dessen Konzept seltsam neugotisch anmutet.
Auch nach 1848 versuchten die Militärs die Stadterweiterung so lange wie möglich hinauszuzögern, konnten sich aber angesichts der aus allen Nähten platzenden Altstadt nicht länger widersetzen. 1849 beschloß Franz Joseph I. die Verlegung der Stadtmauer in der Nähe des Kärntnertors sowie den Bau eines neuen Stadttors und des Hofoperntheaters. Paul Sprenger beschäftigte sich nun zum zweiten Mal mit der Gestaltung der Baupläne aber auch dieses Mal wurden seine Entwürfe nicht verwirklicht. Das gleiche Schicksal ereilte auch die geplante Verbindung des Hofoperntheaters mit der Hofburg (1857).
Ungeachtet dieser früheren, vergeblichen Bemühungen erteilte der Kaiser am 19. Februar 1860 den offiziellen Bauauftrag. Bei den Vorbereitungen bediente man sich der Konstruktionspläne der Opernhäuser von London, Brüssel und Paris, um auf diese Weise einen fundierten Auflagenkatalog zu erarbeiten; Am 15. März 1860 wurde ein Ausschuß gebildet, der die Ausschreibung vorbereiten sollte. Alle Einsendungen wurden anonym beurteilt und bei negativem Bescheid an den Einsender zurückgeschickt, ohne dessen Identität preiszugeben.

Der siegreiche Entwurf

Die Jury prämierte acht Vorschläge mit einem Geldbetrag und kaufte die fünf Entwürfe der folgenden Architekten: Karl Guido Ehrig, Ferdinand Kirschner, Karl von Hasenauer[1] (dritter Preis, 1 000 Gulden), Ernst von Giese und Bernhardt Schreiber (zweiter Preis, 2 000 Gulden) sowie Eduard van der Nüll und August Sicard von Sicardsburg erster Preis, 3 000 Gulden). Da es sich bei diesen Konzepten bereits um sehr detaillierte Baupläne handelte, verzichtete der Ausschuß auf eine zweite Ausschreibungsrunde und beauftragte van der Nüll und Sicardsburg mit der Weiterentwicklung ihres Entwurfs. Ihr Baustil wurde als romantischer Historismus bezeichnet – ein Stil, der im Gegensatz zum Klassizismus der Revolutions-Architekten oder zum späteren Sezessionsstil keinen Bruch mit der Vergangenheit, sondern eine Kontinuität in der Architektur anstrebte und der seinen Höhe- und Schlußpunkt im Hofoperntheater fand. Danach wurde der Historismus strenger und gleichförmiger, um im 20. Jahrhundert schließlich völlig zu verschwinden.
Vor Baubeginn des Hofoperntheaters mußten van der Nülls und Sicardsburg Pläne noch vervollständigt werden. Der ursprüngliche Bebauungsplan sah ein Magazin von 1100–1400 Quadratklaftern vor (das entspricht etwa einem kleinen Fußballfeld), eine Auflage, die vielen Architekten große Probleme bereitete. Van der Nüll und Sicardsburg fanden jedoch eine Lösung: Sie plazierten die Verwaltungsbüros der unteren Angestellten und die Lagerräume neben dem eigentlichen Opernsaal, so daß zwischen den auf diese Weise gebildeten Seitenflügeln und der Oper vier kleine Innenhöfe entstanden. Zahlreiche Eingänge auf der Vorder- und Rückseite des Gebäudes gewährleisteten den freien Zugang zu allen Räumen. Allerdings besaß diese Aufteilung einen Nachteil: Das Hofoperntheater drohte zu einem unförmigen, ausufernden Gebäudekomplex zu verkommen, bei dem das Dach des eigentlichen Theaters von der Seite kaum noch sichtbar gewesen wäre. Im Laufe verschiedener Gespräche erklärten zahlreiche Theaterfachleute jedoch, in unmittelbarer Nähe zur Bühne würden nur etwa 600 Quadratklafter benötigt, von denen sich wiederum 200 Quadratklafter im Souterrain befinden durften. Die restlichen Lagerräume wurden in der eigens dazu umgebauten Albrechtsbastion untergebracht.
Nachdem auch dieses Problem gelöst war, befaßten sich die Architekten erneut mit ihren Bauplänen[2] und entwickelten einen zweiten Entwurf, der zwar auf den ersten Konstruktionsplänen basierte, aber gravierende Neuerungen aufwies. So fielen die beiden vorderen Innenhöfe weg, wodurch sich die Gebäudefassade an der Front und an den Seiten völlig veränderte. Um den Entstehungsprozeß der Baupläne für die Oper besser zu verdeutlichen, werden wir beide Entwürfe miteinander vergleichen.

Der Vergleich der Entwürfe

Der Eingang der an einer Gabelung zweier Hauptstraßen gelegenen Oper weist zur Ringstraße, also zu den neuen Stadtteilen. Ihr zentraler Eingangsbereich besteht aus fünf Travéen, die von zwei schlanken Türmen flankiert werden. Das Ganze bildet eine palladianisch anmutende Galerie mit einer darüberliegenden Loggia, über der sich wiederum ein Überbau und die Balustrade befinden. Diese überragen die dahinter gelegene Eingangshalle nach vorne, welche ihrerseits vor den Seitenflügeln vorspringt.
Die äußeren Enden der Flügel weisen steinerne Kreuzfensterrahmen auf, die durch einen raffinierten Rhythmus mit dem zentralen Eingangsbereich verbunden sind. Diese optische Harmonie wird von den Dachfenstern (2 x 3), den Seitenfenstern (2 x 2) in den Stockwerken der Flügel und der in der Mitte plazierten Schrifttafel mit dem Reichswappen erzeugt. Alle Elemente sind mit einem Rahmen versehen, der auf Vorbildern der französischen Renaissance beruht. Im zweiten Entwurf entfiel aufgrund der Streichung der beiden vorderen Innenhöfe die Notwendigkeit für derartige Akzente: Galerie und Loggia blieben erhalten, dafür wurden die Seitentürme gekürzt. Die Schrifttafel und das Reichswappen verschwanden ebenso wie die dreigliedrigen Kreuzfensterrahmen, die durch zweigliedrige Rundbogenfenster ersetzt wurden. Diese Fenster befinden sich nun entlang des gesamten Hofoperntheaters, da auch die Kreuzfensterrahmen auf der Rückseite des Gebäudes durch Rundbogenfenster ersetzt sind. Außerdem erhielt dieser Gebäudebereich zusätzlich ein Mezzaningeschoß. Die Gliederung der zentralen Auskragung in sieben Travéen wurde beibehalten, während sich auch an der Vorderseite und den Seiten ein Mezzaningeschoß mit darüberliegender Balustrade befindet. Übrigens stimmen die äußeren Stockwerke und Zwischengeschosse nicht mit der Aufteilung der Etagen im Gebäude überein. Ferner fielen die vorstehenden Pavillons an den Seiten im zweiten Entwurf etwas bescheidener aus.
Der zweite Entwurf ist – aufgrund der räumlichen Anordnung der Bauteile sowie der dekorativen Gestaltung – insgesamt klarer und übersichtlicher, insbesondere, wenn man das Gebäude schräg von vorne betrachtet. Natürlich entfielen in den neuen Bauplänen auch die beiden vorderen Innenhöfe sowie der separate Eingang für den Kaiser auf der rechten Seite des (H-förmigen) Grundrisses. Dieser wurde durch eine einläufige, gerade Treppe ersetzt, die dem auf der linken Seite gelegenen Eingang für den Erzherzog gleicht. Die Innenräume erhielten eine prachtvolle Ausstattung mit französischen und italienischen Motiven, und das Treppenhaus für die Besucher spielt auf den deutschen Barock des 18. Jahrhunderts an.
Die Grundsteinlegung der neuen Oper erfolgte im Dezember 1861. Die Eröffnungsvorstellung fand am 15. Mai 1869 statt und verursachte einen Skandal, da es sich nicht um eine Gala-Aufführung, sondern um eine ganz normale Vorstellung für Abonnementbesitzer handelte. Selbst Charles Garnier, dem Architekten der Pariser Oper, den van der Nüll und Sicardsburg mehrfach konsultiert hatten, gelang es nicht, sich eine Eintrittskarte für diese Vorstellung zu beschaffen. Das alte Kärntnertortheater wurde geschlossen und abgerissen.

1 *Hasenauer erhielt später den Auftrag für das kleinere Burgtheater.*
2 *Auch den anderen Preisgewinnern stellte man frei, weitere Entwürfe einzureichen, die mit zusätzlichen 1 000 Gulden honoriert wurden.*

L'Opéra de la Cour, Vienne

La construction de l'Opéra de la Cour, le Hofoper, doit s'étudier dans le contexte des événements de 1848. Même si les troubles qui se déroulèrent dans toute l'Europe cette année-là avaient été matés, il était devenu évident que le pouvoir exclusif de l'aristocratie et du clergé touchait à sa fin. Une nouvelle classe de citoyens aisés et d'esprit libéral, demandait à pouvoir s'exprimer politiquement et à prendre peu à peu une place prépondérante dans la société. Son premier objectif fut atteint, à Vienne, par l'élection de libéraux au conseil municipal, le second, entre autres, par la construction de prestigieux édifices le long du nouveau boulevard périphérique, la Ringstrasse, ou «Ring».

Le Ring et l'expansion urbaine qu'il autorisait enfin étaient nés du désir de quelques hauts personnages, dont le ministre des Affaires Intérieures, Alexander von Bach, de faire de la capitale une métropole moderne, radicalement différente des villes de province autrichiennes. La première étape fut franchie en 1850 avec l'annexion par Vienne de 34 villes et villages de ses environs immédiats. Mais la liaison entre ces satellites et le centre ancien (Altstadt) était compliquée par l'existence d'anciens remparts. Très influente, la caste militaire était opposée à leur démolition et l'empereur François-Joseph Ier, couronné en 1848, avait trop besoin de son appui, en ces temps troublés, pour lui déplaire.
Il ordonna néanmoins de démolir ces murailles en 1857, permettant enfin un développement urbain ambitieux autour de la vieille ville. Une commission d'urbanisme fut constituée en 1859 pour superviser le projet. C'est en bordure du Ring, la voie la plus importante qui délimitait les nouveaux quartiers par rapport au centre, et à l'emplacement d'une ancienne porte, la Kärntnertor, qu'un nouvel opéra fut envisagé pour remplacer l'ancien devenu trop petit. Un concours organisé en 1860 attira 35 architectes plus ou moins renommés. Il était intéressant à plus d'un titre. Tout d'abord, un bâtiment de ce type n'était plus seulement un lieu où voir et être vu. C'était le nouveau symbole de l'influence grandissante des classes moyennes qui pouvaient enfin se rendre dans les mêmes lieux et assister aux mêmes distractions que l'aristocratie et la cour impériale. Le second aspect, lié au premier, était l'opportunité extraordinaire offerte aux architectes de se libérer de multiples contraintes, en particulier financières, à l'occasion de la construction d'un édifice de prestige.
En troisième lieu, le nouvel opéra devait être le centre d'attraction de la nouvelle Vienne, l'une des plus belles villes d'Europe.

Les premiers plans

Plusieurs plans pour un nouvel opéra avaient déjà été proposés depuis les années 1820. Mais le manque de place dans la Vienne intra-muros avait repoussé leur exécution à l'expansion attendue de la cité. Le projet de 1844 de Franz Xaver Lösll, par exemple, incluait l'opéra dans un vaste complexe comprenant un théâtre, une salle de concert et des immeubles d'habitation. D'autres propositions furent présentées au Conseil des Bâtiments de la Cour par Paul Sprenger et Leopold Ernst au cours de la période 1844–1848. La dernière affichait un esprit néo-gothique exubérant. Après 1848, alors que les milieux militaires freinaient toujours l'extension de la ville, le centre ancien semblait prêt à éclater. François-Joseph décida en 1849 de déplacer les remparts près de la Kärntnertor et d'édifier une nouvelle porte et un opéra. Sprenger se vit demander un nouveau projet dont les plans, une fois encore, ne furent pas exécutés. Des propositions pour relier un opéra au palais de la Hofburg (1857) subirent le même destin.

Bien que ces premières tentatives se soient révélées vaines, l'Empereur lança définitivement l'idée d'un nouvel opéra le 19 février 1860. Le 15 mars 1860, la commission du concours fut constituée. Le concours fut ouvert le 10 juillet 1860 et les participants se virent accorder six mois. Il ne leur était pas demandé de plan détaillé: les meilleurs projets seraient achetés et éventuellement précisés par la suite.

Les projets gagnants

Huit projets reçurent des prix en numéraire et cinq furent achetés: ceux de Karl Guido Ehrig, Ferdinand Kirschner et Karl von Hasenauer[1] (troisième prix: 1 000 florins), Ernst von Giese et Bernhardt Schreiber (deuxième prix: 2 000 florins), Eduard van der Nüll et August Siccard von Siccardsburg (premier prix: 3 000 florins). Les propositions remises étant très détaillées, le jury décida qu'il n'y aurait pas de second tour et que van der Nüll et von Siccardsburg pouvaient mettre leurs plans au point. Les deux lauréats n'étaient pas des inconnus. Ils s'étaient rencontrés au cours de leurs brillantes études, l'un à l'Académie des Beaux-Arts, l'autre à l'Institut Polytechnique. En 1838, ils avaient déjà participé ensemble à un concours et remporté une médaille d'or. La bourse qui l'accompagnait leur avait permis de faire un tour d'Europe qui leur donna l'occasion d'étudier l'architecture du XVIème siècle en France, en Italie et en Allemagne. Ils recherchaient une nouvelle approche de l'architecture, une alternative aux styles alors enseignés. Après leur voyage, ils acceptèrent tous deux des postes d'enseignant à l'Académie des Beaux-Arts et continuèrent à travailler de concert sur de nombreux projets. von Sicardsburg était l'ingénieur et Van der Nüll se chargeait des aspects architecturaux et décoratifs. Ils construisirent ainsi ensemble une fontaine, la Schutzengelbrunnen (1843–1846), un établissement thermal, Sophienbad (1846–1847) et l'Arsenal (1849–1856) conçu avec Förster, Hansen et Roesner. Leur style a été qualifié de Romantique historique parce qu'il s'appuyait sur le respect d'une certaine continuité de l'histoire de l'architecture plutôt que sur une rupture avec le passé, cas du néo-classicisme des architectes révolutionnaires et de la future Wiener Sezession. L'Opéra de Vienne marque le pinacle et la fin de ce Romantisme historicisant, qui devait disparaître avec le XXème siècle.
Les plans nécessitaient de multiples améliorations. Dans le cahier des charges, les architectes avaient été priés de prévoir un magasin de 3000 à 4000 m². Cette vaste surface posa un réel problème aux architectes. La solution de van der Nüll et von Siccardsburg fut de lier les bureaux administratifs et le magasin au grand hall, formant ainsi quatre petites cours entre les ailes latérales et la salle d'opéra. L'accès se faisait par des entrées prévues à l'avant et à l'arrière de l'édifice. Son inconvénient était de transformer le bâtiment en une masse informe, le toit en particulier devenant invisible de l'extérieur. Après avoir consulté des experts en théâtre, on décida que 1800 m² près de la scène suffiraient et que les sous-sols fourniraient 600 m² supplémentaires et l'on modifia l'Albrechtsbastion pour gagner les surfaces nécessaires. Ayant résolu ce problème, les architectes retournèrent à leur planche à dessin[2]. Leur second plan, bien que clairement dérivé du premier, s'en différenciait cependant fondamentalement. Les deux cours de la partie avant étaient supprimées, ce qui changeait les perspectives frontales et latérales du bâtiment. La comparaison des deux plans est instructive.

Une comparaison de plans

L'Opéra est situé au carrefour en Y de deux axes principaux qui viennent du centre ville. Son entrée fait face au Ring et à la nouvelle ville. La façade principale compte cinq baies, flanquées de deux tourelles. Elle évoque une galerie palladienne, surmontée d'une loggia se terminant par un parapet. Cette structure est en avant-corps par rapport au hall d'entrée, à son tour en ressaut par rapport aux ailes. Les extrémités de celles-ci possèdent des fenêtres à meneaux de pierre et sont en harmonie avec l'entrée principale grâce au jeu ingénieux des fenêtres de lucarne-attique (deux fois trois), des fenêtres latérales (deux fois deux) des étages supérieurs des ailes, d'une table pour inscription et d'un trophée (au centre). Le style du bâtiment est, en général, inspiré de la Renaissance française. Les deux cours ayant disparu, les ressauts devenaient moins justifiés et si la galerie et les loggias furent conservées, les tours furent raccourcies. La table et le trophée furent supprimés de même que les croisées à deux meneaux, remplacées par des baies cintrées en deux parties. Ce modèle de fenêtres entourait maintenant la totalité du bâtiment, y compris à l'arrière. Un demi-étage fut également ajouté à l'arrière, formant un niveau supplémentaire.
L'articulation du ressaut central, en sept ouvertures fut maintenue et un autre demi-étage, surmonté d'un parapet, apparut aussi en façade et sur les côtés. Comme les niveaux supérieurs intérieurs ne se trouvaient pas sur le même plan que ces nouveaux étages, les pavillons latéraux en avant-corps furent réduits en proportion.
Le plan avait gagné en clarté et en lisibilité, en particulier vu des trois quarts, grâce à la nouvelle relation créée entre les volumes et à un intéressant programme ornemental[3]. Les deux cours en façade avaient été supprimées ainsi que l'entrée séparée de droite, prévue à l'origine pour l'Empereur. Elle fut remplacée par une volée d'escalier droit rappelant l'entrée de l'Archiduc sur la façade latérale de gauche.
De réalisation superbe, l'intérieur était traité avec un grand luxe de détails d'inspiration française ou italienne. Le grand escalier du public devait beaucoup au style baroque allemand du XVIIIème siècle.
Les travaux commencèrent en décembre 1861 et la première représentation du 15 mai 1869 donna lieu à un énorme scandale: elle était réservée aux seuls abonnés! Même Charles Garnier, architecte de l'Opéra de Paris et à ce titre fréquemment consulté, ne put obtenir un billet. L'ancien Kärntnertortheater fut fermé et démoli en 1870.

1 *Hasenauer reçut plus tard la commande du Burgtheater.*
2 *Les autres lauréats furent également interrogés et reçurent chacun 1 000 florins supplémentaires.*
3 *La scène, la salle et l'auditorium sont de hauteur égale, entourés par les bâtiments de service, moins élevés.*

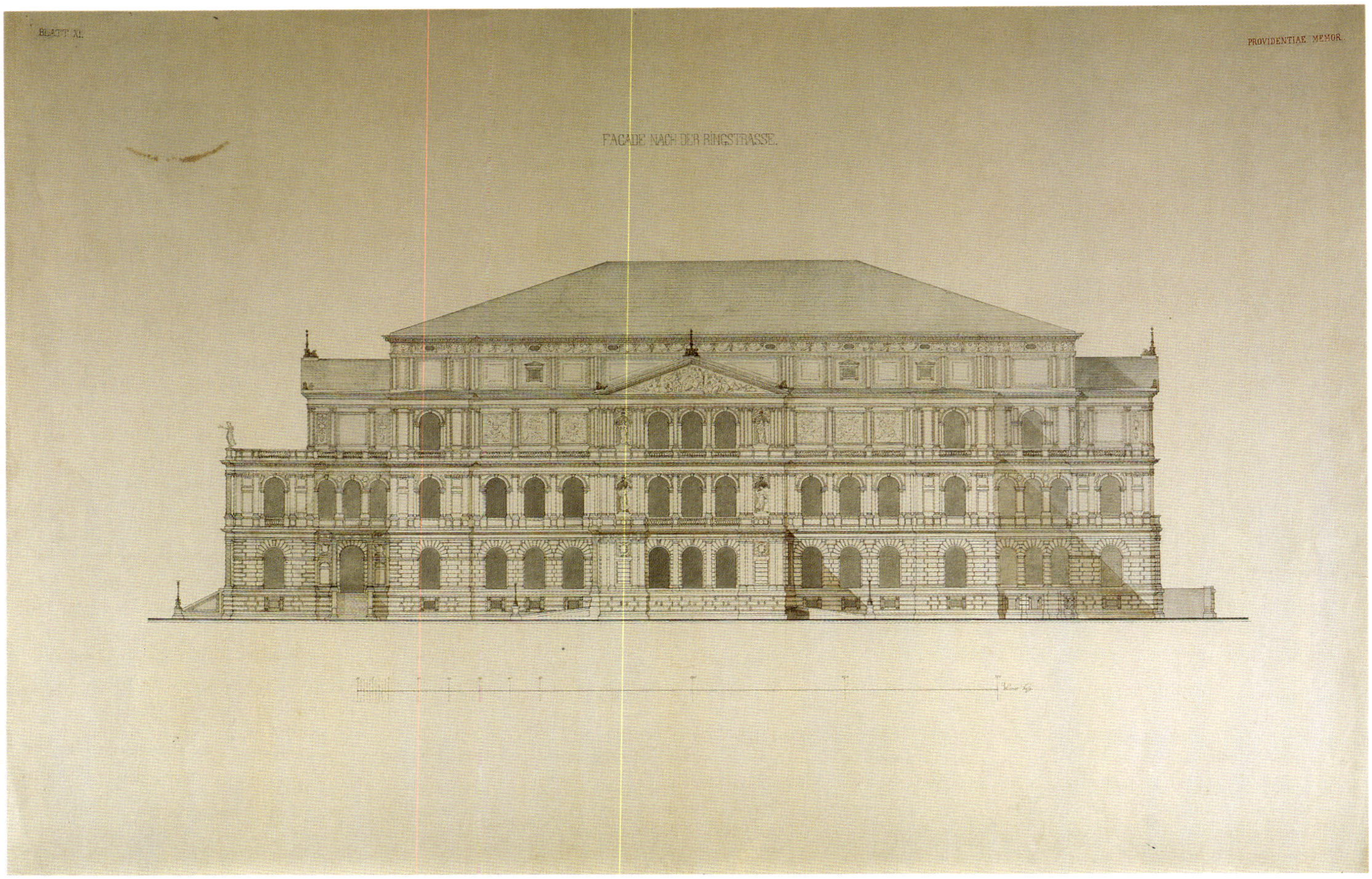
BLATT XI.
PROVIDENTIAE MEMOR.
FACADE NACH DER RINGSTRASSE.

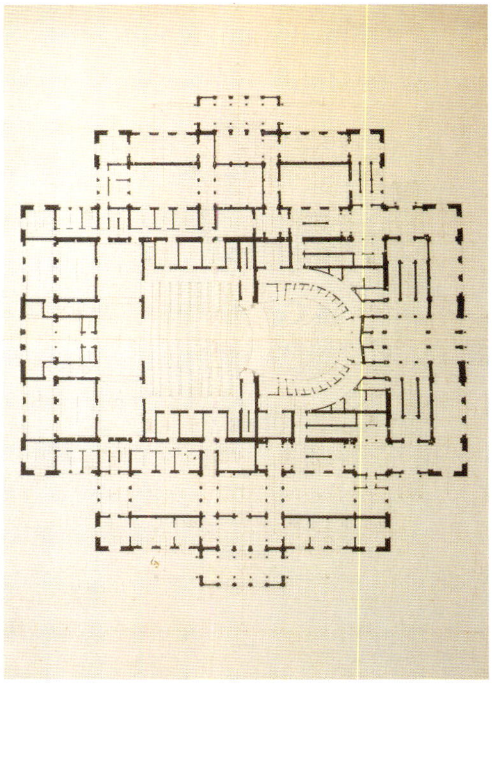

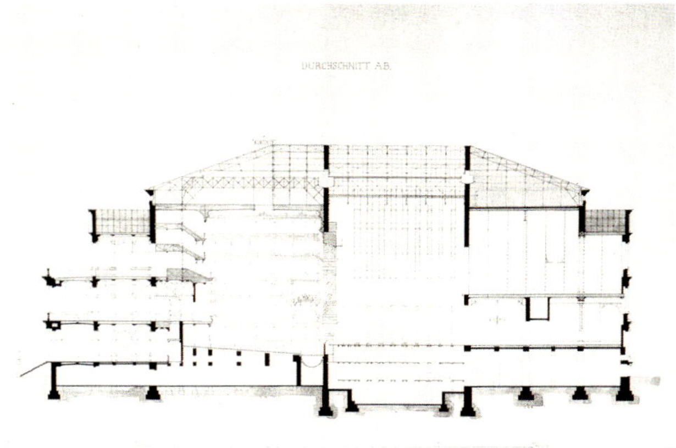
DURCHSCHNITT AB.

Ernst von Giese & Bernhardt Schreiber competition design 1861, front elevation on Ringstrasse, second prize

Ernst von Giese & Bernhardt Schreiber competition design 1861, stalls, second prize

Ernst von Giese & Bernhardt Schreiber competition design 1861, longitudinal section, second prize

Karl von Hasenauer competition design, 1861, basement floor plan, third prize

Karl von Hasenauer competition design, 1861, front elevation on Ringstrasse, third prize

Karl von Hasenauer competition design, 1861, transverse section, third prize

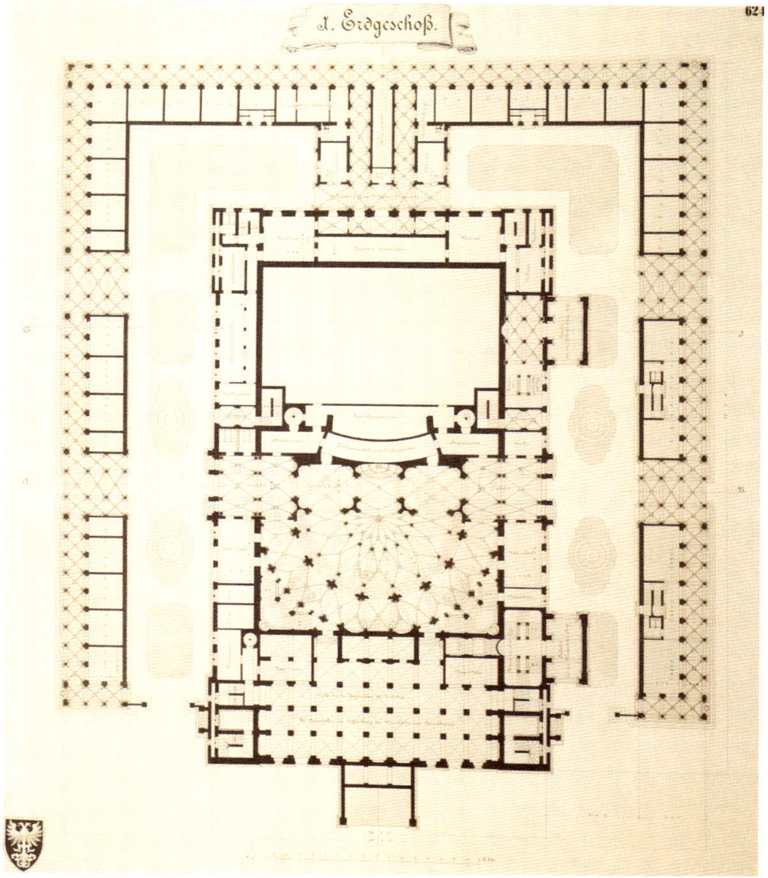

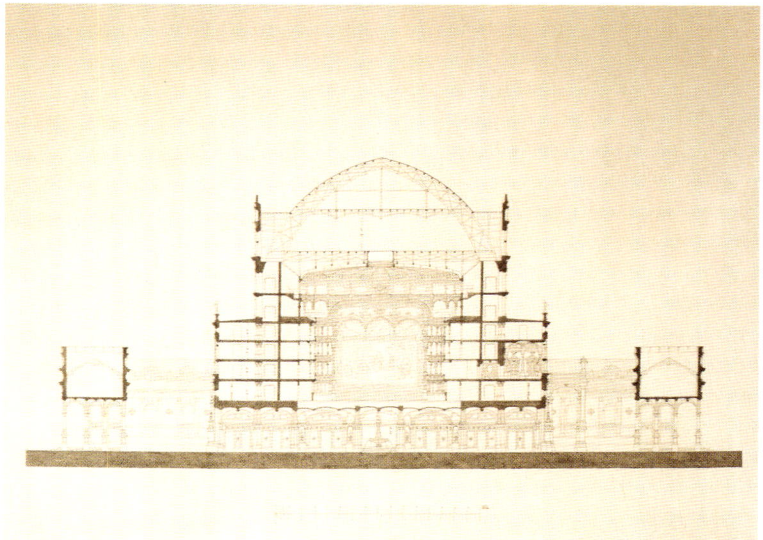

Ferdinand Kirschner competition design, 1861, façade on Ringstrasse

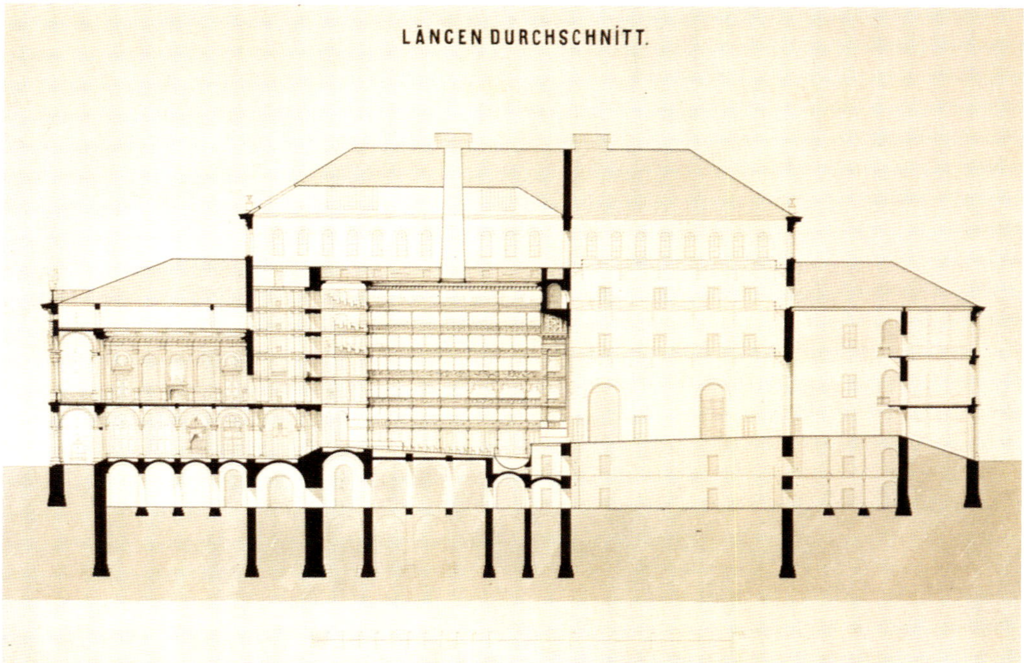

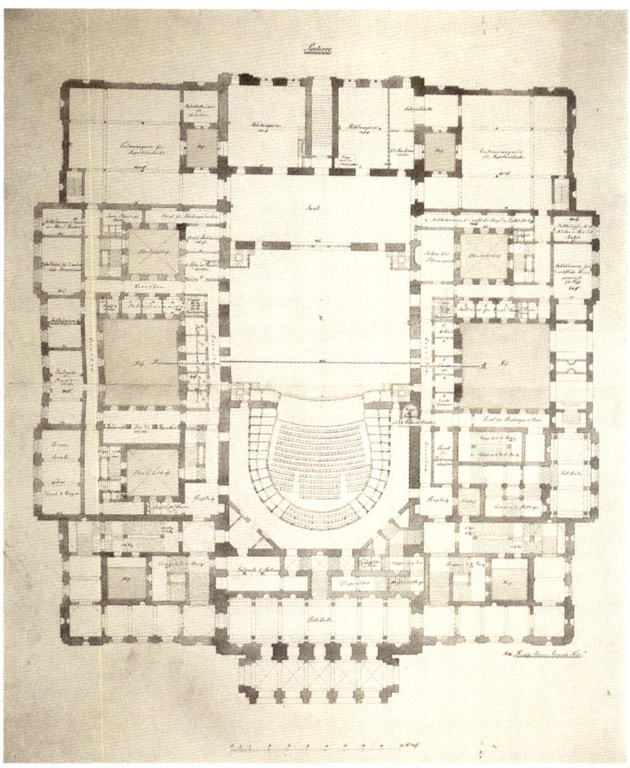

Ferdinand Kirschner competition design, 1861, longitudinal section

Karl Guido Ehrig competition design, 1861, plan of balcony theatre boxes

LE GRAND HOTEL
CAFE DE LA PAIX
LANCEL

Project

Opera

Site

Avenue de l'Opéra, Paris

Dates

First round 29 December 1860 to 31 January 1861 *Second round* March 1861 to May 1861 *Architect appointed* 6 June 1861

Number of entries

171

Jury

A. de Walewski (Chairman), Académie des Beaux Arts: A.N. Caristie, F. Duban, A.H. de Gisors, E. Gilbert (Vice-chairman), H. Lebas, J.I. Hittorf, J.B. Ciceron-Lesueur, H. Lefuel. Conseil des Bâtiments Civils: De Cardeillac (Head of Services), C.A. Questel, L. Lenormand, S.C. Constant-Dufeux

Result

First round P.R.L. Ginain (first prize, 6000 Francs), Botrel & A.C. Crépinet (second prize, 4000 Francs), A.M.G. Garnaud (third prize, 2000 Francs), Louis Duc (fourth prize, 1500 Francs), C. Garnier (fifth prize, 1000 Francs). *Other first round designs* Louet, Uchard, Viollet-le-Duc, Diet, Magne, Barry, Moreau, Rohault de Fleury, Simonet, Tétaz and Hénard. *Second round* Charles Garnier (unanimously chosen)

Commissioned by

Napoleon III and Minister without portfolio De Walewski

Construction

27 August 1861 to 5 January 1875 (Financial problems were the main cause of delays in construction)

Architect

Charles Garnier (1825–1898)

L'Opéra, Paris, 1860–1861

Charles Garnier final design, without date, front elevation on Place de l'Opéra

L'Opéra, Paris

Opinion is divided as to the architectural significance of Garnier's Opera. While one critic (Steinhauser) sees the Opera as marking the end of an era, others (Middleton & Watkin) see it as a turning point. Recently, a more balanced view has been taken by Mead, who sees the Opera as an original reinterpretation of styles from bygone eras. Unfortunately, a detailed architectural-historical account is beyond the scope of this chapter, which will be limited to a review of facts from the past, allowing visitors to the Paris Opera to develop their own opinion concerning this undeniably impressive piece of architecture.

Plans to build a new opera had been in existence since the old opera had burnt down in 1781. In the years that followed, operas were staged at provisional venues, such as François Debret's Theatre le Peletier (1821). However, a change of circumstances was required before a more permanent solution could be found. The long-awaited opportunity presented itself during the reign of Napoleon III. Under the motto that a ruler is great only if he leaves something to posterity, this self-appointed emperor wanted to emphasise his entitlement by building a new opera. He confided his desire to another decisive individual, Baron Georges-Eugène Haussmann (1807–1891). In times of turmoil Haussmann had proved a loyal supporter of Napoleon III and, as a token of his gratitude, the emperor had appointed him "Préfet de la Seine" (1853) when he came to power. Napoleon III had asked Haussmann to turn Paris into a city of imperial grandeur. Furthermore, Napoleon decreed that Paris should have the capacity to accommodate its growing population and that the chance of civil insurrection in defiance of the authorities should be eliminated. Broad, conveniently arranged boulevards, allowing the mounted police room to manœuvre, were seen as a possible solution to the latter problem.

Haussmann's plan

Although a commission had been officially appointed to find a suitable site, Haussmann had already decided in 1858 that the opera would be built in the north-western part of the city. The building order was passed in 1860. Initially, the Minister of Home Affairs, Fould, was in charge of the building, but he was later succeeded by De Walewski, who was head of the Department of Public Works (Conseil des Bâtiments Civils) but indirectly dependent on the emperor. As prefect, Haussmann was in charge of the siting and all aspects of urban development in the area. Originally, Haussmann had had a rectangular square in mind, where the façade of the opera would bound the view from the Avenue Napoleon III (which ended in a T-junction at the Boulevard des Capucines). The radial thoroughfares to the Place Vendôme and the Place de la Bourse (1860) were situated on either side of the opera. Haussmann later altered this design, basing his changes on an existing design for a new opera. This design by Rohault de Fleury, made between 1850 and 1860, would not play a significant part in the competition, which had yet to be organised. However, as so often in the past, this tentative design would later influence the ultimate

Charles Garnier

A title page in "Le Nouvel Opéra de Paris", 1880

Jules-Charles Simonet Le Nouvel Opéra, first round competition design, 1861, exterior view

Eugène Emmanuel Viollet-le-Duc Le Nouvel Opéra, first round competition design, 1861, exterior view

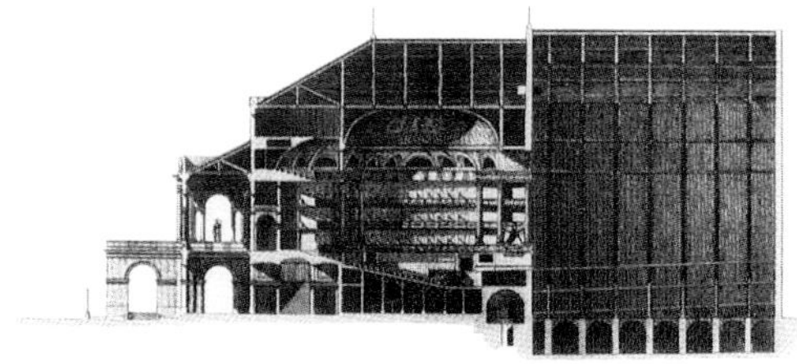

plan. In his final design, which dates from 1860, De Fleury had added two segmented, lateral wings to the rectangular superstructure. In order to let the design coincide with the street pattern, a diamond-shaped floor plan developed. In 1861, this diamond-shaped area formed the basis of the definitive urban development plan around the opera. Haussmann's first design evolved into two symmetrically positioned St. Andrew's crosses, which formed the setting of a priceless jewel: the Opera. The front of the building was chamfered, forming a square as broad as the façade. As a result, the Opera, when viewed from the Avenue Napoleon III (now Avenue de l'Opéra), became a perfect cynosure. It goes without saying that, due to the fire hazard, the Opera was a free-standing building. It was modelled along the lines of Peyre and Wailly's Theatre de l'Odéon.

However, before this stage was reached, a competition had to be arranged. (De Fleury's efforts to obtain a definite commission had been in vain. It has been suggested that the Empress Eugénie had touted her protégé Viollet-le-Duc, to the detriment of De Fleury.) The competition was announced on 29 December 1860. The 171 participants, few of whom had any experience in theatre architecture, had only a month to submit their designs. However, the prestige of the project made participation worthwhile.

During the course of the nineteenth century, the theatre had evolved, particularly under the influence of G. Gottfried Semper. It was no longer a closed and serious building, but had become a more cheerful and open meeting place, where performances not only took place on stage but also in the corridors, where the new middle-class elite, dressed up to the nines, would find themselves in close proximity to the court. As in Vienna, the self-confidence of the middle-classes (and that of the architects) had risen to unprecedented heights. Just as the opera house had been a reflection of power and status for the emperor, so it was for his subjects. This new aspect of theatre found expression in extravagantly capacious stairways and vestibules.

Biased jury

The rather one-sided jury drafted an extremely summary competition programme. All of the jury members had been students of the Académie des Beaux Arts or were still attached to the academy, which automatically implied that the participants should submit designs which were in keeping with the architectural views of this institution. Which implied that any Gothic Revivalist design would probably suffer a resounding defeat at the hands of Neo-Baroque and Neo-Classicist designs. Even Viollet-le-Duc did not dare to submit a Gothic design. Charles Garnier was only awarded fifth prize and his name was hardly mentioned in the press, even though their coverage of the competition had been extensive. De Fleury's design was slated, and he made his exit. Fortunately for Garnier a second round was held. The five prize-winning architects were given two months to develop and adapt their designs. On this occasion they were presented with an extended programme of stipulations. The architects had to take into account specific theatrical features, such as a wardrobe, a tailor's studio, prop storage for the running production and a stage measuring 30 metres from front to back, which could accommodate 300 actors. On the other hand, the audience had to be afforded the best possible freedom of movement within the building: a covered portico, where the audience could step out of their carriages, a separate entrance for season ticket holders, a restaurant and a capacious stairway, where people could meet in an exquisite ambience. In addition, the architects had to include imperial chambers in the design.

During the second, round Duc (fourth prize) dropped out of the competition, while Botrel and Crépinet (second prize) submitted individual designs. It was a vain attempt, because both the jury and the other participants, all of whom had won the Prix de Rome, were classically oriented architects, which Botrel and Crépinet were not.

After the five architects had submitted their new designs, the jury unanimously opted for Garnier, which utterly incensed the first round winner, Ginain, who had arrogantly turned down Garnier's earlier offer of collaboration. Other sore losers were A.M.G. Garnaud (awarded third prize in the first round), who died soon after the result was announced, and Empress Eugénie. It is said that she snarled the following remark to Garnier when he presented his design: *"Qu'est cela, ce n'est pas un style,*

François Debret revised design of Opéra Theatre (Théâtre "Le Peletier"), etching 1821, Top: elevation on "Rue Le Peletier", Bottom: longitudinal section

François Debret "Théâtre Le Peletier", stage and seats, etching 1830, burned down in 1873

Marie-Joseph Peyre & Charles de Wailly Théâtre Français (later Théâtre de l'Odéon), Paris, longitudinal section, built in 1779–1782

Théâtre de l'Opéra, monument for Charles Garnier (in front of "Emperor's Pavilion")

ce n'est ni du Louis XIV, ni du Louis XV, ni du Louis XVI" (What is this? This is not a style. It is not Louis XIV, nor is it Louis XV, and it is not Louis XVI). A telling remark, in terms of both the stylistic preferences of the time and the architectural insight of the empress. Garnier gave the only correct reply: *"Madame, c'est du Napoleon III, et vous plaignez"* (Madame, it is Napoleon III, at your service).
Naturally, if Empress Eugénie had looked further than the decorations alone, she would have realised that Garnier had based his design on Victor Louis' (1772–1780) theatre in Bordeaux, as had all the other participants. Of course Garnier had elaborated upon this prototype, using the competition programme as a guideline. In Garnier's design, the stairway had evolved from a mere thoroughfare into a self-contained architectural feature, which rivalled the auditorium in its grandeur.

Garnier's solutions

Garnier also had to find a way of fitting the Opera into the diamond-shaped floor plan which had developed. He solved this problem by designing a pavilion on one side which would serve as an entrance for season ticket holders. On the other side he envisaged an imperial entrance, also in the form of a pavilion, although in this case it would be accentuated by a monumental double staircase. In this way, Garnier obviated the problems of having two half-hearted triangular squares. The stairways and foyer were designed to allow the audience optimal "circulation" inside the building, although it had been ensured that the auditorium and gallery audiences would never cross each others' paths. Another characteristic problem which Garnier had to solve, was the incorporation of a separate foyer, salon and boxes for the less well-to-do and a double row of first-class boxes to accommodate the growing class of wealthy citizens. Garnier found satisfactory solutions for all these problems. Opinions have differed concerning the style he applied. The debate centred around the Beaux Arts tradition in France and the development of new materials and techniques.

Garnier made numerous references to architectural styles from the past, under the motto: *"Nous regardons, mais nous créons"* (We observe, but we also create). This approach, based on the equality of styles, is characteristically eclectic. Art historians have expressed doubts about this approach, as did Empress Eugénie. What they saw was a copy of Perrault's colonnade in the Louvre, with its famous coupled columns (front side), combined with a free interpretation of an eighteenth century Baroque imperial stairway, Victor Louis' auditorium and a number of other derivative features. However, this view neglects the fact that Garnier certainly did make a contribution to architecture, in terms of his interpretation of the past.

Educated at the Académie des Beaux Arts, first in the tradition of Quatremère de Quincy and later in that of the nascent Neo-styles, Garnier tried to free himself of the stifling restrictions imposed by the prevailing architectural tradition. On the other hand, Garnier was opposed to the French Rationalists, such as Labrouste and Durand, who experimented with new materials and techniques. Although Garnier did make use of such materials (steel framework), he was an expert in concealing them. This skill was a remnant of his tuition at the Académie, as was the symmetrical axial floor plan he used for the Opera. Crafty domes and vaulting conceal the underlying structure, while the vault ribs do not serve as a support but are merely decorative. The statues, murals and other embellishments are in harmony with the architecture, whereby the audience is presented with a vast theatre decor. Garnier saw the audience as an element of the spectacle, which was not only a musical performance but also a social event. Elements from Versailles and Roman architecture (Pompeii) have been incorporated in the decoration programme. The colour scheme is both distinguished and exuberant: gold, deep purple, dark brown and green. Even the façade is colourful. This was a bold move in an era when the use of colour was usually limited to the interior.

In this light, Garnier's apparent eclecticism may be seen as an attempt to break free of the prevailing norms: those of the Académie and those of the Rationalists. The Opera became Garnier's contribution to history and not the emperor's. Napoléon III went into exile in England in 1870 and died there in 1873. Two years later the Opéra opened.

Oper, Paris

Die Bedeutung von Garniers Oper für die Architekturgeschichte ist in der Fachwelt immer noch stark umstritten. Während die einen die Opéra als Endpunkt einer Ära verstehen (Steinhauer), sehen andere dieses Bauwerk eher als einen Wendepunkt (Middleton/Watkin). Hinzu kommt die von Mead vertretene, etwas nuanciertere Meinung, nach der die Opéra als eine naturgetreue Re-Interpretation alter Formen betrachtet wird. Allerdings würde es zu weit führen, in diesem Rahmen auf die architekturgeschichtliche Debatte einzugehen.

Die Pläne für einen Neubau der Oper bestanden bereits seit 1781, als die alte Pariser Oper abbrannte. Seit dieser Zeit fanden die Opernaufführungen in provisorischen Theatern statt, wie z.B. dem Théâtre le Peletier von François Debret (1821). Napoleon III. schließlich regte den Bau einer Oper an, mit der er seine eigene Bedeutung unterstreichen wollte. Unterstützung fand er bei Baron Georges-Eugène Haussmann (1807–1891), der sich auch in unruhigen Zeiten immer als loyaler Anhänger des Kaisers erwiesen hatte und dafür nach dessen Machtergreifung zum Präfekten ernannt worden war (1853). Er sollte Paris zu einer Stadt von wahrhaft kaiserlicher Größe machen. Darüber hinaus verfügte Napoleon, daß in der Stadt genügend Wohnraum für die ständig wachsende Bevölkerung geschaffen werden müsse und daß das Volk keine Gelegenheit mehr erhalten dürfe, die Obrigkeit mit Aufständen und Rebellionen herauszufordern. Dies sollte durch übersichtliche, breite Boulevards gewährleistet werden, auf denen die berittene Polizei schnell für Ordnung sorgen konnte.

Hausmanns Pläne

Obwohl man eine offizielle Kommission berief und sie mit der Suche nach einem geeigneten Baugelände beauftragte, hatte Haussmann bereits 1858 entschieden, daß die Oper im Nordwesten der Stadt gebaut werden sollte. Die endgültige Baugenehmigung wurde 1860 erteilt. Verantwortlich für den Bau waren Innenminister Fould bzw. sein Nachfolger De Walewski, die offiziell die Leitung der Abteilung für öffentliche Bauten (Conseil des Bâtiments Civils) inne hatten, aber indirekt dem Kaiser unterstellt blieben. Haussmann übernahm als Präfekt die Verantwortung für den Bauplatz und die städtebauliche Entwicklung dieses Gebiets. Zunächst plante er einen quadratischen Platz, wobei die Fassade der Oper als optische Begrenzung der Avenue Napoléon III diente (die wiederum im rechten Winkel auf den Boulevard des Capucines treffen sollte). Von diesem Platz aus führten strahlenförmige Durchgänge an den Seiten der Oper vorbei zur Place Vendôme und zur Place de la Bourse (1860). Aber Haussmann änderte diese Pläne wenig später unter dem Einfluß eines bereits bestehenden Entwurfs. Zwar spielte der Bauplan keine Rolle mehr bei der eigentlichen Ausschreibung; aber wie schon oft in der Vergangenheit stellte sich der vorläufige Entwurf als wesentlich für die endgültigen Pläne heraus. In seinem letzten Entwurf von 1860 hatte De Fleury dem ursprünglich rechteckigen Grundriß segmentförmige Flügel an den Seiten hinzugefügt. Um die Straßenführung diesem Bauplan anzupassen, benötigte man ein rautenförmiges Gebäude, das schließlich 1861 die Basis für die städtebauliche Entwicklung rund um die Oper bildete.
Haussmanns erster Entwurf sah eine Straßenführung aus zwei symmetrischen Andreaskreuzen vor, in deren Mitte das neue Juwel der Stadt liegen sollte: die Oper. Die Ecken der Gebäudefront sollten angeschrägt werden, so daß ein Platz in der Breite der Fassade entstehen konnte. Dadurch wurde die Oper zum idealen Blickfang am Ende der Avenue Napoléon III (der heutigen Avenue de l'Opéra). Zudem plante man – aufgrund möglicher Brandgefahren – die Oper als freistehendes Gebäude, ganz im Stil des von Peyre und Wailly entworfenen Théâtre de l'Odéon.
Am 29. Dezember 1860 wurde das Projekt ausgeschrieben. Die 171 Einsender hatten nur einen Monat Zeit, um ihre Beiträge einzureichen, und die wenigsten besaßen Erfahrungen im Umgang mit Theaterarchitektur.
Der Theaterbau hatte sich im Lauf des 19. Jahrhunderts stetig weiterentwickelt. Dank des Einflusses von Gottfried Semper handelte es sich nicht länger um geschlossene, nüchterne Bauwerke. Statt dessen entstanden heitere, offene Begegnungsstätten, in denen nicht nur auf der Bühne, sondern auch in den Wandelgängen gespielt wurde.

Voreingenommene Jury

Die eigentliche Wettbewerbsausschreibung war sehr knapp gehalten und erfolgte durch eine einseitig zusammengestellte Jury: Sämtliche Mitglieder hatten ihre Ausbildung an der Académie des Beaux-Arts abgeschlossen oder waren ihr noch verbunden. Dies führte dazu, daß sich die Teilnehmer den architektonischen Ansichten dieser Institution anpassen mußten: Neugotische Entwürfe waren chancenlos gegen Beiträge im neubarocken oder klassizistischen Stil. Charles Garnier erhielt den fünften Preis und fand kaum Beachtung.
De Fleurys Beitrag wurde völlig verrissen, und er zog sich zurück. Zum Glück für Garnier kam es zu einer zweiten Ausschreibungsrunde, in der die besten fünf Einsender zwei Monate Zeit erhielten, ihre Pläne zu verändern und auszuarbeiten. Allerdings überreichte man ihnen nun auch einen umfangreichen Auflagenkatalog. So mußten die Architekten die speziellen Anforderungen eines Theaters in ihre Planungen einbeziehen: Kostümfundus, Theaterschneiderei, Requisitenkammern für die laufende Vorstellung und eine 30 Meter tiefe Bühne, die Platz für 300 Akteure bot. Auf der anderen Seite sollte sich das Publikum so angenehm wie möglich in und um das Gebäude bewegen können: ein überdachter Portikus, unter dem die Gäste in ihren Kutschen vorfahren konnten, ein separater Eingang für die Abonnementsbesitzer, ein Restaurant und ein geräumiges Treppenhaus, wo man sich in einem angemessenen Rahmen aufhalten konnte. Darüber hinaus mußten auch die kaiserlichen Räumlichkeiten in den Entwurf eingearbeitet werden.
Nachdem die fünf Architekten ihre Pläne ausgearbeitet hatten, fiel die Wahl der Jury einstimmig auf Garnier – zur großen Verbitterung P.R.L. Ginains, des Gewinners der ersten Ausschreibungsrunde, der ein Angebot Garniers zur Zusammenarbeit zurückgewiesen hatte. Garnier hatte sich wie alle anderen Teilnehmer, an Victor Louis' Entwürfen für das Theater von Bordeaux (1772–80) orientiert. Er entwickelte diesen Prototyp weiter, zum Teil anhand der durch die Ausschreibung festgesetzten Vorgaben. So erhob Garnier das Treppenhaus von einem reinen Durchgang zu einem eigenständigen Gebäudeteil.

Garniers Lösungen

Garnier stand vor dem Problem, die neue Oper in die bereits vorhandene rautenförmige Straßenanlage einzupassen. Er fand die Lösung, indem er an einer Seite einen Pavillon entwarf, der als Eingang für die Abonnementsbesitzer dienen sollte. Auf der andere Seite des Gebäudes setzte er – ebenfalls in Form eines Pavillons – den kaiserlichen Eingang, der allerdings durch eine monumentale Doppeltreppe hervorgehoben wurde. Mit Hilfe dieser Anbauten verhinderte Garnier, daß zwei deplaziert wirkende dreieckige Plätze entstanden. Treppenhaus und Foyer waren so angelegt, daß das Publikum frei »zirkulieren« konnte – wobei man natürlich darauf geachtet hatte, daß sich das Saalpublikum und die Zuschauer auf der Galerie nicht begegneten. Zu den anderen charakteristischen Schwierigkeiten, mit denen Garnier sich auseinandersetzen mußte, gehörten die Entwürfe eines separaten Foyers und getrennter Salons und Logen für die weniger Wohlhabenden sowie der Einbau einer doppelten Reihe kostspieliger Logen, um für die ständig wachsende Schicht wohlhabender Bürger genügend Platz zu bieten.
Garnier zitiert in seinen Bauten unzählige Architekturstile vergangener Epochen, getreu dem Motto: *»Nous regardons, mais nous créons«* (Wir betrachten, aber wir schaffen auch neu). Dieser Ansatz, der von der Gleichwertigkeit der Stile ausgeht, stieß bei zahlreichen Kunsthistorikern auf Wierstand. Sie sahen (und sehen) nur eine Kopie von Perraults Kolonnade für den Louvre mit den berühmten paarigen Säulen (Ostfassade), kombiniert mit einer freien Interpretation eines kaiserlichen Treppenhauses im barocken Stil des 18. Jahrhunderts, dem Auditorium von Victor Louis und einigen anderen Beispielen.
Kuppeln und Gewölbe des Baus verbergen geschickt die darunterliegende Konstruktion, wobei die Gewölberippen keine stützende, sondern rein dekorative Funktion haben. Die Statuen, Gemälde und Verzierungen verschmelzen mit der Architektur zu einem harmonischen Ganzen und bilden ein riesiges Theaterdekor für das Publikum. Garnier sah die Besucher als Teilnehmer eines nicht nur musikalischen, sondern auch gesellschaftlichen Schauspiels an. Die Dekorationen gehen zurück auf Versailles sowie römische Vorbilder (Pompeii), die verwendeten Farben wirken zugleich vornehm und überschwenglich: Gold, Dunkelviolett, Dunkelbraun und Grün. Sogar die Fassade ist farbenfroh – sehr gewagt für eine Zeit, in der man Farben im allgemeinen nur für die Inneneinrichtung verwendete.
Soweit Aspekt wirkt Garniers scheinbarer Eklektizismus wie eine Flucht vor den bestehenden Normen, aufgestellt durch die Académie und die Rationalisten. Die Opéra ist Garniers – und nicht Napoleons III. – Beitrag zur Architekturgeschichte: Der Kaiser verlor nach der Grundsteinlegung jegliches Interesse an dem Projekt und setzte niemals einen Fuß in die kaiserliche Loge.

L'Opéra de Paris

Les opinions sur l'importance de l'Opéra de Garnier dans l'histoire de l'architecture sont divergentes. Alors que pour un auteur, Steinhauser, il marque la fin d'une époque, pour d'autres, comme Middleton et Watkin, il représente un tournant. Une vision plus équilibrée a été récemment développée par Mead qui fait de ce prestigieux édifice l'interprétation originale de la rencontre de styles d'époques révolues.

Depuis l'incendie de son théâtre en 1781, la troupe de l'Opéra s'était réfugiée dans différentes salles comme, par exemple, celle du théâtre Le Peletier (François Debret, 1821). Paris avait bien multiplié les plans pour un nouveau bâtiment, mais seul un changement radical de circonstances allait permettre de trouver une solution définitive. L'opportunité tant attendue se présenta avec le règne de Napoléon III. Convaincu que la grandeur d'un souverain se juge aux traces de son passage qu'il laisse à la postérité, l'Empereur souhaitait construire un nouvel opéra. Il confia ce désir à un haut fonctionnaire doté d'une personnalité exceptionnelle, le baron Georges-Eugène Haussmann (1807–1891) L'Empereur lui demanda de transformer Paris en une cité digne de la grandeur impériale et capable d'accueillir une population croissante tout en limitant les risques d'émeutes. De larges boulevards, facilitant les mouvements de troupes, paraissaient apporter une solution à ce dernier problème.

Le plan Haussmann

Bien qu'une commission ait été officiellement nommée pour choisir le site, Haussmann avait décidé dès 1858 que l'Opéra serait construit dans les quartiers nord-ouest de la capitale. La commande du bâtiment fut ordonnancée en 1860. Chargé du projet à l'origine, le ministre des Affaires Intérieures, Fould, fut vite remplacé par Walewski, responsable du Conseil des Bâtiments Civils mais dépendant en fait de l'Empereur dont il était proche. En tant que préfet, Haussmann avait la responsabilité urbanistique de la zone choisie. Au départ, il avait imaginé une place rectangulaire au fond de laquelle s'élèverait la façade de l'Opéra fermant la perspective de l'Avenue Napoléon III qui s'achevait en T sur le boulevard des Capucines. Deux radiales partaient de chaque côté du bâtiment vers la place Vendôme et la place de la Bourse (1860). Il modifia ce projet en fonction d'un plan préparé entre 1850 à 1860 pour l'Opéra par Rohault de Fleury, architecte qui n'allait guère jouer de rôle dans le concours. Cependant, comme souvent par le passé, ces esquisses initiales exercèrent une certaine influence sur la version retenue en final. Dans son dernier plan, daté de 1860, Fleury avait ajouté deux ailes latérales à sa superstructure rectangulaire. Afin d'harmoniser cette forme au schéma des rues, un plan de masse en forme de diamant fut étudié. En 1861, c'est ce projet qui orienta l'urbanisme du futur quartier de l'Opéra.
Le premier projet de voirie d'Haussmann se développait en deux croix de Saint-André symétriques qui formaient le cadre de ce joyau que devait devenir le théâtre de l'Opéra. La façade était dans la coupe du biseau, fermant une place carrée aussi large qu'elle. Vu de l'Avenue Napoléon III (aujourd'hui avenue de l'Opéra), l'Opéra occupait ainsi le centre d'une mise en scène parfaite. Mais il fallait d'abord organiser le concours. (Les efforts de Rohault de Fleury pour obtenir directement la commande avaient été vains. On disait même que l'Impératrice Eugénie avait informé son protégé Viollet-le-Duc, au détriment de Fleury). Le concours fut lancé le 29 décembre 1860 et ses 171 participants, dont peu d'entre eux possédaient une quelconque expérience de l'architecture théâtrale, n'avaient qu'un mois pour soumettre leurs plans. Mais le prestige éventuel de cette commande était tel que beaucoup d'architectes tinrent à y participer.
Tout au long du XIXème siècle, l'architecture du théâtre avait évolué, en particulier sous l'influence de G. Semper. Ce n'était plus un bâtiment fermé et austère, mais plutôt un lieu public, ouvert et chaleureux, dans lequel le spectacle se déroulait aussi bien sur la scène que dans les couloirs où la nouvelle élite bourgeoise, sur son trente-et-un, pouvait enfin se rapprocher de la vie de la Cour. Comme à Vienne, la confiance en soi des nouvelles classes moyennes (dont celle des architectes) atteignait de nouveaux sommets. L'Opéra reflétait la puissance et le statut de l'Empereur mais également celui de ses sujets. Ce nouvel aspect du théâtre s'exprimait en particulier dans des escaliers et des foyers de dimensions extravagantes.

Un jury biaisé

Le jury assez partial avait proposé un programme de concours extrêmement sommaire. Tous ses membres avaient étudié à l'Ecole des Beaux-Arts ou lui étaient encore attachés, ce qui impliquait automatiquement que les participants devaient soumettre des projets en accord avec les conceptions architecturales de cette institution. Tout approche néo-gothique aurait probablement été écartée au profit de projets néo-baroques ou néo-classiques. Même Viollet-le-Duc n'osa pas proposer de plans néo-gothiques. Charles Garnier ne reçut que le cinquième prix et son nom ne fut qu'à peine mentionné par la presse qui s'étendit pourtant longuement sur les résultats. Le plan de Fleury fut écarté pour de bon. Heureusement pour Garnier, une deuxième épreuve fut organisée. Deux mois supplémentaires furent accordés aux cinq lauréats pour préciser et adapter leurs projets à un programme beaucoup plus détaillé qui les obligeait, par exemple, à prendre en compte des équipements spécifiques comme un magasin des costumes, un atelier de tailleur, un magasin de décors pour les productions en cours et une scène de 30 m de profondeur capable de recevoir 300 chanteurs et figurants. Par ailleurs, le public devait pouvoir bénéficier d'une grande liberté de mouvement dans le bâtiment et il fallait aussi prévoir un portique couvert pour accueillir les voitures, une entrée séparée pour les abonnés, un restaurant et un vaste escalier, où les spectateurs pouvaient se retrouver dans un cadre prestigieux. Enfin, les architectes devaient réserver des pièces pour le seul usage de l'Empereur. Lors de cette seconde phase, Duc (quatrième prix) se retira et Botrel et Crépinet (deuxième prix) soumirent chacun de leur côté un plan. Vaine tentative, car le jury et les autres candidats, tous prix de Rome, étaient favorables à une orientation néo-classique que Botrel et Crépinet étaient bien en mal d'offrir.
Le jury choisit à l'unanimité Garnier, à la grande fureur du gagnant de la première phase, Ginain, qui avait repoussé avec arrogance une offre de collaboration du nouveau vainqueur. Parmi les autres perdants, amers et mécontents, figuraient également A. Garnaud (second prix de la première phase) qui mourut peu après la publication des résultats et même l'Impératrice Eugénie. On raconte qu'elle aurait jeté à Garnier, lors de la présentation du projet un *«Qu'est cela? Ce n'est pas un style, ce n'est ni du Louis XIV, ni du Louis XV, ni du Louis XVI»*. Cette remarque en disait long sur les préférences stylistiques de l'époque et les connaissances architecturales de la souveraine. Garnier lui répondit avec à-propos: *«C'est du Napoléon III, Madame!»*.

Les solutions de Garnier

Garnier devait adapter son projet au plan de masse en forme de diamant qui avait été adopté. Il résolut cette difficulté en dessinant deux pavillons latéraux, un pour l'entrée des abonnés, l'autre pour celle du souverain, souligné d'un double-escalier monumental. L'escalier et le foyer étaient dessinés pour permettre une circulation aisée du public à l'intérieur du bâtiment, tout en évitant que les spectateurs de l'orchestre et ceux des galeries supérieures ne se croisent. Il fallut donc créer un foyer séparé, avec salon et loges pour les spectateurs moins aisés et une double rangée de loges de première classe pour les amateurs d'opéra aisés de plus en plus nombreux. Garnier trouva des solutions satisfaisantes. Son style, en revanche, souleva un débat autour du respect de la tradition des Beaux-Arts et du recours aux nouveaux matériaux et aux techniques de la révolution industrielle.
Garnier multiplia les références aux styles architecturaux du passé sur le thème de *«Nous regardons, mais nous créons»*. Cette approche, qui considère tous les styles comme égaux, est celle de l'éclectisme. Les historiens d'art ont exprimé quelques doutes sur la validité de cette démarche, rejoignant en cela l'Impératrice. Ils ont relevé pour la façade une copie de la colonnade du Louvre de Perrault et de ses célèbres colonnes couplées, une interprétation libre d'un escalier baroque du XVIIIème siècle, la grande salle de Victor Louis et un certain nombre d'autres caractéristiques empruntées de-ci de-là. Cette vision critique néglige le fait que l'apport de Garnier réside justement dans cette interprétation du passé.
Ayant étudié à l'Ecole des Beaux-Arts dans la tradition de Quatremère de Quincy puis dans celles des styles 'néo' qui faisaient leur apparition, Garnier essayait de se libérer des contraintes étouffantes imposé par la tradition architecturale dominante. D'un autre côté, il s'opposait aux rationalistes comme Labrouste et Durand qui expérimentaient de nouveaux matériaux et de nouvelles techniques. Bien qu'il n'hésitât pas à se servir de ces matériaux (structures métalliques), il excellait à les dissimuler. Son plan de masse symétrique est un souvenir de sa formation académique. Des dômes et des voussures astucieuses cachent la structure tandis que les arêtes de la voûte sont plus décoratives que fonctionnelles. Les statues, les fresques et autres embellissements sont en harmonie avec l'architecture et offrent au public un vaste décor théâtral. Pour Garnier, les spectateurs faisaient partie du spectacle qui était un événement autant musical que social. On trouve également des citations de Versailles et de Pompéi dans la décoration. Les coloris sont à la fois raffinés et exubérants: or, rouge foncé, brun foncé et vert. Même la façade est polychrome, ce qui était assez osé à une époque où la couleur était réservée aux intérieurs.
L'Opéra aura été la brillante contribution de Garnier à l'histoire de l'architecture comme à celle de l'Empire, même si l'Empereur ne vit jamais ce grand-œuvre terminé.

Charles Garnier final design, without date, Emperors Pavillion, left: west elevation, right: south elevation

Charles Garnier final design, without date, rear elevation on Place de Diaghilev

Charles Garnier final design, without date, front elevation on Place de l'Opéra

Charles Garnier etching from 'Le Nouvel Opéra de Paris', 1880, rear elevation on Place de l'Opéra

Charles Garnier etching from "Le Nouvel Opéra de Paris", 1880, rear elevation on Place de Diaghilev

Charles Garnier etching from "Le Nouvel Opéra de Paris", 1880, transverse section

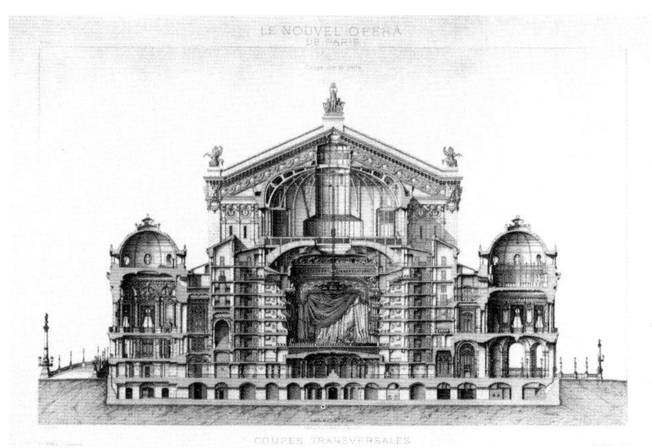

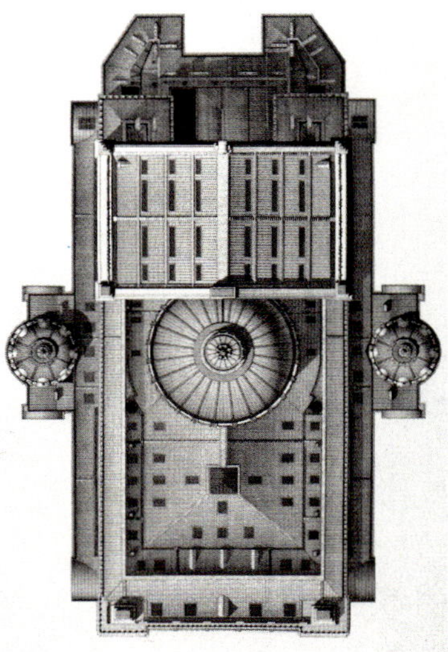

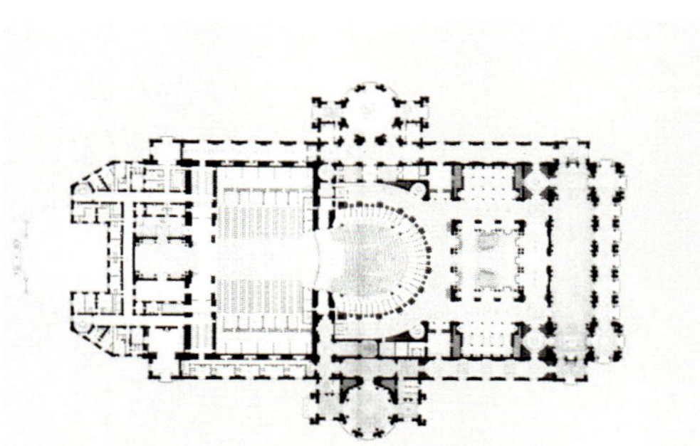

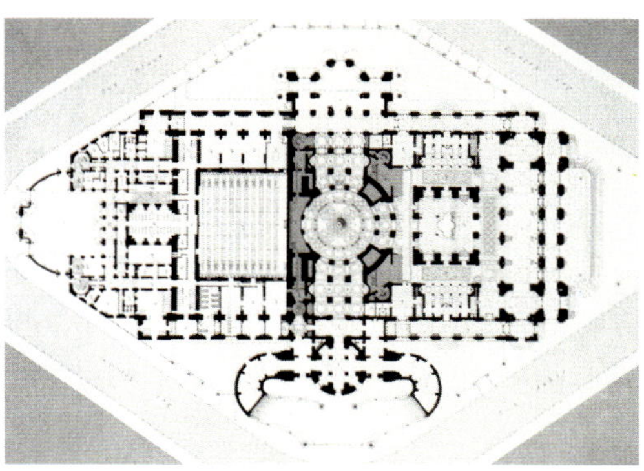

Charles Garnier sketch for final design, without date, exterior view from the south

Charles Garnier final design, alternative, without date, rear elevation on Place de Diaghilev

Charles Garnier etching from "Le Nouvel Opéra de Paris", 1880, foyer plan

Charles Garnier etching from "Le Nouvel Opéra de Paris", 1880, entrance plan

Charles Garnier etching from "Le Nouvel Opéra de Paris", 1880, roof plan

Charles Garnier etching from "Le Nouvel Opéra de Paris", 1880, side elevation on "Place Charles Garnier"

Charles Garnier etching from "Le Nouvel Opéra de Paris", 1880, longitudinal section

Charles Garnier etching from "Le Nouvel Opéra de Paris", 1880, transverse section

Charles Garnier etching from "Le Nouvel Opéra de Paris", 1880, section of the stage

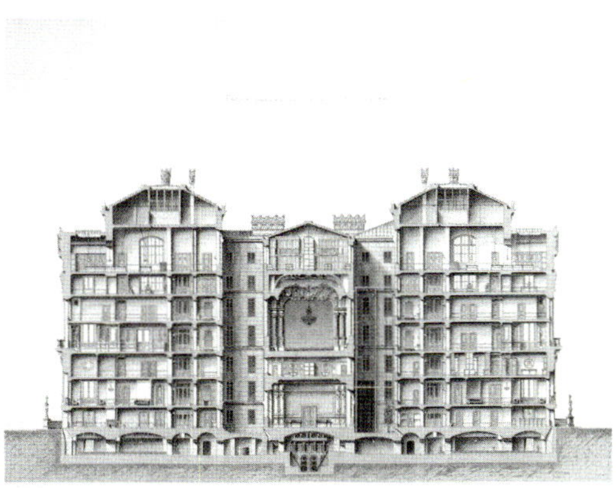

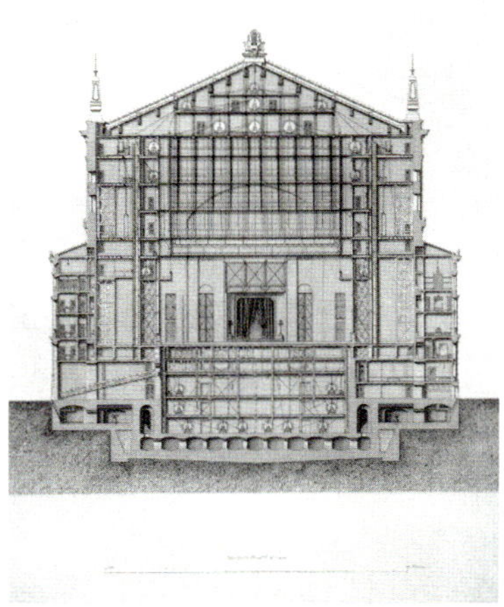

Botrel & Alphonse-Nicolas Crépinet
competitior design, 1861, exterior
view from the south, second prize

Charles Garnier etching from "Le Nouvel Opéra de Paris", 1880, interior view of the Grand Stair Hall

Charles Garnier etching from "Le Nouvel Opéra de Paris", 1880, detail of the side gate

Charles Garnier etching from "Le Nouvel Opéra de Paris", 1880, section of Paradis and Cupola

Charles Garnier etching from "Le Nouvel Opéra de Paris", 1880, section of the Grand Staircase

Project

Museum for the National Art Collection, also National Monument

Site

Stadhouderskade, Amsterdam

Dates

First round April 1863 – 1 February 1864 (private initiative)
Second round 1875 – December 1875 (government initiative)

Number of entries

21 by 19 architects

Jury

First round J.A. Alberdingk Thijm, P.L. Dubourq, W.J. Hofdijk, C.P. van Eeghen, J.P. Six, C. Rochussen, J.W. Kaiser, H.F.C. Ten Kate, all members of the commission whose objective it was to found a museum; W.N. Rose and J.F. Metzelaar, from the Ministry of Home Affairs; A.N. Godefroy, all architects *Second round* Council of eight state advisors from the Ministry of Home Affairs; a special advisory commission; and advice from the chairmen of the painters' societies of The Hague and Amsterdam: Cornelis Springer and Jozef Israëls

Result

First round, first prize Ludwig Lange & Emil Lange *Second prize* P.J.H. Cuypers *Second round* P.J.H. Cuypers

Commissioned by

Ministry of Home Affairs

Construction

1877 to 1885

Architect

P.J.H. Cuypers (1827–1921)

Construction cost

In excess of 2 700 000 guilders

Rijksmuseum, Amsterdam, 1863–1875

Petrus Josephus Hubertus Cuypers
final design, 1877, north-east
elevation on the canal (front)

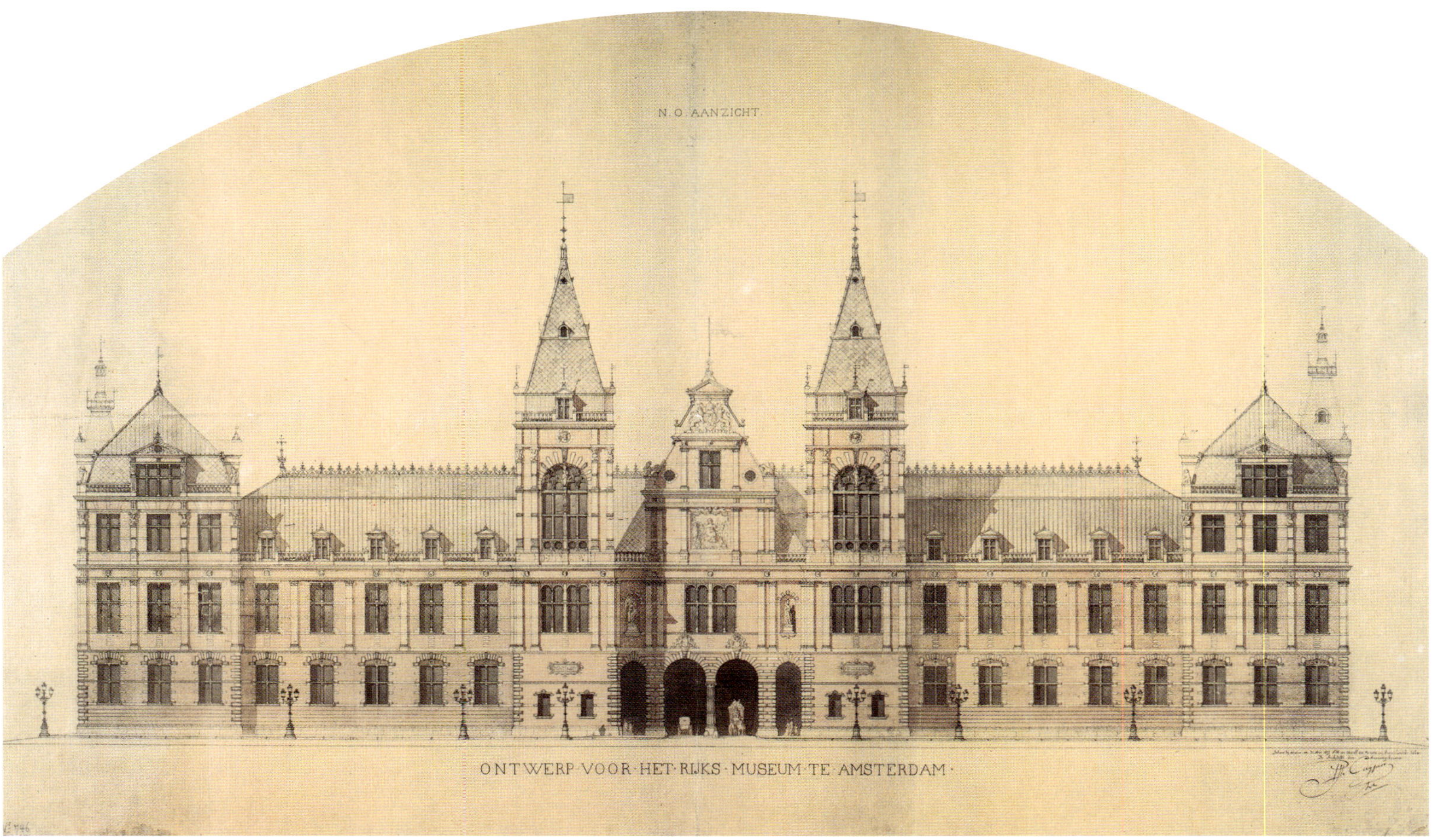

Rijksmuseum, Amsterdam

The design of the Rijksmuseum in Amsterdam was an interesting challenge to the participants for more reasons than one. In the first place, it was interesting because of the building's proposed function. The museum, as a form of architecture, was still being developed in Europe at the time. A number of royal and imperial collections had, of course, already been made accessible to the general public, and the Rijksmuseum was certainly not the world's first new museum building. In fact, the desire for a national museum was to be found in all European countries. Nevertheless, development was in its infancy and a universal museum type had not yet developed.

The prestige of the competition was also enhanced by the fact that the museum would contain the most important Dutch art collection. The Rijksmuseum was to be the most important temple of fine arts in the Kingdom of the Netherlands. A second factor which enhanced the special nature of the competition was the question of the style in which the museum should be built. This was the dominant subject of discussion during almost the entire nineteenth century, not only in the Netherlands. The first initiative for the construction of a national museum had been taken as early as 1862, when a group of Amsterdam dignitaries had formed a commission with the objective of founding a King William I Museum, named after the first king of the Netherlands (1815–1840), who had taken a particularly keen interest in the arts. One of the most important members of this commission was J.A. Alberdingk Thijm, one of the two secretaries. In later years he would prove to be an ardent supporter and advocate of the designs of the architect P.J.H. Cuypers, who hailed from the Catholic south of the Netherlands. The commission was chaired by Dr. W. Vrolik.

State support

It had become high time for attention to be devoted to the museum question. Until then, the collection of paintings had been housed in the Trippenhuis, a 17th century stately home in Amsterdam, or rather, half of the Trippenhuis. The drawbacks of these premises were self-evident. The rooms where the paintings were exhibited were too dark. The building was too small and there was also a fire hazard. It was therefore not surprising that concerned citizens formed a commission. Furthermore, they felt supported by the state, when the statesman Thorbecke announced that a large sum of money would be allocated to the museum. The commission began diligently raising funds and in April 1863 the competition was announced.

The commissioned design was for a national museum which would also serve as a national monument, commemorating the sovereignty gained by the State of the Netherlands in 1813 (which became a Kingdom in 1815). The commission appointed a jury which included eight members of the commission, as well as the architects Godefroy, Rose and Metzelaar. A short programme of requirements was drawn up. The construction site was as yet unknown, but the lay out, size and construction costs (then 500 000 guilders) were stipulated. The style in which the museum would be built had to be in keeping with its function as a national monument and – a subsequent source of conflict – also had to be suitable for a collection of Dutch masterpieces of the sixteenth and seventeenth centuries. In other words, the Dutch Renaissance style or even the Baroque classicism of the latter half of the seventeenth century might be considered as suitable, but not the

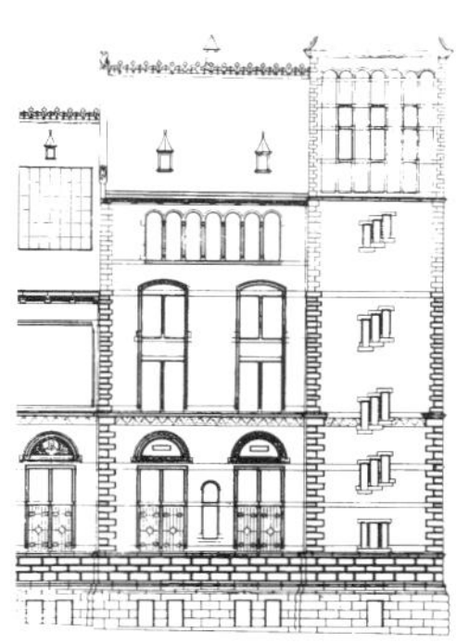

P.J.H. Cuypers Rijksmuseum, detail of the south façade, 1880

Rijksmuseum shortly after completion of construction, front façade on the canal

P.J.H. Cuypers Amsterdam Central Station, front façade

Gothic revivalist style favoured by Cuypers and others. We will return to this subject later on in this chapter.

The first round

A total of 19 architects participated in the competition. Two of them, one of whom was Cuypers, submitted two designs. The entries were submitted anonymously, under a motto. Even after the results were announced, the names of the other participants were not published, so that, unfortunately, little is known about most of their designs.

The first prize, 1500 guilders, was awarded to the Munich architect Lange and his son, who had experience in museum architecture, having designed a museum in Leipzig. The design for Amsterdam was comparable to that for Leipzig, but it could not possibly be considered for a museum for Dutch art. The outstanding features of the design were the dome above the central hall, where the 1813 monument was to be situated, and the Greek portico which marked the entrance. The portico was flanked by two symmetrical wings, in the style of an Italian Renaissance palazzo. Despite the design's first round victory, the style was judged unsuitable for realisation.

Cuypers second

Cuypers was awarded second prize (300 guilders). He had played it safe by submitting two designs, each with a different façade alternatives one in Gothic and the other in Renaissance style. Both floor plans included a central hall where the 1813 monument was to be situated. The jury selected plan A, with the Renaissance façade.

The motto under which Cuypers submitted his design was characteristic: *"Toute forme qui n'est pas indiquée par la structure doit être repoussée"*. This functionalist statement derives from Cuypers' most esteemed model, the French Gothic revivalist architect and theoretician Viollet-le-Duc. Three other architects received an honourable mention: Louis Radoux (Paris), Charles Peignet (Paris) and L.H. Eberson, King's Architect (Arnhem).

None of the designs, however, were considered suitable for actual building. Moreover, jury member Alberdingk Thijm had launched an all-out attack on the winning design, even before the official exhibition of the designs had opened. He had sent letters to newspapers and magazines, anonymously or pseudonymously, slating the "un-Dutch" style of the winner and praising the expertise and artistry of Cuypers, who was his friend and brother-in-law. The entire project was in danger of reaching a stalemate. The commission did try to appease the conflict by asking Godefroy (the jury member) to make an adaptation of Cuypers' and Lange's designs. This proved to be a vain effort, because Godefroy considered it impossible to stay under the stipulated construction cost. A newly formulated brief, given to Eberson, also proved fruitless. Alberdingk Thijm resigned from the commission because the brief had not been given to Cuypers.

New impetus

Nine years after the unsavoury affairs of 1864, the project suddenly gained new impetus and the museum, henceforth referred to as the Rijksmuseum, was listed in the state budget. The municipality allocated a building site, free of charge, and a sum of 100 000 guilders. As of 1874, an Advisory Commission collaborated with the State Advisory Board in order to achieve the proposed objective. The Advisory Commission consisted largely of members of the former commission, while the newly formed State Advisory Board for Historical Monuments and Art was headed by Victor de Stuers. De Steurs was not only considered as the founding father of Dutch monument preservation, but was also the esteemed protector of another prominent member of the board, P.J.H. Cuypers.

The board and the commission suggested to the minister that a new competition should be organised. The minister agreed and the architects C. Outshoorn, Eberson, Cuypers and D.H. Vogel were invited

P.J.H. Cuypers **Rijksmuseum, perspective section, 1885**

H.P. Berlage **Museumplein, project, Amsterdam 1895–1896**

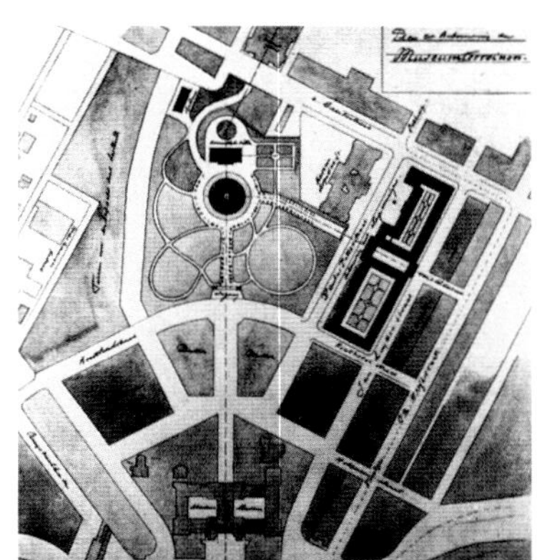

to participate. Lange was already dead and Outshoorn died before he could submit a design. The stipulation that the submitted designs should be suitable for a collection of sixteenth and seventeenth century Dutch art was maintained. Once again, Cuypers submitted a Gothic and a Renaissance design. The latter was chosen, much to the disappointment of the other participants, who suspected that the jury was biased. Eberson's design, however, was not in keeping with another important stipulation: the creation of a passage under the museum leading to the southern part of Amsterdam which had yet to be developed. The design was also considered to be too Greek. The plan that was actually used contained the main features of Cuypers' design, but before (and even after) the first pile had been sunk, he introduced a number of changes. After he had been commissioned, Cuypers saw his way clear, with the support of the Minister of Home Affairs, to set aside the Renaissance design and adopt the alternative Gothic plan, despite the reservations expressed by King William III.

Museumplein, municipal project, Amsterdam, 1891

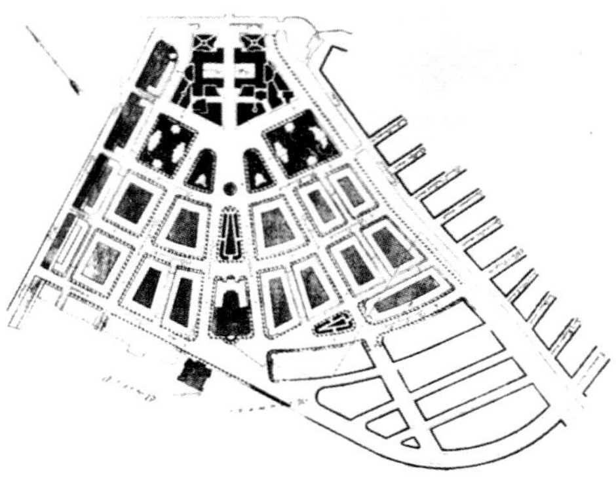

Catholic resurgences

Yet the Rijksmuseum can by no means be described as Gothic, because many Renaissance features have been retained. Many of Cuypers' contemporaries took a different view, however. They considered the design to be too Gothic and therefore too Catholic. They argued that the design did not take into account the other, Protestant part of the nation. This explains why the reactions were often extremely vehement. It was suggested, with some truth, that the Gothic style was a vehicle of Catholic resurgence. And, following the Eighty-Years War against Spain (1568–1648), this was something the Protestants could well do without. It was against this background that Catholicism had been slighted in favour of Protestantism until well into the nineteenth century. The affair was interpreted as a Catholic takeover prepared by Alberdingk Thijm and Victor de Stuers and completed by Cuypers, giving a national museum a Catholic appearance. In political cartoons the museum was referred to as the Bishop's Palace or the Monastery of St. Victor. To top it all, the original construction costs of 800 000 guilders (raised to 1 000 000 guilders during the competition) started to approach the three million guilders mark, which makes the reactions understandable.

However, even though its dual function as a museum and a monument soon lapsed, the Rijksmuseum became truly worthy of the title national museum, particularly due to the focus upon Dutch art in the decoration programme. Later alterations, not executed by Cuypers himself, included the removal of almost all of the colourful interior decorations (murals and terrazzo floors)[1] and the building over of the inner courtyards in 1962 and 1969. However, Cuypers did design the annexes and extensions, such as the Rijksnormaal school (1892), the Rembrandt hall (1904–1906), the south extension (1906–1908) and the Drucker extension (1911–1915). Cuypers had completed the director's residence (free-standing) and the library (attached) at the same time as the museum itself.

1 *It was argued that the quality of art should be self-evident and that excessive decorations would merely distract the viewer.*

Rijksmuseum, Amsterdam

Das Rijksmuseum in Amsterdam stellte eine große Herausforderung für die beteiligten Architekten dar. In erster Linie betraf dies den Bautypus selbst, da die Entwicklung des Museumsbaus als architektonisch eigenständige Form noch nicht abgeschlossen war. Zwar hatte man schon vorher verschiedene königliche und kaiserliche Kunstsammlungen einem breiteren Publikum zugänglich gemacht – und das Rijksmuseum war nicht das erste neue Museumsgebäude der Welt –, aber trotz des in allen europäischen Staaten stark ausgeprägten Wunsches nach einem Nationalmuseum konnte von einem universellen Museumstypus noch nicht die Rede sein. Zusätzliche Bedeutung erlangte die Ausschreibung, weil es sich hierbei um den Bau eines Museums für eine der bedeutendsten niederländischen Kunstsammlungen handelte.

Der zweite Aspekt, der den besonderen Charakter der Ausschreibung unterstrich, betraf die Frage des Baustils. Dieses Thema beschäftigte die Gemüter fast das ganze 19. Jahrhundert hindurch und sicherlich weit über die Grenzen der Niederlande hinaus.
Bereits 1862 war eine erste Initiative zum Bau eines nationalen Museums ergriffen worden. Damals bildete eine Gruppe Amsterdamer Honoratioren eine Kommission mit dem erklärten Ziel, ein »Museum Koning Willem I« zu errichten. Der Name bezog sich auf den ersten König der Niederlande, Willem I. (1815–1840), der als großer Kunstmäzen galt.

Staatliche Unterstützung

In den folgenden Monaten wurde die Errichtung eines neuen Museumsgebäudes immer dringender, da die Gemäldesammlung bis zu diesem Zeitpunkt in einem Gebäudeteil des Trippenhuis, einem Amsterdamer Patrizierhaus aus dem 17. Jahrhundert, untergebracht war. Allerdings waren die Zimmer, in denen die Gemälde hingen, zu dunkel, das gesamte Gebäude war zu klein, und es bestand große Brandgefahr. In der Folge bildeten besorgte Bürger eine Kommission. Sie fühlten sich in ihren Bestrebungen von staatlicher Seite bestärkt, als der Politiker Thorbecke verkündete, daß für das Museum eine beträchtliche Geldsumme bereitgestellt werden müsse. Daraufhin begann die Kommission mit der Sammlung von Geldern und verkündete im April 1863 die offizielle Ausschreibung. Der Bauauftrag umfaßte ein Nationalmuseum, das zugleich als nationales Monument zur Erinnerung an die 1813 erworbene Souveränität des niederländischen Staates dienen sollte (1815 wurde die Staatsform in eine Monarchie umgewandelt). Die Kommission setzte eine Jury ein, der acht der Kommissionsmitglieder angehörten sowie die Architekten Godefroy, Rose und Metzelaar. Obwohl das Baugelände des zukünftigen Museums noch nicht feststand, enthielt die knappe Ausschreibung verschiedene Auflagen bezüglich der Gebäudeeinteilung, des Bauumfangs und der Baukosten (damals noch 500 000 Gulden). Der Baustil des geplanten Museums sollte der monumentalen Bedeutung und Bestimmung gerecht werden und – dies war die Ursache für die späteren Auseinandersetzungen – sich für eine Sammlung niederländischer Kunstwerke aus dem 16. und 17. Jahrhundert eignen.

Die erste Runde

Der erste Preis in Höhe von 1 500 Gulden ging an die Architekten Lange (Vater und Sohn) aus München, die bereits ein Museum in Leipzig konzipiert hatten. Ihr Entwurf für das Amsterdamer Rijksmuseum war dem Entwurf des Leipziger Museums durchaus ebenbürtig, allerdings deutete nichts darauf hin, daß es sich um ein Ausstellungsgebäude für niederländische Kunst handelte.

Der Zweite: Cuypers

Den zweiten Preis (300 Gulden) erhielt Cuypers, der jeden der beiden eingereichten Baupläne mit jeweils zwei Fassadenvarianten versehen hatte – eine Fassade im gotischen Stil und eine im Stil der Renaissance. Beide Grundrisse präsentierten eine zentrale Halle für das Monument 1813. Die Jury entschied sich für Plan A mit der Renaissance-Fassade. Cuypers' Motto zu seinem Entwurf, *»Toute forme qui n'est pas indiquée par la structure doit être repoussée.«*, war typisch für diesen Architekten, dessen funktionalistischer Leitgedanke von seinem großen Vorbild, dem französischen Architekten und Theoretiker der Neugotik, Viollet-le-Duc, stammte.
Dennoch galt keiner der Entwürfe als realisierbar, und das Jurymitglied Alberdingk Thijm begann noch vor der offiziellen Ausstellung der Baupläne einen Privatkrieg gegen den prämierten Entwurf. So schrieb er anonym oder unter einem Pseudonym Briefe an verschiedene Zeitungen und Zeitschriften, in denen er sich über den »unniederländischen« Stil des Gewinners ausließ, während er das fachliche Können und die hohe Kunst seines Freundes und Schwagers Cuypers in den höchsten Tönen lobte. Das Projekt schien in eine Sackgasse zu geraten. Die Jury unternahm zwar noch einen verzweifelten Versuch, das drohende Scheitern des Unterfangens abzuwenden, indem sie das Jurymitglied Godefroy bat, die Entwürfe von Cuypers und Lange zu überarbeiten, doch auch dies führte nicht zum gewünschten Ergebnis: Godefroy hielt es für ausgeschlossen, daß die Baukosten unter der veranschlagten Bausumme blieben.
Auch ein zweiter, an Eberson erteilter Änderungsauftrag blieb ohne Erfolg. Da man Cuypers bei dieser Aktion übergangen hatte, trat Thijm aus der Kommission aus.

Mit neuer Kraft

Erst neun Jahre nach diesen unerfreulichen Ereignissen nahmen die Pläne plötzlich konkrete Formen an, als das Staatsbudget einen eigenen Posten für das neue Museum vorsah, das von nun an »Rijksmuseum« genannt wurde. Die Stadt stellte kostenlos ein Baugelände sowie einen Betrag in Höhe von 100 000 Gulden zur Verfügung, und ab 1874 arbeiteten ein Beratungsausschuß und eine Reichskommission an der Durchführung der Pläne. Der Beratungsausschuß bestand hauptsächlich aus Mitgliedern des alten Gremiums, während die frisch aus der Taufe gehobene Reichskommission für historische Monumente und Kunst unter dem Einfluß von Victor de Stuers stand. De Stuers galt nicht nur als Begründer der niederländischen Denkmalpflege, sondern trat auch als einflußreicher Förderer eines anderen Kommissionsmitglieds hervor: P.J.H. Cuypers.
Beratungsausschuß und Reichskommission wandten sich gemeinsam an das Innenministerium und schlugen eine zweite Ausschreibung vor. Nachdem sich der Innenminister einverstanden erklärte, lud man die Baumeister Outshoorn, Eberson, Cuypers und Vogel ein, sich an dieser Ausschreibung zu beteiligen. Zu diesem Zeitpunkt war Lange bereits tot, Outshoorn starb, bevor er einen Entwurf einreichen konnte. Die Auflage, den Museumsentwurf dem Bestand der Kunstsammlung anzupassen, wurde beibehalten. Cuypers reichte erneut zwei Entwürfe im gotischen bzw. im Stil der Renaissance ein. Zur großen Enttäuschung der übrigen Teilnehmer entschied sich die Jury für Cuypers' Renaissance-Entwurf, was ihr den Vorwurf der Voreingenommenheit einbrachte. Doch hatte sich beispielsweise Eberson nicht an eine weitere Bauauflage gehalten und in seinem Entwurf keine Unterführung vom Museum zu den südlich geplanten Stadtvierteln vorgesehen. Außerdem galt sein Vorschlag als zu »griechisch«.
Cuypers' Entwurf entspricht in groben Zügen den schließlich realisierten Plänen; aber noch bevor der erste Pfahl in den Boden gerammt werden konnte, nahm er die erste von zahlreichen Veränderungen vor. Dank der Unterstützung des Innenministers konnte Cuypers nach der offiziellen Auftragserteilung den prämierten Renaissance-Entwurf zur Seite legen und sich – ungeachtet der Einwände von Seiten König Willems III. – ungehindert seinem alternativen Entwurf im gotischen Stil zuwenden. Dennoch kann das Rijksmuseum nicht als neugotisch bezeichnet werden, denn es weist zu viele Merkmale der Renaissance auf. Die meisten Zeitgenossen Cuypers' dachten darüber anders: Ihnen schien der Entwurf zu gotisch und damit zu katholisch. Folglich wurde er dem protestantischen Bevölkerungsteil nicht gerecht, und es hagelte teils sehr heftige Kritik. Hinzu kam die nicht völlig unberechtigte Vermutung, daß die Katholiken mit Hilfe des neugotischen Stils wieder Einfluß gewinnen wollten. Eine solche Entwicklung war den niederländischen Protestanten ein Dorn im Auge, denn nach den Ereignissen des 80jährigen Kriegs gegen Spanien (1568–1648) hatten sie den Katholizismus bis weit ins 19. Jahrhundert hinein unterdrückt. Nun sah man sich plötzlich einem »Putschversuch« gegenüber, den Alberdingk Thijm und Victor de Stuers vorbereitet und Cuypers ausgeführt hatte – das Nationalmuseum erhielt ein katholisches Äußeres. Das neue Museum wurde in Karikaturen denn auch als »Bischofspalais« oder »Kloster des hl. Victor« verspottet. Diese Reaktionen sind auch durch den Anstieg des Baukosten von ursprünglich 800 000 Gulden (während der Ausschreibung auf 1 000 000 Gulden erhöht) auf knapp 3 000 000 Gulden verständlich.
Auch wenn sich seine Doppelfunktion als Museumsbau und Monument 1813 schnell überholte, entwickelte sich das Rijksmuseum zu einem wirklichen Nationalmuseum, da bei der dekorativen Gestaltung die niederländische Kunst im Mittelpunkt stand. Zu den späteren Veränderungen, die nicht von Cuypers selbst vorgenommen wurden, zählen der Abbruch der bunten Innendekorationen (Wandmalereien und Terrazzoböden)[1] sowie die Bebauung der Innenhöfe in den Jahren 1962 und 1969. Dagegen zeichnete Cuypers selbst für verschiedene Aus- und Erweiterungsbauten verantwortlich – wie etwa die Rijksnormaalschool 1892, den Rembrandtsaal (1904–1906), den südlichen Anbau (1906–1908) und den Drucker-Anbau (1911–1915). Zusammen mit dem Museum hatte er zuvor bereits die Direktorenwohnung (freistehend) und die Bibliothek (dem Gebäude angegliedert) fertiggestellt.

1 *Man vertrat die Ansicht, daß die Kunst für sich selbst stehen sollte und Dekorationen nur die Aufmerksamkeit des Betrachters ablenken würden.*

Le Rijksmuseum, Amsterdam

La conception du Rijksmuseum d'Amsterdam représentait un défi intéressant pour les participants au concours et ce pour de multiples raisons. La première tenait à la fonction même de ce futur musée. A cette époque, en Europe, le musée comme forme architecturale était encore en cours de mise au point. Un certain nombre de grandes collections royales ou impériales avaient déjà été ouvertes au public et le Rijksmuseum n'était certainement pas le premier bâtiment construit pour abriter un nouveau musée. En fait, si le désir d'un musée national se faisait jour dans tous les pays européens, sa mise en œuvre en était encore à ses premiers balbutiements et le concept de musée universel n'avait pas encore été mis au point.

Le prestige de la compétition était encore accru par le fait que le bâtiment allait recevoir la plus importante collection existante d'art néerlandais, et le Rijksmuseum deviendrait de ce fait le temple le plus important jamais consacré aux beaux-arts au Royaume des Pays-Bas.
Le second aspect de ce défi, qui mettait en valeur la nature particulière du concours, fut le problème du style qui pouvait convenir à ce futur musée. Ce fut l'un des principaux sujets de discussion dans ce domaine pendant presque tout le dix-neuvième siècle, et les Pays-Bas ne devaient pas y échapper.

Subventions

La première initiative pour la construction d'un musée national avait été prise dès 1862, avec la formation par un groupe de notables d'Amsterdam d'un comité pour la fondation d'un Musée Guillaume 1er, du nom du premier roi des Pays-Bas (1815–1840, monarque amateur d'art). Il était devenu plus que temps de se préoccuper de la question d'un grand musée pour Amsterdam.
Jusqu'alors, la collection de peintures occupait la moitié de la Trippenhuis, un bâtiment officiel datant du XVIIème siècle. Les inconvénients de cette installation sautaient aux yeux: les salles d'exposition des peintures étaient trop sombres, le bâtiment trop petit et le danger d'incendie réel. Il n'était donc guère étonnant que quelques citoyens pleins de bonnes intentions aient pris l'initiative de ce comité. De plus, ils se sentirent encouragés, lorsque le ministre Thorbecke annonça que l'Etat attribuerait une subvention importante au nouveau musée. Le comité se mit à rassembler des fonds avec diligence, et, en avril 1863, lança le concours.
L'objet en était un musée national qui fasse également fonction de monument commémorant l'acquisition de sa souveraineté par l'Etat des Pays-Bas en 1813 (transformé en royaume en 1815). Le comité désigna un jury de huit membres choisis en son sein ainsi que les architectes Godefroy, Rose et Metzelaar. Un bref cahier des charges fut établi qui, si le site de construction était encore inconnu, précisait le programme, les dimensions et les coûts de construction (500 000 fl).

Le premier round

Au total, 19 architectes participèrent à ce concours. Deux d'entre eux, dont Cuypers, soumirent deux projets. Les participations furent présentées de façon anonyme, sous devise. Même après la publication des résultats, les noms des participants écartés ne furent pas publiés. On ne sait donc malheureusement presque rien de leurs propositions.
Le premier prix récompensa les architectes munichois Lange et fils, qui possédaient une certaine expérience en matière muséale puisqu'ils avaient conçu un musée pour Leipzig. Leur projet pour Amsterdam était comparable à celui de Leipzig mais n'était pas admissible pour un musée d'art hollandais.

Deuxième: Cuypers

Cuypers reçut le second prix de 300 fl. Par sécurité, il avait soumis deux projets, chacun proposant deux alternatives de façade: l'une en style gothique, l'autre en style Renaissance. Les deux plans masse comprenaient également un hall central censé accueillir le monument de 1813. Le jury sélectionna le plan A à façade Renaissance.
La devise sous laquelle Cuypers avait présenté ses projets était significative: *«Toute forme qui n'est pas indiquée par la structure doit être repoussée»*. Cette profession de foi fonctionnaliste était signée d'un des maîtres les plus respectés de Cuypers, l'architecte néo-gothique et théoricien français, Viollet-le-Duc. Trois autres architectes se virent enfin attribuer une mention honorable: Louis Radoux (Paris), Charles Peignet (Paris) et L. H. Eberson, architecte du roi (Arnheim).
Aucun des plans ne fut jugé susceptible d'être réalisé. De plus, un membre du jury, Alberdingk Thijm, s'était lancé dans une attaque virulente contre le projet vainqueur, avant même qu'il ne soit exposé. Il envoya des lettres anonymes ou signées de pseudonymes à la presse, dans lesquelles il pourfendait le style «non-hollandais» du gagnant. D'un autre côté, il louait l'expertise et le talent artistique de Cuypers qui était son ami et même son beau-frère. L'ensemble du projet d'un nouveau musée risquait donc fort d'aboutir à une impasse. Le comité essaya d'apaiser le conflit en demandant à Godefroy (membre du jury) de réaliser une adaptation des projets de Cuypers et de Lange. Cet effort se révéla vain car Godefroy déclara rapidement qu'il lui était impossible de respecter le budget prévu.
Un cahier des charges reformulé, fut confié à Eberson, et se révéla tout aussi infructueux. Mécontent que cette commande n'ait pas été proposée à Cuypers, Alberdingk Thijm démissionna du comité.

Avec de nouvelles forces

Ce n'est que neuf ans après ces malheureuses controverses que l'entreprise rédémarra brusquement avec l'inscription du projet de musée – qui prit alors le nom de Rijksmuseum – au budget de l'Etat. La municipalité offrit gratuitement un terrain ainsi que la somme de 100 000 fl. A partir de 1874, un Comité consultatif collabora avec la Commission consultative d'Etat pour l'Art et les Monuments Historiques pour atteindre enfin l'objectif de la construction. Il était en grande partie composé de membres de l'ancien comité, tandis que la nouvelle Commission consultative d'Etat était dominée par la personnalité de Victor de Stuers qui, en dehors de sa qualité reconnue de père fondateur de la protection du patrimoine en Hollande, était également le protecteur respecté d'un autre membre important de la Commission, P. J. H. Cuypers.
La Commission et le Comité suggérèrent au ministre l'organisation d'un nouveau concours auquel les architectes C. Outshoorn, Eberson, Cuypers et D. I. L. Vogel furent invités à participer. Lange était mort et Outshoorn disparut avant d'avoir pu soumettre son projet. La stipulation selon laquelle les projets devaient être adaptés à la présentation d'une collection d'art hollandais des XVIème et XVII ème siècles fut maintenue. Une fois encore, Cuypers proposa un projet gothique et un de style Renaissance. Le second fut choisi à la grande déception des autres participants qui suspectaient le jury d'avoir été influencé. Il faut cependant noter que les plans d'Eberson ne respectaient pas une autre importante stipulation: la création d'un passage sous le musée conduisant aux quartiers sud de la ville dont on prévoyait le développement. Son style fut également considéré comme trop «grec». Le plan qui fut exécuté respectait les principales caractéristiques du projet Cuypers, mais avant (et même après!) le début des travaux, l'architecte y apporta un certain nombre de modifications. Une fois son projet retenu, Cuypers, vit enfin la voie libre et, avec le soutien du Ministre des Affaires Intérieures, écarta le projet Renaissance pour se lancer avec enthousiasme dans le projet gothique malgré les réserves du roi Guillaume III.
Si le Rijksmuseum ne peut pas pour autant être qualifié de gothique (de multiples détails Renaissance furent conservés), de nombreux contemporains de Cuypers virent les choses différemment. Ils pensaient que ce projet était trop gothique et par conséquent trop catholique. Ils expliquaient que ces plans ne tenaient pas compte de l'autre partie de la nation, les protestants, d'où des réactions souvent extrêmement véhémentes. Il fut suggéré, avec un fond de vérité, que le style gothique véhiculait et illustrait le renouveau catholique. Après la guerre de quatre-vingt ans contre l'Espagne (1568–1648), c'était un mouvement que les protestants voyaient encore d'un mauvais œil. C'est même pour cette raison historique que le catholicisme avait été brimé par les protestants jusqu'à tard dans le XIXème siècle. L'affaire fut prise comme une offensive catholique préparée par Alberdingk Thijm et Victor de Stuers et mise en œuvre par Cuypers: le musée national avait l'air catholique! Dans des dessins humoristiques, il était représenté comme le palais de l'évêque ou le Monastère Saint-Victor. Pour couronner le tout, le budget de départ de 800 000 fl (augmenté à 1 million pendant le concours), commença à frôler les 3 millions de florins, ce qui rendait ces réactions assez compréhensibles.
Cependant, même si sa double fonction de musée et de monument commémoratif national fut vite abandonnée, le Rijksmuseum devint digne de son titre de musée national grâce en particulier à l'accent mis sur l'art hollandais dans le programme de décoration. Plus tard, des modifications, non réalisées par Pierre Cuypers lui-même, supprimèrent presque entièrement la décoration intérieure très colorée[1] (murs et sols en terrazzo) et des salles furent construites au-dessus des cours intérieures en 1962 et 1969. Cuypers, cependant, conçut des annexes et des extensions dont l'Ecole normale royale (1892), le Hall Rembrandt (1904–1906), l'extension sud (1906–1908) et l'extension Drucker (1911–1915). Il réalisa également, en même temps que le musée, la résidence du directeur (indépendante du bâtiment principal) et la bibliothèque.

1 *On pensait que les décorations ne feraient que distraire le spectateur.*

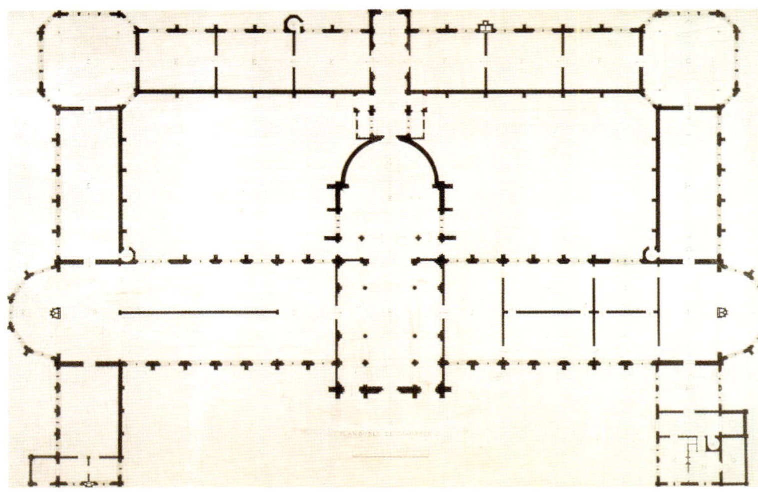

Ludwig Lange & Emil Lange competition design, 1863, project for the "Koning Willem I Museum", 1864, north-east elevation on the canal (front) first prize

Ludwig Lange & Emil Lange competition design, 1863, project for the "Koning Willem I Museum", 1864, transverse section, first prize

P.J.H. Cuypers competition design 1863, project for the "Koning Willem I Museum", alternative B (Neo-Gothic style), 1864, north-east elevation on the canal (front)

P.J.H. Cuypers competition design 1863, project for the "Koning Willem I Museum", alternative B (Neo-Gothic style), 1864, ground floor plan

P.J.H. Cuypers competition design 1863, project for the "Koning Willem I Museum", alternative A (Neo-Gothic style), 1864, exterior perspective on the canal

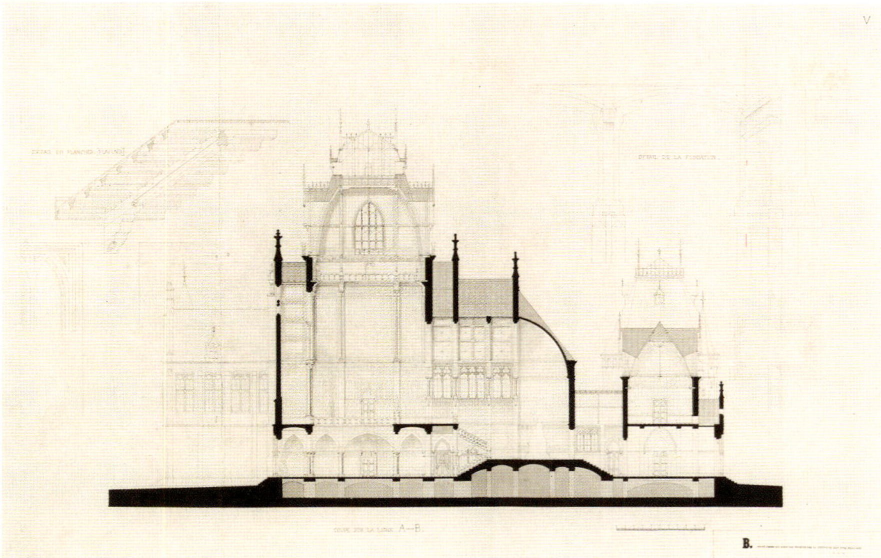

P.J.H. Cuypers competition design 1863, project for the "Koning Willem I Museum", alternative B (Neo-Gothic style), 1864, longitudinal section, detail of ceiling and foundation

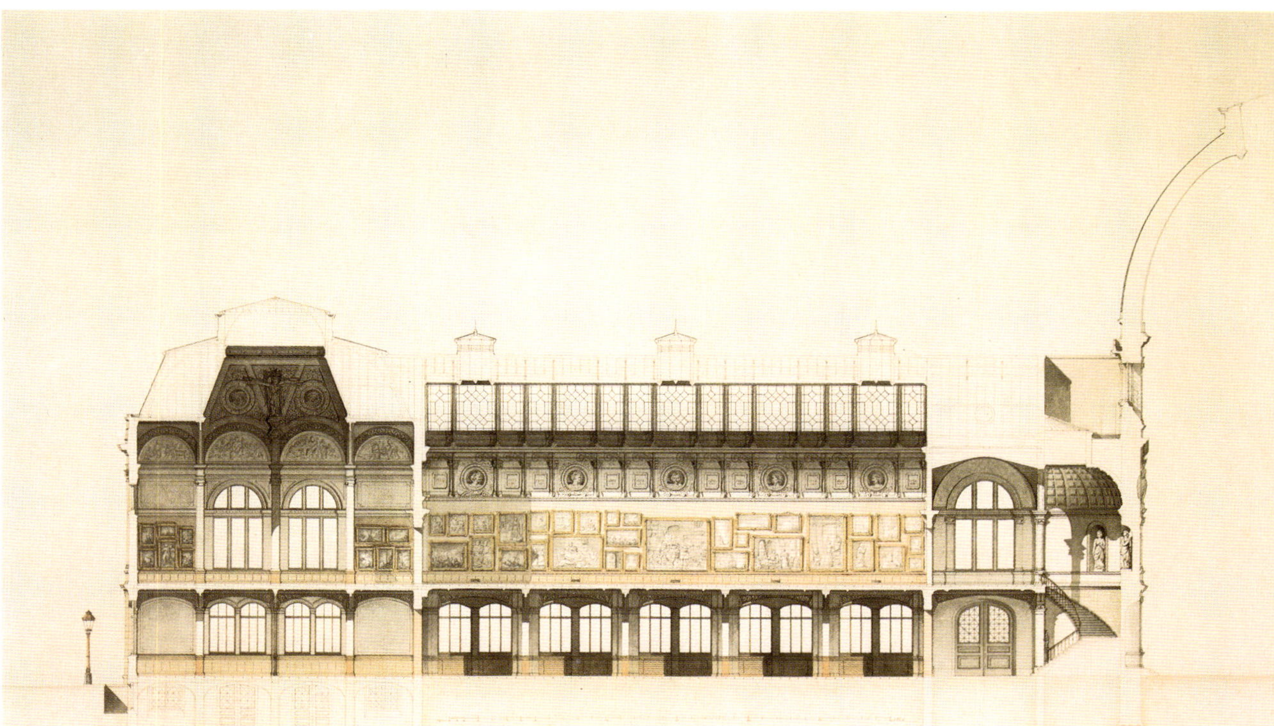

Lucas Hermanus Eberson competition design 1863, project for the "Koning Willem I Museum", 1864, section, honourable mention

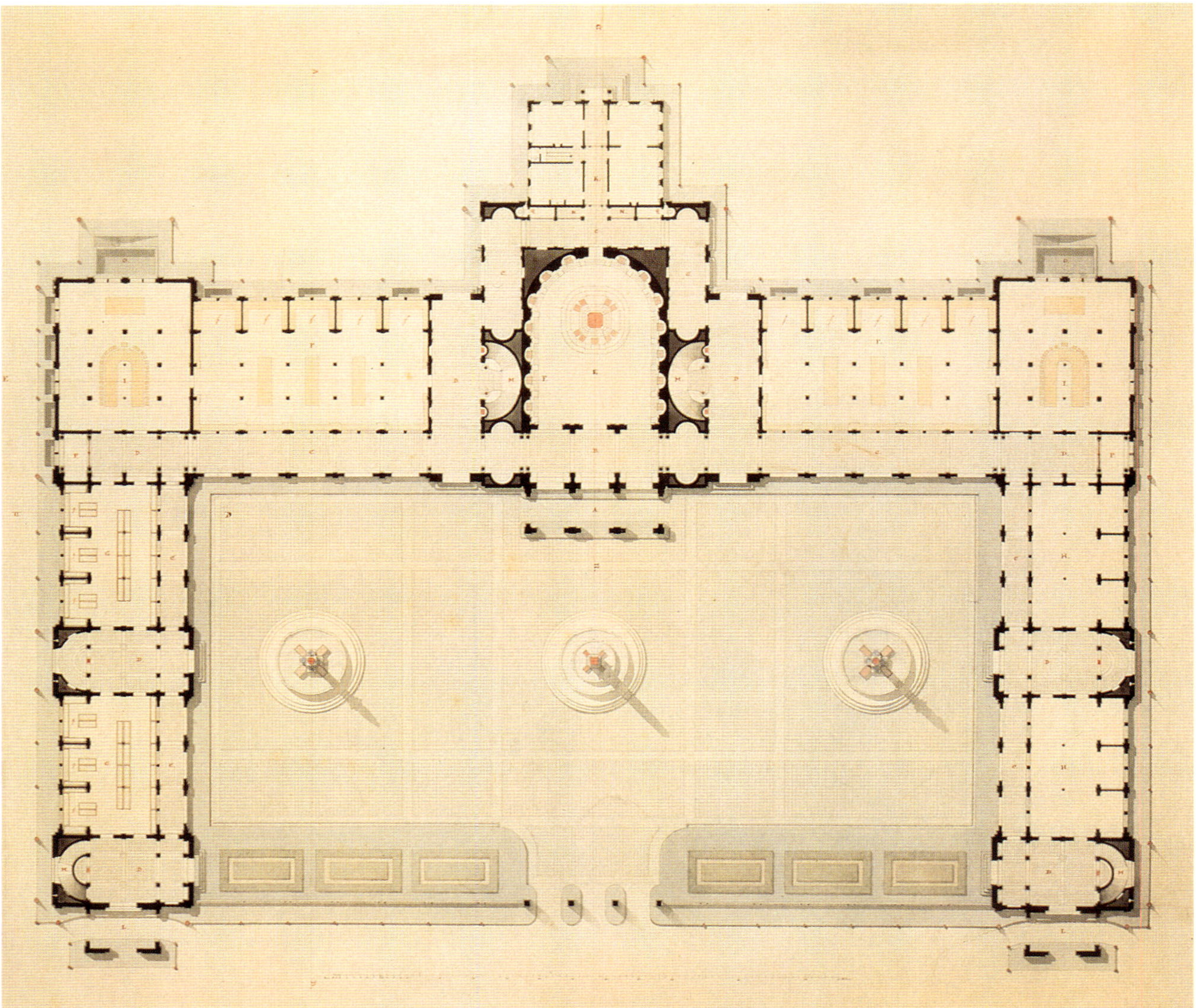

Lucas Hermanus Eberson
competition design 1863, project for the "Koning Willem I Museum", 1864, north-east elevation on the canal (front), honourable mention

Lucas Hermanus Eberson
competition design 1863, project for the "Koning Willem I Museum", 1864, ground floor plan, honourable mention

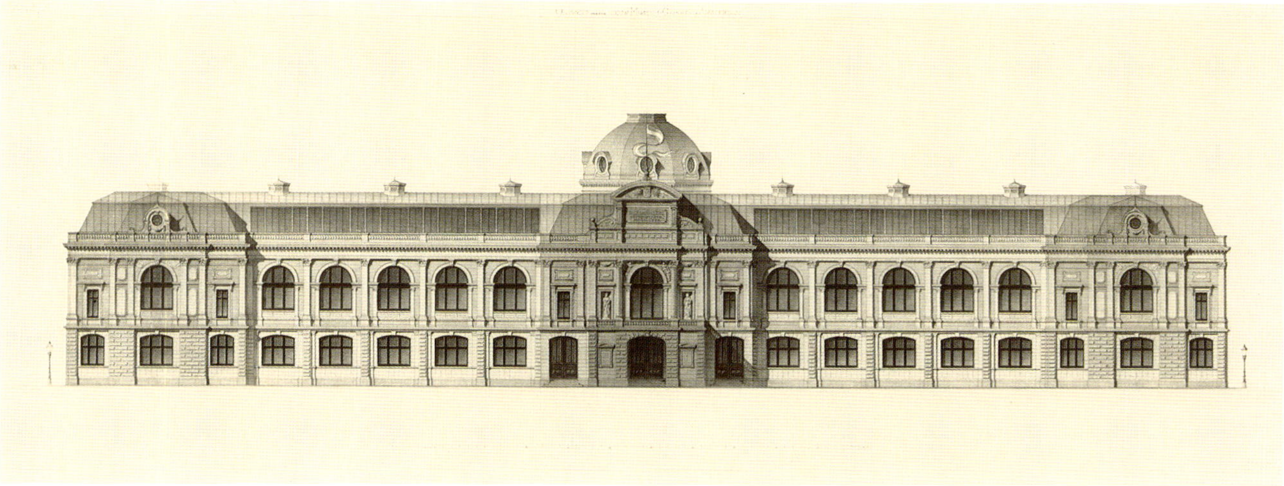

Lucas Hermanus Eberson
competition design 1875, north-east elevation on the canal (front)

Lucas Hermanus Eberson
competition design 1875, longitudinal section

Lucas Hermanus Eberson
competition design 1875, site plan

Rijksmuseum, Amsterdam, 1863–1875

94

P.J.H. Cuypers execution design (16th century style), 1880, part of front elevation on the canal

P.J.H. Cuypers execution design (17th century style), 1877, ground floor plan

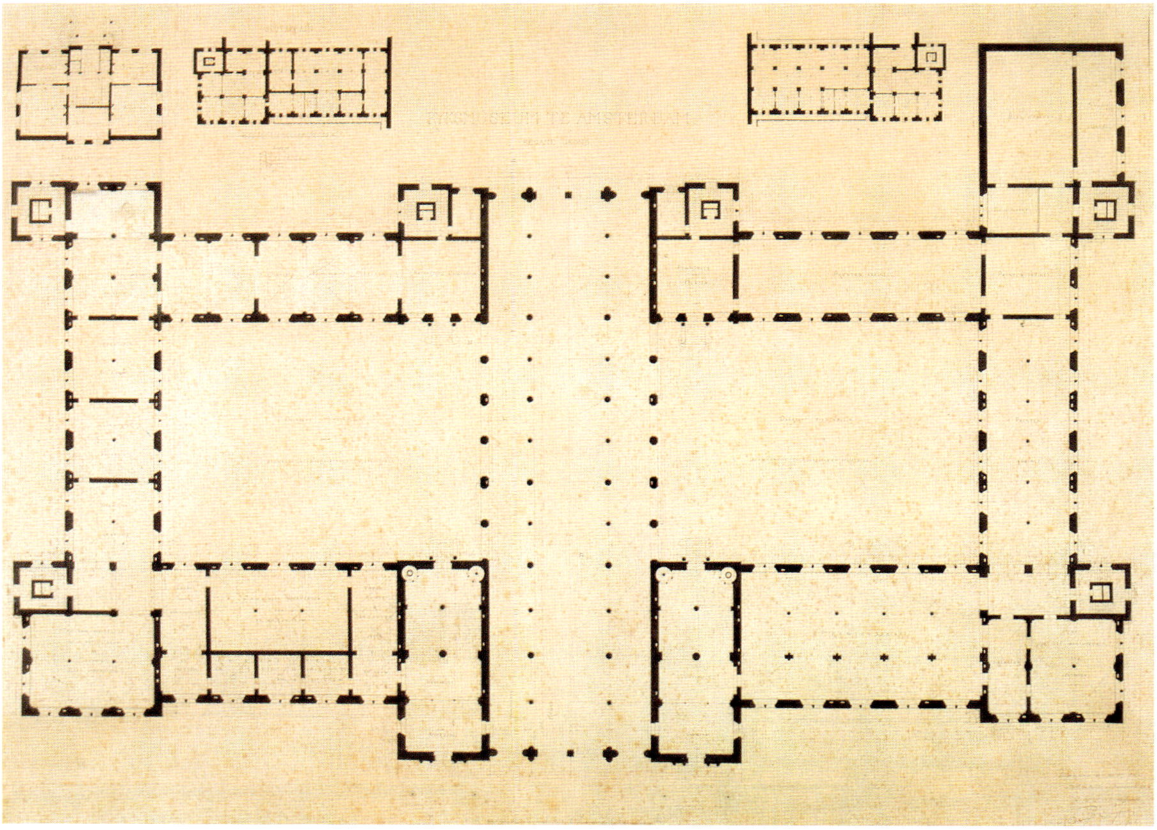

P.J.H. Cuypers execution design (17th century style), 1875, exterior perspective on the canal, first prize

Law Courts, London, 1866

Project

Law Courts

Site

Strand, London

Dates

Competition from 30 April 1866 to 15 December 1866, postponed to 15 January 1867 *Result announced* 29 July 1867 (No official announcement) *Result leaked to the press* 10 August 1867

Number of entries

11 (closed competition), exhibition opened 8 February 1867

Jury

William Cowper (former Commissioner of Works, Chairman), Sir Roundell Palmer and Sir Alexander Cockburn for the Ministry of Justice, William Edwart Gladstone and Sir William Stirling-Maxwell for the Ministry of Finance. Assisted during adjudication by the architects George Pownall and John Shaw

Result

Winners Ewart M. Barry and George Edmund Street *Other participants* George Gilbert Scott, Alfred Waterhouse, William Burges, Henry R. Abraham, John P. Seddon, Thomas N. Deane, Henry B. Garling, Henry F. Lockwood, Raphael Brandon *25 May 1868* Jury decision annulled by government *30 May 1868* Street appointed architect by Ministry of Finance, upon the recommendation of the First Commissioner of Works

Construction

1871 to 1882 (Street died on 18 December 1881)

Architect

George Edmund Street (1824–1881)

Construction cost

1 973 221 pounds (32% more than the 1867 estimate)

Law Courts, London, 1866

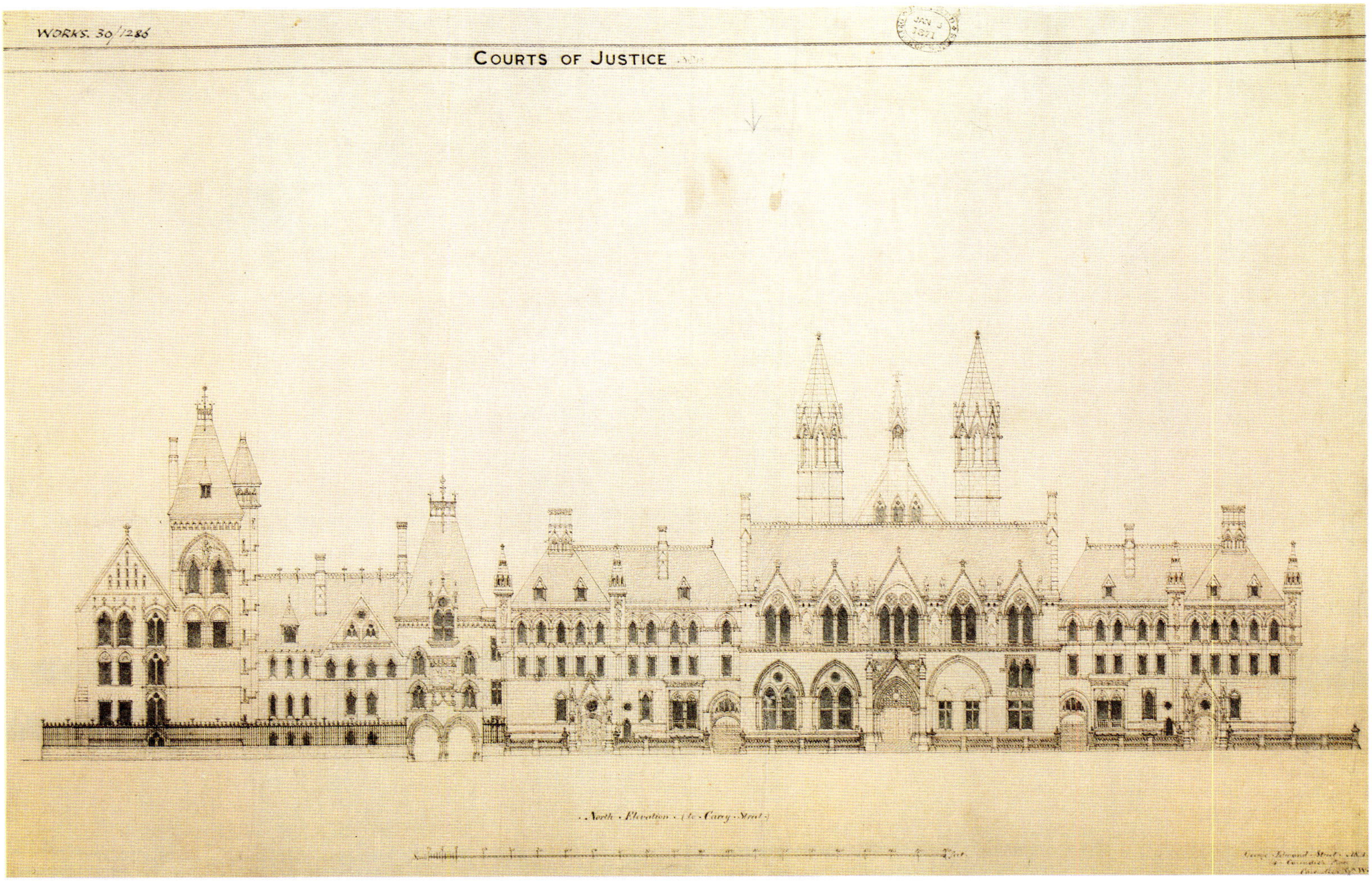

George Edmund Street competition design, 1867, north elevation on Carey Street, first prize

Law Courts, London

Architectural competitions were not uncommon in nineteenth century Britain, but their results were not always equally satisfactory, particularly in cases where the competition concerned prestigious buildings. Notable examples of competitions which may be described as complete fiascos were those for the General Post Office (1819), The Royal Exchange (1838) and the War and Foreign Offices (1856). The debate surrounding the Houses of Parliament may also be added to this ignominious list. The Royal Commission, which was responsible for the new Law Courts, wanted to avoid a repeat performance. However, in spite of their noble intentions, the competition resulted in a debacle.

New law courts had become a necessity because the old buildings in Westminster were too small and expansion in the vicinity was not possible. As early as 1842, Charles Barry, who was working on the Houses of Parliament at the time, submitted a design for the new Law Courts. It was a Classical design, in contrast to the Gothic Revivalist style of the Houses of Parliament. The proposed site at the time was Lincoln's Inn Fields. A second design, drawn up at the request of the Attorney General Richard Bethell (later Lord Chancellor) by his brother-in-law Henry Abraham, was submitted in 1861. Although this plan was never executed, certain sections did form the basis for the competition stipulations. The Law Courts posed an unprecedented architectural challenge. A few weeks after Abraham had submitted his design, the definitive site was announced: the Strand, close to Lincoln's Inn Fields. The existing buildings, mostly old, dilapidated houses, were to be demolished. In 1865, when the necessary permits had been obtained and the land had been procured, the procedure to appoint an architect was set in motion.

Jury selection

With the problems of earlier competitions still fresh in their minds, the Royal Commission had contrived a double-barrelled procedure, which, the members believed, came with the guarantee that there would be no wry faces at the end. This was especially important at the time, because the selection of an appropriate architectural style was a politically sensitive subject, on which the press and public had emphatic opinions. The commission had initially decided that only six architects would be allowed to submit designs, in order to save the jury from not being able to see the wood for the trees. It was also argued that the chosen few would be more motivated. However, the commission itself did not select the architects, but appointed a jury to tackle this task. In an effort to eradicate any chance of prejudice, an all out effort was made to select a balanced jury. The jury consisted of five members. Two were appointed by the Royal Commission, two by the Ministry of Finance and one member was from the Ministry of Public Works: William Cowper (1811–1888), who was also the First Commissioner of Works and the jury chairman. The other jury members were Sir Roundell Palmer (1812–1896), who was Attorney General at the time, and Sir Alexander Cockburn (1802–1880), also from the Ministry of Justice. The Minister of Finance, William Ewart Gladstone (1809–1898) also had a seat on the jury, along with his colleague Sir William Stirling-Maxwell (1818–1878). The former, a political heavyweight who had a particular interest in architecture, would later play a significant part in the competition[1]. Gladstone was personally acquainted with a number of the selected architects and was on particularly good terms with Street. Even though their political views differed, they had a mutual respect for one another and they both believed that architecture and religion were inextricably linked[2]. Both had been influenced by the works of A.W.N. Pugin (1812–1852), in which he argued that Gothic was the only appropriate style for England and that any architect who considered himself a good Christian had a moral obligation to apply this style.

Bias and substitution

Other members of the jury also had ties with the selected architects. It was inevitable that this tangle of interests would lead to the

William Edwart Gladstone

The Royal Courts of Justice (Law Courts)

competition's failure. The first problem arose almost immediately, on 19 February 1866, when the architects were appointed. The chosen six were Edward Barry, Philip Charles Hardwick, George Gilbert Scott, George Edmund Street, Alfred Waterhouse and Thomas Henry Wyatt. Raphael Brandon and Thomas Deane were the possible substitutes. Hardwick and Wyatt immediately decided that they would not participate and they were soon followed by Scctt and Barry. The two vacant positions were immediately taken by Brandon and Deane, and the jury appointed Henry Garling and George Somers Clarke as additional replacements. They declined the offer on grounds of other commitments. The new substitutes were John Gibson and John Seddon. The field now consisted of architects with a preference for Gothic Revival. This was probably one of the reasons why the matter was raised in parliament and a motion was passed that the number of participants should be increased. Their number was raised to twelve and later reduced to eleven. Scott and Barry now agreed to participate. Seddon, the substitute, was invited to participate, along with Henry Abraham (who had already submitted a design in 1861), Henry Lockwood and William Burges. The other substitute, Gibson, had other commitments.

There were now nine Gothic Revivalists in a field of eleven. The selection made by the jury, most of whom were liberals, was proof of the fact that the Gothic Revival was not a specifically conservative style, but a national style with a broad base of support[3].

The task facing the eleven participants was not an easy one. Firstly, there was the problem of organisation: an incredible number of rooms and 23 courtrooms had to be logically incorporated. A related problem centred around the question as to whether a central hall should be included and, if so, what function it should have. Although the competition stipulations mentioned a meeting place, no dimensions had been specified.

Another problem concerned the question as to how the Gothic Style could be suitably applied in a complex of this size. The extended façade along the Strand was seen as particularly problematic. Sufficient light and ventilation were required and the public should not get in the way of the legal community. In addition, the halls and rooms for common law and equity had to be separate. The participants had to solve these problems between 30 April and 15 December 1866, later extended to 15 January 1867. As of 8 February 1867, more than 250 of the submitted drawings were on display in a specially designed building on New Square, Lincoln's Inn (William Burnett). At set times the exhibition was open to the press and public.

All the designs, even those of the Classicists, had been drawn in Gothic Revivalist style, even though a religious building was not in the offing. Whereas twenty years before the Classicists and the Gothic Revivalists were still struggling for supremacy, the latter had now reached the peak of their popularity. However, the press still had objections. Designs with a Gothic appearance, but constructed along Classical lines, bore the brunt of the criticism. Garling, Lockwood and Barry were severely criticised, although an occasional positive voice could be heard in the storm. Another point of criticism concerned the monotony of certain designs, such as Scott's. Burges' design, with its impressive 460 foot (154 metre) high archival tower, was particularly well received and was in keeping with the architectural preferences of the day: not the symmetrical, somewhat rigid Gothic style of Charles Barry's Houses of Parliament, but the asymmetrical Gothic style which had its roots in the thirteenth century.

Street's design was a compromise between the two styles: regular, horizontal façades offset by vertical towers, intentionally positioned asymmetrically. Like most of the other entries, his design included a central hall onto which the courtrooms opened out. Most of the

Joseph Poelaert Brussels Courts of Justice, entrance level plan

Joseph Poelaert Brussels Courts of Justice, main entrance

Joseph Poelaert Brussels Courts of Justice, longitudinal section

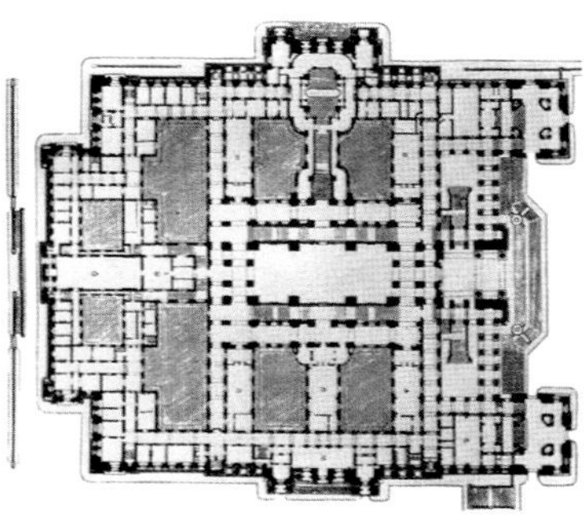

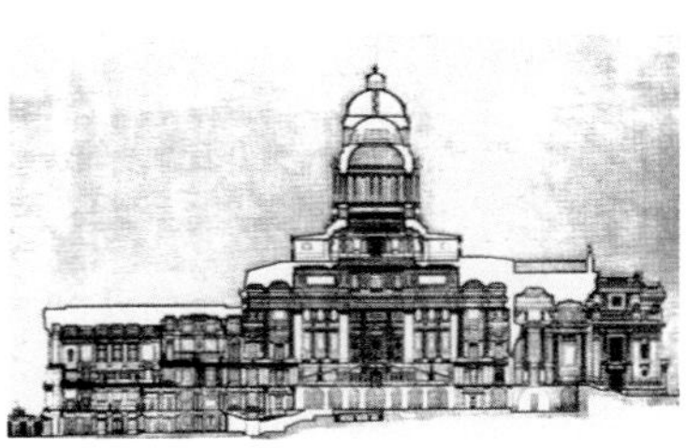

solicitors' and barristers' chambers were situated in a second, wider circle. This too mirrored the designs of the other participants.

Adjudication

In order to ensure the quality of their judgement, the jury called in the assistance of the architects George Shaw and John Pownall. The two architects drafted a report in which they specified how many of the 88 problems presented to the participants had been satisfactorily solved. Barry's was the most successful design, with a score of 41, followed by Scott (25) and Lockwood (9), with Street in eighth place with three (!) points. A commission of advocates and the public prosecutors were also asked to give their opinions. They chose Waterhouse. The jury reached a decision on 29 July and, although it was initially kept a secret, the news leaked out. According to the jury, none of the plans was suitable, but they ruled that Barry's design was the best in terms of the floor plan and the subdivision of the quarters and that Street's was the best in terms of composition. The jury recommended that the two architects should work together on a final design. Although Waterhouse probably had the support of Palmer and Cockburn, it is rumoured that Gladstone and Stirling-Maxwell (Street) had struck a tacit agreement with Pownall and Shaw (Barry) in order to sideline the other three members of the jury. However, the state was not satisfied with the half-hearted result. The Ministry of Finance demanded that the decision should be reconsidered. Not only Barry and Street but also the other participants were understandably indignant at seeing a lucrative commission, already within arm's reach for some (Burges, Waterhouse), slipping away. The press also took a lively interest in the delicate affair, generally expressing their opinions in critical terms. Eventually, the 'winners' were prepared to collaborate. Their change of mind was probably prompted by their fear that the jury would change its decision. Eventually, the unfortunate matter was debated in the House of Commons on 15 May 1868. After all, public funds were at issue.
In the meantime, yet another process had been set in motion by the Royal Commission, who had advised the Ministry of Finance as to which course of action it should take. It was decided that the Attorney General, who had earlier been appointed arbiter, should assess whether Street and Barry could be offered a combined commission and whether the other participants would be allowed to make a further contribution. Barry, however, had changed his mind. He said that he could not possibly collaborate with Street and, on careful examination of the competition stipulations, had concluded that he, and not Street, was most eligible to be offered the commission for the project. Karslake, who was Attorney General at the time, submitted his report on 14 May 1868– the Ministry was under no obligation to uphold the joint commission it had offered to Street and Barry, and the architects could derive no rights from the earlier decision. This gave the Ministry of Finance a free hand in the appointment of an architect.

While the debate in the House of Commons was still in full swing, the First Lord of the Treasury, Benjamin Disraeli, and the Minister of Finance, George Ward Hunt, appointed George Edmund Street as sole architect of the Law Courts, the largest state project of the era. Probably as a consolation prize, Barry won the competition for the design of the National Gallery and Waterhouse was appointed architect of the Natural History Museum. It is worth mentioning that Barry was never commissioned to build the National Gallery. William Wilkins was appointed architect. Street later radically altered his original design. The Strand façade, in particular, which was almost completely symmetrical at first, was later transformed into an asymmetrical and less monumental (i.e. picturesque) façade. He also scrapped the free-standing archival tower and the Italian-looking campaniles. A notable change to the floor plan was that the public hall, which was situated at the heart of the complex in the original design, was moved closer to the Strand, making it more accessible to the public. However, the monumental Gothic style of the hall was retained, forming a rather striking contrast with the modest Strand façade. The original division was removed to form one large hall.
In his later years, Street developed a greater affinity for early English Gothic, as did so many of his younger contemporaries. However, the issue would not occupy him long. He died on 18 December 1881, just before the Law Courts were completed, or, as the Westminster Guardian put it three days later: *"Within sight of the port"*.

1 *This liberal statesman, who was Minister of Finance, later became Prime Minister. His conservative opponent was Benjamin Disraeli (1874–1880), who became Prime Minister in 1868.*

2 *Street had even dedicated his book on Spanish architecture (1865) to Gladstone.*

3 *This view was based on the fiasco surrounding the competition for the War and Foreign Offices.*

Law Courts, London

Im Großbritannien des 19. Jahrhunderts waren Architekturwettbewerbe längst keine Seltenheit mehr, aber sie führten nur in wenigen Fällen zu befriedigenden Ergebnissen. Sowohl die Ausschreibung für das General Post Office (1819) als auch die Architekturwettbewerbe für die Royal Exchange (1838) und die War and Foreign Offices (1856) hatten zu einem Fiasko geführt, und auch die Diskussion um die Ausschreibung für das Parlamentsgebäude (Houses of Parliament, 1835) erwies sich als peinliche Angelegenheit.

Weil das alte Gerichtsgebäude in Westminster Hall längst zu klein und ein Erweiterungsbau in der unmittelbaren Umgebung unmöglich war, benötigte man dringend neue Räumlichkeiten für die königlichen Gerichtshöfe. Bereits 1842 hatte Charles Barry, zu diesem Zeitpunkt mit der Errichtung des Parlamentsgebäudes beauftragt, einen ersten klassizistischen Entwurf für die Law Courts angefertigt, der sich deutlich vom neugotischen Stil seines Parlamentsgebäudes unterschied. Als Standort für die Gerichtshöfe war damals noch Lincoln's Inn Fields vorgesehen. 1861 reichte Henry Abraham – auf Bitte seines Schwagers, Generalstaatsanwalt Richard Bethell (des späteren Lord Chancellor) – einen zweiten Entwurf ein. Obwohl auch diese Konstruktionspläne nicht ausgeführt wurden, dienten sie bei der Ausschreibung als Ausgangspunkt für die Bauauflagen. Wenige Wochen später wurde der endgültige Standort für die neuen Gerichtsgebäude bekanntgegeben: der »Strand«, in der Nähe von Lincoln's Inn Fields. Allerdings mußte die vorhandene Bebauung, hauptsächlich alte Häuser in schlechtem Zustand, dafür abgerissen werden. Als 1865 alle notwendigen Genehmigungen erteilt und das entsprechende Bauland gekauft war, konnte das Verfahren zur Ernennung des Architekten eingeleitet werden.

Die Jury wählt aus

Die Royal Commission beschloß, daß sich nur sechs Architekten an der Ausschreibung beteiligen durften. Auf diese Weise wollte man gewährleisten, daß die Jury alle Vorschläge genau prüfen konnte. Außerdem, so die Argumentation, seien die Auserwählten dann besonders motiviert. Die Kommission überließ die Wahl dieser sechs Architekten einer eigens berufenen Jury, auf deren ausgewogene Zusammenstellung man sehr viel Wert legte, um jeglichen Vorwurf der Bevorteilung auszuschließen. Die Jury bestand aus fünf Mitgliedern. Zwei Juroren benannte die Royal Commission: Sir Roundell Palmer (1812–1896) – zu diesem Zeitpunkt Generalstaatsanwalt – und Sir Alexander Cockburn (1802–1880), ebenfalls vom Justizministerium. Zwei weitere Juroren ernannte das Finanzministerium – Sir William Stirling-Maxwell (1818–1878) und den Finanzminister, William Ewart Gladstone (1809–1898)–, während das Ministerium für öffentliche Arbeiten William Cowper (1811–1888) als Jurymitglied stellte, der zugleich Vorsitzender der Jury und First Commissioner of Works war. Gladstone, eine politische Größe mit besonderer Vorliebe für die Architektur, sollte im weiteren Verlauf der Ausschreibung eine wichtige Rolle spielen. Außerdem kannte er einige der auserwählten Architekten persönlich und stand auf besonders freundschaftlichem Fuß mit Street. Beide waren von den Werken A.W.N. Pugins (1812–1852) beeinflußt, der die Gotik als einzig wahren Stil für England propagierte und sie sogar als moralische Pflicht eines jeden gottesfürchtigen Architekten erachtete.

Ersatzprobleme

Aber auch die anderen Jurymitglieder hatten besondere Beziehungen zu den auserwählten Architekten. Dieser Interessenskonflikt mußte zwangsläufig zum Scheitern der Ausschreibung führen. Das erste Problem stellte sich unmittelbar nachdem am 19. Februar 1866, an dem die sechs Architekten – Edward Barry, Philip Charles Hardwick, George Gilbert Scott, George Edmund Street, Alfred Waterhouse und Thomas Henry Wyatt – benannt worden waren. Auf der Reserveliste standen Raphael Brandon und Thomas Deane. Hardwick und Wyatt lehnten eine Teilnahme an der Ausschreibung sofort ab, kurze Zeit später schlossen sich ihnen Scott und Barry an. Die ersten beiden vakanten Plätze ließen sich durch Brandon und Deane auffüllen, nach den nächsten beiden Absagen entschied sich die Jury für Henry Garling und George Somers Clarke, der dieses Angebot jedoch ebenfalls aus zeitlichen Gründen ablehnen mußte. Auf der neuen Reserveliste befanden sich nun John Gibson und John Seddon, durch deren Nominierung sich der gesamte Teilnehmerkreis ausschließlich aus Architekten mit einer Vorliebe für die Neugotik zusammensetzte. Diese Entscheidung führte zu einer heftigen Debatte im Parlament. Die Zahl der Teilnehmer würde zunächst auf zwölf erhöht und später wieder auf elf Architekten beschränkt. Scott und Barry beteiligten sich nun doch an der Ausschreibung, Seddon erhielt eine Einladung, und Henry Abraham, Henry Lockwood sowie William Burges wurden ebenfalls gebeten, am Wettbewerb teilzunehmen. Der zweite Architekt der Reserveliste, John Gibson, war aufgrund anderer Verpflichtungen verhindert.
In der neuen Teilnehmergruppe favorisierten noch neun Architekten die Neugotik. Diese von einer hauptsächlich aus liberalen Honoratioren bestehenden Jury getroffene Auswahl bewies, daß es sich bei der Neugotik nicht um einen konservativen, sondern um einen nationalen Stil handelte, der in breiten Bevölkerungskreisen auf große Zustimmung stieß.
Alle Entwürfe – auch die der Anhänger des Klassizismus – waren im neugotischen Stil gehalten, obwohl es sich um ein weltliches Gebäude handelte. Während noch 20 Jahre zuvor Klassizismus und Neugotik erbittert um die Vorherrschaft gekämpft hatten, waren die Vertreter des neugotischen Stils, der mit diesem Gebäude seinen Höhepunkt erreichte, in der Mehrheit.

Das Urteil

Bei der Beurteilung der Entwürfe bat die Jury die Architekten George Shaw und John Pownall um fachliche Hilfe. In ihrem Bericht legten sie dar, ob die 88 aufgeführten Problembereiche von den einzelnen Einsendern gelöst worden waren. Barry erreichte mit 41 Punkten die Höchstzahl, mit weitem Abstand vor Scott (25) und Lockwood (9). Street erreichte mit 3 (!) Punkten den achten Platz. Außerdem holte man die Meinung einer Anwaltskommission sowie zahlreicher Staatsanwälte ein, die sich für den Entwurf von Alfred Waterhouse entschieden. Die Jury selbst traf ihre Entscheidung am 29. Juli 1867. Trotz anfänglicher Geheimhaltung sickerte das Ergebnis kurze Zeit später an die Presse durch: Die Jury erachtete keinen einzigen Entwurf als wirklich geeignet, prämierte aber Barrys Pläne aufgrund der räumlichen Aufteilung und Streets Entwurf wegen der kompositorischen Gestaltung und empfahl, die endgültigen Pläne von beiden Architekten gemeinsam erarbeiten zu lassen. Schließlich erklärten sich die »Gewinner« zu einer Zusammenarbeit bereit – ihr Sinneswandel beruhte wahrscheinlich auf der Befürchtung, daß die Jury ihren Beschluß zurücknehmen könnte.
In der Zwischenzeit hatte die Royal Commission beschlossen, die Angelegenheit dem bereits zuvor zum Schiedsrichter ernannten Attorney General vorzulegen. Er sollte entscheiden, ob Street und Barry den Auftrag gemeinsam erhalten würden und ob die anderen Teilnehmer eventuelle Ergänzungen hinzufügen durften. Mittlerweile hatte Barry jedoch seine Meinung geändert und verkündete, daß er unmöglich mit Street zusammenarbeiten könne und – aufgrund einer sorgfältigen Analyse der Bauauflagen – zu der Ansicht gekommen sei, daß nur er und nicht Street für den Bauauftrag in Frage käme. Der zu diesem Zeitpunkt amtierende Generalstaatsanwalt Karslake reichte seinen Bericht am 14. Mai 1868 ein: Das Ministerium sei in keinster Weise an den Doppelauftrag gebunden, und weder Street noch Barry könnten aus der vorherigen Auszeichnung irgendein Anrecht ableiten. Auf diese Weise erhielt das Finanzministerium die Möglichkeit, nach eigenem Gutdünken einen Architekten zu benennen.
Während man im Unterhaus noch heftig debattierte, ernannten der First Lord of Treasury, Premierminister Benjamin Disraeli und der Finanzminister George Ward Hunt den Baumeister George Edmund Street zum alleinigen Architekten der Law Courts, dem größten staatlichen Bauvorhaben der damaligen Zeit. Vermutlich erhielt Barry als eine Art Trostpreis den ersten Platz bei der Ausschreibung für die National Gallery, Waterhouse bekam den Auftrag für das Natural History Museum. Dennoch durfte Barry die National Gallery nicht bauen; der Bauauftrag ging an William Wilkins. Street mußte seinen ersten Entwurf erheblich überarbeiten. So wurde beispielsweise die ursprünglich fast symmetrische Gebäudefront entlang des »Strand« in eine asymmetrische und weniger monumentale (sprich: pittoreske) Fassade verwandelt. Auch der imposante freistehende Archivturm und die italienisch anmutenden Campanilen verschwanden. Ein Blick auf beide Grundrisse zeigt, daß die Public Hall, die sich anfänglich in der Mitte des Gebäudekomplexes befand, zum »Strand« hin verschoben wurde, damit sie für den Publikumsverkehr ungehindert zugänglich war. Allerdings behielt man den monumentalen gotischen Stil für die Halle bei, was angesichts der bescheidenen Fassade am »Strand« verwunderlich erscheint. Die ursprüngliche Unterteilung wurde zugunsten einer einzigen großen Halle aufgehoben.
Während seiner späteren Lebensjahre fühlte sich Street – wie viele seiner jungen Zeitgenossen – stärker zur frühen englischen Gotik hingezogen, der er sich aber nicht mehr lange widmen konnte. Er starb am 18. Dezember 1881, kurz vor der Fertigstellung der Law Courts – oder wie es der Westminster Guardian drei Tage später formulierte: »*Within sight of the port*«.

Le Palais de Justice, Londres

Si les concours d'architecture furent assez fréquents en Grande-Bretagne au XIXème siècle, leurs résultats ne répondirent pas toujours aux attentes, en particulier dans le cas des bâtiments prestigieux. Les concours pour le General Post Office (1819), le Royal Exchange (1838) et le Ministère de la Guerre et des Affaires étrangères (1856) peuvent ainsi être qualifiés de fiascos. Les controverses que suscita celui du Palais de Westminster (Houses of Parliament, 1935) permettent sans doute de l'ajouter à cette liste. La Commission royale, responsable des nouvelles Law Courts (Palais de justice), souhaitait éviter qu'une telle expérience ne se renouvelle. En dépit de ses nobles intentions, son concours se transforma vite en une débâcle.

La nécessité d'un nouveau palais de justice s'imposait. L'ancien bâtiment de Westminster était devenu trop exigu et il était impossible de l'agrandir. Dès 1842, Charles Barry, qui travaillait alors sur le Parlement, avait proposé un plan d'esprit classique, très différent donc du style néo-gothique de son Palais de Westminster pour le site de Lincoln's Inn Fields. Un second projet, à l'initiative du Procureur général Richard Bethell (plus tard Lord Chancelier) et présenté par son beau-frère Henry Abraham fut soumis en 1861. Bien qu'il n'ait pas été retenu, certaines de ses caractéristiques servirent de base au cahier des charges du concours. Ce nouveau palais représentait un défi architectural sans précédent. Quelques semaines après qu'Abraham eût déposé son projet, le site définitif fut annoncé: le Strand, près de Lincoln's Inn Field. Les bâtiments existants, pour l'essentiel de vieilles maisons décrépites, devaient être abattus. En 1865, dès que les permis nécessaires furent obtenus et le terrain dégagé, la procédure de choix d'un architecte fut mise en route.

La sélection du jury

Obnubilée par les difficultés rencontrées lors de précédents concours, la Commission royale mit au point une procédure en deux temps qui, pensait-elle, devait garantir l'objectivité et le bon déroulement du processus. A cette époque, les styles architecturaux faisaient partie des sujets politiquement sensibles sur lesquels la presse et le public défendaient des positions tranchées et l'on ne pouvait prendre trop de précautions. La Commission décida tout d'abord de limiter à six le nombre des participants pour épargner au jury d'être noyé sous les projets et mieux motiver les participants. Néanmoins, elle ne choisit pas elle-même les architectes mais nomma un jury à cet effet. Afin d'éviter tout risque de partialité, on s'efforça d'équilibrer la composition de ce jury de cinq membres. Deux étaient nommés par la Commission royale, deux par le Ministère des Finances et un par celui des Travaux Publics. William Cowper (1811–1888) Premier commissaire des Travaux présidait le jury. Gladstone connaissait personnellement un certain nombre des architectes retenus et entretenait d'excellentes relations avec Street.

Préjugés et substitution

D'autres membres du jury entretenaient, eux aussi, des liens avec les architectes choisis. Il était donc inévitable que cet écheveau d'intérêts ne mène à l'échec du concours. Le premier problème apparut dès le 19 février 1866. Les six praticiens retenus étaient Edward Barry, Philip Charles Hardwick, George Gilbert Scott, George Edmund Street, Alfred Waterhouse et Thomas Henry Wyatt; Raphael Brandon et Thomas Deane étant suppléants. Hardwick et Wyatt décidèrent immédiatement de se retirer, rapidement suivis par Scott et Barry. Les deux places ainsi libérées furent reprises par Brandon et Deane et le jury désigna comme nouveaux suppléants Henry Garling et George Somers Clarke. Ce dernier, pris par ailleurs, refusa la proposition. Les nouveau suppléants furent alors John Gibson et John Seddon. Les architectes choisis étaient tous des adeptes du style néo-gothique. Des pressions se firent alors jour au Parlement pour qu'une motion d'augmentation du nombre des participants soit votée. Leur nombre passa à douze, réduit ultérieurement à onze. Scott et Barry acceptèrent alors de se lancer dans la compétition. Seddon, le suppléant, fut invité à participer ainsi que Henry Robert Abraham (l'auteur du projet de 1860/1861), Henry Lockwood et William Burges. L'autre suppléant, Gibson, avait d'autres engagements. On comptait donc maintenant neuf «néo-gothiques» sur onze. La sélection opérée par le jury, des libéraux pour la plupart, prouvait que le «Gothic Revival» n'était pas un style foncièrement conservateur mais une expression quasi nationale bénéficiant d'importants soutiens .
La tache assignée aux onze participants n'était pas facile et l'organisation de l'espace délicate: un nombre incroyable de bureaux et 23 chambres devaient s'articuler de façon logique. Fallait-il un hall central? Quelle fonction devait-il remplir? Le cahier des charges mentionnait bien un lieu de rencontre, mais sans en spécifier les dimensions.
L'autre grande difficulté résidait dans le style néo-gothique et son application à un édifice de cette taille. La longue façade sur le Strand était particulièrement difficile à traiter. Il fallait aussi régler les problèmes de l'éclairage et de la ventilation et trouver des circulations qui empêchent le public et les hommes de loi de se croiser. De plus, les halls et les chambres pour le civil et le pénal ne pouvaient qu'être séparés.
Tous les projets, même ceux des classiques, avaient été traités en style néo-gothique, bien qu'il ne s'agisse pas d'un bâtiment religieux. Si vingt ans plus tôt, les néo-classiques et les néo-gothiques se battaient encore, ces derniers touchaient enfin au sommet de leur gloire.
La presse n'en émit pas moins quelques objections. Les propositions d'apparence néo-gothique, mais élaborées selon des canons classiques, ne pouvaient que susciter les critiques. Garling, Lockwood et Barry furent dans l'ensemble sévèrement jugés. D'autres reproches s'adressaient à la monotonie de certains dessins, comme celui de Scott. Le plan de Burges, avec son impressionnante tour d'archives de 154 m de haut, fut très bien reçu tant il correspondait aux attentes de l'époque: un style qui ne soit pas le gothique rigide de Charles Barry pour Westminster, mais plutôt un gothique asymétrique prenant ses racines dans le XIIIème siècle.
Le projet de Street était un compromis entre ces deux approches: des façades régulières, horizontales, modulées par des tours verticales, volontairement asymétriques. Comme dans la plupart des propositions, il comprenait un hall central sur lequel donnaient les différentes chambres. La plupart des bureaux des conseillers de la couronne et avocats étaient situés sur un second cercle, plus vaste, formule également employée dans les autres participations.

L'adjudication

Pour conforter la valeur technique de leur jugement, les jurés avaient fait appel aux architectes George Shaw et John Pownall qui notèrent la façon dont les 88 problèmes soumis aux participants avait été résolus. Barry se retrouvait premier avec une note de 41, suivi par Scott (25) et Lockwood (9), Street arrivant en huitième position avec 3 points (!). L'opinion d'une commission d'avocats et de procureurs fut également sollicitée: elle opta pour Waterhouse. Le jury prit sa décision en secret le 29 juillet (mais une fuite se produisit en direction de la presse): selon les jurés, aucun projet n'était satisfaisant, mais celui de Barry était le meilleur en termes de plan de masse et de répartition des fonctions et celui de Street préférable pour sa composition. Le jury recommandait de faire retravailler ces deux architectes. Les «gagnants» étaient prêts à collaborer, craignant sans doute que le jury ne change d'avis. Le sujet finit par être l'objet d'un débat à la Chambres des Communes le 15 mai 1868 puisqu'il s'agissait quand même de fonds publics.
Une autre procédure fut lancée par la Commission royale qui avait conseillé le Ministère des Finances sur la meilleure voie à suivre. Il fut décidé que le problème devait être soumis au procureur général, précédemment désigné comme arbitre. Il devait dire si l'on pouvait offrir une commande commune à Street et Barry et si les autres participants avaient le droit de faire de nouvelles propositions. Entre temps, Barry avait changé d'avis et déclara qu'il ne pouvait en aucun cas travailler avec Street et qu'après avoir attentivement examiné le cahier des charges, il pensait que seul son projet, et non celui de Street, répondait à ses spécifications. Karslake, Procureur général, présenta son rapport le 14 mai 1868: le Ministère n'était pas obligé de maintenir la double commande offerte à Street et Barry et les architectes n'étaient pas fondés de se prévaloir de cette décision. Le ministère des Finances retrouvait ainsi la liberté de désigner son architecte.
Alors que le débat parlementaire battait son plein, le premier Lord du Trésor, Benjamin Disraeli, et le ministre des Finances, George Ward Hunt, nommèrent George Edmund Street unique architecte des Law Courts, le plus ambitieux projet architectural de l'époque. Comme prix de consolation, Barry remporta le concours de la National Gallery et Waterhouse fut nommé architecte du Natural History Museum. En fait Barry ne construisit pas la National Gallery qui revint finalement à Wilkins.
Street allait profondément modifier son premier projet. La façade sur le Strand en particulier, complètement symétrique à l'origine, se retrouva asymétrique et moins monumentale (en un mot plus 'picturesque'). Il supprima la tour des archives et les campaniles dans le goût italien.
Plus tard, comme beaucoup de ses jeunes contemporains, Street allait s'intéresser de plus en plus au Gothique «Early English». Il mourut peu avant que son Palais de justice ne soit terminé ou, comme l'écrivit le «Westminster Guardian», *«en vue du port»*.

1 Cette vue reposait sur le fiasco des concours pour le Ministère de la Guerre et des Affaires étrangères.

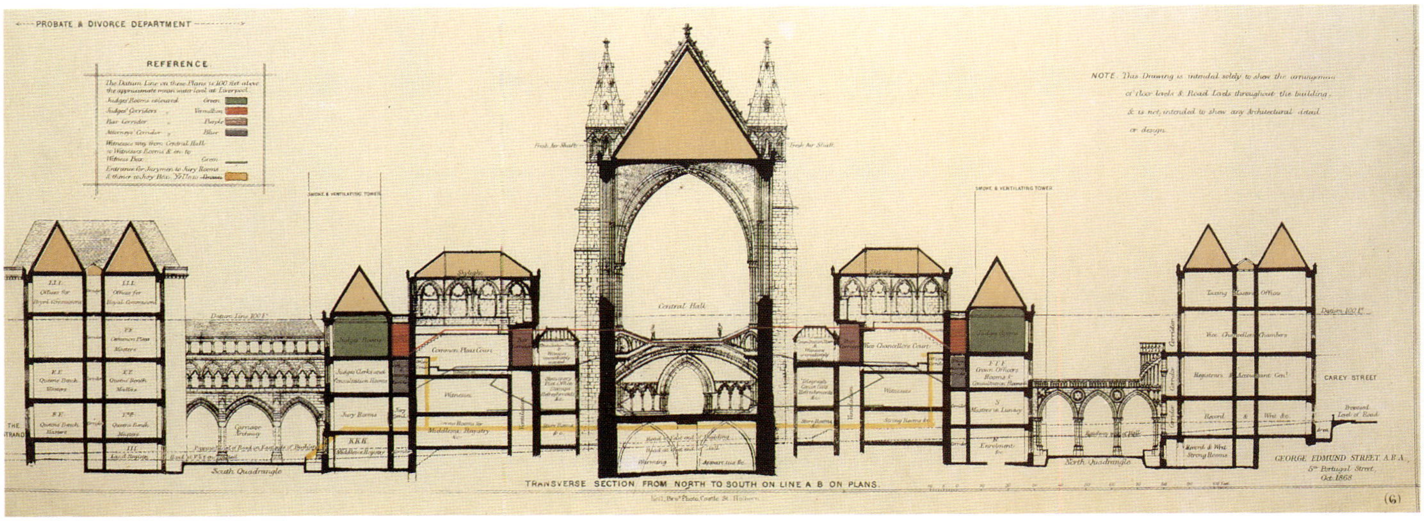

George Edmund Street final design 1868, top: part of section East to West, bottom: part of section North to South, first prize

George Edmund Street competition design, 1867, bird's eye view, first prize

William Burges competition design, 1867, bird's eye view

Raphael Brandon competition design, 1867, interior perspective of the Great Hall

George Edmund Street competition design, 1867, detail of the spire, first prize

George Edmund Street competition design, 1867, ground floor plan

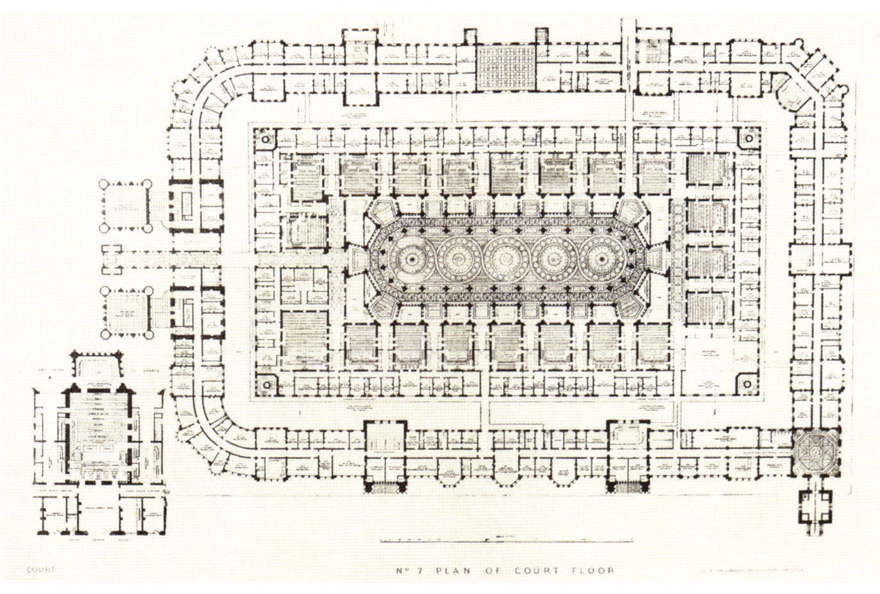

William Burges competition design 1867, interior view, one of the Barristers' Halls

Raphael Brandon competition design, 1867, exterior view

Henry Bayly Garling competition design 1867, exterior view

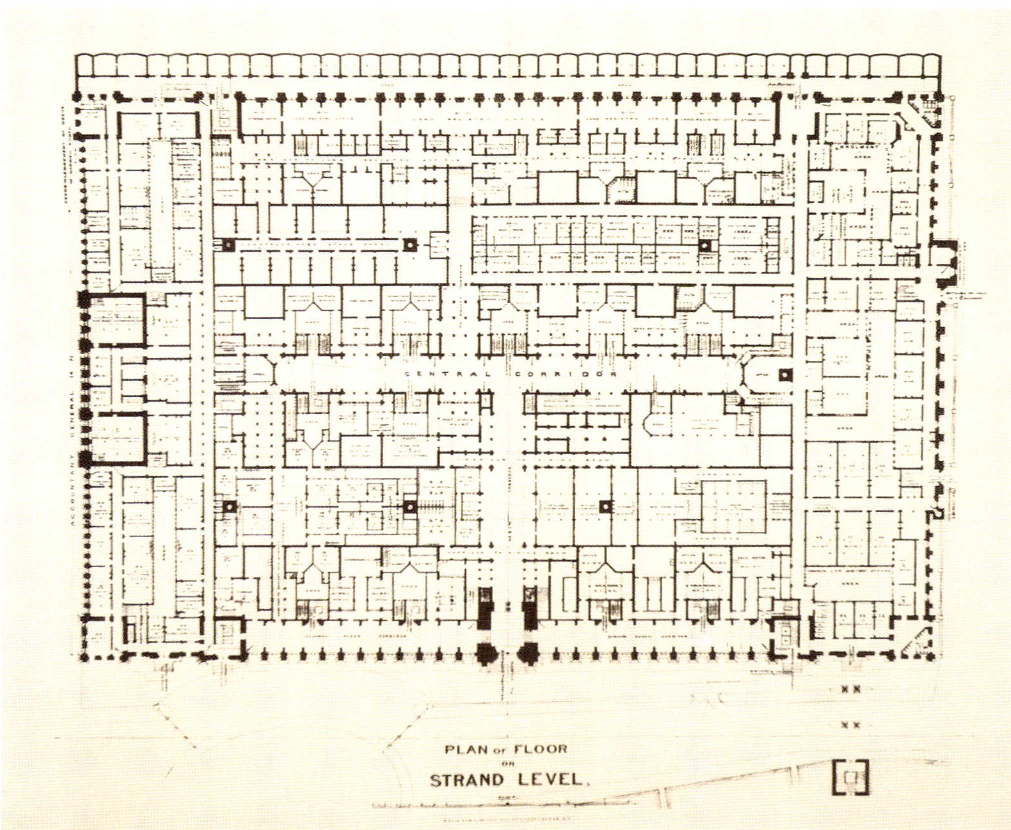

Henry Bayly Garling competition design 1867, ground floor plan, Strand level

Henry Bayly Garling competition design 1867, interior view of the Central Corridor

ヘンリー・ベイリー・ガーリング
設計競技案, 1867年／中央通路内観パース
HENRY BAYLY GARLING
competition design, 1867
Interior Perspective of the 'Central Corridor'

Alfred Waterhouse competition design, 1867, exterior view on the Thames

Henry Bayly Garling competition design 1867, exterior view on the Strand

John Pollard Seddon competition design, 1867, exterior view by E.S. Cole

Reichstag, Berlin, 1872–1882

110

Project

Seat of parliament for the newly formed German Empire

Site

Platz der Republik, Berlin

Dates

First round 24 November 1872 to 15 April 1872 *Second round* 29 January 1882 (officially: 2 February 1882) to 10 June 1882 *Result announced on* 24 June 1882

Number of entries

First round 102 *Second round* 186

Jury

First round Lucae, Hitzig, Friedrich Schmidt, Victor Statz, Gottfried von Neureuther, Gottfried Semper (all architects), Friedrich Drake (sculptor) and eleven members of parliament *Second round* Adler, Persius, J. von Egle, Martin Haller, Max von Siebert, Friedrich Schmidt, Victor Statz (all architects), Anton von Werner, and thirteen members of parliament

Result

First round Friedrich Bohnstedt (additional prizes awarded to Hermann Ende & Wilhelm Böckmann, Heinrich Kayser & Karl von Grossheim, C. Jonas Mylius & Alfred Bluntschli, G.G. Scott & J.O. Scott)
Second round, shared first prize Paul Wallot (nineteen votes to two) and Friedrich Thiersch (eleven votes to two) *Shared second prize* Heinrich Seeling, Kayser & Grossheim, W. Cremer & R. Wolffenstein *Shared third prize* Giese & Weidner, Hubert Stier, Ludwig Schupmann, Busse & Schwechten, Ende & Böckmann

Commissioned by

Ministry of Trade

Construction

1884 to 1894; decoration programme completed in 1900

Architect

Paul Wallot (1841–1912)

Reichstag, Berlin, 1872–1882

Paul Wallot competition design, 1882, exterior perspective on Königsplatz, first prize

Reichstag, Berlin

The historical background of the Reichstag building epitomises the problems faced by German parliamentary democracy in its early days. The German Empire began to take shape during the war of 1870 against France. In 1867, the North German states, with Russia as "Primus inter pares", had united to defeat their common enemy, Austria. In 1871 Wilhelm I (the Prussian king) was crowned emperor of the new Germany. The great statesman Bismarck was appointed Chancellor of the Reich and Berlin became the capital.

During the nineteenth century, Berlin had started to become a European metropolis. Between 1820 and 1850, the population had increased from 186 000 to 419 000, filling the city to capacity. The resulting tension (Kartoffel revolution) indirectly led to the development plans of 1858[1]. During this period, Berlin spread like an ink stain, rapidly absorbing smaller towns in the vicinity. The architecture consisted mainly of tenement blocks. The city was soon furnished with stations, museums, a new city hall and a cathedral. All that was missing was a Reichstag building.

Wilhelm I

The 1872 report of the competition for "Reichstagsgebäude"

PARLAMENTS-GEBÄUDE
BERLIN

New parliamentary seat

The newly established parliament, which was temporarily housed in cramped quarters in the Leipzigerstrasse, had already decided on 28 March 1871 that a new building should be built. A site was soon found at the east end of the centrally situated Königsplatz, near the Brandenburg Gate. It took a little longer before consensus was reached concerning the architectural style, but no insurmountable problems were encountered. Some of the members of parliament considered a plain, functional building to be suitable quarters for the house of representatives. However, the majority saw the Reichstag building as a unique opportunity to build a monument to German unification, featuring works by the best German artists. The programme of architectural conditions and stipulations was soon drawn up and the competition was announced by 24 November 1871. A jury and a building commission were appointed and rapid completion seemed certain but for the fact that parliament had not taken into account the feelings of the diplomat Count Raczynski. The count owned the palace on the chosen building site and the surrounding grounds. It was probably because he had, most inappropriately, learned of the parliamentary plans via the newspapers, that he refused further co-operation until his death. Even though the police prefect assured Wilhelm I that expropriation would be a simple matter, the latter did not give the necessary permission for personal reasons. An agreement was eventually reached with Raczynski's son in 1881. This delay was sufficient cause (or, more accurately, sufficient pretext) for the organisation of a new competition.

In the first round, for which 102 entries were submitted, about a third were from foreign participants, including George Gilbert Scott and his son John Oldrid Scott, for example. Their design was one of the few which had been daringly drawn in the Gothic Revivalist style. The German entries stood in stark contrast. During the nineteenth century, German architects and their teachers at the academy were regular patrons of the Ecole des Beaux-Arts in Paris. With the exception of a few Neo-Renaissance designs (such as that of W. Cremer), most of the designs had been drawn in the Neo-Classicist style (e.g. Lange & Böhlmann and Ende & Böckmann). The first round winner was Friedrich Bohnstedt, whose design seemed largely inspired by the French Baroque and Neo-Baroque. Bohnstedt won by ten votes to nine. The result was probably a consequence of the rivalry between Neo-

Classicists and Gothic Revivalists. Initially, Bohnstedt was not amongst the front runners. However, in a bid to thwart the Neo-Classicists, the Gothic Revivalists, having little opportunity to tout their own preferences, had supported Bohnstedt. The press soon launched an attack upon the competition in general and upon the foreign entries in particular (Bohnstedt hailed from German-Russian stock). However, due to the problems encountered with Count Raczynski, the turmoil had time to subside and ten years later a new competition was organised.

Although Bohnstedt, now advanced in years, did submit an altered design, pro forma, he was one of the first to drop out of the competition. Busse & Schwechten also tried their luck again. Busse's entry met with a storm of protest because he had been involved in drawing up the competition stipulations, which, it must be said, were better defined and less complicated than before. The banqueting halls and the director's residence had been scrapped, reducing the total building area. A new Reichstag Building Commission and a new jury were appointed. The competition was now limited to German-speaking participants. No less than 186 designs were submitted, many of them Neo-Classicist. (The exact number is difficult to ascertain as the designs had to be submitted anonymously.) Striking designs were submitted by Otto Wagner, who was one of the few architects who had not included a dome, and by Heinrich von Ferstel and Friedrich Thiersch, whose domes were excessively large. Von Ferstel's design, in particular, closely resembled St. Paul's Cathedral by Christopher Wren, with added accessories. Oskar Sommer's design was also unlikely to win beauty contests. There was a complete lack of proportional harmony between the façade and the dome, and the two steeples on either side of the dome seemed more than a little inappropriate.

Reichstag front façade on the Platz der Republik (Königsplatz), recent photograph

Reichstag front façade on the Platz der Republik (Königsplatz), Wallot's final design

Ernst von Giese & Paul Weidner
Reichstag, competition design, 1882, exterior view on Königsplatz, third prize

Wallot's appointment

The jury voted nineteen to two in favour of Paul Wallot's design "Für Staat und Stadt" (for state and city), although it required improvement here and there. In the end, only the corner pavilions would remain unchanged. Wallot's selection came as a surprise because he was relatively unknown and had few impressive works to his name. However, he was a gifted draughtsman, a talent which he had perfected under Martin Gropius, for whom he had worked for some time. Gropius, who had also participated in the competition and was the great-uncle of the renowned architect Walter Gropius, went home empty-handed. It is likely that he had had higher hopes, having supervised the alteration of the building on the Leipzigerstrasse.

Demolition of the Raczynski Palace began in 1883. It is interesting to note that the Palace had been designed by Heinrich Strack, who had been Paul Wallot's employer for some time. Strack had also submitted a design for the Reichstag in 1872. The first stone was laid in 1884. Construction was slow and this took its toll on Wallot's patience. The delays were caused by personal and construction problems. The original design was regularly and rigorously changed. The shape and position of the dome, in particular, repeatedly posed a problem.

In Wallot's 1882 design, the dome had been placed above the hall of assembly, but during the adaptation of the plans it was shifted forward, over the entrance hall (October 1883). This monumental hall had developed following the combination, on paper, of several smaller rooms and the stairway, which Wallot had designed earlier. However, Wallot was not pleased with the changes suggested by the building commission and he implored the emperor to allow him to move the dome back to its former position. If the dome were to be placed above the entrance hall, it would disturb the proportional harmony of the façade, due to its size. Wallot's request met with the Emperor's total incomprehension and he waited until the Emperor's death in 1888 before hazarding a second attempt. This time, he had the support of parliament, which had stated that the adapted design looked like a gutted castle. It was suggested that the dome should to be moved to the back and should be smaller and more translucent. It should therefore not be made of stone, but of glass and copper, allowing a greater incidence of light into the hall of assembly. The new emperor gave his consent[2]. Work was started on the dome in 1890, its structure resembling that of a greenhouse.

Further problems and delays

The altered position of the dome did have consequences for the already completed substructure, which had to be reinforced around the hall of assembly. Furthermore, the specifications for the technical installations had to be recalculated. Naturally this caused further delays and increased costs. Another consequence of moving this dominant structure was that the central section of the façade required additional accentuation. The rather disorderly triumphal arch initially envisaged by Wallot was replaced by a Corinthian portico, which was considered suitable for the seat of government power. Wallot also simplified the floor plan by reducing the number of courtyards from four to two.

The problems of a personal nature may be traced back to Wilhelm II. The emperor interfered with all aspects of the construction and, at one point, even wanted to personally add certain 'improvements' to the construction plans, saying: *"Das machen wir so"* (This is how we'll do it). Wallot replied firmly: *"Majestät, das geht nicht"* (Your majesty, that's impossible). As a result, subsequent interaction between the two was icy. The emperor, who was averse to any form of parliamentary democracy in the first place, openly referred to the building as the height of vulgarity. However, Wallot had assured himself of the support of many artists, members of parliament and others. In addition, the motto proposed by Wallot, *"Dem deutschen Volke"* (To the German People), met with Wilhelm's disapproval, which greatly contributed to the emperor's growing unpopularity. It was not until 1916, after lengthy debate, that the motto was finally engraved, based on a typographic design by Peter Behrens. The bronze for the letters came from the cannons which had been used in the Battle of Leipzig (1813).

By 1916, Wallot was no longer involved in the construction of the Reichstag. The criticism of the decoration programme, on top of the problems with the emperor, was more than he could endure and in 1899 he washed his hands of the project and accepted a teaching post.

The building was altered again in 1907, but would only briefly serve its purpose. The German parliament, not known for its firm stance against the emperor and government, was completely sidelined in Nazi Germany. The fire of 1933, started by the Dutch Communist Marinus van der Lubbe in protest against the Nazis, completely gutted the Reichstag. For many years after the war, the building was an ominous symbol, but now, more than a hundred years after its completion, it is to be used again. The architect who will supervise the renovation and the building of new extensions is to be selected by means of a competition.

Reichstag, front façade on the Platz der Republik (Königsplatz)

1 *Kartoffel (Potato) revolution (1847). Hunger and dissatisfaction led to public unrest throughout Europe. In 1848, the Prussian king Friedrich Wilhelm IV founded the "Herrenhaus" (House of Lords) and "Abgeordnetenhaus" (House of Representatives).*

2 *Following the death of Wilhelm I (9 March 1888), his son Friedrich III reigned for 99 days. Wilhelm II was crowned on 15 June 1888. It was the year of the three Emperors.*

Reichstag, Berlin

Die Geschichte des Reichstagsgebäudes steht stellvertretend für die Probleme, die die parlamentarische Demokratie überwinden mußte, um zu einem festen Bestandteil des deutschen Staatswesens zu werden. Mit dem Krieg von 1870/71 gegen Frankreich nahm das Deutsche Reich Gestalt an. Bereits 1867 hatten sich die norddeutschen Staaten unter Führung Preußens zu einem Bund zusammengeschlossen – ebenfalls im Krieg gegen den gemeinsamen Gegner Österreich. 1871 wurden Wilhelm I. zum deutschen Kaiser gekrönt, Bismarck zum Reichskanzler ernannt und Berlin die Hauptstadt des Deutschen Reichs.

Schon im 19. Jahrhundert hatte Berlin begonnen, sich zu einer europäischen Metropole zu entwickeln; die Einwohnerzahl war zwischen 1820 und 1850 von 186 000 auf 419 000 gestiegen, ohne daß die Stadt darauf vorbereitet gewesen wäre. Die hieraus entstehenden Spannungen (sog. Kartoffelrevolution) führten indirekt zu den Expansionsplänen von 1858[1]. In dieser Zeit breitete sich Berlin rasch aus und schluckte die kleineren Dörfer der Umgebung. Die neue Bebauung bestand zum großen Teil aus Mietskasernen. Bald darauf erhielt die Stadt Bahnhöfe, Museen, ein neues Rathaus und einen Dom. Das einzige, was noch fehlte, war ein Parlamentsgebäude.

Der Sitz der neuen Parlaments

Das junge Parlament, das in der Zwischenzeit in zu knapp bemessenen Räumlichkeiten in der Leipziger Straße tagte, beschloß schon am 28. März 1871 den Bau eines neuen Gebäudes. Auch das Baugelände war schnell gefunden: die Ostseite des zentral gelegenen Königsplatzes, direkt am Brandenburger Tor. Über den Baustil debattierte man etwas länger, ohne dabei auf unlösbare Probleme zu stoßen. Zwar gab es Abgeordnete, die für die neue Volksvertretung ein nüchternes, funktionelles Gebäude als passend erachteten, aber die Mehrzahl der Parlamentarier sah in dem neuen Bau eine einzigartige Gelegenheit, die deutsche Einheit mit einem monumentalen Bauwerk zu krönen, an dem die besten deutschen Künstler mitwirken sollten. Die Liste der Anforderungen und Bedingungen, die die Architekten erfüllen mußten, war schnell aufgestellt, und schon am 24. November 1871 erfolgte die Ausschreibung. Eine Jury und eine Baukommission wurden benannt, und eine schnelle Abwicklung schien durchaus realistisch – wenn das Parlament nur die Gefühle des Diplomaten Graf Raczynski besser berücksichtigt hätte. Der Graf war der Eigentümer des gleichnamigen Palais, sein Grundbesitz lag mitten auf dem vorgesehenen Baugelände. Daß er diese Entscheidung – wenig taktvoll – aus der Zeitung erfahren mußte, wird den Grafen wohl dazu veranlaßt haben, bis an sein Lebensende jegliche Zusammenarbeit zu verweigern. Obwohl der Polizeipräfekt versicherte, daß eine Enteignung jederzeit möglich sei, versagte Kaiser Wilhelm I. aus persönlichen Gründen seine hierfür benötigte Zustimmung. Erst mit Raczynskis Sohn wurde 1881 eine Einigung erzielt.
102 Beiträge gingen ein; davon stammte etwa ein Drittel aus dem Ausland, z.B. von George Gilbert Scott und seinem Sohn John Oldrid, die einen kühnen neugotischen Entwurf eingereicht hatten. Die deutschen Wettbewerbsbeiträge standen dazu in einem starken Kontrast, denn die einheimischen Architekten – oder zumindest ihre Dozenten an der Akademie – hatten im 19. Jahrhundert bis auf wenige Ausnahmen die École des Beaux-Arts in Paris besucht. Bis auf einen Entwurf im Stil der Neurenaissance (der von R. Cremer stammte) waren die meisten Zeichnungen (z.B. von Lange und Böhlmann, Ende und Böckmann) im klassizistischen Stil gehalten. Als Gewinner wurde Friedrich Bohnstedt prämiert, dessen Entwurf deutliche Einflüsse des französischen Barock bzw. Neubarock aufwies. Bohnstedt gewann mit zehn zu neun Stimmen, wobei dieses Ergebnis durch die Rivalität zwischen Klassizisten und Neugoten zustande gekommen sein dürfte. Ursprünglich hatte Bohnstedt nicht zu ersteren gehört; aber um einen klassizistischen Entwurf zu verhindern, hatten sich die Anhänger der Neugotik – die keine Chance mehr für ihre eigenen Entwürfe sahen – geschlossen hinter Bohnstedt gestellt. Daraufhin begannen die Zeitungen eine Hetzkampagne gegen den Wettbewerb im allgemeinen und die ausländischen Beiträge im besonderen (Bohnstedt war deutsch-russischer Herkunft). Aber aufgrund der Probleme mit dem Grafen Raczynski kühlten sich die Gemüter ab, und zehn Jahre später kam es zu einer Neuauflage des Wettbewerbs. Eine neue Reichstagsbaukommission wurde ebenso benannt wie eine neue Jury. Am Wettbewerb, an dem diesmal ausschließlich deutschsprachige Architekten teilnehmen durften, beteiligten sich zwischen 186 und 194 Architekten mit hauptsächlich klassizistischen Beiträgen (die genaue Anzahl ist aufgrund der Anonymität der Einsendungen nur schwer festzustellen). Besonders auffällige Entwürfe kamen von Otto Wagner, der als einer der wenigen keine Kuppel zeichnete, sowie von Heinrich von Ferstel und Friedrich Thiersch, die zu große Kuppeln vorschlugen.

Die Wahl Wallots

Die Jury entschied sich mit neunzehn gegen zwei Stimmen für den Plan »Für Staat und Stadt« von Paul Wallot, obwohl er an einigen Stellen noch verbesserungswürdig erschien. Letztendlich sollten nur die Eckpavillons unverändert bleiben. Die Wahl von Wallot überraschte, da dieser Architekt relativ unbekannt war und bisher nur durch wenige Arbeiten auf sich aufmerksam gemacht hatte. Aber er erwies sich als ein begabter Zeichner, der diese Fähigkeit im Büro von Martin Gropius verbessern konnte. Gropius – der Großonkel des später bekannt gewordenen Walter Gropius – nahm ebenfalls am Wettbewerb teil, blieb aber erfolglos. Er hatte sich mehr erhofft, weil nach seinen Plänen der Umbau der Leipziger Straße durchgeführt worden war.
1883 begann man mit dem Abriß des Palais Raczynski. Interessanterweise war der Architekt dieses Gebäudes Heinrich Strack, bei dem Wallot ebenfalls gearbeitet hatte. Auch Strack hatte 1872 einen Entwurf für den Reichstag eingereicht. Die Grundsteinlegung fand 1884 statt, doch die langsam voranschreitenden Arbeiten stellten Wallots Geduld auf eine harte Probe. Der ursprüngliche Entwurf mußte häufig und tiefgreifend geändert werden, Form und Plazierung der Kuppel erwiesen sich als äußerst schwierig.
Wallot hatte die Kuppel 1882 ursprünglich über dem Plenarsaal geplant, aber durch die ständigen Änderungen verschob sich die Kuppel immer weiter nach vorn bis über die Eingangshalle (Oktober 1883). Diese monumentale Halle war durch das Zusammenfügen kleinerer Säle und Treppenhäuser entstanden, die Wallot ursprünglich vorgesehen hatte. Er war mit dieser durch die Baukommission vorgeschlagenen Änderung nicht einverstanden und drang beim Kaiser persönlich darauf, die Kuppel wieder nach hinten zu versetzen. Bliebe die Kuppel über der Eingangshalle, würde sie durch ihre Größe die harmonischen Proportionen der Fassade zerstören. Da der Kaiser diesem Problem völlig verständnislos gegenüberstand, mußte Wallot bis zu dessen Tod 1888 warten, bevor er mit seiner Kritik erfolgreich war. Diesmal erhielt er die Unterstützung des Parlaments, das den Anblick des geänderten Entwurfs mit einer abgebrannten Burg verglich. Die Kuppel sollte wieder nach hinten versetzt und kleiner und leichter werden. Als Materialien boten sich statt Stein Glas und Kupfer an, so daß der Plenarsaal genügend Licht von oben erhielt. Der neue Kaiser[2] stimmte diesem Plan zu, so daß 1890 mit dem Bau der Kuppel – deren Konstruktion an ein Gewächshaus erinnert – begonnen werden konnte.

Weitere Probleme und Verzögerungen

Das Verschieben der Kuppel in dieser Bauphase hatte Folgen für den bereits erstellten Unterbau, der nun rund um den Plenarsaal zusätzlich verstärkt werden mußte. Außerdem wurde eine Neuberechnung der technischen Installationen erforderlich, was zusätzlich Zeit und Geld kostete. Als weitere Konsequenz benötigte der Mittelteil des Giebels einen zusätzlichen Akzent: Der wenig akkurate Triumphbogen, den Wallot anfänglich geplant hatte, mußte einem korinthischen Portikus weichen, der für ein solch mächtiges Regierungsgebäude eher angemessen schien. Darüber hinaus vereinfachte Wallot den Grundriß, indem er aus vier Innenhöfen wieder zwei machte.
Weitere Probleme waren zum größten Teil verknüpft mit der Person Kaiser Wilhelms II., der sich mit allen Angelegenheiten rund um den Bau befaßte und eines Tages sogar eigenhändig die Baupläne »verbessern« wollte. Als Wilhelm II. sagte: *»Das machen wir so«*, antwortete ihm Wallot in festem Ton: *»Majestät, das geht nicht.«* Von da ab waren die gegenseitigen Beziehungen äußerst unterkühlt. Der Kaiser, mit Sicherheit kein Freund der parlamentarischen Demokratie, bezeichnete den Bau öffentlich als Höhepunkt der Geschmacklosigkeit. Wallot dagegen war sich der Unterstützung vieler Künstler, Abgeordneter und Bürger sicher. Auch die von Wallot vorgeschlagene Inschrift *»Dem deutschen Volke«* stieß beim Kaiser auf Widerstand – was übrigens zu seiner wachsenden Unbeliebtheit beitrug. Erst 1916 und nach vielen Diskussionen wurde die nach einem typographischen Entwurf von Peter Behrens entstandene Aufschrift angebracht.

1 *Kartoffelrevolution (1847). Hunger und Unzufriedenheit führten in ganz Europa zu Volksaufständen. Daraufhin befahl der preußische König Friedrich Wilhelm IV. die Gründung eines Herrenhauses und eines Abgeordnetenhauses.*

2 *Nach dem Tod von Wilhelm I. (9. März 1888) regierte dessen Sohn Friedrich III. genau 99 Tage. Am 15. Juni 1888 bestieg Wilhelm II. den Thron (sog. Dreikaiserjahr).*

Le Reichstag, Berlin

Le contexte historique de la construction du siège du Reichstag illustre les difficultés que la démocratie parlementaire allemande dut surmonter pour assurer sa légitimité. L'Empire allemand s'était constitué à l'occasion de la guerre de 1870/1871 contre la France. En 1867, les Etats du Nord de l'Allemagne – la Prusse n'étant considérée que comme primus inter pares – s'étaient unis une première fois pour défaire leur ennemi commun, l'Autriche. En 1871, Guillaume 1er (roi de Prusse) fut couronné Empereur de la nouvelle Allemagne, Bismarck nommé chancelier du Reich et Berlin désignée capitale.

Au cours du XIXème siècle, la ville avait déjà commencé à devenir une métropole d'importance européenne. Sa population s'était accrue de façon exponentielle, passant de 186 000 habitants en 1820 à 419 000 en 1850, ce qui ne manqua pas d'entraîner des troubles (La «révolution des pommes de terre») qui favorisèrent indirectement l'adoption d'un plan d'urbanisme en 1858[1]. Pendant toute cette période, Berlin s'étendit comme une tache d'encre et absorba rapidement les communes voisines. Si son urbanisme reposait essentiellement sur une suite de blocs d'immeubles d'habitation, la cité s'enrichit néanmoins de gares, de musées, d'un nouvel hôtel de ville et d'une cathédrale. Il ne manquait plus qu'un bâtiment pour le parlement.

Le nouveau siège du parlement

Temporairement logé à l'étroit Leipzigerstrasse, le nouveau parlement avait voté le 28 mars 1871 le principe de la construction d'un nouveau siège. Un site fut bientôt trouvé à l'extrémité Est de la Königsplatz, près de la Porte de Brandebourg. Il fallut un peu plus de temps pour que s'établisse un consensus sur le style architectural mais aucun problème insurmontable ne fut rencontré. Certains des membres du parlement voulaient un bâtiment fonctionnel et neutre, mais la majorité voyait dans ce projet l'occasion unique d'élever un monument à l'unification allemande, avec l'aide des meilleurs artistes allemands. Le cahier des charges fut dressé et le concours annoncé dès le 24 novembre 1871. Le jury et la commission des travaux désignés, il semblait que tout allait être rapidement mené à bonne fin. C'était oublier un obstacle imprévu, un diplomate, le comte Raczynski qui possédait tout simplement le palais construit à l'emplacement choisi et les terrains avoisinants. Sans doute parce qu'il n'avait appris les projets du parlement que par les journaux, il refusa toute coopération jusqu'à sa mort. Bien que le préfet ait expliqué à Guillaume 1er que l'expropriation ne poserait aucun problème, l'Empereur s'y refusa pour des raisons personnelles. Un accord fut enfin signé avec le fils de Raczynski, en 1881 et ce retard permit – ou justifia – un nouveau concours.

Pour le premier concours, 102 participations avaient été enregistrées, dont un tiers d'architectes étrangers comme George Gilbert Scott et son fils John Oldrid dont le projet fut d'ailleurs l'un des rares à prôner ouvertement le style néo-gothique. Les participants allemands s'en éloignaient totalement. A l'exception de quelques propositions néo-Renaissance (celle de R. Cremer, par exemple), la plupart étaient de style néo-classique (Lange et Böhlmann, Ende et Böckmann). Au cours du XIXème siècle, les architectes allemands et leurs professeurs de l'Académie étaient très sensibles à l'influence de l'Ecole des Beaux-Arts de Paris. Le lauréat du premier concours, avec dix voix[2] contre neuf, fut Friedrich Bohnstedt dont les plan s'inspiraient du baroque français et du néo-baroque. Sa victoire était probablement la conséquence d'une rivalité: l'architecte ne faisait pas partie des favoris, mais pour empêcher les néo-classiques de gagner, les néo-gothiques, qui ne pouvaient l'emporter, avaient soutenu ses plans. La presse se lança très vite dans une violente attaque contre le concours en général et les architectes étrangers en particulier (Bohnstedt était d'origine germano-russe). Puis, devant les difficultés soulevées par le comte Raczynski, la tempête eut le temps de se calmer et dix ans plus tard, un nouveau concours fut organisé. Bohnstedt, âgé, soumit un projet modifié mais fut l'un des premiers à se retirer de la compétition. Busse et Schwechten tentèrent également leur chance une seconde fois. La participation de Busse souleva de nombreuses protestations car il avait participé à l'établissement de l'appel d'offres par ailleurs moins compliqué et plus précis que la première fois. Les salles de banquet et la résidence du directeur avaient été supprimées ce qui permettait de réduire la surface utile nécessaire. Une nouvelle commission de construction du Reichstag et un nouveau jury furent désignés, le concours étant désormais réservé aux architectes allemands. Pas moins de 186 projets furent présentés, dont beaucoup d'esprit néo-classique (le nombre exact est difficile à connaître car les soumissions étaient anonymes). Des plans étonnants furent soumis par Otto Wagner, l'un des rares architectes à ne pas avoir prévu de dôme, et par Heinrich von Ferstel et Friedrich Thiersch, dont les dômes, en revanche, étaient gigantesques. Un autre plan, celui de von Ferstel, évoquait la cathédrale St. Paul de Christopher Wren, à laquelle auraient été ajoutés des annexes. La liaison entre les façades et le dôme manquait d'harmonie et les deux clochers latéraux semblaient mal placés.

Le choix de Wallot

Par dix-neuf voix contre deux, le jury vota pour les plans de Paul Wallot, «Pour l'Etat et la Cité», même si des améliorations s'avéraient nécessaires. En final, seuls les pavillons d'angle allaient d'ailleurs rester inchangés. Le choix de Wallot fut une surprise car il était relativement peu connu et n'avait guère signé de grandes réalisations. Néanmoins, c'était un dessinateur de talent qui avait étudié sous la direction de Martin Gropius. Celui-ci, grand-oncle du célèbre architecte Walter Gropius, participa au concours mais ne remporta aucun prix bien qu'il ait nourri quelques sérieux espoirs puisqu'il avait supervisé les modifications des bâtiments temporaires du parlement, Leipzigerstrasse.

La démolition du palais Raczynski débuta en 1883. Il est intéressant de noter que cet édifice avait été construit par Heinrich Strack, ancien employeur de Paul Wallot et candidat lui-même au concours de 1872. Si la première pierre fut posée dès 1884, la construction traîna et mit à rude épreuve la patience de l'architecte. Les retards furent provoqués par des problèmes de personnes, mais aussi de construction. Le plan d'origine fut périodiquement bouleversé, en particulier la position du dôme, ce qui souleva de multiples difficultés.

Dans les plans Wallot d'octobre 1883, ce dôme surmontait la salle d'assemblée puis fut avancé au-dessus du hall d'entrée, un vestibule monumental résultant de la réunion de plusieurs salles plus petites et du grand escalier dessiné à l'origine. Mécontent des modifications imposées par la Commission de la construction, l'architecte implora l'Empereur de lui permettre de rétablir le dôme à son emplacement initial: sa taille imposante détruirait l'harmonie de la façade s'il était laissé au-dessus du hall. L'Empereur ne parut pas comprendre et Wallot attendit sa mort en 1888 pour faire une nouvelle tentative auprès de son successeur. Il avait cette fois le soutien du parlement qui pensait que le nouveau plan donnait au Reichstag l'air d'un château en ruines. On suggéra qu'il devait être déplacé vers l'arrière, réduit et plus transparent, en utilisant le verre et le cuivre plutôt que la pierre. Le nouvel empereur y consentit et les travaux du dôme qui ressemblait maintenant à une serre, commencèrent en 1890.

Nouvelles difficultés, nouveaux retards

Le changement de position du dôme obligea à renforcer les infrastructures de la grande salle qui étaient déjà terminées. Toutes les installations techniques durent être revues, ce qui entraîna de nouveaux retards et une augmentation des coûts. Dans le même temps, on s'aperçut que la façade sans dôme était un peu plate. L'arc triomphal échevelé prévu par Wallot fut remplacé par un portique corinthien, mieux adapté, pensait-on, au siège du pouvoir. L'architecte simplifia enfin le plan de masse en supprimant deux cours intérieures sur quatre. Les problèmes de personnes tinrent en grande partie à Guillaume II. L'Empereur se mêla de tous les aspects de la construction et, à un certain moment, voulut apporter lui-même certaines 'améliorations' aux plans en disant *«Das machen wir so»* (Faisons comme ça) auquel Wallot répliqua fermement *«Majestät, das geht nicht»* (Ce n'est pas possible, Votre Majesté). Les rapports entre eux se firent glaciaux et l'Empereur, qui détestait la démocratie parlementaire, qualifia le nouveau bâtiment de 'summum de la vulgarité'. Wallot avait su cependant se gagner le soutien de nombreux artistes et membres du parlement. L'inscription qu'il proposa pour la façade *«Dem deutschen Volk»* (Au peuple allemand) fut désapprouvée par l'Empereur, ce qui contribua grandement à son impopularité. Ce ne fut qu'en 1916, après de fastidieux débats que cette inscription fut finalement mise en place d'après un projet typographique de Peter Behrens. Le bronze des lettres vint de la fonte de canons de la bataille de Leipzig (1813). Mais en 1916, Wallot n'était plus responsable du projet. Faire face aux critiques de son programme de décoration et aux mauvais rapports avec un empereur était plus qu'il ne pouvait supporter et il avait démissionné dès 1899 pour devenir enseignant.

1 *'La Révolution des pommes de terre' (1847). La faim et le mécontentement multiplièrent les troubles dans toute l'Europe. En 1848, le roi de Prusse, Frédéric Guillaume IV, fonda la «Herrenhaus» (Chambre des Seigneurs) et «l'Abgeordnetenhaus» (Chambre des représentants).*

2 *A la mort de Guillaume 1er, le 9 mars 1888, lui succéda son fils Frédéric II pendant 99 jours. Guillaume II fut couronné le 15 juin 1888: ce fut 'l'année des trois empereurs'.*

Ludwig Bohnstedt competition design, 1872, exterior perspective on Königsplatz, first prize

Emil Lange & Joseph Böhlmann competition design, 1872, top: section of the chamber, bottom: site plan

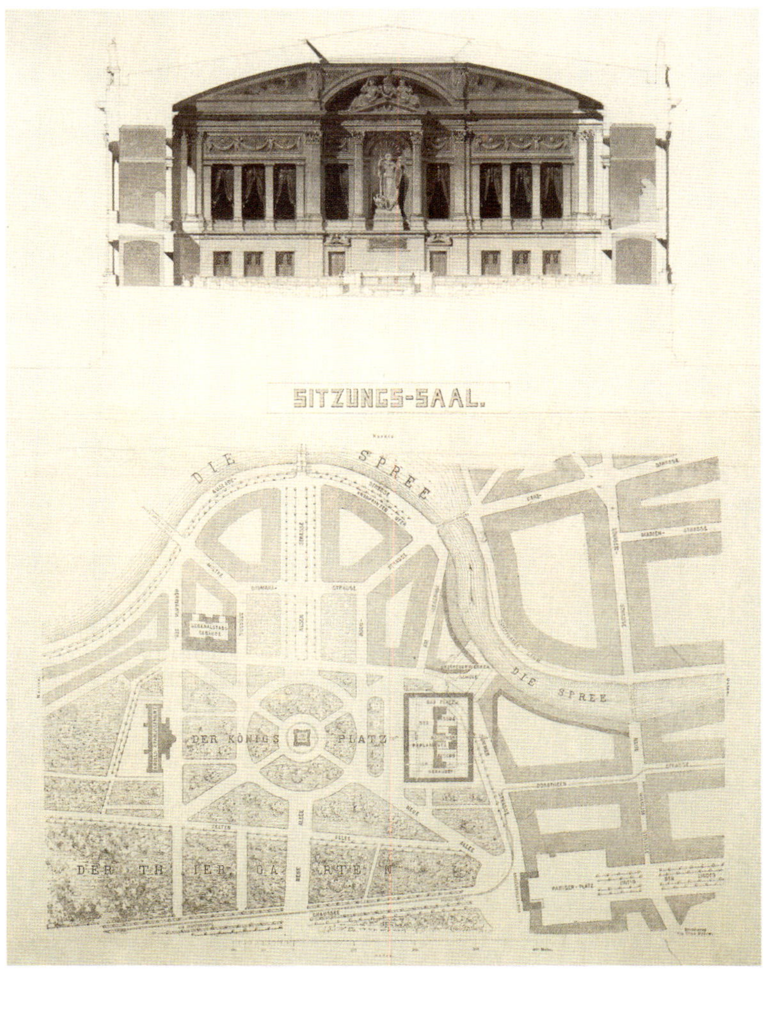

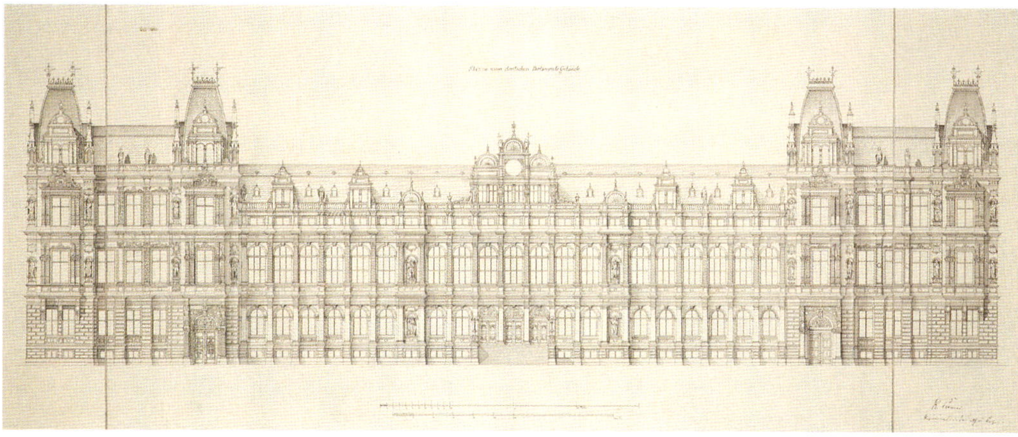

Wilhelm Cremer competition design, 1872, front elevation on Königsplatz

Heinrich Strack & Heinrich Hermann competition design, 1872, exterior view on Königsplatz

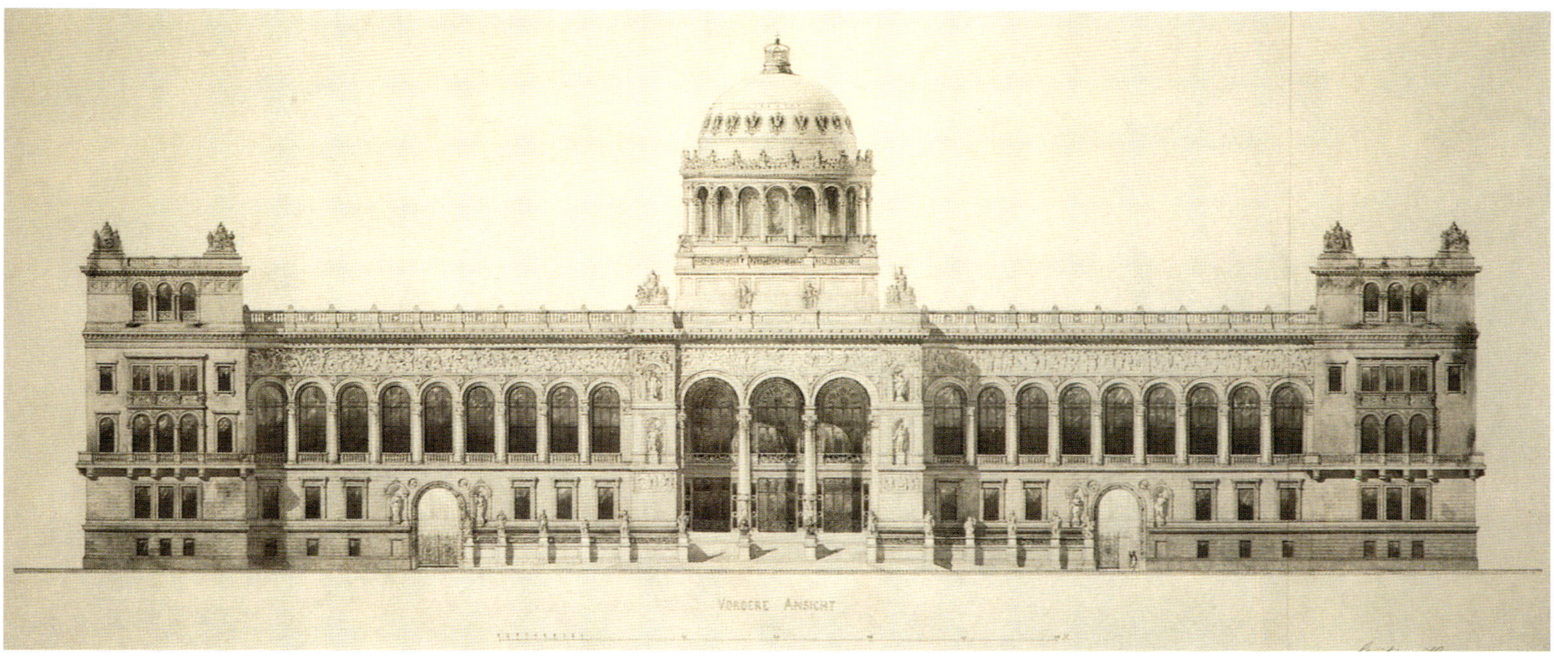

Hermann Ende & Wilhelm Böckmann competition design, 1872, exterior perspective on Königsplatz

Otto Wagner competition design, 1882, exterior view on Königsplatz

Oskar Sommer competition design, 1882, front elevation on Königsplatz

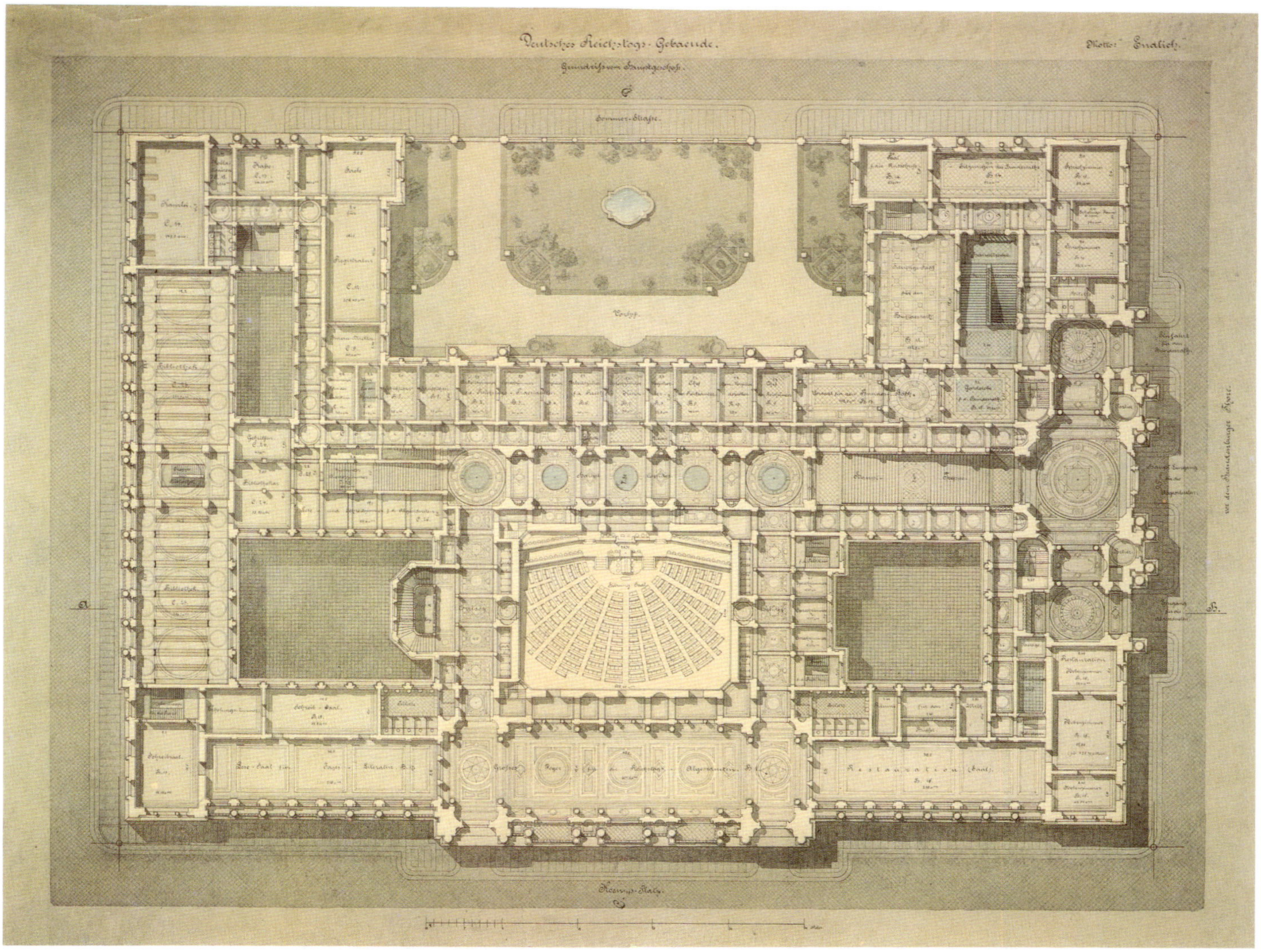

Hermann Ende & Wilhelm Böckmann competition design, 1872, main floor plan

Paul Wallot competition design 1882, front elevation on Königsplatz, first prize

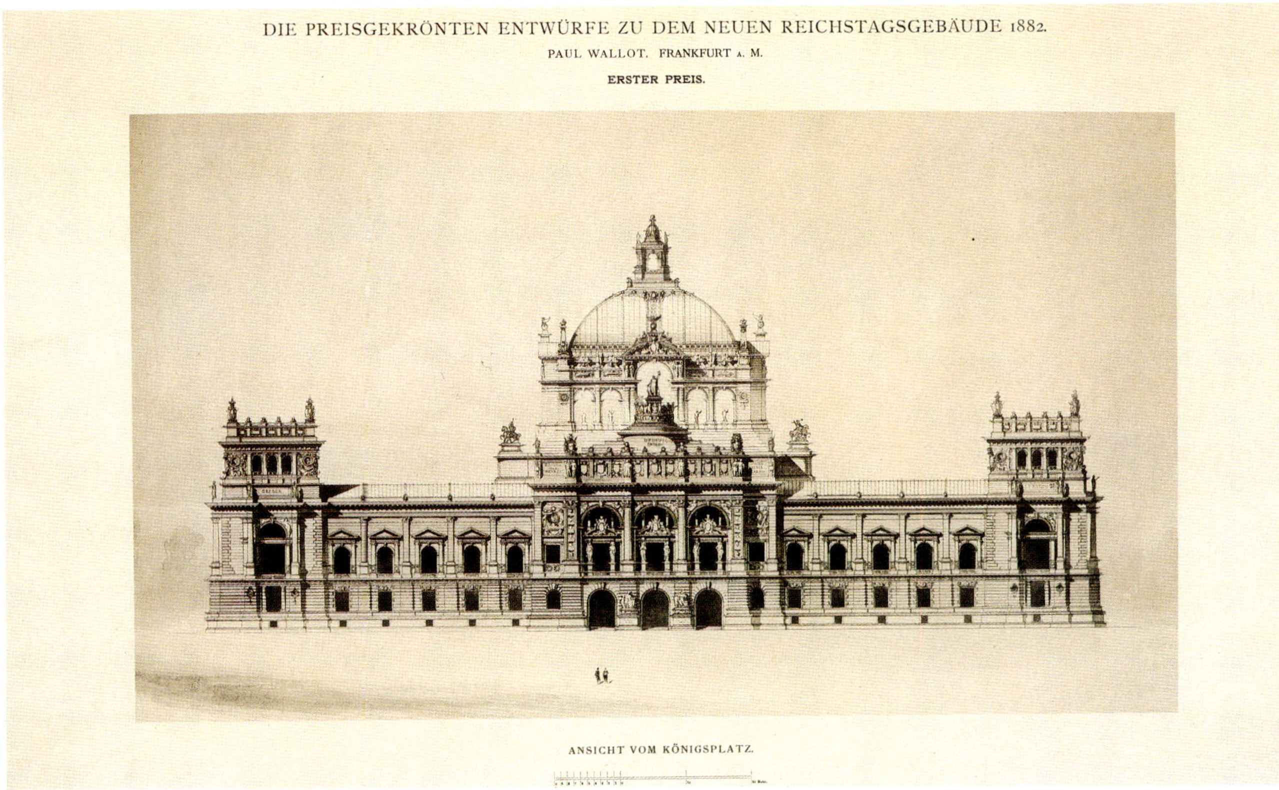

Paul Wallot competition design 1882, main floor plan, first prize

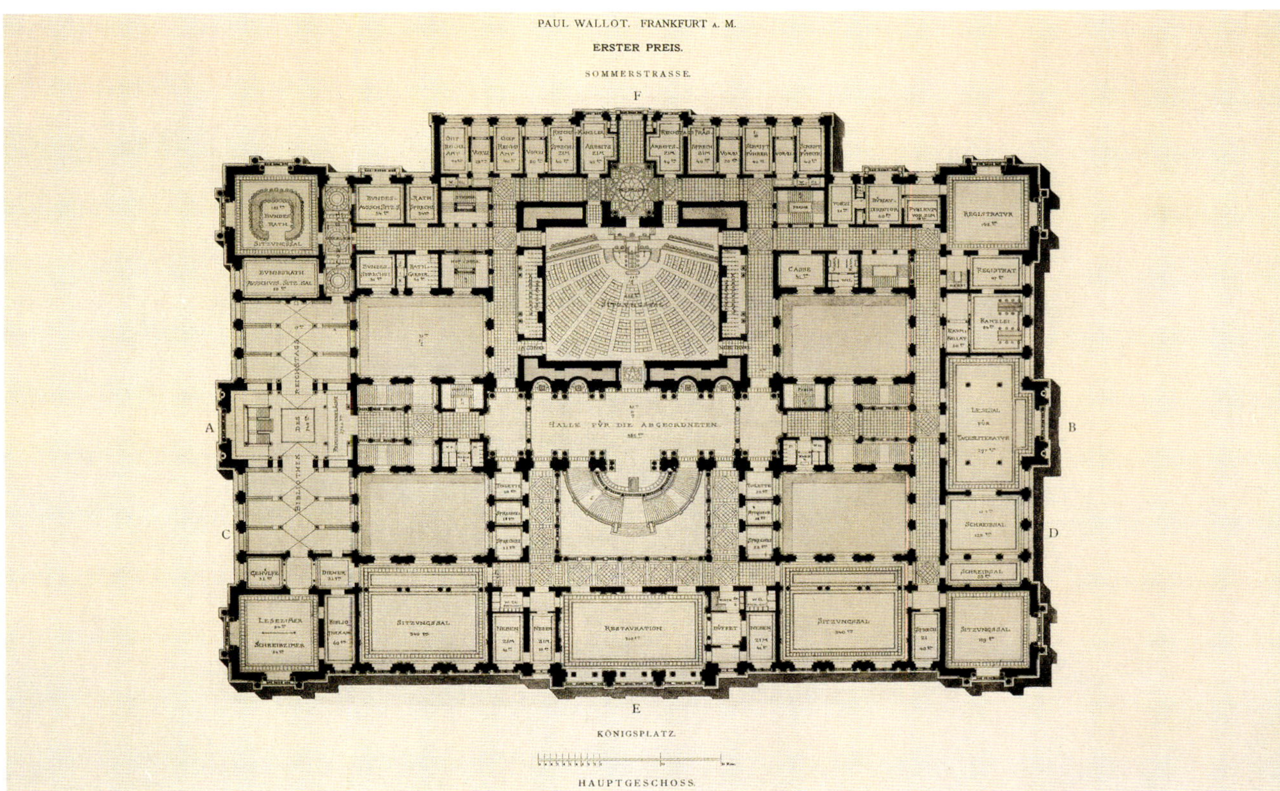

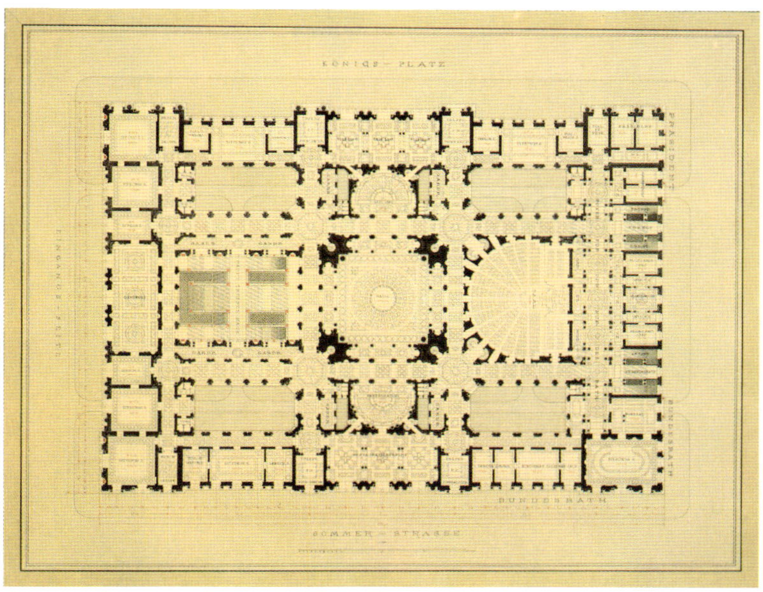

Friedrich von Thiersch competition design, 1882, exterior view on Königsplatz, first prize

Friedrich von Thiersch competition design, 1882, main floor plan, first prize

Franz Schwechten & August Busse competition design, 1882, exterior view on Königsplatz, third prize

Heinrich von Ferstel competition design, 1882, exterior view on Königsplatz

Wilhelm Cremer & Richard Wolffenstein competition design, 1882, exterior view on Königsplatz, second prize

Heinrich Jozef Kayser & Karl von Grossheim competition design, 1882, exterior view on Königsplatz, second prize

Martin Gropius & Heino Schmieden
competition design, 1872, interior
view of the Assembly Hall

Beurs, Amsterdam, 1884

126

Project

Stock Exchange building (commodities exchange, stock exchange, grain exchange, shipping exchange)

Site

Damrak, Amsterdam

Dates

First round 30 June to 1 November 1884 (result announced 15 November 1884) *Second round* Result announced 3 June 1885 *Architect commissioned* 4 February 1896

Number of entries

199

Jury

Eight architects R. Phéné Spiers (London), Paul Sédille (Paris), J.J. van IJsendijck (Brussels), Friedrich von Schmidt (Vienna), Prof. Raschdorff (Berlin) *Three trade representatives* J.R. de Kruyff, L.H. Eberson, P.J.H Cuypers (all Dutch)

Result

First prize Louis Cordonnier *Second prize* John Groll, Hendrik Petrus Berlage *Third prize* Theodorus Sanders

Commissioned by

The Municipality of Amsterdam

Construction

1898 to 1903

Architect

Hendrik Petrus Berlage (1856–1934)

Construction cost

3 000 000 guilders

Beurs, Amsterdam, 1884

Hendrik Petrus Berlage & Theodorus Sanders first round competition design, "Mercaturae", 1884, elevation on Damrak

Beurs, Amsterdam

At first, the Beurs in Amsterdam seemed set to mark the end of an architectural era. Cordonnier's winning design was a typical product of the nineteenth century, a period during which the styles of bygone eras were predominant. His design was lavishly embellished and clearly inspired by the French Renaissance, incorporating characteristic elements of this style. However, all this was not to be. Following a tumultuous competition, the winner was passed over, the construction order was repealed and a new architect, whose design would herald the dawn of a new architectural era, was confidentially approached: Hendrik Petrus Berlage (1856–1934).

However, his official appointment was preceded by one of the most remarkable architectural scandals the Netherlands had ever witnessed. Prior to the announcement of the official competition, the municipality had made a half-hearted attempt to organise the building of a new stock exchange, because the old building, which had been built less than fifty years before, was no longer adequate. The construction of the old exchange had also been preceded by a competition, and here too the winners were passed over and a member of the jury, Zocher, was appointed architect. In 1879, the municipality publicly invited architects to submit designs and suggest possible sites for a new stock exchange building. Participation was entirely free of obligation and there were no prizes to be won. The response to the competition was not astounding (23 designs were submitted), aside from the fact that, based on the architects' suggestions, a future building site was designated: the Damrak (which had to be partially filled in).

The competition begins

Having found a suitable building site, the way was cleared for the organisation of a proper competition. The competition programme was made available for perusal on 30 June 1884. Architects were asked to submit their designs before 1 November. The jury consisted of five European and three Dutch architects, who were to evaluate the designs in pairs. There were 199 entries, one of which was submitted after the closing date, and each design comprised an average of eight drawings. Prizes were eventually awarded to 10 participants. What is remarkable is that none of the selected designs were Classicist. The Neo-Renaissance style was predominant, particularly the Dutch variety, but also French and German derivatives. Partly due to the vaguely specified stipulations, the designs exhibited in the Rijksmuseum elicited a fair amount of criticism, especially from the anti-Cuypers lobby, who saw the all too evident influence of this Catholic architect in many of the selected designs[1]. It soon became apparent that this criticism was not completely unfounded. Five of the ten winning designs were selected for a second round (1884–1885), four of which will certainly have been to Cuypers' liking.
The five designs were by Joh. Vollmer (Berlin), Th. Sanders & H.P. Berlage (Amsterdam), John Groll (London / Amsterdam) & Friedrich Ohmann (Vienna), Ludwig Klinkenberg & Ernst Tauschenberg (Bremen) and Louis Cordonnier (Lille). The following architects dropped out of the competition: A.G. Rives (Paris), Otto Hiesen (Vienna), A. von Wielemans (Vienna), Frans van Deteghem (Lookeren) & J.G. Mouton (The Hague), and Bruno Schmitz & August Hartel. The architects were asked to submit a price estimate with their second round design. The maximum construction cost was set at 2 000 000 guilders. However, this reasonable and generally accepted condition was completely ignored by the jury. All of the participants altered their designs.

W. Kromhout competition design for the Dam Square, "Fancy", 1907

H.P. Berlage & Theodorus Sanders Amsterdam Beurs, first round competition design, "Mercaturae", 1884, left: ground floor, right: first floor

Beurs, interior view

H.P. Berlage Beurs, top: elevation on Damrak, 1896, centre: elevation on Beursplein, 1896, bottom: ground floor plan with Module, 1898

Designs revised

Sanders' and Berlage's design was still clearly inspired by the Dutch Renaissance style of the sixteenth and early seventeenth century, although a number of changes had been made. A particularly noticeable exterior alteration was that the Italian-inspired loggia on the south-facing, short side of the building had been replaced by a more Dutch façade. The interior had undergone even greater change. Nothing remained of the pompous Neo-Baroque style of the original hall of exchange with its lavishly decorative stucco-work and other ornamentation. It had been replaced by a bare brick hall, vaulted by a distinctive roof structure. However, the wall mould seemed a little inappropriate, a problem Berlage would later solve.

Although Cordonnier's design seemed to have been adapted to suit Cuypers' tastes, it had lost none of its original character. It would be more accurate to say that the applied Renaissance style had undergone a shift in accentuation from French to Dutch.

Klinkenberg and Tauschenberg completely altered their design. Their first design, a singularly ponderous, eclectic and probably impracticable stone mass, which had inexplicably survived the first round, was thrown out. Their new design was undoubtedly based on Cuypers' designs for the Rijksmuseum and the Amsterdam Central Station, which was under construction at the time.

The same applies to Groll and Ohmann's second design, which required far less alteration. Their alternative first round design (a rather inappropriate version of Balthasar Neumann's Residence in Würzburg) had by then been completely scrapped. This later led to a row between Groll and Ohmann. The latter had been principally responsible for the scrapped plan.

Finally, Vollmer's design, which had originally combined Dutch Renaissance elements with features of industrial architecture, now looked as though it had been inspired by late Gothic civil architecture, while the interior exuded a more sacral aura.

Winners announced

On 3 June 1885 the jury announced that they had awarded first prize to Cordonnier, ahead of Groll & Ohmann (2) and Berlage & Sanders (3). The announcement caused a certain amount of commotion, because it was rumoured that Cordonnier had copied parts of the Town Hall in La Rochelle (1595–1607) for his design. Moreover, Ohmann began to publicly lament the fact that Groll was getting all the attention. A jury split seemed imminent and the affair received widespread coverage in newspapers and specialist publications. The city council, who were fed up with the bickering, decided to award the prize money on 6 January 1886 and to free itself of any obligation regarding the result. This move was intended to smooth any ruffled feathers. However, on the initiative of alderman Coninck Westerman, the municipal architect Weissman was asked to submit an alternative design which would incorporate the best elements of the top two designs. Naturally, the jury was utterly incensed by this state of affairs, and once again the matter received extensive press coverage. On 2 February, following this rumpus, the municipality thought it best to repeal its decision to build a new stock exchange.

For a while, all was quiet around the new stock exchange. However, the municipality was kept on its toes by the hotel owner W.P. Werker, who inundated the civil servants with plans for a boulevard, the chief purpose of which seemed to be the further enrichment of W.P. Werker. One of the plans is worth mentioning, that of M. Hendriks, which had been submitted on Werker's initiative, under the names A.W. de Flines and J.F. van Glahn. However, this plan was not submitted for the competition.

Berlage's appointment

To everyone's surprise, Weissman was commissioned to alter the old stock exchange building in 1894. Berlage was appointed advisor. A year later a new alderman took charge of the matter: Mr Treub, a personal friend of Berlage's. It was Treub who informally asked Berlage whether he would be able build a new stock exchange for less than 3 000 000 guilders. Following Berlage's affirmative answer, it took until 1896 before he was officially commissioned. The stock exchange which Berlage eventually designed differed radically from all of the previous designs and its preparation was cloaked in total secrecy. So much so, in fact, that De Kruyff[2] et al did not have a clear target for their criticism. The contours of Berlage's design are vaguely reminiscent of the earlier design he had submitted with Sanders. But the similarity ends there.

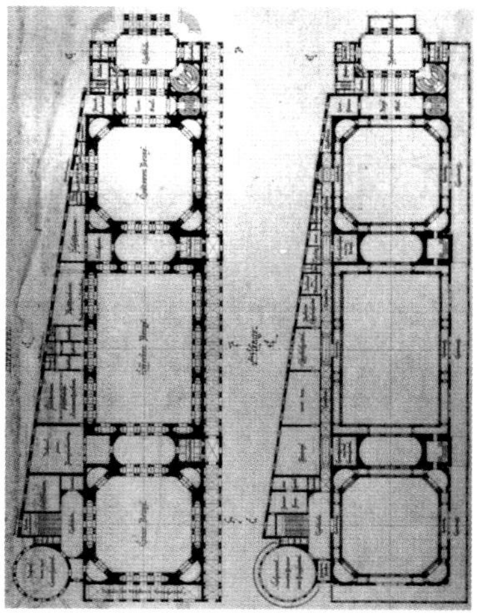

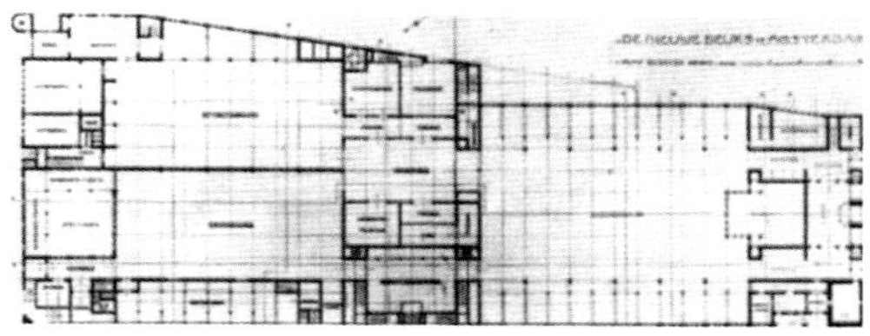

During the gradual process of design, from before April 1896 until construction began in 1898, the stock exchange became more and more austere. Stripped of all excessive decorative features and designed by means of a system of frames, the stock exchange was reduced to its barest brickwork form, in complete contrast to the style of its former rivals in the competition. The difference may best be illustrated by comparing late nineteenth century and early twentieth century stylistic approaches.

De Kruyff had justified the fact that Cordonnier had copied a sixteenth century Renaissance façade, by arguing that this was admissible in terms of the (then) prevailing principles of design. On the other hand, although Berlage's stock exchange was full of references to the past, not a single element was a copy of any feature from a bygone age.

Berlage's version of an Italian urban palazzo, situated on the corner of the Damrak and the Beursplein, has no Italian counterpart. The walls of the commodities exchange vaguely resemble those of a medieval cathedral, yet they are fundamentally different. The rear façade consists of stylised versions of the houses along the Amsterdam canals. And there are many more references of this sort to be discovered. Construction was completed in 1903, but soon thereafter a number of necessary improvements had to be made due to the unstable substratum. This included demi-columns and tie-bars in the commodities exchange on the ground floor.

When the stockbrokers moved to new premises in 1990, Berlage's Stock Exchange was put to good use as a music and exhibition venue.

1 *Cuypers had ruffled some feathers in Dutch architectural circles in the past. See the chapter on the Rijksmuseum for a full account.*

2 *De Kruyff, an extremely critical member of the jury, played an important part in the Stock Exchange affair. This was hardly surprising in light of the fact that he had submitted a design in 1879, together with the city councillor C. Muysken.*

Börse, Amsterdam

Bei Planungsbeginn schien es, als setze die Amsterdamer Börse einen Schlußstrich unter eine Epoche in der Geschichte der Architektur, denn der prämierte Entwurf von Cordonnier galt als typisches Produkt des 19. Jahrhunderts – einer Zeit, in der die Stilmerkmale vergangener Epochen vorherrschten. Cordonniers Entwurf der Börse sah reiche Verzierungen vor und basierte auf Vorbildern der französischen Renaissance, deren Stilelemente das Gebäude kennzeichneten. Nach einer tumultartigen Ausschreibung wurde der Gewinner übergangen, das Bauvorhaben zurückgezogen und in aller Stille ein anderer Architekt beauftragt, der mit seinem Entwurf eine neue Epoche in der Baugeschichte einläutete: Hendrik Petrus Berlage (1856–1934).

Berlages offiziellen Ernennung ging einer der denkwürdigsten Architekturskandale der Niederlande voraus. Schon vor Beginn der offiziellen Ausschreibung hatte die Stadt einen halbherzigen Versuch unternommen, den Bau einer neuen Börse voranzutreiben, da das bisherige, kaum 50 Jahre alte Gebäude den gewachsenen Ansprüchen nicht mehr genügte. Auch der Entwurf für die alte Börse entstammte einer Ausschreibung, bei der die Gewinner nicht berücksichtigt und die Aufträge an ein Jurymitglied (J.D. Zocher) vergeben worden waren. 1879 forderte die Stadt Amsterdam in einer öffentlichen Bekanntmachung zur Einsendung von Entwürfen für ein neues Börsengebäude auf. Die Teilnahme an der Ausschreibung galt als unverbindlich und wurde nicht prämiert. Entsprechend erwies sich keine der 23 Einsendungen als sehr vielversprechend – allerdings entschieden sich die Honoratioren für den zukünftigen Standort der Börse: den Damrak, der teilweise zugeschüttet werden mußte.

Der Wettbewerb beginnt

Da die Stadt nun über ein geeignetes Baugelände verfügte, war der Weg für eine offizielle Ausschreibung frei. Ab dem 30. Juni 1884 lagen die Pläne der Bauvorhaben zur Einsicht aus, die Entwürfe mußten vor dem 1. November eingereicht werden. Die Jury bestand aus fünf europäischen und drei niederländischen Architekten, die jeweils zu zweit die Vorschläge beurteilen sollten. Insgesamt gingen 199 Einsendungen ein (wobei einer zu spät eintraf), die im Schnitt acht Bauzeichnungen enthielten und von denen schließlich zehn prämiert wurden. Erstaunlicherweise war nicht einer der ausgezeichneten Entwürfe klassizistisch. Statt dessen dominierte die Neurenaissance hauptsächlich niederländischer Prägung, aber auch die französische und deutsche Variante dieser Stilrichtung waren vertreten. Die im Rijksmuseum ausgelegten Zeichnungen stießen – vor allem wegen der sehr vage formulierten Baubedingungen – auf heftige Kritik. Dabei trat vor allem eine gegen Cuypers eingestellte Gruppe hervor, die an den prämierten Einsendungen den übermächtigen Einfluß des katholischen Baumeisters bemängelte[1]. Schließlich kamen von zehn Entwürfen fünf in die zweite Ausschreibungsrunde (1884–1885), vier davon fanden Cuypers Zustimmung. Diese fünf Entwürfe stammten von Joh. Vollmer (Berlin), Th. Sanders und H.P. Berlage (Amsterdam), John Groll (London/Amsterdam) und Friedrich Ohmann (Wien), Ludwig Klinkenberg und Ernst Tauschenberg (Bremen) sowie von Louis Cordonnier (Lille). Für die zweite Runde wurde ein Kostenvoranschlag gefordert, der die maximale Bausumme von 2 000 000 Gulden nicht überschreiten durfte. Allerdings ignorierte die Jury diese durchaus übliche Bedingung, woraufhin sämtliche Teilnehmer ihre Entwürfe überarbeiteten.

Veränderte Entwürfe

Der Entwurf von Sanders und Berlage basierte zwar auf der niederländischen Renaissance des 16. und frühen 17. Jahrhunderts, aber sie hatten einige Veränderungen vorgenommen. So wollten sie die auf der schmalen Südseite gelegene Loggia im italienischen Stil durch eine niederländische Fassade ersetzen und die Innenräume neu gestalten. Der Börsensaal im pompösen neubarocken Stil mit seinen reichverzierten Stuckarbeiten und dem üppigen Dekor fiel im überarbeiteten Entwurf einer kahlen Backsteinhalle mit einer charakteristischen Dachkonstruktion zum Opfer. Cordonniers Entwurf schien dem Geschmack des Jurymitglieds Cuypers noch stärker angepaßt, ohne jedoch von seinem ursprünglichen Charakter einzubüßen: Es handelte sich um eine Akzentverschiebung von der französischen zur niederländischen Neurenaissance.

Klinkenberg und Tauschenberg überarbeiteten ihre Baupläne vollständig und ersetzten sie durch ein Konzept, das sehr von Cuypers Rijksmuseum und durch das im Bau befindliche Bahnhofsgebäude der Amsterdamer Centraal Station inspiriert schien. Gleiches galt für den zweiten Entwurf von Groll und Ohmann. Ihr Alternativvorschlag für die erste Ausschreibungsrunde (eine eher mißglückte Anspielung auf Balthasar Neumanns Residenz in Würzburg) verschwand sang- und klanglos und bildete später die Ursache für Auseinandersetzungen zwischen den beiden Architekten, da Ohmann für den verworfenen Entwurf verantwortlich zeichnete.

Vollmers erster Vorschlag – eine Mischung aus niederländischer Renaissance und Zweckbau – wurde durch einen Entwurf ersetzt, der auf die spätgotische bürgerliche Architektur anspielte und dessen Innenräume eine eher sakrale Ausstrahlung besaßen.

Ergebnis bekanntgegeben

Am 3. Juni 1885 verlieh die Jury Cordonniers Entwurf den ersten Preis, während der Vorschlag von Groll und Ohmann auf dem zweiten und der Entwurf von Berlage und Sanders auf dem dritten Platz landete. Diese Entscheidung verursachte heftige Empörung, zumal das Gerücht umging, Cordonnier habe für seinen Entwurf Teile des Rathauses von La Rochelle (1595–1607) kopiert. Der unerfreulichen Auseinandersetzung überdrüssig und im Bestreben, die Wogen zu glätten, beschloß der Stadtrat daraufhin, das Preisgeld zwar am 6. Januar 1886 zu verleihen, ohne jedoch eine Verpflichtung gegenüber dem Gewinner einzugehen. Auf Betreiben des Beigeordneten Coninck Westenberg erarbeitete der städtische Architekt Weissman einen Entwurf, der die besten Elemente der beiden prämierten Pläne (Platz 1 und 2) vereinigen sollte. Dies wiederum empfand die ehemalige Jury als Affront, der bei der Presse auf großes Interesse stieß. Um den Skandal zu beenden, entschied die Stadt am 2. Februar 1888, das gesamte Bauvorhaben zu annulieren.

Danach blieb es einige Zeit ruhig um die Börse, lediglich der Hotelbesitzer W.P. Werker sorgte mit seinen Plänen für einen Boulevard – mit denen er die Stadt jahrelang versorgte und deren vorrangigstes Ziel die weitere Vermehrung seines Vermögens zu sein schien – für regelmäßige Erheiterung.

Zur allgemeinen Verblüffung erhielt Weissman 1894 den Auftrag, die alte Börse den neuen Bedürfnissen anzupassen. Zu seinem Berater wurde Berlage ernannt. Nur ein Jahr später nahm sich der neue Beigeordnete Treub, ein persönlicher Freund Berlages, der Sache an und ließ inoffiziell anfragen, ob Berlage den Bau der neuen Börse für weniger als 3 000 000 Gulden für möglich halte.

Berlage benannt

Nach Berlages Bestätigung erhielt er 1896 offiziell den Auftrag. Die Pläne für das neue Börsengebäude unterschieden sich erheblich von allen bisherigen Einsendungen und Unterlagen strengster Geheimhaltung, so daß De Kruyff[2] u.a. das Ziel für ihre Kritik fehlte. Die Umrisse der neuen Börse erinnern zwar noch an Berlages erste, zusammen mit Sanders entworfenen Baupläne, sonstige Ähnlichkeiten sucht man vergebens. Während der langen Entwicklungsphase, die von April 1896 bis zum Baubeginn 1898 dauerte, zeichnete sich immer deutlicher ab, daß die nach einer Rastermethode entworfene Börse sehr nüchtern ausfallen würde: überflüssige Ornamente verschwanden, und zurück blieb ein kahles Backsteingebäude, das Welten von den Entwürfen der ehemaligen Preisträger entfernt war.

Während Cordonniers Giebelfassade stark an die Renaissance des 16. Jahrhunderts erinnerte und von De Kruyff als Bestandteil der zeitgenössischen Designprinzipien verteidigt wurde, enthielt Berlages Börse zwar ebenfalls zahlreiche Anspielungen auf vergangene Epochen, ohne dabei jedoch auch nur ein Element früherer Stilrichtungen komplett zu verwenden: Berlages Interpretation eines italienischen Stadtpalais auf der Ecke Damrak/Beursplein wäre in Italien undenkbar. Die Wände der Warenbörse erinnern vage an eine mittelalterliche Kathedrale, ohne sie zu kopieren. Auf der Rückseite des Börsengebäudes befinden sich stilisierte Amsterdamer Grachtenhäuser. Weitere Anspielungen auf vergangene Stilrichtungen sind leicht zu finden. Aufgrund seines radikalen Bruchs mit der Vergangenheit gilt Berlage als Vater der modernen niederländischen Architektur.

Die Börse wurde 1903 fertiggestellt, erfuhr allerdings kurze Zeit danach aufgrund des schlechten Baugrundes einige Veränderungen wie etwa die Halbsäulen und Zugstangen im Erdgeschoß der Warenbörse. 1990 wurden die Handelsaktivitäten der Börse verlegt und das Börsengebäude in einen Konzert- und Ausstellungskomplex umgewandelt.

1 *Cuypers hatte die Gemüter in der niederländischen Architekturwelt schon beim Wettbewerb um das Rijksmuseum erhitzt.*

2 *Das kritische Jurymitglied De Kruyff spielte im Börsendrama« eine wichtige Rolle. Dazu trug sicherlich auch die Tatsache bei, daß De Kruyff im Jahre 1879 zusammen mit dem Stadtverordneten C. Muysken selbst einen Entwurf für das neue Börsengebäude eingereicht hatte.*

La Bourse, Amsterdam

Au départ, le concours pour la Bourse d'Amsterdam semblait devoir être l'aboutissement d'une ère de l'architecture. Le plan de Cordonnier, le lauréat, était un pur produit du XIXème siècle, c'est-à-dire d'une époque qui se plaisait à choisir ses références dans les périodes révolues de l'histoire de l'architecture. Le projet s'inspirait clairement de la Renaissance française et son ornementation était élégante, mais rien n'y fit. A l'issue d'un concours tumultueux, le vainqueur fut écarté, la commande repoussée et un nouvel architecte qui, lui, annonçait bel et bien une ère nouvelle, fut discrètement approché: Hendrik Petrus Berlage (1856–1934).

Mais sa désignation officielle allait être précédée du plus bruyant scandale architectural qu'aient jamais connu les Pays-Bas. Avant l'annonce du concours officiel, la municipalité avait déjà essayé, sans conviction, de faire édifier une nouvelle bourse pour remplacer l'ancienne, construite moins de cinquante ans plus tôt, mais déjà inadaptée. Cette ancienne réalisation avait également fait l'objet d'un concours qui avait vu les gagnants mis à l'écart au bénéfice d'un membre du jury, Zocher, nommé architecte du projet. En 1879, la municipalité fit donc une annonce officielle pour appeler les architectes intéressés à proposer le site et les plans d'une nouvelle bourse. Aucune contrainte n'était imposée mais aucun prix ne serait attribué. Les participants ne se précipitèrent pas (23 projets seulement) mais un site intéressant ressortit néanmoins de ce premier tour, le Damrak, qui devait être partiellement comblé.

Les débuts du concours

Le site enfin défini, on pouvait envisager un concours sérieux dont le programme fut publié le 30 juin 1884. Les concurrents étaient priés de remettre leurs projets avant le 1er novembre et le jury désigné se composait de cinq architectes étrangers et de trois néerlandais, qui devaient évaluer les projets en couple. Chacune des 199 proposition comptait environ 8 plans et dessins et 10 prix furent attribués aux meilleures, dont aucune n'était d'esprit classique. Le style néo-Renaissance prédominait, en particulier dans ses variantes hollandaises, françaises et allemandes. En grande partie du fait de l'imprécision du cahier des charges, les projets exposés au Rijksmuseum soulevèrent un bon nombre de critiques, en particulier celles des adversaires de Cuypers qui décelaient l'influence évidente de l'architecte catholique dans beaucoup des projets sélectionnés[1]. Il apparut bientôt que ces critiques n'étaient pas sans fondement. Cinq des projets choisis, dont quatre ne pouvaient que plaire à Cuypers, furent retenus pour un second tour (1884–1885).

Ils étaient signés Joh. Vollmer (Berlin), Th. Sander et H. P. Berlage (Amsterdam), John Groll (Londres / Amsterdam) et Friedrich Ohmann (Vienne), Ludwig Klinkenberg et Ernst Tauschenberg (Brême) et Louis Cordonnier (Lille). A. G. Rives (Paris), Otto Hiesen (Vienne), A. von Wielemans (Vienne), Frans van Deteghem (Lookeren), J. G. Mouton (La Haye) et enfin Bruno Schmitz et August Hartel étaient écartés de la compétition.

Les architectes retenus devaient cette fois soumettre un devis avec leurs plans. Le coût maximum de construction avait été fixé à 2 000 000 de fl., une limite raisonnable qui fut complètement ignorée par le jury. Tous les participants à ce second tour modifièrent leurs plans initiaux.

La révision des projets

Même s'ils lui avaient apporté de nombreux changements, le projet de Sanders et Berlage était encore fortement inspiré de la Renaissance hollandaise du XVIème et début du XVIIème siècle. La loggia à l'italienne de la façade sud, en particulier, avait laissé la place à un dessin plus franchement hollandais. L'intérieur avait été encore plus profondément modifié. Rien ne restait du pompeux style néo-baroque de la grande salle, recouverte initialement de stucs et d'ornements omniprésents. A sa place, Berlage proposait maintenant des murs de brique nue se terminant en une voûte de style assez particulier. La forme des murs semblait un peu inappropriée, problème que Berlage allait résoudre plus tard. Si le projet Cordonnier avait sans doute été modifié pour plaire à Cuypers, il n'avait rien perdu de son caractère original. Son style Renaissance française s'était simplement «hollandisé». Klinkenberg et Tauschenberg transformèrent totalement leurs plans. Leur première proposition, une énorme masse de pierre de style éclectique, sans qualités fonctionnelles qui avait inexplicablement passé le cap du premier concours fut mise à la corbeille. Leur nouveau projet s'inspirait des dessins de Cuypers pour le Rijksmuseum et la gare centrale d'Amsterdam, alors en construction. On aurait pu dire la même chose de celui de Groll et Ohmann, qui nécessitait nettement moins d'adaptations. Leur premier plan, de forme circulaire (version un peu maladroite de la résidence de Balthasar Neumann à Würzburg) avait été complètement refait d'où une dispute entre les deux architectes.

Le projet Vollmer, mêlant à l'origine des éléments néo-Renaissance à des éléments d'architecture industrielle, s'était lui converti au néo-gothique tardif et son intérieur aurait fort bien convenu à une église.

La proclamation des vainqueurs

Le 3 juin 1885, le jury annonça l'attribution du premier prix à Cordonnier, devant Groll et Ohmann, Berlage et Sanders. L'annonce souleva une certaine émotion lorsque se répandit le bruit que le vainqueur avait en partie copié l'hôtel de ville de La Rochelle (1595–1607). De plus, Ohmann se plaignit publiquement de ce que son partenaire Groll monopolisait l'attention. Un éclatement du jury semblait imminent et l'affaire était suivie aussi bien par la grande presse que par les magazines spécialisés. Fatigué de la controverse, le conseil municipal décida de remettre le montant des prix aux lauréats le 6 janvier 1866 et de reprendre sa liberté, espérant ainsi calmer les vanités froissées. A l'initiative du conseiller Coninck Westerman, l'architecte de la ville Weissman, fut prié de travailler à un projet alternatif en se servant des meilleures idées des deux premiers lauréats. Le jury s'enflamma et une fois encore, la presse s'en mêla. Le 2 février, après cet essai malheureux, la ville décida de renvoyer la construction de la nouvelle bourse à des jours meilleurs!

Le calme revint quelque temps. Parallèlement, les fonctionnaires de l'urbanisme étaient inondés par l'hôtelier W. P. Werker de propositions directes pour la création d'un nouveau boulevard et de la nouvelle bourse, dont le but principal semblait d'enrichir encore davantage le sieur Werker. L'une d'entre elles vaut d'être mentionnée, celle de M. Hendriks, proposée sous les noms de A. W. de Flines et J. F. van Glahn, mais il ne participa pas au concours.

Brusquement, à la surprise générale, Weisman fut chargé en 1894 de transformer l'ancienne bourse et Berlage fut nommé pour le conseiller. Un an plus tard, un nouveau conseiller municipal prit le dossier en charge, Treub, ami personnel de Berlage. Il lui demanda officieusement s'il se sentait capable de construire une nouvelle bourse pour moins de 3 millions de fl.

La nomination de Berlage

Berlage ayant répondu par l'affirmative, il lui fallut encore attendre 1896 pour être officiellement désigné. L'édifice qu'il soumit alors différait radicalement de tous les projets précédents et sa mise au point fut entourée du plus profond secret. On voulait éviter de servir de cible aux critiques de De Kruyff[2] et de quelques autres. De façon très générale, le nouveau plan de Berlage rappelait légèrement le premier projet qu'il avait présenté avec Sanders. Mais la similitude s'arrête ici: tout au long des travaux préparatoires qui durèrent d'avril 1896 à 1898, le style de la nouvelle Bourse évolua vers toujours plus d'austérité. Débarrassé de toute ornementation excessive et construit sur un système de trame, le bâtiment choisit la rigueur de la brique nue et se révéla ainsi totalement différent de ses anciens rivaux. Le XXème siècle se confrontait pour la première fois au XIXème siècle finissant.

De Kruyff avait justifié les accusations de copie portées contre Cordonnier en expliquant que l'on pouvait admettre ces emprunts selon les principes de travail alors en cours. Chez Berlage, bien que son nouveau projet ait été chargé de références au passé, aucun élément n'avait été copié sur quoi que ce soit. La version berlagienne d'un palais italien à l'angle du Damrak et de Beursplein n'avait aucun équivalent italien. Les murs pouvaient évoquer ceux d'une cathédrale médiévale tout en étant fondamentalement différents. La façade arrière stylisait une perspective de maisons le long d'un canal d'Amsterdam et de multiples citations de ce genre sont encore à découvrir. La construction s'acheva en 1903, mais très vite des problèmes de résistance du sol se posèrent qui obligèrent à poser des demi-colonnes et des tirants dans la salle des titres du rez-de-chaussée. Lorsque les agents de change quittèrent le bâtiment pour de nouvelles installations en 1990, la Bourse de Berlage fut intelligemment transformée en centre de concerts et d'expositions.

1 *Cuypers avait froissé de nombreuses susceptibilités architecturales dans un passé récent (voir le chapitre sur le Rijksmuseum).*

2 *De Kruyff, membre du jury, très critique, joua un rôle important dans l'affaire de la Bourse, ce qui n'était guère étonnant puisqu'il avait lui-même proposé un projet en 1879 avec le conseiller municipal C. Muysken.*

Hendrik Petrus Berlage & Theodorus Sanders second round competition design, "Mercaturae", 1885, exterior view on Zoutsteeg, third prize

Hendrik Petrus Berlage & Theodorus Sanders second round competition design, "Mercaturae", 1885, interior view, third prize

Louis-Marie Cordonnier first round competition design "Y", 1884, elevation on Oudebrugsteeg

Louis-Marie Cordonnier first round competition design "Y", 1884, elevation on Damrak

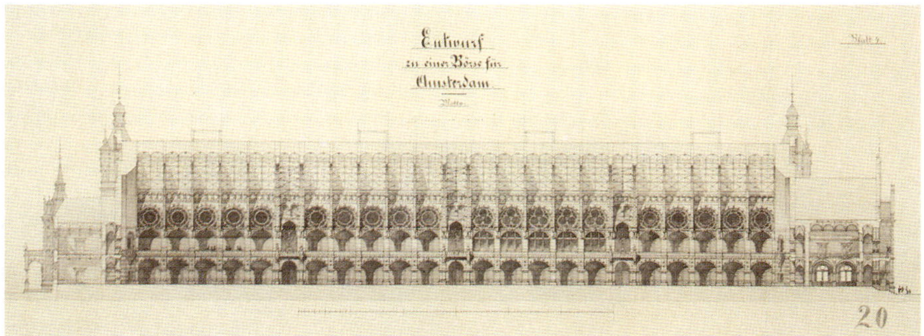

August Hartel & Bruno Schmitz first round competition design, "Lieven de Key", 1884, elevation on Damrak

Johannes Vollmer first round competition design "La Bourse ou la Vie", 1884, longitudinal section

Alexander von Wielemans first round competition design "Neederland", 1884, elevation on Damrak

M. Hendrickx design for Boulevard and Exchange, without date, exterior view on Damrak

F. van Peteghem & J.G. Mouton first round competition design "Persévérance", 1884, elevation on Damrak

F. van Peteghem & J.G. Mouton first round competition design "Persévérance", 1884, elevation on Beursplein

Ludwig Klingenberg & Ernst Tauschenberg first round competition design "Ammerack", 1884, exterior view on Zoutsteeg

Ludwig Klingenberg & Ernst Tauschenberg first round competition design "Ammerack", 1884, elevation on Beursplein

BEVRSGEBOUW TE AMSTERDAM
FAÇADE SUR LE DAMRAK
A·G·R
G

NIEUW BEURSGEBOUW

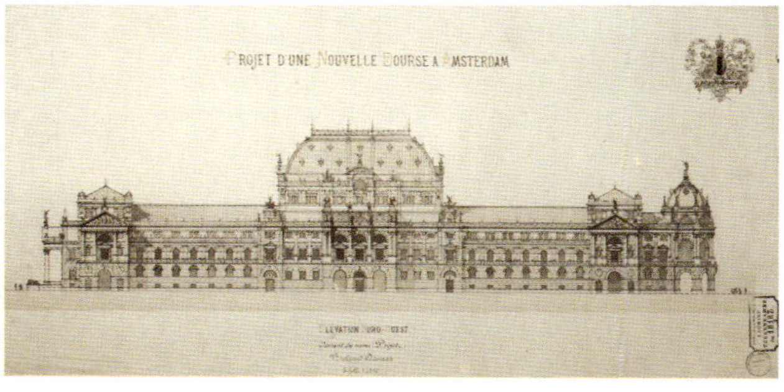
PROJET D'UNE NOUVELLE BOURSE A AMSTERDAM

A.G. Rives first round competition design "A.G.R.", 1884, elevation on Damrak

Otto Hieser first round competition design "Je maintiendrai", 1884, elevation on Damrak

John Groll & Friedrich Ohmann Classicist version of first round competition design "In hoc signo floresco", 1884, elevation on Damrak

John Groll & Friedrich Ohmann Neo-Gothic version of first round competition design "In hoc signo floresco", 1884, exterior view on Damrak

John Groll & Friedrich Ohmann Classicist version of first round competition design "In hoc signo floresco", 1884, exterior view on Damrak

A.W. Weissman Municipal design for the new Exchange, 1887, exterior view on Zoutsteeg

A.W. Weissman Municipal design for the new Exchange, 1887, interior view

John Groll & Friedrich Ohmann Neo-Gothic version of first round competition design "In hoc signo floresco", 1884, elevation on Beursstraat

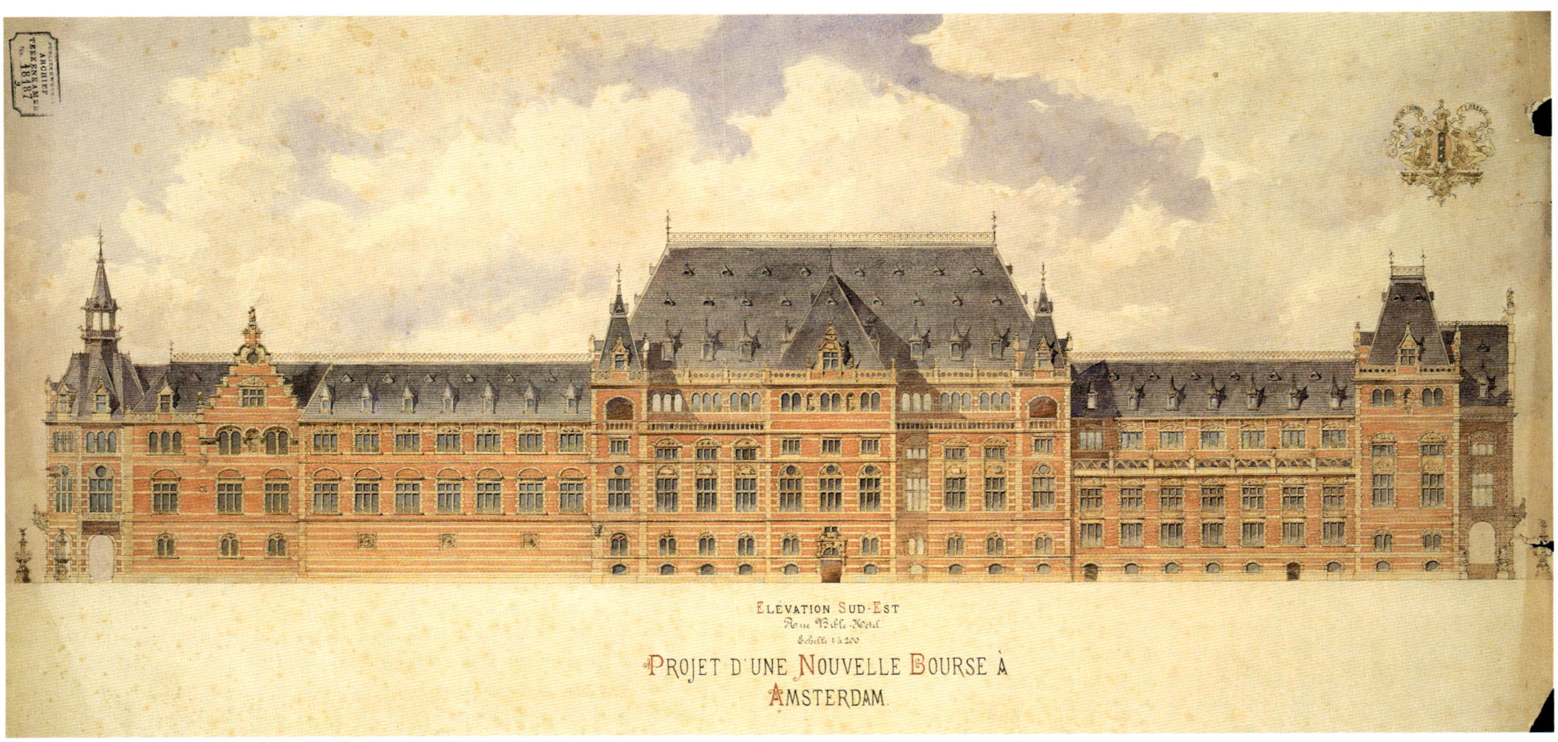

World Exhibition, Paris, 1889

140

Project

World Exhibition, 1889

Site

Champ-de-Mars, Paris

Dates

1 May 1886 to 18 May 1886

Number of entries

107

Jury

J. Alphand (exhibition director, chairman), politicians, scholars, architects, engineers

Result

Joint first prize Gustave Eiffel & Stephen Sauvestre, Jean-Camille Formigé, Ferdinand Dutert

Commissioned by

Ministry of Trade

Construction

1887 to 1889

Architect

Gustave Eiffel (1832–1923)

Construction cost

3 155 000 f (estimated), final cost was 2.5 times higher

World Exhibition, Paris, 1889

Etching from "Le Génie Civile", April 2, 1887, Paris World Exhibition of 1889, bird's eye view of Palace on Champ-de-Mars

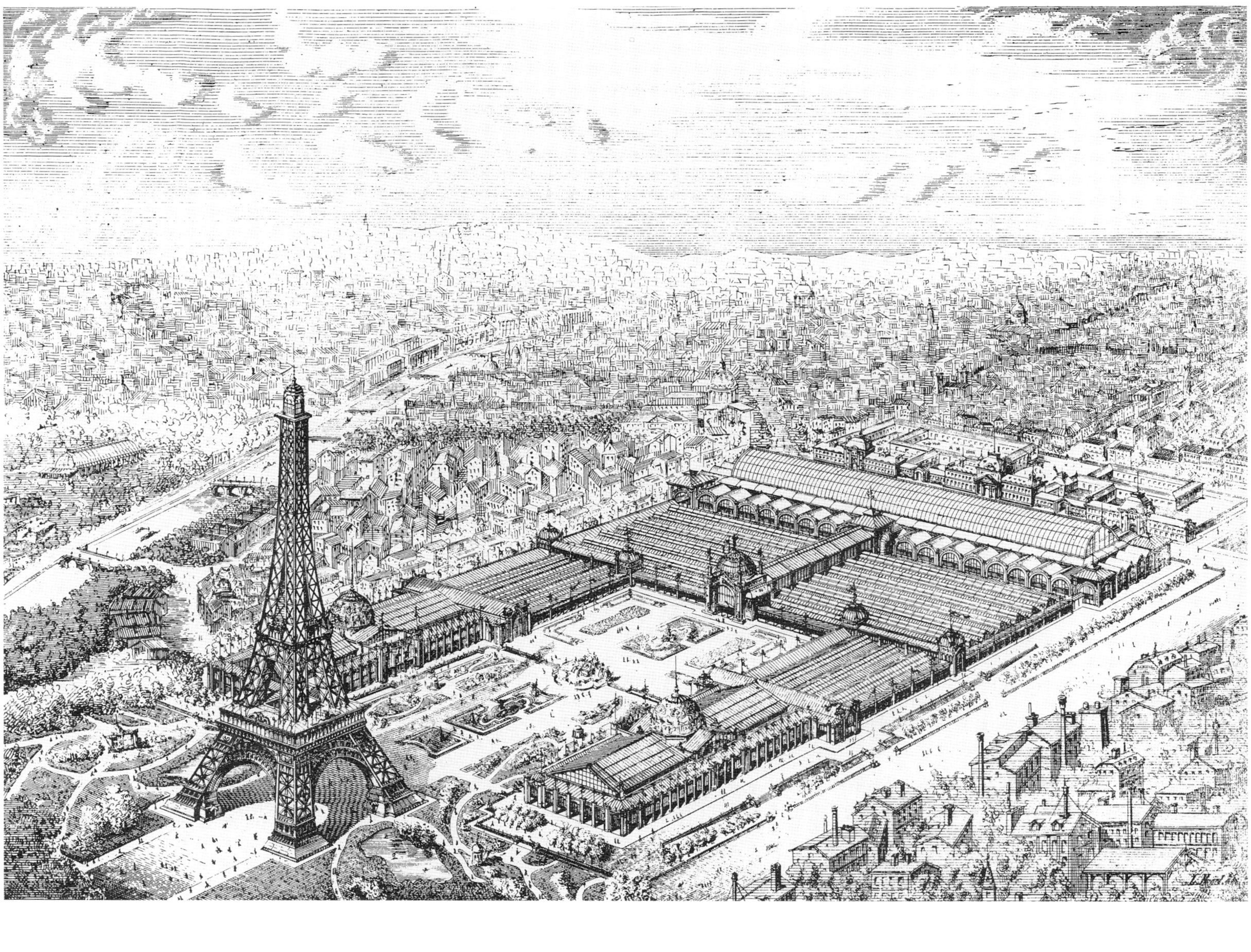

World Exhibition, Paris

The concept of a general international exhibition dates back to the eighteenth century, when a public showcase was sought for the products of trade and industry. The first such world fair was held in 1851 at London's Crystal Palace, which had been specifically designed for this purpose. Participants from 95 countries exhibited the products of their genius, in the hope of being awarded a medal or receiving an honourable mention.

The idea behind organising international exhibitions in the latter half of the nineteenth century was that a joint effort of this sort would lead to greater fraternity between nations, greater unity and free trade. This went hand in hand with a sense of boundless faith in human technical ingenuity. It was the era of the machine and of mass production. Paris prepared for the exhibition of 1889 in the knowledge that it had organised no less than three previous exhibitions. All of these had been as impressive as the first exhibition held in London. This was largely due to the fact that a temporary exhibition presented the perfect opportunity to display new materials and forms of construction by incorporating or applying these in the exhibition halls. The nature of the event implied that large audiences and a wide variety of products had to be accommodated (London 1851: six million, Paris 1900: 48 million) and that the construction and dismantling of the exhibition halls had to be achieved with comparable ease[1].

In 1855, a machine hall measuring 1200 metres had been built along the Seine and at the exhibitions of 1867 and 1888, the Champ-de-Mars had been dominated by giant complexes resembling greenhouses. Due to the growing interest in the exhibition, a large piece of land on the northern bank of the Seine was added to the exhibition grounds in 1878. It was here that the Trocadéro Palace would be constructed (dismantled in 1937). In view of the growing number of visitors, it was inevitable that the exhibition of 1889 should be even grander than its predecessors. This provided sufficient pretext for the organisation of a competition, announced on 1 May 1886, for the design of an exhibition area which would include a 300 metre high iron tower.

A thousand foot dream

The idea for a tower of this height did not come out of the blue. In England and the United States, plans had previously been launched for monuments which would exceed the magical height of a thousand feet (approximately 300 metres). However, for many years, towers higher than the Obelisk in Washington (1848–1885, 169 metres) or the Mole Antonelliana in Turin (1863, 170 metres) seemed to be no more than a Utopian dream, until widespread industrialisation and the development of a railway network brought a new generation of self-confident engineers into the limelight. These engineers, educated at the Ecole Polytechnique, the Ecole des Ponts et Chaussées or the Ecole Centrale, had long been overshadowed by the architects of the Académie des Beaux-Arts or the Ecole Spéciale d'Architecture, for whom they were allowed to make structural designs. These structures were subsequently ingeniously concealed by the architect in question. However, as time progressed, the designer-engineer became emancipated and a growing appreciation for the structure itself started to develop. People were impressed by the technical ingenuity of engineers, who were able to construct a roof for an entire station, a bridge or, indeed, an exhibition hall of monumental proportions. Architects, who occupied themselves with decorative features and the design of annexes, were no longer seen as the engineers' superiors but

Adolph Alphand

Jean-Camille Formigé

Ferdinand Dutert, Portrait by *Jean-Joseph Weerts* 1891

Gustave Eiffel

as their equals. Two of these engineers, Emile Nougier (Ecole des Mines) and Maurice Koechlin (Ecole Polytechnique), deserve credit as the initiators of the plan to build a thousand foot tower for the Paris Exhibition of 1889. Their design, consisting of a number of rough sketches, dates from 1884. They were employed at the offices of Gustave Eiffel.

Eiffel was already a renowned engineer at the time, having designed bridges, viaducts and roofing structures, often of monumental proportions. He had also contributed to the Exhibition of 1878. Eiffel was not immediately convinced by Koechlin and Nougier's plan, which closely resembled the present tower. The tower consisted of four framework posts, placed at the corners of a square base and tapering towards one another at the top. Despite Eiffel's doubts, the two engineers proceeded with their plan, calling in the assistance of the architect Stephen Sauvestre, who was also employed by Eiffel. Sauvestre was to occupy himself with the tower's embellishment. He designed a number of decorative features, including the semi-circular arches on the lower level. Eiffel was impressed by the revised plans and, having paid off both engineers, decided to submit the plans to the organisation in charge of the Paris Exhibition.

Galerie des Machines interior, World Exhibition, Paris, 1889, from "Le Journal Illustré", no. 22, June 1889

Eiffel Tower, man working at 180 metres

Seventeen days

One member of this organisation had already been impressed by Eiffel's expertise: the Minister of Trade, Lockroy. In order to keep up appearances, Lockroy organised a competition, but the seventeens day period set for the submission of alternative designs was hardly likely to produce any serious competition for Eiffel's precisely calculated drawings. Nevertheless, there were 107 entries.

The subject of the competition was the design of the actual exhibition grounds and a tower measuring 300 metres to be built on the exhibition grounds. Many architects saw through the scheme and did not even take the trouble of designing a tower of their own, concentrating on the exhibition area and the most important buildings. M.J. Cassien-Bernard and Francis Nachon, for example, submitted a design in which the tower was not situated on the Champ-de-Mars, but on the continuation of the Dôme des Invalides. Moreover, it had been the organisers' intention to build the tower over the Seine. Eiffel's tower design was simply incorporated into the plans as a set feature. Of course, Eiffel and his engineers had a head start on the other architects, whose designs were often more fanciful than they were technically sound. An example of the latter was the design submitted by Bourdais and Sébillot, which dates from 1884. This round, stone tower was reminiscent of the Tower of Pisa, placed on top of an ancient city gate. Although Bourdais replaced the stones with steel in his competition design, he neither succeeded in gaining the jury's admiration, nor in enhancing the credibility of his design. The same applies to the designs of the other participants.

The jury awarded a joint first prize to Jean-Camille Formigé, Ferdinand Dutert (1845–1906) and Gustave Eiffel. Formigé was commissioned to design the Palais des Arts Libéraux, the large exhibition halls. Taking into account the other first prize winners, this choice was remarkable, because Formigé's design closely resembled the exhibition halls for the 1878 Exhibition. The bombastic, eclectic style of this Beaux-Arts architect stood in stark contrast to the constructive, rational approach of Eiffel, who, as expected, had been commissioned to design the tower. Dutert had submitted a spacious, open plan with Eiffel's tower as a centre-piece. As a result, the main exhibition hall had to be moved to the back end of the Champ-de-Mars and turned ninety degrees, to provide sufficient space for the tower. Consequently, the length of the building lay diagonally across the axis of the exhibition area[2]. The jury commissioned Dutert to design the "Galerie des Machines", for the same site as his proposed exhibition hall. The Eiffel Tower was moved towards the Seine again and Formigé's building was to be constructed in the middle of the Champ-de-Mars, exactly as he had planned.

The Galerie des Machines was to be almost as spectacular as the Eiffel Tower. Dutert (Académie des Beaux-Arts) called in the technical assistance of Victor Contamin (1840–1898), who had gained experience working on the French railway network. Contamin was assisted by the engineers Pierron and Charton. They designed a steel structure with a span of 115 metres, a length of 429 metres and a height of 45 metres. The span of 115 metres almost doubled the existing record for structures which had been built in the past, and not a single extra point of support was required! Joseph Bouvard and Ulysse Graigny were awarded one of the consolation prizes. They were commissioned to design the Pavillon de la Ville de Paris.

Eiffel's contribution

Meanwhile, Eiffel was working on his tower. Although the idea had not been his originally, he did see the project through to completion. The undertaking required an incredible amount of organisational talent and a sizeable investment, because Eiffel personally had to organise most of the financing. Furthermore, Eiffel had to submit a new design for the lifts, for which his original design had been rejected. And lastly, he had to take into account the force of lateral winds and the downward force exerted by the immense weight of the tower. For an engineer of Eiffel's expertise, the latter problem was relatively easily solved. He simply adapted the structural formulas he used for the piles of his bridges to suit the structure of the tower. In this case, the piles were not placed in a row, but at the corners of a square. The lateral force would be counteracted by bending the upright supports and tapering the tower towards the top. The tower's weight was, of course, reduced by the open framework. At first sight, the semi-circular arches designed by Sauvestre seem to form a structural component. However, they have a purely decorative function and, whereas the tower served as its own scaffolding, a special scaffolding had to be constructed to install the arches. Eiffel seemed to have few qualms about the matter. He did not stand in the way of an architect who wanted to add embellishments. However, a number of Sauvestre's other contributions to the tower were rejected on financial grounds. As a result, little remained of the glass pavilions on the first and second floor and an entire floor was scrapped between the second floor and the top. The top itself (at 334,015 metres) is far less grand than that in Sauvestre's design.

The technical challenges presented by the tower were much less of a problem for Eiffel than the challenge of public opinion. There was a particularly vehement outcry amongst the architects, who would have preferred to see "their" man Bourdais get the commission, rather than an insignificant engineer. Artists, writers and composers also raised their voices in protest. Some of them slated this Tower of Babel and saw it as a threat to French art. There was a veritable storm of derogatory comment and some critics even threatened to take the matter to court. Eiffel remained undaunted, convinced of the intrinsic beauty of the structure. The storm of protest certainly did not have an effect upon construction. The tower was completed within 26 months, in good time to serve as the gateway to the World Exhibition, Paris which would reaffirm French status across the globe – if only for the 2.5 million rivets used in the tower's construction.

Jean-Camille Formigé Palais des Arts Libéraux, exterior

Jean-Camille Formigé Palais des Beaux-Arts, entrance hall

1 *Some of the buildings were of a semi-permanent nature and were therefore designed to withstand the test of time.*

2 *Raulin's design also included an exhibition hall which ran parallel to the Seine. This hall was to be situated under the tower.*

Weltausstellung, Paris

Der Gedanke einer Weltausstellung stammt aus dem 18. Jahrhundert, da man bereits damals nach neuen Wegen suchte, Produkte aus Handel und Industrie einer größeren Öffentlichkeit vorzustellen. Die erste internationale Ausstellung datiert allerdings erst aus dem Jahr 1851: Im Londoner Crystal Palace trafen sich Teilnehmer aus 95 Ländern, um ihre Erzeugnisse zu präsentieren und mit etwas Glück eine Medaille oder eine ehrenvolle Erwähnung zu bekommen.

Allen Weltausstellungen in der zweiten Hälfte des 19. Jahrhunderts lag der Gedanke zugrunde, die Völkerverständigung, die Einheit und den freien Handel zu fördern. Dazu kam ein grenzenloses Vertrauen in den menschlichen Erfindungsgeist. Es war das Zeitalter der Maschine und der Massenproduktion. Als man in Paris mit den Vorbereitungen zur Weltausstellung von 1889 begann, hatte die Stadt bereits drei solcher Ausstellungen organisiert, jede mindestens so beeindruckend wie die Messe im Londoner Crystal Palace.
1855 hatte man eine Maschinenhalle von 1 200 Metern Länge am Ufer der Seine erbaut; für die Ausstellungen von 1867 und 1878 waren enorme Glashauskomplexe, die das ganze Champ-de Mars in Beschlag nahmen, errichtet worden. Aufgrund des wachsenden Publikumsinteresses wurde das Messegelände 1878 um ein großes Areal am nördlichen Seine-Ufer erweitert, auf dem das Palais du Trocadéro entstand (1937 abgerissen). Die ständig steigenden Besucherzahlen machten deutlich, daß die Weltausstellung von 1889 noch großartiger ausfallen mußte als ihre Vorgänger. Daher kam es am 1. Mai 1886 zu einer Ausschreibung für das Ausstellungsgelände, in der u.a. auch ein 300 Meter hoher Turm vorgesehen war.

Ein Traum von 300 m Höhe

Die Idee zu einem solchen Turm war nicht von heute auf morgen entstanden. In Großbritannien und den Vereinigten Staaten hatten sich bereits Architekten mit Plänen für ein Bauwerk befaßt, das die magische Höhe von 1000 Fuß (ca. 300 Meter) überschreiten sollte. Aber eine größere Bauhöhe als beim Obelisk von Washington (1848–1885, 169 Meter) oder der Mole Antonelliana in Turin (1863, 168 Meter) erschien jahrelang als undurchführbar. Erst die rasch fortschreitende Industrialisierung und der Ausbau der Eisenbahn brachten eine neue Generation selbstbewußter Ingenieure hervor. Nach ihrer Ausbildung an der École Polytechnique, der École des Ponts et Chaussées oder der École Centrale hatten diese Männer lange Zeit im Schatten von Architekten gestanden, die an der Académie des Beaux-Arts oder der École Spéciale d'Architecture ausgebildet worden waren und für die ein Ingenieur bestenfalls Konstruktionspläne berechnen durfte.
Mit dem technischen Fortschritt jedoch wuchs das Interesse an der Konstruktion von Bauwerken. Ingenieure, die in der Lage waren, das Dach einer Bahnhofshalle, eine Brücke oder auch eine Ausstellungshalle von monumentalen Proportionen zu entwerfen, trafen auf allgemeine Bewunderung. Wenn sich der Architekt mit dekorativen Merkmalen oder dem Entwurf von Nebengebäuden beschäftigte, tat er dies nun als gleichberechtigter Partner und nicht mehr als Vorgesetzter des Ingenieurs. Zwei dieser Ingenieure, Emile Nougier (École des Mines) und Maurice Koechlin (École Polytechnique), konstruierten für die Weltausstellung von 1889 einen 1000 Fuß hohen eisernen Turm. Die ersten Rohskizzen zu ihrem Entwurf stammten aus dem Jahr 1884, als beide für das Büro von Gustave Eiffel (1832–1923) arbeiteten.
Zu dieser Zeit galt Eiffel bereits als berühmter Ingenieur, der Brücken, Viadukte und Dachkonstruktionen von teilweise monumentalen Ausmaßen entworfen hatte. Darüber hinaus war er an der Weltausstellung von 1878 beteiligt gewesen. Koechlins und Nougiers Entwurf – der in groben Zügen bereits mit der heutigen Konstruktion übereinstimmte – stieß nicht sofort auf seine Zustimmung. Der Turm sollte aus einem Stahlgerüst von vier Pfeilern bestehen, die auf dem Erdboden die vier Ecken eines quadratischen Grundstücks bildeten und sich zur Turmspitze hin vereinigten. Trotz Eiffels ablehnender Haltung arbeiteten die beiden Ingenieure ihren Entwurf weiter aus und baten dabei den Architekten Stephen Sauvestre um Hilfe, der ebenfalls für Eiffel tätig war. Sauvestre sollte sich mit der dekorativen Gestaltung des Turms befassen; von ihm stammen u.a. die Rundbögen unterhalb der ersten Plattform. Die überarbeiteten Pläne überzeugten Eiffel schließlich. Er zahlte beide Ingenieure aus und bot danach den Entwurf den Organisatoren der Weltausstellung an.

17 Tage

Zum Organisationskomitee gehörte Handelsminister Lockroy, der sich schon früher von Eiffels Konstruktionen begeistert gezeigt hatte. Zwar ließ Lockroy der Ordnung halber noch einen Architekturwettbewerb ausschreiben, aber der vorgegebene Zeitraum von 17 Tagen war viel zu kurz, um eine ernsthafte Konkurrenz für Eiffels durchdacht ausgearbeiteten Pläne entwickeln zu können. Dennoch gab es 107 Einsendungen. Die Ausschreibung umfaßte den Entwurf zur eigentlichen Weltausstellung sowie die zusätzliche Konstruktion eines 300 Meter hohen Turmes. Viele Architekten vermuteten, daß hier nicht alles mit rechten Dingen zuging, und versuchten sich erst gar nicht am Entwurf eines Turmes, sondern konzentrierten sich auf das Ausstellungsgelände und die wichtigsten Gebäude. M. J. Cassien-Bernard und Francis Nachon beispielsweise reichten einen Entwurf ein, der den Bau des Turms nicht auf dem Champ-de-Mars, sondern in der Verlängerung des Invalidendoms vorsah. Auch waren die Organisatoren ursprünglich von einem anderen Standort (über der Seine) ausgegangen. Schließlich übernahmen die Organisatoren Eiffels Turmentwurf als feste Größe, denn die Pläne seines Ingenieursbüros waren den meisten Architekten weit voraus, die in ihren Vorschlägen eher durch Phantasie als durch technisches Können überzeugten. Ein gutes Beispiel hierfür ist der Entwurf von Bourdais und Sébillot aus dem Jahre 1884. Ihr runder, steinerner Turm erinnerte an den Turm von Pisa, den man auf einem antiken Stadttor plaziert hatte. Für die Ausschreibung ersetzte Bourdais den steinernen Turm durch eine Stahlkonstruktion, konnte aber auch mit dieser Änderung weder die Zustimmung der Jury erlangen noch seinen Entwurf glaubwürdiger machen.
Die Jury prämierte die Beiträge von Jean-Camille Formigé, Ferdinand Dutert (1845–1906) und Gustave Eiffel mit dem ersten Preis. Formigé erhielt den Bauauftrag für das Palais des Arts Libéraux, die große Ausstellungshalle. Angesichts der anderen beiden Preisträger war dies eine bemerkenswerte Wahl, da Formigés Entwurf sehr stark an die Hallen der Weltausstellung von 1878 erinnerte. Der bombastische Eklektizismus dieses Beaux-Arts-Architekten steht im krassen Gegensatz zu den rationellen Konstruktionen Eiffels, der – wie erwartet – den Auftrag zum Bau des Turms erhielt. Dutert hatte einen großzügigen, offenen Entwurf eingereicht, in dessen Zentrum Eiffels Turm entstehen sollte. Um dem Turm genügend Raum zu lassen, verlagerte er die große Ausstellungshalle auf die Rückseite des Champ-de-Mars und drehte sie um 90 Grad. Dadurch lag die Längsseite der Halle diagonal zur Achse des Ausstellungsgeländes[1]. Die Jury beauftragte Dutert mit dem Entwurf der Galerie des Machines, die genau an der Stelle entstehen sollte, an der er seine Ausstellungshalle geplant hatte. Dadurch verschob sich der Eiffelturm wieder zur Seine, so daß Formigés Beitrag seinen eigenen Plänen entsprechend in der Mitte des Champ-de-Mars entstehen konnte.
Die Galerie des Machines sollte ein ebenso spektakuläres Bauwerk werden wie der Eiffelturm. Dutert (Académie des Beaux-Arts) überließ die technische Ausführung Victor Contamin (1840–1898), der seine Erfahrungen u.a. beim Bau der französischen Eisenbahn gesammelt hatte, und der seinerseits die Ingenieure Pierron und Charton als Assistenten verpflichtete. Einer der Trostpreise ging an Joseph Bouvard und Ulysse Gravigny, die den Pavillon de la Ville de Paris erbauen durften.

Eiffels Beitrag

In der Zwischenzeit arbeitete Eiffel an seinem Turm. Obwohl der eigentliche Entwurf nicht von ihm stammte, sollte er das Projekt realisieren. Dies erforderte neben einem enormen Maß an Organisationstalent auch sehr viel Geld, da er einen Großteil der Finanzierung selbst zu tragen hatte. Außerdem mußte er neue Detaillösungen für die Fahrstühle finden, da sein ursprünglicher Vorschlag nicht akzeptiert worden war, sowie das Problem der Seitenwinde und der enormen vertikalen Kräfte lösen, die durch das große Gesamtgewicht entstehen würden. Letzteres war für einen Ingenieur wie Eiffel ein kleineres Problem: Er berechnete seine Konstruktion auf dieselbe Weise wie die Pfeiler seiner Brücken, wobei die Pfeiler in diesem Fall nicht hintereinander, sondern im Quadrat standen. Die seitlichen Kräfte konnten durch die Krümmung der Pfeiler und die sich nach oben verjüngende Spitze aufgefangen werden. Die offene Stahlkonstruktion sorgte dafür, daß das Eigengewicht des Turms relativ niedrig blieb. Die von Sauvestre entworfenen Rundbögen wirken auf den ersten Blick wie ein Element der Konstruktion, dienen aber rein dekorativen Zwecken: Während der Turm sein eigenes Gerüst bildete, mußte für diese Bögen ein zusätzliches Gerüst gebaut werden. Die technischen Herausforderungen, denen Eiffel sich stellen mußte, waren leichter zu überwinden als die öffentliche Meinung. Vor allem die Architekten – die den Auftrag ihrem Kollegen Bourdais gegönnt hatten – äußerten ihren Unwillen; aber auch bildende Künstler, Schriftsteller und Komponisten protestierten im Namen der bedrohten französischen Kunst gegen diesen »Turm von Babel«. Keiner der Proteste konnte den Fortgang der Arbeiten aufhalten, und nach 26 Monaten war der Turm fertiggestellt. Pünktlich zur Eröffnung diente er als Eingangstor zu einer Weltausstellung, die das Ansehen Frankreichs in der ganzen Welt steigern sollte.

1 *Auch der Beitrag von Raulin sah eine Ausstellungshalle parallel zur Seine vor. Diese Halle sollte unter dem Turm errichtet werden.*

Exposition universelle, Paris

Le concept d'exposition universelle remonte au XIXème siècle, période marquée par les débuts du libre échange où l'on cherchait à créer des vitrines pour les produits du commerce et de l'industrie. C'est à Londres, en 1851, que se tint au Crystal Palace, spécialement construit pour l'occasion, la première exposition internationale. Des participants venus de 95 pays y exposèrent les produits dont ils étaient le plus fiers avec l'espoir de remporter des médailles ou des mentions.

En ce siècle confiant dans les bienfaits du progrès, ces manifestations étaient censées promouvoir à la fois le commerce international et une plus grande fraternité entre les nations. C'était l'époque des premiers grands triomphes du machinisme et de la production de masse. Paris se prépara donc pour l'Exposition Universelle de 1889, troisième de ce type à se tenir dans la capitale, dont on espérait un succès encore plus grand. Conçues pour accueillir de vastes publics (6 millions de visiteurs à Londres en 1851, 48 millions à Paris en 1900), ces expositions temporaires étaient l'occasion d'utiliser de nouveaux matériaux, de tester de nouvelles techniques et d'inventer de nouvelles formes de construction. Ces expérimentations étaient d'autant plus faciles que les halls devaient être la plupart du temps détruits[1] à l'issue de la manifestation.

En 1855, une galerie des machines de 1 200 mètres de long avait été élevée le long de la Seine et, en 1867 et 1878, le Champ-de-Mars s'était vu recouvrir d'un gigantesque complexe de verrières. Anticipant le succès de l'exposition, un vaste terrain supplémentaire fut alloué aux organisateurs sur la rive Nord de la Seine en 1878 pour y construire le Palais du Trocadéro, démoli en 1937 seulement. Tout indiquait que la manifestation de 1889, qui coïncidait avec le centenaire de la Révolution, allait remporter encore plus de succès que les précédentes. Un concours fut donc lancé pour concevoir l'exposition qui devait être dominée par une tour métallique de 300 mètres.

Un rêve de trois cent mètres de haut

L'idée d'une tour de cette sorte n'était pas née par hasard. En Angleterre et aux Etats-Unis, des plans de monuments dépassant la hauteur fatidique de 300 mètres avaient déjà été tracés. Mais ils relevaient encore de l'utopie, même si un obélisque de 169 mètres de haut avait été érigé à Washington et le Mole Antonelliana de Turin (1863) atteignait déjà 68 m. C'était sans compter sur une nouvelle génération d'ambitieux ingénieurs, apparue avec l'industrialisation et le développement des chemins de fer. Formés à l'Ecole Polytechnique ou à celle des Ponts et Chaussées, ils avaient longtemps été tenus à l'écart par les architectes de l'Ecole des Beaux-Arts ou même de l'Ecole Spéciale d'Architecture. Ils réalisaient pour eux les plans de structures de plus en plus complexes que l'architecte dissimulait ensuite soigneusement.

Les années passant, les ingénieurs-concepteurs s'émancipèrent et l'on s'intéressa de plus en plus aux structures des bâtiments. Même le public était impressionné par l'audace technique de ces hommes qui pouvaient couvrir une gare d'une immense verrière, jeter un pont spectaculaire, ou monter en quelques mois une galerie de proportions monumentales. Les architectes, obnubilés par l'ornementation et d'obscures controverses stylistiques, perdirent peu à peu de leur supériorité pour devenir leurs égaux.

C'est à deux de ces ingénieurs, Emile Nougier (Ecole des Mines) et Maurice Koechlin (Ecole Polytechnique), employés de l'agence de Gustave Eiffel, que revient le mérite d'avoir imaginé une tour de 300 m pour l'exposition de 1889. Leur projet, assez sommaire, date de 1884. Eiffel était quant à lui un ingénieur renommé, auteur de ponts, de viaducs et de structures couvrantes, souvent monumentales. Il avait déjà travaillé sur l'Exposition de 1878 et ne fut pas d'emblée enthousiasmé par le plan de ses collaborateurs, très proche de la tour qui fut réalisée. Il consistait en une ossature de quatre piliers, disposés en carré et se rejoignant au sommet. Malgré les doutes de leur patron, les deux ingénieurs poussèrent leurs plans avec l'aide de l'architecte Stephen Sauvestre, autre employé d'Eiffel. Il fut chargé de l'embellissement de la tour et conçut certains éléments décoratifs comme les arches semi-circulaires de la base. Eiffel fut enfin convaincu par ces nouveaux plans et après avoir financièrement désintéressé les deux ingénieurs, décida de soumettre le projet aux organisateurs de l'exposition.

Dix-sept jours...

L'un d'entre eux, le ministre du Commerce Lockroy, connaissait et appréciait déjà le savoir-faire d'Eiffel. Pour préserver les apparences, il organisa un concours, mais en ne laissant que dix-sept jours de réflexion aux candidats alors que l'équipe d'Eiffel avait eu tout son temps. Néanmoins, 107 participants présentèrent des projets. L'objet du concours portait sur l'exposition elle-même, y compris la déjà fameuse tour. Beaucoup d'architectes comprirent la manœuvre, ne perdirent même pas le temps de dessiner eux-mêmes une tour, et se concentrèrent sur le plan de masse de l'exposition et les bâtiments les plus importants. Considérés comme incontournables, les plans d'Eiffel et de ses ingénieurs furent tout simplement intégrés dans les projets. M.- J. Cassien-Bernard et Francis Nachon, par exemple, proposèrent même un projet dans lequel la tour n'était pas située sur le Champ-de-Mars, mais dans le prolongement de l'esplanade des Invalides, au-dessus la Seine. D'autres architectes proposèrent cependant des dessins plus fantaisistes mais techniquement aventurés. Bourdais et Sébillot imaginèrent une tour ronde en pierre, rappelant celle de Pise, et surmontant une porte de ville à l'ancienne. Bourdais abandonna les pierres pour l'acier, mais n'emporta pas pour autant l'adhésion du jury.

Celui-ci accorda un premier prix ex-æquo à Jean-Camille Formigé, Ferdinand Dutert (1845–1906) et Gustave Eiffel. Formigé reçut la commande du Palais des Arts Libéraux, l'une des grandes galeries prévues. Par rapport aux autres projets, ce choix était étonnant tant il ressemblait aux galeries déjà construites pour l'exposition de 1878. Le style éclectique et emphatique de cet architecte très Beaux-Arts, contrastait violemment avec l'approche constructiviste et rationaliste d'Eiffel qui, comme on pouvait s'y attendre, reçut la commande de la tour. Dutert avait quant à lui proposé un plan aéré centré autour de celle-ci et repoussant la principale galerie au fond du Champ-de-Mars. Le jury lui demanda de concevoir la Galerie des Machines qui devait être située sur le même site que le hall d'exposition qu'il avait proposé. La Tour Eiffel fut rapprochée de la Seine et les bâtiments de Formigé implantés de chaque côté du centre du Champ-de-Mars.

La Galerie des Machines était presque aussi spectaculaire que la Tour Eiffel. Dutert (de l'Académie des Beaux-Arts) fit appel à Victor Contamin (1840–1898) brillant ingénieur-constructeur du réseau français des chemins de fer. Assisté des ingénieurs Pierron et Charton, il créa une structure d'acier de 429 m de long, 115 m de large et 45 m de haut. La largeur de 115 m doublait le record mondial pour une voûte sans un seul point de soutien central. Joseph Bouvard et Ulysse Graigny reçurent l'un des prix de consolation et la commande du Pavillon de la Ville de Paris.

La contribution d'Eiffel

Pendant ce temps, Eiffel travaillait à sa tour. L'entreprise nécessitait un véritable génie d'organisation et un énorme investissement pour lequel Eiffel s'était personnellement engagé. Bien que ce ne fut pas sa propre idée, il en suivit de très près la réalisation. Par exemple, il proposa un nouveau dessin pour les ascenseurs dont la première version avait été rejetée. Le problème le plus important restait cependant celui de la force des vents et de l'énorme poids exercé par la tour sur un sol meuble en bordure de fleuve. Pour un ingénieur de ce talent, la difficulté fut vite résolue.

Il adapta les formules qu'il utilisait pour les piles des ponts. Dans ce cas particulier, ces «piles» n'étaient pas placées en ligne, mais en carré. Les forces latérales seraient compensées par la courbure des supports verticaux et l'effilement de la tour vers le haut. Le poids de la tour était réduit grâce à son ossature très ouverte. Si, à première vue, les arcs semi-circulaires de Sauvestre semblent faire partie de la structure, ils sont en réalité purement décoratifs. Alors que la tour en s'élevant fonctionnait comme son propre échafaudage, il fallut en réaliser un pour les monter. Eiffel n'était pas très satisfait de cet ajout, même s'il ne tenait pas à s'opposer à un architecte qui voulait apporter des améliorations esthétiques, mais d'autres idées de Sauvestre furent repoussées pour des raisons de coût. Presque rien ne fut conservé de ses pavillons de verre du premier et second étage et un niveau complet fut supprimé entre le second étage et le sommet. Celui-ci, culminant à 334 m, fut moins élaboré que dans le dessin de Sauvestre.

Pour Eiffel, les défis techniques de la tour furent moins délicats à affronter que les critiques du public. Les architectes, qui auraient préféré voir l'un des leurs, Bourdais, décrocher le contrat, plutôt qu'un ingénieur, étaient particulièrement virulents. Des artistes, des écrivains et des compositeurs protestèrent à leur tour. Certains maudirent cette moderne tour de Babel dans laquelle ils voyaient une menace pour l'art français. On assista à une tempête de commentaires acerbes et des tentatives furent évoquées de porter l'affaire devant les tribunaux. Eiffel resta impassible, convaincu de la beauté intrinsèque de sa structure. Les protestations ne ralentirent pas tout au long de la construction qui dura 26 mois. Elle fut réalisée dans les délais et servit de porte triomphale à une Exposition Universelle qui allait réaffirmer l'image de la France à travers le monde. Ce qui éclipsait un devis largement dépassé et les 2,5 millions de rivets qui avaient servi à sa construction.

1 *Certains bâtiments étaient conçus pour être plus durables et furent conservés quelques années. Certains existent encore.*

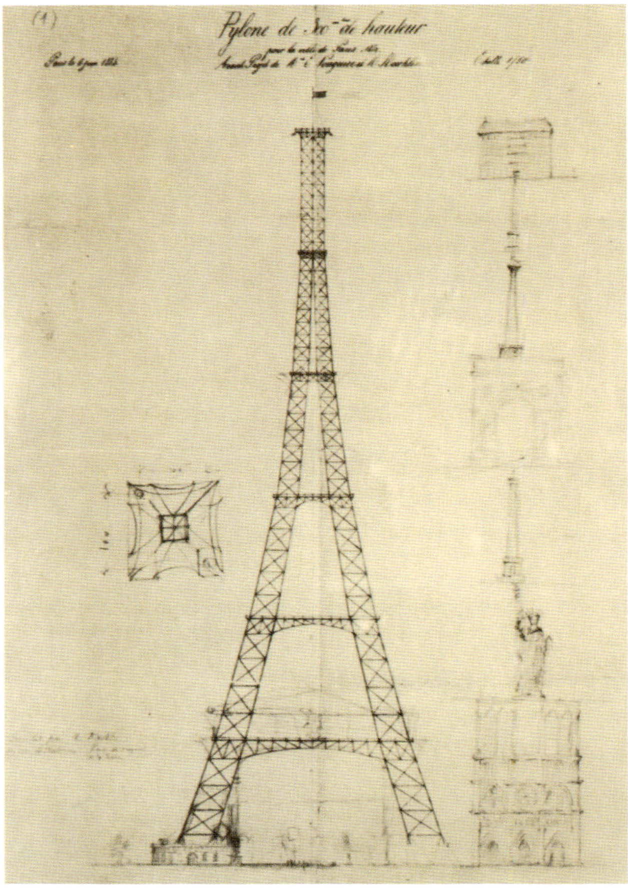

Maurice Koechlin "Pyléne de 300 mètres de hauteur", study of the feature for the World Exhibition Paris by Emile Nougier and Maurice Koechlin, 1884, sketch of the structure

Gustave Eiffel (presenter), Emile Nougier, Maurice Koechlin (engineers), Stephen Sauvestre (architect) "Projet de monument commémoratif à ériger à l'exposition universelle de 1889", etching from "Le Génie Civil", December 13, 1884, exterior view

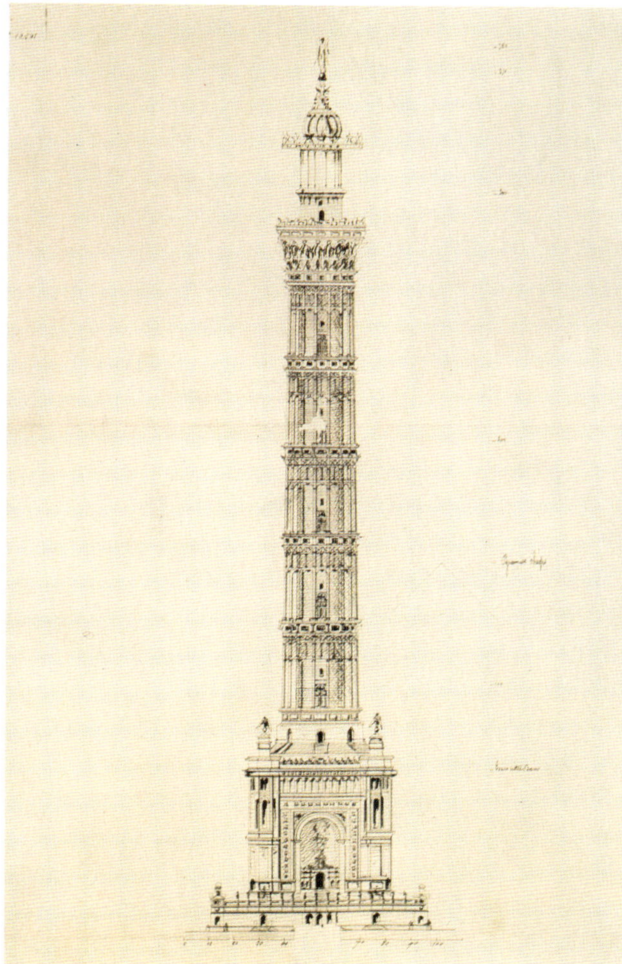

Gustave Eiffel "Tour de 300 mètres", elevation

Jules Bourdais "Projet de phare monumental pour Paris", 1885, elevation

Final design of the "Tour de 300 mètres" in colour, without date, exterior view

Gustave Eiffel & Stephen Sauvestre
"Tour de 300 mètres", without date, montage of arch decoration

Ferdinand Dutert & Victor Contamin
"Galerie des Machines", drawing from monograph by J, Alphand, without date, section

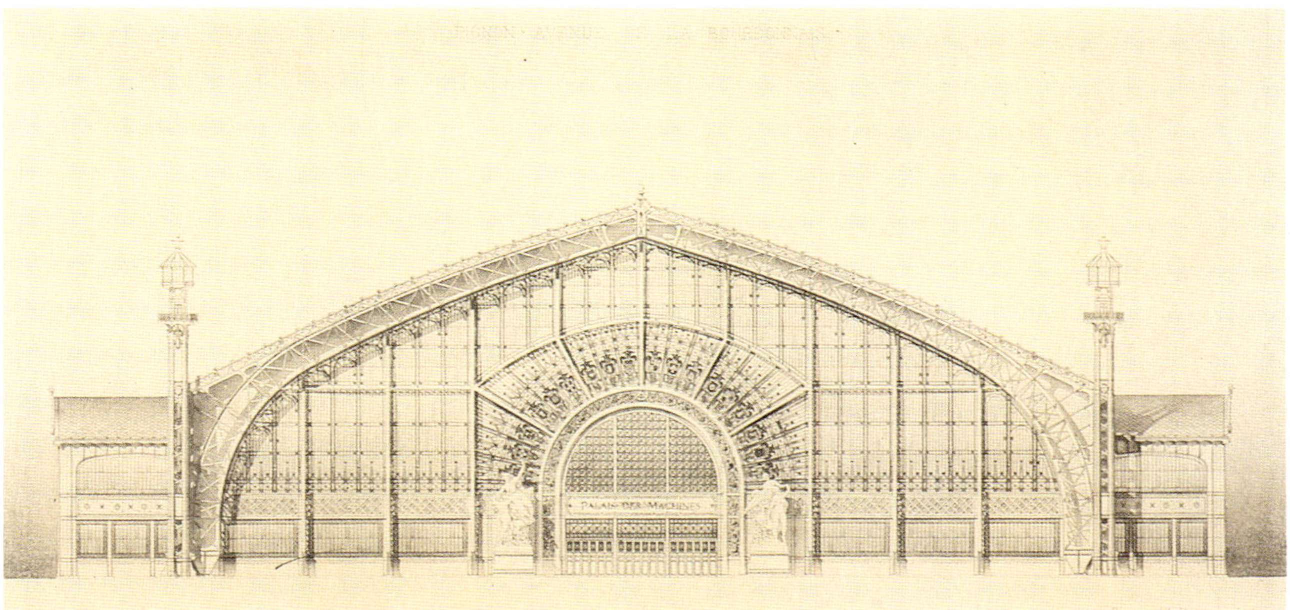

Ferdinand Dutert & Victor Contamin
"Galerie des Machines", without date, elevation on Avenue de la Bourdonnais

Ferdinand Dutert & Victor Contamin
"Galerie des Machines", without date, glass roof of grand entrance hall

Ferdinand Dutert & Victor Contamin
"Galerie des Machines", without date, interior view of grand entrance hall of Galerie des Machines towards Palais des Industries Diverses

Ferdinand Dutert & Victor Contamin
"Galerie des Machines", without date, longitudinal section of grand entrance hall, left: Palais des Machines, right: Palais des Industries Diverses

1789
1855

Joseph Bouvard & Ulysse Gravigny
Pavillon de la Ville de Paris, sketch, without date, front elevation of main entrance

Joseph Bouvard & Ulysse Gravigny
Pavillon de la Ville de Paris, 1889, detail of partition wall

Joseph Bouvard & Ulysse Gravigny
Pavillon de la Ville de Paris, without date, front elevation of main entrance

Joseph Bouvard & Ulysse Gravigny

Pavillon de la Ville de Paris,

without date

M.J. Cassien-Bernard & Francis Nachon competition design for the exhibition grounds, 1886, bird's eye view, second prize

Gustave Raulin competition design for the exhibition grounds, 1886, elevation on the Seine, second prize

Ferdinand Dutert competition design for the exhibition grounds, 1889, bird's eye view, Trocadéro section

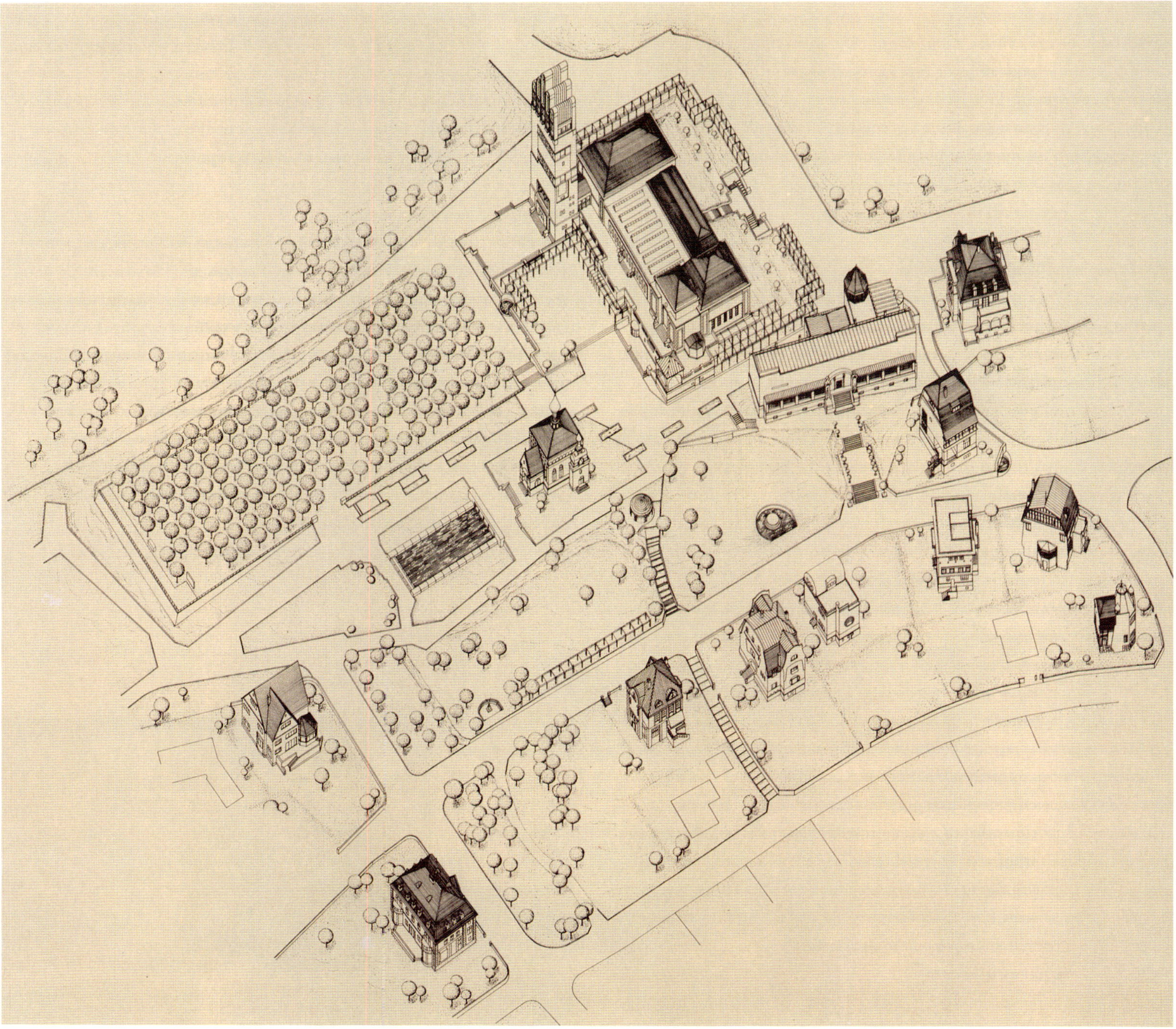

Project

House for a patron of the arts

Dates

Announcement December 1900 *Closing date* 25 March 1901
Result announcement May 1901

Number of entries

36

Jury

Henry van de Velde, Otto Wagner, Martin Dülfer, Joseph Maria Olbrich, Alexander Koch, Von Berlepsch-Valendas, Hans Christiansen, F. Putzer, J. Gräbner, Hans Schliepman, J. Hoffmann

Result

First prize None *Second prize* G. Baillie Scott *Third prize* Leopold Bauer, Oskar Marmorek, Paul Zeroch

Commissioned by

Alexander Koch, Zeitschrift für Innendekoration (Magazine for Interior Decoration)

Haus eines Kunstfreundes, Darmstadt, 1901

Charles Rennie Mackintosh
competition design, 1901, interior view of music room, special purchase prize

Haus eines Kunstfreundes, Darmstadt

Charles Rennie Mackintosh (1868–1928) was one of the leading artists around the turn of the century. In order to understand the significance of his competition design for Haus eines Kunstfreundes, a brief review of the cultural climate in Great Britain and on the Continent is necessary, since Mackintosh played a leading role on both sides of the Channel.

Vienna Secession

At the time, the artistic climate in Europe was dominated by avant-gardist movements such as Jugendstil and Art Nouveau. These allied movements were both intent on conceiving a new form of architecture which dispensed with the eclecticism of the late nineteenth century. This rebellion against tradition also took place in Vienna, where Otto Wagner had succeeded the aged professor Karl von Hasenauer[1] at the Academy of Fine Arts in 1894. Wagner's assistant was Joseph Maria Olbrich (1867–1908) and his best student was Josef Hoffmann. These two young artists founded the Wiener Secession (Vienna Secession) in 1897, together with Gustav Klimt and Koloman Moser. They had Wagner's complete approval. He joined the movement in 1899, which caused a scandal at the time because the Vienna Secession was anti-academic and therefore against the existing order. Olbrich was the most prominent artist in this group, mainly due to the contribution he had made to modern architecture. He designed the exhibition building for the Vienna Secession[2] in 1898 and consequently found himself in a predicament which closely resembled Mackintosh's position in Glasgow: maligned by the conservative population – both Glasgow and Vienna were old-fashioned, "respectable" cities – and revered by the professional community.
Ernst Ludwig, Archduke of Hessen, had also caught wind of Olbrich's fame. This gentleman was a patron of the arts who wanted to make Darmstadt the capital of contemporary art. In order to achieve this, he had established an artists' colony on a hill near Darmstadt, the Mathildenhöhe. The Archduke's new palace had been decorated by the Arts & Crafts artist Baillie Scott and he now asked Olbrich to design the architecture for the artist's colony. Construction was started in 1901 and the result was an unprecedented creative explosion of Jugendstil architecture. Olbrich designed all but one of the villas for the artists[3], the exhibition buildings and the famous "Hochzeitsturm" (wedding tower).

The four Macs

The period marking the breakthrough of the Vienna Secession as an art movement also saw the development of a similar movement in Glasgow. This movement was led by four people (soon known as The Four): Charles Rennie Mackintosh, Margaret Macdonald (Mackintosh's wife), her sister Frances Macdonald and Herbert Macnair (Frances Macdonald's husband). They had met at the Glasgow School of Art and later developed their now famous Glasgow Style. This style was at loggerheads with the prevailing Arts & Crafts movement. The Arts & Crafts movement was trying to counterbalance the detrimental effects of the industrial revolution and wanted to stimulate handicrafts. Sound and simple objects of applied art were to be integrated into everyday life. English rural architecture served as a model. Important members of this movement were C. Voysey and, of course, Baillie Scott, who would later be Mackintosh's "rival" in the competition. Both the Arts & Crafts movement and The Four saw architecture, applied arts and crafts as Gesamtkunstwerk, that is to say, mutually dependent upon one another. Although the movements had similar points of departure and had been influenced by the same tradition[4], their artistic products were completely different. Mackintosh – the only working architect of The Four – later went his own way[5].
In 1896, The Four had submitted work for the Arts & Crafts exhibition. Though initially criticised, their work later met with approval. Between 1897 and 1899, Mackintosh built the Glasgow School of Art.

Joseph Maria Olbrich a poster for the exhibition at the Artists' Colony in Darmstadt in 1901

The opening of the first exhibition at the Artists' Colony in Darmstadt on May 15, 1901, in front of the Ernst-Ludwig-Haus

Consequently, the fame of the Glasgow Style spread to Europe. The Four – who had by now split up into two couples – were invited to submit work for an exhibition of the Vienna Secession in the autumn of 1900. Their style evidently appealed to the tastes of the Viennese artists. Mackintosh's motif of four squares within a square was regularly copied and both Hoffmann and Olbrich were wildly enthusiastic.

Haus eines Kunstfreundes

Mackintosh's fame gained an additional impetus in 1901 when the Zeitschrift für Innendekoration[6] organised a competition for the design of a "house for a patron of the arts". Although Mackintosh did not win the competition – he did not submit all his drawings on time – his design was published by Alexander Koch in portfolio format, along with those of Baillie Scott and Leopold Bauer (Meister der Innenkunst, 1902). Mackintosh later exhibited his drawings at the world exhibition for decorative art in Turin (summer, 1902). None of the three prize-winning designs was ever executed.

The winning designs submitted by Baillie Scott and Mackintosh differed radically. Their drawings perfectly illustrate the differences between the Arts & Crafts style and Mackintosh's characteristic approach. A collection of rural architectural forms is clearly discernible in Baillie Scott's design. The house has French-looking towers on the north side and Dutch clock gables, which break the line of the roof, on the south side. The roof is tiled and the house has high chimneys. All these features contribute to the picturesque character of the design.

A striking feature is the complete symmetry of the two long sides of the building.

Mackintosh's design is completely different, although it does allude to rural styles, particularly the Scottish stately home (Baronial Style). His style of reference, however, is more subtle. He applied similar irregular, asymmetric forms, but turned them into abstract shapes and volumes. Wherever necessary, windows and other elements have been placed asymmetrically within this abstract structure, as is the case in Baillie Scott's design. In order to maintain a certain unity, the line of the apex extends across the entire length of the house. The simplicity of Mackintosh's façades is echoed in his floor plan.

One of the main problems confronting participants was that they had to design a house which offered the cosy comforts of a home but also had to accommodate a large number of visitors. Mackintosh came up with the following solution: a narrow entrance and vestibule lead directly into the hall, which extends upward across both floors. This hall may be almost doubled in size by removing the partition wall between the hall and the dining room. The screen between the reception room and the music room can also be removed, and the hall becomes accessible when the double doors of these rooms are opened. Mackintosh's interior differs radically from Baillie Scott's. The latter created a characteristically rural atmosphere in the best Arts & Crafts tradition. The music room has a wooden floor and a beamed ceiling. The small stage is flanked by timber-framed walls and the programme of decorations seems to have been influenced by Slavic folk art. In his Mackintosh biography, Thomas Howarth remarks, with a touch of bias, that Baillie Scott's music room seems to be a perfectly suitable venue for country dancing, while Mackintosh's music room seems to have been made to perform Beethoven. In Baillie Scott's design, the ingeniously designed objects seem to have been haphazardly positioned, while all the elements in Mackintosh's design are in harmony with one another. The form and colour of the wainscoting and the furniture are perfectly attuned to one another. As always in Mackintosh's designs, the living room and bedrooms have been decorated in light colours, while darker tints have been used for the hall and dining room. The ceilings are smooth and have been fitted with numerous lamps. Mackintosh went to great lengths to create a balance between natural and artificial light. Baillie Scott's dining room opens out through semi-circular arches on columns. The wall, supported by the columns, has been plastered in a stone-and-block pattern which suddenly flows into a peacock frieze. In contrast, Mackintosh's dining room is both stylish and dignified.

Leopold Bauer's design reflected the period of architectural history discussed at the beginning of this chapter. Bauer was educated at the Academy of Fine Arts in Vienna, under von Hasenauer and later Otto Wagner. He excelled in architecture and applied art. He was initially influenced by Olbrich – this is clearly evident in his competition design –

Charles Rennie Mackintosh

Charles Rennie Mackintosh Hill House, 1902, exterior from south-east

Charles Rennie Mackintosh Hill House, 1902, main bedroom

Joseph Maria Olbrich Haus Olbrich in Darmstadt, exterior, 1900

but later took up a position between Historicism and the Secession. He later succeeded Wagner at the Academy, but got bogged down in Biedermeier and eclecticism.

Although Mackintosh's design drew the most attention, he was unable to use this to his own advantage. He was, however, able to use the greater part of his competition design for Hill House (Helensburg, 1902–1906). Even though he enjoyed widespread recognition amongst the professional community, his career was not a success. In 1913, he left Keppie's architectural studio, where he had become a partner. Thereafter, he was commissioned to design a number of buildings, including the new Glasgow School of Art building with its famous library. However, his architectural œuvre is by no means extensive. It bears mentioning that Mackintosh was not only an architect but also one of this century's leading designers. During a period spanning almost ten years he designed no less than four hundred chairs! Towards the end of his life he became a prolific painter of watercolors. He died in 1928 and his wife Margaret died four years later. The contents of their two studios was officially estimated to have "practically no value".

1 *See chapter on the Hofoper in Vienna.*

2 *The building was referred to as the 'house with the golden cabbage', due to its characteristic open-work cupola.*

3 *Peter Behrens designed his own villa. He was a member of the Munich Secession and later became one of Germany's leading architects*

4 *J. Ruskin, W. Morris, A.W.H. Pugin, H. Muthesius: the Picturesque*

5 *As a student, Mackintosh had been employed by architectural agency of Honeyman & Keppie. He built his most important buildings in Glasgow while in their employ.*

6 *Magazine for Interior Decoration.*

Haus eines Kunstfreundes, Darmstadt

Charles Rennie Mackintosh (1868–1928) gilt als einer der herausragenden Künstler der Jahrhundertwende. Um die Bedeutung seines Wettbewerbsbeitrages für das Haus eines Kunstfreundes richtig einschätzen zu können, ist ein kurzer Abriß des damaligen kulturellen Lebens in Großbritannien und auf dem Kontinent notwendig, da Mackintosh auf beiden Seiten des Kanals eine führende Rolle spielte.

Wiener Sezession

Das kunstsinnige Leben Europas wurde in dieser Zeit von avantgardistischen Strömungen wie Jugendstil und Art Nouveau beherrscht. Diese beiden eng miteinander verwandten Stilrichtungen strebten eine neue Formenwelt und Architektur an, die auf den Eklektizismus des späten 19. Jahrhunderts verzichtete. Auch in Wien rebellierte man gegen die gefestigte Ordnung. 1894 wurde Otto Wagner zum Nachfolger von Professor Karl von Hasenauer[1] an die Wiener Akademie der Bildenden Künste berufen. Wagners Assistent Joseph Maria Olbrich und sein Lieblingsschüler Josef Hoffmann gründeten zusammen mit Gustav Klimt und Koloman Moser 1897 die Wiener Secession. Diese Gründung vollzog sich mit Zustimmung Wagners. Als Wagner der Gruppe 1899 beitrat, sorgte er damit für einen Skandal, da die Wiener Secession als anti-akademisch galt und gegen die gefestigte Ordnung eintrat. Den größten Einfluß innerhalb der Gruppe besaß Olbrich, vor allem aufgrund seiner Beiträge zur modernen Baukunst. Nachdem er 1898 das Ausstellungsgebäude der Wiener Sezession (das Gebäude erhielt den Spitznamen »Krauthapel«[2] gebaut hatte, nahm er in Wien eine ähnliche Rolle ein wie Mackintosh in Glasgow: Angefeindet vom konservativen Teil der Bevölkerung – sowohl Glasgow als auch Wien waren traditionsbewußte Städte – und bejubelt von Fachleuten und Kollegen.
Der Ruhm Olbrichs drang bis zu Ernst Ludwig, dem Großherzog von Hessen. Der kunstsinnige Herrscher wollte Darmstadt zum Zentrum der zeitgenössischen Kunst machen und rief auf einem nahegelegenen Hügel, der Mathildenhöhe, eine Künstlerkolonie ins Leben. Ernst Ludwig hatte schon sein neues Palais durch den Arts-and-Crafts-Künstler Baillie Scott einrichten lassen. Nun beauftragte er Olbrich mit dem architektonischen Entwurf für die Künstlerkolonie (ab 1901). Das Resultat war eine kreative Explosion von Jugendstil-Architektur. Olbrich entwarf fast alle Künstlervillen[3] die Ausstellungsräume und den berühmten Hochzeitsturm.

Die vier Macs

Zur gleichen Zeit, als die Wiener Sezession ihren Durchbruch als eigenständige Kunstströmung erlebte, entwikkelte sich in Glasgow eine ähnliche Bewegung. Sie wurde von vier Personen (bekannt als »Mac-Group« oder »The Four«) getragen: Charles Rennie Mackintosh, seine spätere Frau Margaret Macdonald, deren Schwester Frances Macdonald und ihr Ehemann Herbert Macnair. Die vier hatten sich auf der Glasgow School of Art kennengelernt und entwickelten gemeinsam den später berühmt gewordenen Glasgow Style, der sich stark von der vorherrschenden Arts-and-Crafts-Bewegung absetzte. Diese Bewegung wandte sich gegen die schädlichen Auswirkungen der industriellen Revolution und setzte sich für eine Erneuerung des Handwerks ein: Schlichte und solide kunsthandwerkliche Erzeugnisse sollten in das tägliche Leben integriert werden. Als Vorbild diente die ländliche englische Architektur. Zu den wichtigsten Vertretern dieser Bewegung zählten neben C. Voysey auch der bereits erwähnte Baillie Scott, der sich als Konkurrent Mackintoshs an der Wiener Ausschreibung beteiligte. Sowohl die Arts-and-Crafts-Bewegung wie auch die »Mac-Group« sahen Architektur und Kunsthandwerk als voneinander abhängiges Gesamtkunstwerk. Obwohl beide Strömungen in ihren Ausgangspunkten und Einflüssen vergleichbar waren[4], kamen sie zu völlig unterschiedlichen Ergebnissen. Dies gilt insbesondere für Mackintosh, den einzigen Architekten der Mac-Group, der später eigene Wege gehen sollte[5].
Als »The Four« 1896 einige Arbeiten für die Arts-and-Crafts-Ausstellung zur Verfügung stellten, stießen sie auch auf Zustimmung. Von 1897 bis 1899 befaßte sich Mackintosh mit dem Bau der Glasgow School of Art, einem Gebäude, das den Glasgow Style in ganz Europa bekannt machte. Daraufhin erhielten »The Four« – die Gruppe hatte sich inzwischen in zwei Ehepaare gespalten – eine Einladung, einige ihrer Arbeiten für die Ausstellung der Wiener Sezession im Herbst 1900 zur Verfügung zu stellen. Auf diese Weise lernten auch die Wiener Künstler eine Stilrichtung kennen, die ihnen besonders zusagen sollte. So waren Hoffmann und Olbrich vom Glasgow Style begeistert. Mackintoshs Motiv von vier Quadraten innerhalb eines Quadrats wurde von den Secessions-Künstlern häufig kopiert.

Haus eines Kunstfreundes

Als sich Mackintosh 1901 an einem von der Zeitschrift für Innendekoration ausgeschriebenen Architekturwettbewerb beteiligte, wurde sein Name einer breiten europäischen Öffentlichkeit bekannt. Das Thema der Ausschreibung lautete »Haus eines Kunstfreundes«. Obwohl Mackintosh den Wettbewerb nicht gewann – er hatte nicht alle Zeichnungen pünktlich eingeschickt – wurden seine Entwürfe ebenso wie die von Baillie Scott und Leopold Bauer (1872–1938) vom Herausgeber Alexander Koch als Portfolio veröffentlicht[6].
Außerdem erhielt Mackintosh die Aufforderung, seine Pläne der Weltausstellung für moderne dekorative Kunst in Turin (Sommer 1902) zur Verfügung zu stellen.
Die Beiträge von Baillie Scott und Mackintosh, die die meiste Aufmerksamkeit auf sich zogen, unterschieden sich grundlegend voneinander. In den Zeichnungen kommt der Unterschied zwischen der Formgebung der Arts-and-Crafts-Bewegung und dem eigenwilligen Entwurf Mackintoshs gut zum Ausdruck. Schon bei der Außenansicht ist in Baillie Scotts Entwurf deutlich die Kombination ländlicher Bauformen zu erkennen: französisch anmutende Türmchen an der Nordseite, geschweifte, die Dachlinie durchbrechende Giebelformen im niederländischen Stil an der Südseite. Dachpfannen und hohe Kamine verleihen dem Bauwerk einen pittoresken Charakter. Weiterhin fällt auf, daß beide Längsseiten symmetrisch sind.
Mackintosh greift zwar ebenfalls auf ländliche Bauformen zurück – insbesondere die der schottischen Landsitze (Baronial Style) – setzt sie aber geschickter um. Er übernimmt deren unregelmäßige, asymmetrische Formen und abstrahiert sie zu Flächen und Massen.
In diese abstrakte Konstruktion plaziert er Fenster und andere bauliche Elemente nötigenfalls auch asymmetrisch und formt daraus ein strenges, modernes Bauwerk. Die durchgehende Firstlinie verleiht dem Entwurf die nötige Einheitlichkeit, und die Klarheit des Grundrisses korrespondiert mit der Schlichtheit der Außenfassaden.
Als großes Problem für die Teilnehmer erwies sich die Bedingung, daß das Haus einerseits intimen Wohnkomfort bieten sollte, andererseits aber Unterbringungsmöglichkeiten für eine große Anzahl von Besuchern. Mackintosh fand dafür folgende Lösung: Ein schmaler Eingang und ein Vestibül öffnen sich zu einer Halle, die sich über beide Stockwerke erstreckt und die mit Hilfe einer Schiebewand zwischen Halle und Eßzimmer beinahe um das Doppelte vergrößert werden kann. Auch die Wand zwischen Empfangszimmer und Musikzimmer läßt sich entfernen, und die Doppeltüren dieser Räume ermöglichen ebenfalls den Zugang zur Halle.
Mackintoshs Inneneinrichtung unterschied sich ebenfalls grundlegend von den Entwürfen Baillie Scotts. Dieser hatte in bester Arts-and-Crafts-Tradition eine besonders ländliche Atmosphäre geschaffen: Das Musikzimmer besitzt einen Holzboden und eine Balkendecke, die kleine Bühne wird von Fachwerkmauern flankiert, und die Dekorationen zeigen Einflüsse slawischer Volkskunst.
Bei Baillie Scott wirken die kunstvoll gearbeiteten Objekte wie zufällig in den Raum gestellt, während bei Mackintosh alle Einzelteile miteinander in Beziehung stehen. Holzvertäfelung und Mobiliar sind in Form und Farbe sorgfältig aufeinander abgestimmt. Wie immer bei Mackintoshs Entwürfen sind Wohn- und Schlafzimmer in hellen Farben gehalten, Eßzimmer und Halle hingegen in dunkleren Farbtönen. An den glatten Zimmerdecken befindet sich eine Vielzahl von Lampen, denn Mackintosh legte großen Wert auf eine durchdachte, harmonische Balance von Tages- und Kunstlicht.
Mackintoshs Entwurf erregte die meiste Aufmerksamkeit, aber der Architekt war nicht in der Lage, dies zu seinem Vorteil zu nutzen. Zwar erntete er in Kollegenkreisen weithin Anerkennung und konnte den größten Teil seines Wettbewerbsbeitrages für den Bau von Hill House (Helensburg, 1902–1906) nutzen, aber seine Karriere geriet ins Stocken. 1913 verließ er das Architekturbüro, das er zusammen mit Keppie leitete. Er hatte zwar immer wieder Aufträge erhalten – u.a. für die berühmte Bibliothek der Glasgow School of Art –, aber sein architektonisches Oeuvre blieb schmal. Mackintosh war jedoch nicht nur Architekt, sondern auch einer der bedeutendsten Designer dieses Jahrhunderts. In einem Zeitraum von nur zehn Jahren entwarf er 400 Stühle. Gegen Ende seines Lebens beschäftigte er sich intensiv mit der Aquarellmalerei. Nach dem Tode von Mackintosh (1928) und seiner Frau (1932) wurde der Wert ihrer beiden Studios geschätzt. Offizielles Urteil: Sie enthielten »praktisch nichts von Wert«.

1 *Siehe das Kapitel zur Hofoper*
2 *Krautkopf, wegen seiner charakteristischen durchbrochenen Kuppel*
3 *Peter Behrens, Mitglied der Münchener Secession und später einer der bedeutendsten Architekten Deutschlands, entwarf seine eigene Villa*
4 *J. Ruskin, W. Morris, A.W.H. Pugin, H. Muthesius: Picturesque Style*
5 *Als Student wurde Mackintosh vom Büro der Architekten Honeyman und Keppie eingestellt, wo seine bedeutendsten Arbeiten in Glasgow entstanden*
6 *Meister der Innenkunst, 1902*

La Haus eines Kunstfreundes, Darmstadt

Charles Rennie Mackintosh (1868–1928) fut l'un des principaux créateurs du tournant de ce siècle. Pour comprendre l'importance de ce concours pour la «Demeure d'un ami des arts», il est nécessaire de connaître le climat culturel en Grande-Bretagne et sur le continent puisque l'influence de Mackintosh fut aussi profonde d'un côté de la Manche que de l'autre.

La Sécession Viennoise

Le contexte artistique européen était alors dominé par des mouvements d'avant-garde comme le Jugendstil et l'Art nouveau. Proches l'une de l'autre, ces deux tendances cherchaient à mettre au point une nouvelle forme d'architecture qui n'ait plus rien à voir avec l'éclectisme de la fin du XIXème siècle. Cette rébellion contre la tradition était également très vivace à Vienne où Otto Wagner, en 1894, avait succédé au vieux professeur Karl von Hasenauer[1] à l'Académie des Beaux-Arts. L'assistant de Wagner était Joseph Maria Olbrich (1867–1908) et son meilleur étudiant Josef Hoffmann. Ces deux jeunes créateurs fondèrent la Wiener Sezession (Sécession viennoise) en 1897 en compagnie de Gustav Klimt et Koloman Moser et avec l'approbation totale de Wagner. Celui-ci les rejoignit en 1899 provoquant un certain scandale puisque la Sécession s'opposait à l'Académie. Olbrich fut la figure la plus marquante de ce groupe, principalement grâce à ses contributions architecturales. Il dessina le pavillon d'exposition de la Sécession[2] en 1898 et se trouva dans une situation comparable à celle de Mackintosh à Glasgow: honni par les conservateurs – Glasgow et Vienne étaient des villes bourgeoises et «respectables» – et révéré par la communauté professionnelle.
Ernst Ludwig, archiduc de Hesse, avait pris connaissance de la renommée professionnelle de Olbrich. Ce grand aristocrate mécène voulait faire de Darmstadt la capitale de l'art contemporain et, dans ce but, avait fondé sur une colline des environs une colonie d'artistes, Mathildenhöhe. L'archiduc avait fait décorer son nouveau palais par un artiste appartenant aux Arts and Crafts, Baillie Scott, et demanda à Olbrich de concevoir un édifice pour Mathildenhöhe. Cette réalisation allait devenir un chef-d'œuvre sans précédent, exemplaire de l'architecture Jugendstil. Olbrich dessina par la suite les plans de toutes les villas d'artistes, sauf une[3], les bâtiments pour les expositions et la fameuse Hochzeitsturm ou tour des noces.

Les quatres Mac

La période qui vit la Wiener Sezession s'imposer fut également celle de la naissance d'un mouvement similaire en Ecosse, à Glasgow. Il était animé par quatre artistes (The Mac group, the Four): Charles Rennie Mackintosh, Margaret Macdonald (épouse de Mackintosh), sa sœur Frances Macdonald et Herbert Macnair (époux de Frances). Ils s'étaient rencontrés à l'Ecole d'Art de Glasgow et allaient donner naissance à ce qui fut appelé le «Glasgow style», proche mais différent du style Arts and Crafts. Les artistes Arts and Crafts essayaient de contrebalancer les effets nocifs de la révolution industrielle et de promouvoir l'artisanat en prenant souvent pour modèle l'architecture rurale anglaise. Pour eux, des objets simples et bien réalisés, conçus par des artistes, devaient s'intégrer naturellement à la vie quotidienne. C. Voysey et, bien entendu, Baillie Scott, futur rival de Mackintosh lors du concours, étaient les membres les plus représentatifs de ce mouvement. Les Arts and Crafts et le Mac group concevaient l'architecture et les arts appliqués comme un Gesamtkunstwerk, c'est-à-dire une œuvre globale dans laquelle toutes les expressions artistiques dépendaient mutuellement les unes des autres. Bien que les deux mouvement aient des points de départ similaires et aient été influencés par les mêmes traditions[4], leur production artistique différait profondément. Mackintosh, le seul architecte praticien du groupe, devait plus tard suivre sa propre voie[5].
En 1896, le groupe des Quatre avait présenté ses travaux lors d'une exposition Arts and Crafts, contribution critiquée dans un premier temps, puis approuvée. Entre 1897 et 1899, Mackintosh construisit la Glasgow School of Art qui permit au style Glasgow de se faire mieux connaître à travers toute l'Europe. Les Quatre, qui s'étaient séparés en deux couples, furent invités à présenter leurs réalisations lors d'une exposition de la Wiener Sezession à l'automne 1900. Leur style plaisait à l'évidence aux créateurs viennois. Le célèbre motif de Mackintosh, les quatre carrés dans un carré, était copié et Hoffmann et Olbrich étaient enthousiastes.

La maison d'un ami des arts

La réputation de Mackintosh connut de nouveaux développements en 1901, lorsque le Zeitschrift für Innendekoration (Magazine de décoration intérieure) organisa un concours pour la conception d'une «demeure pour un ami des arts». Bien que Mackintosh n'ait pas remporté la compétition – il ne fit pas parvenir à temps l'ensemble de ses projets – ses plans furent publiés en même temps que ceux de Baillie Scott et Leopold Bauer (Meister der Innenkunst, 1902). Mackintosh devait plus tard montrer ses dessins lors de l'Exposition internationale des arts décoratifs de Turin (été 1902). Aucun des projets lauréats du concours ne fut exécuté. Les projets de Baillie Scott et de Mackintosh différaient radicalement. Leurs dessins illustrent parfaitement les oppositions entre le style Arts and Crafts et l'approche du créateur écossais. L'inspiration rurale est clairement discernable dans la proposition de Baillie Scott. Sa maison possède des tours à la française vers le nord et un pignon hollandais, avec horloge rompant la ligne de faîte vers le sud. Le toit est recouvert de tuiles et rythmé de hautes cheminées. Tous ces détails affirment le caractère pittoresque d'un projet marqué d'ailleurs par une parfaite symétrie des deux longues façades.
Le projet de Mackintosh fait également allusion à un style rural qui pourrait être celui des grandes demeures écossaises (Baronial style), mais avec beaucoup plus de subtilité. Il utilise des formes irrégulières qu'il transforme en éléments et en volumes presque abstraits. Lorsque c'est nécessaire, les fenêtres et les autres éléments de la façade sont disposés asymétriquement. Afin de préserver une certaine unité, la ligne de faîte du toit est régulière sur toute la longueur de la maison. La simplicité des façades se retrouve dans le plan de masse. L'un des principaux problèmes auxquels les participants se trouvaient confrontés était d'imaginer une maison qui soit confortable tout en étant capable de recevoir un grand nombre de visiteurs. La solution de Mackintosh fut de proposer une entrée et un vestibule étroits qui débouchaient sur un grand salon (great hall) haut de deux étages. Sa surface pouvait être doublée en faisant glisser les cloisons qui le séparaient de la salle à manger. Un mur-écran pouvait disparaître entre la salle de réception et le salon de musique, eux-mêmes ouvrant sur le grand salon par des double-portes.
Baillie Scott avait recréé l'atmosphère d'une maison à la campagne, dans la meilleure tradition Arts and Crafts. Son salon de musique possédait un plancher et un plafond à poutres apparentes. La petite scène était flanquée de murs recouverts de boiseries et le programme de décoration n'était pas sans évoquer l'art populaire slave. Dans sa biographie de Mackintosh, Thomas Howarth remarque, non sans ironie, que le salon de musique de Baillie Scott convenait parfaitement à une soirée de danses folkloriques alors que celui de Mackintosh semblait mieux convenir à Beethoven. Dans les aquarelles de Baillie Scott, d'intéressants objets sont disposés un peu au hasard, alors que dans celles de Mackintosh tous les éléments sont en harmonie.
La forme et les couleurs des lambris et du mobilier s'accordent parfaitement. Comme toujours, chez Mackintosh, le salon et les chambres sont de couleurs claires, les tons foncés étant réservés au grand salon et à la salle à manger. Les plafonds sont voûtés et équipés de nombreuses sources d'éclairage. Mackintosh apportait toujours un soin particulier à l'équilibre entre lumière naturelle et artificielle. Chez Baillie Scott, l'accès à la salle à manger se fait par une colonnade soutenant des arcs romans. L'entablement est recouvert de plâtre mais avec un effet d'appareillage de pierre se terminant sur une frise de paons. A l'opposé, la salle à manger de Mackintosh est à la fois élégante et digne.
Le projet de Leopold Bauer, quant à lui, reflète cette période de l'architecture exposée au début du chapitre. Bauer avait fait ses études à l'Académie des Beaux-Arts de Vienne, sous la direction de von Hasenauer puis d'Otto Wagner. Il excellait aussi bien en architecture que dans les arts appliqués.
C'est le projet de Mackintosh qui retint le plus l'attention, même s'il ne put être primé. L'architecte utilisa par la suite plusieurs de ses plans pour l'une de ses œuvres majeures, Hill House (Helensburg, 1902–1906). Même si l'importance de son travail fut reconnue par les professionnels, sa carrière ne remporta pas le succès qu'elle eut mérité. En 1913, il quitta le cabinet d'architecture de Keppie dont il était devenu l'associé et réalisa un certain nombre de projets dont la célèbre librairie de l'Ecole d'Art de Glasgow. Il reste que son œuvre architecturale est assez réduite. Créateur prolifique, il ne dessina pas moins de quatre cents modèles de sièges et se tourna vers l'aquarelle et la peinture avant de mourir en 1928. A la mort de sa femme, quatre ans plus tard, le contenu de leurs ateliers fut officiellement estimé 'pratiquement sans valeur'.

1 *Voir le chapitre sur le Hofoper.*
2 *Ce pavillon fut vite qualifié de 'maison au chou-fleur doré' par référence à sa coupole ouverte très particulière.*
3 *Peter Behrens dessina sa propre maison. Membre de la Sécession munichoise, il devint plus tard l'un des plus influents architectes allemands.*
4 *J. Ruskin, W. Morris, A.W.H. Pugin, H. Muthesius, le mouvement «Picturesque».*
5 *Etudiant, Mackintosh avait travaillé dans l'agence de Honeyman et Keppie. C'est pour eux qu'il réalisa ses œuvres les plus importantes à Glasgow.*

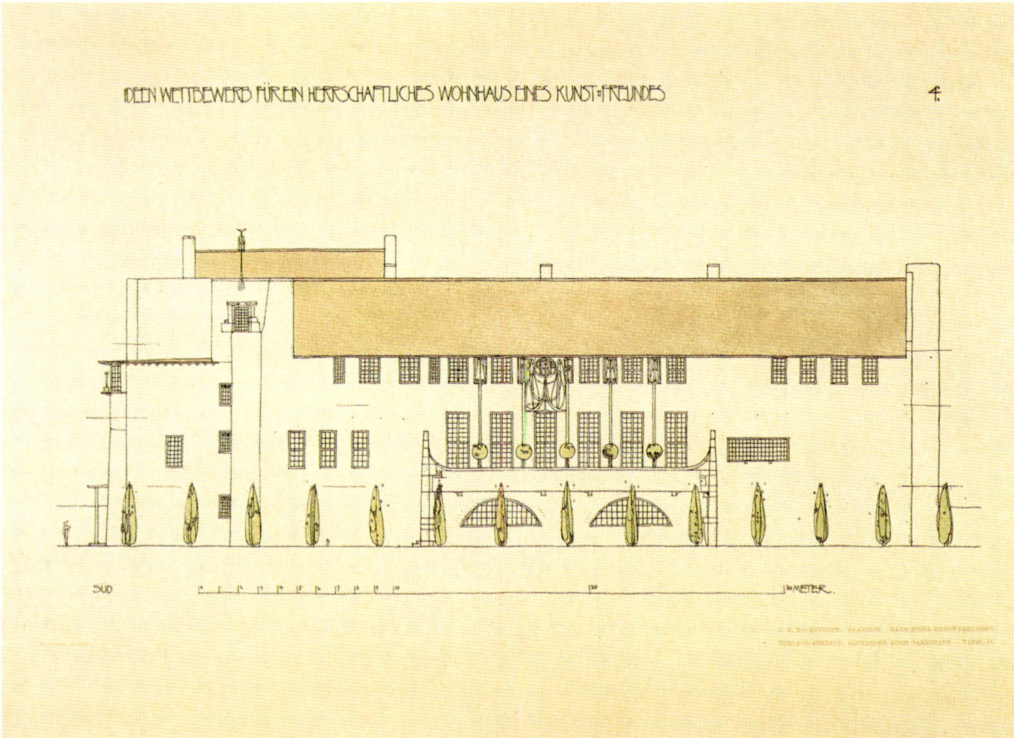

Charles Rennie Mackintosh
competition design, 1901, interior perspective of dining room, special purchase prize

Charles Rennie Mackintosh
competition design, 1901, detail of entrance hall, special purchase prize

Charles Rennie Mackintosh
competition design, 1901, south elevation, special purchase prize

Charles Rennie Mackintosh
competition design, 1901, above: first, second floor plan, below: ground floor plan, special purchase prize

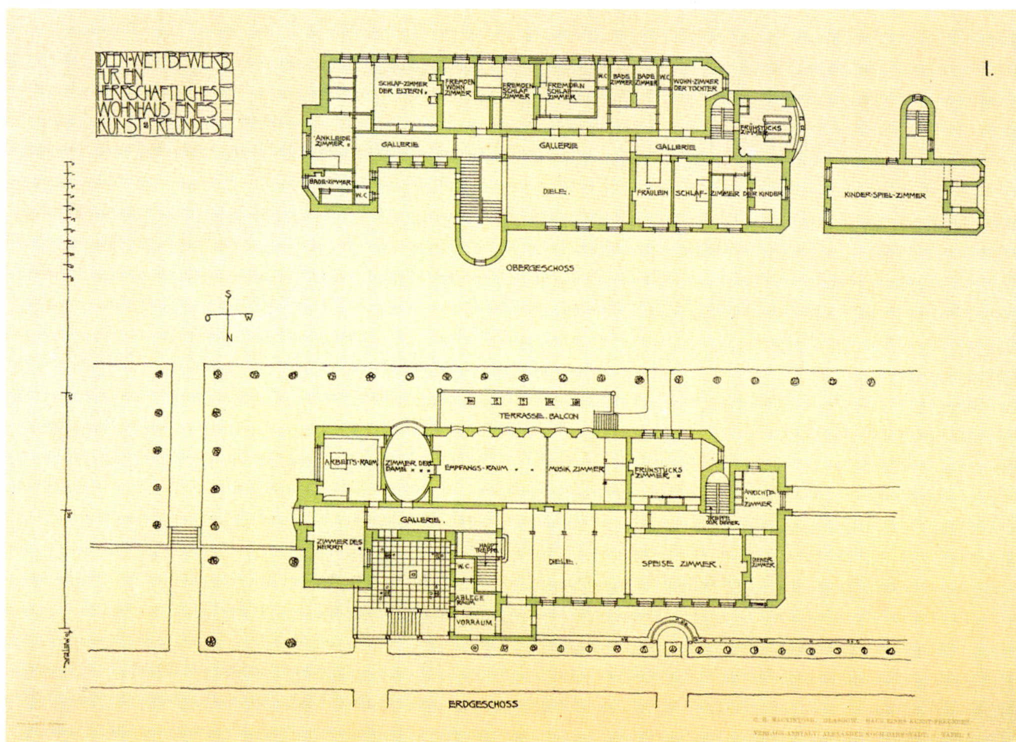

CHARLES

GALLERIES

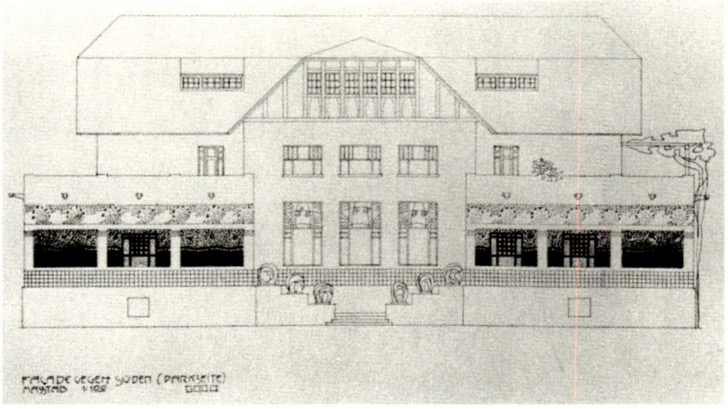

Leopold Bauer competition design, 1901, east elevation

Leopold Bauer competition design, 1901, south elevation

Leopold Bauer competition design, 1901, exterior view from north-east

Leopold Bauer competition design, 1901, interior view of entrance hall

Mackay Hugh Baillie Scott
competition design, 1901, bird's eye view, second prize

Mackay Hugh Baillie Scott
competition design, 1901, above: south elevation, below: west elevation, second prize

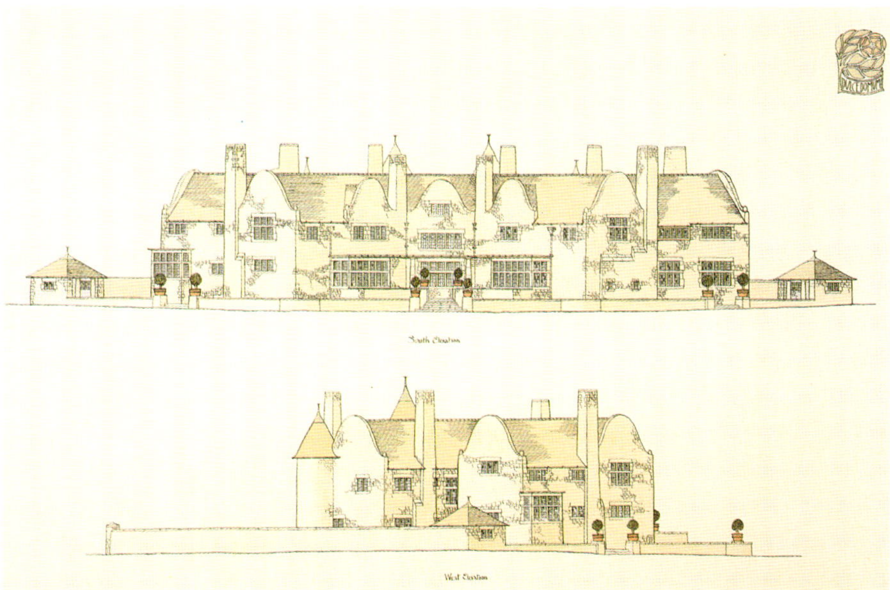

Mackay Hugh Baillie Scott
competition design, 1901, above: ground floor plan, below: first floor plan, second prize

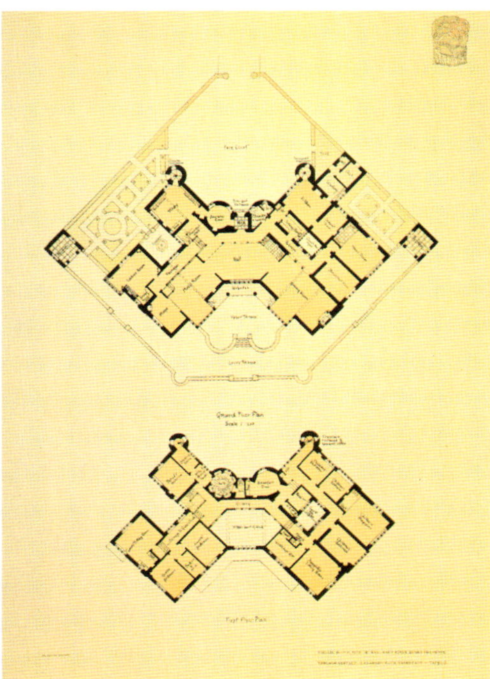

Mackay Hugh Baillie Scott
competition design, 1901, interior view of dining room, second prize

Mackay Hugh Baillie Scott
competition design, 1901, interior view of entrance hall, second prize

Mackay Hugh Baillie Scott

competition design, 1901, interior view of music room, second prize

Leopold Bauer competition design, 1901, interior view of master's room

Leopold Bauer competition design, 1901, interior view of living room with stained glass

Leopold Bauer competition design, 1901, interior view of main dining room

Post Office Savings Bank, Vienna, 1903

Project

Post Office Savings Bank (K.K. Postsparkasse)

Site

Georg Coch Platz, Vienna

Dates

1 February 1903 to 30 April 1903

Result announced

10 June 1903

Number of entries

32

Jury

Mansuet Kosel (Chairman, Director K.K. Postsparkasse), Emil von Förster, Michael Koch, Josef Künstler, Christian Ulrich, Karl von Wiener (civil servants), Georg Niemann (Academy of Fine Arts), Gustav Bamberger, Franz von Neumann, Andreas Streit, Alexander Wielemans, Leopold Bauer (architects)

Result

Joint first prize Eugen Faszbender & Ludwig Fremmel Otto Wagner; Max Freiherr von Ferstel Franz von Krausz & Josef Tölk Theodor Bach

Commissioned by

Ministry of Trade

Construction

12 July 1904 to December 1906 *Extension built* 1910–1913 *Restoration by* Dr. S. Stein 1974–1975

Architect

Otto Wagner (1841–1918)

Construction cost

4 300 000 crowns (Wagner's estimate was 2 900 000).
Extension cost 1 800 000 crowns

Post Office Savings Bank, Vienna, 1903

Otto Wagner competition design, 1903, part of central front elevation on Georg Coch Platz, awarded, recommended for purchase

Post Office Savings Bank, Vienna, 1903

Around the turn of the century, Vienna was one of Europe's leading political and cultural capitals. During the reign of Emperor Franz Joseph (1848–1916), the population of Vienna grew from less than half a million to more than two million inhabitants. The Ringstrasse was constructed, along which impressive buildings such as the parliament, the city hall and the Hofoper[1] were built. The city also boasted a new Stadtbahn (metropolitan railway) and numerous tenement blocks were built. As the capital of the Austrian-Hungarian double monarchy, Vienna drew artists and scholars from all corners of the empire, which extended from South Tyrol to Galicia and from Bohemia to Transsylvania, incorporating cities such as Prague, Cracow, Sarajevo and Budapest.

Vienna around 1900

Vienna was the home of the composers Anton von Webern, Alban Berg, Arnold Schönberg, Gustav Mahler and Richard Strauss. The home of Arthur Schnitzler, Theodor Herzl, Sigmund Freud, Robert Musil, Stefan Zweig and Ludwig Wittgenstein. The standard of fine arts and applied in the city was similarly excellent: Gustav Klimt, Egon Schiele and Koloman Moser enriched the city with their work. Otto Wagner, Josef Hoffmann, Joseph Maria Olbrich and Adolf Loos were the architectural trend-setters. The fame of the Vienna Secession had spread across Europe[2]. In short, the city was booming. However, this era ended abruptly and dramatically in 1916 when Franz Joseph died. The Emperor had been the binding factor between the eleven nations of the double monarchy. In 1918, the empire was divided and Vienna became little more than the capital of an impoverished Austria. During that same year, Klimt, Schiele, Moser and Wagner died.

Otto Wagner

Of all the artists, Wagner probably left his mark most clearly upon fin-de-siècle Vienna, even though he was already in the autumn of his life. Wagner was educated at the Vienna Polytechnic Institute, where he gained technical expertise. He later attended the Royal Academy of Architecture in Berlin (Classically oriented) and the Academy of Fine Arts in Vienna, where he was tutored by Eduard van der Nüll and August Sicard von Sicardsburg, who had built the Vienna Hofoper. Wagner initially gained architectural experience under Ludwig von Förster, who had contributed to the realisation of the Ringstrasse. Between 1863 and 1894, Wagner occupied a teaching post at the Academy of Fine Arts and occasionally did other work. During this period he designed the Länderbank, a tenement and a small palace. His design for the Länderbank incorporated all the elements which he later applied in his design for the Post Office Savings Bank. He also participated in the competitions for the Parliamentary Buildings in Budapest and the Peace Palace in The Hague. In 1893, he won the competition for the Viennese urban development project.
In 1893 Wagner's career gained momentum. He succeeded Professor Karl von Hasenauer at the Academy and was appointed Oberstadtbaurat (municipal architect). He had a seat on the city's Commission for

The cornice and the statue on the front façade

Main entrance and its canopy

Otto Wagner

Traffic Affairs and was charged with the supervision of the water control project on the Danube. Subsequently, Wagner devoted time to larger projects, such as the city tramways and the construction of tenements in the new districts. His assistant on these projects was Joseph Maria Olbrich. Wagner was closely involved in the extensive Viennese development projects, both in his official capacity and as an architect. He contributed to the planning and design of the infrastructure and the necessary architecture.

In 1896, Wagner published his first theoretical work, entitled "Moderne Architektur". In it, he discussed the principles of functional architecture (Nutzstil). Initially intended as a textbook for his students, it was to become one of the most influential architectural dissertations of the twentieth century. Wagner's motto was "Artis sola domina necessitas" (art is ruled only by function). He propagated the use of iron structures and argued that the interior structure of a building should be visible from the outside. Three years later, the aged Wagner scandalised the established art world by joining the Vienna Secession, which rejected academic norms and values. Wagner became the target of a smear campaign, which eventually cost him the commission to design a municipal museum. Nevertheless, he had made a name for himself. His renown probably gave him an edge in the 1903 Post Office Savings Bank competition, because – in contrast to most other competitions – the participating architects were not required to submit their designs anonymously.

The savings bank

The Postsparkasse was a savings bank for the average citizen. The bank was founded in 1883 by Dr Georg Coch, whose bust can still be admired opposite the main entrance. The bank building soon became too small and in 1903 a competition was organised for the design of a new building on the site of the former Emperor Franz Joseph Barracks. The barracks had been demolished to make way for the Ringstrasse. Officially, the competition had been organised by the Ministry of Trade and, as a result, the director of the Savings Bank and quite a number of civil servants had seats on the jury. The competition drew few entries: 32 in total. However, many of the participants were renowned architects. Following a lengthy period of appraisal, the field was narrowed down to five designs, all of which had been submitted by leading architects. Judging from the diversity of the winning designs, the jury had no stylistic bias.

Max Freiherr von Ferstel's design perfectly embodied the spirit of nineteenth century Viennese architecture[3]. He came up with an ingenious solution for the segmented public area on the Biberstrasse. In his design, this part of the building was no more than a single storey high, whereby the bank had an inviting and open character. Unfortunately, his design lacked harmony towards the sides of the bank.

Franz Skowron had also submitted a design in the "Viennese style", which was eliminated during the first round. Theodor Bach had submitted a rather pompous Neo-Baroque design, while Franz von Krausz & Josef Tölk's design was characterised by extreme austerity. Their corner pavilions were the only features which alluded to any Beaux-Arts influence. Unfortunately, they had positioned the banking halls so inappropriately that their design was considered impracticable.

The jury was ecstatic about Wagner's design, which was purchased for execution. This was remarkable, in light of the fact that it was the most modern entry and deviated most from the prevailing tradition. The general public voiced their dissatisfaction by launching a campaign in favour of von Ferstel's design. The architect Peter Paul Brang also proved to be a malcontent. He was the first of the six finalists to be dropped from the competition. He refused to accept the jury's decision and took the matter to court. He wanted the result declared invalid because Wagner had designed a single central hall for the exchange and savings activities, whereas the competition programme had specified 'halls' (plural). A sub-commission was appointed, who ruled

that Brang had a greater right to prize money than Wagner, but also that the bankers were free to buy and execute whichever design was to their liking.

Forerunner of Functionalism

Wagner's bank was subsequently built, although he did have to alter his design here and there. One of the most important changes was made to the raised glass roof over the central section. The raised roof was replaced with two low glass roofs: a lower roof (the "ceiling" of the cashiers' hall) was suspended from the upper (saddle) roof with iron bars. The pillars in the cashiers' hall support the upper roof. This demonstrates how an apparently functional structure may conceal the true structure.

Wagner replaced the raised glass roof with a parapet, set back off the main façade, whereby the accentuation of the mid-section was retained. The public entrance is situated in the mid-section and leads to the banking hall via a vestibule and a stairway. There are small triangular courtyards on either side of the cashiers' hall, through which light and fresh air can enter all parts of the building. The bank's present trapezoidal plan shape developed in 1910, when Wagner was commissioned to design the extension. Two extra courtyards were developed on either side of a new public area, forming an extension to the cashiers' hall. The floor plan is almost entirely symmetrical and – in contrast to the floor plans of Krausz & Tölk and von Ferstel – Wagner included no rounded shapes.

The latter feature is characteristic of Wagner's style, as is the lack of gratuitous embellishments. Wagner only included embellishments if they arose directly from structural features or if they did not interfere with the structure. The former structural aspect is illustrated on the façade, which has protective rusticated granite slabs at its base, above which smooth marble slabs have been mounted. The slabs have been mounted with steel pegs which have a rust-proof aluminium coating. The heads of the aluminium pins form a decorative pattern on an otherwise unadorned façade, which has no mouldings. The bank's public halls are similarly adorned with slabs of marble and glass panes. The well above the banking hall has been done out in white tiles. These features are therefore not only decorative, but also provide the building with a protective outer casing.

The square iron pillars in the banking hall are also aluminium-coated and taper towards the bottom. They have a crown-shaped light fitting at the top, instead of a capital. The rivets in the pillars have the same decorative effect as the aluminium pegs in the façade. The aluminium air ducts are similarly functional and decorative. The pillars and joists have been mounted on reinforced concrete. The building's only striking embellishments are the sculptures representing trade and thrift in the upper corners of the central ressault, created by Othmar Schimkowitz in aluminium. The central heating and electric lighting were intended to enhance the working comfort of the 2700 employees (now only 1900). The offices are light and fresh due to the large windows. On the whole, the Post Office Savings Bank embodies the spirit of the modern era as Wagner envisaged it: democratic, self-assured and functional.

Entrance hall with the statue of the Emperor Franz Josef I by Richard Laks

A spiral staircase

Small hall (for exchange)

Assembly hall with a portrait of the Emperor

Main banking hall with glass roof

Air conditioning shaft in main banking hall

1 *See chapter on Hofoper in this book.*

2 *See chapter on Haus eines Kunstfreundes in this book.*

3 *Von Ferstel was the son of Heinrich Freiherr von Ferstel. See chapter on the Reichstag.*

Postsparkassenamt, Wien

Um die Jahrhundertwende zählte Wien politisch wie kulturell zu den führenden Städten Europas. Während der Regierungszeit von Kaiser Franz Joseph I. (1848–1916) war nicht nur die Wiener Bevölkerung von knapp 500 000 Einwohnern auf über zwei Millionen angewachsen, man hatte auch die Ringstraße mit ihren imposanten Bauwerken – wie etwa dem Reichsratsgebäude (dem heutigen Parlament), dem Rathaus und dem Hofoperntheater (der heutigen Staatsoper[1]) – angelegt und das Stadtbild um die Stadtbahn und etliche Mietskasernen bereichert. In seiner Funktion als Hauptstadt der Österreichisch-Ungarischen Doppelmonarchie übte Wien große Anziehungskraft auf Künstler und Gelehrte aus dem gesamten Kaiserreich aus.

Wien um 1900

Wien war nicht nur die Stadt der Komponisten – Anton von Webern, Alban Berg, Arnold Schönberg, Gustav Mahler und Richard Strauß – sondern auch die Wahlheimat von Arthur Schnitzler, Theodor Herzl, Sigmund Freud, Robert Musil, Stefan Zweig und Ludwig Wittgenstein. Auch die Bildenden Künste standen auf hohem Niveau: Gustav Klimt, Egon Schiele und Koloman Moser verschönerten die Stadt mit Gemälden und Gebrauchsgegenständen, während Otto Wagner, Josef Hoffmann, Joseph Maria Olbrich und Adolf Loos sich auf dem Gebiet der Architektur durchsetzten und die Wiener Secession in ganz Europa bekanntmachten[2].

Von allen Wiener Künstlern des Fin de siècle hat wohl Otto Wagner die Stadt am deutlichsten geprägt. Wagner hatte am Wiener Polytechnikum studiert, wo er die technische Seite seines Fachs erlernte, danach die (klassizistisch orientierte) Königliche Bauakademie zu Berlin besucht und seine Ausbildung an der Akademie der Bildenden Künste in Wien vervollständigt. Zu seinen Lehrmeistern zählten Eduard van der Nüll und August Sicard von Sicardsburg[3]. Seine ersten praktischen Erfahrungen sammelte er bei Ludwig von Förster, der bei der Gestaltung der Ringstraße eine wichtige Rolle gespielt hatte. In den Jahren zwischen 1863 und 1894 arbeitete Wagner als Dozent an der Akademie der Bildenden Künste, erhielt darüber hinaus aber nur wenige Aufträge. Während dieser Zeit entstanden sein Entwurf für die Länderbank – der bereits Elemente seines später entwickelten Konzepts für das Postsparkassenamt aufwies – sowie die Konstruktionspläne für ein Mietshaus und ein kleines Palais. Außerdem beteiligte sich Wagner an zahlreichen Ausschreibungen, u.a. für das Parlamentsgebäude in Budapest und den Friedenspalast in Den Haag.

Im selben Jahr erfuhr Wagners Karriere einen ungeahnten Schub, als er Karl von Hasenauers Nachfolge als Professor an der Akademie antrat und zum Oberstadtbaurat sowie zum Beirat der Kommission für die Wiener Verkehrsanlagen ernannt wurde. Außerdem betraute man Wagner mit der Regulierung des Donaukanals und erteilte ihm den Auftrag für die groß angelegte Stadtbahn sowie für verschiedene Mietshäuser in den neuen Stadtteilen, wobei ihm Joseph Maria Olbrich als Assistent zur Seite stand.

1896 erschien Wagners erste theoretische Abhandlung »Moderne Architektur«, in der er seine Prinzipien zur funktionalen Architektur (Nutzstil) darlegte. Dieses Werk war zunächst nur als Lehrbuch für seine Studenten konzipiert, entwickelte sich aber bald zu einer der einflußreichsten architektonischen Abhandlungen des 20. Jahrhunderts, deren Motto »Artis sola domina necessitas« (Die Kunst wird nur von der Funktion beherrscht) lautet: Wagner propagierte die Verwendung von Eisenkonstruktionen und argumentierte, dab die innere Struktur eines Gebäudes an der Außenfassade erkennbar sein müsse. Drei Jahre später trat der bereits betagte Architekt der Wiener Sezession bei und verursachte dadurch einen Skandal, da die avantgardistische Künstlergruppe der Sezessionisten jegliche akademischen Normen und Werte ablehnte. Dennoch hatte Wagner sich einen Namen erarbeitet, der ihm bei der Ausschreibung für die Postsparkasse wahrscheinlich zum Vorteil gereichte, da der Wettbewerb – im Gegensatz zur üblichen Praxis – nicht anonym verlief.

Eine Sparkasse für den »kleinen Mann«

Die Postsparkasse, 1883 von Georg Coch gegründet, war eine Bank für die »kleinen Leute«. Das Bankgebäude stellte sich schon bald als zu beengt heraus, so daß 1903 die Ausschreibung für einen Neubau erfolgte. Offizieller Auftraggeber des Architekturwettbewerbs war das Handelsministerium, so daß in der Jury nicht nur der Direktor der Sparkasse, sondern auch zahlreiche Beamte saßen. Die Anzahl der eingesandten Beiträge war zwar alles andere als überwältigend, aber bei den meisten Teilnehmern handelte es sich um bekannte Baumeister. Nach langen Diskussionen gelangten schließlich fünf Entwürfe in die engere Wahl, die alle von führenden Architekten stammten und sich durch sehr unterschiedliche Stilrichtungen auszeichneten, was für eine unvoreingenommene Jury sprach.

Der Entwurf von Max Freiherr von Ferstel[4] stimmte am stärksten mit dem Geist der Wiener Architektur des 19. Jahrhunderts überein. Er präsentierte eine wohldurchdachte Lösung für den segmentförmigen, der Öffentlichkeit zugänglichen Bereich an der Biberstraße, der eingeschossig konzipiert ist und so der Bank einen einladenden, offenen Charakter verleihen sollte.

Auch Franz Skowron hatte einen Entwurf im »Wiener Stil« eingereicht, der jedoch schon während der ersten Ausschreibungsrunde aus dem Rennen fiel. Theodor Bach entwarf die Postsparkasse in einem ziemlich pompösen Neubarock, während das Konzept von Franz von Krausz und Josef Tölk ausgesprochen streng und nüchtern wirkte und nur die Eckpavillons den Einfluß des Jugendstils erahnen ließen. Die Lage der Bankschalterräume war jedoch so unglücklich gewählt, daß sich eine Umsetzung der Konstruktionspläne von vornherein verbot. Dagegen stieß Wagners Entwurf bei der Jury auf große Begeisterung und wurde unter den anderen Gewinnern des ersten Preises zur Durchführung ausgewählt. Diese Entscheidung erscheint recht verwunderlich, da er den modernsten Entwurf eingereicht hatte und damit am weitesten von der herrschenden Mode abwich. Die Öffentlichkeit zeigte sich auch entsprechend unzufrieden mit seinen Plänen und leitete eine – jedoch vergebliche – Kampagne zugunsten Ferstels ein.

Vorläufer des Funktionalismus

Wagners Entwurf wurde schließlich doch ausgeführt, allerdings mit einigen Änderungen. Die einschneidendste Wandlung erfuhr das hohe gläserne Dach, das er für den Mittelbereich konzipiert hatte und das durch eine Konstruktion aus zwei flachen Glasdächern ersetzt wurde: Das untere Dach (die Decke der Schalterhalle) ist mit Hilfe von Eisenstangen am oberen Dach (Satteldach) befestigt, das seinerseits von den Pfeilern in der Schalterhalle gestützt wird. Dieses Beispiel zeigt, wie eine auf den ersten Blick funktionale Konstruktion die wahre Konstruktion verhüllen kann.

Statt des ursprünglichen hohen Glasdachs entwarf Wagner eine leicht zurückgenommene Balustrade, so daß der Mittelbereich nach wie vor akzentuiert wird. Hier befinden sich auch der Eingang und die dahinterliegende Eingangshalle sowie eine Treppe, die zur Schalterhalle führt. Dieser Saal wird von zwei kleinen dreieckigen Innenhöfen flankiert, damit alle Räume im Gebäude genügend Licht und Frischluft erhalten. Der heutige trapezförmige Grundriß – mit zwei weiteren Innenhöfen auf beiden Seiten der neu konzipierten, der Öffentlichkeit zugänglichen Halle, die in direkter Verlängerung der Schalterhalle liegt – entstand erst 1910, als man Wagner den Auftrag für den zweiten Teil der Bank erteilte. Dennoch ist dieser Grundriß nahezu symmetrisch und weist keine runde Formen auf – ganz im Gegensatz zu den Entwürfen von Krauß und Tölk sowie Ferstel.

Dieses Merkmal ist für Wagners Stil ebenso typisch wie sein Verzicht auf jegliches überflüssige Ornament: Dekor findet sich nur dort, wo es sich aus der Struktur ergibt oder die Konstruktion es gestattet. Dies zeigt sich am Beispiel der Fassade, die im unteren Bereich aus schützenden Granitplatten in Form von Rustikamauerwerk besteht und darüber mit glatten Marmorplatten verkleidet ist. Die Platten sind mit Hilfe von Stahlbolzen befestigt, die in einer rostabweisenden Aluminiumhülle sitzen. Die den Montagebolzen aufgesetzten Aluminiumköpfe bilden ein dekoratives Muster auf der im übrigen schlichten Fassade, deren Fenster völlig ohne dekorative Rahmen auskommen. Auch die für den Publikumsverkehr bestimmten Räume besitzen eine vergleichbare Gestaltung aus Marmor- und Glasplatten, der Innenhof über der Schalterhalle wurde weiß gekachelt. Auf diese Weise stattete Wagner das Gebäude mit einer zweiten, schützenden Hülle aus.

Die quadratischen, ebenfalls mit Aluminium verkleideten eisernen Pfeiler in der Schalterhalle verbreitern sich nach oben und weisen statt eines Kapitells eine kronenartige Beleuchtung auf, während ihre Nietnägel den gleichen dekorativen Effekt erzielen wie die Aluminiumbolzen der Fassade. Auch die in Aluminium ausgeführten Warmluftausbläser sind zugleich funktional und ästhetisch; bei der Konstruktion der Pfeiler und Querbalken wurde Stahlbeton verwendet. Für den Komfort der 2700 Angestellten (heute 1900 Mitarbeiter) sorgen eine Zentralheizung und elektrisches Licht, während die großen Fenster viel Licht hereinlassen und die Büroräume offen und hell gestalten. Insgesamt umgibt das Gebäude die Aura der Moderne, wie sie Wagner vorschwebte: demokratisch, selbstbewußt und funktional.

Das einzige auffallende Ornament bilden die Skulpturen des oberen Fassadenabschlusses an den Ecken des Mittelrisalits. Diese von Otto Schimkowitz angefertigten allegorischen Figuren symbolisieren Handel und Sparsamkeit – und bestehen ebenfalls aus Aluminium.

1 *Siehe das Kapitel zur Hofoper*
2 *Siehe das Kapitel zum Haus eines Kunstfreundes*
3 *Siehe das Kapitel zur Hofoper*
4 *Heinrich von Ferstels Sohn, siehe das Kapitel zum Reichstag*

Le Postsparkassenamt, Vienne

Au début de ce siècle, Vienne était l'une des grandes capitales politiques et culturelles de l'Europe. Sous le règne de François-Joseph (1848–1916), sa population était passée de 500 000 habitants à 2 millions, la Ringstrasse avait été percée et bordée de prestigieux édifices comme le parlement, l'hôtel de ville et l'opéra[1], un réseau de tramways créé et de multiples immeubles de logements construits. Capitale de la double-monarchie austro-hongroise, la ville attirait des artistes et des universitaires de tous les coins de l'empire qui s'étendait du Tyrol à la Galicie, de la Bohême à la Transylvanie et comptait des villes aussi importantes que Prague, Cracovie, Sarajevo et Budapest.

Vienne en 1900

Pour ne citer que quelques noms, Vienne était la cité d'Anton von Webern, Arnold Schönberg, Gustav Mahler, Richard Strauss, Arthur Schnitzler, Theodor Herzl, Sigmund Freud, Robert Musil, Stefan Zweig et Ludwig Wittgenstein. Les arts plastiques étaient tout aussi bien représentés avec Gustav Klimt, Egon Schiele et Koloman Moser. Otto Wagner, Josef Hofmann, Joseph Maria Olbrich et Adolf Loos animaient la nouvelle tendance de l'architecture et des arts appliqués. Le rayonnement de la Sécession viennoise se faisait sentir dans toute l'Europe[2]. Bref, la capitale était en plein essor. Cette brillante période se termina aussi brusquement que dramatiquement avec la Première Guerre mondiale et la mort de l'empereur François-Joseph en 1916. Le souverain était le facteur de cohésion entre les onze nations de la double-monarchie. En 1918, l'empire fut morcelé et Vienne se retrouva capitale d'une Autriche appauvrie. La même année, moururent Klimt, Schiele, Moser et Otto Wagner.

Otto Wagner

De tous les artistes de cette époque, Otto Wagner est certainement celui qui a laissé la marque la plus évidente sur la Vienne fin de siècle bien qu'il ait déjà atteint à cette époque la dernière partie de son existence. Il avait fait ses études à l'Institut Polytechnique de Vienne, puis suivi les cours de l'Académie Royale d'Architecture de Berlin (traditionaliste) et ceux de l'Académie des Beaux-Arts de Vienne avec, comme tuteurs, Eduard van der Nüll et August Siccard von Siccardsburg, architectes de l'opéra de la capitale autrichienne. Il commença à pratiquer sous la conduite de Ludwig von Förster qui avait participé au projet de la Ringstrasse. De 1863 à 1894, il enseigna à l'Académie des Beaux-Arts sans beaucoup construire. C'est pendant cette période qu'il dessina la Länderbank, un immeuble d'appartements et un hôtel particulier. Ses plans pour la Länderbank préfiguraient déjà les éléments qu'il allait utiliser plus tard pour la Caisse d'Epargne. Il participa également aux concours pour le parlement de Budapest et le Palais de la Paix à La Haye et, en 1893, remporta celui pour le plan d'urbanisme de Vienne.
En 1893, sa carrière s'accélère. Il succède au professeur Karl von Hasenauer à l'Académie, est nommé Oberstadtbaurat, l'équivalent d'architecte de la ville, siège à la Commission municipale de la circulation et est chargé de superviser le programme de travaux hydrauliques sur le Danube. Il se consacre à d'importants projets comme le réseau de tramways et la construction d'ensembles de logements dans les banlieues. Son assistant d'alors est Joseph Maria Olbrich. Wagner est donc impliqué de très près dans tous les projets de développement de Vienne à la fois comme architecte et comme responsable officiel.
En 1896, il publie son premier ouvrage théorique 'Moderne Architektur' dans lequel il décrit les principes de l'architecture fonctionnelle (Nutzstil). Conçu comme un manuel pour étudiants, ce livre devait s'imposer comme l'un des essais les plus importants sur l'architecture du XXème siècle. Sur le thème de «Artis sola domina necessitas», l'art n'est gouverné que par la fonction, il propage l'idée que la structure interne d'un bâtiment doit se comprendre de l'extérieur et l'utilisation du métal dans la construction. Trois ans plus tard, malgré son âge, il rejoint les rangs de la Wiener Sezession, provoquant un scandale dans la mesure ou les Sécessionnistes s'opposaient aux normes et aux valeurs académiques.

La Caisse d'Epargne

La Postsparkasse (Caisse d'épargne de la poste) était un établissement bancaire destiné à une clientèle populaire. Elle avait été fondée en 1883 par le Dr. Georg Coch dont le buste peut encore être admiré face à l'entrée principale. Le bâtiment qu'elle occupait étant trop petit, un concours fut lancé en 1903 pour élever son nouveau siège à l'emplacement des anciennes casernes impériales démolies lors du percement de la Ringstrasse. Le concours était officiellement organisé par le ministère du commerce, et plusieurs fonctionnaires, à côté du directeur de la banque, figuraient au jury. Il n'attira que 32 participants mais pour la plupart de qualité. Le choix se concentra sur cinq projets, tous présentés par des architectes connus, mais dont la diversité prouvait que le jury n'avait aucun a priori esthétique.
Les plans de Max Freiherr von Ferstel incarnaient à la perfection l'esprit de l'architecture viennoise du XIXème siècle[3]. Il avait trouvé une ingénieuse solution pour les espaces ouverts au public sur la Biberstrasse. Cette partie de l'édifice d'un seul étage de hauteur paraissait ouverte et accueillante; malheureusement les choses se gâtaient sur les façades latérales.
Franz Skowron avait également soumis une proposition dans l'esprit viennois. Il fut éliminé lors du second tour. Theodor Bach proposa un projet néo-baroque assez pompeux alors que celui de Franz von Krausz et Josef Tölk se caractérisait par une extrême austérité. Leurs pavillons de coin étaient une discrète réminiscence du style Beaux-Arts, mais leur grande salle des guichets était si mal implantée que leur plan fut rejeté.
Le jury tomba en extase devant les plans de Wagner qui furent immédiatement acquis pour exécution. Cette décision était assez étonnante si l'on considère que son projet était le plus moderne de tous et qu'il rompait avec un certain nombre de traditions alors en vigueur. Une campagne fut lancée en faveur de la solution von Ferstel qui plaisait davantage au grand public. L'architecte Peter Paul Brang manifesta hautement son mécontentement. Premier des six finalistes, il refusa la décision du jury et porta l'affaire devant un tribunal pour invalider le choix de Wagner sous prétexte que celui-ci avait dessiné une vaste salle centrale pour les guichets d'épargne et de change alors que le cahier des charges parlait de «salles» au pluriel. Un sous-comité fut désigné qui déclara que Brang avait plus de titres que Wagner au versement du prix, mais que les banquiers étaient libres d'acheter et de faire exécuter le plan qui leur convenait.

Précurseur du fonctionnalisme

La caisse d'épargne de Wagner fut donc construite après quelques légères modifications. L'un des changements les plus significatifs concerna la grande verrière au-dessus de la partie centrale. Elle fut remplacée par un double toit de verre: un «plafond» translucide suspendu à une verrière en forme de tente. Paradoxalement pour Wagner, une structure apparemment fonctionnelle dissimulait ainsi la vraie structure.
L'architecte dissimula la hauteur de la verrière par un parapet, légèrement en retrait de la façade principale et qui confirmait le ressaut de sa partie centrale. L'entrée du public est située au centre et donne accès à la salle des caisses par un vestibule et un escalier. De petites cours triangulaires de chaque côté de la salle des guichets permettent à l'air frais et à la lumière d'inonder l'ensemble du bâtiment. La banque présente une forme générale de trapèze qui fut complétée en 1910 lorsque Wagner fut chargé de l'agrandir. Deux cours supplémentaires furent alors implantées de part et d'autre de la nouvelle salle d'accueil du public, conçue comme une extension de la grande salle des guichets.
Le plan de masse est presque entièrement symétrique et sans aucune forme arrondie, à la différence des plans de Krausz et Tölk et de von Ferstel.
L'une des caractéristiques du style de Wagner est l'absence de toute ornementation inutile. L'architecte ne prévoyait des ornements que s'ils étaient liés aux éléments structuraux ou s'ils n'interféraient en rien avec la lisibilité de la structure. Cette approche structuraliste est bien illustrée par le traitement de la façade, protégée à sa base par des dalles de pierre rustiquée au-dessus desquelles sont montées des dalles de marbre fixées par des boulons d'acier plaqués d'aluminium pour les protéger de la corrosion. Les têtes de ces boulons forment un motif décoratif élégant sur une façade sans aucune modénature. Les salles du public sont décorées de panneaux de marbre et de verre. Le puits au-dessus de la salle des guichets est carrelé de blanc. Tous ces éléments sont à la fois décoratifs et fonctionnels.
Les piliers métalliques de section carrée de la salle des guichets sont également plaqués d'aluminium et se rétrécissent vers le bas. En guise de chapiteau, ils sont équipés d'un système d'éclairage en couronne. Les rivets des piliers remplissent la même fonction décorative que les têtes de boulons de la façade. Les colonnes d'aération en aluminium sont à la fois fonctionnelles et décoratives.
Les piliers et les solives ont été montés sur du béton renforcé et le chauffage central et l'éclairage électrique assuraient de bonnes conditions de travail aux 2 700 employés (1 900 seulement aujourd'hui). Les bureaux sont clairs et aérés, grâce à de grandes fenêtres. Dans l'ensemble, l'édifice incarne l'esprit de ces temps nouveaux que Wagner aimait à imaginer: démocratiques, volontaristes et fonctionnels.
Les seuls ornements marquants de l'édifice sont les sculptures symbolisant le commerce et l'épargne placées aux angles du ressaut central. Elles furent dessinées par Othmar Schimkowitz et fondues en aluminium.

1 *Voir le chapitre sur le Hofoper.*
2 *Voir le chapitre sur Haus eines Kunstfreundes.*
3 *Von Ferstel était le fils de Heinrich Freiherr von Ferstel. Voir le chapitre sur le Reichstag.*

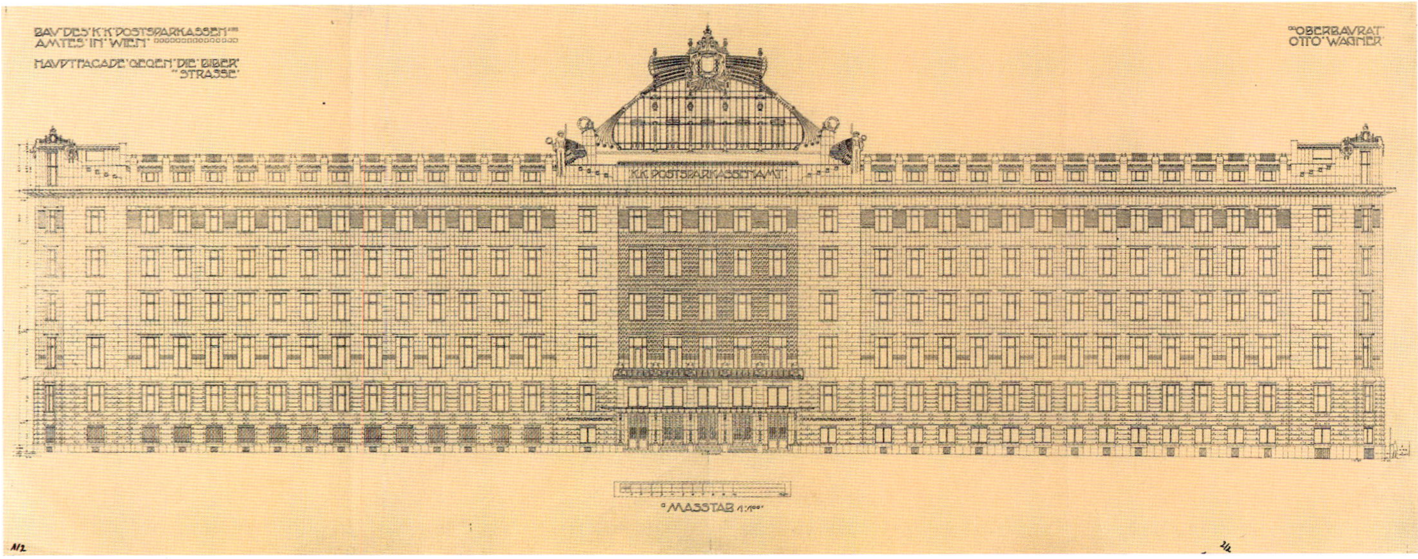

Otto Wagner altered design, 1903, front elevation on Georg Coch Platz

Otto Wagner execution design, 1903, plan of mezzanine

Otto Wagner execution design, 1903, first floor plan

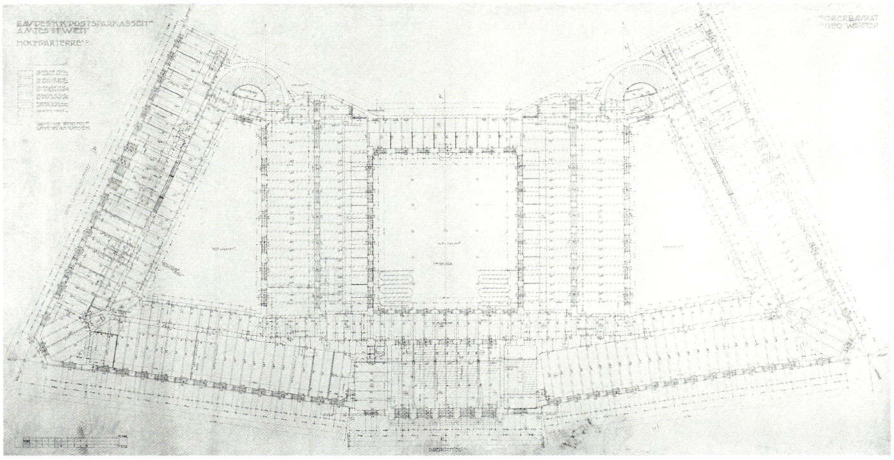

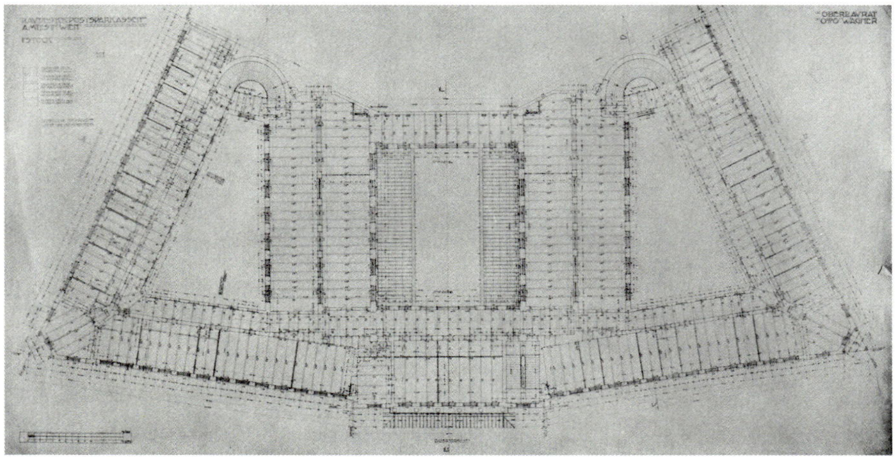

Otto Wagner execution design, 1910, front elevation on Georg Coch Platz

Otto Wagner execution design, 1910, part of central front elevation on Georg Coch Platz

Otto Wagner altered design, 1903, perspective section on Georg Coch Platz

Max Freiherr von Ferstel
competition design, 1903, front elevation on Georg Coch Platz, joint first prize

Max Freiherr von Ferstel
competition design, 1903, left: exterior view on Georg Coch Platz, right: site plan, joint first prize

Max Freiherr von Ferstel
competition design, 1903, plan of mezzanine, joint first prize

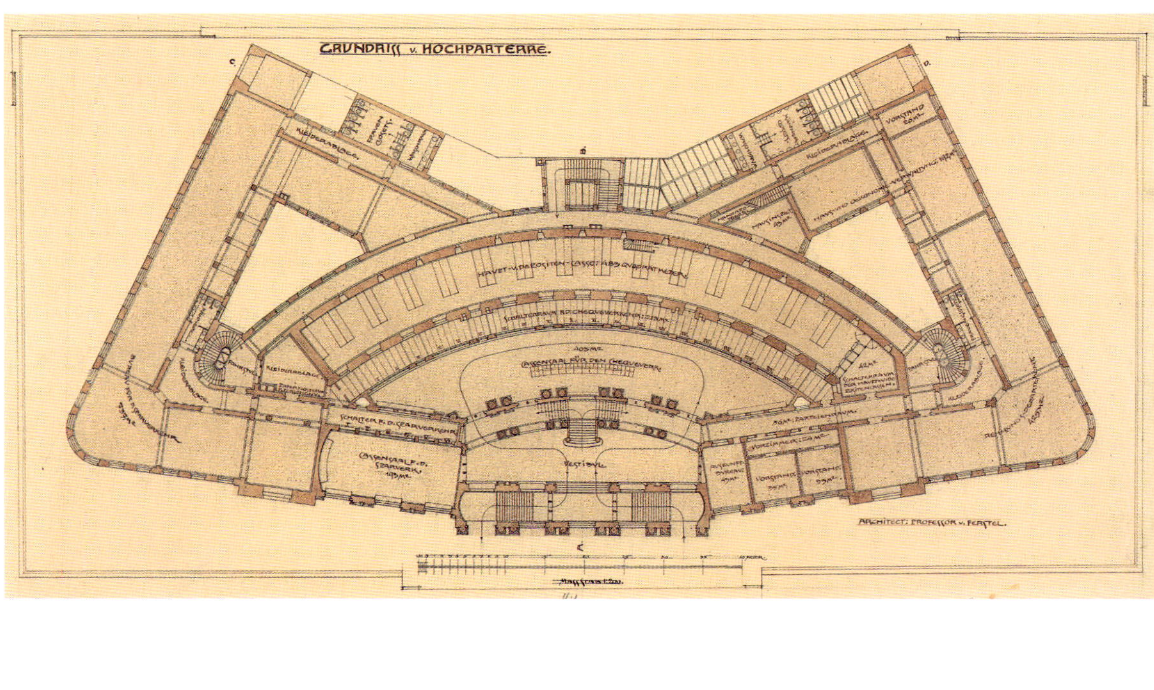

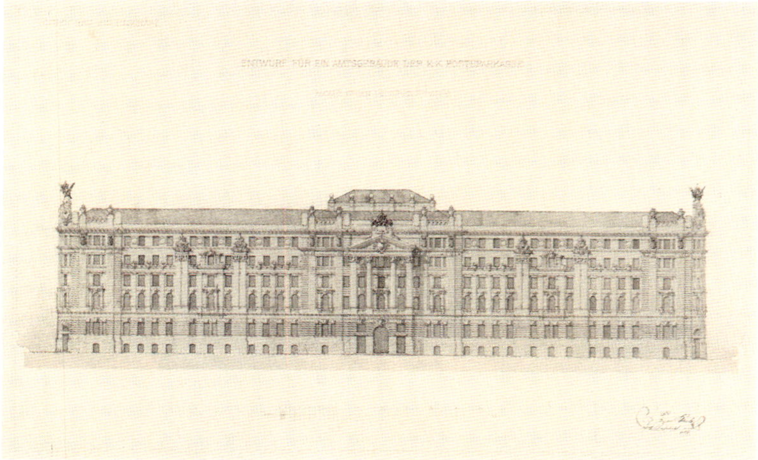

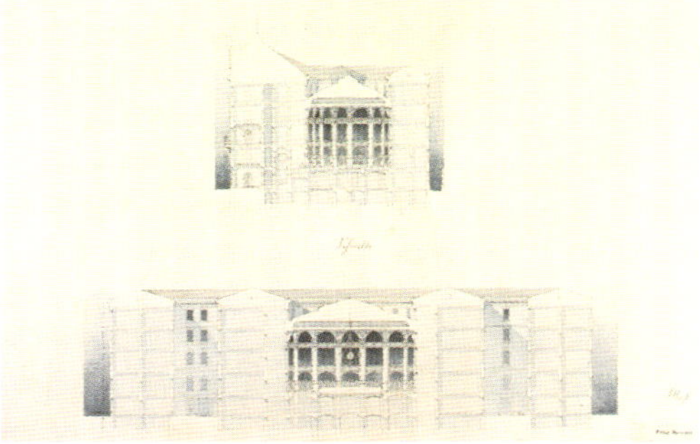

Max Freiherr von Ferstel competition design, 1903, detail of right front elevation on Georg Coch Platz, joint first prize

Theodor Bach competition design, 1903, front elevation on Georg Coch Platz, joint first prize

Franz Skowron competition design, 1903, side elevation on Rosenbursenstraße

Franz Skowron competition design, 1903, above: east-west section, below: north-south section

K·K·POSTSPARKASSENAMT·
MCMIV
WETTBEWERB-ENTWURF
FÜR DEN NEUBAU EINES
AMTSGEBÄUDES DER
K·K· POSTSPARKASSE
FAÇADEN-DETAIL
ARCHITEKTEN
F. v. KRAUSS
J. TÖLK WIEN I
AUERSPERGST. 4

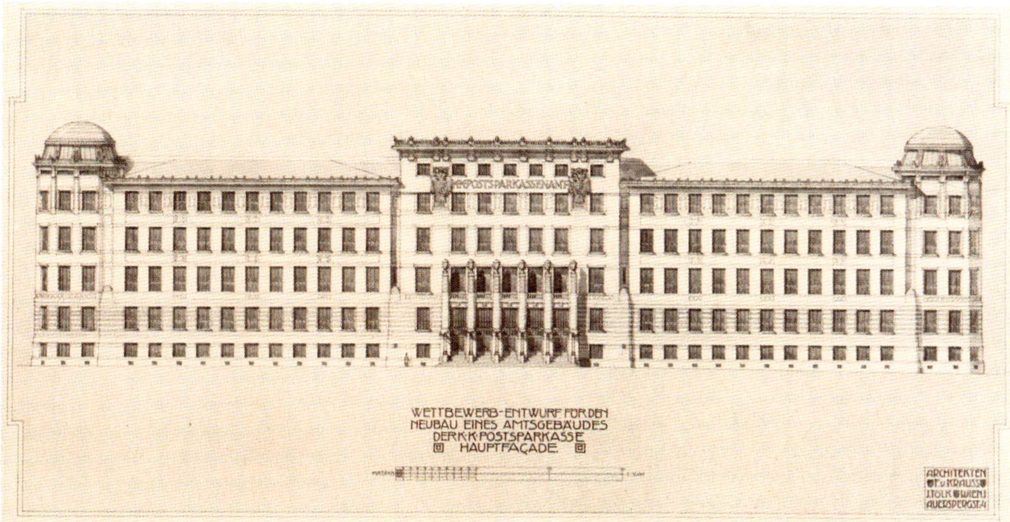

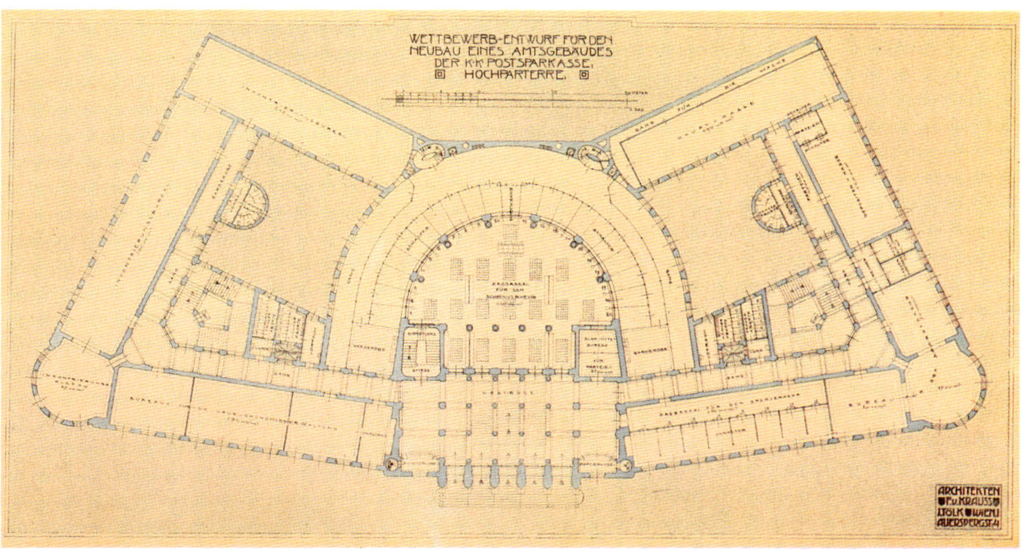

Josef Tölk & Franz von Krausz
competition design, 1903, front elevation on Georg Coch Platz, joint first prize

Josef Tölk & Franz von Krausz
competition design, 1903, plan of mezzanine, joint first prize

Josef Tölk & Franz von Krausz
competition design, 1903, exterior view on Georg Coch Platz, joint first prize

Project

Court-house, later City Hall

Site

Kungsholmen, Stockholm

Dates

First round autumn 1903 to 26 March 1904 *Second round* 11 October 1904 to March 1905

Number of entries

First round 25 *Second round* 5

Jury

Carolus Lindhagen (Chairman, Mayor of Stockholm), Richard Öhnell (Secretary of the Municipal Commission for Architecture), G. Tamm (former Governor of Stockholm), Isak Gustav Clason (architect and chairman of the building sector of the Society of Swedish Architects and Engineers), Martin Nyrop (architect, Denmark), Gustav Wickman (architect)

Result

First prize Ragnar Östberg *Second prize* Ivar Tengbom & Ernst Torulf *Third prize* Carl Westman, Carl Bergsten, Charles Lindholm

Commissioned by

The Stockholm City Council

Construction

1911 to 1923

Architect

Ragnar Östberg (1866–1945)

Construction cost

15 200 000 kronor (art and decoration: 1 677 000 kronor; gardens: 838 000 kronor)

City Hall, Stockholm, 1903

Ragnar Östberg execution design, 1917, north elevation (front)

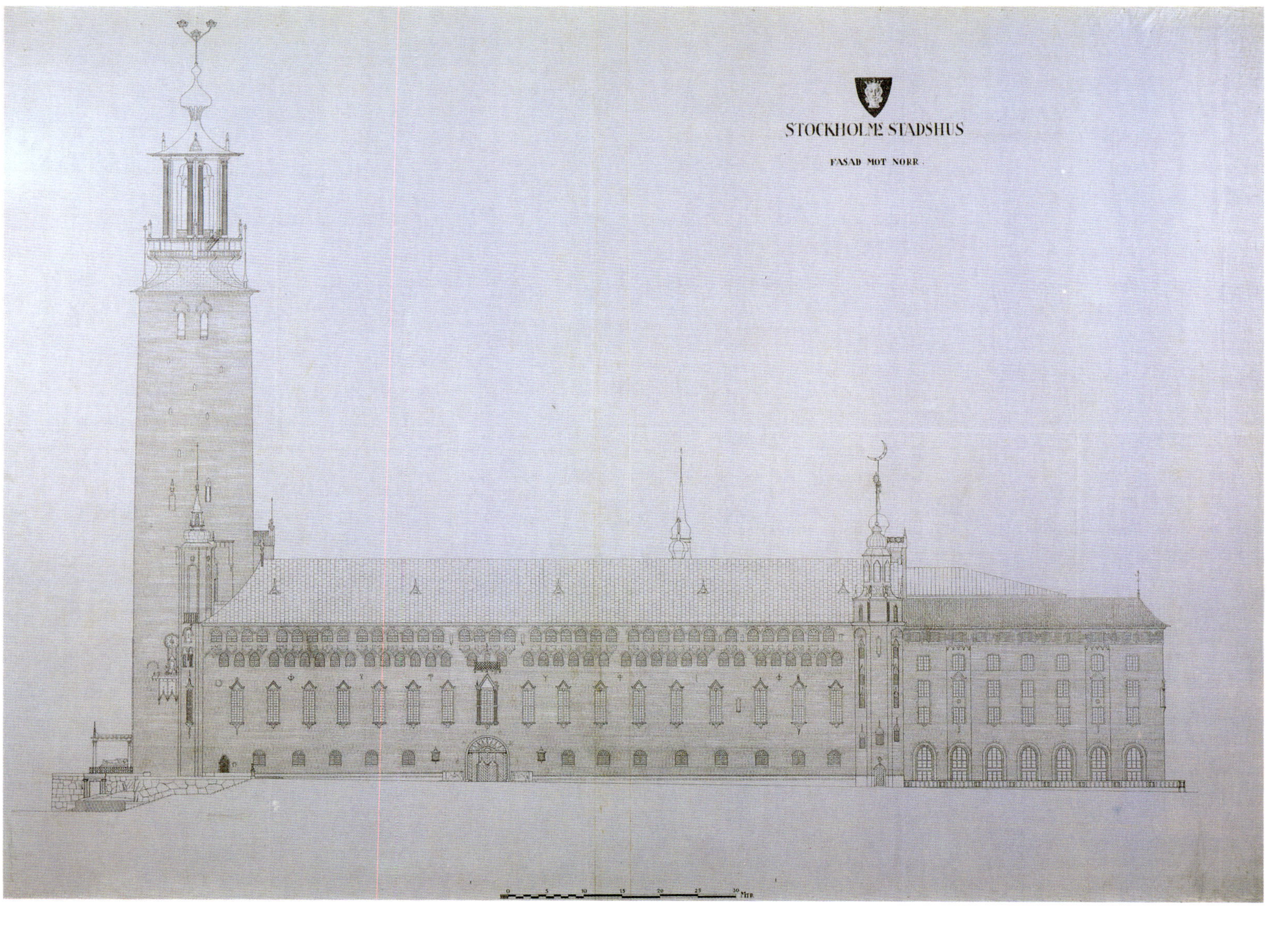

City Hall, Stockholm

The Rådhus (City Hall) in Stockholm may be seen as Östberg's magnum opus. Certainly in comparison to the rest of his œuvre, which is neither extensive nor remarkable, but primarily because Östberg worked on this project from 1893 to 1923. No less than thirty years! Östberg was educated at the Royal Institute of Technology and the Royal Academy of Arts. After graduating, he worked for Isak Gustav Clason for several years. Clason was later appointed chairman of the competition jury. Östberg was just starting out as an architect when he was presented with a perfect opportunity to express his youthful enthusiasm and dynamism. In 1893, the Stockholm Society of Artists invited architects to present their work at the society's annual exhibition for the first time.

The first designs

Östberg exhibited a design for a combined court-house and town hall. The dual-purpose Rådhus was an age-old tradition in Stockholm, where the "rådmän" had a judiciary and governing function. Although this medieval combination of professions had fallen into disuse, a combined judicial and administrative building was still considered to be completely acceptable. Östberg's design evoked a storm of derisive criticism, although he did receive encouragement as well. However, a more significant aspect of the exhibition was that Östberg was introduced to Richard Öhnell, who was a magistrate and Secretary of the Municipal Commission for Architecture. Öhnell was also considering the construction of a new and larger town hall and he informed Östberg of the necessary specifications for a building of this complexity.

Östberg's youthful enthusiasm had apparently made a lasting impression on Öhnell. Eight years after the competition, Öhnell approached Östberg – who had started his own business by then – to discuss the matter further. The old Stockholm Rådhus still had a combined function but had become too small. Öhnell, who had been schooled in the "trias politica" tradition, wanted to house the administrative and judicial sectors in different buildings. However, the deciding factor proved to be of a practical nature. Both the administrative and judicial workload had increased. This implied that there were more decisions to be made, more rules to be followed and that there was more paperwork. As a result, it had simply become too complex to house both sectors in a single building. Öhnell insisted that precedence be given to the court-house.

Öhnell had approached Östberg to discuss the most suitable building site. There were two options. The first option was the old city centre, which still had many medieval streets and buildings. During the exhibition of 1893, Östberg had had this part of the city in mind. The other possible site was the tip of the island Kungsholmen. A narrow stretch of water (Clara Sjö) separates Kungsholmen from the old city, which lies on the island of Staden. The architecture on Kungsholmen stems mainly from the seventeenth century, when Swedish power was at its height. The tip of this island looks out over the old city, Lake Mälar and the granite cliffs of Stockholm's other islands. This part of

Ragnar Östberg

Ragnar Östberg sketch of law Courts and City Hall, lithograph published in the daily newspaper "Aftonbladet" on November 15, 1901

Ragnar Östberg the Law Courts, design in 1902 (before competition), exterior view

Ragnar Östberg the Law Courts, the second competition design "Mälardrott", exterior view

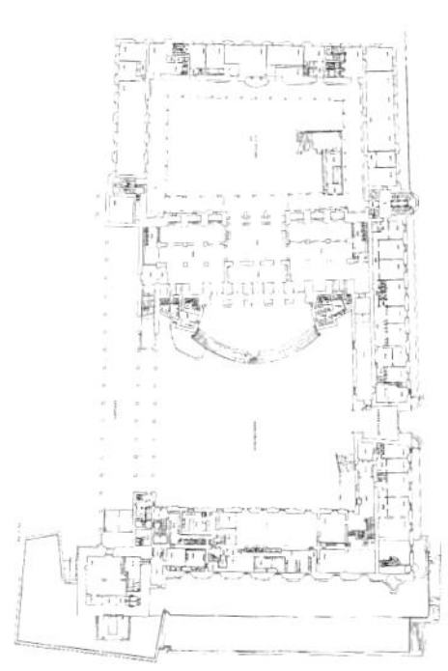

City Hall, ground floor plan, 1979

the island is called Eldkvarnen, which means “steam mill area”. Östberg considered both options and concluded that Eldkvarnen was the most suitable site. In an effort to convince the other council members of this fact, Öhnell asked Östberg to make a preliminary drawing. Östberg had previously published a preliminary design for the Eldkvarnen site in the “Aftonbladet” on 15 November 1901. However, this design was not very detailed.

Return to tradition

In 1902, the council decided to purchase the site, with the intention of building a court-house. To this end, a competition was organised in 1903. The procedure left nothing to chance. All Swedish architects were free to try their luck in the open first round but there was no prize money to be won. The six winning architects from the first round would all be awarded prize money during the second round. The jury consisted of three representatives from the city council (Öhnell was one) and three architects (including Clason and Nyrop, who designed the town hall in Copenhagen). Although the conditions were clearly stipulated, they were so extensive – architects were asked to include a budget – that only 25 architects submitted designs. The designs had to be submitted under a motto. As a result, the names of a number of the participating architects remain unknown to this day. For example, the architect who submitted the design “Leo”. The six winning architects were Axel Ahlberg, Carl Bergsten, Ivar Tengbom & Ernst Torulf, Ragnar Östberg, Carl Westman and Charles Lindholm.

Ahlberg had submitted a rather strange eclectic design under the motto *“non senza dignità”* (not without dignity), but later dropped out of the competition. The other architects, with the exception of Bergsten, had submitted designs which were, to a greater or lesser extent, based on sixteenth and seventeenth century Swedish architecture. The reason for this is fairly obvious: Sweden became a world power during this period[1].

Bergsten's first round design was more in harmony with the medieval city centre than with the Eldkvarnen site. His second round design was clearly inspired by Jugendstil. From the east, the building's silhouette bears a resemblance to the Hagia Sophia. Bergsten even included a minaret. Tengbom & Torulf's first design consisted of a rather massive block with a short, square tower. The tower was situated above the main entrance on the east side. Their second round design was completely different. They had moved the tower and the main entrance to the south side, which featured a gable on the left-hand side. Their revised design seems to have been derived directly from Östberg's earlier drawings. It bears mentioning that the tip of the island was probably the most logical place for the tower. Westman and Östberg's towers stood even closer to the tip of the island than Tengbom & Torulf's. Lindholm's first round design was a boring combination of Louis XIV, Louis XVI and local eighteenth century architecture, which was to be built in stone. Lindholm applied the Swedish Neo-Renaissance style in his second round design. He based this design on the castles of Gripsholm and Vadstena, built by the Vasa kings in the sixteenth century.

Östberg altered his design here and there, but the core concept remained the same. Notable changes were made to the top of the tower, which became a more massive, granite structure with distinct Jugendstil features. His design, submitted under the motto *“Mälardrott”* (King of the Mälar), was awarded first prize (1905). However, this did not automatically imply that he would be commissioned. The city council, probably shocked by the high construction costs, decided to organise a mini-competition between Östberg (estimated cost: four million kronor) and Westman, whose 2.9 million kronor price tag was the lowest of the field. The city council had probably hoped to force Östberg to cut costs in this way. If this was indeed their intention, their ploy was fairly successful. Östberg replaced the granite façades with brick. These building materials were both locally available. Östberg's new budget was still 300,000 kronor higher than Westman's. However, the majority of the council were in favour of Östberg's design, and he was commissioned to build the new court-house in 1906. Östberg set to work, but after a year he was confronted by a new and even greater obstacle.

The court-house becomes a town hall

The competition had received a lot of publicity. The site and the design had an intrinsic appeal and the public thought it a pity that the building would merely be used as a court-house. While Öhnell had been occupied with the court-house, other city councillors had been

View from south (the tower from the back)

considering possible sites for a new town hall. On the initiative of the influential banker K.A. Wallenberg, it was decided (1907) that a City Hall, rather than a court-house, would be built on the Eldkvarnen site. The court-house would be built elsewhere on Kungsholmen. However, Östberg had reached a stage where he was unable to transpose his design to any other site. Carl Westman was therefore commissioned to design the new court-house. The council also decided that the new City Hall would be based on Östberg's design for the court house. As a result, Östberg was faced with the mammoth task of adapting his design (1908–1909). The floor plans, in particular, required extensive changes. However, Östberg was still not sure that he would be commissioned. His appointment was finally verified on 27 March 1911, when Wallenberg and Louis Fraenckel, Wallenberg's friend and a fellow-banker, donated a substantial sum of money to cover the costs of construction, which now amounted to six million kronor.

Work was finally started on Östberg's building. A municipal commission was appointed to supervise construction. Prominent members of this commission were Wallenberg and the Mayor of Stockholm, Carolus Lindhagen, who had also been a member of the jury. The commission had to approve any changes that Östberg intended to make and subsequently had to present these to the city council. The commission was remarkably understanding, which was a stroke of luck for Östberg because a vast number of changes had to be made. The tower underwent the most notable change. It was moved outward and underwent an exterior metamorphosis. Due the fact that Östberg had replaced the granite in the earlier designs with bricks, a less massive tower seemed more appropriate. Consequently, a slender tower developed. The granite top, which had survived the cost-cutting round, was executed in wood with a copper covering. The façade on the east side, which faced the old city centre, was also altered.

Blue hall

A magnum opus completed

On the whole, the City Hall seems to have been based on sixteenth and seventeenth century Swedish architecture. However, the east side was clearly inspired by the medieval city centre of Stockholm. This is not only characteristic of Östberg's work, but also of his progressive Swedish contemporaries. After a lengthy period of internationally-oriented Classicism, this generation rediscovered their own national architecture. Östberg incorporated various features from a variety of Swedish architectural eras in a single building. The red, hand-moulded bricks, used for the exterior, have been laid in a way similar to those in Swedish medieval churches. The machine-made stones in the "blue hall" were later rusticated to give them a rougher appearance. Östberg had initially intended to use blue plaster for the walls. The detail work has been executed in grey and (sometimes) black granite, from local quarries. Rough oak was used for the entrance. There are grey granite columns on the south side, which have been monolithically crowned with an imaginative capital designed by the Swedish sculptor Aron Sandberg. In contrast, the two colossal pillars in the courtyard are clearly of Corinthian origin and may be seen as a reference to sixteenth century Swedish castles, where Renaissance forms and traditional architecture were combined with a certain nonchalance. The onion-shaped pinnacle on the main tower and the smaller towers are also traditionally Swedish, as is the use of copper as a roofing material.

The city hall eventually became a Swedish national monument. The decision to situate it at the tip of the island was evidently made with remarkable foresight.

It would take a while before the building was completed. The First World War caused delays. Wallenberg became Minister of Foreign Affairs but retained his seat on the architectural commission. In addition, the city council decided to reorganise their administration. The reorganisation took some time and Östberg constantly had to adapt his designs. However, when the last stone was laid in 1923, it was evident that Östberg had created a building which would receive widespread praise, both nationally and internationally. Initially, this praise was short-lived, because the Modernist architects were fiercely opposed to this type of architecture. However, in recent years the Stockholm Rådhus has been the subject of renewed interest.

1 *The Swedish empire was founded by Gustave I, who was also the forefather of the Vasa dynasty. The Vasas ruled Sweden from 1523 to 1654. They were also kings of Poland from 1587 to 1668.*

Rathaus, Stockholm

Das Stockholmer Rathaus war Ragnar Östbergs Lebenswerk – nicht nur weil sein restliches Oeuvre kaum als umfangreich oder herausragend bezeichnet werden kann, sondern weil Östberg sich 30 Jahre mit der Gestaltung des Rathauses beschäftigte. Nach seiner Ausbildung am Königlichen Institut für Technologie und an der Königlichen Akademie der Künste war er mehrere Jahre für das Architekturbüro von Isak Gustav Clason tätig, der später den Vorsitz der Jury übernahm. Als 1893 die Stockholmer Künstlervereinigung erstmalig Architekten zur jährlichen Kunstausstellung zuließ, sah der noch junge Architekt Östberg eine willkommene Gelegenheit zur Verwirklichung seines jugendlichen Enthusiasmus und Tatendrangs.

Die ersten Entwürfe

Östbergs Entwurf sah ein Gebäude vor, das sowohl das Rathaus als auch das Gericht beherbergen sollte, und knüpfte damit an die Stockholmer Tradition an, die verlangte, daß der »rådmän« eine zugleich rechtsprechende wie auch administrative Funktion ausübte. Diese mittelalterliche Machtkonzentration gehörte zwar längst der Vergangenheit an, aber die Kombination von Stadtverwaltung und Gericht in einem Gebäude galt als durchaus normal. Dennoch riefen Östbergs Pläne einen Sturm der Entrüstung hervor. Im Zuge der Auseinandersetzungen lernte Östberg Richard Öhnell kennen, der zu diesem Zeitpunkt Sekretär des Ausschusses für städtische Bauten war und als Richter arbeitete. Öhnell spielte selbst mit dem Gedanken, ein neues, größeres Rathaus errichten zu lassen, und informierte Östberg über die Bedingungen, die ein solch komplexes Gebäude erfüllen mußte.
Öhnell muß sehr beeindruckt gewesen sein, denn acht Jahre später suchte er das Büro von Östberg, der sich inzwischen als Architekt selbständig gemacht hatte, auf, um die Gespräche fortzusetzen. Das alte Stockholmer Rathaus, das noch beide Amtsaufgaben in sich vereinigte, war zu klein geworden, und der mit der Maxime der «trias politica» aufgewachsene Öhnell beabsichtigte eine getrennte Unterbringung von Gericht und Rathaus in zwei neu zu errichtenden Gebäuden. Entscheidend für diese Überlegungen waren praktische Gründe: Beide Institutionen waren mit ihren Aufgaben überlastet. Folglich erschien eine Kombination beider Organe in einem Gebäude als zu kompliziert. Auf Drängen des Richters Öhnell gab man schließlich einem Gerichtsgebäude den Vorzug.
Öhnell hatte Östberg kontaktiert, um mit ihm die Frage des geeigneten Baugeländes zu erörtern. Für das neue Gerichtsgebäude boten sich zwei Standorte an: Zum einen das alte Stadtzentrum mit zahlreichen mittelalterlichen Straßen und Bauwerken (dieser Standort hatte Östberg während der Ausschreibung 1893 vorgeschwebt) und zum anderen die Spitze der Insel Kungsholmen, die durch den schmalen Meeresarm Klara Sjö von der ebenfalls auf einer Insel (Staden) gelegenen Altstadt getrennt war. Dieser Teil der Stadt stammte aus dem 17. Jahrhundert, als Schweden sich im Zenit seiner Macht befand. Die Spitze der Insel, die sowohl einen Blick zur Altstadt als auch auf den Mälarsee und die Granitküsten der anderen Stockholmer Inseln ermöglicht, heißt Eldkvarnen (»Feuermühle«, nach der ersten mit Dampf betriebenen Mühle). Östberg unterzog beide Standorte einer eingehenden Prüfung und kam zu dem Schluß, daß sich Eldkvarnen am besten für das neue Gebäude eignete.
Auf Bitten Öhnells fertigte er eine Skizze an, um auch die anderen Ratsmitglieder von diesem Standort zu überzeugen. Bereits am 15. November 1901 hatte Östberg im »Aftonbladet« einen – allerdings nicht sehr detaillierten – Entwurf veröffentlicht, der als Baugelände ebenfalls Eldkvarnen vorsah.

Zurück zur Tradition

1902 entschloß sich der Rat zum Kauf des Geländes, auf dem das neue Gerichtsgebäude errichtet werden sollte. Die Ausschreibung erfolgte 1903, wobei man nichts dem Zufall überließ: Während der ersten (allgemeinen) Ausschreibungsrunde war es jedem schwedischen Architekten gestattet, an diesem Wettbewerb teilzunehmen – allerdings wurden keine Preisgelder ausgeteilt. Erst in der zweiten Ausschreibungsrunde, die sechs von der Jury ausgewählten Architekten vorbehalten war, erwartete die Gewinner eine Prämie. Da die Auflagen zwar genau festgelegt, aber auch sehr detailliert waren (u. a. wurde ein Kostenvoranschlag verlangt), reichten schließlich nur 25 Architekten einen Entwurf ein.
Östbergs Entwurf erfuhr eine Reihe von Korrekturen, blieb im Kern aber unverändert. Besonders auffällig ist die Entwicklung der Turmkrone, die eine sehr viel schwerere Granitstruktur mit charakteristischen Jugendstilelementen erhielt. Sein unter dem Motto '»*Mälardrott*« (König des Mälarsee) eingesandter Vorschlag erhielt zwar den ersten Preis, doch damit bekam Östberg noch lange nicht den Bauauftrag. Da der Stadtrat vor den hohen Kosten zurückschreckte, veranstaltete er einen Mini-Wettbewerb zwischen Östberg, dessen Kostenvoranschlag sich auf 4 Millionen Kronen belief, und Westman, der mit geschätzten Baukosten in Höhe von 2,9 Millionen Kronen deutlich unter den anderen Teilnehmern blieb. Wahrscheinlich wollten die Stadtratsmitglieder Östberg auf diese Weise zu einer Verringerung der Baukosten zwingen, was ihnen auch gelang. Östberg ersetzte die Granitfassade durch Ziegelstein (in beiden Fällen handelte es sich um regionale Baumaterialien). Seine Neukalkulation lag zwar immer noch um 300 000 Kronen über Westmans Kostenvoranschlag, aber ein Großteil des Stadtrats bevorzugte Östbergs Entwurf, so daß er 1906 offiziell zum Architekten des neuen Gerichtsgebäudes ernannt wurde.

Ein Gericht wird zum Rathaus

Die Ausschreibung erfreute sich eines großen öffentlichen Interesses. Aufgrund der ansprechenden Lage und des attraktiven Designs kamen die Stadtväter bald zu der Ansicht, es sei viel zu schade, das Gebäude nur als Sitz des Gerichts zu nutzen. Während Öhnell sich mit diesem Projekt befaßte, beschäftigten sich andere Ratsmitglieder mit der Frage nach einem geeigneten Standort für ein Rathaus. Unter Leitung des einflußreichen Bankiers K.A. Wallenberg beschloß der Stadtrat 1907, auf dem Eldkvarnen-Gelände statt des Gerichtsgebäudes ein Rathaus zu errichten. Das Gericht sollte an einer anderen Stelle von Kungsholmen gebaut werden. Östberg hatte sich allerdings derartig mit dem ursprünglich vorgesehenen Standort seines Gerichts identifiziert, daß Carl Westman den Auftrag für den Entwurf des neuen Gerichtsgebäudes erhielt. Darüber hinaus entschied der Stadtrat, das neue Rathaus solle anhand von Östbergs Entwürfen für das Gerichtsgebäude gebaut werden. Folge: Östberg sah sich vor die Aufgabe gestellt, seine Konstruktionspläne der neuen Situation anzupassen (1908–1909). Insbesondere die Grundrisse erfuhren tiefgreifende Veränderungen. Dennoch konnte Östberg sich der Auftragserteilung immer noch nicht sicher sein. Erst am 27. März 1911 wurde er offiziell zum Architekten ernannt, als Wallenberg und Louis Fraenckel – ein mit Wallenberg befreundeter Bankier – eine beträchtliche Geldsumme zur Deckung der mittlerweile auf 6 Millionen Kronen geschätzten Baukosten zusagten.
Endlich konnte sich Östberg an die Arbeit begeben. Allerdings mußte er jede Abweichung von seinen Plänen gegenüber einer eigens berufenen städtischen Kommission verantworten, die die Bauarbeiten beaufsichtigte. Diese Kommission, der u. a. Wallenberg und Stockholms Bürgermeister Carolus Lindhagen (der bereits in der Jury saß) angehörten, mußte die Änderungswünsche wiederum dem Stadtrat vorlegen. Glücklicherweise zeigte die Kommission viel Verständnis für Östbergs zahllose Korrekturvorschläge, wobei der Turm die größte Veränderung erfuhr: Er wurde nicht nur nach außerhalb des Gebäudes verlegt, sondern auch einer Metamorphose unterzogen. Da Östberg bereits zuvor den Granit durch Ziegelsteine ersetzt hatte, schien ein weniger massiv wirkender Turm angebrachter: Östberg entwarf einen schlankeren Turm, dessen Granitspitze nun aus Holz gefertigt und mit Kupfer verkleidet werden sollte. Auch die Ostfassade gegenüber dem alten Stadtkern wurde abgewandelt.

Vollendung eines Lebenswerks

Während der Gesamteindruck des Rathauses auf Einflüsse der schwedischen Architektur des 16. und 17. Jahrhunderts schließen läßt, ist die Ostseite eindeutig vom mittelalterlichen Stadtkern Stockholms inspiriert. Dies ist nicht nur für Östbergs Arbeiten, sondern auch für zahlreiche andere, fortschrittlich denkende Architekten dieser Zeit charakteristisch. Nach einer langen Periode im Stil des eher international orientierten Klassizismus besann sich diese Generation wieder auf die eigene nationale Baukunst. So lassen sich an Östbergs Gebäude Elemente der verschiedensten Epochen schwedischer Architektur unterscheiden. Der Mauerverband der roten, handgehauenen Ziegelsteine auf der Außenseite entsprach dem Mauerwerk schwedischer Kirchen aus dem Mittelalter, während die maschinell gefertigten Steine der »Blauen Halle« später noch einmal mit dem Meißel bearbeitet wurden, damit sie grober und rauher erschienen. Ursprünglich wollte Östberg die Wände dieses Raums mit blauem Gips versehen. Die Details wurden aus grauem (und teilweise schwarzem) Granit der Gegend gefertigt; für die Eingangspforte verwandte Östberg grobe Eiche. Die mit einem Phantasiekapitell des schwedischen Bildhauers Aron Sandberg monolithisch bekrönten Säulen an der Südfassade bestehen ebenfalls aus grauem Granit – ganz im Gegensatz zu den beiden kolossalen, in korinthischer Säulenordnung ausgeführten Pfeilern im Innenhof, die als Referenz an die schwedischen Schlösser des 16. Jahrhunderts galten: Auch damals hatte man Renaissanceformen und traditionelle Architektur mit einer gewissen Nonchalance kombiniert. Die zwiebelförmigen Kronen auf der Turmspitze des Hauptturms und den kleineren Türmen sind ebenso typisch schwedisch wie die Verwendung von Kupfer für die Dachhaut. Das Stockholmer Stadshuset wurde schließlich zu einem Nationaldenkmal Schwedens.

Hôtel de ville, Stockholm

Le Rådhus (hôtel de ville) de Stockholm est le grand œuvre de Östberg. Non seulement parce qu'il ne construisit rien d'autre de particulièrement important ou remarquable mais parce qu'il n'y consacra pas moins de trente années de sa vie, de 1893 à 1923. Östberg avait fait ses études à l'Institut Royal de Technologie et à l'Académie Royale des Arts. Une fois diplômé, il travailla plusieurs années pour Isak Gustav Clason, futur président du jury du concours. Il débutait à son compte lorsque se présenta à lui l'opportunité de faire preuve de son enthousiasme: en 1893, la Société des Artistes de Stockholm invita pour la première fois les architectes à participer à son exposition annuelle.

Premiers plans

Östberg y exposa le plan d'un édifice associant un palais de justice et un hôtel de ville. Ce double rôle du Rådhus était une ancienne tradition de la capitale suédoise où les «rådmän», les conseillers, exerçaient des responsabilités à la fois administratives et judiciaires. Bien que ce mélange médiéval de fonctions soit tombé en désuétude, l'idée d'un bâtiment réunissant tribunal et mairie semblait toujours envisageable. Le projet d'Östberg s'attira de multiples moqueries et quelques rares encouragements. Cette exposition lui permit cependant d'être présenté à Richard Öhnell, magistrat et secrétaire de la Commission municipale d'architecture qui réfléchissait alors à la construction d'un vaste hôtel de ville et expliqua au jeune architecte les contraintes d'un bâtiment aussi complexe.
L'enthousiasme d'Östberg avait apparemment impressionné le magistrat puisque, huit ans plus tard, il souhaita rencontrer de nouveau l'architecte. L'ancien Rådhus, remplissant l'antique double fonction, était devenu trop petit. Öhnell, partisan de la séparation des pouvoirs, souhaitait que les activités administratives et judiciaires possèdent leurs propres installations, mais le facteur décisif fut de nature plus concrète. Le travail judiciaire aussi bien qu'administratif s'était développé, ce qui entraînait une multiplication des tâches toujours plus complexes qui rendait pratiquement impossible la cohabitation de ces deux activités en un seul lieu. Öhnell insista pour que l'on commence par la cour de justice. Deux sites étaient envisageables. L'un, pour lequel penchait Östberg, dans le centre ancien qui présentait encore un aspect médiéval, l'autre à la pointe de l'île de Kungsholmen séparée de la vieille ville située sur l'île de Staden par un étroit bras de mer.
L'architecture de Kungsholmen datait essentiellement du XVIIème siècle, âge d'or de la puissance suédoise. L'extrémité de l'île, appelée Eldkvarnen (le moulin à vapeur), regarde vers la vieille ville, le lac Mälar et les falaises de granit des autres îles sur lesquelles s'étend la capitale.

Retour à la tradition

En 1902, le comité décida d'acheter le terrain pour construire la cour de justice et de lancer un concours l'année suivante. La procédure ne laissa rien au hasard. Tous les architectes suédois pouvaient tenter leur chance lors du premier tour. Aucun prix en argent ne devait être accordé mais les six lauréats du premier tour recevraient un dédommagement après le second. Le jury était composé de trois représentants du conseil municipal (dont Öhnell) et de trois architectes, dont Clason et Martin Nyrop qui avait conçu l'hôtel de ville de Copenhague. Si les conditions étaient claires, elles étaient si nombreuses et précises (il fallait même détailler les coûts) que 25 architectes seulement soumirent des projets. Leur présentation anonyme explique que le nom de plusieurs d'entre eux soit resté inconnu. Les six architectes vainqueurs du premier tour furent Axel Ahlberg, Carl Bergsten, Ivar Tengbom et Ernst Torulf, Ragnar Östberg, Carl Westman et Charles Lindholm.
Ahlberg avait proposé un édifice éclectique plutôt étrange sous la devise *«Non sans dignité»* (non senza dignita), puis décida de se retirer de la compétition.
Les autres concurrents, à l'exception de Bergsten, s'en étaient tenus à des projets plus ou moins inspirés de l'architecture suédoise des XVIème et XVIIème siècle[1].
Si les plans initiaux de Bergsten convenaient mieux au centre de la vieille ville qu'au site d'Eldkvarnen, son projet du second tour s'inspirait de l'Art nouveau. Vue de l'est, la silhouette de son édifice rappelait Sainte-Sophie et il avait même imaginé une sorte de minaret. Le premier projet de Tengbom et Torulf consistait en un bloc assez massif dont l'entrée principale, à l'est, était surmontée d'une courte tour carrée. Pour la seconde phase du concours, ils avaient apporté d'importantes modifications: l'entrée et la tour passaient sur la façade sud qui s'adornait en plus d'un pignon en partie gauche. Leurs plans révisés semblaient directement inspirés des premiers dessins d'Östberg. La pointe de l'île était l'emplacement le plus logique pour l'édification d'une tour et ce fut la solution retenue par Westman, Östberg et, à un moindre degré, Tengbom et Torulf. Le premier plan de Lindholm était un ennuyeux mélange de styles Louis XIV, Louis XVI et suédois du XVIIIème siècle destiné à être construit en pierre. Pour le second tour, il revint à un style néo-renaissance suédois, inspiré des châteaux de Gripsholm et de Vadstena construits au XVIème siècle par les Vasa.
Östberg transforma légèrement son projet mais en conserva l'essentiel. Ses modifications portèrent sur le sommet de la tour qui se transforma en une massive structure de granit d'esprit Jugendstil. Son projet, proposé sous le nom de *«Mälardrott»* (roi de Mälar), reçut le premier prix (1905) ce qui n'impliquait pas l'obtention de la commande. Le conseil municipal, probablement surpris par le coût de la construction envisagé, décida d'organiser un concours restreint entre Östberg (4 millions de krs) et Westman dont le devis de 2,9 millions de couronnes était le moins élevé de tous. Le conseil pensait sans doute forcer Östberg à réduire ses coûts, ce qu'il fit en remplaçant la pierre par de la brique locale. Bien que son nouveau devis fut encore supérieur de 300 000 krs à celui de Westman, il remporta la commande en 1906 et se mit immédiatement au travail pour se trouver bientôt confronté à un nouvel obstacle.

Le Palais de justice devient hôtel de ville

Le concours avait rencontré beaucoup d'échos. Le site et le projet étaient séduisants et l'idée germa qu'il eût été dommage de se contenter de construire un simple palais de justice en un si bel endroit. Pendant qu'Öhnell se préoccupait surtout de son tribunal, d'autres conseillers avaient étudié le projet d'un nouvel hôtel de ville. Et c'est ainsi qu'à l'initiative de l'influent banquier K.A. Wallenberg, il fut décidé en 1907 d'édifier sur le site d'Eldkvarnen l'hôtel de ville et non le palais de justice pour lequel serait trouvé un autre emplacement. Östberg avait beaucoup avancé et son projet ne pouvait plus être adapté à un autre site. Carl Westman reçut la commande du palais de justice et le conseil demanda à Östberg d'adapter ses plans à la nouvelle mairie. Le plan de masse n'était évidemment pas le même et l'architecte se trouva condamné à un délicat travail d'adaptation qui le mena jusqu'en 1909. Il lui fallut encore patienter jusqu'au 27 mars 1911 pour être certain d'avoir la commande, date à laquelle Wallenberg et son ami et confrère Louis Fraencke offrirent une importante somme d'argent pour couvrir les coûts de construction qui s'élevaient maintenant à six millions de couronnes.
La tour subit les changements les plus visibles. Initialement en pierre, puis en brique, elle fut amincie et son sommet fut monté en bois recouvert de cuivre au lieu de granit. La façade est, vers l'ancienne ville, fut également modifiée.

Un grand œuvre

Dans l'ensemble, l'hôtel de ville paraît inspiré de l'architecture des XVIème et XVIIème siècle suédois, même si sa façade Est rappelle fortement le centre médiéval de la capitale. Son style n'est pas caractéristique du seul Östberg mais également de plusieurs architectes progressistes de l'époque. Après une longue période de néo-classicisme, toute une génération avait redécouvert sa propre architecture nationale. Östberg sut incorporer dans un seul bâtiment de multiples détails empruntés à plusieurs époques différentes de l'architecture suédoise. Les briques rouges des façades, moulées à la main, rappelaient celles des églises du Moyen-Age. Les pierres sciées à la machine du hall furent travaillées pour leur donner une apparence plus brute, et Östberg avait même eu l'intention d'utiliser du plâtre bleu à l'ancienne pour les murs. De nombreux détails sont exécutés en granit gris ou noir de carrières locales et l'entrée est en chêne naturel. La façade Sud est ornée de colonnes de granit gris surmontées d'un chapiteau sculpté par l'artiste suédois Aron Sandberg. Elles contrastent avec les deux piliers colossaux de style corinthien de la cour et font référence à certains châteaux de la région où les formes de la Renaissance et de l'architecture traditionnelle étaient combinées sans se préoccuper de règles académiques. Le pinacle en forme de bulbe de la principale tour comme des petites est d'esprit suédois de même que le cuivre de leur couverture. Spectaculairement situé à la pointe d'une île, cet hôtel de ville, est vite devenu un monument historique.
Mais il fallut de nombreuses années avant qu'il ne soit terminé. La Première Guerre mondiale provoqua des retards. Wallenberg devint ministre des Affaires étrangères tout en conservant son poste à la commission de contrôle, puis la ville réorganisa son administration ce qui contraignit Östberg à revoir de nouveau ses plans.
Lorsque la dernière pierre fut posée, en 1923, il était évident aux yeux de tous que l'architecte avait réussi là un chef-d'œuvre qui serait apprécié aussi bien en Suède qu'à l'étranger. Bien que l'influence d'Östberg ait été vite contrecarrée par le mouvement moderniste opposé à ce type d'architecture, le Rådhus de Stockholm connaît actuellement un regain d'intérêt.

1 *L'empire suédois fut fondé par Gustave Ier, également fondateur de la dynastie des Vasa qui régnèrent de 1523 à 1654. Ils furent également rois de Pologne de 1587 à 1668.*

City Hall, Stockholm, 1903

196

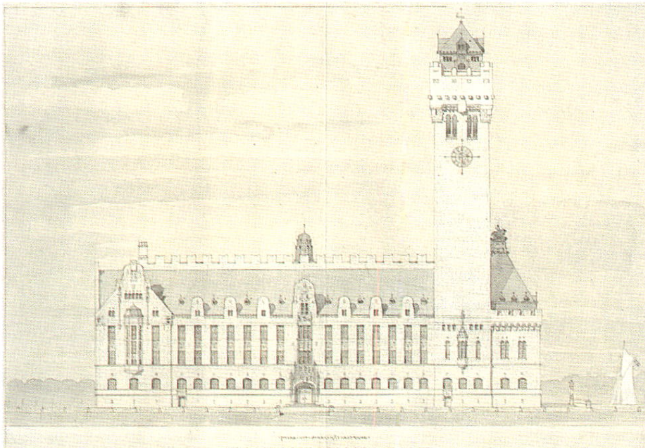

Ivar Tengbom & Ernst Torulf second round competition design "Lilla putte", 1905, south elevation (front), second prize

Ragnar Östberg second round competition design, "Mälardrott", 1905, above: north-south section, below: east elevation of glass roofed court, first prize

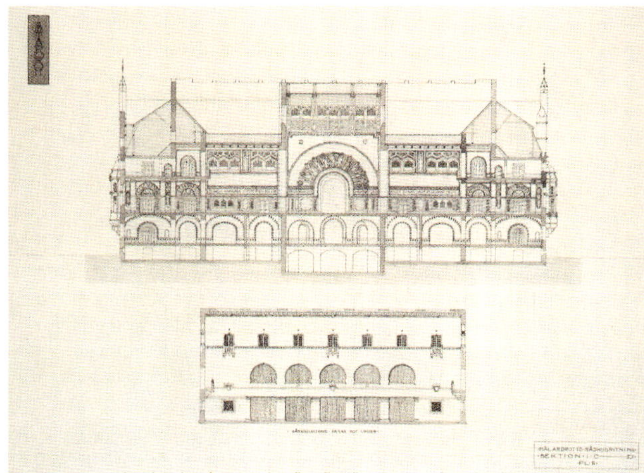

Ragnar Östberg execution design, 1917, east elevation (side)

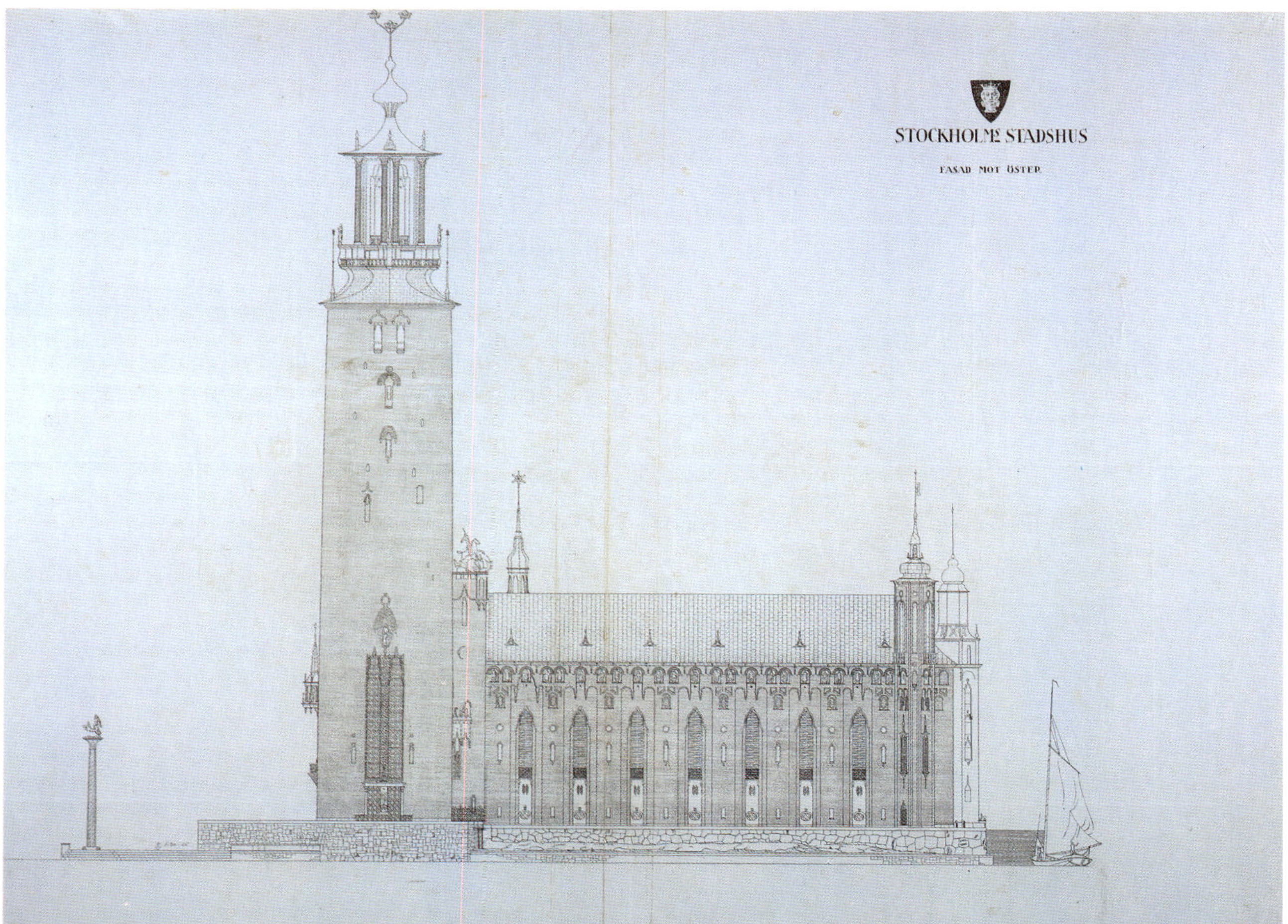

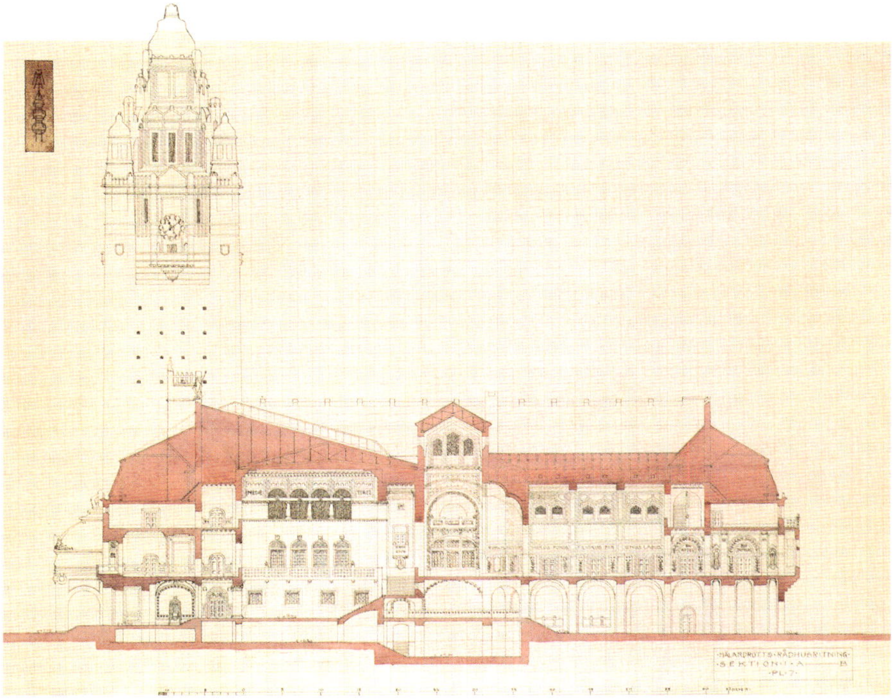

Ragnar Östberg second round competition design, 'Mälardrott', 1905, east-west section, first prize

Ragnar Östberg second round competition design, "Mälardrott", 1905, east-west section, first prize

Ivar Tengbom & Ernst Torulf first round competition design "Lilla putte", 1904, exterior view from south-east, nominated

Ivar Tengbom & Ernst Torulf first round competition design "Lilla putte", 1904, above: north-south section, below: east-west section, nominated

Carl Bergsten second round competition design "Lag och räte", 1905, exterior view from south-east (front), third prize

Carl Bergsten first round competition design "Lag och räte", 1904, exterior view from south-east (front)

Charles Lindholm second round competition design "Justitia", 1905, east elevation (front), third prize

Charles Lindholm second round competition design "Justitia", 1905, exterior view from south-east, third prize

Charles Lindholm first round competition design "Justitia", 1904 east-west section, nominated

Charles Lindholm first round competition design "Justitia", 1904, east elevation (front), nominated

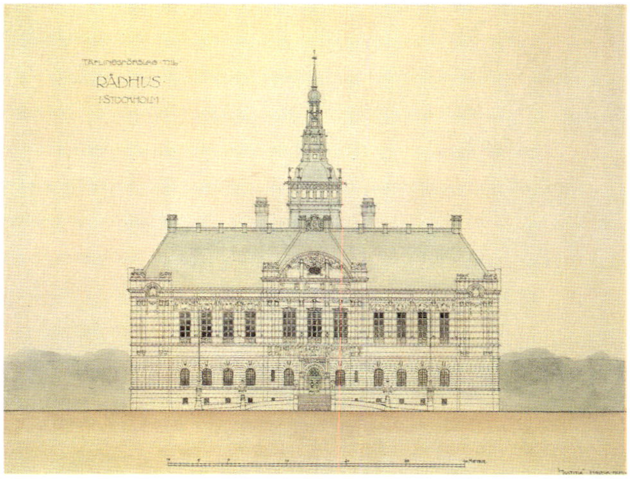

Unknown architect first round competition design "Non senza dignità", 1904, exterior view from south-east, nominated

Unknown architect first round competition design 'Leo', 1904, east elevation (front), nominated

Carl Westman revised design, 1906, north elevation (front)

Carl Westman the first round competition design "Hörn", 1904, north elevation (front), nominated

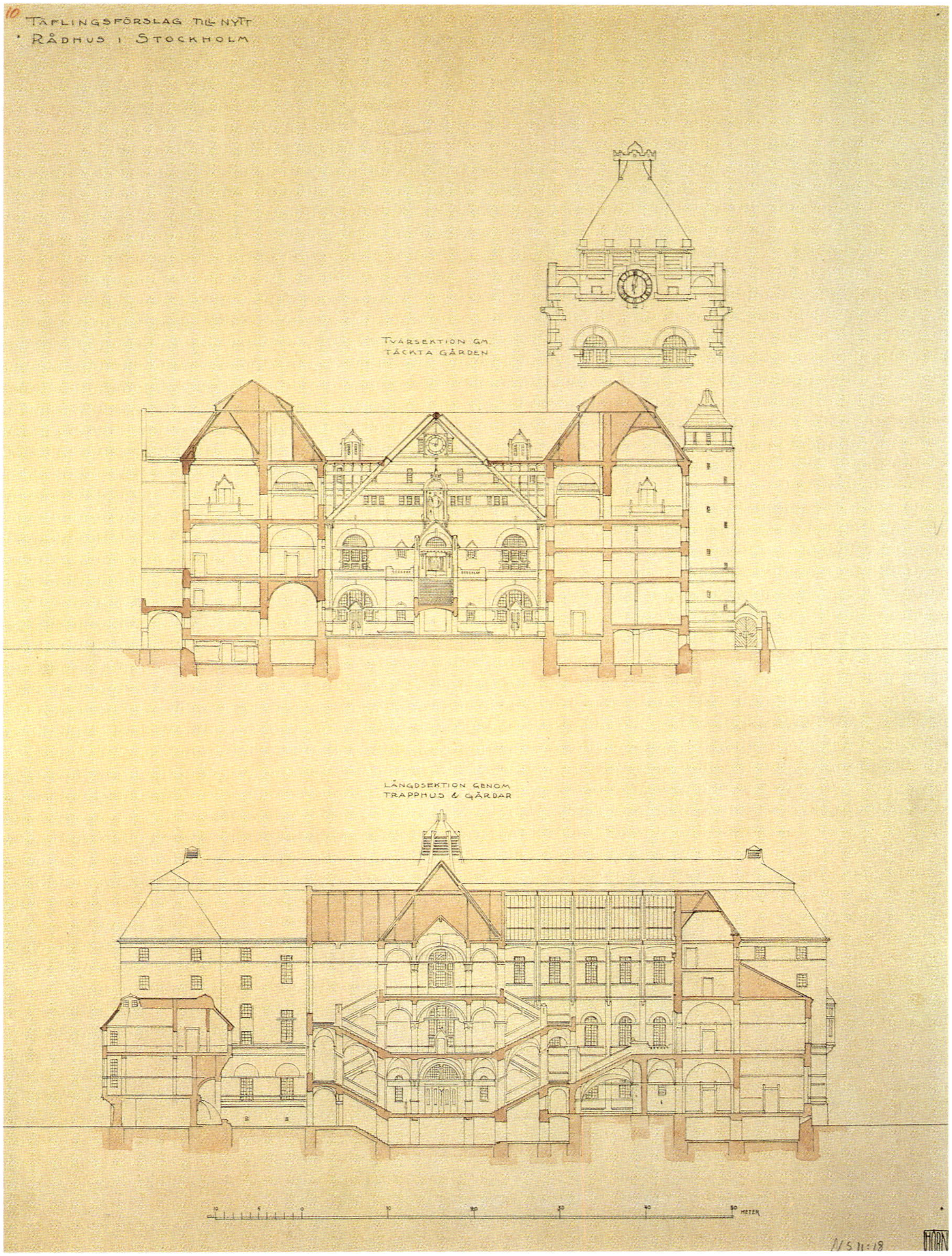

Carl Westman first round competition design "Hörn", 1904, above: north-south section, below: east-west section, nominated

Helsinki Station, 1903

Project

Railway station

Site

Helsinki

Dates

15 December 1903 to 27 May 1904

Number of entries

21

Jury

Sebastian Gripenberg (Director of the National Building Council, architect), Hugo Lindberg, Gustav Nyström (both architects), August Granfelt, Colonel Dratschevski (both representatives for the Finnish Railways)

Result

First prize Eliel Saarinen *Second prize* Onni Törnqvist *Third prize* Hjalmar Åberg, Usko Nyström & Alarik Tavastsjerna *Fourth prize* Paavo Uotila *Fifth prize* Karl Håkan, Einar Lindahl & Valter Thomé

Commissioned by

The Finnish state and railways

Construction

1904 to 1914

Architect

Eliel Saarinen (1873–1950)

Helsinki Station, 1903

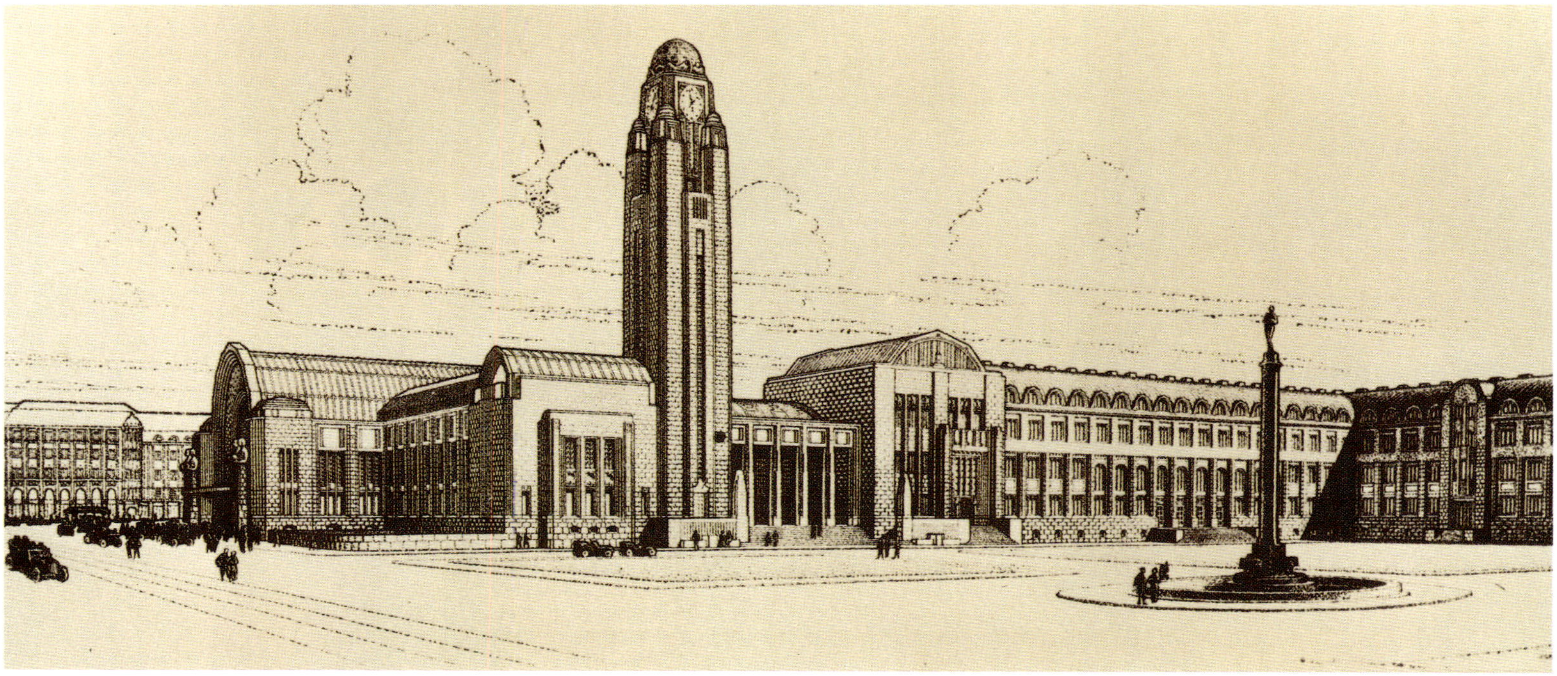

Eliel Saarinen altered design, 1909, exterior view from south-east

Helsinki Station

National Romanticism was the dominant architectural style in Finland around 1900. In order to understand the 'nationalist' aspect of this style, it is necessary to describe the political situation in Finland at the time, which influenced its specific architectural features. At the turn of the century, Finland was little more than a Russian vassal state. For centuries, the country had been a Swedish province, until war broke out between Sweden and Russia in 1809 and Finland was annexed by Russia. Finland became a grand duchy, under Tsarist rule. The Tsar's national representative, the governor-general, ruled the country from Helsinki, which had been the capital since 1812.

Finland between two superpowers

The Finns struggled to retain their culture throughout the nineteenth and early twentieth century. It was not until 1863 that Finnish was accepted as an official administrative and judicial language, next to Swedish. During that same year, the Finnish Landdag (parliament of the people) assembled for the first time since 1809. The Landdag subsequently assembled once every five years. During this period, Finnish culture flourished once again. The period between 1830 and 1860 is referred to as the "Romanticism of Helsinki". During this time J.V. Snellman composed the national anthem and E. Löhnrot compiled the Kalevala epos, a collection of ancient, popular Finnish mythological tales.

Towards the end of the nineteenth century, this cultural revival was brutally interrupted by the Russian Tsars Alexander III (1881–1894) and Nicholas II (1894–1917), who suppressed all forms of nationalism with a heavy hand. In 1899, Nicholas II decided to place the Finnish army under Russian command. When the Landdag refused to give its consent, the Tsar decreed that the body would henceforth only have consultative power. During that same year, Jean Sibelius (1865–1957) composed "Finlandia". The Landdag's resistance was short-lived and in 1901 Finnish soldiers were drafted into the Russian army. The overzealous governor-general at the time, who also imposed Russian as the official language, exacerbated the situation and his assassination by Finnish nationalists heralded a brief period of détente. The Russians maintained a tighter rein until 1917, when the Finns declared themselves independent. However, the threat of occupation by their powerful neighbours remained imminent for many years thereafter.

National Romanticism in Finland

These circumstances formed the backdrop for Finnish architecture around 1900. Architecture was undergoing radical change throughout Europe and architects were shaking off the bonds of academic rules and regulations. Particularly relevant examples are the Art Nouveau, championed by Henry van de Velde, the Vienna Secession (Joseph Maria Olbrich) and the English Arts & Crafts movement. At its inception, the latter movement certainly had a significant influence upon Eliel Saarinen. This is evident in the housing and studio complex at Hvitträsk (1901–1902), which Saarinen designed together with Armas

Eliel Saarinen

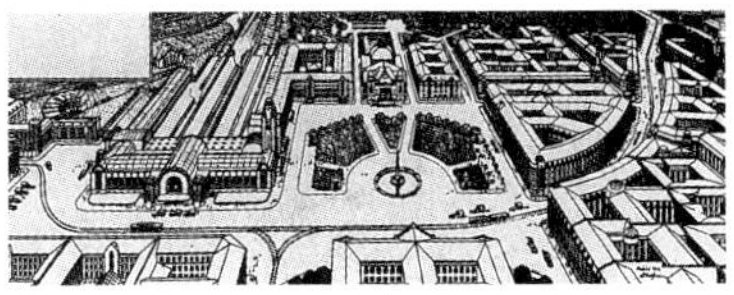

Helsinki Station and Kaisaniemi street, bird's eye view

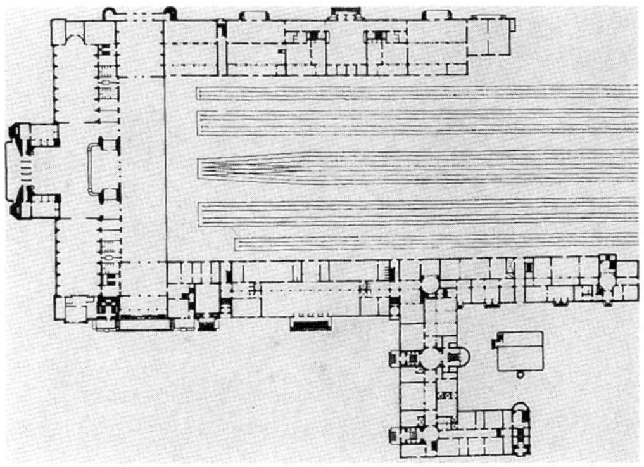

Eliel Saarinen Helsinki Station, ground floor plan

Lindgren and Herman Gesellius. The Arts & Crafts movement, with its emphasis upon handicrafts, medieval Picturesque and "honest" materials, received a warm welcome in Finland.
Finnish historical architecture formed another important source of inspiration. Wood, rusticated stone and saddle roofs are characteristic features of this style. By emphasising their national tradition, the Finns fortified their cultural identity and could withstand Russian domination. The Neo-Classicist style (Graeco-Roman) which had prevailed in the past, was doomed to disappear. Moreover, it was regarded with suspicion because the Russian government buildings had been constructed in this style. It goes without saying that this tendency to delve into "national" (often local) architectural heritage was not limited to Finland alone. However, Finnish National Romanticism did have an added dimension and a special significance.
A fine example of new Finnish architecture is the National Museum in Helsinki, designed by Saarinen, Lindgren and Gesellius. These architects had worked together since 1897 and had gained renown with their design for the Finnish pavilion at the World Exposition in Paris (1899–1900). It is interesting to note that the pavilion was reserved

Helsinki Station, detail of front façade on south

Helsinki Station, main entrance hall from south

solely for the exhibition of works of art. Industrial objects were exhibited in the Russian pavilion.
The competition for the National Museum was held two years before the Helsinki station competition. The jury for the museum competition included the architects Isak Gustav Clason and Martin Nyrop, who had both been members of the competition jury for the Stockholm Town Hall. These architects both had a preference for National Romanticism. It was therefore not surprising that Saarinen, Lindgren and Gesellius were awarded first prize. Their design featured a rusticated stone tower and substructure, with saddle roofs and (semi-circular) arched openings. This National Romanticist prototype left its mark on the competition for the station. The designs submitted by Onni Törnqvist, the team of Håkan, Lindahl & Thomé and Saarinen himself (first design) were all clearly derived from this prototype.

The competition

Due to the intensification of railway traffic between Helsinki and Russia, a new, larger railway terminus became a necessity. The Finnish Society of Architects (Arkitektklubben) and the Finnish Railways were both involved in the project. The Arkitektklubben suggested a complete revamping of the station square, where the station and the National Theatre would become the cynosures. The theatre, completed in 1901, was another example of Finnish National Romanticist architecture. It had been designed by Onni Törnqvist[1], who had clearly been inspired by the works of the American architect H.H. Richardson. The Arkitektklubben tried to influence the choice of architectural style and town planning design by organising a conceptual competition for the layout of the station square (1902).
However, it soon became apparent that they would be unable to influence the town planning design because the Finnish Railways had been working on a new station for some time. This terminus was to have a U-shaped floor plan which "embraced" the tracks (design by C.O. Gleim, 1903). There were no plans for the station square. Bruno Granholm had originally submitted a Neo-Classicist design for the station but a storm of protest cleared the way for the National romanticists. The railways organised a competition for a combined station and administration building, with an imperial waiting room for the Tsar. However, they also stipulated that the architects had to incorporate Gleim's design and Granholm's floor plan.

The designs

The twenty-one entries were submitted anonymously, under a motto. Two designs were disqualified immediately because they did not meet the stipulated conditions. The jury blundered in their adjudication of Usko Nyström and Alarik Tavastjerna's design. They initially concluded that this team had not submitted cross-section drawings, but later discovered that they had been overlooked. In an effort to make amends for their mistake, the jury awarded third prize to this team. Other designs were swiftly eliminated: those of Jung & Bomansen and Gyldén

& Ullberg, and that of Jarl Eklund. Not one of the prize-winning designs reflected European architectural innovation. Sigurd Frosterus had submitted a Jugendstil design and later lodged a complaint against what he termed the conservative bias of the jury. He was to be proved right in time. Saarinen's final design no longer bore any traces of National Romanticism. Saarinen's first design and the other designs described above all featured a tower and had largely been based on the National Museum. Other architects seemed to have based their designs on the works of Richardson. Architects in the latter category included Nyström, whose design also featured a tower, and Paavo Uotila and Hjalmar Åberg, whose towers were less impressive. Without exception, rusticated stone had been used for the façade and the masonry had an irregular pattern, typical of the National Romanticist style. Saarinen discarded this feature in his final design.

The jury unanimously awarded first prize to Saarinen's design. Unfortunately, this led to an awkward situation because Saarinen had also submitted a design together with Lindgren and Gesellius. The jury had recognised the same hand in both designs and had decided to award the prize to the better design. The other design was to be awarded fourth prize, if it later proved to be from a completely different architect. Understandably, the result caused friction within the team, which was disbanded soon thereafter.

Having won the competition, Saarinen made a Grand Tour of Europe in order to gain an insight into station architecture and other architectural developments abroad. One can almost reconstruct his tour on the basis of his final design. Among Saarinen's ports-of-call were Berlin (Behrens) and Darmstadt (Olbrich). It is clear that Saarinen was particularly impressed by Olbrich's Ernst-Ludwig-Haus. Saarinen incorporated a similar horseshoe-shaped entrance, blowing it up to monumental proportions. His station design also featured versions of Olbrich's colossal, flanking sculptures. Four identical statues, sculpted by Emil Wikström, stand solemnly on either side of the main entrance. The conical tower from his earlier design also underwent a metamorphosis. The conical shapes became angular and the tower is reminiscent of the Palais Stoclet by Josef Hoffmann. The saddle roofs were replaced with a reinforced concrete roofing structure, a novelty in Finland. The general character of the station also changed radically. The original design clearly had a rural Finnish character, while the ultimate design was clearly inspired by European Jugendstil.

Departure from Finland

Saarinen's design for the station clearly heralded his departure from National Romanticism towards a more international and modern style. He subsequently emigrated to the United States (1923) and settled there permanently, which seems to have been a logical step to take. Saarinen had become acquainted with American architecture during the competition for the Chicago Tribune Tower in 1922[2]. Saarinen and his famous son Eero, working alone or as a team, went on to play important roles in the field of architecture in the United States.

Helsinki Station, restaurant (now a café)

Museum of Finnish Architecture ed, "Saarinen in Finland", (catalogue of the exhibition), Helsinki, 1984

1 *Törnqvist later changed his name to the Finnish Tarjanne.*

2 *Saarinen had previously participated in the competitions for Canberra, in 1911, and the Peace Palace in The Hague, in 1905 (see chapters on these competitions).*

Hauptbahnhof, Helsinki

Um die Jahrhundertwende beherrschte die Nationalromantik das künstlerisch-kulturelle Leben Finnlands, das kaum mehr als ein Vasallenstaat Rußlands war. Nachdem es jahrhundertelang zu Schweden gehört hatte, war das Land 1809 nach einem Krieg zwischen Schweden und Rußland vom Russischen Reich annektiert worden, dessen Zar es als Großfürstentum unterstand. Die Interessen des Zaren vertrat der Generalgouverneur, der das Land von Helsinki (seit 1812 Hauptstadt) aus regierte.

Finnland zwischen zwei Großmächten

Während des gesamten 19. Jahrhunderts bis weit ins 20. Jahrhundert hinein mußten die Finnen um die Eigenständigkeit ihrer Kultur kämpfen. Erst 1863 wurde Finnisch neben Schwedisch als zweite Amtssprache in der Verwaltung und im Rechtswesen zugelassen; im gleichen Jahr trat erstmals seit 1809 der Finnische Landtag (Volksvertretung) zusammen und tagte von da an alle fünf Jahre. Die finnische Kultur blühte wieder auf. In der Zeit zwischen 1830 und 1860 – die als »Romantik von Helsinki« bekannt ist – komponierte J.V. Snellman die Nationalhymne, und E. Löhnrot veröffentlichte das von ihm zusammengetragene Nationalepos »Kalevala«, eine Sammlung altmythischer Volkserzählungen.
Dieser kulturelle Aufschwung wurde von den russischen Zaren Alexander III. (1881–1894) und Nikolai II. (1894–1917), die seit den neunziger Jahren des 19. Jahrhunderts jede nationale Regung rigoros unterbunden hatten, unterbrochen. Als Nikolai II. 1899 Finnlands Heer der russischen Armee unterstellen wollte und dazu vom finnischen Landtag keine Zustimmung erhielt, beschloß er, daß diese Volksvertretung nur mehr beratende Funktion haben solle.

Die Nationalromantik in Finnland

Die finnische Baukunst der Jahrhundertwende muß vor dem Hintergrund dieser politischen Ereignisse gesehen werden. In ganz Europa war die Architektur großen Veränderungen unterworfen, und zahlreiche Architekten versuchten, sich von den traditionellen akademischen Regeln und Vorschriften zu befreien. Zu den wichtigsten Beispielen dieser Entwicklung zählen der Jugendstil (mit Henry van de Velde als bedeutendstem Vertreter), die Wiener Sezession (Joseph Maria Olbrich) sowie die englische Arts-and-Crafts-Bewegung, die Eliel Saarinen stark beeinflußte. Dies zeigt sich an dem von ihm gemeinsam mit Armas Lindgren und Herman Gesellius entworfenen Wohn- und Atelierhaus Hvitträsk in Kirkkonummi (1901–1902). In Finnland empfing man die Arts-and-Crafts-Bewegung, mit ihrem starken Interesse für das Handwerk, den mittelalterlichen »Picturesque Style« und die »ehrlichen« Materialien, mit offenen Armen.
Neben den avantgardistischen Strömungen des Auslands bildete die finnische Architektur vergangener Jahrhunderte eine wichtige Inspirationsquelle, als deren wesentliche Charakteristika Holz, grober Stein und Satteldächer gelten. Durch eine Betonung dieser nationalen Tradition hofften die Finnen ihre kulturelle Identität zu stärken und der russischen Übermacht zu widerstehen. Der in den Jahren zuvor dominierende Klassizismus (griechisch-römisch) war zum einen im Niedergang begriffen, zum anderen nie beliebt, da die Regierungsbauten der Russen diesem Stil entsprachen.
Ein gutes Beispiel für die neue finnische Architektur ist das Nationalmuseum in Helsinki, das von Saarinen, Lindgren und Gesellius entworfen wurde. Charakteristisch für den Vorschlag sind der Unterbau und der Turm aus unbehauenen Steinen sowie die Satteldächer und die Rundbogenöffnungen. Dieser nationalromantische Prototyp beeinflußte ebenfalls die Konstruktionspläne für den Hauptbahnhof; auch die Entwürfe von Onni Törnqvist, Karl Håkan, Einar Lindahl und Valter Thomé sowie Saarinens eigene (erste) Pläne zeigten sich deutlich von diesem Vorbild inspiriert.

Die Ausschreibung

Aufgrund des stetig anwachsenden Zugverkehrs zwischen Helsinki und Rußland benötigte die Stadt einen neuen, großen Kopfbahnhof, mit dessen Gestaltung sich sowohl die finnische Architektenvereinigung (Arkitektklubben) als auch die finnische Eisenbahngesellschaft beschäftigte. Dem Arkitektklubben schwebte eine völlige Neugestaltung des Bahnhofsplatzes vor, mit dem Bahnhof und dem Nationaltheater als auffälligem Blickfang. Dieses bereits 1901 errichtete Theater gilt ebenfalls als charakteristisches Beispiel für die finnische nationalromantische Architektur. Der Entwurf stammte von Onni Törnqvist. Mit Hilfe eines Ideenwettbewerbs (1902) für die (Neu-)Gestaltung des Bahnhofsplatzes hoffte der Arkitektklubben dessen Baustil und städtebauliche Struktur steuern zu können.
Auf die Gestaltung konnten die Architekten jedoch keinen Einfluß nehmen, da sich die finnische Eisenbahngesellschaft bereits seit längerem mit den Plänen für einen neuen Bahnhof beschäftigte. Der geplante Bahnhof sollte einen U-förmigen Grundriß aufweisen und auf diese Weise die Gleise – im wahrsten Sinne des Wortes – umarmen (Entwurf von C.O. Gleim, 1903). Dabei sollte der bereits vorhandene Platz nicht verändert werden. Ursprünglich hatten die Bauherren an einen klassizistischen Entwurf von Bruno Granholm gedacht, aber aufgrund wütender Proteste wurde der Weg für die Nationalromantiker frei. Derart unter Druck gesetzt, entschloß sich die Eisenbahngesellschaft zu einer Ausschreibung, die mit einigen Auflagen verbunden war: Gleims Pläne und Granholms Grundriß mußten von den Architekten bei der Gestaltung des Bahnhofs nebst Verwaltungsgebäuden und kaiserlichem Wartesaal (für den Zaren) berücksichtigt werden.

Die Entwürfe

Insgesamt 21 Wettbewerbsbeiträge wurden anonym unter einem Motto eingesandt, wovon zwei sofort aus dem Rennen fielen, weil sie die Auflagen nicht erfüllten. Bei dem gemeinsamen Entwurf von Usko Nyström und Alarik Tavastjerna unterlief der Jury ein grober Fehler: Angeblich waren keine Längsschnittzeichnungen angefertigt worden, doch die Jurymitglieder hatten sie schlichtweg übersehen. Schuldbewußt prämierte die Jury diesen Entwurf mit dem dritten Preis. Keine Auszeichnung erhielten die Konstruktionspläne von Bertel Jung und Oscar Bomansen, C. Axel Gyldén und Uno Ullberg sowie der Beitrag von Jarl Eklund. Unter den prämierten Entwürfen befand sich kein einziger Vorschlag, der die europäischen Entwicklungen in der Architektur widerspiegelte. Sigurd Frosterus, der einen Jugendstilentwurf eingereicht hatte, protestierte nach der Preisverleihung gegen die – seiner Meinung nach – konservative Einstellung der Jury. Die Zeit sollte ihm recht geben. Saarinens endgültige Konstruktionspläne hatten nichts mehr gemein mit der Nationalromantik, die seinen ersten Entwurf noch beherrscht hatte. Sie alle erinnerten in groben Zügen an das Nationalmuseum und zeichneten sich durch einen Turm aus. Auch Nyströms Pläne sahen zwar einen solchen Turm vor, waren aber – genau wie die Zeichnungen von Paavo Uotila und Hjalmar Åberg, deren Türme sehr viel kleiner ausfielen – eher von dem amerikanischen Architekten H.H. Richardson beeinflußt. Alle Beiträge hielten sich an die vorgeschriebene Fassadengestaltung aus Naturstein. Diese Auflage beachtete Saarinen in seinem zweiten Entwurf nicht mehr.
Saarinens Entwurf wurde von der Jury einstimmig zum Sieger erklärt. Dies führte zu einer peinlichen Situation, da Saarinen, Lindgren und Gesellius auch einen gemeinsamen Entwurf eingereicht hatten. Die Jury erkannte dennoch Saarinens Handschrift in den Zeichnungen und beschloß, nur dessen eigenen Entwurf zu prämieren; der gemeinsame Beitrag schien ihr nicht so gelungen zu sein. Aus naheliegenden Gründen sorgte das Ergebnis für ein gespanntes Verhältnis unter den drei Architekten, die ihr gemeinsames Büro aufgaben.
Nach der Verleihung des ersten Preises begab sich Saarinen auf Studienreise durch Europa, um sich über die ausländische Eisenbahnarchitektur und andere Entwicklungen in der Baukunst zu informieren. Seine Reiseroute läßt sich nahezu vollständig anhand seines endgültigen Entwurfs rekonstruieren: Saarinen besuchte u. a. Peter Behrens in Berlin und Olbrich in Darmstadt, dessen Ernst-Ludwig-Haus nachhaltigen Eindruck auf ihn gemacht hatte. Bei Saarinens Entwurf für den Hauptbahnhof fand sich ebenfalls ein hufeisenförmiger Eingangsbereich, der allerdings monumentale Ausmaße annahm. Auch Olbrichs kolossale, flankierende Skulpturen feierten in Saarinens Plänen eine Wiederkehr: Vier ehrfurchtgebietende, identische Figuren, angefertigt von Emil Wikström, stehen zu beiden Seiten des Haupteingangs. Der spitze Turm des ersten Entwurfs erfuhr ebenfalls eine Veränderung – die konischen Formen wurden zu rechteckigen; entfernt erinnert der Turm an das von Josef Hoffmann konzipierte Palais Stoclet. Sogar die Satteldächer mußten einer Dachkonstruktion aus Stahlbeton weichen – eine absolute Novität im damaligen Finnland. Der gesamte Charakter des Bahnhofs war einer radikalen Veränderung unterzogen worden. Während der erste Entwurf noch einen ländlichen, finnischen Charakter aufwies, besitzt die endgültige Version eindeutige Reminiszenzen an den europäischen Jugendstil.

Abschied von Finnland

Saarinen hatte sich mit seinem Bahnhofsentwurf unmißverständlich von der Nationalromantik distanziert und sich für einen internationalen, modernen Stil entschieden. Seine Emigration in die Vereinigten Staaten (1923) war folglich ein logischer Schritt, da er sich mit der amerikanischen Architektur bereits 1922 während der Ausschreibung für den Chicago Tribune Tower[1] hatte vertraut machen können. In den folgenden Jahren übernahmen Saarinen und sein Sohn Eero eine führende Rolle in der Architekturwelt der USA.

1 *1905 beteiligte sich Saarinen an der Ausschreibung für den Friedenspalast in Den Haag und 1911 am Architekturwettbewerb für Canberra – siehe die jeweiligen Kapitel*

La Gare d'Helsinki

Vers 1900, l'architecture finlandaise était dominée par le style 'romantique national'. Les aspects proprement nationalistes de ce mouvement s'expliquent en grande partie par la situation politique qui prévalait à l'époque. A la fin du XIXème siècle, la Finlande n'était guère plus qu'un état vassal de la Russie. Pendant des siècles, le pays avait été une province suédoise jusqu'à ce qu'une guerre éclate entre la Suède et la Russie en 1809 et que la Finlande soit annexée par les tsars qui en firent un grand-duché. Le représentant du tsar était gouverneur général et choisit Helsinki pour capitale en 1812.

La Finlande entre deux grandes puissances

Les Finlandais se battirent tout au long du siècle dernier pour préserver leur culture. Ce n'est qu'en 1863 que le finnois fut accepté comme langue administrative et judiciaire officielle, à côté du suédois. La même année, le Landdag (parlement) se réunit pour la première fois depuis 1809. La culture finnoise refleurit et la période de 1830 à 1860 est appelée «romantisme d'Helsinki». C'est à ce moment que J.V. Snellman composa l'hymne national et qu'E. Löhnrot compila l'épopée de Kalevala, un ensemble de légendes mythologiques finnoises.

Vers la fin du XIXème siècle, cette renaissance culturelle fut interrompue par les tsars Alexandre III (1881–1894) et Nicolas II (1894–1917) qui s'opposèrent avec brutalité à toute forme de nationalisme. En 1899, Nicolas II décida de placer l'armée finlandaise sous commandement russe. Le Landdag ayant refusé d'y consentir, le tsar décida qu'il n'aurait plus qu'un pouvoir consultatif. La même année, Jean Sibelius (1865–1957) composa «Finlandia». La résistance du parlement ne dura guère et en 1901, les soldats finlandais furent incorporés dans l'armée russe. Le trop zélé gouverneur général, en partie responsable des événements et qui avait de plus décrété le russe langue officielle fut assassiné par des nationalistes ce qui ouvrit une brève période de détente. Les Russes continuèrent à faire peser leur mainmise jusqu'en 1917, date à laquelle les Finlandais, profitant de la révolution bolchevique, proclamèrent leur indépendance. La menace d'occupation par leur puissant voisin resta cependant très présente jusqu'à une date récente.

Romantisme national en Finlande

Ces circonstances politiques éclairent le contexte de l'architecture finlandaise autour de 1900. Au même moment, l'architecture connaissait des changements radicaux dans toute l'Europe et partout les traditions et les règles académiques étaient remises en question, comme ce fut particulièrement le cas par l'Art nouveau – sous la houlette de Henry van de Velde – la Wiener Sezession et le mouvement des Arts and Crafts en Grande-Bretagne. A ses débuts, cette dernière tendance exerça une influence certaine sur Eliel Saarinen comme en témoigne son immeuble d'appartements et d'ateliers de Hvitträsk (1901–1902) conçu avec Armas Lindgren et Herman Gesellius. Le style Arts and Crafts qui mettait l'accent sur la valeur de l'artisanat et s'appuyait sur une inspiration médiévale et «l'honnêteté» des matériaux fut très bien accueilli en Finlande.

L'histoire architecturale du pays fournit également une importante source d'inspiration. Le bois, la pierre taillée et les toits en forme de carène devinrent caractéristiques de ce style. En célébrant leurs traditions nationales, les Finlandais renforçaient leur identité culturelle et pouvaient ainsi mieux résister à la domination russe.

Le style néo-classique qui avait prévalu par le passé était destiné à disparaître, d'autant plus qu'il était celui des bâtiments officiels russes. Cette tendance à redécouvrir et réhabiliter l'héritage architectural national (souvent même local) n'était pas limitée à la seule Finlande, même si, dans son cas, le romantisme national finnois revêtait une signification toute particulière.

Un excellent exemple de cette nouvelle architecture finlandaise est offert par le Musée National d'Helsinki, de Saarinen, Lindgren et Gesellius. Ces trois architectes travaillaient ensemble depuis 1897 et s'étaient fait connaître grâce au pavillon finlandais de l'Exposition Universelle de Paris (1899–1900), réservé aux seules œuvres d'art, les produits industriels étant présentés dans le pavillon russe.

Le concours pour le Musée National s'était tenu deux ans avant celui de la gare d'Helsinki. Son jury comptait les architectes Isak Gustav Clason et Martin Nyrop, tous deux membres du jury pour le concours de l'hôtel de ville de Stockholm et adeptes du romantisme national. Il n'était donc pas surprenant que Saarinen, Lindgren et Gesellius aient remporté le premier prix. Leur projet comportait un soubassement et une tour en pierre rustiquée, des toits en carène et des ouvertures en arcade. Ce prototype du romantisme national influença la gare, et les plans d'Onni Törnqvist, de l'équipe de Håkan, Lindahl et Thomé, ainsi que de Saarinen lui-même (premier projet) en dérivaient clairement.

Le concours

Avec le développement du trafic entre Helsinki et la Russie, la construction d'une plus grande gare était devenue impérative. L'Association finlandaise des architectes (Arkitektklubben) et les chemins de fer finlandais étaient parties prenantes au projet. L'Arkitektklubben suggéra de revoir complètement le dessin de la place de la gare en fonction des deux monuments importants qui allaient la border: la future gare et le Théâtre National. Celui-ci, terminé en 1901, était également édifié dans le style du romantisme national finlandais. Il avait été dessiné par Onni Törnqvist[1]. L'Association des Architectes tenta d'influencer le choix du style architectural et de l'urbanisme en organisant un concours d'idées pour la place de la gare (1902).

Ces efforts furent vains car les chemins de fer travaillaient à la nouvelle gare depuis un certain temps. Ils souhaitaient un terminus en forme de U, enserrant les voies (Plans de C.O. Gleim, 1903). et ne prévoyaient rien pour la place. Les chemins de fer organisèrent enfin un concours pour une gare comportant un salon d'attente pour le tsar et un bâtiment administratif. Il était précisé que les projets devaient tenir compte des plans de Gleim et du plan de masse de Granholm.

Les projets

Les vingt et une participations furent soumises anonymement. Deux furent immédiatement refusées car elles ne respectaient pas les stipulations du programme. Le jury fit l'erreur d'écarter trop vite les plans d'Usko Nyström et Alarik Tavastjerna sous prétexte qu'ils n'avaient pas fourni de plans de coupe, puis s'apercevant qu'il s'était trompé, accorda le troisième prix à cette équipe. D'autres propositions furent promptement éliminées: celles de Jung et Bomansen et Gylden et Ullberg ainsi que de Jarl Eklund. Aucun des projets lauréats ne reflétait les nouvelles tendances de l'architecture européenne. Sigurd Frosterus qui avait proposé un projet Art nouveau porta plainte contre le jury et ses «préjugés conservateurs» que la suite devait confirmer. Le projet final de Saarinen n'utilisait plus aucun élément de style romantique national. Ses premiers plans comportaient tous une tour et s'inspiraient largement du Musée National. D'autres étaient influencés par l'architecte américain H.H. Richardson, comme, par exemple ceux de Nyström, Paavo Uotila et Hjalmar Åberg dont les tours étaient moins impressionnantes. Sans exception, la pierre rustiquée se retrouvait sur toutes les façades, et la maçonnerie présentait un appareillage irrégulier, caractéristique du style finlandais. Saarinen écarta cependant cette solution dans ses ultimes propositions. Le jury décerna à l'unanimité le premier prix à Saarinen, ce qui provoqua une situation délicate car celui-ci avait proposé un autre projet co-signé par Lindgren et Gesellius. Le jury avait reconnu la même main dans les deux projets et accordé le prix à celui qu'elle jugeait le meilleur, l'autre recevant le quatrième prix s'il était prouvé qu'il était d'un architecte différent. Ce résultat provoqua des frictions au sein de l'équipe qui se dispersa peu après.

Ayant remporté le concours, Saarinen fit un tour d'Europe pour mieux s'informer des développements de l'architecture contemporaine. On pourrait presque reconstituer son voyage à partir de ses plans définitifs. Berlin (Behrens) et Darmstadt (Olbrich) figurent au nombre de ses étapes et il est évident qu'il fut particulièrement impressionné par la Ernst-Ludwig-Haus de Olbrich. Il incorpora à son plan une entrée similaire en fer-à-cheval mais l'agrandit à des proportions monumentales. Son projet pour la gare comportait également une version des sculptures colossales d'Olbrich. Quatre solennelles statues identiques de Emil Wikström se dressent ainsi de la même façon de chaque côté de l'entrée. La tour conique des premières ébauches se retrouva toute en angles et très proche de celle du Palais Stoclet de Josef Hoffmann. Les toits en carène furent remplacés par une structure en béton armé, une nouveauté pour la Finlande. L'allure générale du projet avait évolué radicalement. Si les premiers plans affichaient indéniablement un caractère finlandais, presque rustique, leur version finale témoignaient de la puissante influence de l'Art nouveau.

Départ de Finlande

Le projet pour la gare d'Helsinki marquait donc la rupture de l'architecte avec le style romantique national et son évolution vers un style plus international et plus moderne. Avec logique, il émigra aux Etats-Unis en 1923 où il s'installa de façon définitive après avoir découvert le monde architectural américain lors de la compétition du Chicago Tribune en 1922[2]. Saarinen et son célèbre fils, Eero, travaillant séparément ou en équipe, allaient jouer un rôle majeur dans le développement de l'architecture américaine.

1 *Törnqvist adopta plus tard un patronyme finnois, Tarjanne.*
2 *Saarinen avait également participé aux concours pour le plan de Canberra (1911) et le Palais de la Paix de La Haye (1905). Voir, dans cet ouvrage, les chapitres concernant ces concours.*

Eliel Saarinen competition design, 1904, exterior view from south-east, first prize

Bertel Jung & Oscar Bomanson competition design "F.S.J.", 1904, south elevation

Jarl Eklund competition design "Skenprofil, 1904, exterior view from south-east

C. Axel Gylden & Uno Ullberg competition design, 1904, exterior view from south-east

Karl Håkan Einar Lindahl & Valter Thomé competition design "La Gare", 1904, exterior view from south-east, fifth prize

Usko Nyström & Alarik Tavastsjerna competition design "Stephenson", 1904, exterior view from south-east, third prize

Hjalmar Aberg competition design "Helsingfors", 1904, exterior view from south-east, third prize

Onni Törnqvist competition design "P", 1904, exterior view from south-east, second prize

Sigurd Fosterus competition design "Eureka", 1904, exterior view from south-east

Paavo Uotila competition design "Tunneliaukko", 1904, exterior view from south-east, fourth prize

Peace Palace, The Hague, 1905

216

Project

Peace Palace, International Court of Justice and Library

Site

Carnegieplein, The Hague

Dates

15 August 1905 to 15 April 1906

Result announced

May 1906

Number of entries

216

Jury

H.A. van Karnebeek (Chairman of the Carnegie Foundation), Thomas Edward Colcutt (London, R.I.B.A Chairman), Henri Paul Nénot (Paris), E. von Ihne (Berlin, Oberhofbaurat), Dr P.J.H Cuypers (Roermond, The Netherlands), Prof. C. König (Vienna), Prof. W.R. Ware (Milton, Mass., U.S.A.)

Result

First prize Louis-Marie Cordonnier (12 000 guilders) *Second prize* A. Marcel (9 000 guilders) *Third prize* Franz Wendt (7 000 guilders) *Fourth prize* Otto Wagner (5 000 guilders) *Fifth prize* Howard Greenly & Herbert S. Olin (3 000 guilders) *Sixth prize* Franz Schwechten (3 000 guilders). Cordonnier, Marcel, Wagner and Schwechten had been invited to participate; 17 other invited architects each received 2 000 guilders.

Commissioned by

The Carnegie Foundation

Construction

1907 to 1913

Architects

Louis-Marie Cordonnier (1854–1940) and Prof. J.A.G. van der Steur *Sculpture* W. Retera *Painting* Prof. H. Rosse *Gardens* H. Mawson (selected by closed competition)

Construction cost

Estimated 1 600 000 Gulden

Peace Palace, The Hague, 1905

Louis-Marie Cordonnier
competition design, 1906, front elevation on Carnegieplein, first prize

Peace Palace, The Hague

Around the turn of the century, there was a growing conviction that the nations of the world were tired of being at war. This desire for peace lay at the heart of the plan to build a Peace Palace[1]. It was believed that armed struggle would be a thing of the past if the nations of the world were to discuss their differences before an international court and if the members – that is to say, all the countries of the world – were to uphold the decisions of the court. The Hague was chosen as the seat of the court. This city was the administrative centre of the Netherlands, a country which pursued a policy of strict neutrality. The project was to be financed by the industrial magnate and philanthropist Andrew Carnegie, of American Scottish descent.

An international competition

Carnegie and the Netherlands Ministry of Foreign Affairs had jointly appointed a preparatory commission to select a site and draw up a programme of conditions (September 1903). The preparatory commission was disbanded in June 1904, following the appointment of a board of directors for the newly founded Carnegie Foundation.
In subsequent years, the board of directors took charge of affairs concerning the Peace Palace. They appointed the architect D. Knuttel as advisor. His advice was soon required because almost immediately after the board had been appointed a problem arose concerning the form the competition was to take.
An open competition posed the risk that renowned architects might not participate for fear of losing face. A closed competition therefore seemed a better option. The national federation of architects insisted that participation had to be limited to Dutch architects, thereby ignoring the fact that an international court of law, built with American dollars, was in the offing. The board therefore initially decided to organise a closed international competition. However, the storm of criticism which met this decision was so overwhelming that a compromise was reached: an open international competition, with the emphatic proviso that the board was free to invite certain architects and to reimburse them for their efforts. The twenty-one architects who were eventually invited to participate each received 2 000 guilders.
Even though the above facts were clearly stated when the competition was announced, more than two hundred architects from all over the world submitted designs.
The board appointed a jury of six architects from six different countries (five from superpowers and one from the host nation), all of whom stemmed from architectural traditions firmly rooted in the nineteenth century. The participants were asked to submit the usual series of designs: floor plans, cross-sections and elevations. A remarkable aspect of the competition was that the architects were also asked to submit picturesque, coloured impressions of the building and its surroundings. More often than not, architects were asked to refrain from submitting drawings of this sort, in an effort to stop the best artist, rather than the best architect, from getting an edge on his opponents. However, in this case, a jury of experienced architects had been appointed, who were undoubtedly acquainted with the tricks of the trade.

Andrew Carnegie

Members of the Jury

One of the main problems confronting the architects was the design of a separate library for the Peace Palace. Unfortunately, the competition programme had not specified how separate this library should be. It had merely stipulated a route of connection between the two buildings. The solutions to this problem may be roughly divided into three categories: two separate buildings linked by a corridor, a single building with one or more completely enclosed courtyards to provide the necessary light, and a single building with various wings where light entered the building via an open courtyard. The jury selected plans from each of these categories and presented them to the board of directors. The rest of the competition programme was not very detailed, which accounts for the diversity of designs. Architects were asked to consult Knuttel if they had any questions.

The result

The jury awarded six prizes but refrained from advising the Carnegie Foundation to execute one of these designs. Although the jury had undoubtedly debated the designs at length, this was not evident in their report, which gave brief and superficial comment on the prize-winning designs, four of which had been submitted by invited

architects. It was therefore not surprising that the jury's decision seemed arbitrary. It gave rise to a seemingly endless stream of protests, quarrels and problems concerning the Peace Palace.
Cordonnier was awarded first prize. The jury praised the fact that he had been inspired by sixteenth century Dutch architecture. This was a slap in the face to most of the other participants, for more reasons than one. Firstly, no style had been specified in the competition programme. Moreover, a national architectural style seemed inappropriate for an international court of law. But worst of all, Cordonnier's rendition of the Dutch Renaissance style was considered a total failure. In the press, experts snidely remarked that his design bore absolutely no resemblance to this style. The jury apparently deemed the other designs even less worthy of comment than Cordonnier's design. Comment on Wagner's plan was limited to two sentences and Schwechten's plan was apparently worth no more than a single sentence! It bears mentioning that only one of the prize-winners had submitted a striking design: Wagner. This fact was clearly evident to the public, who had been given the opportunity to view more than three thousand of the submitted designs at Kneuterdijk Palace in The Hague, made available for the exhibition by Queen Wilhelmina.
Cordonnier's design was eclectic and rather gaudy. However, the general quality of the designs had been disappointing. Most of the other designs matched the eclecticism of Cordonnier's design or were insipid products of the Beaux-Arts tradition. Almost all of the participants had applied one of the Neo-styles, even though a wind of change had been blowing through architecture in Europe and the United States for some time. Several participants had submitted fantastical designs, symbolized a united world. Unfortunately, they threw practical architectural knowledge to the winds. Only a few architects took a novel approach: Wagner – whose remark that a new type of building required a new æsthetic form was echoed by the jury – and the avant-garde architects Eliel Saarinen (Finland), Hendrik Petrus Berlage and Willem Kromhout (both Dutch). Other remarkable but regrettably neglected designs were submitted by Jarl Eklund (Helsingfors), W. Molenbroek (The Hague) and G.C.E. Blohm (Hamburg).

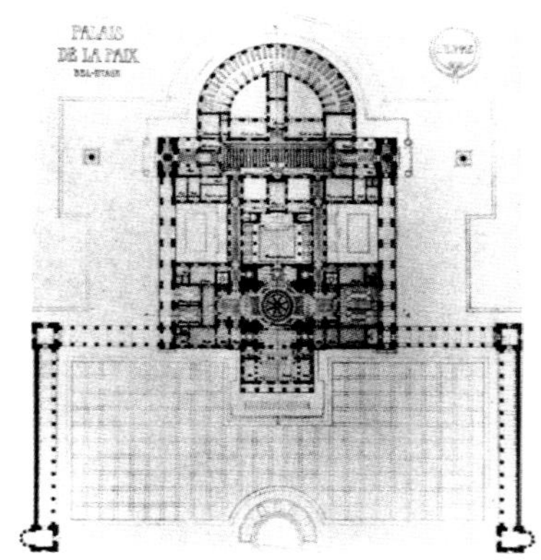

Cordonnier after all

The jury's decision was broadly criticised. The losing architects were understandably disappointed and non-participating architects and even the general public were dissatisfied. The jury advised the board of directors to organise a second round for the six prize-winning designs but the board had had enough. They immediately initiated negotiations with Cordonnier. However, it soon became apparent that the 1.5 million dollars which Carnegie had pledged would not be enough (he had initially been told that a million dollars would be sufficient). It was evident that neither Cordonnier nor the other prize winners had stayed under the 1.6 million guilders budgeted in the competition programme. The board of directors decided to ask Carnegie for more money, arguing that costs had increased because the library had been included in the project. Carnegie initially refused to donate more money. He had, of course, already donated an additional 500 000 dollars and, moreover, he was in favour of a modest building. He had hoped to house a collection of books in the library and had not intended it to become an entire wing, which, unbeknown to him, had been included in the competition programme. This problem took some solving but eventually a compromise was reached and the board of directors were able to proceed with Cordonnier's designs for the Peace Palace and the library.

However, the board were apparently unable to judge the quality of a design from a drawing. They therefore decided to view one of Cordonnier's other works, the town hall in Dunkirk. They were so disappointed by what they saw that they immediately decided to seek alternative options. Greenly & Olin's design, which had won fifth prize, was taken from the shelf, as was Saarinen's design (the jury ignored the fact that this had not been a winning design). But once again the board was unable to reach an agreement and they decided to approach their old friend Cordonnier again.

Cordonnier's problems

Even though the construction budget had been raised to 1.8 million guilders, Cordonnier's extravagant original design required radical alteration. He had probably taken this into account earlier, which explains the fact that his original design was a synthesis of elements from previous designs. He had probably done this to save time. This approach was not unusual. The chance of winning a competition was small and many architects could not afford to spend too much time on detailed designs. They often had the opportunity to implement changes after they had been commissioned and paid.

However, Cordonnier's alterations were still not to the board's satisfaction. Subsequently, a commission of experts[2] was appointed to advise the Frenchman but he was still unable to produce a satisfactory design. The board then appointed a Dutch architect, Prof. J.A.G. van der Steur, who was to work with Cordonnier. The design which eventually got the go-ahead differed considerably from the original design. Two of the four towers had been scrapped. Needless to say, this cut costs.

By now it was March 1907. Construction was delayed by a bill of protest filed by Dutch architects. In truth, the grounds upon which they based their protest were a little thin: they complained about the site, the prize money, the superficial jury report and Cordonnier's design. Naturally, the architects were correct in criticising the way the competition had been run, but their criticism had no legal basis. Nevertheless, by first submitting a bill of protest to parliament and subsequently taking the matter to court, and later the court of appeal, the architects managed to stall Cordonnier and Carnegie's pursuit of their noble endeavour until January 1911. More appropriate beginnings for an international court of law are hard to imagine. A year after the first stone was laid the First World War broke out.

Eliel Saarinen **Peace Palace, first round competition design, transverse section**

Eliel Saarinen **Peace Palace, first round competition design, ground floor plan**

Eliel Saarinen **Peace Palace, first round competition design, exterior view**

Eliel Saarinen **Peace Palace, first round competition design, elevation (front)**

1 *The idea for a Peace Palace idea was first suggested at the Peace Summit of 1899. Tsar Nicholas II had been the initiator of this meeting at Huis ten Bosch in The Hague on 18 May. This had not prevented the Tsar from forcing the Finnish population to take up active service in the Russian army during that same year (see chapter on Helsinki Station).*

2 *The commission included the architects Knuttel and C. Muysken.*

Friedenspalast, Den Haag

Um die Jahrhundertwende war man allgemein zu der Überzeugung gelangt, daß die Völker der Welt genügend Kriege gegeneinander geführt hätten, und die Idee eines Friedenspalastes gewann immer mehr Anhänger. Kriegerische Auseinandersetzungen würden bald der Vergangenheit angehören – so die Überlegungen –, wenn Meinungsverschiedenheiten einem internationalen Tribunal vorgelegt werden könnten und sich die Mitglieder – möglichst alle Länder der Welt – an dieses Urteil hielten. Als Sitz dieses Tribunals wählte man Den Haag. Die Stadt war Regierungssitz der Niederlande, die eine strikte Neutralitätspolitik verfolgten. Die Kosten für das Projekt übernahm der amerikanische Großindustrielle und Philanthrop Andrew Carnegie.

Internationale Ausschreibung

Carnegie und der niederländische Außenminister ernannten im September 1903 gemeinsam eine Kommission, die die Vorbereitungen für die Ausschreibung übernehmen sollte, ins besondere die Wahl eines geeigneten Baugeländes und die Erarbeitung der Bauauflagen. Im Juni 1904 übernahm der Verwaltungsrat der neugegründeten Carnegie Stiftung diese Aufgabe jedoch selbst und entband die Kommission von ihren Aufgaben. Als Berater wurde der Architekt D. Knuttel gewonnen. Sein fachlicher Rat war schon bald gefragt, denn für die Verwaltungsratsmitglieder stellte sich die Frage, in welcher Form die Ausschreibung erfolgen sollte.

Der Bund der Niederländischen Architekten bestand darauf, daß nur niederländische Architekten teilnehmen dürften, obwohl es um den Bau eines internationalen Gerichtshofs (mit amerikanischer Finanzierung) ging. Allerdings machte die heftige Kritik an diesem Vorhaben einen Kompromiß erforderlich: ein öffentlicher internationaler Wettbewerb sollte abgehalten werden, allerdings unter der Bedingung, daß der Rat einige Architekten explizit zur Teilnahme einladen und ihre Bemühungen finanziell vergüten durfte. Man einigte sich auf insgesamt 21 eingeladene Architekten (mit einer Entschädigung von jeweils 2 000 Gulden). Obwohl diese Tatsache bei Bekanntgabe der Ausschreibung nicht verschwiegen wurde, reichten etwa 200 Architekten aus aller Welt einen Entwurf ein.

Das größte organisatorische Problem für die teilnehmenden Architekten bildete der Entwurf einer separaten Bibliothek für den Friedenspalast. Die Bauauflagen ließen nicht erkennen, wie unabhängig diese Bibliothek ausfallen durfte; man wünschte nur einen Verbindungsweg zwischen beiden Gebäudeteilen. Die Lösungen für diese Teilaufgabe lassen sich in drei Gruppen unterteilen: zwei separate Gebäude mit einem Verbindungsgang; ein Gebäude mit mehreren geschlossenen Innenhöfen, die die umliegenden Räume mit dem nötigen Licht versorgen; ein Gebäude, dessen Trakte durch einen offenen Innenhof genügend Licht erhalten. Die Jury wählte aus jeder Gruppe mehrere Vorschläge, um sie dem Verwaltungsrat vorzulegen.

Das Ergebnis

Obwohl die Jury sechs Entwürfe mit dem ersten bis sechsten Platz auszeichnete, enthielt sie sich gegenüber dem Verwaltungsrat der Carnegie Foundation einer Empfehlung, welcher der Beiträge ausgeführt werden solle. Sicherlich hatten die Mitglieder die Konstruktionspläne ausführlich diskutiert, auch wenn dies in ihrem Bericht nicht zum Ausdruck kommt: Das Dokument behandelte die sechs prämierten Entwürfe, von denen vier von eingeladenen Teilnehmern stammten, derart kurz und oberflächlich, daß der Verdacht der Willkür nahelag und der Boden für jahrelange Proteste, Streitigkeiten und Probleme rund um den Friedenspalast bereitet war.

Den ersten Preis erhielt Cordonnier, bei dessen Entwurf die Jury lobend die Inspirierung durch die holländischen Architekten des 16. Jahrhunderts erwähnte. Dies war ein Schlag ins Gesicht der anderen Teilnehmer, denn zum einen enthielten die Bauauflagen keine Angaben über eine vorgeschriebene Stilrichtung, und zum anderen erschien ein nationaler Baustil für einen internationalen Gerichtshof nicht gerade passend. Aber viel schwerer wog die Tatsache, daß Cordonniers Entwurf keineswegs stilistisch sicher ausgeführt war, ja noch nicht einmal in die Nähe der holländischen Renaissance kam – wie Kenner in der Presse spottend bemerkten. Für die anderen Preisträger fand die Jury noch weniger Worte als für Cordonniers Entwurf. Wagners Konstruktionspläne wurden mit zwei Sätzen abgehandelt, Schwechtens Entwurf sogar nur mit einem einzigen. Dabei war Wagners Beitrag der einzige der sechs prämierten Pläne, der sich durch einen außergewöhnlichen Stil auszeichnete. Diese Tatsache fiel auch der breiten Öffentlichkeit auf, die die mehr als 3 000 Zeichnungen in Den Haag im Palais Kneuterdijk, das Königin Wilhelmina eigens für diesen Zweck zur Verfügung gestellt hatte, begutachten konnte.

Nahezu alle Einsender hatten sich einer Neo-Stilrichtung bedient, obwohl die Architektur in Europa und den USA zu diesem Zeitpunkt bereits großen Veränderungen unterworfen war. Einige Teilnehmer hatten Phantasieentwürfe eingereicht, die zwar dem Geist einer vereinigten Völkergemeinschaft entsprachen, nicht aber dem Wissensstand der zeitgenössischen Architektur. Nur einige Beteiligte wagten etwas völlig Neues: der bereits erwähnte Wagner – der in den Augen der Jury zu Recht bemerkte, daß ein neuer Gebäudetypus auch eine neue Ästhetik erfordere – und die avantgardistischen Architekten Eliel Saarinen (Finnland), Hendrik Petrus Berlage und Willem Kromhout (beide aus den Niederlanden).

Es bleibt bei Cordonnier

Das Ergebnis der Jury wurde heftig kritisiert – nicht nur von den anderen Teilnehmern, sondern auch von unbeteiligten Architekten und einer breiten Öffentlichkeit. Daraufhin schlug die Jury dem Verwaltungsrat vergeblich vor, eine neue Ausschreibung zwischen den sechs Preisträgern zu organisieren. Bald wurde deutlich, daß die von Carnegie zugesagte Summe in Höhe von 1,5 Millionen Dollar nicht ausreichte, obwohl ihm die Stadtväter zuvor versichert hatten, daß 1 Million Dollar genügen würden. Weder Cordonnier noch die anderen Gewinner hatten sich an die in den Bauauflagen festgelegten Kosten gehalten. Der Verwaltungsrat entschloß sich daher, Carnegie um mehr Geld zu bitten, mit der Begründung, wegen der zusätzlichen Bibliothek sei alles ein wenig teurer geworden. Carnegie verweigerte dieses Ansinnen zunächst; schließlich hatte er bereits 500 000 Dollar zusätzlich bewilligt. Außerdem bevorzugte er persönlich ein bescheideneres Gebäude, und statt einer Bibliothek in einem eigenen Gebäudetrakt, die ohne sein Wissen in die Ausschreibung aufgenommen worden war, schwebte ihm eine Büchersammlung vor. Dieses Problem erhitzte die Gemüter noch einige Zeit, bis schließlich ein Kompromiß zustande kam und der Verwaltungsrat Cordonniers Konstruktionspläne für den Friedenspalast samt Bibliothek weiterbearbeiten konnte.

Da der Verwaltungsrat jedoch nicht genügend Erfahrung besaß, die Qualität eines Entwurfs anhand von Zeichnungen zu beurteilen, entschied er sich für eine Studienreise nach Dünkirchen, um ein anderes Bauwerk Cordonniers – das Rathaus der Stadt – zu begutachten. Die Enttäuschung über dieses Gebäude war so groß, daß sofort die Suche nach Alternativen begann. Der mit dem fünften Preis ausgezeichnete Entwurf von Howard Greenly und Herbert S. Olin gelangte zu neuen Ehren, und auch Saarinens Konstruktionspläne, bei denen die Jury großzügig darüber hinwegsah, daß sie nicht prämiert worden waren, galten plötzlich als diskutabel. Einmal mehr konnte sich der Verwaltungsrat nicht einigen, und entschied sich – zum dritten Mal – für Gespräche mit einem alten Bekannten: Cordonnier.

Cordonniers Probleme

Obwohl die Bausumme inzwischen auf 1,8 Millionen Gulden erhöht worden war, mußte Cordonnier seinen verschwenderischen ersten Entwurf in vielen Details verändern. Anscheinend hatte er damit gerechnet, denn seine ersten Baupläne bestanden größtenteils aus Elementen, die er bei früheren Bauten schon einmal verwendet hatte; auf diese Weise kostete ihn die Ausschreibung nicht allzu viel Zeit. Diese Vorgehensweise galt keineswegs als ungewöhnlich, da die Chance auf eine Auszeichnung relativ klein war und es sich die meisten Architekten nicht erlauben konnten, viel Zeit mit der Anfertigung detaillierter Konstruktionspläne zu verbringen. Erst nach einer Prämierung und Bezahlung widmeten sie sich den Plänen intensiver.

Der Verwaltungsrat erklärte sich mit Cordonniers Veränderungen jedoch nicht einverstanden, und obwohl eine Expertenrunde[1] zu seiner Unterstützung einberufen wurde, war er nicht in der Lage, einen akzeptablen Entwurf beizubringen. Schließlich beschloß der Rat, ihm den niederländischen Architekten Prof. J.A.G. van der Steur zur Seite zu stellen.

Im März 1907 erhielt der Bau des Friedenspalastes einen bitteren Beigeschmack, als niederländische Architekten offiziell Einspruch erhoben. Aber ihre Einwände standen inhaltlich auf wackligen Füßen: Sie protestierten gegen das gewählte Baugelände, die Geldprämie, den dürftigen und oberflächlichen Bericht der Jury und Cordonniers Entwurf. Zwar war ihre Kritik bezüglich des Ablaufs der Ausschreibung moralisch berechtigt, entbehrte aber jeglicher rechtlichen Grundlage.

Erst mit Hilfe einer offiziellen Protestnote an das Parlament, einer Klage vor Gericht und einer Berufungsinstanz vor dem Gerichtshof gelang es den Architekten, Cordonnier und Carnegie bis zum Januar 1911 an der Ausführung ihrer Pläne zu hindern. Ein Jahr nach dem Ende der Bauarbeiten brach der Erste Weltkrieg aus.

1 Dieser Kommission gehörten u.a. die Architekten Knuttel und C. Muysken an

Le Palais de la Paix, La Haye

Le pacifisme était une idée en vogue à la fin du siècle dernier. On voulait alors croire que les conflits armés disparaîtraient si les nations acceptaient de discuter de leurs différends devant une cour internationale et respectaient les décisions de ce tribunal. Cet idéalisme est à l'origine des projets de construction d'un Palais de la Paix[1]. Capitale d'un pays qui poursuivait une politique de stricte neutralité, La Haye fut choisie comme siège de cette institution. Le grand industriel et philanthrope d'origine américano-écossaise, Andrew Carnegie, s'était engagé à financer l'édifice.

Un concours international

Carnegie et le ministre néerlandais des affaires étrangères constituèrent une commission préparatoire pour choisir un site et établir le cahier des charges du concours (septembre 1903). Elle fut dissoute en juin 1904 dès la nomination du conseil d'administration de la nouvelle Fondation Carnegie chargée de mettre en œuvre le projet. Ce conseil nomma un architecte pour l'assister, D. Knuttel, qui l'aida immédiatement à résoudre le problème de la forme même du concours.

Comme une compétition ouverte à tous risquait d'éloigner des architectes connus qui ne voudraient pas perdre la face, un concours restreint paraissait préférable. Refusant de prendre en compte qu'il s'agissait d'une institution internationale et que les fonds étaient d'origine américaine, la fédération néerlandaise des architectes insista pour que la participation soit réservée à ses membres. Le comité décida dans un premier temps d'organiser un concours international restreint puis, face à une tempête de critiques, opta pour un compromis: un concours international ouvert, mais avec la liberté pour le comité d'inviter certains architectes en les dédommageant de leurs efforts. Vingt et un invités reçurent ainsi chacun 2 000 fl. Malgré ces controverses, plus de deux cents architectes du monde entier décidèrent de tenter leur chance dans cette prestigieuse compétition.

Le comité nomma un jury de six architectes originaires de six pays différents (cinq grandes puissances et la nation invitante), tous imbus des grandes traditions architecturales du XIXème siècle. Comme d'habitude, les participants devaient soumettre des plans de masse, des coupes et des élévations mais également, ce qui était moins fréquent, des représentations en couleur du bâtiment dans son environnement. Dans la pratique des concours, on refusait généralement ce genre de rendu pour éviter de privilégier de pures qualités de dessin sur celles de l'architecture. En l'occurrence, les praticiens expérimentés membres du jury avaient entériné cette demande. Les candidats pouvaient consulter Knuttel s'ils avaient des questions à poser.

Comme le programme n'était pas très détaillé, les solutions proposées furent très diverses. L'une des principales difficultés à résoudre était la présence d'une bibliothèque indépendante du Palais lui-même.

Le programme ne précisait pas la nature de cette autonomie mais stipulait de prévoir une liaison avec le bâtiment principal. Les solutions proposées se répartirent en trois catégories:

- deux bâtiments séparés réunis par un passage,
- un bâtiment unique avec une ou plusieurs cours intérieures pour l'éclairage,
- un bâtiment unique à plusieurs ailes avec cours.

Le jury sélectionna des plans de chacune de ces catégories et les présenta au conseil d'administration.

Le résultat

Le jury décerna six prix sans prendre parti pour l'une ou l'autre des solutions. La longueur de ses délibérations ne transparaît d'ailleurs nullement dans son rapport qui se contente d'un commentaire superficiel et rapide sur chaque projet primé, dont quatre proposés par des architectes invités. La décision parut donc assez arbitraire et déclencha d'innombrables protestations et querelles.

Cordonnier reçut le premier prix et le jury nota avec satisfaction qu'il s'était inspiré de l'architecture néerlandaise du XVIème siècle, ce qui fut jugé comme abusif par la plupart des autres participants. Tout d'abord, aucun style n'avait été recommandé dans le programme; ensuite, un style national semblait peu approprié pour une cour internationale; pire encore, la proposition de Cordonnier était jugée totalement ratée et les experts remarquèrent dans la presse que ce plan n'avait qu'une très lointaine parenté avec le style qu'il invoquait. Les commentaires du jury sur les autres projets étaient encore plus succincts. Le plan de Wagner était expédié en deux phrases et celui de Schwechten en une seule! Wagner avait pourtant présenté un projet remarquable. Le public put d'ailleurs en juger grâce à l'exposition de plus de trois mille plans au Palais de Kneuterdijk à La Haye, à la demande de la reine Wilhelmina.

Si le plan de Cordonnier était éclectique et d'assez mauvais goût, l'ensemble des projets n'était guère enthousiasmant. La plupart se rapprochaient de l'éclectisme du vainqueur ou n'étaient que des sous-produits du style Beaux-Arts. Presque tous les architectes s'étaient orientés vers un style «néo» même si l'on sentait déjà depuis quelques années qu'un vent nouveau soufflait sur l'architecture, en Europe comme aux Etats-Unis. Plusieurs participants s'étaient réfugiés dans des solutions fantastiques irréalisables, symbolisant leur vision de l'universalisme. Seuls quelques architectes se distinguèrent réellement: Wagner, qui avait déclaré que pour un nouveau type de bâtiment il fallait une nouvelle approche esthétique, et des avant-gardistes comme Eliel Saarinen (Finlande), H.P. Berlage et Willem Kromhout, tous deux néerlandais. D'autres projets intéressants furent malheureusement négligés: ceux de Jarl Eklund (Helsingfors), W. Molenbroek (La Haye) et G.C.E. Blohm (Hambourg)

Cordonnier envers et contre tous

La décision du jury fut largement critiquée. Les architectes perdants étaient bien entendu déçus mais même ceux qui n'avaient rien proposé et le grand public étaient insatisfaits. Le jury conseilla d'organiser un second concours réservé aux six architectes lauréats, mais le conseil d'administration était lassé de ces conflits. Il entama immédiatement des discussions avec Cordonnier qui firent apparaître que le 1,5 million de dollars offert par Carnegie était insuffisant, alors que l'on avait affirmé au philanthrope qu'un million conviendrait largement. Il était clair que ni Cordonnier ni les autres candidats primés n'avaient respecté la limite des 1,6 millions de florins du cahier des charges. Le conseil se résolut à demander davantage d'argent à Carnegie sous prétexte de l'inclusion de la bibliothèque dans le projet. Carnegie refusa dans un premier temps: il avait déjà accordé 500 000 dollars supplémentaires et souhaitait que le bâtiment reste raisonnable; il avait voulu abriter une collection de livres dans cette bibliothèque et n'avait pas demandé qu'on lui consacre une aile entière, enfin il n'avait même pas été informé de cette exigence du cahier des charges. Un compromis fut élaboré et le conseil put enfin confier la commande des plans du Palais et de la bibliothèque à Cordonnier. Néanmoins, comme les administrateurs était apparemment incapables de juger de la qualité d'un architecte d'après ses seuls plans et dessins, ils décidèrent d'aller voir de plus près l'une de ses réalisations, l'hôtel de ville de Dunkerque. Déçus par la visite, ils tentèrent de trouver rapidement une alternative. Le projet de Greenly et Olin qui avait remporté le cinquième prix fut réexaminé, de même que celui de Saarinen bien qu'il n'ait pas été primé. Mais une fois encore aucune décision ne fut possible et le conseil se résolut une nouvelle fois à faire confiance à Cordonnier.

Les problèmes de Cordonnier

Bien que le coût de la construction ait été porté à 1,8 millions de florins, l'extravagant plan original de Cordonnier exigeait encore des aménagements. Pris par le temps, l'architecte s'était probablement servi de travaux réalisés pour d'autres projets, ce qui était assez courant pour les concours. Il fallait beaucoup de chance pour remporter ce type de compétition et peu d'architectes pouvaient se permettre de passer de longs mois sur des détails, d'autant plus qu'il était généralement prévu de pouvoir modifier les plans si le projet était retenu dans son ensemble.

Les modifications apportées par Cordonnier ne plurent pas au conseil et une commission d'experts[2] fut nommée pour l'aider, sans résultat tangible et l'on désigna alors un praticien néerlandais, le professeur J.A.G. van der Steur. Les plans finalement acceptés différaient profondément du projet original. Deux des quatre tours furent par exemple supprimées ce qui permit de substantielles économies.

En mars 1907, le démarrage de la construction fut de nouveau retardé par une plainte des architectes néerlandais. Leurs motifs – choix du site, montant des prix, insuffisance du rapport du jury, choix de Cordonnier – manquaient de base légale même s'ils jetaient un éclairage cruel sur la manière dont ce concours avait été mené. En déposant leur réclamation devant le parlement, puis devant un tribunal et enfin en appel, ils réussirent cependant à retarder le projet jusqu'en janvier 1911: intéressant thème de réflexion pour une future cour internationale de justice... Un an après la pose de la première pierre, la Première Guerre mondiale éclatait.

1 *L'idée du Palais de la Paix fit son apparition lors du sommet de la paix de 1899, réuni à la Huis ten Bosch de La Haye à l'initiative du tsar Nicolas II. La même année, le même tsar incorporait de force les Finlandais dans son armée (voir le chapitre sur la gare d'Helsinki).*

2 *Cette commission comprenait les architectes Knuttel et C. Muysken.*

A. Marcel competition design, 1906, part of central front elevation, second prize

Johannes Zimmermann competition design, 1906, exterior view

Otto Wagner competition design, 1906, exterior view, fourth prize

Henrik Petrus Berlage competition design, 1906, exterior view

Franz Wendt competition design, 1906, exterior view, third prize

Franz Schwechten competition design, 1906, exterior view, sixth prize

G. Mancini competition design, 1906, exterior view

Emil Töry competition design, 1906, exterior view

Howard Greenley & Herbert S. Olin competition design, 1906, exterior view, fifth prize

Felix Debat competition design, 1906, front elevation

Willem Kromhout competition design, 1906, site plan

Willem Kromhout competition design, 1906, exterior view from north

Willem Kromhout competition design, 1906, front elevation on Carnegieplein

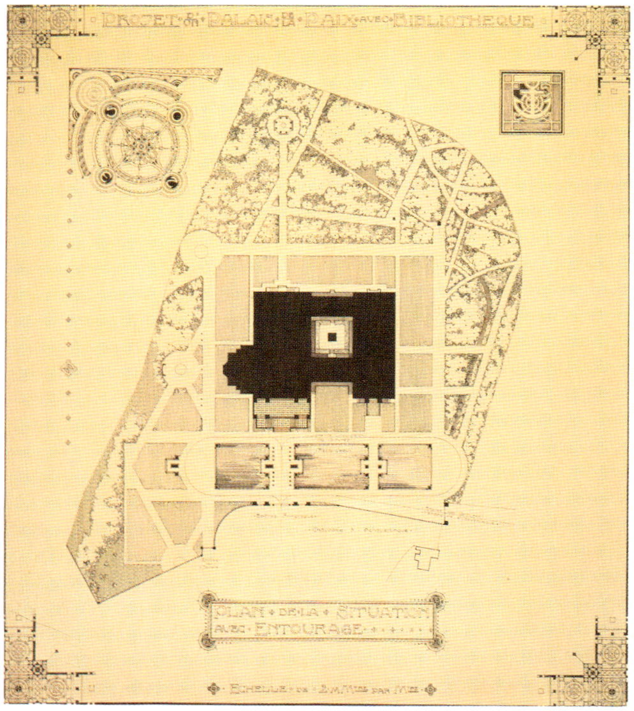
PROJET D'UN PALAIS DE LA PAIX AVEC BIBLIOTHEQUE
PLAN DE LA SITUATION AVEC ENTOURAGE

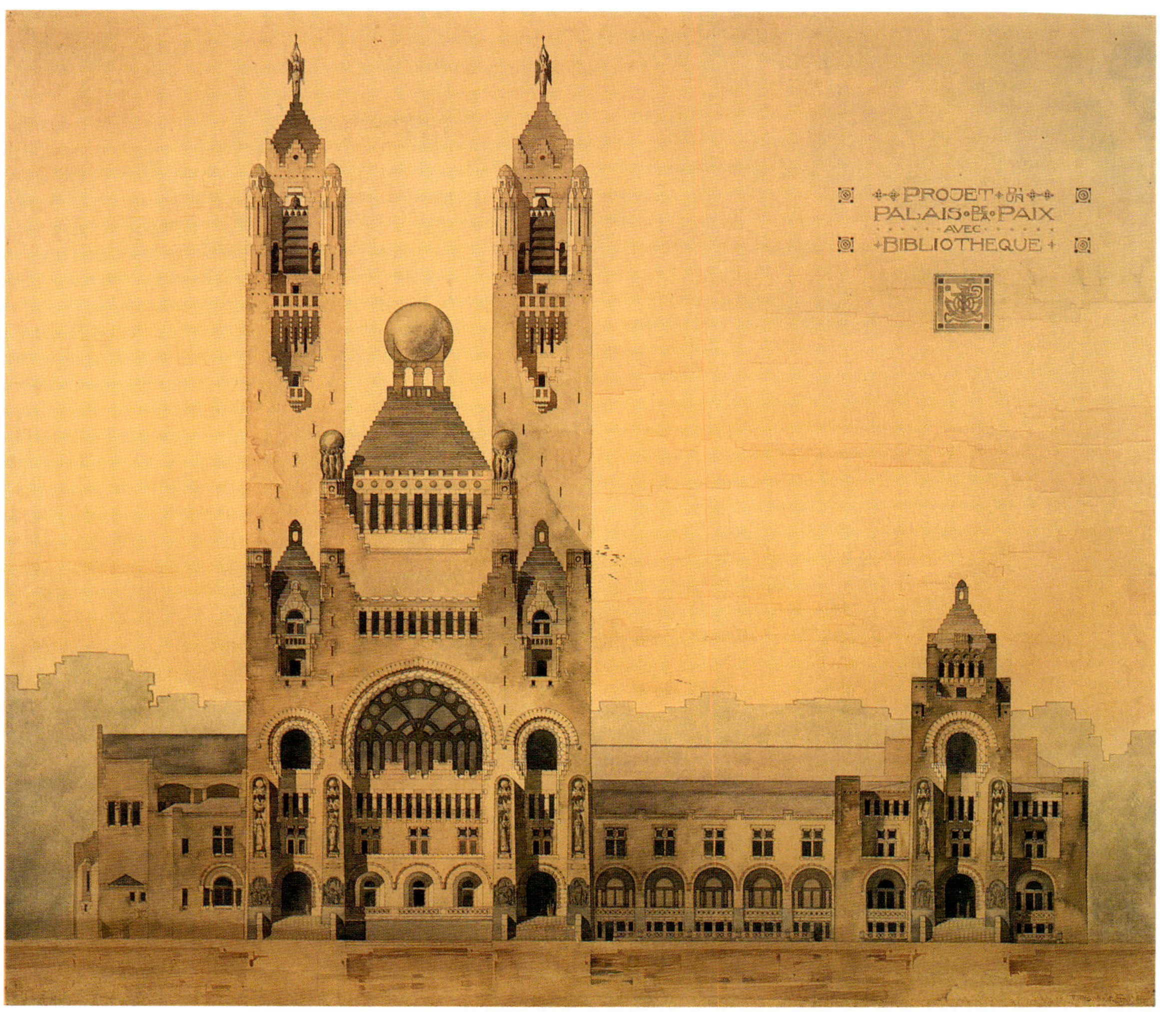
PROJET D'UN
PALAIS DE LA PAIX
AVEC
BIBLIOTHEQUE

Project

Urban development plan

Site

Canberra, a region between Sydney and Melbourne on the banks of the Molonglo river, 110 km from the coast

Dates

24 May 1911 to 31 January 1912

Result announced

23 May 1912

Number of entries

137 (11 were disqualified because they were not submitted anonymously)

Jury

J.M. Coane (engineer, chairman), James Alexander Smith (engineer), John Kirkpatrick (archtitect); The Minister of Home Affairs, King O'Malley, had power of veto

Result

First prize Walter Burley Griffin (USA) *Second prize* Eliel Saarinen (Finland) *Third prize* Donat-Alfred Agache (France)

Commissioned by

The Ministry of Home Affairs

Architect

Walter Burley Griffin (1876–1937)

Canberra City Planning, 1911

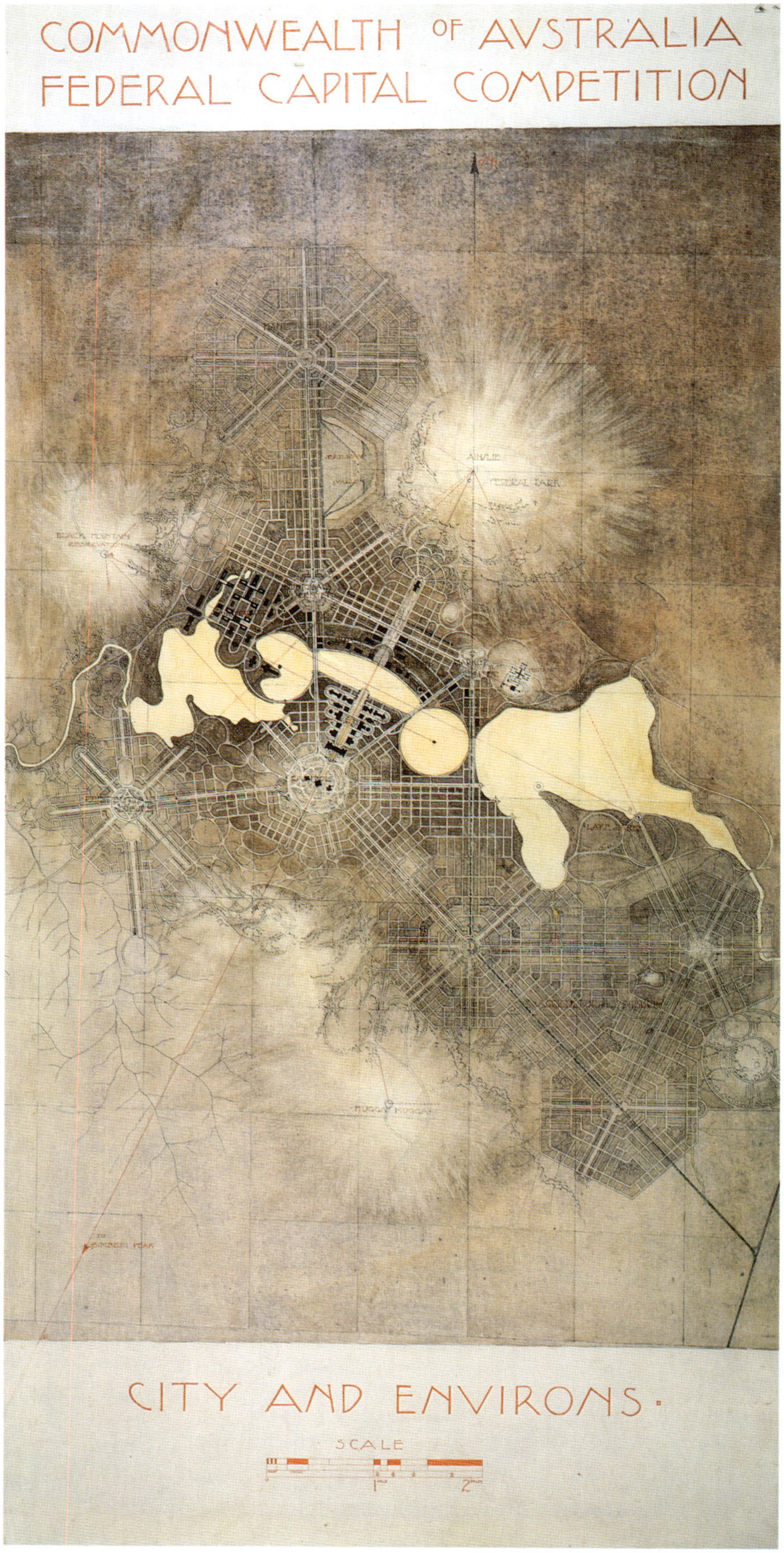

Walter Burley Griffin competition design, 1912, plan of city and environs, first prize

Canberra City Planning

The Australian continent was originally divided into six colonies. It was not until 1901 that these were united to form the Commonwealth of Australia. Naturally, this immense new country was in need of a capital. At the time, the most important cities were Sydney, the capital of New South Wales, and Melbourne, the capital of Victoria. The rivalry between the two cities was intense. Even the width of the railway tracks in the two former colonies differed. It was evident that the two cities were not prepared to give each other an inch. Therefore, the decision was taken to build an entirely new capital. By way of a compromise, Melbourne was chosen as the temporary seat of parliament until the new capital had been completed. The people of Victoria fostered the silent hope that the project would be a failure.

Hills and rivers

It was agreed that a site would be found in New South Wales. One of the conditions was that the site should be at least 100 miles from Sydney, thereby ruling out the chance that the new capital would become a mere satellite city. The task of finding a suitable site was not an easy one. However, in 1918, a region characterised by hills and rivers was eventually designated: Canberra. The rivers were an important source of drinking water, Australia being a dry country. However, Canberra also had a number of disadvantages, such as the total lack of infrastructure and the inferior condition of the soil. In 1909, the exact site was specified and on 24 May 1911 a competition was announced, after an idea by D. Miller, the Secretary of State.
One hundred and thirty-seven architects, from all corners of the globe, requested the competition programme. They each received a comprehensive information package containing layout sketches, maps, soil and climate specifications, and a 12 page list of conditions. In addition, the participants were advised to read "Transactions of the Town Planning Conference", published by the Royal Institute of British Architects (RIBA). It is worth mentioning that RIBA and the Institute of Civil Engineers had exhorted their members not to participate in the competition because the final adjudication was in the hands of a layman, the Minister of Home Affairs, King O'Malley, who was a member of Andrew Fisher's Labour government. The way was thereby cleared for architects from outside England and the Commonwealth. Consequently, the first, second and third prizes were won by an American, a Finn and a Frenchman.

Third-rate fun-fair

Initially, the projected population capacity of the capital was set at 25 000. The city would boast parliament buildings, a National Art Gallery, a State House (including archives), a museum, a theatre, a stadium and a mint. At the time, no one could foresee that these buildings would take another fifty years to materialise, nor that completion of the capital itself would be hampered by numerous delays[1]. The first problems arose when the jury were unable to reach a unanimous decision. The jury chairman, J.M. Coane, was in favour of W. Scott Griffiths' design. The other two members of the jury nominated Walter Burley Griffin, Eliel Saarinen and Donat-Alfred Agache for first, second and third prize.
O'Malley overruled Coane and endorsed the latter result. However, he simultaneously appointed a council of experts to assess the plans as a jury-of-review. One of the members of this council was the above-mentioned Miller. From the start, Miller had intended to create an ideal city by combining elements of various plans. The council liked the idea, set aside the prize-winning plans and subsequently submitted their own plan, which met with O'Malley's emphatic approval. The Minister saw this mixture of urban planning as a brilliant compromise. Thus, the RIBA saw its worst fears materialise and experts in the field were presented with the perfect opportunity to slate this "third-rate fun-fair"[2].

Federal Parliament House

Urban development debacle

Griffin's design was lauded by the professional community, as were those of Saarinen and Agache. It is worth mentioning that Griffin had initially been reluctant to participate in the competition. According to certain sources, he was egged on by his partner, Marion Mahoney, who later became his wife. Griffin and Mahoney had both worked for Frank Lloyd Wright in Chicago. The sketches which had charmed the jury were Mahoney's.

However appealing Griffin's design may have been the headstrong Miller was determined to have things his way. He informed O'Malley that he did not want Griffin interfering. O'Malley had complete faith in Miller and the ministerial plan, and for a long time Canberra seemed set to become an urban development debacle. However, circumstances changed abruptly in 1913. Fisher's government was replaced by a Liberal government under Joseph Cook. A year later, Labour regained power, but Cook, who was also in charge of Home Affairs, organised a meeting with Griffin, together with W.H. Kelly, who later became Minister of Home Affairs. The ministerial council was informed that from then on the project would be based on Griffin's plan and not on the ministerial plan. The tide had thus been turned. The council was disbanded in October 1913 and Griffin was appointed Federal Capital Director of Design and Construction.

The center of Canberra

Griffin's design

Griffin's approach to urban planning developed during a period dominated by two major movements: the "Garden City" and the "City Beautiful". The latter movement was strongly influenced by the French Académie des Beaux-Arts. Griffin had become acquainted with this style during the Chicago Fair of 1893. The decor, which had been specially constructed for this event, mirrored the principles of the City Beautiful style. Monumentality and presentability were its key concepts: urban development was seen as a purely æsthetic issue. Lines of sight criss-cross the street plan, meeting at a triumphal arch, a church or some other monumental building. The old chess-board pattern (Washington) was replaced by varied or symmetrical floor plans, based on triangles or concentric circles. Although the Garden City style, first introduced by Ebenezer Howard, also featured concentric circles, this movement differed in that it was based on the social rather than the asthetic function of a city[3]. Griffin's designs shows traces of both the City Beautiful and the Garden City styles.

The RIBA booklet, which the competition jury had recommended to the participants, contained an article by the English-Australian urban development expert John Sulman. In it, he extolled the virtues of the "spider-web" design, particularly its ingenious structure. In the same article, titled Federal Capital of Australia, he gave examples of a radial plan (circles intersected by radians) and a fan-shaped plan (semi-circles). Griffin shared Sulman's preference for plans of this sort, but added a feature which he had come across while in Chicago: elements of landscape. In traditional concentric plans the lines of sight were often bounded by monumental buildings. Griffin preferred to use elements of the surrounding landscape. This does not imply that he did not plan any buildings at the ends of the lines of sight; he was undoubtedly aware of the fact that no city is complete without monumental buildings, however democratic it may be.

Griffin situated the three most important centres on top of three hills, which lay at the points an equilateral triangle. Capitol Hill was reserved for the Government Centre, the municipality was to have its seat on City Hill (Mount Vernon) and the Market Centre was to be situated around Mount Pleasant and Mount Russel. The triangle was bisected by the so-called land axis - a line of sight which passed from Mount Ainslie through the Government Centre to Mount Bimberi, the highest point of the skyline at 1912 metres. This axis lies at right angles to the line between the Municipal Centre and the Market Centre and runs roughly parallel to the river. It is therefore referred to as the water axis. Griffin planned several bodies of water: a symmetrical body, shaped like a telephone receiver and bisected by the land axis, with two small, natural lakes on either side (these were to be formed by an ingenious system of water management).

A number of satellite centres were developed around the three hills and linked to the city centre by broad, straight roads, whereby a triangular pattern was created. These centres are surrounded by octagonal ring roads. The secondary street pattern is largely regular and block-shaped, but dissolves into less angular shapes here and there (parks).

Griffin had intended to create a city which would embody Australia's exalted democratic qualities. This accounts to a certain extent for the fact that he deviated from the dominant Beaux-Arts approach to urban development. He did, however, adopt the symbolic principles of this movement. Without exception, the buildings were diligently planned and the street names carefully chosen. An equal number of ministries on Capitol Hill have been situated on either side of the land axis, the

Governor-general's house faces that of the Prime Minister and the parliament building is situated on the axis itself.

Griffin had submitted a masterpiece and had deservedly won the competition. However, Saarinen had also submitted an extraordinary design. He had also based his design on two axes at right angles to one another, but around these axes he had projected streets which merged neatly into one another. The rest of the plan was rather stately and cold. Agache had submitted a boring Beaux-Arts design and had completely ignored the surroundings. In contrast, the plan nominated by the jury chairman Coane had taken the surroundings into account and was generally sound. It had been submitted by W. Scott Griffiths, Charles Gibbon Coulter and Charles Henry Casewell, and consisted of an ingenious system of spider webs and triangles. Its elimination, in favour of Griffin's design, was described above.

Execution

Having arrived in Australia, Griffin altered a number of features of his design, thereby making it a little more convenient, without marring the basic concept. The plan was executed at a snail's pace. In the beginning, construction was delayed by the First World War and by the counter-productive attitude of certain civil servants. Griffin was dependant upon the same people who had submitted the ministerial plan. They had been passed over and complained that Griffin interfered in their affairs too often. Fortunately, Griffin was assured of top-ranking support. In 1916, O'Malley was reappointed Minister of Home Affairs and decided to speed up the construction of the new capital. Much to the disappointment of the civil servants, he supported Griffin and demanded complete co-operation. Tragically, Griffin did not live to see Canberra completed. He died in 1937. The Depression had caused additional delays and the Second World War was looming on the horizon. Canberra was completed after the war. The central, man-made lake was completed in 1963. It is called Lake Burley Griffin.

Ebenezar Howard

Ebenezar Howard diagram of the yard and centre of the model garden city

Welwyn Garden City

1 *Only the parliamentary buildings were completed on schedule.*

2 *The words of Patrick Abercrombie, an English urban development expert.*

3 *Howard discussed his theories in Tomorrow – a Peaceful Path to Real Reform, London (1898).*

Städtebauplan für Canberra

Der australische Kontinent war urspünglich in sechs Kolonien aufgeteilt, die sich erst 1901 zum Commonwealth of Australia zusammenschlossen. Dieses riesige neue Land benötigte eine Hauptstadt, wobei als bedeutendste Metropolen Sydney, die Hauptstadt der ehemaligen Kolonie New South Wales, und Melbourne, die Hauptstadt von Victoria, in Frage kamen. Die Rivalität zwischen diesen beiden Städten war so groß, daß sich sogar die Spurbreite der Eisenbahn in den beiden Kolonien unterschied. Da keine Stadt der anderen den Titel der Bundeshauptstadt gönnte, wurde der Bau einer völlig neuen Hauptstadt beschlossen. Solange die neue Metropole nicht fertig war, sollte Melbourne als provisorischer Regierungssitz fungieren. In ganz Victoria hoffte daraufhin die Bevölkerung, der Bau möge nie fertig werden.

Hügel und Flüsse

In New South Wales sollte nach einem geeigneten Baugelände gesucht werden. Bedingung: Das Gelände mußte mindestens 160 km von Sydney entfernt liegen. Mit diesem Beschluß sollte verhindert werden, daß sich die neue Hauptstadt zu einer Satellitenstadt Sydneys entwikkelte. Die Suche nach einem geeigneten Gebiet erwies sich als sehr kompliziert. 1908 fiel die Wahl schließlich auf Canberra, eine Region, die durch Hügel und Flüsse bestimmt wird. Der Wasserreichtum dieses Gebiets war im trockenen Australien von großer Bedeutung. Zu den Nachteilen Canberras zählten das Fehlen jeglicher Infrastruktur und die schlechte Bodenbeschaffenheit. 1909 einigte sich die Regierung auf das endgültige Baugelände. Auf Anraten von D. Miller, Staatssekretär des Innenministeriums, wurde der Wettbewerb am 24. Mai 1911 offiziell ausgeschrieben.

Die 137 Teilnehmer aus aller Welt erhielten ein ausführliches Informationspaket mit Lageplänen, Landkarten, Beschreibungen des Klimas und der Bodenbeschaffenheit sowie eine zwölf Seiten starke Liste mit Auflagen. Außerdem empfahl man ihnen das Studium der Broschüre »Transactions of the Town Planning Conference« (Protokolle der Stadtplanungs-Konferenz), das vom Royal Institute of British Architects (RIBA) herausgegeben worden war. Dasselbe RIBA rief übrigens – zusammen mit dem Institute of Civil Engineers – seine Mitglieder auf, sich nicht am Wettbewerb zu beteiligen, da die endgültige Bewertung der Pläne durch den Innenminister, also einen Laien, erfolgen sollte: King O'Malley, Mitglied der Labour-Regierung unter Andrew Fisher. Durch diesen Aufruf war der Weg frei für die Architekten außerhalb Englands und des Commonwealth; die ersten drei Plätze gingen dementsprechend an einen Amerikaner, einen Finnen und einen Franzosen.

Ein drittklassiger Vergnügungspark

Ursprünglich sollte die neue Hauptstadt etwa 25 000 Einwohnern Platz bieten; dazu kamen verschiedene Regierungsgebäude, die National Art Gallery, das State House (mit mehreren Archiven), ein Museum, ein Theater, ein Stadion und das Münzamt. Zu dieser Zeit konnte niemand ahnen, daß die Gebäude noch etwa 50 Jahre auf sich warten lassen würden und daß die Fertigstellung der Hauptstadt aufgrund zahlreicher Verzögerungen sehr viel länger dauern würde als erwartet[1]. Die ersten Probleme begannen mit dem Unvermögen der Jury, sich zu einigen: Während der Vorsitzende J.M. Coane den Plan des Architekten W. Scott Griffiths favorisierte, votierten die anderen beiden Jurymitglieder für Walter Burley Griffin, Eliel Saarinen und Donat-Alfred Agache. Innenminister O'Malley überstimmte Coane und bestätigte das Urteil der beiden anderen Jurymitglieder, ernannte aber gleichzeitig einen Expertenausschuß, der die Pläne in einer Art Revisionsverfahren noch einmal überprüfen sollte. Ein Mitglied dieses Ausschusses war der bereits erwähnte Staatssekretär Miller. Ihm hatte von Anfang an eine Kombination aus Elementen verschiedener Entwürfe vorgeschwebt, mit denen er die ideale Stadt schaffen wollte. Auch der Ausschuß folgte dieser Idee und wischte die preisgekrönten Pläne vom Tisch, um danach einen eigenen Entwurf vorzulegen – sehr zur Zufriedenheit Millers, der dieses planerische Chaos für einen hervorragenden Kompromiß hielt. Damit war genau das eingetreten, was die RIBA hatte verhindern wollen. Folglich nahmen führende Stadtplaner bei ihrer Kritik an diesem »drittklassigen Vergnügungspark«[2] kein Blatt vor den Mund.

Ein stadtplanerisches Debakel

Ebenso wie die Pläne Saarinens und Agaches wurde auch Griffins Entwurf von seinen Kollegen hochgelobt. Dabei hätte sich Griffin beinahe gar nicht an der Ausschreibung beteiligt – angeblich wurde er von seiner Partnerin (und späteren Ehefrau) Marion Mahoney dazu angetrieben. Griffin und Mahoney hatten sich während der gemeinsamen Arbeit im Atelier von Frank Lloyd Wright in Chicago kennengelernt.

Zunächst jedoch wollte der eigensinnige Miller seine Pläne durchsetzen. Er teilte O'Malley mit, daß er keinerlei Einmischung von Seiten Griffins dulde. O'Malley hatte volles Vertrauen zu Miller und den Plänen des Ausschusses, und es sah lange Zeit danach aus, als ob sich Canberra zu einem städteplanerischen Debakel entwickeln sollte. Doch 1913 änderten sich plötzlich und unerwartet die Umstände: Die Regierung Fisher mußte einem liberalen Kabinett unter Joseph Cook weichen. Zwar kam die Labour-Party bereits ein Jahr später wieder an die Macht, aber in der Zwischenzeit war Griffin von Cook und dem späteren Innenminister W.H. Kelly zu einem Treffen eingeladen worden. Dem Ausschuß wurde mitgeteilt, daß Griffins Pläne und nicht die des Ministeriums als Ausgangspunkt dienen sollten.

Griffins Städtebauplan

Griffin entwickelte seine stadtplanerischen Vorstellungen in einer Zeit, die von zwei Hauptströmungen beherrscht wurde – der »Garden-City« und der »City-Beautiful«, wobei letztere stark von den Ideen der französischen Académie des Beaux-Arts beeinflußt war. Monumentalität und Repräsentatitivität standen im Vordergrund; Städtebau als rein ästhetische Aufgabe: Sichtachsen zerteilen den Straßenplan, begegnen einander an einem Triumphbogen, einer Kirche oder einem anderen monumentalen Bauwerk. Das alte Schachbrettmuster (Washington) wird abgelöst von einer variablen Straßenanlage, deren Ausgangspunkt Dreiecke oder konzentrische Kreise bilden.

Diese konzentrischen Kreise dienten auch als Grundlage für den von Ebenezer Howard eingeführten Garden-City-Stil, der aber im Gegensatz zum City-Beautiful-Stil nicht von der ästhetischen, sondern von der sozialen Funktion einer Stadt ausging[3]. Beide stadtplanerischen Ansätze beeinflußten Griffins Werk.

Während sich im traditionellen konzentrischen Straßenplan die Sichtachsen an einem monumentalen Gebäude (einer Bank, einem Bürogebäude oder einem Bahnhof) treffen, versuchte Griffin, an diesen Punkten landschaftliche Gegebenheiten zu integrieren.

Griffin plazierte die drei wichtigsten Zentren der Stadt auf drei Hügeln, die zusammen ein gleichseitiges Dreieck bilden. Capital Hill war der Regierung vorbehalten (Government Centre). Die Stadtverwaltung erhielt ihren Sitz auf dem City Hill (Mount Vernon), das Market Centre lag rund um Mount Pleasant und Mount Russel. Dieses Dreieck wurde von der sog. Landachse in zwei Hälften geschnitten, einer Sichtachse, die vom Mount Ainslie gerade durch das Government Centre zum Mount Bimberi verläuft. Diese Achse steht im rechten Winkel zu einer gedachten Linie zwischen Municipal Centre und Market Centre, die in ihrem Verlauf den Wasserflächen folgt und daher den Namen »Wasserachse« trägt. Griffin hatte fünf dieser Flächen vorgesehen: einen See in Form eines Telefonhörers, der von der Landachse zweigeteilt wird, und an dem an jeder Seite zwei weitere, natürliche Seen folgen (die durch ein durchdachtes Regulationssystem geschaffen werden mußten).

Rund um die drei Hügel liegt eine Anzahl von Satellitenzentren, die mit dem eigentlichen Stadtzentrum durch gerade, breite Straßen verbunden sind, so daß sich ein dreieckiges Grundmuster herausbildet. Die Zentren selbst sind von oktagonalen Ringstraßen umgeben. Die sekundäre Straßenanlage ist größtenteils regelmäßig und blockförmig, löst sich aber an manchen Stellen (Parks) in weniger eckige Formen auf.

Griffin wollte mit seinem Entwurf eine Stadt schaffen, die die ausgeprägt demokratischen Prinzipien Australiens verkörpert. Dies ist einer der Gründe, warum er der zu dieser Zeit dominierenden städtebaulichen Tradition des Beaux-Arts nicht in allen Punkten folgte. Aber er übernahm die Symbolik dieser Bewegung: Jedes Gebäude war genauestens durchdacht, und auch die Straßennamen wurden mit größter Sorgfalt ausgewählt. Auf dem Capital Hill liegt zu jeder Seite der Landachse die exakt gleiche Anzahl an Ministerien, das Haus des Generalgouverneurs befindet sich direkt gegenüber dem Haus des Premierministers. Das Parlamentsgebäude plazierte Griffin auf die Achse selbst.

Mit diesem Entwurf schuf Griffin ein Meisterwerk; doch auch Saarinens Beitrag verdient besondere Beachtung. Er ging ebenfalls von zwei rechtwinklig aufeinanderstoßenden Achsen aus, ließ aber die Straßen der unmittelbaren Umgebung fließend ineinander übergehen. Allerdings wirkte der übrige Teil seines Entwurfs eher imposant und kühl. Agache reichte einen recht langweiligen Entwurf im Stil des Beaux-Arts ein, der sämtliche landschaftlichen Gegebenheiten außer acht ließ. Im Gegensatz dazu berücksichtigte der von Coane – dem Vorsitzenden der Jury – favorisierte Plan die natürliche Umgebung der Stadt und wirkte solide und durchdacht. Dieser von den Architekten W. Scott Griffiths, Charles Gibbon Coulter und Charles Henry Casewell vorgelegte Entwurf umfaßte einen raffinierten Straßenplan aus Spinnwebmustern und Dreiecken.

1 *Nur das Parlamentsgebäude konnte termingerecht fertiggestellt werden.*

2 *Zitat von Patrick Abercrombie, einem englischen Stadtplaner*

3 *Howard erläuterte seine Theorien in: Tomorrow – a Peaceful Path to Real Reform, London 1898.*

Le Plan de Canberra

Le continent australien avait été divisé par les Britanniques en six colonies qui ne furent unifiées en un Commonwealth d'Australie qu'en 1901. Cet immense pays dont les principales villes étaient Sydney, capitale de l'Etat de Nouvelles. Galles du Sud et Melbourne, celle de l'Etat de Victoria, avait besoin d'une vraie capitale. La rivalité entre les deux cités était intense et même la largeur des voies de chemins de fer des deux anciennes colonies n'était pas la même. Ni l'une ni l'autre n'était prête à accorder un quelconque avantage à son adversaire. La décision fut donc prise de construire une capitale entièrement nouvelle. Melbourne fut désignée siège temporaire du parlement et ses habitants espéraient bien que le projet allait échouer.

Collines et rivières

On s'entendit pour trouver un site en Nouvelles-Galles du Sud mais éloigné de160 km de Sydney au moins, pour éviter que la capitale ne devienne un satellite du grand port. Malgré la difficulté de la tâche, on finit par trouver, en 1908, une région de collines et de rivières: Canberra. Les rivières procuraient une eau douce abondante, ce qui était important dans un pays en grande partie désertique. Canberra présentait cependant quelques graves inconvénients dont l'absence totale d'infrastructure et la mauvaise qualité des sols. En 1909, le site exact fut déterminé et le 24 mai 1911 un concours lancé, à l'initiative de D. Miller, secrétaire d'Etat. 137 architectes du monde entier demandèrent le règlement du concours et chacun reçut un dossier très complet contenant des dessins, des cartes, des informations sur le terrain et le climat et une liste de 12 pages de conditions. Par ailleurs, il était conseillé de lire les comptes rendus de la conférence sur l'urbanisme publiés par le Royal Institute of British Architects (RIBA). Il est intéressant de noter que le RIBA et l'Institute of Civil Engineers avaient exhorté leurs membres à ne pas participer à ce concours pour la simple raison que la décision finale appartenait à un profane, le ministre des Affaires Intérieures, King O'Malley, membre du gouvernement travailliste d'Andrew Fisher. La voie était donc libre pour des architectes n'appartenant ni à la Grande-Bretagne, ni au Commonwealth et les trois premiers prix furent remportés par un Américain, un Finlandais et un Français.

Un parc d'attraction bas de gamme

A l'origine, la population envisagée pour la capitale n'excédait pas 25 000 habitants. La ville devait être équipée d'un parlement, d'une galerie nationale, de bâtiments administratifs (y compris pour les archives), d'un musée, d'un théâtre, d'un stade et d'un palais de la monnaie. On n'imaginait pas à cette époque qu'il faudrait cinquante ans pour mener à bien tous ces projets ni que la construction de la capitale elle-même serait freinée par d'innombrables retards[1]. Les premiers problèmes surgirent lorsque le jury se révéla incapable de prendre une décision. Le président, J.M. Coane, était en faveur du plan de W. Scott Griffith et les deux autres membres penchaient pour attribuer les trois premiers prix à Walter Burley Griffin, Eliel Saarinen et Donat-Alfred Agache.
O'Malley passa par-dessus la tête de Coane et entérina le choix des autres jurés tout en nommant un conseil d'experts pour analyser et évaluer les plans proposés. L'un des membres de ce conseil était Miller, déjà mentionné. Dès le départ, il avait en tête de créer une cité idéale en mariant les meilleurs éléments des divers plans. Le conseil approuva cette idée, écarta le plan vainqueur et poussa en avant son propre plan qui remporta l'adhésion de O'Malley. Le ministre voyait dans ce mélange un brillant compromis. Ainsi, les pires craintes du RIBA se concrétisaient-elles et les experts sérieux brocardèrent à plaisir ce «parc d'attraction bas-de-gamme»[2].

Une débâcle urbanistique

Le plan de Griffin comme ceux de Saarinen et d'Agache avaient été approuvés par la communauté professionnelle. A l'origine, Griffin n'avait pas été très séduit par l'idée de ce concours et il avait fallu toute l'insistance de son associée, Marion Mahoney, qui devait devenir sa femme, pour qu'il fasse acte de candidature. Tous deux avaient travaillé à Chicago pour Frank Lloyd Wright et les dessins qui avaient charmé le jury étaient de la main de Marion Mahoney.
En dépit de la séduction des projets de Griffin, Miller, buté, poursuivit sur sa lancée. Il informa O'Malley qu'il ne voulait pas des interventions de Griffin. O'Malley avait entièrement confiance en Miller, approuvait son plan et pendant longtemps, Canberra courut le risque de se transformer en une débâcle urbanistique totale. Les circonstances changèrent brusquement en 1913 lorsque le gouvernement Fisher fut remplacé par une équipe libérale dirigée par Joseph Cook. Un an plus tard, les Travaillistes revinrent au pouvoir mais Cook, qui était également en charge des Affaires Intérieures, avait déjà organisé une réunion avec Griffin et W.H. Kelly, futur ministre des Affaires Intérieures. Inversion de courant: le conseil fut informé que dorénavant le projet devait respecter les plans de Griffin. Le conseil fut dissous en octobre 1913 et Griffin nommé directeur de l'urbanisme et de la construction de la capitale fédérale.

Le plan Griffin

L'approche urbanistique de Griffin reflète les préoccupations de cette période dominée par deux grands mouvements: la «cité-jardin» et la «belle cité». Cette dernière était profondément inspirée de l'Ecole des Beaux-Arts de Paris. Griffin avait découvert ce style lors de la foire internationale de Chicago de 1893 dont le décor urbain construit pour l'événement illustrait tous les principes de l'urbanisme «Beaux-Arts». La monumentalité et la lisibilité étaient des concepts-clé: l'urbanisme était essentiellement un problème d'esthétique. Le réseau de voirie était animé par des perspectives qui aboutissaient à un arc de triomphe, une église ou tout autre bâtiment d'échelle monumentale. L'ancien plan orthogonal (Washington) était remplacé par un plan plus varié mais symétrique, à base de triangles ou de cercles concentriques.
Si le style «cité-jardin», dont le théoricien fut Ebenezer Howard, faisait également appel à des rues en cercles concentriques, il favorisait les fonctions sociales de la ville par rapport à l'esthétique[3]. Les plans de Griffin témoignent de son intérêt pour ces deux styles.
Le livret du RIBA, dont la lecture avait été recommandée par le jury, contenait un article d'un urbaniste anglo-australien, John Sulman qui s'enthousiasmait pour l'intelligence des structures en toile d'araignée. Dans la même contribution, intitulée «La capitale fédérale de l'Australie», il donnait des exemples d'un plan radial et d'un plan en éventail. Griffin partageait les préférences de Sulman pour ce type de plan mais lui ajouta un élément venu de son expérience de Chicago: le traitement du paysage. Dans les plans concentriques classiques, les perspectives étaient souvent axées sur des monuments. Griffin préférait utiliser le paysage environnant, ce qui n'excluait pas, d'ailleurs, de positionner des édifices à l'extrémité d'une perspective. Il était conscient de ce qu'aucune ville, aussi démocratique soit-elle, n'existe sans monuments.
Griffin implanta les trois plus importants centres d'activité au sommet de trois collines formant un triangle équilatéral. Capitol Hill était réservée au centre administratif, City Hill (Mount Vernon) à la municipalité et Mount Pleasant et Mount Russel aux activités commerciales. Le triangle était divisé en deux par un axe. Une perspective, «Land-axis» (axe de terre), allait du Mount Ainslie en passant par le centre administratif, jusqu'au Mount Bimberi, le plus haut point du site (1912 m). Cet axe coupait à angle droit une ligne reliant le centre municipal et le centre commercial et à peu près parallèle à la rivière, d'où son nom de «Water-axis» (axe d'eau). Griffin avait prévu plusieurs plans d'eau: un grand lac en forme de combiné téléphonique, traversé par le «Land-Axis» et accompagné de deux plus petits sur chacun de ses côtés, alimentés grâce à un ingénieux système de détournement de la rivière.
Quelques satellites étaient créés autour des trois collines et reliés à la zone centrale par de larges avenues rectilignes, selon un motif triangulaire. Ces centres étaient entourés de boulevards de ceinture de forme octogonale. Le réseau de voirie secondaire était essentiellement orthogonal sauf lorsqu'il était interrompu par des parcs.
Griffin avait voulu créer une ville qui incarne et exalte les qualités démocratiques de l'Australie, ce qui explique, dans une certaine mesure qu'il s'éloigna de l'approche Beaux-Arts tout en en conservant certains de ses principes. Sans exception, ses monuments était soigneusement implantés et le nom des rues judicieusement choisi. Le même nombre de ministères se retrouvait sur Capitol Hill de chaque côté de l'axe de terre et la maison du gouverneur général faisait face à celle du Premier ministre tandis que le bâtiment du parlement était à cheval sur l'axe lui-même.
Si Griffin avait proposé un réel chef-d'œuvre et avait mérité de remporter la compétition, Saarinen avait lui aussi soumis un plan exceptionnel. Il s'était également appuyé sur deux axes perpendiculaires, mais avait projeté autour d'eux des réseaux de voirie circulaires. Son plan restait cependant assez majestueux et froid. Agache avait soumis un ennuyeux projet de style Beaux-Arts qui ignorait l'environnement, alors qu'à l'opposé, le plan préféré par le président Coane le prenait largement en compte et offrait beaucoup d'intérêt. Signé W. Scott Griffiths, Charles Gibbon Coulter et Charles Henry Casewell, il mêlait astucieusement des réseaux en triangles et en toile d'araignée.

1 *Seuls les bâtiments du parlement furent achevés dans les délais.*
2 *Expression de Patrick Abercrombie, urbaniste britannique.*
3 *Howard avait explicité ses théories dans Tomorrow – a Peaceful Path to Real Reform, Londres (1898).*

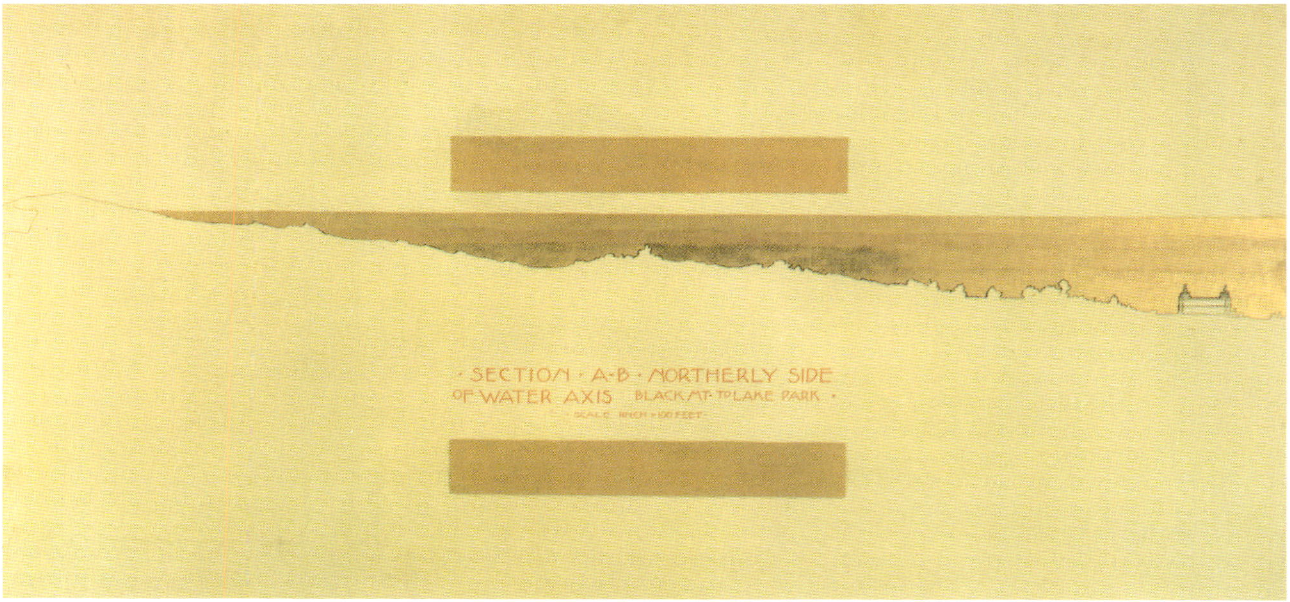

Walter Burley Griffin competition design, 1912, section of northerly side of water axis, Black Mountain to Lake Park, first prize

Walter Burley Griffin competition design, 1912, bird's eye view, first prize

Departmental Board of the Ministry for Home Affairs, execution design, 1912, plan of the central area

Eliel Saarinen competition design, 1912, plan of the central area, second prize

Eliel Saarinen competition design, 1912, map of the central area, second prize

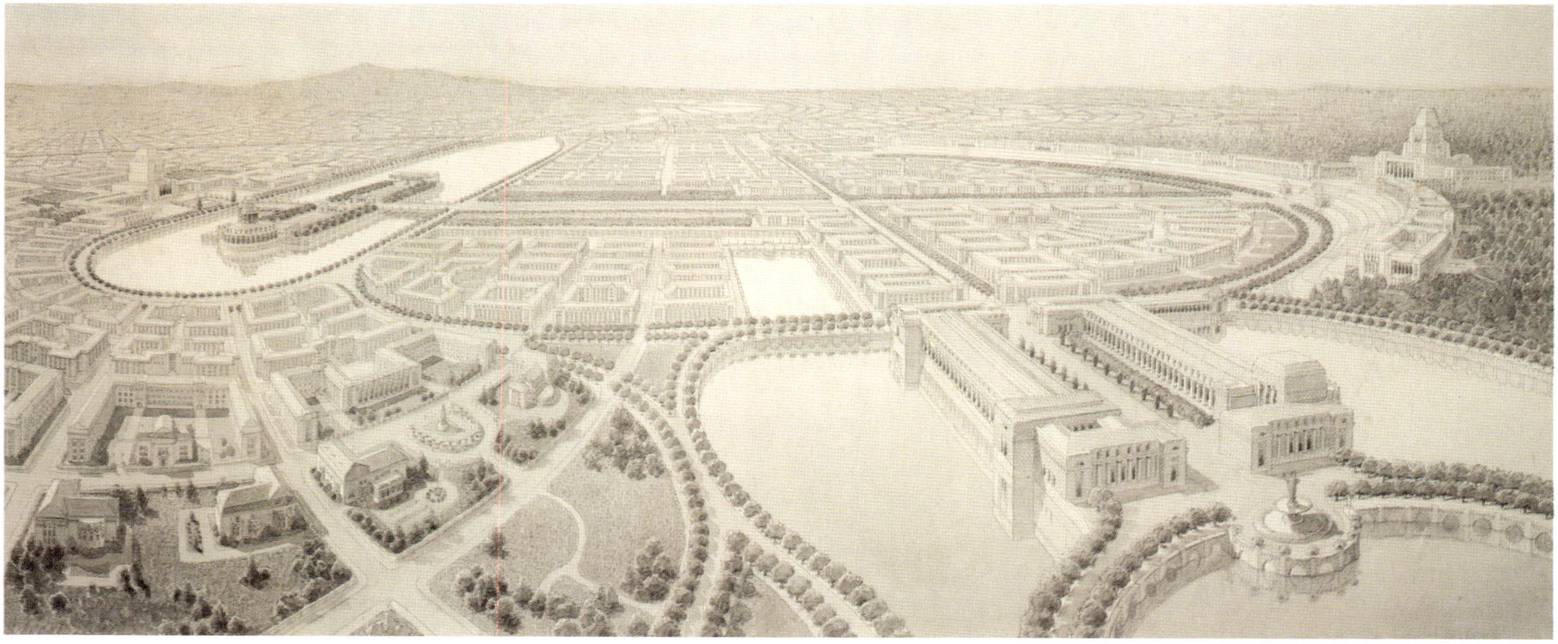

Eliel Saarinen competition design, 1912, bird's eye view, second prize

Eliel Saarinen competition design, 1912, exterior view, front of the Government Centre, second prize

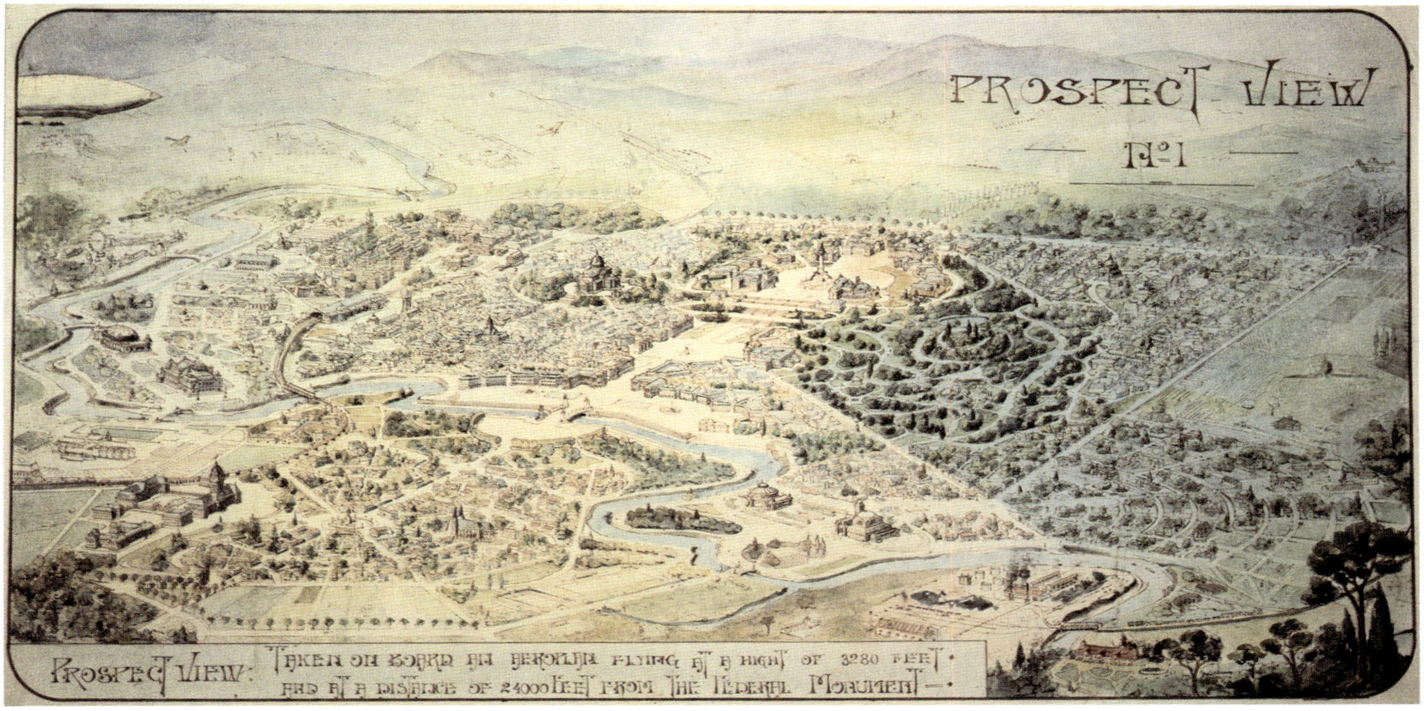

Donat-Alfred Agache competition design, 1912, detail Place of the People's Palace (site plan), third prize

Donat-Alfred Agache competition design, 1912, plan of the central area, third prize

Donat-Alfred Agache competition design, 1912, bird's eye view, third prize

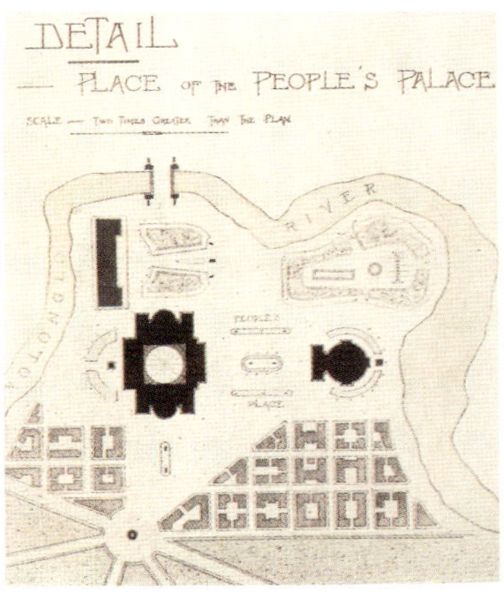

W. Scott Griffiths competition design, 1912, bird's eye view

W. Scott Griffiths competition design, 1912, bird's eye view

W. Scott Griffiths competition design, 1912, plan of the central area

Project

Office building for the Chicago Tribune

Site

North Michigan Avenue, Chicago

Dates

10 June 1922 to 1 November 1922 (1 December 1922 for participants from outside the USA)

Number of entries

263

Jury

Alfred Granger (AIA, Chairman), Captain Joseph M. Patterson, Colonel Robert R. McCormick, Edward S. Beck, Holmes Onderdonk (all Chicago Tribune); Howard L. Cheney (conditions and advice)

Result

First prize John Mead Howells & Raymond M. Hood (50 000 dollar) *Second prize* Eliel Saarinen (Finland, 20 000 dollar) *Third prize* Holabird & Roche (10 000 dollar); A.F. Adams was originally nominated for third prize. 20 000 dollar were divided amongst ten American architects who had been invited to participate

Commissioned by

The Chicago Tribune Company

Construction

1924 to 1925

Architects

John Mead Howells (1868–1959) & Raymond M. Hood (1881–1934)

Chicago Tribune Tower, 1922

John Mead Howells & Raymond M. Hood competition design, 1922, exterior view from south-west, first prize

Chicago Tribune Tower

Skyscrapers were no longer an architectural novelty in the United States when the competition for the Chicago Tribune Tower was held. The Chicago Tribune had not even intended to build the world's highest skyscraper. However, the competition programme had stipulated more than once that the Tower was to be the most beautiful and distinctive building in the world. The Chicago Tribune was one of the largest newspapers in the United States and was naturally more than capable of providing the necessary publicity for the project. This partly accounts for the widespread public interest in the competition. Many European architects also made a bid for first prize. The director of the Department of Architecture at Syracuse University (New York), Frederick W. Revels, even termed the competition the most significant event in architectural history since the professionalisation of architecture.

High-rise building in the United States

Two cities, each with their own style, pioneered skyscraper development in the United States: New York and Chicago. Throughout the history of the skyscraper these two cities alternately took the lead. Chicago deserves credit for taking the first significant steps. This city underwent exponential growth during the nineteenth century, particularly in the industrial sector. However, on 8 October 1871 this prosperity came to an abrupt end when an immense fire razed a third of the city to the ground, leaving one hundred thousand people homeless. In the long run, however, the fire would come to be seen as a blessing in disguise because it presented the opportunity to rebuild the city according to the latest urban planning and architectural principles. The Chicago we know today is largely a product of these principles. A regular, rectangular street pattern with high-rise buildings and skyscrapers.

One of the pioneers of American architecture was William Le Baron Jenney (1832–1907). Having gained technical expertise in the United States, he completed his education at the Académie des Beaux-Arts in Paris. At the time, many American architects boasted similar academic careers. One of Jenney's first successful designs was for the Leiter Building (1879). He incorporated all the features of the later skyscrapers in this building: a steel frame, a curtain wall, concrete floors and a fire-resistant structure. Jenney later embroidered upon this architectural form in his design for the famous Home Insurance Building (1884–1885)[1]. Striking features of Jenney's buildings are their angular austerity and sparse embellishments. His studio employed a number of young architects who later determined the face of Chicago architecture: William Holabird, Martin Roche, Daniel Burnham and Louis Sullivan, who was to become the most famous of the four. Sullivan designed many trend-setting buildings in Chicago, together with Dankmar Adler. Moreover, he was an influential theoretician in search of a new style to embody the spirit of the era. Consequently, Sullivan is seen as one of the pioneers of Modernism. His motto *"form follows function"* has become famous.

Holabird & Roche won third prize in the Chicago Tribune Tower competition. They had been invited to participate, along with a number of other American architects, all of whom were assured of a $ 2 000 participation fee. Holabird & Roche were extremely productive architects, whose firm expanded rapidly during the 1920s. Their high-rise buildings still showed traces of Jenney's influence, but were less innovative in some ways. The same may be said of Burnham's buildings. The latter had also been invited to participate.

Although Jenney, Sullivan and their successors determined the shape of the Chicago skyscraper, the city was also the home of another extremely influential architect: Frank Lloyd Wright (1867–1959). It is remarkable that Wright's influence was initially greater in Europe than in the United States. The American entries for the competition bear little resemblance to Wright's architecture but the designs submitted by their European colleagues show clear traces of an exchange of ideas.

New York

New York had a completely different architectural tradition. Unlike their colleagues in Chicago – who developed a skyscraper with a steel frame and a curtain wall – the New York architects seemed less in search of a new style for a new era. They concealed the structure of their buildings behind imaginative façades which had a distinctly European flavour. Italian palazzi rub shoulders with Gothic cathedral spires. Each skyscraper has its own imaginative pinnacle, ranging from the mausoleum of Halicarnassus to a Graeco-Roman temple or even a simple Egyptian pyramid.

Whereas Chicago was the city of Holabird & Roche and Burnham & Root, New York was the domain of McKim, Mead & White. These architects are better known for the European language of forms they applied in their buildings than for the high-rise buildings they designed. From 1880 to 1882, their firm employed the young architect Cass Gilbert (1859–1934). Gilbert's Woolworth Building in New York was clearly a product of his view that Gothic was the most suitable style for skyscrapers. This luxurious building, which was briefly the world's highest, was the object of widespread admiration.

Thus there were two movements in American architecture. Their champions were to meet during the Chicago Tribune Tower

An advertisement in 'La Libre Belgique', announcing the Chicago Tribune competition

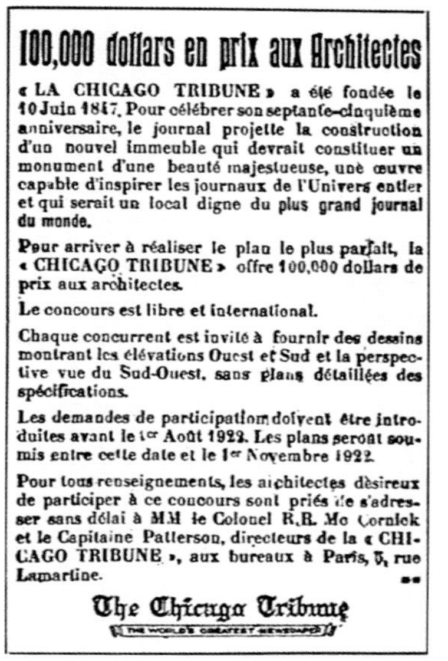

100,000 dollars en prix aux Architectes

« LA CHICAGO TRIBUNE » a été fondée le 10 Juin 1847. Pour célébrer son septante-cinquième anniversaire, le journal projette la construction d'un nouvel immeuble qui devrait constituer un monument d'une beauté majestueuse, une œuvre capable d'inspirer les journaux de l'Univers entier et qui serait un local digne du plus grand journal du monde.

Pour arriver à réaliser le plan le plus parfait, la « CHICAGO TRIBUNE » offre 100,000 dollars de prix aux architectes.

Le concours est libre et international.

Chaque concurrent est invité à fournir des dessins montrant les élévations Ouest et Sud et la perspective vue du Sud-Ouest, sans plans détaillées des spécifications.

Les demandes de participation doivent être introduites avant le 1er Août 1922. Les plans seront soumis entre cette date et le 1er Novembre 1922.

Pour tous renseignements, les architectes désireux de participer à ce concours sont priés de s'adresser sans délai à MM le Colonel R.R. Mc Cormick et le Capitaine Patterson, directeurs de la « CHICAGO TRIBUNE », aux bureaux à Paris, 5, rue Lamartine.

The Chicago Tribune

THE WORLD'S GREATEST NEWSPAPER

Raymond M. Hood

John Mead Howells

competition. The competition itself gave a new impetus to American skyscraper development: 135 of the 263 entries were exhibited in 27 American cities.

The Competition

The competition was announced on 10 June 1922, which was a historic date for the Chicago Tribune because on the same day in 1847 the newspaper's circulation had reached four thousand copies for the first time. In 1902, the newspaper had moved to Madison Avenue but these premises soon became too small. Around 1920, the Chicago Tribune's weekly circulation was four million copies and the newspaper employed 3 100 people.

The Tribune had decided to organise the competition to celebrate the paper's diamond jubilee. The prize money amounted to no less than $ 100 000. The new building was to house all departments of the newspaper, with the exception of the printing presses. These were housed in a building situated in the triangle between the Chicago river and Michigan Avenue. The tower was to be built directly opposite the presses on Michigan Avenue and diagonally across from the impressive Wrigley Building.

The competition was presented as the premier architectural event of the century. The Chicago Tribune's bond with the city was strong and the construction of the most beautiful building in the world seemed to be an appropriate gift. The list of conditions in the competition programme was brief. The building was to be beautiful and impressive and its practical purpose was to be taken into account. It goes without saying that the architects also had to keep to the Chicago building regulations. Although the building area and height were stipulated, the architects were allowed to determine the number of floors. Only one article of the competition programme was devoted to these conditions. The competition regulations were a little more detailed. No less than seventeen articles had been drafted to guarantee that the competition would be fair. For example, it had been stipulated that the winner of the $ 50 000 first prize would not necessarily be commissioned. However, if this was the case, the prize money would be the first installment of the salary. In contrast to many European competitions, the Chicago Tribune Tower competition did not trigger a scandal. Another unique aspect of the competition was that it had been organised by a private company and not by the state.

Entries

Nearly one hundred of the 263 entries had been submitted by architects from outside the United States. Most of these designs were 'modern' and had been submitted by German (39), Italian (12) and Dutch (11) architects. The last architect to submit his design was the Finn Eliel Saarinen. Foreign architects had been given an extra month to submit their designs. Saarinen's design arrived two days before the closing date. Although the jury had already nominated the winners, they were so impressed by Saarinen's entry that they immediately awarded second prize to him. The jury was particularly taken by the unsurpassed harmony of the design.

This left the jury with the niggling problem of the third prize: should they award it to the former runner-up or to the original third-prize nominee. Initially, their decision to nominate the former runner-up, Holabird & Roche, was not unanimous. This was undoubtedly due to the floor plans, although the jury report makes no mention of this fact. The superstructure of this design – a massive statue in a Gothic niche – seems a little ludicrous. The unfortunate third-prize nominee, Arthur Frederick Adams, had submitted a design which consisted of five blocks stacked on top of one another. The blocks decreased in size towards the top. Saarinen had done the same, but Adams' blocks were less well-proportioned.

Adams' design was a free Gothic exercise, as were many of the other American entries. The Woolworth Building and the nearby Wrigley building, designed by Graham, Probst & White (1921), served as prototypes. One of the other designs in this category had been submitted by John Howells and Raymond Hood. Their design featured striking, non-functional sky arches on the pinnacle. Howells and Hood believed that Gothic casing was merely an architectural fad. They therefore concentrated on the floor plan and the structure, which justly deserved the jury's emphatic approval.

Gothic was not the only European style which was applied. Some architects even managed to incorporate all these styles in a single design. Many European architects no longer considered their own

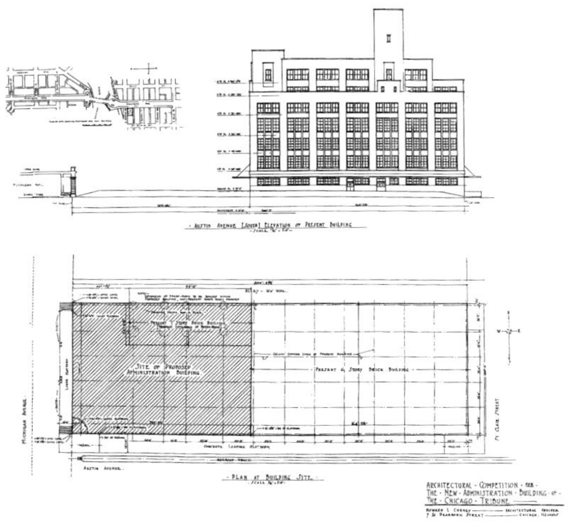

The location for the Tribune Tower, above: elevation on Austin Avenue, (a building on the right hand is the existing plan) below: site plan

Hans Scharoun competition design, sketch (not submitted)

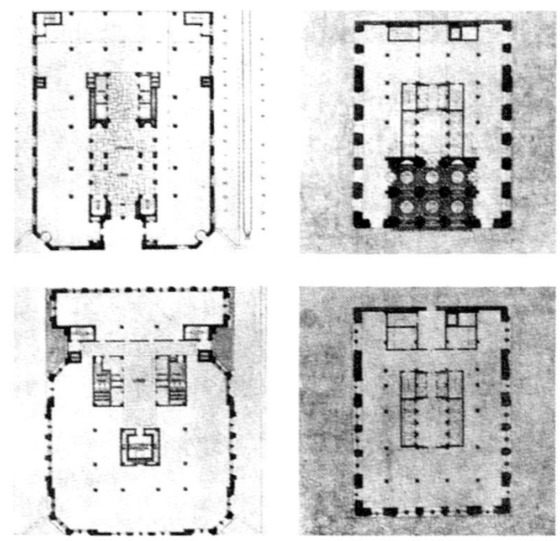

Left: ***John Mead Howells & Raymond M. Hood*** competition design, entrance floor plan (above), typical floor plan, (below)
Right: ***Eliel Saarinen*** competition design, entrance floor plan (above), typical floor plan (below)

culture a challenge and German and Dutch architects, in particular, submitted interesting modern designs.

In their report, the jury made little mention of the foreign architects who had taken the trouble to participate. They patronisingly concluded that the competition had proved the superiority of the American architects. They also mocked the fact that Saarinen had been the only European who was any match for the Americans, though he was from the little country of Finland and not even from one of the renowned cultural capitals in England, France or Italy. It is worth mentioning that the architects abandoned by the jury were certainly not insignificant: Adolf Loos, Walter Gropius & Hannes Meyer, Bruno Taut, Hans Scharoun and J. Duiker & B. Bijvoet. Their designs were exhibited throughout the United States, which is probably the most important aspect of the competition because it presented American architects with the perfect opportunity to become acquainted with Modernism. Although Hood's design certainly also had notable qualities, it no longer appeals to our imagination.

Further events

One of the most significant European skyscraper designs was not submitted for the competition. Nevertheless, Ludwig Mies van der Rohe's (1921) experimental design for a skyscraper in Berlin did become famous. Mies van der Rohe's innovative design was based on reflection against a flat façade, rather than on the interplay between light and shadow. Mies would later educate an entire generation of American architects at the Illinois Institute of Technology in Chicago, thereby perpetuating the Modernist tradition established by Sullivan. The fact that not all architecture in the United States was necessarily angular and modern is borne out by the counter current of architects who clad their new and awesome structures in an old coat, which often, quite remarkably, suited them very well. Raymond Hood was one of these architects.

1 *The steel frame and the curtain wall in the Leiter Building were not entirely to his satisfaction.*

Chicago Tribune Tower

Als die Ausschreibung für den Chicago Tribune Tower veröffentlicht wurde, galten Wolkenkratzer in den Vereinigten Staaten längst nicht mehr als architektonische Novität. Die Wettbewerbsbedingungen sahen daher auch nicht eines der höchsten Bürogebäude Amerikas vor, sondern forderten von den Teilnehmern den Bau des schönsten und markantesten Gebäudes der Welt. Allein der Name des Bauherrn, die Chicago Tribune war eine der größten Zeitungen der USA, sorgte für die nötige Publizität, und das öffentliche Interesse an diesem Wettbewerb war groß. Viele europäische Architekten beteiligten sich an der Ausschreibung; der Direktor des Instituts für Architektur an der Syracuse University, Frederick W. Revels, bezeichnete den Wettbewerb als das bedeutendste Ereignis der Architekturgeschichte seit der Professionalisierung des Berufszweiges.

Hochhausbau in den USA

Zwei amerikanische Städte waren tonangebend in der Geschichte der Hochhausarchitektur: New York und Chicago. Beide prägten ihren eigenen Stil und lösten einander regelmäßig in der Vorreiterposition ab. Chicago kam jedoch die Ehre zu, die ersten Schritte in diese Richtung unternommen zu haben. Die Stadt war im 19. Jahrhundert ungewöhnlich schnell gewachsen; insbesondere auf dem industriellen Sektor. Am 8. Oktober 1871 kam die wachsende Prosperität beinahe völlig zum Erliegen, als ein Großbrand etwa ein Drittel der Stadt in Schutt und Asche legte und 100 000 Menschen obdachlos wurden. Dennoch sollte sich dieser Brand im Nachhinein als ein Segen herausstellen, denn er ermöglichte den Neubau der Stadt nach neuesten stadtplanerischen und architektonischen Gesichtspunkten. Das heutige Stadtzentrum ist ein Resultat dieses Neuaufbaus: eine rechteckige Straßenanlage, bebaut mit Hochhäusern.
Einer der Pioniere der amerikanischen Baukunst war William Le Baron Jenney (1832–1907). Nachdem er in den USA sein technisches Wissen erworben hatte, schloß er seine Ausbildung an der Pariser Académie des Beaux-Arts ab – ein durchaus üblicher Weg für einen amerikanischen Architekten der damaligen Zeit. Zu seinen ersten Bauwerken gehört das First Leiter Building (1879). Bereits hier finden sich alle Merkmale der späteren Wolkenkratzer: ein Stahlskelett, nicht-tragende Außenwände, Betonböden und eine feuerbeständige Konstruktion. Diesen Prototyp entwickelte Jenney in seinem berühmten Home Insurance Building (1884/85) zur Perfektion.
In seinem Architekturbüro beschäftigte Jenney eine Reihe junger Leute, deren Arbeiten das Gesicht Chicagos in späteren Jahren bestimmen sollten: William Holabird, Martin Roche, Daniel Burnham und Louis Sullivan. Holabird und Roche errangen mit ihrem Wettbewerbsbeitrag zum Chicago Tribune Tower den dritten Preis, allerdings gehörten sie zu den zehn eingeladenen amerikanischen Architekten, die ohnehin je 2000 Dollar erhielten. Beide galten als extrem produktive Vertreter ihres Fachs, entsprechend verzeichnete ihre Firma in den 20er Jahren ein rapides Ansteigen der Aufträge. Holabirds und Roches' Hochbauten lassen noch einiges vom Einfluß Jenneys erahnen; dennoch sind ihre Gebäude wenig innovativ.

New York

Im Gegensatz zu Chicago entstanden in New York keine Wolkenkratzer mit einem Stahlskelett und Blendwänden, und die Architekten begaben sich auch nicht auf die Suche nach einem neuen, zeitgemäßen Stil. Sie verbargen ihre Konstruktionen lieber hinter phantasievoll gestalteten, europäisch anmutenden Außenfassaden. Italienische Palazzi stehen brüderlich neben gotischen Kathedraltürmen. Jedes Hochhaus besaß seine eigene charakteristische Bekrönung: Ein Nachbau des Mausoleums von Halikarnassos, ein griechisch-römischer Tempel oder eine schlichte ägyptische Pyramide.

Während in Chicago Holabird und Roche sowie Burnham und Root zu den bekanntesten Büros zählten, galten in New York McKim, Mead und White als führend. Diese Architekten waren weniger für ihre Hochbaukonstruktionen als für ihre Beherrschung der europäischen Formensprache bekannt. Zwischen 1880 und 1882 arbeitete in ihrem Büro der junge Baumeister Cass Gilbert (1859–1934), dessen späteres Woolworth Building (1911–1913) den gotischen Stil in die Hochhausarchitektur einführte. Dieses luxuriöse Bauwerk – für kurze Zeit das höchste der Welt – erregte im ganzen Land große Aufmerksamkeit.

Der Wettkampf

Die Ausschreibung für den Chicago Tribune Tower wurde am 10. Juni 1922 veröffentlicht – an diesem Datum war 1847 die erste Ausgabe der Chicago Tribune in einer Auflage von 4000 Stück erschienen. Um 1920 lag die wöchentliche Auflage bei vier Millionen Exemplaren, und das Blatt beschäftigte 3100 Mitarbeiter.
Zur Feier des diamantenen Jubiläums entschloß man sich, einen Wettbewerb auszuschreiben, dessen Preisgelder rund 100 000 Dollar betrugen. Im neuen Gebäude sollten alle Abteilungen der Tribune Platz finden; nur die Druckerei behielt ihren alten Sitz im Dreieck zwischen dem Chicago River und der Michigan Avenue. Der Vorstand des Verlags entschied sich für ein Baugrundstück an der Michigan Avenue, das der Druckerei genau gegenüber lag, in direkter Nähe zum Wrigley Building.
Der Wettbewerb wurde als das architektonische Ereignis des Jahrhunderts präsentiert: Die Chicago Tribune fühle sich so eng mit der Stadt verbunden, daß sie ihr das schönste Gebäude der Welt zum Geschenk machen wollte. Dieses markante Motto bildete neben den funktionellen Anforderungen an ein Zeitungsgebäude die einzige Auflage, die die teilnehmenden Architekten zu erfüllen hatten. Ihre Entwürfe waren zwar an die Bauvorschriften der Stadt Chicago gebunden, aber die Anzahl der Stockwerke blieb ihnen überlassen. Nur die Grundfläche und Gesamthöhe des Gebäudes wurden vorgegeben. Die gesamten Bauauflagen nahmen in der Wettbewerbsausschreibung einen einzigen Passus ein. Dagegen waren die Wettbewerbsregeln genauer ausgearbeitet: Nicht weniger als 17 Artikel sollten einen fairen und ehrlichen Wettbewerb garantieren. Unter anderem war festgelegt worden, daß der Gewinner der 50 000 Dollar nicht automatisch auch den Bauauftrag erhielt. Falls dies doch der Fall sein würde, sollte das Preisgeld als erster Teil seines Honorars gelten. Im Gegensatz zu vielen europäischen Architekturwettbewerben ging die Ausschreibung zum Chicago Tribune Tower ohne jeden Skandal vonstatten. Außergewöhnlich war auch, daß es sich beim Auftraggeber diesmal nicht um eine staatliche Behörde, sondern um eine Firma handelte.

Die Einsendungen

Von den 263 Einsendungen stammten etwa 100 von Architekten außerhalb der Vereinigten Staaten. Die meisten dieser Entwürfe waren im Stil der Moderne gehalten und kamen vorwiegend aus Deutschland (39), aber auch aus Italien (12) und den Niederlanden (11).
Als letzter Teilnehmer reichte der Finne Eliel Saarinen seine Pläne ein. Ausländischen Architekten war ein zusätzlicher Monat Zeit gewährt worden, und Saarinens Zeichnungen kamen genau zwei Tage vor Einsendeschluß, als die Jury ihre Preisträger schon benannt hatte. Sein Beitrag beeindruckte die Jurymitglieder jedoch dermaßen, daß sie Saarinen auf der Stelle mit dem zweiten Preis auszeichneten; besonders hervorgehoben wurde die Harmonie des Entwurfs.
Nun stellte sich der Jury die knifflige Frage, wer den dritten Preis erhalten sollte – der ehemalige Zweite oder der bisherige Dritte. Durch Abstimmung kam eine Entscheidung für die ehemaligen Zweiten – Holabird und Roche – zustande. Obwohl offiziell nichts darüber bekannt ist, gaben wohl die Grundrisse den Ausschlag zugunsten dieses Entwurfs. Dagegen wirkt der Oberbau – eine gigantische Statue in einer gotischen Nische – beinahe lächerlich. Der unglückliche ehemalige Dritte, Arthur Frederick Adams, hatte ebenso wie Saarinen eine Reihe von fünf immer kleineren Blöcken aufeinandergestapelt; allerdings waren bei Adams die Proportionen nicht so gut gelungen.
Außer Adams beteiligten sich auch die meisten anderen amerikanischen Architekten mit Beiträgen, die an eine freie Übung im Stil der Gotik erinnerten. Das Woolworth Building oder das dem Tribune Tower gegenüber liegende Wrigley Building von Graham, Probst & White (1921) hatten ihnen als Prototypen gedient. Auch der Entwurf von John Mead Howells und Raymond M. Hood gehört in diese Kategorie. Auffällig an ihrem Beitrag sind die funktionslosen Strebepfeiler an der Bekrönung. Howells und Hood sahen die gotische Fassade als eine reine Modeerscheinung und konzentrierten sich auf den Grundriß und die Gliederung, die mit Recht von der Jury gepriesen wurden.
Aber nicht nur die Gotik, sondern auch andere europäische Stilrichtungen traten im Wettbewerb gegeneinander an – einige Beiträge kombinierten sogar sämtliche Stile miteinander. Allerdings waren viele Europäer ihrer eigenen Kultur überdrüssig geworden und sandten moderne Entwürfe ein.
Der Bericht der Jury beschäftigte sich kaum mit den ausländischen Beiträgen, sondern stellte zufrieden fest, daß der Wettbewerb die führende Rolle der amerikanischen Architektur bestätigt hatte. Ein wenig spöttisch merkte man an, daß nur Saarinen sich mit den Amerikanern messen könne – und das, obwohl er aus dem kleinen Finnland und nicht aus einem bedeutenden kulturellen Zentrum wie England, Frankreich oder Italien stamme. Dabei waren es nicht die schlechtesten Namen, die von der Jury übersehen wurden: Adolf Loos, Walter Gropius und Hannes Meyer, Bruno Taut, Hans Scharoun sowie J. Duiker und B. Bijvoet. Die Entwürfe dieser Architekten wurden in zahlreichen Städten der USA ausgestellt. Dadurch erhielten amerikanische Architekten die Möglichkeit, sich ausführlich mit der Moderne auseinanderzusetzen. Obwohl Hoods Entwurf sicherlich eigenständige Qualitäten besaß, hat er heute an Anziehungskraft verloren.

La Tour du Chicago Tribune

Les gratte-ciel n'étaient déjà plus une nouveauté aux Etats-Unis lorsque se déroula le concours pour la Chicago Tribune Tower. Le journal n'avait pas l'intention de construire la tour la plus haute du monde mais le programme précisait à plusieurs reprises que cette tour devait être «le plus bel et plus élégant édifice de l'univers». Le Chicago Tribune était l'un des plus grands journaux des Etats-Unis et donc en mesure d'assurer la publicité nécessaire au projet, ce qui explique sans doute son retentissement national auprès du grand public. Le directeur du département d'architecture de l'Université de Syracuse (New York), Frederick W. Revels, le qualifia même de «plus important événement de l'histoire de l'architecture depuis qu'existe la profession d'architecte».

Les immeubles de grande hauteur aux Etats-Unis

Deux villes, New York et Chicago, chacune dans son propre style, ouvrirent la voie au développement des immeubles de grande hauteur aux Etats-Unis. Chacune d'entre elles mena alternativement la course, mais Chicago doit être créditée des premiers vrais débuts de ce type d'immeuble. La ville, qui avait connu une croissance exponentielle au XIXème siècle, en particulier pour les activités industrielles, avait vu sa prospérité brusquement compromise le 8 octobre 1871 par un gigantesque incendie qui détruisit un tiers de sa surface, faisant cent mille sans-abri. Cette catastrophe apparut par la suite comme une sorte de bénédiction puisqu'elle permit de reconstruire la cité selon des principes urbanistiques et architecturaux modernes. Le Chicago d'aujourd'hui, son plan orthogonal et ses grands immeubles, est né de cet événement.

William Le Baron Jenney (1832–1907) fut l'un des pionniers de l'architecture américaine. Après avoir appris son métier en Amérique, il partit se perfectionner à l'Ecole des Beaux-Arts de Paris. A l'époque, de nombreux architectes américains étaient fiers de pouvoir bénéficier d'une formation européenne. L'un des premiers succès de Jenney fut le Leiter Building (1879) dans lequel se retrouvent déjà toutes les spécificités des futurs gratte-ciel: ossature d'acier, mur-rideau, niveaux en béton et structure résistant au feu. Jenney déclina cette forme architecturale dans son plan pour le célèbre immeuble de Home Insurance (1884–1885)[1]. Son agence employa plusieurs des jeunes architectes qui allaient bientôt changer le visage de la ville: William Holabird, Martin Roche, Daniel Burnham et Louis Sullivan.

Holabird et Roche, invités parmi d'autres à concourir contre une indemnité de 2 000 $, remportèrent le troisième prix du concours du journal.

Si Jenney, Sullivan et leurs successeurs déterminèrent la forme du gratte-ciel de Chicago, la ville était aussi la terre d'élection d'un autre grand architecte, Frank Lloyd Wright (1867–1959), dont l'influence fut au début plus grande en Europe qu'aux Etats-Unis. Les projets américains pour le concours ne portaient guère la marque du style Wright alors que ceux venus d'Europe reflétaient certaines de ses idées.

New York

La tradition de New York était toute différente. Alors que leurs confrères de Chicago inventaient le gratte-ciel à ossature d'acier et mur-rideau, les New-yorkais paraissaient moins intéressés par la mise au point d'un style contemporain. Ils masquaient les structures de leurs immeubles derrière des façades dans le goût européen, très décorées, évoquant tantôt un palais italien, tantôt une cathédrale gothique, flèche comprise. Chaque gratte-ciel se terminait ainsi par une touche personnelle qui pouvait rappeler aussi bien le mausolée d'Halicarnasse, qu'un temple gréco-romain ou une pyramide égyptienne.

New York était le domaine réservé de McKim, Mead et White, architectes plus connus pour leur habileté à manipuler les formes architecturales européennes que pour leurs immeubles de grande hauteur. De 1880 à 1882, leur agence employa Cass Gilbert (1859–1934) dont le fameux Woolworth Building (1911–1913) reflétait cette conception étrange qui voulait que le gothique soit le style par excellence des gratte-ciel. Cette luxueuse tour, brièvement la plus haute du monde, était fort admirée.

Deux mouvements coexistaient ainsi dans l'architecture américaine. Leurs champions allaient s'affronter à l'occasion du concours du Chicago Tribune qui se proposait aussi de donner une nouvelle impulsion au développement des immeubles de grande hauteur: 135 des 263 projets présentés furent d'ailleurs exposés dans 27 villes américaines.

Le concours

La Tribune avait décidé d'organiser un concours d'architecture doté d'un budget de $ 100 000 pour célébrer son jubilé de diamant.

La compétition fut annoncée le 10 juin 1922, date historique pour le Chicago Tribune puisque le même jour, en 1847, sa diffusion avait atteint 4 000 exemplaires. En 1902, le journal avait déménagé pour Madison Avenue dans des locaux devenus vite trop petits. Vers 1920, sa diffusion hebdomadaire s'élevait à 4 millions d'exemplaires et il employait 3 100 personnes. Le concours était présenté comme le grand événement architectural du siècle. Le lien entre le journal et sa ville était très fort et la construction du plus beau bâtiment du monde pouvait presque apparaître comme un cadeau à la cité.

L'immeuble prévu devait accueillir tous les départements du journal à l'exception des presses, installées dans un bâtiment situé dans le triangle entre la Chicago River et Michigan Avenue. La tour devait être construite sur Michigan Avenue, face à l'imprimerie et non loin de l'impressionnant Wrigley Building.

La liste des stipulations du programme était brève mais il va sans dire que les architectes devaient respecter les règlements de construction de la ville. Si le site et la hauteur leur étaient bien précisés, ils restaient libres de déterminer le nombre de niveaux. Un seul article du cahier des charges avait trait aux contraintes techniques.

Le règlement du concours était en revanche plus détaillé puisque pas moins de 17 articles garantissaient l'objectivité de la compétition. Il était indiqué, par exemple, que le lauréat qui gagnerait les $ 50 000 ne remporterait pas forcément la commande, mais que si c'était le cas, son prix serait considéré comme une avance sur honoraires. A la différence de nombreux concours européens, celui du Chicago Tribune, organisé par une société privée et non par un Etat ne s'acheva pas dans un scandale.

Participations

Presque cent des 263 participations furent soumises par des architectes étrangers qui disposaient d'un mois de plus que les Américains pour travailler: 39 par des Allemands, 12 par des Italiens et 11 par des Néerlandais. La plupart de ces projets étaient d'esprit moderniste.

Le dernier reçu – deux jours avant la date de clôture – fut celui du Finlandais Eliel Saarinen. Bien que le jury ait déjà désigné les gagnants, il fut si impressionné par cette nouvelle proposition et sa merveilleuse harmonie qu'il lui accorda immédiatement le second prix.

Que faire alors pour le troisième prix? Fallait-il l'attribuer au titulaire du second prix d'avant l'irruption de Saarinen ou au suivant? La décision de donner le second prix à Holabird et Roche n'avait pas été pas unanime. Les réserves des jurés tenaient indubitablement au plan masse, même si le jury ne l'avait pas mentionné et la superstructure, ornée d'une massive statue logée dans une niche gothique, semblait légèrement ridicule. Le malheureux troisième prix avait proposé un plan consistant en cinq blocs de taille décroissante, empilés les uns sur les autres. C'était un peu la proposition de Saarinen, la qualité des proportions en moins.

Comme beaucoup de projets américains, le plan d'Adams était une libre improvisation sur le style gothique. Le Woolworth Building et le Wrigley Building de Graham, Probst et White (1921), tout proches, l'avaient visiblement inspiré. L'un des autres projets de cette catégorie avait été envoyé par John Howells et Raymond Hood. Il se caractérisait par son sommet couronné d'une étonnante armature purement décorative. Howells et Hood pensaient que le gothique n'était qu'une lubie architecturale et s'étaient plutôt attachés au plan de masse et à la structure pour se gagner l'intérêt du jury.

Le gothique ne fut pas le seul style européen mis à contribution et certains projets combinaient toutes les sources stylistiques de la tradition. En revanche, les citations culturelles ne faisaient déjà plus partie des préoccupations des architectes européens. Les Allemands et les Néerlandais, en particulier, soumirent d'intéressants projets modernes.

Dans leur rapport, les jurés ne mentionnèrent guère les concurrents étrangers. Sur un ton suffisant, ils conclurent que le concours avait prouvé la supériorité américaine. Ils se moquèrent même de ce qu'un seul étranger, Saarinen, ait égalé les Américains alors qu'il venait de la petite Finlande et non pas de l'une des grandes capitales européennes. Ces commentaires s'appliquaient à des architectes aussi importants qu'Adolf Loos, Walter Gropius et Hannes Meyer, Bruno Taut, Hans Scharoun ainsi que J. Duiker et B. Bijvoet. Leurs projets furent cependant retenus pour l'exposition itinérante du concours qui donna à beaucoup de praticiens américains la possibilité de se familiariser avec le modernisme.

Si le projet finalement retenu, celui de Hood, présentait de réelles qualités, il ne parle plus guère aujourd'hui à notre imagination. Toute l'architecture américaine n'était pas nécessairement moderne et d'esprit cubiste. Un fort courant continua quelque temps à revêtir des structures techniquement très modernes et de taille impressionnante avec les vieux habits de la tradition, ce qui leur allait parfois très bien. Raymond Hood se rattache à ce mouvement.

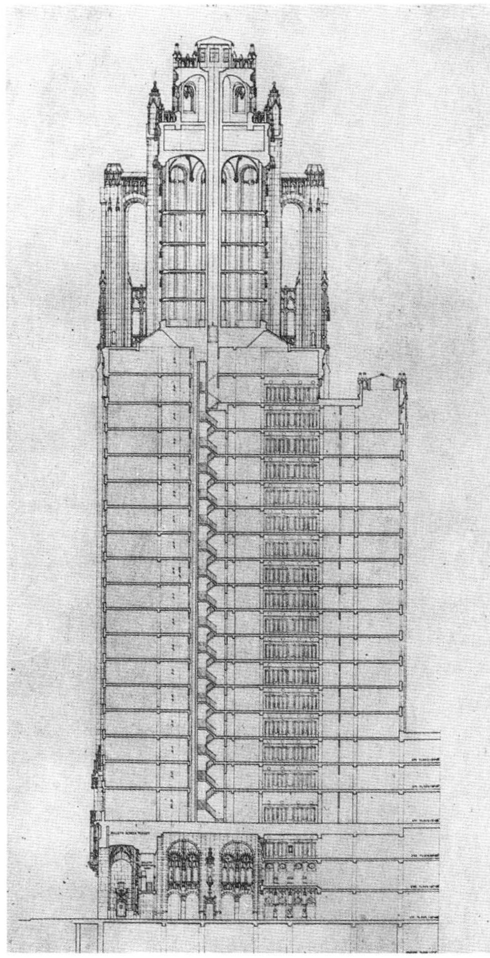

John Mead Howells & Raymond M. Hood competition design, 1922, elevation on Austin Avenue, first prize

John Mead Howells & Raymond M. Hood competition design, 1922, east-west section, first prize

Eliel Saarine competition design, 1922, east-west section, second prize

Eliel Saarinen competition design, 1922, elevation on Michigan Avenue, second prize

Eliel Saarinen competition design, 1922, exterior view from south-west, second prize

Holabird & Roche competition design, 1922, exterior view south-west, third prize

Walter Burley Griffin competition design, 1922, exterior perspective

Max Taut competition design, 1922, exterior view

CHICAGO
TRIBUNE

Walter Fischer competition design, 1922, exterior view

Bertram G. Goodhue competition design, 1922, exterior view, honourable mention

Albert J. Rousseau competition design, 1922, exterior view, honourable mention

Rudolph Eckmann competition design, 1922, exterior perspective

Adolf Loos competition design, 1922 exterior view

Alfred Fellheimer & Steward Wagner competition design, 1922, exterior view, honourable mention

Frank Fort competition design, 1922, exterior view, honourable mention

Walter Gropius & Adolf Meyer competition design, 1922, model

Gerhard Schroeder competition design, 1922, exterior view

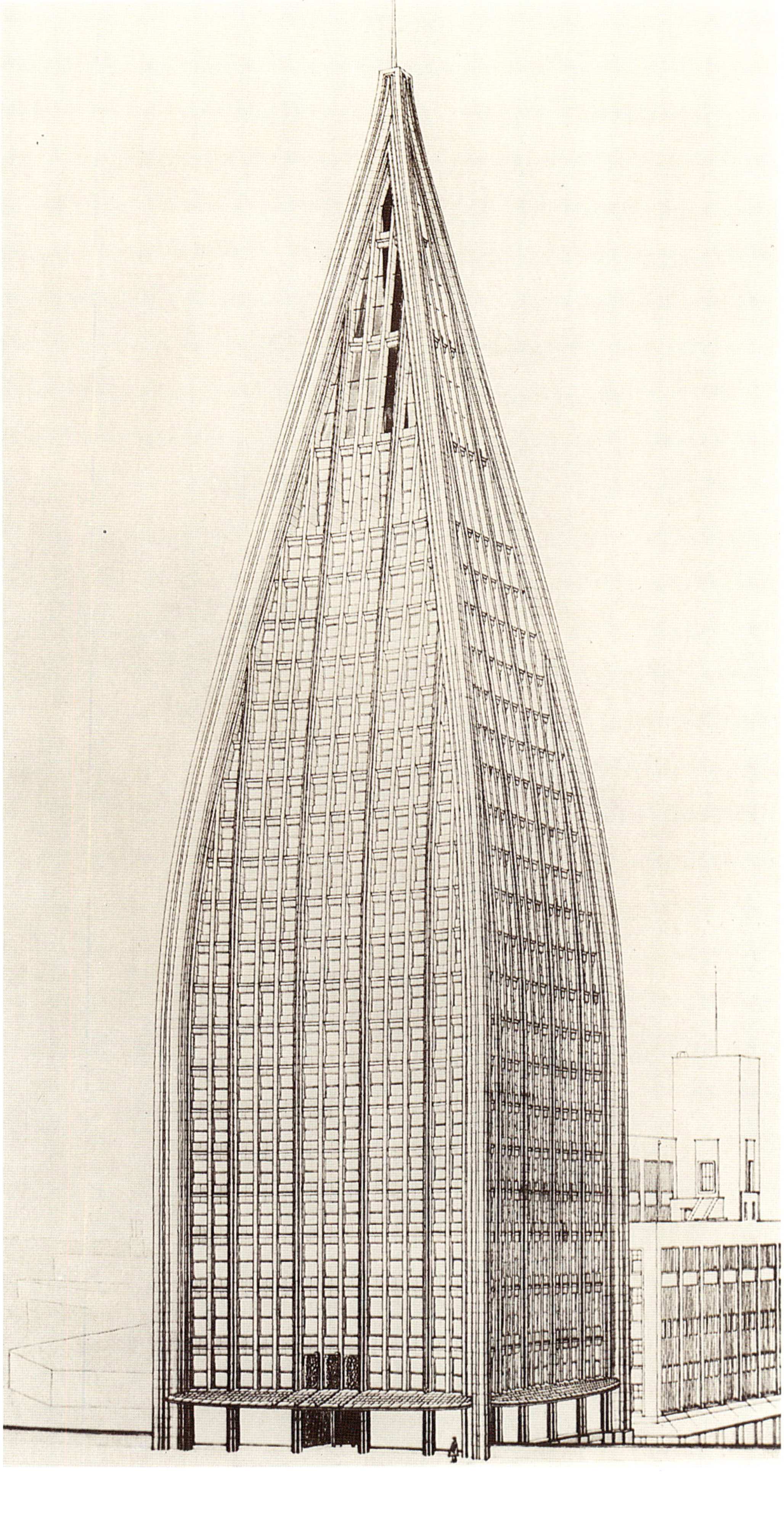

Bruno Taut, Walter Gunther & Kurz Schutz competition design, 1922, exterior view

Frank Herding & W.W. Boyd Jr. competition design, 1922, exterior view

Anonymous competition design, 1922, exterior view

Project

League of Nations Headquarters

Site

La Perle du Lac, Geneva (later renamed Parc de l'Ariana)

Dates

April 1926 to 25 January 1927

Result announced

5 May 1927

Number of entries

377

Jury

Victor Horta (Brussels, Chairman), H.P. Berlage (The Hague), Charles Henri Camille Lemaresquier (Paris), John J. Burnet (London), Koloman Moser (Zurich), Carlos Gato (Madrid), Attilio Muggia (Bologna), Josef Hoffmann (Vienna), Ivar Tengbom (Stockholm)

Result

Le Corbusier & Pierre Jeanneret (Paris); Nils Einar Eriksson (Stockholm); Emil Fahrenkamp & Albert Deneke (Dusseldorf); Henri Paul Nénot (Paris) & Julien Flegenheimer (Geneva); Carlo Broggi, Giuseppe Vaccaro & Luigi Franzi (Rome); Camille Lefèvre (Paris); Erich zu Putlitz, Rudolf Klophaus & August Schoch (Hamburg); Georges-Antoine-Pierre-Albert Labro (Paris); Giuseppe Vago (Rome). In addition, nine designs received a honourable mention as first runner-up and nine designs received a honourable mention as second runner-up

Commissioned by

The League of Nations

Construction

1929 to 1937

Architects

Henri Paul Nénot & Julien Flegenheimer; Carlo Broggi; Camille Lefèvre; Giuseppe Vago

League of Nations Building, Geneva, 1926

Le Corbusier & Pierre Jeanneret
competition design, 1927, elevation
on Lake Leman, first prize

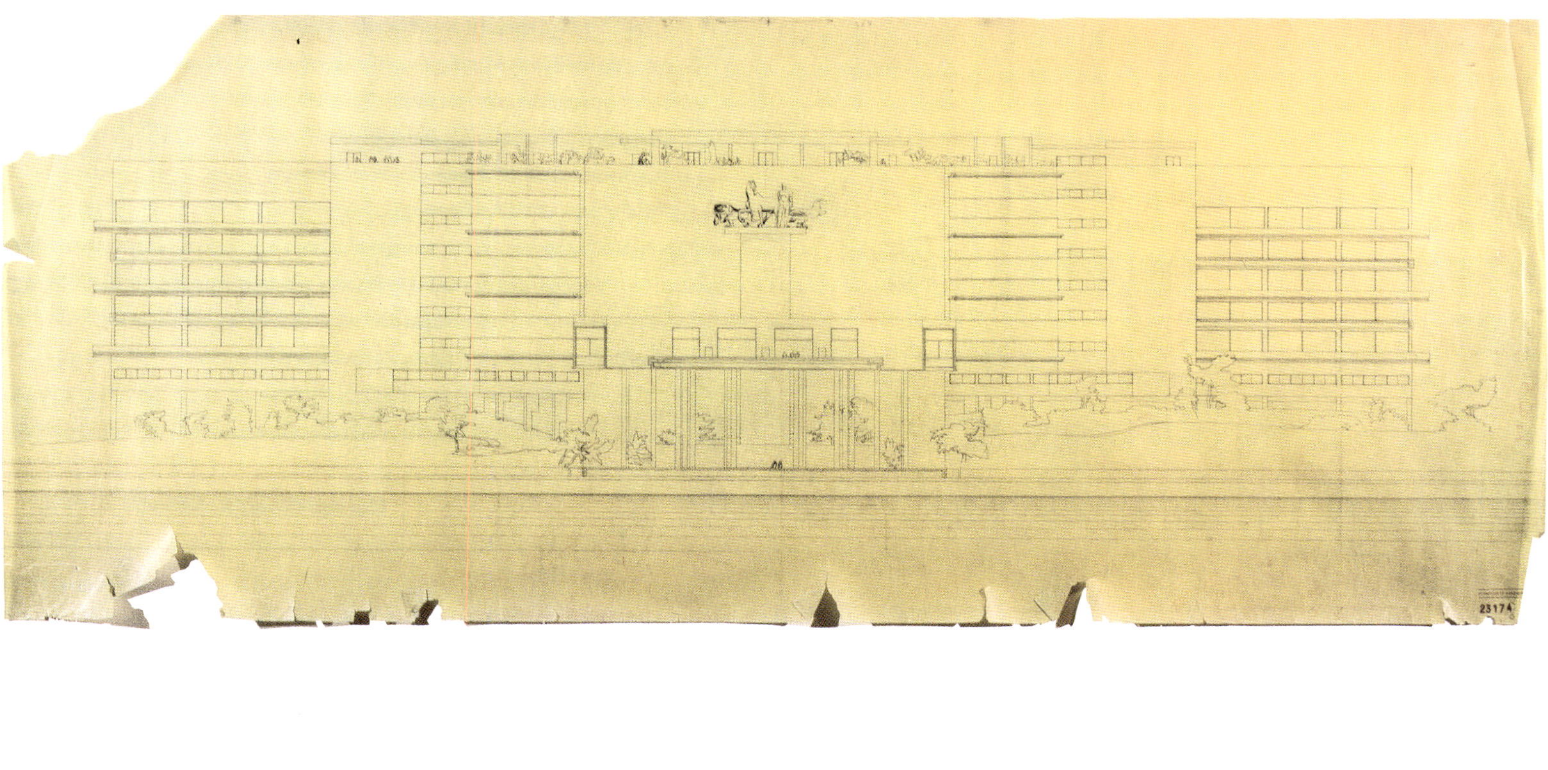

League of Nations Building, Geneva

The competitions for the League of Nations Building and for the Peace Palace were marked by a similar course of events. Both buildings were to be symbolic of the endeavour to establish greater international harmony and world peace. The exalted objectives of the resident institutions were to be embodied in the architecture. Unfortunately, both competitions were a complete disaster. They provoked international incidents and caused a world-wide scandal. Modern architecture, embodying the spirit of the new era, was rejected in favour of an old-fashioned style. By the time construction was completed, the institutions were outdated too. The First World War broke out soon after the inauguration of the Peace Palace. The Second World War broke out two years after the completion of the League of Nations Building.

Prelude

When the League of Nations was founded in Paris in 1919, permanent quarters had yet to be found. However, from the beginning, the city of Geneva had tried to persuade the organisation to establish its seat in the Swiss capital. Initially, the city had proposed building an entirely new town near Creux-de-Genthod, a mere stone's throw from Geneva. The League of Nations, which was meeting in London for the time being, rejected this proposal. However, they did decide to purchase the Hotel National in Geneva. Soon thereafter, in 1923, the city donated the adjacent plot of land to the organisation. This proved to be a godsend because the nineteenth century Hotel National provided insufficient and unsuitable quarters.

In 1923, the League decided to organise a competition. Prior to that, the Swiss architect Marc Camoletti had been commissioned to design a new conference hall which was to be linked to the hotel where the Secretariat was to have its quarters. The League tentatively proposed Camoletti's design as a model for the competition assignment. They were subsequently confronted with the age-old dilemma of choosing between a closed national or an open international competition. They chose the latter option, thereby accepting the risk that every amateur in the world might participate. However, in light of the nature of the organisation, this was a logical decision.

The competition programme was based on guidelines which had been drafted for a competition organised by the Society of Swiss Engineers and Architects (S.I.A.). One of the leading members of this society was Henri Paul Nénot. He had helped to draw up the society's guidelines and later submitted a prize-winning design. Throughout the competition, the S.I.A tried to maintain its grip on the proceedings.

A jury of six, from six different countries, was appointed. During their first meeting, they decided that more money should be made available for the project and that an entirely new and coherent complex should be built, rather than hazarding the awkward extension of the Hotel National. A larger building site was therefore required. At this point, Hendrik Petrus Berlage (The Netherlands), Carlos Gato (Spain) and Ivar Tengbom (Sweden) joined the jury, which had initially consisted of Victor Horta (Belgium), Josef Hoffmann (Austria), Charles Henri Camille Lemaresquier (France), John J. Burnet (England), Koloman Moser (Switzerland) and Attilio Muggia (Italy).

The jury, chaired by Horta, gained almost complete control over the proceedings. Without prior consultation, they selected a building site near Lake Geneva, outside the city centre. The competition regulations and construction programme were drafted in April 1926. The jury decided to limit the amount of prize money, hoping to dissuade many novice architects from trying their luck in the competition. The jury explicitly stated that the building was to be symbolic of world peace. They would therefore evaluate not only the explicit features of the designs but also the underlying conception of the architects. The international press was wildly enthusiastic and exhorted the architects to defend the honour of their respective countries.

Sir James Eric Drummond, the first secretary-general of the League of Nations

Façade of the League of Nations Building, Hotel National

Le Corbusier

Le Corbusier & Pierre Jeanneret
Centrosoyuz, exterior perspective, Moscow, 1928–1936

Le Corbusier & Pierre Jeanneret
Centrosoyuz, axonometric, Moscow 1929

Le Corbusier & Pierre Jeanneret
Centrosoyuz, plan 1928–1936

The struggle begins

A total of 2400 competition programmes were requested and dispatched to private architects and various states. The participants were asked to submit eighteen detailed drawings within six months. The competition closed on 25 January 1927, even though many architects had requested extra time. Designs continued to arrive in dribs and drabs from all corners of the globe. By 13 April the jury had completed the mammoth task of hanging up all the drawings, and adjudication of the 377 entries could begin. The jury met behind closed doors and announced the result on 5 May. Not one of the designs was considered practicable. One of the jury's main problems was that almost all of the designs were too expensive to execute. Le Corbusier and Jeanneret were the only architects who had stuck to the budget. Unfortunately, their drawings did not meet the stipulated technical specifications. Having informed the Secretariat of their dilemma, the jury announced a result which was as unique as it was bizarre.
Each of the nine jury members had selected a winner and two runners-up. The result epitomises the impotence and the limitations of the League of Nations. The jury members were all Western Europeans. The four members from Northern European countries – Moser, Berlage, Hoffmann and Tengbom – all selected modern designs. The Englishman Burnet and the four Southern European members – Horta, Gato, Muggia and Lemaresquier – all selected Traditionalist designs. Not one of the 27 nominated architects was selected more than once. Although the designs had been submitted anonymously, jury members selected a total of eleven designs made by their fellow-countrymen. The Northern members chose Northern architects and vice versa. The Englishman, Burnet, was the only member of the jury whose choice was not predictable. Twenty-seven designs from eight different countries were selected from a field of 377. Each of these countries had a representative on the jury. England was the only country without a 'champion'. On the victory platform, nine architects from five different countries were jointly awarded first prize.

Modernists launch attack

In his book "Oeuvre complet 1910–1929" Le Corbusier ignores the fact that he was one of a group of nine prize-winners, and presents himself as the sole victor. Le Corbusier's interpretation of the result was evidently a question of personal conviction. This is borne out by his attempts to convince the jury and the League of Nations of his superiority. He was aided in this endeavour by the jury member Moser, who sent letters in support of Le Corbusier to a number of people, including the Secretary-General of the League of Nations, Sir James Eric Drummond. Within a short time, Le Corbusier became the Modernist champion. He received widespread support: if a Modernist was to design a building of such international significance, this would be beneficial for the Modernist movement throughout the world. Rumours and insinuations about Traditionalist and Modernist architects fanned the flames of rivalry. Le Corbusier even went so far as to engage in "confidential" consultation with Berlage and Lemaresquier. In a letter to Berlage, he mentions a meeting with Lemaresquier. Le Corbusier writes that he had offered to appoint Lemaresquier project supervisor, but only if he and his brother Pierre were commissioned for the project. Le Corbusier added that he had two additional supervisors in mind: Moser and Berlage.
The jury was unable to reach a decision and a second round seemed inevitable. At this point, the League of Nations intervened. On 10 September 1927, five diplomats were assigned the task of cutting the Gordian knot. In a rare display of insight, the League selected jury members who were not from one of the prize-winning countries: Adatci (Japan, Chairman), Osusky (Czechoslovakia), Politis (Greece), Urrutia (Colombia) and Young (England). This inexperienced and equally incompetent jury called in the assistance of experts. Not one of the prize-winning designs was considered suitable for execution. Adding insult to injury, the jury slated Le Corbusier's design, saying that it closely resembled a factory and that it did not adequately embody the spirit of its purpose. Nevertheless, two of the five jury members, Urrutia and Politis, nominated Le Corbusier. Young nominated Vago, as had his compatriot, Burnet.
The new result was as bizarre as the first. By way of a compromise, the French-Swiss team of Nénot and Flegenheimer were commissioned to produce a new design, together with three other first-prize nominees (Vago, Broggi and Lefèvre)[1]. The four commissioned architects all hailed from the Traditionalist clique. The only Traditionalist who had not been commissioned subsequently demanded his portion of the prize

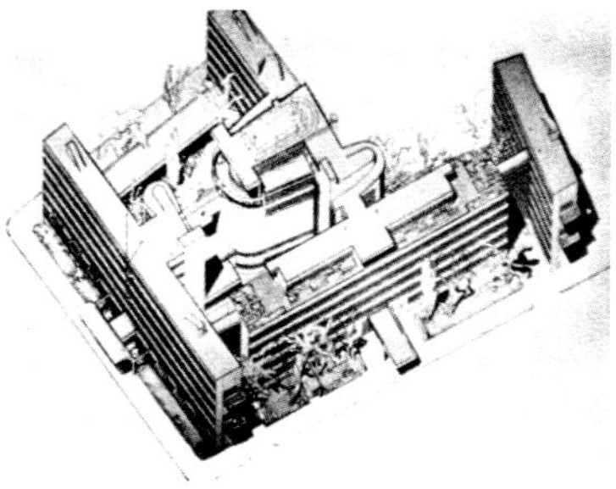

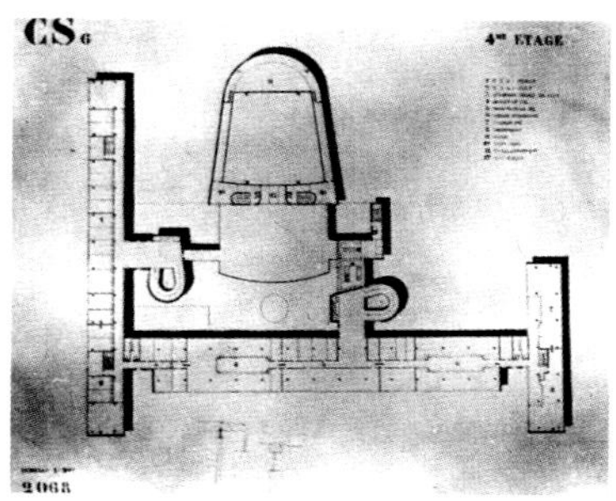

	First prize	First runner-up	Second runner-up
H.P. Berlage (Netherlands)	Fahrenkamp/ Deneke (Germany)	Van Linge (Netherlands)	Rosen (Denmark)
J. Hoffmann (Austria)	Zu Putlitz/ Klophaus/ Schoch (Germany)	Fischer/Speidel (Germany)	Ahlberg (Sweden)
K. Moser (Switzerland)	Le Corbusier/ Jeanneret (France/ Switzerland)	Bonatz/Scholer (Germany)	Meyer/Wittwer (Switzerland)
I. Tengbom (Sweden)	Eriksson (Sweden)	William/ Olsson (Sweden)	Birch/Lindgren (Sweden)
V. Horta[2] (Belgium)	Lefèvre (France)	Guidetti (France)	Hendrickx/De Ligne (Belgium)
J. Burnet (England)	Vago (Italy/ Hungary)	Wijdeveld (Netherlands)	Laverrière/ Thévenaz (Switzerland)
C. Gato (Spain)	Nénot/ Flegenheimer (France/ Switzerland)	Boileau/ Le Bourgeois (France)	Lambert/Legendre/ Camoletti (France/ Switzerland)
C. Lemaresquier (France)	Labro (France)	Patouillard (France)	Luthmann/Wouda (Netherlands)
A. Muggia (Italy)	Broggi/Vaccaro/ Franzi (Italy)	Boni/(Italy)	BoariPiacentini/ Rapisardi/Mazzoni (Italy)

money. He based his demand on the S.I.A. regulations, which stated that prize winners who were not commissioned had to be awarded prize money.

Last offensive

Le Corbusier did not take the result lying down and blithely continued to harass the members of the jury and other officials of the League of Nations. In September 1928, fate lent him a hand. Rockefeller, the American millionaire, pledged a sum of money for the building of a library, which meant that a larger building site had to be found. The designated site was Parc de l'Ariana. In order to obtain permission to build on this site, the League required one last signature. That of Hélène de Madrot, who had hosted a meeting held by angry Modernists at La Sarraz castle from 25 to 29 June 1928. At this meeting, the Modernists had founded the C.I.A.M. in an effort to counteract the S.I.A. and the Traditionalist members of the competition jury. De Madrot made it clear that she would only give her permission if all the prize winners were given the opportunity to submit a new design for the new site. Furthermore, the five jury members would have to give Le Corbusier the opportunity to clarify various aspects of his design to them.

The League reluctantly agreed to give the architects a little more time. However, only two architects made use of this opportunity: Le Corbusier and Erich zu Putlitz. Their efforts were in vain. In April 1929, the jury met with Le Corbusier but decided to stand by their earlier decision. Le Corbusier continued his campaign. He demanded compensation for damages and accused the four appointed architects of plagiarism. It goes without saying that Le Corbusier was convinced of his own superiority and was a bad loser – a fact borne out by his book "Oeuvre Complet". Nevertheless, he was unable to turn the tide. The first stone of the Palace of the Nations Building was laid in 1929. The actual building took place between 1932 and 1937. The building itself is of little architectural interest. It certainly bears no resemblance to Le Corbusier's original design, nor to his design for the Parc de l'Ariana. However, Le Corbusier did not have to shelve his plans completely. In 1928 he was commissioned to design the Ministry of Light Industry (Centrosoyuz) in Moscow. His design for this building, completed in 1934, was based largely on his drawings for the Geneva competition.

1 *It is interesting to note that, in his unrelenting lobbying via various political channels, Le Corbusier had suggested to Nénot that they should make a joint bid to obtain the commission.*

2 *Although Horta was not really a Traditionalist, he did select Classicist designs. Berlage, Hoffmann, Moser and Tengbom are Modernists, the last four are Traditionalists.*

Palais des Nations, Genf

Der Architekturwettbewerb zur Gestaltung eines Sitzes für den Völkerbund stand unter ähnlichen Voraussetzungen wie die Ausschreibung zum Friedenspalast: In beiden Fällen ging es um ein Bauwerk, das als Symbol für die menschliche Eintracht und den Willen zum Frieden dienen sollte. Leider entwickelten sich beide Wettbewerbe zu Fehlschlägen, die zu internationalen Zwischenfällen führten und für einen Skandal sorgten. Man entschied sich nicht für ein gelungenes Beispiel moderner Baukunst, sondern wählte altmodische Entwürfe, die bei ihrer Fertigstellung ebenso überholt waren wie die Institutionen, die sie beherbergen sollten. Kurz nach Einweihung des Friedenspalastes brach der Erste Weltkrieg aus, zwei Jahre nach Beendigung der Arbeiten am Völkerbundpalast begann der Zweite Weltkrieg.

Vorbereitungen

Als der Völkerbund 1919 in Paris gegründet wurde, hatten sich die Mitglieder noch nicht auf einen festen Sitz geeinigt. Von Anfang an bemühte sich jedoch die Stadt Genf, diese Organisation in ihre Stadtgrenzen zu holen. Unmittelbar nach der Gründung bot sie an, bei Creux-de-Genthod – in unmittelbarer Nähe Genfs – eine neue Stadt für den Völkerbund zu bauen. Dem zu dieser Zeit noch in London residierenden Bund sagte diese Idee nicht zu, aber man entschloß sich zum Ankauf des Genfer Hotel National. Daraufhin erklärte sich die Stadt bereit, dem Völkerbund auch die Nachbargrundstücke des Hotels zu schenken (1923) – eine kluge Entscheidung, da das im 19. Jahrhundert erbaute Gebäude für seine neue Aufgabe eigentlich viel zu klein und damit ungeeignet war.

1923 entschied sich der Völkerbund, einen Architektenwettbewerb auszuschreiben. Das Wettbewerbsprogramm basierte auf den Richtlinien, die der Schweizer Ingenieur- und Architektenverein (S.I.A. bzw. C.I.A.) für Architekturwettbewerbe aufgestellt hatte. Einer der führenden Köpfe dieser Vereinigung war Henri Paul Nénot. Er gehörte nicht nur zu den späteren Preisträgern, sondern versuchte mit dem S.I.A., den Wettbewerb zu beeinflussen.

Als nächstes wurde eine sechsköpfige Jury mit Vertretern aus sechs Ländern ernannt. Ihre Mitglieder plädierten während der ersten Sitzung dafür, einen größeren Geldbetrag zur Verfügung gestellt zu bekommen, so daß statt eines zweifelhaften Anbaus an das alte Hotel National ein neuer, zusammenhängender Komplex geschaffen werden konnte. Natürlich war dafür auch ein größeres Baugelände vonnöten. Darüber hinaus wurde die bis dahin aus Victor Horta (Belgien), Josef Hoffmann (Österreich), Charles-Henri-Camille Lemaresquier (Frankreich), John J. Burnet (England), Koloman Moser (Schweiz) und Attilio Muggia (Italien) bestehende Jury durch die Architekten Hendrik Petrus Berlage (Niederlande), Carlos Gato (Spanien) und Ivar Tengbom (Schweden) ergänzt.

Der Jury – unter Vorsitz von Horta – gelang es, die Initiative zu übernehmen: Ohne vorherige Absprachen entschied sie sich für ein Baugrundstück außerhalb des Zentrums, in der Nähe des Genfer Sees. Im April 1926 stellte sie Reglement und Bauauflagen zusammen.

Der Kampf beginnt

Auf Anfrage wurden insgesamt 2 400 Wettbewerbsprogramme verschickt. Als am 13. April alle Zeichnungen vorlagen, begann die Jury mit der Beurteilung der 377 Einsendungen. Die Beratungen fanden hinter verschlossenen Türen statt und dauerten bis zum 5. Mai. Dennoch wurde kein Entwurf als ausführbar erachtet. Größtes Problem: Alle Projekte stellten sich nach kurzer Berechnung als zu teuer heraus. Nur Le Corbusier und Pierre Jeanneret blieben im Rahmen des vorgesehenen Etats, aber ihre Zeichnungen genügten den technischen Anforderungen der Jury nicht. Nachdem sie das Sekretariat als Vertreter des Völkerbunds über dieses Problem informiert hatte, traf die Jury ihre ebenso bizarre wie einzigartige Entscheidung. Jedes der neun Mitglieder wählte einen ersten Preisträger und zwei weitere Ankäufe. Das Resultat war bezeichnend für die Ohnmacht und die Grenzen des Völkerbundes. Kein einziger der 27 nominierten Architekten wurde doppelt genannt.

Die Modernisten greifen an

Obwohl Le Corbusier zu den neun Preisträgern gehörte, stellte er sich in seinem Buch »Oeuvre Complet 1910–1929« als den einzigen Gewinner dar. Allerdings war er auch schon während des Wettbewerbs dieser Auffassung, was sich in mehreren leidenschaftlichen Versuchen niederschlug, die Jury und den Völkerbund von seiner Überlegenheit zu überzeugen. In diesen Bemühungen unterstützte ihn sein Landsmann Moser, der sich bei einer ganzen Reihe von Personen für Le Corbusier einsetzte und sich auch an den Generalsekretär des Völkerbunds, Sir James Eric Drummond, wandte. Auf diese Weise entwickelte sich Le Corbusier in kürzester Zeit zur Gallionsfigur der Modernisten, die ihn von allen Seiten unterstützten: Falls ein Vertreter der Moderne den Auftrag für ein Bauwerk von solch internationaler Bedeutung erhielte, bedeute dies einen entscheidenden Durchbruch für die moderne Baukunst.

Die Jury war nicht in der Lage, sich zu einigen, und eine zweite Ausschreibungsrunde schien unvermeidbar. An diesem Punkt griff der Völkerbund ein: Am 10. September 1927 wurden fünf Diplomaten bestimmt, die eine endgültige Entscheidung treffen sollten. Durch die bisherigen Erfahrungen klug geworden, benannte der Völkerbund nur Jurymitglieder, die nicht aus einem der preisgekrönten Länder stammten: Adatci (Japan, Vorsitzender), Osusky (Tschechoslowakei), Politis (Griechenland), Urrutia (Kolumbien) und Young (England). Diese ebenso unbefangene wie unerfahrene Jury ließ sich bei ihrer Entscheidung durch Experten beraten und lehnte alle Entwürfe der bisherigen Preisträger ab. Dabei teilte sie noch einen Seitenhieb gegen Le Corbusier aus: Sein Entwurf erinnere viel zu sehr an eine Fabrik und sei keinesfalls repräsentativ. Dennoch entschieden sich zwei der fünf Jurymitglieder für Le Corbusier: Urrutia und Politis.

Das neue Endergebnis war ebenso bizarr wie die erste Entscheidung: In einer Art Kompromißblösung erhielt im Dezember 1927 die französisch-schweizerische Kombination Nénot-Flegenheimer den Auftrag, zusammen mit drei anderen Gewinnern des ersten Preises (Vago, Broggi und Lefèvre) einen neuen Entwurf auszuarbeiten. Alle vier Preisträger stammten aus den Reihen der Traditionalisten. Daraufhin forderte der einzige preisgekrönte Traditionalist, der keinen Bauauftrag erhalten hatte, einen Teil des Preisgeldes für sich ein, indem er sich auf das S.I.A.-Reglement berief.

Schlußoffensive

Le Corbusier gab sich mit diesem Ergebnis nicht zufrieden und bedrängte weiterhin die Jurymitglieder und andere Funktionäre des Völkerbunds. 1928 kam ihm der Zufall zu Hilfe: Der amerikanische Millionär Rockefeller spendete einen großen Geldbetrag für den Bau einer Bibliothek, was zur Folge hatte, daß ein größeres Baugelände gefunden werden mußte. Man entschied sich für den Parc l'Ariana (Arianapark). Für die Baugenehmigung wurde die Unterschrift von Hélène de Madrot benötigt. Madame de Madrot war Gastgeberin eines Kongresses auf Burg La Sarraz, wo sich vom 25. bis 29. Juni 1928 zornige Modernisten getroffen hatten, um als Gegengewicht zur S.I.A. und den Traditionalisten der Jury die S.I.A.M. zu gründen. Sie sagte ihre Unterschrift nur unter der Bedingung zu, daß alle Preisträger der ersten Runde eine Chance zur Entwicklung neuer Entwürfe für das neue Gelände erhalten sollten. Darüber hinaus mußte die Jury Le Corbusier empfangen und ihm die Gelegenheit geben, seine Pläne ausführlich zu erläutern.

Widerstrebend gestand die Jury den Architekten einen knappen Zeitraum zur Überarbeitung ihrer Pläne zu. Nur Le Corbusier und Erich zu Putzlitz traten erneut an, doch ihre Bemühungen blieben umsonst: Nach der Anhörung Le Corbusiers im April 1929 bekräftigte die Jury ihr altes Urteil. Le Corbusier gab immer noch nicht auf. Er forderte von der Jury Schadenersatz und beschuldigte die vier preisgekrönten Architekten des Plagiats. Trotz allem konnte er den Bau nicht aufhalten: 1929 fand die Grundsteinlegung zum Palais des Nations statt, das zwischen 1932 und 1937 erbaut wurde. Architektonisch ist das Gebäude von nicht allzu großem Interesse. Es ähnelt in keinster Weise dem Projekt Le Corbusiers und ist weder mit seinem ersten Entwurf noch seinen umgearbeiteten Plänen für den Parc de l'Ancona zu vergleichen.

Le Corbusier fand für seine Entwürfe eine neue Verwendung: 1929 erhielt er den Auftrag, das Ministerium für Konsumgüterindustrie (Centrosojus) in Moskau zu bauen. Die Entwürfe für das 1934 fertiggestellte Gebäude basierten größtenteils auf seinen Zeichnungen für den Genfer Wettbewerb.

Le Palais des Nations, Genève

Les concours pour le Palais des Nations de Genève et celui de la Paix à La Haye se déroulèrent à peu près selon le même schéma. Les deux bâtiments étaient tous deux chargés d'exprimer l'espérance d'une plus grande harmonie universelle et de la paix mondiale mais leurs concours se transformèrent en complets désastres. Ils provoquèrent même des incidents diplomatiques et un scandale international. L'architecture moderne, qui incarnait l'esprit de l'ère nouvelle, fut mise à l'écart en faveur de styles dépassés. A l'achèvement de la construction, l'une des institutions que ces palais devaient abriter était déjà dépassée, et la Seconde Guerre mondiale éclata deux ans après l'inauguration du Palais des Nations.

Prélude

Fondée à Paris en 1919, la Société des Nations se préoccupa immédiatement de se trouver un siège digne d'elle. Très tôt, la ville de Genève avait tenté de la persuader de s'établir dans ses murs et avait même proposé de construire une ville nouvelle proche de Creux-de-Genthod, pratiquement sa banlieue. La Société, qui se réunissait alors à Londres, rejeta cette proposition et décida à la place d'acquérir l'Hôtel National, à Genève. Peu après, en 1923, la ville offrit un terrain adjacent, générosité qui tombait à point nommé, tant l'hôtel répondait mal aux besoins.
La Société décida la même année d'organiser un concours, bien que l'architecte suisse Marc Camoletti ait déjà reçu commande d'une salle de conférence reliée à l'hôtel. L'administration tenta d'intégrer les plans de Camoletti au cahier des charges et se trouva vite confrontée au dilemme d'avoir à choisir entre un concours national restreint ou une compétition internationale ouverte. Elle opta pour la seconde solution en prenant le risque de voir affluer les projets d'amateurs mais cette décision était plus dans l'esprit de sa vocation internationale.
Le programme du concours reposait sur des directives mises au point par la Société des Ingénieurs et Architectes suisses (S.I.A.). L'un de ses principaux membres était Henri Paul Nénot qui avait participé à l'établissement du cahier des charges et plus tard soumis un projet primé. La S.I.A. devait tenter par la suite de conserver un regard sur le concours .
Un jury de six membres originaires de six pays différents fut désigné. Dès sa première réunion, il réclama un financement plus important et la construction d'un bâtiment entièrement nouveau plutôt que de tenter la solution d'une extension de l'Hôtel National qui ne présentait que des inconvénients. Il fallait donc commencer par trouver un terrain plus vaste. A ce moment Berlage (Pays-Bas), Gato (Espagne) et Tengbom (Suède) rejoignirent le jury composé au départ de Horta (Belgique), Hoffmann (Autriche), Lemaresquier (France), Burnet (Grande-Bretagne), Moser (Suisse) et Muggia (Italie). Ce nouveau jury, présidé par Horta, prit le contrôle des événements. Sans consultation préalable, il choisit un site proche du lac, en dehors du centre-ville. Le règlement du concours et le cahier des charges furent établis en avril 1926 et le montant des prix fut volontairement limité pour dissuader les architectes novices de tenter leur chance. Le jury précisa explicitement que l'édifice devait symboliser la paix universelle et qu'il ne jugerait pas seulement les plans mais également les concepts.
La presse internationale était enthousiaste et exhorta les architectes du monde entier à défendre les couleurs de leurs pays.

Début des combats

2 400 règlements et cahiers des charges furent demandés et expédiés dans de nombreux pays. Les participants devaient soumettre dix-huit plans détaillés dans les six mois. Le concours fut clos le 25 janvier 1927, bien que de nombreux concurrents aient demandé une prolongation du délai. Des projets de toutes sortes arrivèrent de tous les coins du monde. Le 13 avril, le jury termina enfin l'accrochage des dessins des 377 participants et l'adjudication put commencer. Le résultat fut proclamé le 5 mai. Aucun des projets n'était retenu, ne serait-ce que parce que tous se révélaient trop coûteux à construire. Le Corbusier et Jeanneret étaient les seuls à tenir dans les limites budgétaires même si, malheureusement, leurs plans ne respectaient pas les stipulations techniques.
Après avoir informé le Secrétariat de la Société des Nations de leur problème, le jury prit une décision aussi bizarre qu'originale qui mettait en lumière l'impuissance et les limites de la Société des Nations: chacun des neuf jurés sélectionnerait un premier gagnant et deux seconds prix. Tous les membres du jury étaient européens. Les quatre jurés de l'Europe du Nord – Moser, Berlage, Hoffmann et Tengbom – penchaient pour des projets modernistes alors que le Britannique Burnet et les quatre juré de l'Europe du Sud avaient choisi des plans classiques. Aucun des 27 candidats retenus n'avait été retenu par plus d'un juré. Bien que les projets aient été anonymes, chaque juré avait sélectionné des plans proposés par ses compatriotes. 27 projets venant de huit pays différents furent donc sélectionnés et chacun de ces pays était représenté au jury. Seul le choix du Britannique était inconnu et la Grande-Bretagne se retrouvait sans champion. En final, neuf architectes de cinq pays différents reçurent le premier prix ex-æquo.

Contre-attaque moderniste

Dans son livre «Œuvre complet, 1910–1929», Le Corbusier ignore ce premier prix ex-æquo accordé à 9 architectes et se présente comme le seul vainqueur. Cette conviction toute personnelle tient sans doute à ses tentatives de convaincre le jury et la Société des nations de la supériorité de ses idées. Il fut aidé en cela par un juré, Koloman Moser, compatriote suisse allemand, qui envoya des lettres de soutien à Le Corbusier dont une au Secrétaire général de la Société des Nations, Sir James Drummond. Très vite, Le Corbusier s'imposa comme le champion du modernisme et reçut des appuis de tous côtés car si un moderniste pouvait remporter un concours d'une telle importance internationale, le mouvement tout entier en bénéficierait. Des rumeurs et des insinuations sur les architectes des deux camps se répandirent et entretinrent la rivalité. Le Corbusier alla jusqu'à consulter «confidentiellement» Berlage et Lemaresquier. Dans une lettre à Berlage, il mentionna sa rencontre avec Lemaresquier et écrivit qu'il lui avait proposé de le nommer superviseur du projet si lui et son frère Pierre étaient retenus. Il ajoutait qu'il avait pensé à deux autres personnes: Moser et Berlage.
Le jury ne put se décider et un second concours parut inévitable. C'est à ce moment que la Société des Nations intervint et chargea, le 10 septembre 1927, cinq diplomates de trancher ce nœud gordien. Perspicaces, ils sélectionnèrent un jury dont aucun membre n'appartenait à un pays ayant remporté le premier prix: Adatki (Japon, président), Osusky (Tchécoslovaquie), Politis (Grèce), Urrutia (Colombie) et E.H. Young (Grande-Bretagne). Ce jury inexpérimenté et incompétent s'entoura d'experts. Aucun des plans présentés ne fut jugé réalisable. Ajoutant l'insulte à la blessure, il fustigea le projet Le Corbusier, précisant qu'il ressemblait à une usine et ne traduisait pas ce qu'on lui avait demandé. Néanmoins, deux des cinq jurés Urrutia et Politis, choisirent Le Corbusier. Young opta pour Vago, comme l'avait fait précédemment son compatriote Burnet.
Le nouveau résultat était aussi curieux que le premier. A l'issue d'un compromis, l'équipe franco-suisse de Nénot et Frankenheimer reçut commande d'un nouveau projet ainsi que trois autres titulaires du premier prix: Vago, Broggi et Lefèvre[1]. Les quatre architectes distingués appartenaient tous aux milieux traditionalistes. Le seul conservateur non retenu réclama sa part du prix en s'appuyant sur les règlements de la S.I.A. qui stipulaient que les concurrents primés mais dont les plans ne seraient pas réalisés recevraient un dédommagement.

Dernière offensive

Le Corbusier ne resta pas sans réaction et continua inlassablement à harasser les jurés et les responsables de la Société des Nations. En septembre 1928, le destin lui prêta la main. Rockefeller, le milliardaire américain, offrit une somme importante pour la création d'une bibliothèque, ce qui nécessitait un nouveau terrain, plus vaste. Le nouveau site retenu fut alors le parc de l'Ariana. Mais pour obtenir le permis de construire, la Société devait obtenir une dernière signature, celle de Hélène de Madrot, qui avait organisé une réunion de modernistes au château de La Sarraz, du 25 au 29 juin 1928. C'est à cette occasion qu'avait été fondé le C.I.A.M. pour contrer la S.I.A. et les traditionalistes du jury. Madame de Madrot fit clairement comprendre qu'elle ne donnerait son autorisation que si l'ensemble des architectes primés pouvait présenter un nouveau plan pour le nouveau site et si les cinq membres du jury offraient à Le Corbusier l'opportunité de clarifier certains aspects de sa proposition.
La Société accepta sans enthousiasme de donner un peu plus de temps aux architectes. Deux d'entre eux seulement profitèrent de cette chance – Le Corbusier et Erich zu Putlitz – mais leurs efforts furent vains. En avril 1929, le jury reçut Le Corbusier mais refusa de revenir sur sa décision. L'architecte, convaincu de sa supériorité et mauvais perdant, poursuivit sa campagne, réclama des compensations pour dommages et accusa les quatre architectes retenus de plagiat. Il ne put inverser le courant et la première pierre du Palais des Nations fut posée en 1929. La construction débuta en 1932 pour s'achever en 1937. L'édifice en lui-même offre peu d'intérêt architectural et ne ressemble certes en rien au premier projet de Le Corbusier, ni à celui qu'il avait dessiné pour l'Ariana. Le Corbusier réutilisa partiellement ses plans. Choisi, en 1928, pour construire le ministère de l'industrie légère (Centrosoyuz) à Moscou, il s'inspira beaucoup de ses dessins pour le concours de Genève.

1 *Lors de son offensive pour tenter d'influencer le jury, y compris auprès des milieux politiques, Le Corbusier avait suggéré que Nénot et lui s'allient pour obtenir la commande.*

S.d.N
14

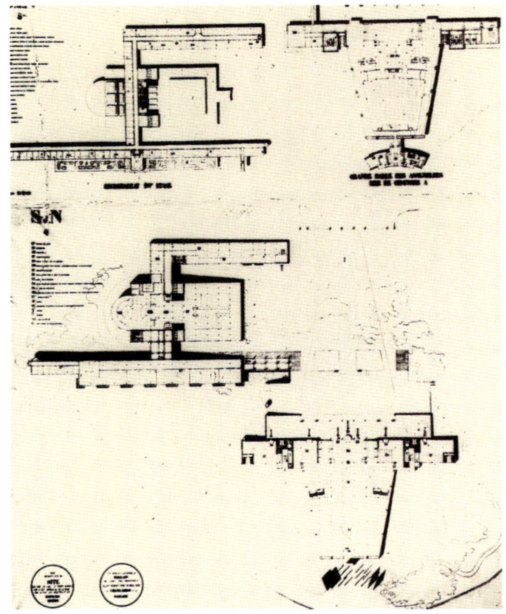
S.d.N

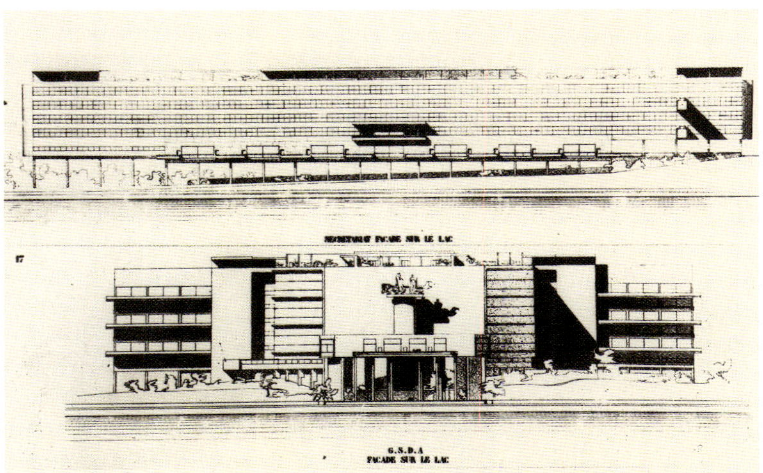
17
FACADE SUR LE LAC

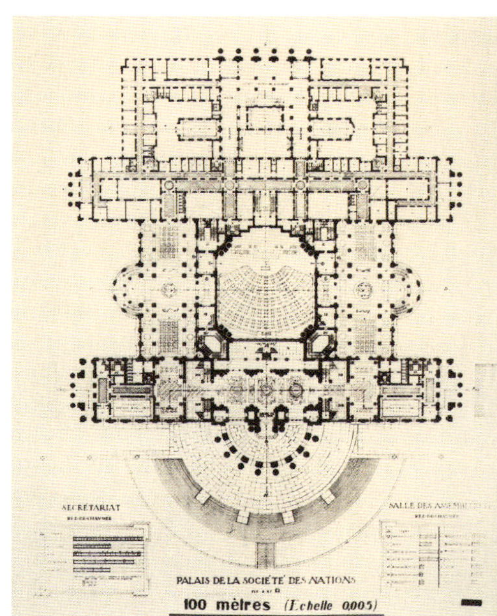
SECRÉTARIAT
PALAIS DE LA SOCIÉTÉ DES NATIONS
100 mètres (Echelle 0,005)

Le Corbusier & Pierre Jeanneret competition design, 1927, axonometric, first prize

Le Corbusier & Pierre Jeanneret competition design, 1927, above: elevation on the secretariat building on Lake Geneva, below: elevation on Grand Assembly Hall on Lake Geneva, first prize

Le Corbusier & Pierre Jeanneret competition design, 1927, plan, first prize

Carlo Broggi, Giuseppe Vaccaro & Luigi Franzi competition design, 1927, exterior view from Lake Geneva, first prize

Carlo Broggi, Giuseppe Vaccaro & Luigi Franzi competition design, 1927, ground floor plan, first prize

Giuseppe Vago competition design, 1927, bird's eye view, first prize

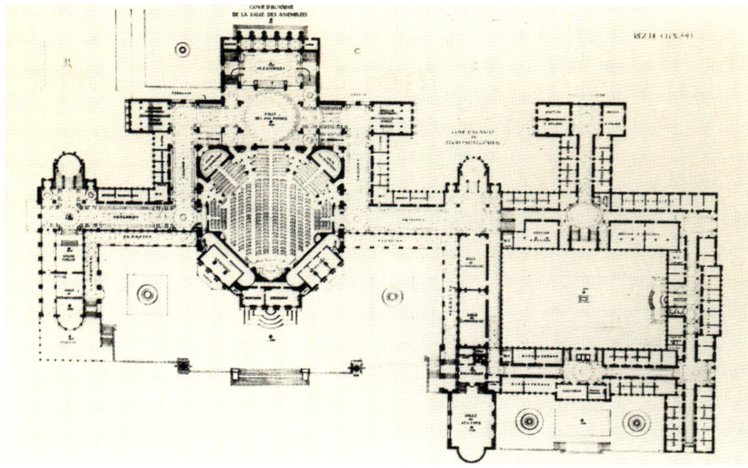

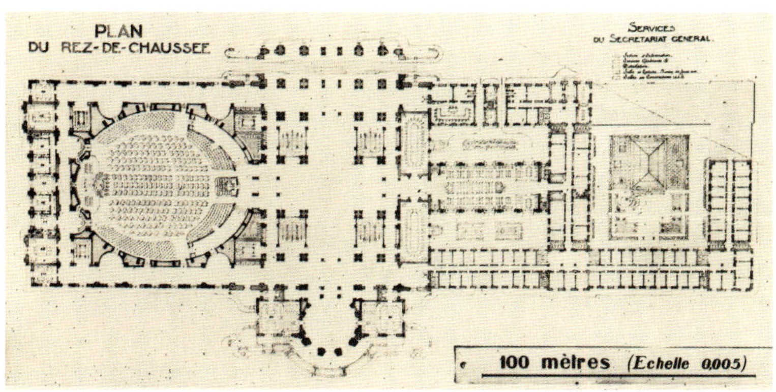

Camille Lefèvre competition design, 1927, above: elevation on Rue de Lausanne, below left: elevation on Parc Mon Repos, below right: elevation of the secretariat building, first prize

Camille Lefèvre competition design, 1927, ground floor plan, first prize

Giuseppe Vago competition design, 1927, ground floor plan, first prize

Erich zu Pulitz, Rudolf Klophaus & August Schoch competition design, 1927, exterior view from Lake Geneva, first prize

Henri Paul Nénot & Julien Flegenheimer competition design, 1927, elevation on Lake Geneva, first prize

Emil Fahrenkamp & Albert Deneke competition design, 1927, bird's eye view, first prize

Nils Einar Eriksson competition design, 1927, bird's eye view, first prize

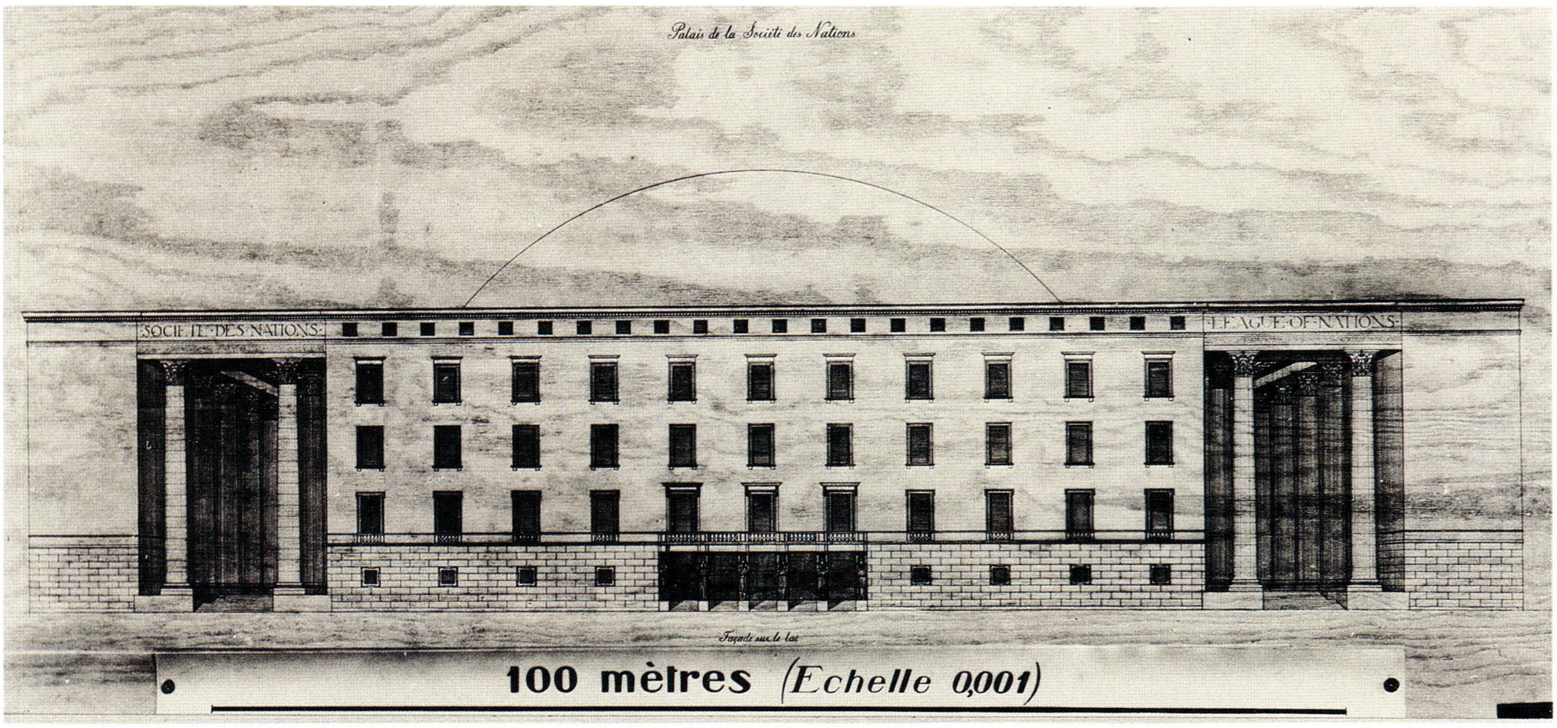

Carl Martin Tage William-Olsson
competition design, 1927, elevation on Lake Geneva, honourable mention, class I

René Patouillard-Demoriane
competition design, 1927, elevation on Lake Geneva, honourable mention, class I

Pierre Giudetti & Louis Giudetti
competition design, 1927, elevation on Lake Geneva, honourable mention, class I

Alfred Fischer-Essen & Richard Speidel competition design, 1927, first floor plan, honourable mention, class I

Alfred Fischer-Essen & Richard Speidel competition design, 1927, elevation on Lake Geneva, honourable mention, class I

Hendrikus Theodorus Wijdeveld competition design, 1927, ground floor plan, honourable mention, class I

Hendrikus Theodorus Wijdeveld competition design, 1927, elevation on Lake Geneva, honourable mention, class I

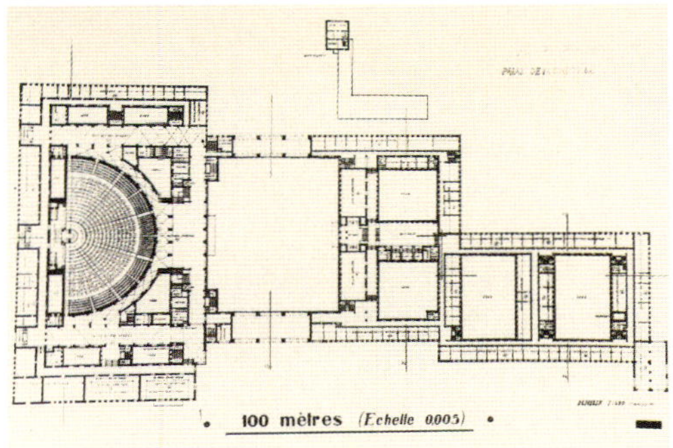

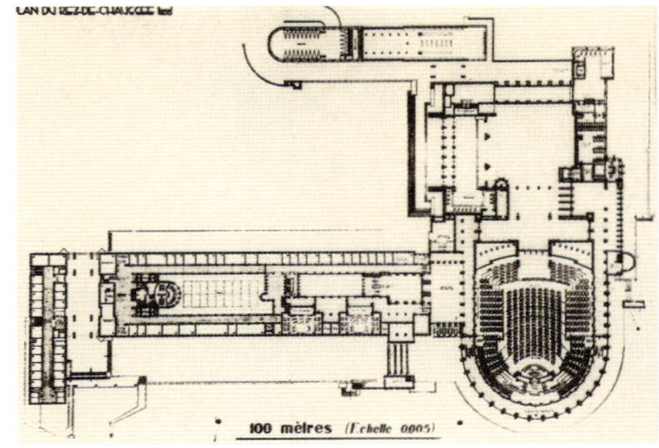

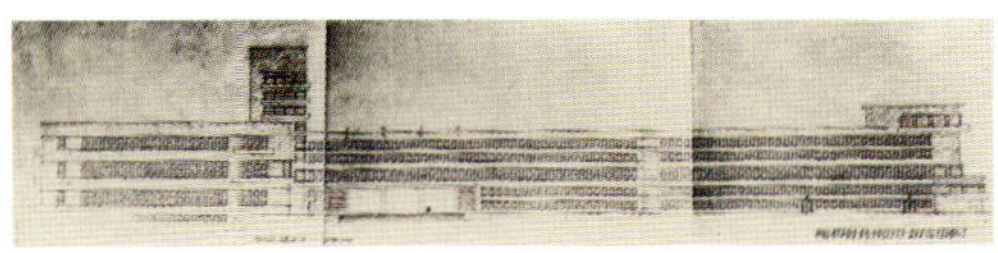

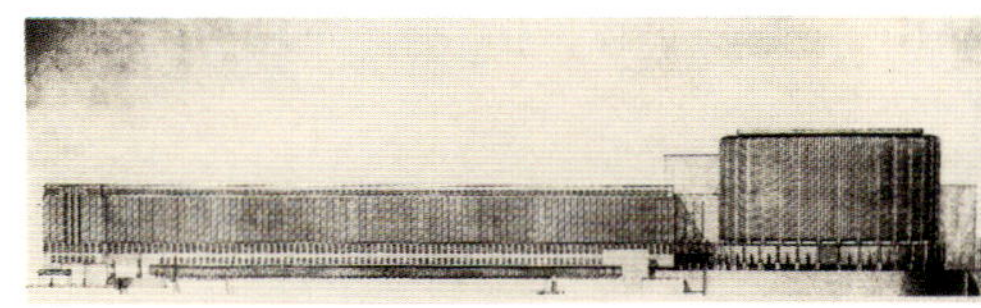

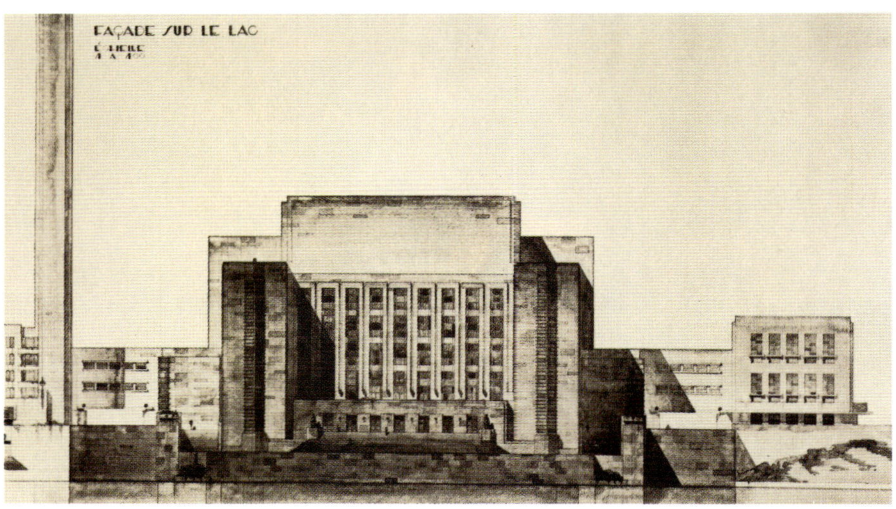

J.M. Luthmann & H. Wouda competition design, 1927, elevation on Lake Geneva, honourable mention, class II

Anton Rosen competition design, 1927, elevation on Lake Geneva, honourable mention, class II

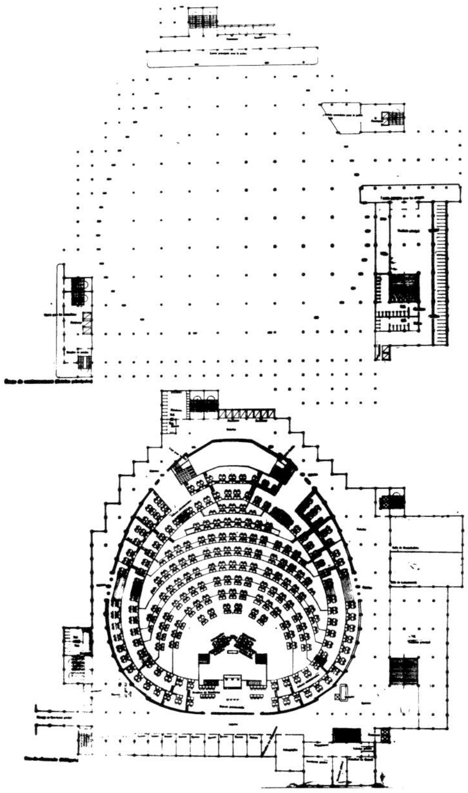

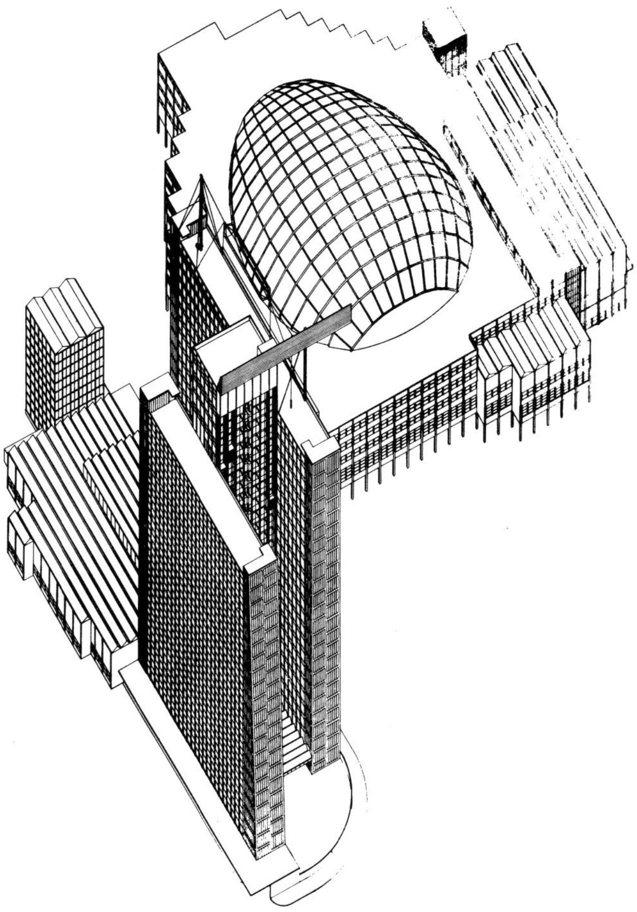

Hannes Meyer & Hans Wittwer
competition design, 1927, above: ground floor plan, below: plan of assembly hall level, honourable mention, class II

Hannes Meyer & Hans Wittwer
competition design, 1927, axonometric, honourable mention, class II

Lenin Library, Moscow, 1928

Project

Library

Site

Kalinin Prospekt, Moscow

Dates

1 January 1928 to 2 April 1928 *Result announced* November 1928

Number of entries

First round, open competition 10 *Second round* 4 (all invited: Alexei Viktorovich Shchusev Viktor Alexandrovich Vesnin & Alexander Alexandrovich Vesnin Ivan I. Rerberg Vladimir Shchuko)

Jury

P. Smidovich, Anatoly Luchanarsky, K.V. Ukhanov (all state representatives), G.B. Krasin (city engineer), I.I. Diumulen, I.P. Mashkov, I.V. Rylsky, V.N. Semionov, E.V. Shervinsky (architects), V.I. Nevsky and D.N. Egorov (libraries), a number of other expert advisors

Result

First round D.S. Markov, D.F. Fridman & V.I. Fidman (open competition); A.V. Shchusev; V.A. Vesnin & A.A. Vesnin; V. Shchuko (all invited)
Second round V. Shchuko

Commissioned by

The Peoples' Commissariat for Enlightenment (Narkompros)

Construction

Completed in 1941

Architect

Vladimir Alexeyevich Shchuko (1878–1939)

Lenin Library, Moscow, 1928

Vladimir Alexeyevich Shchuko
competition design, 1928, interior view of main reading hall

Lenin Library, Moscow

During the post-revolutionary 1920s, Soviet architects and other artists enjoyed relative freedom of expression. The avant-garde movement appealed to the tastes of the Communist leaders and artists saw themselves as part of a chosen generation who were to give form to a new period in history. It was an era marked not only by Modernism and fantasy, but especially by optimism[1]. However, there was also a traditional, more hierarchically Classicist undercurrent in Russian architecture. This undercurrent gradually became the official form of state architecture as the Communist regime became more repressive. The circumstances surrounding the competition for the Lenin Library accurately illustrate this course of events.

Post-revolutionary optimism

Initially, the architectural climate was determined by the avant-gardists, who had formed two separate movements. The Association of New Architects (Asnova) was founded in 1923 by Nicolai Ladovski (1881–1941) and Vladimir Krinski. Their form of Rationalism was based on the concept that form, colour and space influenced the human mind. The Union of Contemporary Architects (OSA), which soon became more famous than Asnova, was founded in 1925 by the architects Alexander A. Vesnin (1883–1959) and Moisei Ginzburg (1892–1946) and the Constructivist artists Alexander Rodchenko and Alexei Gan. The Rationalists of Asnova and the Constructivists of OSA both sought a scientific basis for architectural issues. The Rationalists based their designs on the floor plan. This "form follows function" approach led naturally to asymmetrical forms. The Constructivist approach – derived from the works of Vladimir Tatlin and other early examples – was based on the concept of visible structure[2].

Unfortunately, this period of Soviet history was not only marked by the freedom to fantasize, but also by a lack of funds. As a result, most of these imaginative designs were never executed. However, the nascent state naturally required new buildings and new types of architecture. The hierarchic Traditionalism of the pre-revolutionary era was considered to be too reminiscent of Tsarist despotism and a totally inappropriate style for the new society.

One of the new types of building was the workers' club. The workers were the linchpins of the new system and had to have their own buildings: a facility which would contribute to their cultural development. The architect Konstantin Melnikov (1890–1974), who had close ties with Asnova but was not a member, designed a truly impressive club building in Moscow (Rusakov Workers' Club, 1927–1929). However, the Constructivists also had their champion, Ilya Golosov (1881–1945), whose Zuev Workers' Club had made a profound impression (Moscow, 1928–1929).

Besides Golosov, Melnikov, Ginzburg, Ladovski and the brothers Vesnin, many other architects proved to be ardent supporters of the Modernist movement. As a result, the status of this movement took on immense proportions in the Soviet Union. In addition, the Russian architects had become acquainted with the work of German and Dutch

K.S. Melnikov **project for the competition of the Palace of Labour, bird's eye view, 1922**

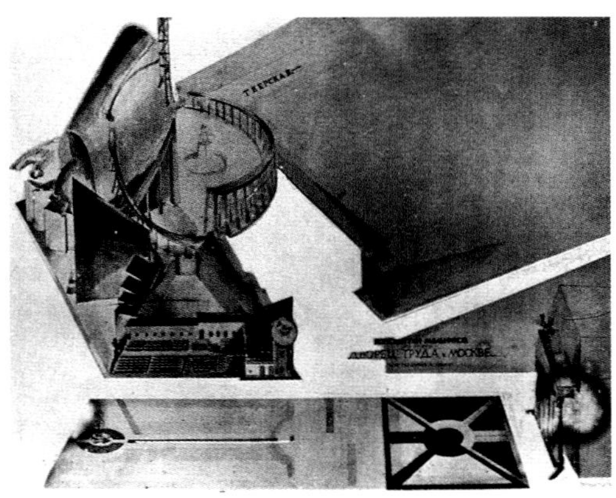

architects, such as Walter Gropius, Bruno Taut, Max Taut and Mart Stam. These architects had even been invited to the Soviet Union on a number of occasions to give technical and asthetic advice.
There was also another category of buildings which had a completely different function. They were not intended for the workers but for the collective, the Soviet. Examples of this type of architecture are the Palace of the Soviets and the Peoples' Commissariat for Heavy Industry, both of which were preceded by competitions[3]. Prior to that, competitions had been held for a Workers' Palace (1923) and the Lenin Library (1928). The latter was to serve as an intellectual centre for Socialist ideology, where the collected works of Marx, Engels and Lenin could be studied, just as the bible had been studied in monasteries during the Middle Ages.

Final exam project

The library administration had initially contrived an inexpensive and uncomplicated ploy to obtain a suitable design for a new building (1927). They had asked the directors of Moscow's leading school of architecture (Vkutein) to make the Lenin Library the final exam project. But, as was to be expected, their ploy did not produce a practicable design. However, the student Ivan Leonidov (1902–1969) did distinguish himself. Although Leonidov's subsequent design œuvre was not extensive, his written works and visionary drawings made him one of the most important Russian architects of his time[4]. Aside from this opportunistic ploy, the library had also asked the architects P.N. Andreev, B.A. Kondrashov and D.S. Markov to submit preliminary sketches. The library did not make use of these preliminary sketches, but Markov later hazarded a second attempt.

Open and closed competitions

He got his second chance on 1 January 1928, when the Peoples' Commissariat for Enlightenment of the Russian Republic organised an official competition. The library was evidently a prestigious project. A prime site near the Kremlin had been made available and the competition programme had been drafted in an excessively pompous tone. The building would not only be a monument to Lenin and his ideology but also a cynosure for the capital. The programme also included the remarkable stipulation that the library had to be in keeping with its historical surroundings. Furthermore, shelf space for six million books had to be provided.
An open and a closed competition were run simultaneously. Four architects had been invited for the closed competition: Alexei Shchusev (1873–1949), Vladimir Shchuko (1878–1939), the brothers Vesnin and the engineer Ivan Rerberg. The ten architects who participated in the open competition all submitted Modernist designs, while the invited architects were more inclined towards Traditionalism. Markov, assisted by D.F. Fridman and V.I. Fidman, won the open competition. Rerberg was dropped from the closed competition and Markov faced three invited architects in the second round (closing date: November 1928).

Reading hall of Lenin Library

I. Golosov competition design, 1928

Surprisingly, these architects all altered their plans to compete with Markov's Modernism. With the exception of the brothers Vesnin, of course, who had been founder members the Modernist movement and had submitted a design which reflected their beliefs.

The jury decided to commission Shchuko, who was the most traditional of the four. The decision unleashed a storm of protest from both OSA and Asnova. However, neither the jury nor the library took any notice of this outcry. After altering his plans several times, Shchuko built the Lenin Library together with the architect Vladimir Gelfreikh (1886–1967).

Stripped Classicism

Although Shchuko's first design was certainly not that of an arch-conservative, it does not bear comparison with the designs of the brothers Vesnin, Melnikov and the other Constructivists. His style may be described as a form of Classicism, stripped of most of its decorative features, leaving a handful of embellishments, such as Lenin's bust and the double frieze on Kalinin Prospekt. In his second design the friezes had been replaced with the inscriptions "S.S.S.R" and "Lenin". Although the building had been made less massive, it still lacked the spark of true Modernism.

To a certain extent, the same applies to Shchusev's design. He radically altered his first design, which was extremely hierarchic, Classicist and characteristically massive. In contrast, he had completely assimilated the principles of Modernism in his second design. The "pilotis" (free-standing columns) and the extended windows are particularly striking. The differences between the first and second designs of the brothers Vesnin are less radical. Both designs are clearly Modernist.

Shchuko's Lenin Library was only completed in 1941, but at least his design had escaped the fate of many other prize-winning Russian designs, most of which were never executed.

1 *The best known example of the fruitful exchange of ideas between artists and the state is the monument for the Third International designed by Vladimir Tatlin (1919). However, the esteem was also mutual in the fine arts field, where Casimir Malevich paved the way.*

2 *As always, there were combinations of these two schools, and architects who belonged to neither movement. It is for this reason that the two movements are generally referred to as Modernism here.*

3 *Described elsewhere in this book.*

4 *See also the chapter on the Peoples' Commissariat for Heavy Industry.*

Lenin-Bibliothek, Moskau

In der post-revolutionären Sowjetunion der 20er Jahre besaßen Architekten und andere Künstler ein hohes Maß an Freiheit. Die kommunistischen Führer waren beeindruckt von den avantgardistischen Auffassungen der Zeit, und die Künstler sahen sich selbst als Teil einer auserwählten Generation, die einem neuen Zeitalter Form verleihen durfte. Es war nicht nur die Zeit des Modernismus und der phantastischen Architektur, sondern vor allem die des Optimismus[1]. Daneben existierte in der russischen Baukunst der damaligen Zeit eine eher traditionell und hierarchisch klassizistisch ausgerichtete Strömung, die sich unter der immer repressiveren kommunistischen Führung mehr und mehr zur offiziellen Staatsarchitektur zu entwickeln begann. Die Ereignisse rund um den Architekturwettbewerb zur Lenin-Bibliothek sind beispielhaft für diese Entwicklung.

Post-revolutionärer Optimismus

Das architektonische Klima der jungen Sowjetunion wurde von den Avantgardisten beherrscht, die in zwei separate Gruppierungen zerfielen. Die Vereinigung Neuer Architekten (snowa) bildete sich 1923 um die Architekten Nikolai Ladowski (1881–1941) und Wladimir Krinski; ihr Rationalismus war eng verbunden mit dem Einfluß von Form, Farbe und Raum auf die menschliche Psyche. Die andere Gruppierung, die die snowa schnell an Bekanntheit übertreffen sollte, entstand 1925, als die Architekten Alexander A. Wesnin (1883–1959) und Moisej Ginsburg (1892–1946) zusammen mit den Konstruktivisten Alexander Rodschenko und Alexei Gan die Vereinigung Moderner Architekten (OSA) gründeten. Sowohl der Rationalismus der snowa als auch der Konstruktivismus der OSA gingen von einem wissenschaftlichen Unterbau ihrer architektonischen Themen aus. Die Entwürfe der Rationalisten basierten auf einem formalistischen Konzept, und dieser Gedanke des »form follows function« führte wie von selbst zu asymmetrischen Formen. Dagegen leitete sich der Konstruktivismus von Wladimir Tatlin und früheren Vorbildern ab und ging von der Sichtbarkeit der Konstruktion aus[2].
Leider war diese Periode in der Geschichte der Sowjetunion nicht nur geprägt von der Freiheit der Kunst, sondern auch von einem Mangel an Geld. Aus diesem Grunde wurden nur die wenigsten der phantasievollen Entwürfe imgesetzt. Auf der anderen Seite benötigte der junge Staat dringend neue Gebäude und Gebäudetypen, denn der hierarchische Traditionalismus der prärevolutionären Ära war viel zu sehr mit dem despotischen Zarismus verbunden.
Einer der neuen Gebäudetypen war der Arbeiterclub. Der Arbeiter als das zentrale Element des Staates mußte sein eigenes Gebäude haben, um sich auch kulturell entwikkeln zu können. Konstantin Melnikow (1890–1974), ein der snowa eng verbundener Architekt, entwarf mit dem Arbeiterclub Rusakow (Moskau 1927–1929) ein imposantes Bauwerk dieses Typus; aber auch Ilja Golosow (1881–1945) beeindruckte mit seinem Arbeiterclub Suew (Moskau, 1928–1929).
Außer Golosow, Melnikow, Ginsburg, Ladowski und den Gebrüdern Wesnin gab es noch eine ganze Reihe anderer Architekten, die sich als glühende Anhänger des Modernismus erwiesen. Diese Strömung setzte sich in der Sowjetunion auch deshalb durch, weil die Werke deutscher und niederländischer Architekten wie Walter Gropius, Bruno und Max Taut sowie Mart Stam frei zugänglich waren; in vielen Fällen lud man die ausländischen Baumeister auch in die Sowjetunion ein, wo sie Beraterdienste leisteten.
Neben den bereits erwähnten Clubs gab es noch eine andere Kategorie von Gesellschaftsbauten, die nicht den einzelnen Arbeiter, sondern das Kollektiv – den Sowjet – in den Mittelpunkt stellten. Solche Bauwerke waren beispielsweise der Palast der Sowjets und das Volkskommissariat für die Schwerindustrie, für die jeweils Architekturwettbewerbe ausgeschrieben wurden[3]. Auf dieselbe Weise ermittelte man die Architekten für den Palast der Arbeit (1923) und die Lenin-Bibliothek (1928). Diese Bibliothek sollte zum intellektuellen Zentrum der sozialistischen Lehre werden, wo die gesammelten Werke von Marx, Engels und Lenin studiert werden konnten, ähnlich wie man in den Klöstern des Mittelalters die Bibel studiert hatte.

Der Examensentwurf

1927 unternahm die administrative Abteilung der Bibliothek einen ersten Versuch, auf einfache und preiswerte Art und Weise an einen geeigneten Entwurf für ein neues Bibliotheksgebäude zu gelangen. Man bat die Leitung der bedeutendsten Architekturschule Moskaus (WCHUTEMAS) die Lenin-Bibliothek als Projekt für das Abschlußexamen auszuschreiben. Wie zu erwarten war, brachte diese Idee keine brauchbaren Resultate. Allerdings tat sich Iwan Leonidow (1902–1969) hervor. Obwohl nach dem Ende seiner Ausbildung nur wenige Bauwerke von Rang realisierte, gilt er aufgrund seiner Schriften und visionären Skizzen als einer der bedeutendsten russischen Architekten seiner Zeit[4].
Desweiteren ließ die Bibliothek von den Architekten P.N. Andrejew, B.A. Kondraschow und D.S. Markow eine Vorstudie anfertigen, die jedoch nicht weiterverfolgt wurde.

Offen und geschlossen

Markow erhielt eine zweite Chance, als am 1. Januar 1928 das Volkskommissariat für das Bildungswesen der Russischen Republik einen offiziellen Wettbewerb ausschrieb. Daß es sich bei dieser Bibliothek um ein Prestigeobjekt handelte, zeigte bereits die Wahl des Baugeländes in unmittelbarer Nähe des Kreml. Das Bauwerk sollte nicht nur ein Ehrenmal für Lenin, sondern auch eine Zierde der Hauptstadt werden. Außerdem enthielt die Ausschreibung die bemerkenswerte Forderung, daß das Gebäude seiner historischen Umgebung anzupassen sei. Darüber hinaus mußte Platz für sechs Millionen Bücher vorhanden sein.
Gleichzeitig mit der offenen Ausschreibung forderte man fünf Architekten auf, sich an einem geschlossenen Wettbewerb zu beteiligen: Alexej Schtschusew (1873–1949), Wladimir Schtschuko (1878–1939), die Gebrüder Wesnin und den Ingenieur Iwan Rerberg. An der offenen Ausschreibung nahmen nur zehn Architekten teil, deren Entwürfe alle im Stil der Moderne ausfielen, während die fünf Eingeladenen eher zum Traditionalismus neigten. In der ersten Gruppe erhielt Markow der seinen Entwurf mit Unterstützung von D.F. Fridman und V.I. Fidman ausgearbeitet hatte, den ersten Preis. In der zweiten Gruppe schied nur Rerberg aus, so daß Markow in der zweiten Ausschreibungsrunde (Einsendeschluß: November 1928) eingeladenen Architekten gegenüberstand, die sich nun seinen Vorstellungen anpaßten und ihre Entwürfe im Stil der Moderne überarbeiteten. Eine Ausnahme bildeten die Gebrüder Wesnin: Sie waren Modernisten der ersten Stunde und hatten von Anfang an Pläne vorgelegt, die ihrer Überzeugung entsprachen.
Die Jury vergab den Bauauftrag an Schtschuko, den traditionellsten der vier Architekten. Diese Entscheidung hatte einen Proteststurm von seiten der OSA und der snowa zur Folge. Aber weder die Jury noch die Bibliothek und das Volkskommissariat ließen sich durch die empörten Reaktionen beirren. Nach wiederholter Umarbeitung der Pläne begann Schtschuko – in Zusammenarbeit mit dem Architekten Wladimir Gelfreich (1886–1967) – mit dem Bau der Lenin-Bibliothek.

Entblößter Klassizismus

Schtschukos erster Entwurf ist sicher nicht als übermäßig konservativ zu bezeichnen, aber er unterschied sich deutlich von der Baukunst der Gebrüder Wesnin, Melnikows und der anderen Konstruktivisten. Im Grunde handelte es sich um eine Form des Klassizismus, dem nahezu alle dekorativen Elemente fehlten, mit Ausnahme einiger Verzierungen wie der Büste Lenins oder dem Doppelfries am Kalinin Prospekt, das im zweiten Entwurf durch die Aufschriften »S.S.S.R.« und »Lenin« ersetzt wurde. Obwohl die überarbeiteten Pläne weniger massiv wirken, fehlt ihnen der Geist des echten Modernismus. In gewissem Maße gilt dies auch für die Entwürfe Schtschusews. Seine beiden Beiträge unterschieden sich deutlich voneinander: Während der erste Entwurf stark hierarchisch, klassizistisch und wuchtig erscheint, zeigt der zweite sämtliche Prinzipien des Modernismus. Auffällig sind vor allem die »pilotis« (freistehende Säulen) und die durchgängigen Fenster. Dagegen unterschieden sich die Pläne der Gebrüder Wesnin weniger stark voneinander: Beide Entwürfe waren deutlich modernistisch. Die Bauarbeiten an der Lenin-Bibliothek waren erst 1941 abgeschlossen.

1 *Das bekannteste Beispiel für eine Integration der Künste ist das Denkmal der Dritten Internationale von Wladimir Tatlin (1919). Aber auch auf dem Gebiet der bildenden Kunst konnte von einem gegenseitigen Ideenaustausch gesprochen werden: Hier ist vor allem Kasimir Malewitsch als Wegbereiter zu nennen.*
2 *Auch hier gab es Zwischenformen und Architekten, die sich nicht in eine der Strömungen einteilen ließen, daher wird im Text hauptsächlich der Sammelbegriff »Modernismus« verwendet.*
3 *Siehe entsprechende Kapitel*
4 *Siehe auch das Kapitel zum Volkskommissariat für die Schwerindustrie*

La Bibliothèque Lénine, Moscou

Tout au long de la période post-révolutionnaire des années 20, les architectes et les artistes soviétiques bénéficièrent d'une liberté d'expression à peu près sans limite. L'avant-garde avait séduit les responsables communistes et les artistes se voyaient en élus chargés de donner une forme à cette nouvelle étape de l'histoire de l'humanité. Ce fut une ère marquée à la fois par le modernisme, l'imagination, l'enthousiasme et l'optimisme[1]. Mais au sein de l'architecture russe, le puissant mouvement traditionaliste plus classique, plus discret n'avait pas baissé les bras. Il allait s'imposer comme architecture officielle au fur et à mesure de la transformation du communisme en régime répressif. Les circonstances qui entourent le concours de la Bibliothèque Lénine illustrent cette évolution.

Optimisme post-révolutionnaire

Initialement, le contexte architectural était dominé par les avant-gardistes divisés en deux mouvements distincts. L'Association des Nouveaux Architectes (Asnova), avait été fondée en 1923 par Nicolaï Ladovsky (1881–1941) et Vladimir Krinsky. Leur rationalisme reposait sur l'idée selon laquelle la forme, la couleur et l'espace étaient influencés par l'esprit humain. L'Union des Architectes Contemporains (OSA), devenue rapidement plus célèbre qu'Asnova, fut créée en 1925 par les architectes Alexander A. Vesnine (1883–1959), Moisei Ginzbourg (1892–1946) et les artistes constructivistes Alexander Rodchenko et Alexei Gan.
Les rationalistes d'Asnova et les constructivistes d'OSA recherchaient tous deux une base scientifique pour tenter de résoudre les problèmes de l'architecture. Les rationalistes attachaient une importance fondamentale au plan de masse en privilégiant la fonction aux dépens de la forme, ce qui conduisait naturellement à des asymétries marquées. L'approche constructiviste, issue des œuvres de Vladimir Tatline et de quelques expériences antérieures, reposait sur le concept de visibilité de la structure[2]. Malheureusement, cette période de l'histoire soviétique marquée par la liberté de l'imagination le fut tout autant par un manque critique de moyens financiers et la plupart des projets merveilleusement créatifs de cette période ne furent jamais réalisés.
Il n'en restait pas moins que l'Etat nouveau avait besoin de bâtiments neufs et de nouvelles formes d'expression architecturale. Le traditionalisme hiératique de l'époque pré-révolutionnaire apparaissait trop marqué par le despotisme tsariste et tout à fait inapproprié à la nouvelle société.
Le Cercle des travailleurs était l'une de ces nouvelles applications de la recherche en architecture. Le travailleur était l'élément fondateur du nouveau système et méritait de disposer de son propre lieu qui, idéalement, devait contribuer à son développement culturel. L'architecte Constantin Melnikov (1890–1974) qui entretenait des liens étroits avec Asnova sans en être membre, imagina un remarquable Cercle pour la ville de Moscou (Cercle des travailleurs Rusakov, 1927–1929). Les constructivistes, quant à eux, avaient leur propre champion en la personne d' Ilya Golosov (1881–1945) dont le cercle Zuev avait fait une profonde impression (Moscou, 1928–1929).
En dehors de Golosov, de Melnikov, de Ginzbourg, Ladovsky et des frères Vesnine, de nombreux autres architectes se firent les ardents soutiens du mouvement moderniste dont l'importance prit des proportions toutes particulières en Union soviétique. Les architectes russes s'étaient aussi familiarisés avec les travaux de leurs confrères allemands ou néerlandais, comme Walter Gropius, Bruno Taut, Max Taut et Mart Stam qui avaient même été invités en Union Soviétique à un certain nombre d'occasions pour donner un avis technique ou esthétique.
Une autre catégorie d'édifices répondait à une fonction toute différente. Elle n'était pas destinée aux travailleurs, mais à la collectivité, aux soviets. Le Palais des Soviets et le Commissariat du Peuple pour l'Industrie Lourde, tous deux objets de concours[3], en sont deux bons exemples. Mais auparavant deux grandes compétitions avaient été organisées pour le Palais des Travailleurs (1923) et la Bibliothèque Lénine (1928), centre de l'idéologie soviétique où les œuvres de Marx, de Lénine et d'Engels pourraient être étudiées, comme la Bible dans les monastères du Moyen-Age.

L'examen final du projet

L'administration de la bibliothèque avait préalablement tenté de mettre au point un projet simple et économique (1927). Elle avait demandé aux directeurs de la principale école d'architecture de Moscou (Vkutein) de faire de la bibliothèque le thème de l'examen de fin d'études. Le professeur Ivan Leonidov (1902–1969) se distingua. Bien qu'il n'ait rien réalisé de notable, ses écrits et ses dessins visionnaires avaient fait de lui l'un des plus importants théoriciens de son temps[4]. En dehors de cette tentative opportuniste, la bibliothèque avait également demandé à P.N. Andreev, B.A. Kondrachov et D.S. Markov de soumettre des plans préliminaires dont elle ne fit aucun usage, même si Markov, par la suite, tenta sa chance une seconde fois.

Concours ouvert et restreint

Le 1er janvier 1928, le Commissariat du Peuple pour L'Edification de la République Russe organisa un concours officiel pour la bibliothèque Lénine (six millions de livres), grand projet de prestige pour lequel un premier site avait été libéré non loin du Kremlin.
Le cahier des charges était rédigé dans un style excessivement pompeux. Le bâtiment ne serait pas seulement un monument à Lénine et à sa philosophie mais également un des points de mire de la capitale. Le programme mentionnait la stipulation assez déroutante que la bibliothèque devait s'harmoniser à son environnement historique. Un concours ouvert et un concours restreint furent lancés simultanément. Quatre architectes furent conviés à la compétition restreinte: Alexei Chtchoussev (1873–1949), Vladimir Shchouko (1878–1939), les frères Vesnine et l'ingénieur Ivan Rerberg. Les dix architectes qui avaient participé au concours ouvert avaient tous soumis des projets modernistes alors que les invités penchaient davantage vers le traditionalisme. Markov, assisté de D.F. Fridman & V.L. Fidman, remporta le premier concours. Rerberg fut écarté du concours restreint et Markov se retrouva face à trois architectes invités pour le second tour clos en novembre 1928. Ces concurrents modifièrent leurs plans pour concurrencer le modernisme de Markov, à l'exception des frères Vesnine, bien sûr, qui, membres fondateurs du mouvement moderniste en Russie, restèrent fidèles à leurs convictions.
Le jury opta pour Shchouko, le plus classique des quatre. La décision souleva une tempête de protestations, à la fois de l'OSA et d'Asnova dont ni le jury ni l'administration ne tinrent compte. Après avoir modifié ses plans à plusieurs reprises, Shchouko construisit la bibliothèque Lénine avec l'architecte Vladimir Gelfreikh (1886–1967).

Un classicisme dépouillé

Bien que le premier projet de Shchouko n'ait pas été celui d'un conservateur, il ne supportait pas la comparaison avec les dessins des frères Vesnine, de Melnikov et des autres constructivistes. Son style peut se décrire comme une forme de classicisme dépouillé de la plupart de ses éléments décoratifs, mais préservant cependant quelques ornements, tels le buste de Lénine ou la double frise de la façade sur la perspective Kalinine. Dans sa seconde proposition, les frises avaient été remplacées par une inscription «URSS» et «Lénine». Bien que l'édifice ait perdu de sa massivité, il lui manquait encore la vivacité du vrai modernisme.
Dans une certaine mesure, le même commentaire peut s'appliquer au projet Chtchoussev . Il modifia complètement son premier plan extrêmement hiérarchisé, classique et massif, et se rallia, dans sa seconde proposition, aux principes du modernisme. Ses «pilotis» (colonnes) et les vastes fenêtres sont particulièrement frappants. Les différences entre le premier et le second dessin des frères Vesnine sont moins radicales mais leurs deux projets sont définitivement modernistes.
La Bibliothèque Lénine de Shchouko ne fut terminée qu'en 1941, mais son projet avait au moins échappé au triste destin de nombreux grands noms de l'architecture soviétique dont les projets ne furent jamais réalisés.

1 *Le meilleur exemple des fructueux échanges entre l'Etat et les artistes est sans doute le monument à la Troisième Internationale dessiné par Vladimir Tatline (1919). Dans le domaine des Beaux-Arts s'imposa de même la personnalité de Malévitch.*
2 *Comme toujours, on trouve des combinaisons de ces deux approches et des architectes qui n'appartenaient à aucun de ces deux mouvements. C'est pour cette raison que nous nous référons ici à la notion de 'modernisme', regroupant ces deux approches.*
3 *Ces concours sont décrits dans d'autres chapitres de cet ouvrage.*
4 *Voir également le chapitre sur le Commissariat du Peuple pour l'Industrie Lourde.*

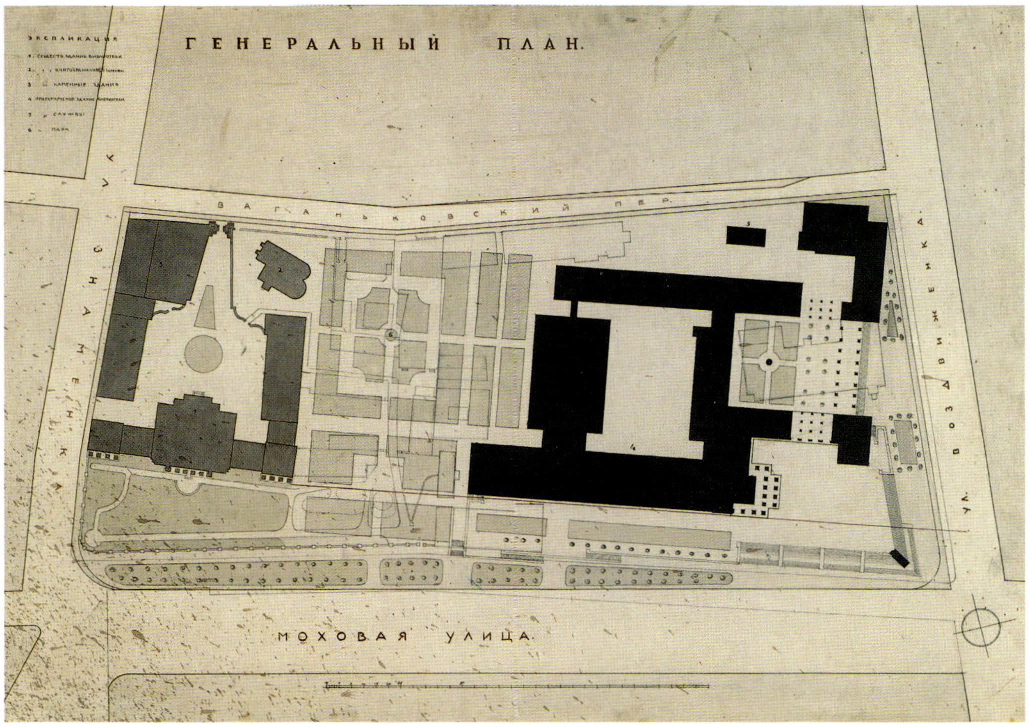

Vladimir Alexeyevich Shchuko
competition design, 1928, site plan

Vladimir Alexeyevich Shchuko
competition design, 1928, north elevation

Vladimir Alexeyevich Shchuko
competition design, 1928, east elevation

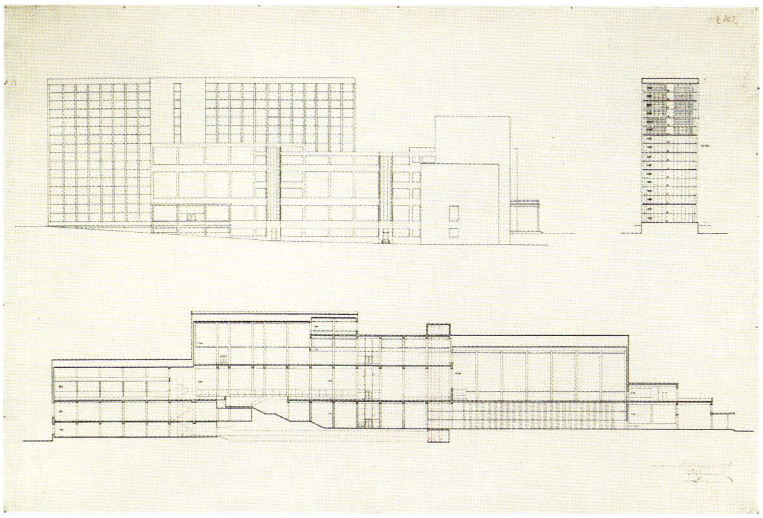

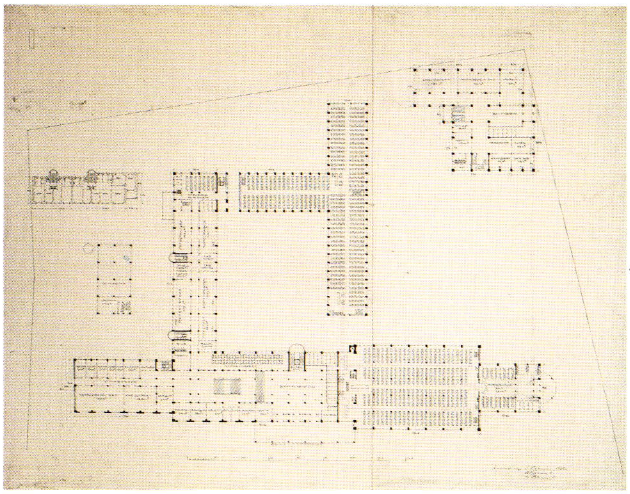

Alexander Alexandrovich Vesnin
& Viktor Alexandrovich Vesnin
competition design, 1928, sections

Alexander Alexandrovich Vesnin
& Viktor Alexandrovich Vesnin
competition design, 1928, ground floor plan

Alexander Alexandrovich Vesnin
& Viktor Alexandrovich Vesnin
competition design, 1928, east elevation

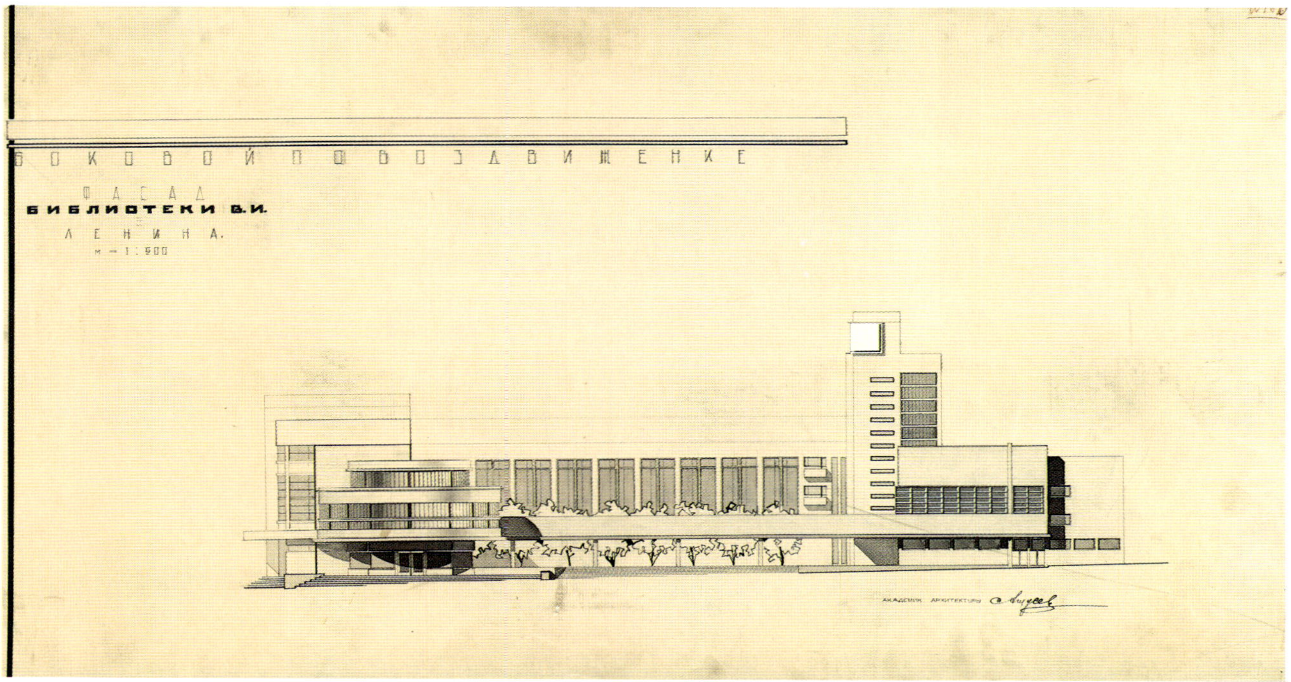

Alexei Viktorovich Shchusev
competition design, 1928, north elevation

Alexei Viktorovich Shchusev
competition design, 1928, site plan

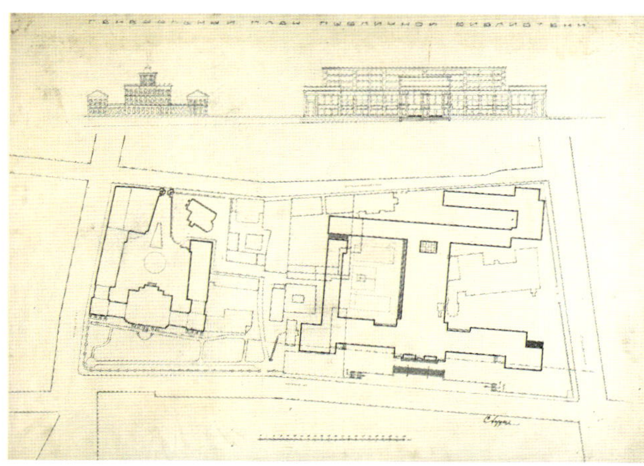

Alexei Viktorovich Shchusev
competition design, 1928, ground floor plan

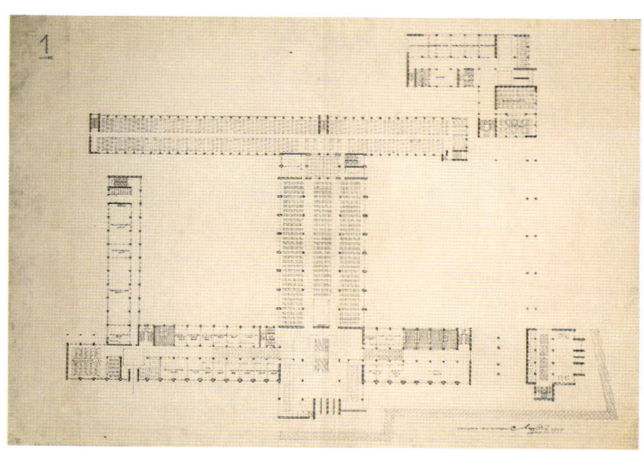

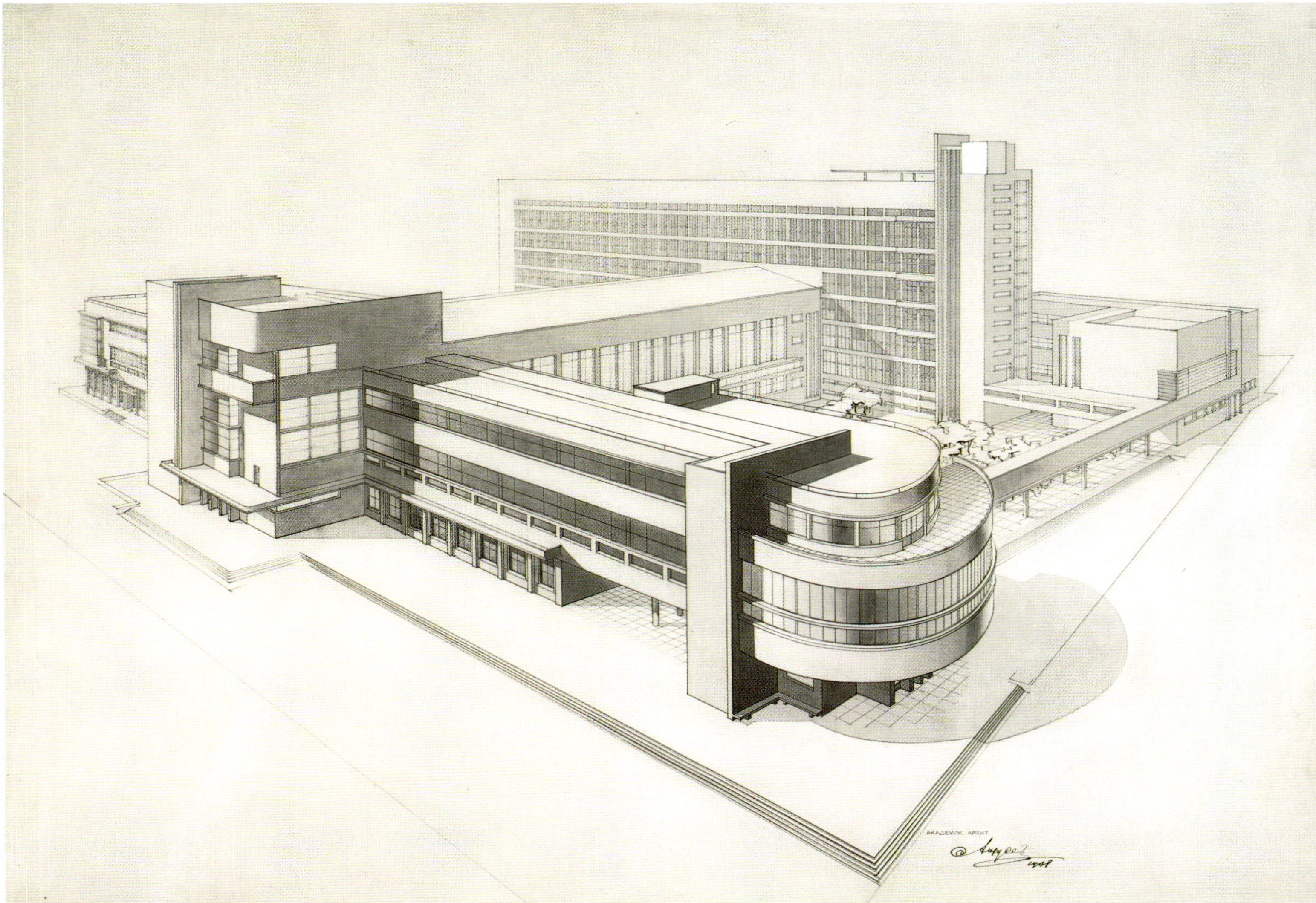

Alexei Viktorovich Shchusev

competition design, 1928, exterior perspective from north-east

Project
Palace of the Soviets

Site
Kropotkinskaya Nab., Moscow (next to Kremlin)

Dates
Closing date preliminary round February 1931 *First round* 18 July 1931 to 20 October 1931 (later postponed to 1 December 1931) *Result announced* 28 February 1932 *Second round* March 1932 to July 1932 *Third round* August 1932 to February 1933 *Result announced* 10 may 1933. B.M. Iofan and V.A. Shchuko & V.G. Gelfreikh were commissioned on 4 June 1933 (the exact dates of the competition are the subject of debate)

Number of entries
Preliminary round 15 *First round* 272 (160 complete designs and 112 partial designs) *Second round* 22 (12 invited) *Third round* 5 (Karo S. Alabjan, B.I. Simbirtchev, Arkadi Mordvinov & G.V. Kochar, L.A. Vesnin & V.A. Vesnin, B.M. Iofan, I.V. Zholtovsky & A.V. Shchusev, V.A. Shchuko & V.G. Gelfreikh)

Jury
Gleb Krzhizhanosky (Chairman), Anatoly Lunacharsky, Maxim Gorki, Constantin Stanislavsky, Vsevelod Meierkhold, and the architects M.V. Kriukov, A. Kozelkov and N.P. Zapetlin

Result
First round Ivan V. Zholtovsky, G.O. Hamilton

Commissioned by
The Palace Construction Council

Construction
The construction of the Palace was postponed when the Second World War broke out; the construction plans were later cancelled

Palace of the Soviets, Moscow, 1931–1933

ДВОРЦА СОВЕТОВ СССР
-КОНЕ - ВОЗВЫШЕНІЕ-
·другой конец· подобный·
VII
„ПРОСТОТА„ ПРЕДЛАГАЕТ

Palace of the Soviets, Moscow

During the 1930s, Stalin gradually tightened his hold on all aspects of Soviet life, including the arts. However, avant-garde artists continued to express their ideas. The competitions for the Palace of the Soviets and for the Peoples' Commissariat for Heavy Industry[1] both attracted a deluge of designs from Modernist-Constructivist architects. Hardly any of these architects ever saw their designs executed, although they were not barred from participating in intellectual life. Regrettably, this too would change. The architects, including foreigners such as Mart Stam and Le Corbusier, who had hoped to make a contribution to the new society, saw their dreams shattered with a heavy hand. State architecture became more pompous and Neo-classicist, and the housing more monotonous, as the Communist regime redoubled its drive to establish its authority.

A palace for the people

The competition for the Palace of the Soviets embroidered upon an idea which had developed in the early 1920s. The building, then referred to as the Workers' Palace, was to be the seat of the Supreme Soviet, symbolising the power of the people. Lenin was personally involved in the realisation of the palace, which was to be a monument for the new city and for the new, revolutionary Russia. The innovative architecture of the Constructivists was considered the most appropriate style for the building. The competition attracted designs from many Modernist architects, including Constantin Melnikov (1890–1974) and the team of Viktor Vesnin (1882–1950) & Alexander Vesnin (1883–1959). However, these architects saw the winner's laurels being snatched from under their noses by Nicolai Trotzky. Trotzky was an architectural cameleon who alternately submitted Modernist and monumental Neo-classicist designs, depending on the circumstances. He had become proficient in the latter style under the scholar I. Fomin. However, following Lenin's death the plans were shelved, due to lack of funds.
Eight years passed before a new competition was organised. Once again the avant-garde architects submitted their designs and faced the challenge of the Traditionalists. However, the climate had changed. Socialist realism had become the dominant art form and there had been a shift of emphasis from the people to the state. The building to be constructed was now referred to as the Palace of the Soviets, rather than the Workers' Palace. A subtle yet significant change. The power of the state, rather than the glory of the people, had become paramount. The Communist Party intended to show the world what great deeds it was capable of, regardless of the costs. Stalin contrived megalomaniac plans. Moscow was to rival New York and Chicago in its grandeur, regardless of the fact that it was a wooden city around the turn of century, with the exception of a few churches and the Kremlin.
Stalin's ambition was comparable to that of the Nazis in the 1930s. In Germany, a totalitarian regime had sought a monumental form which would embody its ideology. The Bauhaus in Dessau was closed down and Albert Speer became the Reich's architect. Speer's plans for Berlin and Stalin's plans for Moscow were two sides of the same coin. Yet, in 1931, the Russian avant-garde had not even considered the fact that

G.O. Hamilton **the first round competition, 1931, elevation, first prize**

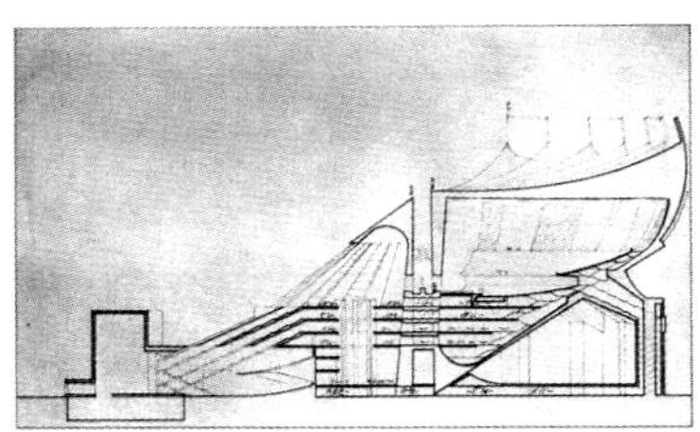

K.S. Melnikov **competition design, 1931, section, first round**

Le Corbusier **the first round competition, 1931, forum under the assembly for 15.000, interior perspective**

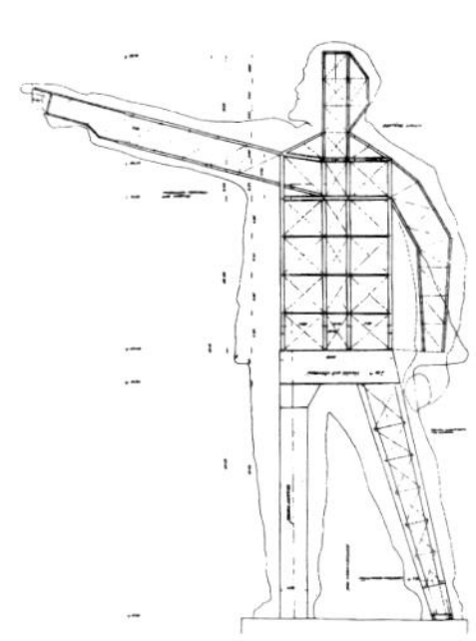

The statue of V.I. Lenin on the top of the Palace of the Soviets, section of the structure, 1934

there would be no freedom of innovation in a society governed by absolutists. Innovation, artistic or otherwise, meant change, and change was a threat to those in power.

Colossal architecture

An informal preliminary round was held in early 1931. A number of architects had been invited to submit designs, and others had submitted designs of their own accord. The architectural societies Asnova and SASS (formerly OSA) had also submitted designs, which served as a guideline for the official first round. Initially, the first round closing date was 20 October 1931 but this was later changed to 1 December. No less than 272 designs were submitted, including plans for parts of the complex. The field of participants included Le Corbusier, Mendelsohn, Walter Gropius, Auguste Perret and Hans Poelzig, all of whom had been invited to participate. These Modernists were held in high esteem by their Russian colleagues.
The competition programme was similar to that drafted for the Lenin Library. The Communist ideology was to be monumentally embodied. Other than that, the programme was quite summary. The building was to have two large halls (which could accommodate 15 000 and 6 500 people respectively), a gallery for 2 000 people, and two "small" halls, which could each accommodate 500 people. In addition, the building was to house a restaurant, a broadcasting studio and a library. To top it all, an entrance was required through which 25 000 people could pass at the same time! The competition programme did not stipulate the exact reasons for admitting crowds of this size to the building. But the mass reverence of their beloved leaders seems to be the most probable explanation.
Although prizes were awarded, the first round did not produce a design that was suitable for execution. The two main prizes were awarded to the Traditionalist architects Ivan Zholtovsky (1867–1968) and the American Hector Hamilton, both of whom had been invited to participate.

The second and third round

The conditions for the second round were slightly different. The programme no longer included the ludicrous stipulation that 25 000 people should be able to enter the building at the same time. A style was not specified but the architects were asked to seek a synthesis between the novel and the traditional. Twelve architects and teams from the first round were invited to participate, along with ten other invitees. The foreign architects were thanked for their efforts and dismissed. Although the Communist elite were in favour of megalomaniac Traditionalist buildings, there was still something for the lover of architecture. The first group of twelve invitees included the Vesnin brothers and Moisei Ginzburg (1892–1946). The second group included Ilya Golosov (1881–1945) and Nicolai Ladovsky (1881–1941). The architectural teams led by A.F. Zhukov and Vladimir A. Shchuko (1878–1939) had also been invited to participate[2]. Besides these avant-

gardist pioneers, the field of invitees included a number of extremely conservative architects. They were given from March to July 1932 to submit their designs.

In the third round, seven teams and individual architects were assigned to five teams. They were given until February 1933, to develop their plans. On 10 May 1933 the jury announced that Boris Iofan (1891–1976) was to be appointed project supervisor and that Shchuko and Gelfreikh (1886–1967) were to be his assistants. Construction was to be based on Iofan's design. The jury also announced that a colossal statue of Lenin would grace the roof of the building. The glorification of the Soviet leaders had started to take on excessive proportions. Iofan and his assistants were still developing their plans in 1941. However, the Second World War stood in the way of execution and the project was officially cancelled in 1954.

Rivalry

The architects had been asked to seek a synthesis between the old and the new. However, towards the end of the competition the chasm between the Traditionalist and Modernist movements was even greater than during the competition for the Lenin library. The movements had been divided from the start and it is therefore remarkable that both the Traditionalist and the Modernist architects incorporated the same symbolic elements in their designs. The mass parades of workers or soldiers bearing red banners seem to be symbolically appropriate. However, the imagery also included planes or shadows of planes.

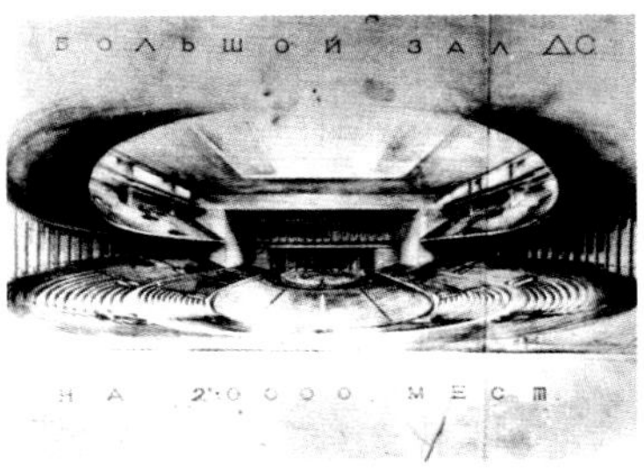

I.V. Zholtovsky **competition design, 1932. elevation, second round**

A.V. Vlasov & students of the VASI (school of architecture) **competition design, 1932, elevation, second round**

A.V. Shchusev & I. Zholtovsky **competition design, 1932, grand hall for 20 000 people, third round**

B.M. Iofan **competition design, 1931, elevation, first round**

B.M. Iofan, V.A. Shchuko, V.G. Gelfreikh **final design, 1935, bird's eye view**

N.A. Ladovsky **competition design, 1931–1932, elevation, second round**

To illústrate the "tribal warfare" in Russian architecture, let us compare the third round design of Shchuko[3] & Gelfreikh with that of the Vesnin brothers .

Shchuko & Gelfreikh's design was even more eclectic than the work they had produced in the past. The Palace itself was an over-sized version of the Palazzo Ducale in Venice, almost completely symmetrical and involving many repetitive features. For example, the horizontal articulation is identical on all four sides. The classically designed square is dominated by a massive column which combines the best features of the Siegesäule in Berlin, Trajan's column and the Tower of Pisa. Although the exterior of the palace and the column may lead one to conclude otherwise, both structures were to be constructed in reinforced concrete. The architects clearly concentrated on the visual aspects of their design, and it is debatable whether an edifice of this sort met the necessary technical and budgetary requirements.

The design submitted by the Vesnin brothers also contained repetitive elements, but was more asymmetrical. The proportional harmony between the cubic volumes, rather than the façade articulation, was taken as a point of departure. The underlying structure was also a basis for design. The "pilotis" (free-standing supports) and the free façade arrangement were clearly derived from the works of Le Corbusier.

The other designs may be compared in a similar manner. They were either ludicrously megalomaniac, traditionalist structures or examples of the best that the Modernist movement had to offer during this century. The two categories are on a par in terms of scale and imaginativeness. However, if the designs of the Traditionalists, such as Iofan and Zholtovski, are to be termed impressive, then those of Modernists, such as Karra and Ginzburg, must be characterised as breathtaking.

1 *The competition for the Peoples' Commissariat is discussed in the next chapter.*

2 *See chapter on the Lenin Library in this book.*

3 *Shchuko had won the competition for the Lenin Library.*

Palast der Sowjets, Moskau

In den 30er Jahren wurden in der Sowjetunion die Repressionen Stalins in allen Bereichen des täglichen Lebens – also auch in der Kunst – immer spürbarer. Dennoch hinderte dies die avantgardistischen Architekten der Zeit nicht an der Verbreitung ihrer Ideen. Sowohl der Wettbewerb für den Palast der Sowjets als auch die Ausschreibung zum Volkskommissariat für die Schwerindustrie[1] hatten eine Flut von modernen, konstruktivistischen Entwürfen zur Folge. Obwohl für die Architekten eine Realisierung ihrer Projekte nahezu unmöglich geworden war, ließen sie sich nicht daran hindern, nach wie vor am intellektuellen Leben teilzunehmen.

Ein Palast für das Volk

Der Wettbewerb für den Palast der Sowjets entwickelte sich aus einer zu Beginn der 20er Jahre entstandenen Idee. Damals plante man einen »Palast der Arbeit«, der als Sitz des Obersten Sowjet und zugleich als Symbol für die Macht des Volkes gedacht war. Lenin selbst setzte sich für diesen Palast ein, der ein Monument der neuen Stadt und des neuen, revolutionären Rußland werden sollte. Die Architektur der Konstruktivisten schien zur Umsetzung dieser Vorstellungen am besten geeignet. Dementsprechend gehörten Konstantin S. Melnikow (1890–1974), Viktor A. Wesnin (1882–1950) und Alexander A. Wesnin (1883–1959) zu den Teilnehmern an der Ausschreibung für den Palast der Arbeit. Doch sie mußten mitansehen, wie ihnen Nikolai Trotzki den ersten Preis vor der Nase wegschnappte. Trotzki galt als architektonisches Chamäleon, das den Umständen entsprechend entweder moderne konstruktivistische oder monumentale klassizistische Bauten entwarf. Nach Lenins Tod wurden Trotzkis Pläne ad acta gelegt, nicht zuletzt aus Mangel an finanziellen Mitteln.

Als acht Jahre später ein neuer Architekturwettbewerb ausgeschrieben wurde, sandten die Konstruktivisten erneut ihre Beiträge ein und nahmen den Kampf mit den Traditionalisten auf. Aber das Klima hatte sich verändert: Der sozialistische Realismus war zur beherrschenden Kunstform geworden, und das politische Gleichgewicht verschob sich vom Volk zum Staat. Man sprach nicht mehr vom Palast der Arbeit, sondern vom Palast der Sowjets – ein kleiner Unterschied von großer Bedeutung. Nicht der Ruhm des Volkes, sondern die Macht des Staates stand im Vordergrund. Die Welt mußte erfahren, zu welchen Leistungen die Kommunistische Partei imstande war. Stalin schwebten megalomane Bauten vor. Moskau, das gegen Ende des 19. Jahrhunderts bis auf den Kreml und einige Kirchen völlig aus Holz bestand, sollte sich in Größe und Glanz mit New York und Chicago messen können.

Kolossale Bauwerke

Die Ausschreibung begann 1931 mit einer informellen Vorrunde. Einige Architekten war zur Teilnahme eingeladen worden, andere reichten aus eigener Initiative ihre Entwürfe ein, auch Beiträge aus den Architekturvereinigungen (u.a. von der snowa und der in SASS umbenannten OSA) waren darunter. Die gesammelten Entwürfe dienten als Richtlinie für die offizielle erste Runde des Wettbewerbs. Einsendeschluß war zunächst der 20. Oktober, später der 1. Dezember 1931. 272 Beiträge wurden eingereicht, von denen einige nur für einen Teil des gesamten Komplexes gedacht waren. Unter den Einsendern befanden sich die offiziell eingeladenen Architekten Le Corbusier, Erich Mendelsohn, Walter Gropius, Auguste Perret und Hans Poelzig. Diese Vertreter der Moderne genossen in der UdSSR hohes Ansehen.

Die Wettbewerbsbedingungen ähnelten den Auflagen beim Bau der Lenin-Bibliothek: Der Palast der Sowjets sollte kommunistische Ideologie in monumentaler Form verkörpern. Ansonsten waren die Forderungen recht knapp gefaßt. Der Palast sollte zwei große Säle mit genügend Platz für 15 000 bzw. 6 500 Personen, eine Galerie für 2 000 Personen und zwei kleine Säle für 500 Personen enthalten; desweiteren mußten die Architekten ein Restaurant, ein Rundfunkstudio und eine Bibliothek in das Gesamtkonzept integrieren. Außerdem war ein Haupteingang verlangt, durch den 25 000 Menschen zugleich in den Palast strömen konnten.

Die erste Ausschreibungsrunde brachte keinen Entwurf hervor, der sich zur Umsetzung eignete. Dennoch wurden mehrere Beiträge prämiert: Am 28. Februar 1932 vergab die Jury die beiden Hauptpreise an Iwan Scholtowski (1867–1968) und den Amerikaner Hector G.O. Hamilton, die zu den Eingeladenen zählten und Entwürfe im traditionalistischen Stil eingereicht hatten.

Weitere Ausschreibungsrunden

Für die zweite Runde des Wettbewerbs wurden die Bedingungen überarbeitet. Als erstes fiel die Forderung nach einem Eingang für 25 000 Menschen. Obwohl kein bestimmter Stil vorgeschrieben war, sollten die Architekten bei ihren Entwürfen Neues und Traditionelles miteinander verbinden. Als Teilnehmer an der zweiten Runde waren zwölf Architekten und Teams aus der ersten Runde zugelassen; zudem wurden zehn weitere Baumeister zur Teilnahme eingeladen. Die Entwürfe sollten von März bis Juli 1932 ausgearbeitet werden, ausländische Teilnehmer waren nicht mehr zugelassen. Trotz der Vorliebe der Machthaber für megalomane, traditionalistische Bauwerke bot der Wettbewerb dem Architekturliebhaber einige Überraschungen. Die Gebrüder Wesnin und Moisej Ginsburg (1892–1946) gehörten zu den zwölf Eingeladenen; unter den zehn anderen Architekten befanden sich Ilja Golosow (1881–1945), Nikolai Ladowski (1881–1941), A.F. Schukow und Wladimir A. Schtschuko (1878–1939), wobei die beiden letzteren jeweils mit einem Partner zusammenarbeiteten[2]. Neben den Avantgardisten der ersten Stunde gehörten äußerst konservative Architekten zu den Teilnehmern.

Die 22 Teilnehmer wurden in fünf Gruppen eingeteilt, die ihre Pläne bis zum Februar 1933 weiter ausarbeiten sollten (dritte Runde). Am 10. Mai 1933 ernannte die Jury Boris Jofan (1891-1976) zum Chefarchitekten und Schtschuko sowie Wladimir G. Gelfreich (1886–1967) zu seinen Assistenten; Jofans Entwurf sollte beim Bau als Planungsgrundlage dienen. Darüber hinaus stellte die Jury die Bedingung, daß der Palast von einer kolossalen Statue Lenins gekrönt werden solle – ein Zeichen für den immer stärkeren Personenkult in der Sowjetunion. Jofan und seine Assistenten arbeiteten noch bis 1941 an den Plänen, aber der Zweite Weltkrieg verhinderte die Durchführung. 1954 wurde das Projekt eingestellt.

Konkurrenzkämpfe

Obwohl die Wettbewerbsauflagen eine Symbiose von neuem Stil und Traditionalismus gefordert hatten, war der Gegensatz zwischen beiden Strömungen in der Schlußphase des Wettbewerbs noch größer als bei der Ausschreibung für die Lenin-Bibliothek. Beide Bewegungen hatten einander von Anfang an unversöhnlich gegenübergestanden. Interessanterweise verwandten sowohl traditionalistische als auch moderne Architekten in ihren Entwürfen dieselben Symbole: Marschierende Massen von Arbeitern, Soldaten mit roten Fahnen, aber auch Flugzeuge und deren Schatten wurden als Ausdruck einer bestimmten Atmosphäre herangezogen.

Um die »Stammesfehde« innerhalb der russischen Architektur zu illustrieren, lohnt ein Vergleich des Entwurfs von Schtschuko und Gelfreich mit dem der Gebrüder Wesnin[3]. Beide Projekte stammen aus der dritten und letzten Ausschreibungsrunde.

Der Entwurf von Schtschuko und Gelfreich ist im Vergleich zu ihrem bisherigen Schaffen als äußerst eklektizistisch zu bezeichnen. Ihr Palast erinnert an eine aufgeblasene Version des Palazzo Ducale in Venedig. Das Gebäude ist von nahezu symmetrischem Aufbau. Es zeigt eine Reihe repetitiver Elemente und ist in seiner horizontalen Gliederung nach allen vier Seiten identisch. Auf dem nach klassischem Vorbild angelegten Platz steht eine riesige Säule, die in sich die schönsten Elemente der Berliner Siegessäule, der Trajanssäule und des Turms von Pisa vereinigt. Obwohl die Außenfassaden des Palastes und die Säule es nicht vermuten lassen, sind beide Konstruktionen aus Stahlbeton angefertigt. Die Architekten setzten sich ausschließlich mit den visuellen Aspekten ihres Bauwerks auseinander. Offen bleibt, ob ein derartiges Gebäude auch anderen (d.h. technischen und ökonomischen) Ansprüchen genügt hätte.

Der Entwurf der Gebrüder Wesnin zeigt ebenfalls repetitive Elemente, ist aber asymmetrisch in seinem Aufbau. Ansatzpunkt war hier nicht die Gestaltung der Außenfassaden, sondern das gegenseitige harmonische Verhältnis der kubischen Volumen. Auch die eigentliche Baukonstruktion wurde zum Ausgangspunkt des Designs. Die freistehende Stützpfeiler und eine freie Fassadengestaltung zeugen vom starken Einfluß Le Corbusiers.

Die anderen Entwürfen waren entweder groteske, megalomane, traditionalistische Bauten, oder sie gehörten zum Besten, was die moderne Bewegung in diesem Jahrhundert zu bieten hatte. In punkto Maßstab und Phantasie stehen beide Richtungen einander in nichts nach. Während die Entwürfe der Traditionalisten Jofan und Scholtowski vor allem imposant wirken sollen, sind die Projekte der Modernisten wie Karra und Ginsburg atemberaubend.

1 Die Ausschreibung für das Volkskommissariat wird im nächsten Kapitel beschrieben

2 Siehe das Kapitel zur Lenin-Bibliothek

3 Schtschuko und Gelfreich hatten den Wettbewerb für die Lenin-Bibliothek gewonnen

Le Palais des Soviets, Moscou

Au cours des années 30, alors que Staline resserrait peu à peu sa mainmise sur tous les aspects de la vie soviétique, y compris la culture, les artistes d'avant-garde tentaient encore de s'exprimer. Les concours pour le Palais des Soviets et le Commissariat du Peuple pour l'Industrie Lourde[1] attirèrent tous deux une avalanche de projets modernistes et constructivistes, mais aucun de leurs auteurs ne vit jamais le moindre de ses projets réalisés. La liberté de participer à la vie intellectuelle leur fut petit à petit retirée et leurs rêves, y compris ceux d'étrangers comme Le Corbusier ou Mart Stam, furent brisés. L'architecture officielle devint encore plus pompeuse et plus conservatrice, les immeubles de logements encore plus monotones et le régime communiste redoubla d'autoritarisme.

Un palais pour le peuple

Le concours pour le Palais des Soviets naquit d'une idée lancée au début des années 20. L'édifice, alors appelé Palais des Travailleurs, devait être le siège du Soviet suprême et symboliser le pouvoir du peuple. Lénine s'impliqua personnellement dans le projet qui devait aussi constituer le principal monument de la nouvelle capitale et de la Russie révolutionnaire. On pensa tout d'abord que seule une approche aussi innovatrice que celle des constructivistes pouvait permettre d'atteindre un tel objectif. Le concours vit donc affluer les participations de nombreux modernistes dont Constantin Melnikov (1890–1974), l'équipe des frères Viktor Vesnine (1882–1950) et Alexander Vesnine (1883–1959). Mais ces brillants créateurs se virent ravir les lauriers qu'ils attendaient par Nicolaï Trotzky. Architecte-caméléon qui alternait les projets classiques ou modernistes, selon les circonstances, il s'était perfectionné dans ce dernier style sous l'influence du Professeur Fomine. Néanmoins, après la mort de Lénine, ses plans furent écartés pour des raisons financières. Huit années passèrent avant qu'un nouveau concours ne soit organisé. Une fois encore, les architectes d'avant-garde soumirent des projets pour tenter de relever le défi des traditionalistes. Mais le climat avait changé. Le réalisme socialiste était en plein essor et l'Etat pesait déjà plus lourd que le peuple. Glissement sémantique significatif, le bâtiment s'appelait maintenant Palais des Soviets au lieu de Palais des Travailleurs.

Le parti communiste voulait alors prouver au monde qu'il était capable de mener à bien de grands projets, quel qu'en soit le coût. Staline imagina des plans mégalomanes, dans lesquels Moscou rivalisait de grandeur avec Chicago ou New York, oubliant que sa capitale était encore une ville construite en bois, à l'exception de quelques églises et du Kremlin.

L'ambition stalinienne était comparable à celle des nazis. En Allemagne, le nouveau régime totalitaire était à la recherche d'une forme monumentale qui incarne son idéologie. Le Bauhaus de Dessau avait été fermé et Albert Speer nommé architecte du Reich. Ses plans pour Berlin et ceux de Staline pour Moscou étaient de la même nature. En 1931, l'avant-garde russe n'avait pas encore compris qu'il n'y avait plus de place pour la liberté d'innovation dans une société totalitaire. Innovation signifiait changement et tout changement ne pouvait être qu'une menace pour les hommes en place.

Une architecture colossale

Un premier concours informel fut organisé début 1931. Quelques architectes avaient été invités à soumettre des projets et d'autres concouraient de leur propre initiative. Les associations d'architectes, Asnova et SASS (ex OSA) avaient de leur côté proposé des plans qui servirent de cadre au concours officiel. La date de remise des projets, fixée au 20 octobre 1931, fut repoussée au 1er décembre. Pas moins de 272 projets furent envoyés dont plusieurs pour certaines parties du complexe seulement. Parmi les participants, on remarquait Le Corbusier, Mendelsohn, Walter Gropius, Auguste Perret et Hans Poelzig, tous invités, et représentatifs d'un modernisme très apprécié par leurs confrères russes.

Le cahier des charges était semblable à celui de la Bibliothèque Lénine. Si l'idéologie communiste devait bien entendu trouver en cet édifice sa matérialisation monumentale, les spécifications étaient assez succinctes. Le palais devait être équipé de deux vastes salles de 15 000 et 6 000 auditeurs, d'une galerie pour 2 000 personnes et de deux petites salles de 500 places. A cela s'ajoutait un restaurant, un studio de radio et une bibliothèque. Le hall d'entrée quant à lui devait pouvoir accueillir 25 000 visiteurs en même temps. Si le concours ne précisait pas les raisons de tels chiffres, la fascination que les grands nombres exerçait sur les hauts responsables en était sans doute l'explication la plus plausible.

Des prix furent accordés, mais aucun plan réalisable ne sortit de ce premier tour. Les deux principales récompenses furent accordées le 28 février 1932 à l'architecte classique Ivan Zholtovski (1867–1968) et à l'Américain Hector Hamilton, tous deux invités.

Deuxième et troisième tours

Les conditions du second tour furent légèrement différentes. Le programme ne comportait plus ce chiffre un peu absurde de 25 000 personnes pour le hall d'entrée, le style n'était pas spécifié mais les hommes de l'art étaient incités à trouver une synthèse entre modernisme et tradition. Douze participants du premier tour furent conviés ainsi que dix nouveaux invités. Ils avaient de mars à juillet 1932 pour soumettre leurs projets. Les architectes étrangers furent remerciés pour leurs efforts et priés de repartir. Même si l'élite communiste favorisait les plans mégalomanes et traditionnels, une petite place était encore faite aux vrais créateurs. Le premier groupe de douze participants comptait en effet les frères Vesnine et Moisei Ginzbourg (1892–1946), le second, Ilya Golosov (1881–1945) et Nicolaï Ladovsky (1881–1941). Des équipes conduites par A. F. Zhoukov et Vladimir A. Shchouko (1878–1939) avaient également été conviées[2], mais en dehors de ces pionniers de l'avant-garde, le choix des invités révélait une nette tendance vers un plus grand conservatisme. Les 22 participants au troisième tour furent répartis en cinq équipes et eurent jusqu'à février 1933 pour mettre au point leurs plans. Le 10 mai 1933, le jury annonça que Boris Iofan (1891–1976) serait superviseur du projet, assisté de Shchouko et Vladimir Gelfreikh (1886–1967) et que la construction serait basée sur le plan de Iofan. Détail montrant les proportions que commençait à prendre le culte de la personnalité: une statue colossale de Lénine s'élèverait au sommet du bâtiment. Iofan et ses assistant en étaient encore à mettre au point leurs plans en 1941 lorsque la guerre interrompit leur travail. Le projet fut officiellement abandonné en 1954.

Rivalité

Bien que les architectes aient été conviés à rechercher une synthèse entre l'ancien et le nouveau, la fracture entre les traditionalistes et les modernistes fut encore plus marquée à la fin du concours que lors de l'affaire de la Bibliothèque Lénine. Mais même si les deux mouvement s'opposaient dès le départ, les architectes des deux écoles n'en incorporèrent pas moins des éléments décoratifs symboliques identiques dans leurs projets: parades de travailleurs ou de soldats arborant des drapeaux rouges et souvent avions ou profils d'avions.

La comparaison entre les plans de Shchouko et Gelfreikh et ceux des frères Vesnine[3] illustre l'état de guerre «tribal» de l'architecture russe de cette époque. Les plans de Shchouko et de son associé étaient encore plus éclectiques que les œuvres qu'ils avaient signées dans le passé. Leur palais était une sorte de version surdimensionnée de celui des Doges. Le bâtiment était presque complètement symétrique et faisait largement usage de la répétition. Par exemple, son articulation horizontale était identique sur les quatre côtés. La place carrée était très classiquement dominée par une colonne massive qui mélangeait des éléments de la Siegessaüle de Berlin, de la colonne de Trajan et de la tour de Pise. Malgré le soin pris à le dissimuler, la colonne comme le Palais étaient en ciment armé. Les architectes s'étaient à l'évidence concentrés sur la séduction visuelle de leurs dessins et l'on peut se demander si un tel édifice respectait les contraintes techniques et budgétaires.

Les plans des Vesnine contenaient également des éléments répétitifs, mais tout en étant plus asymétriques. L'harmonie des proportions entre les volumes cubiques et la structure générale plus que l'articulation des façades avait été prise comme point de départ. Les «pilotis» de la façade venaient tout droit des travaux de Le Corbusier.

Les autres plans peuvent être comparés de la même façon. C'étaient tantôt des exemples ridicules ou colossaux de structures traditionnelles ou l'illustration de ce que le mouvement moderniste pouvait offrir de mieux. Pour leur échelle et leur créativité, les deux catégories de plans se valaient, mais autant les projets classiques de Iofan et de Zholtovski impressionnaient, autant ceux des modernistes comme Karra et Ginzbourg coupaient le souffle.

1 *Traité dans le chapitre suivant.*
2 *Voir le chapitre sur la Bibliothèque Lénine.*
3 *Shchouko et Gelfreikh avaient remporté le concours de la Bibliothèque Lénine.*

Vladimir Georgievich Gelfreikh &
Vladimir Alexeyevich Shchuko
competition design, 1932, exterior view, second round

Ivan Vladislavovich Zholtovsky competition design, 1932, exterior view, second round

G.O. Hamilton competition design, 1931, section, first round, first prize

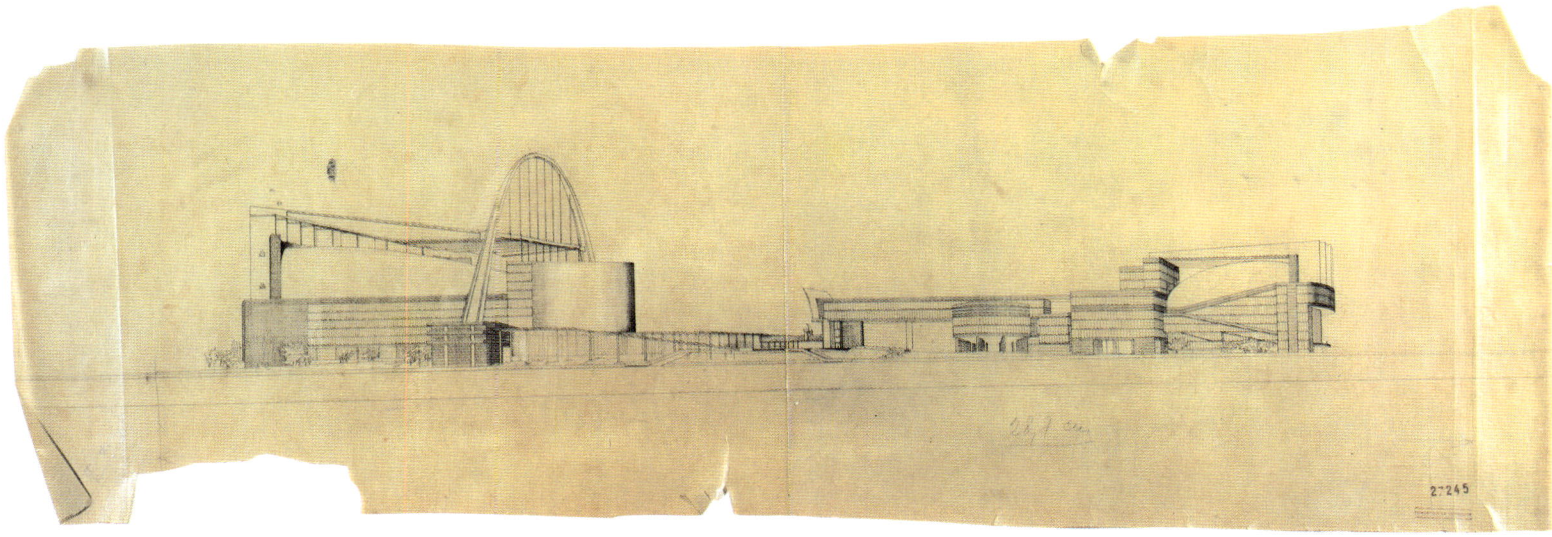

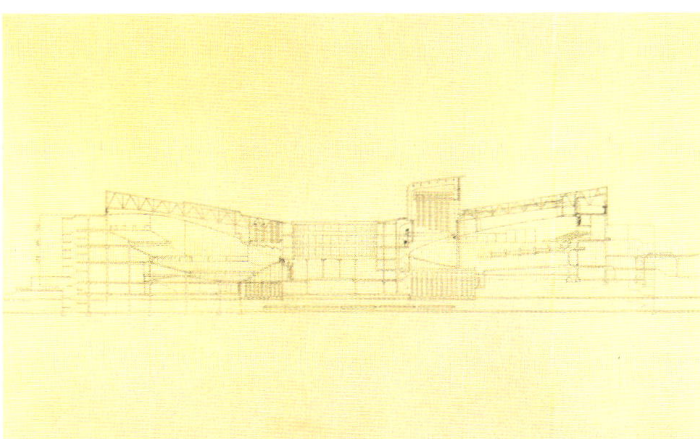

Le Corbusier competition design, 1931, exterior view, first round

Walter Gropius competition design, 1931, longitudinal section, first round

Walter Gropius competition design, 1931, exterior view of entrance, first round

Walter Gropius competition design, 1931, plan, first round

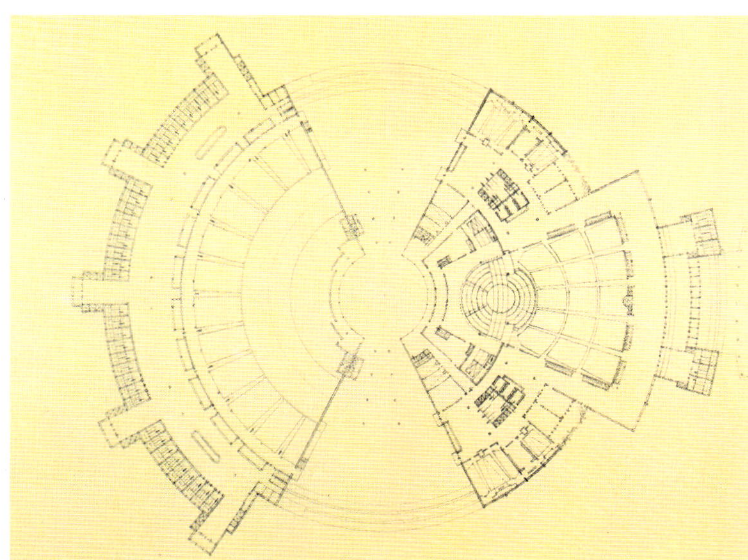

Alexander Alexandrovich Vesnin, Viktor Alexandrovich Vesnin & Leonid Alexandrovich Vesnin
competition design, 1933, exterior perspective, third round

Alexander Alexandrovich Vesnin, Viktor Alexandrovich Vesnin & Leonid Alexandrovich Vesnin
competition design, 1933, interior perspective, third round

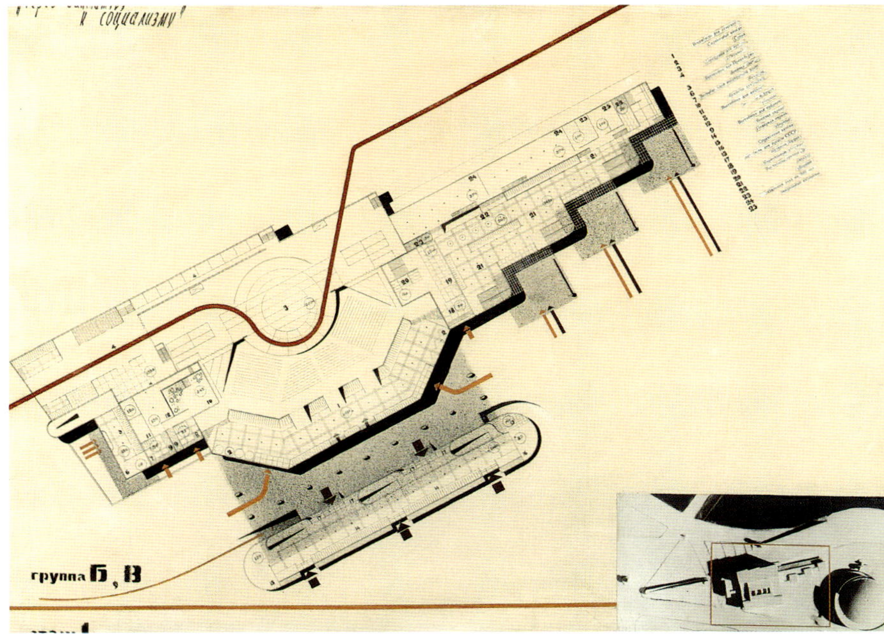

VOPRA (All Union Society of Proletarian Architects), N. Baranov, K. Ivanov, V. Notes, B. Rubanenko, M. Rusakov & F. Terekhin competition design, 1931, axonometric, first round

VOPRA (All Union Society of Proletarian Architects), N. Baranov, K. Ivanov, V. Notes, B. Rubanenko, M. Rusakov & F. Terekhin competition design, 1931, plan, first round

Moisei Yakovlevich Ginzburg, G. Gassenpflug, S. Risagor & Arthur Ferdinandvich Loleit competition design, 1932, elevation, second round

Alexander Jakovlevich Karra competition design, 1931, axonometric, first round, second prize

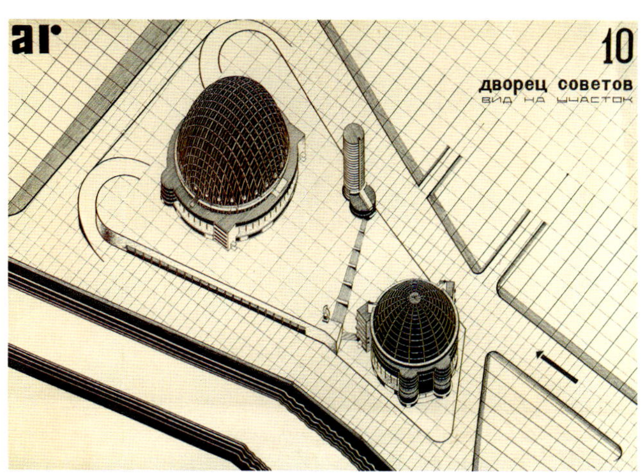

Team belonging to ARU (Union of Architect Urbanists): Georgi T. Krutikov, Valentin S. Popov & Vitaly A. Lavrov competition design, 1931, exterior view, preliminary round

Boris Mikhailovich Iofan, Vladimir Georgievich Gelfreikh & Vladimir Alekseevich Shchuko variant after competition, exterior view

People's Commissariat of Heavy Industry, Moscow, 1934

Project

Peoples' Commissariat for Heavy Industry (Ministry)

Site

Red Square, Moscow

Dates

1934, 1935 and 1936

Number of entries

1934 10 (V.A. & A.A. Vesnin; M.J. Ginzburg & S. Lisagor; V.M. Lebedev & C.S. Melnikov; I.I. Leonidov; P.A. Golosov; B.A. Korshunov & A.A. Zubin; A.M. Zaslavsky & A.M. Faifal; D. Fridman & V. Fidman; I.I. Trankvillitsky & N.A. Khokhriakov; I. Fomin & M. Minkus) *1935* 8. (A.V. Shchusev; V.A. Shchuko; V.A. & A.A. Vesnin; D.F. Fridman & D.M. Kogan; A.G. Mordvinov; M. Gunger; G.P. Domshlak & F.F. Gursky; a team from the Leningrad School of Art) *1936* Unknown

Jury

Unknown

Result

No winner

Commissioned by

The Peoples' Commissariat for Heavy Industry

Construction

Postponed to a later date due to the outbreak of the Second World War, later cancelled completely

People's Commissariat of Heavy Industry, Moscow, 1934

Alexander Alexandrovich Vesnin
& Viktor Alexandrovich Vesnin
competition design, 1934, exterior
view on Red Square

People's Commissariat of Heavy Industry, Moscow

The competition for the Peoples' Commissariat for Heavy Industry followed a pattern similar to other Russian architectural competitions of the 1920s and 30s. An almost identical series of events marked the competition for the Palace of the Soviets, which was not nearly settled in 1934. It is important to note that any comparison of the two competitions should be considered with a certain amount of circumspection in view of the fact that many records have disappeared and many more facts remain unknown to us. All matters pertaining to architectural competitions were treated as classified information in Stalinist Russia.

Modernism versus Traditionalism

The obscure manner in which competitions were organised in the Soviet Union, especially with respect to adjudication, is quite intriguing. A recurrent theme in all competitions was the rivalry between the Modernists, who may be roughly categorised as Rationalists or Constructivists, and the Traditionalists (Neo-Classical and Neo-Renaissance). Initially, the Modernist movement prospered. They were closely involved in the revolution and supported Communism. However, in spite of their revolutionary principles, the new leaders were not always equally taken by the avant-garde. They preferred to keep to the beaten track and more often than not they commissioned architects of the old school.
Nevertheless, modern architecture flourished as never before, partly because competitions were frequently organised. However, after Lenin's death in 1924, Stalin rose to power and the Communist Party gained an ever stronger grip on cultural life. Architectural competitions were either organised directly by the Party or by Party members, who dictated the course of events in the organisations involved. It is interesting to note that both Traditionalists and Modernists were always explicitly asked to participate. However, the winning design usually stemmed from academic circles. This was the case in the competition for the Lenin Library, won by V.A. Shchuko (1878–1939), and in the competition for the Palace of the Soviets, won by B.M. Iofan (1891–1976). However, Modernist architects continued to submit uncompromising, innovative designs. The competition for the Peoples' Commissariat for Heavy Industry proved to be a turning point, marked by growing scepticism.

Communist hobby-horse

The Palace of the Soviets and the Peoples' Commissariat were to embody the glories of Communism. Lenin had initiated the industrialisation of agrarian Russia and in 1929, Stalin launched his first five-year plan, which ended prematurely in 1932, the year in which the Peoples' Commissariat was established. Stalin had hoped to boost Soviet heavy industry – a Communist hobby-horse – to a level comparable with that of the USA, making Moscow one of the world's leading capitals.

Constantin Stepanovich Melnikov (1890–1974)

Ivan Ivanovich Leonidov (1902–1969)

A. Dushkin Mayakovskaya Station, Moscow, 1938

Platform of the underground station, Moscow, 1935

Stalin evidently believed that no metropolis was complete without a comprehensive infrastructure, and that no infrastructure was complete without a subway. Naturally, it had to be the world's safest and most beautiful subway. It was to reflect the glory of the new Moscow. Its stations were to serve as Workers' Palaces. This immense project was mainly executed during 1934 and 1935. The competition for the Peoples' Commissariat was held during the same period. The stations and entrances were designed by Modernists (Ladovski), Neo-Classicists (Fomin) and Socialist Realists (A.N. Doushkin). Without exception, these architects did their utmost to make the Moscow subway something out of the ordinary. In contrast to their colleagues working above ground, they did so with consummate success.

Moscow was to be completely redesigned. The Palace of the Soviets and the Peoples' Commissariat were to be the most important buildings, both architecturally and ideologically. Both buildings were to be conveniently situated near the Kremlin. A site for the Peoples' Commissariat had even been made available on Red Square. The site specified in the competition programme is the block where the GUM department store now stands. This block was to be demolished and it was left up to the architects to suggest what was to be done with the surrounding buildings. It was a question of conscience, certainly in view of the fact that the continued existence of the historical heart of the city (Kitaj-Gorod) was at stake. The most significant cynosure in this area was St. Basil's cathedral. The architects Golosov, Fridman and, surprisingly, the scholar Fomin, were amongst those in favour of demolishing the cathedral. The Vesnin brothers and Ivan Leonidov incorporated the cathedral in their urban development plans, as an optical copes stone for the Red Square. Another fixed feature which the architects had to take into account was Lenin's Mausoleum, designed in an angular Modernist style (1926–1930) by the architectural chameleon Alexei Shchusev (1873–1949). This little building was oriented towards the Kremlin, which had certain consequences for the situation of the Peoples' Commissariat.

Three very closed competitions

Of the three Russian competitions discussed in this book, the least is known of the competition for the Peoples' Commissariat. The first round was held in 1934. Most of the spectacular designs, which were in keeping with the wishes of the regime and the visionary ideas of the architects, stemmed from Modernist circles. The Peoples' Commissariat was to have a conference hall, with a capacity to seat up to 1 500 representatives from the different republics. There would also be a number of smaller halls (seating capacity: 300) and areas for other facilities, such as a hotel, a library, clubs, cafeterias, restaurants and the like. The most important areas were reserved for those in power. In short, the Peoples' Commissariat was an authoritarian, hierarchic public body.

In 1935, a second round was organised for unknown reasons. A select group of architects was asked to submit designs, as in the first round.

A.V. Shchusev **Mausoleum of Lenin, above: exterior perspective, middle: ground floor plan, below: elevation, Moscow Red Square, 1929–1930**

However, in this instance, the sole avant-garde architects were the Vesnin brothers. It is interesting to note that, although the Vesnins almost always participated, they hardly ever won a competition. Even less is known of the third round, except that the Vesnins' design was highly praised.

Soon after the third round the authorities decided that the Red Square was not a suitable location. All major construction plans were cancelled when the Second World War broke out. The war left 25 million people homeless in the Soviet Union and housing became the top priority on the construction programme. Aesthetics were no longer considered important, let alone costly, prestigious projects. The Peoples' Commissariat was never built.

1932

The year 1932 marked a turning point in Soviet architectural history and was a significant milestone in the economic history of the country. An important top-level decision was implemented, at a time when the Modernist movement was flourishing and architects such as Hannes Meyer (Bauhaus) and Ernst May (renowned for his Modernist housing and urban planning designs) were working on their competition designs for the new Moscow.

At the congress of the Association of Soviet Architects it was established that Socialist Realism was to be the corner stone of art. This implied that architects should strive to combine an optimal

M.A. Ginzburg competition design,
1934, exterior view

I.A. Fomin competition design,
1934, exterior view

I.L. Leonidov typographical feature
in SA 1926, number 3, declaring:
"Architects! Do not imitate the forms of technology but learn the method of the engineering designer"

quality and frugality with artistic simplicity and expressive power. In fact, this was little more than a hollow reiteration of the words spoken by the first architectural historian, Vitruvius, two thousand years before. In practice, however, this heralded a return to unwieldy Classicism, intended to impress the people and glorify the state. Whereas in previous competitions European architects had been invited to participate – usually for reasons of prestige – the competition was now limited to Russian architects.
The Association of Soviet Architects was founded after the Communist Party had intervened in a quarrel between various architectural societies. Subsequently, these societies became part of the new Party-oriented association. The number of Modernist buildings constructed in Moscow gradually diminished, even though Moisei Ginzburg (1892–1946) and Ladovski were members of the board. The Association reached rock bottom in 1937, when Constantin Melnikov (1890–1974) was expelled. The official reason given for his expulsion was that he was too "formalistic", which was inconsistent with the principles of Socialist Realism. Formalism, in this case, was merely another word for "senseless individualism". Melnikov was no longer permitted to pursue his profession and only managed to avoid slipping into total obscurity towards the end of his life.

Volkskommissariat für die Schwerindustrie, Moskau

Die Ausschreibung zum Volkskommissariat für die Schwerindustrie verlief nach einem ähnlichen Muster wie die meisten anderen russischen Architekturwettbewerbe der 20er und 30er Jahre. Insbesondere der Wettbewerb zum Palast der Sowjets, der 1934 noch nicht abgeschlossen war, weist eine Reihe von Parallelen auf. Allerdings sind genaue Aussagen darüber nur schwer zu treffen: Da Architekturwettbewerbe im stalinistischen Rußland wie Staatsgeheimnisse behandelt wurden, sind viele Dokumente verschwunden und einige Umstände bis auf den heutigen Tag ungeklärt.

Moderne kontra Traditionalismus

Der undurchsichtige Ablauf solcher Wettbewerbe in der Sowjetunion und die unklaren Umstände, unter denen die Jury ihre Entscheidungen traf, sind bis heute Gegenstand der Forschung. Wie ein roter Faden zog sich durch alle Ausschreibungen der Gegensatz zwischen Traditionalisten (Neo-Klassizismus und Neurenaissance) und Modernisten, die ihrerseits in Rationalisten und Konstruktivisten gespalten waren. Anfänglich gaben die Modernisten in der sowjetischen Architektur den Ton an: Sie unterstützten den Kommunismus und waren eng mit der Revolution verbunden. Trotz aller revolutionären Ideale zeigten sich die neuen Führer nicht immer begeistert von der russischen Avantgarde. Lieber griffen sie auf Vertrautes zurück und bevorzugten Architekten der alten Schule.

Dennoch erlebte die moderne Baukunst in der damaligen Zeit eine nie gekannte Blüte – auch aufgrund der vielen Architekturwettbewerbe. Als nach Lenins Tod 1924 der Aufstieg Stalins begann, wurde der Einfluß der Kommunistischen Partei auf das kulturelle Leben immer spürbarer. Die Initiativen zu Architekturwettbewerben gingen meistens von der Partei oder von Parteimitgliedern aus, die dann in den Organisationsgremien den Ton angaben. Interessanterweise wurden zu jedem Wettbewerb neben den Traditionalisten auch Modernisten eingeladen, doch die Gewinner kamen meist aus dem Kreis der akademischen Architekten. Dies gilt ebenso für die Lenin-Bibliothek von W.A. Schtschuko (1878–1939) wie für die Ausschreibung zum Palast der Sowjets, die B.M. Jofan (1891–1976) gewann. All das hielt die Anhänger der Moderne nicht davon ab, bei den Wettbewerben ihrem Stil kompromißlos treu zu bleiben. Erst mit der Ausschreibung zum Volkskommissariat für die Schwerindustrie deutete sich eine Änderung dieser Haltung an, was für eine wachsende Skepsis in den Reihen der Modernisten spricht.

Ein Steckenpferd der Kommunisten

Ebenso wie der Palast der Sowjets sollte das Volkskommissariat zum Monument für den Sieg des Kommunismus werden. Nachdem Lenin mit der Industrialisierung des agrarischen Rußland begonnen hatte, stellte Stalin 1929 seinen ersten Fünfjahresplan für die Schwerindustrie vor. Damit wollte er diesen Industriezweig, dem sein besonderes Augenmerk galt, auf das Niveau der Vereinigten Staaten bringen und aus Moskau eine Weltstadt machen. Der Plan endete vorzeitig – 1932, im Jahr der Errichtung des Volkskommissariats.

Stalin war überzeugt, daß keine Metropole von Weltrang ohne angemessene Infrastruktur und eigene Untergrundbahn auskommen könne. Natürlich sollte die Moskauer Metro die schönste und sicherste Bahn der Welt werden, mit Stationen, die wie wahre »Arbeiterpaläste« den Glanz der neuen Stadt auch unter der Erde widerspiegelten. Das gewaltige Bauvorhaben wurde größtenteils 1934/35 umgesetzt, also zeitgleich zur Ausschreibung für das Volkskommissariat. Die einzelnen Stationen und Eingänge entwarfen Modernisten wie Nikolai A. Ladowski (1881–1941), Neo-Klassizisten wie I.A. Fomin und sozialistische Realisten wie A.N. Duschkin.

Die Stadt Moskau sollte von Grund auf neugestaltet werden, wobei das Volkskommissariat und der Palast der Sowjets sowohl in architektonischer wie in ideologischer Hinsicht als zentrale Gebäude gedacht waren. Dies deutete sich auch in der städtebaulichen Planung an: Beide Bauwerke sollten in unmittelbarer Nähe des Kreml entstehen, das Volkskommissariat war sogar direkt am Roten Platz geplant. Die Wettbewerbsausschreibung sah als Baugelände einen Häuserblock vor, in dem sich heute das Warenhaus GUM befindet. Dieser Block hätte abgerissen werden müssen. Den Architekten blieb es freigestellt, wie sie mit der übrigen umgebenden Bebauung – dem historischen Stadtkern (Kitai-Gorod) mit der Basilius-Kathedrale als bekanntestem Bauwerk – verfahren wollten. Architekten wie P.A. Golosow und D.F. Fridman, aber auch der Akademiker Fomin sprachen sich für den Abriß der Kathedrale aus. Dagegen integrierten die Gebrüder Alexander A. Wesnin (1883–1959) und Viktor A. Wesnin (1882–1950) sowie Iwan I. Leonidow (1902–1969) die Basilius-Kathedrale in ihren städtebaulichen Entwurf und benutzten sie als optische Krönung des Roten Platzes. Die zweite vorgegebene Konstante, die die Architekten bei ihren Plänen in Betracht ziehen mußten, bildete das Lenin-Mausoleum. Dieses Gebäude war zwischen 1926 und 1930 nach einem streng modernistischen Entwurf des architektonischen »Chamäleons« Alexei V. Schtschusew (1873–1949) entstanden, seine Ausrichtung zum Kreml hin hatte Auswirkungen auf die mögliche Lage des Volkskommissariats.

Drei geschlossene Wettbewerbe

Von den drei in diesem Buch vorgestellten Moskauer Architekturwettbewerben ist über das Volkskommissariat am wenigsten bekannt. Die erste Ausschreibungsrunde fand 1934 statt. Von seiten der Modernisten wurden aufsehenerregende Entwürfe eingereicht – ganz in Übereinstimmung mit den Wünschen des Regimes und den visionären Ideen der Architekten. Das neue Volkskommissariat sollte einen Sitzungssaal für 1 000 bis 1 500 Delegierte aus den Sowjetrepubliken erhalten. Dazu kam eine Reihe kleinerer Säle (für etwa 300 Personen) und Platz für ein Hotel, eine Bibliothek, verschiedene Clubs, Cafeterias, Restaurants usw., wobei bestimmte Räumlichkeiten ausschließlich der höchsten Führungsebene vorbehalten bleiben sollten.

1935 wurde ohne Angabe von Gründen ein zweiter Wettbewerb ausgeschrieben, zu dem man – wie schon in der ersten Ausschreibung – eine Handvoll Architekten exklusiv einlud. Allerdings waren diesmal von den avantgardistischen Baumeistern nur die Gebrüder Wesnin übriggeblieben: Sie erhielten zu jeder der größeren Ausschreibungen eine Einladung, wurden aber mit ebenso großer Regelmäßigkeit bei der Preisvergabe übergangen. Es fand sogar noch eine dritte Ausschreibungsrunde statt, von der aber kaum etwas an die Öffentlichkeit drang.

Bereits kurz nach Ende der dritten Runde entschied sich die sowjetische Führung gegen den Roten Platz als geeigneten Standort. Der Ausbruch des Zweiten Weltkriegs sorgte für eine zeitweilige Einstellung aller großen Bauvorhaben, worunter auch das Volkskommissariat fiel. Nach Kriegsende gab es 25 Millionen. Obdachlose in der Sowjetunion, so daß der Wohnungsbau oberste Priorität erhielt. Ästhetische Aspekte waren in dieser Zeit ebensowenig gefragt wie teure, prestigeträchtige Bauprojekte. Folge: Das Volkskommissariat wurde nie gebaut.

1932

Das Jahr 1932 nimmt sowohl in der sowjetischen Architektur – wie auch in der Wirtschaftsgeschichte eine Schlüsselrolle ein. Während die modernistische Bewegung auf dem Höhepunkt ihres Schaffens stand und Architekten wie Hannes Meyer (Bauhaus) und Ernst May (bekannt für seine modernen Wohnungsbauten und städtebaulichen Entwürfe) sich mit den Plänen für den Neubau der Stadt Moskau beschäftigten, kam es auf oberster Ebene zu einer folgenschweren Entscheidung.

Der Kongreß des Verbandes der Architekten der UdSSR legte fest, daß der sozialistische Realismus die Grundlage jeder Kunst bilden müsse. Für die Architektur bedeutete dies: höchstmögliche Qualität, Wirtschaftlichkeit sowie Klarheit und Ausdruckskraft der baulichen Gestaltung. Im Grunde handelte es sich bei diesem Beschluß um eine hohle Variation dessen, was der erste Architekturhistoriker Vitruvius schon vor 2000 Jahren gefordert hatte. In der Praxis bedeutete es eine Rückkehr zu einer plumpen Form des Klassizismus, die vornehmlich darauf bedacht war, das Volk zu beeindrucken und den Staat zu verherrlichen. Während die Führung bei früheren Wettbewerben noch Architekten aus anderen europäischen Ländern eingeladen hatte – allerdings mehr aus Prestigegründen –, beschränkte sie sich in folgenden Jahren auf sowjetische Baumeister.

Der Verband der Architekten der UdSSR war entstanden, nachdem die Kommunistische Partei in die Streitigkeiten zwischen den verschiedenen Architektenvereinigungen eingegriffen hatte. Die Partei löste alle anderen Vereinigungen auf und gründete einen neuen, parteinahen Verband unter Leitung von Moisej Ginsburg (1892–1946), Ladowski u.a. Dennoch entstanden in und um Moskau immer weniger Gebäude im modernen Stil. Der Ausschluß von Konstantin Melnikow aus dem Verband bildete einen weiteren Höhepunkt staatlicher Einflußnahme. Offiziell wurde Melnikow des '»Formalismus« beschuldigt – womit ein »sinnloser Individualismus« gemeint war, der in heftigem Widerspruch zum sozialistischen Realismus stand. Melnikow erhielt Berufsverbot und erlangte erst kurz vor seinem Tod Anerkennung.

Le Commissariat du Peuple pour l'Industrie Lourde, Moscou

Le concours pour le Commissariat du Peuple pour l'Industrie Lourde se déroula de la même façon que les autres grandes compétitions d'architecture en Union Soviétique durant les années 20 et 30. Des incidents presque identiques émaillent celle du Palais des Soviets qui n'avait pas encore abouti en 1934. Toute comparaison entre les deux concours ne peut d'ailleurs se faire qu'avec prudence, la plupart des archives ayant disparu. Sous la Russie staliniste, tout ce qui avait trait à ce type de compétition était classé confidentiel.

Modernisme contre traditionalisme

Si le secret qui entourait les concours, et plus encore les adjudications, rend toute analyse difficile, il reste que la rivalité entre les modernistes (rationalistes ou constructivistes) et les traditionalistes (néo-classiques et néo-renaissance) se manifesta à chaque fois. Au départ, le mouvement moderniste eut le vent en poupe. Ses membres étaient très impliqués dans le processus révolutionnaire qu'ils soutenaient. Mais les nouveaux responsables politiques, aussi révolutionnaires soient-ils dans leurs principes, n'étaient pas toujours séduits par l'avant-garde. Ils préféraient des voies plus sûres et favorisèrent souvent les architectes de la vieille école. Grâce à l'organisation de multiples concours, on assista cependant à une véritable explosion de l'architecture moderne. Après la mort de Lénine, en 1924, et avec l'arrivée de Staline au pouvoir, le parti communiste renforça son emprise sur la vie culturelle. Les concours furent directement organisés par son intermédiaire ou par certains de ses membres qui influençèrent leur déroulement. Si l'on invita toujours des modernistes et des traditionalistes, les projets lauréats émanèrent la plupart du temps des cercles les plus conservateurs. Ce fut le cas de la Bibliothèque Lénine (V.A. Shchouko, 1878–1939) et du Palais des Soviets (B.M. Iofan, 1891–1976). Les architectes modernistes n'en continuèrent pas moins à proposer des projets remarquables. Le concours pour le Commissariat du Peuple pour l'Industrie Lourde marque un tournant dans cette histoire, placée sous le signe d'un scepticisme grandissant.

Le cheval de bataille des communistes

Le palais des Soviets et le Commissariat du Peuple pour l'Industrie Lourde devaient témoigner de la gloire du communisme. Lénine avait lancé l'industrialisation d'une Russie jusqu'alors essentiellement agricole et, en 1929, Staline avait décrété le premier plan quinquennal prématurément achevé en 1932, année de la création du Commissariat. Le dictateur voulait pousser l'industrie lourde, un des chevaux de batailles communistes, au niveau de celle des Etats-Unis et faire de Moscou l'une des premières métropoles du monde. Il fallait pour cela complètement redessiner la capitale.
Staline savait qu'il devait améliorer les infrastructures de la ville et en particulier créer un métro dont le besoin se faisait cruellement sentir. Bien entendu, ce devait être le plus sûr et le plus beau métro du monde reflétant la puissance du nouveau Moscou. Ses stations devaient être de véritables palais. Cet immense projet fut réalisé pour l'essentiel entre 1934 et 1935, dates du concours pour le Commissariat du Peuple pour l'Industrie Lourde. Les stations et leurs entrées furent dessinées par des modernistes (Ladovsky), des néo-classiques (Fomine) ou des réalistes-socialistes (A.N. Douchkine). Ces architectes s'efforcèrent de faire de ce métropolitain une réalisation exemplaire et, à la différence de leurs confrères travaillant à la surface, y réussirent parfaitement.
Le Palais des Soviets et le Commissariat du Peuple pour l'Industrie Lourde devaient compter parmi les principaux bâtiments, architecturalement comme idéologiquement. On avait même prévu pour le Commissariat un site sur la Place Rouge, l'emplacement du grand magasin GUM condamné à la démolition. Le sort des bâtiments environnants était laissé à l'initiative des architectes. C'était leur poser un problème de conscience puisqu'il ne s'agissait rien moins que du cœur historique de la cité (Kitajgorod) et en particulier de la cathédrale Saint-Basile. Les architectes Golosov, Fridman et – surprise – le professeur Fomine étaient partisans de la détruire. Les frères Vesnine et Ivan Léonidoff l'intégraient dans leurs plans d'urbanisme comme une sorte de clef de voûte optique de la Place Rouge. Il fallait aussi prendre en compte le mausolée de Lénine réalisé dans un style moderniste désséché (1926–1930) par ce caméléon de l'architecture qu'était Alexei Chtchoussev (1873–1949). Le petit édifice était orienté vers le Kremlin, ce qui n'était pas sans conséquences pour l'implantation du Commissariat.

Trois concours très restreints

Des trois concours soviétiques abordés par cet ouvrage, le moins connu est certainement celui du Commissariat pour l'Industrie Lourde. Le premier tour se déroula en 1934. Le cahier des charges spécifiait une salle de conférence pour 1 500 délégués des différentes républiques, un certain nombre de petites salles de 300 places et des services comme un hôtel, une bibliothèque, des clubs, des cafétérias, des restaurants etc. Les espaces les plus importants étaient réservés aux dirigeants. A l'évidence, le Commissariat du Peuple reflétait déjà l'autoritarisme du régime. La plupart des projets les plus spectaculaires qui alliaient les souhaits du régime aux idées visionnaires des architectes provenaient des cercles modernistes.
En 1935, un second tour fut organisé pour des raisons inconnues. Comme lors du premier tour, on demanda à certains architectes de soumettre des projets, les frères Vesnine étant cette fois les seuls représentants de l'avant-garde. Ils ne manquaient d'ailleurs pas de persévérance puisqu'ils ne remportèrent jamais un seul concours, malgré leurs nombreuses participations. Le troisième tour est encore moins documenté, même si l'on sait que le projet Vesnine fut cette fois très apprécié. Peu après ce troisième tour, les autorités décidèrent que la Place Rouge n'était pas le site idéal et tous les grands projets urbanistiques furent annulés dès le début de la guerre. Celle-ci laissa 25 millions de sans-abri en Union Soviétique et le logement devint la priorité absolue. L'esthétique perdit de son importance et l'on oublia les projets de prestige. Le Commissariat du Peuple ne fut jamais construit.

1932

En 1932, la faveur dont jouissait le modernisme était au plus haut et des architectes comme Hannes Meyer (Bauhaus) et Ernst May (célèbre pour ses immeubles de logement et ses plans d'urbanisme) participaient aux concours du nouveau Moscou. C'est pourtant cette même année que fut prise, au plus haut niveau, une décision qui allait marquer un tournant dans l'histoire de l'architecture soviétique comme dans celle du pays.
Au congrès de l'Association des Architectes Soviétiques, il fut décidé que le réalisme socialiste serait la nouvelle base théorique de la création artistique. Ceci impliquait pour les architectes de s'efforcer de combiner une qualité et une recherche de l'économie optimales dans le cadre d'une recherche expressive laissant de côté tout individualisme. En fait ce n'était que la réitération creuse des écrits du premier historien de l'architecture, Vitruve, deux mille ans plus tôt. Concrètement, le réalisme soviétique se traduisit par un classicisme pompeux, conçu pour impressionner le peuple et glorifier l'Etat. Alors que dans les premiers concours, certains architectes européens avaient été incités à participer, généralement pour des raisons de prestige, les architectes russes furent les seuls invités des compétitions ultérieures.
L'Association des Architectes Soviétiques avait été fondée à l'issue d'une intervention du parti communiste dans une querelle entre les différentes associations professionnelles qui furent alors regroupées dans une seule structure contrôlée par le parti. Le nombre des immeubles modernistes construits à Moscou diminua peu à peu, même si Moisei Ginzbourg (1892–1946) et Ladovsky participaient à la direction de l'association. Celle-ci tomba au plus bas en 1937, avec l'expulsion de Constantin Melnikov (1890–1974) pour la raison officielle que son trop grand «formalisme» ne correspondait pas aux principes du réalisme socialiste. Dans ce cas, formalisme voulait simplement dire «individualisme dénué de sens». Melnikov ne put continuer à exercer sa profession et n'échappa à l'oubli total que vers la fin de sa vie.

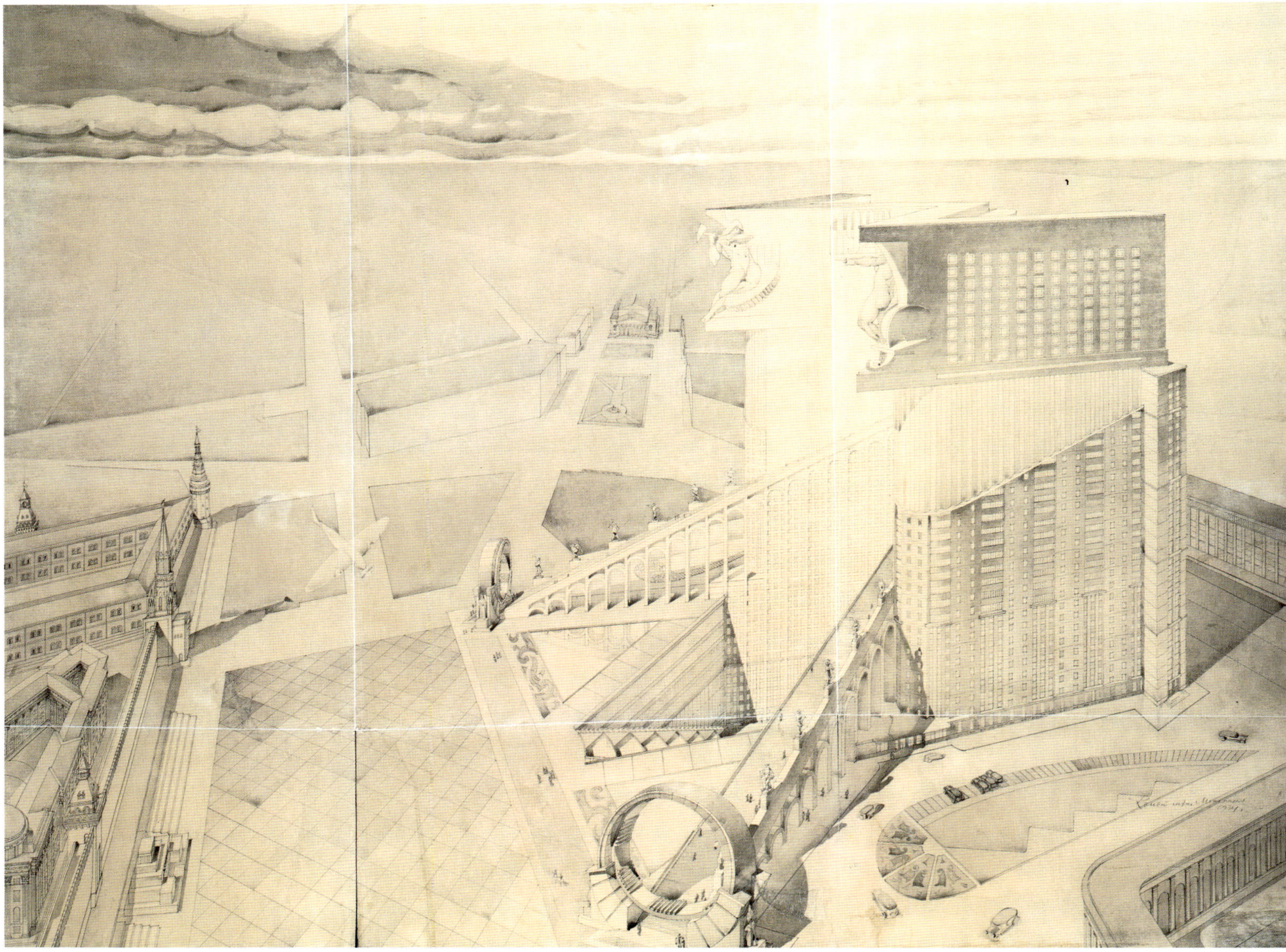

Constantin Stepanovich Melnikov

competition design, 1934, bird's eye view

Constantin Stepanovich Melnikov
competition design, 1934, site plan

Constantin Stepanovich Melnikov
competition design, 1934, exterior view of entrance

Alexander Alexandrovich Vesnin
& Viktor Alexandrovich Vesnin
competition design, 1934, exterior
view by night

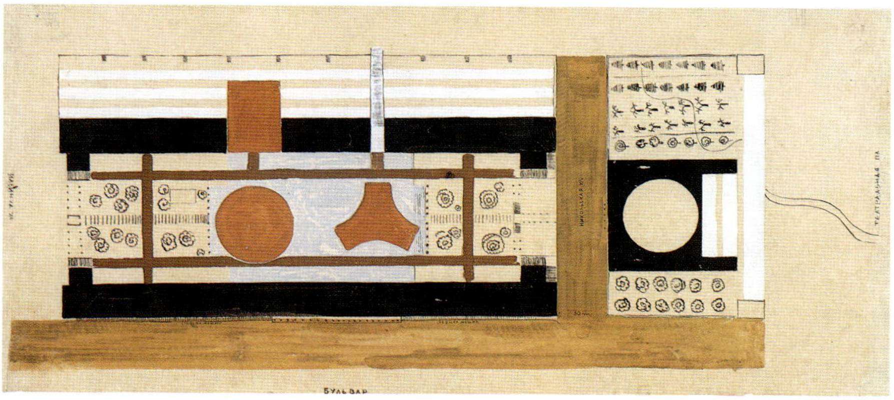

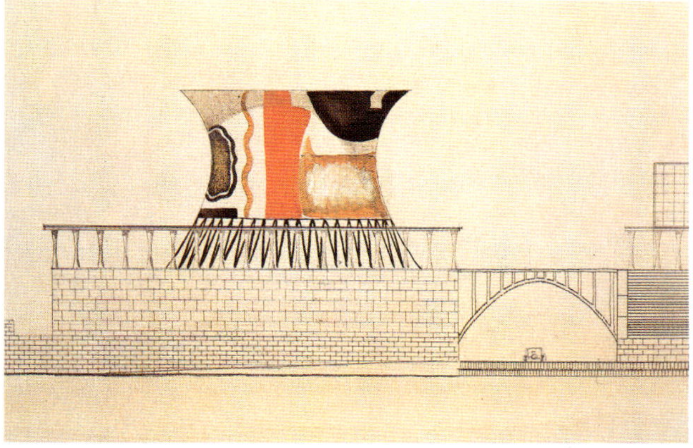

Ivan Ivanovich Leonidov
competition design, 1934, site plan

Ivan Ivanovich Leonidov
competition design, 1934, Workers' Club for Narkomtiazhprom employees

Ivan Ivanovich Leonidov
competition design, 1934, exterior view of Upper Part

Ivan Ivanovich Leonidov view out into Red Square and towards the Lenin Mausoleum from the central vestibule under the stepped spectator tribunes

Ivan Ivanovich Leonidov sketch with the Kremlin

Ivan Ivanovich Leonidov competition design, 1934, elevation on Red Square

Project

City Hall

Site

Frederiksplein, Amsterdam

Dates

First round December 1936 to 10 August 1937 *Result announced* 20 December 1937 *Second Round* 23 March 1938 to 1 December 1938 *Result announced* Early 1939 *Third round closing date* 7 November 1941 *Result announced* 7 January 1942

Number of entries

First round 225 *Second round* 4 *Third round* 2

Jury

W. de Vlugt (Chairman and Mayor of Amsterdam), S. de Miranda (Alderman, Amsterdam), A.R. Hulshoff (Head of Municipal Services), M.J. Granpré Molière, H. van der Kloot Meijburg, L. van Ravensteijn, A. van der Steur, P. Vorking (all architects)

Result

First round H.T. Zwiers, M. Duintjer & A. Komter; J.F. Staal & A. Staal; J.F. Berghoef & J.J.M. Vegter (all selected for the second round) *Second round* M. Duintjer & A. Komter; J.F. Berghoef & J.J.M. Vegter (selected for the third round) *Third round first prize* J.F. Berghoef & J.J.M. Vegter, *Second prize* M. Duintjer & A. Komter

Commissioned by

Amsterdam City Council

Project

City Hall in combination with a music theatre, after a suggestion by Wilhelm Holzbauer

Site

Waterlooplein, Amsterdam

Dates

First round closing date 30 November 1967 *Result announced* February 1968 *Second round closing date* 7 October 1968 *Result announced* 22 November 1968

Number of entries

804

Jury

H.A. Maaskant (chairman), Prof. J. Schader (Switzerland), Sir Robert Matthew (England), F.J. van Gool, P. Zanstra (all architects)

Result

First round Seven designs selected for the second round. *Second round first prize* Wilhelm Holzbauer *Second prize* Bernardo Winkler, Friedrich Hahmann & Hanna Hahmann *Third prize* Group GIA *Honourable mention* L.J. Heijdenrijk

Commissioned by

Amsterdam City Council

Construction

1982 to 1987

Architects

Wilhelm Holzbauer (1930–), Cees Dam (1932–), B. Bijvoet (1889–1979) & G.H.M. Holt (1904–1988)

Amsterdam City Hall, 1936–1967

Wilhelm Holzbauer & Cees Dam
execution design for combined project, City Hall and Opera House, 1981, view section through the Opera House

Amsterdam City Hall

Initially, two competitions had been organised. One for a city hall on the Frederiksplein and one for an opera house in the Amsterdam working class district "De Pijp" (The Pipe). Both projects reached an impasse after the Second World War. A new competition for a city hall, organised in 1967, also produced an unsatisfactory result. It was not until 1979 that the Austrian architect Wilhelm Holzbauer came up with the idea of combining the two buildings, using a selection of the best designs submitted in the past, one of which was his own[1].

The first competition

Amsterdam had been debating the city hall question for more than a century before the first competition was organised in 1936. The city had once boasted one of the most impressive city halls in the world. This building, which had replaced a medieval jumble, had been designed by Jacob van Campen in 1648. It was situated on the Dam, the historical centre of the city, overlooking a splendid square. During a brief period of French occupation at the beginning of the nineteenth century, the city hall was requisitioned by the new king, Louis Napoleon. After that, the city hall on Dam square never quite regained its former stature.

The city hall became a royal palace which the city sold to the state in 1935. The city council had been housed at the Prinsenhof in another part of the city for some time. In the late 1920s, an austere extension was added to these premises. This extension, designed by N. Lansdorp and A.R. Hulshoff in the stark Amsterdam School style, mirrored the architectural tastes of the era. The architects, who both worked for the Department of Public Works, had commissioned a select group of sculptors and decorators, including Hildo Krop (the municipal sculptor), W. Penaat and J. Thorn Prikker. However, these premises soon became too small. Moreover, the city hall was anything but presentable and gave the passer-by the impression that it was inaccessible.
The council therefore decided to organise a competition for a new city hall in 1939, to be built on Frederiksplein. This square had been the site of the former Paleis voor Volksvlijt (Palace for Popular Industry), a permanent exhibition venue, similar to Crystal Palace in London. However, the similarity between the two buildings does not end there. In 1929, the Paleis voor Volksvlijt was also destroyed by fire.

The competition drew no less than 225 entries, 28 of which were from foreign participants. The jury consisted of the Mayor W. de Vlugt and Alderman S. de Miranda, who were assisted by a number of rather conservative architects. Even though Functionalism was gaining popularity throughout Europe – with Amsterdam in a leading role – a jury of Traditionalists had been appointed. It seemed likely, therefore, that designs in the Delft and Amsterdam School styles had the best chance of winning. Having diligently assessed the vast number of entries, the jury came to the disappointing conclusion that not one of

Exterior view from river Amstel

M. Duintjer & A. Komter competition design, 1938, exterior view from Frederiksplein, second round before war

Engraving of the Dam (c. 1750), former City Hall designed by Jacob van Campen (left), Gothic Nieuwe Kerk (centre)

the designs was suitable for execution. However, three designs were selected for a second round (1938) on the basis of particular qualities. The nominated architects were H.T. Zwiers, M. Duintjer & A. Komter, J.F. Staal & A. Staal and J.F. Berghoef & J.J.M. Vegter. Zwiers' design was inspired by the city hall in Stockholm and Staal senior and junior had submitted a quasi-modernist design with Neo-Baroque features. Berghoef and Vegter's design was clearly Delft School inspired, as was Zwiers'. This Traditionalist school was based on rural (particularly Scandinavian) architecture and had a preference for natural materials such as wood and brick. One of the theoretical champions of this school, who was also a member of the jury, was Professor Granpré Molière of the Faculty of Architecture at the University of Delft. Although Duintjer and Komter's design was the most austere, it was a far cry from Modernist architecture. A number of Modernist designs, including that of G.H.M. Holt and J.P. Kloos, had been submitted. However, these designs stood little chance with this jury.
The nominated architects had been given a list of stipulations to be incorporated into their second round designs. However, once again the jury were unable to choose a winner. Duintjer & Komter and Berghoef & Vegter were given a chance to submit a third design. Berghoef & Vegter submitted a rather tasteless and conformist design in 1942, which was chosen ahead of Duintjer & Komter's new design. After the Second World War, the council decided to proceed with the former team.

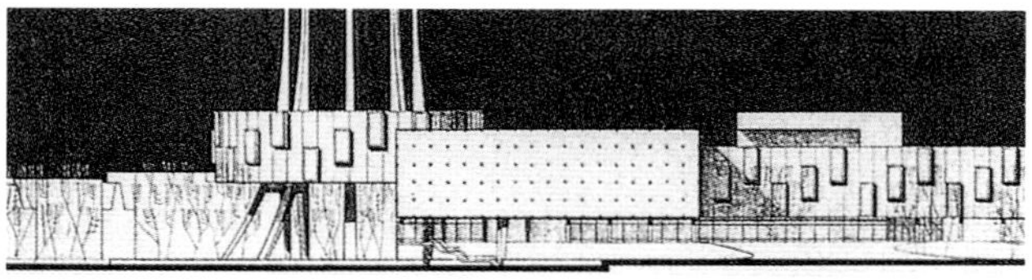

Anonymous competition design, 1967, elevation, first round, after war

Anonymous competition design, 1967, bird's eye view, first round, after war

Second chance

A new site was designated for the city hall: Waterlooplein, in the city centre near the Amstel river. Berghoef and Vegter blithely continued to develop their city hall plans. In 1961, they eventually produced what they believed to be the definitive design until certain Dutch architects began to interfere. Aldo van Eyck, who was then an architect of the up-and-coming generation, launched a remarkably fierce attack on the design. He referred to it as an *"unbelievably childish piece of provincial Fascism"*. Other architects, such as the aged H.Th. Wijdeveld, were unable to suppress the urge to submit new designs, uninvited. This state of affairs came to an end in 1964, when the city council decided not to execute the plans of the unfortunate architects. Instead, a new competition was organised in 1967.

The competition drew no less than 804 designs, submitted under a motto, as in the previous competition. It is rumoured that the jury had come across a design in which they recognised the hand of the famous Finnish architect Alvar Aalto. They promptly awarded first prize to this design, only to discover that it had been submitted by the relatively unknown architect Wilhelm Holzbauer. Holzbauer's design differed radically from the four prize-winning designs submitted thirty years before. It was a colossal, concrete edifice. However, this spectacular product of a Functionalist mind failed to impress the Amsterdam architects.

It was the era of political participation and civil disobedience. Holzbauer's design was seen as a symbol of government power and authoritarian rule. It was also the era of "modest" architecture. The Structuralist designs of Herman Hertzberger, Piet Blom and Aldo van Eyck were anti-hierarchical and small-scale. In contrast to the Functionalists, who occasionally designed on a massive scale, they preferred to design a number of small, equal units. Hertzberger, Heijdenrijk and the team of Davidson, Rijnboutt & Zwarts all submitted Structuralist designs. Holzbauer and Arne Jacobsen submitted Functionalist designs.
The council weathered the storm and decided to uphold the jury's decision at a meeting in 1970. Unfortunately, Amsterdam was unable to obtain financial support for the project from the government, and Holzbauer's design for the city hall was subsequently shelved.

Music theatre

The history of the music theatre was equally grim. It had been the dream of the Dutch Wagner Society to build a venue similar to that in Bayreuth where the operas of this celebrated composer could be performed. Plans for a theatre of this sort had previously been submitted by Hendrik Petrus Berlage in 1910 but these were never executed. Thereafter, Berlage had always maintained an interest in the matter. He had been a member of the jury for the closed competition organised in 1916. The architects Blaauw, Gratama, van der Mey, Slothouwer, Staal and Wijdeveld had been invited to participate.

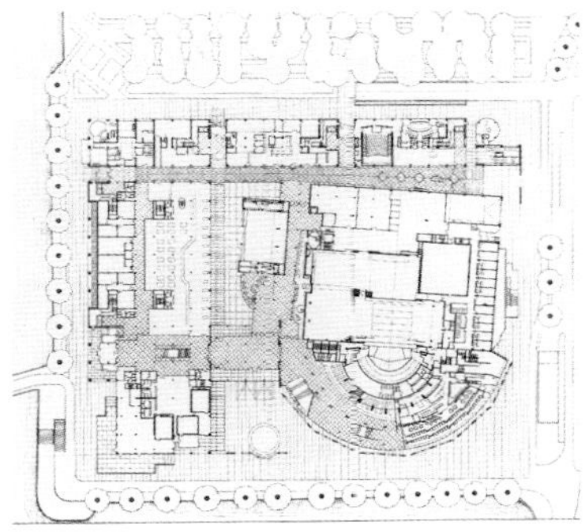

Wilhelm Holzbauer **competition design, 1968, above: interior view of the hall, below: model, second round, after war**

Wilhelm Holzbauer **design of combined City Hall and Opera House, above: ground floor plan, below: model, 1981**

Almost all of these architects were of the Amsterdam School. Staal won the competition by a unanimous vote, but the municipality thwarted the plan, even though the Wagner society had pledged a sizeable sum of money. The Depression and the Second World War put paid to any further developments.
After the war, repeated attempts were made to organise the building of an opera house. There was incessant bickering about the most suitable site and the municipal architects Holt and Bijvoet submitted plan after plan. At one stage, the plan to build a music theatre even seemed set to be scrapped completely. Objections were alternately raised by the council, who wanted to give priority to housing projects and social welfare, and residents from the surrounding areas. The wave of democratisation had clearly broken over Amsterdam.
It was April 1979 and a solution had yet to be found, when Wilhelm Holzbauer came up with a plan. During a ramble through Amsterdam, a vision of the Stopera had suddenly occured to him.

In sight of the end

Holzbauer's plan to combine the city hall and music theatre was unique. In fact, it was so unique that Holt and Bijvoet were more than a little sceptical at first. However, the two architects and the national and regional politicians soon grew accustomed to the idea and enthusiasm for the plan mounted. Bijvoet and Holt, both of whom had experience in theatre architecture, agreed to collaborate with Holzbauer. However, their collaboration was not always optimal. The municipal architects both hailed from the pre-war Functionalist tradition. Holzbauer was an architect of the new generation. These problems and the objections raised by the public and the architectural fraternity eventually overwhelmed the aged Bijvoet. He died on 27 December 1979. Holt took the opportunity to call in the help of his son-in-law, Cees Dam. Holzbauer considered the latter to be something of a Trojan horse. Both architects had to effect a number of changes in their designs, partly due to the protest raised by a group of artists, championed, once again, by Aldo van Eyck. Residents from the surrounding areas also caused delays by sabotaging machinery and damaging building materials. However, construction progressed slowly but surely and nothing could stand in the way of completion.
There was, however, an unsavoury twist in the tail. A dispute developed between Dam and Holzbauer as to who should take creative credit for the design. The L-shaped city hall, which "embraces" the opera, was undeniably Holzbauer's idea. Which of the two architects contrived the interlocking rings[2] seems irrelevant in light of the fact that the idea was derived from the designs of Carlo Scarpa and is also an ancient wedding symbol.

1 *The Dutch word for city hall is "stadhuis". In combination with the word "opera" the new term "Stopera" developed. This term was perhaps a little imprudently chosen, because it may also be seen as a combination of the words "stop" and "opera". Groups opposed to the building used this in their protest campaign.*
2 *This motif is also to be found on the walls of the wedding room.*

Stopera, Amsterdam

Zunächst handelte es sich um getrennte Wettbewerbe für das neue Rathaus (auf dem Frederiksplein) und das Operngebäude, das im Amsterdamer Stadtviertel De Pijp errichtet werden sollte. Nach dem Zweiten Weltkrieg gerieten beide Projekte in eine Sackgasse, und ein erneuter Architekturwettbewerb für das Rathaus (1967) brachte keine befriedigenden Ergebnisse. Erst 1979 verfiel der österreichische Architekt Wilhelm Holzbauer auf die Idee, beide Ausschreibungen miteinander zu verbinden und für den neuen Gebäudekomplex die besten in der Vergangenheit eingereichten Entwürfe – unter denen sich auch sein eigenes Konzept befand – zu verwenden.[1]

Erste Ausschreibung für das Rathaus

Amsterdam hatte bereits seit etwa 100 Jahren mit dem Gedanken an ein neues Rathaus gespielt, als es sich 1936 zu einer Ausschreibung entschloß. Dabei besaß die Stadt einst eines der schönsten Rathäuser der Welt, ein 1648 von Jacob van Campen entworfenes Gebäude, das ein mittelalterliches Sammelsurium ersetzte und auf dem Dam entstand – dem schönsten Platz der Stadt mitten im historischen Zentrum. Während der relativ kurzen französischen Besatzungszeit zu Beginn des 19. Jahrhunderts wurde das Rathaus vom neuen König Louis Napoléon konfisziert und erlangte nie wieder die alte Bedeutung. 1935 verkaufte die Stadt das inzwischen zum Königlichen Palast umgewandelte Rathaus an den niederländischen Staat. Der Sitz des Stadtrats befand sich bereits seit einiger Zeit in einem Gebäude am Prinsenhof, das zwischen 1926 und 1928 nach einem Entwurf von N. Lansdorp und A.R. Hulshoff ergänzt worden war. Dieses Gebäude erwies sich jedoch schon bald als zu klein; außerdem machte es von außen einen seltsam unzugänglichen Eindruck und war wenig repräsentativ.
1936 beschloß die Stadtverwaltung eine Ausschreibung für das neue Rathaus, das am Frederiksplein entstehen sollte. Daran beteiligten sich 225 Architekten, darunter 28 Teilnehmer aus dem Ausland. Der Jury gehörten neben Bürgermeister W. de Vlugt und dem Beigeordneten S. de Miranda nur Architekten an, die eine recht konservative Bautradition vertraten. Während sich in ganz Europa der Funktionalismus immer größerer Beliebtheit erfreute, hatte man für diesen Wettbewerb eine rein traditionalistische Jury benannt. Daher war davon auszugehen, daß die Entwürfe der Delfter und der Amsterdamer Schule die größten Aussichten auf Erfolg besaßen. Nach sorgfältiger Beratung kam die Jury zu einem enttäuschenden Ergebnis. Trotz unzähliger Einsendungen war nicht ein einziges Konzept zur Ausführung geeignet. Allerdings hatten die Juroren die vier bemerkenswertesten Konstruktionspläne für eine zweite Ausschreibungsrunde (1938) ausgewählt. Zu den nominierten Architekten gehörten H.T. Zwiers, M. Duintjer und A. Komter,
J.F. und A. Staal sowie J.F. Berghoef und J.J.M. Vegter. Die nominierten Architekten befaßten sich nun mit den von der Jury näher definierten Bauauflagen. Aber auch nach dem Ende der zweiten Runde konnte man sich auf keinen Gewinner einigen. Zwar erhielten Duintjer und Komter sowie Berghoef und Vegter noch eine weitere Chance, aber der von Berghoef und Vegter eingereichte Entwurf (1941–1942) wirkte geschmacklos und konformistisch. Dennoch erhielten diese Pläne den Vorzug gegenüber dem neuen Konzept von Duintjer und Komter, so daß der Stadtrat nach dem Ende des Zweiten Weltkriegs die Zusammenarbeit mit ihnen fortsetzte.

Eine zweite Chance

Der zentral an der Amstel gelegene Waterlooplein war neuer Standort für das geplante Rathaus. Berghoef und Vegter arbeiteten eifrig an ihren Plänen, und 1961 schien endlich ein definitiver Entwurf vorzuliegen – bis sich einige andere niederländische Architekten der Konstruktionspläne annahmen. Besonders scharfe Kritik übte Aldo van Eyck, der damals zu der aufstrebenden Generation junger Architekten gehörte. Er bezeichnete den Entwurf als ein *»unglaublich kindisches Produkt eines provinziellen Faschismus«*. Daraufhin fühlten sich Architekten wie etwa der hochbetagte Baumeister H.Th. Wijdeveld dazu aufgefordert, einen neuen Entwurf einzureichen. Erst als sich der Stadtrat 1964 entschloß, auf eine Durchführung der Pläne von Berghoef und Vegter zu verzichten, beruhigten sich die Gemüter. 1967 kam es zu einer erneuten Ausschreibung.
Diesmal gingen 804 Beiträge ein, die wie beim ersten Wettbewerb unter einem Motto eingereicht werden mußten. Die Jury ordnete einen Entwurf dem berühmten finnischen Architekten Alvar Aalto zu und prämierte ihn prompt mit dem ersten Preis. Aber es stellte sich heraus, daß die Pläne von dem relativ unbekannten Wilhelm Holzbauer stammten. Sein Konzept unterschied sich erheblich von den vier Entwürfen, die 30 Jahre zuvor nominiert worden waren: Holzbauer plante einen wuchtigen Betonklotz. Doch auch dieses kühne Produkt eines funktionalistischen Geistes fand vor den Augen der Amsterdamer Architekten keine Gnade.
Es war die Zeit der Proteste und des bürgerlichen Ungehorsams, und Holzbauers Entwurf galt als Symbol der Staatsmacht und der autoritären Regierungsgewalt. Aber es war auch die Zeit der »bescheidenen« Architektur. Der Strukturalismus eines Herman Hertzberger, Piet Blom und Aldo van Eyck war anti-hierarchisch und kleinformatig; und im Gegensatz zu den Funktionalisten planten sie nicht im großen Stil, sondern stellten ihre Entwürfe aus einer Anzahl kleinerer, gleichartiger Einheiten zusammen. Während Hertzberger, L.J. Heijdenrijk und H.F.D. Davidson, K. Rijnboutt und M.E. Zwarts die zweite Richtung vertraten, zählten Holzbauer und Arne Jacobson zur ersten Kategorie.
Der Stadtrat ließ sich nicht beirren und beschloß 1970 in einer Versammlung, dem Urteil der Jury zu folgen. Da die Stadt Amsterdam keine finanzielle Unterstützung vom niederländischen Staat bekommen konnte, verschwanden auch Holzbauers Pläne wieder in der Schublade.

Musiktheater

Der Bau der Oper stand ebenfalls unter keinem glücklichen Stern. Es war immer der Traum der niederländischen Wagner-Gesellschaft gewesen, ein Podium zu besitzen, auf dem wie in Bayreuth die Opern des berühmten Komponisten aufgeführt werden konnten. Bereits 1910 hatte Hendrik Petrus Berlage Pläne für ein solches Theater angefertigt, die jedoch nicht verwirklicht wurden. Als Jurymitglied der Ausschreibung von 1916 war er nach wie vor an dem Projekt beteiligt. Eine Einladung erhielten die Architekten C.J. Blaauw, J. Gratama, J.M. van der Mey, D.F. Slothouwer, J.F. Staal und H.Th. Wijdeveld – alle Vertreter der Amsterdamer Schule. Staal wurde einstimmig zum Sieger des Wettbewerbs erklärt, doch obwohl die Wagner-Gesellschaft eine finanzielle Beteiligung anbot, versagte die Stadt ihre Zustimmung. Die Depression und der Zweite Weltkrieg verhinderten den Bau.
In der Nachkriegszeit nahm man die Pläne zur Errichtung einer Oper wieder auf. Nach endlosen Querelen wegen eines geeigneten Standortes und zahllosen Entwürfen der städtischen Architekten G.H.M. Holt und B. Bijvoet schien der Weg zu einem eigenen Musiktheater endgültig verbaut zu sein. Entweder war es die Stadt, die die Pläne zugunsten anderer Projekte (Neubauwohnungen) oder aus sozialen Erwägungen zurückstellte, oder es kam zu Beschwerden aus der Nachbarschaft.
Als sich im April 1979 immer noch keine Lösung abzeichnete, überraschte Holzbauer mit einem Vorschlag: Während eines Spaziergangs in Amsterdam war ihm vor seinem inneren Auge die Vision der »Stopera« erstanden.

Ein Ende in Sicht

Holzbauers Idee einer Kombination von Rathaus und Oper zu einem Gebäudekomplex kann mit Recht als einzigartig bezeichnet werden. Der Plan war so ungewöhnlich, daß Holt und Bijvoet zunächst äußerst skeptisch blieben. Aber nachdem sich die verantwortlichen Politiker in Stadt und Regierung mit dem Gedanken vertraut gemacht hatten, wuchs die Zustimmung für eine solche Idee. Die beiden Architekten, die Erfahrung mit Theaterarchitektur besaßen, erklärten sich zur Zusammenarbeit mit Holzbauer bereit. Leider gestaltete sich die Kooperation nicht immer zur gegenseitigen Zufriedenheit. Die städtischen Architekten standen in der funktionalistischen Tradition der Vorkriegszeit, während Holzbauer einer neuen Generation von Baumeistern angehörte. Dieser Gegensatz und die heftigen Proteste seitens der Bevölkerung und der Architektenvereinigungen überforderten den hochbetagten Bijvoet: Er starb am 27. Dezember 1979. Holt nutzte die Gelegenheit, um das Projekt an seinen Schwiegersohn Cees Dam weiterzugeben, der in den Augen Holzbauers eine Art trojanisches Pferd darstellte. Beide Architekten mußten ihren Entwurf in der Folge noch mehrfach überarbeiten, u.a. aufgrund erneuter Proteste einer Künstlergruppe unter Führung von Aldo van Eyck. Auch die Bewohner des Stadtviertels sorgten für weitere Verzögerungen, indem sie Maschinen sabotierten und Baumaterial beschädigten. Dennoch konnte der Bau 1987 endgültig fertiggestellt werden.

1 *»Stopera« setzt sich zusammen aus dem niederländischen Wort für Rathaus »stadhuis« und »opera«. Böse Zungen (meist Gegner dieses Projekts) verwendeten den Begriff allerdings auch in der Bedeutung von »stop« und »opera«.*

Le Stopera, Amsterdam

Au départ, deux concours furent organisés, l'un pour une mairie sur Frederiksplein et l'autre pour un opéra dans le quartier populaire «De Pijp». Les deux projets s'enlisèrent après la Seconde Guerre mondiale. En 1967, une nouvelle compétition pour l'hôtel de ville ne donna pas plus de résultats et ce ne fut qu'en 1979 que l'architecte autrichien Wilhelm Holzbauer proposa la solution de marier les deux projets à partir des meilleurs plans existants, dont l'un était sa création.

Le premier concours

Les édiles d'Amsterdam débattaient de la nécessité d'un nouvel hôtel de ville depuis plus d'un siècle lorsque le premier concours fut lancé en 1936. Pendant longtemps, la cité s'était enorgueillie de posséder l'un des plus beaux hôtels municipaux du monde. Construit sur une belle place, le Dam, et remplaçant un ensemble médiéval compliqué, il avait été dessiné en 1648 par Jacob van Campen. Pendant la courte période d'occupation française du début du XIXème siècle, il fut réquisitionné par le nouveau roi, Louis Napoléon et ne retrouva jamais sa fonction première.

L'hôtel de ville resta donc palais royal que la ville vendit à l'Etat en 1935. Le conseil municipal s'installa pendant un certain temps au Prinsenhof, dans un autre quartier de la ville, auquel il fut ajouté une extension à la fin des années 20, œuvre austère de N. Lansdorp et A.R. Hulshoff, dans le plus pur style 'Ecole d'Amsterdam' alors à la mode. Les architectes qui travaillaient tous deux pour le département des Travaux Publics avaient fait appel à un groupe de sculpteurs connus, dont Hildo Krop (sculpteur de la ville), W. Penaat et J. Thorn Prikker. Mais rapidement ces nouvelles installations se révélèrent insuffisantes.

En 1936, le conseil décida donc d'organiser un concours pour la construction de son nouvel hôtel sur Frederiksplein. Cette place était le site de l'ancien Paleis voor Volksvlijt (Palais de l'industrie populaire), une exposition permanente similaire à celle du Crystal Palace de Londres. La similarité entre les deux édifices ne s'arrête pas là puisque le «Paleis» disparut également dans un incendie, en 1929.

Le concours n'attira pas moins de 225 concurrents dont 28 étrangers. Son jury était composé du maire, W. de Vlugt et du conseiller municipal S. de Miranda, assistés d'un certain nombre d'architectes plutôt conservateurs. Même si le fonctionnalisme marquait des points dans toute l'Europe – Amsterdam jouant un rôle de premier plan dans ce mouvement – un jury assez traditionaliste avait donc été désigné et il semblait probable que les projets dans l'esprit de l'Ecole d'Amsterdam ou de Delft aient toutes les chances de l'emporter. Après avoir diligemment étudié les multiples propositions, le jury en arriva à la conclusion décevante qu'aucun des plans soumis ne lui convenait. Trois projets furent cependant sélectionnés pour un second tour (1938), sur la base de leurs qualités intrinsèques.

Les architectes retenus étaient H.T. Zwiers, M. Duintjer et A. Komter, J.F. et A. Staal ainsi que J.F. Berghoef et J.J.M. Vegter. Les plans de Zwiers rappelaient l'hôtel de ville de Stockholm tandis que les Staal, père et fils, avaient soumis une proposition quasi moderniste non sans quelques détails néo-baroques. Berghoef et Vegter s'étaient clairement inspirés de l'Ecole de Delft, de même que Zwiers. Cette école traditionaliste s'inspirait de l'architecture rurale (en particulier scandinave) et appréciait les matériaux naturels comme la brique et le bois. L'un des théoriciens de cette école, également membre du jury, était le professeur Granpré Molière, de la Faculté d'Architecture de l'Université de Delft. Bien que les projets de Duintjer et de Komter soient les plus austères, ils étaient encore bien loin de la modernité. Quelques projets modernistes, dont ceux de G.H.M. Holt et de J.P. Kloos avaient également été soumis même s'ils n'avaient guère de chances face à un tel jury.

Pour cette seconde étape, les architectes reçurent un cahier des charges plus précis. Mais une fois encore, le jury se révéla incapable de choisir un vainqueur et demanda à Duintjer et Komter, Berghoef et Vegter, de soumettre un troisième projet. Après la Seconde Guerre mondiale, qui survint entre-temps, l'assemblée municipale décida de conserver cette dernière équipe.

Seconde chance

Un nouveau site fut alors choisi, Waterlooplein, au centre de la ville et tout près de la rivière Amstel. Berghoef et Vegter se remirent avec entrain à leurs plans et, en 1961, présentèrent ce qui, dans leur esprit, était le projet final. C'est à ce moment que certains architectes néerlandais intervinrent. Aldo van Eyck, brillant représentant de la nouvelle génération, lança une attaque frontale. Il qualifia le projet d *«incroyable morceau d'architecture fasciste provinciale»*. D'autres hommes de l'art, comme H.Th Wijdeveld, alors âgé, ne purent se retenir de soumettre des projets bien qu'on ne le leur ait pas demandé. Toute cette agitation s'apaisa en 1964 avec la décision du conseil municipal de ne pas exécuter les plans retenus et un nouveau concours fut annoncé pour 1967.

Cette nouvelle compétition attira 804 propositions, soumises une fois encore anonymement. On raconte que le jury crut reconnaître dans un des projets la main d'Alvar Aalto et lui décerna le premier prix pour découvrir ensuite qu'il était signé d'un architecte quasi inconnu, Wilhelm Holzbauer. Les plans de celui-ci se distinguaient radicalement des quatre lauréats du concours de trente ans plus tôt. C'était un colossal édifice de béton. Aussi spectaculaire soit-il, ce pur produit du fonctionnalisme n'impressionna guère les architectes d'Amsterdam.

C'était l'époque de la participation et de la désobéissance civile. L'idée de Holzbauer fut perçue comme un symbole du pouvoir et de l'autoritarisme alors que l'architecture du moment se voulait 'modeste'. Les projets structuralistes de Herman Hertzberger, Piet Blom et Aldo van Eyck étaient anti-hiérarchiques et de taille réaliste. A l'opposé des fonctionnalistes qui créaient parfois à énorme échelle, ils préféraient de petites unités à taille humaine. Hertzberger, Heijdenrijk et l'équipe de Davidson, Rijnboot et Zwarts soumirent tous des projets structuralistes; Holzbauer et Arne Jacobsen en restèrent au fonctionnalisme.

Le conseil municipal laissa passer la tempête et décida de renvoyer la décision du jury à une réunion en 1970. Malheureusement, la ville ne put obtenir les subventions gouvernementales nécessaires et le projet d'Holzbauer fut enterré.

Un auditorium

L'histoire de l'opéra est tout aussi confuse. La Société Wagner néerlandaise avait rêvé de construire un lieu semblable au Festspielhaus de Bayreuth pour y jouer les œuvres de son compositeur favori. Des plans furent proposés par Hendrik Petrus Berlage en 1910 mais ne furent jamais exécutés. Berlage continua néanmoins à s'intéresser au projet. Il avait été membre du jury pour le concours restreint organisé en 1916 qui avait vu les architectes Blaauw, Gratama, van der Mey, Slothouwer, Staal et Wijdeveld invités à participer. Presque tous étaient représentatifs de l'Ecole d'Amsterdam. Staal remporta la compétition à l'unanimité, mais la municipalité garda le projet sous le coude bien que la Société Wagner ait réussi à réunir des fonds importants. La grande dépression et la Seconde Guerre mondiale mirent fin à son rêve.

Après la guerre, des tentatives répétées furent lancées pour construire un opéra. Des controverses sans fin s'élevèrent autour du choix du site, et les architectes de la ville, Holt et Bijvoet, soumirent plan sur plan.

En avril 1979, la solution était encore à trouver, lorsque Wilhelm Holzbauer proposa un plan original: au cours d'une promenade dans Amsterdam, la vision du 'Stopera' s'était brusquement imposée à lui...

Une issue en vue

Le plan de Holzbauer de combiner un hôtel de ville et un opéra était original. En fait, il l'était tellement que Holt et Bijvoet se montrèrent assez sceptiques au départ. Les deux architectes et les responsables politiques, que ce soit au niveau national ou régional, s'habituèrent cependant peu à peu à cette idée et un certain enthousiasme en sa faveur commença même à se dessiner. Bijvoet et Holt, qui avaient tous deux l'expérience de l'architecture de théâtre, acceptèrent de travailler avec Holzbauer, même si leur collaboration ne fut pas toujours sans nuage. Ces difficultés de cohabitation et les objections soulevées par le public et certains confrères furent mal supportées par un Bijvoet âgé qui mourut en décembre 1979. Holt saisit l'opportunité pour faire appel à son gendre, Cees Dam, qu'Holzbauer considéra vite comme une sorte de cheval de Troie. Les deux architectes durent apporter un certain nombre de modifications à leurs dessins, en partie pour répondre aux protestations d'un groupe d'artistes, animé, une fois encore, par Aldo van Eyck. Les habitants du quartier provoquèrent de nouveaux retards en sabotant des équipements et en endommageant des matériaux de construction, mais les travaux progressaient, lentement mais sûrement. Rien ne pouvait plus les arrêter.

Les choses s'envenimèrent néanmoins entre Dam et Holzbauer lorsque chacun prétendit s'attribuer le crédit du projet. L'hôtel de ville en L qui «embrasse» l'opéra était indéniablement l'idée de Holzbauer. Mais lequel des deux architectes pensa le premier aux cercles croisés[2] semble sans importance d'autant plus que ce très ancien symbole du mariage se retrouve également dans un dessin de Carlo Scarpa.

1 *Le terme néerlandais pour hôtel de ville est «stadhuis». Le mot de Stopéra est ainsi né du rapprochement de «stadhuis» et d'opéra. Néologisme légèrement maladroit, il fut utilisé dans un autre sens par les opposants au bâtiment, qui y virent la contraction de «stoppez l'opéra».*

2 *Ce motif se retrouve également sur les murs de la salle des mariages.*

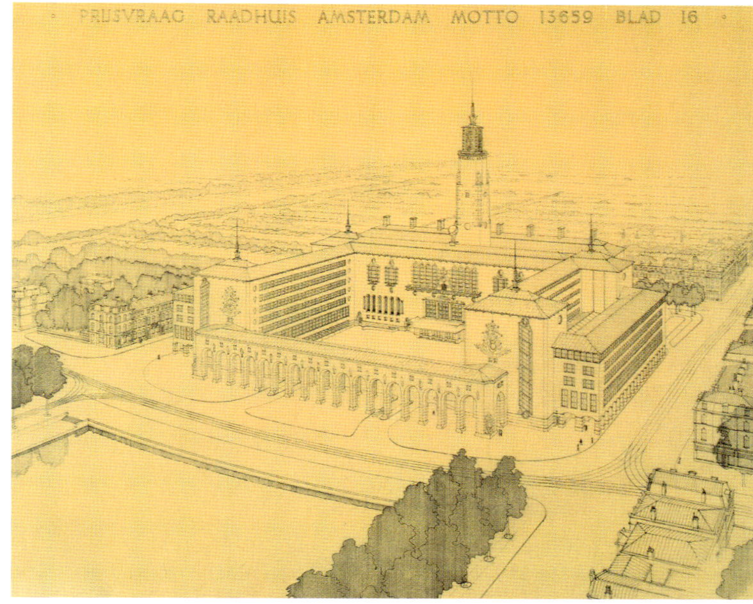

G.H.M. Holt & Jan Piet Kloos competition design, "Arp", 1937, bird's eye view, first round before war

H.T. Zwiers competition design, "13659", bird's eye view, first round before war

Jan Frederik & Arthur Staal competition design, "Anangkè", 1938, exterior view of façade, second round before war

Jan Frederik & Arthur Staal competition design, "Anangkè", 1938, top: interior view of oval civic hall, bottom: interior view of entrance hall, second round before war

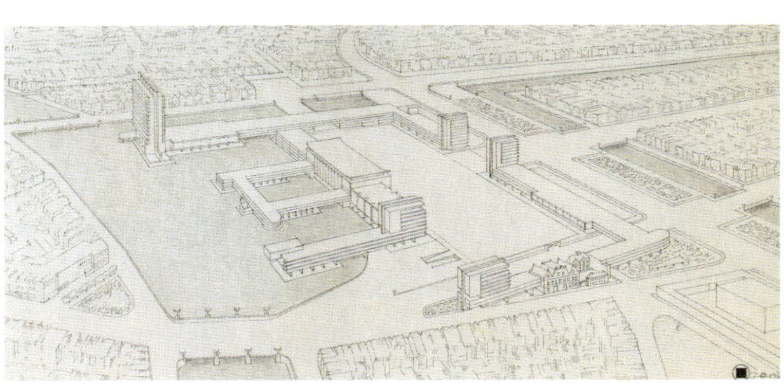

Johannes F. Berghoef & J.J.M. Vegter altered design, 1961, exterior view from the River Amstel

Johannes F. Berghoef & J.J.M. Vegter competition design, "Belfort", 1938, front elevation, first prize, second round before war

M. Duintjer & Auke Komter competition design, "Meron", 1938, exterior view of façade, second round before war

Hendrikus Theodorus Wijdeveld alternative design, 1961, bird's eye view

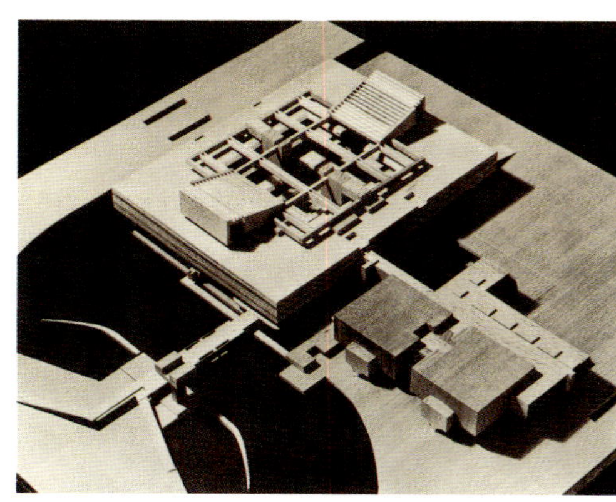

José Rafael Moneo competition design, 1967 elevation of main entrance, first round after war

Jan Hoogstad, M.C. van Deudekom, W. Schulze & A.S. van Tilburg competition design, 1967, model, first round after war (3rd examination)

Shoichi Kondo competition design, 1968, model, first round after war (4th examination)

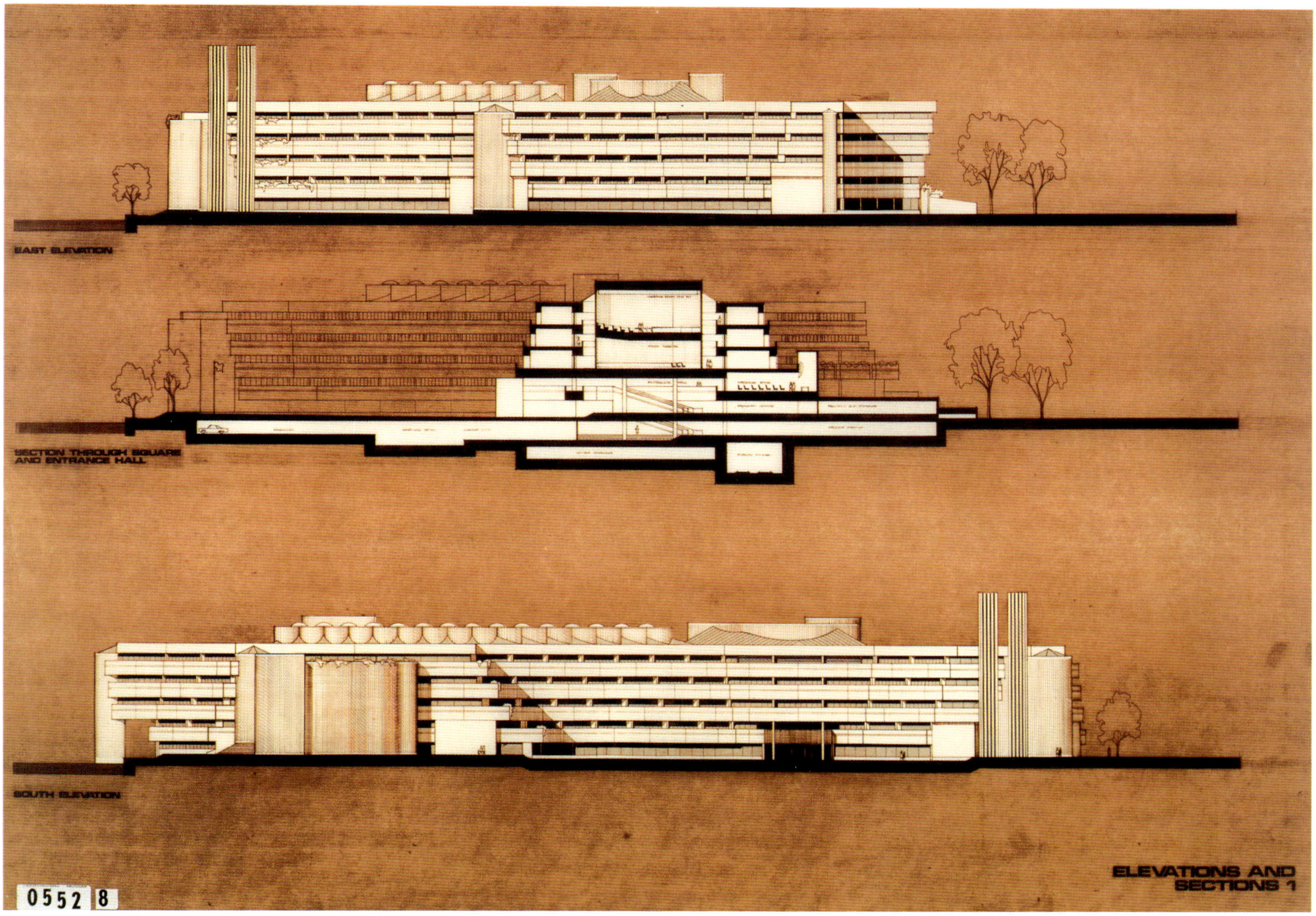

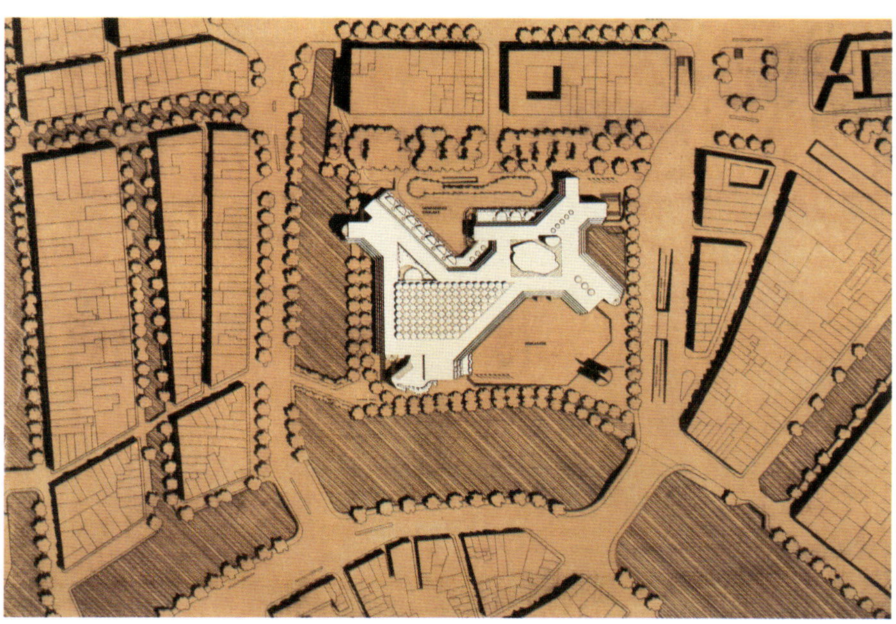

Robert Fairfield & Macy DuBois competition design, 1967, above: east elevation, middle: north-south section, below: south elevation, second round after the war (2nd examination)

Robert Fairfield & M. DuBois competition design, 1967, site plan, first round after the war (2nd examination)

Arne Jacobsen competition design, 1968, model, first round after war (4th examination)

Arne Jacobsen competition design, 1968, site plan, first round after war (4th examination)

P
M

L.J. Heijdenrijk competition design, 1968, site plan, special mention, second round after war

L.J. Heijdenrijk competition design, 1968, from top: elevations, section, left: plan of level 0.0., right: plan of lever 3.60, special mention, second round after war

L.J. Heijdenrijk competition design, 1968, model, special mention, second round after the war

Wilhelm Holzbauer & Cees Dam execution design, combined project City Hall and Opera House, 1981, exterior view on the River Amstel

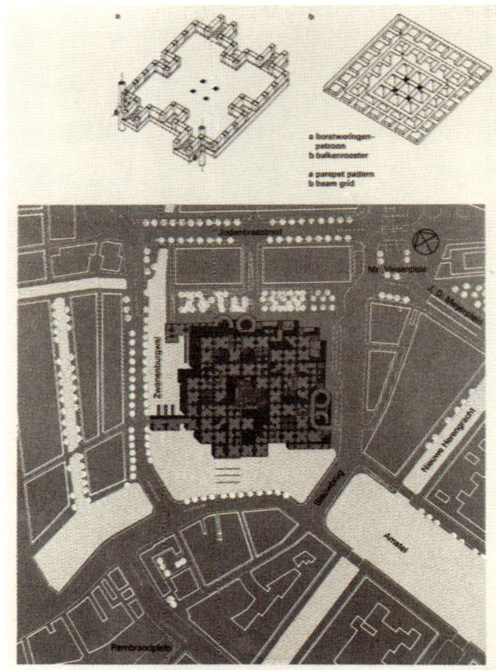

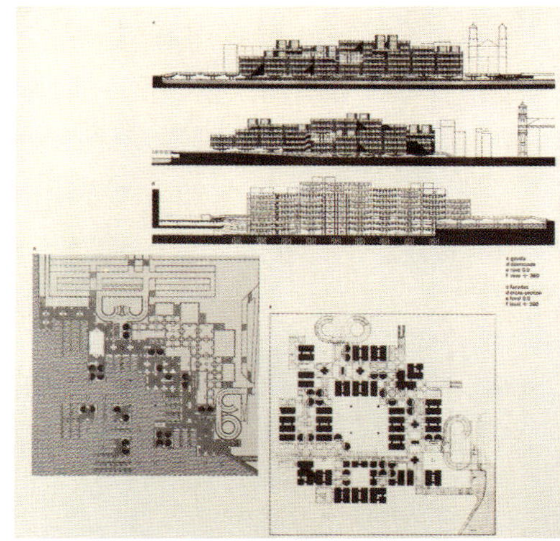

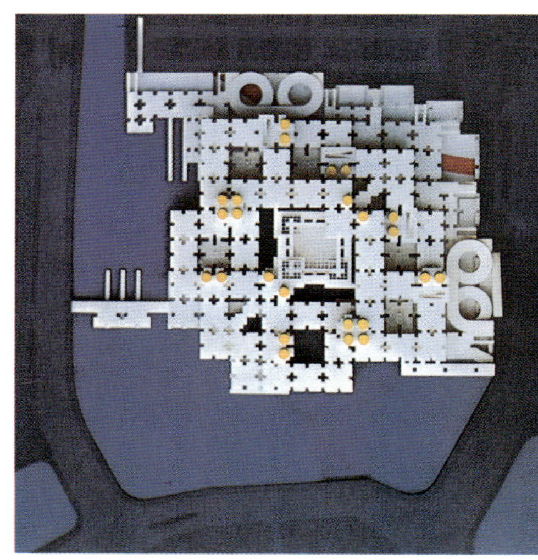

Project

Central station with offices

Site

Piazza dei Cinquecento, Rome

Dates

February 1947 to 30 June 1947 *Result announced* 31 October 1947

Number of entries

40

Jury

G. di Raimondo, G.C. Pamieri, A. Gianelli, E. Le Cigno, R. Narducci (Railways), M. Visentini, R. Marino, G. Nicolosi (state), A. Maccari (representative of the City of Rome), M. Urbinati, M. Paniconi (National Society of Italian Engineers and Architects), R. Regnoni (secretary of the research committee)

Result

First prize Leo Calini & Eugenio Montuori; Massimo Castellazzi, Vasco Fadigati, Achille Pintonello & Annibale Vitellozzi *Second prize* Vittorio Immirzi, Luigi Cosenza, Francesco della Sala, Adriano Galli, Guglielmo Ricciardi & Raffaello Salvatori; Saul Greco; Claudio Longo Gerace *Third prize* Cesare Pascoletti; Bruno Ronca & Carlo Mutinelli; Alfredo Scalpelli, Pietro Lombardi & Marco Fagioli; Achille Petrignani, Constantino Forleo & Nello Ena; Eugenio Rossi & Alberto Tonelli; Mario Ridolfi, Ludovico Quaroni, Aldo Cardelli, Mario Fiorentino, Giulio Ceradini & Enrico Caré; Leonato Favini & Mariano Pallotini; Robaldo Morozzo dalla Rocca & Carlo Domenico Rossi

Commissioned by

Railways, state and the City of Rome

Construction

1948 to 1951

Architects

Leo Calini, Eugenio Montuori, Massimo Castellazzi, Vasco Fadigati, Achille Pintonello & Annibale Vitellozzi

Termini Station, Rome, 1947

Leo Calini & Eugenio Montuori competition design, 1947, exterior view from Piazza dei Cinquecento, first prize

Massimo Castellazzi, Vasco Fadigati, Achille Pintonello, Annibale Vitellozzi competition design, 1947, exterior view from Piazza dei Cinquecento, first prize

Termini Station, Rome

Station architecture had been developing for more than a century when the competition for Termini Station was organised in 1947. The first stations were built in the style of the prevailing tradition. Even though these buildings had an entirely novel purpose, the architects applied existing styles, such as Gothic Revival (particularly in England) and Neo-Renaissance. However, the roofing structures over the tracks were often splendid examples of state-of-the-art engineering. These steel and glass roofs were particularly popular during the latter half of the nineteenth century.

Development of station architecture

In some cases, separate shelters for passengers were constructed over each platform instead of a single roof covering the entire station. Many railway terminus buildings had a characteristic U-shaped floor plan, with two wings on either side and one wing at the head of the tracks. The front of the station, which is often situated at the head of the tracks, faces the station square. In this way the station may also form a magnificent cynosure within the architectural surroundings. This approach to station architecture was the one taken in both Helsinki[1] and Rome.

The clear-cut distinction between engineering (the roof and tracks) and architecture (the station building) gradually disappeared during the nineteenth century. The two professions slowly started to merge. The engineers, self-assured and confident of their expertise, started to adopt a more independent attitude and revealed the asthetics of structures to the public (e.g. Eiffel). Especially in new forms of architecture, the architects increasingly emphasised the structural aspects of their work instead of trying to conceal the structure with lavish embellishments. This development continued into the early twentieth century.

An example of this modern approach to station architecture may be found in Stuttgart. This building, which dates from 1911, was designed by Paul Bonatz and Friedrich Scholer and has a characteristic austerity. One of its dominant features is a tower, which gives the building a certain stature. Hierarchic symbolism of this sort was probably an eyesore for many Modernists during the 1920s and 30s, but at least the pompous stations built in some arbitrary Neo-style were a thing of the past. The architects now saw stations as an element of the engineering and transport sector and took this into account in their designs.

Exterior view of entrance hall on Via Giovanni Giolitti

Interior view of entrance hall

All tracks lead to Rome

Termini Station in Rome endured all of the developmental phases described above. The first station, designed by Salvatore Bianchi, was completed between 1864 and 1879. A temporary building had previously served as a station. Although the station itself underwent a metamorphosis, it would always remain perched on top of the city's highest hill. This remarkable site had been chosen for purposes of property speculation. Bianchi's design was a typically eclectic product of his time. A central roof loomed above the low entrance façade.

Identical annexes in Neo-Palladian style were built on either side. Upon completion, Bianchi's station was almost immediately outdated and provided insufficient capacity to cope with the increasing number of passengers. The Pope's city-state had become the capital of united Italy in 1871 and from then on all tracks led to Rome. However, extension of the station was put off until 1905 because the city did not have the funds to commission projects of this magnitude, even though Rome was the capital. In terms of commerce, the city had been left far behind by the Northern Italian cities of Milan and Turin.

The former Termini Station shortly after this completion

When Mussolini came to power, the dilapidated and impractical station was demolished. The dictator wanted to restore Rome to its former glory, reminiscent of the magnificent metropolis of classical antiquity. In his delusions of grandeur, he saw the Fascists as direct successors to the Roman Empire. Rebuilding Rome would boldly underscore this theory. The style Mussolini had in mind was a blend of Classicism and Modernism. His preference for Classicism was not illogical – there were more than enough examples of it lying around – but Modernism also appealed to the tastes of those in power. The prime example of this blend of styles is the Casa del Fascio in Como, built in 1934 by G. Terragni.

Impetus for new building

In 1937, Mussolini decreed that a new station would be built on the old site. He commissioned the chief architect of the Italian Railways, Angiolo Mazzoni (1894–1976), who submitted his design in 1938, a year after Bianchi's station had been demolished. Construction was started in 1939. Mazzoni was held in high esteem at the time. He had already designed approximately thirty railway stations and post offices. Occasionally, he had applied a somewhat boring Classicist style, usually at the request of his clients. However, he had also applied his own futuristic style. Mazzoni was one of the publishers of the futuristic newspaper "Sant'Elia"[2] and a champion of the Italian modernist movement.
Mazzoni's design for Termini Station was of the Classicist variety. He envisaged a monumental portico which dominated the station square. This central block was flanked by two lateral wings, on which construction was started in 1939. However, due to the outbreak of the Second World War and the waning power of the Fascists, construction was stopped at this stage. During Mussolini's reign, the trains ran on time but there was no station...

Heritage of the past

Naturally, the city was still in need of a new station after the war. In January 1947, an open competition was organised. The participants had to take a fairly extensive programme of conditions into account. Mazzoni's wing annexes were to be retained and the architects were also advised to make use of the leftover building materials which had been ordered for Mazzoni. This was the extent of the heritage of the past.

In addition, the number of tracks had to be increased and the central building had to be moved towards the square, so that the building as a whole would be situated in front of Mazzoni's wings. The central building was to house various offices which had previously been situated in different parts of the city. The lateral wings would also contain offices and the side entrances were to be sealed off. The ticket office and restaurant were to be situated in front of the central office block. A central axis was envisaged between the office block and the lateral wings, which would link the restaurant, the ticket office and the platforms.
There was also one other problem. Not a single stone of the Ager Servianus, Rome's ancient city wall, was to be moved, even though the restaurant and ticket office were to be situated on the square where it stood, at an angle to the tracks. This little wall, no more than ten metres in length and a few metres high, proved an almost insurmountable obstacle.

Two winning designs

No more than forty architects and architectural teams submitted designs, many of which continued pre-war trends. The jury had both classical designs – with impressive, Mazzoniesque porticos – and modernist designs to judge. The latter category fared better. The first category was probably a little too reminiscent of the Fascist past, which the nation was trying to forget. First prize was jointly awarded to two teams of architects, that of Leo Calini and Eugenio Montuori and that of Massimo Castellazzi, Vasco Fadigati, Achille Pintonello and

Paul Bonatz & Friedrich Scholer
railway station, Stuttgart, 1911

Annibale Vitellozzi. Both teams had impressed the jury by submitting austere, modernist designs. Seventeen other teams and individual architects were awarded prizes or given an honourable mention. In the apparent belief that the combination of two good designs would produce an even more magnificent result, the jury decided to award a joint commission to the two teams. This proved to be an astute decision. The resulting station easily met the stipulated conditions and is also an exceptionally beautiful piece of architecture.

The station square is dominated by the long, uninterrupted façade of the office building, which is five floors high. The horizontal articulation consists of alternating lines of windows (two lines per floor) and slabs of stone. The restaurant and ticket office, which are situated in front of the office block, are separated by the Ager Servianus. The corbelling roof of the ticket office ingeniously mirrors the irregular silhouette of the wall, which is visible through the glass side-wall. Costly materials, such as red and pale-pink granite, have been used for the interior of the ticket office. The office building is not attached to Mazzoni's lateral stone wings. The three blocks are in harmony with one another because they are of equal height and have been constructed with similar materials. The roof covering the area between these three sections creates a certain unity and forms a hall leading to the most important sections of the station. This hall also forms a passage between the Via Marsala and the Via Giovanni Giolitti. On the platform side, the roof is supported by extremely slender posts, whereby an "open" space is created, similar to that in the ticket office. The hall also gives access to the subway and the public areas under the restaurant. At this subterranean level, one can marvel at the foundations of the Ager Servianus. In this way a piece of modern architecture makes a deep bow to the distant past. Fortunately, this architectural eulogy is far more creative than Mussolini's attempts to rewrite history.

1 See chapter on Helsinki station in this book.
2 Sant'Elia was founded in 1932 by F.T. Marinetti and was of course named after the Futuristic architect of the same name.

Stazione Termini, Rom

Als 1947 die Ausschreibung für den Stazione Termini in Rom erfolgte, konnte die europäische Eisenbahnarchitektur bereits auf eine 100jährige Geschichte zurückblicken. Die Architektur der ersten Bahnhöfe entsprach dem jeweils vorherrschenden zeitgenössischen Stil, denn obwohl es sich bei diesen Bauwerken um einen neuen Gebäudetypus handelte, griff man meist auf bekannte Stilrichtungen wie die Neugotik (hauptsächlich in England) und die Neurenaissance zurück. Die Dachkonstruktionen aus Glas und Stahl, die sich über die Gleise spannten, zeugten von meisterhafter Ingenieurskunst und erfreuten sich in der zweiten Hälfte des 19. Jahrhunderts großer Beliebtheit.

Die Entwicklung der Bahnhofsarchitektur

Einige der ersten Bahnhofsgebäude besaßen statt einer durchgehenden Dachkonstruktion für alle Gleise und Bahnsteige jeweils einzelne Dächer über jedem Bahnsteig, um die Reisenden vor dem Wetter zu schützen. Bei den Kopfbahnhöfen lag ein U-förmiger Grundriß nahe, der die Gleise von drei Seiten umschloß. Die Frontseite dieses Bahnhofstypus' befand sich meist am Ende der Schienen mit Blick über den Bahnhofsplatz. Auf diese Weise übernahm der Bahnhof auch die Funktion eines herausragenden städtebaulichen Blickfangs – wie etwa beim Hauptbahnhof von Helsinki[1] und in Rom. Die strikte Trennlinie zwischen technischer Ingenieurskunst (Dachkonstruktion und Gleise) und Architektur (Bahnhofsgebäude) verschwand gegen Ende des 19. Jahrhunderts immer mehr, da beide Berufsgruppen einander annäherten. Auf der einen Seite standen die Ingenieure, die – selbstbewußt und von ihren eigenen Fähigkeiten überzeugt – immer unabhängiger wurden (z.B. Gustave Eiffel) und der Öffentlichkeit die Schönheit ihrer Konstruktionen vermittelten. Auf der anderen Seite befanden sich die Architekten, die sich mehr und mehr für Konstruktionen und technische Details interessierten und bei neuen Gebäudetypen auf eine überflüssige, verhüllende Ornamentik zu verzichten versuchten. Diese Entwicklung setzte sich bis ins 20. Jahrhundert fort.

Alle Gleise führen nach Rom

Die Gestaltung des Stazione Termini in Rom zeichnet alle genannten Entwicklungsphasen nach. Der erste Bahnhof an dieser Stelle wurde zwischen 1864 und 1879 nach einem Entwurf von Salvatore Bianchi fertiggestellt; davor hatte ein provisorisches Gebäude als Bahnhofsstation gedient. An der Lage des Bahnhofs auf dem höchsten Hügel der Stadt – das Baugelände war aufgrund von Bodenspekulationen ausgewählt worden – sollte sich im Laufe der Zeit nichts mehr ändern. Allerdings durchlief die Planung des Bahnhofsgebäudes verschiedene Stadien. Bianchis Entwurf entsprach ganz dem eklektizistischen Stil seiner Zeit: Hinter dem niedrigen Eingangsbereich erhob sich ein zentrales Dach, auf beiden Seiten des Hauptgebäudes befanden sich zwei identische Anbauten im neopalladianischen Stil. Doch bereits kurz nach seiner Fertigstellung erwies sich der Bau als veraltet und zu klein für den stark angestiegenen Reiseverkehr, denn der Stadtstaat des Papstes war 1871 zur Hauptstadt Italiens ernannt worden. Von nun an sollten alle Gleise nach Rom führen. Dennoch wurde der Bahnhof erst 1905 erweitert, da Rom zwar die Hauptstadt Italiens war, sich aber derart große und kostspielige Projekte nicht leisten konnte. Wirtschaftlich lag Rom weit hinter den norditalienischen Städten wie Mailand und Turin zurück.
Erst nach Mussolinis Machtergreifung wurde der baufällige und unpraktische Bahnhof abgerissen. Der Diktator wollte Rom wieder zu der prachtvollen Metropole machen, die es in der Antike gewesen war. In seinem Größenwahn betrachtete er die Faschisten als direkte Nachfolger des Römischen Reichs, und ein in neuem Glanz erstrahltes Rom sollte diesen Anspruch untermauern. Als Baustil schwebte Mussolini eine Mischung aus Klassizismus und Moderne vor. Seine Vorliebe für den Klassizismus lag auf der Hand, da die Stadt mit Bauwerken dieses Stils übersät war. Aber auch die Moderne entsprach dem Geschmack der Machthaber – man denke beispielsweise an das berühmte Casa del Fascio in Como, 1934 von G. Terragni erbaut.

Planung eines Neubaus

1937 erteilte Mussolini dem Chefarchitekten der italienischen Eisenbahn, Angiolo Mazzoni (1894–1976), den Auftrag zum Bau einer neuen Station auf dem Gelände des ehemaligen, inzwischen abgerissenen Bahnhofs. Mazzoni reichte seinen Entwurf 1938 ein, und bereits ein Jahr später begannen die Bauarbeiten. Der monumentale Portikus des Gebäudes sollte den gesamten Bahnhofsplatz beherrschen und von zwei Seitenflügeln flankiert werden. Die Bauarbeiten an diesen Gebäudeteilen begannen 1939, wurden aber durch den Ausbruch des Zweiten Weltkriegs und die schwindende Macht der Faschisten schon bald unterbrochen. Während Mussolinis Herrschaft fuhren die Züge zwar pünktlich, aber es gab keinen Bahnhof.
Nach Kriegsende benötigte die Stadt einen neuen Bahnhof und entschloß sich im Januar 1947 zu einer öffentlichen Ausschreibung. Die Teilnehmer mußten eine Reihe von Auflagen berücksichtigen. Die von Mazzoni entworfenen Seitenflügel sollten erhalten und die für den damaligen Bahnhof bestellten Baumaterialien verwendet werden. Über dieses Vermächtnis der Vergangenheit hinausgehend, verlangten die Auflagen einen Ausbau der Gleise sowie eine Verschiebung des Hauptgebäudes in Richtung Bahnhofsplatz, damit sich der neue Bahnhof vor Mazzonis Seitenflügel befand. Das Hauptgebäude sollte genügend Platz für die Verwaltungsräume bieten, die bis zu diesem Zeitpunkt noch über die Stadt verstreut waren. Darüber hinaus mußten die Seitenflügel in Büroräume verwandelt und die Seiteneingänge zugemauert werden. Den Fahrkartenschalter und das Restaurant wollte man vor das Hauptgebäude plazieren, während zwischen dem Verwaltungsgebäude und den Seitenflügeln eine zentrale Achse verlaufen sollte, die als Verbindung zwischen Restaurant, Fahrkartenschalter und Bahnsteigen diente.
Aber es gab ein Problem: Obwohl sich Restaurant und Fahrkartenschalter auf der Seite des Bahnhofsplatzes befinden sollten, durfte an der alten Stadtmauer, der Agger Servianus, nichts verändert werden. Die kleine, nur wenige Meter hohe und etwa zehn Meter lange Mauer verlief schräg zu den Gleisen mitten über den Platz und bildete ein beinahe unüberwindliches Hindernis.

Zwei Entwürfe auf dem ersten Platz

Nur etwa 40 Architekten und Architektenteams hatten sich an der Ausschreibung beteiligt; die Mehrzahl hielt in ihren Entwürfen an den Stilrichtungen der Vorkriegszeit fest. Die Jury mußte sich sowohl mit klassizistischen Konzepten – mit imposanten Portiken, ähnlich wie bei Mazzonis Vorschlag – als auch mit modernistischen Konstruktionsplänen befassen, wobei diese größere Zustimmung fanden. Die klassizistischen Entwürfe erinnerten noch zu stark an den Faschismus, von dem man sich deutlich distanzieren wollte. Den ersten Preis erhielten zwei Architektengemeinschaften – Leo Calini und Eugenio Montuori sowie Massimo Castellazzi, Vasco Fadigati, Achille Pintonello und Annibale Vitellozzi – deren Konzepte die Jury durch ihr strenges, modernistisches Design beeindruckt hatten. An 17 weitere Architekten und Architektengemeinschaften wurden Preise und ehrenvolle Erwähnungen vergeben.
Die Jury ging offensichtlich davon aus, daß die Kombination zweier guter Konstruktionspläne zu einem noch besseren Ergebnis führen würde und beschloß, die Gewinner einen gemeinsamen Entwurf erarbeiten zu lassen. Ein weiser Entschluß: Das fertige Bahnhofsgebäude erfüllte nicht nur alle Auflagen, sondern galt auch als außergewöhnlich gelungenes Bauwerk.
Der Bahnhofsplatz wird von der langen, durchgehenden Fassade des fünfgeschossigen Verwaltungsgebäudes beherrscht. Die horizontale Gliederung besteht aus einander abwechselnden Fensterreihen (zwei Reihen pro Etage) und Natursteinplatten. Restaurant und Fahrkartenschalter befinden sich vor dem Verwaltungsgebäude, werden von ihm aber durch die Agger Servianus getrennt, wobei das auskragende Dach des Fahrkartenschalters auf meisterhafte Weise dem unregelmäßigen Verlauf der Mauer folgt, die durch die Glaswand weiterhin sichtbar ist. Für die Innenausstattung des Verkaufsraums wurden teure Materialien wie roter und blaßrosafarbener Granit verwendet. Das Verwaltungsgebäude ist nicht mit Mazzonis Seitenflügeln verbunden, doch die Verwendung des gleichen Materials (Naturstein) und die identische Geschoßhöhe gewährleisten ein Gleichgewicht zwischen den drei Gebäudeteilen. Die Fläche zwischen den einzelnen Teilen wird von einem durchgehenden Dach überspannt, was dem Entwurf Einheitlichkeit verleiht und eine Verbindungshalle zwischen den wichtigsten Räumen schafft. Darüber hinaus dient diese Halle als Passage zwischen der Via Marsala und der Via Giovanni Giolitti. Da das Dach auf der Bahnsteigseite von sehr dünnen Stützpfosten getragen wird, entsteht – wie beim Fahrkartenschalter – ein »offener« Raum. Durch ihn erreicht man außerdem die U-Bahn sowie die öffentlich zugänglichen Räume unter dem Restaurantbereich mit Blick auf die Fundamente der Agger Servianus. Hierdurch erweist ein äußerst modernistisches Gebäude der fernen Vergangenheit seine Reverenz.

1 Siehe das Kapitel zum Hauptbahnhof, Helsinki

La Gare Termini, Rome

L'architecture ferroviaire avait déjà plus d'un siècle d'existence lorsque le concours pour la gare Termini fut organisé en 1947. Bien que la fonction de ces bâtiments eût été entièrement nouvelle, les architectes avaient appliqué aux premières gares les styles qui avaient leur préférence comme le néo-gothique (surtout en Angleterre) ou le néo-Renaissance. Les structures de couverture des quais et des voies témoignaient néanmoins du haut niveau technique et du talent de toute une nouvelle génération d'ingénieurs. Leurs immenses verrières furent particulièrement appréciées pendant toute la seconde moitié du XIXème siècle.

Le développement de l'architecture de gare

Dans certains cas, les architectes préféraient des abris séparés courant au-dessus de chaque quai à la couverture d'une seule volée de la totalité de l'espace des voies. De nombreux bâtiments de gare suivaient un plan en U avec une aile principale perpendiculaire à l'extrémité des voies et deux ailes latérales. Située généralement en bordure d'une vaste place, la gare remplissait une fonction monumentale, comme ce fut le cas à la fois pour Rome et Helsinki[1].

La distinction, voire l'opposition, entre les ingénieurs (voies et verrières) et les architectes (la gare elle-même) disparut peu à peu au cours du siècle dernier. Les deux professions fusionnèrent graduellement. Conscients de leur expertise, les ingénieurs adoptèrent une attitude plus indépendante et n'hésitèrent plus à affirmer l'esthétique de leurs structures (Eiffel, par exemple). Dans cette nouvelle mise en pratique de leur art, les architectes mirent de plus en plus en valeur les aspects structuraux de leurs créations au lieu de tenter de les masquer sous des ornements. Cette évolution se poursuivit au début du XXème siècle et Stuttgart offre à cet égard l'exemple d'une approche moderne de l'architecture ferroviaire. Sa gare, réalisée par Paul Bonatz et Friedrich Scholer en 1911, affiche une austérité toute personnelle. L'une de ses principales caractéristiques est une grande tour qui lui confère toute son allure. Cette affirmation symbolique de puissance ne devait pas plaire aux modernistes des années 20 et 30, mais ils pouvaient au moins être contents de la disparition des pompeuses gares de style «néo». Les gares relevaient maintenant de l'ingénierie et du secteur des transports, et les architectes surent prendre en compte ces nouveaux paramètres dans leurs projets.

Tous les chemins mènent à Rome

La gare Termini, à Rome, passa par toutes les phases que nous venons de décrire. Succédant à un bâtiment temporaire, la première vraie gare, conçue par Salvatore Bianchi, fut construite entre 1864 et 1879 sur un site qui allait rester inchangé, la plus haute des collines de Rome. Cet emplacement remarquable avait été choisi dans une optique de développement immobilier. Les plans de Bianchi étaient typiques de l'époque, en un mot éclectiques. Un vaste toit central dominait la façade principale assez basse et deux annexes latérales identiques, de style néo-palladien. A peine terminée, la gare était à la fois démodée et trop exiguë pour le nombre grandissant de voyageurs qu'attirait la cité papale devenue capitale de l'Italie en 1871. Néanmoins, aucune transformation ne fut entreprise avant 1905 car la ville n'était pas assez riche pour se lancer dans une réalisation de cette ampleur. L'expansion économique de la cité était restée très en arrière de celle de Milan.

Lorsque Mussolini arriva au pouvoir, la gare vétuste et mal commode fut démolie. Le dictateur voulait rendre à Rome sa gloire antique et dans ses rêves de grandeur, il voyait dans les fascistes les successeurs des Romains. Reconstruire Rome concrétiserait sa théorie. Le style que Mussolini avait en tête était un mélange de classicisme et de modernisme. Sa préférence pour le premier n'était pas illogique – les modèles originaux abondaient autour de lui – mais le modernisme plaisait également aux nouveaux dirigeants. Le premier exemple de ce mariage stylistique fut la Casa del Fascio, à Côme (1934) dont les plans sont dus à G. Terragni.

La volonté de construire

En 1937, Mussolini décréta qu'une nouvelle gare serait construite sur l'ancien site. Il fit appel à l'architecte en chef des chemins de fer italiens, Angiolo Mazzoni (1894–1976) qui soumit un premier plan en 1938, un an après la démolition du bâtiment de Bianchi. La construction débuta en 1939. Mazzoni était très estimé à l'époque et il avait déjà conçu environ trente gares et hôtels des postes. Il avait appliqué à l'occasion un style classique un peu ennuyeux, la plupart du temps à la demande de ses clients, mais préférait cependant un style futuriste personnel. N'était-il pas l'un des éditeurs du journal futuriste «Sant'Elia»[2] et l'un des champions du mouvement moderniste italien?

Ses plans pour la gare Termini relevaient de son style classique. Il envisageait un portique central monumental dominant la place et flanqué de deux ailes latérales dont la construction démarra en premier. L'éclatement de la guerre et l'affaiblissement puis la disparition du pouvoir fasciste mirent vite fin à ces travaux. Si les trains arrivaient à l'heure sous Mussolini, ils n'avaient pas toujours une gare pour ce faire...

Héritage du passé

Après la guerre, la capitale avait toujours autant besoin d'une nouvelle gare. En janvier 1947, un concours fut organisé. Les participants devaient prendre en compte un ensemble complexe de contraintes héritées du passé. Ils devaient en particulier conserver les ailes déjà édifiées par Mazzoni et se servir des matériaux de construction qu'il avait commandés. Le nombre de voies était augmenté et le bâtiment principal devait être avancé vers la place pour se trouver en avant par rapport aux ailes de Mazzoni. Il abriterait divers bureaux jusqu'alors dispersés dans toute la ville. Les ailes latérales accueilleraient également des bureaux, et leurs entrées seraient supprimées. La billetterie et le restaurant seraient situés en avant du bloc central administratif et l'on pouvait imaginer un axe central, entre les bureaux et les ailes reliant le restaurant, la billetterie et les quais.

Dernière difficulté, pas une seule pierre de l'enceinte de Servius, l'ancienne muraille de Rome, ne devait être déplacée, bien que le futur restaurant et la billetterie fussent situés à son emplacement, perpendiculairement aux voies. Les ruines de ce rempart, de quelques dix mètres de long et de deux ou trois de haut, se révélèrent un obstacle presque insurmontable.

Les deux plans vainqueurs

Quarante architectes ou équipes d'architectes seulement concoururent, dont beaucoup exprimaient encore les tendances stylistiques de l'avant-guerre. Le jury se trouvait face à des projets classiques, avec de vastes portiques mazzoniens et d'autres d'esprit moderniste. Cette seconde catégorie avait d'autant plus de chances de gagner que la première rappelait sans doute trop un passé fasciste que le pays s'efforçait d'oublier. Le premier prix fut attribué à deux équipes, celles de Leo Calini et Eugenio Montuori d'une part et de Massimo Castellazzi, Vasco Fadigati, Achille Pintonello et Annibale Vitellozzi d'autre part. Toutes deux firent une forte impression sur le jury avec des projets austères et modernistes. Dix-sept autres participants reçurent des prix ou une mention honorable.

Le jury pensa que la combinaison de deux plans de qualité donnerait naissance à un projet plus magnifique encore et décida d'attribuer conjointement la commande aux deux équipes. Cette décision se révéla judicieuse puisque la gare née de cette collaboration,œuvre architecturale particulièrement remarquable, remplit les multiples conditions du concours.

La place de la gare est dominée par la longue façade ininterrompue de l'immeuble des bureaux, haut de cinq étages. L'articulation horizontale se fait grâce aux lignes de fenêtres alternées (deux lignes par niveau) et de dalles de pierre. Le restaurant et les guichets situés en avant des bureaux sont séparés par l'enceinte de Servius. Le toit en encorbellement de la salle des guichets reflète ingénieusement la silhouette irrégulière de l'ancien rempart, visible à travers le mur de verre latéral. Des matériaux de prix, granit rouge ou rose pâle sont abondamment utilisés dans la salle des guichets. Le bâtiment des bureaux n'est pas lié aux ailes de pierre de Mazzoni, mais ces trois blocs de hauteur égale et construits dans des matériaux similaires restent cependant en harmonie. Le toit qui recouvre la surface définie par ces trois parties apporte également une certaine unité et forme un hall qui ouvre sur les zones de la gare les plus actives. Il fait également office de passage entre la Via Marsala et la Via Giovanni Giolitti. Côté quais, le toit est soutenu par des poteaux extrêmement fins qui déterminent un espace ouvert, similaire à celui de la billetterie. Du hall, on accède au métro et aux espaces publics implantés sous le restaurant. Au niveau souterrain, on peut encore admirer les fondations de l'enceinte de Servius, hommage d'une œuvre architecturale du XXème siècle à un lointain passé. Cette louange architecturale s'est révélée avec bonheur beaucoup plus créative que les tentatives mussoliniennes de réécriture de l'histoire.

1 *Voir plus loin, le chapitre sur Helsinki.*

2 *Le magazine Sant'Elia fut fondé par F.T. Marinetti et intitulé d'après le nom du grand architecte futuriste, Antonio Sant'Elia (1888-1916).*

Saul Greco competition design, 1947, exterior view from Piazza dei Cinquecento, second prize

Claudio Longo Gerace competition design, 1947, exterior view from Piazza dei Cinquecento, second prize

Cesare Pascoletti competition design, 1947, exterior view from Piazza dei Cinquecento, third prize

Leonato Favini & Mariano Pallottini competition design, 1947, exterior view from Piazza dei Cinquecento, third prize

Mario Ridolfi, Ludovico Quaroni, Aldo Cardelli, Marion Fiorentino, Giulio Ceradini & Enrico Care competition design, 1947, exterior view from Piazza dei Cinquecento, third prize

Robaldo Morozzo della Rocca & Carlo Domenico Rossi competition design, 1947, exterior view from Piazza dei Cinquecento, third prize

Achille Petrignani, Constantino Forleo & Nello Ena competition design, 1947, exterior perspective from the Piazza dei Cinquecento, third prize

Alfredo Scalpelli, Pietro Lombardi & Marco Fagioli competition design, 1947, exterior perspective from Piazza dei Cinquecento, third prize

Bruno Ronca & Carlo Mutinelli competition design, 1947, exterior perspective from Piazza dei Cinquecento, third prize

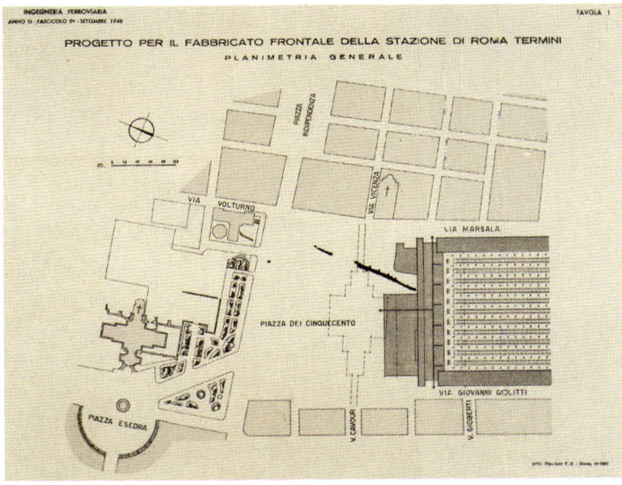

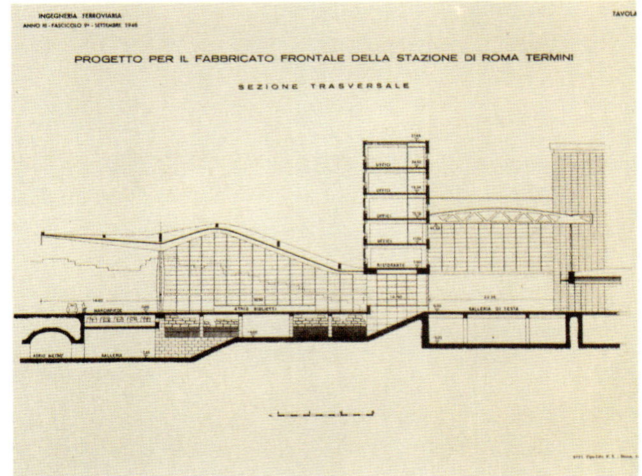

Leo Calini, Eugenio Montuori, Massimo Castellazzi, Vasco Fadigati, Achille Pintonello & Annibale Vitellozzi execution design, 1947, site plan

Leo Calini, Eugenio Montuori, Massimo Castellazzi, Vasco Fadigati, Achille Pintonello & Annibale Vitellozzi execution design, 1947, longitudinal section

Leo Calini, Eugenio Montuori, Massimo Castellazzi, Vasco Fadigati, Achille Pintonello & Annibale Vitellozzi execution design, 1947, interior view of Galleria di Testa

Leo Calini, Eugenio Montuori, Massimo Castellazzi, Vasco Fadigati, Achille Pintonello & Annibale Vitellozzi execution design, 1947, exterior view from Piazza dei Cinquecento (model)

Leo Calini, Eugenio Montuori, Massimo Castellazzi, Vasco Fadigati, Achille Pintonello & Annibale Vitellozzi execution design, 1947, ground floor plan

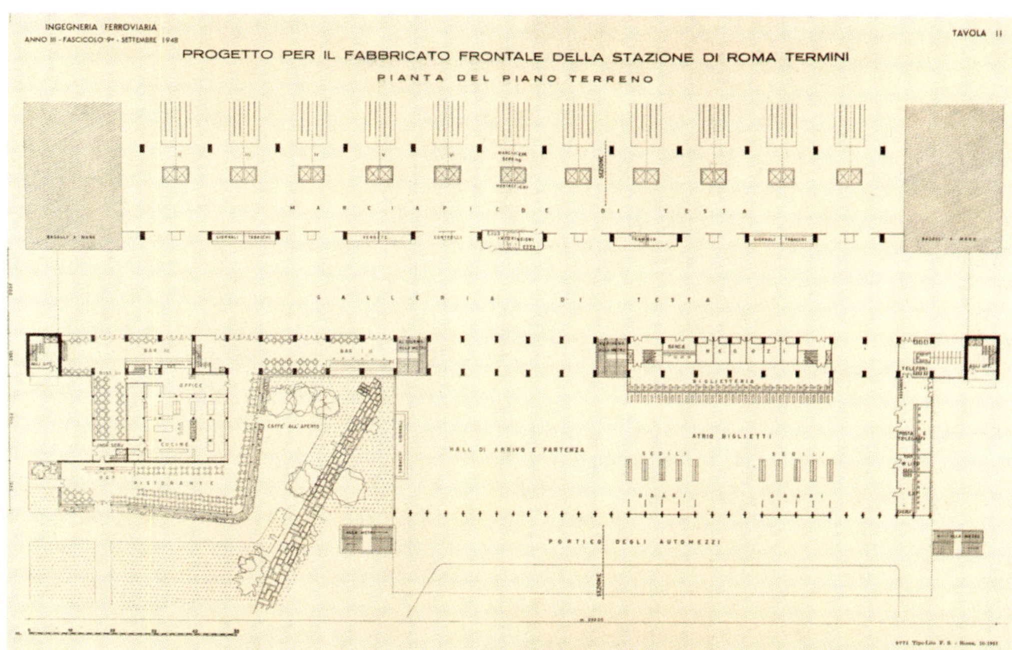

Chief editor

Cees de Jong, V+K Publishing, Naarden

Design

Cees de Jong, José K. Vermeulen, V+K Design, Naarden

Illustration research co-ordinator

Emmanuelle Kramps, Naarden

Production co-ordinators

Cees de Jong, Emmanuelle Kramps, Naarden
Jochen Dilling, Cologne

Editor

Erik Mattie, Amsterdam

Assistant editor

Michiel Pestman, Amsterdam

Translator – English

Richard de Nooy, Amsterdam

Translator – German

Franca Fritz & Heinrich Koop, Cologne

Translator – French

Jacques Bosser, Paris

Architectural Competitions is based on an idea developed by Cees de Jong, V+K Publishing, Naarden, The Netherlands.
In 1988, V+K Publishing published an international co-edition *Architects in Competition.*
In 1991, V+K Publishing published *Architectural Politics as seen in Competitions* in a set of seven volumes, especially for the Japanese market.
In 1994, this publication *Architectural Competitions* is completely edited and written by Cees de Jong and Erik Mattie.

Caudan Waterfront is the highlight in the capital Port Louis. When visiting the city, a detour to Chinatown and the market is definitely worth a visit.

Die „Caudan Waterfront" ist das Highlight in der Hauptstadt Port Louis. Wenn man schon in der Stadt ist, lohnt sich auch ein Abstecher nach Chinatown und zum Markt.

Foto: Mienny istock

The Rochester Waterfall in the south west is surrounded by sugar cane and banana plantations and is the widest waterfall in Mauritius.

Inmitten von Zuckerrohr- und Bananenplantagen liegt der breiteste Wasserfall von Mauritius, der Rochester Waterfall im Südwesten.

Foto: amriphoto istock

Foto: Pictures Shutterstock

Mauritius offers wunderful beaches, is a paradise for golfers and a colourful mixture of different cultures.

left page: Temple of Socaligum Minathi Amen near Port Louis

photo left: colonial style house from 1872 „Le Domaine des Aubineaux" south of Curepipe

above: Ile Aux Cerf Beach island golf club

Mauritius bietet traumhafte Strände, ist ein Paradies für Golfer und ein bunter Mix verschiedenster Kulturen.

1

Constance
Prince Maurice

MAURITIUS EAST COAST

A place where luxury blends with extraordinary design – the 'Constance Prince Maurice' is the place to be. Housed in an exclusive 60 hectare private peninsula on the tranquil North Eastern corner of Mauritius the luxury resort provides a stunning setting. Families love the beach villas and the complementary Constance kids club, while golf pros can retreat to the two 18-hole championship golf courses. Designed by masterminds Jean Marc Eynaud and David Edwards, the Constance Prince Maurice creates the essence of sheer luxury close to the water. Blending perfectly in the beautiful surroundings, the hotel is inspired by Feng Shui principles to fulfil the perfect sense of harmony: all beds stand high above floor level to help and increase the circulation of Qi. Seven restaurants and two bars offer international and creole cuisine.

Wer einem Ort sucht, wo Luxus mit außergewöhnlichem Design verschmilzt, für den ist das „Constance Prince Maurice" genau das Richtige. Auf einer 60 Hektar großen Privathalbinsel in der ruhigen nordöstlichen Ecke von Mauritius, offenbart das Resort ein beeindruckendes Szenario. Für Familien sind die Beach-Villas und der „Constance Kids Club" ideal, Golfer können sich dem 18-Loch-Golfplatz widmen. Das Resort mit seinen 89 Suiten und Villen, gestaltet von Meister-architekt Jean Marc Eynaud und Designer David Edwards, bietet die Essenz des puren Luxus – harmonisch in die Lagunenlandschaft eingefügt und nach Feng-Shui-Prinzipien gestaltet. Kulinarisch werden die Gäste in sieben Restaurants und zwei Bars mit internationaler und kreolischer Küche verwöhnt.

The intimate location surrounded by lush vegetation creates an ultimate cocoon of luxury with dedicated service.

Die ruhige Lage des Resorts inmitten einer üppigen Vegetation ist ein perfekter Rückzugsort mit Luxus und hingebungsvollem Service.

Foto: Constance Hotels

Foto: Constance Hotels

Foto: Constance Hotels

Designed by masterminds Jean Marc Eynaud and David Edwards, the Constance Prince Maurice creates the essence of sheer luxury close to the water.

Das „Constance Prince Maurice“ mit seinen 89 Suiten und Villen, gestaltet von Meisterarchitekt Jean Marc Eynaud und Designer David Edwards, ist Luxus pur direkt am Wasser.

Foto: one&Only

2

One & Only

Le Saint Géran

MAURITIUS EAST COAST

The One&Only Le Saint Geran Resort has become a legend thanks to its history, charm and unique location amidst a thriving tropical paradise with small water courses and over 4,000 palms. After a lavish renovation, a combination of new and traditional elements characterise the current design of the resort. The colonial style is complemented by inspiration from the local lifestyle and the architecture of the island. The sugar kilns and palm-thatched roofs are reminiscent of manor houses on local plantations. The one-, two- and three-bedroom suites from 110 m^2 to 250 m^2 promise first-class luxury overlooking the sea, the white sand beach or the magnificent lagoon.

Die einzigartige Lage in einem blühenden tropischen Idyll mit kleinen Wasserläufen und über 4.000 Palmen sowie die Historie und Charme des Resorts machten das One&Only Le Saint Géran zu einer Legende. Nach einer aufwendigen Renovierung prägt eine Kombination aus neuen und traditionellen Elementen das Design. Der Kolonialstil wird durch Anlehnungen an den lokalen Lifestyle und die Architektur der Insel ergänzt. Zuckerrohröfen, palmblattgedeckten Dächer und Gebäude erinnern an die Manor Houses auf den örtlichen Plantagen. Die One-, Two- und Three-Bedroom-Suiten von 110 bis 250 m^2 mit Blick auf das Meer, den weißen Sandstrand oder die herrliche Lagune versprechen erstklassigen Luxus.

The new rooms are elegant with spacious living areas, modern, timeless designs with a touch of island flair. The furniture, fabrics and colours used such as white marble, teak and grey tones set the scene for the lush green tropical landscape, the intense turquoise of the Indian Ocean and the white sand on the beaches. The addition of natural materials such as wood, stone, leather and custom-made furniture and lithographic prints by local artists create an atmospheric space. The resort's Villa One is a secluded island hideaway with two bedrooms for up to four adults and two children and not only offers complete privacy, but breathtaking views of the sea.

Die neuen Gästezimmer präsentieren sich elegant mit großzügigen Wohnbereichen in modernem, zeitlosem Design mit einer Prise Inselflair. Mobiliar, Stoffe und Farbgebungen wie gedeckte weiße Marmor-, Teak- und Grautöne setzen die üppig grüne Tropenlandschaft, das kräftige Türkis des Indischen Ozeans und den strahlend weißen Sand an den Stränden in Szene. Hinzu kommen natürliche Materialien wie Holz, Stein, Leder und Leinen, individuelle Möbel und Lithografien örtlicher Künstler. Ein Höchstmaß an Privatsphäre bietet die „Villa One" des One&Only Le Saint Géran, ein abgeschiedenes Inselrefugium mit zwei Schlafzimmern für bis zu vier Erwachsene und zwei Kinder und einem atemberaubenden Meerblick.

Foto: one&Only

Foto: Le Telfair

3

Golf & Wellness Resort

Heritage Le Telfair

MAURITIUS SOUTH COAST

In the unspoilt South of Mauritius 'The Heritage Le Telfair' offers the ultimate combination of beach, nature, relaxation and adventure. The resort radiates the elegant and refined style of former sugar plantation properties on Mauritius. Hidden in one of the most beautiful spots of the island, the Domaine de Bel Ombre stretches from the hills down to the preserved lagoon. Heritage Le Telfair provides real gourmet experiences throughout the twelve restaurants of the Domaine de Bel Ombre with all the multicultural tastes Mauritius has to offer. For an active day the Heritage Golf Club invites guests on a European Tour branded and sustainable golf course, awarded three years in a row as best golf course in the Indian Ocean at the World Golf Awards.

Im unberührten Süden von Mauritius bietet das „Heritage Le Telfair" die ultimative Kombination aus Strand, Natur, Erholung und Abenteuer. Das Resort strahlt das elegante und raffinierte Flair der ehemaligen Zuckerplantagen auf Mauritius aus. Verborgen an einem der schönsten Plätze der Insel, erstreckt sich die Domaine de Bel Ombre von den Bergen bis hinunter zur Lagune. In den zwölf Restaurants bietet das „Heritage Le Telfair" Gourmeterlebnisse inklusive der ganzen Geschmackspalette, die Mauritius zu bieten hat. Für einen aktiven Tag lädt der Heritage Golf Club die Gäste zu einer Europameisterschaft auf den Golfplatz ein, der drei Jahre in Folge bei den World Golf Awards als bester Golfplatz im Indischen Ozean ausgezeichnet wurde.

Surrounded by water – the Indian Ocean is never far away at 'Le Telfair'.

Vom Wasser umgeben – das "Le Telfair".

Foto: Le Telfair

Foto: Le Telfair

Interiors at the 'Heritage Le Telfair' are classical – pale walls draped with silks, set against dark wood floors and period furniture, with roll-top baths in Junior Suites and paintings of the Irish naturalist Charles Telfair.

Die Einrichtung im „Heritage Le Telfair" ist klassisch: helle Wände, mit Seidenstoffen drapiert, dunkle Holzböden und antike Möbel. Die Roll-Top-Bäder in den Juniorsuiten und die Gemälde des irischen Naturforschers Charles Telfair geben dem Ganzen eine besonders charmante Note.

4

The Residence Mauritius

MAURITIUS EAST COAST

Situated on the one mile stretch of immaculate white sand, fringed by the azure Indian Ocean and tropical gardens, 'The Residence Mauritius' is an idyllic retreat for unsurpassed relaxation. Inspired by the island's stately turn-of-the-century plantation houses, this luxurious Mauritian resort blends modern elegance with classic, colonial style enveloping guests in an endearing sense of nostalgia. The rooms radiate luxurious comfort and charm combined with highly-personalised, intuitive service. Reminiscent of a bygone era, the resort is a jewel of elegant refinement, offering a beautiful symphony of modernity and tradition.

An einem kilometerlangen Strand gelegen, verbindet das Resort moderne Eleganz mit klassischem Kolonialstil. In den luxuriösen, geschmackvoll eingerichteten Zimmern fühlt man sich zurückversetzt in vergangene Zeiten. „The Residence Mauritius" verbindet Tradition mit Moderne auf elegante und raffinierte Weise.

The resort's 135 rooms and 28 suites are intimate spaces for relaxation, decorated with an inspired blend of simplicity and elegance. Sunlight sifting through the shutters creates a melody of light and shadow on the soft palette of white and delicate shades of beige. Large marble bathrooms add a touch of decadence.

Eingerichtet im Stil simpler Eleganz bieten die 135 Zimmer und 28 Suiten des Resorts Entspannung pur. Die Sonne schimmert durch die Fensterläden und malt eine Melodie aus Licht und Schatten aus Weiß und zartem Beige. Große Marmorbäder fügen einen Hauch von Dekadenz hinzu.

Foto: The Residence

Foto: The Residence

Foto: The Residence

'The Plantation' restaurant reminds of the verandah of a private sugar cane plantation house from the past. Excellent food, attentive service and spectacular ocean views.

Im „Plantation" Restaurant speist man wie auf der Veranda einer Zuckerrohrplantage – mit ausgezeichneter Küche, aufmerksamem Service und einer spektakulären Aussicht auf den Indischen Ozean.

5

Shangri-La's
Le Touessrok

MAURITIUS EAST COAST

After an extensive renovation, 'Le Touessrok' has reopened in November 2015. The resort offers an unrivalled standard of privacy and in an atmosphere of refined island luxury. Thoughtfully renovated in accordance with plush contemporary design, every room and suite incorporates indigenous island touches, features postcard-perfect views of turquoise waters and embodies sophistication and style. In addition, with fashionable restaurants, bars and entertainment venues that are set against the backdrop of a dramatic tropical landscape the resort is the perfect address for renowned traditions, bespoke gastronomic experiences and holistic wellness.

Im November 2015 hat das „Le Touessrok" nach einer umfangreichen Renovierung wieder eröffnet. Das Resort bietet einen unvergleichlichen Standard der Privatsphäre, kombiniert mit raffiniertem Inselluxus. Sorgfältig renoviert mit exklusivem zeitgenössischen Design, bieten die Zimmer und Suiten dezente einheimische Noten und einen perfekten Ausblick über das türkisfarbene Meer. Mit modischen Restaurants, Bars und Unterhaltungsmöglichkeiten vor einer dramatischen tropischen Kulisse bietet das „Le Touessrok" einzigartige Eindrücke und Luxus auf höchstem Niveau.

Foto: Shangri-La's Le Toussrok

Foto: Shangri-La's Le Toussrok

The resort features five restaurants that serve finest Western and Asian cuisines with the spices and fragrances of India and fresh ingredients of Japan. Overlooking Hibiscus Bay, 'Safran' for example is a refined dining restaurant offering a blend of authentic Indian and Mauritian cuisines. The menu was conceived by internationally acclaimed Chef Ramesh Bundi and provides an array of popular Indian dishes served family-style. In 'Kushi' one will be transported to the Far East with the restaurant's red, sensual Geisha-inspired design, including an impressive centrepiece made of hundreds of kushi combs.

Fünf Restaurants bieten feinste westliche und asiatische Spezialitäten mit den Aromen der indischen und Zutaten der japanischen Küche. Im „Safran" wird eine Mischung aus authentischer indischer und mauritischer Küche serviert. Die Speisekarte wurde von dem international gefeierten Chef Ramesh Bundi konzipiert und bietet eine Reihe von beliebten indischen Gerichten, serviert im „Familien-Stil". Im „Kushi" wird man mit dem roten sinnlichen Geisha-inspirierten Design des Restaurants in den Fernen Osten transportiert. Das Herzstück des Restaurants besteht aus Hunderten von Kush-Kämmen.

Foto: Shangri-La's Le Toussrok

Each one of the 200 rooms and suites and three beach villas provide guests with a personalised sanctuary in a newly defined, elegant island chic. Tasteful furnishings have been carefully curated to complement the surrounding natural beauty and local culture. Indigenous materials and contemporary style are seamlessly mixed to create a beautiful and chic atmosphere.

Die 200 Zimmer, Suiten und drei Strandvillen sind ein individuell gestaltetes Refugium, ein neu definierter, eleganter Insel-Chic. Die exklusive Einrichtung greift Elemente der Natur und Kultur von Mauritius auf, lokale Materialien und zeitgenössischer Stil gehen nahtlos ineinander über und schaffen eine schicke Atmosphäre.

Foto: … 's Le Toussrok

6

Four Seasons
Resort Mauritius at Anahita

MAURITIUS WEST COAST

Lush gardens of exotic flowers and warm Indian Ocean breezes create an instant sense of freedom. With all pool villa accommodation split across the meandering coastline and a private 11 acre island, this stylish resort offers boundless space for escapism, and discovery along intertwining cycling pathways. Unrivalled children's and teen facilities and spacious Residence Villas make this the perfect family retreat, while romantic tranquility caters to the desires of couples and honeymooners. Three secluded beaches invite relaxation and are home to complimentary water-skiing and non-motorised watersports. Further activity is offered on the 'Ernie Els Design' 18-hole championship golf course and regionally inspired treatments ease away tension in the overwater treatment suites of the Afro-Indian inspired Spa.

Das stilvolle Resort bietet viele Möglichkeiten zum Ausspannen und für Entdeckungstouren auf den verschlungenen Radwegen in den üppigen Tropengärten der 11 Hektar großen Insel. An den weitläufigen Stränden liegen auch die Poolvillen. Kinder- und Jugendeinrichtungen sowie geräumige Residenzvillen sind ideal für Familien. Paare und Hochzeitsreisende werden vor allem die romantische Ruhe auf der Insel schätzen. Wer gern am Strand liegt oder Wassersport betreiben will, hat drei einsame Strände mit diversen Wassersportmöglichkeiten zur Auswahl. Freunde des „grünen Sports" werden von dem „Ernie Els Design"-18-Loch-Championship-Golfplatz begeistert sein. Wer dann noch mehr Entspannung sucht, findet sie im das afro-indisch inspirierten Spa.

Foto: Four Seasons Kent Seet

...ur Seasons Kent Seet

Four Seasons Resort Mauritius at Anahita offers a variety of unique fine dining options from sushi served at the poolside to the finest gourmet Italian and more. From a casual sushi lunch to a multi-course dinner under the stars, the chefs put creativity, and attention to detail into every aspect of the resort's cuisine. A number of premiere chefs are specialized in different types of cuisine – Italian, Indian, Chinese and Mauritian – for restaurant menus as diverse as the island itself.

Mehrere exklusive Restaurants mit kreativer Küche vom lässigen Sushi am Pool bis zum Multi-Gänge-Dinner unter den Sternen verwöhnen die Gäste mit Spezialitäten der italienischen, indischen, chinesischen und lokalen Küche.

Foto: Four Seasons Kent Seet

The resort offers a wide range of luxurious suites and villas from the 'Sanctuary Beach Villa' to the Five-Bedroom 'Royal Residence Villa'. Inspired by local elements and using traditional materials to contemporary effect, the villas design seamlessly melds generous indoor and outdoor living space with external features including landscaped terraces, al fresco shower, infinity edge plunge pool and private tropical gardens.

Eine breite Palette luxuriöser Suiten und Villen von der „Sanctuary Beach Pool Villa" bis zur Five-Bedroom "Royal Residence Villa" erfüllen unterschiedlichste Ansprüche. Inspiriert von regionalen Elementen und traditionellen Materialien verbinden die Villen großzügige Innen- und Außenbereiche mit Features wie Landschaftsterrassen, Al-Fresco-Dusche, Infinity-Pool und private tropische Gärten.

Foto: Four Seasons Kent Seet

7

St. Regis

MAURITIUS SOUTH-WEST COAST

Whether in need of action and adventure, or tranquility and relaxation, the St. Regis offers both at the highest level. Situated on a beautiful stretch of white sand on the Southwest coast of the island, the resort is flagged by the famous UNESCO world heritage site of Le Morne mountain. Tucked away between lush palm trees and the turquoise blue waters of the Indian Ocean, the resort was named 'Best Spa Resort in Mauritius' by the World Travel Awards in 2015. The St. Regis Mauritius Resort is not only famous for the extraordinary combination of sophistication and modern sensibility, but also for its outstanding cuisine and its legendary butler service and great water sport facilities. The St. Regis Villa – a private resort within the resort – is nestled in lush tropical surroundings, with the ocean lapping literally at its toes. The private entrance opens out into an elegantly furnished living accommodation, including dining areas, outdoor and indoor lounges, office rooms, private pools and direct access to a 143-meter beach front.

Ob Abenteuer oder Ruhe und Erholung, das St. Regis bietet beides auf höchstem Niveau. Das Resort erstreckt sich über einem langen weißen Sandstrand an der Südwestküste am Fuße des Le Morne. Zwischen üppigen Palmen und dem türkisblauen Wasser des Indischen Ozeans versteckt, wurde das Resort im Jahr 2015 von den World Travel Awards als „Best Spa Resort in Mauritius" bezeichnet. Das St. Regis Mauritius Resort ist nicht nur für die außergewöhnliche Kombination aus Raffinesse und moderner Sensibilität berühmt, sondern auch für seine hervorragende Küche, den legendären Butlerservice und den vielen Wassersportmöglichkeiten. Die St. Regis Villa – ein privates Resort im Resort – liegt im tropischen Garten mit dem Ozean direkt vor der Tür. Der private Eingang öffnet sich in eine elegant eingerichtete Wohnanlage mit Essbereich, Außen-und Innen-Lounges, Büroräume, private Pools und direkten Zugang zu einem 143 Meter langen Strand.

The five-star luxury resort welcomes guests with a magical setting: breathtaking views to the soft white sands of Le Morne Beach with its turquoise lagoon.

Foto: St. Regis Mauritius

The spacious suites create a relaxed, tropical ambience with exquisitely appointed interiors, refined fittings and delicate textures. Each suite has a full, direct ocean view and opens up to a private timber deck or balcony, with private sun loungers and direct access to the beach.

Die geräumigen Suiten schaffen ein entspanntes, tropisches Ambiente mit exquisit ausgestattetem Interieur, raffinierten Armaturen und zarten Texturen. Jede Suite verfügt über einen bezaubernden Blick aufs Meer und öffnet sich zum privaten Holzdeck oder Balkon mit direktem Zugang zum Strand.

The 172 rooms and suites, are designed and fitted to the highest standards; from Junior Suite (above) to the St Regis Villa. Some bathrooms are equipped with private plunge pools and facades sliding away to reveal ocean views stretching as far as the eye can see.

Die 172 Zimmer und Suiten, von der Junior Suite (oben) bis zur St. Regis Villa, sind auf höchstem Niveau gestaltet, die Bäder zum Teil mit privaten Tauchbecken. Verschiebbare Fassaden ermöglichen den Blick über den Ozean bis zum Horizont.

8

Dinarobin
Beachcomber Golf Resort & Spa

MAURITIUS SOUTH-WEST COAST

In a stunning setting, at the base of Le Morne, guests have access to three world-class golf courses. Water landscapes with small islands covered in flowers, spacious wooden decks and tropical gardens, full of the rich green of exotic trees, make the Dinarobin Beachcomber a symbol of Mauritian elegance. With the adjoining sister hotel 'Paradis Beachcomber Golf Resort & Spa' the grounds stretch along the Morne Beach. 'Sports Beachcomber', the largest sports school in the Indian Ocean, offers guests an extensive range of land- and water activities. Guests can meet for a sundowner at the pool, and stroll to the 'Mahogany Bar' for some post dinner atmospheric live music.

In spektakulärer Lage am Fuße des Le Morne, haben die Gäste Zugang zu drei Weltklasse-Golfplätzen. Wasserlandschaften mit kleinen Inseln voller Blumen und großzügigen Holzdecks, Terrassen mit Meerblick sowie tropische Gärten, begrünt mit exotischen Bäumen, machen das Resort zum Symbol tropischer Eleganz auf Mauritius. Mit dem benachbarten Schwesterhotel „Paradis Beachcomber Golf Resort & Spa" erstreckt sich die Anlage entlang des kilometerlangen Le-Morne-Beach. „Sports Beachcomber", die größte Sportschule im Indischen Ozean, bietet den Gästen ein umfangreiches Angebot an Land- und Wasseraktivitäten. Abends trifft man sich zum Sundowner am Pool, nach dem Dinner zu stimmungsvoller Lifemusik in der „Mahogany Bar".

Foto: bechcomber

In accordance with the cultural diversity of the population, the cuisine is a mixture of French, Italian, Chinese and Creole aromas. The culinary highlight is, without doubt, the restaurant 'Umami', where surrounded by fine wood and stone, Asian Fusion cuisine is served. Situated right on the beach, one can visit 'Le Morne Plage', and, with your feet in the sand, enjoy a light lunch of snacks, fresh fish and seafood.

Entsprechend der kulturellen Vielfalt der Inselbevölkerung mischt die Küche französische, italienische, chinesische und kreolische Aromen. Das kulinarische Highlight ist zweifellos das „Umami". Umgeben von edlem Holz und Stein wird asiatische Fusion-Küche serviert. Direkt am Strand gelegen, trifft man sich im „Le Morne Plage" zum legeren Lunch mit den Füßen im Sand zu Snacks, frischem Fisch und Meeresfrüchten.

Foto: bechcomber

Foto: bechcomber

The colonial style interior decor is characterized by warm colors and elegant wooden furniture. The emphasis is on light and lots of space. For golfers, the golf suites offer a golf package for the Paradis Golf Club. The spacious senior suites offer plenty of space, comfort and an unobscured sea view.

Die stimmungsvolle Inneneinrichtung im Kolonialstil ist von warmen Farbtönen und eleganten Holzmöbeln geprägt mit Betonung auf Licht und viel Platz. Für Golfurlauber bieten sich die Golf Suiten mit Golfpaket für den Paradis Golfclub an. In erster Meereslinie liegen die geräumigen Senior Suiten mit viel Platz und Komfort.

Foto: The Oberoi

9

Hotel & Resort
The Oberoi

MAURITIUS NORTHWEST COAST

15 kilometres north of the capital Port Louis, 'The Oberoi' is embraced by twenty acres of sub-tropical gardens, bursting with fragrant frangipani and flaming red flamboyant trees, Buddha statues, palm-lined infinity pools and six hundred metres of combed, white sandy beaches. The Restaurant specialises in classic European and Asian dishes, as well as local Creole cuisine. A dinner in the 'Gunpowder Room' which dates back to French colonial times with rustic, brick walls, rough stone floors and antique wine barrels, makes for an unforgettable evening. Secluded by indigenous trees and framed by a lush garden, the spa therapies include Ayurvedic, Western, Thai, Balinese and 'Oberoi signature treatments' that harmonise modern science and ancient philosophies.

Fünfzehn Kilometer nördlich der Hauptstadt Port Louis liegt das „Oberoi". Von 20 Hektar üppigen subtropischen Gärten umgeben, mit duftenden Frangipani und feurig roten Bäumen, Buddha-Statuen, palmengesäumten Infinity-Pools und einem 600 Meter langen weißen Sandstrand. Das Restaurant ist spezialisiert auf klassische europäische, asiatische und kreolische Küche. Aus französischen Kolonialzeiten stammend, fasziniert der „Gunpowder Room" mit rustikalen Ziegelwänden, rauen Steinböden und antiken Weinfässern. Der Spa-Bereich liegt in einem üppigen tropischen Garten. Ayurvedische, westliche, thailändische und balinesische Behandlungen und die „Oberoi signature treatment" werden hier angewendet, wo moderne Wissenschaft und alte Philosophie aufeinandertreffen.

Foto: The Oberoi

Lots of space to relax at six hundred metres of combed, white sand beaches at Turtle Bay.

Viel Platz zum Entspannen am 600 Meter langen weißen Sandstrand in der Turtle Bay.

The pavillons and villas of 'The Oberoi' feature rustic oak and natural cane furniture, wall-to-wall windows and marble bathrooms which look out onto the private garden and pools.

Die Pavillons und Villen des „Oberoi" beeindrucken mit rustikalen Rattanmöbeln, großen bodentiefen Fenstern und Marmorbädern mit Blick auf die privaten Gärten und Pools.

Foto: Oberoi

10

Beachcomber Golf Resort & Spa
Trou aux Biches

MAURITIUS WEST COAST

The concept of the modern five-star village-style resort, manages to combine tropical elegance, contemporary style and comfort in an impressive way. It is set in gardens which run along the two kilometre sandy beach and have been carefully nurtured for decades. The resort was built in accordance with the requirements of international ecological organisations. The spa, with its own pool, consists of a series of individual pavilions amongst palms and exotic plants, and is surrounded by rippling pools - making it perfect for families, couples and honeymooners. And by the end of 2017, there will also be an 18-hole golf course 'Mont Choisy', pleasing lovers of the green sport.

Das Konzept des modernen 5-Sterne-Dorfstil-Resorts in einer über Jahrzehnte eingewachsenen und sorgsam gepflegten Gartenanlage entlang dem zwei Kilometer langen Sandstrand vereint tropische Eleganz, Modernität und Komfort. Das Resort wurde nach den Anforderungen internationaler ökologischer Verbände gebaut. So besteht der Spabereich mit eigenem Pool aus einer Reihe von einzelnen Pavillons zwischen Palmen und exotischen Pflanzen, umgeben von plätschernden Wasserbecken. Perfekt für Familien, Pärchen und Honeymooner – und ab Ende 2017 nach Fertigstellung des 18-Loch-Golfplatzes „Mont Choisy" auch für Freunde des grünen Sports.

The six resort restaurants look after the culinary desires of the guests, who can enjoy the beach feeling of Le Deck or indulge in Thai dishes in the Asiatic 'Blue Ginger'. Guests can explore the range of indian spices in 'Mahiya' where scents of cumin, curcuma and cardamon transcend the airwaves. Situated directly by the sea and with dreamy views 'La Caravelle' is especially romantic. Two bars invite you every evening to a Sundowner of a homemade 'Rum arrange'.

Gleich sechs Restaurants kümmern sich um das leibliche Wohl der Gäste: Im Strandrestaurant „Le Deck" mit echtem Beachfeeling, mit Thai-Gerichten im asiatischen „Blue Ginger" und im „Mahiya" ganz indisch. Hier duftet es nach Kreuzkümmel, Kurkuma und Kardamon. Mit Traumblick direkt am Meer ist es im „La Caravelle" besonders romantisch. Zwei Bars laden allabendlich zum Sundowner oder hausgemachten „Rum arrangé" ein.

Foto: Beachcomber

The suites are integrated in the spacious tropical garden. The beachfront suites with their private pool are a perfect combination of elegant and modern style.

Die Suiten sind in die großzügige Gartenanlage integriert. Die Beachfront-Suites mit eigenem Pool sind eine perfekte Kombination aus Eleganz und Modernität.

Foto: Beachcomber

11

Beachcomber Luxury
Royal Palm

MAURITIUS WEST COAST

Here guests can experience luxury at its highest level. The white beach stretches along the turquoise-blue Grand Baie, in the restaurant haute cuisine is served by award-winning chefs and in the 'Clarins Spa' ones body and spirit will experience complete relaxation. The first member of the 'Leading Hotels of the World' in the Indian Ocean receives its guests with colonial charm, timeless elegance and heavenly peace. The hotel complex, with 69 luxurious suites and two natural stone pools, is situated within tropical gardens along the picturesque bay. Since the extensive renovation in 2014, guests can choose from nine different categories of suites, from the Junior Suite to the Royal Suite on three floors with a total of 300 m^2. For exclusive private excursions the hotel's own yacht 'Royal Princess' is available.

Hier wird Luxus auf höchstem Niveau zelebriert. Der weiße Strand erstreckt sich entlang der türkisblauen Grand Baie, im Restaurant wird Haute cuisine vom preisgekrönten Küchenchef serviert und im „Spa by Clarins" erfahren Körper und Geist vollkommene Entspannung. Das erste Mitglied der „Leading Hotels of the World" im Indischen Ozean empfängt seine Gäste mit kolonialem Charme, zeitloser Eleganz und himmlischer Ruhe. Nahe der Grand Baie liegt die Hotelanlage mit 69 luxuriösen Suiten und zwei Natursteinpools inmitten einer tropischen Gartenanlage entlang der malerischen Bucht. Nach der umfangreichen Renovierung 2014 kann der Gast aus neun verschiedenen Suite-Kategorien wählen – von der Junior-Suite bis zur Royal-Suite auf drei Etagen mit insgesamt 300 m^2. Für exklusive private Ausflüge steht die hauseigene Hotelyacht „Royal Princess" zur Verfügung.

Foto: Beachcomber

Foto: Beachcomber

In the restaurant 'La Goélette' the top chef, Michel de Matteis, winner of the 'Meilleur Ouvrier de France', will spoil the guests with star-quality cuisine, using mainly local ingredients, of course. In 'La Brezza' Italian cuisine is served in a relaxed atmosphere, and 'Le Bar Plage' offers light cuisine in the shade of a giant tropical Bardamier tree above the beach, accompanied by the chatter of birds and the sound of the waves.

Im Restaurant „La Goélette" verwöhnt der mit dem „Meilleur Ouvrier de France" ausgezeichnete Chefkoch Michel de Mattéis die Gäste mit sternemäßiger Küche – unter Einbeziehung heimischer Zutaten natürlich. Im „La Brezza" wird in ungezwungener Atmosphäre italienische Küche serviert und im „Le Bar Plage" im Schatten eines riesigen tropischen Bardamier-Baumes oberhalb des Strandes bei Vogelgezwitscher und Wellenrauschen leichte Küche.

Varying color concepts transform the roomy suites into a warm atmosphere of classic elegance, with a hint of colonial style. The combination of indoor- and outdoor elements is complemented by spacious sun terraces with a sea view.

Unterschiedliche Farbkonzepte tauchen die großzügigen Suiten in eine warme Atmosphäre aus klassischer Eleganz mit einem Hauch von Kolonialstil. Das Setup von Indoor- und Outdoor-Elementen wird durch großzügige Sonnenterrassen mit Meerblick ergänzt.

Foto: Beachcomber

Maldives
Equator
Zanzibar
Seychelles
Madagascar
Mauritius
La Reunion
Tumbatu Island
2
Mnemba Island
1
Stone Town 102 – 113
1
Zanzibar City
Michamvi Beach 98
Rock Restaurant 118
3
4
Beach 96
5
Jozani Forest 122, 124
6
Makunduchi 116
TANSANIA
TANSANIA
10 km

Zanzibar

Hotels

1	**Emerson on Hurumzi**	
2	**Mnemba Island Resort**	
3	**Zawadi Zanzibar**	The Zanzbar Collection
4	**Baraza Resort & Spa**	The Zanzbar Collection
5	**The Palm**	The Zanzbar Collection
6	**The Residence Zanzibar**	Cenizaro Hotels & Resorts

Golf Courses

1	**Sea Cliff Resort**	9 hole

Area:	*2,461 km²*
Highest mountain:	*133 m*
Population:	*1,155,000*
Religion:	*98.9 % Islam* *0.6 % Christianity* *0.5 % Indigenious*
Language:	*swahili, arabic, english*
Government:	*Federacy*
Independence:	*1963*
Currency:	*Tanzanian Shilling*

The people of Zanzibar stem from an amalgamation of cultures, from Africans, Indians, Persians and Arabs, and are particularly happy and friendly people.

Die Sansibari, ein bunt gemischtes Volk aus Afrikanern, Indern, Persern und Arabern sind ein außergewöhnlich fröhliches und herzliches Volk.

Karibu Sana, meaning welcome on the Spice Island of Zanzibar, has a romantic ring to it - it sounds like unspoiled, white sandy beaches, turquoise blue water and relaxing in a hammock in the shade of a coconut tree. In line with oriental romance it exudes the magic of Africa and instantly enchants its visitors. Although the real magic is down to its residents; the cheerful Jambo Jambo of the locals impresses and captivates guests, like a spell, immediately transforming the holiday into something truly special.

A visit to the historic centre of Zanzibar City, the stone town, is a must. With its crumbling buildings and the many shops, the UNESCO world heritage site is an unforgettable attraction. Tacky tourist souvenirs are a rarity, instead genuine hand crafts are on offer. Shoes, pictures, a variety of materials, furniture, accessories and traditional style masks are made in the store, on the street or in the backyard. That one can eat well on the island of spice goes without saying. With an Oriental flair and spectacular views over the rooftops of the city, one can enjoy what the rooftop restaurants, such as 'Emerson Spice', have to offer. For spectacular scenery reserve a table during sunset, and when all the city's mosques call to prayer in unison, one feels as if transported to a different world.

In the countryside the huts are simple, with little or no comforts. For most people electricity remains a dream and running water something unimaginable. Luckily, food is plentiful thanks to the gardens where fruit and vegetable appear to grow easily. However, life can be hard and yet the people of Zanzibar are a happy and very friendly community. The locals highly depend on tourism and the associated jobs it brings. Visitors often travel to Zanzibar for a few days after a safari tour in Africa, yet even for a longer period it offers the opportunity for a memorable holiday, with a perfect combination of nature, beaches and welcoming people.

Karibu Sana! „Herzlich willkommen" heißt das auf der Gewürzinsel Sansibar im Indischen Ozean. Klingt romantisch und nach unberührten weißen Sandstränden, nach Hängematte unter Kokospalmen und türkisblauem Wasser, nach orientalischer Romantik aus 1.001 Nacht und nach dem Zauber Afrikas. Und genauso ist es auch. Sansibar verzaubert. Wobei den wahren Zauber die Menschen ausmachen. Andauernd tönt dem Besucher das fröhliche Jambo-Jambo der Einheimischen entgegen. Ein Zauber, der sich auch auf den Besucher überträgt und den Urlaub zu etwas ganz Besonderem macht.

Einen Besuch der Altstadt von Sansibar-City, Stone Town, sollte man unbedingt einplanen. Mit seinen maroden Gebäuden und den landestypischen Geschäften ist das UNESCO-Weltkulturerbe ein unvergessliches Erlebnis. Den üblichen Touristenkitsch findet man wenig, dafür unverfälschte Handwerkskunst. Schuhe, Bilder, Stoffe, Möbel, Accessoires und alte Masken werden direkt im Laden oder auf der Straße gefertigt. Dass man auf der Gewürzinsel gut essen kann, liegt auf der Hand. Mit orientalischem Flair und toller Aussicht über die Dächer der Stadt und das Meer am besten in einem der Dachrestaurants wie „Emerson Spice" zum Beispiel. Wenn dann zum Sonnenuntergang aus allen Moscheen der Stadt zum Gebet gerufen wird, ist man angekommen – in einer ganz anderen Welt. Auch in einer Welt, wo die Menschen in einfachsten Verhältnissen leben. Auf dem Land in pittoresken Lehmhütten, oft nur ein Dach über dem Kopf und ohne jeden Komfort. Strom ist für viele unerschwinglich, fließendes Wasser kaum bekannt. Zu essen gibt es zwar genug, denn viele haben einen Garten, in dem einfach alles wächst. Aber hart ist das Leben trotzdem. Und doch sind die Sansibarer ein fröhliches und herzliches Volk. Ein Volk, das auf Tourismus angewiesen ist. Oft wird Sansibar im Anschluss an eine Safari auf dem afrikanischen Kontinent gebucht. Aber auch als direktes Ziel bietet Sansibar beste Voraussetzungen für einen erlebnisreichen Urlaub mit einer idealen Kombination aus Natur, Strand und herzlichen Menschen.

In addition to spices, Zanzibar is especially known for its endless, snow-white sandy beaches as shown here on the east coast at the hotel Baraza.

Neben Gewürzen ist Sansibar vor allem für seine endlosen schneeweißen Sandstrände bekannt wie hier an der Ostküste beim Hotel „Baraza".

Foto: The Zanzibar Collection

A natural artwork the coast near Michamvi

Ein Kunsterk der Natur: die Küste bei Michamvi

The dhow has been the traditional sailing boat of Zanzibar for centuries and is still used today.

Seit Jahrhunderten ist die Dhau das traditionelle Segelboot auf Sansibar.

Foto: mango1778 Shutterstock

Stone Town is the colourful yet somewhat morbid historic centre of Zanzibar and a UNESCO World Heritage site since 2000. Life pulsates through the narrow streets with a blend of Oriental and African flair.

Bunt und morbid zugleich wirkt Stone Town, die Altstadt von Sansibar-City und seit dem Jahr 2000 UNESCO-Weltkulturerbe. Hier pulsiert das Leben auf den engen Gassen, orientalisches und afrikanisches Flair verschmelzen zu einem Gesamtkunstwerk wie aus 1.001 Nacht.

BREAKING
NEWS

Even at night Stone Town remains safe

Selbst nachts ist man in Stonetown sicher

KARIBU ZANZIBAR

Tacky tourist souvenirs are seldom, instead genuine crafts are offered here. Shoes, pictures, various materials, furniture and accessories are made in the store, on the street or in the backyard.

Den üblichen Touristenkitsch findet man wenig, dafür überwiegend unverfälschte Handwerkskunst. Schuhe, Bilder, Stoffe, Möbel und Accessoires werden im Laden, auf der Straße oder im Hinterhof gefertigt.

Artist on the street of Stonetown

Künstler auf der Straße in Stonetown

Authentic arts and crafts can be purchased in Stone Town. These are made to protect against ghosts as well as to remember departed family members.

In Stone Town kann man noch echte Handwerkskunst erstehen. Die Masken werden sowohl als Schutz gegen Geister als auch zur Erinnerung verstorbener Familienangehörige gemacht.

A visit to the market of Zanzibar City is definitely an experience – although it may be a bit much at times for delicate souls.

Ein Besuch im Markt von Sansibar-City ist ein Erlebnis, die Fleischabteilung ist allerdings nichts für zarte Gemüter.

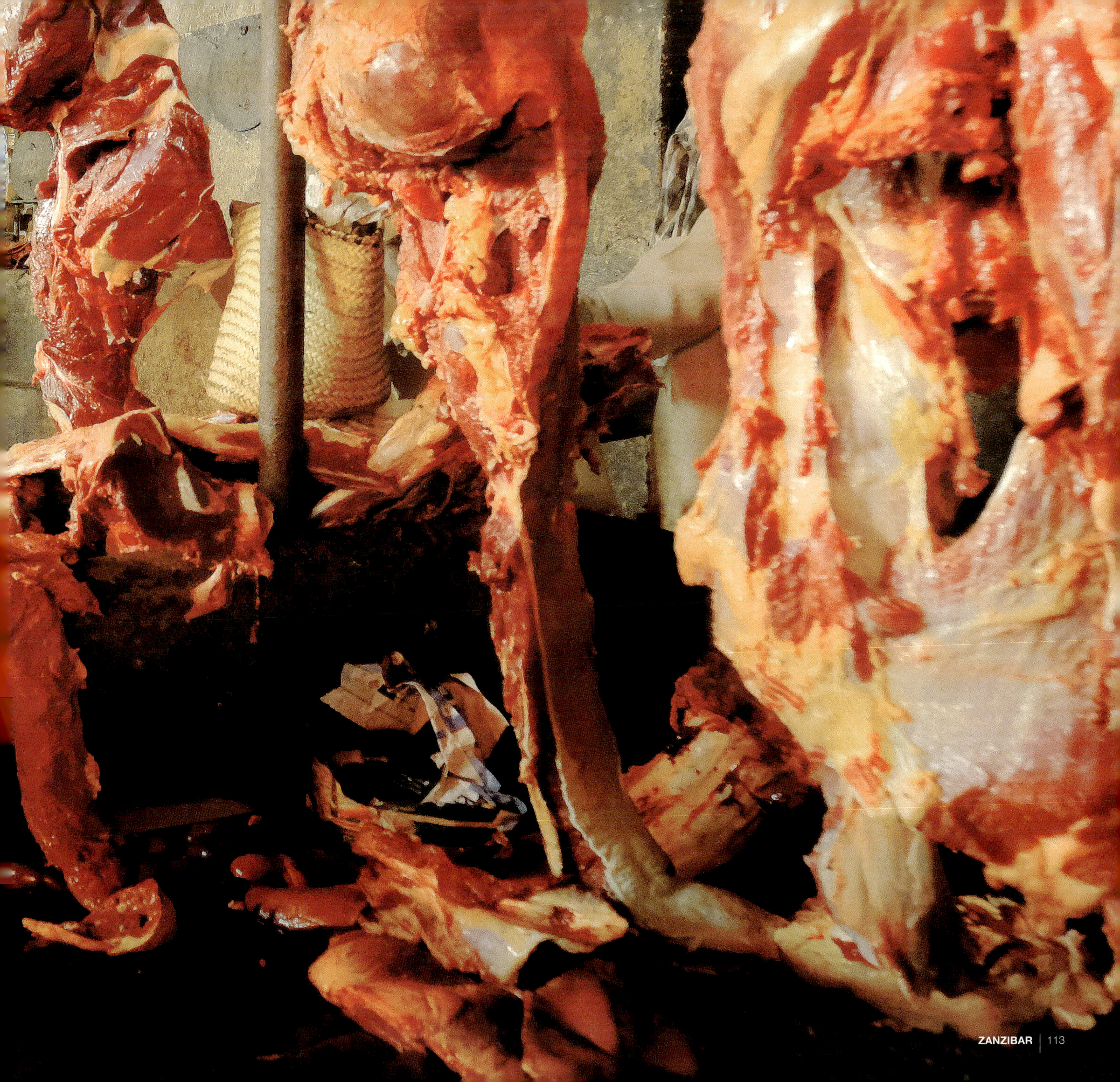

For hundreds of years Zanzibar has been the hub of spices, supplying their goods to the world. Healing and medicinal properties of spices and herbs is general knowledge amongst the population and the foundation of many medical treatments.

Seit Jahrhunderten versorgt die Gewürzinsel Sansibar die ganze Welt mit Gewürzen. Das Wissen über die Heilkraft der Kräuter und Gewürze ist in der Bevölkerung weit verbreitet und ist Basis vieler medizinischer Behandlungen.

Makunduchi, on the south west coast, is one of the many authentic villages where people still live in simple mud huts.

Makunduchi an der Südwestküste ist eines von vielen authentischen Dörfern, wo die Menschen noch in einfachen Lehmhütten leben.

One must wait for a low tide to get to the 'Rock Restaurant' at the east coast at Pingwe by foot, otherwise guests can travel by boat.

Zum „Rock Restaurant“ an der Ostküste bei Pingwe kommt man nur bei Ebbe trockenen Fußes, ansonsten werden Gäste mit dem Boot abgeholt.

Mass tourism is unknown on Zanzibar, the beaches are idyllic and untouched.

Massentourismus ist auf Sansibar unbekannt, die Strände sind noch idyllisch und naturbelassen.

In the Jozani Forest visitors can meet the Colobus Monkeys, endemic to Zanzibar.

Im Jozani Forest trifft man die zutraulichen Colobus Monkeys, die nur auf Sansibar vorkommen.

The 'Blue Monkeys' are everywhere - in some hotels they can be seen queuing up for breakfast at the restaurant in the morning.

Die „Blue Monkeys" sind überall anzutreffen, in manchen Hotels stehen sie morgens am Restaurant Schlange.

Some sandbanks disappear completely during high tide.

Manche Sandbänke versinken bei Flut vollkommen im Meer.

Foto: nicolny shutterstock.com

The Spice Island of Zanzibar has been supplying the whole world with spices for centuries. The healing power of the herbs and spices is widely appreciated in the population and has become the basis of many medical treatments. The cheerful lifestyle on Zanzibar is made up of a combination of centuries-old African and Oriental cultures. Already back in the year 800, Arab merchants from Oman and Yemen engaged in trade with the coastal regions of Kenya and Tanzania.

Auf Sansibar verbinden sich jahrhundertealte afrikanische und orientalische Kulturen zu einem fröhlichen Lebensstil. Schon seit dem Jahr 800 betreiben arabische Kaufleute aus Oman und Jemen regen Handel mit den Küstenregionen Kenias und Tansanias.

Foto: scoopysue shutterstock.com

1

Emerson on Hurumzi

ZANZIBAR STONETOWN

The hotel and restaurant is situated in the heart of Stone Town in an exotic yet curious building with historical significance. The recent refurbishment combines the elegance of the time it was built with period antique furnishing and the colour and comfort of the 21st century.

Das Hotel und Restaurant befindet sich mitten in Stonetown in einem exotischen Gebäude mit historischer Bedeutung. Bei der jüngsten Renovierung wurden der der damaligen Epoche mit antiken Möbeln und dem Komfort des 21. Jahrhunderts gelungen miteinander verbunden.

Ten double rooms and three suites plus two large apartments provide a mixture of an authentic oriental and african atmosphere. At the rooftop tea house restaurant the cuisine is designed to marry the culture and style of the building with the distinct culinary heritage of the era.

Zehn Doppelzimmer, drei Suiten sowie zwei große Appartements bieten eine Mischung aus authentischer orientalischer und afrikanischer Atmosphäre. Die Küche im Rooftop-Restaurant verbindet die Kultur und den Stil des Gebäudes mit dem unverwechselbaren kulinarischen Erbe der Epoche.

Foto: Mnemba Island DOOK

2

Mnemba

ZANZIBAR MNEMBA ISLAND

Mnemba Atoll is situated just five kilometers north of Zanzibar. Here the diverse marine-life encompasses dolphins, turtles and over 600 different kinds of coral – a colourful paradise for divers. The charismatic villas of the Luxury-Lodge are crafted from natural products such as wood and palm leaves, creating a luxurious ambience with laid-back barefoot charm. The five star service and welcoming atmosphere make 'Mnemba Island' a truly special experience.

Fünf Kilometer nördlich vor der Sansibar gelegen, ist das Mnemba-Atoll mit über 600 Korallenfischarten, mit Delfinen und Schildkröten ein Paradies zum Tauchen, Schnorcheln und vielem mehr. Aus natürlichen Materialien wie Holz und Palmblätter gefertigt, sind die Villen der Luxuslodge perfekt für einen romantischen Urlaub im Stil des „Barfuß-Luxus". Zusammen mit dem exklusiven Service und familiärem Ambiente ist „Mnemba Island" ein ganz besonderes Erlebnis.

Foto: Mnemba Island DOOK

Hidden in the tropical island jungle, all ten villas boast private beach access as well as private areas for relaxing in the sun or shade. The exclusiveness of Mnemba is evident in every aspect of this dreamy hideaway.

Die zehn Villen sind versteckt im Tropenwald der Insel, alle mit direktem Strandzugang, privaten Sonnen- und Schattenliegen. Privatsphäre und Exklusivität auf höchstem Niveau inmitten traumhafter Hideaway-Atmosphäre ist hier das Motto.

Foto: Mnemba Island DOOK

Foto: Mnemba Island DOOK

Foto: The Zanzibar Collection

3

Zawadi Zanzibar

ZANZIBAR EAST COAST

The all-inclusive Zawadi Hotel is the 4th property of "The Zanzibar Collection", opened in August 2016. Located on a beachfront cliff the 'Zawadi' with its magnificent views over the sea and the white beaches, hotel impresses is very impressive. Access to the sand cove is by a short hewn staircase – guests are able to swim and snorkel in the ocean directly in front of the hotel, even at low tide. A 'Barefoot Retreat' with only nine private spacious luxury cottages serves as a perfect hideaway. Minimum age 16 years.

Das im August 2016 eröffnete All-inclusive-Hotel ist das vierte Haus der „Zanzibar Collection". Auf den Klippen gelegen, begeistert das „Zawadi" mit einem atemberaubendem Blick über das Meer und einem privaten weißen Sandstrand. Gäste können auch bei Ebbe im Ozean direkt vor dem Hotel schwimmen. Ein „Barefoot"-Refugium mit nur neun privaten, geräumigen Luxusvillen für entspannte Eleganz. Mindestalter 16 Jahre.

A fusion of cultures in Zanzibar has created an exotic cuisine which blends local spices and flavours featuring the best of the island's produce.

Die Verschmelzung von verschiedenen Kulturen in Sansibar hat im 'Zawadi'eine exotische Küche geschaffen, die das Beste der Insel mit lokalen Gewürzen und Aromen vermischt.

The nine private 100 m^2 villas, with en-suite bathrooms directly overlooking the ocean, large spacious terrace and surrounded by bougainvillea and palm trees offer a stunning panoramic view over of the Indian Ocean.

Neun private 100 m^2 große Villen mit En-suite-Meerblickbadezimmer, großer Terrasse und umgeben von Bougainvilleen und Palmen bieten einen phantastischen Panoramablick auf den Indischen Ozean.

4

Baraza
Resort & Spa

ZANZIBAR EAST COAST

The thirty villas of this glamorous, fully inclusive boutique resort, evoke the island heritage dating back to the era of Sultans. The resort is a fusion of Arabic, Swahili and Indian styles with lovely antiques and unique handmade furniture. It is located on a beautiful unspoiled white beach which was chosen by 'Condé Nast Traveller' as one of the 30 top island beaches in the world. As part of 'The Zanzibar Collection' (a privately owned collection of small deluxe hotels), Baraza offers an unparalleled standard of luxury on the island of Zanzibar.

Die glamourösen Villen des All-inclusive-Boutiqueresorts erinnern an das Erbe der Insel aus der Ära der Sultane. Eine Mischung aus arabischen, swahilischen und indischen Stilen prägt das Dekor der Antiquitäten und handgefertigten Möbel. Der weiße Strand wurde von „Condé Nast Traveller" als einer der 30 Topinselstrände der Welt gewählt. Als Teil der „Zanzibar-Collection", einer privat geführten Sammlung von kleinen Luxushotels, bietet das „Baraza" Luxus auf höchstem Niveau.

Foto: The Zanzibar Collection

The cuisine at 'Baraza' is inspired by Arabic, Indian, Persian, Asian and Swahili flavors using the local spices for which the island is famous. Every evening features a different influence, showcasing the islands produce and spices.

Eine Fusion aus arabischen, indischen, persischen, asiatischen und Swahili-Aromen prägt die Küche im „Baraza". Jeden Abend wird eine Fusionsrichtung gewählt und mit Hilfe lokaler Produkte und Gewürze serviert.

The one and two-bedroom villas characterise classic Swahili architecture featuring luxury interiors, beautiful fabrics, hand carved furniture, brass lanterns and more.

Die Ein- und Zwei-Zimmer-Villen verkörpern die klassische Swahili-Architektur mit luxuriöser Einrichtung, edlen Stoffen, handgeschnitzten Möbeln, Messinglaternen und vielem mehr.

5

The Palms

ZANZIBAR EAST COAST

'The Palms' is the ultimate retreat providing a stunning hideaway for the discerning traveler. The six fully inclusive private villas are beautifully designed, creating an atmosphere of relaxed understated elegance. It is a sanctuary for those in search of tranquility, a place to stimulate the senses and to experience the very best of the magical island of Zanzibar. Minimum age 16 years.

„The Palms" ist der ultimative Rückzugsort für den anspruchsvollen Reisenden. Die sechs privaten Villen sind sehr schön gestaltet und schaffen eine Atmosphäre entspannter Eleganz. Hier werden die Sinne stimuliert, die Magie der Insel kann bis ins kleinste Detail erlebt werden. Ab 16 Jahre.

Foto: The Zanzibar Collection

'The Palms' consists of six private villas each over 130 m² with a living-room, a master bedroom with a full en-suite master bathroom and walk-in dressing-room, a second smaller bedroom with its own en-suite bathroom, a large furnished terrace with a view of the garden and the ocean and its own plunge pool. Each villa also comes with its own beach banda to enjoy maximum privacy also when at the beach.

Auf jeweils über 130 m² bieten sechs Villen mit Pool, Master-Bedroom, Bad-en-suite, begehbarer Ankleide sowie einem weiteren Schlafzimmer mit wunderbarem Blick auf den tropischen Garten und das Meer. Für maximale Privatsphäre am Strand ist jede Villa mit einem eigenen Beach-Bungalow ausgestattet.

Foto: The Zanzibar Collection

6

The Residence Zanzibar

ZANZIBAR WEST COAST

Set against a sparkling seascape backdrop, the lush palm tree forest hideaway of 'The Residence Zanzibar' combines a mix of elegant sophistication and island charm. At the two restaurants international dishes with Indian, Arabic and Mediterranean influences are offered. With smiles as warm as the sun, the welcoming hospitality of the Swahili people embraces guests with gracious charm as mystical as the beauty of the spice island of Zanzibar. Retreat to a world of divine relaxation where five-star luxuries sit harmoniously alongside nature's untouched beauty.

„The Residence Zanzibar" kombiniert eine gelungene Mischung aus eleganter Raffinesse und Inselcharme mit Ausblick auf den Indischen Ozean, umgeben von einem üppigen Palmenwald. In den beiden Restaurants werden beste internationale Gerichte mit indischen, arabischen und mediterranen Einflüssen gereicht und immer verzaubert die swahilische Crew die Gäste mit ihrer herzlichen Gastfreundschaft. "The Residence" ist eine harmonische Kombination aus 5-Sterne-Luxus und unberührter Natur.

Foto: The Residence Zanzibar

Foto: The Residence Zanzibar

The interiors are influenced by the island's history and Swahili, Omani, British and Indian influences.

Ein spannender Mix von luxuriösem Understatement und Inselcharme: Das Interiordesign des Resorts ist inspiriert von den vielen Kulturen, die auf Sansibar aufeinandertreffen.

The hotel's sandbank tour is a truly unforgettable experience for snorkeling and swimming before a stylish lobster-lunch, surrounded by the tourquoise waters of the Indian Ocean.

Ein unvergessliches Erlebnis ist die Sandbank-Tour des Hotels zum Schnorcheln, Baden und stilvollen Lobster-Lunch, umgeben vom türkisblauen Wasser des Indischen Ozeans.

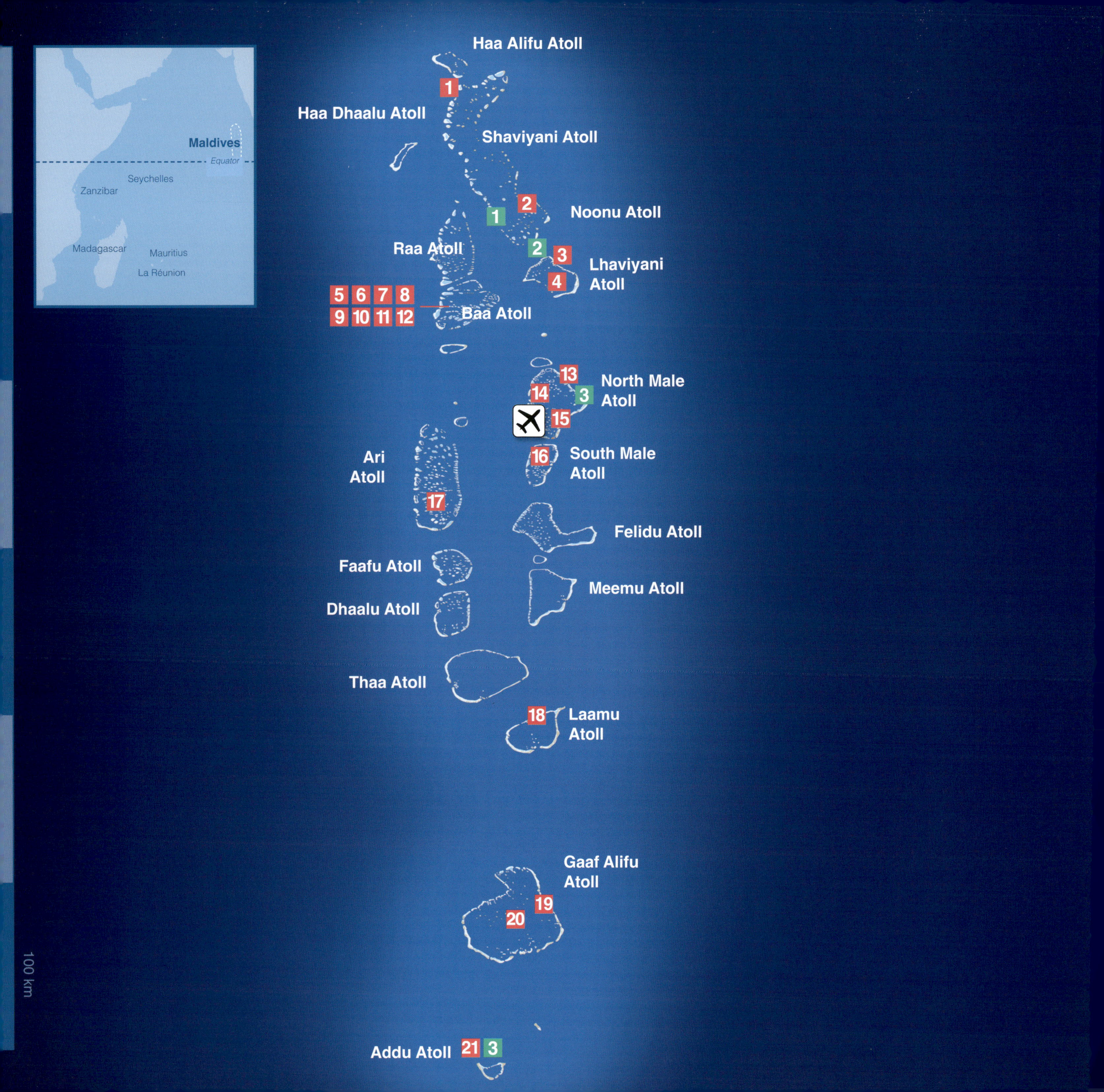

Maldives
Equator
Seychelles
Zanzibar
Madagascar
Mauritius
La Réunion
Haa Alifu Atoll
Haa Dhaalu Atoll
Shaviyani Atoll
Noonu Atoll
Raa Atoll
Lhaviyani Atoll
Baa Atoll
North Male Atoll
Ari Atoll
South Male Atoll
Felidu Atoll
Faafu Atoll
Meemu Atoll
Dhaalu Atoll
Thaa Atoll
Laamu Atoll
Gaaf Alifu Atoll
Addu Atoll
1
2
3
4
5
6
7
8
9
10
11
12
13
14
15
16
17
18
19
20
21
1
2
3
3
3
100 km

Maldives

Hotels

1	**St. Regis Vommuli Resort**	Starwood Hotels	Dhaalu Atoll
2	**Soneva Jani**		Noonu Atoll
3	**Hurawalhi**		Lhaviyani Atoll
4	**Kanuhura**	Sun Resorts	Lhaviyani Atoll
5	**Landaa Giraavarua**	Four Seasons Resorts	Baa Atoll
6	**Voavah Private Island**	Four Seasons Resorts	Baa Atoll
7	**Amilla Fushi**	The Small Maldives Island	Baa Atoll
8	**Finolhu**	The Small Maldives Island	Baa Atoll
9	**Kihavah**	Anantara Hotels · Resorts · Spas	Baa Atoll
10	**Coco Privé Kuda Hiti**	Coco Palm	Baa Atoll
11	**Milaidhoo Island**		Baa Atoll
12	**Soneva Fushi**		Baa Atoll
13	**Gili Lankanfushi**		North Malè Atoll
14	**Reethi Rah**	One & Only Resorts	North Malè Atoll
15	**Kuda Huraa**	Four Seasons Resorts	North Malè Atoll
16	**Vittaveli**	Jumeira Hotels & Resorts	South Malè Atoll
17	**Moofushi**	Constance Hotels	South Ari Atoll
18	**Laamu**	Six Senses Hotels · Resorts · Spas	Laamu Atoll
19	**The Residence**	Cenizaro Hotels & Resorts	Gaaf Alifu Atoll
20	**Dhevanafushi**	Jumeira Hotels & Resorts	Gaaf Alifu Atoll
21	**Villingili Resort & Spa**	Shangri–La Hotels & Resorts	Addu Atoll

Golf Courses

1	**Velaa Private Island**	Golf Academy
2	**Kuredu Resort**	6 hole
3	**Meeru Island**	9 hole
4	**Villingili Resort**	9 hole

Area:	*298 km²*
Islands:	*1,119*
Highest peak:	*2,54 m*
Population:	*420,000*
Religion:	*100 % Islam*
Language:	*dhivehi, english*
Government:	*unitary presidential constitutional republic*
Independence:	*1965*
Currency:	*Maldivian rufiyaa*

The population of the 220 inhabited islands are from malay, arabic and indian descent. There is little daily contact between the local islands, where everyday life is centred around fishing and the catch is sold at the market in Male.

Die heutigen Einwohner der 220 Inseln stammen von malaiischen, arabischen und indischen Vorfahren ab. Zwischen den Inseln gibte es wenig Kontakt. Der Alltag ist vom Fischfang geprägt und die Fischer sind lange Zeit unterwegs zum Fischen und um den Fang in Male zu verkaufen.

Like droplets of pearls the 1190 coral islands are dotted 800 kilometers from north to south in the Indian Ocean – like glistening jewels floating in the turquoise waters. The islands have a diameter on average of only 200 to 300 meters, and therefore are the ideal location for a tranquil, romantic getaway. The 'one island – one resort' philosophy creates an array of luxurious possibilities, a world away from crowded beaches. No cars, only serenity to appreciate the moment. The pristine white beaches disappear into the infinite blue where below the surface colourful and exotic sea life create a wonderland for snorkelers and divers alike. The aquatic world is a spectacle alone. The coral extract minerals from the sea water which builds the reef, whose delicate ecosystem houses colourful and curious swarms of fish, moraines, whale sharks, turtles and the elegantly gliding giants known as manta rays.

Not only the underwater world invites visitors from all over the world, but the 150 resorts of varying styles and categories attract guests on a global scale to indulge in luxury, nature and relaxation. The offerings are plenty; exquisite cuisine, wellness and water sports programs, sailing, surfing and of course dolphin cruises.

The capital city (and island) Malé houses approximately 320,000 people and has been the centre-hub of the Atolls for 800 years. Due to overpopulation the island had to be artificially enlarged several times already, and due to few attractions Malé remains an area for transit to the resort via seaplane or speedboat for most visitors.

Wie Perlen an einer 800 Kilometer langen Kette reihen sich die 1.190 Koralleninseln der Malediven von Nord nach Süd im Indischen Ozean aneinander. Meist nur wenige hundert Meter im Durchmesser sind die kleinen Inseln ideal für einen entspannten, romantischen Urlaub, denn nach dem Prinzip „eine Insel – ein Resort" gibt es hier keinerlei Massentourismus. Und keine Autos. Nur Erholung. Pur. Weiße Strände wie aus Puderzucker und Tauchgründe, die zu den besten der Welt zählen. Wobei selbst die Schnorchelausrüstung schon ausreicht, um das bunte Unterwasserleben zu beobachten. Doch ein paar Tauchgänge sollte man hier schon einplanen. Der Fischreichtum und die Korallenwelt sind ein unvergessliches Erlebnis. Und ein sensibles Ökosystem. Die Steinkorallen entziehen dem Meerwasser Mineralien, um Kalk abzuscheiden, und bauen dadurch das Riff auf. 200 verschiedene Arten dieser Nesseltiere haben die Riffe der Malediven gebildet und sind die Basis für eine sensible Welt mit farbenprächtigen Fischschwärmen, 15 Meter langen Walhaien, Schildkröten und gemächlich dahinschwebenden Mantas.

Doch nicht nur die Unterwasserwelt zieht Erholungssuchende aus aller Welt an. 150 Resorts unterschiedlichster Kategorien bis zum 6-Sterne-Resort verwöhnen ihre Gäste vom Feinsten. Mit exzellenter Küche, einem umfassenden Wellness- und einem großartigen Wassersportprogramm. Neben Schnorcheln und Tauchen kann man sein Glück auch beim Fischen versuchen, Katamaransegeln, Surfen und mit dem Boot Dutzende Delfine beobachten. Oder einfach alle Vier gerade sein lassen und den Moment genießen.

Zentrum des Inselstaates ist seit über 800 Jahren die Hauptstadt Malé auf der gleichnamigen Insel mit rund 130.000 Einwohnern. Aufgrund einer enormen Überbevölkerung mußte die Insel bereits mehrmals künstlich vergrößert werden. Aufgrund mangelnder Sehenswürdigkeiten dient die Hauptstadt meist nur als Transitstation zum Wasserflugzeug oder zum Motorboot für die Weiterfahrt zum Resort.

Luxury can be so simple: white sands and clear waters…

Ein schöner Strand, klares Wasser – Luxus kann so einfach sein . . .

Foto: Jumeirah Vitavelli

With up to thirteen meters in length and a mouth three meters wide, whale sharks are the largest of all living fish. They feed on plankton and small fish such as mackerel and small tuna. Depending on the region, guests are able to witness these gentle giants all year round.

Walhaie sind mit bis dreizehn Meter Länge und einem drei Meter breiten Maul die größten lebenden Fische. Auf dem Speiseplan stehen Plankton und kleine Fische wie Makrelen und klein Thunfische. Auf den Malediven sind die Riesen je nach Region ganzjährig zu beobachten.

Foto: Peter Marshall for Soneva Fushi

The Indian Ocean is famous for its vast sea life and hosts endless species of colourful fish of all shapes and sizes.

Der Reichtum an Fischen aller Größen und Farben im Indischen Ozean ist legendär.

Foto: Alph[illegible] Island

Turtles have been roaming these tropical waters for 200 million years. To bury their eggs, the females swim thousands of miles to return to their place of birth. Many resorts run their own conservation programs in order to protect the endangered turtle species of the Maldives.

Seit 200 Millionen Jahren tummeln sich Meeresschildkröten in tropischen Gewässern. Zum Eier legen kehren sie zu ihrem Geburtsort zurück und legen dabei oft tausende Kilometer im Meer zurück. Viele Resorts auf den Malediven fördern den Bestand der Wasserschildkröten mit eigenen Programmen und Schildkrötenfarmen.

May until October is known as 'manta season' in Baa Atoll – due to large amounts of plankton swarms of mantas regularly visit 'cleaning points' where little fish remove parasites from the mantas' bodies and excess food from their mouths. Manta rays can have a wing span of up to seven meters and feed mainly on plankton.

Wenn zwischen Mai und Oktober besonders viel Plankton in das Baa Atoll treibt, tummeln sich viele Mantas und kommen regelmäßig zu den "Cleaning points", wo ihnen kleine Putzerfische Parasiten von der Haut fressen. Mantas können eine Spannweite von sieben Metern erreichen und ernähren sich ausschließlich von Plankton.

Sascha Caballero shutterstock

The combination of pristine white sand, turquoise water, dramatic sunsets, the most colourful underwater world and first class service make a holiday in the Maldives an unforgettable experience.

Die Malediven vereinen schneeweißen Sand, türkisblaues Meer, glutroten Sonnenuntergang, eine farbenreiche Unterwasserwelt und First-Class-Service zu einem unvergeßlichen Urlaubserlebnis.

1

St. Regis Maldives Vommuli Resort

MALDIVES DHAALU ATOLL

Set out to redefine 'barefoot luxury', the St. Regis Maldives Vommuli embraces an unexpected blend of traditional island-inspired design, with modern curves and simplistic shapes. The futuristic architecture combined with natural elements creates a unique personality; creative and luxurious. The range of dining options includes signature beachfront restaurant Alba, which offers the finest Italian flavours in a picturesque setting by the pool. At Orientale, guests can enjoy asian cuisine such as curries and biryanis from the Indian and Pakistani grill to sushi and sashimi from the Japanese bar.

Der Begriff „Barfuß Luxus" wurde vom „St. Regis Maldives Vommuli" neu definiert – mit einer unerwarteten Mischung aus traditionell inspiriertem Design, modernen Kurven und vereinfachten Formen. Die futuristische Architektur in Kombination mit natürlichen Elementen schafft eine kreative und luxuriöse Atmosphäre. Kulinarisch bietet das Resort ein breit gefächertes Angebot aus der italienischen Küche, asiatische Spezialitäten vom indischen und pakistanischen Grill sowie Sushi und Sashimi von der japanischen Bar.

The 'Whale Bar' is an architectural feat in its own right, inspired by the shape of a whale shark. Above turquoise waters guests can enjoy a la carte tapas dishes or five course menus created by the talented chefs.

In der "Wal-Bar" werden Tapas und Fünf-Gänge-Menüs serviert.

Fotos: St. Regis Vommuli

The Resort provides a wide range of villas and suites from the Beach Villa (140 m²), the Over Water Villa (182 m²) and the Over Water Suites (282 m²) to the Two Bedroom Family Villa (334 m²) and the Two Bedroom Beach Suite (531 m²). The resort is also an excellent joice for larger groups wishing to accomodate family and friends in one luxurious estate like the Caroline Astor Estate (620 m²) and the John Jacob Astor Estate (1,540 m²).

Das Angebot an Villen und Suiten reicht von der Beach Villa mit 140 m² über die Over Water Villa mit 182 m², die Over Water Suites mit 282 m² bis zur Zweibett-Familien-Villa mit 334 m² und der Zweibett-Strandvilla mit 531 m². Für große Familien oder Urlaub mit Freunden stehen das Caroline Astor Estate mit 620 m² und das John Jacob Astor Estate mit 1.540 m² zur Verfügung.

Architectural highlight of the resort: the 'Whale Bar'

Architektonisches Highlight des Resorts: die "Wal Bar"

Fotos: St. Regis Vommuli

St. Regis Maldives Vommuli is also an excellent choice for larger groups wishing to accommodate family and friends in one luxurious estate such as the 'Caroline Astor Estate' (620 m²) or the 'John Jacob Astor Estate' (1.540 m²).

Für größere Familien oder für den Urlaub mit Freunden ist in den Privatresidenzen „Caroline Aster Estate" mit 620 m² im „John Jacob Astor Estate" mit 1.540 m² ausreichend Platz.

Fotos: St. Regis Vommuli

The 620 m² "Caroline Astor Estate" is situated in a prime location on the pristine sands meters from the ocean and boasts a 67 m² private pool. Modern floor-to-ceiling glass doors and windows fill the interior with ample natural light, and the bright wooden floors and lofty ceilings create a spacious, harmonious atmosphere.

Das 620 m² große Caroline-Astor-Estate mit mit seinem großen Pool liegt direkt am Strand und erstreckt sich über zwei Etagen. Raumhohe Glastüren bieten einen beeindruckenden Panoramablick auf den Indischen Ozean.

Fotos: St. Regis Vommuli

2

Soneva Jani

MALDIVES NOORU ATOLL

The newcomer to the Nooru Atoll, Soneva Fushi's sister resort 'Soneva Jani' opened in 2017. With a 5.6 km private lagoon that surrounds it, Jani's fresh perspective and simply extraordinary architecture exude youth and playfulness. Jani's lighthearted luxury continues into its dining offerings such as at the Midnight Astronomy Picnic or at the Maldives' first overwater observatory and restaurant 'So Starstruck'.

Das Schwesterresort von „Soneva Fushi", „Soneva Jani", eröffnete im Jahr 2017 und ist der Newcomer im Noonu-Atoll. Mit einer 5,6 Kilometer langen privaten Lagune und außergewöhnlicher Architektur besticht „Jani" durch frisches und verspieltes Design. Weißes Holz und bodentiefe Fenster harmonieren mit den türkisfarbenen Wellen des Ozeans. Im „Midnight Astronomy Picnic" und im Restaurant „So Starstruck", dem ersten Überwasser-Observatorium der Malediven, setzt sich der unbeschwerter Luxus des Resorts fort.

The contemporary minimalist interior is elegantly styled in white-washed wood and clean lines, surrounded by glass windows revealing a splash of turquoise hues.

Die zeitgenössische, minimalistische Einrichtung überzeugt durch Eleganz und klare Linien, die mit weiß gewaschenem Holz und bodentiefen Fenster eindrucksvoll mit den türkisfarbenen Wellen des Ozeans harmonieren.

Foto: Richard Waite

3

Islandresort & Spa
Hurawalhi

MALDIVES LHAVIYANI ATOLL

A haven for adults, regardless of whether above, below, or on the water, Hurawalhi is a 5-star indulgence with a wonderful mixture of peace and busyness. Large villas, all-inclusive service, luxurious spa treatments, beautiful coral reefs and turquoise lagoons. The highlight is the impressive and world's largest, fully glazed underwater restaurant. While the beautiful world of the Indian ocean passes by the shimmering panoramic glass domes, guests can enjoy a menu of international cuisine made from purely organic products.

Ein Zufluchtsort nur für Erwachsene, egal ob über, unter oder am Wasser – Hurawalhi ist ein 5-Sterne-Genuss mit einer wunderbaren Mischung aus Ruhe und Geschäftigkeit: große Villen, All-inclusive-Service, luxuriöse Spa-Behandlungen, zauberhafte Korallenriffe und türkisfarbene Lagunen. Das Highlight ist das imposante und weltweit größte, komplett verglaste Unterwasserrestaurant. Während die Meereswelt des Indischen Ozeans an schimmernden Panoramaglaskuppeln vorbeizieht, genießen die Gäste Menüs der internationalen Küche aus rein organischen Produkten.

The beach and over water villas are all elegantly furnished and offer exactly what you are looking for in the Maldives: peace and seclusion.

Die Beach- und Over-Water-Villen sind zum Sonnenaufgang aus- und elegant eingerichtet. Sie bieten genau das, was man auf den Malediven sucht: Ruhe und Abgeschiedenheit.

Foto: Hurawalhi

The atmospheric decor sets the tone for Hurawalhi's architecture.

Das stimmungsvolle Dekor wird in Hurawalhi gekonnt in Szene gesetzt.

Foto: Hurawalhi

All 90 beach and water villas are stylishly decorated and furnished: quiet and atmospheric decor meets dark, wooden floors and modern décor, private sun terraces offer a unique panoramic view over the Indian Ocean.

Alle 90 Villen am Strand und über Wasser sind stilvoll gestaltet und eingerichtet: Ruhiges und stimmungsvolles Dekor trifft auf dunkle, hölzerne Böden und modernes Interieur, private Sonnenterrassen eröffnen einen einzigartigen Panoramablick über den Indischen Ozean.

4

Sun Resorts
Kanuhura

MALDIVES LHAVIYANI ATOLL

The Kanuhura Maldives celebrates life in creating a Bohemian chic, yet elegant ambience by combining the gipsy and jet-set lifestyle. Thus, the eighty bungalows and villas are decorated with precious natural materials, colorful elements and pretty patterns, as well as lamps made of shell chains. The guests can expect to be spoiled in seven restaurants and three bars with international, Italian and Brazilian cuisine.

Mit dem Konzept des Gypset, einer Kombination aus Gipsy und Jetset, zelebriert das „Kanuhura Maldives“ das Leben in Verbindung mit Bohemian-Chic, aber dennoch elegantem Ambiente. So sind die 80 Bungalows und Villen mit edlen Naturmaterialien und Elementen in bunten Farben und Mustern sowie Lampen aus Muschelketten gestaltet. Kulinarisch werden die Gäste in sieben Restaurants und drei Bars mit internationaler, italienischer und brasilianischer Küche verwöhnt.

All the villas have a covered terrace with sea view of at least 59 m^2 to allow guests to enjoy both sunrise and sunset. The semi-open bathroom with bathtub and external shower allows a bath under the stars.

Teils der Sonnenaufgangs-, teils der Sonnuntergangsseite zugewandt, haben alle Unterkünfte eine Größe von mindestens 59 m^2 und verfügen über eine überdachte Terrasse mit Meerblick. Besonders romantisch ist ein Bad unter den Sternen im halboffenen Badezimmer mit Wanne und Außendusche.

Foto:Kanuhura

5

Four Seasons Resort at Landaa Giraavaru

MALDIVES BAA ATOLL

The five-star facilities and world class cuisine make the established Landaa a true luxury experience whilst the pristine vegetation and impeccable sands make exploring the luscious island a little adventure in itself. Should the turquoise waters or picturesque sunsets ever become boring, guests can turn their stay on their heads, with some upside down yoga classes or play with the elements with outdoor adventures like kiteboarding, jetblading, wake-surfing, parasailing and much more.

Die 5-Sterne-Anlage mit ihrem tropischen Garten und einer Weltklasseküche macht das etablierte Landaa zu einem Luxuserlebnis mit umfangreichen Aktivitätenprogrammen wie Yoga, Kiteboarding, Jetblading, Wakesurfing, Parasailing und vielem mehr.

Foto: Four Seasons Seet Ken

Foto: Four Seasons Seet Ken

Landaa's vast natural wilderness incorporates 103 thatched bungalows and villas of contemporary Maldivian design. Hidden behind traditional turquoise gates, all land-based accommodations have their own beach access, pool, and lush private gardens.

Die großzügige Naturlandschaft von Landaa umfasst 103 strohgedeckte Bungalows und Villen in zeitgenössischem maledivischen Design. Versteckt hinter traditionellen türkisfarbenen Toren haben alle landgestützten Unterkünfte ihren eigenen Strandzugang, einen Pool und üppige, Privatgärten.

Foto: Four Seasons Seet Ken

Foto: Four Seasons, Seet Ken

6

Voavah
Four Seasons Private Island

MALDIVES BAA ATOLL

Situated on its very own island, this private seven-bedroom resort is the world's first exclusive-use UNESCO hideaway. As remote as can be, this private paradise houses its own PADI 5-star dive centre, gym, Ocean of Consciousness Spa and 62-foot luxury yacht, surrounded by pristine sand and a beautifully colorful reef. Guests can also easily visit the Four Seasons Resort Maldives at Landaa Giraavaru, only 20 minutes away, or the nearby Hanifaru Bay for seasonal Manta snorkelling.

Das sieben-Zimmer-Privatresort erstreckt sich über die gesamte Insel und ist das weltweit erste "UNESCO-Hideaway". Das private Paradies ist mit einem eigenen PADI 5-Sterne-Tauchzentrum, einem Fitnessraum, Spa und einer 62-Fuß Luxus-Yacht ausgestattet. Umgeben ist das Ganze von einem unberührten Sandstrand inklusive einem traumhaft bunten Riff.

Situated on its very own island Voavah, this private seven-bedroom resort is the world's first exclusive-use UNESCO hideaway.

Die Privatinsel Voavah mit dem Sieben-Zimmer-Resort ist das erste exklusiv nutzbare UNESCO Hideaway.

Foto: Four Seasons

NOMAD

Foto: Four Seasons Seet Ken

Foto: Four Seasons Seet Ken

The resort consists of a beach villa with a lounge, dining room, library, gym, guest kitchen and pool deck, as well as a two-bedroom water villa including a master bedroom with attached study/children's room and an additional separate king-sized bedroom pavilion. The air-conditioned living room opens onto an al fresco living deck with a 17-meter-long sunset pool, loungers and hammocks. Two Mezzanine Suites flank the Loft Lounge, a lovely in-the-eaves chill zone complete with comfy seating, a pool table and views that stretch forever. Just off the lounge, the Bunk Room has beds for up to four children, creating a great kids' floor for larger groups.

Das Resort besteht aus einer Strandvilla mit Lounge, Esszimmer, Bibliothek, Fitnessraum, Gästeküche und Pool-Deck sowie einer Zwei-Zimmer-Overwater-Villa mit einem Hauptschlafzimmer, einem angeschlossenem Arbeits- bzw. Kinderzimmer und einem zusätzlichen separierten Pavillon. Die Türen des klimatisierten Wohnzimmers öffnen sich zu einem al fresco Wohn-Deck mit 17 Meter langem Pool und Blick auf den Sonnenuntergang. Neben der Loft Lounge liegen zwei Mezzanine Suiten, eine Chill-Zone mit Billardtisch und wunderbarem Fernblick sowie eine Kinderetage mit vier Betten.

Guests can enjoy the captivating Maldivian sunset in serene privacy, whilst enjoying flavours tailored to their desires. The effortless elegance of the interior design allows guests to relax in their home from home with island ease, with no distractions but the endless ocean.

Die lässige Eleganz der Inneneinrichtung, ein Mix aus natürlichen Materialien mit modernem Design und den Farben des Indischen Ozeans, ist der perfekte Rahmen zum Relaxen und Entspannen.

Foto: Four Seasons

Foto: Amilla Fushi

7

Amilla Fushi

The Small Maldives Island Company

MALDIVES BAA ATOLL

The philosophy at Amilla is simple – high end luxury and holiday feeling, but with the comfort guests are used to at home. The luxury resort offers modern 'homes' over crystal clear waters and meters away from the magnificent house reef. Manta rays at the nearby Hanifaru Bay offer a memorable snorkel experience for guests who alternatively can explore the colourful house reef at their own leisure right on their doorstep.

Die Philosophie hinter „Amilla" ist einfach: Highend-Luxus mit dem Komfort des eigenen Zuhauses. Die modernen Unterkünfte thronen über dem kristallklaren Wasser des Indischen Ozeans. Nur wenige Meter entfernt liegt das Hausriff, dessen Farbpracht zum Erkunden einlädt. In der nahegelegenen Hanifaru-Bucht wird das Schnorcheln mit Mantarochen zu einem unvergesslichen Erlebnis.

67 homes over water and on the beach boast their own private pool, showcasing stylishly modern interior. Alternatively guests can stay in one of the Wellness Treehouses, at 12 meters high amongst the treetops or the Miami-style Residences with a range from four to eight bedrooms.

Die stilvollen 67 Over-Water und Strand-Villen mit eigenem Pool sind modern eingerichtet. Ein ganz besonderes Erlebnis sind die Baumhäuser 12 Meter über dem Boden im "Miami"-Stil mit vier bis acht Zimmern.

Foto: Amilla Fushi

The contemporary interior is sleek and modern with playful elements, and many of the overwater homes embrace an open-plan layout, where bathroom and bedroom are cleverly separated with furniture rather than walls.

In dem offen gestalteten Layout der Villen verschmelzen die einzelnen Zimmer ineinander. Anstelle von Wänden, dienen Möbel als räumliche Trennung zwischen Bad und Schlafzimmer.

The 'food Baazaar' is centred around the pool, offering diverse culinary experiences from around the world and Amilla's signature overwater restaurant 'Feeling Koi' spoils the guests with a unique blend of Japanese dining. The most recent Destination Dining addition is Mystique Garden; a secluded enchanted garden, with beautiful sculptures designed and built by the islanders which are lit up theatrically.

Der „Food Bazar" am Pool bietet diverse kulinarische Erfahrungen aus der ganzen Welt. Das Over-Water-Restaurant „Feeling Koi" verwöhnt die Gäste mit ausgewählten japanischen Gerichten. Die jüngste kulinarische Ergänzung ist der versteckte „Mystische Garten" mit Skulpturen lokaler Künstler.

Foto: Amilla Fushi

8

Finolhu

The Small Maldives Island Company

MALDIVES BAA ATOLL

This retro-inspired island is a unique voice within the industry – the funky vibe and lively spirit are evident from the moment the speedboat arrives in its quintessential turquoise lagoon, dubbed 'Finolhu blue' amongst the locals. With a modern spin, Finolhu embraces the iconic 1950s era with a playful mix of music and style from the 70s and 80s. The perfect spot for couples who like to mingle in the evenings, and families alike – with plenty of activities for the kids. The 125 rooms are tastefully decorated in pastels and textures, and gentle 'retro touches' add that special charm to this 'beach club haven'.

Kaum angekommen in der türkisfarbenen Lagune, verspürt man die ausgefallene und lebhafte Stimmung dieser retro-inspirierten Insel. Finolhu verkörpert die ikonische 1950er-Ära mit einer spielerischen, modernen Mischung aus Musik und Stil der 70er- und 80er-Jahre. Ein perfekter Ort für Paare und Familien, die sich abends gerne unter Leute mischen. Die 125 Zimmer sind geschmackvoll in Pastellfarben gehalten und mit verschiedensten Stoffen dekoriert. Zarte Retro-Elemente runden den Charme dieses himmlischen Beachclubs ab.

The main dining area, 'Baa Baa Beach Diner', consists of multiple live cooking stations serving different specialities each night, varying from hearty Italian specialities, seafood extravaganzas to oriental influences. Guests can enjoy fresh seafood at The Fish & Crab Shack on the 1.8 km sandbank. Finolhu's signature overwater restaurant, Kanusan, is centred around a stunning duck oven, and it's open kitchen displays its cuisine centre stage. The iconic dark wood architecture and red touches add to the theatricality of its asian spices. It's overwater bar is the perfect place to enjoy a sunset cocktail before indulging in cantonese or Indonesian flavours.

Vier Restaurants und eine Bar servieren täglich das Beste aus dem Ozean: Krebs, Krabbe und Krake vom Feinsten. Dazu mixen prämierte Bartender abends Cocktails, der hauseigene DJ sowie Künstler und Artisten sorgen für entspannte Lounge-Atmosphäre am Pool. Im „Baa Baa Beach Diner" werden auf mehreren Live-Kochstationen verschiedenste Spezialitäten serviert: internationale, herzhaft italienische und orientalische Inspirationen. Oder frischer Fisch und Meeresfrüchte auf der 1,8 Km langen Sandbank in der „Fish & Crab Shack". Gourmets werden im „Kanusan" mit einem „Enten-Ofen" auf den Geschmack kommen.

Foto: Finolhu

Overwater and beach villas feature unique furniture designs like crystal chandeliers, retro cain seating and marshall speakers, whilst some of the two bedroom villas have their own retro telephone, with a 'Press for Champagne' button.

Bei der Einrichtung der Überwasser- und Strandvillen setzen ausgefallene Einrichtungselemente wie Kronleuchter, Retro-Rattansessel und Marshall-Lautsprecher dominante Akzente.

Foto: Finolhu

9

Anantara Kihavah

MALDIVES BAA ATOLL

Derived from ancient Sanskrit, the word Anantara means 'without end' – evoking the freedom and limitless luxury the resort lives by. Located on the doorstep of Hanifaru Bay, guests can snorkel with mantas and watch these gentle giants in all their glory feeding on the seasonal supply of plankton. 79 private villas from 260 to 2,700 m² are situated on the white beach or poised over turquoise water.

Direkt vor der Hanifaru-Bucht gelegen, ist das Resort ideal, um die Unterwasserwelt des Indischen Ozeans zu erkunden. 79 private Villen mit zwischen 260 und 2.700 m² liegen am weißen Sandstrand oder auf Stelzen über dem türkisfarbenen Ozean.

The quartet of restaurants 'Salt', 'Sea', 'Fire' and 'Sky' offer over- and underwater dining, setting it apart as a one-of-a-kind experience – fish swim by in their natural habitat whilst guests enjoy their romantic dinner under the sea.

Die vier Restaurants, „Salt", „Sea", „Fire" und „Sky", verwöhnen über und unter Wasser. Bei einem romantischen Abendessen unter dem Meer können die Gäste die farbenfrohe Fischwelt ungestört in ihrem natürlichen Lebensraum entdecken.

Foto: Anantara Kihavah

10

Coco Privé
Kuda Hithi

MALDIVES BAA ATOLL

Like all resorts of the Coco Collection, the Coco Prive Kuda Hiti also stands for paradise-like nature, absolute exclusivity and ecologically sophisticated luxury. The private Island of Coco Prive (1,4 hectares) consists of a large main villa – the Palm Residence (468m2), along with 5 villas (38 -178m2) accomodating ten adults and two children in total.

Wie alle Resorts der Coco Collection steht auch das „Coco Privé Kuda Hithi" für paradiesische Natur, absolute Exklusivität und ökologisch durchdachten Luxus. Auf der 1,4 Hektar großen Privatinsel mit dem 468 m^2 großen Haupthaus „Palm Residence" und fünf weiteren Villen von 38 bis 178 m^2 ist Platz für zehn Erwachsene und zwei Kinder.

Foto: Coco Privee Kuda Hiti

Pure white tones meet earthy and pastel colors with plenty of wood and stone elements, refined with romantic lighting and state-of-the-art high-tech equipment. A harmonius combination of mature, luxury and modern design.

Vom preisgekrönten Architekten Guz Wilkinson entworfen, bieten die Villen eine perfekte Mischung aus Eleganz und Komfort sowie stilvoll gestaltete Innenräume mit atemberaubenden Aussichten. Puristisches Weiß trifft auf erdige und pastellige Farben, viel Holz und Stein sowie raffiniert gesetzte indirekte Beleuchtungselemente und eine Hightechausstattung auf dem neuesten Stand. Eine harmonische Verbindung aus Natur, Luxus und modernem Design.

Foto: Coco Privee Kuda Hiti

11

Milaidhoo Island

MALDIVES BAA ATOLL

The beautiful, tiny island, abundant with tropical greenery, measures just 300 m by 180 m and is fringed by soft deep white sand beaches. Guests at Milaidhoo are not viewed as holidaymakers, but as storywriters – crafting their dream holiday in the luxury five star resort. They lose themselves in the heart of nature in Baa Atoll's UNESCO Biosphere reserve, and dolphins, turtles and mantas only add to their adventure. Three restaurants and two bars focus on authentic, light food with clean flavors.

Von tropischen Pflanzen bedeckt und schneeweißen Sandstränden umgeben, misst die Insel gerade mal 300 x 180 Meter. Und doch verliert man sich hier schnell im Herzen der Natur. Drei Restaurants und zwei Bars setzen auf authentische, leichte Kost mit kräftigen Aromen.

All villas offer their own private freshwater pool on the sundeck, and are light, airy and beautifully decorated with beach chic wood and a creative combination of textures.

In den hell und luftig eingerichteten Villen mit schicken Holz- und bunten Stoffakzenten kann man wunderbar entspannen.

Foto: Milaidhoo Island

12

Luxury Resort
Soneva Fushi

MALDIVES BAA ATOLL

The philosophy at the eco-friendly island is simple: "no news, no shoes" – an idea the guests at Soneva Fushi happily submit to. The resort's down-to-earth vibe is reflected in its nature-inspired wooden structures and the spectacular star-gazing observatory allow one to forget about civilization for a while. This Robinson Crusoe feeling blended with a one-of-a-kind luxury experience is the ideal choice for anyenvironmentally-conscious traveler who enjoys world-class treetop dining and five-star service, without too much glitz and glam.

Das Motto auf der umweltfreundlichen Insel ist einfach: „No shoes, no news", also „Keine Schuhe, keine Nachrichten". Bei den Gästen kommt der bodenständige Charakter gut an und spiegelt sich auch in den natürlichen Holzstrukturen wider. Ein einzigartiges Luxuserlebnis mit Robinson-Crusoe-Atmosphäre, ideal für den umweltbewussten Reisenden, der Weltklasse-Treetop-Restaurants und 5-Sterne-Service genießt ohne zu viel Glanz und Glamour.

The villas exude as much character as the main areas, with tasteful wooden accents to an airy playful layout, such as the charming two-storey beach villas which have a little bridge leading from the four-poster bed to the upstairs terrace.

Geschmackvolle natürliche Akzente und ein luftiges Layout der Villen schaffen Robinson Crusoe-Feeling. So auch die zweistöckigen Strandvillen mit kleinen Brücken vom Himmelbett bis zur Terrasse im Obergeschoss.

Sandro Brücklmeier

Surrounded by tropical banana trees, Soneva's "Fresh in the Garden" is a dining experience not to be missed. Set in the treetops, this architectural feat allows guests to dine above herb and vegetable gardens with a breathtaking panorama.

Sonevas „Fresh in the garden" ist ein besonderes kulinarisches Erlebnis in den Baumkronen über Kräuter- und Gemüsegärten und umgeben von Bananenstauden.

Foto: Richard Waite

Soneva Fushi's luxurious beachfront private residences are available for purchase, each of which are made from sustainable materials and are surrounded by luscious foliage for maximum privacy and tranquility. The detached living areas are joined by wooden walkways, and the rooms are washed in the abundant natural light with breathtaking views of the ocean. Each private residence is bespoke and customizable and all furniture is specifically designed for each villa.

Soneva Fushi's luxuriöse Privatresidenzen können käuflich erworben werden. Die Villen sind aus nachhaltigen Materialien erbaut und von grüner Natur umgeben – Ruhe und Privatsphäre garantiert. Die freistehenden Wohnräume sind über Holzbrücken miteinander verbunden, die Räume in natürliches Licht getaucht mit atemberaubenden Ausblicken auf den Ozean. Wer gerne mit großer Familie oder Freunden verreist, findet in einer der elf luxuriösen „Private Residences" Privatsphäre auf höchstem Niveau.

Foto: Richard Waite

Foto: Gili Lankanfushi

13

Gili Lankanfushi

MALDIVES NORTH MALÈ ATOLL

The resort with its 45 over water villas was one of the first to implement the concept of "no shoes, no news" consistently. Plastic basically doesn't exist here and all the villas are built from natural materials in luxurious eco-designs. This is an extraordinary achievement, even for the Maldives. With your feet in the sand, or right above the water, you can enjoy fresh fish and meat specialties as well as international cuisine with Asian and Japanese influences.

Das Resort mit den 45 Over-Water-Villen hat als eines der ersten das Konzept "No Shoes, no News" konsequent umgesetzt. Plastik existiert hier so gut wie gar nicht, alle Villen sind ausschließlich aus natürlichen Materialien in luxuriösem Öko-Design erbaut. Selbst für die Malediven in dieser Konsequenz außergewöhnlich. Mit den Füßen im Sand oder gleich über dem Wasser genießt man frische Fisch- und Fleischspezialitäten sowie internationale Gerichte mit asiatischen und japanischen Einflüssen.

Foto: Gili Lankanfushi

Foto: Gili Lankanfushi

The over water villas have a very spacious terrace with direct access to the water, an open plan living room with sitting and dining areas overlooking the sea, a sleeping area and a bridge leading to the bathroom. The roof terrace with sunbeds invites guests to enjoy the romantic sunset. The turquoise-blue sea is omnipresent in all of the rooms.

Die Over-Water-Villen verfügen über eine sehr große Terrasse mit direktem Zugang ins Wasser, einen offenen Wohnbereich mit Sitz- und Essbereich mit Blick auf das Meer, einen Schlafbereich und über eine Brücke erreichbares Bad. Die Dachterrasse mit Tagesbett lädt zum romantischen Sonnenuntergang ein. In allen Räumen ist das türkisblaue Meer allgegenwärtig.

Foto: One&Only

14

One & Only
Reethi Rah

MALDIVES NORTH-MALÈ ATOLL

The six kilometer long island is a paradise for divers, with over 2,000 species of fish waiting to be explored in the colorful reef. The complimentary KidsOnly and OneTribe programmes are tailored to younger guests ages 4 - 11 years, allowing parents to enjoy the unprecedented privacy and transcendent luxury the island exudes. The latest addition to One&Only's dining experiences is Botanica – a unique organic restaurant. The serenity of the island, and sheer vastness, sets Reethi Rah apart from many resorts. With its pristine landscape and elegant design, it is a world in itself.

Die sechs Kilometer lange Insel ist mit über 2.000 Fischarten ein Paradies für Taucher. Die kostenlosen KidsOnly- und OneTribe-Programme sind speziell auf jüngere Gäste im Alter von 4 bis 11 Jahren zugeschnitten. Im Bio-Restaurant „Botanica" erleben Gäste einen Abend im Orchideenhaus oder im Schatten des Banyan-Baumes mit hundertprozentigen Bio-Produkten. Die Ruhe und Weite der Insel hebt Reethi Rah von vielen anderen Resorts ab und ist mit seiner unberührten Natur und der eleganten Architektur eine Welt für sich allein.

Foto: One&Only

Directly spaced along the water's edge, shrouded in foliage for unrivalled privacy, the beach villas open onto an expansive veranda with a stretch of private beach.

Direkt am Wasser gelegen, vom tropischen Garten umhüllt, öffnen sich die weitläufigen Terrassen zum privaten Strand.

Foto: One&Only

Foto: Kuda Huraa

15

Four Seasons Resort Maldives at
Kuda Huraa

MALDIVES NORTH MALÈ ATOLL

The garden island with its traditional village charm is the perfect destination offering; diving and snorkeling, a palm-lined lagoon and a magical mixture of Maldivian culture, friendly people and tropical romanticism. This magnificent natural setting is the perfect backdrop for inspiring menus: four restaurants celebrate the flavors of fine Indian cuisine, modern Italian cuisine and Asian delicacies.

Die Garteninsel mit traditionellem dörflichen Charme begeistert durch ihre bunten Riffs zum Tauchen und Schnorcheln, eine palmengesäumte Lagune und eine zauberhafte Mischung aus maledivischer Kultur, freundlichen Menschen und tropischer Romantik. Diese großartige natürliche Umgebung bildet die perfekte Kulisse für inspirierende Menüs: Vier Restaurants zelebrieren die Aromen der feinen indischen Küche, moderne italienische Speisen und asiatische Delikatessen.

Foto: Kuda Huraa

From the straw roofs and rustic wooden floors to the more typical white stone walls, all architectural details were built by craftsmen from the region using local materials. The techniques used here are centuries old and reflect the true spirit of the Maldives.

Von strohgedeckten Dächern und rustikalen Holzböden bis hin zu den typischen weißen Steinwänden wurden alle architektonischen Details von Handwerkern aus der Region mit heimischen Materialien erbaut. Die dabei verwendeten Techniken sind jahrhundertealt und spiegeln den Geist der Malediven hautnah wider.

Foto: Kuda Huraa

The imposing Entrance to the Indian fine dining restaurant Swarna.

Foto: JUmeirah

16

Jumeirah Vittaveli

MALDIVES SOUTH MALÈ ATOLL

Only a 20-minute ride on board a luxurious catamaran from Male the house reef is the prime spot for snorkelling, for the more adventurous explorers some beautiful underwater treasures await in the nearby wreck dives. The architecture of the resort is a kombination of traditional and modern elements. The iconic shape of the villas and buildings create a magical setting for a luxury holiday. At the restaurants guests can flavour indian spices and fine dining french cuisine.

Nur 20 Minuten von Malé entfernt, ist das Hausriff der Insel der bevorzugte Ort zum Schnorcheln. Abenteuerlustigere können sich auf schöne Unterwasserschätze in dem nahegelegenen Wrack freuen. Architektonisch ist das Resort eine Kombination aus traditionellen Elementen mit modernen Stilmitteln. Die ikonischen Formen der Villen und Gebäude kreieren eine zauberhafte Kulisse für einen Luxusurlaub. In den Restaurants können Gäste die verschiedenen indischen Gewürze oder hochwertige französische Küche genießen.

Aerial View of Jumeirah Vittaveli from the Southeastern side of the island

Foto: JUmeirah

The wooden architecture and design of the villas are inspired by traditional Maldivian villages, whilst embracing the modern style of the resort.

Die von traditionellen maledivischen Dörfern inspirierte Architektur der Villen prägt den eleganten Stil des Resorts.

The resort comprises 89 villas and suites each with their own swimming pool and direct access to the beach or lagoon. Highlights are the free-standing Ocean Suites, located only a heartbeat away from the main island and accessible by complimentary boat service.

Das Resort verfügt über 89 Villen und Suiten, jede mit eigenem Pool und direktem Zugang zum Strand oder zur Lagune. Das Highlight sind die frei-stehenden „Ocean Suites", die mit einem Bootservice bequem von der Hauptinsel erreichbar sind.

Foto: JUmeirah

Foto: Constance Hotels

17

Constance Moofushi

MALDIVES SOUTH ARI ATOLL

The trendy designed resort combines flair and 'barefoot' atmosphere with a real Robinson Crusoe feeling. The three lagunes are ideal for swimming and almost all sorts of watersports. Two restaurants and two bars offer a diversified cuisine with local meals up to a culinary trip around the world. Ymalia's innovative bio marine spa offers relaxing treatments.

Das Resort in trendigem Design verbindet viel Flair und Barfuss Atmosphäre mit einem echten Robinson Crusoe Feeling. Die drei Lagunen sind ideal zum Baden und ermöglichen nahezu alle Wassersportarten. Für den kulinarischen Genuss bieten zwei Restaurants und zwei Bars eine abwechslungsreiche Küche von regionalen Gerichten bis hin zu einer kulinarischen Reise um die Welt. Für Entspannung sorgt Ymalias innovatives Bio Marine Spa mit seinen wohltuenden Behandlungen.

Die 110 Beach- and Over-water-villas from 57 to 94 m² are designed in the typical style of the region in harmony with nature.

Die 110 Beach- und Overwater-Villen von 57 bis 94 m² sind im landestypischen Stil in farblichem Einklang mit der Natur eingerichtet.

18

Six Senses Laamu

MALDIVES LAAMU ATOLL

With its ecologically construction, the resort has 96 villas with stunning sea views. The innovative restaurants, bars and leisure activities combine recreation with excellent gastronomy concepts; be it in the tropical jungle, on the beach or above the turquoise water. The culinary experience offers creative menus from both hemispheres. There are plenty opportunities to relax; whether it's in the middle of the organic garden, in a glass tower or on glass floor directly above the waves. The Six Senses Spa, offers further relaxation, with its five secluded treatment rooms and two "nestlets" in the middle of the natural island vegetation. Most of their treatments apply lifestyle and holistic methods such as reflexology, acupressure, reiki or shiatsu.

Das Resort verfügt über 96 Villen in ökologischer Bauweise und mit wunderbarem Meerblick. Die innovativen Restaurants, Bars und Freizeitaktivitäten verbinden Erholung gekonnt mit hervorragenden Gastronomiekonzepten; sei es im tropischen Dschungel, am Strand oder über dem türkisblauen Wasser. Die innovative Erlebnisgastronomie bietet kreative Menüs von beiden Hemisphären – entspannt im Liegen, mitten im organischen Garten, in einem gläsernen Turm oder auf einem Glasboden direkt über den Wellen. Zum Entspannen steht auch das „Six Senses"-Spa mit seinen fünf abgeschiedenen Behandlungsräumen und je zwei „Nestchen". Lebensstilgestaltung und ganzheitliche Methoden sind die Schwerpunkte der Behandlungen. Bei der Innenausstattung der Beach- und Over-Water-Villen liegt der Schwerpunkt auf natürlichen Materialien, die ein sanft anmutendes und gleichzeitig modernes Refugium schaffen.

Foto: Philip David Clark & Anthony Paul Clark

Foto: Jorg Sundermann

Foto: PetrinaTinslay

The interior of the beach and over-water villas focuses on natural materials that create a comfortable, modern refuge.

Bei der Innenausstattung der Beach- und Over-Water-Villen liegt der Schwerpunkt auf natürlichen Materialien, die ein sanft anmutendes und gleichzeitig modernes Refugium schaffen.

19

The Residence Maldives

MALDIVES GAAFU ALIFU ATOLL

The villa resort is located just 20 kilometers north of the equator. The 94 straw-covered villas are located directly on the beach or stand on stilts over the water. The simple yet elegant vibes easily impress visitors, who are spoiled by a fabulous 360 ° panorama and every imaginable comfort. One of the highlights is the hotel's Spa by Clarins, which is the only spa in the Maldives, which only uses products by Clarins. For diving and snorkeling offers the PADI 5 *-Centre offers divers and snorkelers of all skill levels the opportunity to explore the rich underwater world around Falhumaafushi.

Das Villenresort liegt nur 20 Kilometer nördlich des Äquators. Die 94 strohgedeckten Villen befinden sich direkt am Strand oder stehen auf Stelzen über dem Wasser und beeindrucken durch ihr schlicht-elegantes Ambiente, einen 360°-Rundumblick und jeden nur erdenklichen Komfort. Eines der Highlights ist der hoteleigene “The Spa by Clarins” – der einzige Spa auf den Malediven, in dem ausschließlich Produkte von Clarins verwendet werden. Zum Tauchen und Schnorcheln bietet das PADI 5*-Tauchzentrum bietet Tauchern und Schnorchlern aller Erfahrungsgrade die Möglichkeit, die reiche Unterwasserwelt rund um Falhumaafushi zu erkunden.

Foto: The Residence

Traditional Maldivian architecture along with custom made furnishings create an elegant atmosphere. Two restaurants and a bar offer modern interpretations of Asian and Indian cuisine, as well as fresh seafood and fish accompanied by fine wines from around the world.

Traditionelle maledivische Architektur mit individuell angefertigten Möbeln schaffen eine elegante Atmosphäre, in der zwei Restaurants und eine Bar modern interpretierte asiatische und indische Küche in Begleitung erlesener Weine aus aller Welt bieten.

Foto: The Residence

Foto: JUmeirah

20

Jumeirah Dhevanafushi

MALDIVES GAAFU ALIFU

Dhevanafushi consists of a hotel island and an upstream water settlement called Ocean Pearl, and can only be reached from the main land, by boat. The feeling of casual luxury is combined with perfect seclusion here.

Dhevanafushi besteht aus einer Hotelinsel und einer vorgelagerten Überwasser-siedlung namens „Ocean Pearl“, die von der Hauptinsel aus nur per Boot zu erreichen ist. „Luxus legere”, kombiniert mit vollendeter Abgeschiedenheit, ist hier das Urlaubskonzept.

13 Beach Revives Villas (206 m^2 each) are situated on the main island surrounded by the Indian Ocean, while the seven Island Revives (306 m^2 each) are embedded in the middle of the rich flora of the island Interior. All villas have an extra work room, and one almost 100 m2 large bathroom area with an outdoor shower. Ocean Pearl is a very special hideaway. The 16 water-villas are built on stilts surrounded by a coral reef and located 800 meters away and not connected to the main island. All Jumeirah Villas are equipped with panoramic views on the sea or in nature with floor-length panoramic glass walls.

Auf der Hauptinsel liegen 13 Beach-Revives-Villen mit je 206 m^2 direkt am Indischen Ozean. Die sieben Island-Revives-Villen mit 306 m^2 sind inmitten der reichen Flora des Inselinneren eingebettet. Alle Villen verfügen über ein zusätzliches Arbeitszimmer und einen fast 100 m^2 großen Badezimmerbereich mit Außen- dusche. Das ganz besondere Hideaway ist „Ocean Pearls". Die 16 Wasservillen liegen rund 800 Meter ohne Verbindung zur Hauptinsel entfernt mitten im Indischen Ozean, auf Stelzen gebaut und von einem Korallenriff umgeben. Alle „Jumeirah"-Villen sind mit bodentiefen Panoramaglaswänden mit Panoramablick in die Natur oder auf das Meer ausgestattet.

Foto: JUmeirah

Foto: JUmeirah

Foto: JUmeirah

All revives and sanctuaries have sunbeds on a terrace with a private swimming pool, direct access to the beach and lagoon and a 24-hour butler service.

Alle Revives und Sanctuaries verfügen über einen privaten Pool, direkten Zugang zu Strand und Lagune, Day Beds auf der eigenen Terrasse sowie 24-Stunden-Butlerservice.

Foto: Shangri-La's Villingili

21

Shangri-La's Villingili Resort & Spa

MALDIVES ADDU ATOLL

The two-kilometer white sand beach invites guests to take full advantage of this romantic island. However, Villingili has far more to offer: twelve hectares of lush vegetation with 17,000 palm trees and old banyan fig trees, three natural lagoons as well as nature trails above and under water. Amidst this beautiful location, Shangri-La's Villingili Resort & Spa features tree-house villas with pool decks, measuring 218 m^2 and 3 m high.

Inselromantik finden die Gäste an dem zwei Kilometer langen weißen Sandstrand zur Genüge. Doch Villingili hat weitaus mehr zu bieten: Zwölf Hektar üppige Vegetation mit 17.000 Palmen und alten Banyan-Feigenbäumen, drei natürliche Lagunen sowie Naturlehrpfade über und unter Wasser sowie die 218 m^2 großen und drei Meter hoch gelegenen Baumhausvillen mit Pooldeck.

Foto: Shangri-La's Villingili

There are 132 villas of various categories, measuring between 133 and 1,000 m^2. Dr. Ali's Restaurant has three themed rooms, serving specialities from the cultures of the Indian Ocean, the South China Sea and the Arabian Gulf. The spa complex, with eleven spa villas on 16,700 m2, is one of the largest in the Maldives. The applications are based on philosophies and rituals from China and the Himalayas. The element analysis is especially characteristic and is based on the Chinese philosophy of Yin and Yang. Villingili also offers a variety of activities including 25 dive sites, an underwater path on the house reef, and the 140 m wreck of the 'British Loyalty'.

Insgesamt stehen den Gästen 132 Villen verschiedener Kategorien zwischen 133 und 1.000 m^2 zur Verfügung. Auch Gaumenfreuden genießen hier einen hohen Stellenwert. In drei Restaurants werden Gerichte aus den Kulturen des Indischen Ozeans, des Südchinesischen Meers und des Arabischen Golfs serviert. Mit elf Spa-Villen auf 16.700 m^2 ist die Spa-Anlage eine der größten der Malediven. Die Anwendungen beruhen auf Philosophien und Ritualen aus China und dem Himalaya. Charakteristisch ist die Elementanalyse, die auf der chinesischen Philosophie des Yin und Yang basiert. Villingili bietet außerdem eine ganze Reihe an Aktivitäten wie 25 Tauchgründe, einen Unterwasserlehrpfad am Hausriff und das 140 Meter lange Wrack der „British Loyalty".

Foto: Shangri-La's Villingilli

The highlights of the resort: the 218 m^2 and 3 m high tree-house villas with pool decks.

Die Highlights des Resorts: die 218 m^2 großen und drei Meter hoch gelegenen Baumhausvillen mit Pooldeck.

Foto: Shangri-La's Villingili

Guests can choose out of 132 villas in aight categories: the 'Ocean View Tree House' in 3 meters hight, water villas and beach villas or the deluxe pool villas and two residential villas.

Gäste haben die Wahl zwischen 132 Villen in acht Kategorien vom „Ocean View Tree House", in drei Metern Höhe auf Pfählen gebaut, über Wasservillen auf Stelzen und Beachvillen am Strand bis zu Deluxe-Poolvillen und zwei Präsidentenvillen.

Foto: Shangri-La's Villingili

Maldives
Equator
Zanzibar
Seychelles
Madagascar
Mauritius
La Reunion
Saint Denis
1
Le Port
Cap Noir 304
Saint Paul
Saint Gilles les Bains
2
Cirque de Mafate
Cirque de Salazie
Saint Benoit
Trou de Fer 312, 314
Maido 308
Hell Bourg 332
Cirque de Cilaos
Bois Court 324
Rivière de Remparts 326
Piton de la Fournaise 328, 330
3
l'Etang Salé les Bains 320
Saint Louis
Cascades Trou Noir 318
Saint Pierre
Saint Joseph
10 km

La Réunion

Hotels

1 Lodge Roche Tamarin & Spa
2 LUX* Saint Gilles
3 Palm Hotel & Spa

Golf Courses

1	Golf Du Bassin Bleu	18 hole
2	Golf Du Colorado	9 hole
3	Golf De Bourbon	18 hole

Area:	*2,512 km^2*
Highest Mountain:	*Piton des Neiges, 3,069 m*
Population:	*850,000*
Religion:	*86 % Christianity* *14 % Hindi, Islam*
Language:	*réunion-creole, french*
Government:	*department of France*
Currency:	*Euro*

On La Réunion influences from Africa, Asia and Europe create a very unique amalgamation of cultures.

Auf La Réunion vereinen sich Einflüsse aus Afrika, Asien und Europa und machen es zu einem wahren Schmelztiegel der Kulturen.

The volcanic island in the Indian Ocean is the perfect location for those looking for a more varied holiday. Three-thousand-meter-high mountains, thousand-meter-deep ravines, a wide variety of climates, one of the most active volcanoes in the world, beaches on the Atlantic coast, alpine meadows and tropical rainforests tempt locals and visitors every day. Hiking, mountain biking, kite surfing, canyoning, paragliding, diving, whale-watching, lying on the beach and a nightlife that is reminiscent of the Côte d'Azur, topped with French cuisine and way of life. The French Department is a meeting place for the active as well as gourmet fans.

Most visitors come to hike in the prehistoric-looking nature. The Three Valley Basin, the Cirque Gordon, the Cirque of Cilaos and the Cirque of Salazie, with dramatically towering mountain cones and up to 1,000 meter-deep gorges form the center of the island strongly remind of Spielberg's Jurassic Park. Dense cliffs drop steeply, up to a thousand meters in depth. Cascading waterfalls, the deep green of the jungle and the sharp rugged edges of the mountains shape the Green Valley. The Vulkan Piton de la Fournaise in the south-east combines alpine pastures and arid lunar landscapes, just a short drive away from each other. Early risers are clearly at an advantage here: for the best visibility one should visit at the crack of dawn, as from early morning onwards the peaks of the mountains are hidden in the clouds.

Saint Gille-les-Bains, on the west coast, is the perfect place for those wanting an active holiday combined with beach and nightlife. The lagoon with its kilometer-long beach and numerous beach bars bet- ween Saint Gilles-les-Bains and l' Étang brings back memories of the French Atlantic coast and the nightlife at the Cote d'Azur. One can indulge in a variety of water sports in the idyllic Marina of Saint Gilles-les-Bain, take a stroll or enjoy a sundowner at one of the beach bars. Between July and October, humpback whales come to visit, and are sometimes so close to the beach that one could nearly skip any whale-watching tours. Being at the foot of the Piton Maïdo makes a trip to the spectacular mountain world is a must. It's a curvy trail along 2,200 meters, typically lasting just over an hour. You'll never forget the views in the Cirque de Mafate with its over 500 meter high mountain cones. Those wanting to experience more of the natural treasures of the island, should consider combining their stay with a stopover in the mountains. Ideally, in a traditional rustic cabin on the volcano with a panoramic view over the island, or in one of the many guesthouses on the island.

Wer einen abwechslungsreichen Urlaub mit unvergesslichen Eindrücken sucht, ist auf La Réunion genau richtig. Über dreitausend Meter hohe Berge, tausend Meter tiefe Schluchten, einer der aktivsten Vulkane der Welt, Strände wie an der Atlantikküste, alpine Almwiesen und tropische Regenwälder begeistern Einheimische und Besucher täglich aufs Neue. Canyoning, Wandern, Mountainbiking, Kitesurfen, Paragliding, Tauchen, Whalewatching, Am-Strand-Liegen und ein Nachtleben, das fast an die Côte d'Azur erinnert. Alles garniert mit französischer Küche und Lebensweise. Das französische Departement und südlichster Teil der Europäischen Union ist ein Treffpunkt für Aktive und Genießer.

Zur der Insel zwischen Mauritius und Madagaskar kommen die Besucher vor allem zum Wandern in der prähistorisch anmutenden Natur. Drei Talkessel, der Cirque de Mafate, der Cirque de Cilaos und der Cirque de Salazie, mit drastisch aufragenden Bergkegeln und tiefen Schluchten bilden die Inselmitte – wie ein Mix aus Spielbergs „Jurassic Park". Tosende Wasserfälle, dichter Urwald und schroffes Zickzack-Gebirge, tiefgrün und mit scharfen Kanten, prägen die immergrünen Talkessel. Der Vulkan Piton de la Fournaise im Südosten vereint alpine Almwiesen und karge Mondlandschaften nur wenige Fahrminuten voneinander entfernt. Frühaufsteher sind hier klar im Vorteil, denn ab vormittags sind die Gipfel meist in Wolken gehüllt und lassen das schönste Postkartenmotiv verblassen.

Die Westküste bei Saint-Gilles-les-Bains ist ideal, um Strand und Berge mit einander zu kombinieren. Die Lagune mit dem kilometerlangen Strand und zahlreichen Bars zwischen Saint-Gilles-les-Bains und l'Etang weckt Erinnerungen an die französische Atlantikküste und das Nachtleben der Côte d'Azur. Den verschiedensten Wassersportarten kann man hier frönen, im idyllischen Yachthafen von Saint-Gilles-les-Bains flanieren oder sich an einer der Strandbars den Sundowner reinziehen. Zwischen Juli und Oktober kommen Buckelwale zu Besuch, manchmal so nah am Strand, dass man sich die Whale-watchingtour fast sparen könnte. Aber eben nur fast. Von hier, zu Füßen des Piton Maido, ist ein Ausflug in die spektakuläre Bergwelt ein Muss. Gut eine Stunde geht es kurvenreich auf 2.200 Meter hinauf. Die Aussicht in den Cirque de Mafate mit seinen über 500 Meter aufragenden Bergkegeln vergisst man nie mehr. Wer mehr von den Naturwundern der Insel erleben will, kombiniert seinen Aufenthalt am besten mit Zwischenstopps in den Bergen – auf einer urigen Hütte auf dem Vulkan oder in einem der vielen Gästehäuser.

The panoramic view from the Kiosque du Cap Noir (accessible from Le Port on the northwest coast) offers beautifully picturesque views into the Cirque de Mafate with the towering Piton Cabris, visible in clear conditions.

Der Panoramablick vom Kiosque du Cap Noir (über Le Port an der Nordwestküste aus erreichbar) bietet an wolkenfreien Tagen spektakuläre Postkartenblicke in den Cirque de Mafate mit dem steil im Talkessel aufragenden Piton Cabris.

Not much has changed since the creation of the island two to three million years ago; the plant life had plenty of time to envelop the volcanic landscape.

Seit der Entstehung von La Réunion vor zwei bis drei Millionen Jahren hat sich hier nicht viel geändert und die Flora hatte genügend Zeit, die Insel ungestört zu erobern.

Maxim K. istock

From Saint-Gilles-les-Hauts on the west coast the 2,205-meter-high Piton Maido is about an hours' drive along winding roads. The view into the Cirque de Mafate and it's towering cliff walls is breathtaking.

Von Saint-Gilles-les-Hauts an der Westküste aus ist der 2.205 Meter hohe Piton Maido über eine kurvenreiche Straße in gut einer Stunde zu erreichen. Die Aussicht in den Cirque de Mafate mit seinen steil aufragenden Felswänden ist atemberaubend.

To experience La Réunion's theatrical landscape is like a journey back in time. What appears like a grass lawn from a distance, is indeed an impenetrable jungle of gigantic tropical trees and flora.

Eine Reise nach La Réunion ist wie eine Zeitreise zurück in die Urzeiten der Erdgeschichte. Was von der Ferne wie ein Rasenteppich wirkt, ist in Wirklichkeit ein undurchdringlicher Dschungel aus riesigen tropischen Bäumen.

Maxim K. istock

There is no want for water on the island. The many waterfalls plummet down the cliffs to depths of hundreds of meters such as here at the 'Trou de Fer'.

An Wasser mangelt es auf La Réunion nicht. Überall stürzen die Wassermassen hunderte Meter in die Tiefe wie hier am „Trou de Fer" und nähren die üppige Pflanzenwelt.

Yggdrasil istock

The hike from the 'Gîte de Bélouve' through the rainforest to the Trou de Fer offers three highlights: a magnificent panoramic view at the hut on the Cirque de Salazie, a unique flora with up to twenty-meter-high ferns and with any luck, even a glimpse inside the Hellmouth, the Trou de Fer.

Die Wanderung von der „Gîte de Bélouve" durch den Regenwald zum Trou de Fer bietet gleich drei Highlights: einen grandiosen Panoramablick bei der Hütte auf den Cirque de Salazie, eine einzigartige Flora mit bis zu zwanzig Meter hohen Farnen und beim Ziel mit viel Glück einen Blick in den Höllenschlund, den Trou der Fer.

Foto: Marzena Martij shutterstock

The hike to the 'Trou de Fer' leads through almost permanent fog and along natures' own works of art.

Die Wanderung zum „Trou de Fer" führt durch permanenten Nebel vorbei an bizarren Naturkunstwerken.

The waterfalls 'Cascade de Trou Noir' are an attraction in the south of the island near Saint Joseph.

Eine Attraktion im Süden der Insel: die Wasserfälle "Cascade de Trou Noir" bei Saint Joseph.

The only black sand beach on the island at Etang Salé les Bains is also very popular with locals.

Der einzige schwarze Sandstrand der Insel bei l'Étang-Salé-les-Bains ist vor allem bei Einheimischen sehr beliebt.

The humpback whales (measuring 12 to 16 meters) visit La Reunion from May to September. Whale-watching excursions leave from Saint Gilles les Bain.

Die zwölf bis sechzehn Meter langen Buckelwale kommen von Mai bis September auf La Réunion zu Besuch. Whalewatchingtouren starten zum Beispiel von Saint Gilles les Bain aus.

Foto: Andrey Gudkov-shutterstock

The plateau at the base of the Piton de la Fournaise seems almost biblical.

Fast biblisch wirkt die Hochebene am Fuß des Vulkans mit den üppig bewachsenen Ausläufern des Piton de la Fournaise.

On the way to the volcano, one can enjoy the fantastic panoramic views into the gorge of the 'Rivière ds Rebparts'.

Auf der Fahrt zum Vulkan eröffnet sich auf über 1.770 m Höhe der fantastische Panoramablick in die Schlucht der „Rivière ds Remparts".

The sand layer on the high plateau of the 2,632-meter-high volcano came into being 65,000 years ago. The volcano is one of the most active volcanoes in the world and even erupted leaking lava in August 2017. Continuing on from Bourg Murat, the road takes travels through a landscape similar to that of the Tyrolean Alps. Black and white cows graze on lush pastures before the scenery abruptly changes into the barren moon-like landscape.

Die Sandebene auf dem Hochplateau des 2.632 m hohen Vulkans entstand vor 65.000 Jahren. Der Vulkan zählt zu den aktivsten Vulkanen der Welt und hatte im August 2017 wieder Eruptionen mit austretender Lava. Die Fahrt von Bourg-Murat aus führt weiter oben durch eine Landschaft wie in den Tiroler Alpen. Schwarz-weiße Kühe grasen auf saftigen Weiden, bevor sich die Landschaft oben abrupt in die karge Mondlandschaft verwandelt.

The martian landscape composed of black basalt almost looks sinister. Travellers with a bit more time and wishing to explore the landscape can spend the night in the 'Gité de Vulcan' and enjoy the unique sunrise before the first clouds appear.

Gespenstisch wirkt die Mondlandschaft aus schwarzem Basalt. Wer ohne Zeitdruck die Landschaft erwandern möchte, kann in der „Gîte du Volcan“ übernachten und einen einmaligen Sonnenaufgang erleben, bevor die ersten Wolken aufziehen.

Many years ago slaves who managed to escape hoped to find refuge in the inaccessible mountains of La Réunion. Today, it has become the small village of Hell-Bourg with colourful, traditional Creole houses.

Ursprünglich hatten hier entlaufene Sklaven Zuflucht in der unzugänglichen Bergwelt von La Réunion gesucht. Heute ist das Dörfchen Hell-Bourg mit hübschen Häusern im kreolischen Stil daraus geworden.

The four elements – earth, fire, water and air – are omnipresent on La Réunion and serve as the breeding ground for the unparalleled vegetation found on the island.

Die vier Elemente, Erde, Feuer, Wasser und Luft, sind auf La Réunion allgegenwärtig und der Nährboden für eine weltweit einmalig üppige Vegetation.

1

Palm
Hotel & Spa

LA RÉUNION SOUTH-EAST

The 'Palm Hotel & Spa' is a part of the new generation of high-end hotels, which blend designer comfort, subtle luxury and a Zen atmosphere. Situated in the heart of an authentic and preserved environment, close to Saint-Pierre City and the volcanic cirque and peaks it is the ideal starting point when visiting the island's main tourist attractions. One of the unique features of the hotel is its beach suspended between sky and sea, with a panoramic view over the Indian Ocean. Two pools, a spa and other facilties further contribute to an unforgetable stay. Three restaurants and a lounge bar spoil guests with international cusine, complemented by Creole influences.

Das „Palm Hotel & Spa" gehört zu einer neuen Generation exklusiver Hotels, die Komfort und diskreten Luxus bieten. Nahe Saint-Pierre, dem Vulkan und den Bergen in einer wunderbaren Naturlandschaft gelegen, ist das Hotel idealer Ausgangspunkt zu den Hauptattraktionen der Insel. Eine Terrasse wie ein „hängender Strand" zwischen Himmel und Meer mit Blick über den Indischen Ozean sowie zwei Pools und ein Spa machen den Aufenthalt zu etwas Besonderem. Kulinarisch werden die Gäste von drei Restaurants und einer Lounge-Bar mit regionaler und internationaler Küche verwöhnt.

The rooms and the suites are located in charming Creole villas, set in the heart of a 3.5-hectare tropical garden. The lodges, on stilts, nestled together on the cliff's edge give a unique and spectacular view over Grand Anse Bay and the Indian Ocean.

Die Zimmer und Suiten liegen in kreolischen Häusern im Herzen eines 3,5 Hektar großen tropischen Gartens. Die Lodges thronen über dem Indischen Ozean am Rand einer Klippe. Auf Pfählen errichtet, bieten sie einen fantastischen Ausblick über die Grande Anse auf den Indischen Ozean.

Foto: LUX* Resorts & Hotels

2

LUX* Resorts & Hotels
LUX* Saint Gilles

LA RÉUNION EAST COAST

The only 5-star hotel on La Réunion with direct access to one of the most beautiful beaches, lies on the sun-washed west coast and is ideal for relaxing and exploring the spectacular nature. The Cap Noir, Cirque de Mafate, the volcano in the south and two golf courses are also not far away.

Das einzige 5-Sterne-Hotel auf La Réunion mit direktem Zugang zu einem der schönsten Strände liegt an der klimatisch günstigen Westküste und ist ideal zum Entspannen am Meer und zum Erkunden der spektakulären Natur. Das Cap Noir, der Cirque de Mafate, der Vulkan im Süden und zwei Golfplätze sind von dort schnell erreichbar.

Foto: Lux Saint Gilles les Bain

Guests can cool down in the refreshing turquoise blue lagoon or in the 1,100 m^2 pool, which is the largest on the island. The one kilometre beach of L'Ermitage is regarded as the most beautiful of the island, ideal for a walk, swim or to go snorkelling in the protected reef. A few steps further and one is in the idyllic Marina of Saint-Gilles-les-Bains.

Zur Erfrischung stehen Gästen die geschützte türkisblaue Lagune und mit 1.100 Quadratmetern der größte Pool auf La Réunion zur Verfügung. Der kilometerlange Strand von L'Ermitage gilt als der schönste der Insel, ideal zum Schwimmen und Schnorcheln innerhalb des geschützten Riffs mit seinen tropischen Fischen. Nur ein paar Schritte weiter gelangt man zum idyllischen Yachthafen von Saint-Gilles-les-Bains.

Foto: Lux Saint Gilles les Bain

The elegant suites (34 to 68 m²) in the colonial-style villas are surrounded by the beautiful tropical gardens of the resort, overlooking the sheltered lagoon of L'Ermitage. A few steps through the greenery lead directly to the beach and the pool. Three restaurants, a pool bar and a beach bar offer guests Creole, French and international cuisine of the highest level.

Die eleganten Suiten (34 bis 68 m²) in den Kolonialstilvillen fügen sich harmonisch in den tropischen Garten des Resorts mit Kokospalmen und Blick über die geschützte Lagune von L'Ermitage ein. Ein paar Schritte durch den Garten führen direkt zum Strand und zum Pool. Drei Restaurants, eine Poolbar und eine Strandbar verwöhnen hier die Gäste mit internationalen, französischen und kreolischen Gerichten auf höchstem Niveau.

Lodge Roche Tamarin
VILLAGE NATURE
Hotel-Lodges 4*
Restaurant & Spa
Lodge Tamarin
Spa Body Harmonie
Prestations 2013

3

Lodge Roche Tamarin & Spa

LA RÉUNION NORTH

Immersed in the heart 15,000 m² of tropical flora, the 'Lodge Roche Tamarin & Spa' enjoys splendid views of the Indian Ocean. Walkways meander the grounds and connect the 20 Lodges and Suites built on wooden stilts, surrounded by nature. The gourmet restaurant offers a refined cuisine with local and international dishes. The hotel is a unique little paradise with charm and atmosphere.

Im Herzen eines tropischen, 15.000 m² großen Gartens mit Blick auf den Indischen Ozean ist „Lodge Roche Tamarin & Spa" ein kleines Paradies mit Charme und Atmosphäre. Die 20 Lodges und Suiten, auf Pfählen errichtet, sind über Wege verbunden und umgeben von Natur pur. Das Gourmetrestaurant bietet eine raffinierte regionale und internationale Küche.

Decorated with refinement, the chalets of solid wood logs are cozy and comfortable, each with its own private terrace, sheltered from prying eyes and facing the ocean of course.

Die aus aus Holzbalken erbauten und mit natürlichen Materialien eingerichteten chalets sind gemütlich und komfortabel, alle mit privater terrasse und Blick auf den Ozean.

Maldives
Equator
Seychelles
Zanzibar
10
Madagascar
Mauritius
La Reunion
CURIEUSE
368
Anse Lazio 358
6
1
Anse Volbert
PRASLIN
Valle de Mai 370
7
FÉLICITÈ
LA DIGUE
Grand Anse
354, 356
Anse Source d'Argent
364, 372, 374
5
NORTH
ISLAND
362
SILHOUETTE
FRÉGATE
8
Beau Vallon
Victoria
9
ROUND
ISLAND
2
MAHÈ
3
4
1
Anse Intendance 360
Anse Takamaka 366
10 km

Seychelles

Hotels

1	**Banyan Tree**	Banyan Tree	Mahé
2	**Ephelia**	Constance Hotels	Mahé
3	**Maia Luxury Resort**	Tsogo Sun	Mahé
4	**Four Seasons**	Four Seasons	Mahé
5	**North Island**		North Island
6	**Lèmuria**	Constance Hotels	Praslin
7	**Zil Pasyon**	Six Senses	Félicité
8	**Frégate Island**	Oetker Collection	Frégate Island
9	**Enchanted Island Resort**	JA Resorts & Hotels	Round Island
10	**Alphonse Island**		Alphonse Atoll

Golfcourses

1	**Lémuria Golfcourse**	18 Hole

Area:	*455 km²* *115 islands*
Highest mountain:	*905 m*
Population:	*97,000*
Religion:	*86.8 % Christianity* *2.4 % Hinduism* *1.6 % Islam*
Language:	*creole, english, french*
Government:	*unitary presidential republic*
Independence:	*1976*
Currency:	*Seychellois Rupee*

Most of the inhabitants of the Seychelles are descendants of slaves and from other immigrated colonial settlers.

Die Bevölkerung der Seychellen besteht überwiegend aus Nachfahren von Sklaven und der aus anderen Kolonialgebieten eingewanderten Siedler.

The 115 islands of the Seychelles are famous for their endless, untouched white sand beaches with gigantic rock formations. The inner islands around Mahé, Praslin and La Digue, and the outer islands consisting of a group of flat coral islands are unique worldwide. The French were the first to recognise this, and inhabited the islands in 1756. In 1794 the English came to the same conclusion and occupied the Seychelles, as part of the Commonwealth, until its independence in 1976. The roots of the African and Asian populations, combined with the French and British way of life, have formed a lively and peaceful society over the centuries. The different regions with their colourful houses are lovingly cared for and on Sundays one is expected to dress festively for church, followed by a barbecue on the beach with friends and family. The combination of the lush jungle, the secluded beaches and the granite rocks, make the Seychelles a memorable natural experience, under strict protection by the government. The beaches are completely natural, with only a few exceptions. Hotels, or even sunshades or sunbeds are not allowed on the beaches to preserve the beauty of this paradise. Even restaurants directly on the beach are a rarity.

The main island of Mahé with 90,000 inhabitants and 65 beaches is very versatile. Most visitors land in the north, on the island's longest beach, Beau Vallon. Here, along the bay, one is spoilt for choice with numerous accommodation possibilities, restaurants, shops and diving centers. However, if you are looking for peace, the south of the island is the place to be. The beaches Police Bay, Anse Intendance and Anse Takamaka, flanked by huge granite rocks, are among the most beautiful in the world. In the west, the Morne National Park, the Bay of Port Glaud and the fairytale island of Terese, surrounded by turquoise shimmering lagoons, are popular destinations for day trips. A romantic lunch or sundowner in the beach restaurant 'Del Place' is an unforgettable experience. The second largest island, Praslin, has hardly changed in the last 20 years. The main attraction is the Vallée de Mai, a dense palm grove where the Coco de Mer grows. The most beautiful beaches are Anse Lazio (with beach restaurant) and Anse Georgette in the north. In contrast to the tranquil Praslin, the third island, La Digue, has developed into a true tourist magnet. Although some cars are now permitted on the famous Cyclist Island, the bike is still the main means of transport. The Anse Source d'Argent beach with its giant compositions of granite, sand and palm trees and the Sundown Dinner in the 'Bellevue' restaurant with a magnificent panorama view from the 333-meter-high mountain Nie d'Aigle provide unforgettable moments.

Die 115 Inseln der Seychellen sind wegen ihrer endlosen, unberührten weißen Sandstrände mit den gigantischen Felsformationen weltberühmt. Aus Granit mit bis knapp über 900 Meter hohen Bergen bestehen nur die inneren Inseln um Mahé, Praslin und La Digue. Die äußeren Inseln sind dagegen flache Koralleninseln. Als erstes verfielen die Franzosen dem Reiz der Inseln und verleibten sich 1756 die Inseln ein. 1794 kamen dann die Engländer auf den Geschmack. Bis zur Unabhängigkeit im Jahr 1976 waren die Seychellen ein Teil des Commonwealth. Die Wurzeln der afrikanischen und asiatischen Bevölkerung in Kombination mit der französischen und britischen Lebensart haben über die Jahrhunderte eine lebendige und friedliche Gesellschaft gebildet. Die Orte mit ihren bunten Häusern sind liebevoll gepflegt, sonntags geht es festlich gekleidet in die Kirche und anschließend mit Familie und Freunden zum Barbecue an den Strand. Zusammen mit dem üppigen Urwald, den wunderbaren Stränden und besagten Granitfelsen sind die Seychellen ein unvergessliches Naturerlebnis, was die Regierung auch eisern schützt. Bis auf ganz wenige Ausnahmen sind die Strände der Seychellen vollkommen naturbelassen. Kein Hotelkasten stört die Idylle, nicht einmal Sonnenschirme oder Liegen sind am Strand erlaubt und selbst Restaurants direkt am Strand sind eine Ausnahme.

Vielseitige Aktivitäten bietet die Hauptinsel Mahé mit 90.000 Einwohnern und 65 Stränden. Die meisten Besucher landen im Norden am längsten Strand der Insel, Beau Vallon. Entlang der Bucht gibt es hier zahlreiche Unterkünfte, Restaurants, Läden und Tauchbasen. Wer Ruhe sucht, ist im Süden der Insel richtig. Die von gewaltigen Granitfelsen flankierten Strände Police Bay, Anse Intendance und Anse Takamaka zählen zu den schönsten der Welt. Im Westen sind der Morne-Nationalpark und die Bucht von Port Glaud mit türkis schimmernden Lagunen und der vorgelagerten Bilderbuchinsel Térèse beliebtes Ziel für Tagesausflüge. Ein romantischer Lunch oder Sundowner im Strandlokal „Del Place" runden den Ausflug ab. Die zweitgrößte Insel, Praslin, hat sich in den letzten 20 Jahren kaum verändert. Hauptattraktion ist das Vallée de Mai, ein dichter Palmenwald, in dem die berühmte Coco de Mer wächst. Die schönsten Strände auf Praslin sind Anse Lazio (mit Strandrestaurant!) und Anse Georgette im Norden. Im Gegensatz zum beschaulichen Praslin hat sich die dritte Insel, La Digue, zu einem wahren Touristenmagnet entwickelt. Der Strand Anse Source d'Argent mit seinen gigantischen Kompositionen aus Granit, Sand und Palmen und das Sundown-Dinner im Restaurant „Bellevue" mit grandiosem Panoramablick von dem 333 Meter hohen Berg Nid d'Aigle bescheren unvergessliche Momente.

The beauty of the remote beaches is rarely disrupted by hotels, such as at the Grand Anse on La Digue.

Kaum ein Hotel stört die Schönheit der Strände auf den Seychellen wie hier am Grand Anse auf La Digue.

Foto: Alohaflaminggo/Shutterstock

Due to strong currents swimming is prohibited at beaches such as here at Grand Anse on La Digue Island. Some brave it nevertheless.

Wegen starker Strömung ist an einigen Stränden wie hier am Grand Anse auf La Digue das Schwimmen verboten. Auch wenn es manche trotzdem versuchen.

The beach bar at Anse Lazio on Praslin is famous for its creole cuisine.

Anse Lazio auf Praslin ist vor allem wegen der Strandbar mit kreolischer Küche beliebt.

Foto: Alpinenatur Shutterstock

Anse Intendance on Mahé is amongst its most beautiful beaches and not to be missed. Those wanting to extend their stay on the Island can book into the noble Hotel 'Banyan Tree'.

Anse Intendance ist einer der schönsten Strände auf Mahé. Wer dort länger bleiben will, quartiert sich im Edelhotel „Banyan Tree" ein.

Guests of the 'Barefoot Luxury Resort' on North Island can enjoy this vast beach of pristine white sand.

Die Gäste des "Barfuß-Luxus-Resorts" North Island auf der gleichnamigen Insel können sich über einen Sandstrand wie Puderzucker freuen.

Foto: North Island

One can find these world-famous stone giants at the Anse Source d'Argent on La Digue.

Am Anse Source d'Argent auf La Digue stehen die in der ganzen Welt berühmten Felsgiganten.

Anse Takamaka is located in the peaceful south of the main island of Mahé with a hotel built in the typical local style and a beach bar serving good food.

Im ruhigen Süden der Hauptinsel Mahé liegt der Strand Anse Takamaka mit einem Hotel in landestypischer Architektur und einer Strandbar mit guter Küche.

The beautiful beach on Curieuse Island is only a 10-minute boat ride from Praslin.

Nur zehn Minuten sind es mit dem Boot von Praslin zu diesem traumhaften Strand auf der Insel Curieuse.

The famous Coco de Mer grows in the Vallée de Mai, which is a unique palm forest on Praslin. Weighing around 25 kilos it is the heaviest fruit in the world.

Im Vallée de Mai auf Praslin, einem einzigartigen Palmenurwald auf Praslin, wächst die weltberühmte Coco de Mer. Mit rund 25 Kilo ist sie die schwerste Frucht der Welt.

Granite rocks such as these are solely found in the inner islands of the Seychelles. As a by-product of continental drift they came into being around 200 million years ago, when India started shifting from Africa towards Asia, leaving rocks along the way.

Granitfelsen wie hier auf La Digue gibt es nur auf den inneren Inseln der Seychellen. Entstanden sind sie vor 200 Millionen Jahren bei der Kontinentaldrift, als Indien von Afrika nach Asien wanderte und ab und zu ein paar Felsen liegen ließ.

Stark contrasts: granite boulders at the Anse Source d'Argent on La Digue

Spannende Kontraste: die Felsen am Anse Source d'Argent auf La Digue

Foto: leoks Shutterstock

Foto: alphonse Island

The Seychelles combine nature, culture, water sports and luxury hotels, creating an unforgettable experience. Not only are the Seychelles famous for their beautiful diving sites with a visibility of up to 40 meters, but the Creole lifestyle with a hint of French charm, endless white beaches and the world-famous granite rocks make it a unique destination.

Die Seychellen verbinden Natur, Kultur, Wassersport und edle Hotels zu einem unvergesslichen Urlaub. Kreolische Lebensweise mit einem Schuss französischem Esprit, die schönsten Tauchgründe der Welt mit bis zu 40 Meter Sichtweite, einmaliges Revier für Sportfischer wie auf dem Alphonse-Atoll, endlose weiße Strände und die weltberühmten Granitfelsen sind die Zutaten.

Foto: North Island

1

Luxury Resort North Island

SEYCHELLES – NORTH ISLAND

'Barefoot luxury' in combination with a nature reserve. Three granite mountains, lush vegetation and the brilliant turquoise ocean set the scene of about 3.4 x 2.2 kilometer wide island creating a tropical paradise with a variety of plants and animals. Surrounded by the impressive landscape of granite rocks, the gleaming white beaches, the dense forest and the gently swaying palm trees offer a unique and elegant place for a romantic honeymoon or family vacation. In two restaurants and one bar meals with French, Creole, mediterranean and Japanese influences are served.

„Barfuß-Luxus" in Kombination mit Naturschutz. Drei Granitberge, eine üppige Vegetation und der türkisfarben leuchtende Ozean bestimmen das Bild der etwa 3,4 x 2,2 Kilometer großen Insel und machen es zu einem tropischen Paradies mit einer Vielfalt an Pflanzen und Tieren. Eingebettet in die beeindruckende Landschaft, sind die leuchtend weißen Strände und der dichte Palmenwald ideal für romantische Flitterwochen oder einen Familienurlaub. In zwei Restaurants und einer Bar werden Gerichte mit französischen, kreolischen, mediterranen sowie japanischen Einflüssen serviert.

In keeping with the islands theme of building sustainably, the eleven guest villas were built using local, recycled, natural materials. Luxury and simplicity blend into an impressive architectural style, with a nautical-themed interior, where rough and soft textures are combined. Bleached branches decorate the railings and stairways. Mussel shells and many other natural materials of the island have also been incorporated in the decor and design of the lodges.

Die elf Gästevillen wurden aus lokalen, im Rahmen der Inselsanierung recycelten Naturmaterialien erbaut. Luxus und Schlichtheit vermischen sich hier zu einem eindrucksvollen Architekturstil, der das Interieur im maritimen Farbenspiel aus rauen und weichen Texturen verbindet. Verbleichte Äste zieren Geländer und Treppenaufgänge, angeschwemmte Muscheln und andere Naturmaterialien der Insel wurden in die Architektur und das Design der Lodges eingearbeitet.

Foto: North Island/Andrew Howard

The ten presidential villas with 450 m² living space are located along East Beach, all with direct access to the beach. The 11th villa is the biggest villa with 750 m² living space. Perched on the granite rock at the far end of East Beach it is the epitome of privacy and seclusion. The villa extends over several levels and has private access to the beach over a leadwood bridge through a beautiful palm garden.

Die zehn, 450 m² großen, Presidential Villas entlang des East Beach haben alle direkten Zugang zum Strand. Die elfte, und mit 750 m² größte Villa, thront auf den Granitfelsen am äußersten Ende von East Beach – der Inbegriff von Privatsphäre und Abgeschiedenheit. Die Villa erstreckt sich über mehrere Ebenen durch einen Palmengarten mit privaten Strandzugang über eine Brücke aus Leadwood-Holz.

Constance Lèmuria

SEYCHELLES – PRASLIN

The lavish hotel on the Praslin island's northwest coast and member of "The Leading Hotels of the World" is edged by three incredible stretches of pristine sands. The 105 suites and villas are spread over several levels adapting themselves to existing rocks, trees and hilly terrain. Luxury, space and elegance are combined to offer the perfect island hideaway.

Das luxuriöse Hotel, Mitglied der „Leading Hotels of the World", liegt von drei weißen Sandstränden umgeben an der Nordwestküste von Praslin. Die über über mehrere Ebenen verteilten 105 Suiten und Villen sind in die hügelige Umgebung mit Gramitfelsen und Palmen integriert. Die Kombination aus Raum, Luxus und Eleganz hat hier ein perfektes Hideaway erschaffen.

A wide range of outdoor activities are provided by three white sandy beaches, including the most beautiful beach on Praslin – Anse Georgette, and the only golf course of the Seychelles, with 18 holes.

Die drei Sandstrände, darunter auch der schönste Strand auf Praslin, Anse Georgette, und der einzige Golfplatz der Seychellen, bieten eine breite Palette an Outdoor-Aktivitäten.

Foto: Constance Hotels

Seychellois' flavours can be savoured in the three restaurants and bars of the hotel. The suites and villas are richly furnished in a cool colonial style, using wooden furniture with stone and marble nestled elegantly in its environment. To create a cocoon of luxury amidst vibrant nature, materials such as wood, stone, pink granite, marble and thatch palm have been used to create a modern yet warm feel.

Die Suiten und Villen sind in einem frischen Kolonialstil eingerichtet und perfekt eingebettet in die Umgebung. Mit natürlichen Materialien wie Holz, Naturstein, rosa Granit, Marmor und Dächern aus Stroh wurde ein Luxusnest mit moderner, aber warmen Atmosphäre geschaffen.

Foto: Constance Hotels

3

Oetger Collection
Frégate Island

SEYCHELLES – FRÈGATE ISLAND

The former pirate hideout is one of the last entirely unspoiled island hideaways worldwide with seven white, sandy beaches and a tropical vegetation. With only sixteen residences there are only ever a handful of people on the island at the same time. Fregate Island provides a reception with a boutique, library, main restaurant, a wine-tasting cellar, the charming Pirates Bar beach hut, two common pools, the Plantation House (with an exquisite dining ambiance) and a museum with a fascinating treasure chest of artefacts. Weddings can be celebrated in the island's own chapel, decorated in an authentic Creole style. For a truly magical and unforgettable stay, Fregate Island offers the opportunity to have the entire island to oneself.

Das ehemalige Piraten-Versteck ist eines der letzten völlig unberührten Insel-Refugien weltweit mit sieben weißen Sandstränden und einer üppigen grünen Vegetation. Mit nur sechzehn Residenzen ist die Anzahl der Besucher auf der Insel auf eine Handvoll Gäste begrenzt. Eine Rezeption mit Boutique, Bibliothek, Hauptrestaurant, Weinkeller, die charmante Piraten Bar, zwei Pools, das Plantation House Restaurant mit einer exquisiten Atmosphäre und ein Museum mit einer faszinierenden Schatztruhe mit Artefakten machen den Aufenthalt zu einem besonderen Erlebnis. Hochzeiten können in der Insel-eigenen Kapelle im authentischen kreolischen Stil gefeiert werden.

Sixteen beautifully crafted residences of african Chamfuto teaxwood and mahogoni, each 400 m² – 700 m² big and all with grand private pools ensuring a memorable and exquisite holiday in the middle of a unique nature reserve. The highlight of the resort is the Banyan Hill complex with three separate sleeping villas, superbly located on a hilltop overlooking the harbour, beaches and a large part of the island. Guests can meet and dine in the large, architecturally stunning main building with an open living area and grand dining space.

16 Residenzen mit afrikanischem Chamfuto Teakholz und Mahagoni eingerichtet, jede 400 - 700 m² groß und mit privaten Pools, bieten einen unvergesslichen Luxusurlaub in der Mitte eines einzigartigen Naturreservats. Das Highlight des Resorts ist der Banyan Hill Komplex mit drei separaten Schlafvillen, herrlich gelegen auf einem Hügel mit Blick auf den Hafen, die Strände und einen großen Teil der Insel. Die Gäste können sich im großen, architektonisch beeindruckenden Hauptgebäude mit offenem Wohnbereich und großem Speisesaal treffen und gemeinsam das Abendessen genießen.

Foto: Oetger Collection

Foto: JA Resorts

4

JA Resorts Enchanted Island Resort

SEYCHELLES ROUND ISLAND

The luxurious hideaway in the middle of a designated National Marine Park is located on an island blessed with five acres of white sand, rock formations and lush vegetation, only fifteen minutes by speedboat from Mahé. Ten exclusive villas are hidden in the island's jungle, each with a private walkway to the beach. The 'Bounty Restaurant' and the 'Castaway Bar' spoil the guests with international and Creole cuisine and tropical cocktails.

Das luxuriöse Hideaway liegt nur 15 Minuten mit dem Schnellboot von Mahé auf einer Insel, umgeben von fünf Hektar weißem Sand, Granitfelsen und üppiger Natur. Zehn exklusive Villen sind in dem Inseldschungel versteckt, jede mit privatem Zugang zum Strand. Die beiden Restaurants "Bounty Restaurant" und "Castaway Bar" verwöhnen die Gäste mit internationaler und kreolischer Küche sowie tropischen Cocktails.

Foto: JA Resorts

Ten exclusive villas, each with a private walkway to the beach provide one and two bedroom units designed to reflect the unique heritage and colonial past of the Seychelles Islands, with modern day comforts and technology.

Zehn exklusive Villen mit privatem Strandzugang und wahlweise ein oder zwei Schlafzimmer-einheiten, spiegeln das einzigartige Erbe und die koloniale Vergangenheit der Seychellen wieder.

Foto: JA Resorts

The Private Pool Villa is an idyllic getaway for two adults and one child between eight to fifteen years of age.

Die private Villa mit Pool ist ein idyllisches Refugium für zwei Erwachsene und ein Kind zwischen acht und fünfzehn Jahren.

5

Constance Ephelia

SEYCHELLES – MAHÈ

Constance Ephelia, on 120 hectares of land in the Northwest of Mahé, is situated on two of the most beautiful beaches of the island, overlooking the Marine National Park of Port Launay and consists of 41 spacious, modern villas and 224 suites surrounded by lush greenery and glistening lagoons. On two of Mahé's most scenic beaches, guests can indulge in one of five restaurants with Arabic, French, Italian and Creole cuisine, varying from a more casual, sandy-beach atmosphere to a more elegant, romantic setting.

41 großzügige, moderne Villen und 224 Suiten, umgeben von üppiger Vegetation und glitzernden Lagunen – das ist „Constance Ephelia" auf 120 Hektar Land im Nordwesten Mahés gelegen mit Blick auf den Marine-Nationalpark von Port Launay. An zwei der schönsten Strände von Mahé gelegen, werden die Gäste in fünf Restaurants mit arabischer, französischer, italienischer und kreolischer Landesküche von leger auf Sandboden bis edel und romantisch sowie in fünf Bars verwöhnt.

Foto:Constance Hotels

Suites in various categories, from 62 m^2 and villas from 185 m^2 to 370 m^2 offer every imaginable comfort. The highlight is the 980 m^2 large presidential villa (photo above - right) with magnificent views of the Indian Ocean, a perfect retreat for families and holiday with friends.

Suiten in verschiedensten Kategorien ab 62 m^2 und Villen von 185 m^2 bis 370 m^2 bieten jeden erdenklichen Komfort. Das Highlight ist die 980 m^2 große Presidential Villa (Foto oben u. rechts) mit Traumblick auf den Indischen Ozean, ein perfekter Rückzugsort für Familien und Urlaub mit Freunden.

Foto:Constance Hotels

Foto: Banyan Tree

6

Luxury Resort
Banyan Tree

SEYCHELLES – MAHÈ

The former residence of ex-Beatle George Harrison was converted to the luxury resort Banyan Tree, while preserving the authenticity of the architecture and culture of the place. 60 charming and luxuriously equipped villas with breathtaking views of the Indian Ocean are picturesquely nestled in the lush tropical landscape - only a few steps to the beach where the iconic rock formations cushion the coast. Guests can also enjoy award-winning Thai cuisine, consisting of South-East Asian specialities, as well as international and Creole culinary delights.

Der frühere Wohnsitz von Ex-Beatle George Harrison wurde unter Wahrung der authentischen Architektur und der Kultur des Ortes zum Luxusresort umgebaut. 60 charmant und luxuriös ausgestattete Villen mit atemberaubendem Ausblick auf den Indischen Ozean liegen malerisch eingebettet in die üppige Tropenlandschaft. Zum Sandstrand mit den typischen Granitfelsen sind es nur ein paar Schritte. Kulinarisch werden die Gäste von einer preisgekrönten thailändischen Küche, von südostasiatischen Spezialitäten sowie internationaler und kreolischer Küche verwöhnt.

Foto: Banyan Tree

In the villas, the architecture of the Seychelles is inspired and elaborated by colonial French and English design aspects. The villas with their high, slanted ceilings, airy verandas and open doors exude the flair of the past colonial era.

In den Villen wurde die Architektur der Seychellen aufgegriffen und durch koloniale französische und englische Designaspekte erweitert. Die Villen mit ihren hohen, schrägen Decken, luftigen Veranden und offenen Türen verströmen so das Flair der vergangenen Kolonialepoche.

7

Six Senses
Zil Pasyon

SEYCHELLES – FÉLICITÈ

Félicité is one of the most dramatically beautiful islands in the 115-island nation and features massive granite boulders and picture-perfect beaches. Occupying less than one third of the total land, Six Senses Zil Pasyon is the only resort on the island. Considered as one of the satellite islands of La Digue (as well as Grande Soeur, Petite Soeur, Coco and Marianne), Félicité offers the ultimate island hopping experience. These architectural masterpieces are truly inspirational and beckon guests seeking an uncompromising level of comfort and style. They present a bold vision, are environmentally conscious plus offer stunning views of the sea.

Félicité ist eine der spektakulärsten Inseln der 115-Insel-Nation und verfügt über massive Granitfelsen und Strände wie aus dem Bilderbuch. Das „Six Senses Zil Pasyon" ist das einzige Resort auf der Insel und nimmt weniger als ein Drittel der Gesamtfläche ein. Als eine der Satelliteninseln von La Digue bietet Félicité das ultimative Inselhopping-Erlebnis. Die architektonischen Meisterwerke sind wirklich inspirierend und ziehen Gäste an, die ein kompromissloses Maß an Komfort und Stil suchen. Zusätzlich zu dem atemberaubenden Ausblick über das Meer überzeugen sie auch mit kühnem, umweltbewusstem Denken.

© Thomas Foucourt

© John Athimaritis

'Six Senses Zil Pasyon' includes 28 one-bedroom pool villas and two two-bedroom pool villas ranging from 200 m^2 to 500 m^2, as well as several private residences. Every villa offers seclusion amidst tropical vegetation and spacious surroundings, unsurpassed vistas of the ocean, a private infinity pool and a personal butler service.

Das „Six Senses Zil Pasyon" umfasst 28 Ein- und zwei Zwei-Zimmer-Poolvillen mit Größen von 200 bis 500 m^2 sowie mehrere private Residenzen. Jede Villa bietet Ruhe und Abgeschiedenheit inmitten großflächiger tropischer Flora. Komplett mit einem unübertroffenen Ausblick auf den Ozean, einem privaten Infinity-Pool und einem eigenen Butler-Service lassen diese Villen keine Wünsche offen.

The Island Café offers breakfast and dinner inspired by flavors from the Seychellois spice route, a melting pot of European, Asian and African fare. Meat-free oceanside dining for lunch and dinner, with a fresh and simple cuisine from local waters, is available in the Ocean Kitchen. Drinks and refreshments are served throughout the day in two bars; the traditional Lakanbiz bar, with a selection of flavored and aged rums as well as cuban cigars and Koko Bar, located beside the ocean. The setting of the omnipresent majestic rock formations in combination with the locally inspired décor create a unique atmosphere.

Das Inselcafé bietet Frühstück und Abendessen, inspiriert von Aromen der Seychellen – ein Schmelztiegel europäischer, asiatischer und afrikanischer Kost. Zwei Bars, die traditionelle „Lakanbiz Bar“ mit einer Auswahl an aromatisierten und alten Rumsorten sowie kubanischen Zigarren und die „Koko Bar“ direkt am Meer servieren den ganzen Tag Getränke und Erfrischungen.

© John Athimaritis

The setting of the omnipresent majestic rock formations in combination with the locally inspired décor create a unique atmosphere.

Die einzigartige Lage inmitten der majestätischen Felsformationen schafft in Kombination mit dem lokalen Dekor eine besondere Atmosphäre.

© John Athimaritis

COLOR

© Peter Vitale

8

Four Seasons
Resort Seychelles

SEYCHELLES – MAHÈ

This remote, hillside retreat embraces the natural simplicity of treetop living in an isolated position overlooking the idyllic bay of Petite Anse. The resort covers a secluded area of 170 acres and comprises 67 villas and suites and 27 residences that descend down a lushly forested incline to the private, horseshoe beach of Petite Anse. Creole-inspired design complements the dramatic topography, with granite boulders lining the powder-white beach, steep jungle slopes and a shoreline protected by the horseshoe-shaped bay. Two restaurants offer Mediterranean and Creole and South-East Asian cuisine as well as Japanese specialities.

Etwas abseits am Hang gelegen, verkörpert dieses Refugium mit 67 Villen und Suiten sowie 27 Residenzen die natürliche Einfachheit des Baumkronen-Lebens mit spektakulärem Blick auf die idyllische Bucht von Petite Anse. Kreolisch inspiriertes Design ergänzt die dramatische Topographie, wo Granitfelsen den schneeweißen Strand säumen. Zwei Restaurants bieten mediterrane, kreolische und südostasiatische Gerichte sowie japanische Spezialitäten.

The tree-house villas and suites are perched on stilts amidst a jungle of coconut, mango, jackfruit and cinnamon trees. Standard features in all villas include: an infinity-edge plunge pool, open-air shower, glass-walled bathroom and expansive, private outdoor living space with sunset views over the Indian Ocean or surrounding tropical landscape. High above the bay, the hilltop spa epitomises the sense of tranquility and seclusion found throughout the resort.

In den Baumhausvillen und -suiten inmitten eines Dschungels aus Mango-, Kokosnuss- und Zimtbäumen kann man den Abend mit Blick auf den Sonnenuntergang über dem Indischen Ozean oder der umliegenden tropischen Landschaft ausklingen lassen. Hoch über der Bucht berauscht das Hilltop-Spa mit einer atemberaubenden Aussicht.

9

Maia
Luxury Resort & Spa

SEYCHELLES – MAHÈ

The hotel with its blossoming tropical garden is nestled within a beautiful landscape of granite cliffs, on a peninsula in the south-west of Mahé with direct access to the beach. A team of five chefs conjure up Creole, Indian, Japanese, Thai and Mediterranean cuisine. Snacks and drinks are available at the sunset pool bar, which is an idyllic place to enjoy the sunset with an evening drink.

In exponierter Lage auf einer Halbinsel im Süden von Mahé mit direktem Zugang zum Badestrand schmiegt sich das Hotel in einem blühenden Tropengarten in die von Granitfelsen geprägte Landschaft. Ein Team aus fünf Küchenchefs zaubert Spezialitäten aus der kreolischen, indischen, thailändischen, japanischen und mediterranen Küche. Für Snacks und Drinks ist die idyllisch von Granitfelsen umgebene „Sunset Pool Bar" der ideale Ort, um den Sonnenuntergang bei einem abendlichen Drink zu genießen.

Foto: Maia Luxury Resort & Spa

Foto: Maia Luxury Resort & Spa

Thirty open-plan villas each with a private infinity pool and a shaded outdoor pavilion equipped with sunbeds, a dining area and kitchen are located on the hillside with views of the Indian Ocean or directly on the beach. Noble materials and fabrics, warm earth tones, bright colors and some colorful accents define the interior. Tasteful black and white photographs, depicting scenes from the life of the Seychellois serve as decoration for the exclusive bedrooms with king size beds.

Die dreißig offen gestalteten Villen mit eigenem Infinity-Pool und überdachtem Außenpavillon mit Essbereich, Küche und Tagesbett liegen am Hang mit Blick über den Indischen Ozean oder direkt am Strand. Edle Materialien und Stoffe, warme Erdtöne, helle Farben und einige bunte Akzente bestimmen das Interieur. Geschmackvolle Schwarz-Weiß-Fotografien mit Szenen aus dem Leben der Seychellois dienen als Dekoration für die exklusiven Schlafzimmer mit Kingsize-Bett.

Foto: Alphonse Island

10

Alphonse Island

SEYCHELLES – ALPHONSE ATOLL

The Alphonse Atoll Group is considered one of the most pristine, untouched Edens of the world. The magnificent island threesome comprising Alphonse, St. Francois and Bijoutier lies in the very heart of the Indian Ocean as part of the Seychelles outer island group. Beautiful white beaches line the edges of the dense natural forest, interspersed with the remnants of old coconut groves. Guests will find ancient ambling tortoises, scurrying crabs and an interesting array of bird species.

Die Alphonse-Atoll-Gruppe ist ein absolut unberührtes Paradies. Der Insel-Dreier mit Alphonse, St. Francois und Bijoutier ist Teil der äußeren Seychellen-Inseln. Weiße Strände umranden den dichten Naturwald mit den Resten einer Kokosnussplantage und Schildkröten, Krebse und eine Reihe interessanter Vogelarten als Bewohner der Insel.

The sheer drop offs, rich currents and abundant sea life that surrounds the Alphonse group of atolls makes it one of the most diverse diving destinations in the Seychelles. The pristine sites are famous not only for their great visibility, but also its unbleached corals and a diverse range of fish species comprising of reef, pelagic and shark species. The fifteen dive sites are suitable for all categories of divers, beginners as well as advanced divers.

Die steilen Abhänge, Strömungen und das reichhaltige Meeresleben macht das Alphonse Atoll zu einem der aufregendsten und abwechslungsreichsten Tauchziele auf den Seychellen. Die unberührten Tauchspots sind berühmt für ihre großartige Sicht und ungebleichte Korallen sowie eine Vielzahl von Fischarten wie Riff-, Ozean- und Hai-Arten. Die fünfzehn Tauchplätze eignen sich für Anfänger wie erfahrene Taucher.

Foto: Alphonse Island

Foto: Alphonse Island

The central dining and bar area allows guests to socialize alongside the sparkling pool and shoreline, with diverse cuisine inspired by the sensuous island atmosphere and complemented by a comprehensive wine list. Entwining the influences of local Seychellois Creole and French cuisine, the dishes overflow with inspiration from all corners of the Indian Ocean.

Die Küche bietet eine Vielzahl an Gerichten, inspiriert von der sinnlichen Inselatmosphäre und ergänzt durch eine umfangreiche Weinkarte. Die Gerichte sind geprägt von der kreolischen und französische Küche mit Einflüssen aus allen Ecken des Indischen Ozeans.

Foto: Alphonse Island

Alphonse Island features a single resort comprising of Beach Bungalows and Suites built alongside the water's edge, each with scenic ocean views. Freedom of movement around the island on foot or bicycle permits self-discovery of the wonders of this special place.

Alphonse Island verfügt über ein einziges Resort mit Strandbungalows und Suiten direkt am Meer. Zu Fuß oder mit dem Fahrrad kann man auf der Insel auf Entdeckungstour gehen.

Comores
Baie d'Emeraude 460
Antsiranana
Nosy Be
1
Maldives
Equator
Zanzibar
Seychelles
Madagascar
Mauritius
La Reunion
Mananara
MOZAMBIQUE
Sainte Marie
1
2
Geysire at Analavory 442
Tsingy de Bemaraha Strict Nature Reserve 440
Antananarivo 458
3
4
Antsirabe
Baobab Allee 438
Parc national de l'Isalo 444
Toliara
2
3
100 km

Madagascar

Hotels

1 **Constance Tsarabanjina** — Constance Hotels & Resorts
2 **Manafiafy Beach & Rainforest Lodge** — Madaclassic
3 **Mandrare Rivercamp** — Madaclassic

Golf Courses

1 **Foulpointe Golf Club** — 9 hole
2 **Golf ny Rova** — 18 hole
3 **Malaza Golf Club** — 9 hole
4 **Golf Club d'Antsirabe** — 9 hole

Area:	*587,295 km^2* *1,580 x 580 km*
Highest Mountain:	*Maromokotro, 2.886 m*
Population:	*24 Mio.*
Religion:	*52 % indigen, Animism* *41 % Christianity* *7 % Islam*
Language:	*malagasy, french*
Government:	*semy presidential republic*
Independence:	*1960*
Currency:	*Ariary*

The twenty million inhabitants of Madagascar are made up of eighteen individual tribes, each preserving the country's cultural beliefs and traditions.

Die zwanzig Millionen Einwohner von Madagaskar setzen sich aus achtzehn verschiedenen Volksstämmen zusammen, die ihre Traditionen sorgsam bewahren.

No beach clubs, no hotel silos, no mass tourism. Instead, the island off the southern coast of Africa offers great treasures such as dense rainforests, dry steppes, tropical beaches, the typical baobab trees, unique wildlife and extremely friendly people. Madagascar consists of diverse landscapes and climates; hot tropical forests, temperate zones and dry, hot steppes. In the hilly, barren highlands in the center lies the capital, Antananarivo. The climate here is temperate with warm rain from November to April and cooler temperatures from May to October. At elevations above 1,800 m there is even night frost. Although Madagascar belongs to Africa, it is not purely African. While the dry landscape of the south seem typical for Africa, the rice terraces are more reminiscent of Asia. It is even hotter and more humid in the tropical north.

Due to the enormous number of endemic animals and plants on the island, this fourth largest island in the world is sometimes also referred to as the sixth continent. From the 200,000 species, 150,000 are endemic. The best known are the cute lemurs with their black and white curled tails. There are over 50 species of lemurs, and they are all only found on Madagascar. 36 genera of birds, 99% of frog species and half of all chameleon species worldwide also live on Madagascar and 80% of the 12,000 plant species are endemic. Madagascar is also famous for its Baobab Tree, of which there are ten different types in the world, six of which are exclusively found here. One can also discover the incredible flora and fauna in several national parks in the island.

Madagascar offers a variety of nature to explore, like hardly any other region of the world. But traveling in Madagascar is not easy. It has not yet been developed for tourists and travelling alone is basically impossible due to the lack of infrastructure on the 1,580 km long and 580 km wide island. Also time-wise, it would be impossible to explore the island in two weeks. One would need to allocate two months or more. The island of Nosy Be with kilometer-long beaches and luxurious hotels is a preferable target for a first visit. And the former pirate island Sainte Marie, off the east coast of Madagascar, with beautiful small coves, sandy beaches is a hotspot for whale-watching.

Keine Beachclubs, keine Hotelsilos, kein Massentourismus. Dafür bietet die Insel vor der Südostküste Afrikas große Schätze wie dichte Regenwälder, trockene Steppen, tropische Strände, die typischen Baobabs, eine einzigartige Tierwelt und freundliche Menschen. Madagaskar besteht aus verschiedensten Landschaften und Klimazonen: tropisch heiße Waldgebiete, gemäßigte Zonen und trockene Steppen. Im hügeligen, kargen Hochland im Zentrum liegt die Hauptstadt Antananarivo. Das Klima hier ist gemäßigt, mit warmem Regen von November bis April und kühleren Temperaturen von Mai bis Oktober. Über 1.800 Meter kann es auch mal Nachtfrost geben. Madagaskar gehört zwar zu Afrika, ist aber nicht rein afrikanisch. Die Reisterrassen erinnern eher an Asien, die trockene Landschaft des Südens ist dagegen typisch afrikanisch. Noch heißer und feuchter ist es im tropischen Norden.

Aufgrund der enormen Anzahl endemischer Tiere und Pflanzen wird die viertgrößte Insel der Welt auch als „sechster Kontinent" bezeichnet. Von über 200.000 Tierarten sind 150.000 endemisch. Die bekannteste Art sind die niedlichen Lemuren mit ihrem schwarz-weiß gekringelten Schwanz. Über 50 Arten von Lemuren gibt es, und sie alle leben nur auf Madagaskar. 99 Prozent der Froscharten leben auch auf Madagaskar, 36 Gattungen von Vögeln und die Hälfte aller Chamäleonarten. Von den 12.000 Pflanzenarten sind 80 Prozent endemisch. Die berühmteste Pflanze Madagaskars ist der Baobab, der Affenbrotbaum. Von zehn Arten weltweit existieren sechs nur hier.

Madagaskar bietet eine Naturvielfalt wie kaum eine andere Region der Welt. Doch das Reisen in Madagaskar ist nicht einfach. Touristisch noch kaum entwickelt, sind individuelle Reisen aufgrund fehlender Infrastruktur auf der 1.580 Kilometer langen und 580 Kilometer breiten Insel sehr beschwerlich und kosten viel Zeit. In zwei Wochen mal die Insel zu erkunden, ist unmöglich – in zwei Monate schon eher. Bevorzugte Ziele für einen ersten Besuch sind die Insel Nosy Be mit luxuriösen Hotels und kilometerlangen Traumstränden und die ehemalige Pirateninsel Sainte Marie vor der Ostküste Madagaskars mit schönen kleinen Buchten, Sandstränden und einem Hotspot zum Whale Watching.

The Baobab Alley is a conspicuous group of carob trees on the road from Morondava to Belon'i Tsiribihina in the west of Madagascar. Its bark and roots are fire resistant and are used in the manufacture of cloth and rope, while its leaves can be used as a spice or even medicine. The fruit serves as an important supply of vitamin C. The tree can store hundreds of liters of water, and can reach 1,500 years of age.

Die Baobaballee ist eine auffällige Gruppe von Affenbrotbäumen an der Straße von Morondava nach Belon'i Tsiribihina im westlichen Madagaskar. Rinde und Stamm des Baobab sind feuerfest und werden für die Herstellung von Tuch und Seil, die Blätter als Gewürz und Heilmittel verwendet. Die Frucht liefert wichtiges Vitamin C. Hunderte Liter Wasser kann der Baum speichern, über 1.500 Jahre wird er alt.

Foto: Alex Ship Shutterstock

The "Tsingy de Bemaraha Strict Nature Reserve" is a karst landscape of striking limestone formations.

Das „Tsingy de Bemaraha Strict Nature Reserve" ist eine Karstlandschaft mit auffälligen Kalksteinformationen, den Tsingy.

Foto: Denis an de Water, Shutterstock

The geysers of Andranomandraotra are made from the carbon dioxide in the sewage of nearby mines. The effluent of the mine picks up iron and limestone from the pipes on the way to a river and surfaces in Andranomandraotra. In doing so, limestone is deposited over the course of time and forms the present-day geysers.

Die Geysire von Andranomandraotra sind durch das kohlensäurehaltige Abwasser aus nahegelegenen Mineralminen entstanden. Das Abwasser der Minen löst auf dem Weg zu einem Fluss Eisen und Kalk aus den Rohren und sprudelt in Andranomandraotra wie bei einem kleinen Geysir an die Oberfläche. Dabei lagerte sich im Laufe der Zeit Kalkstein ab und bildete die heutigen Geysire.

Foto: Ducarev Mikhail, Shutterstock

Bizarre sandstone formations in the 815 km² Isalo National Park of Madagascar
Bizarre Sandsteinformationen im 815 km² großen Isalo-Nationalpark

Foto: Denis an der Water Shutterstock

Madagascar belongs to the poorest countries in the world, yet the people are genuinely cheerful individuals. About 70% of the population can neither read nor write, but in rural areas the family structures work well and provide children safety and security.

Eigentlich haben sie nichts zu lachen. Madagaskar ist eines der ärmsten Länder der Welt und doch sind die Menschen auf Madagaskar von Natur aus fröhlich. Rund 70 % der Bevölkerung können zwar weder lesen noch schreiben, aber in ländlichen Regionen funktionieren die familiären Strukturen gut und geben Kindern Schutz und Sicherheit.

The peninsula Masoala in the north of Madagascar accommodates a rainforest of 2,400 km² which is home to some of the greatest biodiversity in the world.

Die Masoala-Halbinsel im Norden Madagaskars beherbergt einen 2.400 km² großen Regenwald mit einer der höchsten Artenvielfalt der Erde.

57 species of chameleons, half of all deposits worldwide, live in the Isalo National Park in Madagascar. Depending on the type, they can range from three centimeters to one meter in length.

57 Arten von Chamäleons, die Hälfte aller weltweiten Vorkommen, leben auf Madagaskar und sind je nach Art von drei Zentimeter bis zu einem Meter groß.

Foto: Mogens Trolle Shutterstock

Today, there are about 60 species of lemurs endemic to Madagascar. The nocturnal Prosimians can be found across the island as well as in the National Park.

Heute gibt es rund 60 Arten von Lemuren, die ausschließlich auf Madagaskar leben. Die nachtaktiven Halbaffen leben verstreut auf der ganzen Insel und sind am besten im Nationalpark zu finden.

Foto: LVV Shutterstock

Madagascar has the highest intake of rice worldwide, second only to Vietnam. Per person approximately 120 kg are consumed each year, and for every kilo of rice, 2,000 liters of water are needed.

Auf Madagaskar wird – nach Vietnam – mit 120 kg pro Kopf und Jahr am meisten Reis der Welt gegessen. Für ein einziges Kilo Reis sind 2.000 Liter Wasser nötig.

Foto: Dudarev Mikhail/Shutterstock

Madagascan ground is covered in a clay layer about 20 meters deep, painting the villages a bright ochre-red. Life in rural areas is very difficult due to the lack of electrical power and running water. Even in the capital running water is not always available.

Eine bis zu zwanzig Meter dicke Schicht roter Erde bedeckt Madagaskar und taucht manche Dörfer in leuchtendes Ocker bis Rot. Ohne elektrischen Strom und fließendes Wasser ist das Leben in den ländlichen Regionen sehr beschwerlich. Nicht einmal in der Millionenstadt Antananarivo ist fließendes Wasser überall vorhanden.

Foto: Luke Wait, Shutterstock

The capital Antananarivo consists of over 1.8 million people, making it by far the biggest city in Madagascar.

Die Hauptstadt Antananarivo ist mit über 1,8 Mio. Menschen auch mit Abstand die größte Stadt Madagaskars.

Foto: Dudarev Mikhail, Shutterstock

Unfortunately Madagascar's oceans have not been spared from overfishing. The amount of fish caught in Madagascar over the past 50 years has been twice as much as officially documented. Especially international fishing fleets roam the coastal waters, leaving them empty for local fishermen. The European Union also maintains various fishing agreements with African States and pays to be allowed to fish in Madagascan waters. The fish ends up in European fish restaurants and less and less in the nets of local fishermen.

Die Überfischung der Weltmeere lässt leider auch Madagaskar nicht verschont. Die Fangmengen in Madagaskar sind in den vergangenen 50 Jahren doppelt so hoch gewesen wie offiziell dokumentiert. Vor allem internationale Fangflotten fischen die Bestände vor der Küste leer. Ganz offiziell. Auch die Europäische Union unterhält diverse Fangabkommen mit afrikanischen Staaten und zahlt dafür, vor Madagaskar fischen zu dürfen. Der Fisch landet dann in europäischen Fischrestaurants und immer weniger in den Netzen der lokalen Fischer.

Until now, the globalization of Madagascar has passed almost without a trace. Madagascar is a world of its own. A bizarre world, with 150,000 animals and 9,200 plant species, that only exist in Madagascar.

Bis jetzt ist die Globalisierung an Madagaskar so gut wie spurlos vorübergegangen. Denn Madagaskar ist eine Welt für sich. Eine bizarre Welt mit 150.000 Tier- und 9.200 Pflanzenarten, die es nur auf Madagaskar gibt.

Foto: Constance Hotels

1

Constance Tsarabanjina

MADAGASCAR NORTH COAST

An truly relaxing holiday experience, where guests can get close to the undisturbed nature of Madagascar. This luxury barefoot resort is located on a small island 60 kilometers from Nosy Be on the north-west coast of Madagascar.

Eine extrem entspannte Urlaubserfahrung, in der die Gäste die unberührten Natur Madagaskars unter und über Wasser erleben können. Das luxuriöse Barfuß-Resort liegt auf einer kleinen Insel 60 Kilometer von Nosy Be an der Nordwestküste von Madgaskar.

The 25 Villas on the North and South Beach are thatched and airy, elegantly decorated with four-poster beds, facing the Indian Ocean.

Die 25 reetgedeckten Villen am Nord- und Südstrand sind luftig und elegant eingerichtet mit Blick auf den indischen Ozean.

Foto: Constance Hotels

Foto: Constance Hotels

Foto: Constance Hotels

The elegant decor of the 25 thatched villas combines rosewood floors, sky beds and wooden furniture into a stylistic whole. There is no TV, telephone or wifi in the villas.

Die elegante Einrichtung der 25 Villen vereint Rosenholzböden, Himmelbetten und Holzmöbel zu einem stilistischen Ganzen. Kein TV, Telefon und Wifi in den Villen.

Foto: manafiafy Lodge

2

Manafiafy
Beach & Rainforest Lodge

MADAGASCAR SOUTH

With sparkling blue seas, verdant rainforests, abundant wildlife and distant mountains this small and intimate lodge offers a choice of serenity and adventure. Nestled into a forest fringed cove, each bungalow offers a private terrace just inches from the sea. The thatch-roofed rooms lead directly onto pristine white sand beaches and the azure waters of the Indian Ocean.

Nahe am Meer gelegen, vom tropischen Regenwald umgeben und mit zahlreichen Wildtieren, bietet diese kleine und intime Lodge eine große Auswahl an Möglichkeiten zum Entspannen und Entdecken. Von den Terrassen der strohgedeckten Bungalows ist es nur wenige Meter zu den unberührten weißen Sandstränden und den azurblauen Gewässern des Indischen Ozeans.

Foto: manafiafy Lodge

Four luxury bungalows and one family villa are discreetly tucked along the edge of the forest, all with private wooden terraces and stunning views across the bay. These rooms meld local wood, ravinala thatch and stone with modern comforts to create the perfect 'Robinson Crusoe' experience.

Vier luxuriöse Bungalows und eine Familienvilla liegen geschützt am Waldrand mit herrlichem Blick über die Bucht. Holz und Stein der Umgebung, kombiniert mit modernem Komfort, schaffen die perfekte „Robinson-Crusoe-Idylle".

Foto: manafiafy Lodge

Foto: manafiafy Lodge

3

Mandrare
Rivercamp

MADAGASCAR SOUTH

Guests dine together around hand carved pallisandre tables in the warm glow of hurricane lamps. Mandrare is a great place to explore the unique spiny and gallery forest in the search for something previously unseen. There are five species of lemur that you can discover during your stay.

Mandrare ist der perfekte Ort, um den Stachelwald im Süden Madagaskars, eine weltweit einzigartiege Ökoregion, zu erforschen. Außerdem können fünf verschiedene Arten von Lemuren während des Aufenthaltes entdeckt werden.

Set overlooking the river and a golden sunrise, the fully equipped, bespoke tents allow guests to relaxe and invigorate the soul. The ornate wooden furniture in the tents is individually hand carved to depict a different local wildlife theme: Chameleon, Lemur, Gecko, Baobab, Radiated Tortoise and Heron.

Mit Blick auf den Fluss und einen goldenen Sonnenaufgang können Gäste in den voll-ausgestatteten Zelten entspannen und die Seele beleben. Die Holzmöbel in den Zelten sind handgeschnitzt und zeigen verschiedene regionale Wildthema zu zeigen: Chamäleon, Lemur, Gecko, Baobab, Schildkröte und Reiher.

Translation:	Lisa Dite Sara Loiperdinger Ania O'Leary
Proof reading german:	Monika Thiele
Proof reading english:	Ania O'Leary Sara Loiperdinger
Final editing:	Sara Loiperdinger
Photo editing:	Ruben Kabalo
Map illustrations:	Ruben Kabalo
Publisher:	Travel Publishing GmbH 82031 Grünwald, Germany

www.travelpublishing.de
sl@travelpublishing.com